CALTOUN HILL
St. James's Square
Leith Walk
Leith Street
Register Office
Caltoun Burying Ground
Orphan Hospital
College Church
Old Physic Garden
North Back of the Canongate
Charity Workhouse
Canongate
Foot of the Canongate
Easter Road to Leith
Abbey Close
Chapel
Holyrood House
Flesh Market
Bridge Street
HIGH STREET
Nether Bow
CANONGATE
St. John's Street
South Back of the Canongate
High School
Adams Square
Royal Infirmary
College
Richmond Street
Chapel Street
Cross Causeway
London Road by Dalkeith
Buccleugh Place
Buccleugh Street
Archers Hall
MEADOWS
PARK
SALISBURY CRAGS
D1577504
To The Right Honourable David Steuart Esq.
Lord Provost of the City of Edinburgh
This Plan is most humbly Dedicated by
His Lordship's most Obed.t Ser.t John Ainslie

EDINBURGH
The Golden Age

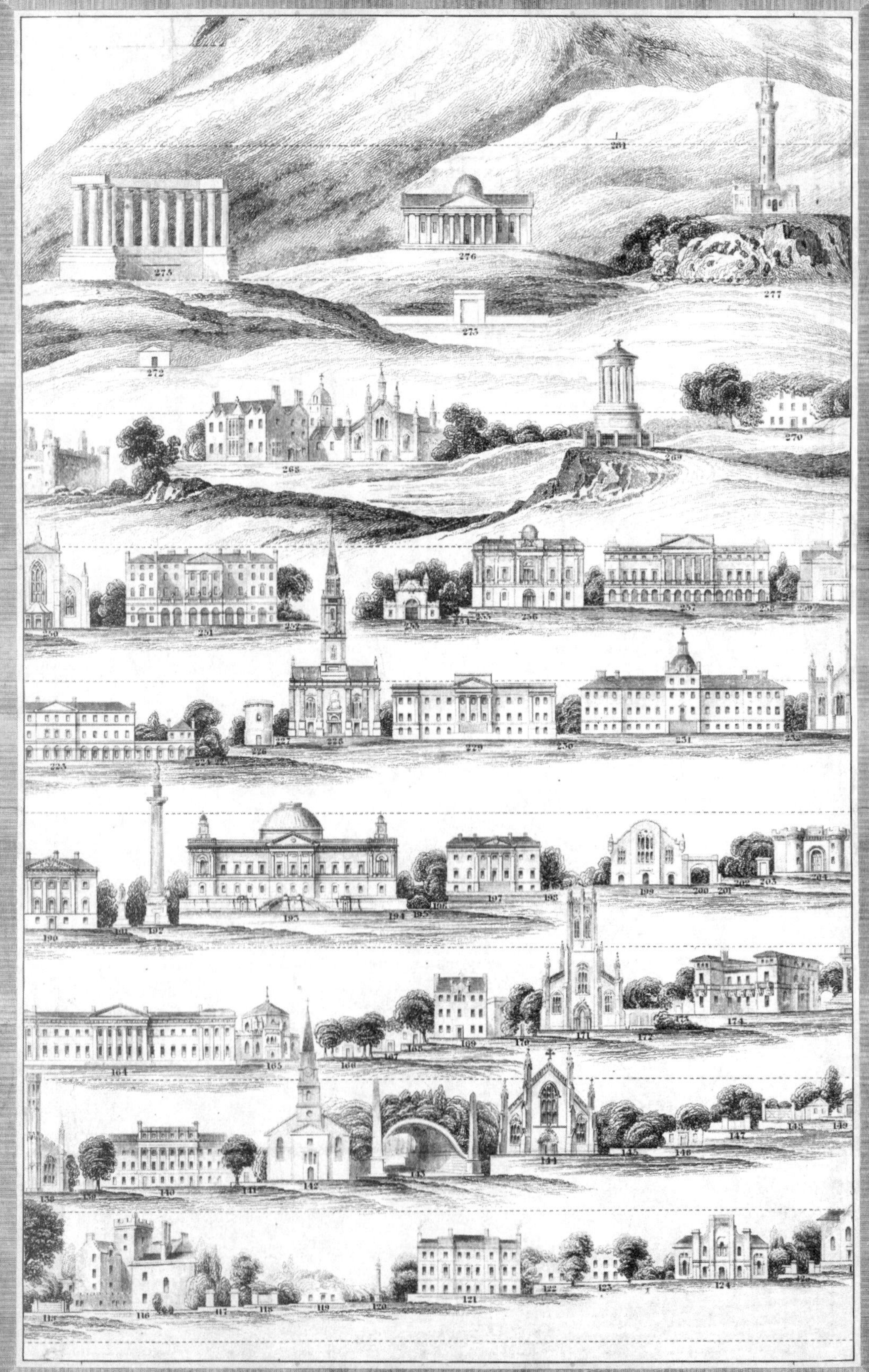

275
276
277
272
268
269
270
251
256
257
228
229
231
223
195
197
199
200
201
190
192
164
165
169
170
171
172
174
140
141
142
144
147
116
117
118
119
120
121
124

EDINBURGH
The Golden Age

Mary Cosh

JOHN DONALD PUBLISHERS
EDINBURGH

First published in 2003 by
John Donald Publishers, an imprint of
Birlinn Limited
West Newington House
10 Newington Road
Edinburgh
EH9 1QS

www.birlinn.co.uk

ISBN 0 85976 571 7

British Library Cataloguing-in-Publication Data
A catalogue record for this book is available from the British Library

Front endpaper: John Ainslie, City of Edinburgh (1780), showing the Old Town and the partially completed New Town

Back endpaper: Robert Kirkwood, Plan and elevation of the New Town of Edinburgh (1819)

Frontispiece: Detail from William Moffat, The geometrical and geological landscape . . . from . . . Leith to . . . Edinburgh (1837)

All maps reproduced by permission of the Trustees of the National Library of Scotland

Typesetting and origination by Brinnoven, Livingston
Printed and bound by Creative Print and Design, Wales

CONTENTS

ACKNOWLEDGEMENTS

Many people have my grateful thanks for their help in the writing and production of this book. First, Ian Gow who urged me to write it several years ago – though the book he visualised was a fairly short of account of how removal to the large houses of the New Town changed Edinburgh's social life. He gave further encouragement as the work progressed, as did friends who read parts of the book in draft: James Davis, Philippa Toomey, and Professor Aubrey Manning. Alison Weir not only read and commented on the whole but kindly undertook research into many queries raised, and Kitty Cruft provided useful checks and answers from her wide knowledge of Edinburgh.

I am most grateful to Hugh Andrew, at that time of Canongate Books, now Birlinn Publishers, for taking on the publication, and wish to thank the staff of the National Library of Scotland for their help during the research, and the resourcefulness of London Library staff in tracking down elusive works.

During the later stages, the two highly-informed readers were Andrew Fraser, who corrected many errors and repetitions, notably in the chapters on the University and medical/surgical history, and John Beaton who also pointed out numerous queries and obscurities, while David Greenhalgh had the laborious task of the index. Michele Le Roux supervised assembly of the many illustrations, and Jan Rutherford undertook publicity. To all these I owe heartfelt thanks. Above all I thank Andrew Simmons for his unfailing help, efficiency and tireless labours during the months of arduous work in preparing the book for publication.

The whole has been a rewarding if occasionally frustrating enterprise, and the history of Edinburgh's New Town is an enthralling subject. Remaining errors and imperfections are my own.

Mary Cosh
Islington, London
November 2002

INTRODUCTION

To many people Edinburgh is incomparably Britain's most beautiful city, even beyond such likely competitors as York, Bath or Oxford. It is a *capital* city, a working city, a stone city; a city built on hills and set in a staggering landscape. Its approach from the south-east is still alluring today, a second Athens with its Acropolis, even in spite of its now despoiled prospects. Old and New Towns still make their arresting contrast, however swallowed up in large conurbations.

How much greater was the effect two hundred years ago, when the proto-New Town first faced the Old from its long, windswept ridge – and how dramatically the vista of castle, rock and High Street struck the visitor of, say, Wordsworth's day. Stranger after stranger records admiration, and even the most prosaic are moved to near-poetry.

The sixty or so years between Edinburgh's first vestigial new northern suburb and the death of Sir Walter Scott in 1832 comprise a memorable period of such splendour that it is surprising that they have not yet received a full-length study of the city's life, experience and ideas. Architecture has received its due, poets and public men have their biographies. This book is the biography of the city – the new city between its inception in 1769 and the eventual irruption of the railway and industrial age, and the era of Reform, which changed it radically: the years of Modern Athens in full flower.

Important figures of the period include not only such obvious lions as Sir Walter Scott, Lord Cockburn, Henry Brougham, Thomas Carlyle and (especially) Francis Jeffrey of the *Edinburgh Review*, but less expected though equally celebrated figures like Sydney Smith and Thomas De Quincey, and leading English poets like Southey and Shelley, Coleridge and Wordsworth. There were distinguished ladies, their stockings tinged to whatever degree with blue – Mrs Grant of Laggan, the beautiful and accomplished Mrs Fletcher, Mrs Somerville the astronomer, and spinster authoresses like Susan Ferrier, society figures such as the famous Duchess of Gordon and Elizabeth Grant of Rothiemurchus. And there was an amazing infiltration from the New World, with young gentlemen of the Eastern states on their European travels or attending the celebrated University, and later, Washington Irving,

James Fenimore Cooper, other literary lights such as George Ticknor, distinguished visiting clergy, and notabilities from politics, philanthropy, medicine – from Benjamin Franklin and Benjamin Rush to others less well known.

There were pillars of the Church, leading academics, pioneers in medicine and surgery . . . the list seems endless.

In time the fine broad, straight streets of the New Town, rising in face of the Old, would generate an entirely new life-style. By degrees it was to make Edinburgh a place of pilgrimage for scholars, savants, poets, doctors and scientists from all over the world, on whom the renowned New Town made an indelible impression of splendour and dignity, learning and romance.

PART I

THE NEW TOWN'S INCEPTION, TO 1802

'When I was a boy nearly the whole vicinity of Edinburgh was open. Beyond the Causeway it was always almost Highland. Corstorphine Hill, Braid Hill, Craiglockhart Hill, the Pentland Hills, the seaside from Leith to Queensferry, the riverside from Penicuik to Roslin and Hawthornden to Lasswade, the valley of Habbie's How, and innumerable other places, now closed, and fast closing, were all free . . .'

Journal of Henry Cockburn, 1831–1854, 22 Jan. 1845; Edinburgh, 1874

'The New Town Is very Beautifull all new stone very fine with a handsome Square call'd St Andrews Cheifly inhabited by Nobility. there is a fine Square in the Old Town Called St Georges also inhabited by Nobility. The Churches are Numerous of the Scotts establishment, only two of the English which are finely Decorated with Paintings and each a good Organ, but most of the Scotts very Plain Building.'

Anon., *Journey to Scotland*, 1786, 23 Feb. 1786; NLS MS 10991

'An uninterrupted series of information and rational amusement. The society of men of Learning, to some of whom he had the happiness of being introduced, the chearful hospitality, and the elegant conviviality which he experienced among them, the Public Buildings, the noble views . . . the singular contrast between the Old and New Towns . . .'

James Bailey, *A Journey in Scotland*, July 1787; NLS MS 3294–5

'Nothing is wanting in Edinburgh but a fine climate to make it the place in which I should prefer, before any that I have seen, to pass my life, if I were obliged to pass it in any town. Nothing can surpass the beauty of the country around it, which is rich, highly cultivated, well-wooded, well-peopled, mid bounded in the different sides with the sea or with mountains.' (1793)

Memoirs of the Life of Sir Samuel Romilly written by himself . . . London, 1840, II.23

1
A DARING CONCEPT

'Look at those fields . . . You, Mr Somerville, are a young man, and may probably live, though I will not, to see all those fields covered with houses, forming a splendid and magnificent city . . . Nothing more is necessary than draining the North Loch, and providing a proper access from the old town.'

Provost Drummond to Henry Thomas Somerville, in Dr Thomas Somerville, *My Own Life and Times, 1741–1814*; Edinburgh, 1861, 47–48

'Mark my words, not one of you will live to see this square finished.'

David Hume on St Andrew Square; quoted by the Rev. John Sinclair, *Memorials of the Life and Works of the late Rt Hon. Sir John Sinclair Bart*, Edinburgh, 1837, I.189

'A city that possesses a boldness and grandeur of situation beyond any thing I had ever seen . . . The view of the houses at a distance strikes the traveller with wonder; their own loftiness, improved by their almost aerial situation, gives them a look of magnificence not to be found in any other part of Great Britain.'

Thomas Pennant, *A Tour in Scotland, MDCCLXIX*; Warrington, 1774, 49

A party of intrepid young Englishmen, venturing on a foreign tour to Scotland in 1705, when the last Scottish Parliament was debating the Treaty of Union with England, was so awed by the prospect of entering this savage dominion that, on reaching the border in Northumberland, they dismounted from their horses, solemnly embraced one another, and mutually wished themselves good fortune in their desperate expedition.[1]

The small capital city these youths visited was confined to the top of a narrow ridge of rock, sloping downwards from its castle's high peak on the west, past the Kirk of St Giles and the Tolbooth, to the Canongate, a separate burgh with its own Kirk and Tolbooth. At the eastern limit was the old Palace of Holyroodhouse. The extent from end to end was one mile. From the central High Street, centipede legs bestrode the hill in the form of wynds and closes, few broad enough to accommodate even a horse, let alone cart or carriage. On the north, below the sheer rock, a stagnant loch defended the town, on the south a wall and town gates. So constricted was the area that its inhabitants had had to build high, in tenements or lands whose narrow, winding common stairs climbed ten or a dozen storeys – or even more – with seven or eight families to a stair: 'perpendicular streets', Benjamin Franklin called them. The families on a single stair were often unknown to one another, and living was neither convenient nor clean.

For half a century following the young Englishmen's visit at the time of the loss of its Parliament, Edinburgh stagnated, no longer a city with a Government, and outwardly changing very little. Yet even as early as 1725 one notable citizen had expansive ideas. George Drummond, a merchant who, personally far from appealing, was nevertheless to serve six times as Lord Provost, had a breadth of civic vision far beyond most contemporaries. For a generation he contemplated the idea of a fine new suburb beyond the brackish Nor' Loch, on the bleak slopes of Bearford's or Barefoot's Parks, but not until 1752 did he achieve adoption even of debatable proposals. Drummond's visionary extension would in time lead to the creation for Edinburgh of what even he scarcely dreamed of, a whole new town.

A simple grid of parallel streets was the sum of modest beginnings proposed. To achieve even this small suburb, the city must accept the principle of extending its 'Royalty', or area held of the Crown by royal charter, and before this was secured by Act of Parliament opposition must be overcome, after which the first step towards extension could take physical shape by bridging the Nor' Loch gulf.

Many years later the theologian Dr Thomas Somerville recalled in old age how, as a young man, he was looking one day from a top window in the house of Provost Drummond's son-in-law, the Rev. John Jardine, across the loch towards the windswept hillside and so-called 'parks', then well-nigh uninhabited; and Drummond spoke to him of his belief that in Somerville's lifetime – though not in his own – the loch would be drained and access created to those naked slopes. Then, he said, the world might see 'all those fields covered with houses, forming a splendid and magnificent city'.[2] Drummond almost certainly did not foresee how that ideal city would slowly but inexorably change the whole character of the town he knew. The bridge, begun in the 1760s, and the suburb it heralded, eventually shifted Edinburgh's focus of business and, more particularly, society; although even then the city's main functions, the law and the college, remained in their old surroundings.

Progress was long hampered by Scotland's state of near-bankruptcy at the time of the Union with England. Partly from dissatisfaction at the downgrading of both country and capital, and disappointment over the expected improvement in trade, Jacobitism ebbed and flowed; but after

Prince Charles's resounding defeat at Culloden, and the subsequent settlement, both population and trade increased. Edinburgh felt the pressure, and plainly now had to expand.

Before 1770 expansion northwards, given the deep gulf of the brackish and smelly swamp, seemed an impossibility, and north of the loch was only St Ninian's Row, a poor quarter at the foot of the west side of Calton Hill, inhabited by 'the lowest class of artificers', chiefly shoemakers.[3] The only direction for growth was south, where there was space below the central ridge, and the only existing houses were in the short Bristo Street and narrow Potterrow. On the west was Portsburgh, an equally mean street of poor houses and dirty alleys, with one fine survival, Wrights Houses, said to have been built by King James IV for his mistress, by now demolished and its name adopted by a neighbouring tenement.

Although the old city had lost little of its medieval appearance – the Flodden Wall of 1513 was still standing in Walter Scott's day – throughout the eighteenth century several old features disappeared. In 1744 a small wicket was opened in the city wall, not far from the West Port, allowing easier acces,[4] and although the city was walled from the castle to Holyrood, many were already living outside, not only in the old burgh of Canongate, incorporated into Edinburgh in 1636, but round the Portsburgh area outside West Port, along the Glasgow road and in Dalry.

Natural pressure, then, was towards the area outwith the Flodden Wall boundary, east of Potterrow. Beyond this Lady Nicolson built some of Edinburgh's first single detached houses, on land inherited by her late husband which had become popular among the college youths for football games. This new street commanded fine vistas towards the Forth and Salisbury Crags, and at its northern end the lady erected a 25-foot Corinthian obelisk, inscribed in Latin and English to her husband's memory. So Nicolson Street was born; though in time the memorial column was unfortunately removed to make way for new houses.[5]

More fashionably, Edinburgh began to build new squares after the English manner. In order of creation they were, within the city walls, Alison's and Argyle Squares in the 1730s and Brown's Square in the 1760s, and well beyond the walls was the largest, 27-acre George or George's Square, begun by James Brown in 1766. While its substantial east and west sides were of uniform height with fairly regular fronts, their effect was demeaned by a relatively low, irregular north side, poorly finished in a chequering of blue whin limestone.[6] The south side was at first left open, and built up in the 1770s with grander houses. George Square, boasting a view of the Braid and Pentland Hills, soon became a sought-after address for leading men of law, and as town houses for lairds whose estates lay in that direction.[7]

In place of the simple spinal ridge, the mid-eighteenth-century city had become of roughly mushroom shape, the long narrow rectangle of the High Street and Cowgate at the north tapering away to a narrow stalk, the triangle to the south between Bristo Street and the Pleasance, where the terrain had dictated the western part as suitable for development. Nicolson Street formed the extension's central spine. Brown's and Argyle Squares extended west, just south of the Cowgate; the grander George Square, and the later Buccleuch Street to the south again, filled a large space adjoining the site of the drained Borough Loch. All this was going on as private development, just when the New Town was being officially projected to the north, and the City missed a profitable opportunity by not taking up the property when it was available for a relatively small sum.

One could regard the New Town as having its origins when southwards expansion began. James Boswell, writing in 1763 to his friend John Johnston, was disparaging about what was already happening to 'Edina's lofty towers'. 'What a grotesque heap of building! What a Smoak. See how the City stretches away to the Southeast while new houses are every day rising to increase it.'[8] But although Mrs Piozzi, visiting in 1789, referring to the new squares and streets south of the High Street, states categorically that Edinburgh was 'built, and all the Environs of it beautified into the state we find it, since the year 1745', the real expansion belongs to the period after the bridging of the valley allowed access to the bare fields to the north.[9]

Hope Park, another fashionable area, was a meadow named after Thomas Hope of Rankeillour, who had leased the land surrounding the South or Borough Loch, drained it in 1722 and built a house at the north-east end. He also laid out a tree-planted gravel walk of some mile-and-a-half circumference which became a popular Mall, the Meadows. Later, Lord Swinton, of Brown's Square, and others, raised a subscription to improve the walks, but in the process they felled some of Hope's best trees. Further, the ground was ill-drained, with smelly ditches, and in time the park was outrivalled by the New Town's amenities. Hope's house itself (observes Henry Mackenzie censoriously) was 'ornamented so much beyond the practice of that period' that it was admired 'rather more . . . than good taste would have warranted'. The owner, however, displayed a defensive legend: '*Spectator fastidiosus sibi molestus*'.[10]

In the 1760s the magistrates made a decision to bridge the Nor' Loch valley, in the teeth of land-owners, who foresaw the Royalty's extension and subsequent northern expansion as spelling ruin to their properties, and the extension was not ratified until 1767. Long before that, however, the necessary work was begun, the loch was drained and its mud dug out. In October 1763 George Drummond laid the bridge's foundation stone – nearly two years before even the all-important contract was ready. Its architect was William

Mylne, younger son of the mason Deacon Mylne and descendant of a long line of King's Master Masons. The bridge was to be completed by Martinmas 1769; a clerk's suggestion of appointing a supervisory overseer was rejected as an implied insult.

The bridge rose 95 feet above the vale and had three arches. In March 1766, when it was 'in great forwardness', plans for the intended northern suburb were invited by advertisement. The chosen site in Bearford's Parks was small enough, its low ridge a minor-key echo of the spine of the old city, and the proposals by a young architect, James Craig, generally accepted in July 1767 out of some half-dozen entries, were fairly basic.[11]

Given the site and Edinburgh's topography, there was no great scope for variation. As early as 1760 the Irish traveller Richard Pococke, Bishop of Meath, had recorded that 'the first hill . . . to the north is to be divided into three streets from East to West, and the houses to be only three stories high' – a complete contrast to the old city – remarking later that 'A street along the top of each of these hills with hanging gardens on each side, and a street at the east end of them extending to the west end of Leith would make it a most glorious City.'[12]

Craig's winning plan had the three broad parallel streets straddling the ridge, the outer two nearly a mile long, the main central street along the summit leading at either end to a large square, each dominated by a church. Cross-streets intersected the parallels, dividing the building plots into regular blocks. Only the central street of the three would be built on both sides: to the north would be an unbroken vista downhill to the Forth and across to the hills of Fife, while to the south, Craig proposed an ornamental canal in place of the former loch, with an uninterrupted view of the magnificent skyline of the existing town.

Minor changes were made both to Craig's plan and to the street names, but a set of loyal Hanoverian titles was agreed, with homage to the Union (Rose and Thistle) and to Scotland (St Andrew); and building of the suburb began at the east or new bridge end with part of St Andrew Square and the first houses of Princes Street, where many gentlemen took up feus and built privately.

The town's labour pangs were unexpectedly painful. In August 1769, when the new bridge was almost complete and already open to pedestrians, to universal dismay it suddenly collapsed, killing five people in the crash.

Blame inevitably fell on the architect, who was accused of skimping the work to cut costs, and who took to his bed with the shock. The bridge piers as built were in fact several feet lower than in the contract, but Mylne had miscalculated the height required to match the descent from the High Street, and in raising the piers to compensate he overloaded their weight. The foundations, not on virgin ground but on piled 'travelled earth', were unable to take the extra load, and part of the south abutment gave way. Disputes, expense and rebuilding deferred the bridge's opening until 1772.[13]

The fall of the bridge might have been regarded as a portent, especially by those believing in planetary influence. It was the year of the transit of Venus, visible in Edinburgh only for seconds at a time, and during early September people regularly gathered in open spaces or gazed from upper windows in hope of a sighting. In this Thomas Somerville appears to have been lucky, but not so Henry Mackenzie. The latter, allowed to sup with Dr James Hutton and distinguished astronomers, and to accompany them to the house of yet another, Dr Bryce, minister of Kirknewton, was expecting to view the phenomenon through an instrument made by Dr Lind. Although he stayed up all night watching from Dr Hutton's bedroom, young Henry reporting every few minutes to the geologist, who was in bed, the morning proved too dark and cloudy, and none of the party saw anything at all.[14]

There was vexed argument over treatment of the south side of Princes Street. Feuars who had built 'genteel houses' here conformed to a regular style, only to find that their expected view of the Old Town was already spoiled. A coach-builder named John Home had acquired from the Council the land south-east of the new street to a depth of 500 feet (the site of the Balmoral Hotel), and was raising a row of 'mean and irregular buildings, and work-houses for tradesmen', running steeply down to the loch bed at right angles to Princes Street. Worse, with similar purpose Home combined in 1770 with the upholsterers Young and Trotter to secure more land to the west. At this point the gentlemen feuars objected strongly, and several of them, including Sir William Forbes, and David Hume, who now had a house in North St David Street, brought a Bill before the Court of Session to arrest further building (October 1771).[15]

Although when feuing the ground the Council had forbidden building so much as a chimney above the level of Princes Street, it now invoked an Act of 1767 which implied that houses *might* be built opposite the feuars' houses, at a minimum distance of 96 feet. The feuars claimed ignorance of this Act, but the Court found for the Council. However, in 1772 the House of Lords reversed the decision, and Lord Mansfield forcefully criticised the Corporation as 'misguided'. Still the case went back and forth, while Home's houses – wrights' shops, warehouses, a coach-yard – continued to rise. Not until 1776 was the final decreet arbitral pronounced, allowing completion of any houses then building, but ordaining that, apart from some workshops west of the present-day Waverley Steps, the south side of Princes Street must remain open as far as the site of Hanover Street, 'preserved in perpetuity as a pleasure ground'. So the shape at least of Princes Street survives to this day – but in the hollow west of the bridge, for many years, the steep, unsightly little St Anne's Street remained.[16]

The New Town's earliest feuar was not, it so happened, any of the Princes Street gentry but a wright named John Young, who already in 1767 had taken up three lots and by 1779 built most of Thistle Street (now Young Street) with small semi-detached villas in open ground. The little street had work-shades adjoining, and some fourteen years later this too was to prove a great embarrassment to the Town Council. But when Young started building the New Town was still barely even a plan.[17]

Another far-sighted individual who had quickly seized the chance of a fine site was Sir Laurence Dundas, self-made son of a bankrupt baillie, who had made a fortune as Commissary-General to the army in Flanders. Even before Craig's plan appeared in 1767, Dundas bought land outside the then Royalty, and then for £450 secured from the surprisingly unsuspicious City a further feu, expressed vaguely as 'an Area in the East Square'. It was in fact where Craig had planned to place his vista-closing church. Consequently the new St Andrew Square terminated unintentionally in a grand free-standing mansion, and the church had to be fitted in later as a mere adjunct to the George Street frontage.

Dundas's house, however, designed by William Chambers, contributed handsomely to the new townscape, elegantly Palladian, three-storeyed with central pediment and four Corinthian pilasters. It occupied only part of the feu, the rest remaining open as garden.[18]

Sir Laurence was among seventeen others who took up feus in the same year; next year there were eleven.[19] Most opted for the fashionable spaciousness of St Andrew Square, in the manner of most new building on the south side of the city. The common method was for masons and wrights to take up the feus, build houses and sell them to clients. In this way William Jameson, a mason, had bought two of the Square lots in 1767, and in 1770 an adjacent lot in St David's Street, built houses and sold them respectively to a Mr Hunter, Patrick Crawford of Auchinames, and Dr David Hume.[20]

Hume had formerly lived in James Court, one of Edinburgh's early small 'squares' off the Lawnmarket, with 'mean' houses 'occupied by persons of inferior rank', except for its north side, which consisted of a single large building entered from the Lawnmarket, four storeys and garrets, increasing by three more below on its north front where the cliff fell away. It was divided into two, each side containing two flats occupied by fashionable families, and on the north side commanded an extensive view over Princes Street and the new buildings. (Here Boswell lived and was to entertain Johnson.)

In September 1771 Hume was just returned to his new home from an inaugural visit to Inveraray Castle, where the new 5th Duke of Argyll and his beautiful Duchess had entertained their first large and light-hearted house-party. The weather was phenomenally bad, with hurricanes and gales. A month or so later Benjamin Franklin, of Philadelphia, on his first visit to Britain since an extended stay in the 1750s, arrived in Edinburgh late one evening from Ireland, 'thro' storms and Floods'. He found his old lodgings in Milne Square altered, their east end demolished for the building of the new bridge, and had to put up in 'miserable' lodgings at an inn, probably in the Grassmarket.[21] As soon as Hume, 'that excellent Christian', heard of his plight he invited Franklin to stay at his new house, and Franklin accordingly changed quarters, crossed the new bridge over the drained Nor' Loch, and had his first sight of houses of the New Town, as reported by Hume, 'in a short Interval between two Hurricanes'. Because of the continued bad weather, he stayed longer than the intended fortnight, 'most happily', visiting Lord Kames at Blair Drummond, the Carron Works and other sights, and returning once more to 'the hospitable Roof of the good Samaritan'.[22] Franklin may well have been Hume's first guest under his new roof, managed by his martinet old cook Peggy Irving, whom he had brought from James Court and had trained to make certain dishes for which his table was renowned. Since he and she could make famous soups, his hope that the new house might become both a culinary and an intellectual centre was well launched by the arrival of Dr Franklin. Hume, indolent rather than fiery despite what his writings might suggest, was mild and moderate in temperament, a typical Tory/Jacobite anti-enthusiast, opposed to the attitudes of Fanatics and Cromwellians. A convivial and lively host, he enjoyed entertaining and liked whist, as a thinker's game based on observation.[23]

Certainly at Hume's table Franklin met many of the academic, medical and theological celebrities, though hardly a hint survives of the memorable conversations in which they must have indulged. He noted, incidentally, that Hume's house was very like his own in Philadelphia.

When Franklin finally left by post-chaise for Preston on the way to London, floods again hindered him, and the Carlisle road was blocked. His friend Marchant, following the same road later, called it 'The greatest flood in the memory of man, scarcely a bridge in this part of England [all stone-built though they were] but were in part or whole destroyed'.[24]

Hume's house in what is now called St David Street, though left unnamed when first built, was an address he used in a letter to Baron Mure in 1775. The name was reputed to be the result of a joke played on him by Nancy Ord, daughter of the Chief Baron of the Exchequer, whom Hume, although he remained a lifelong bachelor, at one time fancied he might have married had she not considered him too old. One evening Miss Nancy chalked the name 'St David Street' on his gable, and Hume consoled his indignant servant, who thought it an affront as well as vandalism, with a tolerant 'Never mind, lassie, many a better man has been made a saint without knowing it.' St David's Street it remained.[25]

At the eastern end of the New Town site was the austere St James' Square, also laid out if not designed by Craig, and built between 1775 and 1790 on ground belonging to Walter Ferguson, a lawyer. It was glowingly advertised as convenient of access and healthy in position with extensive views, near to all public buildings and markets and, being outwith even the extended Royalty, free of city taxes. Only the architecture was not so good. More regular than St Andrew Square, its gaunt four storeys were also considerably more stark, and its history was not to be particularly distinguished – apart from Robert Burns living there briefly in 1787,[26] and later, the painters Nasmyth and Andrew Geddes. Rocks and steep hills introduce odd features into cities which grow up round them, and despite the careful grid plan of Edinburgh's successive phases of building, its layout became unavoidably eccentric. St James' Square was the earliest of several developments spliced on to the plan at peculiar angles, springing out north-east along the road to Leith, behind the new Register House. Above it to the east, on the craggy face of Calton Hill, in 1776 an observatory was begun to Craig's design, and (supposedly at Robert Adam's suggestion) resembling a low, mildly castellated fortification.

A threat to New Town building progress was competition from a successful rival in a different area, James Brown's fashionable George Square. The magistrates, having earlier improvidently let this slip through their fingers, were now mean enough to offer to buy back the ground from Brown at a derisory price. The square had attracted leaders of society as residents, notably the lively Duchess of Gordon and the Countess of Sutherland, the politician-paramount Henry Dundas, and the notorious judge Lord Braxfield. Almost next door to the last lived a less celebrated lawyer, Mr Walter Scott, father of a young family of whom one was his namesake. For years George Square remained Edinburgh's most élite address, many people finding its comparatively sheltered site and spacious layout more attractive than a house on the windswept hillside of the New Town, approached only by the crazy – perhaps still insecure – bridge. Brown had also enhanced the area by creating walks in the nearby Meadows, had built Charles and Crichton Streets, and secured a further large plot on which he built the broad Buccleuch Place.[27]

To date the New Town was making little enough impact. In July 1769 Edinburgh had had a visit from Thomas Pennant, doyen of gentlemen travellers, whose writings long formed the bible – indeed quarry – of his successors. He arrived very shortly before the collapse of Mylne's new bridge, the beauty of whose triple arches Pennant admired. A single paragraph, however, was enough for him to describe 'the new town, which is planned with great judgment, and will prove a magnificent addition to Edinburgh'. House prices in St Andrew Square, he noted, ranged upwards from a minimum of £1800 to £2000, a couple being valued as high as £4000 or £5000, 'all built in the modern style . . . free from the inconveniencies attending the old city'. Pennant's was perhaps the first outsider's account of new Edinburgh, bald predecessor of scores of glowing descriptions that poured out as the town took shape.[28]

Contemporary with the bridge and New Town, yet part of neither new nor old, was the birth of Edinburgh's first custom-built theatre. The City's love-hate relationship with the stage stemmed from early clerical antagonism, and the first eighteenth-century attempts to establish a theatre were soundly trounced. Even in 1756 staging of the nobly patriotic play *Douglas* led to virtual excommunication from the Kirk of its young clergyman author John Home, and certainly to his having to resign his living. Struggling against the stigma of moral turpitude and illegality, a theatre had managed to maintain itself in one hovel-like hall after another, off the High Street in Carrubers Close, the Cowgate, the Canongate, bedevilled by quarrels among the companies as well as by the thunderings of the clergy. When the law was invoked against them, various methods of evasion were evolved, such as the device used by most unlicensed theatres of calling each performance 'a concert of music'. But on the passing of the Act which extended the Royalty, a clause was included which enabled a licensed theatre to be built, and the censorious clergy were silenced.

When play-acting was thus legalised the proprietors disposed of the patent to David Ross, formerly of Covent Garden and then manager at the Canongate. Nothing was to be straightforward however. For one thing, the new patentee had to take over all existing debts. Ross paid up, fixed the new site, and raised a subscription to pay for the building, a total of £5000 including costumes and scenery.[29]

Matters were not helped by the collapse of the bridge, which would be the new theatre's main approach from the town, three days before its planned opening in November 1769. Direct access was thus impossible for some weeks. The first audiences had to approach through Leith Wynd and other alleys: with scarcely any houses yet existing on the New Town site the surroundings were not inviting.

Ross's chosen site was a field in the valley belonging to the Orphan Hospital where George Whitfield the evangelist had preached during his missionary visit in 1744.[30] The theatre was built appropriately facing the non-existent New Town and almost below the bridge. It finally opened on 9 December 1769, with *The Conscious Lovers*, followed two days later by *The Beaux' Stratagem*. The plain rectangular building, sometimes compared with the one at Bristol, received little but abuse. 'Simple and commodious' were among the few words of praise, and for some time lack of funds prevented much decoration of the interior either. The auditorium, lit by wax candles, had a *parterre* in the French style, intended for gentlemen not in full dress, with a discreet partition for ladies should the house be crowded. In the early years pit and boxes cost three shillings, later raised to five; the galleries two shillings and a shilling. A full house was variously quoted at £130 and £140, and they played on three or four nights a week.

Although the scenery was well painted, poor stage machinery limited the repertoire, and Ross could not afford good actors. Well into the next century bitter complaints were made of the companies' inferior quality. This and Ross's own indolence were responsible for two unsuccessful first seasons, and Ross then leased the theatre for three years at £500 a year to Samuel Foote. Foote was Edinburgh's first notable actor, known as 'the English Aristophanes', and Garrick's chief rival.

So far, entrance to the New Town was not very dignified. Until 1778 the east end of Princes Street was a makeshift muddle, a 'grim little enclosure', in form roughly square, with the theatre standing isolated on its north side, its back abutting on the Orphan Hospital's enclosing wall.[31] The rest was a hotch-potch of taverns, oyster-houses, and lodgings.

But Princes Street itself was progressing well, and St Andrew Square and the connecting streets were nearly finished. The fine stone brought from Craigleith quarry, west of the town, was well suited for both building and paving and earned praise from the discerning. In addition to an excellent view and efficient sewerage, the gentle southern slope provided an ample water supply from a new reservoir on the Castle Hill. Stylistically, however, the new houses were undistinguished. A clause in the 1768 Building Act had admitted that 'people's taste in building is so different' that fixed rules for the frontages were impossible, and each feuar might build as high or wide as he pleased. The early houses, therefore, were inclined to be irregular and roughly finished.[32]

One contrast probably not anticipated between old and new was that, whereas the tall, closely-built city was partly sheltered from the violent local winds, on the bleak new site gales raged unchecked. The new houses, exposed on all sides, were assailed by whirling dust eddies, sometimes so strong that one could barely stir out of doors. Sedan chairs were overturned, and the combined efforts of three or four men might be needed to force a front door shut. The new bridge added to the hazards, as violent air currents, generated by the sea and surrounding hills, roared across the long valley to buffet passengers trapped on the draughty balustraded bridge, open at both ends, as if by a pair of bellows. The English visitor Edward Topham was greatly entertained one wild spring day, claiming to have 'had the pleasure of adjusting a lady's petticoats which had blown almost entirely over her head', while a passing gentleman, transfixed by the sight, was rewarded by losing hat and wig in the next gust.[33]

The Edinburgh historian and advocate Hugh Arnot comments on the 'no uncommon circumstances of houses blown down, large trees torn up by the roots, people carried off their feet, and beat down upon the pavement'. Indeed, one January day in 1778 the whole Leith guard – a sergeant and twelve men of the 10th Regiment – were blown off Castle Hill, and some of them badly hurt.[34]

The streets long continued vulnerable to gale-like winds – today fairly confined to the Waverley Steps – with few protections from walls or balustrades. Much later, about 1832, the newly appointed Professor of Clinical Medicine Robert Christison, one very stormy Sunday, was on his way to the Infirmary for noontide duty, when the streets were, advisedly, empty. He was completely bowled along by a sudden gust, and a friend who saw him from the opposite side of the street told him afterwards that at every step he was blown about three feet above the level of the 'stones' supporting the lamp-posts. Flying faster and faster, on the point of being dashed to the ground he was able to reach for a lamp-post, was thrown down and rolled in the gutter, badly hurting his knee. When he got his breath back he was amazed to see how far he had left his friend behind. At last someone watching from a window was able to struggle out and rescue him, and he was laid up with his injury for some weeks.[35]

Open streets, and 'houses to themselves', were indeed an almost indecent innovation for citizens accustomed all their lives to the cosiness of dark upper-storey apartments in cramped tenements. In 1775 Topham claimed that 'one old lady fancies she should be lost . . .; another, that she should be blown away in going over the new Bridge'.[36]

But the New Town was now becoming an entity: first the theatre, now the founding of a public building. This was the Record Office, Robert Adam's Register House at the eastern end of Princes Street. Creation of the office might be thought to have some priority, Scottish records having been kept for decades in the laigh rooms of the Inner Sessions House, gnawed by rats, mice and beetles, and their rehousing had been under discussion off and on for nearly half a century. Some were said to have been brought from England at the time of the Union, and lain unexamined ever since for want of storage space. In 1765, when it was plain that no local funds would be available for a suitable building, the Lords of Session and Barons of the Exchequer secured a Treasury grant of £17,000 from the sale of the forfeited Jacobite estates.

The first site proposed, inevitably on Edinburgh's south side, was the grounds of Heriot's Hospital, but the magistrates discarded this for its inconvenient distance, and they let the matter rest for several years. Creation of the bridge brought a different area into view, and Craig had incorporated into his plan a site on the eastern boundary, facing the bridge and entry to the old town. Part of the ground was presented free by its owners, the City; the rest was purchased.

Robert Adam's design was voted excellent, its cost estimated at £25,000; Mr James Salisbury was appointed mason and overseer, and at a slightly shabby ceremony on 27 June 1774 the Lord Register, Lord Frederick Campbell, laid the foundation stone.[37] James Boswell, who was present, was scornful at the lack of spectacle. Although a crowd of well-dressed spectators turned out besides the usual 'mob', there was 'no procession, no show or solemnity of any kind upon such an occasion' and the judges and even the Lord Provost were invited in a private capacity, appearing not in their robes but in ordinary dress, some even in unpretentious bob-wigs.[38]

Perhaps it was better so. For lack of funds, fourteen years were to pass before enough of the building could be completed for even part-occupation, and the remainder was hardly finished before 1800.

In 1776 a more modest public addition was begun near the south-east end of George Street: the Physicians' Hall, designed by Craig. Its porticoed frontage was correctly Palladian, though the Royal College complained of internal inadequacies, while Craig in turn complained of their failure to pay the extra costs incurred by rising wages and additional fittings.[39] The Hall had a short life, existing only until the 1840s, and no actual building designed by Craig now survives in Edinburgh.

There was perhaps more building activity on Edinburgh's south side, where in 1775 an abortive attempt was made to improve access. Wishing to rival the magistrates' new bridge, the gentlemen developers secured an Act of Parliament for another, to connect the High Street and Nicolson Street, without further extending the Royalty. The object was to attract builders and profits at the expense of the northern extension, which was paying interest on the debt. The bridge's estimated cost, £8600, might be recouped through a toll, but the county lairds overreached themselves by trying to make this a general toll on all city streets, to the tune of £3000 a year. Strong objections from both trade incorporations and the public forced them to drop the scheme, and it was not resolved for nearly a decade.[40]

The New Edinburgh was very much a suburb of the future. Although on paper it extended to the present West End and straddled the crest of the ridge both south and north, well into the 1770s it was a mere scattering of the carcases of houses standing starkly in unfinished streets, marked out on the despoiled hillside. The western part of the axial streets was slow to be built up, and Charlotte Square remained unfinished for many years, a mere concept of an unrealised square at the western end of George Street. As late as 1796 when John Peter Grant of Rothiemurchus, as a very young husband, acquired number 5 on the north side, the only other houses standing were those of his immediate neighbours, 'Agricultural Sir John's' son Sir George Sinclair, and the Redfearn family.[41]

In spite of Hume's prediction that St Andrew Square would never be finished, in 1778 the square and adjoining streets were nearly complete and the rest laid out, to this extent fulfilling Craig's plan. Robert Adam therefore produced a plan for a westward extension, to be realised by building Charlotte Square, Edinburgh's handsomest square – the more so had Adam's St George's Church, designed as part of the square, been executed to his proposals.[42]

But although St Andrew Square was habitable and a source of pride, otherwise the New Town was a building site and rubbish dump. Fitful glimpses illuminate it from incongruous sources. It was an open invitation for such as James Boswell, whose house was in James' Court, to live down to his deplorable instincts. Despite subsequent moral anguish he could seldom resist moments of dubious 'pleasure' by slipping into its darker corners with Old Town whores. Late in 1776 he admits to a mad fling with 'a young slender slut with a red cloak' in what he still refers to as Barefoots Parks, and scarcely a week later he is skulking with Peggy Grant, 'a plump hussy', 'in a mason's shade in St Andrew's Square'. On sobering up, Boswell remorsefully confesses the lapse to his long-suffering wife; yet a couple of months later, several dinners out and too much drink again inflame him to lug 'a big fat whore' to the same dark corner and lie on 'a stone hewing in a mason's shade just by Dr Hume's House'.[43] Boswell does not clarify for posterity whether his unworthy bed was on an unbuilt stance or in the central enclosure. (And what might David Hume have said?)

At this time inhabitants of Princes Street could look west of the castle towards open country, while Queen Street was an Esplanade, a favourite airy promenade on summer evenings, overlooking the unenclosed land of a thatched farmhouse, downhill towards Stockbridge. Here Willy Wood, who farmed for his old father, shot pigeons and rooks over the fields planted with oats, where Heriot Row now runs.[44]

At the foot of the hill were the small, closely packed cottages of the mean hamlets of Stockbridge and Canonmills, and Silvermills, remnant of a short-lived venture to refine silver found in Linlithgowshire, once backed by King James IV. (Finding it unprofitable, the King withdrew.) A lane known as Gabriel's Road[45] had long wound uphill to connect the hamlets with the old city, behind the future West Cumberland Street, past the end of Queen Street gardens – to this day irregular for that reason – and at last diagonally behind Register House, where the new road lines similarly became fixed at an angle. In the 1770s, when the New Town began building, a few people were living along the lane: a merchant, a minister, a plasterer, their homes gradually drawn into the developing area.

2

THE OLD TOWN AND HIGH STREET LIVING

'Remember that this is the city of ancient Scottish royalty; that there is not a close or alley in the Old Town, and hardly a street in the New, that has not memories of the great and quaint attached to it.'

Daniel Masson, *Edinburgh Sketches and Memories*, London/Edr, 1892, 163

'[Houses] built, as it were, one upon another . . . each Story being a compleat House, consisting of Parlour Kitchen Lodging Rooms &c and containing separate Families'.

John Pease, 'Journal of a Traveller', 1795, in *Scottish History Review*, 1957

The chequer'd chairs, in seemly circle placed,
The Indian tea, with Indian china graced;
The red-stone Tea-pot with its silver spout;
The Tea Spoons numbered, and the tea *fill'd out* . . .
Hapless the wight, who, with a lavish sup,
Empties too soon the Lilliputian cup!
Tho' patience fails, and tho' with thirst he burns,
All, all must wait till the last cup returns.

Simon Gray [Sir Alexander Boswell], *Edinburgh or The Ancient Royalty*, Edinburgh, 1810

For a long time the theatre was the New Town's sole functioning public building. It was many years before the shift to the large and spacious new houses made any significant impact on social habits, and meanwhile Edinburgh's town life continued in its old mode.

In the 1760s that style, though socially lively, was relatively simple. In the restricted area of tenement flats and small wainscoted rooms, large dinner-parties were difficult to accommodate, and Edinburgh's customary entertainments were ladies' tea-parties and informal suppers. In the fashionable Lawnmarket, where the street widened out above St Giles' and Parliament House, ladies would walk to social gatherings, rarely more than a couple of hundred yards from their own apartment. Many of course took a chair, borne by a pair of muscular Highlanders – transport that had its hazards. Addresses were easily confused where houses abutted on a different wynd at front and back, as in Niddry's and Merlyn's Wynd south of the High Street.

One day a lady was deposited by the chairmen at the wrong door, in the wrong wynd, and was shown up to the wrong drawing-room. Retreating with an apology, she boarded her chair again and ordered the bearers to the other wynd. But somehow they ended up at the back door of the same house, and she a second time in the wrong drawing-room.[1]

The famous Jane, Duchess of Gordon, as a girl lived with her mother, Lady Maxwell of Monreith, and sister, in Foulis Close, a dark passage. It was a household not uncommon among distinguished families in old Edinburgh. 'You passed the kitchen door going to the parlour', notes Charles Kirkpatrick Sharpe, and 'there were generally in said passage the fineries of her beautiful daughters, hung on a screen after washing.' The sister (later Lady Wallace) 'used to be sent to the Fountain Well with the tea-kettle, for water for tea'.[2]

Furnishings in these houses were not rich. Carpets even in leading households were found only in their best rooms; clocks were limited to the larger houses, and apart from the occasional tea-table, mahogany was little known. Rooms were panelled in natural oak, in larger mansions hung with tapestry or cheaper materials depicting scripture scenes, hunting or sports. In the cramped space the best bed had often to be set up in the drawing-room, and lesser bedrooms might have no space for grates: such as there were, of polished brass, were removable. Box beds were in general use, whose sliding sides kept out the air, and it was usual even for strangers to double up in the same bedroom.

At table, even the clergy used wooden platters such as were common on farms, and the gentry used pewter, their delft and china reserved for a second course, in those houses where (says Somerville) they could 'afford pretentious 3 o'clock dinners'. The usual dinner hour was 12 or 1, and no later than 3 o'clock in fashionable households. In the kitchen the joint would be cooked on a spit-roast turned not by a roasting-jack but by a sweating servant, sometimes by a dog – the wretched animal being bundled into the box that held the large wooden wheel, if he was so unlucky as not to have spotted the preparations in time to run off and hide.[3]

Greater show was reserved for one's dress. Gentlemen's full dress was elaborate even to ostentation, resplendent with gold and silver lace, wigs, and laced cocked hats – velvet caps for indoors – and the sword indispensable at all times. Ladies wore their silk gowns for receiving company, fringed riding habits with gilt buttons for taking exercise, and for church a loose silk plaid. They still patched their faces, though the fashion was passing. According to Topham Scottish ladies conformed to Parisian taste, and, unlike their men, were never ill-dressed; though Somerville claims that in *un*dress both sexes appeared 'coarse and slovenly', men in threadbare coats or dressing-gowns (called nightgowns), covering their cropped heads with a greasy nightcap – women with aprons over their worsted gowns. Older ladies would encase their heads in large linen caps tied under the chin. Clergymen's full dress was by preference blue, while informally they wore coats of coarse materials in different colours.[4]

The gentlemanly footman John Macdonald claimed to have first introduced the Frenchified fashion of the umbrella. This dandyish young man, who had worked with the nobility and gentry in various parts of Scotland, and later in Ireland and London, was often referred to as 'Frenchman' for his fastidious ways, and returning to London in 1778 after some years in India, the East, and Portugal, he appeared very smartly dressed. In the rain his 'fine silk umbrella' occasioned his being called after in the street: 'Frenchman! why do you not get a coach, Monsieur?' – to his sister's embarrassment, while he answered the vulgarians in French or Spanish. However, other foreigners were emboldened to follow his lead, and at last the English too. 'Wearing' the umbrella eventually moved to the Scottish capital.[5]

For the poor the roughest garments served. Stockings were almost unknown, and even in high-ranking households maidservants mostly went barefoot for their rough work early in the day. In larger houses, a master tailor and journeyman attended regularly for a day's make-and-mend, and as shoes seemed to wear out remarkably fast, shoemakers were among the most important tradesmen, living north of the Canongate in the unsavoury area below Calton Hill.

The authoress Mrs Mary Anne Hanway's English delicacy was shocked to see in the streets 'the lower class of women, that wear neither shoes nor stockings, nor can it fail to strike any female, with an air of poverty'. This was about 1775. That it was partly a matter of taste did not impress her, certainly not on hearing a young Highland girl say that, while she was now getting used to the hated shoes, she would never be reconciled to stays.[6]

Convivial meetings were frequent, with men drinking to excess, for example at the popular citizens' clubs where each man stood a round in turn. Because of the lack of public rooms, business meetings were generally held in taverns, and gentlemen seeking legal advice usually retired with their advocates to the dram-shops or coffee-houses round Parliament Square – so the first item in the lawyers' bill was likely to be the tavern account. Business done, drinking went on far into the night, while the end of a lawsuit would be celebrated by a tavern supper.[7]

Since the Union with England, politicians of both Lords and Commons had spent most of the year in London, returning only in the summer to their Scottish estates or Edinburgh houses – and even town-dwellers usually deserted it for a country retreat. Edinburgh's great function as a city after losing its Parliament was as home of the law and the university. The courts centring on old Parliament House rose in July, and by mid-August everyone with any pretension to gentility was off to the country house or villa, often only a few miles away. Shopkeepers' business slowed to a trickle and the streets were almost empty.

Besides her numerous clergy and the university professors, whose most distinguished members were of the medical and surgical faculties, Edinburgh's leading citizens were judges of the Court of Session, advocates, and lower down the hierarchy writers to the signet. Most young men of family were trained in the law, for which many more were qualified than ever chose to practise. Members of the courts, wigged and gowned, cut a far more distinctive figure in the area round the courts than did the ill-paid professors or even the college students, who had never worn academic dress since its foundation in 1580. Hence students blended with the populace far more easily than those of Oxford or Cambridge, with consequently less tension between 'town and gown'. Nor did these youths live in halls of residence, but had to fend for themselves in often spartan lodgings; Edinburgh was full of the sons of poor families in distant parts of Scotland who had scraped to send them to be educated. And by the late eighteenth century the College, particularly its medical faculty, had achieved such high international repute that students came, not only from all over Europe, but from America as well.[8]

Edinburgh's poor were poor indeed, in times of scarcity finding little help from charities: as late as 1783 any form of public relief met with opposition. The rich regularly gave to the poor, feeding them in their kitchens, scattering coins as they left an inn, and responding to personal appeals, but it was an era of individual gestures, not public charity.[9]

By contrast the family bond was remarkably close, extending even to distant relatives, known impartially, however remote, as Uncle, Aunt or Cousin; and hospitality, though simple, was bountiful to callers. No notice was required and vagrants were regularly admitted to houses for alms of bread and meal, or a supper of porridge.

Edinburgh, with its grid of narrow lanes, noisy, dirty and crowded, was a confusing place for the stranger. To his rescue came the 'caddies', a hardy race of porter-messenger usually recruited from Highlanders, whose activities extended to every field. Their street knowledge made them a repository of unlimited information, and did one want (says the young English writer Topham) 'a *valet de place,* a pimp, a thief-catcher, or a bully', the caddy would find one. Thanks to them, it was claimed, Edinburgh had fewer burglaries and street robberies than other comparable cities – certainly a stolen watch or purse might be returned by means of a judiciously-passed reward.[10]

A service greatly lacking well into the time of the New Town was the food shop. For daily supplies old Edinburgh was wedded to street markets. Flesh, fruit and vegetables were sold near the Tron, cattle at the King's Stables end of the Grassmarket, fish at Fishmarket Close – a steep, stinking wynd from whose top end grubby boys and women dragged the supplies thrown from delivery carts, and, for lack of a water supply, sold them unwashed from 'old, rickety, scaly wooden tables, exposed to all the rain, dust and filth'. The fruit tables were little better, while vegetables were merely stacked on the ground to be sold by 'a college of old gin-drinking women'. Cockburn recalls 'not half-a-dozen' shops of any kind west of St Andrew Street, even in 1810, probably not a single fruiterer's before 1815, nor a fishmonger's before 1822. The great change from market sales to full-blown, modern-style food shops began only in the 1820s.[11]

Another notorious feature of Edinburgh's daily life, not repeated in the spacious New Town, and by the nineteenth century phased out of the old, was the nightly street baptism of the unwary by the day's soilage. Any town with space for a backyard would also have space for a necessary house privy – not of course a water closet – but constricted Edinburgh was denied this basic amenity. Waste of all kinds was, therefore, by logical process disposed of at a certain hour from the windows to the street below, with the elegant warning of '*Gardez l'eau*', long Scotticised to '*Gardy loo!*'. Being dowsed from above, as strangers or the forgetful often were, was called (as noted by the American Benjamin Rush) 'being *naturalised*'. 'As yet', he added, 'I have escaped being made a freeman in this way.' His friend Jonathan Potts, who had come over with him from Philadelphia, 'gained the honor' first.[12] Topham claimed in 1774 that the custom was 'now outlawed', but even if the prohibition was observed in the High Street it did not apply in the narrow wynds. 'Many an elegant suit of clothes has been spoiled; many a powdered well-dressed macaroni sent home for the evening.'[13]

Even worse, perhaps, than the danger of dowsing was the failure to cleanse the filth for days on end. Visiting in 1775, Mrs Mary Anne Hanway complained bitterly of streets filthy from the frequent rains, which made Edinburgh 'a truly disagreeable place to live in'. Whereas the New Town was being built with individual houses 'after the English model', she plainly disapproved of the old, with its towering ten- and even fourteen-storey tenements, dark and gloomy from their height and closeness. 'Dirty, dismal, and irregular', Edinburgh had for Mrs Hanway 'a poverty, and a sort of northern misery in the very features of the commonality'. She preferred Glasgow, 'well built, with broad, well-paved streets, with a "*metropolitan*" dignity'.[14]

Others were more favourably impressed. Edward Topham, an observant, articulate 23-year-old, born in Yorkshire and educated at Eton and Trinity College, Cambridge, has left the earliest detailed account of this Edinburgh life. He settled there for no discernible reason in November 1774 and remained until at least the end of the following May. Easy and elegant in manner, companionable and outgoing in society, and with considerable literary talent, this young man of the world noted and recorded every aspect of the city's life, with and without approval, in a series of (possible apocryphal) letters, and though these are certainly the better for a Ciceronian polish, and inevitably contain inaccuracies – as Henry Mackenzie was quick to point out – they cover Edinburgh society from the quality of its housing to its entertainments, meals, manners and standards of education. [15]

Topham declared himself on the whole enchanted by Edinburgh customs. Their good manners, the ladies' pretty salute of a kiss, their courtesy in punctuating even impassioned argument with a polite phrase, 'My dear sir' – their engaging diminutives like 'doggy', 'manny', 'wifey' – even 'booky' or 'housey' – all charmed him. If only that Scottish accent (he thought) had not lent their statements such disagreeable pomposity!

The language used by these citizens varied considerably, from a now-vanished 'pure classical Scots . . .very agreeable', as Mackenzie claimed, to the coarse, broad patois of the uneducated.[16] Scots who attended the English Parliament habitually strove to excise their more blatant Scotticisms, and Thomas Sheridan, father to the playwright, settled in the city in 1763 to give lessons in English diction. Even so, to modern ears their Scotticism would still be very pronounced. Boswell, ever snobbish about diction and provincialism, later expressed his annoyance at his own daughters' being 'at no pains to acquire the English pronunciation', and was disgusted when his old friend Temple came to London to seek promotion 'at having found his language and manners as Scotch and coarse as ever'. [16]

Many leading nobles and judges spoke a strong lowlands brogue. The more polished, however, considered their pure vowels and exact enunciation superior to that of the English themselves. [17]

Topham was impressed by the learning that gentlemen displayed, and their 'spirit' similar to the French – whose culture, traditionally, had been imbibed by the Scots far more than by the English. While outward manners might seem rough, Scots were 'temperate, careful, and parsimonious, proud', jovial in company if inclined to the bottle – deplored by Topham, a non-drinker, but explained as the combined effect of excellent wine imports and a cold climate. They were great readers, and even well down the social scale illiteracy was rare; but he complained of a lack of humour and inability to laugh at ridicule.

Women, though modest, appeared 'fond of admiration, and flattery, and pleasure'; agreeably free in manner – perhaps too free in hospitable inquisitiveness about strangers, and in revelation of their own circumstances. They were educated to develop inner resources, not in idle pursuits but in pastimes to exercise the mind. 'The young people paint, draw, are fond of music', and enjoy reading and mental accomplishments. Here were no superficial elegancies of an English miss, but young ladies educated in morality and virtue, and introduced early into polite company. Needlework they might learn, but not to waste hours over it, and they read more widely and deeply than the English.

In early youth (said Topham) girls were beautiful and blooming, but their freshness withered early, their voluptuousness coarsening even after twenty. The 'common people', however, he found extremely ugly, deploring the effect of a rough open-air life on 'haggard looks, meagre complexions, and bodies that are weakened by fatigue'.[18]

Men's appearance in general Topham found large and clumsy, and their long,[17] saturnine faces expressed national character to an almost ludicrous degree. In vain would these powerful, sinewy young giants attempt the graceful minuet, more suited to the Italians and French. Topham complained of the young men's over-developed legs and ankles, and even of ladies' legs disproportionate to their upper figures, at the expense of 'that fine tapering form which is so essential to real beauty'.[19]

Perhaps for that reason dancing masters in Edinburgh were two a penny. Mackenzie notes that in his boyhood there were three leading masters. Most fashionable was the courtly Lamotte, better with the ladies than with men. For the latter Picq excelled: he was grandfather to that Picq who later made famous pirouettes in London, and was for a time supported by his son. This son came to an unfortunate end when, demonstrating steps to the officers on board a man-of-war in Leith Roads, in a high leap he fatally struck his head on a nail in the cabin ceiling. The third teacher, Downie, a muscular Highlander from Strathspey, taught the energetic traditional Scottish dances at his school in Niddry's Wynd, but from him one learned little grace of movement.[20]

Children, indeed, displayed grace and beauty that surprised Topham, and with neither French foppery nor English slovenliness, performed well at the masters' balls, vying against each other at the Assembly Rooms, when the clumsy farce of minuets alternated with nimble mastery in the complex figures of Scottish dances. An Irish onlooker exclaimed that he'd 'never seen children so handy with their feet' – the limb most in use.

Adult balls were another matter altogether. The Assembly Rooms, in a close off the High Street, were so cramped that only two sets of twelve couples could dance at a time, strictly arranged by rank, by the Lady Directress of the evening. A line of chairs separated the sets, one dancing minuets (prescribed by the ticket handed out by the lady), the other country dances. The succeeding pairs of sets followed until all had had their turn, when the process was repeated, thus maintaining order without crowding; but the young ladies complained that they seldom had a chance to dance even twice.

The Assembly Rooms were managed by seven Directors and seven Directresses – especially the latter – as arbiters of society. One lady acted as Mistress of Ceremonies for the evening. In the 1770s it was Mrs Murray, sister to Lord Mansfield, universally respected for courtesy, good-humour, and fairness in dealing with the crowd of aunts and other chaperones who beset her for tickets the moment she arrived. Once her term of office ended she would be hard to follow; yet her departure led to a campaign for larger rooms.

These were the public balls. Weekly balls were also held by various societies and groups of subscribers, and married ladies would hold a ball for the unmarried. Some, like those of the Capillaire Club, included elegant suppers with ices and so forth, after which the gentlemen regrettably betook themselves to a private room to drink bumpers, actually changing into less formal clothes to increase their enjoyment.[21]

As for music, a weekly concert was held at the handsome St Cecilia's Hall, small but perfect of its kind. The concert tradition dated from as early as 1728, when an amateur or Gentlemen's Concert was launched at St Mary's Chapel in Niddry's Wynd. Masters were later employed, and the larger St Cecilia's, built nearby in 1761–3 by Robert Mylne, drew more subscribers, hence better performers' salaries that attracted London musicians – mostly Italian. First came Signor Doria, then Signora Corri, wife to Domenico, himself only an indifferent singer; and the popular Tenducci, who delighted audiences with the sweetness of his simple rendering of Scots airs.

The vocal tradition was strong in Scotland, and young ladies almost universally learned the plaintive harmonies and tender words of songs; but in 'modern' composition the Scots did not excel, too easily seduced by imitations of the Italian style. This was popularised by Tenducci, who lived some time in Edinburgh before 'fleeing' from Britain, presumably for debt, so that music became a favourite subject of both entertainment and conversation. Topham regretted that the arts of painting, architecture, poetry and drama were all neglected while 'philosophers, professors of science, and respectable characters [disputed] over the merits of an Italian fiddle, and the preciseness of a demiquaver'.[22]

St Cecilia's elliptical shape at first created a displeasing echo, which was later counteracted by building pilasters round the sides. Tickets were distributed by the managers to 'people of fashion'. This was a jealously guarded privilege, and in 1773 when the cellist George Schetky arrived in Edinburgh with his younger brother, the pair were somewhat cavalierly refused entrance at the concert hall until it was realised that he was their distinguished new performer.[23]

The less sophisticated hours kept in early days demanded a concert at 6 p.m. It was later progressively put back, eventually to 9 or 9.30 p.m. Dress was informal, so that men of business – namely lawyers – found it easy to slip in, such as Lord Kames, a regular attender, and the daughters of Lord Chief

Baron Ord, all good Italian linguists as well as musical, who wanted to sit close to the performers. Young Henry Mackenzie joined in about 1778, and some ten or a dozen years later became a director, along with the governor Lord Haddington and others.[24]

A place of entertainment often mentioned, and described by Topham in some detail, was the oyster cellar, an Edinburgh phenomenon which gradually died out as the New Town expanded. Responding one evening to an invitation from a lady, in expectation (he claims) that it might be a secret rendezvous, Topham was perhaps disappointed to find it an occasion of innocent respectability. Down a basement stair in the Old Town he entered a room filled with 'a large and brilliant company of both sexes' including 'a dozen very fashionable women', seated round a large table covered with dishes of oysters and pots of porter. These disposed of, no more food was brought in, but a punchbowl was produced and the hitherto dull conversation livened up, the ladies especially quick in repartee.

To one of Topham's formal English background it seemed odd to be mirthfully 'regaling in a cellar' with such 'innocent freedom'. Dancing of reels next followed, until one man fell and hurt himself, and the ladies began to consult watches and summon carriages. Left to themselves, the gentlemen turn to pipes and politics, and Topham becomes bored and bows himself off. He comments on the remarkably low cost of the entertainment to this smart company, two shillings a head; moreover, in London (he observes) such a private rendezvous would soon become a place of intrigue, while in Edinburgh it was pure enjoyment.[25]

Topham does not mention the venue of this gathering, but Sir John Sinclair, observing that Adam Smith was among its frequenters, reveals that the party originally met at a stabler's 'second-rate inn' in the Grassmarket, but that as it became better known it removed several times to maintain secrecy, ending at a small inn in the Cowgate. Members included distinguished doctors, Hutton, Black and Adam Ferguson, John Clerk 'the naval tactician', and even at one time Robert Adam.[26]

According to Charles Kirkpatrick Sharpe, the chief oyster parties were held in a house in the Cowgate. Ladies used to persuade the 'oyster wenches', who though 'known to be of the worst character' were excellent dancers, to dance in a ballroom, under the convenient name of '*frolic*' and as for the gentlemen, they were happy to have the wenches as their only female company at balls in the oyster taverns. ('How much Edinburgh is improved in some particulars', observes Sharpe frostily in the 1820s.[27])

An oyster feast was a snack, not a meal. Scottish cuisine in general was considered barbarous, and drew varying degrees of opprobrium. Even

Topham remarked drily that their hospitality outstripped their cookery. At one multi-course dinner, recommended by Lord Kelly and other reputed gourmets, he first sampled a haggis, highly praised by Fortune, the restaurateur. Whether from its plebeian associations – a sheep's stomach, resembling 'a bullock's paunch, which you often meet in the streets of London in a wheel-barrow' – or from its unappetising presentation, stuffed like a football with entrails and oatmeal, Topham could bear scarcely more than a taste, proceeding with better hopes to the cocky-leeky. After watching his host extract an elderly boiled fowl from a tureen filled with leeks, he reckoned that it tasted exactly what it sounded like. The company eagerly awaited his verdict, but Topham afterwards admitted that the bird was 'impenetrable . . . a warrior cock' that seemed to require the stomach of an ostrich'. The Scots, however, devoured it with a will, though the ladies took only the broth.

The next dish, a black sheep's head, doubtless a rarity, he prudently by-passed, although his neighbour reassured him that the colour was due to singeing off the wool, after which the head was merely boiled.

The *pièce de résistance* was a solander goose. Topham was honoured with a hunk of the breast, blackish but tender, 'something better than a tern or a sea-gull but with a strong, oily, unpalatable flavour'. Now ravenous, he actually snatched a mouthful or two. Abundance of good claret and conversation had to make up the deficiency, but after this feast, reminiscent of Porthos and the *procureuse,* he determined in future to avoid 'dinners of the highest taste'.[28]

Henry Mackenzie, unlike the squeamish Topham, considered Scottish cookery superior to the English who (he said) could only roast – and that to a pretty raw stage – and boil, with the 'savage accompaniments' of 'blood and butter', whereas the Scots had acquired French habits, including their excellent soups. Besides the dishes named by Topham he mentions hodge podge, hare soup, lamb's stove and pan kail, the *soupe maigre.* Hare soup was made from cut joints simmered with the blood, preferably from a hung shot hare, better than the English jugged version. Lamb's stove, presumably Topham's 'black sheep's head', was cooked with spinach, sometimes with prunes. Cocky leeky was improved by including a piece of beef, but as the leeks were almost whole it was admittedly hard to eat 'without offence against delicacy by some slobbering' (hence the ladies taking only the broth). Mackenzie also remarks that the solander goose fell out of favour in time because of its strong smell, and like the herring for the same reason it was banished from fashionable households.[29]

Other favoured delicacies were barley broth, beef stewed in pearl barley with green vegetables; cabbiclaw – codfish slightly salted, but not dried like other salt fish, and boiled with parsley and horseradish; and friar's chicken – small pieces boiled in a strong beef broth with parsley, cinnamon and eggs.[30]

Most of these dishes show a noticeable lack of greenery, yet Topham remarks on the profusion with which vegetables grew in the area round Edinburgh, in an especially favourable soil. Root vegetables were indeed plentiful, and in winter the poor could be sure of potatoes, carrots, turnips and cabbages. The great shortage, in a climate cursed with a sharp north-east wind, was fruit. No exotics such as figs, mulberries or vineyard grapes could be grown; apricots, peaches and nectarines were of poor quality, and while apples and pears were common, only one good apple orchard was found near Edinburgh, and cherries, except on walls, were unsuccessful. On the other hand gooseberries were good, and fine strawberries grew in profusion round Roslin, hardly outdone by Switzerland, adding to its fame for summer excursions.

The lack of fruit was oddly compensated for (claims Topham) by small turnips or neeps, 'eaten with as much avidity as if they had been fruit of the first perfection'. The gentry, indeed, could boast of hothouses fired by cheap local coal, in which grew melons, pineapples and grapes to perfection. [31]

Edinburgh's bread was highly esteemed at this time, but towards the end of the century it deteriorated through a shortage of yeast, monopolised by the brewers. When the exiled French court was in sanctuary in Holyrood during the 1790s the Comte d'Artois' mistress, Mme Polestron, showed a local baker named Greig how to make a palatable flat leavened loaf, which he named after her in compliment; but when the royal family left Edinburgh he lost or abandoned the art, and bread became bad again. [32]

Party catering was plentiful but not elegant: joints were mainly mutton, lamb and veal, the animals in winter were still often killed off and salted for lack of winter forage, and a rare treat for servants and labourers. Winter fare was limited to a standing menu of barley broth, salt beef, boiled fowl and greens, the barley being neither milled nor scaled but coarsely bruised in a trough by the cook. Home-brewed ale and brandy were the daily drink, claret and brandy-punch being drinks of ceremony.[33]

For entertaining, while there were – necessarily small – formal dinners, the favourite amusement was supper, relaxed and friendly like the French *petits soupers*, limited by the size of the rooms to seven or eight people, with the advantage that conversation could be general. During the prolonged supper the ladies drank rather more than an English lady could accommodate, which helped to enliven the occasion. After supper they would sing, with 'a plaintive simplicity, tantalisingly attractive from a pretty girl'. Many were proficient on the guitar or harpsichord. All excelled with 'vivacity and agility' in Scottish country dancing and reels; not so good was their fondness for formal minuets, at which they were so ungraceful.

Complementary to suppers were the ladies' own small parties, where cards were played for small sums – far more popular here than the large 'routs' common in London. Afternoon tea was a fairly recent innovation, though tea was already served by the middle-classes at breakfast.

The popularity of tea as a 'meal of ceremony' produced a great choice, said to run to more than fifty, of light 'tea-breads' and 'milk bakes', in which the Scots excel to this day, and every afternoon at 5 o'clock, as the ladies made their way to their hostesses' drawing-rooms, the maid-servants were crowding at the door of Scott, the baker in Forrester's Wynd.[34]

Tea-parties had their own sets of rules. Woe betide the buck who drank off his cup of tea too fast, and expected more: none would be served until all were ready. The lady then ceremonially refilled every cup and passed it down, each teaspoon numbered to ensure that the right cup reached the right guest.[35]

With the growth of the New Town, however, the tea party as a form of entertainment gradually disappeared, probably because the new, larger houses could better accommodate dinners than the old. Already in 1783, wrote William Creech, tea invitations were no longer issued: 'ladies and gentlemen meet only at dinners or suppers', and after a long dinner, followed often by a late supper, card parties might be held. By then for some twenty years tradesmen had been selling a great deal more wine rather than spirits. The fashionable dinner hour, moreover, was moving forward, and instead of shutting shop briefly in the middle of the day, businessmen began to knock off work altogether from the new dinner-time onwards.[36]

There were some notable figures who were remembered well into another generation. The team of formidable sisters, daughters of Sir John Sinclair of Ulbster, was known variously as 'the Great Sinclairs', 'the Six Beauties', or in their old age less kindly as 'Plague, Pestilence, Famine, Battle, Murder and Sudden Death'. They could not marry, as it was feared that any man who sought the hand of one would be lumbered with the lot, and for that reason even to cross the road where they lived in George Street was shunned as 'the Giants' Causeway'.

Helen Graham recounts this sad fate of the spinster sisters in 1823, and three years later Mrs Grant of Laggan, visiting Blackford House with her 'good old lady' friend Miss Trotter of Mortonhall, meets (she suppresses the name, or more likely her publisher-son suppresses it) 'one of six fair vestals, none of them young' and still with an antique mother.

'What a history is theirs,' she exclaims. 'Two distinguished beauties, two wits, and two ingenious damsels full of rare devices, who drew, and played, and worked all manner of cunning workmanship . . . Great was their celebrity some thirty years since, and much were they caressed and sought after among the nobles of the land', yet they remained single – 'all very cheerful and intelligent. I begin to think that those sensible contented women, who have outlived the turbulence and flutter of expectation and admiration, and think of nothing but being pleasant companions and good aunts . . . have more unmixed enjoyment, than we whose hearts are always either mourning the departed, or aching with fear and anxiety for the living.' The six sisters themselves may not have seen it quite that way.[37]

A more exotic character to be encountered in the 1770s in the New Town was the Princess Dashkoff (Yekaterina Romanovna Vorontsova, 1744–1810), patron of the literary arts in Russia, a close associate of Catherine the Great and one of those instrumental in putting her on the Russian throne in 1762. Having fallen out with the Empress, during the late 1760 and 1770s, she lived much in the West, placing her sons at school at Westminster and in Edinburgh.[38]

Charles Kirkpatrick Sharpe relates that the Princess lived at the corner of St Andrew Square. In the largest room she held her parties, when only ladies were provided with chairs, 'the gentlemen stood or acted as waiters'. She was said to have had an affair with the MP Daniel Campbell of Woodhall, and to have fleeced him of his family diamonds. 'As tutor for her son she employed Mr Greenfield, at whose flat in Middleton's Entry in Potterrow Lady Stafford, as a girl, went to take tea with her grandmother Lady Alva in order to meet the Princess. The latter came with a bodyguard, 'quite covered with costly furs and diamonds'.

A portrait of the Princess by S. Ponci in the Hermitage shows her as anything but handsome, and indeed suggests she might almost pass for Madame Defarge. Nevertheless, this lady not surprisingly made a great sensation in Edinburgh, making the most of her title to show rank – though in Russia it was inferior to Duchess. Having taken precedence of the Duchess of Buccleuch, the latter, 'not much pleased at this breach of ceremony', determined on the next occasion to leave the room first, but the Princess, guessing her intention, 'just as they were going to move came up to the Duchess and took hold of her familiarly with "*allons, ma chère duchesse, point de cérémonie*".'[39]

3
THE FABRIC OF EDINBURGH SOCIETY

I The Church

> 'During the time of Kirk you scarcely see any body in the streets, or loitering away the time of prayer in wantonness and excess; though, at other times . . . there is no crime they would scruple to commit. To be seen in the street after the summons of the bell, or to read any book on a Sunday which has no relation to religion, seems wicked and abominable to the most abandoned.'
>
> Edward Topham, *Letters from Edinburgh*, London, 1776, 190

> 'I thought the whole congregation felt wearied with the having two complete services at one time.' (1796)
>
> *Memoirs of the Rev. Charles Simeon, MA*, Rev. William Carus (ed.); 3rd edn, London, 1848, 91

Scottish life was much influenced by the Kirk and its ministers. Edinburgh itself having as its *raison d'être* both the seat of the law and its now world-famous college, the three institutions of kirk, courts and university between them formed the bulk of society. Although many ministers came from a lower social stratum, and in status and stipend ranked lower than the professors, their influence was paramount.

The governing body of the Kirk, as it were its Parliament and judiciary, was the annual General Assembly held in May, to which 350 delegates were sent by presbyteries throughout the country. As Scotland's supreme ecclesiastical court it handled cases referred from the lower Kirk courts. The Lord High Commissioner, appointed by the King as his representative, sat as its Convenor but could neither debate nor vote. The assembly sat for a week at the 'New Kirk', a specially equipped aisle of St Giles'.

The Sabbath in Scotland was strictly observed. Topham and others remark on Edinburgh's 'glum' Sundays, contrasting with its weekday liveliness. While the nobility often kept their own chaplains for private worship, for the rest, failure to attend the long church services was considered 'disreputable', although by the 1790s William Creech and others were complaining of a great falling-off – the effect of new philosophies and revolutionary ideas. All sects without exception inclined to bigotry, and resisted any form of joint worship.

A picture of even greater restriction, given in retrospect by Benjamin Rush, a Philadelphian studying medicine in Edinburgh in the late 1760s, shows how hard it is to generalise. Rush describes an overall Puritanical rectitude, so that he was

> often struck in observing the moral order which prevailed among all classes of people. Silence prevailed in the streets of that great city after 10 o'clock at night. The churches were filled on Sundays. I never saw a pack of cards in either a public or a private place. Dancing supplied the place of silence or insipid conversation in all large evening companies. Swearing was rarely heard in genteel life, and drunkenness was rarely seen among the common people. Instances of fraud were scarcely known among servants. But integrity descended still lower among the humble ranks of life . . .

and he quotes a notice displayed at the playhouse door, requesting 'the Gentleman who gave the orange-woman a guinea instead of a penny last night' to call for it at the check office. Such 'universal morality', he thought, must spring from the teaching of the conscientious clergy: or possibly it denoted a natural Scottish feeling for right standards.[1]

The focal point of the Presbyterian church service was of course the sermon. It is hard today to appreciate the enthusiasm with which society in general flocked to listen eagerly to sermons that might easily last two hours, often twice in a day, and the adulation, almost hero worship, lavished on preachers of the time. Congregations hung on their every word, and good preachers were discussed with as much earnestness as fine actors, their doctrines dissected, their delivery critically analysed and their every foible and idiosyncrasy – facial detail, hair, expression, changing emotions – implacably noted. Religious writings are full of meticulous accounts of the incumbents of every church, sometimes in merciless terms.

Throughout the eighteenth century the standard of preaching, emerging from the school of ranting Covenanters, had gradually improved. In the 1690s, when many of the Episcopal clergy resigned their livings rather than accept the new church settlement under William III, their places were often filled, with scant judgement, by half-educated or even near-illiterate zealots. Years were to pass before this legacy of intemperate dogmatists and intolerant anti-Episcopals worked its way through the Kirk, though the missionary journeys of George Whitfield and John Wesley later helped to disseminate a gentler spirit.[2]

The previous century's fanaticism largely died down, and Church and State were no longer at odds. A group known as 'Moderate' clergy formed, eager to co-operate with the Government in maintaining political stability rather than keep up the old aggressive arguments. Milder Moderatism gradually dropped some of the more extreme manifestations of zeal such as national repentance and scripture examinations of parishioners by the clergy, not to mention the old stool of repentance, but towards the end of the eighteenth century it was showing signs of tired support of an unreformed Establishment.

The established Kirk had been riven by dissension, especially over the Patronage Act, which since 1713 had revived the privilege of land-owners to appoint ministers in their parish, and over the years a number of Presbyterians seceded: usually those of a sternly Puritan disposition and often from among the artisans.

The Kirk was split between the Moderates, orthodox supporters of the Dundas interest, and the more fanatical Evangelicals or 'high-flyers', who by degrees attracted more reform-minded members while remaining within the Kirk.

Moderate clergy's sermons shifted away from theology towards morality and tolerance, and considered society and its needs. They were more liberal in interpreting Calvinist dogma, less anxious to sniff out heresy. It was this that made the Kirk in time adopt a more benign attitude to popular entertainments, drink, dances and even the theatre. Several members held university professorships, and under the Principal, Dr William Robertson, they exerted a strong influence in church affairs.[3]

There was a minority of Episcopalians and Catholics, though the latter were few outside the Highlands until the nineteenth century, when Irish immigration began. The penal laws aimed at suppressing non-conformity were not abolished until 1792. An attempt in 1779 to bring in a Bill applying to the United Kingdom, repealing the statutes against Catholics, aroused a violent outcry and led to one of Edinburgh's not infrequent riots. Hostile resolutions and petitions were presented to the Town Council, which eventually agreed to lay a recommendation before the Lord Advocate that the Bill, so far as it applied to Scotland, should be dropped. 'Inflammatory' pamphlets were circulated, and the Catholics were accused of exaggerating the dangers of mob action. A mob did burn the Bishop's house in Trunk Close in the belief that it was a Catholic chapel, and next day burned another priest's house. Even Principal Robertson's house was threatened, and dragoons and Fencibles were called out to patrol the streets, until arrival of a Government assurance, that the Bill was not after all to be introduced.[4]

Among the many famous preachers towards the latter end of the century was Dr Hugh Blair, minister of the High Church, for whom a Professorship of his great subject, Rhetoric, had been created in 1762. Blair, an eminent Moderate, inclined to believe that a religious life was its own reward, and that piety culminated in a peaceful, even joyful, death. His preaching was marred by stiff, formal delivery, which people like Dr Somerville thought even affected. In personality he was vain and foppish, walking to his High Kirk services in frizzed and powdered wig, carefully arranged gown and exquisitely clean and neat turn-out. He was once said to have destroyed a portrait newly painted of himself because he objected to its 'smirk'.[5]

At the Tron Church the minister was Dr George Wishart, principal Clerk to the General Assembly and a dean of the Chapel Royal. Practical and accurate, he was popular among the more educated members of society for his moral teaching, mild and elegant address, and 'meek apostolic countenance'.[6]

The historian Dr Robertson, Principal of the University, was also minister of Old Greyfriars. He eschewed any address to the 'passions', and in sensible, logically argued sermons he excelled in applying scriptural history to life. His austere Greyfriars colleague, Dr John Erskine, was perhaps most practical of all, fervour and sound arguments making up for a harshly monotonous delivery, which lacked the elegant presentation beloved of pulpit admirers. Scott, who used to attend his church in youth, describes Erskine in *Guy Mannering*.

Among other ministers were Dr Robert Dick of College Church, a graceful preacher undermined by poor health; and Mr Robert Walker of the High Church, who softened the harsh Calvinistic doctrines with sweet tones and 'simple Addisonian language'.[7]

Dr McKnight, a minister at the Old Kirk, was among those not considered good preachers. Arriving at church one day soaked with rain, the flustered minister was soothed by the greeting, 'Never mind, Doctor, when ye get to the pulpit ye'll be dry enough'.[8]

Towards the end of the century the Moderates were losing ground to the Evangelicals, of whom the most famous was Sir Henry Moncreiff of Wellwood, minister of the West Kirk, although as a preacher he was thought orthodox; his sermons (according to Cockburn) were 'sensible and practical'. To Cockburn he was 'the oracle of the whole Church in matters not factious, and the steady champion of the popular side': as leader of the Evangelicals no-one came near him. In 1785 he was elected Moderator of the General Assembly, thus putting that party into greater prominence. Edinburgh could then boast half a dozen distinguished clergy, but of these a generation later only Moncreiff remained and until the rising like a comet of Thomas Chalmers, no-one had appeared to take the place of the rest.[9]

Cockburn gives a pleasant account of Sir Henry's old fashioned Sabbath habits: he would dine between the two services, usually without wine; walk to church from his small house at the east end of Queen Street 'with his bands, his little cocked hat, his tall cane, and his cardinal air', return after church in the same style, take tea at 5 o'clock and then be alone in his study. At 9 there were family prayers, to which he welcomed his sons' friends, after which all would sit down to a 'substantial hot supper' at which – according to Mrs Somerville – Sir Henry was a host par excellence, with 'roasted fowls, game, or lamb', when wine and good conversation flowed 'without a shade of austerity'. [10]

A noted Episcopalian clergyman from England, the Rev. Daniel Sandford, provides an objective view of both the Kirk and Edinburgh society. Sandford (who was to become Episcopal Bishop of Edinburgh in 1806) was a clergyman's son, born near Dublin in Dr Delany's house at Delville, and his first vacations at Oxford were spent with the widowed Mrs Delany at Windsor. He was early recognised as an accomplished scholar, and incidentally a keen botanist.

Moving to Edinburgh with his family in 1792, as offering a likely opportunity for an Episcopal chapel living, Sandford was struck by the difference from English life and society. This was the time of Hudson and Blair, whose ideas strongly influenced taste and principles, the distinguished Rev. John Erskine, and early days of Professors Stewart and Playfair, though the most famous characters were still to come. Looking back some thirty years later (that is, with hindsight), Sandford considered that Edinburgh's reputation in philosophy, although already eminent for both its standard and its professors, was yet 'extremely questionable'. A disturbingly alluring scepticism had seeped in among the students, stimulated by the French revolution and propagated here.

The apparent intellect of these new doctrines even attracted older thinkers, and 'the young men, fond of speculation, and vain of limited attainments, were easily smitten'.

To Sandford, fresh from conventional England, this intellectually brilliant society, where originality was all, was almost alarming. English formality, regulated by etiquette, appearances and constricting ideas, was here replaced by paradoxes and unusual glosses, clever and witty, but in his view sometimes 'unsound and insidious'.

The nineteenth-century religious stranglehold had not yet taken over, and at this period many people had become either sceptics or indifferent, religious doctrines being but feebly expounded. Sandford was welcomed as a grave and sober preacher, and his small congregation (mostly English) was soon greatly increased. So was his chapel. The new Charlotte Chapel was built by subscription, and here he served from 1797 to 1816.[11]

It was often the English visitors who recorded their church-going impressions, in much the way that they described the round of sightseeing and socialising. Although the painter Joseph Farington, in Edinburgh in the summer of 1788, was chiefly interested in recording weather and scenery, he described an attendance at St Giles' in some detail, at the 10.30 Sunday morning service. Dr Greenfield, then Professor of Rhetoric, was preaching, though unlike other visitors Farington says nothing of the sermon. Having expected a 'sour and mortifying appearance' in a Scottish church, he was agreeably surprised at the grandeur of St Giles' fittings. A gallery encircled the area, in which on the right sat the Lord Provost with the chief council officers; opposite them were seats for the Lords of Session, in their black silk robes with crimson tassels. That day Lord Braxfield, Lord Alva, and two other judges attended. In the centre of the gallery, facing the pulpit, was the royal seat under a pillared canopy, used during the General Assembly by the Royal Commissioner. Farington and his companion were admitted to the Provost's seats, and invited to dine with him after the second service at 2.15.

Farington not only remarked on the length of the prayers, like most English, but timed them, at fifteen, five and twelve minutes, and the sermon, comparatively short, at forty-four. There were two psalms, sung by the clerk and a choir, who sat in the gallery opposite the pulpit. Great decorum was observed throughout. [12]

A Mr Willis from London, in a not particularly original diary of his Edinburgh visit with a friend probably in 1793, says in one typical entry:

> I went with my friend, Mowbray, with all due decorum to church. We were disappointed in not hearing Dr Blair, though a more popular preacher, Mr Greenfield, filled the pulpit. The form of service was to me completely novel, all falls upon the preacher, except the psalmody. Both prayers and sermon are his extempore effusions, they were both energetic, but diffuse; but his delivery was monotonous and soporific; and his manner too much in the spirit of John Knox . . .[13]

Some four years later came Lady (Maria) Stanley, whose husband of a year, Sir John, had been ordered to Scotland with the Cheshire militia because of the disturbances. Lady's Stanley's report of a service was similar to Mr Willis's: Greenfield was 'the next in request after Blair. He gave us an excellent discourse. The prayers I liked much, and particularly the exhortation preparatory to the Sacrament, which is here only twice a year.' Although she found it 'more solemn and impressive than ours', still 'there is more psalm singing than I like . . . I think the prayers better'. [14]

The length of sermons even then was felt to be excessive, when congregations were particularly devout. The Rev. Charles Simeon, a clergyman of exceptional piety, ready to attend church or to preach almost daily if required, found on a preaching tour in 1796 that because of lengthy sermons, at one church not only most of the congregation but he himself nodded off, or were at least very inattentive: and as it was the day before the Sacrament there were two sermons, one lasting one and a quarter hours, the other one and a half.[15]

To most visitors the differences in service and the amount of extempore prayer brought the added interest of novelty, and there is almost an element of appreciating good showmanship, like attending a popular play to see a favourite actor – which years later comes to a head in the days of Thomas Chalmers and the very different Edward Irving.

Topham described funerals as very solemn. They did not hire mourners from the undertakers, but in the French style sent cards to friends and near relations, who appeared dressed in black, with 'weepers' and long strips of muslin hung from collar to waist, which they wore throughout the mourning period. They were less pompous than in England, eschewing plumes and strings of carriages, limiting themselves to a single carriage following the hearse.

Dr Somerville described the traditional funeral procession. A death was announced by the ringing of the passing bell, and the beadle, head bared, would walk slowly through the streets ringing his hand-bell. Before the funeral a nightwatch, or lyke-wake, would be held, and although the ceremony was attended by crowds, this did not include women relatives, who would follow the procession only as far as the kirk gate and then disperse.

The lower orders regularly went in for processions, the coffin carried by four men, preceded by the minister and followed at a solemn pace by the friends and relations – who in the country might be so numerous that they extended the length of a main street. As deaths of the numerous relatives were so frequent, families might seldom be out of mourning. The first visit after a death was always in mourning.[16]

II The Law

> 'Every man who has nothing to do, and no better name to give himself, is called Advocate.'
>
> Edward Topham, *Letters from Edinburgh,* London, 1776, 315

After the Union of the two Parliaments in 1707, sixteen of the Scottish nobility, elected as representative Peers, attended the Parliamentary sittings at Whitehall, sometimes accompanied to London by their wives. The forty-five Scottish Members of the Commons, themselves often younger sons of aristocratic families, did the same. Members of the landed classes not in Parliament might live in Edinburgh, or more often on their estates, coming to their capital city for the season and returning when the Court of Session rose in July.

Those connected with this court, Scotland's supreme court and court of appeal, the backbone of Edinburgh society, formed the hierarchy of the Law, from the Lord President of Session, the Lord Justice Clerk, the judges, the

Solicitor General and Lord Advocate, to the numerous advocates, Writers to the Signet and officials of the court. Some of these last might be of relatively humble background, struggling with their families to maintain what was regarded as an appropriate gentleman's life.

The fifteen Lords of Session united the powers held in England by the Court of King's Bench and the Court of Chancery. Their decisions were subject only to the House of Lords. Appointment was by Royal Warrant, and the minimum qualification was five years as an advocate or principal clerk of session, or ten years as WS. The court's privileges extended to all members from highest to lowest, and all were exempt from paying ministers' stipends and duty on goods carried to and from Edinburgh. The rest of the country was covered by circuit courts which travelled the different districts in April and October, each with two judges sitting in specific burghs which had their own court-houses.

Revenue cases were heard by the Court of Exchequer, run by the Chief Baron and four ordinary barons who were qualified as either Scottish advocates of five years' standing, or English barristers. They too had the privileges of Lords of Session. The Commissioners of Customs and Excise and their staff, said to be notorious for perjury, came under this court.

Then there was the Commissary Court in Parliament Close, presided over by four judges appointed by the Crown, dealing with wills, divorce and other marital cases. Poky, dark and dirty, it was reached by a dismal winding stair. In the same close was the Baillies' Court, which met thrice weekly for minor civil and criminal cases; elsewhere were the Dean of Guild's Court for mercantile cases, and the Sheriff's Court for small debts.

Dr Somerville, who often used to attend the Court of Session in the mid-century, was not impressed by the standard of legal debate, either for elegance or for correct language; many speeches were verbose, dictatorial, superficial, and poor in delivery. On paper, however, a number of speakers excelled: the two Dalrymples, Sir David and Sir John, Lord Kames and Lord Monboddo were all highly regarded for their writings if not for the spoken word.[1]

Topham thought the Scottish judicial system mild compared with the savageries practised in England, though duelling laws were theoretically strict. One of the most ludicrous laws was that which entrapped many an unsuspecting young man into unintentional matrimony. Without seeking his consent, a woman might bring two witnesses to swear that he had addressed her as his wife (or even wished she was), or had spent the night with her, and provided others could be brought to believe it, the marriage was confirmed without ceremony.

'By the law of this country . . . marriage is a *consensual* contract,' wrote Peter Halkerston in 1827 in *A Digest of the Law of Scotland*. 'The *consent of parties*, if they are of lawful age, and not disabled otherwise, is the essence and only indispensable requisite . . . It may either be express or tacit . . . The subsequent acknowledgment of it by the parties is sufficient to support the marriage, if it appears to have been made not in a jocular manner, but seriously, and with deliberation.' Unfortunately for some foolish young men, who claimed 'jocularity', this did not save them.[2]

The Court of Session sat in the old Parliament House, up and down whose Hall aspiring young advocates daily perambulated, hoping for a brief or at least passing the time chatting to friends. It opened at 10, though the officials and young hopefuls had to be there from 9, and rose at 2 o'clock when all left their dry work and went home to dinner.

Although most young men of good family became qualified advocates, only a fraction of them practised.[3] The Session lasted from October until July, and whereas the sittings themselves might be hours of uninterrupted drudgery, there was ample time for a rich social life, with one's friends mostly within easy walking distance or at least a short journey by chair.

The nineteen-year-old Walter Scott, on completing his apprenticeship with his father in about 1790, decided not to accept his kind offer to continue in a partnership, but to aim for the bar, preferring its greater interest and seeming independence to the better-paid WS's office where he would be tied to clients. Aware that he made a poor showing as a speaker, he and his bright, but indolent, friend William Clerk moved on to the wider studies of Civil Law and the Municipal Law of Scotland. The latter class was then conducted by David Hume, junior, nephew to the historian, whose lectures in exposition of development from feudal regulations were clear and penetrating.

Walter and William evolved a course of study. Scott joyfully took possession of a small parlour at home for the only period (he admitted) in which he 'applied to learning with stern, steady, and undeviating industry'. He and Clerk were to meet alternately at each other's houses every morning except Sunday, to study the points of law required for the examination. Unfortunately William proved incapable of waking in time to walk the two miles from his home at the far end of Princes Street to Scott's in George Square, so it was Walter who punctually made the daily walk. In this way they got through the texts of institutes over two summers, duly passed their Civil Law examinations on 30 June 1791 and Scots Law on 6 July 1792, were received as advocates and assumed their gowns.[4]

On being raised to the Bench, a new judge took the title of Lord and a territorial name, usually if not always from his estate. His wife might be addressed his 'Lady', but their children still bore the family surname.

The talents and personalities of Scottish judges ranged perhaps uniquely wide, from plodding to highly gifted and often sheerly eccentric. There was Henry Home, Lord Kames, who died in 1782 at the age of eighty-six, by temperament as much an agriculturist as a philosopher. In 1762, when he had been a judge for ten years and had already published several works, he produced his three-volume *Elements of Criticism,* a landmark in aesthetics, drawing a parallel between beauty and what is agreeable to the senses; while in 1776 he produced *The Gentleman Farmer.* In Mackintosh's patronising opinion, though he inspired 'literary ferment', his natural genius never matured into specialisation, and he 'wrote many bad books, full of ingenuity'.[5] Home lived at the edge of the Old Town in an ornamentally-fronted house in New Street. He was said to be as coarsely facetious in speech as he was elegant in writing.

Many a judge was mild and dull, such as John Swinton who became Lord Swinton in 1782, heavy in person as he seemed in personality, though as Cockburn points out, he had originality enough to propose a standard weights and measures scheme (1779) and to suggest a more efficient organisation of the courts (1789) – neither reform implemented in his own lifetime.[6]

Swinton, who became extremely deaf, was also capable of some ingenuity. Chambers relates that when Burns was staying in Edinburgh (between 1787 and early 1789) they were both invited to a dinner which included Henry Erskine, who as usual was keeping the table in fits of laughter. The old judge, unable to hear the jokes, unobtrusively asked his neighbour, 'Is that my friend Harry?' On learning that it was, 'he burst into as hearty a laugh as the best of them' and kept up his merriment through the evening. A lady to whom Burns related this next day said disapprovingly that it cast a poor light on Swinton as a judge, to which Burns rejoined, 'My dear madam, you wrong the honest man; he acts exactly as a good judge ought. He does not *decide* before he has *heard* the *evidence*.'[7]

At the other extreme was the notorious Robert McQueen, Lord Braxfield, Lord Justice Clerk, whose reputation long outlived his time. Dark, powerfully built, with rough brows, threatening eyes and mouth and a harsh voice growling out deliberately exaggerated Scotticisms, he inspired terror into most hearts. Uncouth as he was, and distinctly lacking in learning, he was even thought by some to be all but illiterate: his strength lay in a naturally sound understanding and high-principled if bigoted approach. Braxfield died in 1799, when the age had become considerably more refined than that in which he had been brought up, but Cockburn, whose view is said to be partisan and over-stressed (not having met the judge himself), describes him as almost deliberately indecorous. 'His habits were all gross.' He was ignorant, 'illiterate and without any taste for refined enjoyment', to an extent that shocked even his coarsist contemporaries. In his leisure he was 'devoted to claret, whist, and less pure enjoyment', and treated the Bench as 'a place for privileged brutality'. As for women, he succeeded in 'making most women uneasy who had the misfortune to be within his reach'.[8]

Braxfield's judgments were undeniably harsh, even cruel, accompanied by aggressive taunts and criticism. Many an anecdote was preserved of his uncompromising, down-to-earth comments, and many more squeamishly suppressed by a later generation. One of the milder was his exclamation to his butler when the latter gave notice because of his mistress's constant abuse: 'Lord! ye've little to complain of: ye may be thankfu' ye're no married to her.'[9]

Braxfield's successor as Lord Justice Clerk (head of the Criminal Court) was David Rae, Lord Eskgrove, already seventy-four years old, sound and acknowledged as a lawyer though far short of Braxfield in reasoning power. His absurdities and extraordinary appearance rather than his abilities were popularly supposed to have gained him the post. Imitating Eskgrove was a favourite sport among young law-men, not least of them Scott: anyone heard 'talking slowly, with a low muttering voice and a projecting chin, amid roars of laughter', was bound to have Eskgrove as subject. Henry Brougham, whose wit was ever on the cruel side, went out of his way to needle him – an easy target indeed.

> Esky's vast nose, huge nether lip and chin, and scurfy complexion, variously red or blue, were accompanied by a low mumble in which he drew out syllables and even short words, 'King-g', 'impossi-bill', 'simpel-l', 'humbel-l', 'yeternal'. He was stooped, with a sly and stealthy walk – not a preposessing appearance. Over-punctilious in legal detail, he would keep juries standing (as the letter of the law dictated) for hours while he harangued them, as Cockburn recalled, even at midnight, 'still going on, with the smoky unsnuffed tallow candles in greasy tin candlesticks, and the poor despairing jurymen . . .'[10]

Some judges, especially those famed for the bottle, were a fund of bibulous anecdote. Even John Clerk, Lord Eldin, regarded as 'chief luminary of the bar', was recorded as staggering home after a drunken evening and muttering vaguely to a passer-by, or perhaps the Town Guard, 'Where's John Clerk's house?' – 'Why, *you're* John Clerk!' was the astonished answer. 'Yes, yes! but it's his house I want.' Another time, seen leaving a house at what seemed an unusually early hour, he was asked, 'Done with dinner already?' – 'Ay, but we sat down yesterday.'

Lord Eldin, lame and badly dressed, was an odd figure, with strong grim features and jutting black brows; quarrelsome on the Bench, he was weighty but always to the point in speech, in the strong Scots still the norm for the educated. He would sit with his lame foot stretched on a stool and a huge cat settled on his shoulder. He ran a large legal practice from his house at 16 Picardy Place, which was filled with pictures, books and *objets d'art* such as china, clocks and snuff-boxes. (It was here that in 1833, on the last day of the sale of his possessions, there happened the disaster of the floor's collapse under the great crowd.) Eldin himself, having spent lavishly, died almost poor. [11]

Old James Burnet, Lord Monboddo, had in younger days been a fine lawyer, but tended to dissipate his talents in fondness for the classics and rather wild metaphysics, and society especially in the form of his famous entertainments and fine conversation. His house in St John Street was renowned for early-evening 'learned suppers', held every fortnight for carefully chosen wits and thinkers, on the model of the 'Attic banquet' at a table strewn with roses, Horatian-style. Even though his guests laughed at some of his follies, Lord Monboddo's house was famed for agreeable hospitality. [12]

The Scottish bar had been noted for violent party spirit. Henry Erskine, younger brother of Lord Buchan, was sacked in favour of Dundas as Dean of the Faculty of Advocates simply for attending a peaceful meeting to petition against Pitt's and Grenville's Sedition Bills, although he had personally urged the group to disperse quietly(1796). His colleagues, under Dundas's influence, voted him off by a majority. Just as one of them, a personal friend, cast his vote against, it was said, the clock struck 3 and Lord Eldin audibly murmured, 'Ah! when the cock crew thrice Peter betrayed his master.'

Twice Lord Advocate, and Dean of the Faculty, Erskine never became a judge, doubtless because of his known Whig principles. He had been educated in Edinburgh though, as the snobbish noted, without acquiring its accent or provincialism. Cultivated, a good, concise speaker and arguer, agreeable in manner and without affectation, he was sometimes too witty for his own good.

Cockburn thought him a man of considerable charm, 'liberal, judicious, and considered beloved', but dominated by the tougher John Clerk who was considered wildly eccentric. Erskine, unlike other Whigs, was always welcome in Tory households for his gaiety and sense of humour. When Boswell was leading Dr Johnson round Edinburgh in November 1773, Erskine pressed a shilling into his hand, explaining that it was 'for the sight of your bear'. He was so popular a speaker that once, rising to start his speech with 'I shall be brief, my Lord', the judge hastily interrupted, 'Hoots Harry! dinna be brief!' He was also a terrible punster, so much so that one day a friend pretended to be in fits of laughter over an imaginary book called *The New Complete Jester, or every man his own Harry Erskine.* A number of his recorded sayings are, however, too arcane or topical to have worn well. [13]

When Erskine became Lord Advocate under the short-lived Whig Government of 1783, the outgoing Lord Advocate Henry Dundas suggested rather acidly that he might as well borrow his gown, as 'for the short time you will want it' a new gown was hardly worthwhile. Erskine responded that while he had no doubt Dundas's gown was made to fit any party, 'it shall never be said of Harry Erskine that he adopted the *abandoned habits* of his predecessor'.

Indeed he had little use of it: the Coalition administration shortly ended and Ilay Campbell succeeded him. This time he told his successor: 'My Lord, you must take nothing off it, for I'll soon need it again.' 'It will be bare enough, Harry,' answered Campbell, 'before you get it again.' (In fact it was twenty years.)[14]

Erskine was renowned for good looks, brains, kindness, and a fine, powerful voice. He was also noted for a yellow chariot drawn by black horses. He lived next door to the Scotts, at 24 George Square.

III The Schools

> 'Few universities in Europe have had more famous teachers in a shorter time, and . . . in few high schools have so many skilled men been educated for the State and for the sciences in recent times.'
>
> *Svedenstierna's Tour, Great Britain 1802–3,* Travel Diary of an Industrial Spy, trans. E. L. Dellow, David & Charles, 1973, 123

> 'Six hours a day, staring idly at a page, without motion and without thought.'
>
> Henry Cockburn on the High School, *Memorials of His Time*, Edinburgh, 1876, 4

Most boys, at least of the middle class, attended Edinburgh's High School during their formative years, but preceding that there were many privately run classes of disturbingly varied standard. George Combe the phrenologist, whose father was a brewer living at Livingston's Yards, an insalubrious area below the Castle Bank, besides growing up in these thoroughly unhealthy surroundings, first went to Mr Waugh's school among entirely working-class boys in Portsburgh, one of Edinburgh's lowest suburbs. Studying in its dark rooms soon affected his sight, and he had to be sent to recuperate at Prestonpans for a spell of sea-bathing.

Later he attended another small working-class school off Bristo Street, run by Mr Campbell, a poor young 'stickit minister' and a mediocre Latin scholar, glad enough to be given his tea by George's mother. Here George did learn to read without understanding the meanings, and with a broad Scots accent, and it was years before he was able to interpret the words he read in a book.

He also formed a habit of inattention, especially during church services, because he was unable to understand the sermon, though in that he was surely no different from many a Scottish child.[1]

The High School, or Grammar School, then near the Infirmary, was long notorious for discipline rather than learning. The syllabus was limited to Latin, and that by rote. The boys sat on backless, free-standing benches from 7 to 9 a.m., 10 until noon, and 1 to 3 p.m.; in winter from 9 to 11 and 12 to 2. (Accounts differ, but the total was much the same.) There was no intervening exercise to relieve the day's endless repetition of lessons.

It was not a healthy regimen for growing boys, many of them (like George) living in airless quarters at home and with not enough to eat. Cold feet, thin clothes, nothing to distract the mind, and almost no food – except at the hour's breakfast break, perhaps for porridge and stale buttermilk, and a penny roll at noon, until the home dinner-hour at about 2.30 in the afternoon – promoted listlessness and indigestion.

High School boys, like many others of their time, habitually wore brown corduroy breeches tied at the knee with 'a showy knot', a shirt tied at the neck with a black ribbon, without ruffles except on 'dress days', a single-breasted jacket which later (as our source, Henry Cockburn, tells us) was lengthened into a tail-coat, and a wide double-breasted cloth waistcoat, convenient to change over when one side became dirty. These last were always of 'glaring colours', and Cockburn recalls his pride in a combination of scarlet waistcoat and bright green coat. They wore worsted stockings in winter, blue cotton in summer, and white for 'dress'; and clumsy buckled shoes which were actually intended to be worn on either foot, swapped daily. Completing the ensemble was a round black hat.[2]

For four endless years the boys repeated the lesson they had learned without much understanding, followed by grammar and translation. The better-off were helped by evening tutors. The top boy or dux started the translating, then came the next down in turn, who would also try to fill any gaps in the previous ones' knowledge.

It is hard to equate the High School and its brutal master as experienced by Combe with the apparently kindly regime experienced by Scott. Many have left their recollections of their education, but these two seem at opposite poles.

Walter Scott started at the High School in 1778 under Luke Fraser. He was described as worthy and scholarly.[3] Boys were allocated to places according to their stage of progress and Scott's early poor health and long absences from Edinburgh put him at a disadvantage. Once fallen behind, it was difficult to get ahead, particularly as those at the bottom tended to be apathetic over progress and indifferent to learning, whereas the dux and next highest scholars often went on in adult life to positions of distinction.[4]

Scott, as he himself said, 'glanced like a meteor' from bottom to near top and back again according as he showed, or not, flashes of talent. Among the boys, even if they were the ones 'somewhat dull of head', his game efforts to counteract his lameness, and his genius at telling gripping tales, soon gained him popularity.

George Combe was sent to the High School in 1797 at the age of nine, enrolled as was customary in Luke Fraser's Latin class; his father respected Fraser for 'plying the tawse', and this was how the lesson usually ended.

George had not at first the benefit of an evening tutor to help him on, but he managed to move up gradually to a safer position than the foot of the class. It was 'when the incapables were reached' as he recalled in later life, 'that beating took the place of teaching. Mr Fraser exhausted his muscular strength, which was great, in inflicting blows.'

On one terrible day in his third year, Fraser resorted to incessant beatings, when no less than fifteen boys were standing in the middle of the room stripped of their breeches and awaiting punishment, and with the door (as was Fraser's custom on these occasions) ready locked. Suddenly in the nick of time a knock was heard, and like lightning the master called, 'Put up your breeches, my dears', before opening the door to find Lord Meadowbank, whose son James Maconochie was one of his pupils, arrived on a visit. Fraser received the judge 'with smiles and honeyed tones, which appeared like a burst of sunshine', and luckily the visitor stayed on until it was time for their dismissal, so for once the boys escaped.

Hand strokes or 'palmies' were a scarcely less painful punishment, savage enough to evoke screams, accompanied by Fraser's unctuous 'It is all for the good of your soul and body, my dear'. That year he exchanged his rod for a gamekeeper's riding-whip with a short, thick handle, whose knotted cord lash twisted round the victim's hand, bringing up red scores and even drawing blood.

'All this torture was a substitute for teaching,' recalled Combe feelingly. The sole instance of profitable instruction seems to have been a few blessed days when Fraser would bring out a model 'brig' to illustrate Caesar's method of crossing the Rhine, and while this was being demonstrated the boys, who looked forward keenly to the respite, could not only actually learn something but also avoid the lash. It never occurred to Fraser to interpret this.[5]

George's purgatory ended in 1801, but he could never see Fraser afterwards without dread. Yet when his brother Andrew came to the school in 1809, although Fraser had succeeded to the rectorship on Dr Adam's death, the monster had become so old and enfeebled that his rule was now lax, and the boys slacked and played truant with impunity.

Henry Cockburn was another who suffered torments at the High School. He recalls his justified terror on the first day, fairly dragged along by his tutor when just eight years old, at the start of four useless years. No matter how well prepared in the pointless tasks, he escaped for scarcely ten days without a flogging, and six hours a day were spent 'staring idly at a page, without motion and without thought, and trembling at the gradual approach of the merciless giant'. Like George Combe, he found the whole structure of learning irrelevant, and absorbed not a particle of feeling for the Latin language.

In his next two years, under the Rector, his education was transformed: Dr Adam 'was born to teach Latin, some Greek, and all virtue', inspired the backward, and expressed delight in signs of talent. He was said to devote all his spare time to classical scholarship, verifying quotations in the small hours, and once not succeeding in joining his family in the country during the whole long vacation, through being sidetracked into further research.[6]

Walter Scott was among those whose fathers engaged a tutor to supplement the narrow school syllabus. In 1782, from James Mitchell, a fanatical young man trained for the church, young Walter learned French, and some divinity and church history – in the process becoming a fervent Tory, pro-Cavalier, anti-Presbyterian and anti-Whig.

The years under Fraser were followed by graduation to the class of the Rector, Dr Alexander Adam, in Scott's case within three years, in Combe's four. Here Scott began to enjoy Latin literature and even began to make verse renderings from Horace and Virgil, and the Rector's praise (and criticism) went far to counterbalance the boy's earlier indolence. He made it to the top class, and in later years Adam never ceased to pique himself on his contribution to Scott's achievements, as he did with all his ex-scholars, recalling the fate of every boy at the school during his fifty years of teaching and ascribing their success or failure in life to their attention or otherwise.[7]

George Combe moved up to this milder regime in 1801. It was a great contrast to Fraser. Adam was benevolent and conscientious but also dynamic, and was the author of respected publications such as *Roman Antiquitie,* and several dictionaries. But although Dr Adam actually taught his boys, George was by then incapacitated for learning except by rote, and stayed well down the class. He did not comprehend what he read at school or at home when on dreary Sunday evenings the family intoned New Testament verses in turn, without explanation. By the time he left school in 1802, George had actually begun to respect his teacher and to absorb reading with pleasure; but some four or five formative years of education had been largely thrown away. Except for the bright boys who showed early promise, or those whose families could afford tutors to offset the High School drudgery, this must have been the common experience of the Edinburgh boy in the late eighteenth century.

Dr Adam suffered from the enmity of William Nicol, an under-master, 'a savage fellow' whom the magistrates (claims Lockhart) encouraged to undermine his authority.

John and Charles Schetky, sons of the cellist, one day played truant from the High School and went out in a Leith fisherman's boat. On the way home they were unfortunately spotted sneaking past Willie Nicol's house, and even more unfortunately, their father was there on a visit. Dire threats were uttered by parent and master, and the boys were only spared by the spirited intervention of another visitor. He was Robert Burns.

Nicol was a good classical scholar, and thanks to his convivial humour a good friend of Burns, but also 'worthless, drunken, and inhumanly cruel to the boys'. Once he was said to have waylaid Dr Adam in the dark and knocked him down, but his own toadying to the Council lost Adam their favour for some time, especially at the outbreak of the French Revolution. Adam was rash enough to support the revolutionaries, and his freely uttered political opinions shocked even the boys, most of whose families were strongly Tory and anti-Revolution. [8]

These difficulties past, however, Adam continued with honour in his class until 1809, when he suffered a stroke during a class, and died not many days after.

In order to learn anything other than Latin, boys (and a few girls) attended daily classes run privately, often by clergymen. George Combe, at the age of about eleven (1799), went for two further hours a day after High School hours for the usual subjects of writing and arithmetic, to Mr Swanston's High Street school at the Cross, considered one of the best of its kind. Here not only was there no corporal punishment but the pupils had a better chance to learn. The girls, who sat separately, had a civilising effect on the uncouth boys, who except for any sisters probably had had little contact with girls before.[9]

The ordeals suffered by girls at school were different but no less distressing than boys'. Mary Fairfax, daughter of Admiral William Fairfax, as Mrs Somerville was to become a uniquely famous lady astronomer, but nothing in her imposed education contributed to this. She was growing up 'wild and ignorant' until the age of nine, when her father with good intentions sent her to Miss Primrose's, an expensive school in Musselburgh, where she was 'utterly wretched'. The other girls were mostly older, and the shy, timid girl was always in dread of the schoolmarm's habitual frown. Her account of her woes is harrowing. [10]

> A few days after my arrival, although perfectly straight and well-made, I was enclosed in stiff stays with a steel busk in front, while, above my frock, bands drew my shoulders back till the shoulder-blades met. Then a steel rod with a semi-circle which went under the chin, was clasped to the steel busk in my stays. In this constrained state I, and most of the younger girls, had to prepare our lessons. The chief thing I had to do was to learn by heart a page of Johnson's dictionary, not only to spell the words, give their parts of speech and meaning, but as an exercise of memory to remember their order of succession. Besides I had to learn the first principles of writing, and the rudiments of French and English grammar. The method of teaching was extremely tedious and inefficient.

Their play included ball, marbles, and a game called 'Scotch and English', in which each side raided the other for their playthings, and needless to say the smaller girls lost out again, the older ones unloading on them the 'degrading' part of the English. Even Mary's Saturdays, when her mother's cousin Lady Hope, a frosty lady in poor health, often invited her to Pinkie, were not very happy. The stout, loud-voiced Sir Archibald had a passionate nature and was chiefly interested in hunting, and Mary spent a lonely time in the grounds, dodging a frighteningly aggressive turkey-cock.

On Sundays Miss Primrose tackled the difficulty of some of her pupils being Presbyterian and others Episcopalian by taking the whole school to kirk in the morning, and to church in the afternoon.

Mary's purgatory lasted for a year that must have seemed endless, and she returned home still unable to spell, keep accounts or even write legibly – the subjects her mother thought all-important.

When she was thirteen, about 1793, her mother rented a small Edinburgh apartment for the winter so that the girl could attend the usual writing school and arithmetic lessons. But her uncle William Charters, newly back from India, gave her a pianoforte, and this meeting her mother's approval Mary took music lessons from an old lady living at the top of one of the highest Old Town tenements. She continued all these lessons next year and, staying at her uncle's in Edinburgh, also went to dancing-school. Mr Strange, the master, was like a stage character, tall and thin, with a powdered wig and pigtail and 'cannons' (cylindrical curls) at his ears. 'Ruffles at the breast and wrist, white waistcoat, black silk or velvet shorts [i.e. breeches], white silk stockings, large silver buckles, and a pale blue coat completed his costume. He had a little fiddle on which he played, called a kit.' The first accomplishment he taught Mary was the royal curtsy.

On Saturdays Strange took all his pupils, boys and girls, to the George Street Assembly Rooms, in full evening dress, to learn the minuet, reels and country dances. Young officers and idlers about town, drawn by the prettiness of the older girls, came to lounge around, while the pupils had to endure the humiliations of clumsy mistakes before this uninvited audience.

Mrs Fairfax's desires for her daughter's education were rewarded when Mary became interested in drawing after a visit to their house by Miss Melville, a talented miniature painter. She was then allowed to attend Alexander Nasmyth's classes at his new academy for ladies – 'proof of the gradual improvement which was taking place in the education of the higher classes'. Nasmyth had many pupils, but in later years he told a lady that Mary Fairfax was 'the cleverest young lady he had ever taught'.

Mary's own genius began to be revealed when her interest in education was stirred by her discovering algebra. She still enjoyed music, getting up early to play the piano for four or even five hours; she had lessons from Signor Corri, but thought him careless. He did not correct her bad habit of thumping so hard as to break the strings, and she herself at length corrected this. From him she learned fashionable pieces by Mozart, Clementi, her favourite Beethoven and others, sometimes accompanied by Robert Burns's friend George Thomson, and often by Stabilini.

Pleased with this (though not by the algebra and her late hours of study), her old-fashioned mother rounded things off by sending Mary to learn to cook by daily lessons from a pastrycook. With the pretty Miss Moncreiff, daughter of Sir Henry Moncreiff of Wellwood, a current belle, she learned to make 'jellies and creams for little supper parties, then in fashion', as her mother liked to keep a good, though not extravagant, table.

All this kept her mentally stimulated, although one day when her mother praised her daughter's watercolours, which she had hung on the walls, to a rich widowed cousin, the latter's crushing response was that she was glad Mary showed 'any kind of talent' by which to earn, 'for everyone knows she will not have a sixpence'.[11]

Although Admiral Fairfax was knighted after the Battle of Camperdown, he received little reward otherwise, and they remained poor and living quietly. Mary was, however, spared from having to earn her living, by marrying in 1804 a cousin Samuel Greig, Commander in the Russian Navy. Her memoirs are reticent about their happiness or otherwise, except for a telling remark that he did not encourage her studies. Widowed after three years with two young boys, she resumed mathematical study, and in her later marriage to William Somerville went on to a brilliant career in astronomy in a happy intellectual partnership.

Mary Fairfax was like many Scottish children in enjoying a certain freedom in early years, and grown-up young ladies of the time had still more so. Many a visitor to Edinburgh, especially female, remarked with pleasure on the way ladies could walk alone or with each other, without chaperone, in the fashionable streets, where they might even be joined by their dancing partners. Topham remarks on this in 1775, not just from the women's point of view but on street safety in general. Housebreakers, footpads, even street brawls, he thought rare – not through the virtue of the populace but rather the City Guard, 'very terrible looking men', who not only paraded daily in the High Street but kept 'night stations', well trained and regularly relieved. Topham also thought the indispensable services of the caddies might contribute to this feeling of order.[12]

Ladies needed no chaperone except to attend the theatre or concerts, and often went to a ball alone in a chair. They might be accompanied by a footman, but Mary Fairfax, because her parents could afford only a couple of maidservants, in spite of their comparative poverty, was able to attend balls, alone in a chair as her mother (who herself would never 'go into society' if her husband was away) had perfect confidence in the Highland bearers. At her first ball Mary was introduced by their relative, the old Countess of Buchan, when her first partner was Gilbert Elliot, later 1st Earl of Minto, and Erskine cousins could always go with her if required. Indeed she was likely to know everyone in the room, but 'liked to have some one with whom to enter and to sit beside . . . I was fond of dancing, and never without partners, and often came home in bright daylight'. Not surprising: small and graceful, with her well-set little head, she was much admired – 'beautiful complexion, bright, intelligent eyes, and a profusion of soft brown hair'. This beauty she retained into old age. She used to make all her own dresses, even her simple but elegant ball-gowns.[13]

The sociability and freedom shown by ladies so admired by Topham seems to have remained an element in Edinburgh life. Almost half a century later in the anonymous *Letters written for the Post, and not for the Press* (1820), the nineteen-year-old 'Lady Lucy' is writing to a friend of her delight 'that with a brother, sister, or female friend, a young woman may walk through the whole of this town with perfect propriety'.

Revelling in her first experience of this new-found liberty, 'oh! how I danced along Prince's Street, my bonnet and hair all blown about with the wind', and everywhere one could see groups of young people 'all mirth and bloom' and lively chatter in an enjoyment 'quite unknown to our circle of *haut ton* in the South', and the ladies walking with an 'active bounding step' contrasting with English ladies' London dawdling parade with their footmen and lapdogs. Lady Lucy did not even notice any such upper-class dogs in the streets, presumably because their owners came out without the servants who would exercise them.[14]

The enlightened and liberal Mrs Fletcher (Eliza Dawson), who at twenty-one had married an advocate more than double her age and formed the centre of an intellectual circle, had in all seven children, whom at one time she was thought to indulge almost too unconventionally. She had employed a governess, Miss R—, highly recommended by the blue-stocking writer Mrs Elizabeth Hamilton, but, apart from her piety and industry, found in her 'a sternness and a want of sympathy', and though she continued to employ her, she bitterly regretted the unnecessary discipline applied to the children. Her own treatment was more relaxed, and before breakfast at their house in North Castle Street at one time she would take the little ones on a walk, 'not a very common [custom] with Edinburgh ladies', each carrying a small tin to be filled with milk at a dairy-woman's field along the Queensferry Road. 'These morning walks in spring were an emancipation from schoolroom rigidity, which they and I enjoyed together exceedingly.'[15]

Yet the Fletchers seem to have thought little of leaving some or all of the children with a relative or governess while they travelled or even lived elsewhere, and at least one of them, Bessy (and later apparently Grace as well), was taken at the age of eight to live at Tadcaster with a Dawson aunt. The boys went to the High School, but Miles, the eldest, fell among idle companions there, and in 1802 they removed him to join a group of six boys for tuition with a clergyman near Hamilton. From here he successfully went on to the College.[16]

There was of course great variation between families. Lord Woodhouselee adored his tribe of unruly children, the girls having no governess but learning sporadically from the various masters. He saw no particular deficiency in his son Patrick's poor showing at school, and his 'principle', to which their indulgent mother yielded, was 'They are the kind of children with whom it will answer best'.[17]

No matter what shortcomings and limitations existed in Scottish schools, they were esteemed enough to attract English families to live in Edinburgh, both for the society and for their children's education, especially in adolescence.[18]

One of the more rumbustious of the city boys' outdoor activities, tolerated by the authorities, was the 'bicker'. Probably the fullest account was that eventually published by Sir Walter Scott in his General Preface to the Waverley Novels, and quoted *in extenso* by Lockhart in his biography, but it was evidently taken direct from a 'Narrative' compiled by another author, Miss Ann Fraser Tytler, daughter of the judge, Lord Woodhouselee. The judge's lively son Patrick, an inattentive though not unsuccessful High School pupil, was an eager participant of these street fights. The bicker tended to be between upper- and lower-class boys, not apparently from any particular class-attitude but simply the way the boys fell into groups. The fights were fairly tough, one side charging while the other stood fast, sticks, stones and fists flying and sometimes causing serious injuries. Walter Scott and his George Square contemporaries naturally formed a company, or side, and the lady who later became the Duchess-Countess of Sutherland even presented them with colours. Their regular opponents were a 'suburban' team from Crosscauseway, Bristo Street and Potterrow, hardy, barefoot and 'rugged antagonists'. A fight might last a whole evening, one side repulsed but then turning the tables with reinforcements. When the George Square boys were in trouble, elder brothers, servants and any able-bodied residents were pressed into service. They never seemed to learn the names of the enemy, except for obvious nicknames.

One lively fourteen-year-old, chief of the suburban side, was known as Green-breeks from his old livery breeches (arms, legs and feet usually bare), with his height, blue eyes and long fair hair like a young Goth, but described by Miss Fraser Tytler more romantically as 'the Achilles of the

Cross-causeway'. He once nearly seized the George Square colours, but was violently struck down by an opponent with a dagger-blow to the head. All fled, the local watchman 'took care not to know' the attacker, the weapon was flung into a ditch in the Meadows and all were sworn to secrecy; but then the boys learned to their alarm that he had taken Green-breeks to the Infirmary. The victim gallantly refused to reveal the assailant, and when he came out of hospital, Scott and his friends made peace with him over a feast of gingerbread from the baker's: he proudly refused a purse of money, though apparently he later accepted a pound of snuff for his grandmother. The parties could never become friends, being too wedded to the stirring idea of the bicker, but the affair cemented their mutual respect.[19]

Mrs Somerville notes that sometimes when the bigger boys joined in, such serious fights took place that the magistrates called out the City Guard – upon which, of course, both sides united against the common enemy. Patrick Tytler so dearly loved the sport that one day, covered with bruises and streaming with blood, he rushed into the family's Princes Street home shouting to his youngest sister, 'Wash my face, quick! put a key down my back, and let me out again to the bicker!'[20]

A regular bicker-ground where almost every evening from the early part of the war with America the skirmishes started before dusk and continued until it was too dark to see, was on the ground below Calton Hill where the Bridewell was built in 1791. By that time several age-groups had grown up and passed on to other things. According to Alexander Campbell, many of the youths joined the Edinburgh Volunteers when the city raised the 80th Foot against the Americans in 1778.[21]

IV Edinburgh Societies

'A preparatory school for public speaking.'

Henry Mackenzie on the Speculative Society, in H. W. Thompson (ed.), *Anecdotes and Egotisms*, Oxford, 1927, 37

'There is a variety of clubs among the men, in which hard drinking is still kept up, though not to such excess as formerly.'

Thomas Newte, *Prospects and Observations on a Tour in England and Scotland*, London, 1791, 376

'One may easily conceive what powerful motives of emulation these societies present, where your fellow comrades are judges . . . more severe than men of more advanced age.'

L. A. Necker de Saussure, *Travels in Scotland; descriptive of Manners, Literature, and Science*, London, 1821, 16

Edinburgh University was a nursery for debating societies, which covered most imaginable subjects. The Academical Society flourished from 1796 to 1816, meeting in Professor Playfair's shabby little classroom, 'the great receptacle of youthful philosophers and orators', according to Cockburn[1] – eventually destroyed for the building of the new Library.

Walter Scott joined his first society in his seventeenth year (about 1788) and soon made up for the social disadvantages caused by his long periods of illness with his wit, enthusiasm and keen observation of character, although he was not a particularly brilliant speaker unless on a subject that inspired him, and he was still untutored in the art of composition, unable to condense his huge quantity of 'ponderous and miscellaneous knowledge' to precision or relevance.[2]

The most famous, long-established and exclusive Speculative Society had been founded as long ago as 1764, by William Creech, later Lord Provost, and five other students, and rapidly became a forcing-house for future eminent lawyers and politicians. This too met in the Old College, but in its own private hall, and when that too was demolished it was allotted a new hall in the east block designed by Robert Adam.

Its rules were strict: membership was limited, hence greatly prized, no strangers were admitted, and attendance was compulsory. Members were expected to work for their privilege.[3] It was long the custom for young advocates, either just before or just after being called to the bar, to spend their new leisure in the practice of debate in the Speculative Society. Many a future statesman, including Lord John Russell, became a member while studying at Edinburgh. Walter Scott was admitted in January 1791, and within a year he had produced essays on the origin of the feudal system, the authenticity of Ossian's poems, and the origin of Scandinavian mythology; he also joined in debates on whether the poor should be given regular support, should there be an established religion, should the slave trade be abolished and was the execution of Charles I justifiable, the last a subject which came up again the following year. Scott was soon elected librarian and later, secretary and treasurer.

Francis Jeffrey admitted to being struck by his first sight of Scott, seated at the foot of the table wearing a large woollen nightcap – for which he apologised, as he was suffering from toothache. His essay on ballads so interested Jeffrey that he got himself introduced, called on Scott next evening in his small book-lined den in the basement of the George Square house, and went to supper with him at a tavern. Thus began a gradually deepening friendship.[4]

In the 1790s a notorious dispute, even schism, arose over Mr Emmett, who was implicated in the Irish rebellion and was expelled. A proposal to end the society's long-standing connection with the sister society in Dublin brought about a violent political disagreement.

Former members such as Charles Hope and the younger Hume returned to take part, but the young Whig members, Jeffrey, Henry Brougham, Francis Horner and others, initiated debates which for the best part of a session brought in the whole college and the city too. The old party was at length worsted, and some resigned. Unfortunately the dispute deterred many able young Tories from joining, and the brilliant young Whiggish orators now in the lead sometimes found their audiences rather thin. Henry Cockburn, who joined in 1799, not long after this fracas, disclaims his own qualities as 'decidedly the worst and most unpromising', and picks out Brougham as the most dazzling and keenest of the day.[5]

Henry Brougham was one of those who excite admiration or antipathy; what some saw as sarcasm and arrogance others took to be youthful high spirits and *joie de vivre.* He had a strong streak of vanity, a showy manner and liked people to know of his exploits, whether exuberant practical jokes or intellectual achievements. Hard work at law studies was punctuated by 'high jinks' at the Apollo Club or, after oysters at Johnny Dow's, horseplay by a gang of students or even advocates parading through the New Town to wrench off the brass bell-handles. These were a New Town innovation, and the streets 'abounded in sea-green doors and huge brazen devices, which were more than our youthful hands could resist'.

Brougham bragged of having a whole closet-full of these prizes under lock and key – for indeed what could he do with them? One of the last such exploits was a rowdy evening when they fêted the intensely serious Francis Horner on his departure for London. After dining at Fortune's they reeled off to the North Bridge, where at Manderston's the druggists Brougham (of course) climbed on the shoulders of the tallest and thence to the top of the doorway, and twisted off the huge brazen serpent which formed the shopman's sign. They had a hard run for it to escape the City Guard.[6]

A rather worthier evening which ended in the lock-up was an affray on the South Bridge, when Brougham and friends, again returning home from a supper party, found a crowd of bakers showering some unfortunate woman with blows. The friends charged in and started a free fight. 'All the watchmen within hail were about our ears in an instant', writes Sir Arthur Brook Faulkener, who was among them, 'and, in return for our chivalry, lodged us in the watch-house.' Brougham profited from the occasion by learning the history of an old soldier who had fought in the American war, and in the morning by some judicious talk he got them all freed, 'by a sort of general jail delivery'.[7]

Similarly it was Brougham who baited the wretched Robert Heron during the sole performance of his execrable drama *St Kilda in Edinburgh.* The friends were noisy enough through a couple of impatiently received 'dreadful acts', until there came the proposal of a toast in a dinner scene, at which the lanky Brougham rose from the pit and shouted, 'We'll drink good afternoon, if you please!' After that it was pandemonium, and despite a few helpless appeals from the manager, the curtain had to fall among shouts of execration.[8]

When he was a student in 1794 Brougham claimed that Professor Playfair had one day called him back after a class to tell him that in his latest exercise he, Brougham, 'had hit upon the Binomial Theorem', to which the sixteen-year-old Brougham modestly replied that he had done so entirely 'by induction'.[9] Some ten years later, after he had joined Jeffrey and Sydney Smith in launching the *Edinburgh Review,* he was quick to claim that it was he, Brougham, who had contributed the most essays to the first issues.

Brougham undoubtedly had a deeper side, as he showed in his later political life. He was deeply affected by his brother Peter's death in 1800 in a duel with Campbell of Shawfield, and became so distracted that after taking his law examinations he was totally put off his chosen profession. He then spent much of his time in literary and scientific pursuits, and regularly spoke at Speculative Society meetings. With the launch of the *Review* in 1802 he found an immediate outlet for his talents.

Another noted member of the Speculative Society was the versatile Sir James Mackintosh, son of an Inverness-shire laird and already a graduate of Aberdeen University, who came to Edinburgh to study medicine in 1784 at the age of nineteen. At that time Edinburgh seemed at the pinnacle of academic fame, though its most brilliant days were still to come. The split between 'Cullenians' and 'Brunonians' was at its height (see p. 74). At the same time the geologist and metaphysician Dr James Hutton, then in his late fifties, was working on his theory of the origins of the earth, and in 1785 his views appeared in the Edinburgh Royal Society's *Transactions* as 'Theory of the Earth, or an Investigation of the Laws observable in the composition, dissolution, and restoration of land upon the globe', which ten years later he was to publish, expanded into two volumes. Briefly, it was a confutation of the influential Wernerian doctrine of 'Neptunism' which argued that all rocks were originally precipitated from a solution in water. Hutton's 'Plutonian' theory demonstrated that geological features were produced by slow change and not as the result of catastrophe, and that certain types had been molten and then cooled. Like the Brunonian theory, this too excited violent controversy, but Hutton was eventually accepted as correct.[10]

On the lighter side, during that session 1784–5, Edinburgh lectures were attended by a notorious London quack named Graham, whose claim to sensation was to be buried up to the neck for hours on end, demonstrating an 'earth-bath' cure. But the crowds who came to watch tended to laugh rather than admire.[11]

Other members joining the Speculative Society in 1784 who later became famous included the seventeen-year-old Benjamin Constant, at that time usually known by his title Baron Constant de Rebecque; Charles Hope, later Lord Justice Clerk and Lord President; and the historian Malcolm Laing.

During his three years at Edinburgh at this eventful time, James Mackintosh, being disputatious himself, took against Drs Gregory and Cullen, to both of whom he had been warmly recommended, and fell under Dr Brown's influence. Brown's theories were seductively simple; he was anti-authority and almost paranoiac about Edinburgh's leading teachers, and his method required little background study: he thus strongly appealed to the young. There are also hints, typically undefined by contemporaries, at 'Bacchanalian orgies', and all this drew the rebellious Mackintosh. 'I was speculative, lazy and factious, and predisposed to Brunonianism by all these circumstances,' he writes, and was quickly elected to the faction-ridden Royal Medical Society before he had even gained much medical knowledge. Always silver-tongued, Mackintosh was fluent in out-arguing complex questions.

At this time among Edinburgh philosophers, metaphysical enquiry was all. 'Accurate and applicable knowledge was deserted for speculations not susceptible of certainty, nor of any immediate reference to the purposes of life,' writes Mackintosh's biographer, his son Robert. As eager as the rest to run ahead of proof, he abandoned dry practical study for the speculative. He became so suspect for his anti-authority behaviour, so indolent, preferring the easy option of desultory reading and speculation to attending lectures, and falling into 'dissipation' and poetry-reading, that friends called him 'an honorary member of the classes'. He even turned up late for his examination, but retrieved the gaffe by his quick and ingenious answers. Mackintosh left Edinburgh in 1787, not returning until 1812.[12]

V The University

> 'Scotland has produced, within these modern times, learned men and writers of great reputation, who cannot but excite the jealousy of their southern neighbours.'
>
> Fredk Augustus Wendeborn, *A View of England towards the close of the 18th century*, London, 1791, II.172

> 'There is no part of the world where so general an education can be obtained as in Edinburgh . . .
>
> 'There are few places where a polite education can be better acquired than in this City; and where the knowledge, requisite to form a Gentleman, and a Man of the World, can be sooner obtained.'
>
> Edward Topham, *Letters from Edinburgh,* London 1776, 217, 218

'We were grieved to see the new college in the imperfect state in which it now appears, and more so to learn that it is not likely ever to be finished.' (1804)

Joseph Mawman, *An Excursion to the Highlands of Scotland and the English Lakes*, London, 1805, 103

Edinburgh had for two centuries been renowned for its university, founded in 1583 in the reign of James VI – though younger in age than Scotland's other universities at Aberdeen, St Andrews and Glasgow. Its fine library, a year or so older, had been bequeathed to the Town Council by Clement Litill and later removed to the college, thence further enriched by the statutory deposit of all new books registered at Stationers' Hall.

Viewed from the standpoint of Oxford or Cambridge, Scottish universities had many idiosyncrasies. Edinburgh's professors were appointed by the City magistrates, a practice which, particularly later, led to semi-political controversy and was eventually abolished in 1858.[1]

At the time of its foundation, students were by statute to wear gowns, speak Latin and keep out of the taverns, although such rules became abandoned, and in spite of attempts at enforcement the boys never wore gowns. Nor had they halls of residence, but lived in private lodgings in the town, often in great poverty or at least frugality. These factors may well have contributed to the lack of town *v* gown hostility always such a feature of, say, Oxford. As for taverns, most youths were poor enough to need to keep out of them. Their fees were paid individually to their professors, each of whom (by the eighteenth century) received three guineas per student per session and issued a ticket for each course. This represented almost the sole professorial income. When Henry Brougham registered with the Chemistry Professor Dr Black in about 1792, he was surprised to see a kind of brass weighing instrument, which the professor explained was really a safeguard with students he did not personally know, some of whom were not above trying to pass off 'light' guineas.[2]

The lack of a professorial stipend was a result of the university's poor endowment, and their tenuous income, thought the German traveller Wendeborn (1791), was presumably why they took such pains over their lectures, the better to attract more students.

Edinburgh students were enrolled at a very early age, fifteen or sixteen, or even less – Alexander Dalzell and Sir John Sinclair were only thirteen – because the university was seen as an important intermediate step between school and Oxford or Cambridge, taken for example by Lord John Russell and Henry Temple, later Viscount Palmerston.

There was precious little to be obtained in grants from the alma mater. In 1775, when it cost the Council £2000 a year to run, there were fifty-one 'poor' students qualifying for grants of up to £10 a year, a maximum to which only five, presumably poorest of all, were entitled.

Only the Principal was resident, in a house on the site of Kirk o' Field just outside the old city walls, where Lord Darnley had been blown up in 1567. The 'ancient and irregular' college, whose buildings survived in increasing decrepitude until the end of the eighteenth century, consisted of three courts on different levels, with small lecture rooms.

Dr Johnson considered the age of entry too young for students to learn adequately, but this may have been his natural prejudice against the Scots. English students were often as young and, as Wendeborn observed, with such brilliant lecturers as they had by then at Edinburgh, they could not fail to learn.

The academic year was not divided into individual terms but was a single session running for eight months from October to June (with minimal break over the turn of the year), which, being less interrupted than English universities, many thought had the advantage.

Student behaviour was also superior to that current in English universities, where scions of the nobility extravagantly idled their time away. The Scots, of whatever rank, often came from poor families and were eager to further a professional career, usually for their families' sake.[3]

The syllabus was very different from the English which required a wider knowledge of Greek and Latin, including composition in those languages, whereas the Scots, coming on from the narrow High School teaching with no Greek, required only translation. The second year took one on to mathematics and the third might include political economy, including of course Smith's *Wealth of Nations*. Then came the top Greek class, and broader mathematics including trigonometry and geometry.

The mid-eighteenth century was not outstanding for the university's achievement. In 1756 when Thomas Somerville entered, at the usual age of fifteen, it was far below the reputation it was to earn in the next generation. He records that the classes were backward (Greek), dry (logic), limited (natural philosophy), or just poorly taught (mathematics) and thinly attended (Latin and moral philosophy). Divinity, he conceded, fared somewhat better![4] The medical side alone had achieved brilliance under the celebrated Dr Alexander Monro, Primus, as first Professor of Anatomy.

Within a few years, however, Scotland's universities had attained a reputation in philosophy and history thanks to the works of Hume, Robertson, Adam Smith and Dugald Stewart – and a little later, hardly less to their outstanding scholars, Brougham, Horner, Jeffrey, and later still, Lord John Russell and William Lamb (Lord Melbourne).[5] There were those who already foresaw a future for an Edinburgh expanded far beyond its present limits. As early as 1762 the painter Allan Ramsay was writing from London to his friend Sir Alexander Dick at Prestonfield,[6] enthusiastic at what might seem a trivial development, an Academy of Riding: 'A few more such institutions will render Edinburgh the Athens of Britain' – a perspicacious forecast in itself, for the Athens analogy did not generally arise for some thirty years. This, he thought, would counteract 'the awkward and monkish pedantry of the old-fashioned Universities', exercising young gentlemen in 'all these liberal accomplishments which qualify a man to appear in the distinguished spheres of life'. He also praised the proposal for the new College of Physicians' library, which 'join'd to the Advocates Library, gives an advantage which this opulent City of London is hardly able to exhibit'.[7] That year, 1762, was the year of the appointment as Principal of Dr William Robertson, clergyman and historian, a post that he held for thirty-one years until his death.

The most comprehensive description of the university in its time of expansion is, once again, that of the gentlemanly Edward Topham, who was much impressed by the professors, so worthy of their 'setting an example of civility and good manners, as of morality and virtue . . though all of them are men of letters, and skilled in the sciences they profess, they are not less acquainted with the world, and with polite behaviour, than with polite literature'. One senses here an implicit criticism of contemporary Oxford.[8]

The old fashion of teaching only Divinity had given way to professorships in 'all the liberal arts', totalling eighteen sciences and twenty-one professors, as divinity, mathematics and Greek each had two; and the highest salary was a mere £150, for the Professor of Law of Nature and Nations, the lowest only £33 (supplemented, of course, by the students' individual fees).

By now Edinburgh's philosophy and literature schools were celebrated throughout Europe, drawing a huge number of students from all over Britain and beyond. Students were inclined to dissipate their attention by signing on ambitiously for too many classes, with a zeal for 'universal knowledge' which prevented true achievement in a single subject. To this Topham ascribed the 'mediocrity of learning' complained of in Scotland by Dr Johnson.

The chance to learn, however, spread to outsiders as well. Lectures were open to all on payment of the necessary fee, so that anyone, in any walk of life, could educate himself (provided he could spare the time) – 'the reason why the middle degree of people are not in such a state of ignorance as in England and in other countries'.

Topham attended a number of the courses and found them inspiring, apart from the students' rather unpolished manners and their general lack of cleanliness. No doubt he found them smelly. Only the professors wore gowns, standing or sitting in the middle of the lecture room surrounded by students' benches furnished in front with desks for note-taking.

The English universities, he thought, dwelt too much on higher education's social and worldly advantages. In Scotland all subjects carried equal value and over-specialisation was avoided. Literature, modern languages, music, fencing, riding and dancing could all be learned to a high degree of excellence. Even the 'low amusements' of wrestling and quoit throwing were valued by some.[9]

On a higher plane, Wendeborn in 1791, fairly scathing about English universities, considered the Scottish superior: 'and Scotland has produced, within these modern times, learned men and writers of great reputation, who cannot but excite the jealousy of their southern neighbours . . .'[10]

At the time of Wendeborn's visit, Edinburgh had six to seven thousand students and twenty-three professors, one for 'each branch of literature' and for the scientific and medical subjects: nearly half the students were studying medicine.

Taking a year at random, 1784, the senior members of the university excluding the Principal Dr Robertson were as follows: in the medical field William Cullen, medicine; Joseph Black, medicine and chemistry; James Gregory, institutes of medicine (i.e. physiology); Francis Home, materia medica; John Hope, medicine and botany; Alexander Monro Secundus, anatomy. In the humanities Andrew Hunter, divinity; Robert Cumming, church history; Adam Ferguson, moral philosophy; John Robison, natural philosophy; Hugh Blair, rhetoric. The rest were James Robertson, Hebrew; Alexander Fraser Tytler, civil history; Allan Maconochie, law of nature and nations; Dugald Stewart, mathematics; Andrew Dalzell, Greek; Robert Dick, civil law; and William Wallace, Scots law.[11]

Principal Robertson (1721–93) had early made a name as historian with his *History of Scotland* in 1759, a year before he became joint minister at Greyfriars Church. Appointed Principal of the University in 1762, he was Moderator of the General Assembly in 1763 and became the Historiographer Royal for Scotland.

He also published the first complete to date *History of America* (1777), and his earlier *History of the Reign of Emperor Charles V* (1769) was highly praised by both Gibbon and Voltaire and was the original on which Schiller partly based his *Don Carlos*. In style he was described as 'elegant and picturesque', in conversation 'polite and entertaining'. Like a number of the famous Edinburgh lecturers he was praised for various qualities but not for profundity or originality.[12]

Dr Joseph Black, Professor of Chemistry since 1766, excelled in experiments, especially towards the end of his lecturing career which ended in 1795 – in illustrating his simple and clear verbal explanations, in a seemingly effortless presentation, with basic notes, low but audible voice, steady hand and unwavering eye. 'I have seen him', says Brougham, 'pour boiling water on boiling acid from a vessel that had no spout, into a tube holding it at such a distance as made the stream's diameter small, and so vertical that not a drop was spilt.'[13]

Henry Cockburn, whose family at one time lived near him, describes

Black as 'so pale, so gentle, so elegant, and so illustrious' that even 'the wildest boy' respected him. His appearance was 'striking and beautiful . . . tall, very thin and cadaverously pale', large dark eyes like deep pools and his thin hair powdered and drawn back into an exiguous queue. He dressed meticulously in black, with silk stockings and silver-buckled shoes, and carried 'either a slim green silk umbrella, or a genteel brown cane'. This 'attenuated philosophical gentleman' had so tranquil a death in 1795, seated with a bowl of milk on his knees, that when he ceased to breathe the milk was quite unspilt.[14] The art of a steady hand unthreatened by spillage he carried from life into death.

Towards the end of the century the two most distinguished professors were undoubtedly Dugald Stewart and John Playfair, very different in temperament but universally highly esteemed.

Stewart (1753–1828), son of a Professor of Mathematics, and educated at both Edinburgh and Glasgow Universities, was appointed assistant to his father in 1774; but with amazing virtuosity he took on Professor Ferguson's moral philosophy class when the latter was in America, besides astronomy and mathematics; notified on a Thursday that he must also take a metaphysics class he started the teaching on the following Monday, working out the arguments while walking up and down in the small garden of his father's house in the college, and then lecturing, as he always did, extempore.

'The most remarkable among the literary young men in Scotland,' wrote Benjamin Vaughan in August 1783 to John Jay, then in the American diplomatic service in France. 'He is already their first rate mathematician and moral philosopher; and as his diligence and abilities and connections are equal to any thing, there is no knowing where he will stop . . . he wants nothing but a little longer period of life to make him somewhat famous.' (Stewart was then travelling with Lord Lothian's heir Lord Ancram.[15])

He married, was elected a Member of the Royal Society of Edinburgh, and on his father's death in 1785 succeeded to the chair of mathematics, but exchanged this with Ferguson, now in poor health, taking on his moral philosophy class, which he held until 1820. His wife died, and in 1790 he made a remarkably happy second marriage to Helen d'Arcy Cranstoun, daughter of the Hon. George Cranstoun.

He next concentrated on metaphysics, and wrote and published prolifically, the 400-page *Elements of the Philosophy of the Human Mind* (1792), a biography of Adam Smith (1793), and a students' philosophy textbook being only the start.

Stewart studied political economy, was widely read in literature, and being so clear-minded and his ideas so well arranged, he was often called on to stand in for colleagues who were ill: natural philosophy, Greek, mathematics, logic and once even belles lettres. He also opened his house to those likely to make their way in the world and showing early signs of distinction, as well as to many visiting foreigners, since he regarded the formation of manners and taste a vital part of education: his evening parties, of the lively and learned of all ages, therefore became famed for their variety and brilliance.

Like many professors, he took in aristocratic students to his household, including the young Henry Temple, whose talents and industry Stewart praised, adding that he was both amiable and a model for his age. In the same year, 1800, came Thomas Chalmers, who was to have a brilliant future in the Church.

Stewart was the chief exponent of the 'commonsense' school of philosophy, seeing it as a scientific discipline, with affinities between mathematical axioms and the laws governing thinking. His complete works, published in the 1850s, filled eleven volumes.[16]

Whether from a fashionable need to express their own intellectualism by criticising, many felt the urge to point out that Stewart and other noted Edinburgh lecturers were not themselves original or profound, but rather excellent teachers and expounders of the views of others. Thomas Chalmers was one of these critics, finding Stewart (1800) disappointing in avoiding difficult discussion, offering only 'detached hints and incomplete outlines', and lacking a 'masterly and comprehensive whole'. At the same time Francis Horner, attending Stewart's thrice-weekly political economy classes, found his great merit in delivery and unfolding of the argument, liberal and enlightened in 'chaste and impressive language'. In Archibald Alison's opinion Stewart's own sound judgment and high principles made him an unrivalled critic, while Alexander Dalzell's admiration never ceased, claiming that in his philosophical works Stewart was one of the few to keep to scientific principles and not stray into prejudice and intolerance. Sydney Smith, meeting him in 1798, noted that he was 'generally considered to be one of the first men' in the university.[17]

In 1799 Stewart became one of Thomas Campbell's earliest patrons, and his backing when Campbell published *Pleasures of Hope* contributed to the poet's success. He introduced Campbell to Lord Minto, who invited him to his Roxburghshire seat and was among those who gave him letters of introduction when Campbell moved to London.[18]

Although equally a figure in society, Stewart was a contrast to the more worldly and urbane Playfair: simple and unostentatious in habits, and with his gifted wife displaying unaffected, heartfelt kindness and hospitality. This continued when they removed to Kinneil, some twenty miles from Edinburgh.

John Playfair (1748–1819), five years Stewart's senior, was of a very different mould. Eldest son of a Forfarshire minister, to whose living he eventually succeeded (having entered the church in 1785), he was educated at Aberdeen University where he twice almost obtained a professorship, one at the age of eighteen. At thirty, he presented a paper on 'Impossible quantities' to the Royal Society of London, spent some time as a tutor to Fergusson of Raith, and in 1784 became a member of the Royal Society of Edinburgh, in whose *Transactions* he published extensively. In 1785 he was elected Joint Professor of Mathematics to serve with the ageing Fergusson, who became titular professor on the exchange with Stewart. In 1795 Playfair published *Elements of Geometry*, and in 1797 on the death of the famous geologist James Hutton compiled his memoir, which led on to *Illustrations of the Huttonian Theory of the Earth*, an improved presentation of Hutton's own somewhat ill-organised exposition. This work occupied him five years (1797–1802).

In 1805 Playfair exchanged mathematics for natural philosophy, succeeding to Dr Robison's chair and surrendering his own to the unpolished John Leslie. This transaction caused a fierce division between the Provost and magistrates and the Church. On Leslie's standing for the post, the Church party tried to denigrate him because he had supported Hume's theory of causation, and entered their own undistinguished clergyman candidate, the Rev. Mr Thomas MacKnight, an assistant of Dr Robison's. Thomas Chalmers also offered himself, but both Playfair and Stewart strongly opposed the appointment of a clergyman, arguing that the post was incompatible with a clerical vocation and, further, that the Scottish variety was not remarkable for achievement in either Mathematics or Philosophy. A prolonged pamphlet-winging contest ensued, including an essay by Thomas Brown attacking the Church faction, and one by Chalmers against Stewart. Eventually Chalmers decided to stand down and MacKnight also withdrew, and Leslie was duly elected.[19]

John Leslie was one of those remarkable characters thrown up by rural Scotland to become academic prodigies. Of a humble Fife family, and once working as a shepherd on Fergusson of Raith's estate, he taught himself mathematics from an *Edinburgh Encyclopaedia*, and was discovered working on a problem scratched on a piece of slate, befriended by Lord Kinnoull and helped to an education. Professor John Robinson of St Andrews sent him to see Dugald Stewart, who was visiting at the time, and Stewart considered him 'of real genius and obstinate as a mule'.

Leslie was assisted in various ways to study mineralogy and meteorology, and published an essay on 'the solution of indeterminate problems', which was attacked in the *Monthly Magazine.* Experimenting in heat and cold, he eventually succeeded in producing artificial ice. One day in 1799 the 21-year-old Francis Horner, as a student of privileged background and early noted for his precocious talents, was surprised while walking with Professor Stewart to see him meet and talk to 'a vulgar looking man of a very homely physiognomy . . . of very low birth'. This was Leslie, then aged thirty-three, whose talents and achievements by self-help Stewart then revealed to the naïvely astonished Horner. Poor Leslie was so unprepossessing – 'one of the coarsest looking men I ever knew', says Mrs Somerville – that William Clerk of Eldin was inspired to make a clay model of 'his ungainly figure'. When his hair went grey he tried dyeing it, but it merely turned purple. He kept on trying, so that 'the professor's hair was often white at the roots and dark purple at the extremities'. Leslie never failed to hope he might find his ideal woman, and regularly fell in love with young ladies, whom he asked Mrs Somerville to bring along for him to meet, but they never responded, and the poor fellow died a bachelor. (His public career was more successful; in 1819 he transferred to the Chair of Natural Philosophy in succession to Playfair – a not unusual change – and was knighted in 1832, shortly before his death.[20])

Playfair was Professor of Natural Philosophy until the end of his life. Jeffrey, in the *Edinburgh Magazine* (August 1805), described him as 'sure though not brilliant', notable for clear presentation of others' theories, hence a sound and enthusiastic teacher. His accuracy in learning combined with clarity in composition rendered him unsurpassed in exposition. Archibald Alison called him 'Able rather than original', 'eloquent rather than profound' and 'an incomparable disciple' rather than a creative genius.

A man of easy, polished manners, Playfair moved in high society, always welcomed for his learning matched with unaffected courtesy. He never married, but was a great favourite with the ladies, particularly the famous Miss Berrys, whom he met some time in the 1790s and visited regularly in London over more than twenty years. 'The darling of women, the favourite of children', as Alison put it, he was considered a great flirt.[21]

One young lady of twenty who was greatly influenced by meeting Playfair was Maria Dundas, a cousin of the Berrys, who became Maria Graham (and later Lady Callcott), author of *Little Arthur's History of England.* Contrary to what one might expect, she was not only highly intelligent – an unconscious blue-stocking – but almost self-taught, her intractable passions when at school in England having prevented her acquiring any orthodox learning. She was also then considered plain and ugly, certainly had no fashionable airs and graces, and having lost her mother early in life entered society with no inhibitions about young-lady-like behaviour. Her father, Captain William Dundas, was captain of a revenue cutter, and in 1805 and 1806 she made a prolonged stay in Edinburgh with the family of her uncle James Dundas, Clerk to the Signet, living in St Andrew Square, with whom her father had a delighted reunion.

At her uncle's house Maria met her uncle's former school-mates or fellow students, Dugald Stewart, John Leslie and Dr Thomas Hope, as well as Professor Playfair, and made a great impression on them all. Having 'a fearful notion of metaphysics' she was astonished, after an evening at Stewart's, that Professor Thomas Brown of moral philosophy had called her 'Metaphysics in Muslin'. The professors were staggered by her conversation. Yet to her (as she told them) 'it was simple reasoning on moral points, such as the nature of truth . . . I did not die of fright, nor did I leave off going to Dugald Stewart's. On the contrary, I seized every opportunity of being there.'

It was Playfair, however, who impressed her most; then in his late fifties (she judged him more), he showed her great kindness from the start, would always talk and answer questions, and recommended useful books which he then readily discussed. 'I think if there was one quality for which Playfair was more remarkable than another it was his singular candour. No spirit of party ever seemed to disturb his calm and clear understanding', and he steered a moderate course between the fanatical extremes of the 'Neptunists' and 'Platonists' whose controversies were then tearing philosophers apart.

The plain Playfair and even plainer John Leslie, both unmarried, were devoted to children, who equally adored them. She describes Playfair graphically as 'short and square', his unremarkable features further disfigured by the smallpox, with small, deep-seated grey eyes which no-one except perhaps his family ever saw without his spectacles. 'His voice was low and pleasing, his conversation remarkably cheerful, though he had not the smallest pretensions to wit, or liveliness of manner. He was a great admirer of wit in others.'[22]

Playfair's younger brother was James the architect, who secured the patronage of Henry Dundas, and studied in France and Italy. James worked extensively in England and Scotland, and in Edinburgh designed St Peter's Episcopal Church in Roxburgh Place (1790–91), but died prematurely in Edinburgh in 1794 at the age of only thirty-nine. He was the father of the better-known architect William Playfair (1790–1857).[23]

Maria Dundas was less impressed, incidentally, by the famous chemistry professor Dr Hope: very clever, she admitted, and noted for 'neat' experiments, but spoilt by affectation, and 'the first specimen of a dandy philosopher' she had met. He was an assiduous attender at balls, arriving first and leaving last, and she knew well that he often had to lecture at 11 in the morning after staying to dance until 3 a.m.[24]

It was not uncommon for a second, joint professor to be appointed to a chair whose existing holder was ageing, sick or perhaps absent on travels. The first Alexander Monro's son acted as Joint Professor of Anatomy towards the end of his father's tenure; and Andrew Dalzell, son of a tenant farmer at Kirkliston near Edinburgh, in 1772 at the age of thirty, after some years acting as tutor to the Lauderdale family, was appointed joint Professor of

Greek with Professor Robert Hunter, who was anxious to retire. For the junior partner the appointment was seldom lucrative, as the financial rewards often stayed with the senior, but in this case although Dalzell paid Hunter £300 capital, he shared the salary such as it was, and kept the students' fees, which were expected to reach £200.

This turned out profitably for him as the Greek class had dropped to a low level and his teaching soon reclaimed numbers to at least 110, then the highest ever, 180 in 1784 and still continuing to rise, so that his classroom had to be redesigned to accommodate them.

Dalzell compiled and published a grammar for his students (1782), and later a collection of Greek prose authors, with scholarly notes in Latin. As a lecturer he was unpretentious and unaffected, not concerned with philosophical enquiry, and concentrated on the class, the students, and re-establishment of the Greek language.

In 1778 Dalzell achieved a revival of the degree presentation and its formalities, though only in the shabby common hall, but at Dugald Stewart's suggestion he launched a course of poetry lectures for a two-guinea fee, whose proceeds went towards the magistrates' restoration of the hall, ceremonially reopened by Dalzell with a Latin harangue. His colleagues were impressed, his reputation was made. Dr Monro said that he had rescued Greek from 'going fast down-hill'.

Dalzell's career was an uninterrupted success story. He was already elected to the Royal Society of Edinburgh when the University Librarian Dr Robertson, Professor of Hebrew, resigned and the magistrates offered him the post, although the salary would still be paid to Robertson during his lifetime. Eager to restore order to the collection and records, Dalzell accepted: 'I look upon myself to be at the summit of my academical ambition.' His classes were still increasing, he published more Greek works, contested the Clerkship of the General Assembly against Dr Alexander Carlyle and secured the office on a re-count.

He married Annie Drysdale, a childhood friend and daughter of Mary Adam, sister of the Adam brothers. In 1790 their house was demolished for the rebuilding of the college and they removed to new quarters: the library too was rebuilt, and Dalzell started re-ordering the books on the lines of Cambridge and the King's Library at the British Museum. He travelled with Lord Lauderdale, son of his early patron, and in his nineteenth teaching session in 1791 continued with 'no diminution of vigour'. In 1793 on the death of Principal Robertson, Dalzell was asked by his son to help with the official biography, which Dugald Stewart actually wrote.

In 1802 Dalzell contributed a paper to the revived *Scots Magazine*; but his health was now beginning to fail. Henry Cockburn, who started at the college in 1793, felt that the ever-enlarging class had outrun itself, and that

Dalzell was unequal to dealing with such numbers. On the other hand, only Stewart had as much influence on Cockburn as Dalzell: kindly and gentle, 'mild, affectionate, simple', but enthusiastic and a favourite lecturer. He was then living in Bonnington Road and evidently not very practical: Cockburn's last recollection of him was his 'trying to discharge a twopenny cannon for the amusement of his children' but he was so awkward and scared himself that he terrified the children too, and at last had to retreat behind a washing-tub and set it off by a match on a long stick.

One of Dalzell's last public actions was in 1805, when the Presbyterians contested the election to the Mathematics chair on Playfair's exchange. The Town Council hastened on the decision, in which Dalzell took part, meeting at his own house as by then he was too ill to attend the Library. On his retirement his classes were taken over by others including Dugald Stewart, who read his own written lectures, and Dalzell died in December 1806, aged sixty-four. [25]

VI Medicine and Surgery

> 'There are no public disputations and all degrees are disregarded except that of Doctor of Medicine.'
>
> Sir John Carr, *Caledonian Sketches*, London, 1809, 95

> 'Every meeting in the University and in the Infirmary and every visit to and walk with [other students] was productive of more or less knowledge upon some subject of taste or science'
>
> George W. Corner (ed.), *The Autobiography of Benjamin Rush*, Princeton UP, 1948, 44

> '. . . now in the zenith of its glory. The whole world I believe does not afford a set of greater men than are at presented united in the College of Edinburgh.'
>
> Benjamin Rush to Jonathan Bayard Smith, 30 April 1767, in L. H. Butterfield (ed.), *Letters of Benjamin Rush*, Princeton UP, 1951, 41

Edinburgh University was to become as famous for its medical school and colleges as for its philosophers. King James VI and Oliver Cromwell had both tried to initiate a College of Physicians, though neither made any progress. In 1681 the Royal College of Physicians of Edinburgh was actually founded at the instigation of Sir Robert Sibbald, when King Charles II's brother James, as Duke of York, briefly held court at Holyrood. Three titular professors of medicine, including Sibbald, were appointed in 1685, though none gave lectures, and the initiative foundered.[1] Another of these 'professors' was the Jacobite Archibald Pitcairne, who died in 1713, famous for having been Professor of Medicine at Leyden in 1692.[2]

Sibbald and Sir Andrew Balfour also started the famous Physic Garden in 1670 at Holyrood, and from 1675 at a site between the Nor' Loch and the nearby Trinity College. In 1763 this garden was removed to the west side of Leith Walk, where it remained until the present Royal Botanic Garden was founded off Inverleith Row in 1824.[3]

The surgeons of Edinburgh had been established as a craft incorporation in 1505, initially as the Incorporation of Barber Surgeons, and had close links with the Town Council until they were granted a charter as the Royal College of Surgeons of Edinburgh in 1778.[4]

It was, however, well into the eighteenth century before this led anywhere, and it was George Drummond, during his first provostship, who effectively launched a new medical school in 1726, on the basis of the earlier abortive attempts.

A theatre for anatomical demonstrations had been built as early as 1697 in Old Surgeons' Hall, Surgeon Square, and continued in use until 1725. The first Alexander Monro began giving anatomy lectures here in 1720, and four doctors who, like him, had studied in Leyden under Herman Boerhaave joined him at the theatre in teaching theory and practice of medicine, and chemistry.[5] They were always short of 'subjects' for dissection, only the bodies of executed criminals being allowed and usually barely three available in a year: even at that time there were angry suspicions of graves violation, for example at Greyfriars. Riots were barely avoided, and to prevent further threat to the building Monro obtained permission to move his class into the university. Provost Drummond, impressed by the success of his teaching, determined to promote the medical school, and to appoint staff – not through influence, the usual university method at the time, but on merit.[6] In 1726 the Town Council granted Monro's colleagues professorial appointments, thus founding the University Medical Faculty, providing a full course of instruction and leading to the award of the MD degree.

At that time it was usual for young Scots to study medicine in Holland with Boerhaave, and the passing of pre-eminence from Leyden to Edinburgh during the eighteenth century was due to a series of brilliant physician-professors. Dr William Cullen, Professor of the Practice of Medicine, his successor Dr James Gregory, Dr Joseph Black, Professor of Chemistry, and the first two of the three generations of Alexander Monros, together laid the foundations of Edinburgh's medical reputation. By 1770 large numbers of students were attending the medical classes, and about twenty a year followed the full course and graduated MD.

The city's Infirmary, founded in a small house in 1729, was another product of Provost Drummond's, jointly with the first Alexander Monro, who was Professor of Anatomy until 1759. This was a national charitable institution, accepting patients from all over the country, not run by the Town Council but financed by subscription. A new building, completed in 1748, accommodated 228 patients, and provided such amenities as hot and cold baths, of which one, of marble, was open to non-patients. It served for many years as Edinburgh's sole public bath and is said to have been used by King George IV in 1822. The Infirmary's central staircase leading to the wards and the operating theatre in the attic was designed of a width to admit patients arriving in sedan chairs. In 1828 the building was expanded to absorb the adjoining Old High School, when the latter moved to its new site on Calton Hill.[7]

Hospital treatment was supervised by six physicians, attending in turn as physician in ordinary on a two-month rota and dispensing medicines from their own supply. Surgeons, who had a separate Incorporation and were not at first included, opened their own Surgeons' Hospital, but after 1738 when the two professions united, they too became eligible to join the Infirmary staff. The rota system later came under close scrutiny during the acrimonious feud between Dr Gregory and Dr John Bell.[8]

An important innovation at the Infirmary was introduced as early as 1748 when Dr John Rutherford, Professor of the Practice of Physic (clinical medicine), began lecturing on cases *in situ*, expounding 'the Diagnosis, Prognosis and Method of Cure'. This was the first use of clinical instruction which has continued to modern times.[9]

Establishment of a variety of University chairs in medicine and its sub-specialities was not matched in surgery, whose teaching remained in the hands of the Professor of Anatomy. During the mid-eighteenth century, despite Scotland's poverty and unsettled political state before and after the '45, 'Monro Primus' built up Edinburgh's medical school's reputation before resigning the chair to his equally brilliant son in 1759. 'Monro Secundus' had studied in London, Leyden, Paris and Berlin, and on his return to Edinburgh his father invited leading citizens to attend his first lecture, which the younger Alexander had memorised by heart. When the time came he was seized with such panic that he forgot his words; but recovering, he managed to give the lecture extempore, to such effect that he never afterwards spoke from notes.

Monro Secundus himself held the chair for fifty years and retired in 1808/9. His lectures were so popular that in 1764 he built a new octagonal Anatomy theatre seating 200 students in the College garden; and it was he who laid the foundation stone of a new anatomy theatre in the north-west corner of Robert Adam's new University building on 31 March 1790, and opened it in October 1792 at the start of the winter session. Besides his major publications on the brain and nervous system, he built up a museum, which in

1800 he presented to the University with his catalogue. This presentation was accompanied by the condition that his son, 'Alexander Tertius', continued to have the use of it – which ensured his succession to the chair.

Throughout his academic career Monro found time to run Edinburgh's leading physician's practice, and according to his famous colleague and younger rival James Gregory (1753–1821) he was in all ways head of his profession – as physician and consultant and as teacher and anatomist. Also a skilled consultant in surgery (not in its practice), in 1777 he successfully defended his formal title of Professor of both Anatomy and Surgery.

An athletic man of middle height, with a large head and expressive features, Monro was fond of social life and the theatre, and was a keen gardener and improver of the estate he bought in 1773 at Craiglockhart. He believed in sharing academic posts with younger colleagues, which in youth he had himself found valuable with his father. During his last ten active years he was joint professor with his son 'Alexander Tertius', although it was he who still gave most of the lectures in place of his less gifted son. The three Monros between them taught for 126 years (1720–1846).

Under Monro II medical student numbers increased steadily. In 1807, shortly before he retired, Professor Monro reckoned that in forty-eight years from 1759 total student attendance had been 13,404, nearly two-fifths of them (5831) from outside Scotland: from England, Ireland, Europe and America.[10]

The Medical School having achieved one of the highest reputations in the civilised world by the 1760s, it became accepted practice for young American colonists to study in Edinburgh, especially medicine under the great Dr Cullen and chemistry from 1776 under Dr Joseph Black, and then take back their skills to start medical schools in New Jersey and Pennsylvania. By 1776, forty-two of the 393 graduates were American, mostly medical students, and this practice continued well into the nineteenth century, even long after the founding of their own institutions such as in Philadelphia and New York. Many of these Edinburgh graduates went on to distinguished careers after their return to America.[11]

'The whole world I believe', wrote the Pennsylvanian Benjamin Rush in 1766, when ardently studying under Cullen and Black, 'does not afford a set of greater men than are at present united in the College of Edinburgh'; so much so that he was loth to move on to London, fearing that even Hunter and Fordyce might prove poor copies of these great masters. (In the event he was agreeably surprised.)[12]

Benjamin Franklin not long afterwards expressed reservations, on writing to advise his Philadephia friend Dr Thomas Bond in July 1771 where to send his son to study. 'Most of our young men have depended on Edinburgh and

London for their education. The School of Edinburgh seems at this Time to be better calculated to please the Fancy, than to form the Judgement; and indeed the many extraordinary Novelties inculcated there, would be a Barr to public Confidence in this Part of the World.' [13]

A few months later Franklin, back in London, was advising Bond that he considered physics and surgery as good in London as anywhere, with the best practitioners, and providing hospital attendance as well as anatomy lectures. 'And yet the general Run is at present to Edinburgh, there being at the Opening of the Schools when I was there in November last, a much greater Number of medical Students than had ever been known before.' He admitted that their professors were highly regarded, and he, as a layman, had at all events found them 'very sensible Men, and agreeable Companions'. [14]

Topham in 1775 regarded Drs Cullen, Black and Monro Secundus as equal in their fields, of 'physic', chemistry and anatomy, though not necessarily so as lecturers: Cullen he felt lacked energy in delivery, with a 'dryness and insipidity'; Black was 'too diffident', and his statements were sometimes so loaded with content as to choke utterance, though this aside, 'its propriety and strength more than reward your expectation', and his experiments were 'outstanding'. Monro, teaching the basic subject for medical students, was 'the most frequented', and a great orator, his well-rounded statements forcefully delivered. The rhetoric professor, Dr Blair, spoke with fire, and also in harmonious and well modulated terms.

These were only the best: in his view all excelled. 'There is no part of the world where so general an education can be obtained as in Edinburgh.' So much so that no degree below doctor carried any weight. [15]

The syllabus was distinctly tough. The full medical school programme, as outlined in 1771 by a first-year student, Thomas Ismay, a Yorkshire vicar's son, was formidably concentrated. From 9 to 2.30 p.m., punctuated by a bell between each class, there were hourly lectures by Dr Home (materia medica), Dr Cullen on physic, Dr Black (chemistry), Dr Gregory (physiology), Dr James Russell on natural philosophy, and Professor Monro II on anatomy, the last being allotted one and a half or even two hours. One hour was allowed for dinner between 3 and 4 (for which most students hurried back to their nearby lodgings), followed by Dr Young on Midwifery at 4. Between 5 and 7 Professor Monro's subject of the day was recapitulated by his dissector, Dr Innis. As if this were not enough, at 6 o'clock on Tuesday and Friday there was a chemistry class, and on Monday and Thursday Rae lectured on surgery at Surgeons' Hall, having somehow or other also fitted in a session on teeth in the morning. During the hour before his own class Professor Monro used to walk the Infirmary wards with Dr Innis, accompanied by the physicians and surgeons and followed by a trail of students.

In order to fit in all this study, young Ismay rose at 7 and read until 9 a.m., attended Dr Cullen's class and then returned home for breakfast and to transcribe his notes. At noon he followed Monro in walking the Infirmary, and then attended his lecture. By dinner-time 'as you may suppose I am very hungry'. He went to Dr Young at 5, again wrote up his notes and then went to Innis's 'private demonstrations' from 7 to 9 p.m., copying lecture notes which a fellow student had lent him, which saved having to buy them at three guineas. After supper at 9, he continued his lecture notes until midnight, joined by a young final-year student from Holland. In addition he went to the twice-weekly clinical lectures.

All this industry used up so many quill pens, besides five or six sheets of paper a day, that he had to write home for more.

His fees, like the work, mounted up: three guineas apiece to Professors Cullen, Monro and Young, another guinea to the dissector Innis, half a guinea to the lying-in ward, three more to 'walk' the Infirmary, 6s 6d to the various servants, a shilling to the college porter, half-a-crown to the Library, and three guineas for a copy of Cullen's and Gregory's lectures on the patients. Thomas told his family that his adviser Mr Williamson, a gifted surgeon, had four apprentices who paid him one hundred guineas each. This when a journeyman in Edinburgh earned a mere £4 a year.

Thomas was very pleased with the course and admired the professors, especially the brilliant Monro, lecturing in his fine theatre to some three hundred students: 'very good natured' and available for help and advice at any time. Cullen, however gifted, he thought, 'dwells too much upon Theory', and Dr Gregory, using theory only to illustrate practice, was more appreciated.

Thomas lodged opposite the college with an old gentlewoman, widow of a professor, who had two other boarders, one of them a student from Aberdeen. The charge was £10 a quarter for full board excluding washing, the lowest possible figure to be 'boarded in a genteel manner': some students paid £12. For this he was provided with tea twice a day, and a hot dinner and supper. Dinner was usually 'a large Tirene of Soup, which I like extremely well, a Dish of Boiled Meat and another of roast. Their Mutton and Beef is very good . . . Puddings only one'. Supper might be fish, eggs, beef-steaks 'or what you please'. He found Edinburgh living very dear, and so kept 'very retired', studying too hard for the good of his health. Sadly, this dedicated and promising student died in May 1772 in his twenty-second year. [16]

Benjamin Rush was more fortunate, and was much praised, especially by Dr Black, who befriended him with many 'marks of favour'. His professors naturally expressed interest in their model ex-student's returning to establish medical schools in Philadelphia – the more important because (writes Rush already in 1768) 'Boarding is now become so excessive high in Edinburgh that few students will be able to come here hereafter from America'. [17]

There was certainly a rise in the cost of living. In mid-century a young colonial student, John Moultrie, son of a laird of Roscobie, Dunfermline, who had emigrated to Charleston early in the century and become both a doctor and an indigo planter, paid only thirty shillings a quarter for lodging and £4 for dinners. He attended anatomy and materia medica lectures at the usual £3 per session, and early in February 1748 joined Rutherford's new lectures on Infirmary cases, 'very valuable and serviceable'.[18]

In the 1760s Andrew Dalzell and Robert Liston, who were to become, respectively, Professor of Greek at Edinburgh and a distinguished foreign diplomat (not to be confused with the later surgeon of that name), shared lodgings, living frugally on eggs and potatoes, probably brought from Andrew's family's farm at Kirkliston.[19]

Teaching took place in a group of buildings resembling a broken-down schoolhouse or 'pile of old stables', which – as Rush pointed out in 1786 to the Trustees of the Dickinson College in Philadelphia, whose establishment was in much the same condition – did not detract from Edinburgh's illustrious academic standing. A Virginian student, Thomas Tudor Tucker, noted that the old, irregular building was 'too mean to merit a description', and in any case he thought students used it only for reading and were mostly with their tutors or studying at home.[20] The shameful old building survived until long after Robert Adam's new college was begun in 1789, which remained unfinished until 1834.

In time the quality of medical teaching deteriorated to match. A generation after Benjamin Rush's eulogies, his own son James was thoroughly disillusioned by the standard of teaching which under the third generation of Monros had become a travesty of the great days.

In 1772 James Rae, Deacon of the Incorporation of Surgeons, started an independent extramural surgery lecture course at Surgeons' Hall, to which cases were referred by the College of Surgeons. Rae thus became founder of clinical surgery teaching in Edinburgh so successfully that in 1776 the College requested the magistrates to establish a formal University professorship. In 1778 the surgeons acquired a Royal Charter as the Royal College of Surgeons of Edinburgh.[21]

This school was renowned, paradoxically, for being soundly based on anatomy, or the theory of surgery; for practical study students were still advised to go to Paris.

A surgeon's training started with a five-year apprenticeship from the age of fifteen, living in a surgeon's house and attending his operations and house visits to the richer patients: the youth himself was probably soon put in charge of lower-class patients and carried out such useful and instructive 'drudgeries' as acting as hospital dresser or clerk, meanwhile attending the university lectures. On completing his apprenticeship, if he could afford it he would travel or study abroad or perhaps serve in the army, afterwards returning usually to Edinburgh where he was already familiar with the hospital practice, enter himself as FRCS with the President of the Royal College, and sit three examinations. He was then received as a surgeon at the hospital on payment of £200, and for the next few years would assist at or attend every consultation and operation.[22]

Hospital conditions, however, in no way mitigated the traumatic ordeal of unanaesthetised operations. At least until the end of the century the suffering patient had to be carried up several flights to an uncomfortable, gloomy, low-ceilinged room under the dome at the top of the Infirmary, overhearing meanwhile the cries of whoever was already under the knife. The surgical wards were crowded with curious, chattering onlookers and idle students. Infection was rife, and even small wounds or ulcers were usually attacked by a notorious 'hospital sore', about twice a year turning into a kind of epidemical 'hospital gangrene' which infected even the nurses. According to Dr John Bell, at certain seasons no operations were safe.[23]

Most surgeons were young, and by 1800 all the relevant chairs, anatomy, chemistry, midwifery and materia medica were also occupied by young men. According to Bell, however, the one quality not essential to a surgeon was experience. Knowledge of anatomy, he said, was all, and an operation was just like a dissection: practice had made surgeons perfect before they ever wielded a knife on a living subject. Surgery was a mechanically 'sure' art, and the long 'drudgery' practice during training paid dividends once the surgeon was qualified. Clinical medicine, on the other hand, he argued, was an uncertain science and for this experience was all-important.[24]

Surgeons also worked as general practitioners. 'Father of the surgical school' and first of Edinburgh's so-called 'scientific surgeons' was Benjamin Bell (1749-1806) (no relation to John), of Covenanter descent, eldest of fifteen children of a poor but gifted Dumfries man. At Edinburgh Bell studied under Monro I and II for clinical surgery and anatomy respectively, Dr Cullen, and others. He became an FRCS in 1770, completed his studies in Paris, and at the age of twenty-four was appointed a surgeon to the Royal Infirmary and became Scotland's leading practitioner. His six-volume *System of Surgery* was long the standard work.

As shown in Kay's *Portraits*, John Bell (who was an ancestor of Joseph Bell, said to be the original of Sherlock Holmes) was short and thick-set, with good features, clean-shaven and with thick wavy hair. His manner was mild and pleasant, and he was a well-informed conversationalist. Dr Bell, Dr Sandy Wood and others customarily wore the traditional doctor's formal dress, which continued long after it generally went out of fashion: knee breeches, lace-ruffled long-tailed black coat, silk stockings and silver-buckled shoes, and a broad-brimmed beaver hat; they carried the customary physician's gold-headed staff.[25]

Benjamin Bell unfortunately met an untimely death, never fully recovering after a fall from his horse, although treated at Liberty Farm by Dr Sandy Wood. He carried on with his profession until deteriorating health and increasing financial problems obliged him to limit his practice to a few patients, and he died on 5 April 1806 at Newington House, aged only fifty-seven.

Dr Alexander Wood, or 'Lang Sandy' (1725-1807), was also a leading figure, for rather different reasons, tall and striking, usually seen on his rounds with a tame raven and followed by a pet sheep. *Pace* John Macdonald, he seems to have been the first person in Edinburgh to carry an umbrella.

It was said that, when trying to convince his future father-in-law of his 'means', he produced his lancet-case with the confident assertion, 'We have nothing but this'.

It was Lang Sandy who was often called to aid the ladies who had fainted from enthusiasm at Mrs Siddons's performances. In fact Lang Sandy was almost better known for convivial eccentricity than for his surgery, and as co-founder of Edinburgh's various medico-social societies he lightened the profession. Lang Sandy Wood was commemorated for years after his death in 1807. Byron records of him in *Childe Harold*,

> Oh for an hour of him who knew no feud –
> The octogenarian chief, the kind old Sandy Wood.

while the distinguished Professor Andrew Duncan, who published *Poems* in 1818, wrote of his High Street tavern high-jinks,

> Here lies Sandy Wood, a good honest fellow,
> Very wise when sober, but wiser when mellow;
> At sensible nonsense by no man excell'd,
> With wit and good humour dull care he repell'd.
> Shed no tears my good friends, wear no garments of sable;
> Sandy Wood is not dead, but laid under the table.[26]

Another convivial medico was John Bennet, a polished and agreeable man who set up a carriage, the gift of a grateful patient, and became involved in one of the duels which were almost as common in the medical world as in the literary. He fell into an argument over a repair to his carriage with Field, partner of the famous coach-builder Crichton. Field challenged him, but Bennet refused as Field's 'rank was not that of a gentleman'. Crichton himself then turned up with a challenge, being colonel of the East New Town Company of the Edinburgh Volunteers, and this Bennet could not refuse. (He himself had been surgeon to the Sutherland Fencibles.) They therefore met, and Bennet shot Crichton through the right pectoral muscle, the ball passing through and emerging near his shoulder-blade. Though severely wounded, Crichton fortunately recovered.

Another medical duel was in 1805 between a pair of students, Romney and Leckie, son of the chief magistrate of Londonderry. Leckie was hit four times in the groin, and died of the first of these wounds, but had time to shake hands with his opponent and warned him, the surgeon and the seconds that he knew the wound was mortal and urged them to escape, which they did. John Bennet attended Leckie, and for his services was given the freedom of Londonderry. That same autumn, however, out on a shoot with his dog from a friend's house, he accidentally shot himself and died.

Bennet was regrettably fond of practical jokes. One fairly harmless one was when, as forfeit in a wager, he had to dine a party of friends and treat them to the opera. All went well, but on leaving the theatre they found among an astonished crowd, instead of carriages, a line of hearses to carry them home.[27]

In the great year 1784 Edinburgh was in the throes of the Cullenian/Brunonian controversy. The orthodox medical teaching of Dr William Cullen was challenged by his former pupil, the disputatious Dr John Brown, three times President of the Royal Medical Society. To it he expounded his simplified theory of medicine: that diseases and their treatments could alike be reduced to sthenic and asthenic, or strong and weak, treated respectively by stimulants and sedatives. This naturally produced fierce debates which soon extended from Edinburgh to the Continent. The eccentric Brown, having fallen out with everybody and supposedly led a 'dissipated' life, and ended not long afterwards in poverty. He died of his own remedies, excess of alcohol and opium.[28]

In Professor Monro Secundus' class was John Bell, small, neatly turned-out, intelligent-looking and alert, a former apprentice of Sandy Wood, who had once carried out a difficult operation on his father. John Bell complained ruefully of the shortage of dissection practice, with so few anatomical subjects available for study – unless 'there be a fortunate succession of bloody murders'.

This prize student, considerably more gifted than Monro III, was versed both in the classics and modern literature, a skilful musician and artist and a political speaker – more vivid than was usual in the Edinburgh school. The versatile Bell travelled in Northern Europe and Russia after graduating, and on his return in 1786, still aged only twenty-three, was entered as FRCS. Next year he started lecturing on midwifery, and in 1788 secured a site near Surgeons' Hall on which he built at his own expense a small anatomical school. He thus became the first true extra-mural anatomy lecturer, to ever-increasing numbers thanks to his vivid, polished presentation. His career was, however, marred by the notorious enmity of Dr James Gregory, Professor of the Practices of Medicine.[29]

At the end of the century a bitter controversy arose between Bell and James Gregory, who pursued a personal vendetta against him, starting with a paper war. One of Gregory's vitriolic pamphlets, signed by 'Jonathan Dawplucker' and entitled 'Review of the writings of John Bell, Surgeon in Edinburgh', was displayed all over the city, on the gates of the Infirmary and the College and even on the door of Bell's lecture-room, descending to such scurrilities as a claim that any patient 'should as soon think of calling in a mad dog, as Mr John Bell'. Gregory's object, in which he eventually succeeded, was to exclude Bell from the Infirmary, by attacking 'young surgeons' and changing the rules so that six surgeons would now serve for a two-year period instead of the two-month rota.

Gregory's lengthy attack provoked more than one reply. Longest was Bell's *Letters on the Education of a Surgeon and the Duties and Qualifications of a Physician, addressed to James Gregory,* in 650 pages, and the less unwieldy *Answer for the Junior Members of the Royal College of Surgeons, of Edinburgh . . .*[30]

Gregory attacked the arrangement by which every member of the Royal College of Surgeons was eligible to take his turn as operating surgeon of the Infirmary. He was incensed that only four of the twenty-three senior surgeons had so attended, while only four of the seventeen juniors had not, claiming that this violated the agreement originally made.

Thus in spite of attempts at change, surgery was now generally carried out by the youngest and least experienced. Even the students (he claimed) strongly disapproved, and a few years earlier there had been such a 'violent explosion' that the managers had had to intervene and enforce the rules by expulsions for 'indecent behaviour'. Young surgeons could not acquire enough experience in two months, yet sometimes a succession of them had been carrying out the operations for up to three years, resulting, in his view, in too many with poor qualifications. In an uncannily 1990s fashion Gregory further argued that Edinburgh was over-provided with surgeons and had more than double the necessary number – as also of physicians and lawyers. It was to this argument that John Bell responded that surgeons needed skill rather than experience. He lost the battle, however, despite the bulky published polemics on both sides, and Gregory secured the exclusion of Bell and others from the Infirmary rota, depriving poorer patients of their services and interrupting Bell's promising career after thirteen years as a lecturer, when he was only thirty-six.[31]

The colourful and contentious Bell continued, however, for nearly twenty years longer as Edinburgh's chief consulting and operating surgeon, with patients all over Europe, and he completed his *Principles of Surgery* in three volumes between 1801 and 1808. 'He was the reformer of surgery in Edinburgh, or rather the father of it', was one judgment. He made valuable contributions by reducing bleeding and gangrene, and by a treatment of wounds that often avoided amputation. But his judgment was sometimes warped by professional animosity, and he also fell out with Benjamin Bell. In 1816 he travelled abroad, received with acclamation everywhere, but his health deteriorated and in 1820 he died in Rome, in his fifty-seventh year.[32]

VII Tories and Revolutionaries

> 'The Scotch are not that civil and polite people they are reputed to be; if they are fauning it is only to bite you – They are excellent Flatterers and more make their Fortune by it than the English by their Industry, instance Dundas.'
>
> John Pease, 'Journal of a Traveller', 1795, in *Scottish History Review,* 1957

> 'A country without political life, without public meetings, without newspapers, without a hustings: could any endurable existence be lived in such a set of conditions – could any good come out of it?'
>
> David Masson, *Edinburgh Sketches and Memories*, London/Edinburgh, 1892, 160

> 'Scotland will be a thorn in the side of Government till it is newly represented. This whole country considers Lord Melville as its *chief;* and well they may, after 30 years' reign and entire power.'
>
> Lady Minto to Lord Minto, 30 May 1806, *Life & Letters of Sir Gilbert Elliot . . .*, 1874, III.383f

Edinburgh might appear to be run by Church, Law and University, but its effective ruler, and Scotland's itself, was Henry Dundas, created Viscount Melville in 1804. Younger brother of Robert, Lord President, he was born in 1741, educated in Edinburgh, qualified in the law, and in 1774 was elected MP for the county. Next year he was appointed Lord Advocate during Lord North's Government, continuing in office under Rockingham and Shelburne. His next post, as Treasurer of the Navy, he resigned on formation of the North/Fox coalition; but he had become a close friend of the younger Pitt, who was eighteen years his junior, and Pitt when forming his first ministry in December 1783 returned Dundas, then forty-two, to his Navy office. In 1787 he became MP for Edinburgh City and was responsible for several of its improvements; and was in turn President of the Board of Control for Indian Affairs, Home Secretary, Secretary for War, and First Lord of the Admiralty.

According to his nephew, Henry Cockburn, Dundas was 'handsome, gentlemanlike, frank, cheerful, and social . . . a favourite with most men, and all women'. And to Brougham: 'a plain, business-like speaker rather than an orator; a reliable friend, a hilarious companion' (one of the bonds between Dundas and Pitt might have been their mutual fondness for port), kind and good-natured.[1]

Throughout Pitt's premiership Dundas was effectively 'King of Scotland' (familiarly known as 'Harry the Ninth') – a position of power without defined office, such as had also been enjoyed for many years by Archibald, Earl of Islay and 3rd Duke of Argyll, who had died in 1761. He was constantly moving between Edinburgh and London. The whole legal administration of Scotland was in his hands, and all office and preferment came through him: judges, senior legal offices, sheriffs, Customs and Excise officials, university professors, and clergy held their places through his approval. Scotland, and Edinburgh, were ruled by a Tory oligarchy. Fifteen of Scotland's forty-five MPs represented burghs, or rather (excepting Edinburgh) districts of several burghs, and were elected by the Town Councils or their delegates. Edinburgh itself had just thirty-three voters. The rest 'represented' counties, elected by little more than 2,500 voters between them. Government control under such circumstances was not difficult and the English, traditionally ignorant of Scotland and the Scottish, were happy to let its affairs be delegated to a single minister.[2]

Under Dundas's jurisdiction there was in fact no representation of the people. With Town Councils self-elected and self-perpetuating, the Kirk established and without rival, juries usually voting according to the direction of the county sheriffs, and prosecuting counsels picked by judges for their likely submission to the establishment, all was imposed from above. There were no public political meetings, and had any been attempted, official revulsion would have seen them quickly dispersed.

On the plus side, Dundas mitigated several of the anti-Scot, anti-Jacobite restrictions imposed half a century earlier: in 1782 the proscription of Highland dress and the pipes was repealed, and in 1784 most of the forfeited estates were restored to their owners. He also sponsored Acts for the improvement of Edinburgh, such as that for building the College.

The press was limited to a handful of journals: the old-established *Caledonian Mercury* and *Courant*; the short-lived *Gazetteer*, launched in 1792 but suppressed on prosecution for reporting the activities of the Friends of the People; and the *Scots Chronicle*, an attempt at a literary and political bi-weekly which ran only from 1796 to 1806. The only semblance of a literary paper was the *Scots Magazine*, again long-established, which survived until 1826 after it had been taken over and its style much altered by Archibald Constable.[3]

Almost all the landed classes, and three-quarters of Scotland's population, were Tory.[4] Even the mild liberalism of those few professional and working men who opposed the Tories was regarded as dangerously seditious, though their influence was too small for organised political dissension or debate, and with no important newspaper as a vehicle for ideas, and a well-nigh incestuous relationship among the ruling classes, a narrow provincialism prevailed.

Yet the social structure was less rigid than in England. Scotland's small population and relative poverty allowed for a more fluid interchange between elements, and the remnants of the clan system put the humble on a less unequal footing with their chiefs. Further, cadets of the nobility and gentry were not limited to the armed services or the church. The law, whether practised or not, offered a regular training, and for many generations the youngest members of families had become merchants and bankers, who were therefore often well connected. The high standing of the University, too, meant that its senior staff, however poorly paid, moved in the same social circles as families of rank. In Edinburgh society distinguished doctors and professors were the friends of the usual nobility, land-owners and Members of Parliament, along with judges and advocates, heads of the Customs, Excise and Board of Exchequer, army and naval officers, men about town, and the favourites of the literary profession – these last often of quite humble birth. Even leading theatrical figures had a respectable social standing.

It was, however, a time of great political rancour, when entrenched Tories regarded almost with horror the Whiggish antagonism to the war and sympathy with French revolutionaries. Young Whigs had little chance of a successful career in the law, and in some cases had to abandon it. Edinburgh's corrupt and all-powerful council controlled everything in the city: 'our light, water, education, paving, trade, including the port of Leith, the poor, the police'.[5]

Particularly in the 1790s the Dundas rule was absolute. In the 1796 election he was calculated to control thirty-six of Scotland's forty-five constituencies, and of the representative Peers only three opposed him. Opposition was growing, however, among a group of Whig advocates, led by Henry Erskine, Dean of the Faculty of Advocates, and joined by Dundas's own nephew Henry Cockburn.

As the ideas of the French Revolution permeated through Scotland's more radical and discontented elements, one effect was the formation in 1792 of the 'Society of Friends of the People' – and on the other hand, the employment by a nervous Government of spies and secret observers. A leader among the 'Friends' was Thomas Muir, a young Glasgow advocate, who solicited other enlightened men to become members. Among these was the advocate Archibald Fletcher, husband of the brilliant Elizabeth Dawson, whose modest household in Hill Street had become the centre of advanced thinkers and philosophers. Mrs Fletcher heard them one day in another room at 'high words', but Fletcher, though a great lover of liberty, active for burgh reform and in hopes also of parliamentary reform, while approving Muir's enthusiasm, considered him lacking in judgment. 'These violent reformers will create such an alarm in the country', he observed with foresight to his young wife, 'as must strengthen the Government.'[6] Most 'Friends' in fact tended to be skilled workers in the provincial towns, and members kept in touch with others in England, Ireland and France.

Among the contentious issues between the ruling party and the 'Friends' was the question of reform in the Scottish Burghs, and because of Dundas's opposition, in 1792 the magistrates received anonymous warning of a planned demonstration during the traditional King's Birthday celebrations. A posse of dragoons was therefore ordered out on the morning of the Birthday, who rode furiously through the streets with drawn swords, producing only hoots and hisses from the crowd. In the afternoon the magistrates assembled as usual at Parliament House to drink the loyal toasts, with the City Guard drawn up outside to fire a volley to accompany each toast. They were assailed by a mob which gathered to throw dead cats at the Guard and each other. This was not uncommon behaviour for an Edinburgh mob, but they were further incensed by the unwise appearance of some dragoon officers, insulted them and were driven away for their pains, throwing a few last stones as Parthian shots.

The following evening they turned up outside Dundas's mother's house in George Square with a straw figure to burn him in effigy, and threatened two of his friends who, also unwisely, came out in an attempt to stop them. After breaking a few windows, they went on to the Lord Advocate's for the same treatment. A party of soldiers was sent out from the castle and the Sheriff read the Riot Act, followed by repeated warnings, but the mob refusing to disperse, the soldiers fired and wounded several men. For this deed the two majors of the Queen's Dragoons and the 53rd Foot were later made Burgesses of Edinburgh.

Undeterred, the mob re-assembled next evening, Wednesday, in Queen Street to attack Lord Provost Sir James Stirling's house. Signal guns were then fired at the castle to alert the marines on the *Hind* frigate at Leith, and the 4th Dragoons who were quartered a short distance out at Musselburgh. When they appeared, the crowd drew off.[7]

A ludicrous accident had occurred at the North Bridge while the crowd was on its way up to Queen Street. They overtook a tall, thin, black-clad old gentleman in a cocked hat, who in the flickering oil street-lamps looked so like the hated Sir James that several of them seized and hoisted him up, all ready hurl to him over the bridge. The poor gentleman roared out in a panic, 'Set me down, ye deevil's callants! – I'm no Sir Jeems, but Lang Sandy Wood!' And indeed he was that well-loved Sandy, or more formally the great Dr Alexander Wood, head of Edinburgh's medical profession, clad in his traditional doctor's garb. The mob released him at once, with cries of 'Och, it's gude Sandy Wood – let him gang!'[8]

That same evening in a distant part of Edinburgh, the boys at Mr Taylor's exclusive Musselburgh school were woken by the sound of the 4th Dragoons' trumpets in the street below. Springing out of bed they rushed to fling open the windows and cheer the soldiers. The Dragoons, mounted on sturdy black carthorses whose tails swept the ground, cheered back. To the boys they were a splendid sight, in scarlet uniforms faced with green and silver, yellow plush waistcoats and breeches and black knee-boots, their cocked hats bound with white braid, and armed to the teeth: straight basket-hilted swords, a brace of pistols on the saddle, and long muskets whose muzzles rested in a leather socket, by their feet. This rousing scene was summarily ended by the appearance of unsympathetic school ushers, themselves armed with leather tawse, who quickly scourged the boys back to bed.[9]

After this slightly farcical occasion the situation soon became uglier. The Government, deeply alarmed that the principle of monarchy should become subject of debate in Britain, began arresting potential radicals for sedition,[10] in a period of repression even harsher in Scotland than in England. Maurice Margarot and Joseph Gerrard, English delegates, were arrested and transported to Australia.

A trial which excited a great deal of high feeling was that of Thomas Muir, the Friend who had been agitating for a Scottish Convention and reformed suffrage, and had rashly made overtures to French thinkers and to a fellow-society in Dublin. In 1794 he was sentenced by Lord Braxfield to fourteen years' transportation, but died four years later at Botany Bay at the age of thirty-three.

Then there was Watt, a former Government spy who, apparently discontented with his pay, changed sides and ended as a fanatical supporter of the revolutionary cause. He and his fellow-conspirator Downie, a 'mechanic', were jointly accused of a plot to organise an Edinburgh rising, seize the castle and bank, take hostage the judges and declare a provisional republican Government. They were apparently in league with the London conspirators Hardy, Thelwall and Holcroft who were arrested shortly before them, but unlike the English revolutionaries, Watt and Downie were condemned to death. Downie was later reprieved, but Watt was executed in September 1794, when his behaviour was considered 'unmanly', in contrast with his earlier bold demeanour. The savagery of these trials at the outset of a period claiming enlightenment is a reminder of the element of barbarity not all that far from the surface of this civilised city.[11]

The orthodox Tory reaction to the sedition trials was typical of that expressed by the poet James Beattie, writing to Mrs Montagu:

> Sedition is still busy in North Britain . . . the jury unanimous in finding the charge proved, and the Court unanimous in banishing the criminals for 14

> years . . . A Society in and about Edinburgh has had the impudence to make some appearance under the name of the 'British Convention', and to adopt all the French gibberish of *civism* and *incivism*, *organisation*, *bulletin*, etc . . . There are but few of them, and they are all low people, weavers chiefly, I think I have heard of only one man of rank among them who no doubt wishes to do mischief . . .[12]

Similarly Walter Scott, who came back specially from Kelso to attend Watt's trial, thought it revealed 'the most atrocious and deliberate plan of villany . . . in the annals of Great Britain'. A fervent Loyalist, he saw in the evidence of the witnesses only 'equivocations and perjury', and in the arguments of the King's Counsel Anstruther, patience matched with skill.

During Watt's trial, the more interesting of the two, Scott sat in court from 7 one morning until 2 a.m. the next, fortified by cold meat and a bottle of wine he had brought with him. It appeared that the theatre disturbances by the 'Irish' gang were connected with the Friends. Scott doubted whether the conspirators would have achieved more than initial success, in some perhaps considerable blood-letting and seizing the banks, and he noted that at the time of the trial 'the people' appeared quiet, no matter how much they might have earlier supported the rebels.[13]

The treason trials were followed up by further repressive measures, the Treason and Sedition Bills (known as the Dumb and Padlock Bills). By the perverse political logic of the time, the official view was that representative government was contrary to the traditional British establishment, so that to agitate for it therefore amounted to treason. In 1795 the Circus at the top of Leith Walk was borrowed for taking signatures to a petition against the Bills. Two men stood at the door holding torches to alert passers-by, and inside, two copies of the petition were laid out on each of three tables; but although six men could thus sign at a time, it was usually necessary to queue for about half-an-hour. John Pease, a young Quaker businessman from Newcastle, travelling with an older member of his firm, was one who not only lined up to sign his name, but returned eagerly next day to follow progress, and was pleased that even from far off he could see a crowd 'as large and respectable as the day before': more than 2000 men signed the petition that day before noon.[14]

The trial of Watt was one of the earliest occasions on which the Edinburgh Volunteer Corps was called in. In 1794 a group of able, eager young men met to enlist in a corps to defend their city and country against revolutionaries, and by the next year had amassed 700 members. Over the next few years they were to play a conspicuous and picturesque if not truly warlike part.

The volunteers, who were to act in support of the regular regiments stationed at the castle, met to exercise for four hours almost daily, and were subject to military discipline. Scott's brother Tom joined the Grenadiers who, he noted, were all over six feet tall and made a most spectacular appearance; but the volunteers, weighed down with heavy uniform, still managed to appear 'martial and warlike',[15] and their proficiency in firing and manoeuvring supposedly surprised the regular soldiers.

Political unrest of course continued, and on the King's Birthday in 1796 Edinburgh suffered 'a formidable riot'. Nearly a thousand of the gentry, among them Scott, volunteered to the magistrates as special constables, and were issued with batons, assembling in the aisle of the New Church for some reason for claret and 'sweetmeats'; the mob chased Sir John Whiteford, and Scott, his brother Tom and one or two others rescued him, hustling off the aggressors with their batons. The Lord Justice Clerk's windows were broken by a gang of youths but a party of constables and pressed men arrived and were disappointed to find the mob departed. All in all the occasion was considered fairly peaceful, but the very quiet suggested worse to come. [16]

The 'association' then met to be divided into districts, and their captains appointed and places of rendezvous fixed. The summons to action was to be the hoisting of a flag on the Tron steeple and ringing of all the bells, upon which the men had to assemble within five minutes.

By 1797 the threat of a French invasion seemed imminent. A troop of London Light Horse had already been raised, but in Edinburgh it appears to have been to some extent Scott's enthusiasm that inspired the formation of a troop of mounted volunteers aged between sixteen and sixty. His own lameness made the prospect of a cavalry troop, armed with sabres, the more desirable. [17] On 14 February a group of friends met and officially agreed to serve anywhere in Scotland if invaded, as the Edinburgh Volunteers. The Duke of Buccleuch as Lord Lieutenant of Midlothian passed the proposal to the Government. Charles Maitland of Rankeillour was elected Major-Commandant, (Sir) William Rae of St Catharine's captain, and there were two lieutenants, two cornets, an adjutant, and Walter Scott as 'Paymaster, Quartermaster, and Secretary' – an over-ambitious combination which was soon docked off the Paymaster's duties. That had been especially chosen to spare Scott's lameness, but in fact he was a skilled and fearless rider, seemingly impervious to fatigue, his enthusiasm infecting the rest, and he was always able to set them laughing: all of which offset the tedium of the long hours of drilling, especially for those quite unaccustomed to regular discipline. The others called Scott 'Earl Walter', and he was always ready for a joke when there was a break in the exercises.

In the spring and summer there were continuous exercises for some weeks, when the troops took up quarters at Musselburgh and dined together every day in mess; but duties had to be fitted in with people's professions, so that the drills started at 5 a.m., after a few hours of which Scott, for example, had to appear gowned and wigged in the Parliament House for the hours until 2 p.m. He was also running a small legal practice, and there seems to have been no let-up in his literary work, which in these early days was chiefly translations from the German.

Scott's detailed notes of the items required for his military portmanteau are revealing: two shirts, a black handkerchief, a woollen nightcap, a pair of blue pantaloons, a sleeved flannel shirt, a pair of flannel drawers, a waistcoat and a pair of worsted stockings. In the cover he stacked a shaving-case, combs, knife, fork and spoon, 'a German pipe and tobacco-bag, flint, and steel', pipe-clay and its implements, 'a pair of shoes or hussar-boots', and a shoe-brush. There were also items for cleaning down his horse: overalls, jacket, a horse-sheet and other things. In his cartouche-box were 'a screw-driver and picker for pistol', and spare flints.

Not all his friends admired this single-minded military zeal, and one Whiggish acquaintance commented sarcastically on his becoming 'the merest trooper that ever was begotten by a drunken dragoon . . . Not an idea crosses his mind, or a word his lips, that has not an allusion to some damned instrument or evolution of the Cavalry'.[18] Cockburn too remarked on his 'absolute passion' in their activities in 1804/5, gratifying 'his feudal taste for war, and his jovial sociableness. He drilled, and drank, and made songs, with a hearty conscientious earnestness which inspired or shamed everybody within the attraction.'[19]

It was, incidentally, later in the summer of the Volunteers' formation that, holidaying in the Lake District with friends after the ending of his unrequited love affair,[20] Scott met and shortly became engaged to a second-best, Miss Charlotte Carpenter, née Charpentier, of French extraction, a ward of the Marquess of Downshire. A rather wayward young lady, she was a match of which not all Scott's friends approved. Once her guardian's consent was received, however, the lady's letters became less capricious, and the pair were married on 21 December 1797.

George Combe, who heard a seamier side of military and naval life from the men working at his father's brewery, who were all vulnerable to call-ups and the press gang, relates how the first regiment of Volunteers were 'gentlemen', providing their own uniforms, and supplied only with their muskets and belts with the ammunition. There were also three or four regiments of 'inferior' rank, who were given their uniforms. This service exempted its members from militia call-up, but others not exempt were liable for service between the ages of eighteen and forty-five, unless they paid a premium of up to £50 for a substitute. As militiamen were always volunteering to join regiments of the line, there were frequent ballots to fill their ranks from the townspeople, who could only plead exemption if they had three children and an income of less than £50. The humbler ranks were also at the mercy of the press gang, and pay for a man-of-war was far worse than in the merchant navy. George could feel for these men, knowing that young midshipmen or ensigns were recruited straight from the brutalised atmosphere of the High School and hence, as he saw it, the norm was 'flogging as the substitute for moral and intellectual influence'.

Although, being at school at this period, George did not personally witness the brutality, he knew that punishment parades were held in the castle between 9 and 11 a.m. several mornings a week, in the space between the castle wall and the new barracks begun in 1796.[21] This was just above the brewery, and the victims' screams could be heard all too clearly down below. Spectators, mostly women, crowded the barrack windows to watch with ghoulish interest.

Punishment for small civil offences was commonly flogging through the Old Town at the cart's tail; and there were frequent hangings, in the afternoons between 2 and 4 o'clock, sometimes of women. George, caught up one day in the Lawnmarket and trapped between the Luckenbooths and St Giles's, was an involuntary witness of the execution of a letter-carrier, condemned for stealing from the mails. The man, respectably dressed in a black suit, had a white cap pulled over his face, and was handed the white handkerchief whose drop was his signal to open the trap. The bolt was drawn, he fell, and after a pause began his ghastly death-struggles, which lasted for four or five minutes. The coarse jokes heard around him, and expressions of sympathy for the condemned man's family, did nothing to lessen the shattering effect on the boy, and this harrowing experience added to the superstitious terrors which haunted his childhood.[22]

At a time when in England the young Wordsworth and Coleridge were inflamed with a passion for liberty and proclaiming it in their writings, it was not surprising that a Scottish poet should be fired with enthusiasm.

Thomas Campbell, of a West Highlands family, at the age of fifteen in 1794 had been much affected by attending the Edinburgh trial and condemnation by Lord Braxfield of Margarot and Gerrard, to which he purposely walked from Glasgow. Campbell shortly began to earn his living as a tutor in Mull and Argyll, and suffered many early disappointments, including in love. Handsome and athletic though short in stature, as time went on he was increasingly victim to moods and depressions, struggling to write poetry and dabbling in a variety of part-time jobs. Mrs Fletcher, who befriended him when he was lodging in Rose Street, was impressed by the 'ardent, enthusiastic' boy in whom the Dugald Stewarts, Brougham, Cockburn and others also fancied they could detect a spark of genius.[23]

This unpretentious youth (as his painter acquaintance Somerville thought him), 'quaint, queer, desultory, comic, occasionally querulous and sarcastic, but always rather the reverse of poetical', was inclined to take offence easily, subject to mercurial, almost suicidal, changes of mood. Judge, then, the Edinburgh world's astonishment when, after many reluctant revisings and plunges into gloom, Campbell's four hundred-line poem *Pleasures of Hope* was published in 1799 and rocketed him, at the age of just under twenty-two, 'like a star from his obscurity' as (claimed the press) a 'new and interesting light over the literary horizon'.

The poem, dedicated and idealistic, in style reminiscent of Pope, Gray and Goldsmith, ranged over the Revolution, the partition of Poland and massacre of patriots during the capture of Warsaw, the evils of slavery and European barbarities in India – and the influence of Hope.

Great men quickly became interested patrons. Dr Gregory casually picked up a volume at the publisher's and, his attention caught by one passage, turned back to the beginning and did not stir from the counter until he had read the whole first Part. Then, 'Mr Mundell!' he exclaimed, 'This is poetry! Where is the author to be found? I will call upon him immediately'. And did, apparently overlooking a patient's appointment to do so. The praise of a cultured and widely travelled man like Gregory, versed in literature and the friend of genius, was valuable indeed.

Walter Scott, whom the poet had already met, gave Campbell a dinner at which the bashful youth was all but overcome by the guests' distinction and sparkling conversation. But then Scott, as soon as the cloth was removed and the loyal toasts were drunk, rose to pay a handsome compliment to the new poem and to propose a toast to its author, whom he now introduced to the company. Campbell was made.[24]

In the political atmosphere of the time, the Lord Advocate thought *Pleasures of Hope* dangerously 'democratical'.

On the other hand the still young Scott, a fervent Tory, had begun to make his name with poetry of a very different sort. Based on ballad traditions and medieval Scottish history, it rapidly became dear to latent Whig as well as Tory hearts. *The Lay of the Last Minstrel* a few years later was to establish Scott as a poet, and by that time he was also in a secure – though still underpaid – legal career.

VIII Theatrical Progress

> 'To my chagrin, every thing conspired to make it disgusting. It is hard to say which were most execrable, the acting, the scenes, the dresses, or the fiddling. Decorations there were none.'
>
> 'The Ghost' [Dr Constantia], Glasgow and London, 1796, No. 5

> [The building has a] 'double effect of disgusting spectators by its own deformity, and of obstructing the view of the Register-House, perhaps the handsomest building in the Nation.'
>
> Hugo Arnot, *History of Edinburgh*, 1788, 371

> 'The house is neat, but not what would be expected in the New Town of Edinburgh. The heat was very great and the audience called to have the green curtain drawn up . . . it did not seem to have the advantages of dress and scenery that it enjoys in London . . . To compare Mr Home to Shakespeare is injustice to him [but] . . . he may always be mentioned as one of the brightest ornaments of the Drama.' (11 July 1799)
>
> 'The Journal of a Tourist in the 1790s', in Ian Ousby (ed.), *James Plumptre's Britain*, Hutchinson, 1992, 130

The early theatre managers, unable because of the high annual rents to afford good costumes or stage machinery, let alone good actors, found it hard to make ends meet. Samuel Foote's company was better than his predecessor Ross's. He brought his whole company of twenty men and eight women from the Haymarket in London and – an innovation – opened for the whole winter season: normally the licence had been limited to the summer. His first season in 1770–1 was a financial success, and he actually cleared £1000. The company's first good comedian was the versatile mimic Henry Woodward, who was generally admired and able to have the first benefit night that Edinburgh had voluntarily supported.

James Boswell was appreciative: 'We have been kept laughing all this winter by Foote, who has made a very good Campaign of it here', through Woodward's invaluable support, for 'Mr Foote's drollery cannot entertain long in a Town where there is not a Variety of audiences'. In fact Edinburgh could not understand the London jokes, and the leading lady, Mrs Jewel, had a poor figure and an 'aukward inanimate action'. In general Foote did not like Edinburgh, where the weather was bad, his satires on the recently dead George Whitfield were attacked by the clergy and his own lifestyle was criticised by the locals as luxurious: his carriage and livery-servants were jeered by the mob with derisive shouts of 'There goes the *play actor!*'. Losing a legal dispute with Ross, he finally decided to sell the remaining two years of the lease at a loss, and left Edinburgh.[1]

The new takers were West Digges, a well connected gentleman, and John Bland, an ex-Templar who had served in the army at Fontenoy and in the '45, and now proved a stage favourite for twenty-three years; he was, incidentally, uncle to Mrs Jordan. The fashionable Digges had no London experience but had acted at the Canongate, as one of those gentlemen whose youthful extravagances drove them to the desperate expedient of the stage. The new managers concentrated on tragedy, and did so well that when their two years were up they renewed the lease for a further five years.

Although Digges was successful both as actor and manager, his company were, as Topham charitably puts it, 'foils to himself': that is, inferior, and he changed them every year, not for the better. His own acting, not being based on other models, was patchy but original. His best roles were Sir John Brute in *The Provok'd Wife,* Cardinal Wolsey in *Henry VIII* and (Boswell thought) the best ever Macheath, but he was obliged to play all the main parts himself, not all of them suitable. His expression was unattractively severe and his voice had a rough timbre – perfect no doubt for Pierre in *Venice Preserv'd.* Meanwhile his wretched company existed on pittances, sometimes as little as a guinea a week, in a city where the cost of living was considered as high as London.

According to Topham, the start of the theatre season was dictated by 'genteel' society, so polite that nobody would dare be seen there before a due date had been agreed for their first attendance. Topham was also struck by the number of ladies in the audiences, and the taste and judgment they displayed over Digges's choice of plays. Moreover the galleries, or Gods, were better behaved than in London, more like the French, and refrained from showering the stage with rotten fruit. Their disapproval was shown simply by lack of applause.[2]

'Everybody' went. Boswell was a fairly frequent attender and used to meet Digges on friendly terms, while young Henry Mackenzie was a regular theatre fan and self-appointed critic, sending a running commentary to his cousin Elizabeth Rose, and often sitting in and contributing his views at auditions. The theatre had acquired social respectability. Lawmen had supported it since Canongate days, but now the aristocracy were also regular supporters, and the 6.30 performances conveniently followed on after the usual 4 o'clock dinner-hour.[3]

There were ups and downs. Mrs Yates and her husband, engaged for two seasons at a high fee in the spring of 1773, gave the theatre a boost, but proved too expensive; two years later a low-paid company performed no better than could be expected, and their poor acting drove audiences to the concert-hall instead. Then in 1775 Digges was inspired to stage a ridotto in the theatre, whose advertisement brought all Edinburgh and its neighbouring lairds and families to attend at a guinea a head. The Kirk, which would have denounced a masquerade, did not disapprove of a ridotto. It was held on 10 March.[4]

For that enchanted evening the stage was covered over, as at the London opera on such occasions; wine, ices and other refreshments were served in the side boxes, while orchestra and singers were massed at the top of the stage. Above the stage boxes were landscapes painted by Edinburgh's leading artist, Alexander Runciman; above the other boxes heads of poets were illuminated, and other 'elegant ornaments' completed the scene. After a staid opening with sets of minuets in different parts of the auditorium, lively country dances took over. Music accompanied the refreshment interval, and finally there was a performance of French horns and clarinets provided by gentlemen of the regiment quartered in Edinburgh. The public's behaviour on this occasion was considered admirable – with no unseemly over-indulgence even after the ladies had left.[5]

Edinburgh's rival entertainments were of varying quality. The leading musical attraction was the weekly recitals of high standard at St Cecilia's concert hall. Scottish voices being thought poor, Italian singers were usually engaged, made fashionable by Tenducci, who was succeeded in 1770 by Luciani, whose voice was more powerful but with less feeling and expression; on the other hand, Henry Mackenzie thought him 'a better man, temperate, devout', and less likely to be spoiled by the city life. Next year came the handsome Signora Corri, with a 'hard unmellow'd voice', best suited to burletta singing.[6] In 1772 John Christoff Schetky came over and settled in Edinburgh, becoming the chief cellist at St Cecilia's.

Signor Domenico Corri, music master, composer and publisher, at this time lived largely in Edinburgh. In July 1776 he opened a new 'Ranelagh Garden' near the West Kirk at Kirkbraehead, with music, transparencies, cascades, fireworks and all the other displays proper to a pleasure garden. Corri regularly held concerts at which his pupils performed, two of them being Boswell's daughters (1785). He was evidently considered socially acceptable, for early in 1786 Boswell invited him to dine, along with Lunardi the balloonist, 'at the earnest desire of my children'. Lunardi had made an ascent from Edinburgh in December, but fell into the sea and was almost drowned.[7]

Corri later moved to London, set up his own carriage and declared to Boswell that he would not return to Edinburgh for any consideration (1789), though he evidently changed his opinion later.

In 1777 a show at a 'Grand Museum' off the Netherbow offered such novelties as automata, including an activated elephant and a horseless machine. Those up-to-date displays like the Panorama and the Circus took a few more years to become established, while in 1788 the historian Arnot notes that the venture Comely Garden was merely 'a wretched attempt to imitate Vauxhall, for which neither the climate nor the gardens are adapted'.[8]

During years of prosperity at the theatre Digges was able to engage Mrs Bellamy, Mrs Barry, Sheridan and occasionally Foote, as well as the Yateses, the last actually receiving 100 guineas for the 'fag-end of a season'. There were special occasions, such as an evening devoted to raising funds for a bridge at a dangerous ford over the river Carron, when Mr Nicholson Stewart, a gentleman of fashion, acted Richard III. He was judged a good actor but with a weak voice: the 'polite audience' nevertheless filled the theatre, and paid five shillings for the privilege.

Digges himself ran into trouble at last, and handed over to another well-connected successor, John Jackson, who had joined the stage for his own pleasure and published a useful if rather dull *History of the Scottish Stage.* Jackson's management initiated a more glittering period of some eleven years, notably because in his second year he engaged the new comet who had just taken London by storm – Mrs Sarah Siddons. Jackson followed the actress from London to her next assignment in Dublin, and engaged her for the Edinburgh season. She first appeared there on 22 May 1784, as Belvidera opposite Joseph Woods as Jaffier.[9]

Sarah Siddons was then twenty-nine. A stranger to Edinburgh, she was unaware of the gravity of their audiences, which Mrs Barry, Mrs Yates and others had suffered before her. Edinburgh people customarily held back their applause until they had determined that it was fully earned, so for some time the lady performed to total silence, as if, it was said later, she was speaking to stones. At length, in a particularly moving speech, she threw herself into it heart and soul, resolving that should this fail, she would never come to Edinburgh again. She ended, and paused. The audience was still silent . . . then suddenly a single voice was raised: 'That's no bad!' A gale of laughter convulsed the house, followed by storms of applause.[10]

It was a triumph. Mrs Siddons played for three weeks and gave twelve performances, including as Mrs Beverley and Isabella, while Edinburgh could think and speak of nothing else. People came from as far afield as Newcastle. Crowds formed at the theatre hours before it opened, so that the management agreed to let them in as early as 3 p.m., then in order to get in at 3, they started turning up at noon. One group of men-about-town paid the manager £200 to guarantee their seats and thus obtained specially early admittance. Families sent their servants, or engaged porters to camp in the street on stools and palliasses. Even the clergy were won over, and the General Assembly, then sitting, was actually persuaded to time its meetings to avoid clashing with performances, its younger members cleverly arguing that Mrs Siddons's pure diction was a valuable lesson for clerical eloquence. The theatre, which held 630, one day had 2557 applications for seats. In the frantic struggles for entrance military detachments had to be called to guard the gallery doors – even with bayonets – while wigs, hats, shoes, watches and pocket-books were lost or pilfered, and rumour had it that when word got to London, its thieves had hurried up to Edinburgh for the pickings.

The scenes inside were no less dramatic. The effect of the actress's more moving scenes on staid Scottish ladies was staggering. Swoons and hysterics accompanied some passages, especially in *Isabella, or The Fatal Marriage,* where the heroine, persuaded into remarriage believing her husband, Biron, is dead, finds he is alive: a scene which so exhausted Mrs Siddons herself that one night she had to be carried from the stage. Miss Gordon of Gight, a young Aberdeenshire heiress, was also carried, screaming, from her box, shouting hysterically for 'her Biron'. (Oddly enough the next year Miss Gordon received and of course accepted a proposal from the Hon. John Byron, of whom she had not then even heard, and they became the parents of Lord Byron the poet. How much had Mrs Siddons unconsciously influenced that acceptance?) So many people fell ill with the excitement that doctors diagnosed the combination of fatigue and emotion as 'Siddons fever'.[11]

The sportsman Colonel Thornton, about to set out on a Highlands shooting tour with friends, and prolonging their Edinburgh stay on the news of some riots, found among the city's upper classes 'a commotion almost as great' over Mrs Siddons. Meeting acquaintances dining at Fortune's, he wanted to procure them all seats, but to his surprise they affected boredom, having seen the lady so often already, and offered only to turn up for the farce and ogle the audience. Two of Thornton's party, however, secured a box, when he was astonished at the 'long murmurs, deep sighs, and tearful handkerchiefs . . . plentifully displayed by the ladies', which he dismissed as fashionable affectation as the house was so full that he reckoned most of the audience 'could scarcely hear a syllable'. When they started fainting, despite his admiration for the actress he began to wish himself back at Dun's hotel. They returned after the play to Fortune's, however, and found the party they had left still at table and courteously ready to order them supper.[12]

Throughout Edinburgh, politics and other subjects had been forgotten: all the talk was of Mrs Siddons. The critics were in raptures, of course, and one journal actually urged audiences to follow the Drury Lane rule (not then used in Edinburgh) of regularly withholding applause until the end of each scene, in order not to destroy the emotional effect.

All this benefited the actress to the tune of nearly £1000, £350 of it from her benefit night, besides a night's profits given to the Charity Workhouse. On her second Edinburgh visit in 1788 Mrs Siddons was presented with a piece of plate by the Faculty of Advocates, as 'an acknowledgment of respect for eminent virtues, and of gratitude for pleasure received from unrivalled talents'; while on her 1792 visit she cleared £1253 in ten nights and £154 from her benefit.[13] This was only the start of her and her family's long association with the Edinburgh theatre.

The 1784 summer season was generally more crowded than usual, and the theatre's success kept people longer in the city, despite disconcertingly changeable weather, ranging from uncomfortable heat at Leith races in August to rain and thunder followed by piercing cold. The Duchess of Buccleuch, who went to see Congreve's *Mourning Bride,* was not much pleased even with Mrs Siddons as Zara, the supporting company being so tiresomely bad; she hoped for better things next night with Vanbrugh's *Provok'd Husband*, in which surely the actors 'cannot be so bad in comedy as in tragedy'.[14] The following week the actress moved on from Edinburgh, the Court of Session rose, the shooting season began and at last 'we shall be quiet for some time'. The 'Siddonian rage', as Colonel Thornton called it, died down.[15]

Mrs Siddons was of course lionised by society, and was carried off to stay at the eccentric Lord Buchan's. Here she met the poet James Beattie, who had been lucky enough to get one of the best seats in the theatre through the efforts of the Buchans and the Duchess of Gordon. For Beattie, the occasion was a 'dinner-party' extending to a night or two's hospitality, and during his stay Mrs Siddons sat for her portrait to Lady Buchan, while the Earl's brother entertained the party with his violin, and Beattie accompanied the actress on the violoncello in the Scots airs she loved, one of which brought her to tears. He thought her appearance – barring that of his glamorous patroness the Duchess of Gordon – the most beautiful he had ever seen, with her black brows and deep dark eyes.[16]

Sir Gilbert Elliot of Minto, who met the lady in London in 1787, remarked to his wife that 'she is very beautiful in a room, but of the strong powerful sort of beauty that reminds one of a handsome Jewess'. She spoke little, and modestly at that, in so slow and studied a way that it seemed like acting, always theatrical.[17] (She was later described as even asking for a dish at supper tense with drama.)

There was meanwhile a particular form of music in Edinburgh, experienced by Faujas de St Fond during his visit in 1784. While meeting all the 'savants' and literati, he saw most of the 'venerable philosopher' Adam Smith, with whom he struck up a strong rapport as Smith had travelled in France and lived in Paris, and knew Voltaire and Rousseau. He one day invited St Fond to a concert which he thought would test his musical judgment, and escorted him to 'a spacious concert-room, plainly but neatly decorated, and full of people'. These gentlemen (the ladies sat elsewhere), sitting on benches in a circle, were competition judges, all land-owners from the Highlands and Islands, and thus natural connoisseurs of what they were about to hear.

Meanwhile there was no sign of music. They waited for half-an-hour, and at last the folding doors opened and St Fond was amazed to see no one enter but a Highland piper 'in his costume of Roman soldier . . . walking up and down the empty space with rapid steps and military air, blowing the noisiest and most discordant sounds from an instrument which lacerates the ear'. St Fond, with no means of judging his skill, and distinguishing 'neither air nor design' in what he heard, except that the work was divided into three parts, was further astonished that the 'insupportable uproar' received such great applause. The next performer was even more enthusiastically received, and 'grave men and high-bred women shed tears'.

The Frenchman listened to eight of these versions of the same work, eventually grasping that part one was a kind of military march, part two described a bloody battle and was therefore faster and noisier, with histrionic gestures and shouts, all present being enthralled by 'this fine disorder'; finally 'a kind of andante' as lament for the dead. Musically he could make nothing of it, and was forced to interpret it as a form of history, works not being written down but handed on in this way from generation to generation. All lay in the skill of the performers, treated equally whether laird's son or shepherd.

The competition ended, the judges set to their assessment, while the performers played airs and others danced, then they marched out two by two to the foot of the castle rock, and played an air in honour of Mary, Queen of Scots. The winner was presented with a fine set of ivory-mounted pipes. All in all, the performance was wasted on St Fond; but then, his own tastes lay almost wholly in the field of mineralogy and natural history.[18]

Aside from Mrs Siddons's triumphs, the chief theatrical success during this period was a six-night visit in July 1789 by Mrs Jordan, then aged twenty-seven and not yet the mistress of the Duke of Clarence. On this occasion the Duchess of Buccleuch, who kept Lady Louisa Stuart, her cousin by marriage, informed of the Edinburgh season (and weather) was often more concerned with the conditions than the play. She was pleased with the performance though not with the cold and changeable weather. After the Leith races the playhouse was not very full and therefore not too stifling, and she conceded in passing that Mrs Jordan 'always delights me'. But when her young family went next night it turned uncomfortably hot.[19] The young Samuel Rogers, already known as a poet and lively conversationalist, on his first Edinburgh visit was scarcely more informative. On 20 July, after dining with Adam Smith, where he met Henry Mackenzie ('very soft and pleasing manners'), they all went on to a dull meeting of the Royal Society to find only seven gentlemen present, and Adam Smith fell asleep. Eventually they landed at the theatre, and sat in the stage box, shut in, 'in the Italian style', with a lively party including the Piozzis and Miss Thrale. Of the play, *Hippolyta,* Rogers remarked merely that 'Mrs Jordan directed herself to the box'.[20]

The playhouse itself, so often criticised for its unimpressive exterior, was in 1788 rendered more distinguished by a pedimented portico bearing the town's arms, and by a statue of Shakespeare above with figures of Comedy and Tragedy on either side.[21]

Few theatre managers came to a happy end. David Ross was negotiating for renewal of his patent in 1781, but a few years later, in June 1786 Boswell saw him in London lame and poor, subsisting on an annual gift from an anonymous donor. His wife Fanny Murray, a famous courtesan, had died in 1778.[22]

Jackson's own management ended with a complicated dispute, and he left the Edinburgh theatre in 1791.

Other famous names appear. One feature of Jackson's tenure of the theatre was an improvement in the scenery when about 1787 the versatile young artist Alexander Nasmyth turned his hand to occasional scene-painting. Nasmyth, son of a successful builder and architect, born in the Grassmarket in 1758 and educated at the High School, had learned mathematics from his father (precious little to be gleaned at the school), and early showed a talent for art. Apprenticed to Crichton's the coach-builder's, he painted the expensively decorated coach panels, and at night attended Edinburgh Drawing Academy, where he so impressed the grumpy master, Alexander Runciman, that he actually framed and hung one of Nasmyth's studies. At sixteen he was discovered by Allan Ramsay, now Court Painter to the King, who persuaded or bribed Crichton to transfer his indentures and carried the boy off to London to paint clothes and props for his portraits. Late in 1778, with Ramsay's lifelong friendship behind him, Nasmyth returned to Edinburgh and set up as a portrait painter himself.

By 1787 he had married, befriended and painted Robert Burns, and helped the rich banker Patrick Miller of Dalswinton in pioneer experiments with a steam-driven pleasure-boat on Dalswinton Loch – with Burns as one of the passengers and Henry Mackenzie watching from the shore. Besides giving painting lessons at his house, Nasmyth enjoyed a busy social and club existence. He liked studying Edinburgh's architecture and discussed road layout with the builders and architects, such as consulting with Sir James Nesbit over building the new Dean Bridge; he also designed St Bernard's Well in the vale of the Water of Leith. His turn at scene-painting for the theatre in 1787 was just another extension of his wide-ranging talents. The younger David Roberts learned the art from him and adopted his style.

Nasmyth was similarly commissioned by the next theatrical luminary, Mrs Siddons's younger brother Stephen Kemble, who had come to run the theatre from 1789. On Jackson's retirement, however, Kemble was unsuccessful in applying for the patent, which was secured by Mrs Esten, herself a talented actress, and another lady. He then fitted up a 'New Theatre', a building known as the Circus at the head of Leith Walk, which he opened on 18 January 1793, and employed Nasmyth to paint the scenery. The venture almost collapsed because of the Theatre Royal's monopoly of the licence. Although Mrs Esten secured a court decree against plays acting at the rival theatre, it remained a competitor for some years. In January 1794 Kemble regained the patent and lease of the Royal which he kept for the next six years.[23]

While the theatre itself had attained a respectable footing in society, rival forms of entertainment such as pantomime, or equestrian shows, remained unsuccessful.[24]

Strolling players who gave unsophisticated performances in the suburbs offered no serious competition. Philip Ainslie, as a schoolboy at Mr Taylor's in Musselburgh, was one of those whom the master allowed to attend a performance at the local Town Hall, temporarily fitted up as a theatre. The inexperienced youths, faced with their first (very topical) play, *The Last Days and Execution of Louis XVI*, could hardly distinguish between fiction and fact, especially when they recognised among the extras 'the town drummer, and the baker's prentice', clumsily tripping over their cloaks as they tried to bear off the King's corpse; and they treated the executioner to such a storm of threats and abuse, ending in near-riot, that the school's bullying usher drove the bemused boys from the hall with his cane.[25]

One traditional annual event, too much the prerogative of high society to be affected by the theatre or other forms of entertainment, was the Leith Races, run early in August on Leith Links. They were often attended by more than 300 carriages, and 'an immensity of riders and spectators', usually very smartly attired. In 1781 Sir Alexander Dick noted that his daughter Janet ('Jessie') turned up with her Guardsman brother in a gig wearing a fashionable scarlet habit. Indeed, in a dull year for racing, as Lady Carlow complained it was, fashion and spectacle made the event: 'It was a very uncommon sight to see the shore crowded with people, and millions [sic] of carriages and servants upon the sands. You must know everybody piques themselves upon having a number of attendants and smart liveries upon these occasions.'[26]

Leith races were an event of the season, as in England Ascot and Henley were to be later. A stand for the Lord Provost and magistrates was built by the winning-post, and opposite was 'a magnificent purse decorated with a large bunch of ribbons', which was supposed to hold the town prize. Scaffolds of seating were put up for the spectators, and crowds of ballad singers, bagpipers, organ grinders, wild beast shows and, in the 1790s, recruiting parties on the lookout added to the throng.

The races were run on the sands east of the port. Its daily tides made it a 'heavy' course, so that owners could not enter any of their more valuable horses. They started on a Monday at (say) 9 a.m. when the tide was low and the sands dry, and moved on an hour everyday as the tide changed. On Tuesday was the King's Plate, with a prize of £100; otherwise the prizes were £50. According to Philip Ainslie, who as a schoolboy in the 1790s was to his joy allowed a week's holiday to join his handsome ex-dragoon father there, the races were not over-patronised and their chief supporters were the Duke of Hamilton, Baird of New Baith, Hamilton of Wishaw, Sir Archibald Hope, Mr Cathcart, and Sir Hedworth Williams – this last the only 'southerner' to enter his horses in Scottish races.

To the gay and animated scene the Lord Provost and magistrates arrived in old-fashioned style in a glass coach-and-six driven by the expert old John Hay, said to be the only Edinburgh coachman then able to drive a four-in-hand. Even their postilion was old and portly, dressed in buckskins and boots, with a blue coatee, red waistcoat and black cap, carrying a long, stout riding-whip held upright like a sabre. Four servants in the town livery were up behind, wearing large cocked hats.

The start of the races was signalled by a bell. The course was always along the 'back sands', and young Philip would be screaming support for his favourite. During the intervals friends like his father's former brother-officers would come to chat. Among the colourful crowd might be seen Francis, the 'English Sitwell', who had the first four-in-hand driven by a gentleman to be seen in Edinburgh. He was married to Anne, daughter of Sir Ilay Campbell, Lord President, and became 'a leader of the *haut ton* in Edinburgh'.[27]

Philip, beside himself with joy at this exciting occasion, remembered the scene in great detail. Race-week was the highlight of the summer season, and was accompanied by grand evening assemblies, not to mention the Piping competition, strictly for addicts. Philip was far from being the only one who found the 'awful skirling' 'really dreadful', wishing himself a hundred miles off, until the reel-dancing began. For the schoolboys this junketing came at the end of the school holidays, as their long school slog soon began again.[28]

The theatre could by now certainly be rowdy. The rather starchy Mr Willis complained in 1790 that he 'could hear nothing for the obstreperous noise of those pests of society, ycleped bucks. (N.B. – This town swarms with these vermin.)'[29]

During the revolutionary days of 1794 a real riot took place at the theatre when a performance of *Charles I* excited the extremism of a gang of fiery Irish, anti-Government medical students in the pit, known as 'croppies' from their revolutionary hair-styles. The conformist young advocates in the audience demonstrated their loyalty by rising and demanding the National Anthem, but the dissidents obstinately kept their seats, and their hats, shouting instead for 'seditious tunes'. On the first such evening there was no serious violence, but a couple of nights later the loyalists, who included the 23-year-old Walter Scott, newly qualified in the law, turned up armed with cudgels and the 'Irish' with shillelaghs, and a violent struggle broke out as the Anthem began. The lawyers won, and Scott was reputed to have felled three of the enemy. He afterwards used to recall the affray with pride, though he and the rest of the victors were bound over for their pains.[30]

The cropped hairstyle, incidentally, was highly symbolic. Mary Fairfax rashly said in her father's hearing that she admired short hair in men and wished they would all cut off their ugly pigtails. But as this was a Liberal fashion, and therefore suspect, her fervently Tory father the Admiral declaimed fiercely, 'By God, when a man cuts off his queue, the head should follow it!'[31]

In spite of such outbreaks, Kemble and his sister Mrs Siddons between them kept the theatre on a good footing; it was remarked how young women could even attend alone or at least only with a chaperone, and the actors' morals were considered excellent.[32] But even reservation of the boxes for a complete season did not spell financial success, and in 1795 Mrs Siddons had to act in order to bail Kemble out of gaol. For years the theatre continued loaded with debt which prevented the engaging of good supporting actors and thus continued the vicious circle.

Stephen Kemble was himself an indifferent actor, and his clumsy, stocky figure militated against his suitability for parts other than those physically appropriate, such as Falstaff – which he could actually play without padding. He had the Kemble family's expressive features and commanding voice, but overdid the violent gesticulations. At the end of the century the theatre was still criticised as 'not what would be expected in the New Town of Edinburgh'.[33]

The Rev. Sydney Smith, in Edinburgh in his capacity of tutor to the schoolboy Michael Hicks-Beach, wrote to his pupil's parents in 1799 that he was surprised that in Passion Week 'these wicked people are . . . going to tragedies and comedies'. He was really more concerned at the reportedly ludicrous performances, Kemble spending much of his time on stage prompting the rest of the cast. 'The other evening he was stabbed, and he was forced to put his assassin in mind that it was time to stab him.' Smith in any case determined to stay away as long as Kemble had 'a group of wretched strollers at his heels'.[34] Later that season things improved when in July Mrs Siddons made her first appearance as Lady Randolph in *Douglas*.

Not all the company were hacks, even during the bad times. Certain actors maintained an unbroken connection with the theatre for many years. Both Mr Woods, who took 'high-class parts', and Mrs Charters, player of old ladies, continued for thirty years, respectively from 1792 to 1822, and from 1777 to 1807, while the latter opened an unbroken succession over nearly eighty years, being followed by Mrs Nicol, who in turn was followed in 1834 by her daughter, until the theatre closed in 1859.[35]

There were also compensations for the audience of a non-theatrical sort. Andrew Clephane, one of Henry Brougham's group of friends, noted at Christmas 1800 that the theatre was 'now some amusement', the players (he thought) now quite good, but his main object in going was to chat up the dowager Lady Grant of Monymusk, since he heard she gave good parties and usually had a young heiress in tow – which had drawn 'a vast quantity of particles of sighing matter' to her magnet, among them Patrick Fraser Tytler.[36]

The rival entertainments were not flourishing. Signor Corri leased the Circus for concerts, while Signor Urbani tried cards and music at the Assembly Rooms. Corri was so regularly unsuccessful that he began to think himself cursed, and complained that, for example, if he turned baker people would actually give up eating bread. One foreign visitor suggested that the failures were due to Scotland's relative lack of money, since even the most distinguished were on low incomes. There was even a reputed ghost at the theatre, when sounds of acting could be heard from the apartment above the theatre, long after it was closed.

In this troubled time, John Jackson took over the management from Kemble with Mr Ayckin from Liverpool (1800), but at first little change or improvement appeared.[37]

4
BUILDING A NEW TOWN

'For sale: "That large and elegant house . . . 3 and 4 rooms on a floor, with double coach house, stable, laundry, coachman's room, harness room, &c. in the detached offices.

"On the first floor are lobby, eating room, back parlour, closet and butler's pantry. On the second, small ante-room, drawing-room, second room or bed chamber, and dressing room. Above stairs, large nursery and closets, family bed chambers, with dressing room, and all conveniences; and another small bedroom and closets. In the garret floor, independent of servants' apartments, is a larger room with a Venetian window, commanding a most beautiful view of the coast, which many families might prefer for a nursery. On the ground floor, large kitchen and pantries, housekeeper's room, store room, and servants' hall.

"The principal rooms are upwards of 30 ft by 21, The stair and passages are all of stone."'

Advertisement for Col. Campbell's house, west end George Street, *Edinburgh Evening Courant,* 9 Jan. 1790

'Edinburgh begins to surmount its numerous misfortunes; manufactures and commerce, the true sources of wealth, are in some degree resumed. This city is considered as the modern Athens, in politeness, science and literature. The writings of its professors, divines, and lawyers, are every where read and admired. In the healing art it hath been long and justly celebrated.'

John Knox, *A View of the British Empire, more especially Scotland,* 3rd edn, London, 1785, II.576

'Such are the amusements of this rising city, – salubrious air, variegated and extensive prospects of land and water; provisions and vegetables cheap and plentiful; spirits and wines unadulterated; coals at 8s or under, per ton; respectable schools for both sexes; a celebrated university . . .; literary societies; a flourishing botanic garden; an observatory; public libraries, and all the fashionable amusements.'

Ibid., II.583

'Edinburgh has made considerable strides even since I was here two years ago. The new [south] bridge will be a fine thing at worst, but it seems bungled & I believe might have been the finest thing in the world.'

Sir Gilbert Elliot to Lady Elliot, 1 July 1787, Minto MSS, NLS 11045/190/1

'It is an amazing thing how our new town has extended itself, from Princes Street to Queen street in breadth, it shoots along till almost opposite to the Castle rocks, compact buildings and streets the whole way.'

Innes of Stow MSS, 1787; SRO GD 113/5/75b

'Within these last 20 Years have grown up in this great City Public Edifices which do honour to their Skill in Architecture, & private Dwellings of a uniform & symmetrical Beauty sought for elsewhere in vain; Square of uncommon Magnitude, and Streets unrivalled . . . both for Construction & Space . . .

'Truth is, the general Appearance resembles no other Town I have run over; and of all other Towns perhaps least resembles London . . . Some Buildings put some of us in mind of Bath too, but neat Elegance & delicate Gayety are the Characteristics of that Place – Symmetrical Singularity and Dignity of Appearance distinguish this.'

Mrs Piozzi, journal, Rylands Eng.MS 623, Thrale MSS 1789

'No Days are long enough to admire its Situation or new Buildings, the symmetrical beauties of which quite exceed my expectations, while the Romantic Magnificence of the first is such as gives no notion at all of the other . . . as we have Engagements for every Day, one should be ungrateful not to like the Scots too.'

Mrs Piozzi to Miss Penelope Weston, 10 July 1789, in Oswald G. Knapp (ed.), *The Intimate Letters of Hester Piozzi and Penelope Pennington 1788–1821*, London 1914, 20–21

In 1781 St Andrew Square was complete, and about half of the Craig New Town plan had been realised, that is as far as Hanover Street. That year at the suggestion of Sir James Hunter Blair, a former Lord Provost, the Council accepted the need for a church to serve families already living there, and to encourage others to move in; also partly in the hope of raising money for a Poor House from church collections. Unfortunately as the intended site for the terminating vista to the east end of George Street and the Square had long been pre-empted by Sir Laurence Dundas, they had to settle instead for the north side of the street, a position with less townscape significance opposite Craig's Physicians' Hall. This was part of the ground already feued to John Young, and in buying it back the city had to accept restrictions imposed by their own feuar.[1]

The architect David Kay won a ten-guinea prize for a joint design with a gentleman amateur, Major Andrew Fraser, chief engineer for Scotland, and the church was built in 1782–85. A narrow, tapering spire was added by William Sibbald in 1786–87.[2]

Alexander Campbell in 1801 criticised St Andrew's as 'so strangely constructed . . . so new in the order of its parts, that, although the workmanship is excellent, yet one is at a loss whether to bestow praise or blame on the architect of so peculiar a structure. The portico and spire are admirable', but he damned the bells as 'sadly out of tune, and wretchedly rung' to the annoyance of all, especially when on their way to church on Sundays.[3]

The only other public building was a new Assembly Rooms, also in George Street, designed by John Henderson and built by public subscription between November 1784 and 1787, though its grand projecting Tuscan portico was added only in 1818, by William Burn. The first-floor ballroom, 92 feet long and 42 feet wide, with a set of imposing lustres, at last provided a dancing area adequate for Edinburgh society.

In 1784 a spate of building activity launched the next phase of Craig's plan. 'Building of houses has been going on with amazing rapidity', wrote Professor Alexander Dalzell.[4] Feuing started in Hanover Street, and two years later in Frederick Street. When these were nearly built, Castle Street was begun in 1792, while the three spinal streets kept pace. Completion of the western end and Charlotte Square presented site difficulties, because the curious angle of the property's boundary line required an awkward junction with Princes Street (Hope Street). The property adjoining north of the square was the Earl of Moray's, where the ground dropped away dramatically to the wooded gorge of the Water of Leith, while to the west, nearly a mile from the town, was the estate of Drumsheugh House. The land west of Castle Street was not even acquired until 1785. In 1791 an agreement with Lord Moray was urgently concluded, and Charlotte Square could go ahead.

Uniform height and monotonous plainness had hitherto been the order of the day: praise of New Town 'elegance' was based on its good stone, sound masonry work and fine ashlar finish, and its notable contrast with the Old Town's forbidding, tower-like tenements. To the discerning eye George Street was especially disappointing, its houses too low in proportion to its generous width (115 feet). In a totally new departure, for Charlotte Square a more distinguished and unified design was proposed, for which Robert Adam was called in. He had already in 1780 designed number 8, Queen Street for Chief Baron Ord of the Exchequer.

The Charlotte Square plan had four corner exits leading north and south, besides the axial entry from George Street to be centred on the western church, St George's. Adam's north (first built) and south sides were intended to be identical. All houses, of three storeys, with attic and basement, neatly combined a rusticated ground floor, broad round-headed fanlights above the front doors, circular panels surrounding the drawing-room windows, and a modicum of carved decoration in friezes below the balustrades. The central house on either side would have a pediment carried on four half-columns, balanced in their two adjoining houses with paired columns, while a dignified battalion of advancing chimney-stacks completed a standard not hitherto aimed at in Edinburgh.

But although Charlotte Square's first north-side house was built by 1792, Britain's war with France inhibited further building, and Adam's death that year ended any control he might have exercised over the completion of his design. Only five more houses, on the same side, were built between 1796 and 1798, and by the end of the century old Provost George Drummond's grand conception had still reached only part of even James Craig's plan.[5]

In 1785, meanwhile, it had appeared as if the city's South Side might forge ahead when an Act was passed authorising construction of a South Bridge, and building beyond it of the much needed new University college. Professor Dalzell observed ironically to his friend Robert Liston when building began that 'when the *posteriors* of the College are exposed, people will be shamed into building a new College'.[6] This new bridge provided the vital southern access whose lack had hampered full development, and by spanning the deep valley of the Cowgate carried a north/south road from the partly-built Register House directly towards the Nicolson Street area. Thomas Newte, the Oxford scholar and traveller, who witnessed the laying of the bridge's foundation, thought the new means of direct communication with the city's centre 'not only highly conducive to convenience, but will have a very handsome appearance', and considering that 'Edinburgh is not a commercial city', he was impressed by the number of other new public buildings intended.[7]

The bridge was completed in 1788.[8] In the small adjoining Hunter Square between 1788 and 1790 John Baxter's Merchants' Hall was built in a style echoing Adam, with a rusticated ground floor and Doric pilasters. The college, again designed by Robert Adam, was begun in November 1789; but like so many of Edinburgh's grand projects it was long to remain unfinished, this time for a quarter-century.

Intended to replace the old seventeenth-century buildings, its foundation was laid in November by Francis, Lord Napier, in the usual impressive ceremony watched by a large crowd. The ground beyond the bridges was open land and an uninterrupted view was to be had. The magistrates turned out in their robes, the Principal and professors in their gowns, and their students with their hats decked with laurel. Freemasons, bearing the insignia of their order, were drawn up in order of seniority of lodges.[9]

The new college was intended by Adam to have two courts; the earliest part to be built was the north-west corner, and the centre of the east façade facing the main street; the huge entrance with its monolithic pillars of stone brought from Craigleith was completed in 1791. Work continued for another three years until funds ran low, and before long both Principal Robertson and Robert Adam were dead. The grand new University building remained unfinished for another twenty years.

For long enough only a few forward-looking residents made a New Town move. The chief shops and businesses, the offices, law courts, main churches, everything, were still centred in the old city. Many people believed that the scheme would fail, and that the New Town would have insuperable disadvantages however much might be built. One WS, who decided to move from Brown's Square to George Street, was warned by a string of friends that he would ruin his business.[10] And many even still feared that the bridge might fall again.

There was also a sense of inhibition by frugal householders who supposed that with a move to the larger, more distant houses, ceremonial teas must give way to dinners, suppers to routs, and what had seemed a perfectly genteel income while living in an Old Town close would be shown up for poverty in Princes Street or St Andrew Square.[11]

Yet Edinburgh, though still in a state of creation, was at last graduating into modernity. Robert Burns on his second visit in 1788 (during which he was crippled by a serious fall from a coach) noted its lively state of 'houses building, bucks strutting, ladies flaring, blackguards sculking . . . &c in the old way'.[12] And Professor Dalzell wrote to Liston in January 1787, 'You will scarcely be able to know "Auld Reekie", now it is undergoing such a change. The New Town is extended to the West Church, and the bridge over the Cowgate to the south has been passable for some time. There is likewise a mound of earth raised across the Nor' Loch, opposite to the Lawnmarket, by the earth which is dug from the foundations of the new houses in the New Town, and which is now open for foot passengers . . . The additional number of families that come to town is prodigious.'[13]

This is one of the earliest references to new Edinburgh's probably most controversial feature, the 'Earthen Mound' which had begun to take shape in 1783. An irremovable problem with which the city had to come to terms, it was at first almost continually sinking and having to be filled up. Some 1800 cartloads of rubble from old houses thrown down, and more particularly of soil from New Town dug foundations, were tipped there daily, more than a quarter of a million so far.

The draining of the Nor' Loch had left a spongy morass, into the centre of which the spoil from foundations of Princes Street and other New Town streets were tipped by contract, free of charge. This controversial site, which over the decades has long come to be taken for granted, was said to have been originally the idea of George Boyd, a Lawnmarket shopkeeper, who liked to cross from Old Town to New to observe building progress. To make a short cut instead of the tedious circuit round by the North Bridge, he had suggested that he and a few neighbours pay for stepping-stones across the middle of the old loch's swamp. He next persuaded builders to bring over the earth from the new foundations, creating by degrees 'a tolerable footpath', jocularly known as 'Geordy Boyd's Brig'. Once the magistrates saw its likely public value they officially authorised its use as a rubbish dump, and with parliamentary permission, opened up an entrance to the Lawnmarket by demolishing a few houses there. To Boyd's mortification, one of these was his.[14]

The idea was not entirely new. Some years earlier the 8th Earl of Lauderdale had pointed out that if builders and others were statutorily obliged to shoot rubbish at an agreed spot, at small cost they would in a few years raise 'a ridge or earthen bank'. As often, the seer was not the one to bring about this useful change. The perennial question over the Mound was, what to do with it?[15]

By 1785 Thomas Newte, referring to the 'offensive marsh' of the Nor' Loch's last days, was praising the effect now that the site had already been planted with shrubs and was contributing to the surroundings. Besides the 'magnificent bridge' linking the two towns, he said, they were 'making a terrace, which is every day enlarged . . . formed by the rubbage of old houses, and the earth which is dug up in laying the foundation of new ones . . . the contrivance of a very judicious and cool-headed citizen'. According to Newte it was popularly named after the Provost, as 'Provost Grieve's Brigg'. Unlike the North Bridge, being solid it could be in no danger of being 'overturned but by some earthquake or inundation'.[16]

The following year Stebbing Shaw saw the mound 'brought almost to a level . . . a very surprising undertaking, and the abundance of earth already buried is beyond conception'.[17] In the same year Innes of Stow writes of the spoil-heap partly filling the gap left by draining the loch. 'There is also raised an immense mound of earth which runs from Princes Street in a straight line to James Court, filling up the gap of the Nor' Loch and rendering it a level road not much less broad or high than the North Bridge.'[18]

In 1799 the carping John Stoddart added to a list of complaints on the New Town that the mound, 'lumpish and ugly', would by the completion of a street over it, joining the two towns, destroy the beauty and contrast of the crowded, irregular old town and fine houses of the new, 'entirely of fresh stone . . . regular, light, and simple in their construction'. A simple improvement, he suggested, would be to dress and plant the sides of the mound, or slope them with an even, regular verdure', the top making 'a rampart, perhaps with battlements and watch-towers'.[19]

In general the 'Earthen Mound', as it was usually called, came in for years of criticism because of the uncompromisingly solid visual barrier that it had formed across the valley.

Despite the visible progress, Philip Ainslie later recalled how limited in 1788 the New Town still was, Princes Street extending only five houses west of Castle Street, the other two streets not quite so far.[20] Beyond the site of Charlotte Square the open ground of Brae's Foot Parks extended as far as the entrance to the Queen's Ferry road at Kirk Brae-Head Toll. The Lang Gate, a thoroughfare between the ferry road and Calton Hill, ran through here.[21]

Eastwards, Queen Street ended at North St David Street, and beyond St Andrew Square was the suburb of Broughton. Fields covered the sites of York Place, Dundas Street, and the area of Picardy Place, named after Huguenot damask weavers who had settled there. At the foot of the hill was Bellevue, seat of General Scott of Balcomie, on the site of Provost Drummond's villa, its park-like grounds extending as far as Canonmills.[22]

In a medieval city, with houses built of wood and crammed close together, fire was always a hazard and one hard to deal with. Edinburgh's old town was subject to serious fires, with its packed closes and wynds, and multi-storeyed lands surviving from Stuart times. Chimneys alone were responsible for many outbreaks. But the first recorded fire in a New Town house was not until September 1786, in George Street, and although at first alarming was soon brought under control and contained in the apartment where it started. This was a good advertisement. 'Nothing can more clearly show the excellency of the present mode of building,' was the *Scots Magazine*'s approving comment.[23]

The next to occur, just two years later in the cramped area of Rose Court behind St Andrew's Church, was less lucky, and the owner's house and possessions were 'totally consumed' despite the combined efforts of magistrates, military and city guard, firemen and tradesmen and plenty of water; but the nearest engine was at Castle Hill and took an hour to arrive. In the confined space the throng must have been quite formidable.

The Old Town at this time was unluckier, and in 1791 it was noted that more fires had occurred in months than over several years to date. And from 1795 to 1824, the year of greatest disasters, fires broke out on average almost once a year. Of these, four were in or off Parliament Close, and in the New Town three were near the North Bridge: one at the former GPO, caused by a bucket of smouldering ashes, one in a watchmaker's shop, and the third in a row of old wooden shops sole survivors of Cap and Feather Close, which had been mostly demolished for building the bridge in 1767. Their survival had been considered a disgrace, so that their burning in 1819 was a godsend, and they were replaced by a row of soundly-built modern tenements. The one regret was that the close had been the home of poor young Robert Fergusson, the vernacular poet whom Burns had much admired.[24]

Although every celebrity in Britain seems to have visited Edinburgh at some time, and most recorded their impressions, some of the more famous perversely left us no account: particularly tantalising when their visits were in the earlier days of the New Town. Edmund Burke came in both 1784 and 1785, on both occasions as an offshoot of his installation as Rector of Glasgow University, but we know of his movements only circumstantially, and of his impressions almost not at all. Boswell, who had fondly imagined he could use Burke's influence to secure legal office in Edinburgh, only to be told diplomatically that Burke had very little pull in these matters, had assiduously cultivated the politician by letter. After several false starts he at last succeeded in meeting him in Glasgow one morning in April 1784, when Burke delighted him by 'admirable behaviour', but he did not succeed in his plan to give Burke an elaborate supper in Edinburgh. (His characteristically Boswellian attempts at pursuit, with mutual mishaps, finally succeeded in Burke's dining with him in London in 1788.)[25]

The day after Burke's arrival in Edinburgh Lord Maitland, who 'attended him constantly', and Adam Smith took him to Professor Dalzell's, who thought him 'the most agreeable and entertaining man in conversation I ever met with'; they all dined at Hatton, stayed overnight for Good Friday, and went together to the Glasgow installation. Dalzell and Smith saw more of him than anyone (poor Boswell!), and learned that 'Edinburgh, as well as Glasgow, greatly exceeded his expectations'.[26]

During his 1785 visit Burke dined with the Hon. Henry Erskine at a 'turtle feast' at Fortune's, the turtle being a gift from Sir Thomas Dundas of Kersey; this was apparently followed a day or so later by 'a quiet supper in the College' with the Principal, Dr William Robertson. Even these few details are found only in references by others, and Burke enlightens us with not a single comment about either his Rectorship ceremony, his Edinburgh junketings, or his 1785 travels in the Highlands with William Windham, dismissed carelessly as having 'Seen the works both of God and man in some new and striking forms'.[27]

Only a few years after Edward Topham's strictures on Edinburgh's cuisine, Mrs MacIver opened a school of cookery instruction for young ladies, and

Topham would have entered feelingly into her conviction that it was 'a necessary branch of female education' and have felicitated her on its success. It was 1783 when, yielding to pressure by many ladies, Mrs MacIver published *Cookery and Pastry*, and in 1787 a second edition followed.[28] In the revised work she added 'Bills of Fare' of between five and fifteen dishes for family dinners, ranging from seven simple menus including plum-pudding and roast beef with potatoes and pickles, roast mutton with kidney beans and sliced cucumber, to main dishes of fish, veal, boiled pork, stewed tongue or haricot mutton. Higher up the scale came four seven-dish menus, and at the top, the most elaborate:

Soup removed,
Boiled Turkey with Oyster Sauce

Stewed Pease	Hen's Nest	Scotch Collops and Lettuce
Ratafia Cream	Syllabubs	Raspberry Cream
Apricot Tart	Orange Pudding	
Blanc-mange Jelly in a Cheap	Egg Cheese	
Fricassée Roast	Pig Wild Fowls	

The apparently odd arrangement refers to the setting of the table, not the order in which dishes were served: the only change being of course substitution of the turkey for the soup.

Bearing in mind that dinners were large and heavy, suppers seem almost equally over-nourished, running to beef steaks, roast chicken, duck, hare, boiled tripe, sausages, white meat fricassées, stewed giblets and cold fowl or hare, with a variety of vegetables, spinach, asparagus, peas, artichokes or salads, celery and potatoes; followed by blancmanges or trifles. 'Have always some garden dishes', she directs, 'according to the seasons at supper', before going on to 'buttered crabs in the shell, commonly called *parton pies*', and pancakes.

Fruit was of course strictly seasonal: strawberries and cherries from mid-May until July, gooseberries and currants lasting a little longer; apples and pears all the year round, and indeed the only fruit between February and April. Peaches and quinces came in September/October, figs and grapes from August until January. Oranges are not mentioned.

Surprisingly, there seems to have been no lack of vegetables, in addition to the inevitable roots, even in winter: sorrel, broccoli, spinach, endive, salsify, several herbs, and more exotically, cardoons, scorzonese, skirret, burnet and rape. Even marigold leaves are recommended. But of course many of these suggestions might have been the author's wish to educate ladies in their use.

Joints that figured throughout the year were beef, mutton and veal, and different qualities of lamb. Seasonally, there was venison, buck from June to September, doe from October to December. There was also a fine choice of game, partridge, woodcock, pheasant and snipe, with tame pigeons and rabbits in winter; and in season no lack of crayfish, prawns, lobsters and oysters.

After Mrs MacIver's death her colleague Mrs Frazer followed on with *The Practice of Cookery, Pastry, Pickling, Preserving, &c.*, of which 'arts' she claimed to be 'sole teacher in Edinburgh'. First published in 1791, Mrs Frazer's book sold 10,000 copies, then ran into several editions, the seventh, enlarged, appearing in 1820. It was more elaborate than Mrs MacIver's, like a proto-version of the much later Mrs Beeton, with her frontispiece of a table-setting of her largest menu of nineteen dishes, but describing dishes for 'all ranks and conditions', pouring scorn on other books 'fraught with extravagant and useless receipes' and inaccurate into the bargain. The seventh edition included marketing, cookery being now so essential to 'Female education'.

Starting like Mrs MacIver with a five-dish menu, but replacing plum-pudding with bread pudding, and adding such delicacies as green pease soup, giblet pie, roast veal, and scalloped oysters (but a noticeable lack of vegetables), Mrs Frazer works up to a luxurious fifteen-dish menu including beef à la mode, crimped haddocks, marrow pasty, Italian cheese and potted pigeons – but only two puddings. The remarkably heavy nineteen-dish dinner, presumably for winter, as shown in the frontispiece, included haricot mutton, two ragouts, macaroni pie, and veal olives.

Mrs Frazer also advised on how to dress a table, warning that for a large number even a one-course dinner must be laid with 'good substantial dishes', borrowing a choice from the other courses, with soup served at both ends and removed by fish. A generous interpretation of a single course.

Three-course dinners would end with desserts or 'ornamental' dishes, a variety of fruits including 'artificial, or preserved', with 'custards, cheesecakes, fritters, meringues, wafers, &c.' 'Artificial' fruits were a kind of mousse or 'French flummery', set in peach-moulds lined in colour so that they looked like real peaches, and decorated with bayleaf stalks and leaves. 'Creams' included ratafia, almond, steeple (set with jelly from boiled calf's foot), ices and syllabubs, blancmanges made with isinglass, trifles, and floating islands in jelly.

'The grand object', adjured Mrs Frazer, was to furnish the table with 'the best of meals, well dressed, and arranged with taste and judgment'. The hostess's part in all this was likely to be limited to supervision, and perhaps turning out the elegant desserts (like those learned by Mary Fairfax). At all events the product had left far behind the crudity of menus endured by Edward Topham some forty years earlier. [29]

These were stirring times for Edinburgh. Seventeen eighty-four, the year of Burke's visit, the year of Mrs Siddons, the year of renewed building activity in the New Town, was also a year in which many promising young students enrolled at the University and joined the Speculative Society. According to Robert Gillies, looking back on the 1780s more than half a century later, Edinburgh, while maintaining its old tradition of jovial hospitality and good living, was still limited in culture and customs. He recalled its lack of poetic life, due at least in part to the narrow, Latin-bound High School education based entirely on the dull construing of Caesar, Nepos and so on. Burns's contribution to literature seemed in Edinburgh comparatively little regarded, James Beattie was unsuccessful and melancholic, and as for fiction, writers were striving to achieve the statutory three volumes with very flimsy material.

David Hume had died in 1776, and the literary leaders were still Principal Robertson, Lord Kames and the mannered Henry Mackenzie who, whatever his preciosity as a writer, was a fair-minded critic, eager to promote talent in others, and quite devoid of envy or self-conceit. Henry Home, Lord Kames, died in 1782, much honoured despite Mackintosh's rude dictum.

In the University, the leading thinkers (says Gillies) were Dr Joseph Black, 'father of modern chemistry', too retiring to be as valued as he deserved, Dr Cullen, almost rivalling Boerhaave and Hoffman as Europe's leading medical teacher but now just past his zenith, the 'elegant and picturesque' if not profound historian Robertson, Dr Adam Ferguson the Moral Philosopher, of 'masculine energy and mature dignity of style', Dr Robison the mathematical philosopher, and the accomplished young Dugald Stewart.[30]

Charles Kirkpatrick Sharpe in 1825, gratefully recording Edinburgh's then good fortune 'in being free from such nuisances as Hume, Arnot &c', describes the young men of their day as 'free-thinkers from fashion; they took no time to examine the truth of the doctrines most conducive to happiness both here and hereafter, but pinned their faith upon the sleeves of a set of metaphysical mountebanks' (in Hume's *Essays*) 'and imagined that they were men of genius because they laughed at all religions'. This was fortunately ended, he claims, by 'the horrors of the French Revolution', and a generation later 'they were thought fools for their pains'.[31]

A bridge is perhaps the most complete disguise conceivable to a landscape or townscape, even if unintentional. In London when the Fleet valley was spanned in the nineteenth century, it was doubtless not intended to be visually obliterated to the point of extinction, but so it turned out. With the building of Edinburgh's North Bridge, so long opposed not for environmental but for economic and political reasons, the moment the valley of the Nor' Loch was successfully spanned in 1769, the view changed. The eye instead of travelling downwards into the valley was now involuntarily drawn across. A few years later, completion of the new street across the South Bridge, and finally King George IV Bridge (1827–34), and the infilling of the Mound with similar visual effect, flattened vistas and changed for ever the townscape of old Edinburgh, even as seen from the New Town.

The once fashionable Cowgate thus became a dingy canyon, indeed easily overlooked when traversing the bridge above. The lower reaches of Edinburgh, plunging through the gulfs below the North Bridge or, better still, the Waterloo Arch, are distinctly romantic, but these were mostly a later creation of Modern Athens, and it is now all but impossible to imagine how the two cities appeared to an observer before, say, 1820.

For half a century the New Town consisted of Craig's grid. Robert Reid's 'Second New Town' immediately north of Craig's, was begun in 1802 and only partly completed by 1825; the grand ceremonial approach from the London Road by Regent Bridge and Waterloo Place began in 1815; and outlying developments such as the building up of the Moray estate, Stockbridge, Broughton, Bellevue, Coates and its surroundings, came mostly in the 1820s and later. During that half-century, when much of Edinburgh's life was still rooted in the old city, only the more fashionable or avant garde householders and members of society moved out, many, as we have seen, in the psychologically less daring transfer to the south side.

Thus guidebooks and visitors' descriptions during those years still describe city and social life in terms of the romantically spectacular old city, merely tacking on a few comments to describe the new additions.

Henry Skrine, on a first visit in 1787, foresaw a splendid future for Edinburgh after decades of civic inactivity, 'like the insect bursting from its chrysolis', as 'all the blessings of industry began to pour their benign influences on this newly awakened people'. More specifically, the grandeur of 'the southern parallel eminence' made the most striking city approach one could imagine, with the magnificence of the (intended) new college, the bridges and sudden huge increase in New Town building, which seemed to portend a future southern entry to 'vie in ancient magnificence with any street in Europe'.[32]

This rosy prospect faded somewhat in the chill 1790s. Returning in the bleak year 1793, Skrine detected sad changes. In the stagnation following the French Revolution, Scotland's economy was affected even more than England's, with over-extended paper credit.[33]

The Rev. Daniel Sandford, who moved to Edinburgh from England in 1792, questioned its present reputation as a 'seat of philosophy', despite its thinkers Playfair and Stewart. In an interim before the rise of later luminaries, it was affected by doctrines from France. He found a preponderance of 'sceptical opinions dressed in an attractive style . . . by the genius of their authors', and young men – even some older men – 'fond of speculation, and vain of limited attainments', were lured by the new, original doctrines of independence. Edinburgh society, intellectual and brilliant, differed from England, where 'conventional rule was supreme . . . prescription was every thing', whereas in Scotland 'originality was the zest of conversation', and in contrast to the etiquette and mannerisms so regarded by the English, here 'one might hazard any thing which he had abilities to defend'.

As for religion, 'if men were not sceptical they were indifferent', and Sandford was almost embarrassed to find himself soon appreciated as a serious preacher of 'the truth'. In 1797 a subscription was raised to build him the Episcopal Charlotte Chapel, where he remained preacher for twenty-one years.[34]

Meanwhile, the 'spirit of improvement' was not to all people's liking: arbiters of taste like Stoddart and the painter Joseph Farington were full of criticism. Farington, who came to Edinburgh to paint in the same year as Stoddart's visit (1792), thought that architects of the public buildings showed little taste, and that the new buildings were ill-regulated. 'In the New Town in George street there is a strange jumble of different styles of design, in the Physicians Hall the capitals are a third too large for the pillars. The New Church under the west end of the Castle [St Cuthbert's] is equally deficient in taste.' George Street, he considered, reversed the usual fault of giving insufficient width to fine streets in new towns: here it was 'so wide [115 feet] in proportion to the height of the buildings, that in the declining line of perspective they appear like barracks'.[35]

That all was not progress unsullied was shown by Mrs Piozzi, who visited with her husband in the summer of 1789. She began by pouring forth a stream of mannered panegyric on Edinburgh buildings such as might befit a travel brochure. 'Squares of uncommon Magnitude, and Streets unrivalled so far as my Experience has carried me', and 'an Air of Dignity unrivall'd by any City I have seen yet', reminded her of Paris. Some of the parallels were less agreeable. 'The Love of Dirt is another Continental Taste.' She joins the list of the many foreign visitors, like Edward Topham and Benjamin Rush, who expressed amazement that 'The Scots have never turned their Thoughts towards making a Common Sewer . . . Every thing most odious is brought & thrown out before the owners door at 10 o'clock of an Evening without Shame or Sorrow – Carts being provided to carry it off before Morning, leaving only the Smell behind – as Not a Privy is yet used in Edinburgh. In Contradiction to all this I never saw People so fond of Flowers in my Life . . .'[36] This even suggests the New Town's modification – into pollution at front doors. The Old Town habit of emptying slops from above seems evidently to have died hard.

Later, having meanwhile visited Glasgow, Mrs Thrale remarks that in both cities grandeur scarcely makes up for the filth, and 'I have now found a most discreditable Reason why Passengers walk up the Coach way . . . 'tis because People used to throw Ordure &c out of the Windows, and Foot folks rationally enough chose rather to hazard being run over.'[37]

The 26-year-old Samuel Rogers arrived in Edinburgh in July 1789, soon after the Piozzis; like most other young travellers he was primed with introductory letters, and kept a notebook of terse jottings on the lines of Boswell's daily records before they were worked up into his polished Journal. The Piozzis, who were staying at the same hotel, when they saw that Rogers's introductions had brought Principal Robertson, Adam Smith and Henry Mackenzie to call, decided (or doubtless she decided) he must be worth their calling too. Adam Smith, whom Rogers found at breakfast a couple of days later, remarked that he did not know Mrs Piozzi but that he 'believed her to be spoiled by keeping company with odd people'. Smith, sitting with a plate of strawberries, a famous local fruit and his favourite summer diet, 'said that Edinburgh deserved little notice; that the old town had given Scotland a bad name; that he was anxious to move into the new town, and had set his heart on St George's Square; that Edinburgh was entirely supported by the three Courts – the Exchequer, the Excise, and the Judiciary Courts . . . Said that in Paris as well as in Edinburgh, the houses were piled one upon another . . . Spoke contemptuously of Sir John Sinclair, but said that he never knew a man who was in earnest and who did not do something at last.'

On the Sunday Rogers, finding Smith about to step into his chair for an airing, was invited for dinner next day with Mackenzie. 'Who could refuse?' (This was when they all ended up at the play.)

Rogers gives other thumbnail sketches: Dr Robertson, who came into his parlour to receive him 'trumpet in hand', did not look like his portrait by Reynolds. 'His dress was remarkably neat, and his countenance very open and pleasing . . . His eye has lost much of its fire, and age has given a stoop to his figure . . . He said Edinburgh contained little worth notice' – two bad opinions in two days! – 'but that its situation was very romantic.' He also advised Rogers that on his Highland tour he should reverse Gilpin's route, and took the trouble to fetch down a map of Scotland and kneel on the floor to trace it for him. On the Sunday Rogers heard him preach. 'His manner striking, but not graceful; his voice not unpleasing. He spoke and looked like a good man.' Rogers thought he directed his sermon particularly at him and the Piozzis – but then, at the theatre he fancied Mrs Jordan did the same. Dr Blair in the afternoon spoke 'not distinctly. A hoarse, unpleasant voice. A very neat elegant sermon on "Censoriousness". Afterwards bowed to the corporation in the gallery on the right.' The rest of his notes, like many English travellers' diary-jottings, merely list those whom he met without any enlightening comments, except that Adam Smith thought Junius was probably 'Single-Speech Hamilton'.[38]

There were celebrities of a different sort from those whom Rogers and the Piozzis met, for Edinburgh had some famous beauties who included the demi-monde. Among them was Miss Burns (or Matthews), who claimed to be the daughter of a rich Durham merchant who after a 'ruinous' second marriage had fallen on hard times, luckily not until his daughter had had a good education. To capitalise on this and her looks, she came to Edinburgh when scarcely twenty in about 1789, lodging in Rose Street – opposite the back of Lord Swinton's George Street house. The fashionably beautiful girl with her fine figure quickly attracted attention, especially during the evening Queen Street promenades, but such attention was not thought desirable, and she was sent before the magistrates. The strait-laced Baillie Creech warned her away from Edinburgh under penalty of being drummed through the streets and sent to the House of Correction, which evoked some ribald squibs, against him, not her, with a story (to his rage) that he intended to marry her. Robert Burns – no relation – who had been some time in Edinburgh before his namesake's arrival, and had had acrimonious business dealings with Creech, wrote an appreciative verse:

Cease, ye prudes, your envious railing
Lovely Burns has charms, confess:
True it is, she had one failing,
Had a woman ever less?

The poor girl did not plague the city long, but 'fell into a decline', perhaps TB, perhaps more sinister, and after 'a few years of unenviable notoriety' died in 1792 at Roslin in her early twenties.[39]

At about the time when the States General were meeting in Paris, starting a chain of events that would eventually change the style and conception of Governments throughout Europe, a voyage was undertaken from Leith to Europe's very fringe. John Stanley, then a bachelor, after a winter's preparation in Edinburgh fitted out a ship and gathered a party for an expedition to Iceland. He started with a series of misfortunes over his partners. On the eve of departure he quarrelled with Dr Hume, the physician recommended by Principal Robertson who had assisted with his preparations, and Hume cried off, a great disadvantage for the voyage. Watkin Williams Wynn, who was studying in Edinburgh, having asked to join the party had to cancel at a late stage because of the death of his baronet father. However, Stanley's botanist, Dr William Wright, also from Edinburgh University, was able to join them.

The expedition lasted from May to October, and on the return voyage they weathered a terrible gale. They reached Leith safely, however, saluting the harbour with eleven guns as they approached, bringing out a large crowd which acclaimed their arrival, and they were allowed to land free of duty. Among their trophies, Dr Wright's collection of dried plants was later presented to Sir Joseph Banks.

Stanley had also been asked to bring from Iceland the ingredients for a celebratory dinner to be given for him by the Oyster Club, but it proved a gastronomic failure. As Stanley's wife later wrote in her memoirs, 'the philosophers left everything almost untouched. It was like a *Festin de Pierre.*' The squeamish 'philosophers' included Adam Smith, Dr Hutton, Dr Joseph Black, Sir James Hall, Henry Mackenzie and Dugald Stewart.[40]

Stanley became MP for Wootton Bassett, and in 1796 married Maria Josepha Holroyd, a remarkable young woman who shared in all her husband's scientific interests. In October 1797, three months after the birth of the first of their seven children, they returned for a time to Edinburgh when the Cheshire Militia, in which Stanley served as a volunteer, was ordered there because of the danger of riots. Stanley, who maintained his friendships with Edinburgh scientists, succeeded to his father's baronetcy in 1807.

The war with France had an immediate impact besides the hospitality given to an exiled royal family and a few visiting frigates in Leith Roads. There was also the particular excitement of the arrival of a Russian squadron of eight ships of the line and four frigates, anchoring in the Roads for a fortnight, late from Archangel and bound next for Kronstadt. The Rev. Sydney Smith, in Edinburgh with his charge Michael Hicks-Beach, wrote to his patron the boy's father in December 1799, 'The town is overun with Russians in green coats, with ugly faces and lice. They are very sick aboard Ship but are not allowed to Land to form an encampment, only to come ashore in the day-time.'[41] For the locals their greatest curiosity was the way they would shin up the street-lamps on the road to Leith, illuminated with colza-oil (a product of rape-seed), to drain off the oil for cooking their cabbage. The squadron was not, it happened, manned entirely by Russians: many of the officers were Scots from Kirkcaldy and Culross, who had joined the Russian navy under its 'founder' Admiral Greig.

The bands of the troops on board were sent into the city to perform at the Assembly Rooms, and curious crowds appreciated hearing their Russian songs. Even more popular were their trios, quartets and the choruses sung 'in so masterly a style as to surprise every one that heard them'.[42]

Edinburgh Castle, always a garrison, was from 1796 also a prison for captured French soldiers. They used to exercise on the old castle archery ground; otherwise they passed their idle time in making toys and trinkets, 'dominoes, scent boxes, little ships', from the beef-bones of their rations, and would display them for sale on Sundays when sympathetic Edinburgh people visited the castle after the forenoon service. One or two liked to show off signs of former grandeur (Philip Ainslie tells us), such as the man known as

'M. Le Marquis', who 'appeared every Sunday *en grande tenue,* his coat and every part of his dress being made of paper, painted to imitate silk . . . and completed by his chapeau bras under his arm, and his *solitaire* and ruffles at breast and wrists; his manners were an excellent imitation of a Frenchman of fashion of the ancient regime.'[43]

The song-writer Charles Dibdin, during one of several short visits to Edinburgh (mostly to perform his entertainment 'Sans Souci' at the theatre), went to the castle with his family, when the prisoners 'performed for us a grand ballet in a capital style'. He spoils his compliment with patronising comments. 'I found these prisoners what I never ceased to find Frenchmen, full of design, impudence, and adulation . . . We bought their baubles, saw their show, paid them handsomely, and came away.'[44]

There were excitements such as the festivities on news of victories, like Camperdown and Aboukir in 1797. George Combe went with his family to see the Camperdown illuminations and had never seen anything so brilliant. There was a dramatic discharge of artillery from the Castle esplanade, far above the crowds watching from the New Town. 'The upper air was dark over the North Loch and every flash shone like lightning in the sky . . . In a moment again all was dark around the guns, and the echoes rolled away among the hills . . .' Further illuminations celebrated the victory of the Nile in 1799. There was also a panorama of the storming of Seringapatam, displayed in an open space near the college, which enlightened George, for one, on the horrors of war.[45]

Then there was the sad procession to the city bringing back the bodies of wounded officers landed from the ships at Leith; but probably the highlight in Philip Ainslie's young life was the escape of several French officers during a violent snow-storm in February 1799. Roads were blocked and mails delayed; at Comrie in Perthshire there were even earthquake shocks. At this unpropitious point several of the French had succeeded in mining under their floor to reach a drain running under the walls and in a very long, steep descent down the rocks of the castle hill, before it connected with an outlet in the old Nor' Loch. 'How the prisoners could endure the dreadful stench and want of air in the drains was wonderful.' They did endure it, however, and on making their way out split up to range over the countryside north of Edinburgh towards the sea. The next morning, Sunday, their escape was discovered and some of the Shropshire militia were sent out to scour the country after them.

That day Philip, now fourteen, was with his father on their way to dine with the Rocheids at Inverleith House. As they arrived at the avenue, an armed soldier appeared on top of the garden wall, and Sir Philip stopped the carriage to ask what he was doing. He was Jem Corbet, and he was 'out to catch them there wagabond French prisoners, who broke their padrole, and escaped down the drains (the dirty rascals)'.

Dinner passed off without interruption, but was barely over when there was a commotion outside, and a servant came in to announce that they had found a Frenchman hiding in the dog-kennels, and Jem Corbet had him in charge. Philip was called on as interpreter (his father evidently pleased to have included French in his education), and learned that Jem had discovered the man when the dogs started growling, found him hiding among the pointers, prodded him with his 'bagonet' and made him surrender. The Frenchman, Pierre, then told how he was from the Haute Garonne, with three years' service in General Hoche's army, and that having escaped from the Castle he and his companions became lost and separated on this side of Edinburgh; *'j'apercu ce château, et me suis refugié dans le chenil'*. Of course he complained bitterly of hunger and thirst, and on Philip's reporting this back to the dining-room, Mr Rochead ordered both prisoner and guard to be fed.

A little later Philip found Pierre trolling love-songs to the women-servants, and full of *politesse* to Sheriff the butler, and even to Jem . . . *'Morbleu! quel bon boeuf! – quel bière forte!'* – and with profuse thanks to the *'seigneur'* for his *'traitement superbe'*, he was busy making up to a maid-servant before the indignant Jem lugged him away. The rest of the escaping party were picked up in various places, and meanwhile, it had made Philip's evening.[46] In due course all the prisoners were freed through an exchange with the enemy.

The approach of the new century inevitably roused moral, philosophical and generally contemplative ideas. By 1800, when Edinburgh's New Town had existed at least partially for some thirty years and was largely complete, the country was at war with a detested tyrant, and revolutionary ideas were rife: but patriotic young men of all classes were ready to defend their country to the death, flocking to join the volunteer Fencible regiments, don uniforms and endure hours of drilling.

Already in 1794 there had been a grand summing-up of a generation's change. William Creech, bookseller and magistrate, in the volume on the Lothians he contributed to Sir John Sinclair's *Statistical Account of Scotland*, had taken stock of Edinburgh during the preceding thirty years.

'So remarkable a change is not, perhaps, to be equalled, in so short a period, in any city of Europe; nor in the same city for two centuries, taking all the alternatives together . . .' Thinking back to 1763 and recalling the constricted city, with an empty space, Ross Park, on the site where George Square now stood, and farther south, fields and orchards covering the now populous Nicolson, Bristo and Buccleuch Streets and St Patrick's Square, he reminded readers of the New Town's unexpectedly slow start. Yet whereas for some years after the collapse of the North Bridge in 1769 few had had the courage to build or settle in the sparsely built new site, in little over the next twenty years some £3 million sterling had been spent on it, rents had doubled and by 1791 more than tripled. The new South Bridge of 1785–86, though demolishing many of the Cowgate's oldest and most historic buildings, made properties beyond so desirable that values rocketed to the region of £100,000 per acre.

Creech was at pains to point out improvements and otherwise, mostly the latter. Needless to say, the younger generation had deteriorated. Young men's education, manners and principles had gone by the board, and today's were three-bottle men, swearing, gaming and drinking, quarrelsome and anti-religious. Young ladies were no longer educated in housewifery, and even tradesmen's daughters now reprehensibly wasted hours with milliners and perfumers, leaving the housekeeping to servants and spending their leisure in expensive music lessons or just reading novels. Moreover, whereas earlier girls could safely walk abroad, they must now be protected from 'insolence'. (This view was at odds with the experience of many young ladies.) Divorced women were received in society; bastardy fines had annually increased, as had the number of 'disorderly females' – there were now twenty times more brothels, promoting theft and crime. As for so-called 'sport', within the past ten years the deplorable pastime of cock-fighting had taken hold,[47] while a school for boxing lessons had been opened – by an *English* pugilist.

Creech complained that the old Assembly Room, decorous in dress and manners and strictly controlled, closing promptly at 11 p.m., had been abandoned to the City Guard and removed to the fashionable new rooms, disgraced by men who came straight from the tavern, dressed anyhow, and romped through the dances until 3 or 4 in the morning. As for the stage . . . long gone were the days when no clergyman might be seen at a play, and the prosecution of the Rev. John Home for his chaste drama *Douglas*. Present-day displays were indecorous, especially on Saturdays, actors being interrupted by 'impudent buffoons' and scenes that would once have been hissed off the stage were now applauded by the gallery!

Sad times indeed. Religion had similarly suffered. Sects such as the Unitarians, which formerly conformed to the laws, now flourished openly. No longer did the established clergy visit and instruct families, to the present detriment of manners if nothing worse. Strict Sunday observance, servants meekly following their families to church, generous collections for the poor and home services if families could not attend – thinking it a disgrace to be seen in the streets during service-time – had yielded to neglect of the churches, especially by men, while servants now thought it 'ungenteel' to attend their employers. Collections had fallen, and far from thinking it shame, people had made Sunday a day of relaxation. 'Looseness, dissipation and frivolity have succeeded' and few blushed at what was once thought a crime.

The list seemed endless. One of the smaller lapses was the perennial moving forward of the dinner-hour, from 2 o'clock at the latest, when businessmen closed their offices between 1 and 2, to 4 or even 5 for those in the 'higher and midranks', their working hours ending completely at dinner-time, and sitting down to the main meal of the day considered 'a very serious business'.

Wages appeared to have risen relatively little, but Creech complained that, whereas the maidservants of 1763, earning £3 or £4 a year, dressed soberly in dark cloaks or plaids, now they were 'almost as fine as their mistresses' of thirty years earlier, while the affectation of employing a manservant (paid proportionately more, of course), had increased among 'almost every genteel family'. On the credit side, Edinburgh, formerly only able to lodge strangers in 'a dirty uncomfortable inn', could now entertain them 'like a prince'.

In economic and educational matters Creech saw great changes for the better. The five hundred university students of 1763 had by 1791 and 1792 increased to 1255 and 1360 respectively; the two hundred boys of the High School had swelled to five hundred and the school was claimed as Britain's largest. The couple of small-scale newspapers of the 1760s had risen to four, and in 1792 six, full-size despite heavy new duties on paper and advertisements: the *Courant, Mercury, Advertiser, Herald, Caledonian Chronicle* and *Gazetteer*. Traffic, whose increase was at that period considered a good thing, had risen almost four-fold, with 1427 four-wheeled carriages, besides the thousands of wains and carts not formerly counted. Quality, too, had improved: the upper classes used to have carriages built in London or, better still, Paris, but now Edinburgh could produce not only as fine as anywhere but also 'stronger and cheaper', and was even exporting to north-east Europe, St Petersburg and the Baltic.

For the ladies, haberdashers, milliners, linen-drapers, glovers and especially perfumers, once totally lacking, had become almost Edinburgh's commonest tradesmen. In the clothing trade, while the manufacture of shawls and buttons had been unknown, and only a small amout of starch had been produced, now factories had been established in the city in great 'perfection', and some 250,000 pounds of starch were being made, much of it for hair powder (a change less of economics than of fashion). For men, there had always been plenty of barbers and wigmakers of a sort, but their number had now tripled, and on Sundays they were, deplorably, busiest. There was even a 'professor' of hair-dressing advertising his 'academy'.

Of more general manufactures, Scotland could formerly boast only a single iron foundry, the Carron Company, and that fairly recent; there were now several, especially near Edinburgh, while cast iron was made in sufficient quantities for export. Glass bottle-making, starting in Leith in a small way, had risen by 1790 to six firms making 'as fine chrystal and window glass as any where in Europe'. Output of soap and candles, the former hitherto always imported, had similarly increased enormously. Indeed, back in 1763 tallow from St Petersburg had been imported by a single ship, whereas now several hundred plied the Baltic up to three times a year and Leith had become almost the leading British Baltic port.

The three paper mills near Edinburgh had also considerably increased production (though still employing the uneconomic method of bringing stamped paper from London, whose carriage alone cost £700 a year). Printing houses had risen from six to sixteen, printed cotton manufacture had increased by the staggering figure of more than 250,000 yards, and finally, bank capital had risen, up to fourfold.

Less admirably, in Creech's view, the small distillery industry had almost trebled production, to 1,696,000 gallons. A lower duty on malt liquor and higher on spirits would be beneficial, he considered, spirits being 'hurtful to the health, industry, and morals of the people'.[48]

In 1796 James Gillespie of Spylaw, a rich man with no family, endowed a hospital to be built for old men and women, with a free school for boys. In 1801, when the building began, it was given a Royal charter. It was designed by the mason Robert Burn (father of the architect William Burn), who at about the same time designed a group of streets at Edinburgh's east end: Picardy Place, Union Street, Forth Street and Broughton Street, built between 1804 and 1810. Gillespie's Hospital, in a castellated gothic style, was on the south-west border of the city.[49]

A blind asylum and a Magdalen Asylum to reclaim 'fallen women' were also projected, largely sponsored by Dr Johnstone, of Leith. The latter, founded in 1805 with the Prince of Wales as patron, was the first such institution founded in Scotland.

'Handsome and very commodious', it was being built while Sir John Carr was in Edinburgh in 1807. Well-intentioned ladies, headed by the Duchess of Buccleuch, opened a shop known as 'The Repository', for selling fine needlework executed by 'ladies in straitened circumstances'. This was considered a paragon of delicacy for the provision of 'the necessities of the fair sex who may require it'.[50]

The old Tolbooth had been supplemented by a House of Correction in Bristo Port, a low, cramped building which by the 1790s had become too small for its purpose. The foundation stone of a new Bridewell, designed by Robert Adam, was laid in 1791 on the Calton Hill on part of the favourite bicker-ground of schoolboys and apprentices, a semi-circular building, completed in 1795. New prisons at this time were inspired by the enlightened approach of the philanthropist John Howard, and Sir John Carr, who saw the Bridewell in 1807, considered it the best adapted to its purpose that he had seen, 'a perfect model for a correctional house'. He was impressed by its clean kitchen and by the prisoners' health, with only four deaths in its twelve years of existence to date. Carr listed the daily diet, which governors were always eager to have publicised. Breakfast and supper were oatmeal porridge with small beer, and dinner appears to have been only broth, though with bread and extra porridge for those who had exceeded their work quota. Meat was served only on Sundays, and this appears to have provided the prisoners' only protein.[51] The Bridewell was demolished in about 1884.

Water supply, always a problem in Edinburgh, had been first piped to the city in 1681 by Bruschi, a German engineer, from Comiston, three-and-a-half miles to the south-west. Another pipe of half-inch bore, added in 1722, proving still inadequate, in 1787 and 1790 two more were added at some expense of five and seven inches, connecting more distant springs. By now Edinburgh and Leith had the Castle Hill reservoir of three hundred tons' capacity, and a new one nearly as large at Heriot's Hospital, fed by good springs.[52]

Best of the improvements, perhaps, were the sums now being spent on charities and popular education. The handsome, commodious high school [Infirmary Street, 1777], built by subscription, and the half-dozen charitable foundations, such as Watson's for seventy boys, Merchant Maiden and Trades Maiden for eighty and sixty girls respectively, and Trinity Hospital, for fifty-four old people, were only the start of generously endowed institutions.[53]

These improvements had to service a greatly increased population, risen from little more than 19,000 (estimated) within walls in 1687 to nearly 83,000 in 1775, not including the inmates of hospitals and poorhouses: a fourfold increase and still rising.

Philip Ainslie, who seems to have retained an almost photographic recollection of his boyhood in Edinburgh, leaves a picture of its privileged society at the very end of the century. By the 1790s society had taken up the New Town, living in St Andrew Square or Edinburgh's earlier squares, George or Brown's, and otherwise in Princes Street, George Street and Queen Street so far as they were built (a little beyond Castle Street): Charlotte Square was away on the far limits. An attractive fare of theatre, concerts and assemblies was on offer, and formal dinners and private balls were still in fashion, though country dances and reels had taken over from old-style formal minuets and cotillions (and it was well before the age of the waltz). Sedan chairs were still preferred to carriages: the chairs were parked at their owners' houses, usually on the ground floor at street corners, carried by the hardy, trustworthy Highlanders from Badenoch and Atholl, always to be found whether in snow, frost, hail or rain. Parking was easy in the spacious front halls of the new houses, enabling ladies to embark and return without damage to their elaborate toilette, especially while powdered heads and ostrich feathers were in vogue, along with the immense trains which they skilfully manoeuvred even while dancing. Neil Gow was still the favourite composer on the violin, whether for a personally commissioned Strathspey, a dance for a wedding or a particular reel. By now the George Street, as opposed to George Square, Assembly Rooms had triumphed.

The streets were still regarded as safe: the Town Guard was on duty only during the day, and after midnight out of doors was completely silent apart from an occasional 'drunken roarer' wending homewards.

And beyond the new houses, petering out at the northern and eastern edge, were fields where later York Place and Dundas Street would be built, with General Scott of Balcomie's mansion of Bellevue in its park-like grounds, later to be covered by Drummond Place.[54]

Young Philip used to learn shooting from Willy Wood, Lang Sandy's younger brother, who farmed for their old father, over the open land between Castle Street and Frederick Street. Philip would stay overnight at Inverleith with kind Mrs Rocheid, the friend of his dead mother and a granddaughter of Lord Reay, and after a solitary early breakfast of bread and butter with currant jelly fed him by the motherly housekeeper, he and Willy would range all day with the pointers Bob and Sal over potato and turnip fields, by Pilton and Muirhouse, as far as Wester Pilton or even Royston, Philip at first learning by watching Willy, and only carrying the game, and later beginning to shoot. About 4 o'clock he returned home to change from his muddy clothes into a dinner suit.[55] Such were the pleasant rural pursuits of new Edinburgh's northern limits at the end of the eighteenth century.

5
THE FRENCH EXILES

'The officers of the jurisdiction, the constables of the bounds, the Abbey guards, and the whole inhabitants are bound to turn out to protect the debtor.'

Peter Halkerston, *A Treatise on the History, Law, and Privileges of the Palace and Sanctuary of Holyroodhouse*, Edinburgh, 1831, 53f.

'The Comte was observed to eye [the Volunteers], as they made their bows, with a more than usual expression of countenance; some believing it proceeded from a feeling recollection of the resemblance which our volunteer gentry bore to the French national guard.'

Alexander Campbell, *A Journey from Edinburgh through Parts of North Britain*, London, 1802, 1.140

No King had visited Scotland since before the Union, and afterwards the only royalty to stay at Holyrood had been James VII when Duke of York and his wife in 1681, and Prince Charles Edward Stuart in the '45. Because of a curious legal situation, in 1796 and later at intervals, and again in 1830, Edinburgh became the home of a *ci-devant* French Prince.

Holyrood Palace had from medieval times been a place of sanctuary, limited after the Reformation to sheltering debtors, and it was now the only sanctuary in Scotland. The Abbey Court maintained this privilege under a Baillie appointed by the Duke of Hamilton, Hereditary Keeper, as senior peer. The rules were similar to those of an English debtors' prison: resident debtors, once established, were free from arrest, but allowed outside the precincts only on Sundays and official fast days of the Kirk.

In December 1795 Louis XVIII's brother Charles, Duc d'Artois, the titular Monsieur since the death of the boy King Louis XVII, was dispatched to seek English quarters for his brother, who however then felt obliged to accept the Tsar's pressing invitation to stay in Russia. Monsieur set off for London with an appeal to the Government to aid a Royalist attack on Brittany, but the émigrés were defeated, and he found himself dunned for payment by the suppliers of the Prince de Condé's army, so that although he denied the debt, he was at first unable even to land at Portsmouth. He was advised not to contest this and, to avoid a lawsuit, to sail 'secretly' to Edinburgh and take sanctuary in Holyrood until the British Government decided how to act. The Prince of Wales offered him the use of the Royal apartments, and had them refurbished to lessen their decided gloom.

D'Artois, now thirty-nine, who had been Marie Antoinette's favourite brother-in-law, was good-looking, frivolous and socially minded. His marriage to Princess Thérèse of Savoy had foundered among mutual amours after it had produced two sons, the Duc d'Angoulême and the Duc de Berri. Mme de Polastron, sister of Queen Marie Antoinette's friend the Duchesse de Polignac, was his most lasting love.

The Prince landed at Leith from HM frigate *Jason*, on the afternoon of 6 January 1796, to be greeted by a salute of twenty-one guns. He was received by Lord Adam Gordon, younger son of the 2nd Duke of Gordon, Commander of the Forces in Scotland, who in that capacity had lived at Holyrood since 1789, and was now in his seventies. The royal party was driven to Holyrood, the Prince in Lord Adam's carriage, his small suite following in other carriages, arriving to a second twenty-one-gun salute but dispensing with other intended ceremonies. The streets were lined with crowds the whole way, and windows were decorated, to mark the novel experience of a passing Prince – and probably also to indulge many a secret Jacobite tendency.[1]

Until Lord Adam's residence as C-in-C, Holyrood had all but decayed; he had restored it so far as to be at least habitable, but it was still described as 'cold, damp, cheerless'. The Royal apartments were on the east front and included part of the south wing. However, Lord Adam now[2] conducted the Royal party from the palace gate to his own apartments, as the Royal suite was still unfinished, and several of the nobility joined them at dinner. The following day the Prince, who decided to hold his levées on Mondays and Thursdays at noon, held his first when he received the Duke of Buccleuch and his son the Earl of Dalkeith, officers of the Hopetoun Fencibles and staff, and the Sheriff of Midlothian, among others. At the next leveé he received official Edinburgh: the Lord President, Lord Advocate, Lord Provost, magistrates and others, and was then escorted by Lord Adam, the Lord Advocate and the Provost, Sir James Stirling, to view his new quarters.

Lord Adam, besides making much-needed repairs, had had the old carvings and panelling painted white and removed some untidy outbuildings. Monsieur was allowed an income of £6000 a year by the British Government, having refused any help from his brother, but the costs of maintaining his small court (to start with he was accompanied only by two close friends, Comte François Descars and the Chevalier de Puysegur), supporting his followers, and running his secret courier service to the Continent, kept him poor, and he had to limit himself to one carriage.

Once his position became known he was joined by members of the Court who had earlier fled to Russia, Germany or London. They thought Edinburgh dismal and the Palace worse, with its citadel-like situation and dreary rooms in one of Edinburgh's seediest quarters. After a couple of weeks his 21-year-old son d'Angoulême arrived, who had to stay in Lord Breadalbane's apartments until his own were ready, and probably for reasons of economy held his own levées at the same time as his father.[3]

The courtiers lived in houses surrounding the Palace, among them the Duc and Duchesse de Guiche, the Prince's long-standing mistress the shy Mme de Polastron, the Marquis de Polignac and his wife, the Duc and Duchesse de Gontaut with the Duchesse's mother. Monsieur was full of polite regrets that, not being in his own home (doubtless a euphemism for his poverty), he could not accommodate his friends but must lodge them in what became this small French colony in 'the square'. For example, on arrival of the Gontauts, he explained that his modest establishment allowed him only to invite the ladies for tea in the evenings though he insisted that the Duc dine with him at any time.

However, on the arrival of his former boon-companion the Vicomte de Vaudreuil with his much younger wife, much straitened for funds and living on only £10 a month, of which four had to pay for their lodging, Monsieur sent them two *plats* every day from the royal dinner.

The atmosphere must have been rather like that of Napoleon's later household on St Helena – strenuous efforts were made at entertainment, and any new arrival was an event. Before long they were joined by the Duc de Berri, remarked on as 'a stout country-looking curly-headed stirring boy', who brightened their daily life with music and comedies. Lady Louisa Stewart, who met the Royal court a few years later, describes father and son in dispassionate terms. Monsieur was handsome and healthy-looking, of middle size and well made, appearing younger than his age, with his chief defect a too short upper lip which prevented his mouth from closing properly, but with a princely, well-bred and gracious manner, product of 'the politest court in Europe'. As for his unfortunate son, 'nobody would find him out for a prince or gentleman, and less of a soldier than either'. Lady Louisa continued mercilessly, 'his appearance is against him; he is little, thick, stumpy and slouching, with a very ugly brown face that might be 50 years old, and a sullen dour look'. The lady conceded, however, that he appeared sensible and intelligent.[4]

Monsieur, as the Comte de Ségur had reported of him in happier days, 'liked the great world, was fond of society, theatre, hunting, and fêtes'.[5] He was fashionable as well as handsome, as Henry Mackenzie recalled him in Paris when splendidly accoutred at a military review. At Holyrood his fondness for comedies was partly satisfied by amateur court productions in which his entourage acted the parts (the audience were mostly the servants).

One was held on his birthday, another on his fête-day. There were also little concerts, in which the ladies sang with some talent.

Good French speakers were of course welcome. Christison relates how the French teacher Mylne, who prided himself on his fluency, and Christison's brother John, were much in the court circle. One evening Mylne, not being a good whist player, in cutting for partners fell to the lively Mme Boyd, and when she ironically congratulated herself he innocently remarked '*Madame, je ferai votre plaisir toute la nuit.*' To which unintended *galanterie* the lady with unruffled aplomb replied, '*Oh monsieur, la soirée suffira.*'[6]

Six months after Monsieur's arrival there was an election of the sixteen Representative Peers, which was always held at Holyrood, and he was able to witness this ceremony which dated from the Union of 1707. Many fashionable ladies were present, including the Countesses of Breadalbane and Glasgow, and those Peers who were elected afterwards held a party at Fortune's new tavern in Princes Street for the garrison officers, officers of the law, and the French court which of course the Prince himself could not attend. Some of the courtiers in fact felt slightly guilty at accepting hospitality, as the Prince was obliged to stay so much in retirement.[7]

Not suffering the same restrictions as he did, they were able to visit freely among the Scottish aristocracy, whom they found hospitable and kind. Among their most generous friends were the Duchess of Buccleuch, her daughter-in-law Lady Dalkeith, and the Duke of Hamilton and his family. Other ladies included the Wedderburns – the Jacobite Lady Hope and her sister-in-law Lady Wedderburn, of Inveresk. Monsieur made his carriage available, since he could use it only on Sundays. The Comtesse de Boigne, married very young to a disagreeable General old enough to be her father, found herself much fêted, especially by the Hamiltons, and the old husband, seeing her in fashion, became temporarily less surly: 'he treated me diplomatically, as he saw that society welcomed me', and all in all, this period of exile turned out one of the more pleasant experiences of her youth.[8]

When the Loyal Volunteers were formed, it was said that their blue uniforms with red facings reminded Monsieur too much of the National Guard in Paris for comfort so that he was quite put out when their commander and staff appeared at a levée.[9] The Duc d'Angoulême, however, turned up to drill with the troop. Poor fellow, he can have had little else to do.

Among the Prince's visitors from England was the Duke of Rutland, travelling with an entourage of young clergymen, Mr King, Mr Culling Smith and Mr Hayes, who were in Edinburgh in August 1796. They waited on the Prince at 11 o'clock one morning – not the usual time of a levée – falling in with Sir Godfrey Webster on the same mission. Monsieur was playing billiards with a few of his court: they included the old Duc de Ferrand, whose two sons had been killed in the disastrous Quiberon Bay expedition.

The visitors were pleased with the Prince's 'affable and easy demeanour' and admired his 'apparent resignation, and even cheerfulness'; d'Angoulème, who was able to enter into Edinburgh society, had 'conciliated the esteem and attachment of the whole neighbourhood'.[10]

Henry Mackenzie, introduced to the Prince by the latter's own desire, was presented at a levée by Lord Adam Gordon and much impressed by the Royal charm. 'His manners were affable tho' princely, his bow . . . most graceful. He spoke to everyone in the circle and seemed to know a great deal of matters both foreign and domestic.' He regarded the Prince, naïvely, as a reformed man, 'very regular and temperate in his habits' and 'likely to be a great King . . . not showy and expensive'.[11] A forecast fairly wide of the mark. In his extravagant youth the Prince had been much blamed for the unpopularity of the Queen and her Austrian friends, whose insolent self-indulgence had earned so much criticism.

Lord Adam, in charge of the Holyrood entertainments, and presenting suitable persons at the levées, was much handicapped by his poor knowledge of French: for example, his version of a Highland chief, or 'montagnard', came out deplorably as 'un gentilhomme sauvage'. Among those presented, and whom Monsieur visited (on Sundays, of course), was Lord Chief Baron Dundas, to whom he gave his portrait which was afterwards kept at Arniston. He and his party also went shooting at General Wemyss's, gunning down the partridges in a volley, French-fashion, to the gamekeeper's horror.[12]

Monsieur's old mistress, Mme de Polastron, was about as inhibited as Louise de la Vallière, and partly to satisfy the guilt-ridden lady he agreed to employ a simple and pious almoner, who 'will dine with my first *valet de chambre* . . . but he must never expect to act as my confessor'. For this position Monsieur preferred 'a good Scotch Catholic' free of political or conspiratorial tendencies. The Vicomtesse de Vaudreuil recommended the Abbé Jean Baptiste Latil, a poor young priest of humble birth. The court was able to attend mass at St Andrew's, a small Catholic chapel in Blackfriars Wynd. The Prince, not being in the least religious himself, was embarrassed by the fervour of Scottish Catholics, and on one occasion was much disconcerted at having to travel some twenty miles to attend a religious festival, and spend several hours in a devout family's private chapel. To avoid such ordeals in the future he had a chapel fitted up at the end of the Palace gallery.

Latil greatly influenced the holy-minded Mme de Polastron, and by means of her own rigid ideas, disseminated through the little court, its members also became narrowly pious. Although Monsieur mocked, friends like the Duchesse de Guiche, who had vainly tried to intrigue with the First Consul before joining him in Edinburgh, were greatly affected, and the Duchesse herself died an 'exemplary' death, attended by her cousin the penitent Mistress, who was herself falling victim to phthysis.

The de Guiches lived with Mme de Polastron in a small white-washed house 'on the left of the Chapel looking into the park', where Monsieur joined her every evening for a game of whist; there was also her eleven-year-old son Louis, who was supposed also to be Monsieur's. While the French happily accepted the lady's irregular position, the Scots raised their eyebrows, especially as Madame, the Prince's wife, was not with the court but living in Turin.[13]

Until his mistress became ill, the social Monsieur continued his visits to noblemen's houses and enjoyed entertainments at his court. In August 1798, for example, he was treated to a surprise performance of a farce, *Le Sourd*, staged in the rooms of the Duc de Berri, who had been ill. When his father came in to visit him he found the place transfomed by screens and curtains, lighted with wax candles from the billiard room and with an audience of maids and footmen. The play, in which de Berri played a rich bourgeois, made the Prince laugh a great deal – apparently an infrequent occurrence.[14]

This was in the nature of a parting entertainment, however, for on 5 September de Berri and his suite left Holyrood, sailing for Hamburg in order to join the Prince de Condé's army.

The Royalist debt seems never to have been paid, but by the Aliens Act passed in 1798 any person fleeing from tyranny in France was not only offered asylum but specifically freed from liability to arrest for related debts. This was an *ad hoc* ruling, and further legislation on the Prince's behalf was sought in 1801. Yet thirty years later he was still pursued by creditors and the same situation arose again.[15]

Once the Act was passed and he became, at least for the present, free of debt, Monsieur was able to return to London, where he joined the Prince Regent's circle. Although far from an admirable character, his grace and polish were much noted, with the distinguished manners that seemed second nature to a French leader of fashion – far outshining the Regent, who 'seemed nothing more than his caricature'. Although the English Prince was at that time more handsome, Monsieur 'had greater grace and dignity, while his bearing, his dress, and his mode of entering and leaving a room were incomparable'. His debonair manner, which made him appear eager to please, and earned the devotion of all who met him, brought him many friends for whom, to be honest, he cared nothing in return.[16]

Before he left Scotland he visited the many chiefs of clans and other friends who had shown so much kindness during his exile, to express his thanks. Some of his court followed him to London (1801), others remained and continued their friendship with the Buccleuchs. Holyrood remained the Prince's headquarters for the next two years, and he travelled between Edinburgh and London several times.

The mad Tsar Paul ordered Louis XVIII to leave Mittau, where he had been living, and d'Artois, then in Edinburgh, hastened to London to raise money for his brother, and to persuade the Government to grant him a pension similar to his own. This not surprisingly helped bring about a reconciliation between the estranged brothers, and d'Artois also achieved pardon for the Orléans Princes, disgraced by Philippe Egalité's complicity with the execution of Louis XVI.

These Princes also visited Scotland in 1801, and in September attended the Circuit trials in Glasgow. Monsieur's Scottish sojourns in 1801 and 1802 were much freer since he was no longer under threat of arrest, and he was also better off financially. Nobody at that time would forecast, first, that it would take more than a dozen years for the Bourbons to be restored, nor that in about thirty years' time Monsieur would be back at Holyrood, this time as an exiled King.[17]

Some years after their departure Lady Bessborough, on an Edinburgh visit, 'quite knock'd up with walking to Arthur's Seat, and afterwards all round Edinburgh', on reaching Holyrood was surprised, as she rested leaning against an archway, to be accosted by an old woman who told her that just alongside was the grave of the Duchesse de Gramont, 'who was embalm'd, and lies there till her friends can fetch her over again'. The woman further recalled the duchess's 'little smiling figure . . . and all her kindness. She lov'd life so, poor little thing!'[18]

The French royal apartments were afterwards shown to visitors, who were mostly unimpressed. Holyrood generally struck people as dismal and melancholy, and its garden was full of weeds. The Comte d'Artois' room was still identified by the name 'Monsieur' on the door, and contained his bed and other furniture, also a portrait of the Princesse Elizabeth, whose elaborate costume now seemed excessive and antiquated. The chapel fitted up for the French on a platform at the end of the long gallery appeared makeshift, and the altar, covered by a cloth, was revealed by the inquisitive as 'a common sideboard'.[19]

Foreign visitors, especially of course the French, showed much curiosity. Charles Nodier in 1822 draws the obvious parallel: 'What a subject for historical meditation – the Bourbons taking refuge in the tragical palace of the Stuarts! . . . A picture which represents the family of Charles I after his execution, was the first object which, on his rising, struck the eye of the brother of Lewis XVI.'[20]

6
INTERREGNUM

One obviously arbitrary date for the end of the New Town's first phase would be 1800, closing the old century, with the first New Town virtually complete – although Princes Street was still unfinished. There was now talk of an extension towards a terminating circus, improving the exit road to Glasgow by a road across the new bridge over the Water of Leith at Bell's Mills.[1]

There are better milestones, however, than a round date: for example, the ill-conceived, short-lived peace in March 1802, which lured hundreds of people to visit the continent, only to stream back again little more than a year later when war was resumed. Then, too, Lord Melville's impeachment in 1805 signalled a new era in politics, when although he was acquitted it was the end of his power career in Scotland. (The Dundas influence, however, continued under his son.) There was the death of Pitt in January 1806, Fox's brief premiership – the first Whig government for twenty-three years – and the Grenville interlude on Fox's own death.

All this had a profound effect for Scotland, even though in 1807 Tory rule was reinstated in Britain for a further quarter-century. Furthermore, the older generation of lawmen, academics, thinkers and writers was passing, and in 1806 younger Whigs succeeded into office, Dundas of Arniston becoming Lord Chief Baron, and Charles Hope obtaining the Lord Justice Clerkship on old Lord Eskgrove's death.

Shortly before the temporary peace with France was signed in 1802, Lady Minto wrote with her characteristic articulacy and perceptiveness to her husband, from the pleasant vantage point of the upper classes: 'This country has arrived at the true pitch of comfort and happiness . . . People meet together to be pleased, cheerful, and easy. Even the Scotch pride has its uses by putting the poor often on an equal footing with the rich. Their education is equally good, their society the same, their spirit and love of their country possibly much greater . . . At the present time I think the race very superior to the English.' Except for the last sentence, the poor perhaps did not view affairs in quite this sanguine way.[2]

Yet the next stage in Edinburgh's development may most appropriately be dated from 1802, when a fresh breeze began to blow with the launching of a new periodical, by a group of brilliant and enterprising young Whigs. The *Edinburgh Review,* from the first day of its publication, was to have a profound effect for at least the next century on literary, political and social ideas.

PART II

1802–1815

INTRODUCTION

By 1800 Edinburgh was on the brink of three decades of its most brilliant history. The war had concentrated society within Britain: the Continent was for most of the first fifteen years of the century out of bounds. In Edinburgh's newly enlarged capital city were now gathered some of the greatest thinkers, philosophers and literati it had ever known: of the old guard Henry Mackenzie and Fergusson were still alive, and of the younger men, Jeffrey, Cockburn, Brougham, Horner and Sydney Smith were the chief of its glittering luminaries.

Meanwhile the Volunteer regiments which drew in all the keen young men of the upper and professional class provided a closeness and camaraderie which long survived – and though the force was disbanded with the Peace of Amiens, it had precipitately to be revived in 1803.

Walter Scott, who had worked on *Border Minstrelsy* while serving as Sheriff of Selkirk, in his search for ballads had met and befriended James Hogg, a self-educated shepherd a year younger than himself and a natural poet.

Changes in the legal establishment were instigated when the Lord Chief Baron, Sir James Montgomery, resigned his office in 1801 and was succeeded by Robert Dundas of Arniston, while Charles Hope became Lord Advocate, an office which he described as comprising all the state powers, military and civil, inspiring a newspaper to report: 'Arrived at Edinburgh, the Lord High Chancellor of Scotland, the Lord Justice General, the Lord Privy Seal, the Privy Council, and the Lord Advocate, all in one post chaise, containing only a single person'.[1]

Hope had an uncontrollable temper, as Henry Cockburn records, and it was perhaps fortunate that in 1804 he was appointed Lord Justice Clerk on the death of old Lord Eskgrove.

The century started disturbingly with food shortages and 'meal-mobs' both in Edinburgh and Glasgow, arising from a poor oat-harvest which was Europe-wide. Even the unpopular Provost, Sir James Stirling, attempted to mollify malcontents by advising use of wheat and barley as substitutes; luckily the 1800 harvest was somewhat better. Meanwhile the Council had secured a £10,000 assessment through Parliament in order to relieve the poor. In 1801 Stirling was succeeded by Sir William Fettes of Comely Bank.

Renewed fear of invasion was seen in 1801, hence great activity by the Edinburgh Volunteers, now numbering over 3000, drilling, exercising and being reviewed on the links at Bruntsfield and Leith. In September a small earthquake, which might or might not have been seen as portentous, its epicentre at Crieff or Comrie, was felt in the New Town. Among public works in May Robert Dundas of Melville, Depute Grand Master of Masons, laid the foundation of a new harbour at Leith, following an Act of 1799 authorising the magistrates to borrow the funds. The engineer for the works, which continued until 1806, was John Rennie. Meanwhile a plan to give employment to the poor was launched when the Council resolved to drain the Meadows. Here the Volunteers paraded on 13 October 1802 when the proclamation of peace was ratified, whence they marched to Princes Street to fire a *feu-de-joie* before many spectators, answered by the castle guns. Bells rang and the city was illuminated in the evening, and transparencies were displayed. Better still, the prisoners in the castle, 208 French and twenty-four Dutch, were freed and sailed home from Leith.

The city was now to be further enlarged, with a Bill in 1802 to extend the Royalty and include the lands of Bellevue on the north, to extend York Place and make further improvements. A subscription was opened to build a canal to Edinburgh from the west of Scotland, while arguments raged over its route. On the King's sixty-fourth birthday, what with the usual royal salute, afternoon collation given by the magistrates for the nobility and gentry, and an evening assembly, no one could recall such untroubled celebrations, the newspapers hoping that in future Edinburgh might be spared 'those dangerous and filthy demonstrations of tumultuous joy' which endangered innocent citizens. But by November the police reported a rise in robberies, street and domestic, warning that now Edinburgh had so increased in size, the Town Guard had become ineffective. In view of the peace, however, the Volunteers were to be disbanded.

And in 1802, the *Edinburgh Review* was launched.

7
THE YOUNG WHIGS AND THE *EDINBURGH REVIEW*

'I do not believe that either London or Paris ever saw so much genius in our days. It is, indeed, seldom that so many young men of distinguished talents have sprung up at one time or in one place.'

Mrs Elizabeth Hamilton, letter to a friend, 1802, in *Memoirs*, 1.163

'Perhaps there is at present no spot upon the earth where religion, science, and literature combine more to produce moral and intellectual pleasures than in the metropolis of Scotland.'

Benjamin Rush in Philadelphia to his son James, then a medical student at Edinburgh, 19 March 1810; *Letters of Benjamin Rush*, 1038

At the beginning of the nineteenth century a mercurial, restless and dissatisfied young man – rising advocate, member of the Speculative Society, committed Whig, and friend of most literary aspirants – was reviewing his twenty-seven years of life and finding them wanting.

He was Francis Jeffrey, son of a rather gloomy, intolerant father of medium rank at the Court of Session as Depute Clerk. Small, dark and vigorous as a child, Francis never grew very much, maturing into a wiry little man compact of energy.

A clever scholar at the High School,[1] anxiously ambitious, before he turned fourteen he was studying Greek, Logic and Moral Philosophy at Glasgow University, hating the drudgery of writing and recording his already acute critical insights in an illegible scrawl.

Next he attended law classes in Edinburgh, lonely, but with his quick intelligence prolifically turning out essays and tales. James Boswell, whom one night he helped lug to bed in a drunken stupor, told him next day that he was a 'promising lad', and that 'if you go on as you've begun, you may live to be a Bozzy yourself yet'.[2]

In a third spell at a university, Jeffrey went for a single academic year to Oxford, lonelier still and striving mainly to achieve an English accent. The result, neither English nor Scots, offended his friends with its fast, almost affected gabble, high-keyed and sharp in pronunciation.

Jeffrey completed law studies in Edinburgh (1789–91), under its leading professors Hume, Tytler and Stewart, and here 'from a lounging, idling, unhopeful kind of fellow, I have become a most persevering and indefatigable student'.[3] Joining the Speculative Society, he became friends with Francis Horner, Henry Brougham, John Murray and Walter Scott, never kept silent during meetings and read five papers in three years. Yet while he revelled in this stimulus to the mind, at twenty he was all too conscious of a waste of 'unprofitable years, without use, distinction, or enjoyment'. At that time, too, he hated Edinburgh, 'disturbed with its filth, and debauchery, and restraint, without having access to much of the virtue or genius it may contain'.[4]

Still assiduously writing, he even dabbled in verse, believing for a time that this might be his vocation.

Scotland, and Edinburgh, were in the doldrums of 'Dundas-ism'. Politically corrupt and restricted, the outlook still strictly limited in the church, it offered no outlet either in politics or even in a literary or journalistic field.

Jeffrey now embarked on a career in the law where some of the liveliest and keenest thinkers practised. He had a mixed reception. He was skilled at the written pleadings required by the Scottish courts (until 1825), a talent offset by his Whiggish principles, affected-seeming English manner and sarcastic style of arguing. After two years he felt that those few members he knew did not care for him, apart from the high-principled Archibald Fletcher, always an opponent to oppression, and Henry Erskine. To his shame, when Erskine was voted out by the Faculty in 1796, Jeffrey did not openly join the thirty-eight members who supported him, but was one of the younger, less experienced advocates who abstained rather than fall foul of their parents' rigid prejudices.

Still unsatisfied, in his solitary walks he worried at his 'dismally stupid and inactive' life, and wished he could marry. He met and was stimulated by contemporaries newly arrived from England, Lord Webb Seymour and the Rev. Sydney Smith. He could not afford to travel, but went to St Andrews, 'bathed, and lounged, and fell in love with great assiduity'. This was in 1800. Although his love's father, Dr Wilson, died the following year, he and his Catherine were able to marry, and settled in a house (that is, a tenement) in the new-built Buccleuch Place, beyond the South Bridge. He was earning little; he wanted to write. But what?[5]

About this time Jeffrey became a close friend of Archibald Alison, whose family moved to Edinburgh in 1800 when the father, the Rev. Archibald Alison, became senior minister at the Episcopal chapel in the Cowgate. They lived in a charming villa at the top of Bruntsfield Links, then nearly two miles outside the city. This spared the two sons, Archibald and William, from attending the High School, and they studied at home with a tutor, yet they still learned by the limited Scottish method, with no Latin verse, and no Greek at all. Archibald became a great friend of the judge Lord Woodhouselee's son Patrick, of that cultivated family the Fraser Tytlers, eighteen months older than himself and hence seeming vastly superior. The youths spent their spare money at auctions, buying etchings, and Archibald began building up a library to supplement his father's of mostly French and Italian works.

When Jeffrey was a rising young advocate, Alison thought that Thomas Campbell, a great friend while he was living in Edinburgh, showed more of 'genius and sensibility', though in conversation he did not shine except when gripped by strong emotion. Whereas Jeffrey could speak 'lightly and felicitously on every subject' – literature, philosophy, poetry, politics, the arts – to Alison it seemed superficial. 'No deep wells of thought or feeling existed in Jeffrey' (naïve assumption); 'he was judicious and candid in criticism, and lenient and considerate in judgment, but had scarcely an original thought or profound reflection in his mind.'[6] As Alison was barely thirteen when the two boys first met at the college, his judgment might be thought a little premature.

Among Jeffrey's brilliant young contemporaries Francis Horner was much admired by his friends. Born 1778, he was the son of an Edinburgh merchant living in St David Street, where as an infant he used to play with Henry Brougham; he did well at the High School and university, studying the Classics, mathematics, philosophy and French, and with Brougham became a leading member of the Juvenile Literary Society. Intending to become a public speaker, he was sent to England – like Jeffrey, to lose his accent as well as to study, but (under the Rev. John Hewlett, of Shacklewell) found it difficult to 'feel the difference between the rhythm of their conversation and mine'. Not to mention the problem of attending House of Commons debates and returning at night with five miles' walk each way. He was disappointed, anyway, by MPs' 'cant' and poor speaking.

Horner, an assiduous scholar with a clear mind and retentive memory, was of solemn, though reasonably cheerful, disposition, and friends called him 'the sage' and 'the ancient Horner'. Armed with his impeccable English accent he returned to Edinburgh in 1797 to study law, joined the Speculative Society along with Brougham, missed only three meetings in three years and was president for two. Early in 1799 he met Lord Webb Seymour and started a programme of discussions with him in order to sharpen his reasoning skills. Horner was then twenty-one, the more plodding Lord Webb was twenty-two. Horner's serious study plan included three hours a day at law, forcing himself to rise early, attend Allen's 'Animal Economy' lectures in the middle of the day, then walk until the dinner hour. He and Seymour spent much time looking at rock formations round Edinburgh, and also visited the Highlands.[7]

Horner's accomplishments were the more remarkable that none of his family either came near him in talent or were even of a literary inclination. His father, though well-informed, was not intellectual; Francis maintained a 'constant and high principled affection' for his parents and a cheerful affection for his siblings. For a man of understanding he was unusually modest, ready to test his views by comparing with others. Nor could he tolerate a joke on serious subjects. His friends Sydney Smith and Lord Dudley one day pretended to argue that the Government were justified 'in stealing the Danish fleet', but Horner angrily bolted from the room, and although they flung up the window and shouting with laughter assured him they were only joking, he made off and 'it took a fortnight of serious behaviour before we were forgiven'.

When Sydney Smith met Horner, 'feeble-minded people' tried to warn him of his 'violent political opinions', but this the more attracted Smith, who regarded him as 'among the most conspicuous young men in that energetic and infragrant city', and he soon grasped that Horner 'loved truth better than he loved Dundas', at that time the tyrant of Scotland. Thenceforward they were constant friends.[8]

So patently honest and sincere was Horner that Smith believed he could get away with any crime. 'The commandments were written on his face . . . no judge or jury would give the smallest degree of credit to any evidence against him . . . you saw at once that he was a great man, whom nature had intended for a leader of human beings'.[9]

The suspect group of young Edinburgh liberals, which now included Horner, Brougham and Jeffrey, fell foul of the younger Hume, the historian's nephew, who considered them disloyal and irreligious. He unwisely summoned a meeting of professors at a tavern, in order to propose that seven of them be expelled from the city. Dr Gregory, Dr Hunter and others were outraged. Gregory in particular praised the group as 'the flower of the College', pointing out by the way that one of them (Copeland) was his own nephew. The meeting broke up.

When news of this academic threat reached the group, they determined that it must come to a duel, and cast lots for which of them should challenge Hume. The lot fell on Jeffrey – a curious prefiguring of his encounter with Moore half a dozen years later – who chose Horner as second. But Frank Horner was ill with a sore throat which Lord Webb innocently aggravated by keeping him talking until he became feverish. Meanwhile the story reached the Sheriff's ears, and when Frank recovered, his father was called to answer for him to the court, and Frank was bound over to keep the peace.[10]

The gentle, unassuming and studious Lord Webb Seymour was younger brother to Edward, 11th Duke of Somerset. After studying at Oxford, at Christ Church, where he became devoted to science and philosophy, in 1798 at the age of twenty-two he decided to settle in Edinburgh. He rapidly became one of the Jeffrey–Horner circle, which also included Professor Dugald Stewart, the now elderly Henry Mackenzie and the new arrival, the Rev. Sydney Smith.

Seymour, thoughtful and reserved, had a frail, distinctly unrobust constitution which gave him a certain lethargy. He lived much with Professor John Playfair and Sir James Hall, working with them on mathematics and the physical sciences, especially geology. He and Playfair made a congenial pair, affectionately known as husband and wife, apparently without the significance which would probably be attributed today. Developing his passion for geology, for some three years after his arrival Seymour worked on the *Novum Organum* with the equally serious Horner, who saw in him 'an ardent passion for knowledge and improvement', with 'the truly philosophical qualities of scrupulous caution, unconquerable patience, unclouded candour' (a favourite contemporary word, its meaning sometimes obscure), and ready to devote his life to philosophy and speculation.[11]

Horner, 'not sure that his genius is of a high order', diagnosed Seymour's studiousness as 'intense almost to plodding – a mild, timid, reserved disposition'.[12] His lack of physical energy, and perhaps also of imagination made him rather slow of comprehension. He possessed everything requisite for a philosopher except 'inventive genius', and in his passion for knowledge limited himself to one subject at a time. The perennial student, he worked at Greek, chemistry, mineralogy, botany in turn, then mathematics, and his judgment of character was equally impressive. But 'I never knew a person read so slowly', observed Horner, 'and with such circumspection'. Hardly a day passed 'in which he has not made some intellectual improvement'. Horner, Seymour and his brother the Duke, who made a return visit to Edinburgh (he had toured Scotland in 1795), discussed forming a Philological Society with a chosen few.

In 1800, when young Lady Stanley met Lord Webb with Playfair visiting a salt pit, she wrote to her Aunt Serena, 'I never met with a more pleasing young man, in regard to the universal knowledge he had acquired, and the total absence of a conceit notwithstanding.'[13]

In the same year Lord Webb's zeal for knowledge made him experiment with nitrous oxide with the chemist Dr Hope, and he recklessly inhaled the gas several times before prudence prevailed. 'Though the first time I laughed, yet it was in a great measure from a consciousness of my ridiculous appearance'; and he continued innocently, 'The second time I felt still more strongly the state of orgasm . . . I said, I felt as if I was going to knock a man down.'

This curious reaction soon passed off, however, to be succeeded the same evening by two hours of placid 'philosophic conversation with Horner'.[14]

In June 1798, about the same time that Lord Webb Seymour came to live in Edinburgh, Sydney Smith, a lively, witty young clergyman of distinctly different temperament, arrived for what proved to be a ten-month first stay. He was at that time established in a Wiltshire curacy, and his present mission was to supervise the studies of the eldest son of his squire, Michael Hicks-Beach. During their Edinburgh residence Smith regaled his employers with pungent comments on young Michael's progress, on the city and on its leading figures. Although the vacation was just beginning and the town was therefore 'empty', Smith soon met Lord Webb, Professor Dugald Stewart – 'generally considered to be one of the first men in [the university]' – also the Greek professor, Andrew Dalzell. Dugald Stewart and his wife became great friends, and the professor greatly admired Smith's preaching.

Before long tutor and pupil removed to lodgings at 38 South Hanover Street, cheap, convenient and pleasant, 'in the centre of the finest street I have yet seen in Great Britain', with a view of the Firth and its shipping and the shores of Fife. 'We have the whole floor, a kitchen, a Servant, and every kind of furniture found us for about £12 sl [sic] a week. The boarding Tables are very objectionable here . . .'

More objectionable still was Edinburgh sanitation, or lack of it: 'No Smells were ever equal to Scotch Smells. It is the School of Physic; walk the Streets, and you would imagine that every Medical man had been administering Cathartics to every man, woman and child in the Town.' (Little improvement on Mrs Piozzi's strictures ten years earlier.) Smith was balanced between disgust and his admiration for Edinburgh's 'uncommnly beautiful' appearance.[15]

He employed a cook at 6d a day, and a maid-servant who received only her board. He had also brought with them a valet, Mithoffer, who attended to their housekeeping, but was not very skilled in marketing – or in pastry-making. Smith had to buy their butcher-meat, and the three of them, including the cook, made sad business of a pie.

The Rev. Sydney liked the Scots, noting them as larger in frame than the English, the women handsomer and their 'dialect very agreeable'; poorer than the English, cautious and discreet. He also noted how the 'common people' were well versed in the scriptures, and people generally were much in earnest over religion, though seemingly rather less so now than they had been, despite the strong clergy influence. Indeed, he was impressed at how well informed they generally were.[16]

Meanwhile they had met Baron (of the Exchequer) Norton, and Charles Hope, great-grandson of the 1st Earl of Hopetoun and shortly before he became Lord Advocate (1801), and his wife Lady Charlotte Hope whose father had become 3rd Earl in 1781.

Michael Hicks-Beach proved a fairly average scholar, but enjoyed his daily dancing lessons and playing Scottish songs, while his tutor occasionally preached at the Episcopal Charlotte Chapel in Rose Street. Michael also showed alarming signs of falling in love, but soon got over it.

Smith was shocked to meet a poor schoolmaster, 'starving to death with his wife and 4 children' – because Scotland had no outdoor poor relief. Not long before, 'the poor man had had to exist from a Sunday evening to Thursday noon on nothing but 2 little bits of tobacco . . . a few scraps of barley bread he kept for his family . . . He gets bread once in 24 hours.' Yet this man was accomplished in Latin, Greek and French. Smith and Michael planned to keep the family supplied with broth.

He soon found out about the workhouse. The sole funds available for the poor were the Sabbath church-door collections, but so great was resistance at this time to any form of organised relief that these amounts were small. There were about three times as many beggars as in England. (Eventually the poor were provided thrice weekly with soup at a penny a quart, not much to their taste as they had expected oatmeal; but once used to it they found they quite liked it. Wheat was still a delicacy among them.)

Despite Smith's distress at the hardships of the poor, 'This place rather grows upon us both, we are extremely comfortably situated, and have thoughts of never coming back . . .' He was to change his mind before long, because their social contacts had proved so few, 'all University business [is] so compleatly at a Stop in the Summer', and even by early December the city seemed still deserted of 'company'. He was also in a quandary whether to keep on the lodgings, or give notice, because as soon as the town began at all to fill again their hitherto civil landlady became anxious to get rid of them unless Smith raised the monthly rent to twelve guineas. She was all for pushing them out at once with a string of insults, but Smith stood his ground, threatening justice in the courts of England and 'from thence to Russia' until of course she gave in, became amiable and apologetic, and was persuaded to sign a witnessed agreement.

More domestic trouble arose on New Year's Eve, when every servant became drunk on ale or rum, and the housemaid, who had multiple suitors, insisted on going out to celebrate with the rest.

A little later it was young Michael who became drunk, Smith having allowed him to entertain two schoolmates from Eton while he himself was dining out, and on his return found them rowdy and boisterous. However, he was sure that this was not Michael's personal choice, his thoughts being less on drink than on dancing. 'He turns up the carpet and capers away for the hour together.'

Smith was struck by the absence of any observance of Lent, or even of Easter, shops staying open on Good Friday (a custom widely held at least until the 1960s), and with none of the English Easter customs such as appropriate prayers, let alone hot cross buns.[17]

At last tutor and pupil had to leave Edinburgh, and in May 1799 set off for England with the loan of a coach to London but in great hopes of a second pleasurable year in the Scottish capital. In fact they were back again in October, better lodged this time at 19 Queen Street, at much the same rent. Michael, now greatly improved, took three hourly French lessons a week, with a work total of five or six hours a day.

Arriving this time in the autumn, they were quickly showered with introductions, and invited to many a supper, 'to the infinite delight of Michael. I am almost ashamed to say we were invited out every day last week to Supper'; but at least this was after Michael's study hours. 'In the meantime Michael gains manners, and I a headache.' And also meantime, Smith was delivering many sermons. Michael fell in love again, with the lady at number 30, who invited him several times to her house, 'rather singular for an unmarried lady'. But in June 1800 it was the Rev. Sydney Smith's own impending marriage which this time took them away from Edinburgh.[18]

Smith was soon back, however. On 2 July 1800, at Cheam, he married Catherine Pybus, whose father had been a banker. Bride and groom returned to Edinburgh about the end of August, this time with the Hicks-Beaches' younger son William, and they set up at 46 George Street for Smith's longest spell yet, not returning to London until 1803.

They quickly found a good cook and housemaid, and were looking out for a third servant. William, well-behaved but shy, soon met several 'respectable and gentlemanly young men', though Smith at first feared he 'found Edinburgh a little dull, a fault which diminishes every day'.[19]

Smith was delighted to resume relations with 'the aged Horner, and the more aged Seymour: I love the Sages well'. As for Jeffrey, 'We will pass many evenings together, arguing and joking amidst eating and drinking; above all being stupid when we feel inclined, a rare privilege of friendship.'[20]

His pleasure in the autumn was saddened by the death of his mother in England. It was also at this time that King George's mysterious malady returned, causing a political crisis that made less impact in these northern parts than in the south. 'We are as ignorant of what happens in London as if we were in heaven.'

Assuming that William would stay until he entered Oxford next year, the youth was embarked on a curriculum that included botany lectures, lessons in drawing and fencing, and an autumn tour of the Highlands 'with some very eligible companions, and a Mentor'. He also did well at mathematics. In December the household was joined by Alexander Gordon, 'a charming young man', natural son of the 3rd Earl of Aberdeen, who had just died at the age of eighty.

At sixteen Alexander had been brought home from an English academy and had lived for a time 'immured with his father'. Smith felt he would be 'a prodigious acquisition to William', in spite of the extra burden on his household – albeit with the sweetener of a £400 fee.[21]

In March 1802 Catherine Smith was brought to bed of their first child, a girl, Saba, the confinement leaving her so weak that sadly she had to give up nursing her. Smith had to take over the household management: 'with a set of strange servants and in a foreign land, I have been forced to be head nurse and head everything'.[22] By June, however, thanks to a stay in the sea air at Burntisland, beautifully placed 'under the high woods of Aberdour, Lord Morton's property', she was fairly recovered, so that Smith prophesied that the small town, famous for cured herrings, would now be renowned 'for the cure of Wives'.[23]

The Burntisland stay, in a primitive 'cabin', was an interlude of abandon. 'We have barrels for tables', wrote Smith to Caroline Fox, 'tongs for bells, and ropes to tie our doors instead of Locks . . . Everything is vicarial and suppositious.' In July he was describing to Mrs Beach how they contrived. 'Our meat larder is a hamper and is hung to a beam; Mrs Smith's dressing-table a herring barrel; her bell is a pair of tongs tied to a rope passed through the door. The books are kept in the corner cupboard with the yellow pickles . . .'[24]

Meanwhile he had been helping his friend John Allen, a learned, sensible man and skilled but impoverished physician, to a post as travelling companion to Lord Holland's family on a visit to Spain. Allen, then a little over thirty, was described by Smith as 'civil, unaffected and good-natured' and (he pointed out) having lived in Scotland was free of the 'politeness which consists in attitudes and flexibilities'. ('What to compare his French to', he warned, 'I know not . . . I never heard a sound as dreadful.')[25] For better or worse, Allen's career was made. For many years he was the treasured aide at Holland House, and devoted to the tyrannical Lady Holland, who treated him almost as her slave.

It was before the Burntisland jaunt, in March, on an evening at Jeffrey's apartment in Buccleuch Place that there was a momentous gathering of the group of talented youth, Smith, Horner, John Allen and Thomas Brown, all aspiring to a writing career, and with a certain amount of time on their hands, to discuss the idea of launching a literary review. Not entirely literary either, but to embrace politics, philosophy, science . . . all subjects which at that time any cultured man had to some extent at his fingertips.

The initiative appears to have come from Sydney Smith (who in his account of the occasion exuberantly adds a few floors to Jeffrey's third-floor tenement: the new-style Edinburgh 'land' was nothing like as towering as the old).

The idea was not sudden or spontaneous, the venture having been turning over long enough in their collective mind, and this 'tempestuous evening', as Jeffrey called it, was to crystallise the idea in serious discussion. Out-of-doors the tempest seems to have been real, and they had 'some merriment at the greater storm they were about to produce'.[26]

Of the group, Allen, at thirty-two, and Smith, at thirty-one, were the oldest. Jeffrey was not far behind at twenty-nine, while Horner and Brown were twenty-four and the prodigy Brougham, who was soon clamouring to join, was a mere twenty-three.[27]

Jeffrey and his wife shortly abandoned the historic birthplace of the *Edinburgh Review*, and removed in May to 62 Queen Street in 'an uproar with painters, and chimney-sweeps, and packages of old books, and broken china, that I have scarcely had time to eat my dinner, or to find out where my pens and paper were laid till yesterday . . .'[28] They were now considerably nearer their friends and, like Smith the previous year, able to enjoy the beautiful open view to the Forth and Fife hills. That same month Jeffrey made his first speech in the General Assembly, and though it was, as Cockburn says, a 'paltry' cause, his appearance caused some sensation and added to his reputation.[29]

Many years later Jeffrey told Robert Chambers that they had had several consultations on the *Review* at his flat, consisting of Smith, Horner, Dr Thomas Brown and Lord Murray (as he later became). Lord Webb Seymour, Dr John Thomson and Thomas Thomson sometimes joined them. It was agreed that the financial risk, and the cost, be carried by their publisher, Archibald Constable. They had no particular editor in mind, and indeed the first three issues were mutually put together 'in a dingy room of Willison's printing office, in Craig's Close'; they read their own proofs and (for later issues) discussed contributions from outsiders.[30]

The bookseller and printer Constable, chosen as the most appropriate publisher, had already published the *Scots Magazine*, and was later to undertake the *Edinburgh Philosophical Journal* and publications of, among others, the Highland Society, the Royal Society of Edinburgh and the Wernerian Society. In 1802, the first year of the *Review*, he published *The Lay of the Last Minstrel* for Scott, and in 1808 *Marmion*.

Producing the *Review* was never plain sailing. They ambitiously planned to launch it as early as June, but entries somehow evaporated before the chore of actual writing. Long before even the proposed publication date Jeffrey was writing apologetically to Horner that rather than begin, or even confess his embarrassment, he had been driven to the usual writer's delaying tactics – in this case sitting trimming his quill. 'I have written none of my reviews yet, and I was afraid to tell you so.' But having now practically begun his article on Monnier he was so filled with virtue that he could 'confess all my enormities . . . We are in a miserable state of backwardness', to an extent that might even prove fatal to publication. But there is progress: 'Smith has gone through more than half his task. So has Hamilton. Allen has made some progress: and Murray and myself, I believe . . . are *almost* ready to begin'. On the other hand Thomson is ill, Brown would undertake nothing, and Brougham having 'cheerfully' promised has backed out. And so forth.[31]

They had to delay the *Review*'s first appearance until September, then October. When at last the first number appeared on the 10th, it included seven papers by Sydney Smith (all contributions were of course anonymous), four by Horner, and five by Jeffrey, including the opening article on Monnier's work on the influence of the French Revolution.[32]

Jeffrey feared that they had already missed the tide for success, and was not hopeful, doubting that they could survive longer than the four numbers for which contributions were already pledged. In his characteristic lapses from lively cheerfulness to gloomy pessimism, he was convinced that, like most 'grand projects', it would fail.

He was wrong.

'The effect was electrical' (writes Cockburn). 'The force of the shock was increased on each subsequent discharge. It is impossible for those who did not live at the time . . . to feel, or almost to understand, the impression made by the new luminary, or the anxieties with which its motions were observed . . . The learning of the new Journal, its talent, its spirit, its writing, its independence, were all new.'[33]

That it should appear in Edinburgh, so remote from London and apparently without long premeditation, was also astonishing. Edinburgh had had no critical journal worth consideration since the 1750s, when an earlier *Edinburgh Review* had survived for just two issues; while in England, current reviews were not only trivial but confined to literary subjects. The new *Edinburgh Review*'s scope by contrast was universal; there seemed no limit to the subjects these brilliant young men were able to cover.

And its timing was not after all so unpredictable: rather, with hindsight, almost inevitable. The repression and intolerance of the Tory government, pitted against the Revolution in France, and general resentment towards the old European regimes, the desire for reform with as yet no means of working for it (except by revolution itself) other than through the press – all made the hour, and the production, appropriate.

For the first three issues the contributors received no fee – the usual custom for literary reviews. This, and the lack of a central control, soon led to problems, and the group asked Jeffrey to become editor. The decision cost him a struggle. '£300 a year is a monstrous bribe to a man in my situation'; on the other hand, there were the trials and vexations of an editor's life. But he had started the venture with a set of men whose character and situation in life must deserve the honour thanks to the 'excellence of its criticism'. Being quarterly, it allowed time for contributors to work up an essay, and with the added lure of pay, it was a great temptation especially to aspiring young writers.[34]

At much the same time as Jeffrey and friends were producing the first *Review*, Walter Scott, then living at 30 Castle Street and Lasswade, had begun to compose his first long original poem, *The Lay of the Last Minstrel.* He read over some stanzas to his friends William Erskine and George Cranstoun (he was not a very accomplished reader), who listened in silence. This misled Scott into throwing them into the fire. When he understood that their silence was of stunned approval, he wrote them again.

He continued composing the poem throughout the Musselburgh autumn manoeuvres until, at last completing the last canto, he decided he ought to abandon the law and concentrate on writing. Fortunately for himself, he did not do so.[35]

Scott, a well-known Edinburgh character, now at the age of thirty-nine became a famous literary one. *The Lay* printed 750 copies which quickly sold out, and as quickly ran to fourteen impressions – a record for poetry. In the next decade Scott composed *Marmion* (1806–7), published in 1808 by Constable, *The Lady of the Lake* (1810), and *Rokeby* (1812), and having until then limited himself to the collection and editing of traditional ballads, now seemed set for permanent success as a poet.

He was also on the way to making a fortune, and would doubtless have maintained it indefinitely had he not become putty in the hands of the Ballantyne brothers, James and John, lending them money and prolonging the loans, although it was another decade before he began to feel the effects.

Jeffrey was not the only one who hitherto had felt discontented with his career. Surprisingly, on the eve of the launch of the *Review* Henry Brougham had been writing to his friend James Loch (20 August) that he felt uncertain of his future, dissatisfied with his Edinburgh prospects, but loth to try the English bar, which was 'tedious' and its people 'disagreeable . . . of brutal manners and confined talents'. As a last resort for 'incurables' there was always the army![36]

Horner, who had finished several short pieces and his essay on Thornton on paper credit, in September 1802, notes in his diary how the *Review* had been 'concerted, about the end of last winter, between Jeffrey, Sydney Smith, and myself', and at once shared with Murray, Allen and Hamilton. 'Brown, Brougham, and the two Thomsons, have gradually been made parties.' He was dissatisfied at having to send his work unedited, in 'rude form': 'my style of writing is too formal and not sufficiently correct'.[37]

When the first number came out he was still dissatisfied, noting in his diary that 'upon the whole, I do not think we have gained much character by it: it is considered as respectable enough in point of talents, but the severity, in some of the papers it may be called scurrility, has given general dissatisfaction. In the next number, we must soften our tone, and be more indulgent to folly and to bad taste.'[38]

Horner, always the purist, was right, but underestimated the value of the shock effect on readers of so original and daring a work. They might be angered, but mostly came back for more. It was a talking point.

However, Horner, no mean judge, was pleased to tell Loch in January 1803 that their second number seemed almost free 'from some of the objections that were most strongly, and all of them justly' fired at the first: 'the general train of criticism less abusive . . . the opinion of our friends has made a considerable impression upon us'.[39] All the same, it was chiefly its astringency that gave the *Review* its enduring fame.

Jeffrey, who had to get up at all hours in order to complete his articles, answered a later criticism from Horner of 'fastidiousness' with the claim that he was in truth a great *admirer*; but that perversely, 'I have a sort of consciousness that admirers are ridiculous, and therefore I laugh at almost everything I admire . . . I meant no contempt to Wordsworth . . . I classed him with Southey and Coleridge who were partners once, and have never advertised their secession.' They were deluged with poetry for review, including Scott's *Lay* with which many readers were 'infatuated', such as William Erskine, who thought it 'inimitable' and probably had persuaded Scott it was too; but 'justice must be done'.[40]

Alexander Murray, commenting to Archibald Constable on the journal's progress in March 1803, remarked that the latest number showed 'much genius'. 'Their spirit is excellent. They point out the leading face of two great societies to admiration . . . Your correspondents are very severe, but I think they are, in general, just . . . I think our Reviewers are much more solid and judicious than their southern brethren. Their taste is better.'[41]

Jeffrey as editor proved as severe as he was a critic. 'Jeffrey is inexorable to my prayers and tears', writes Thomas Thomson on 24 December 1803, 'and of a truth hath no bowels of compassion within him. He certainly dashes away himself with marvellous rapidity, though I think . . . he does not always touch the ground.' The grouse was over 'this cursed review of Bentham – the most ungrateful task I ever engaged in', to complete which he had to give up his Christmas holidays.[42]

The perceptive Lady Stanley wrote to Aunt Serena, wondering who ran the *Review*. 'It is extremely clever, and conducted in a very superior style . . . perhaps they are right in the severity with which they expose and lay open the defects of every author. But I think they are sometimes too severe and illiberal in the style of their wit. They are likewise sworn enemies to sentiment . . .'[43]

Sydney Smith had been reluctant to admit Brougham to the writing cabal, considering him too indiscreet for their still fairly clandestine venture. He was let in however, and was a prolific contributor. Meanwhile, Thomas Brown lasted for only two issues, parting from the *Review* after a disagreement over alterations which Smith made to his work. 'Nothing of the kind occurred ever after', notes Cockburn rather optimistically.[44]

Brougham admitted casually that he had recently 'been writing a few articles for a new Review here, which, of course, you have heard of', notably writing up his personal researches on the West Indies, in a review of a recent pamphlet. He had, however, found himself so at odds with its author Stevens, that he abandoned the *Review* and embarked on a more general paper for independent publication, on Britain's colonial policy. This was eventually published by Longman.

So that, whereas in June he had been looking frustratedly on his literary efforts as 'little better than waste of time', by the time the *Review* reached its second issue in November Brougham was working on this and his legal employment at Parliament until the small hours, 'more cheerfully than if I had a wife to go to bed with at that late hour'.[45]

All did not yet go smoothly for him, for at the end of January, 1803, with his book nearly ready for the press, 'that damned, blasted, b[uggerin]g, brutal *Review* stopped it for a whole calendar month'. He had to drop everything and, he complained, while not even being the editor, had to contribute '100 pages of print'. 'My chief articles are: all the *Mathematics* (except one), all the *Chemistry* or *Physics*, and a long one on the *Balance of Power*, 37 pages.'[46] (All articles being unsigned, readers and/or victims often had to guess at the author who had slaughtered, or otherwise, their work.)

In 1803 Jeffrey counted himself lucky to include as contributors not only Horner, Sydney Smith and Brougham but Peter Elmsley, an Oxford clergyman and friend of Robert Southey's, 'full of jokes and erudition', Alexander Hamilton, 'two ingenious advocates' Thomas Thomson and John Murray, and, most illustrious among some dozen 'occasionals', 'young Watt of Birmingham, and Davy of the Royal Institution'.[47]

Having taken Edinburgh, and the further reaches of the two kingdoms, by storm, the rest of the coterie unfortunately did not survive in the city much more than two years. Horner moved to London and later entered Parliament as MP for St Ives (1806); James Reddie, a promising young lawyer contributor, soon moved to Glasgow. Sydney Smith himself had to return to England in 1803, though he kept continuously in touch. Jeffrey wrote reproachfully to Horner, 'I console myself with believing that you have all committed a great mistake in leaving . . . we have here capabilities of happiness that will not so easily be found any where else.'[48]

'We are all gathered together again for the winter', he wrote again to the deserter in London in November, 1804, 'but I miss you terribly still . . . nothing but emigration to London: my great friend Charles Bell is about to follow your cursed example.'[49]

Jeffrey's editorial sufferings were fairly standard. For the January number of 1805, for example, he told Horner bitterly, 'this number is out, thank heaven, without any assistance from Horner, Brougham, Brown, Allen, Thomson, or any other of those gallant supporters.'[50]

Jeffrey's personal life was at this time for some years emotionally distressed. The renewal of war against Napoleon in May 1803 depressed him immeasurably. A new corps of riflemen was being raised in which he might get a company, though he was encouraged to notice that there was now more disillusion than enthusiasm over the earlier 'boyish prating about uniforms, and strutting in helmets'.[51] He was soon in a company, however, tiring himself out with the mornings' drill on top of his other responsibilities.

Except for his happiness when his wife's sister married the Episcopal minister Robert Morehead in November 1804 – when 'my life is taken up with contracts and flirtations', he had little but sadness. In September 1802 his wife Kitty gave birth to a son who lived only a few weeks. In May 1804, when he was just back from a lively visit to London, where he was fêted with his new fame, his sister Mrs Napier died. They had been in almost daily contact since infancy, and the shock was overpowering. Returning from her deathbed at sunrise, 'the birds were singing gaily, as I sobbed along the empty streets. I thought my heart would have burst'.[52]

The young Moreheads lived in a modest house at 21 Hill Street, and having finished his day's work and before going home to dress for dinner, Jeffrey used to visit daily on the way back from his afternoon ride. It was some substitute for the daily visits he had made to his sister before she died. They discussed topical events, 'public, social, literary, private, personal', on Jeffrey's side with (said Morehead) 'that sparkling vivacity which, witnessed, was never forgotten'.[53]

Then came the final blow, when his beloved wife Kitty, who was again pregnant, died in his arms on 8 August 1805. They had thought the pregnancy was the cause of her poor health, but she developed 'excruciating headaches', water on the brain was diagnosed, and she ended in a coma. 'I doted upon her . . . after four years of marriage, was more tenderly attached to her than on the day which made her mine.' Cheerful and affectionate despite her frequent illnesses, she was adored by all, her servants, her doctors, the shopkeepers, the very chairmen who used to carry her. Jeffrey was desolated. Though of such mercurial temperament he was never again to feel such loneliness and misery. 'I am inwardly sick of life', he wrote to Horner (12 Oct. 1805), '. . . my heart is dead, and cold': his apparent gaiety in society was wholly superficial.[54] For a time it seemed he could scarcely struggle on with his successful career, but calmness and his principles eventually prevailed, when the *Review* became a distraction, and social life an antidote.

8

THE SECOND NEW TOWN[1]

'When the plans at present in contemplation are completed, Edinburgh will be the most beautiful and picturesque city in the world.'

> Wm Creech, *Letters . . . respecting . . . Edinburgh, in 1763, and since that period*, Edinburgh 1793, in Sir John Sinclair (ed.), *Statistical Account 1794*, Vol.II

'The New Town is by far the most complete and elegant I ever saw. In various towns of England and Scotland, I have indeed seen some good streets, and many good houses, but in this the whole is uniformly fine; not one house, much less a whole street, that can be termed indifferent in the whole town.'

> *Memoirs of the 45 First Years of the Life of James Lackington, Bookseller, Finsbury Square, London, written by himself*, new edn, London, 1803, 302

'The new town presents its fair front, divided into square battalions, covered with the buckler of their roofs, *en tortue*, separated, by regular intervals, in straight lines,- and at right angles. All is order, light, and neatness, the very reverse of the old town.'

> Louis Simond, *Journal of a Tour and Residence in Great Britain* . . ., 1st edn, Edinburgh, 1815, 1.270

'What could have induced the original founders of this city, to chuse so irregular a situation?'

> Stebbing Shaw, *A Tour, in 1787, from London, to the Western Highlands of Scotland*, London 1786, 187

'With this Town I am delighted and surprised, tho' it is as offensive to the nose as it is delightful to the Eye.'

> Sydney Smith to Mrs Hicks-Beach, 16 June 1796, in Nowell G. Smith (ed.), *Letters of Sydney Smith*, Oxford 1953, 1.18

Edinburgh's second New Town was launched in the same year as the *Edinburgh Review*. Sited immediately north of the first, it was separated by garden ground downhill from Queen Street; and although of similar size, shape and to a certain extent layout, it was a very different venture from Craig's, from whose problems and limitations much had been learned.

While it too started with a plan, which over the years was much modified, unlike Craig's Edinburgh its execution was controlled by contract and the style, standard and building restrictions were clearly set out. Its final design was by two architects, and building went on for about twenty years. Hence the new streets north of Queen Street were considerably more regular than those which had preceded them decades earlier.

The land on which the second New Town was built was owned by George Heriot's Hospital. It was the work of Robert Reid and William Sibbald, but the idea had been around for years before either was consulted, for the first plan was drawn as early as 1792 by a rich merchant banker, recently Lord Provost, David Steuart, youngest son of John Steuart of Dalguise in Perthshire. He was cultivated, literary, and far-sighted. In 1782 he moved to number 5 Queen Street, near its eastern end and almost next door to the house Robert Adam had designed for Chief Baron Ord (number 8). In the following year he bought two acres opposite his house from the Heriot's Hospital Trust.

This rural area, part of the old Barony of Broughton, had been used by Heriot's since 1636 and let to farmer tenants, including in the eighteenth century Lang Sandy Wood's father Thomas Wood. During the century the Hospital sold about thirteen acres at the eastern end, on which a small mansion was built, then bought by Provost George Drummond who renamed it Drummond Lodge. He eventually owned more than thirty acres.

Some years after Drummond's death the property was sold (1774) to a rich major-general, John Scott of Balcomie, who rebuilt the house on a slightly different site as Bellevue House. Long attributed to James Brown, the George Square architect, this house is now known to have been based on a design by Robert Adam.[2]

It was later acquired by the City and enlarged to serve as a Customs House. Through this acquisition it was possible to extend plans to build to the east of the New Town.

While that New Town was still creeping westwards, David Steuart began to buy with a view to later development, starting with the garden ground north of his own garden (the area where Abercromby Place was later built). This encouraged the Heriot Trust to commission a survey of their remaining land (1785), with a plan of possible streets 'in the view of the same becoming building ground'. They then let the idea rest for several years.

Steuart bought up Baron Ord's garden and other land, and in 1787 commissioned his own survey and plan of the site opposite his house, which is shown as surrounded by trees, with a pond in one corner and the rest chiefly under grass. He had in mind its development as 'Steuartown'.

All these surveys and proposals were well away from Queen Street, and downhill from land which it had always been intended to keep open. For one thing, any new town plan would echo Craig's own layout which was bounded by open space north and south, this space on the north and the Nor' loch on the south, forming two ornamental stretches the length of the building area.

For another, Queen Street having quickly established itself as a fashionable promenade, no one was likely to countenance the destruction of its fine view across to the Forth and beyond, so that new building must take place well below. All the land in this stretch was feued as garden.

Steuart somewhat blotted his copybook by allowing two young cabinet makers to run up a workshop on part of his land, which stirred his neighbours to complain to the Trust. Finding that he had not sought their authorisation – although he claimed that he had acted in good faith, and hoped to bring them revenue – because the Queen Street residents were pressing to preserve their view, the Trust decided to advertise the ground.

David Steuart thereupon drew up a plan for the joint property in 1792 with the aid of the Trust's surveyor William Sibbald, a builder. Nothing is known of Sibbald's earlier life save that he came from Inverness. In 1787 he had designed the spire for St Andrew's Church, and in 1790 was appointed Superintendant of Works for the City.[3]

All this involved adjustment to boundaries as well as demolition of the offending workshop. The Sibbald/Steuart plan, approved by Heriot's Governors in 1793, which differed in several respects from what was eventually built, in conception echoed main features of Craig's plan. These included a circus (germ of Royal Circus but surrounding a 'bason') at the western limit, and at the eastern end a square (Drummond Place), to be built round the grounds of Bellevue House. Further, on the northern boundary a proto-Royal Crescent was proposed.

The governors paid half the cost of 1000 engravings of this plan but took no action on it. The death in 1797 of the long-established farmer Thomas Wood, by which his land became available, led Steuart to urge them on; but now they were more interested in the easterly lands, what was to become Duke Street (now Dublin Street) and York Place. Steuart, who had given up banking and was now a merchant in Leith, was in financial trouble, and tried to persuade the Trust (1799) to extend the line of York Place to include his own ground, offering to share the rents. The Hospital, however, refused to allow building in the Queen Street area. Steuart became bankrupt and had to sell his lands (1800), advertised as likely to 'bring a considerable price for building stances', with his own garden – then let out as gardens and nurseries – as a separate lot.[4] Perhaps because of the bankruptcy people appeared shy of the risk, and the land sold only in 1802.

Meanwhile the Council had stepped in, buying the five-acre Bellevue property, including the mansion, with the object of taking a hand in the development.

They had the land cleared and the trees felled, robbing Edinburgh without warning of pleasant woodland vistas,[5] and in October 1800 advertising a competition for a plan, first prize 100 guineas, second prize 50, within two months 'for laying out in streets, squares etc. for building', not only their Bellevue grounds but Steuart's and Heriot's to the west, up to the boundary of the Earl of Moray's lands of Drumsheugh. Bellevue House was to be incorporated in the design. Of numerous plans submitted, four, decided as of equal merit, shared the prize-money. One of these was by James Elliot (1770–1810), younger brother of Archibald and director of their Edinburgh architects' office.[6]

Alexander Nasmyth had entered a plan which John Paterson judged by far the best, and most suited to the ground, directing the streets to 'central points'. Baxter rated it only sixth of the dozen plans submitted, however, and Reid fourth.

Nasmyth's and Crichton's plans, instead of sticking to a grid *à la* Craig, were adapted to the steep contours. Crichton used open spaces, Nasmyth concentrated on vistas, proposing a main square with a central church and crescents behind, and a grander, convex crescent beyond. 'Spectacular vistas' were proposed to Arthur's Seat and the Calton Hill buildings, with a public garden and walks.[7]

Some of the plans incorporated features of the Sibbald/Steuart layout: a circus at one end and a square or other space at the other, surrounding Bellevue, with a wide connecting street. Only in 1801 did the governors decide to adopt a plan, and even then asked for further revision. Eventually the young Robert Reid was offered the job.

Reid was born in 1774 when the first New Town was already in its infant stages, son of Alexander Reid, mason and builder in the Tron Kirk parish, who had been Deacon of the Masons from 1787 to '91 and had feued areas in Craig's New Town. Like Sibbald, nothing has been discovered of his early life or training, and apart from a design for houses in Marshall Street, Perth, in 1801, this major assignment appears to have been his first. Now aged twenty-seven, he lived at 18 South Castle Street.

Robert Reid was evidently influenced by the style of Robert Adam, who had died a decade earlier, although his houses are simpler than Adam's in Charlotte Square. The Adam influence was to appear particularly in the new Law Courts fronting Parliament Square, which the Trustees for Public Buildings in Edinburgh commissioned Reid to design in 1803, and on the strength of this he was in 1808 awarded the (wholly honorary) title of 'King's Architect and Surveyor in Scotland'.

By the end of 1801 Reid had produced a sketch-plan which, except for part of the Bellevue ground on the north-east, was approved by the Heriot governors, and at their order he and Sibbald completed a large version which again was approved (February 1802). The governors shortly agreed to include their lands north of Queen Street in the new extended Royalty, and the Reid/Sibbald plan went ahead. Many features of the earlier plans being incorporated, notably the open spaces at either end linked by the wide (Great) King Street; but the quadrants originally proposed for the western circus had been simplified to two deep crescents, not quite semi-circles, with broad openings east and west, allowing a vista to a church on the west. (This was subsequently much modified, and no church was built on this site.) At the east end Reid altered the proposed oval to a square, with an apsidal extension to include Bellevue Lodge. He also included three crescents, not symmetrically placed. One, dictated by the ground slope on the north-east limit, Reid kept from earlier plans, and designed another (Bellevue), as a neater termination to the development almost back to back with it; finally, Abercromby Place was given a shallow curve to avoid cutting into the protected Queen Street gardens. As the first of the area's three crescents to be built, and Edinburgh's earliest curved street, it became very fashionable.[8]

On the strength of his achievement, Reid was commissioned to design elevations for the chief new streets (1802–6): that is, the three parallels Heriot Row, Abercromby Place, Great King Street/ London Street, and Drummond Place. To maintain symmetry in Abercromby Place he divided its crescent down the middle by altering Nelson Street to an angle-iron plan.

The grandeur of these streets, notably Heriot Row and to a lesser degree Abercromby Place, with their finely cut rusticated blocks on the ground floors and 'rock' finish for the basements, contrasts with the shoddier work of much of the first New Town, though houses in the cross streets such as Dundas and Dublin Streets, plainer in finish, were often as large or even larger, striding down the steep hill in stepped blocks.

The limits of the development were to be Fettes Row, Royal Crescent and Scotland Street on the north, India Street on the west, and Bellevue Crescent on the east, with Dundas Street a continuation of Hanover Street, cleaving down the centre as a main south-north artery.

Heriot's and the Council then jointly offered the land for sale, the former turning down a last-minute proposal by Steuart that the Heriot Row houses should be a storey higher. There was a delay when several of the governors (unsuccessfully) demanded more churches. Steuart's hand in the development finally ended when he and/or his creditors disposed of his land to new owners, who apparently had no interest in it and in 1804 sold on, to buyers who included the architects who were now building the Dublin Street area,[9] whose proposed alterations for Abercromby Place were put to the governors. A revised contract was at last signed in February 1806, consisting largely of essential detailed regulations as to stone, strictly limited building heights, basements, sewers and water supply, and that each individual elevation must be first approved by the Council and Dean of Guild. The details were probably largely supervised by Sibbald.[10]

Building began in 1803, but spread over twenty years until 1823, starting with Heriot Row and Dublin Street, both finished in 1808. Northumberland Street and Jamaica Street (demolished in the 1960s) followed in 1807–19, while Abercromby Place was built only in 1814–19, Great King Street 1814–23, and India Street and Royal Circus were not even begun until after the Napoleonic Wars.[11]

The only important changes in plan were made in Royal Circus. Although earlier plans had included an essential link on the west side with Stockbridge, Reid's 1802 plan did not, and this defect was not remedied until 1819 - 20, when the Circus was still unbuilt, and the layout was modified by William Playfair at Heriot Hospital's request.

This new town planning venture – 'by far the largest single scheme' in Georgian Edinburgh[12] and its largest uniform development – was thus initiated by a private individual, David Steuart, and ended as a joint achievement by the City and Heriot's Trust. Its controlled plan and use of architect-designed main streets were an advance on the first New Town, and were to serve as an example for developments such as the Moray estate, Raeburn's in Stockbridge, and the Walker estate at Coates.[13]

The chief contrast with Craig's New Town, which centres on the long ridge of a hill and descends north and south to its secondary parallels, is the Second New Town's uniformly steep descent from south to north, losing some of the sense of symmetry. This loss is also felt in the modified Royal Circus, or rather two crescents, with its deeply splayed entrances east and west.

Further, in any planned town the effect will be partly lost when the young trees planted by its designers grow to a sometimes overpowering maturity and obscure the vistas.

An interesting picture of the new developments on Heriot's Hospital land is given in the summer of 1803 by Jessy Allan, daughter of the banker-proprietor of the *Caledonian Mercury,* Robert Allan, and recently married to the keen water-colour painter John Harden. The couple were then still living with her father at 63 Queen Street. A letter to her sister Agnes relates that the row opposite their house is nearly completed, but only 'just under Lady Blairs Field so that our situation is still very open for a Town', and the two rows intended below these will probably be delayed by the war. 'You would be astonished to see the improvements in that part of the town; there is now a handsome street instead of the old beggarly houses that used to be inhabited by the Weavers in Picardy, its called Forth Street, and in a short time York Place will be continued to Hillside or rather Forth Street will join them. Mrs Scots House is enlarged and converted into the Excise Office . . . Charlotte Square too is at last going on tho' rather slowly.'

She also mentions the 'very expensive Bank' now building nearly opposite the Mound, and 'a very neat Street heading from it to the High Street . . . a very great improvement particularly now when the lucken booths are coming down. The houses there are all condemned and emptied except Creeche's and the Prison which are allowed to remain a year or two still.' This pious hope was not to be fulfilled for some years.[14]

Edinburgh's increase in size brought the inevitable criticisms. Henry Brougham's friend Andrew Clephane complained bitterly of the prospect of new building. 'The consequence . . . is that it spoils Queen Street as a Terrace entirely, and they never can get a street half so handsome, as the lowest of the three rows will be down in the Mill Dams and will hardly have any view at all excepting the Mill wheels and the rats swimming up and down.'

Clephane was also discontented with Reid's proposals for the Law Courts in the Old Town. The Court of Exchequer was removed and its site incorporated in the Inner House, to make it higher and more convenient; alterations to the Bench would also enlarge the room. 'I cannot much commend the taste of the Scotch architects of the present day' (Clephane complained), who proposed to replace the beautiful ceiling of the Exchequer Chamber by 'a common plain roof' – but were vigorously opposed by an indignant Faculty. On the burnt-out site of old Goldsmith's Hall, on the west side of Parliament Square, a new room was built to enlarge the Library. 'With all these Improvements we shall at least have a good appearance . . .'[15]

9
A MECCA FOR VISITORS

> 'I like what I have seen of Scotland so much, and I am bribed to do so, for they call Rollo a bonny wee thing, and me *Lassie*, which, Heaven help me! I have no claim to.'
>
> Lady Bessborough to G. Leveson-Gower, 27 Aug. 1808, in *Private Correspondence of Ld Granville Leveson-Gower, 1781–1821*, London, 1916, II.323

> 'Taken altogether, I do not know any town where it would be pleasanter to live. It is, in a great degree, the Geneva of Britain.'
>
> Louis Simond, *Journal of a Tour and Residence in Great Britain*, 1st edn, Edinburgh, 1815, II.65

> 'The best houses in Edinburgh are very inferior certainly to those of the same rank in London, yet the difference of the materials, a bright crystallized stone, instead of dingy bricks, gives them a look of superior consequence and cheerfulness; the variety of views also, and the proximity to the country, without the fag-end of suburbs, are invaluable advantages.'
>
> *Ibid.*, II.152

The city meanwhile was continuing to attract more visitors and part-time residents. Edinburgh is 'for its size the most dissipated place existing, and seems every year to grow more so; this may indeed be owing to the increasing influx of strangers.' So wrote Andrew Clephane to James Loch in 1803. That spring, he says, was 'unexampled for the demand of houses and lodgings', so that neither the Duke of Atholl nor the Earl of Breadalbane, visiting in March, could find lodging, and had to stay for two nights at the Black Bull Inn. This was at the very inception of the second New Town. 'From the immense number of New Buildings one would think that some part of the city would be thinned of its inhabitants', Clephane went on, 'but this does not seem to be the case.'[1]

Many illuminating commentaries on Edinburgh come from the people who grew up there and in later life compiled memoirs for a new generation. One of the most famous is the gifted Elizabeth Grant of Rothiemurchus, whose father John Peter Grant, kinsman to the Grants of Grant, had settled in Edinburgh in 1796 soon after his marriage to Jane Ironside, a lady from County Durham. At number 5 on the north side of Charlotte Square, one of its only three houses then complete, in 1797 Elizabeth, their eldest child, was born, who many years later wrote her reminiscences for the benefit of her own children. At this time the Grants were well-to-do and enjoying a lively social existence, but in 1800 they left Edinburgh for some years.[2]

The start of Edinburgh's fame as a Mecca for poets, philosophers, scientists and politicians is inextricably combined with the shock-waves caused by the *Edinburgh Review.* In its first issue, its barbed criticisms included one on Robert Southey's *Thalaba*, attacked as the work of a member of the hated 'followers of simplicity'. This referred to Wordsworth's 'manifesto that preceded one of their most flagrant acts of hostility' that their capital object was 'to make use in poetry of the ordinary language of conversation'.[3] Wordsworth, who incidentally claimed that he never read reviews, not unnaturally took this as an attack on himself as much as on Southey.

It so happened that in autumn 1803 Wordsworth, his sister, and Samuel Coleridge, all visited Edinburgh. Coleridge, who was ill, had had to leave the Wordsworths at Loch Lomond after a Highland tour and was in Edinburgh for only a couple of days, finding Walter Scott was at Lasswade and feeling too unwell to make the walk to visit him. He was impressed, however, by Scott's 'divinely situated' Castle Street house (he wrote to Southey on 11 September), 'it looks up . . . a new magnificent street, full upon the Rock and the Castle'.

The Wordsworths, who later rejoined Coleridge at Jedburgh, had more luck in Edinburgh, and were able to visit Scott. Both Lake poets were smarting from a sharp critique by Henry Tytler, not as it happened in the *Review* but in the *Scots Magazine*: 'illiberal', wrote Wordsworth to Southey, whom he shortly met for the first time at Keswick and who now had to review a poem by his critic, 'so no mercy for poor Tytler . . .' Tytler could not expect much, having dismissed 'Southey, Coleridge, or any other Imaginationist' as far inferior to Pope or 'the Ancients'.[4]

Dorothy Wordsworth, writing later to Lady Beaumont, recalled their visit to Scott at Lasswade. On the strength of his Border ballads and antiquarian studies, Scott was already a celebrity. 'He is a man of very sweet manners, mild, cordial and cheerful', and despite his lameness almost from birth, 'he is very stout and tall but I think does not look healthy'.[5] (This was written in May 1805, and that August Scott was able to visit the Wordsworths at their home, where to their pleased surprise they were also joined by Humphrey Davy, whom Coleridge had met in Somers Town and later in Bristol.)

Wordsworth had little to say on Edinburgh, but happily Dorothy recorded their impressions of the romantic city. Their short stay began before sunset on a September evening when they put up at the quiet, reasonably priced White Hart in the Grassmarket, eschewing as ever the lure of a more fashionable quarter. They quickly visited the historic sites, castle, Holyrood, the chapel and Arthur's Seat, and their view of the castle looming through damp mist, with the city itself half hidden in a pall of black smoke, added to its grandeur.

'It was impossible to think of anything that was little or mean, the goings-on of trade, the strife of men, or every-day city business . . . it was visionary.' Holyrood, with its modern-seeming, regular exterior, lighted by sash windows, looked too like a service-men's hospital to please them; but in walking 'industriously' through the city streets, they were delighted with 'its irregular houses, stage above stage . . . in the obscurity of a rainy day [it] hardly resembles the work of man, it is more like a piling of rocks, and . . . high as my expectations had been raised, the city of Edinburgh far surpassed all expectation'.[6] The streets of the New Town, on the other hand, appear not to have merited their notice.

If Dorothy Wordsworth's response was poetic, Coleridge's, ill though he was, was epic. In the day he spent exploring Edinburgh, he was ravished by its beauty, even from the moment the coach entered the town:

> What a wonderful City Edinburgh is! – What alternation of Height & Depth! so enormously *stretched-up* are the Houses! . . . I cannot express what I felt – such a section of a wasp's nest, striking you with a sort of bastard Sublimity from the enormity & infinity of it's littleness – the infinity swelling out the mind, the enormity striking it with wonder . . . I have seen huge Quarries of Lime or Free-stone, in which the Shafts or Strata have stood perpendicularly instead of horizontally . . .

Climbing to Arthur's Seat at sunset, whence he saw the Forth crowded with shipping and counted fifty-four mountain-tops and the smoke from ten thousand houses, 'then all at once turning my Eyes down upon the City, it and all its smokes & figures became all at once dipped in the brightest blue-purple . . . The passing a day or two, quite unknown, in a strange City, does a man's heart good . . .'[7]

An acquaintance of the Lake poets who fared badly this year both in Edinburgh and at the hands of the *Review* was the radical John Thelwall, who had been arrested for treason a decade earlier with Horne Tooke and sent to the Tower. In 1803 he published a second edition of poems, which Jeffrey (anonymously) slated in the *Review*, even sneering unfairly at his birth – his father was a silk mercer – and at his imprisonment for treason.[8] In December, after staying in the Keswick area, Thelwall came to Edinburgh to give a series of lectures on elocution. According to Henry Cockburn this proved such a disaster that he was laughed off the stage.[9]

The angry Thelwall dashed into print with *A letter to Francis Jeffrey, Esq., on Certain Calumnies and Misrepresentations, etc.*, advertised for publication in January 1804, in which he charged Jeffrey with conspiring to obstruct his lectures and even signalling to the audience from behind a screen. The disruption had actually been caused – but not from behind a screen – by Scott's friend William Erskine, who regarded Thelwall as a traitor. Jeffrey, advised to reply, made an anonymous denial. Thelwall fired another salvo from Glasgow, where he was giving further lectures (*Mr Thelwall's Replies to the Calumnies*).[10]

Wordsworth, having already warned Thelwall of 'enemies in wait for you at Edinburgh', wrote sympathetically, congratulating him on the 'drubbing' his pamphlet had given to Jeffrey.[11] Such were the hazards incurred by the more vitriolic items in the *Review*.

The paper war raged on, Jeffrey regularly attacking 'disciples' of 'the peculiar manner of that new school of poetry', notably the Lake Poets and their friend Charles Lamb, and in turn being reviled for immorality in admiring Virgil's Alexis, in his Second Eclogue ('we care very little about the character of its author, still less about the chastity of the fair one to whom it was addressed'), which excited Wordworth's rage against the *Review*'s 'wicked and abstract opinions'.[12] Southey, sore from the criticism of *Thalaba*, had written scathingly to Coleridge, 'the Edinburgh Review will not keep its ground, it consists of pamphlets instead of critical accounts. There is the quantity of a three-shilling pamphlet in one article on the Balance of Power.'[13]

To satisfy his curiosity about Edinburgh, which so many people told him was 'the finest place in the world', Southey came to visit in October 1805 with the Rev. Robert Elmsley, intending to stay three weeks but rather cavalierly deciding that one was enough. Back at Keswick he described it in measured prose to the MP Watkin Williams Wynn (20 October):

> It is certainly a magnificent city. The New Town resembles Bath in the regularity, the cleanliness, and the silence of its streets, and in the colour of its buildings; but the houses, being only of ordinary height, are dwarfed by the old city. There they are commonly 6, 7, or 8 stories on the one side; 10, 12, or 13 on the other; and this height increased by the chimneys, which rise like a sort of turret from the front of the house, instead of the gable-end. The famous view of Leith and the river, which the Scotch boast of so loudly, is nothing to one who has seen Lisbon . . . but that from Princes Street is truly surprising. You cross a valley (once a loch) by a high bridge, and the back of the old city appears on the edge of this depth – so vast, so irregular – with such an outline of roofs and chimneys, that it looks like the ruins of a giant's palace. I never saw anything so impressive as the first sight of this.[14]

Southey and Elmsley spent three days with Walter Scott, now living at Ashestiel, and Southey admitted that he admired his ballads apart from their mingling of 'modernism of thought and language turns' with 'antique words'. He considered Scott a man of genius. *The Lay of the Last Minstrel* had brought him fame, and Southey liked it 'for it is poetry', but at the same time criticised its stiffness of language.

Scott himself he thought 'a much superior man, whom it was impossible not to like'. Scott, with a mind less honed to criticism, was always unstinting with praise, and his generous admiration of Southey's manuscript of *Madoc*, a copy of which he proposed should be sent to the Advocates' Library, naturally endeared him to the fellow-poet. As for the famed wits and philosophers, he was scathing: 'Of Edinburgh society I think very little. Elmsley very justly observed that, of the three faculties of the mind, judgment is the only one which they cultivate or value. Jeffrey is amusing from his wit; in taste, he is a mere child; and he affects to despise learning, because he has none . . .'[15]

The memorable meeting between Southey and Jeffrey was at supper at Thomson's rooms; Brougham was also there. Although Southey was predisposed against him because of his attack on Coleridge as well as on himself, he confessed himself somewhat softened to tolerance by Jeffrey's 'gentlemanly conduct' in sending him an advance copy of his review of *Madoc*, which Thomson brought him before they met. 'The review is very unfair and very uncivil, though mixed up with plenty of compliments' – besides, even bad publicity is publicity.

He determined, therefore, to meet his critic 'with perfect courtesy, just giving him to understand that I have as little respect for his opinions as he has for mine'. In the event he was put into superior good humour by Jeffrey's diminutive size. How could he quarrel with 'a thing not more than five foot two'? (Elsewhere he goes one better: 'an homunculus of five foot one' with features so small as to be 'pretty'.) Southey, like others, was struck by Jeffrey's accent, 'eenunciating his words'. When after supper they talked of taste, 'how he flourished about, endeavouring to imply an apology without making one and talking *at* what he did not talk of . . . Upon my soul, I cannot feel offended with a thing so insignificant. He has wit and readiness, but in taste and learning so mere a child, and so utterly feeble in intellect . . .' To John Rickman he wrote, 'In argument he was quick, conceited and as shallow as heart could wish', too tiny in all ways to be angry with, 'and so we are very good friends'.[16] This was Southey's idea of tolerance.

He particularly found fault with Jeffrey's 'immoral trade' and the 'cleverness' which made him damn books in print which he praised in private, being 'a good-natured man who only writes malignantly because it gratifies his vanity and sells his review'. Southey met all the more celebrated 'Reviewers' except Sydney Smith, and of them all 'I think little, perhaps too little. But having lived with Coleridge and Wordsworth and William Taylor, it is impossible not to perceive that these Scotchmen are very feeble indeed.' Poor citizens, in fact.

Southey's sneers sound malicious, especially as Jeffrey joined them in the stage coach returning to the Lakes, and supped with his fellow travellers 'so you see we are good friends'.[17] It is arguable whether Jeffrey saw through the assumed friendliness and imperviousness to his own criticism.

One celebrity of whom Southey was less dismissive was Mrs Fletcher, who tickled his fancy by her judgment that he was 'all that was intellectual, but that it was plain from every feature in his face that he was a man acquainted with woe!'[18]

In general Southey thought more of the city than of its pundits. This evidently included the bookshops, for having had no new coat or hat for some time he was expected by his wife to visit the Edinburgh shops for clothes and boots but instead he laid out all his spare money on books.[19]

Despite his praise of its architectural and topographical beauty he looked back afterwards 'with a sort of shivering antipathy to the long cheerless streets of your new town', raked by fierce winds.[20]

A couple of years after his visit, when Scott was trying to persuade him to review for Jeffrey and be uniquely highly paid for such 'unpleasant sort of work', Southey told him that although he had no animosity against Jeffrey despite their opposite views, he could not excuse his 'bitterness', of the sort 'which tends directly to wound a man in his feelings and injure him in his fame and fortune'. While he could be courteous to Jeffrey as a man, as a reviewer he must think of him as of 'a bad politician, a worse moralist, and a critic, in matters of taste, equally incompetent and unjust'.[21]

In short, Southey did not wish to write for the *Edinburgh Review.*

Thomas Campbell, who had returned to Edinburgh by sea in 1801 after continental travels and a triumphant stay in London, had the humiliation of learning that a story was current of his arrest for high treason – much to the alarm of his recently widowed mother. First thing next morning he waited on the Sheriff, Mr Clerk, whom he found in the hands of his barber, and inclined to believe the story, because, as he gravely explained once the barber had gone, there was a warrant for the poet's arrest. Courteously he warned him to keep a low profile. 'Do I live to hear a sensible man like you', exclaimed Campbell, 'talking about a boy like me [he was now twenty-four] conspiring against the British Empire?'

He had frequented Jacobin clubs in Hamburg, said Clerk, and come home in the same ship as the Irish patriot Donovan, who had fought at Vinegar Hill. But he had never heard of such clubs! Campbell retorted, and as for Donovan, being on the same ship was mere coincidence.

Next afternoon he attended a 'rigorous examination' at the Sheriff's office, when his answers were taken down by a clerk. But a box of 'treasonous' papers impounded at Leith proved on examination completely innocuous. 'This comes of trusting to a Hamburg spy,' exclaimed the exasperated Sheriff. 'This is a cold wet evening – what do you say to our having a bottle of wine, during the examination of your treasonous papers?'[22]

The affair ended on a friendly note. Campbell had become more tolerant of English institutions since living abroad, and his European adventures proved of great interest to Edinburgh friends such as Dugald Stewart, Mr Fletcher, and the Rev. Archibald Alison. But he had found his now fatherless family much impoverished, and had to rely on his writings to maintain his mother and invalid sisters.

Edinburgh was still in the midst of a time of serious famine and shortage after the crops had failed in 1799, aggravated by heavy war-time taxes, oatmeal doubled in price, and the quartern loaf now risen to 20d. The poor in desperation raided meal-carts, ripped open the sacks and carried away the meal. Carters could not feed their horses and had to take them to the tanners for slaughter. Brewers, like George Combe's father, were nearly ruined as the poor could no longer afford ale or beer. Even the farmers were attacked on market days, and many small firms became bankrupt.[23]

During this national privation when even basic necessities fetched high prices and not only the poor but professional families felt the pinch, Campbell imprudently took out a high-interest loan which proved hard to pay off, and he was driven to raising subscriptions to re-issue his *Pleasures of Hope*. During the summer he witnessed food riots or 'meal-mobs', but the magistrates were loth to prosecute Newhaven and Musselburgh fishwives – who therefore seized the chance to form gangs to break into bakers' and meat-stores. Campbell recorded some of his impressions in *The Mobiade*.

Luckily in the autumn at Dugald Stewart's he met Lord Minto, back from serving as Envoy Extraordinary in Vienna. Interested in Campbell's own experiences, he invited him to Minto, valued his comments and encouraged his poetry. Campbell was able to return to London with a fistful of introductory letters, doing light secretarial duties for Lord Minto, staying in the latter's Hanover Square house in a special 'Poet's Room', and enjoying London society.[24]

Back in Edinburgh for the summer (1802) in poor health with 'languor' and 'lassitude' – which, however, seem to have helped his composition of poems like 'Hohenlinden' – Campbell worked up a good subscribers' list and prepared for publication. During a morning call at the Stewarts he read Mrs Dugald the manuscript of 'Lochiel', to which she listened attentively, then went to him and laid her hand reverently on his head, with the solemn pronouncement, 'This will bear another wreath of laurel yet!'[25]

At the age of twenty-five Campbell was described as 'scrupulously neat', and was habitually seen in 'a blue coat, with bright gilt buttons, a white waistcoat with cravat: buff nankeens, and white stockings, with shoes and silver buckles'. He unfortunately suffered premature baldness and took to wearing a wig, which he never afterwards left off. In spite of his dandified tendency, he was absent-minded enough often to set off for a dinner-party having forgotten some vital item, such as cravat or waistcoat, and would have to call on a friend to lend it.[26]

He used to frequent the North Bridge with fellow-poets or others who, like him, had achieved 'early and permanent fame', and his own success gave him a rather irritating conviction of superiority which offended the older and more established when he expressed free opinions too arrogantly. But this failing was offset by his wit, his sound critical views, and his warm-heartedness.[27]

Campbell returned to London in February 1803, and though homesick for Edinburgh, rarely returned in the following years. Oddly enough he did not shine at a dinner at Longman's at which guests included Walter Scott, Humphrey Davy, George Ellis and Thomas Young. He seems to have been too keen to appear to advantage to succeed in doing so.[28]

In September 1803 he married his cousin Matilda Sinclair, daughter of a rich merchant originally from Glasgow, in spite of the father's misgivings about his poetic career. His petite, dark-eyed wife, almost like a Spaniard, was vivacious but inclined to irritability; and Thomas himself had bad health, largely caused by nervous tension and money worries, with his Edinburgh family to support and, from 1804, a child of his own. Friends long canvassed for a state pension, and £200 a year was granted him by the King in 1805, which probably saved Campbell from a debtor's prison. Horner, Sydney Smith, Lord Webb Seymour and others raised a subscription to help support him.[29]

Horner, having determined to read for the English bar, at Lincoln's Inn, had settled in London in the autumn of 1803 and joined the Temple. Early in 1806 Lord Minto offered him a place on the Board of Commissioners for the East India Company, and, after lengthy consultation with his father and knowledgeable friends, decided with some misgivings to accept, as it must lead to a seat in Parliament.[30]

This was a time of political turmoil, with William Pitt's death in January 1806, Lord Melville's trial (and acquittal) in May, and Fox's death in September. In October Lord Kinnaird put up Horner for a seat in St Ives; he went down to canvass and in November was elected. This confirmed what Horner had already decided on some time before, a permanent life in London; and although he maintained his writing for the *Edinburgh Review*, except for occasional visits to his home town, London remained his base until his health seriously failed in February 1816.[31]

Henry Brougham, meanwhile, had soon made his name. His *Enquiry into the Colonial Policy of the European Powers,* published in 1803, in which he attacked the slave trade, made a great impression. 'A man of extraordinary talents and acquirements' was how a friend's father, Dr Thomas Percival, described him to William Wilberforce. Papers on mathematics and physics had earned him membership of the Edinburgh Royal Society, but his preference was for 'polite science'. His *Colonial Policy,* Percival noted, showed 'great accuracy and extent of research, as well as acuteness of observation'.[32]

A couple of years later Wilberforce recommended Brougham to William Pitt for diplomatic business, for 'perhaps you could not in the whole kingdom find any one in all respects so well qualified': fluent in French and other languages, and better still, 'of uncommon talents and address' and, for a man of twenty-six, of knowledge too. He also had 'great resolution, strength of Constitution, &c.'[33] This resolution and these talents were not always in his career to be addressed to the most altruistic ends.

A character who some years later was to make a notable mark on Edinburgh literature and academic life, as 'Christopher North' and as Professor of Moral Philosophy, was John Wilson, who first appears in Edinburgh in 1801. Born in 1785, he was fourth of ten children of a rich Paisley gauze manufacturer, and was descended through his mother Margaret Sym from the Marquesses of Montrose. Of a sunny, extrovert disposition, he grew up muscular and athletic. From 1797 to 1803 he attended Glasgow College, but his father having died at the beginning of the boy's studies the family moved to Edinburgh, where he joined them on vacations.

They lived at 53 Queen Street and evidently enjoyed a full social life, for in January 1801 John records in his diary that on 2 January they gave a ball, when he danced with 'the Misses M'Donald, Corbett, Fairfax, Chartres, Balfour, Brown, Lundi, Millar, Young'. An energetic evening.[34]

As this might suggest, John Wilson was tall, strong, active, sporting and extrovert – though unusually for an athlete he was also notable academically and dabbled in poetry. With his fair, reddish hair and florid complexion, by any standards he was a striking figure.[35]

In 1802 he wrote a long, adulatory letter to Wordsworth on the *Lyrical Ballads,* whereas when an Oxford student at Magdalen, from 1803 to 1808, he was an athlete, leading sportsman, and pugilist. The powerfully-built, muscular Wilson made quite an impression at Oxford. Broad-chested, about 5 ft 10 inches tall, he sported 'a great profusion of hair and *enormous* whiskers', the latter then unusual especially at Oxford, and was generally regarded as 'the strongest, most athletic, and most active man' in the university.[36]

Regrettably, he was also a patron of cock-fighting at both Oxford and Edinburgh, where it was popular for a time, and a main was fought between the Lanark and Haddington 'teams' in the still unfinished kitchen of the new Assembly Rooms.[37]

He spent his long vacations on walking tours, such as to the Highlands in 1807, starting from Stirling; and meanwhile was madly in love with a young lady living at Dychmont whom, for some reason, obstacles prevented him from marrying, and the two had to part. For a time he hovered between suicide and accompanying Mungo Park to Timbuctoo.

Wilson early formed a love for the Lake District, and in 1805 bought land near Windermere where he lived in a charming cottage called Elleray, gradually extending it and keeping it as a country home until 1825, although he began a large house in 1808. On leaving Oxford he settled there, sailing, wrestling (Cumberland fashion), and cultivating the Lake Poets. He became friendly with the Pennys, a Liverpool family who moved to the area, and in 1811 at the age of twenty-six married their daughter Jane, the local belle in a gay social life.[38]

Wilson's ideal was the Hellenic, combining athletic physique with the mind of a philosopher. He therefore seriously took up poetry.

Dorothy Wordsworth, who spent Christmas 1809 at Elleray with her brother, Coleridge and De Quincey, was much impressed with Wilson. 'He is a very interesting young man', she told Lady Beaumont, 'of noble dispositions, and fine ingenuous feelings', still only twenty-four but, she thought, idle to date, having been left comfortably off by his father and too easily influenced 'to see virtues that do not really exist in minds greatly inferior to his own'. This did not apply to Wordsworth, whom he greatly admired.[39]

Another who was to figure largely if often vicariously in Edinburgh's history, was a young scientist who began to make a noise in the English world when the *Edinburgh Review* was in its birth-throes. Humphrey Davy, a Cornishman who early showed signs of genius, was at the age of twenty appointed laboratory superintendant at the 'Pneumatic Institution' in Bristol (1798), where Coleridge first met him.[40] He specialised in chemistry, especially galvanism and the gases (and nearly died from breathing carburetted hydrogen during an experiment in 1800). From 1801 Davy was at the Royal Institution in London, first as director of the chemical laboratory, and from 1802 as Professor of Chemistry.

Government ministers in London, and later in Edinburgh, flocked to hear Davy lecture. Early that year Lord Minto heard him speak on galvanism and chemistry, and judged him 'not an orator; still less so than Dr Hope [in Edinburgh], but he is remarkably clear as well as simple'. Francis Horner attended a lecture on the fashionable subject of 'animal substances' in an audience of more than two hundred men *and women*, and was impressed by Davy's modest, unassuming presentation, 'without theatrical quackery', but thought his style awkward. A few days later, however, meeting him in company, Horner was pleased to note 'great softness and propriety of manner, which might be cultivated into elegance', besides a 'poetic feeling' in his facial expression.[41]

Davy evidently retained a boyish appearance, for in 1807 the painter Benjamin Haydon, meeting him at dinner at Sir George and Lady Beaumont's, described him as 'a little slender youth [he was twenty-nine] . . . his hair combed over his forehead, speaking very dandily and drawlingly'.[42]

Thomas De Quincey, who met Davy at the *Courier* office in 1808 or 1809, wrote of him, 'nowhere . . . have I seen a man who had so felicitously caught the fascinating tone of high-bred urbanity which distinguishes the best part of the British nobility . . . what chiefly distinguished him from other men was the captivating – one might call it the radiant – courtesy of his manner . . . graceful, and at the same time, gracious.'

Coleridge, on the other hand, thought him 'effeminate and sycophantic to fashionable women' and that he tried to please society too much, adapting his Royal Institution experiments to an amateur audience.

Davy was barely of medium height, elaborately and fashionably dressed, perhaps too youthfully. His appearance increased the charm of his manner. 'Ladies would exclaim audibly in the lecture-room, "Oh those eyes! Those brilliant eyes!" at which he was as pleased as an adolescent.'[43]

The distinguished amateur geologist and chemist Sir James Hall (1761–1832) met Davy in Edinburgh in 1804, spending two days with him and 'Mr Phillips' who had arrived with an introduction from Dr Marcet in London. Phillips was presumably William Phillips (1775–1828), another amateur mineralogist and geologist, working in London as a bookseller and printer but devoting his spare time to geology. In 1807 he was made FGS, and in 1827 FRS.

'Our Huttonian doctrines were examined in all points of view', records Hall. Phillips had studied the Huttonian theory in greater depth than most, and Hall hoped he would now feel the force of their arguments. The Edinburgh men demonstrated the local scenery as proof of their theory, but Hall feared that this 'transient impression' had yielded to the later 'opinions with which he [Phillips] has been since surrounded'. However, Hall was impressed by Phillips's almost unique fairness in discussion – not to mention his agreeable company. Phillips on his side was impressed with the physical make-up of the scenery round Edinburgh, though his theories were at odds with Davy's and Hall's.

Meanwhile 'we are all highly delighted with the acuteness & clearness of Mr Davy whose head seems to be calculated beyond all others for discovery'. Both he and Phillips had been surprised at the state of knowledge of the subject in Edinburgh, and admitted that 'we are possessed of a multitude of facts hitherto unnoticed by the rest of the world'.[44]

Hall had long been working on the effects of heat under compression, and wrote triumphantly from his seat at Dunglass on 18 September how he was 'at last safely delivered of a secret which has tormented me and interested me during many years'. He read a short paper on his experiments, a copy of which he submitted to Dr Pictet for the latter's *Bibliothèque.* He had further imparted his success to Playfair and Davy. Gratefully supplied with porcelain tubes and crucibles from William Cary, mathematical instrument maker in the Strand he had been able to continue experiments, and was defending Hutton and his discovery of formerly unobserved or neglected facts.

He repeated his praise of Davy, 'the acutest man I have ever conversed with', who had quickly understood and respected his reasoning: 'But the field is a vast one. I battled myself during three years with old Hutton before I began to see his system in any favourable light.' But he was now disillusioned with Pictet, who had dismissed with contempt both his and Playfair's ideas.[45]

Hall, one of Edinburgh's leading 'Plutonian' or 'Huttonian' scientists, had undertaken experiments in both Scottish and Continental rock formations to refute the Wernerian theory, named after the German geologist Abraham Werner who proclaimed an aqueous origin of rocks. Sir James became President of the Royal Society of Edinburgh, and was MP for Mitchell in Cornwall from 1807 to 1812. His wife was the sister of the Earl of Selkirk.[46]

Sir John and Lady Stanley, great admirers of Hall, often entertained him and other Edinburgh philosopher-scientists in London, not always without embarrassment. One evening in May 1809 a dinner for Sir James, Davy, Playfair and Lord Webb was temporarily disrupted when unexpectedly 'the most unphilosophical of all peers', Sir John Stanley's relative Lord Sheffield, wandered in, which to everyone's consternation seemed likely to prevent all serious conversation. Luckily, he found even their general subjects beyond his comprehension and, after sitting silently in a corner took a precipitate leave. So at last the philosophers, who had been specially invited to talk to each other, 'did begin, and continued the subject until 11'.

A couple of weeks later Lady Stanley suffered a more personal embarrassment. After 'the pleasantest imaginable' dinner-party, joined afterwards by Sir James, when 'they all talked like men of sense and knowledge, yet not too scientific' she was mortified when having attacked the criticism of *Corinne* in the latest *Edinburgh,* she found that 'poor Playfair', seated on her right, had written the review. 'How could I suppose that a professor of mathematics would condescend to review a novel?'[47]

While poets, scientists and other travellers were beginning to converge on Edinburgh, the university continued a favourite for aspiring students. The seventeen-year-old Henry Temple, heir to the 2nd Viscount Palmerston, entered the College in the same autumn that the Wordsworths visited, 1803, and was shortly joined by a group of fellow-Harrovians and other friends. His father had chosen Edinburgh for intermediate studies before sending him to Cambridge, rather than keep him at Harrow a further year, particularly as he felt him to be 'still a boy' rather than a budding young man.[48]

Temple naturally tended to meet the leading Whigs such as Lord Henry Petty (later 3rd Marquess of Lansdowne), Brougham, Sydney Smith, and Gilbert Elliot (later 2nd Earl of Minto), son of his parents' closest friend, who, however, lived at the other side of Edinburgh. Temple lodged with Dugald Stewart along with the unprepossessing Richard Barre Dunning, Baron Ashburton; and had been preceded there by John Ward, later Earl of Dudley, and Laurence Sulivan. The latter, 'Lazy Laurence', grandson of a nabob, was to become Temple's brother-in-law.

Henry Temple was later joined in Edinburgh by his brother William, and the two went on from there to Cambridge. So far as debating societies went, Henry was unable to join the Speculative Society (though William did), and had to content himself with 'the puerile domestic imitations arranged by Professor Stewart in his own house'. At Cambridge the brothers were to have better luck.[49]

The poet Southey was pleased when his own idle brother Henry Herbert, who had entered Edinburgh College in the same year as Henry Temple, 'against my opinion, without my uncle's knowledge and against the approbation of his friends', shortly turned out 'a very fine young man'. So much so that in 1804 he was elected the youngest-ever President of the Medical Society – not to mention becoming President of the Speculative Society which had not admitted Temple. Henry was doing almost too well, was almost too handsome, a new matter of anxiety to his elder brother.[50]

Lord Minto, on return from his Vienna mission, sent his namesake son to the University, to study chemistry and philosophy (under Dugald Stewart). He also hired a house for the winter and after Parliament rose, satisfied with Gilbert's progress, in 1802 joined the classes himself. Enterprising for a 51-year-old, though it was quite usual for mature men to attend the lectures in Edinburgh.

The two would walk to the college. 'We sit together at the chemistry class, we lounge together the hour that intervenes between that class and Mr Stewart's', often also with Temple, who was studying chemistry. Both attended Stewart's first-year class, and for good measure, under colour of observing his son's progress, Minto 'steals a little instruction of the private masters': with Gilbert for geometry and algebra, with Harry Temple and his daughter Anne for drawing, and Catherine for dancing and spelling.

The younger Gilbert's programme included first-year classics, second-year philosophy and science, and he was then to go to Oxford. His father meanwhile planned to study in turn history, law and politics, finding it a stimulating experience. He claimed that his ambition was to keep up with the 'learned Viscountess [Palmerston] and her accomplished daughter'. He joined Dr Hope's chemistry lectures, and learned of the professor's experiment, already performed before the Palmerstons, to prove how cold was transmitted between two concave mirrors and hence 'must be a matter'.[51]

Dr Hope, the 'dandy philosopher' whose experiments were admired for their brilliance, was later in life a great asthma sufferer, and had to sleep propped upright, a problem which he solved by wearing 'a pair of woollen-plush breeches' to prevent him from slipping down the bed. Apparently his mentioning this to Lady Mansfield greatly shocked the lady, presumably for breaking the taboo on the unmentionable word 'breeches' – or perhaps even the word 'bed'.[52]

Hope admitted to Lord Minto his own admiration for Lady Palmerston 'as a virtuoso, and a very agreeable lady'. Lord Minto was delighted to pass on this information to her, together with the merits of Harry, who his hosts the Stewarts agreed was 'the only young man they know with whom it is impossible to find any fault': diligent, kind, cheerful, with 'perfect sweetness' and 'total freedom from vice'. Queen Victoria in later years would doubtless have been delighted to know of the youthful charm of her beloved Lord Palmerston. Lady Minto too thought him faultless apart from a 'want of spirits' unusual for his age; though at one 'solemn' party at Professor Stewart's he did display the liveliness to leap over his hostess's 'Gothic couch in the middle of the drawing-room' – and sprained his ankle for his pains.[53]

The conclusion of a peace signalled noisy and colourful celebrations. On 1 April 1802 London news reached the Lord Provost of 'a peace (but not with *whom*)' Lady Minto drily remarked. Everyone had already been woken in the morning of a beautiful day by 'a parcel of boys drawing the mail-coach through the square, and all about the town'. The Provost ordered a 'general illumination' of the city for 7.30 in the evening: there happened to be no play at the theatre, and most citizens turned out for the sight. 'The Castle guns were fired and all the regiments fired volleys from the Castle Hill; the volunteers lined Princes Street, and formed a line over the mound to the castle.'

Lady Minto, her sons, with Lady Douglas, Lady Montagu and Harry Temple drove around admiring the illuminations, which they thought the best ever. '*Everywhere* in the town had candles or lamps or transparencies three stories high and the tall houses in the old town to the tops; the streets were perfectly light . . . as full as they could hold, but as orderly and quiet as if perfectly empty' – more like a fête than a celebration, she thought, for nobody seemed really 'elated'. They might well have had a premonition that this could not be a true peace; indeed it was to last only fifteen months.[54]

The Elliot youth were soon on close terms with the Stewarts, Playfair, Jeffrey, Horner, John Murray and Lord Webb Seymour. They also met Thomas Campbell and Walter Scott at this early point in their famous careers. Scott they admired for his 'originality, agreeableness, and lame leg'. Campbell, whom Lord Minto was about to help launch into improved prosperity, was invited, along with Scott, to his country seat (September 1802).[55]

Despite his host's personal and unaffected kindness, Thomas Campbell found the stay at Minto an uneasy experience. His aristocratic fellow-guests were uncomfortably prone to 'in-talk', 'a slang of conversation among themselves, as unintelligible to plain, sober beings, as the cant of the gipsies'. Even worse than their fashionable snobbishness was their boring lack of intellect. 'I declare I have not heard a sentence of either good sense or amusing nonsense from any of our guests, except from Lady Malmesbury, who is a shrewd and liberal-minded woman.'[56]

In 1800 more than 1000 young men were registered at the University from almost all over Europe and most of the USA. Between 1768 and 1788 the number had nearly doubled. The Medical School, still in high repute, showed perhaps the highest rise. In 1766, when Dr John Gregory had succeeded Dr Rutherford as Professor of Medicine, the average attendance was ninety. Gregory's son and successor Dr James Gregory, in whose favour Dr Cullen had resigned in 1789, had had between 220 and 240 students.[57]

Between 1720 and 1800 the total of students in the Medical School was 15,930, of whom 3130 attended in the ten years 1790 to 1800. In these eighty years the Monros, father and son, had occupied the chair of medicine, anatomy and surgery. 'Monro II's anatomy and surgery demonstrations usually drew nearly double the attendance of the other medical departments except for chemistry and physics practice. More than half the students at the anatomy theatre went in for a career as surgeon or apothecary, and many entered the army or navy as surgeons or assistants.'[58]

In 1803 the Rev. James Hall, travelling in Scotland for six months, while in Edinburgh contrived by means of a small tip to attend a dissection class. 'They were dissecting a man that had been kept in spirits for some months, having been hanged for murdering his wife. The body had but little smell. When we entered it was lying on a table in the middle of the room, covered with a clean linen cloth, and seemed hard and shrivelled, from having been so long in spirits.'[59]

As dead malefactors such as this victim formed the only legal supply for subjects for dissection, and as, despite the savage penal laws, there were not nearly enough to satisfy the students' desires, by degrees there grew up the scandalous system of grave robbery and in notorious cases, in the late 1820s, deliberate murder.

Louis Simond, visiting in 1810, likened the University to 'the Birmingham of literature, – a new place, which has its fortune to make': a curious conclusion, in view of its antiquity and established fame; but he remarked that while Oxford and Cambridge were resting on their laurels, Edinburgh was making its reputation.[60]

10
POLITICAL AND SOCIAL CHANGE

'This country has arrived at the true pitch of comfort and happiness. The people are full of information, are natural, unassuming, and social, but with a mixture of occupation . . . Even the Scotch pride has its uses by putting the poor often on an equal footing with the rich . . . their education is equally good, their society the same, their spirit and love of their country possibly much greater . . . I think the race very superior to the English, who are too far gone in luxury and dissipation to be agreeable or happy.'

Lady Minto to her husband, 21 Feb. 1802, *Life and Letters* . . . III.235-6

In 1805 the astounding news went round that Viscount Melville (the title Henry Dundas had borne since 1802), now First Lord of the Admiralty, had been suspended from office and was to be impeached for malversation of funds. His apparently eternal system of Scottish Government suddenly collapsed with his overthrow as central pillar of the political structure.

The impeachment took place next year. 'Scotland will be a thorn in the side of Government till it is newly represented', wrote the percipient Lady Minto to her husband (30 May). 'This whole country considers Lord Melville as its chief, and well they may, after 30 years' reign and entire power.' The Dugald Stewarts and Lord Webb Seymour, visiting her at Minto, warned that were he acquitted, the people were determined to hold illuminations in Edinburgh, Glasgow and other cities, and this aroused the fury of his opponents.[1]

Lord Melville, though accused of negligence in allowing disgraceful mismanagement by his underlings, was acquitted of the main charges, and his supporters in Scotland were jubilant, his enemies in despair. 'The Land of Cakes has really gone crazy,' said Lady Minto. The Lord Provost, who had already sanctioned the illuminations, was warned of disapproval especially among the people of Leith, and for fear of a mob had to countermand the order 'and so the candles were ordered to be snuffed out'.[2]

A celebratory public dinner was held, however, attended by the Lord Justice Clerk (Charles Hope since 1804), most of the judges, the Barons of the Exchequer, and the Commissaries and Boards of Customs and Excise. All the officers of Government, in fact. The press cautiously stopped short of publishing details of the songs and toasts, one of which, proposed by a Commissary Court judge, ran, 'May the oppression of the House of Commons ever be repressed by the House of Peers'. This the company judged of such merit that they drank it three times over. Walter Scott, who was present, imprudently 'led away by the hue and cry' (wrote Lady Minto, 6 July), 'and so blind to the effects it would produce against him', composed a song in Melville's honour which inevitably gave great offence to the Whigs and Radicals, but on the occasion was so loudly applauded that silence could not be restored for a quarter of an hour.[3]

The event brought home to Government Ministers Scotland's deep political division, the Tory majority triumphantly 'glorying in their protector having completely defeated the malice, as they call it, of Ministers, Lords, and Commons'. So wrote Lady Minto again (5 June); and next month, 'England has no idea of the state of Scotland' (as she could probably have written two hundred years later).[4]

Despite the acquittal, Melville's impeachment spelt the end of his political career, and he lived his last years in Edinburgh in (honourable) retirement.[5] Yet the Dundas system survived for years: on Melville's death in 1811 his son and nephew took over management, though the rule was no longer secure. Melville's many admirers eventually saw to it that a handsome monument was raised to him in St Andrew Square.

We now get first glimpses of several ladies whose residence or visits in Edinburgh contributed to its literary fame. First came the Irish novelist Maria Edgeworth, who made several visits to England with one or other of her siblings by her much-married father, or with her latest stepmother (who was younger than she). She twice visited Edinburgh, the first time in 1803 when she was thirty-six, with her parents and half-sister Charlotte. The occasion was the illness of her brother Henry, who was then a medical student at the University (as his brother Lovell had been). The family stayed nine days, and saw 'wonders', including the famous 'Irish Giant'. Henry did not seem so ill that they did not meet a 'delightful society of friends', including the Dugald Stewarts; who although Miss Edgeworth thought was reputed reserved and serious, towards them he was warm, easy in conversation, and even 'surpassed all that I had expected'. His 'grave, sensible face' reminded Maria of the head of Shakespeare.

Mr Edgeworth attended Stewart's public lectures, at which women were not allowed. Stewart's wife had 'for years wished in vain for the pleasure of hearing one of her husband's lectures'. Maria found her, as did everyone who knew her, extremely lovable, and she had been very kind to Henry.[6]

During the following years, although often in England, and meeting numerous celebrities from Edinburgh, and although her brother Sneyd went to the University in 1808, Miss Edgeworth did not revisit the city until the time of her famous meeting with Scott in 1823.

A serious authoress whose connection with Edinburgh ranged, with long intervals, over a number of years, was Miss Elizabeth Hamilton (or Mrs, as she was known from middle life). She was born in 1758 to a respectable Woodhall family, whose grandfather Charles was financially unlucky, and his son, having married a beautiful girl in Dublin, died of typhus only a year after his youngest child Elizabeth's birth. At the age of four she was sent to live with her aunt Marshall, who had married (so her biographer tells us) a man 'of low birth but superior intelligence'. With them she spent a happy youth near Stirling, and was educated at both Glasgow and Edinburgh.

Having been educated to think, she was eager to write. For some years she lived with her now widowed uncle in quiet, restricted pursuits, amid a genteel circle of medium fortunes, and corresponding with her older sister and brother. In 1785 she succeeded in having essays published in *The Lounger,* although the editor knew nothing of her beforehand.

In 1786 Miss Hamilton's brother returned from distinguished service with the East India Company, with a commission to translate the Medaya, or Mohammedan code of laws. His arrival widened his sister's limited social life, and she was stimulated to study the East. In 1788 they visited London, where Elizabeth's talents became appreciated, and after Mr Marshall's death the family settled there. Her brother, too, died untimely in 1792 and the sisters lived in seclusion in the south of England, and Elizabeth at length followed her desires to become a writer.

Her *Hindoo Rajah* in 1796 had great success, though she was too modest to seek publicity, and she continued writing despite illness, living in Bath and publishing at first anonymously *(Memoirs of Modern Philosophers,* 1800), until encouraged to admit her identity. Among works which made her famous were her *Letters on Education* (1801), praised by Dugald Stewart. During the next couple of years the sisters travelled extensively in Britain.

They arrived in Edinburgh in December 1802, at the pressing invitation of the Stewarts. Staying in North Hanover Street, and later in George Street, Miss Hamilton was at once plunged into 'agreeable engagements' and had to lay aside her work on 'the Agrippinas', whose first volume she had submitted to the judgment of Stewart. She had also been introduced to Professor Playfair.[7]

The authoress enjoyed Edinburgh society, even a ball. She was admired by Mrs Fletcher, met and became friendly with Miss Edgeworth, and wrote of the city approvingly: 'I do not believe that either London or Paris ever saw so much genius in our days. It is, indeed, seldom that so many young men of distinguished talents have sprung up at one time, or in one place.'

Edinburgh society was superior to anything she had yet known. 'Seldom indeed are so many people of eminent talents to be met with in one friendly circle. Few days have passed in which we have not seen some persons of distinguished abilities' and (unusually in society generally) none of the parties she attended had been a mere waste of time.[8]

The pleasant tenor of a blue-stocking existence was established. Spending the mornings in study, at 2 o'clock Mrs Hamilton (by which courtesy title she was now known) descended to the drawing-room to receive callers and friends. In the evenings, on the rare occasions when there was no social engagement she would enjoy hearing a book read aloud, even for hours on end. On Mondays she held a kind of morning levée which continued until quite a late hour, attended by some of Edinburgh's most brilliant thinkers, but although her manner was frank and cheerful, Mrs Hamilton showed up best in private, when she shone with entertaining anecdotes and vivid narrative.

A lady writer was still a phenomenon to draw attention, for although most Scottish ladies were educated in taste and reading, few cared to risk their reputations in authorship. 'Her house', wrote a friend, 'was the resort, not only of the intellectual, but of the gay and even of the fashionable; and her cheerfulness, good sense, and good humour, soon reconciled every one to the literary lady', overcoming society's 'vulgar prejudices against literary women'.[9]

An eager sponsor was the Stirling poet Hector McNeill,[10] who knew and encouraged her from youth and helped to bring her into society. She in turn was generous and encouraging towards the aspirations of other women and young people. By the spring of 1803, however, Mrs Hamilton had already found that 'the dissipation of an Edinburgh winter has proved very adverse to study'. Many families had now left and 'the rage for visiting has ceased', large formal parties being succeeded by small and more intimate gatherings. As it was accepted that she would not see people in the mornings, it was now up to her to settle down to writing.

Having completed half of *Agrippina* she gave it to Dugald Stewart to read, who assured her that 'it is written in a far more masterly manner than any of my former productions and pronounces biography to be my forte'. As she feared male prejudice in judging the period too classical for a woman writer, Stewart recommended balancing ancient and modern characters. She duly picked on James VI and I's daughter the Princess Elizabeth, who married the Elector Palatine.

Mrs Hamilton's health, however, was now giving trouble: she found the Edinburgh air too keen and piercing, although the famous east wind, traditionally such a problem in the New Town, for two or three years had scarcely troubled them. Professor Playfair gave the strange explanation that according to some philosophers the east and west winds were 'accidental', and that in the late spring they were equally free from the north wind. Playfair, 'as much beloved by the young as esteemed by the old', continually delighted Mrs

Hamilton, with 'the amiable simplicity of his manners and the acknowledged superiority of his talents'.

While enjoying the view of the fields from their windows, as yet still unbuilt over, as the second New Town was barely begun – giving an illusion of being in the country – the sisters preferred to spend time in July in Stirlingshire, and in August, 'after the summer heat', retreated to the milder climate of Bath. Here about a year later Mrs Hamilton was able to complete *Agrippina* and submitted it to Dr Stewart for his approval.

In the autumn of 1804 they again settled in Scotland, when Mrs Hamilton reluctantly accepted a post to superintend, as friend and adviser, the education of a widowed nobleman's children, being allowed full control and a separate establishment. From this experience she compiled the much praised *Letters to the Daughter of a Nobleman* (1806).

Mrs Hamilton became active in Edinburgh's House of Industry, in which several ladies had set up a school for 'females of the lowest class'. Limitation of levées to once a week was partly due to her poor health, and also in order not to interrupt this charitable and committee work in distributing the funds. Her popular book, *Cottagers of Glenburnie* (1808), was an outcome of her interest in the poor.[11]

The Edinburgh society in which these ladies and their contemporaries moved had modified considerably since the century began, as living in the New Town became more established, and changes were to become more noticeable by the end of the decade.

Informal dinner invitations could be made at virtually no notice to the household: a house containing the usual number of a married couple with three or four (or more) children, and aides and servants of varying ranks, necessarily catered for many people every day. (The waste must have been alarming.) For example, Walter Scott dropped an impromptu suggestion to his young friend Robert Gillies on his way home from the Parliament House, that he come back with him at once, dinner on the table at 4.30 p.m., not to bother to change as there was nobody but themselves. 'Nobody' turned out to be his amanuensis Weber and a legal colleague Malcolm Buchanan, neither of whom could count as anybody; and on ascending to the drawing-room for tea, besides Scott's two daughters there was the lady who taught them music and similarly did not count.[12]

Dinner menus were usually bountiful, except for the meagre desserts, which were best supplemented in the strawberry season. Sir John Carr in 1807[13] noted with approval that gentlemen were not obliged to drink too much. A small glass of Highland whisky would be served at the end of dinner.

It was Scott's idea, in 1803, to form a gentlemen's social club, nominally limited to Edinburgh but open to visitors, for 'all the literary and social persons in the city'. It started with Scott's and Jeffrey's friends, sixteen in number: eventually the top limit was fixed at thirty. It was prosaically known as the Friday Club from the day of its weekly meetings at 4 p.m., and according to Henry Cockburn it formed the basis of Jeffrey's friendships for the next forty years.[14]

Besides Scott and Jeffrey, members included Dugald Stewart, Sydney Smith, William Erskine and George Cranstoun, both later judges (Lords Kinneder and Corehouse), the Rev. John Elmsley from Oxford, Thomas Thomson the antiquary, afterwards Clerk of Session, Professor John Thomson, physician, the geologist Sir James Hall, Alexander Irving, afterwards Lord Newton, the Rev. Archibald Alison, and of course Professor Playfair and Henry Mackenzie. On learning that Lord Webb Seymour was expecting to return to Edinburgh for the winter, Jeffrey urged Horner in London (8 August) to convince him that 'without being a member of the said club, it is impossible to have any tolerable existence in Edinburgh'.[15]

They dined or supped at Bayle's in Shakespeare Square (at the corner of the present Leith Street), and also at Barry's nearby in Princes Street (site of the later North British Hotel). The cost averaged £1.18 to £2.5s a head, probably including the wine, and dinner was often followed by the fabled Edinburgh 'high jinks'. There was the time when Sydney Smith, Playfair and Thomas Thomson went out to steal the head of Galen from Gardiner's shop in George Street, when 'the perfidious Brougham' (as Cockburn recalls) called the watch and had them arrested. So much for his own pilfering of brass knockers not many years earlier. At Barry's, Jeffrey and Playfair would worship before the graven image of a hideous New Zealand god over the chimney-piece, and Brougham would brew a dangerous concoction, 'a stiff punch of rum, sugar, lemon, marmalade, calves-foot jelly, and water'.[16]

Yet it was not a rowdy club, and it was certainly not formal. New members were introduced 'silently', and the evenings were expected to be spent in relaxed enjoyment with 'talk, and good wine'. At first they supposedly foregathered for Edinburgh's favourite convivial meal, the supper, and afterwards lingered until up to 2 o'clock in the morning. In due course they introduced a monthly 'banquet', served at 6 p.m., and although the suppers continued, dinners were also introduced. Their secretary for three years was Mr Richardson, succeeded on his removing to London in 1806 by Henry Cockburn. Jeffrey, Playfair and Thomson, who never missed, were the most constant members, and Scott seldom did. Only in later years did age, illness and death thin the ranks.[17]

Many visitors commented on the Scots' passion for dancing. The Assembly Rooms in George Street, completed in 1787, generally came in for ponderous criticism for their 'heavy and inelegant' appearance (before William Burn added the portico in 1818), though the magnificent interior was praised. The principal ballroom, described by Sir John Carr as 'a noble room', was 92 by 42 feet, and 40 feet high, lighted by eleven splendid lustres and with an organ at one end. The ball Sir John attended was held in another room, directed by an aristocratic lady and accompanied by an orchestra directed by the son of the famous Neil Gow. 'Insensible must that heart be', says Campbell (1801) 'which feels not the influence of female charms, while beholding a select party of Scottish ladies on the night of an assembly.' Carr much admired the beauty of the women, and both sexes danced with taste and skill, especially in the favourite Scottish dances; but like others, he was struck by 'the national gravity' of their expressions, especially the young men's. By contrast concert nights at the Assembly Rooms were significantly attended by an audience 'neither so select nor so brilliant'.[18]

Susan Mein, who first visited Edinburgh in 1801 at the age of eighteen, and again about 1804, describes in detail how one organised a private ball, a service which seems to have changed little in two centuries. Her naval uncle Captain James Mein gave a dance in return for the hospitality he had received, and the arrangements were made entirely by a leading confectioner (Susan does not say which). All the firm needed to know was the number of guests. On the morning of the ball they would come to the house, 'take up the carpet, bring forms and decorate the rooms; the floor of the dancing room would be beautifully chalked; the music engaged . . . Not a servant in the house needed to be employed in these rooms during the evening, nor a single article of plate, glass or anything else used but what belonged to the person who supplied the rooms for the evening.' The supper, tea and coffee were all brought in, charged per head; the music was charged according to the size of the band. 'In the morning you would find your rooms in the same order as before.'

On that particular evening most of the guests were young people, few married couples being invited. To spare their shyness Susan's relative Mrs Smail, her hostess in Dublin Street, acted as 'Matron'. The acknowledged belles of the evening were the Misses Grierson, outshining everyone in dress, and looking as if they expected it. Their outfits, commented Susan, were 'indeed somewhat fantastical . . . and would have suited the stage better'. Margaret, the younger, very high-spirited and lively, was a real town girl. When visiting friends outside Edinburgh she used to declare 'she would not live in the country for the world'.

This lovely girl suffered a great misfortune when one evening, heated after dancing, she caught a chill from an open window which caused 'a slight eruption on her face'. Concealing this with one of the lethal cosmetics of the day, she so damaged her complexion that for more than two years she refused to see anyone but her family. When at last she reappeared she was totally changed, her beauty 'transferred to her mind', thoughtlessness transformed into pleasing manners, and her once extravagant dress now 'neat and lady-like'. She had taken a religious turn, wrote edifying works for children, and produced improved plans for schools, for which she became sought after by clergy and landowners.

Margaret Grierson in fact ended more happily than her elder sister, who made 'a most unfortunate marriage' while she, though physically and mentally so changed, now led a useful life.[19]

The less dangerous cosmetics, listed by the diligent Rev. Mr Hall, included Hungary water, Italian paste and other exotics for the wealthy, but if money did not stretch to these, skin impurities were treated by boiling sowens, 'a well-known Scotch dish . . . a strong drastic, and which cleans and whitens what it covers, astonishingly'. Ladies used it at night, soaking a cloth with holes cut out for the eyes, nose etc., and covering their faces while they slept.

As for dress, at this period 'indecency', a legacy from the free ideas spread by the French Revolution, was still the fashion. The Rev. James Hall remarked that Edinburgh ladies emulated London fashion in appearing with bosoms and backs almost bare, sometimes wearing little more than a thin muslin gown. Young men were equally indecent, who in summer especially 'display their shapes . . . in thin, light flesh-coloured silk pantaloons, reaching from their ankles almost to their neck'.[20]

Some ladies, especially eccentric spinsters, dressed in a bizarre style. Susan Mein notes how at a private ball in about 1804 Captain Mein, six foot two inches, led off with their hostess Miss Ainslie who was only about four feet tall, and dressed 'in a most extraordinary way – everything was so conspicuously fine. That evening she had a gold net on her head that hung down behind with a gold tassel, with a bird of paradise in front, perfectly out of proportion to her height. Unfortunately, at supper, a button on the coat of one of the servants caught in the net as he was hurrying past, and in an instant the little bald head was partly exposed to view. She had a wig on.' Uncle James diplomatically did his best to adjust it and pretend that all was well, but everyone had to stifle giggles at the little lady's 'coquettish' attempts to carry off the mishap.[21]

Another spectacle was witnessed by the novelist Susan Ferrier, who was a year older than Susan Mein: her father James Ferrier was legal agent to the 5th and 6th Dukes of Argyll, and she therefore spent much time with him at Inveraray, source of many of her observations of the aristocracy at home. On this occasion it was at an Edinburgh concert when she was confronted by 'Widow Bell' (January 1802). 'She looked so queer and so vulgar, that I was fain to fight shy. She came bobbing along, sticking out at all points and places, keys and *coppers* jingling in her pockets, led in triumph by a frightful male creature with a large *bow window* bound in blue and buff, and a pair of pea-green *upper legs.* I thought I should have swooned in shame when she stopped and stared at me.'[22]

The other Susan notes for us the more restrained fashions of the day-time, and coming from London, she astounded her Edinburgh cousins by her advanced style. In general Edinburgh ladies dressed with taste, in the English fashion but less expensively. London's morning dress that summer (1802) was a white 'curricle dress': 'a short open garment showing the petticoat in front, which was trimmed in the same way as the dress with short sleeves, the body open and low, showing an embroidered "French habit shirt" [chemisette] . . . and a small white chip hat, gipsy shape, around which was a wreath of small pink roses'. Describing all this many years later for her descendants, she of course laughs at the thought of 'short sleeves and low dress in the forenoon'. Afternoon or evening dress was similar but in 'thin plain or figured muslin, the petticoat of silk or satin trimmed with lace, as was the upper dress'.[23]

The contrast of dress between the classes was extreme, as many observers noted. Already in Newcastle Susan had remarked on the difference in costume of the 'lower class of people', the women bare-legged, 'no caps, short petticoats, and bedgowns with short sleeves'. Everyone remarked on working women's bare legs and feet in Edinburgh, which they preferred to the tyranny of shoes, and many comment unsympathetically on their coarse appearance. Their costume was perforce fairly unchanging in style, and their laborious lives and constant exposure to the weather, especially the fish-wives, offered little alternative. 'Short and brawny', notes Joseph Mawman in 1804, 'with arid skins and tarnished complexion, without . . . any pretensions to beauty.'[24]

Susan Mein was a keen observer. A naval doctor's daughter from Cornwall, after leaving school in Bath in 1800 she mostly lived at Eildon, where her parents had moved, or in London. Her remarks on her travels are to the point. Newcastle, incidentally, was 'a most dirty, horrid place . . . a queer primitive sort of Town'. From Melrose, near their house, Greenwells, there was no coach service to Edinburgh, only the 'three Legged Fly', with two lean, lame horses with 'only three serviceable legs between them', which plied the eleven miles from Drygrange to Lauder, so that the total of thirty-six miles to Edinburgh took a long day. She and her sisters stayed with their cousins in the newly built Dublin Street.[25]

Susan recorded a case of the iniquitous Scottish marriage-trap as encountered by her gregarious uncle Captain James Mein. One evening (probably in 1804) at the Assembly, while he was nonchalantly propping up a chimney-piece, an unknown lady engaged him in conversation, and invited him to her house to supper. Etiquette-wise this seemed rather bold, and on mentioning it to his friend Captain Ross he learned that the lady was 'Mrs John Dalrymple', the determined winner of an unguarded husband through the infamous practice. As Miss Johanna or 'Jackie' Gordon, daughter of Charles Gordon of Cluny, she had flirted one day at a large dinner-party with Captain John Dalrymple, when the gentlemen had returned to the drawing-room in exceptionally merry mood. Dalrymple happened to make a stupid joke such as 'This shall be my wife', and one way or another the girl's relations managed to insist that the so-called declaration of matrimony must stand. The gentleman was so disgusted at the lady's part in this trickery that 'he left the house immediately and never saw her afterwards, but he had to make a settlement on her'. This marriage was in fact eventually annulled (1820), but when the 'husband' became the 7th Earl of Stair the lady, who had always used his name, contrived to be known as the Countess, until her death in 1847.

This lady was well-known in Edinburgh for her 'capital suppers' – so Captain Ross recommended Mein to accept her invitation, because he would meet a great company there. She was also a regular attender of the Duchess of Gordon's parties, with her sister who had married Captain Sir John Lowther Johnstone of Westerhall (and in 1820 married Richard Weyland), and was considered 'the most lady like in her appearance of the three [sisters], but all alike noisy and bold in their manner'.[26]

Matrimony-wise, sometimes the boot was on the other foot. The Rev. Mr Hall relates dining in 1803 with a gentleman who, as 'a handsome young captain' stationed at St Andrews, had seduced a clergyman's daughter and left her pregnant. The girl, afraid to tell her father, wrote to her lieutenant brother in England, who quickly came to her help. Learning the culprit was in Edinburgh, he took leave of absence, hastened there with his sister in a carriage and traced the errant captain to 'a respectable coffee-house, in the New Town'. Here the brother turned up with his sister and a clergyman in tow, summoned the captain from a drinking session with fellow-officers, and locking the door behind them, confronted him with his sins. The flabbergasted captain was given an ultimatum: 'As you are unmarried, and there is a clergyman in waiting, by God, if you do not marry her before you leave this room. I will blow out your brains!'

Pausing only to make sure (rather belatedly?) that the trembling Bess was willing, the brother summoned the minister and a couple of witnesses, and a marriage sufficient in Scots law was solemnised. The lieutenant then took up his hat and left, with the parting injunction that 'By all that is sacred, if you are uncivil to her, I will kick you out of the world.'

Surprisingly, perhaps, the marriage proved not unsuccessful and the young captain was an affectionate spouse. The story is plausible, though how the Rev. Mr Hall came by the unsavoury facts (and how much he exaggerates) he does not explain.[27]

A case which worked out well at least for the lady concerned, though causing a great furore at the time, was in 1809 when Sir Arscott Molesworth, of an influential Cornish family and by all accounts a rather thick-witted young man, was packed off with a friend for a Highland tour 'to keep him out of harm's way'. During the mere two days they spent in Edinburgh on their way north they were invited to a ball, where Molesworth danced with (writes his great-aunt Lady Lucan) Miss Mary Brown, 'a simple, pleasant virgin of about 30 years of age, who was kind enough to make no objection to his being but eighteen'. The morning after he returned from the Highlands he was informed that the lady and a parson were awaiting him. 'Up got my dear nephew, followed the man like a goose, and *was married* like an idiot . . . He says he proposed to her at the ball, but she refused to marry him then . . . without witnesses, etc.', but said she would give him time to reflect. The boy seems naïve enough to deserve what he got. He kept quiet about it even to his travelling-companion, until a letter arrived (to his family?) from the bride. Lady Lucan remarked sniffily 'The name of Brown is not one of the illustrious of Scotland', but it was quite a respectable match, her father Captain Brown, 'a distinguished warrior', having left money which she would inherit from her mother. The marriage certainly endured, and the couple's eldest son, Sir William, became a Radical politician.[28]

Elizabeth Grant mentions Lady Molesworth in 1816 as one of the go-getting would-be leading Edinburgh hostesses, and recalls how, as 'the fast daughter of a managing manoeuvring mother, very clever, no longer young', she ran off with this rich young man 'and made him an admirable wife – for he was little beyond a fool'.[29]

Sir John Carr, incidentally, as well as others, remarked on the unusual disparity in age of many marriage partners: old husbands of much younger wives were much commoner in Edinburgh than elsewhere – 'but the old men are tall and vigorous, and have sound stamina': witness the large families of their prolific wives, who quite often produced up to ten or a dozen children.[30]

Returning to the enterprising Captain Mein, one evening at the theatre with his niece Susan he was attracted by the hearty laughter of their neighbour in the box, 'a most cheerful ruddy-faced, elderly person'. As they talked in the interval he was interested to learn that this was Alexander Cunningham the jeweller, formerly Burns's great friend. Cunningham had never got over his love for the beauty Anne Stewart, who in 1789 had married a rival, Forrest Dewar; and although he himself married a few years later, he still used to haunt the street where she lived in the hope of seeing even her shadow on the blind. If ever he did, he would burst into tears.

So relates the romantic Susan, who, however, on leaving the theatre that evening was bundled into a sedan by her uncle so that he could accept Cunningham's invitation to supper. During his visit Cunningham showed him Burns's black marble punch-bowl, a wedding-present from Jean

Armour's father, which she had given Cunningham after Burns's death, mounted in silver and engraved with a verse by the poet. Cunningham filled the bowl with whisky toddy and, at first to his guest's delight, began to relate anecdotes of Burns, but then, beginning to reminisce about his long-lost love, became lacrymose. The extrovert Captain Mein unsympathetically told him he ought not still to grieve for a girl so obviously unworthy; but the anecdote ends here and Cunningham's reaction is not recorded.[31]

Another observant young lady, who appeared in Edinburgh in about 1805, was the twenty-year-old Maria Dundas, 'Metaphysics in Muslin' who caused such a sensation more for her intelligence than looks. Staying with her uncle James Dundas and his wife Elizabeth Graham of Airth in St Andrew Square, their affectionate meeting included the eight young children, and three maiden aunts, aged from fifty upwards. 'As we walked along the streets,' says Maria, 'it seemed to me that I was introduced to every third person we met, and that two out of every three declared him or herself to be a cousin' (not surprising in the wide-ranging Dundas family); all greeted her warmly, the more elderly with a kiss. ('They are grown finer now', she recalled thirty years later, and while still kind, were 'cooled down to more than London carelessness'.[32])

Despite her hostess's poor health which prevented her chaperoning Maria and thus accepting certain invitations, the girl was able to meet 'Edinburgh society' at dinner-parties with her father and uncle, and during the six weeks of her father's stay they met more relatives and friends, and James Dundas took her and her father on long walks to show them 'the improvements of Edinburgh, which even then seemed marvellous to him'.

Introduced by degrees to the Edinburgh world, Maria was especially interested in 'the literary and scientific society which at that time rendered it so particularly agreeable', and it was at her uncle's house that she met those eminent professors, Dugald Stewart, Playfair, John Leslie and Dr Thomas Hope, all of whom had been at school with him, and on whom she made such a remarkable impression.[33]

Her schooldays, unlike those of more conventional young ladies, had given her no preparation for the fashionable world. Loving literature, she envied men their classical learning (little did she know of the strait-jacket methods of the High School), and innocently supposed that anyone with common interests must be free to talk of them like brothers and sisters. Having no mother to introduce her to society, and her aunt being semi-invalid, she found herself discoursing easily with men and women alike in a way that some found quite shocking, and eager to talk on any subject of which she knew anything. Although she was invited to Edinburgh balls, being a poor dancer and usually partnered by a young schoolboy or student cousin, she preferred sitting out and talking with the professors – Playfair being one of her favourites – and the professors loved it. Gossips accused her of flirting, when she sought only knowledge, and was certainly too innocent to know or care about young gentlemen's rank or income.

Maria's first Edinburgh year, with enjoyable visits to castles and mansions, and appreciation of Highland scenery even before Scott had made it so fashionable, ended abruptly with a long and serious illness which undermined her former robust constitution and for a time seemed likely to cause her death. She was attended by the noted Dr Gregory, who used to come and read to her in the evenings, as his family were away. His attention and the care of many friends and relatives eventually steered her to a surprising recovery, assisted by a voyage home to her father in Richmond in a Berwick smack.[34]

Maria Dundas's intellect caused a sensation, yet many English and foreign visitors commented on the Edinburgh ladies' literary articulacy, equal to the men's, sensible in their conversation rather than superficial like many English ladies: 'they manage a point of intellectual disputation', remarked Sir John Carr, 'with equal talent and delicacy'. He thought their parties resembled the conversazioni of France and Italy: for example Lady Charlotte Campbell presided over gatherings which combined 'learning with politeness, and philosophy with gaiety', crowned by her own famous beauty and charm.

Carr praised the ladies for their frankness, a happy medium between English reserve and French excessive freedom. They were friendly yet modest, also accomplished, though less well educated than the English in music. The gentlemen he found unaffectedly polite, if punctilious over rank, and remarkable too for literary and general knowledge, thanks to their educational grounding. They were 'well bred, yet moral; brave, yet courteous; highly cultivated, but unassuming'.[35]

Towards the end of the decade the style of entertaining was noticeably changing. Mrs Fletcher noted that the old-style large dinner-parties were now less common, and that the 'hot supper' so beloved of old Edinburgh was practically given up. The new style was the evening party, sometimes too large even for the New Town rooms in which they were held, and card playing had given way to 'music or conversation'. Parties ran from 9 until midnight, with tea or coffee handed round on arrival, and later, cold light refreshments served at table, but the object was not to eat, 'but to talk and listen' in respectful circles, gathered round, say, the brilliant Jeffrey, Dr Brown supported by Professor Playfair, or the now old Henry Mackenzie relating anecdotes of past times.[36]

In 1811 Jeffrey's brother-in-law, the Rev. Robert Morehead, an Episcopal clergyman, similarly noted that the traditional dinner party had been supplemented by an assembly of 'a number of people collected in a small room', whose entertainment was similar to a twentieth-century party – 'to go from one person to another, and converse with perfect ease and freedom'. As the guests were likely to be Edinburgh's leading lights it made for a very pleasant occasion. And afterwards, notes Sir John Carr, walking along the Queen Street promenade was popular until a late hour, especially by moonlight.[37]

Few visitors comment on the appearance of the houses or their furnishings, unless perhaps those of humbler rank whose talents had brought them into society, like James Hogg, who in his new periodical *The Spy* (mostly his own composition), in the guise of a visiting 'foreigner', comments unfavourably on fashionable occasions. Whereas more worldly travellers merely remark on Edinburgh's furnishings as being simpler than London's, the still unsophisticated Hogg is clearly impressed, but he has far less to say on this than he does of the rooms' occupants' snobbery and vanity. The drawing-room, 70 or 80 feet long, is beyond anything he has seen in a house, superbly adorned with crimson velvet for curtains, sofas and chairs. 'The room was in a blaze of light, and what I could see of the floor was painted with beautiful devices.' Indeed the crowd was too great to see much.[38]

Rents were considered over-priced. In 1800 Mrs Dunmore, removing with her family from Stirling, took a Princes Street house for £52 a year, 'besides horrid taxes'. At that date there were still few streets to choose from. However, she thought herself well housed: 'three stairs up and a very narrow steep stair but its a pleasant situation looks over to the old town and up to the Castle. I have a kitchen a dining room drawing Room 2 Bedrooms on the first floor, but they are all very small indeed . . .; up a kind of trap stair we have 2 very good Rooms and 2 very small ones I can accomodate our whole Family and has a good spare Bed Room'. Despite the rent, she thought that expenses would in the long run prove less than in the country.[39]

These houses, notably the large, well-equipped Queen Street buildings, in 'the best part of Edinburgh', by 1810 were selling for £3000; others almost as good for £2500. In the lesser streets good houses went for £1800, or could be rented for £100 a year, plus £30 taxes. Land was valued disproportionately high and rented 'exorbitantly' at £10 an acre, or was feued on perpetual lease at £8. [40]

Of the servants who ran these establishments, a female cook was then paid £12 a year, a manservant £40, a maidservant only £8. There would be considerably more space for them to sleep than in the old days in the Old Town.[41]

In the streets, while the sedan chair was still a major means of transport, there were now far more carriages. Stage coaches were a fairly recent introduction. In 1763 a modest service of two coaches covering the mile-and-a-half to Leith had been established, running hourly from 8 a.m. to 8 p.m. and taking a whole hour for the journey. Each had a coachman, a postilion and three horses. At that time Scotland was linked with London by only a single monthly stage, taking sixteen to eighteen days for the near-four-hundred-mile journey. But by 1807 a perfect stream of local, short- and long-distance coaches connected the Scottish capital with Leith, Musselburgh, Dalkeith, Stirling, Glasgow, Kelso and Aberdeen. London was served by a mail and two coaches. The total number in service was forty-two, of different types, mostly running daily.[42]

Carriages had been manufactured in Edinburgh for many years, though for obvious reasons in small numbers. In 1763 the few to be seen had been imported from London, but twenty years later good vehicles were being made in Edinburgh and already exported, even to Paris – Louis Simond recalled seeing a long procession of Scottish-built carriages, after unloading from the ship, travelling from Rouen for sale in Paris.[43]

By the early nineteenth century the coachworks of a Lt-Colonel of the Volunteers named Crichton, on the road between Edinburgh and Leith, were considered 'of great respectability and ingenuity'. Crichton had invented a 'machine' for the speedy transport of troops, and another to ease travel for wounded soldiers. At his works a handsome display of Scottish-made carriages, well-built, light and elegant, was on show. Sir John Carr in 1807 comments that by then many were exported to the West Indies, and although hampered by the war with Napoleon, before the naval blockade they had supplied several European countries.

As for serving as local Edinburgh transport, while in 1787 there had been only eight hackney carriages, by 1807 there were eighty-six, generally better than the beat-up, cast-off versions serving London. And Edinburgh-built private carriages were considered very fine, especially for their 'cabinet' and upholstery work, forming part of the city's small high-quality luxury trade. A carriage, including all furniture, cost £250.[44]

The sedan chair with its Highland bearers was still the popular, and most convenient, vehicle, even long after the wide streets of the New Town had made wheeled traffic more practicable. It could present hazards. When Susan Mein was staying with her cousins in 1804, she had an alarming adventure returning from the theatre on her family's last evening in Edinburgh. The party had taken a carriage to the theatre but after the play decided to cover the short distance to Dublin Street by chair.

Thomas the footman having engaged chairs for Susan, her sister Kitty, and the other ladies, they all set off, her uncle, Admiral Sir Archibald Dickson, accompanying them on foot. Most of the chairmen turned up through St Andrew Square, but Susan's bearers carried on along Princes Street. Before long the chair began to sway so alarmingly that she realised they were drunk, and tapped urgently on the window to be let out. They stopped, one of the men opened the top and she jumped out, but he seized her by the arm to push her back again. In a panic she screamed for Sir Archibald, and in no time a passer-by had knocked down the chairman and several gentlemen rescuers were crowding round offering their services. But Sir Archibald quickly came hurrying to her assistance, and the prudent Susan of course modestly declined any escort but his. The affair ended without further trouble, and her sick father never got to hear of it.[45]

A similar adventure with drunk carriers is recorded much later by Helen Graham, one night in 1825 returning from Lady Scott-Douglas's. Mrs Graham with the footman took the first chair, Helen the second, General Graham bringing up the rear. The journey to her aunt's house at 67 George Street seemed very long, and Helen was fairly sure they had missed the way. They stopped, the chairman ascended a stair, found it was either General Maxwell's or the Sinclairs of Ulbster's, and called 'Back! Back!' in an 'inebriated voice'. Back they went, tried another stair – 'Ineffectual'.

Helen called in exasperation to let her out. 'Met the lacquey flying without his hat. Said I was going home, left them to settle *comme ils se plaisaient.* Mama sitting in the dining-room. Had been in some time. Said hers flew like lamp-lighters and seemed to slice the air . . . Papa then appeared. Said he did not know where he had been, but the chairmen had taken several rests by the way, complained of his weight, and one said he was "upwards of seventy. Kent his honour weel"', and seemed inclined to reminisce. This for a party of three, whose carriers were not only drunk but lost them as well.[46]

Sedans used to be brought into the house and parked in the large entrance hall for passengers to board, thus avoiding any danger of getting wet, cold or muddy; the husky Highlanders then shouldered their burden and shambled away. They may well have engendered a special form of travel sickness. Many years later the prickly ornithologist John Audubon, never lacking in initiative, tried one for the first and last time one snowy March Sunday in 1827, to go to church after breakfasting with Mr Newbold. It proved a great mistake. 'I like to try everything which is going on . . . But so long as I have two feet and legs, I never desire to try one of these machines again: the quick up-and-down, short-swinging motion, reminded me of . . . the great earthquake in Kentucky.' (A fine sermon from Sydney Smith helped to console him.)[47]

Despite Edinburgh's small size, chairmen were less encyclopaedic in their topographical knowledge than today's London taxi-driver. The absent-minded Lord Minto, on another snowy occasion, once ordered a chair to carry him to dine on the other side of the town. On his boarding, the men said they would have to ask the way as they went along. 'Oh no, I'll show you', said the obliging politician, and quite forgetting what the chair was there for, walked in his immaculate evening dress and shoes the whole way across the city, the men carrying the chair behind him.[48]

Street lighting in the city was distinctly parsimonious, the streets being lighted only in winter, and then not well. One dark July night Sir John Carr had literally to feel his way from George Square over the North Bridge almost to St Andrew Street, nearly a mile. Despite that, he thought there were few street robberies, implying a natural honesty among the Scots![49]

The oil used in the lamps was whale or train oil – the same for which the Russian sailors had shinned up them to drain for their cooking, plunging Leith and Leith Walk into darkness. Oilmen were therefore among the most important shopkeepers.

Thomas Smith, known as 'Leery Smith', an ingenious young tinsmith of Potterrow, long had the lighting contract for the city, and proposed a system of reflectors to improve the effect, which the city rejected. He then, with Robert Stephenson (who married his daughter), evolved a method which was eventually adopted by the Board of Northern Lights, the mechanics and supplies being taken over by Smith and his sons.

The lamp-lighters, or Leeries, used to parade daily in Hunter Square to be supplied with the oil and wicks for the cruises, and the flambeaux – tin tubes like police batons stuffed with tow and saturated with oil at the top, with which to light the lamps. When gas lighting took over, Leerie Smith lost the lighting contract, the lighters' parade ceased, and train oil consumption was reduced, even for kitchen use. But for many years the same type of flambeau was still used to light the gas lamps, until they were superseded by small lanterns with openings at the bottom.[50]

Smith & Co. were now restricted to trade with county families who used wax candles, and handsome lamps which burned colza (rapeseed) oil. Domestic lamps had been greatly improved. In 1808 Charles Kirkpatrick Sharpe bought a drawing-room lamp at a sale for £10 that was worth £25, very elegant and with four burners, 'which will set a larger room than yours in a perfect blaze', he proudly told his mother. For another £3 he could get a brass chain to hang it from, rope being cheaper but, of course, less fashionable.[51]

Gas took some time to become established, at first used experimentally in kitchens and lobbies, and when that appeared not catastrophic, in dining rooms and parlours, eventually even in bedrooms.[52]

The water supply was at this time quite good, a new reservoir near Heriot's Hospital supplementing the three hundred-ton tank on the Castle Hill. From the reservoirs, water-carriers bore barrels on their backs for Old Town inhabitants, while in the New Town, piped water was supplied to those households which paid a rate. There was also a spring west of the castle, beside the Lothian Road, which was running to waste, and a proposal had been made to pipe this for watering the streets, cleansing the filthy markets and supplementing sewers.[53]

This was a welcome accent on cleanliness. In 1803 the Rev. James Hall had noted with disapproval that formerly the magistrates had spent £80 a year on removing 'filth' from the streets, whereas now they were actually paid hundreds of pounds for the privilege of removing it for use as manure. Someone had evidently nosed out a handy source of profit. In 1811 the Old Town streets were still 'a melancholy spectacle', according to Louis Simond, and the tradition, or myth, of the street-cry 'Gardy-loo!' died hard, for although he confessed that he had never heard it, and was assured that it had not been used for years, he insisted that the Old Town was full of filth thrown from windows, as in Marseille, and that not only underfoot but even the walls of side-streets and wynds were disgusting to behold.[54]

Unlike other Scottish towns Edinburgh never developed much industry, though there was plenty of activity in its environs. The Swedish industrialist Erik Svedenstierna, as an 'industrial spy' picking up hints from British manufacture, noted in 1803 the large distillery and a biscuit-porcelain painting manufactory. Coal-mining was carried on round Dalkeith, Lasswade had a paper mill, and at Cramond were Cadell & Sons' iron-works. Svedenstierna does not mention Edinburgh's extensive printing industry, carried on by the booksellers.

Much of the production was centred on the road to Leith, which as a busy port by contrast boasted numerous works: glass-makers, foundries, salt boilers, soap and soda factories, and paper mills. The glassworks outside the town were famous for 'the clearest and purest crystal glass . . . which surpasses in beauty all other, in England as well as in France'. Among other factories was Jameson's soap works: its owner was brother to the mineralogist Robert Jameson, who after studying at Edinburgh University had gone on to study with Werner in Freiburg.[55]

Joseph Mawman, a visitor the next summer (1804), landing at Leith found it a dirty town like most seaports, but already with some fine modern stone houses. He also records its contribution to Scottish prosperity by its convenient shipping to London, besides the recent increase of trade with Russia and Oporto, and the herring and Greenland whale fisheries.[56] Until the end of the eighteenth century it was on the whole a port of crowded, mean and comfortless houses, with narrow streets and lanes. The several elegant houses built on its outskirts by about 1800 were significant of its merchant inhabitants' increasing wealth.[57] From about 1798 the lighting of Leith Walk at night brought a great improvement.

The port's trade was chiefly in timber, tar and iron imported from the Baltic, flax and its seed from Holland, wine and spirits from Portugal and the Mediterranean, apples from England, and, from a few vessels trading with the West Indies, rum and sugar. It was limited by the shortage of exportable Scottish manufactures – except for the Edinburgh-built carriages – and during the Napoleonic Wars the blockade curtailed trade. But once the fine docks, begun in 1801, were completed trade would much increase.[58]

The foundation stone of Leith new docks was laid on 14 May 1801, by Robert Dundas of Melville in the absence of the Grand Master Mason, the Earl of Dalkeith. The engineer was John Rennie. Finance was to come from a loan authorised to the magistrates by an Act of 1799. The usual ceremonies accompanied the stone-laying ceremony, a masonic and civic procession marching from the Assembly Rooms to the south-west corner of the first dock's outer wall, and the stone was laid with the customary mementoes deposited in the cavity.[59]

In 1810 Louis Simond compared industries and products with a previous generation much as Creech had done in the 1790s. Export tonnage from Leith had tripled in eight years, but as there were no rich products and no major navigable river, all was achieved by 'industry, frugality, and good order'. Glass, paper and carriages were the main manufactures.[60]

One great increase, not for the common good, was in the production of spirits at the expense of the brewing industry. In 1708, 51,000 gallons of spirits were distilled in Scotland, in 1791, more than a million and a half gallons, while by contrast some half a million barrels of beer brewed in 1720 had sunk in 1784 to less than 10,000. Scottish whisky production was found to be far greater than spirit alcohol in London, when in 1787 it was demonstrated that they discharged their stills daily – then believed to be the maximum economic output – while in 1799 it was reported to the Treasury that a single 43-gallon still could discharge every 2½ minutes, or nearly twenty-two times an hour.[61] Some, like Sir John Carr, regarded this feat as 'pernicious and deleterious', and likely seriously to retard 'the improvement of the lower classes of the people'. All the same, he admitted to seeing few examples of drunkenness during his visit in 1807.[62]

By 1810, at the height of the war with Napoleon, the whole country was in distress, especially the manufacturing towns: the effects were seen even in Edinburgh which was outwith the usual run of trade. Glasgow suffered exceedingly, and even the tenant farmers were failing, banks were calling in loans, and many were forced to sell their land at a loss. For example, a 620-acre estate between Glasgow and Edinburgh, beneath which were coal seams, originally valued at £60,000 and later at £57,000, sold in the winter of 1810–11 at a mere £35,000.[63]

11
A CITY IN A LANDSCAPE

'One of the chief gratifications derived from Edinburgh, as a place of residence, is that of great variety with regard to walks, rides, short excursions into the country, and rambles in the very bosom of solitude, and all within a very short distance of the capital.'

A. Campbell, 11.2881

'What a wonderful City Edinburgh is! – What alternation of Height & Depth! – a City looked at in the polish'd back of a Brobdingnag Spoon, held length-ways so enormously stretched-up are the houses! . . . such a section of a wasp's nest . . . the infinity swelling out of the mind, the enormity striking it with wonder . . .'

S.T. Coleridge to Robert Southey, 13 Sept. 1803, *Collected Letters . . .*, II.988f.

That Edinburgh was very much a half-finished city, the uncompleted buildings of the new College and the Register House were for years a constant reminder. It was also a city set in the country, as its hilly topography and the nearness of the Forth with the Fife hills beyond make it, to some extent, to this day. When Coleridge admired Scott's Castle Street house in 1803 it was because it was so 'divinely situated', with its view on one side towards the castle and on the north 'down upon cultivated fields, a fine expanse of water . . . & low pleasing Hills beyond – the Country well-wooded & chearful'.[1] In the same year Elizabeth Grant, as a small girl old enough to register visual impressions, admired the city when they stayed at Blackwood's Hotel at the Princes Street corner of the North Bridge on the way north. Their visit was 'long enough for an abiding impression of that beautiful city to be made on a young mind. The width of the streets, the size of the houses, the brightness and the cleanliness . . . impressed me . . . It was then very far from being what it became a few years later. The new town was but in progress, the untidy appendages of building encumbered the half finished streets, and where afterwards the innumerable gardens spread [the Queen Street gardens], there were then only unsightly greens abandoned to the washerwomen.'[2] That impression of grandeur was to remain with the writer all her life.

Louis Simond in 1810 made the interesting comment that this 'singular town . . . created all at once, within the memory of half its inhabitants', was 'placed in the middle of a beautiful and fertile country, without suburbs, or shabby approach, like other towns which have grown by degrees'.[3] Unfortunately this phenomenon did not survive more than half a century.

In 1801 Alexander Campbell had compared the view from above the hamlet of Dean to a composition by Claude, the Water of Leith winding through the valley between wooded banks, with St Bernard's Well on the right bank as 'the chief ornament of this delightful valley'. On the left bank, among trees, contrasting with the classical temple was the Gothick tower of Dean-haugh and behind, Stockbridge and the house of the painter Henry Raeburn. And farther off, towards the shore, were the villas of Inverleith, Warriston, and 'many snug boxes resorted to in the summer months as sea-bathing quarters', among 'gardens, corn-fields, hedgerows, and inclosures'. Stockbridge itself, known as the village of the Water of Leith, was wretchedly built with the crowded houses that had been common thereabouts until some forty years earlier.

In the glen, St Bernard's Well of medicinal waters, a small circular temple in Roman Doric on a heavily-rusticated base containing the pump room, had been built in 1789 by Alexander Nasmyth. Sir John Carr, during his visit in 1807, liked to walk in the evenings from the centre of the city to admire the scene: Lord Gardenstone's temple above, the well whose water 'mineralised . . . by sulphurated hydrogenous gas', could be sampled on payment of a small sum to the attendant, though it was now rather going out of fashion. The 'verdant banks, elegant villas, the shallow rocky bed of the river, and the little woods' in their rural setting were within hailing distance of the lofty bakers' mills of the Dean.

Henry Raeburn's house, on the north side of the water, had formerly been owned by Walter Ross, WS, keen botanist, collector and man of taste. In a field was 'Lord Gardenstone's tower', a two-storey affair with an outside stair and incorporating fragments of sculpture from the old Edinburgh Cross, a font from St Ninian's Chapel, and other antiquities. In the middle of the field Ross had up-ended a huge block of partly dressed stone, carved with the beginnings of an equestrian figure, reputedly the rudiments of a statue of Oliver Cromwell which the magistrates had diplomatically countermanded at the Restoration. It was said to have lain neglected for 150 years until Ross acquired it.

Ross was troubled by vandals and predators, and when a warning that his property was protected by man-traps and spring-guns had no effect, he procured a human leg from the Infirmary, dressed it in a stocking and buckled shoe, and had it hawked round the village by the local crier, with the story that it had been found in the grounds the previous night and the owner was welcome to have it back.[4]

Cross-country to the east, the road from Leith to Edinburgh was by degrees being built up on both sides with 'elegant rows'; on the west side was the Botanic Garden, removed from its former site within the city. Enclosed by high walls, and overhung by large willows, it contained most indigenous British plants and many exotics, arranged on the Linnaean system. Dr John Hope, late Professor of Botany, had erected a monument to Linnaeus there, in a sequestered, tree-ringed spot.[5] In 1803 the Rev. James Hall complained that although the garden seemed to surpass Oxford's, in the matter of exotics it contained neither Indian corn, sugar cane, coffee, tea, rice nor indigo, all of which he reckoned might have been grown in frames; while neither Edinburgh nor Oxford boasted a cotton plant.[6]

At the city's opposite, western edge, where the chasm of the old Nor' Loch came to an end, was St Cuthbert's, an all-but suburban parish below the castle rock. It consisted of small buildings among gardens, orchards and fields, and had no proper highway. There had been much discussion on how to deal with this, until (according to Alexander Campbell) at the end of the eighteenth century 'a gentleman' (that is to say Clerk of Penicuik) made a trifling wager that, for the sake of being able to drive safely over the ground in his carriage, he was willing to make a straight road about three-quarters of a mile long and twenty paces broad, in a single day's labour.

Amid much scepticism, and in secrecy to avoid appeals and demands for compensation, he laid his plans. It was winter, and there were plenty of laid-off labourers available, glad of a day's pay. At sunrise the men appeared on the ground in hundreds, and were organised into parties for special jobs: to demolish little houses, pull down dykes, root up hedges, fell trees. The ruthless task of destruction continued without cessation through the day, and by nightfall, as wagered, it was accomplished. Once done, the new proto-Lothian road was recognised to be of general 'public utility', not merely to its quixotic creator.

During its eventful creation a 'ludicrous incident', related by Campbell without noticeable sympathy, concerned an old milk-woman living there who in the morning had milked her cows and set off to serve her customers, leaving her 'kail-pot of sheep's-head broth' simmering on the fire. Returning at noon, she found 'neither pot, nor fire, neither house, byre, nor cows', all swept away during the morning's destruction. Campbell does not bother to add whether the poor old soul received any recompense.[7]

Unfortunately for the veracity of this picturesque anecdote, Dr Margaret Wood has demonstrated that it is fantasy from beginning to end. The 'absurd' tale is contradicted by the evidence of the Council's own proposed route. The road was first considered in 1783, was 60 feet wide and nearly completed in two years. The 1804 map shows it then extended as far as Tollcross.

The new road would lead towards, or past, George and Andrew Combe's father's brewery in the insalubrious area below the castle. By the west gate 'lowering basalt rocks' contrasted with 'an area on the right, strewed with the skeletons of horses, the remains of carcases devoured by the swine and dogs of the neighbourhood; a nuisance which calls loudly for removal'. Campbell adds that the pigs were sold to local butchers, who displayed their meat as 'country-fed pork'. Beyond this 'wretched suburb' were the West Port and Grassmarket.[8]

According to the direction from which one approached Edinburgh, therefore, one might pass through pleasant rural areas or dismally poor quarters.

In the New Town itself, no-one could fail to notice that the earliest, eastern end was inferior to later building. The more development progressed westwards, the more elegant the houses, many of them completed 'in the best style of modern architecture'. So judged John Stark, commenting on progress street by street, in his *Picture of Edinburgh* of 1806. By then the First New Town 'wants only a few houses at the western extremity', while the Second was advancing to east and north. The axial George Street, Stark affirmed, 'has no rival in Europe, or perhaps in the world, for the grandeur of its appearance, the elegance of its architecture or its exact uniformity'. Charlotte Square was unfortunately still not complete.

Thistle and Rose Streets, the service streets for 'shopkeepers and others', were of course built in a simpler style. At the far end, Stark declares the half-finished Register House 'a most superb building', the Theatre opposite he dismisses, like everyone else, as small and mean, 'unworthy of the general grandeur of the Scottish metropolis'.

With St James' Square on the rising ground to the east, the standard fell again; not being included in the plan of either First or Second New Town, it had been built more like the Old Town tenements and taller than the rest.

The infilling of 'the great road' to Leith on either side would in a few years (thought Stark) join the capital and its sea-port. 'And, when the present plans are completed, the Scottish metropolis will undoubtedly excel, in grandeur of appearance, in regularity of plan, and in elegance of architecture, every other city in Europe'.[9] For not only was there now more New Town to admire, but its plan, architecture and stone alike won praise. The Swedish industrialist Svedenstierna in 1803 remarked on the broad, straight streets and of course – in contrast to brick-built London – on the dressed stone of most buildings 'in a higher and nobler style than in the English towns'. In this quarter were the houses of the rich and well-born, especially lairds from the nearby countryside, who stayed part of the year in the city. Svedenstierna also observed that the rapid expansion and the new link between Leith and Edinburgh bore witness to the growth of trade and industry.

In 1804 Joseph Mawman also admired the 'excellent white stone', and its building 'agreeable to modern rules of symmetry and elegance, for uniformity, elegance and taste is hardly to be paralleled'.[10] The Swede, in an envious comment on the quantity of fine sandstone and limestone available, with rock deposits below the shallow topsoil, described the British method of preparing mortar, unknown to him, by slaking freshly burnt lime and sand in the open air, leaving it in large heaps for several weeks to 'ripen' on site. 'Now whether the firmness of the plastering and the masonry which were noticed here, stem from this method of preparation or from the nature of the lime . . . it far surpasses anything of ours.' In further contrast to what he saw as the bungling methods of Swedish master builders and workmen, English and Scottish bricklayers used stiffer mortar, spread more thinly and usually with greater care.[11]

As regards house fittings, Sir John Carr commented that Scottish plantations were too recent to provide native timber for New Town houses. All came from the Baltic, the usual source for their houses built in the eighteenth century and later. He also remarks on the 'cheerless look of unpainted wainscots' even in 'respectable houses', which he puts down to 'Caledonian economy', because painted surfaces (he claims) rotted more quickly.[12]

This was adding up to a satisfying whole. As Alexander Campbell, ponderously appreciative, prosaically put it,

> The uniformity of the straight line is happily varied by the transverse sections of the streets, that on either side branch off at right angles and join Queen Street on the north and Princes Street on the south . . . a prospect, than which, when properly illumined in sun-shine, for uniformity pleasing and attractive, cleanliness, neatness, appearance of comfort, and populousness without bustle, hurry, or confusion, hardly such another is any where to be met with.[13]

Yet nearly a decade later Louis Simond noted how besides the college, shops, tradesmen and labour were still mostly in the Old Town, though 'learning begins to be attracted by politeness, and the professors come to live in the region of good dinners and fine ladies'.

As usual (he said) the new had been 'deplored by the old but lauded by the young', and among New Town advantages were its spacious, clean houses, and the changes in entertaining, 'dining at the hour in which they used to sup', and taverns giving way to the playhouse and concert rooms. Even the modern use of umbrellas, in this rainy country, seemed worthy of comment. As for the Old Town's finest houses, Lord Drumore's had been occupied by a chairman – who then moved out because he found it too small; the Duke of Douglas's was now a wheelwright's, and the Marquess of Argyll's was rented out to a hosier.[14]

There was always the problem of the Mound. Campbell in 1801 felt it spoiled the view towards the striking feature of the North Bridge, so like a Roman aqueduct. The Mound's 'heavy and formal appearance distorts the picture'.

Since its inception in 1783, it had been built up to about 800 feet across, and was over 90 feet wide at the junction with the Old Town and 58 on the north side. The west side gradually sank under the weight of soil by about 80 feet, thus absorbing about half of the rubbish. According to Stark in 1806, it was calculated to contain 300,000 cubic yards of earth, and including the half that sank would total 450,000 cubic yards; estimated at three carts per cubic yard this represented 1,350,000 [sic] cart-loads. Pursuing his calculations, Stark reckoned that at 6d a cart its creation would have cost the city £13,750 – but in fact cost 'nothing but the expence of spreading the earth'.[15]

Farther east, throwing down rubbish from Old Town foundations into the Nor' Loch valley had long been common practice, and it was this which had created the mass of 'travelled earth' on top of the natural clay leading to the collapse of the new bridge in 1769. The building in 1806 of the Bank of Scotland beside the Mound, designed by Robert Reid and Richard Crichton, caused similar problems. No permanent footing could be found, only more 'travelled earth', and so much had to be dug out that neighbouring houses became undermined and rents appeared in the walls. When at last they reached base, about as much stone footing had to be laid below ground as above. The bank's protective 'dead wall' on the north side was ornamented with a balustrade.[16]

Louis Simond in 1810 reckoned that the cartloads of earth recorded in 1792 had by now probably doubled. Of this 'stupendous causeway . . . projected *en talus* across the immense ditch' Simond, never slow to find complaint, claimed that because of the lack of buildings here, a violent wind, at times well-nigh a hurricane, swept across both causeway and North Bridge, and that but for the protective wall, seven or eight feet high, built along the causeway, and the infilling of the bridge balustrades, pedestrians would be regularly bowled over.[17] The 'Earthen Mound' was the source of love-hate feelings in the city for many years.

12
LITERARY REVENGES

'The manner in which reviews are in general conducted, has given occasion to much complaint. Indiscriminate praise is concealed censure; censure at random is envy in disguise. The Edinburgh Reviewers have hitherto avoided these extremes . . . an impartiality which no party zeal has yet pretended to call in question . . . risen to be the first publication of the kind in Britain or in Europe'.

J. Stark, *Picture of Edinburgh*, Edinburgh, 1806, 255

'That on which I chiefly rest my contempt of the *Edinburgh Review* is its utter *feebleness* . . . as intellectual power in all those parts of knowledge which are employed about the indefinite . . . Their papers on mathematics, I am told, have gained them much credit, but I must ask *with whom*?'

Thomas De Quincey to his brother Henry, 8 June 1811, Alec H. Japp, *De Quincey Memorials*, London, 1891, II.112f.

The *Edinburgh Review* continued to arouse controversy, more rather than less as years passed, and literary passions in general were so high during the first decades of the nineteenth century that at least four famous duels were fought, none actually in Edinburgh but all concerned with its writers. If the word farcical can be applied to a duel, that between Francis Jeffrey and the poet Thomas Moore was probably the nearest event, or non-event, of 1806. Although it happened not in Edinburgh but on the outskirts of London it was of cardinal importance to Edinburgh's history. The literary world must have been full of gentlemen itching to point a pistol at Jeffrey, and Moore was the one who did.

The Irishman Tom Moore,[1] who loved his encounters with the aristocracy, was in London in July 1806 awaiting the *Review*'s latest issue, with a critique of his new *Odes and Epistles,* but he did not see a copy until he reached Lady Donegal's in Worthing. The contempt with which Jeffrey dismissed his poems so infuriated him that he wound himself up by degrees to the pitch of contemplating a duel. Poet and critic had never met. The review, written in a spirit of irony, would have offended the mildest of men. It claimed that Moore 'may boast, if the boast can please him, of being the most licentious of modern versifiers, and the most poetical of those who, in our own times, have devoted their talents to the propagation of immorality. We regard his book, indeed, as a public nuisance.'[2]

When the furious poet returned to London, he found that by coincidence Jeffrey had also arrived on a short visit, and enlisting his friend Dr Thomas Hume as second, he wrote Jeffrey a challenge, on the grounds of accusing Moore of 'a deliberate intention to corrupt the minds of my readers'. To make his point doubly sure, he added, 'To this I beg leave to answer, You are a liar; yes sir, a liar.'[3]

There was always only one response to such an accusation. Jeffrey referred Hume to Francis Horner (who would have acted for him in the abortive duel with David Hume the younger), and the two seconds fixed a meeting for the very next day at the rural area of Chalk Farm, much used for duels. Both parties were complete innocents in the matter of duelling or even of pistols. Moore asked Samuel Rogers to lend him a pair, but Rogers refused, so he applied to his friend William Spencer.[4] Eventually Moore was referred to a shop in Bond Street. He spent some time writing valedictory letters, including to Viscount Strangford, to whom he drank a last health, and to his friends Mary Godfrey and Lady Donegal.[5]

After a solitary dinner he went out and bought powder and bullets 'in such large quantities . . . as would have done for a score of duels'. Then back to Spencer who had procured pistols, which he gave to Moore with the warning that they were really too good for the job. On to Hume, where he spent the night, though knowing that Hume had no spare linen, he first took a hackney back to his own lodgings and surreptitiously purloined his own sheets, to avoid arousing suspicion of the illegal duel.

Tommy actually slept so soundly that he had to be awoken by Hume, who had engaged a surgeon to go with them in the hired chaise. At Chalk Farm they found Jeffrey and Horner already arrived, with John Murray and one or two other friends ('no man, I believe', observed the marvelling Moore, 'could ever boast of a greater number'), all hanging around to await the fatal moment. The appropriate bows and formalities were exchanged.

'Then it was that, for the first time, my excellent friend Jeffrey and I met face to face. He was standing with the box which contained the pistols in his hand, while Horner was looking anxiously around.' They seemed already to have found a suitable place, screened by trees on one side, and the two seconds went aside to try and load the pistols, at which they were lamentably inexpert. The duellists, who took a liking to one another on sight, were left alone.

Jeffrey broke the silence. 'What a beautiful morning it is!' – 'Yes,' agreed Moore with a rueful smile, 'a morning made for better purposes.' Jeffrey's response was a sigh.

They walked about, but found themselves in sight of the 'operations', and

Moore nervously related a similar occurrence at a duel of the Irish barrister Billy Egan, when his fiery little antagonist angrily shouted to him to keep away. 'Don't make yourself unairy, my dear fellow,' said Egan, 'sure isn't it bad enough to take the dose, without being by at the mixing up!'

To this Jeffrey barely had time for an answering smile before their seconds, who had been measuring the distance, came to place the sworn contestants, both short men, and hand them their guns.

At this breathless moment, with the seconds retired, guns raised and aimed, and the two nervous duellists awaiting only the signal to fire, some police officers who had crept up unseen, in the nick of time rushed from behind a hedge and bore down on them. One struck with his staff from behind Jeffrey, knocking his pistol into the field, another ran to seize Moore. The crestfallen, or more likely relieved, group were then ordered into their carriages and escorted back into London to Bow Street.

On the way Hume told Tom Moore that, as Horner knew even less about pistols than he did, he had had to load them both. On arrival at Bow Street they sent to friends who could provide bail, Moore sending for Spencer. Neither party had suggested they be separated, and they were shown into the same waiting-room.

The encounter now took an even more bizarre turn. Jeffrey, stretching himself out on one of the benches, was soon launched into a literary discussion, the subject that came naturally to his mind now the anxieties of the duel were behind him. Moore, not at the time much of a literary talker, said little, and the ebullient Jeffrey poured forth fluently in his odd hybrid accent, 'in every variety of array that an ever rich and ready wardrobe of phraseology could supply'. He admitted afterwards that he had taken a fancy to Moore from the first moment they met in the field, and as Moore felt the same, the Bow Street runners' arrival was greatly to be blessed.

Samuel Rogers, according to his own account, was with Spencer when Moore's message came to bail him out, having called to learn the latest about the duel. Spencer said pettishly that he could not go to Bow Street, 'for it was already 12 o'clock, and he had to be dressed by 4!' Hence it was Rogers who went to the police to offer bail.[6]

In the hustle of arranging bail and leaving the police station, the pistols were forgotten. Hume was off to the country, so that Moore had to return and collect them, but at Bow Street he was given a 'not entirely civil' refusal, on the grounds that on examining them, the magistrates had had suspicions. The awkward truth was that while Moore's pistol was found to contain a bullet, Jeffrey's was not. It looked like some kind of underhand conspiracy.

The dismayed Moore hastened to Horner's chambers and luckily found him at home, and reassuring: 'Don't mind what these fellows say. I myself saw your friend put the bullet into Jeffrey's pistol, and shall go with you instantly to the office to set the matter right.' They went together, Horner's statement was accepted and the pistols were returned to them, with the one bullet (which Moore's publisher Carpenter later begged as a memento). It seems likely that the bungling Hume had been unable to lodge both bullets securely and that one had simply fallen out.

Reaction now set in. Moore's eloquent envoi the previous day to Miss Godfrey being 'all gone for nothing' he had to write again feeling 'very like a ninny'. It emerged that Spencer, though sworn to secrecy, had told Lord Fincastle[7] at dinner, and the latter had alerted Bow Street. The police gave the story to the papers, including the matter of the single bullet, and the press made the most of it; one Irish reporter maximised – or rather minimised – the affair by calling it a 'pellet', that is, of paper. Horner signed a statement to correct the errors, but Hume took fright and refused to counter-sign, causing an estrangement with Moore which lasted for years. As the statement never appeared, the ill-natured gossip continued.

There was still a question whether the duel should go ahead. General Fitzpatrick assured Rogers that even if Moore sent a second challenge, Jeffrey ought not to accept. Luckily the argument was pre-empted by a reconciliation. By arrangement with Rogers and Horner the pair met at Rogers's house, and shook hands in his back garden.[8]

Jeffrey made Moore a handsome apology and admitted that many 'exceptionable' things appeared in the *Review*, though he maintained it was fair in judgment. Moore later recounted to Joseph Atkinson how Jeffrey told him in the most friendly way that 'if he had known the least of the character which I hold . . . he never should have written such an article . . . and in short was very sorry it had ever appeared'. He followed this up in another article, an appropriate letter was published in the *Post*, and Moore was at last both relieved of resentment and happy at acquiring a valued new friend. Jeffrey, he declared, was 'a most excellent, gentlemanlike fellow', and hoped people would tell everyone so.

Miss Godfrey, having heard the whole story, wrote back delightedly in October that the most pleasing aspect was how 'Jeffrey took a great fancy to you from the first moment he saw you in the field of battle, pistol in hand to kill him'; and that his conduct had won Moore general praise. 'But never take a pistol in your hand again while you live!'[9]

There were several postscripts to the affair, one as late as 1809, when Byron published 'English Bards and Scotch Reviewers', in which he wrote sarcastically of Jeffrey and made the most of the duel libel:

Can none remember the eventful day,
That ever glorious, almost fateful fray,
When Little's leadless pistol met his eye,
And Bow-Street Myrmidons stood laughing by?[10]

This work was anonymous, but when Moore discovered the author he wrote to Byron from Dublin (1 Jan. 1810) to challenge – almost literally – his accuracy. Another duel might well have resulted.[11] As Byron left England soon afterwards Moore was not even certain that he had received the letter, and as long as twenty months later (October 1811) he begged Byron to write a friendly explanation as he would be 'uncomfortable' unless he put the record straight. Byron, however, replied that the verses really concerned 'my worst literary enemy' (presumably Jeffrey), and that he could not retract a falsehood he had never uttered. In the uneasy, reproachful correspondence that followed Moore became as prickly as Byron, until they referred the matter to Samuel Rogers, who once again arranged a dinner and the misunderstandings were settled – without resorting to a duel.[12]

13
THE LITERARY SCENE

'The genius of Scott and of Jeffrey had made [Edinburgh] the seat at once of the most popular poetry, and the most brilliant criticism, that then existed.'

Henry Cockburn, *Life of Jeffrey*, 1.160, f.n.

'She is a literary lady, a complete *Blue stocking* . . . we are all afraid of *her*; even the men are quite jealous of her metaphysical skill and political knowledge.'

[Fictitious description] in James Hogg, *The Spy*, No.34, 20 April 1811

'[There are] the *Philosophers*, who are also wits, and the *Enthusiasts* who are also Loyalists . . . with such a sentiment to which your virtuous Falkland and our great Montrose fell victims. To this party, my friends more particularly belong. The Philosophers, whom we consider as disguised republicans, value themselves on their prejudice against prejudices, and on general incredulity. We, again, believe all that our fathers believed; . . . Now this enrages the Sophs beyond measure; their literary pride is all in arms at the very idea that gentle manners or generous sentiments should precede the existence of the sciences . . . on the same principle they treat female genius and female productions with unqualified scorn, never mentioning any thing of the kind but with a sneer.'

Mrs Grant of Laggan to John Hatsell, 27 Nov. 1806, *Memoirs & Correspondence*, London, 1844 I.81

This was the viewpoint of the blue-stocking author Mrs Anne Grant of Laggan,[1] then living in Stirling, after a visit to Edinburgh in the year of the Jeffrey-Moore duel.

The *Edinburgh Review* was in its glory. Despite the 'absurd' attacks on Wordsworth, whose poems Robert Gillies supposed Jeffrey had never really read, it was now generally seen as the most original periodical ever to appear in the city, and one designed to be as enduring as literature.

Mrs Grant's summing-up was more than a little tongue-in-cheek. In particular, the ladies had begun to make an impressive showing in the literary field, although nothing as dramatic as Jeffrey's duel enlivened the time. In the spring of 1808 a new figure on the scene was the playwright Joanna Baillie, with her sister Agnes. Miss Baillie (neither sister married), born in 1762 and educated in Glasgow, published her first verses in 1790, followed over the years by three collections of plays in 1796, 1802 and 1812.

During their Edinburgh visit in 1808 the sisters stayed with the Scotts in Castle Street. In 1810 Miss Baillie wrote her most famous play, Scott's great favourite, *The Family Legend.*

Like several contemporary women (and men) writers, Miss Baillie was very short. Plainly dressed, 'small, prim, and Quaker-like looking', she had few personal attractions, insignificant to the point of commonplace and with a 'mean and shuffling gait'. On the other hand, she had a pleasingly gentle, 'well-bred' manner, with none of the affectations displayed by certain blue-stocking ladies.[2]

Jeffrey's criticism of Miss Baillie in 1803 had aroused much resentment, and Scott in particular felt that his caustic wit and erudition sorted ill with works of imagination (1808). During Miss Baillie's visit, both Mrs Elizabeth Hamilton and the Duchess of Gordon tried to arrange a 'conversation' – as Rogers had with Jeffrey and Moore – by which they could be reconciled, but the lady coldly declined. Yet three years later Jeffrey made amends by comparing her with Southey, Wordsworth and Coleridge (1811).

The success of *The Family Legend* in 1810 established Miss Baillie's reputation, and while she and her sister mostly lived in London, she became equally well-known in Edinburgh.

Unlike Elizabeth Hamilton, Joanna Baillie never adopted the courtesy title of 'Mrs' affected by many unmarried lady writers. Mrs Hamilton and her sister (another pair who never married), after living some time in Bath, also revisited Edinburgh in 1808, dividing the time between there and the Lake District. In November Mrs Hamilton writes from 53 George Street, possibly the home of cousins, where she spent a season almost continuously until the following June. Then Edinburgh's easterly winds, which it boasted in such 'perfection', returned with a severity that caused widespread illness.

Mrs Siddons was then performing at the theatre, and, although families were leaving and closing their houses for the summer, her audiences seemed just as great. Mrs Hamilton, except when she did not feel well enough, took a stage-box for every evening's performance, in order to study Mrs Siddons's acting as closely as possible. She thought her more admirable than ever, especially as Queen Catherine in *Henry VIII.* Meanwhile she was occupied in the tedious revision and condensing of her *Letters on Education* for a cheap edition.[3]

Much of Mrs Hamilton's life-story is admittedly a chronicle of recurring illness (attacks of gout, bad colds and so on) and uneventful travels with her sister throughout the British Isles, usually staying with friends. When in Edinburgh they lived in George Street and her letters show that, for example, when the Bishop of Moray and his family took a house one season just opposite, in spite of his being armed with the usual letter of introduction, the author's poor health prevented any acquaintance beyond 'an exchange of messages and notes'.[4]

In Ireland in 1813 the sisters met Miss Edgeworth, who in the same year as *Cottagers of Glenburnie* (1808) had published her *Tales of Fashionable Life*, an instant success and highly praised in the *Review* by Jeffrey for its 'sober sense and inexhaustible invention' even asserting the stories' superiority to much of the history and 'solemn philosophy' that came his way.[5] On her side Miss Edgeworth thought *Cottagers* 'will do a vast deal of good, and besides it is extremely interesting, which all good books are not . . .' When they met, she felt her fellow-authoress even improved on acquaintance, 'so good-humoured, so cheerful, so little disposed to exact attention . . . so ready to give everybody their merits . . . and so hopeful of the reformation of even the faults and vices of the world.'[6]

Mrs Hamilton's *Cottagers,* however, did not altogether please. Charles Kirkpatrick Sharpe complained to his mother that although 'very just and very amusing . . . she hath written it in such bad grammar that I am grieved to the heart about it, for she is an excellent woman', but that 'in this case she must be condemned and executed without mercy'.[7]

In the summer of 1814, cold and dismal, 'more than two months of bitter east-wind, and continued drought' were followed by cold rains in July. Green crops and soft fruit were quite destroyed, to the ruin of the poor who relied on growing strawberries to increase their income. 'Some who pay hundreds of rent will not sell ten pints of berries this season.' Further, with the end of the war (as it seemed to be) sending people to France in droves, it was a mis-fortune for Scottish innkeepers. In the Trossachs not an English voice was to be heard. Mrs Hamilton was much amused by the conflicting accounts of those who had returned, and hoped for more sensible comments from the Rev. Archibald Alison's sons, Patrick Fraser Tytler and 'Mr S.A.'[8]

Poor health prevented her own wish to visit France, and her last years were spent largely in Edinburgh. 'But the better I become acquainted with the French character and manners, the less do I feel inclined to their society.' The sisters were also detained in Edinburgh by making a home for the brother of unmarried cousins, who had lived in France with friends of his mother's since he was a child, and was now at Edinburgh University; meanwhile one of his sisters was still with them.

In 1815 when they were living at 114 George Street, Mrs Hamilton's sister's health was giving concern, and she benefited from a seven-week stay at Pitcaithly Wells near Perth. The brother-and-sister cousins returned to them in the autumn, and 'Mr C.' felt he learned more from the Edinburgh lectures than those in Paris. 'Nothing appears to be more astonishing', wrote Mrs

Hamilton, 'than that any people in their senses should take their children to France for their education. It is, however, not seldom done.' This crisp maxim is in the last of Mrs Hamilton's surviving letters.[9]

She loved helping young people, especially in developing their minds. During her last years, gouty, rheumatic and deaf, she sketched another novel, but was physically sadly limited, turned to religious works with a practical object, and in 1815 published *Hints* addressed to the patrons of schools, recommending the Pestalozzi teaching method.

It was her last completed work. The deaths of several friends saddened her closing years, as did a depression caused by a serious eye complaint affecting her whole system. In May 1816 the sisters proposed to settle for a time in England, but once arrived at Harrogate Mrs Hamilton was so exhausted that they had to rest, and despite treatment she gradually sank, dying there, barely in her sixtieth year, on 20 July.

Charles Kirkpatrick Sharpe, antiquarian, writer, collector, eccentric, was a close friend of Scott, who was ten years his senior. He was born in 1781, one of the twelve children of Charles Sharpe, of Hoddam, Dumfriesshire, and Eleonora Renton, of Lammerton, who had been married at Drummond Lodge in Edinburgh in 1770. Descended from the Earls of Mar and Lennox, with distant Stuart connections, Sharpe was also a great-grandson of the famous Susanna, Countess of Eglintoun. He completed his education at Oxford, and from youth amused himself in composing satirical verse.

His first overture to Scott was written in 1802 from Hoddam Castle, offering two ballads for inclusion in *Border Minstrelsy,* which he had read 'with much delight'. One was 'The Twa Corbies', written down by Miss Jean Erskine of Alva from an old woman's recitation. Scott replied cordially and they continued to correspond, but the third intended volume took a long time to appear. They first met in 1803 when Sharpe, by then a BA, was still at Christ Church, and Scott called on his way to London and was invited to breakfast. 'He is dreadfully lame', wrote Sharpe, 'and much too poetical. He spouts without mercy' and paid high-flown compliments. Initially it was Scott who got the better impression, promising Sharpe a copy of the new book and inviting him to Lasswade. Sharpe accepted, which he admitted to his mother was 'a little fib'.[10]

A couple of years later, however, he was 'in raptures' over Scott's *Lay.* Despite imperfections 'the beauties so far exceed the blemishes, that I wish to forget the latter exist'.[11] Shortly before *Marmion* was published in 1808, Sharpe produced *Metrical Legends,* which earned Scott's congratulations. 'The first literary child always gives most trouble and anxiety'.[12] Sharpe on his side used to send Scott useful material and amusing sketches, notably his caricature of Queen Elizabeth, 'the inimitable virago', as Scott called her, being tossed in the air dancing the *lavolta* with Lord Leicester.[13]

As he grew older Sharpe grew more freakish, and was oblivious to his appearance. The style of clothes – perhaps the very same ones – he had worn at Oxford at the beginning of the century served him until his death years later. There were his famous 'green umbrella, the crosier-shaped horn handle, and its long brass point; . . . thread-stockings . . . pumps, tied with profuse ribbon; with his ever-faded frock-coat, and his cravat of that downy bulging character which Brummell repealed', and an 'ante-Brummellite neckerchief (not a tie) which projected in many wreaths like a great poultice'.[14] When everyone else was wearing top-boots, he still preferred stockings and 'pumps of early Oxford cut', and a blue surtout. Even his light-brown wig was of the 'Brutus' style of his youth. It was a mystery how these clothes, including the umbrella, had always seemed old and worn. Yet despite his outer garments' 'frousy mouldiness', Sharpe's linen was always scrupulously white, matched by his mind, which in age retained an 'internal freshness . . . an ever-blooming garden of intellectual flowers', while his manners like his tastes were stately and old-world.[15]

Thomas Campbell, meanwhile, completed *Gertrude of Wyoming*, begun in 1806 and taking well over two years to reach proof stage. He had hoped Constable would publish his *Selections from British Poets*, which he had commissioned but seemed to have forgotten, and wrote anxiously at tedious length, first to Jeffrey and then, when he had no reply, to beg Henry Cockburn to intervene lest he had offended Jeffrey by saddling him with a troublesome task: he was more concerned at losing Jeffrey's regard than Constable's. Early in 1809 it turned out that Jeffrey, far from offended, had asked Constable to reply direct, and it was the latter who had done nothing. At this stage Campbell released himself from the Constable commission and sought another publisher.[16]

In April Jeffrey was highly complimentary over *Gertrude*, criticising only its shortness and over-refinement – it needed 'some of the tough pearls of your fancy'. The Rev. Archibald Alison was also delighted with it, and when he passed it to Dugald Stewart to read, Stewart took it away to study in solitude and (said Alison) 'returned to them as pale as a ghost, and literally sick with weeping', while Mrs Stewart was rapturous, and unlike the others thought the length perfect. They were probably the more emotionally affected because of the recent death of their son. Jeffrey's tribute in the *Review* was glowing: 'a polished and pathetic poem in the old style of English pathos and poetry', comparable to 'The Castle of Indolence', or to Spenser. The new collection included shorter poems, such as 'Lord Ullin's Daughter'. Some thought the obscurer parts of *Gertrude* almost unintelligible, and so they remained, for Campbell hated revising once anything had reached print. He earned equal praise for the work from America.[17]

This was and continued to be a time when not only genius flourished but talent from however circumscribed beginnings would find its way. The shortlived Alexander Murray, born in 1775, was son of the second marriage of a poor Galloway shepherd – a background not unlike John Leyden's, his exact contemporary, and like him he was nine before he went to school. Like him, too, Murray early showed a passion for reading, and spent much time with Leyden when, later than most students, he went to the University. He had a natural gift for languages, a talent spotted by an uncle who sent him to school, and in spite of a serious illness and sporadic attendance Murray learned Latin, Greek, Hebrew and French, discovered Milton's poetry, and attempted an epic on King Arthur.

In 1794, through friends' interest, he entered Edinburgh University, when Dr Baird and colleagues who examined him were astonished at his fluency in languages and even in a Hebrew psalm. A bursary, eked out by private teaching, launched Murray on a successful career.[18]

He contributed to the *Scots Magazine,* and succeeded as editor in 1802 when Leyden retired. Constable commissioned him to write the memoir and edit the Abyssinian travels of James Bruce of Kinnaird, and for ten months he stayed at Bruce's house, an uneasy guest because of his awkward manners: his host complained when he wanted to remove valuable papers to Edinburgh, and generally he treated the house 'as an inn'. Murray eventually succeeded in the task, however, and the work published in 1805 enhanced his reputation. In 1806 he became minister of Urr. In January 1807 he analysed the current state of the *Edinburgh Review.*[19]

In 1812 Murray was appointed Professor of Oriental languages at Edinburgh, and wrote a history of languages, which was published posthumously, for unfortunately he died only the next year.

James Hogg, born in Ettrick on the Borders in 1770 and employed as a shepherd, had tried and failed farming in Dumfriesshire and returned to his native Ettrick. By the age of thirty he had begun to publish verses and in 1807 began to make a name for himself with *The Mountain Bard*, but did not move to Edinburgh until 1810. Much earlier he had made the acquaintance of Walter Scott, and contributed material to his *Border Minstrelsy.*

He first visited the Scotts in 1802, when Scott unintentionally alarmed the socially untutored poet by warning him that his wife was 'a foreigner . . . As dark as a blackberry and does not speak the broad Scots so well as you and me'. Hogg, picturing 'a kind of blackamore' whom Scott had presumably married for money, was taken aback when confronted by 'one of the most beautiful and handsome creatures . . . A brunette certainly with raven hair and large black eyes . . . I found her quite affable and she spoke English very well', except for pronouncing 'th' as 'd' and being unable to sound an 'h'. She regularly addressed the poet as 'Mr 'Og'. While Hogg could understand her, it was his replies that Scott had to interpret for his wife.

The homely Hogg was always made welcome in her house, but Mrs Scott was cold to many celebrities, and Jeffrey and especially Brougham she detested. To Jeffrey, after his unfavourable review of *Marmion*, she would never even speak.[20]

14
THE LAW AND THE OFFICES

'This city has advantages, including its being the capital of Scotland, its old reputation, and its external beauties, which have enabled it, in a certain degree, to resist the centralising tendency, and have hitherto always applied it with a succession of eminent men.'

Henry Cockburn, *Life of Jeffrey*, 1.160

'From about 1800, everything purely Scotch has been fading.'

Ibid., f.n.

Walter Scott's daily job, which sustained him alike through his years of affluence and ruin, was his prosaic law appointment. In the eighteenth century, and for some time after, the majority of young Scots of the professional and upper classes studied law and qualified as advocates, whether or not they intended to practise – which often they did not. The Parliament House, centre of legal Edinburgh, was a kind of parallel to the University, a venue for young aspirants as well as drudges. During the session, from October until July, with brief holiday intervals, the profession was on duty there every day.

Thomas Carlyle vividly describes how he first saw it in November 1809, when he and an older schoolfellow, Tom Smail, arrived in Edinburgh on foot after an 81-mile walk from Ecclefechan. Smail, though described by the censorious nineteen-year-old Thomas as lacking scholarship and 'very innocent, conceited, insignificant, but strict-minded orthodox', was at least more familiar with the city than Thomas, a total stranger. It was afternoon, and having secured cheap but clean lodgings in the poor quarter of Simon Square, south of the town, the youths set off to explore. They came to the High Street, the Luckenbooths, St Giles', and at length Smail took Thomas into the Parliament House.

He was amazed at the dimly lit interior, with its bustling throng of men of the law, many in their wigs and black gowns, advocates eagerly conversing with judges in red velvet sitting on little enclosed thrones, and over all a 'grinding din'. The criers of the court contributed 'wildly plangent lamentable' calls. At this busiest period of the courts' existence the crowd was far greater than it would be in later years, after many of its functions had been transferred to county jurisdictions.

When the morning session ended at two o'clock many advocates and officials would have left the court, and the only distinguished figure Carlyle could identify was John Clerk, by his 'grim strong countenance with its black far-projecting brows and look of great sagacity'. Yet for all he knew, the throng might have included Jeffrey, Cranstoun, Cockburn or Walter Scott.[1]

Scott, as Clerk of the Session, would indeed probably have left at two. This post had long been held by George Home until his health broke down under the job, and Scott was appointed his successor by Pitt's Government, ratified in 1807 by the short Whig ministry. The circumstances were peculiar, and unsatisfactory for Scott, because Home nominally retained the office and for several years still drew the whole salary, until at last he retired on a pension in 1812, and Scott thereafter had the not unreasonable salary of £1500.

The work, which occupied him every forenoon during the Session from 9.30 a.m., consisted in taking down the decisions of the court, seated below the bench, and signing various papers. Scott's rapid, legible writing was ideal for the task, which although dry and exacting left him free during the legal vacations, especially in summer, and every day from the afternoon onwards.[2] Then he would delight in meeting a regular stream of visitors and showing them Edinburgh's historical sights. At the same time his fertile mind was engaged in antiquarian research, editing, reviewing, biography and history, not to mention the narrative poems which established his fame, the *Lay* in 1805 and *Marmion* in 1808. At Constable's suggestion Scott even worked on an eighteen-volume of Dryden which encompassed a memoir and a history of English literature of the age. But Constable being a Whig publisher, the devoted Tory Scott decided to join with John Ballantyne, who, eager to start business in Edinburgh, took up new and handsomely equipped offices which far outshone Constable's dingy High Street shop. To Constable's annoyance, Scott became virtually a partner of the Ballantyne brothers.

John Ballantyne also took a house in South Hanover Street, and at his dinner parties Scott, whose disposition had not a little of the peacock, would sometimes 'parade in full dress, with white silk stockings, a scarlet silk under-waistcoat, and uniform coat of the Border Club'. The guests were usually distinguished in the musical and theatrical world, such as John Kemble, and Henry Mackenzie, always a theatre buff; there were also Sir Brooke Boothby,[3] William Erskine, later Lord Kinedder, and others. It was walking back one day from Ballantyne's shop with Robert Gillies that Scott invited the young man to dine, promising to read him the start of his new poem and ask his opinion.

On this occasion Scott was laughing at the pedantry of the blue-stocking writer Anna Seward, and his amanuensis Weber classed Boothby, now living in Edinburgh, as of the same 'Della Cruscan School', but Scott disagreed as he judged Boothby to write with simple good taste. He went on to talk of aspiring poets who pestered him to read their trashy verses, and of resolutely non-poetic readers like Lord Hermand, who was said to have only got as far as line 2 of 'The Lady' and boggled over the identity of Monan's rill, quite forgetting the poem. Another was Malcolm Laing, who was solely interested in spotting errors.

As promised, Scott read them his 'Don Roderick', written in a new style, but as a reader he was dreadfully monotonous. They talked of ghosts, including one Scott said he had seen near his house at Ashestiel. Weber returned to his labours, and the others, having disposed of a magnum (except for Buchanan, nervous of the gout, joined Scott's young family upstairs, and were charmed by the rendering of Scottish airs on the harp by the visiting lady music teacher. By about 8 o'clock Scott was ready for 'Don Roderick' once more, and was all for Gillies staying with the family and talking about books until they took supper at 10 o'clock; but Gillies had to leave for another engagement. Knocking at Scott's library door on his way out to borrow a book, he found the poet busy writing and correcting. Scott reckoned that before he left for his office next day he would have completed eight or ten more stanzas.

Gillies was one of the few for whom Scott broke his rule of not entertaining on Sundays or Mondays, when he was always busy and his 'stout coachman' was directed to say he was not at home; but for Gillies, 'I don't mind you; because you make no botheration, and seldom stay long.'

Lord Buchan's brother Henry Erskine thought highly of Charles Hope, who was an outstanding speaker and probably the most eloquent of his fellow-advocates. Hope's English education had conferred on him 'pure' diction – unlike Jeffrey's – a self-possessed manner and sound professional knowledge. Pitt and Fox both admired his speech in his own defence as Lord Advocate.[4] In 1804 when the Whigs took office, Hope was automatically offered the top legal office of Lord Justice Clerk. At that time he generously insisted that Henry Erskine ought to have it, and personally took the news of the offer to him. Erskine, however, following his party's advice, declined the office. So it went to Hope after all, and Erskine was greatly impressed by his gesture.[5] Erskine briefly succeeded Henry Dundas as Lord Advocate in 1783, but was then superseded by Ilay Campbell (1784).

In 1806 John Clerk succeeded as Solicitor General.

The career of Erskine's younger brother Thomas, who died in 1823, was more continuously successful; he served in both army and navy, and after studying at Lincoln's Inn was called to the English bar, where he took on important libel cases and defended politicians and reformers in treason trials. He was a sound jury lawyer, and a valuable counterbalance to the savage repression following the French Revolution. In 1783–84 and again from 1790 to 1806 he was MP for Portsmouth until created 1st Baron Erskine (1806), and briefly became Lord Chancellor.[6]

Another advocate was to make a useful career in a different official field. At the end of the eighteenth century Scotland's public records had deteriorated to such disarray that in 1800 a Select Committee of the House of Commons recommended their complete reorganisation. Nobody, however, knew how to undertake such a task, certainly not the Commissioners then appointed, who included William Pitt and Chief Baron Dundas, and would have been content to publish a hastily compiled scrap-book of items. Dundas urged Lord Frederick Campbell, who had the sinecure of Lord Clerk Register, to find a qualified editor.

James Ferrier, who was one of the Sub-Commissioners, recommended the advocate Thomas Thomson, a friend of Scott, Jeffrey and the legal circle;[7] in accepting, Thomson warned the Commissioners that the job would require much time and care. The Commissioners, who consistently under-estimated the time needed, expected him to produce an 'authentic' publication of the Scottish Acts which they could then present to Parliament.

Thomson soon earned Lord Frederick's respect for his professional approach, but only his detailed explanation to Lord Glenbervie,[8] who was spending a few months in Scotland, eventually convinced the Commission (1805) of the danger of too precipitate action. Manuscripts had to be assembled from such various sources as foreign libraries, fellow-scholars must be consulted. Then there was the condition of the manuscripts themselves, many of which had not been examined for years; some had been 'farmed out' by sinecure office-holders, and many were damaged, unbound, or incomplete.

Thomson's researches meanwhile took him to London, where he was happy to have a reunion with Francis Horner and Sydney Smith (1804). Horner, at first suspicious of Thomson's 'desultory' initial knowledge of the subject, now praised his 'excellent judgment, in the selection of the best sorts [of documents]. Then his temper is so manly and cheerful. . . .'[9]

It had need to be. To the detriment of his law career, the work now kept Thomson in Register House, where his inevitable clean sweep earned the opposition of old-established clerks, who resented intrusion into their unreformed office. Thomson, unable to find anyone locally qualified to bind documents, employed Mrs Weir, an old lady from London. A more durable paper for copying was introduced by degrees, and a new permanent ink, invented by Dr Hope and Sir George Mackenzie.

Thomson was fortunate in his clerk, Mr A. Macdonald, an experienced antiquarian, skilled in the orderly arrangement of records. In his capacity as Thomson's aide for nearly forty years, it was said there was never a cross word between them.[10] By degrees the pair trained a team of qualified assistants.

When in January 1806 the Commissioners agreed to create a permanent, salaried post of Deputy to the Lord Clerk Register, to be offered to an advocate, Lord Frederick formally proposed Thomson, and the commission was executed that June.

He was already working on an abridgment of 'retours' (returns to the Chancery of Services of heirs), dating from the seventeenth century, eventually published between 1811 and 1816; and on a compilation of recorded charters from Robert the Bruce to James I in 1424, to be published in 1814 as *Registrum Magni Sigilli.*

When Thomson embarked on his job the Register House, like the University, was standing unfinished. It had already been twice abandoned, first in 1788 when the funds granted from the forfeited estates ran out; then, although work was resumed with a further grant, left still incomplete when Robert Adam died in 1792. So it was to remain until after the war ended. At this time about two-thirds of the building was finished: the main front, half of each wing, and the dome, under which was installed Mrs Ann Damer's marble statue of King George III. The office was already equipped to take the records removed from the Session House, where they had lain for many generations.

Lord Glenbervie proved a valuable ally and frequent correspondent. In the spring of 1809 Thomson secured the passing of an Act for better regularising the Public Records of Scotland, and thereafter until 1819 presented annual reports.[11]

Glenbervie consulted Thomson over the further education of his young son Frederick,[12] sending him to study at Edinburgh in the winter of 1805–06, and then on to take a degree at Oxford. Meanwhile (November 1809) he put him to study under Playfair and Stewart, to learn 'as much Scotch law as his time will allow'.[13] Frederick brought three other Oxonians, Lord Dysart, Mr Fazakerley and Mr Hartop, to join in studies with Stewart; but he then fell seriously ill, when Thomson looked after him. On his recovery his father asked Thomson to persuade the youth to join the Speculative Society, as good practice in 'courage to bear failing, and to try and try again'.[14] Frederick's early death while still in his twenties ended a promising career.

15
SCHOOLS, STUDENTS AND APPRENTICES

'From the time of Hume and Robertson, we have been fortunate in Edinburgh, in possessing a succession of distinguished men, who have kept up this salutary connection between the learned and the fashionable world . . . how superior the society of Edinburgh is to that of most other places of the same size, and how much of that superiority is owing to the cordial combination of the two aristocracies, of rank and of letters – of both of which it happens to be the chief provincial seat.'

Edinburgh Annual Register, 1819, 324 [on biography of John Playfair]

'What would I not give, to pass a month, a week, or even a day in that city!'

Benjamin Rush to his son James, then a student in Edinburgh, 17 Aug. 1809, *Letters*, II.1015

Private schools and teachers continued to flourish in Edinburgh side by side with the High School, whose limited curriculum they supplemented. Robert Christison, whose father became Professor of Humanity and was himself to become a famous toxicologist and Professor of Medical Jurisprudence in Edinburgh,[1] was born in 1797 and sent at the age of six to the 'English School' in Drummond Street under Mr Mylne.[2] Mylne in the Old Town and Mr Fulton in the New shared the reputation of Edinburgh's best teachers, the former as grammarian, the latter as elocutionist. Mylne, a short, sturdy man of 'great energy, and a powerful squint', was 'a fair classical scholar, a dabbler in science, a squire of dames . . . a man of wit, not without a dash of eccentricity'.

Later at the High School, both Robert and his brother John did well under its new master George Irvine, an amiable man with the then rare ability to rule well but kindly. Their contemporaries included the usual bunch of future celebrities and sons of existing celebrities, among them two of the Dundases: David, third son of John, WS, who later became a QC, Judge-Advocate General in England and a Privy Councillor, and Robert, eldest son of the Chief Baron, who was to inherit Arniston. There were also John Dalzell, youngest son of the Professor of Greek, who became an advocate but died young; and the delicate, generally loved Andrew Combe, 'a constant valetudinarian'.

Not all the boys were so bright. Christison instances the four sons of a local carver and gilder, 'who sat all steadily on the booby form, and occasionally shoulder to shoulder at the end of it'. As they did at school, so (he claims) they did later in life.[3]

The senior school experienced some upheaval. Robert missed the start of the term through a scalded foot, and had to catch up from the booby place; he then had only two months under Dr Adam before the latter's death. In the ensuing interregnum Luke Fraser, now old and effete, was called from retirement, taken back by the Town 'in an ill-omened hour'. Attempting to redeem his former reputation for tyranny Fraser introduced a curious 'honour-code' which only led to difficulties (Christison is vague on the subject). It would be during this second Fraser regime that Andrew Combe found him so mild compared with the savagery his brother George had experienced.

In their free time boys played a variety of games. When Robert was six the Christisons moved to a house in the Pleasance, then bordered only by the large park and the quiet Dumbiedykes Road, 'a beautiful rural suburb' with fields on either side. In the evenings there was plenty of scampering about Arthur's Seat. The favourite sports were shinty, clacken, played with a light wooden bat held in one hand, football, jumping and wrestling, racing, and for less energetic moments, tops, peeries or pegtops, bools (marbles), and papes (cherry-stones).

The cherry-stones essential for papes were robbed from local trees. They were arranged against a wall in 'castles' of three, a fourth resting on top. Each boy in turn, stepping from ten feet away, tried to hit a castle with one of his own papes – the biggest he could get. It was 'really dexterous, quiet, and unfrolicsome'.

The most exciting occasion for this was on 1 August, the annual examination day before the school holidays, when the Town Council in their robes, with halberdiers in attendance, walked from school gate to hall flanked by dense rows of several hundred boys, who showered them with handfuls of papes, especially the Lord Provost. All the trophies they had won during the summer were flung away in seconds. This reception, says Christison, 'was bestowed as an exceeding great honour!'[4]

Like most boys, Christison also went to a nearby private school for tuition in arithmetic and writing. He curiously approved the High School's concentration on the classics that had obtained for so many years, whereas George Combe was active in public meetings and a press campaign for change. In Christison's view the young mind could not cope with too great a variety of subjects: better, then, to limit study to a few.

In 1810 James Pillans was appointed to the Rectorship, at thirty-two young for the post, and after the Fraser interlude had some difficulty in establishing authority. He took over 'the most mutinous and unbridled pack of boys', and in the end even he had to resort occasionally to the tawse and exert strict control. After a couple of years, in place of the endless deadly grind over the classics endured by so many boys who by now had become famous in the professions, Pillans introduced the monitorial system, for the teaching of Latin, Greek and Ancient Geography. By this means he was able to carry on the teaching of at least 230 boys from the age of twelve to sixteen assisted only by the boys themselves, applying to advanced education a method hitherto limited to its lower branches. Edward Bulwer Lytton 'recorded hearing from Pillans that, compared with the teaching of the same class under Dr Andrew Adam, in his own boyhood, and his own first two years as Headmaster, he had found that the monitorial system increased a teacher's resources both in improving the boys' education and in forming their minds and morals'. (In 1820, on the death of Professor Christison, Pillans became Professor of Humanity and Laws at the University, and shortly afterwards introduced the same system, first in his junior, then in his senior class – with a success that surprised even himself.)[5]

Andrew Combe, who was then a pupil, said afterwards that all he learned from this was that Pillans was abler, stricter than his former teachers, 'and more of a gentleman withal'.[6]

Andrew was fifteenth in the family of eventually seventeen children of the brewer George Combe, thirteen of whom survived at least until 1807. He and his elder brother George had very different school and work experiences.

University studies began for many boys at so young an age that afterwards, still immature, they might go on to an apprenticeship. George, who, after his restricted, unhealthy childhood and traumatic early High School sufferings, entered the University in November 1802 (at the same time as the privileged and glamorous Henry Temple, Lord Palmerston's son), found himself quite unprepared for Professor John Hill's Humanity (Latin) classes. He sat passively at the back, unable to do much more than read (and enjoy) the texts. At home his education could receive no help, but his father began to employ him to teach the younger children, and having no better experience himself, George had to use the old limited method, by rote. He claimed in later years that his evident deficiency in all creative arts, drawing, music, dancing, or crafts, was demonstrated by the science of Phrenology, of which he was to become so noted a disciple; but he was already aware of an unfulfilled urge to *do good*.

In 1804, at sixteen, shabby, feeble and delicate of constitution, George narrowly escaped being apprenticed by his father to a woollen and flannel dealer in 'a small, dark shop near the head of Warriston's Close'. Mr Pattison luckily, after one good look, pronounced him unsuitable. A few days later, bound with his father on a similar errand to Yule and Abernethy, cloth merchants on North Bridge, by good fortune they fell in with Baillie William Arnott, Mr Combe's brother-in-law, who strongly advised him to apprentice George to a Writer to the Signet. The brewer had neither money nor influence to achieve this, but through Arnott's help the boy was eventually apprenticed to Alexander Dallas, armed to his own amazement with a certificate from Professor Hill stating that he had studied Humanity for two years 'with great diligence and success'. Dallas, a Highlander, whose office was on the east side of Frederick Street, had become the partner of his former master, John Alexander Higgins of Newck. [7]

This apprenticeship was a turning-point in George's so far wholly unpromising life. Feeling that 'no future could be worse than the past', he was willing to try anything that might both offer an opportunity and ease the family finances. The senior apprentice downstairs in the Frederick Street office was George Hogarth, a farmer's son, who many years later became music critic to the *Morning Chronicle* and father-in-law to Charles Dickens.

Hogarth was kind to the blundering George, who conspicuously failed to handle the paper-work or legal language, and this was the first real teaching he had ever had, while Hogarth was the first to recognise in him any potential. To improve George's slovenly diction and lack of background reading, Mr Dallas sent him in the evenings to 'a refined, natural gentleman', old Mr Scott, in a class of some half-dozen youths in North Bridge Street. They read from their master's own collection of elegant extracts, *The Beauties of Eminent Writers,* and George's fellows were convulsed with laughter by George's choice, for personal reading, Milton on Satan. Scott supported him, telling them that it was one of the finest passages in *Paradise Lost* – unaccustomed praise to the awkward boy.

The long office hours, 10 a.m. until 4 p.m., followed by an hour at Mr Scott's, and then office again from 6 until 8 p.m., sometimes even 10, did not improve George's weak health, allowing no time to digest his dinner and no exercise unless he was sent on a welcome errand. [8]

Andrew Combe was born in 1797. By nature lively and active, from his restricted life, especially on Sundays, in the dreary house in that unhealthy area of Livingston's Yards, he became shy and reserved. Like most of his siblings he was at first reared in Corstorphine by a jolly, energetic tailor's wife, who habitually took in so-called middle-class infants until they were weaned.

A revealing anecdote of Andrew's early childhood describes an adventure at St Bernard's Well, where he was sent one day when aged seven or eight, along with another boy called Inglis, with a penny and a bottle to collect medicinal water, presumably for his own well-being. The mill-stream, later enclosed in a stone aqueduct, was then carried along a wooden channel where there was no footpath, only stepping-stones. On these slimy green stones, covered by flood-water, Andrew slipped and was carried downstream, while Inglis, behind him, screamed for help. But nobody was about, and the struggling boy was sure he must be drowned. Then in shallow, broken water about thirty yards down he struck a large stone and managed to scramble to safety – on the wrong side.

Drenched, shivering and with neither bottle nor penny he now had to walk up to the bridge at the village, cross it and walk back. He then trudged about miserably for a few hours until he was dry, terrified to go home, as such childish mishaps were put down to carelessness and usually drew severe parental punishment. As it turned out, when he got home it was supposed he must already have drunk the water, and nothing was said. The misadventure determined Andrew that when he grew up he would 'induce parents to study and act in harmony with the faculties of their children'.[9]

Andrew's first school was Mr Brown's English Academy in Frederick Street, where he was sent at the age of five. Brown was decent but commonplace, and he learned little; at the High School from the age of eight, he found the new master, Fraser's successor Irvine, a sound but routine teacher, inspiring 'no ardour'. Andrew did not do badly, however, keeping between fifteenth and twenty-fifth place in a class of 120, in his fourth year moving sometimes to second place, and in examinations fifth or sixth. He went on to the Rector's class in 1809, shortly before Dr Adam died which led to the temporary reinstatement of the now much modified Luke Fraser.

About the time he went to the High School Andrew attended the usual writing and arithmetic classes, and later algebra and geometry with 'old Mr Gray'. His brother George taught him French, and on his advice Andrew studied for a quarter with M. Dufresne, one of Edinburgh's best teachers, and another with Dr Gardiner. As for literature, or science, there was not the barest suggestion. The daily speech of boys and family was vernacular Scots, and the subjects talked of at home were commonplace. On the other hand, at home they had the good example of duty, constant activity, and endurance.

Andrew moved on to the college in 1810 in order to study medicine and surgery. To start with, however, he had two more years of Latin and Greek, when Professor Christison's teaching was so monotonously sleep-inducing that all he achieved was to forget what he had learned before.

When asked about his future, all Andrew would admit to was a stubborn double negative: 'I'll no do *naething*' – taken to mean that he did have ambition. In the end his father decided to apprentice him to Henry Johnston, a Princes Street surgeon. This was in April 1812. Andrew had endured a non-stop grind over the past year, without the customary holiday with their

Corstorphine cousins at Redheughs, and as for leaving home, except for sea-bathing at Portobello, he had not been away at all. Then, the thought of going to work for some 'grand doctor' in one of those 'self-contained' Princes Street houses filled him with dread. He dug his toes in. On the due day, despite all appeals he would not budge. Even George, nine years older, begging him to try it for a day had no success. At last they forcibly got him into his best clothes and, his father and George propping up his shoulders and James pushing from behind, they lugged him from the house, through the brewery, and a few hundred yards along the high road before he even put a foot to the ground. At last he felt so ashamed that he agreed to walk quietly, and his father left him at the surgery.

After this mutual misunderstanding due to total lack of communication between boy and parents, Mr Combe felt a strong prick of conscience when Mr Johnston hoped that Andrew had been willing to come.[10]

When George qualified as a Writer to the Signet he moved to 11 Bank Street, near the open land by the new Bank of Scotland, in a healthy situation and with a fine view over the New Town. Here he was joined by Andrew and their sister Jean, who was to look after them, which relieved the pressure on their crowded home and eased their own life. Andrew now benefited from his brother's support.

Mr Johnston's apprentices had a dull life. Their official hours were from 10 in the morning until 3.30 and again from 6 till 8 p.m., but except for delivering medicines they might have almost nothing to do, especially in summer, when they gazed for hours wistfully through the iron-barred windows and longed for freedom. They received no guidance or teaching, and got through the days playing cards or reading. Andrew read novels, chiefly trash, which corrupted not his character but his reading habits so that he later found it hard to concentrate. However, he became 'disgusted' by the works he borrowed from the Subscribing Library, and as a change tried a variety ranging from biography, tales of voyages and action, to medical works.[11]

Andrew grew up with a strong feeling of inadequacy, but a total antipathy to any kind of violence. Overcoming his sullen tendency he resolved tearfully 'to be forever kind and good, no matter how others might treat me'. In place of affection his Calvinistic family doled out principles of integrity and duty, and their minister at the West Kirk, the Rev. David Dickson, presented the world in terms of sin and misery – by nature kindly and genial, but in the pulpit bent on retribution and hell-fire. Even Andrew's normally cheerful, contented mother would quash any natural expression of enjoyment with a warning that *things did not last*.

His most positive influence was George, who tried to encourage the humble Andrew, almost the youngest in the family and accustomed to being called a blockhead, full of inferiority feelings and, however much George reproached him, silent in company. Neither of them could see much of a prospect for him.[12]

At the University poor students lived frugal and restricted lives, but did not have to be poor to be uncomfortable to the point of misery. The writer Robert Pearse Gillies, who was born in 1788, makes the most of his sufferings, relating in vivid detail what he endured not in the classes but in his dismal lodgings, 'in one of the obscurest and most ill-famed streets in the oldest part of the new town': he does not say where, but possibly St James' Square, or elsewhere near the Theatre. Here he lived for his first 'six wretched months' in 1806. The lodgings were run jointly by a St Andrews graduate and a French teacher, who took in four students.

The house was a 'land' of six or seven storeys, ascended by the usual dingy common stair, their flat being on the fourth or fifth level. Isolated at the very top lived a low-grade writer or King's Messenger (equivalent to a bailiff), 'truculent and merciless' in his job. Edinburgh lodgings bore brass name-plates, and the better-off kept 'a winking lamp', or a rush-light, fed by train-oil, over the door, though only on winter nights.

The lodging boasted a dining parlour with a fine view across to the Old Town, a drawing-room facing the street – 'a cold ghastly-looking apartment' used on state occasions but containing a sofa-bed for their hefty landlord. Of the three other rooms, one was the monopoly of the senior student, Gillies shared the second with the others, and the third the owner kept locked. He employed two sturdy-looking women servants, but where they dwelt, unless in the small kitchen, was a mystery.

His first evening was etched on the miserable Gillies's mind. Two of his fellow-students were busy at their French exercises, at a table covered with ragged green baize and lit by 'two dusky lank mutton candles', while the senior student sat by the fire immersed in 'the British Constitution'.

At 9.30 the French 'maître' came in, gleeful at having completed his lessons for the day, and summoned them (in French) to supper. Preparations for this consisted in removing the candles and writing materials, snatching the baize from the table while he bawled (also in French) for the maid to serve. Gillies minutely describes the dismal menu: on the worn table-cloth were laid 'a so-styled omelette at one end', fried potatoes at the other. In reality this meant hard-boiled eggs cut into halves and swimming in 'some dingy milk and water, like floating islands', while the *pommes frites* were cold boiled potatoes thinly sliced, and warmed until blackened on a gridiron. This being considered 'a fête night', 'we were indulged with six little square morsels of cheese, and a plate of raw apples', very indigestible. The crowning treat was a bottle containing a small quantity of whisky distilled from potatoes, of which each pupil was allowed three teaspoonfuls in a wine-glass, with hot water and *cassonade.* The maître served himself a larger measure; the powerfully built master of the house took none.

During Gillies's stay the food continued uniformly awful, its cost averaging about 3½d a head. The other boys had little experience of anything better, being the sons of a country gentleman who, although he had become rich, maintained a prudent economy. Gillies declared he had nothing in common with the boys.

His own studies suffered under the regimen; the others sneered at his desire to read the classics, and the two masters had no interest beyond their own course. Poetry, because it 'proved nothing', was out. Gillies admitted that his own tastes were narrow, having no interest in 'politics, law, natural philosophy, chemistry, maths, engineering, land-surveying, navigation, and so forth'.

It was November. On his first cold foggy morning Gillies woke early, listening to two lugubriously reiterated street-cries in 'that vile district'. Perhaps to impress him, breakfast that day was served in the drawing-room, where he could admire its deal chairs painted to simulate bamboo, and cushions and curtains of chintz. It seemed an uninspiring start to a course at a world-famous university.

Gillies had been advised to study with Leslie, Dunbar and Christison. Leslie he admitted was a genius, but by his own fault he was bored with the lectures, and Dunbar's on Greek seemed to him organised against common sense. 'Why any youth should be doomed to trudge along the streets in the cold, dark, dismal, winter mornings, before 8 o'clock, in order to attend a service of Greek . . .', not to mention a second at two in the afternoon, was beyond his comprehension. 'We might have rain, hail, snow, frost, hurricane, or, as it often happened, a *mélange* of all five together', yet the student, once entered on the register, had no choice but to attend. The professor, calm and pale, sat patiently between 'two dingy tallow candles' while the shivering students were either restless or half asleep. 'Snores, protracted yawns, and other indecorous noises, with practical jokes of divers kinds, wore through the long hour.' Professor Christison in the Latin class, though no better, at least did not lecture until 11 a.m., when a wintry sunshine filtered into the 'dreary and unfinished college'. One must remember that the bored youths were virtually schoolboys, mostly still in their middle teens. And further, studying year after year in a half-built, semi-abandoned college probably engendered more apathy than inspiration.[13]

John Leslie, to whom Gillies warmed somewhat, while still uncouth in manner, had risen amazingly quickly to a professorship which the admiring Gillies felt 'demonstrated the pre-eminence of Genius', but was elected to the chair of mathematics in 1805 after a bout of canvassing, pamphleteering, and a battle with the magistrates, who regarded him as heretical, anti-John Knox and a danger to youth. A reference in Leslie's *Experimental Inquiry into the Nature and Properties of Heat*, published in 1804, to Hume's doctrine of cause and effect, which he condemned as 'an indirect attack on the First Cause', created a great furore. (Hume, in arguing that *post hoc* did not mean *propter hoc*, had carried his doubt of causes to doubt of their effects: doubting, that is, even the existence of the perceived world and substituting ideas existing in the mind; thus, since the mind 'does not exist' except as 'simple modification of matter', he was reasoning away all certainty.) Leslie's supposed heresy led the clergy to violent opposition to his election. The academics and literati sprang to his defence, Dugald Stewart writing 'with great severity', John Playfair 'with keen irony' and Dr Thomas Brown 'logically'. Leslie's supporters won, and he was duly appointed Professor of Mathematics.[14]

The problem for his students was that he was too brilliant for the more run-of-the-mill. To him the curriculum, indeed the whole science, was so natural that he would launch at once into complex problems, while his 'grotesque physiognomy' lit up at some mathematical concept of which all but one or two of his class had not the least understanding. Blissfully unaware of the failure in communication, Leslie would carry on with his discourse unperturbed.

He was very helpful, however, when students came to his rooms for enlightenment, and explained their difficulties with patience. Furthermore, as his knowledge also comprised chemistry, optics, astronomy and natural philosophy, he would impart all this with 'such a hopeful, buoyant, youthful spirit' (he was then forty) that, says Gillies, 'I regarded him as one of the best humoured and happiest of mortals'.[15]

Professor Leslie, unexpectedly, was socially inclined, and a convivial dinner guest (as Maria Dundas and others had found), not spurning even the miserable fare at Gillies's lodgings. His conversation was full of quirky originality, and he would often launch into some extraordinary, even undreamed-of theory.[16]

The boredom of lectures unfitted Gillies (as he saw it) for serious study, returning to the dreary lodging miserable, disappointed and tired. However, on most afternoons he spent a couple of hours at his kinsman Dr Tytler's house in the suburbs.[17]

Tytler was seeking a publisher for his *Silius*, and the pair would rail at literature and patronage in Edinburgh, praise the cleverness of the *Review* and dismiss the pretensions of the *Edinburgh Monthly Magazine*. Gillies toyed with the idea of a new monthly miscellany with Lord Buchan's support, to be written by himself, Buchan, Dr Tytler and the latter's daughter Margaret.[18]

Dr John Black, then a layman, whom Gillies met at dinner with Malcolm Laing, MP for Orkney, was an author devoted to poetry and romance, especially Italian, and had published a life of Tasso. At this time he was in a sinecure, that is as tutor to a young Orkney laird so uninterested in learning that Black was free to do much as he liked. Impervious to the ridicule aroused by his unfashionable Italian researches, and knowing no one in the literary world except Laing and Lord Woodhouselee (chief of Edinburgh's few Italian scholars), he lived retired in a secluded two-floor house of large rooms, 'low down in the broom' of the ravine below Calton Hill, looking out only on 'green sward and a few blighted trees'.[19]

An acquaintance who disappointed Gillies was the arrogant Rev. J. Mullens, who coming from Oxford seemed likely to help extend Gillies's studies. But his mind ran in a different groove. All that the cynical Mullens did for him was fill him with disgust for Edinburgh. 'He censured almost everybody, and every thing' – except for Jeffrey, Bishop Sandford, Alison and Robert Morehead; for Scotland in general he had only 'contemptuous vituperation of the state of manners, morals, literature', while he wrote off Gillies's wretched 'land' as 'the *rummest* specimen of an academical establishment that he had ever seen'. In this at least he was probably right.

Mullens's unfavourable contrast of Edinburgh with Oxford quickly made him enemies. He also made himself sartorially ridiculous, walking in the streets on Sundays dressed ostentatiously in full 'canonicals' and adorned by 'insignia as chaplain to a nobleman, and member of a college'. On weekdays he was the dandy, sporting top-boots and 'brilliant buckskins' as if on his way to follow the hounds, except that 'unluckily, there were at the time no hounds to follow'.[20]

After six months at the University, in the spring of 1807 Gillies's health broke down, and after a nearly fatal bout of fever he had to return home, where for some months he studied with his uncle Dr James Gillies. In November he reluctantly returned to the University during an early winter of frost and snow, but this time found better lodgings with 'two parlours on a *rez de chaussée* of the veritable new town', and he signed on for Stewart's, Playfair's and Finlayson's lectures.

His fellow-lodger that winter was Spencer Stanhope, and in an exceptionally lively season – because the celebrated Duchess of Gordon was in town – he enjoyed a pleasant life writing poetry and collecting old books and paintings, and almost every evening dining or attending a party.

Dr Finlayson, the Professor of Logic, fell ill from a disease that shortly carried him off; but logic was not at the time thought of as a great loss to the curriculum. Of his other professors, Gillies often met Playfair in society, though not knowing him well: in his view this social, equable philosopher oddly had a rather dry, reserved manner belied by his good-natured facial expression.[21]

Apart from his fastidious literary taste Playfair was very unlike Dugald Stewart, who was then at the height of his reputation. Stewart's name alone brought scholars to the University from all civilised countries, and his classes were crowded long before his lectures started. Members of the nobility so competed for his tutorship of their sons that he was said to have refused £2000 for a single pupil. On the other hand, some criticised his 'courtier's' manners, and his preference for retirement – for he so desired country life that in Edinburgh he lived as near the country as possible, in Whitefoord House, an old Canongate mansion which had been subdivided and was shared with Lord Bannatyne. It stood well back from the street in more than an acre of ground, secluded by walls and gates, and with tall, ancient trees housing a rookery. Stewart had his library at the back overlooking Calton Hill.

He was happiest when studying or writing, and was inclined to refuse social invitations, only occasionally attending a dinner or rout – and was so painstaking a worker that (Gillies tells us) he would 'mould and re-mould the same sentence fifty times over'. A page of metaphysics supposedly took him as much trouble as would the work of a poet.

Stewart was very hospitable, however, and he and his wife made strangers feel at home by their cordial reception. Gillies recalls his first dinner at Whitefoord House 'on a dark evening in December 1807 . . . I remember the drawingroom lighted only, but quite sufficiently by a blazing fire . . . over the most common place chitchat' – because after a taxing day exercising his intellect Dr Stewart wanted total relaxation. His wife, who was sister to the noted Countess Purgstall, and was equally original and entertaining, perfectly complemented her husband, her quiet, even tones contrasting with his 'enthusiastic, poetical, romantic sentiments'.

On that evening there were few guests: the mathematical teacher Mr Jardine, and two students, one of them a foreigner who had brought the usual letter of introduction. There was nothing learned in the table-talk, which was light and cheerful, giving Gillies an impression of perfect domestic harmony.[22]

Sadness clouded Stewart's life in 1809 with the death of his beloved son, making him want to retire altogether. Henry Holland,[23] then a student, reported to the Edgeworths in Ireland that at the end of his season's lectures (December 1809) Stewart reviewed his thirty-eight years' service at the University, implying that they were about to end, 'most pathetic and impressive'.[24] He was persuaded to resume, and at his first reappearance the classroom was crowded to the doors, and many could not get in at all. This was when the eccentric Lord Buchan characteristically 'made a spectacle' of his own respect for the great man by taking a seat beside him – and Stewart then courteously resigned him his own.

He never recovered from his son's loss, and in 1812 gladly accepted the Duke of Hamilton's offer of Kinneil, one of his own houses near Queensferry on the Forth, and retiring there he gradually resumed his studies. Sadly Gillies, one of those whom Stewart invited to visit them there, was himself at the time living a retired life and did not go, and after 1811 they met only once.

He praises Stewart's 'humane, indulgent, and kindly disposition', love of literary work and indifference to distinction or reward, devoted only to achieving 'lucidity and harmony of style'.[25]

After Stewart's retirement Louis Simond reckoned (1811) that the most popular professors were Playfair on natural philosophy, Stewart's successor Brown on moral philosophy, Hope on chemistry, Gregory on medicine, Thomson on surgery and John Leslie on mathematics. Many who attended the lectures were adult, even quite old, and at least half of the audience of Mr Coventry, Professor of Agriculture, were farmers; but as unfortunately he was quite inaudible, even from the third row, he lost up to one hundred students – Scottish agriculture, as Simond drily put it, losing the more. Dr Gregory, whom Simond heard lecturing on the liver, spoke without notes, in a conversational tone, with his hat on and constantly playing with his spectacle case. He had five hundred students in a vast amphitheatre.[26]

In March 1808, meanwhile, Gillies again had had to leave Edinburgh for Kincardineshire because of the serious illness of his father, who died in July. The following winter he returned unwillingly to take up a profession. The eighty-mile journey took him three days, having to travel with his own horses because of a lack of post-horses on the road. Even near the end, it was quite usual to wait for a crossing of the River Forth for up to three hours – a 'perilous voyage' indeed, which Lord Gardenstone, for one, would never risk but always went round by Stirling.

That winter Gillies enjoyed no social life because of prolonged bad health, and he concentrated on qualifying for the bar. In December, however, he was elected to the Speculative Society, at which Jeffrey and other past members still sometimes put in an appearance.[27]

The political bias of elections to professorships had at last begun to wane. 'I consider the election of professors Leslie, Christison, Brown, and some others, as an actual series of victories over the old corrupt system of giving the Chairs . . . to middling unqualified men in preference to those of far superior merit.'[28]

In the year 1808 University prizes were offered for the first time. That April Alexander Alison carried off the top Greek prize for an essay on Athenian eminence in the arts and sciences, which he exuberantly explained by applying Adam Smith's law of supply and demand. For the mathematics prizes there were four leading competitors, including Alison again and Edward Irving. Alison found the first day difficult, but on the second solved all the problems, and shared the first prize with Borthwick of Crookston.[29]

Alison was intended by his clergyman father for the ministry, but like a number of students changed his career intentions while at the University.

His work on economics, and preliminaries for an essay on population, so impressed his father that he was entered for the bar and spent a further year under the two philosophers, Stewart on moral, Playfair on natural, which Alison regarded as 'the most fortunate event . . . in my education'.[30]

He was also typical of contemporary students, when he left the University at eighteen, in being unable to write either Greek composition, Latin verse or good Latin prose, at which an English youth might have been adept. But unlike such an English contemporary he was not full of distaste for the classics and had read all the authors. He knew French and Italian literature, and had also learned trigonometry, conic sections, natural and moral philosophy, chemistry, mathematics and astronomy. In all these achievements he was not regarded as outstanding or even unusual: many others surpassed him.

Alison considered that in Scotland education was aimed at the middle classes, who needed to succeed in a profession, whereas the object in England was both more general and more particular, training 'the great and affluent', whose fortunes had already been made by their ancestors.[31]

Apart from Dr Gregory, Edinburgh's medical school had meanwhile deteriorated. The Philadelphian Benjamin Rush was delighted to send his son James to follow in his footsteps there in 1809, envying his chance to bask in 'the agreeable and enlightened society of Edinburgh. What would I not give, to pass a month, a week, or even a day in that city!' He urged James to make himself known to some of his own contemporaries, including the now ageing William Creech the publisher, Thomas Hogg, who he was surprised and pleased to hear was still living, Hogg's daughters whom he had known as children, and 'the worthy Mr Scott Moncreif'. He was touched that James, when he first attended the Tolbooth Church, recognised his father's description of it and the pew where he used to sit. He had not expected Mrs Hogg or Mrs Fletcher to be alive (the latter surprisingly, she being only in middle age), or would have written him introductions; and he urged his son to 'do homage in my name to their goodness, and thank them over and over for their kind remembrance of me'. Feelingly he remarked, 'What a contrast between an evening at Mrs Hamilton's or Mrs Fletcher's, or a seat at the table of the venerable Mrs Hogg, or a chair next to Miss A. Hogg,[32] and the convivial dinners and insipid tea parties of Philadelphia'.

Benjamin Rush named many other personalities kind to him during his own studies, including 'the good Lord and Lady Buchan', and reminded James that when he left Edinburgh he should give them all small presents, 'a knife, a breast pin, or a pencil', to preserve his own memory until yet a third generation of Rushes arrived.[33]

But in the medical school, the third generation of Monros caused sad disillusionment to young Rush. By 1810, too, the state of the medical school in general proved to have gone downhill, through dissensions aroused by rivalry and malice between the physicians. James was disgusted at the poor standard of teaching, although his father was not surprised, having expected little of the principles then taught there, but he reminded his son that the University existed not merely to teach but to cultivate 'the man, the scholar, and the gentleman'.[34]

Dr Rush wrote to John Adams in America (8 Sept. 1810) that James, disgusted with the degenerate medical school, 'treats the lectures there with great contempt, as do all the young men who have studied there after studying in Philadelphia'. Here was a volte-face in the course of a generation, indeed. 'They all . . . believe there would be no great diminution of medical knowledge if that university were annihilated.' James's colleague Thomas Fuller Jr, who had accompanied him to Europe, wrote to Dr Rush confirming James's account of 'the dissensions of the Edinburgh physicians' and Rush quoted Dr Gregory's father in saying that 'nothing could exceed the rancor of rival physicians', worse even than that of rival authors.

He was also disgusted by the Edinburgh reviewers' censure of the opinions adopted by Philadelphia's medical experts, and their general prejudice against American authors. As he told John Adams, as long as his own publications were accepted by every doctor in Philadelphia, he could scarcely give credence to reviewers who fulminated against his principles. The worst criticisms came from other doctors, 'for teaching a system of medicine that robbed them by its simplicity of cargoes of technical lumber by which they imposed upon the credulity of the world'.[35]

On the other hand, early in 1813 Rush was urging the Trustees of Pennsylvania University to bring their syllabus and administration more into line with Edinburgh's three-year degree course of medical lectures, besides the scientific background and modern and ancient languages which most of its students had acquired. Further, whereas Philadelphia courses lasted only four months, or eight in a course of only two years, Edinburgh lecture sessions lasted six months, totalling eighteen in the three-year course. Finally, Philadelphia should follow New York and Boston in setting up a botanic garden, Edinburgh's being of paramount importance, and there any physician ignorant of botany was considered not 'completely educated'. Rush dismissed with scorn any pretence that lengthening the course would send students elsewhere. Edinburgh, with four rival medical schools not far distant, had never suffered from this.[36]

16
THE CHURCH AND CHURCHMEN

'Perhaps there is at present no spot upon the earth where religion, science, and literature combine more to produce moral and intellectual pleasures than in the metropolis of Scotland.'

Benjamin Rush to his son James, 19 March 1810, *Letters*, II.1038

Religion had become fashionable in the mid-1790s, and amid the universal zeal even actors turned preacher. Sabbath observance had indeed fallen off, and Sunday was seen by many as simply a day for relaxation, but on the other hand religious societies were being formed for gospel missions, tabernacles were built, and according to Stark in 1806 Edinburgh was 'flooded' by itinerant English preachers[1] such as Rowland Hill. St Cecilia's, after closing as a concert hall, was converted to a meeting house, and two others opened near the Circus at the head of Leith Walk.[2]

Yet the New Town remained very short of churches, with only St Andrew's in George Street, and the medieval St Cuthbert's originally serving a country parish, rebuilt in 1774 with a steeple added in 1790. There was also an Episcopal chapel, St George's in York Place – Gothick, a rare style yet in Edinburgh – in a strange octagonal design by James Adam of 1794.[3]

Robert Adam's plan for a large church for the west side of Charlotte Square was abandoned after his death for financial reasons, along with the unfinished square. Not until 1810 did the City determine to proceed, employing Robert Reid as architect. His estimated cost, £18,000, was eventually met by borrowing, but after building began in 1811 it was plain that this was quite inadequate, and before St George's was completed in 1814 it had cost £23,675.[4]

Adam's design had had a free-standing pedimented portico crowned by statues, with paired Corinthian columns, and elegant miniature temples on top of the corners. Reid's design was heavier, keeping Adam's outline and central dome, heightened and considerably changed in detail, but completing the main building with four large Ionic columns *in antis* and surmounted by a heavyish balustrade.

St George's first minister was Dr Andrew Thomson, of New Greyfriars

Church. At this time when Moderatism was still almost unchallenged, the Evangelical Thomson came like a bombshell, denouncing society's hypocrisies and preaching the doctrine of redemption by atonement. His fiery, practical sermons drew crowds, who struggled for seats even in the lobby and passages. Concerned at the lack of education among his parishioners, Thomson also established a school. In 1811 he launched and edited *The Christian Instructor*, a paper which became very influential and ran until 1840. As for patronage, he announced that he preferred congregations to choose their own clergy (the view to which Chalmers and others eventually came).[5]

Edinburgh in general was enjoying some unusual preachers. James Grahame (1765–1811) was educated at Glasgow, qualified as a WS, an advocate and an Episcopal clergyman. He was also an eclectic writer whose publications, at first anonymous, included *The Sabbath* (1804), *Birds of Scotland* (1806), *British Georgics* (1809) and other books of verse. His first living was a curacy in Somerset and he then applied for St George's Church in Edinburgh. Mrs Grant thought he preached gracefully, without contentious or 'adventurous' ideas. She records attending an afternoon service in May 1810 (after her usual orthodox attendance at 'the High Church', that is St Giles'). A great crowd had turned up out of curiosity, 'to see and hear the amiable, poetical, sabbatical, and once anti-prelatical, James Grahame, reading the Litany in a surplice, fearless alike of the ghosts of John Knox and Jenny Geddes', but perhaps more fearful of 'his brother advocates and writers – not to mention the reviewers' (who had spurned his *Sabbath*).[6]

Equally unorthodox was the eccentric dissenting preacher Rowland Hill, brother of a controversial baronet Sir Richard Hill, and descendant of an eighteenth-century diplomat. Hill, born in 1744 and educated at Shrewsbury, Eton and St John's College Cambridge, decided to become an itinerant preacher, and was for that reason refused orders. From 1783 he had held services and Sunday schools at the Surrey Chapel in London, and in 1803 he preached in and around Edinburgh. The Rev. James Hall, visiting the city at that time, relates numerous anecdotes of his life and preaching. Hill's audiences were extravagantly reckoned as anything up to 10,000 (but how could they hear?) He was one of the preachers who employed 'groaners' whose lamentations punctuated their sermons to add dramatic effect, though some of them (says Hall) unfortunately 'made the most noise when . . . there was least occasion for it'. One such woman, described as looking cleaner and better dressed than she had been for years, whispered to a friend that now she was employed as a groaner, she had 'besides victuals and drink, clothes, and a weekly allowance'.

Hall was impressed chiefly by a sense of the ridiculous in Hill's tones and gestures, and his choice of language, not to mention religious views, which suggested that he 'has more zeal than knowledge. It is his peculiarities more than his parts, that seem to draw attention.' A great crowd awaiting the preacher's arrival, many there out of curiosity, others (he thought) either fanatics or hypocrites, tired themselves with psalm-singing until someone sent to find out if he was ever coming. When at last he turned up, he mounted the pulpit waving a large blood-stained handkerchief, and then spread it over the Bible, with the tame explanation that his nose had been bleeding. The congregation appropriately struck up with a new hymn on the Blood of Christ.

Hill's domestic habits, if quirkish, were kindly meant. Hearing his maids quarrelling one day while he breakfasted, about who should wash the passage, he called for a mop and water and started the job himself, saying as it must be done, he would do it. The girls of course rushed to take over. Another time he overheard his coachman on a rainy evening refusing to go out for oysters, arguing closed-shop rules. Mr Hill rang for John, had the coach put to and ordered him to drive the maid for sixpenny-worth of oysters, with the moral injunction that as he would not voluntarily 'step out' with an umbrella, 'you must take the trouble to drive her thither'.[7]

Another exponent of a free church at the turn of the century was James Haldane (born 1768), youngest son of Captain James Haldane of Airthrey, who after serving as a midshipman in the East India Company's service, settled in Edinburgh in 1794. In 1797 he founded the Society for Propagating the Gospel at Home, and in 1799 founded Scotland's first Congregational church, and also became a prolific religious writer. For fifty years until his death in 1851 he officiated at a tabernacle in Leith Walk, built for him by his brother Robert.

According to Henry Cockburn, Haldane was an Anabaptist, but by 1808 he was certainly Baptist, and even before that led his flock 'to Stockbridge to be washed every Sunday by scores'. Cockburn observed in the winter of 1806 that 'T'other day there were about 2000 spectators: the glass stood at 30'. Somebody remarked that 'he would rather not be saved than immerse on such a day'.[8]

The great Thomas Chalmers was now beginning to make his mark as a preacher in Edinburgh, although for a long time the course of his career was unresolved. Born in 1780 at Anstruther in Fife (he never lost a strong Fife accent) to a prosperous ship-owner and merchant, he was educated in St Andrews and formed a strong taste for mathematics. He was licensed as a preacher in 1799 – though not yet ordained – studied for two years in Edinburgh, especially mathematics with Playfair, and planned an academic career. He was actually appointed Assistant Professor of Mathematics at St Andrews in 1802, and not long afterwards was nominated minister of Kilmany in Fife.

Dismissed from the St Andrews post he set up for a time as an independent lecturer there in mathematics and chemistry, and applied unsuccessfully in 1805 for the vacant chair in Edinburgh: the subject strongly appealed to him for its realities, being neither literary, critical nor imaginative. As he was later attracted by natural philosophy, he became a 'mathematico-physicist'.

Still pulled in several directions, at one time he fancied becoming a military engineer, and when already a young minister he rather recklessly became a captain of volunteers, wearing the scarlet uniform under his clerical robes, an eccentricity for which he was rebuked by a colleague. As a student he had been much influenced by the radical Whig reformers such as John Leslie, and even after he was ordained was inclined to atheism. He also tried chemical experiments at home (including a mild form of whisky), and in 1807 on a visit to London was intrigued by current experiments with gas.[9]

Visiting Edinburgh in 1806 as a guest of Robert Gillies, Chalmers with his energy and versatility seemed to forecast a clerical career. His manner was natural, and he could pour forth streams of ideas on innumerable unrelated subjects. He could easily have followed several different careers with equal success, versatile like John Leslie and equally enthusiastic in theology, poetry, politics, metaphysics and mathematics. The following winter (1807), when Gillies had escaped from his ghastly first lodgings, Chalmers sometimes passed an evening with him, enthusing over Gillies's growing collection of black-letter books, and in ecstasies over Gavin Douglas's translation of the *Aeneid*, while they discussed old Scottish poetry, and *Marmion*, celebrated even before it was published.[10]

In 1808 Chalmers published an *Enquiry into the Extent and Stability of National Resources,* and in 1809 made his first appearance at the General Assembly. Here his maiden speech, on the dry subject of clergy stipends, was enlivened with humour, sense and powerful reasoning. Dr Campbell asked his neighbour if he knew the man, 'surely a most extraordinary person'; others were soon thinking the same. Breakfasting next morning with Dr Brewster, who had been his contemporary at St Andrews, Chalmers was congratulated by his host on his brilliant speech, but answered despondently, 'But what did it signify? – it had no effect.' He was right, as his supporters on the subject were ignorant of Assembly protocol. At length, following the advice of many admirers, he published the work. Yet his career seemed as undirected as ever.[11]

David Brewster, a year younger than Chalmers, pale, pensive and quiet, had become a licensed preacher in 1804 but soon abandoned it for law, mathematics and natural philosophy.[12] Another St Andrews contemporary was that wayward genius the other Thomas Thomson, snappish and suspicious-minded, a brilliant chemist, who took his MD in Edinburgh in 1799 and opened what was reputedly the first chemical laboratory in the country to be used for teaching.[13] Of the three, Chalmers was to make by far the greatest impression.

Brewster, who in 1807 had become editor of the *Edinburgh Encyclopaedia,* engaged Chalmers to contribute an item on trigonometry, to which at his own request Chalmers added Christianity, his research having by now inclined him again to faith. Shortly after the deaths and illnesses of siblings, and recovery from a serious illness from which he fully expected to die, at the age of thirty he turned fully to religion, a deep spiritual change having charged him with a spirit of mission. His conviction grew, and by early 1812 he determined to devote himself to the ministry and enrolled at Edinburgh University in Moral Philosophy for the session 1812–13. This was Dr Thomas Brown's third year in the subject, and excitement at his brilliance was still high.

Chalmers now became increasingly sought-after as a preacher, especially for 'public sermons', for example in the autumn of 1812 and again in April 1813 to the Destitute Sick Society. His sometimes controversial theological publications aroused great interest, and when in November 1814 he was elected to the Tron Church in Glasgow the news caused great interest in both cities, adding further fame to his published work.[14]

Interesting comments on the Church are made by a visiting American, Benjamin Silliman, not a student but a mature young man of twenty-five, already admitted to the bar in Philadelphia, and when only twenty-three appointed to its new professorship of chemistry and natural history. Having taken up the post in 1804, in 1805 he sailed for England to study with foreign scholars, and to buy books and apparatus for his university.

It was not therefore meant as a 'Grand Tour-style' visit, and his object was not to be introduced to society; nevertheless when in Scotland he met everyone who was of interest to him, including Humphrey Davy, Dr David Brewster and the geologist Dr Thomas Hope.[15]

Silliman, who was considered to have charm as well as scholarship, was handsome, tall, well-built and vigorous. Always courteous, he went down well with his British associates, but was also deeply religious, indeed strait-laced. Visiting Vauxhall when in London, while at first he was greatly impressed by the spectacular illuminations and entertainments, as the evening wore on it was spoiled for him by what he considered the shocking freedom and immoderate behaviour of the light ladies whose dancing incited young gentlemen to abandon their respectable parties and join them.

In December 1805 Silliman attended the dignified service of thanksgiving at St Giles' after the Battle of Trafalgar (5 December). The grand trappings had greater appeal than the sermon. The Lord Provost, Lords of Session, magistrates, military officers and members of the nobility and gentry were assembled, in scarlet-covered seats, while in the front gallery sat Lord Moira,

C-in-C for Scotland, of particular interest to the young American because of his gallant service at the Battle of Camden in South Carolina (1780).

The disappointing sermon, by a leading churchman, though appropriately on the subject of war was (Silliman thought) sentimentalised, bombastic and 'with inflated style and puerile ornaments'.

On another level he was astonished that a member of the minor aristocracy, Sir Henry Moncreiff of Wellwood, should have entered the church. To him it seemed almost comic, that 'a titled man should voluntarily become a preacher'. He conceded, however, that the baronet was not 'tinctured with enthusiasm' but showed 'rational though ardent piety', sign of 'a sound and excellent mind'.[16]

He remarked how some clergy fell into 'refined speculative theology' and 'metaphysical systems, elaborated with great subtelty of reasoning' rather than expounding the 'plain dictates of the word of God'. There was sometimes, he felt, too much attempt at intellectual superiority and not enough benevolence.

At Lady Glenorchy's private chapel, which Silliman attended in January 1806, to take the sacrament, he noted similarities with American forms of Presbyterianism, though in Scotland communion was less frequent than in America. The method was to issue metal tokens at a previous service, or on the same morning, which were handed in by the communicant at the celebration. This was taken at tables set up in the aisles, at which parties took their place in turn, and of course no one left the church during the ceremony. While communion was going on ministers offered prayers, and made exhortations usually addressed to the congregations' 'hearts and consciences'.[17]

No one at this date seems to have described an Edinburgh wedding in detail, but in 1811 Louis Simond was much impressed by the grandeur of a funeral, especially as it was for a poor woman who had died in the upper storey of his lodging. The cortège started from outside the house: 'A coach and six covered with black cloth, and surmounted with plumes of feathers of the same colour'; more carriages followed, and were preceded and followed by hired mourners on foot, all in black and carrying black plumes of feathers.

Such a sight could indeed be witnessed daily in streets and highways in both England and Scotland, somewhat to Simond's disapproval, 'making grief a show' – yet generally ignored by the passing crowds, and its followers splashed by passing carriages.

Benjamin Silliman expressed surprise during his visit at receiving a written notice of the death of a distinguished clergyman friend. It was, indeed, normal to send notices of the time and place of a funeral, which were taken as an invitation to attend. Funerals were not attended by women.[18]

17
THE PAINTERS

'Painting, sculpture, Engraving, and Music, I am sorry to say, are not well understood in this capital.'

The Ghost (Dr Constantia), Glasgow & London, 1796, No. XI

'The elegant and useful arts are, perhaps, as far advanced in Edinburgh as any where in Europe.' (1803)

The Rev. James Hall, *Travels in Scotland, by an Unusual Route*, London, 1827, 582

Foreigners, including the English, generally commented on Scotland's poor showing in art. In the eighteenth century most Scottish painters studied in Italy, for example Alexander Runciman (1736–85) and his younger brother John. In 1772 Alexander was appointed first Master, at a salary of £120 a year, of the 'Academy of Drawing' set up by the Trustees of the Manufacturers to train boys and girls in draughtsmanship, for the encouragement not of art but of manufacture. Runciman was succeeded in 1785 by David Allan, a painter of peasant life, who likewise had studied in Rome, and was known as 'the Scottish Hogarth' by virtue of his scenes of the Venetian Carnival exhibited at the Royal Academy in London in 1779. On Allan's death in 1796 a competition was fraudulently won by John Wood, who was accordingly dismissed and a historical painter John Graham was appointed in his place.

Graham (1754–1817), trained as a coach painter, had turned to painting in oils, a skill which he introduced to the Academy. His new ideas inspired the students, though they were destined on the whole to jobs like embroiderers and damask-weavers, and their practice was mostly limited to drawing plaster casts of the antique. Under Graham, several gifted students, including David Wilkie and William Allan, were able to branch out into art.

Alexander Nasmyth had attempted to found an academy of the fine arts in 1791, and another attempt was made in 1797, but it was Nasmyth's gifted pupils who managed to spread artistic taste in Scotland.[1] And later Nasmyth and Henry Raeburn, Nasmyth's pupil, opened their studios to the public. There were also the portrait painter George Watson, and the landscape painter Hugh Williams.[2]

David Wilkie, who trained under John Graham, was a minister's son, descendant of tenant farmers, born in Fife in 1783. From earliest years he had a passion for drawing, and in November 1799 his father agreed to send him to the Trustees' Academy in Edinburgh, conveniently available to 'mechanics as well as artists'. At first he was refused by the secretary George Thomson, but luckily an introduction to the Earl of Leven secured the influence to gain his entrance in 1800.

Wilkie's bashful, countrified exterior and slow manner concealed ambition. He worked industriously, and having a natural feeling for character and expression, used to sketch people he saw at fairs and trysts. He lived frugally and studied hard, working at the Academy up to twelve hours a day. He also painted at home in his Nicolson Street lodgings, and in spare hours would wander through the streets watching people as they worked, to exercise his powers of observation.

At his lodgings, up two pairs of stairs, he followed a Spartan regimen: he possessed a plain table and chairs, his bible and fiddle, a copy of Allan Ramsay's 'Gentle Shepherd' (which he was re-copying) and for painting, just his brushes and palette – no easel or lay figure such as richer students possessed. He was his own model, and would go on painting even when he was numbed with cold, or when fellow-students called.

To the antics of his boisterous fellow-students (says his biographer Allan Cunningham), training to be 'house-painters, engravers, weavers, pattern-makers' and full of horse-play and crude jokes, the serious and dedicated Wilkie was immune. He, John Burnet the engraver, and George Thomson's brother David, were regarded as Graham's leading students, with Thomson perhaps the favourite. Wilkie entered a rendering of the murder of Lady Macduff for a new ten-guinea premium for the best painting in oils, but it was Thomson who won. In 1803 Wilkie did win, with 'Calisto in the Bath of Diana'.

Wilkie was never robust and was far from handsome, a 'tall, plain, thin Scotsman', red-haired and with bright blue eyes, short nose and humorous mouth. In 1804 he left the Academy, armed with Graham's praise, and after struggling to work at home in Fife between portraits and (his personal preference) country scenes, secured his family's reluctant consent next year to study at the Royal Academy in London, aged nineteen and a half. There he found his reputation had preceded him, and on his account Benjamin Haydon signed on as a student as well, and the two became friends.

Early struggles were eventually rewarded, and apart from occasional visits Wilkie did not return to Edinburgh, in London meeting celebrities from Lady Hamilton to Joanna Baillie and Sir George Beaumont, and in 1809 Walter Scott ('a very rich mind'). Dubbed 'the Scottish Teniers', he remained unaffected, modest, good-natured and pleasant.[3]

In 1811, at the age of twenty-five, Wilkie was elected to the Royal Academy, and the following year after his father's death settled with his family at 24 Phillimore Place. This was 'a new and handsome house', barely finished, equipped – like most Edinburgh's modern houses – with piped water, but (he told his sister Helen) when complete would outstrip equivalent Edinburgh houses and be 'fitted up in a much neater manner, and have much better accommodation'.[4]

Another talented young painter who went to London for a career was Andrew Robertson, a miniaturist like his brother Archibald, of an Aberdeen family; he sailed to London from Leith in 1801 after making contact in Edinburgh with Raeburn and Nasmyth, both of whom praised his work as better than the Edinburgh miniaturists, and told him he charged too little. In London he spent much time at the Royal Academy exhibition, and went to see Sheridan's *Pizarro* at Drury Lane, whose scenery he thought inferior to Nasmyth's. He joined the Academy, where a fellow-student and miniature-painter was Vaughan, whom he had met at Nasmyth's.

Robertson's struggle for a career was crowned with success, and though normally in debt he had distinguished sitters including Benjamin West, then President of the Academy, the Duke of Gordon and his family, and in due course, members of the Royal Family. In December 1805 he was appointed Miniature Painter to the Duke of Sussex. When possible he would spend the winter, or at least part of the year, in Aberdeen, taking in visits to the highly approving Nasmyth and Raeburn in Edinburgh. Anxiety caused the poor man to lose his hair at the age of thirty, in 1806, and like Thomas Campbell he had to take to a wig.[5]

In 1806, to Robertson's delight, Nasmyth and his son Peter visited London. Praising Wilkie and his success, Robertson urged Nasmyth to help rescue Scotland from the myth of being unable to to produce genius in the fine arts, whereas 'in poetry and music I think we stand our ground'.[6]

Royal connections continued, and eventually Robertson was concerned in the founding of a Scottish orphanage in London, mooted in 1808 but a bungled project until he was called in as convenor.[7]

Several Scottish painters from poverty-stricken backgrounds made the most of their talent against all the odds. David Roberts, who was to become famous for his paintings in Egypt and the Holy Land, was first of the five children of a poor shoemaker, himself a farmer's son, and was brought up in the humble village of Stockbridge where he was born in 1796.[8] The local men, 'a godless race', as he recorded later, were chiefly outdoor workers, masons, carpenters, quarrymen and carters, and the village boasted a few little shops kept by old women. The Robertses though poor were hardworking and religious. At first the small boy went to school with an old village woman for 3d or 4d a week, more to keep him out of the way than to educate him, and later in Edinburgh. He does not say where, but probably the High School, for he records feelingly how 'like other boys at that period, I was very cruelly treated, getting the skin flayed off my legs and fingers'.

The origin of David's art apprenticeship has two versions. He early showed a fondness for the pictures in halfpenny books, such as Little Red Riding-Hood. Then, on his way back from school he would pass the Earthen Mound, where the Panorama was then set up (on the site of the present Royal Scottish Academy), and leased to a wild beast show. David would earnestly study the lively, crude animal paintings outside the wooden huts, and once he got home would try for his mother's benefit to reproduce what he had seen, scratching on the whitewashed kitchen wall with a burnt stick, or with charcoal and keel (red ochre).

According to the more romantic story, one day a gentleman collecting his shoes from David's father remarked on the spirited drawings of lions and tigers. 'Hoot!' says the father, 'it's our laddy Davie, he's been up at the Mound seeing a wild beast show.' So what would he do in life? asks the gentleman; and learning he must just sit beside his father 'and learn to mak and mend shoon', he said positively, 'Nature has made him an artist. He must be a painter!'

The combined efforts of this benefactor and David's own determination got him an apprenticeship to a celebrated house-painter, Gavin Beugo. David's own more prosaic account was that 'a lady' interested in his aptitude for copying drawings showed his work to John Graham, and suggested he become a pupil at his Academy. Graham, however, saw apprenticeship as a more practical outlet for the son of such poor parents, and with an ornamental house-painter he could earn while studying, and go on to the Academy when his time was out.

David served his seven years with Beugo, for the first year earning two shillings a week, rising by 6d a year. To start with his winter hours were 5 a.m. to 6 p.m., when (presumably as the junior apprentice) he had to go to Beugo's house near Silvermills to pick up the shop key, knocking loudly until the irascible painter opened the window and hurled the heavy key almost on his head. Then he must walk up to the shop in West Register Street to open it at 6 o'clock, nauseatingly stuffy with the smell of oils and paints from being closed overnight. All day he would grind colours, with an hour off for breakfast and dinner, for which he usually had to run the mile to his father's and back again. Summer hours were much easier, from 9 until 4, when he was able to use the long evenings in drawing and reading. This he did alongside his father, whose business also kept him up late, so that there was always 'a well-trimmed lamp' for their joint labours.

Customers used to exclaim wonderingly at Davie's drawings, but the shoemaker father was not very interested. His mother was proud of him, however, and even more so when, showing his portfolio to a neighbour, she found what seemed to be a £1 note inside. How could he have come by this large sum? Davie explained 'with a loud guffaw' that he had copied it from one he had from Beugo to pay a merchant, and so admired the design that he had made this almost perfect facsimile.[9]

Beugo, tyrannical and passionate, was an unpredictable master. He allowed David time to practise drawing, but he employed more apprentices than men, and tended to favour the latest, so that when a new boy came David's chances lessened. 'Kicked and cuffed at work', and with little support at home he used to study the products of the other boys, such as William Kidd, who later became a good painter, and William Mitchell, half brother to John Dick, who liked to create romantic scenes such as Queen Mary's escape from Loch Leven. Mitchell, who sometimes used to grind Dick's colours, during the breakfast break might gather the boys to show them his small oil paintings, and David would go home with him, to draw together at William's widowed mother's laigh or basement flat in Picardy Place. David's own first painting was framed for him for half-a-crown by another Mitchell brother who was a frame-maker, paid off at 6d a week. His pictorial achievement gave David 'supreme happiness'.

The Mitchells later moved to a large, gloomy tenement below Royal Exchange Buildings alongside the Mound, whose north window faced a back green and a dark passage below the offices. Keen youths foregathered for drawing practice in the evenings. After trying a donkey as model, whose braying in the night disturbed all the neighbours, the boys took to acting as model by turns. They even produced enough work to hold an annual exhibition for a few years. But nothing ever overcame David's dread at descending the dark, sinister staircase to the close beneath, with a row of massive cobwebby, padlocked doors 'said to have been shut ever since the great plague', and popularly believed to contain the victims' skeletons.

Meanwhile David improved his reading by spending part of what his father gave him for a midday roll at the village library, where for a penny fee he worked by degrees through Arnot's *History of Edinburgh,* Scott's *Border Ballads, Gil Blas, Don Quixote,* all a great influence in his later life.

He ended his apprenticeship without regret, went to Perth as foreman to a London decorator, Mr Conway, who was working on Scone Palace, and after a year returned for a stint in Edinburgh in the spring of 1816.[10]

Besides painters who struggled from Edinburgh to succeed in London, there were others living and studying in London who frequently came to Edinburgh. The gifted and ambitious, but moody and generally unlucky, historical painter Benjamin Haydon, ten years older than David Roberts, gained his first London success in 1807 with the approval of Sir George and Lady Beaumont. Invited there to dinner with Wilkie, full of nervous anxiety, among the fellow-guests he met Humphrey Davy whom he found 'very entertaining'. At this early date Davy was politically shrewd enough to suggest that, by advancing in Poland, Napoleon must inevitably come up against Russia 'and there probably will begin his destruction'. As Napoleon at the time seemed an eternal and irremovable fixture in Europe, Haydon was sufficiently impressed to make a note of it in his journal.

That year the argumentative Wilkie, prudent in his living habits, returned for a time to Scotland. Haydon was amused in meeting a fellow-Academy student, George Callender from Edinburgh, to find him so like Wilkie that he might have been his brother: a thorough Edinburgh man, 'where they never snuff the candles at a meeting without addressing the chair and appointing a sub-committee to take the propriety of the act into consideration'.[11]

A new and topical spectacle was provided in Edinburgh in 1803, during the short peace with France, by the visit of the French wax model-maker Mme Marie Tussaud, who had been in England since the previous November. After a very rough passage lasting nearly a fortnight she disembarked at Leith on 10 May: even the captain confessed to never having experienced such terrifying waves, and it took Mme Tussaud several days to recover.

She was accompanied, along with her numerous packing-cases, by her five-year-old son Joseph, befriended by all the passengers, who christened him 'Little Bonaparte'. Her business partner and chief, Philipstal, with whom she was on bad terms, had allowed her only £10 travel expenses and would not pay for crates, which the captain refused to unload until 'Mr Charles', a ventriloquist acquaintance then presenting a show in Edinburgh, lent her £30, £18 of which went on redeeming the baggage.

Once at Edinburgh things improved. Lodgings were found with a French-speaking landlady at 38 Thistle Street, a large display space was hired at Bernard's Rooms, and Mme Tussaud opened on 18 May to good audiences. 'Everybody was amazed at my figures', she wrote, though while enjoying Edinburgh and its still snow-covered surrounding hills she was sometimes too tired to eat. She met compatriots at the castle, including a 'lady-in-waiting', presumably the wife of an official, while Joseph was able to play with the French boys there.

When Philipstal arrived, jealous of her success, luckily for her there was no space for him at the Rooms, and he had to show his automata and 'Phantasmagoria' at Corri's, meanwhile claiming half her takings and paying no expenses. Madame felt obliged not to show under her own name, advertising under that of her uncle with 'the accurate models from life in composition from the great Curtius in Paris'. Her exhibitions, open from 11 to 4 and 6 to 8, admission two shillings, attracted up to 150 a day.

'Nothing like them has been seen in this city', she claimed – and indeed her figures were extremely topical, including the then First Consul Napoleon and his wife Josephine, the *ci-devant* French Royal Family, including the unfortunate Princess de Lamballe, Voltaire, Rousseau, and such international celebrities as Frederick the Great and Benjamin Franklin. Her son Joseph was also a popular subject.

The advertisements are revealing. Mr Charles had been advertising his 'Invisible Girl', who 'Speaks & sings English, German, and French &c.' already to the admiration of the Prince of Wales, Monsieur, and 'the most distinguished Personages and Philosophers in England and Scotland', at 63 South Bridge Street opposite the College. It included a preliminary puff for Madame's 'BONAPARTE' forthcoming, with Republican 'dignitaries' in 'proper costume', as shown at the Lyceum in London before the Royal Family (not to mention a mummy supposedly brought from Alexandria by Napoleon), albeit attributed to 'The Great Curtius of Paris'.

They were not the only curiosities on show. At the same time in North College Street was James de Maria's Panorama of Paris, explained by a guide, and claimed to be drawing 'an assembledge no less of Fashion than of Lovers of the Arts'; and this was shortly followed by a rival at the Calton Hill Observatory, of Nelson's victory at the Battle of the Pyramids, and in June by Barker's Contantinople.

When Philipstal arrived he took top billing for his 'pieces of Mechanism' and 'unparalleled Experiments in the Science of Optics'. Notices of Madame's figures were always placed second.

Philipstal met with disaster, however, having promised to open thrice weekly on 11 June with two life-sized automata, a Spanish rope-dancer, a small boy, a mechanical peacock which could not only eat and drink but answer questions, and an optical illusion which was to 'do away with the belief of the Vulgar in Ghosts' – backed up by fireworks and perspective views. But having taken a fortnight to set up his show, when he did open his 'magic lantern' broke down so that his experimental explanation of ghosts by 'the Science of Optics' was initially a failure.

He had to publish an apology for his faulty mechanism and promise to reopen thrice weekly, which he did only in July – when according to Mme Tussaud he was considered a charlatan, and she a great lady.

It seemed a signal to strike for her independence. Turning down a partnership with Mr Charles, after acrimonious dispute she bought herself out from Philipstal for £150 taken from the receipts, plus £100 to return the original advance.

When war resumed and the ports were closed again, exhibition visitor numbers fell, and admission was reduced to a shilling. But she lingered until October, before moving on to equal success in Glasgow.

After further travels, Mme Tussaud returned to Edinburgh in 1810–11, showing at the Panorama at the top of Leith Walk. Of her repertoire, Josephine had given way to the Empress Marie-Louise, and Napoleon, his generals and the French revolutionaries were joined by the English King and Queen, Admiral Nelson and Sir John Moore. More sensational exhibits included Mary Ann Clarke, cause of the army pay scandal – and a show of flea-drawn carriages.

Mme Tussaud was never to return to France. She showed again in Edinburgh in 1824, in 1828 included Burke and Hare in her figures at Gibbs' Rooms in Waterloo Place, and continued an itinerant life with her two sons before finally settling in London in 1854.[12]

Except as amateurs, Scottish lady painters do not appear in Edinburgh, though in 1804 a Miss Linwood had held an exhibition of forty-nine paintings at Laurie's Rooms in the unassuming Thistle Street. She had already exhibited in London, but her talent seems to have been limited to copying such masters as Raphael, Ruysdael, Reynolds, Wilson, Hoppner and Morland. Each item in the exhibition was accompanied by some lines of poetry, from Shakespeare, *Paradise Lost*, Pope and so on, which seems to place her work in the category of 'gift' or 'souvenir'.[13]

18
THE THEATRE

The Theatre is so small that it is altogether out of proportion with the grandeur of the city. But as the drama is very little cultivated in Edinburgh, it has not been found necessary to construct a new theatre. Society in Edinburgh presents so many resources, that the inhabitants do not feel the want of theatrical amusement.

L. A. Necker de Saussure, *Travels in Scotland; descriptive of Manners, Literature, and Science*, London, 1821, 20

'The Edinburgh theatre is diminutive, paltry and little frequented.'

Louis Simond, *Journal of a Tour and Residence in Great Britain, during the years 1810 and 1811*, 1st edn, Edinburgh, 1815, 1.373

The Edinburgh Theatre was uniformly condemned for its mean, unattractive exterior, though admitted to be better inside. Its inferior appearance was no bar to the quality and fame of some of its actors, and the theatre was regarded as a stepping-stone to the London stage. In 1804 and 1805 the boy actor William Betty, 'the young Roscius', played to packed houses. Joseph Mawman, who saw him in 1804, noted with astonishment that although only thirteen he seemed more like sixteen, 'a phaenomenon, as well from his powerful action, as from his commanding articulation, his just apprehension of character, and the perfect recollection and delivery of his part'. That part, amazingly, was Richard III.[1]

Robert Southey, on his disgruntled visit in October 1805, had the unexpected luck to see Betty, in the part of Young Norval in Home's *Douglas*. Although he confessed to a little disappointment, Southey thought him 'incomparably the best actor I have ever seen'.[2] Betty, son of a linen-draper, had been brought up in Ireland, became stage-struck as a child, and started a stage career at the age of eleven with tours in Ireland, Glasgow, Edinburgh, Birmingham and so forth. His youth, looks, grace and feeling diverted public attention from the established leading actors. John Home felt that he realised his own vision of the part of Young Norval, which he played at Covent Garden,[3] and while

John Kemble and his sister Mrs Siddons 'wisely withdrew' from competing, the showy but quarrelsome George Cooke whose besetting sin was the bottle, unwisely allowed himself to be cast as the villain Glenalvon.

Cooke, a man of great charm when sober, had been forty-five when he acted in Edinburgh in 1801 during an extended British tour in a series of Shakespearean parts – Shylock, Iago, Othello, Hamlet, Macbeth. He was warmly praised, but tended to damage his own career through drunken bouts. He acted again in Scotland in the summer of 1807, and then again from December, starting in Glasgow and arriving in Edinburgh in January 1808, where he stayed at M'Gregor's Hotel in Princes Street. As Shylock he was 'received in a flattering manner, by a brilliant and crowded audience', spent a good deal of his time rehearsing as Kitely in Garrick's adaptation of *Every Man in His Humour*,[4] was several times displeased with his own performance, and dined out possibly more than he wished, including with the manager Mr Rock.

His notebook records briefly that at a Mr and Mrs White's and elsewhere he met a Miss Lamb, from Newark, whom he subsequently met again in London and married (November 1808). One evening he, Mr White and Mr Dubuisson went to Corri's Rooms for the latter's 'own night', where they heard singers, and 'a concerto on the violin by Master Gattie, a promising boy of eleven years of age from London'. Cooke left Edinburgh by mail coach on 4 March.[5]

Rock evidently gained some credit for securing so well-known an actor in winter, when the London season was in full swing and usually kept the best of them employed. The truth was that thanks to his proverbial drunkenness Cooke had had few engagements during 1807 and spent much of the time in the debtors' gaol at Appleby in Cumberland (where he kept a journal). He corresponded with Rock in Edinburgh, presumably with appeals for help, and Rock in return for a certain number of performances agreed to settle his debt and free him from prison. While in Edinburgh Cooke played with Charles Young, now a leading tragedian.

Cooke's stage appearances suffered so often from drink that in London a press campaign was launched against him, sadly at odds with his popularity and public acclaim. Yet he continued with touring engagements, and in July 1809 was in Edinburgh again, when during race week he blamed himself for *giving* the managers two nights, 'which was wrong'. He had time for day expeditions, including twice to Roslin, once with a party of ladies including Mrs Rock and Mrs Young, ending with dinner at Dalkeith, 'A very pleasant day in every sense.' He finally appeared in the theatre at Perth, then set off via Edinburgh for Liverpool, but when only twenty-two miles from departure, at Backhouse[6] 'received so severe a fall, that I was constrained to return thither'. Although he does not say so, this was probably due to drink, and he had to stay another twelve days to recover before taking the mail coach for London (9 September).[7]

Actors tended to have unusual lives, and the tragedian Charles Mayne Young, who became friendly with Walter Scott, was no exception. Born in 1777, he was the son of Thomas Young, an eminent London surgeon and anatomist described as selfish, profligate, irascible and overbearing. He was also a gambler and callous spendthrift. Charles as a small boy spent a year in Denmark with his father's sister, who had married the King's physician Professor Müller, and he became such a favourite with the Danish royal family that they begged in vain for the boy to stay on, and afterwards kept up a correspondence with him.

Charles was educated at Eton and Merchant Taylors', but his father's cruel tyranny made for an unhappy family life, and when Young senior determined to set up his mistress in their house, his wife and sons left home. Having no means of their own, they now lived a restricted life with the wife's unmarried sister, but all the sons went on to make successful careers and Charles, after working as clerk to a business firm, quickly transferred to the stage. He started in Liverpool with a part in *Douglas* (1798), then went to the north of England and Glasgow; later in 1802 and 1803 he played often as a leading tragedian in Edinburgh, where audiences made much of him.

Throughout its existence of almost a century the Edinburgh Theatre had associations with all its literary celebrities, and many of its painters. Scott, a great theatre lover, was one of the pioneers, and had barely set up house before he was entertaining leading actors. Young was one of the first of these, whom Scott praised in 1803 as 'a valuable addition to the Society of Edinburgh'. For the rest of his life, whenever playing in Edinburgh, Young regularly visited Scott.[8]

Young met his wife, Julia Grimani, whose background was more picturesque than his own, at the Haymarket Theatre in 1804. Both of good birth, handsome, talented, and adopting their dramatic career from a necessity to support relatives, they had much in common. They married in Liverpool in 1805 and lived briefly in 'unchequered bliss' too good to last: Julia died of fever that July, shortly after giving birth to a son.[9]

The desolate husband left the infant for six years in the care of a naval captain's daughter, while he pursued a successful acting career at the Haymarket under George Colman, with the recurring misfortune of his malicious father's too frequent attendance in order to hiss his son.[10] In 1807 and February 1808 he returned to Edinburgh, playing to 'ecstatic' audiences. 'Praise . . . follows you everywhere', wrote Colman, on learning that Charles had earned £500 on his benefit night, and ticked him off for making complaints: may he freeze 'on the top of Calton Hill, a north-easterly wind blowing the intensest frost that ever cut the bare breech of a Scotchman!'

Scott, who remained a good friend to Young, in later years was able to advise him on his son Julian's education at St Andrews University.[11]

In March 1808 Mrs Siddons made one of her several 'last' Edinburgh appearances, with a single performance of each of her most famous parts. Everyone was anxious to see her celebrated Lady Macbeth. Robert Gillies came across Professor Stewart in the lobby, unable to reach the box to which he had been invited because it was already crowded out. Gillies himself had to climb up and find an uneasy perch in the slips.[12]

Charles Kirkpatrick Sharpe met Mrs Siddons at a dinner at Walter Scott's, and was disillusioned that she could behave so like an ordinary person. 'You cannot imagine', he told his sister Isabella, 'how it annoyed me to behold Belvidera guzzle boiled beef and mustard, swill streams of porter, cram up her nose with handfuls of snuff, and laugh till she made the whole room shake again.' Worse, she had been putting on weight and was 'really now so broad in the pockets that she is a great shame to be seen'.[13]

That same summer, the dramatic actor R. W. Elliston, on tour after a poor showing in Dublin, 'made ample amends' in Edinburgh where (he wrote to his wife) 'my reception was quite an hurrah! I have already remitted £610 to my bankers . . . But who can tell how long this tide of popularity will last . . .' He was particularly impressed on meeting some of the professors with their 'great kindness', by the literary class of Edinburgh, which he dubbed its 'aristocracy'. 'There is no better society, nor should there be'. 'This is highly honourable to the Scotch character.'[14]

The theatre's progress was complicated by the rise and fall of rival establishments as well as general dissatisfaction about the building. Henry Siddons celebrated his take-over by leasing Corri's Rooms at the former Circus in Leith Walk, and transferring the Royal sanction to what he now opened as the 'New Theatre Royal'. Redecorated in the 'Gothic' style – '*gingerbread* work', as some criticised it – it was opened with *The Honeymoon,* in which both the Siddonses played leading parts, on 14 November 1809. The first night was crammed.

There was some criticism of the new venue. Access was awkward, complained the *Monthly Mirror*: 'You must make the complete circle of the house, and ascend one or two flights of steps before you arrive at the box lobby', and the St James' Square entrance was reserved for chairs, coaches being directed via Leith Walk.

Unfortunately Siddons was overreaching himself; converting Corri's Rooms cost between £4000 and £5000, which he had leased for three years at £800 a year. Meanwhile he was still paying rent for the old theatre.[15]

As a result, they were able to remain in their new premises only until August

1811, and in November Siddons was obliged to reopen at the old Shakespeare Square premises. There were some valuable additions: Scott's friend Daniel Terry first appeared, at the new theatre, a fortnight after it opened, and in 1810 Mrs Siddons's brother William Murray, a competent accountant, was first employed as stage manager. But Siddons found it hard to keep up the standard of productions: in a small theatre a full house could raise scarcely £200, with top prices for boxes at only four shillings, three for the pit, and the galleries a shilling. This was a disadvantage when some celebrity, or successful play, appeared. For example, there were the brilliant comedian Charles Mathews in August 1813, Mr Betty as Douglas in November, and both Mathews and Charles Kemble (for the first time in fifteen years), in 1814. The soprano Catalani sang at the old theatre in December 1811, several times, before moving to the Assembly Rooms under Corri's management. The theatre would regularly be closed for weeks at a time, the season running from November until May, and then with intervals until August.[16]

During his regime Siddons acted Belcour in Cumberland's *The West Indian* and Charles Surface in *The School for Scandal*; the older Daniel Terry played Sir Peter Teazle, Sir Anthony Absolute and Lord Ogleby. Chambers recounts that Mason played 'stern guardians and snappish old men', Berry low comedy, and of the ladies, Mrs Henry Siddons acted Lady Teazle, and Belvidera in *Venice Preserv'd,* Mrs Nicol was Mrs Malaprop and other elderly aunts, and Mrs William Penson played breeches parts and uncouth girls, such as Audrey in *As You Like It*, Priscilla Tomboy in Bickerstaffe's *The Romp* and William in *Rosina.*[17]

In 1810, the great sensation at the new theatre was Joanna Baillie's *Family Legend,* produced to open the season on 29 January and running for thirteen consecutive nights. Terry acted the Earl of Argyll and Siddons John of Lorne. The prologue was written by Scott, the epilogue by Henry Mackenzie, and scenery was painted by Alexander Nasmyth and J. F. Williams. Although Miss Baillie had written it for the Edinburgh theatre, its acceptance was thanks to Scott – who admired it greatly – as acting trustee for the proprietors.[18]

The Lord Provost expressed an unexpected interest in this play, when he discovered that his own firm of stocking-weavers had provided all the Campbell and Maclean tartans and hose. The *Scots Magazine* criticised the scenery, complaining with some justification that the interior of old Inveraray Castle ought to have been Gothic, not 'Corinthian' or Neo-Classical. Nasmyth, who had visited the *new* Inveraray, had perhaps been influenced by its uncompromisingly modern interiors.[19]

No play had caused such a sensation in Edinburgh since the first production of *Douglas,* and like *Douglas,* its attraction probably lay more in the Scottish theme than in its dramatic skill. The house was full every night, and all Edinburgh's fashionable society turned up, so that it was 'the only subject of town talk'. It was very long, too long, lasting until 10.30 at night, and some less powerful scenes were later cut. Scott, sitting anxiously in the audience on the first night, praised it highly, and was pleased that in the fight scene at Inveraray the garrison was swelled by Volunteers, raised by his brother's Highland recruiting party, giving a convincing effect 'as they mustered beneath the porch of the castle, and seemed to fill the courtyard beneath'. His young family, whom he took to see the play, gratifyingly sobbed heartily at the more affecting passages.[20]

Theatrically, 1810 was glittering. On 14 March Mrs Siddons opened her return season with *Macbeth*, as brilliant as she had been in her 'great parts' twenty-six years earlier. At the end of the month she played Jane to her nephew's De Monfort in Miss Baillie's play of that name written in 1800, and this too earned great applause.[21]

In June Mrs Jordan played for a chequered three weeks, staying at Fortune's Hotel, but despite its 'very elegant rooms & good accomodations in every respect', found more to grumble at than to please in Edinburgh. She paid twenty-five guineas for the first ten days for lodgings and other expenses, 'they charge here for everything enormously'. Her impression of the city's beauty was at once nullified by a string of complaints at being over-worked and underpaid. She had no evening off until Friday, and even then had to rehearse, and had to forgo a bathe, which she would have dearly liked, being too tired to get up at 7 a.m. to fit one in. She did find time to visit Holyrood, but thought it 'but a poor thing', while the castle must be missed because continuous 'bustle and worry' affected both her spirits and her sleep.

She was playing at Henry Siddons's New Theatre, and once her presence was known her reception was all that could be wished. She thought the theatre 'miserable', and on meeting Scott was so jaundiced that she was impatient at his 'fine speeches', even countering his flattery at her supposedly unchanged appearance with a tart retort that that was extraordinary, since he was reputed so 'sharp-sighted'. This sally was much appreciated, and generally passed around. She felt angry with Scott, who though a proprietor had not advanced money towards the new theatre.

Everything irritated Mrs Jordan, even the acoustics; even her successful first night, which left her immensely fatigued with a relaxed throat and sore mouth. The ninth of June was the King's birthday, and the city's loyalty was apparent, but their 'salutations' woke her at 4 a.m. The King's birthday dinner at the Parliament House ended in a drunken brawl and, worse from her point of view, half emptied the theatre or at least its boxes, usually the best attended.

Even when the house was good and receipts heavy, she complained that figures were fiddled to suit managers rather than actors. (Glasgow, she was told, was even worse.) She admitted that the poor houses were partly her own fault, having not ascertained that this would be an 'empty time of year'. Pushing herself to clear her debts, she was for a time inclined to accept Siddons's invitation to play a further twelve nights following her Bath engagement, at the height of the season. Ending this 'disagreeable and unprofitable engagement' without regret, she observed with some satisfaction that Siddons had been 'reprobated' by Edinburgh's 'liberal' elements for deceiving her into believing that the time of year made no difference, claimed rather smugly that 'the whole town' thought Siddons had 'played the Jesuit with me', and ended with a certain amount of spite that she would not now play in Newcastle – nor even go to Portobello, because it was so expensive.

Heavy suspicion over his division of the benefit night profits, and Mrs Jordan's conviction that she had lost heavily over the booking, ended her season as it had gone on, as she parted from 'the most *grovelling* and ungrateful wretch that ever was seen'. To do her justice, she found others inclined to share her opinion.

Even at the end there was dissatisfaction, as confusion in booking Miss Duncan in Glasgow lost Mrs Jordan two nights in Edinburgh. She ended her stay in the part of Lady Teazle with the waspish comment that the town was so empty that the boxes had been occupied nightly by 'the same sort of people . . . I certainly was not born to combat with the Kemble family'. She never returned to Edinburgh.

It was perhaps a little naïve to find that at last, having doubtless made her displeasure strongly felt, as she would not relent over booking a return visit, the Siddonses turned insolent, 'even amounting to rudeness'. One wonders precisely what she had said to them.[22]

James Hogg, discussing the actors in his short-lived magazine *The Spy*, concluded that the company still lacked 'a dashing buck' and a 'tender passionate lover'; the current younger leads, Mrs Henry Siddons's brother the newcomer William Murray, Brooke, Thomson and Halliwell were all insipid. Their lack of tragedians, however, as Hogg pointed out, mattered less to Scottish audiences who were 'naturally gay, and fond of humour'. Siddons himself Hogg rated highly.

As for the orchestra, this chauvinist writer complained that national music was neglected for the 'false taste' imposed on them by 'Italian tirlie-whirlies', 'chattering and trilling at their foreign airs'. Yet in the *Family Legend* (he said), how popular the Highland music had proved![23]

Clementina Drummond remarked how that year Catalani, Mrs Siddons, Mrs Jordan, John Kemble and Henry Siddons were all in Edinburgh together. Catalani they met several times, nearly every Sunday at Lord Maurice's old friend Lord Fingall's. With her elegant manners she was admired in society and was still in splendid voice. 'When she sang in church', Clementina recalls, 'the crowd was so great that it was not only difficult to get standing room, but many persons invariably fainted.'

They also met Mrs Jordan, socially as well as on the stage, and used to go personally to collect tickets which were advertised as obtainable from her lodgings. She had pretty features and beautiful eyes, but, noted the sharp-eyed Clementina, was disfigured by smallpox, and while lively and animated, seemed 'rather too old and too fat for some of her favourite parts' – especially *The Romp*, in which she was playing (she was nearing forty-nine).[24]

Lady Clem was nearly disappointed of seeing Mrs Siddons, which she had longed for, especially after meeting her one evening with her father at Lady Maurice's. Lord Maurice, who had acted at the Trianon and Versailles with Marie Antoinette, was charmed with both Mrs Siddons and Kemble, especially as they understood French acting, and could discuss it with him in French.

As soon as their performance was announced every seat and box was snapped up. Lady Wemyss invited the Drummonds senior, but not Clementina or even her own daughter, perhaps thinking them too young. Clementina was desolate. The situation seemed to be saved when her cousin Mrs Drummond Burrell, who was staying at a St Andrew Square hotel and who had a box, despatched another cousin from the theatre especially to fetch her. But the ground was covered with snow – no wheel traffic could venture over it! A chair was at last found, but only one porter. The kind cousin, Sir William Stuart, took the second pole and at last they succeeded in reaching the theatre just as *The Gamester* was beginning.

When they had met at her mother's, Clem had thought Mrs Siddons 'anything but young, and much too stout to be elegant', despite her 'inimitable grace, that easy *pose*'. Now, seeing her on stage, she forgot everything – even that she was playing opposite her own son Henry as hero. She was spellbound. 'When at last, the Gamester was carried in apparently lifeless, and Mrs Siddons, as Mrs Beverley, in an attitude of terror . . . fell down on her knees before him . . . and at last with one piercing shriek, exclaimed "He is dead!" I screamed too.'

Good acting made the audience forget the actor. Later she was deeply impressed by John Kemble in *Coriolanus* and the 'statuesque grandeur of his acting', and forgot the oddity of his niece acting his mother Volumnia. 'She was pretty, and acted her part charmingly.' There was evidently no further difficulty in Clementina's attending the theatre, for she also saw Mrs Siddons in *Macbeth*, which she found less riveting, for in this case 'I did not, to the same extent lose sight of her identity!' In the sleep-walking scene, for example, with the words 'this little hand', she could not help noticing how very large Mrs Siddons's hands were. Yet this was considered the actress's most memorable part.[25]

Clementina was extremely lucky to have seen Mrs Siddons then, almost the last opportunity. Though still very young to go into society (especially in her mother's view), her time of ball-going now started, and she was probably diverted.

A great devotee of the theatre, a taste inherited from his father, was Archibald Alison. Alison senior had known Kemble at Oxford, and Archibald thought him a better actor even than Mrs Siddons – 'a natural genius . . . a powerful countenance, a fine figure; and a thorough antiquarian knowledge of the costume'. Nothing could be finer than his Roman characters, Brutus, Cato, Coriolanus, especially when he entered as the last, 'his step on the stage . . . in his Roman costume, with a dazzling helmet on his head'.

The family always went to see Mrs Siddons, and now for her swan song Archibald contrived to see her thirty-five times (so he claims – she could scarcely have appeared that many times). Still handsome in her late middle age, cut out for a tragedy queen, she could still convincingly play Desdemona or Juliet. 'A tall and commanding figure, a profusion of black locks, a Roman style of countenance, and an expression of poetic inspiration.' Again, though her figure was now unwieldy, he found it was quickly forgotten in her brilliant presentation.[26]

The year 1811 proved less star-spangled. Louis Simond saw 'the excellent English actor' Charles Bannister, but in 'one of their wretched modern plays', *The Battle of Hexham*: 'the plot most absurd, and with a total want of taste', redeemed only by Bannister. The theatre was almost empty, the boxes completely so, though this could be explained by the rival lure of the singer John Braham performing in a concert elsewhere. Simond believed that in Britain generally the theatre was considered 'a rather vulgar amusement', an odd inference in Edinburgh at least, where it was always the talk of society.

He saw Bannister in other plays, including the 'low and improbable' *Bold Stroke for a Wife* which, however, he preferred to 'modern' works. Bannister was actually a comedian, who excelled in 'harlequin' roles involving frequent, fast changes of costume and character. At audience request he would often give a song between the play and the farce. One favourite mentioned by Simond 'in the genuine national taste', was plainly a nonsense song, quite untranslatable, a string of unconnected words or even mere 'uncouth sounds', absurdly set off by Bannister's talented buffoonery.[27]

As actor-manager Henry Siddons was popular and a happier chapter seemed to be opening for the theatre, apart from his error of judgment in trying to set up in the Leith Walk building. He invested in much-needed improvements, new decorations and scenery, creating a light, elegant impression so far unfamiliar to Edinburgh audiences.

His wife endeared herself to the public. Lord Glenbervie praised her as 'one of the most amiable and best, pretty looking, modest creatures that can be, and a very pleasing actress', and he also raved about her qualities as wife and mother, and her 'two little cherubs' of daughters. 'She is worth ten thousand Abingtons', and Edinburgh ought to take good care of her.[28]

Siddons's reign unfortunately lasted only a few years, and he died untimely in 1815 at the age of forty-one. There had been a rumour of his declining health, and a suggestion that the Kembles might succeed him, but he stayed on and their period of bad luck seemed to be ending. On 1 March 1815 Mrs Henry had her benefit, with her husband, in *The Wild Indian,* in what proved to be Siddons's last appearance ever, for only a few weeks later he died.[29]

Though he was sorely missed, his widow carried on as manager, her brother William Murray acting as stage manager and maintaining the quality of the company and visiting players; and his mother, Mrs Siddons the elder, her powers scarcely diminished at sixty-two, returned for occasional benefit nights in aid of the family. That August the beautiful Miss Eliza O'Neill, her successor as tragedienne, made her first Edinburgh appearance, which led to scenes reminding old stagers of Mrs Siddons's own Edinburgh début: the Highland porters camping out for seats and sometimes coming to blows over places, while fashionable families left their breakfast tables to watch the skirmishes.[30]

The city's other forms of entertainment endured even patchier fortunes. Corri's Rooms, Siddons's ill-starred venture as a theatre, was at the head of Leith Walk in St James' Square, near the former village of French weavers called Picardy.[31] Having started in 1788 as The Circus (apparently strictly as an amphitheatre), and not proving very profitable, it had been converted in 1792 to a playhouse, and by 1801, while still used on week-nights for riding exhibitions, tight-rope dancing, tumbling and pantomime – a 'synagogue of Satan' – on Sundays it housed religious services, and at least by 1806 ran subscriptions for foreign missions. According to Campbell it was 'a huge unshapely mass of building'.[32]

Re-converted from a chapel to amusements and dancing, and used by Signor Natale Corri as a music-room, 'Corri's Rooms' became Edinburgh's fashionable concert-hall after St Cecilia's descended to the bourgeois. Corri as director engaged reputable performers, and in winter staged balls there.[33]

A panorama, at the Assembly Rooms,[34] was possibly the one published in 1825 by J. & R. Burford, 'from Drawings taken by them from the Summit of Calton Hill'. It is to be hoped that the original was better than the crudely executed print forming the frontispiece, a poor rendering of the city, though it shows buildings like the new gaol and other institutions. Many important buildings, though indicated by a number, are invisible, and there is no sign of the Theatre or St James' Square in the foreground. Rather more interesting is the view to the east, showing the foundation stone of the National Monument in its solitary state, and the all-but-empty country north and east of the city.[35]

Miss Edgeworth saw presumably the same Edinburgh Panorama in Dublin in 1812. 'I never saw a sight that pleased me more: Edinburgh was before me – Princes Street and George Street – the Castle – the bridge over dry land . . . At first a mistiness, like what there is in nature over a city before the sun breaks out; then the sun shining on the buildings, trees, and mountains.'[36] The effect would have been not unlike the much later camera obscura.

Panoramas were usually exhibited on the Earthen Mound, for example, one of the Banks of the Thames, in February 1811, advertised as in a new building and painted by Mr F. Gibbon, which was claimed to contain 'every remarkable feature . . . from Gravesend up to Windsor'. However, one advertised with much gusto in March 1808 of the Battle of Agincourt was shown 'in a large Wooden Building, erected for that purpose, in Drummond Street, Immediately behind the Royal Infirmary'. Robert Ker Porter's work was on 3500 square feet of canvas and was claimed as the largest in Europe. It was too large for the Mound, and the proprietor, Parkes, could find nowhere spacious enough to accommodate it, so at the request of friends he built expensively in wood, whose price having greatly risen he had to charge two shillings for entry instead of the usual one. As it was only advertised between 5 and 12 March, and not written up in a newspaper report (though this was not unusual), it may have proved a financial failure.[37]

At the same time, and rivalling the singer Braham's appearance, Bannister at the Theatre, and the menagerie, was Mr Cartwright's 'Amusements' in the more genteel setting of Fortune's 'Tontine', 'on the Musical Glases and Display of Philosophical Fireworks', of which to please those ladies and gentlemen who found it difficult to get home at night, he offered two morning performances in the week besides the regular evenings. This did earn the notice of a reporter, described as 'the favourite resort of fashion and elegance', and praised for 'the neat manner in which he has fitted up the room, and the comfort and warmth he studies to give it'. A week later there was further praise for 'the ingenuity and beauty of the philosophical fireworks, which gain universal applause' – without, unfortunately, defining what they were.[38]

Early in the century this seems to have been joined by the menagerie, set up in caravans and wooden huts, painted on the outside with the pictures on canvas of the animals to be seen inside, which so fascinated the boy David Roberts. In the severe winter of 1811, when Edinburgh suffered heavy snow and high winds, the timber menagerie seemed in imminent danger. Louis Simond, who from Dumbreck's hotel had it in full view, toyed with the idea that, should it be blown down, 'the people of Edinburgh might see at large in the streets two lions, two royal tigers, a panther and an elephant, besides monkies, and other underlings of the savage tribe'.[39]

Music in Edinburgh was at a fairly low ebb. The great days of St Cecilia's

Hall were long past. After its successful and fashionable early years, it had already run into financial trouble in the 1770s, and was further affected when families began to move away from the Old Town to the New. The opening of the George Street Assembly Rooms in 1787 ended its lure as a fashionable venue, as the new rooms proved more convenient for New Town dwellers for concerts. In 1801 the Musical Society was wound up.[40]

The Society's concerts had been conducted since 1771 by Domenico Corri, invited to Edinburgh the year after Charles Burney had met him in Italy; he settled in the city as a singing master and publisher in partnership with his brother Natale. His wife, though educated as a miniaturist, proved to have such a fine singing voice that she was then trained as a singer and joined her husband in Edinburgh, and despite having a young family devoted herself to the art. She was the first woman singer engaged by the St Cecilia directors.

Some saw the decline of music in Edinburgh from the 1770s as the result of 'vitiated taste', which preferred 'mere rapidity, noise, and unmeaning sounds' to such classics as Handel, Haydn and so on. In other words, a preference for the 'modern'. According to Campbell, even in 1777 it was seen as due to the development of instrumental music, and to the 'contagion' which in his own day led people of fashion to affect connoisseurship in painting, music and poetry. In 1804 John Stark also claimed that the 'decay' of music was partly due to a decline in taste.[41]

Natale Corri, besides opening the Circus as a concert hall, which was for a time the only hall offering winter concerts, directed weekly performances at the Assembly Rooms. After a shaky start, these improved when he engaged the gifted violinist George Pinto, Lambeth-born grandson of the famous Pinto mentioned by Charles Burney, who was met with some acclaim.

His brother Domenico, meanwhile, who could have been a good singer like his wife, dissipated his talents in concentrating on often unsuccessful 'projects', such as a hare-brained attempt to launch an Edinburgh 'Vauxhall', and another to run a theatre at the Circus. He proved better as a singing-master to young ladies, including the Ladies Montagu, and as a music-seller, including of his own works.[42]

Not surprisingly Corri was considered more than a little eccentric. In fact when he called one day to ask the novelist Monk Lewis [?early in 1803] to write the dialogue for *The Travellers,* or *Music's Fascination,* from his manner, conversation, and 'the extreme absurdity of the plan', Lewis thought him quite mad. His music was not very good either (so Lewis thought). The Buccleuchs, who had been Corri's patrons in Edinburgh, were 'highly amused with his oddities' and related several anecdotes which unfortunately the Monk did not bother to repeat.[43]

In 1811 the famous tenor John Braham[44] appeared in Edinburgh, but Louis Simond, who heard him in a poor performance of *The Siege of Belgrade* in which apparently he sang as a counter-tenor, thought it so bad that even 'the British public' could not listen with patience. Braham had a fine voice and his technique was then uncommon – clear and powerful 'but he wants simplicity and feeling'. Further hearings did not change Simond's opinion. 'It is not music you hear, but only fine sounds.' One must bear in mind that this was a time when it was the fashion for every man of taste to set himself up as a critic of all the arts and even of scenery, and to enlighten the world with his views.

As for the old theatre building, it remained 'diminutive, paltry' and according to Simond 'little frequented' – the last possibly a temporary lapse in view of a second-rate production. He thought, not very convincingly, that in contrast with France people preferred evenings at home.[45]

Of instrumentalists, for some years Signor Puppo had been First Violin at St Cecilia's Hall. His successor was Stabilini, whom the directors invited from Rome in 1783 and for seventeen years was unrivalled as performer and composer. He pleased the Scots by setting songs in the national style, a favourite being 'Sandie o'er the Lee', which evoked Campbell's rapture: 'What brilliancy! what pathos! what expression! Oh, exquisite, exquisite.'[46]

Dancing never lost its hold, and the professional teachers staged displays at specially arranged balls, thanks to their leading light David Strange. His successor Charles Stewart, a former pupil, followed him with equal popularity for a quarter of a century.[47]

The Assembly Rooms in George Street, completed by public subscription in 1787 – though still lacking William Burn's Tuscan portico on rusticated arches – was a popular venue, despite the heavy criticism of self-appointed visitor critics. Its grand saloon, 24 feet square, was supplemented by two card rooms, a tea room used for dancing during card assemblies, and other facilities. In the main dancing saloon the orchestra sat in a circular recess at the side. In winter two assemblies were held each week, one for dancing, one for cards. Rooms built in George Square to serve the city's south side proved unsuccessful after a few seasons and were converted to housing.[48]

Paramount in popular affection, needless to say, were the bagpipes, and in 1807 Sir John Carr endured a piping contest with much the same grim distaste as Faujas de St Fond twenty-three years earlier. Professing his love of music was his undoing, for friends promised 'a rich treat' when, as a great favour, he was invited to a rehearsal in the Assembly Rooms. 'I shall never forget it!'

There was the usual ritual of the judges taking their places, the folding doors opening to admit a kilted piper, his pipes decked with ribbons. With a volley of sounds 'loud and horrible . . . comparable only to those of the eternally tormented', he stalked to loud plaudits in his stately march.

All the competing pipers were finely-built, shown to advantage by their dress; many were prize-winners come from long distances, for example from Mull and Skye. Carr, who could not even distinguish between 'the gathering of the Macdonalds' and a depressing and (to him) discordant lament, welcomed the all-too-short intervals of Highland dancing, though this again seemed to him to demonstrate agility without grace. Most of the audience meanwhile were impatiently awaiting the pipers' return.

After enduring in common politeness (he claimed) for three whole hours, Sir John left in a state of near-collapse.[49]

Yet he had not wholly escaped. At the end of the Leith races, the fashion was to go on to the theatre, and here Carr again witnessed pipers and dancers, remarking prudishly on the effect of their 'springs and caperings' on the men's philabegs, which he thought must surely wound the delicacy of ladies in the pit. The winner of the silver-mounted pipes was piper to the Laird of McNab and Breadalbane.

Carr managed to slip out before the end, and later met several Scots who actually confessed distaste for the pipes. 'Whilst refinement is rapidly spreading,' he concluded, 'the bagpipe is amongst the very few remaining barbarisms of Scotland.'[50]

Far more to his taste was a silent exhibition of reading and writing by the pupils of Mr Paton in Corri's concert rooms. Well-dressed, good-looking children sat at desks and illustrated their proficiency at writing, and stood in the orchestra space to display on slates an astonishing arithmetical skill. Mr Paton was said to have introduced a new method of calculating simultaneously in pounds, shillings and pence. Gratified at the number of genteel spectators, Carr was convinced that such public exhibitions must excite a salutary spirit of competition, to national good effect.[51]

19
ECCENTRICS AND OTHERS

'There are whimsical people every where . . . A gentleman at Edinburgh of rather a whimsical turn, some time ago used to curl and powder his horses tails and their manes after they had been well frizzed and pomatumed; and, having built a house, had almost the one end of it, from the foundation to the top, of glass, thinking this by far the best way to light a house, and save the window tax.'

Rev. James Hall, *Travels in Scotland, by an Unusual Route*, London, 1807, II.581

Edinburgh's supply of remarkable characters extended well beyond the literary, artistic and academic worlds. One of the most extraordinary was the elder brother of the advocate Henry Erskine – David, 11th Earl of Buchan, a noted egotist whose contemporaries seemed unsure whether to regard him as pompous braggart or eccentric near-genius. Archibald Constable admired him, despite his absurdities, for 'sterling excellence, both mental and moral', as a sincere friend even to excess, certainly to Constable with whom he was close for nearly thirty years.[1]

Born in 1742, under his courtesy title of Lord Cardross he had been a diplomat, but resigned on inheriting his father's title in order to cultivate the family estates. By living on a limited income he contrived to rid the inheritance of financial encumbrance and to educate his brothers Henry and William, whose potential he recognised – a generosity never forgotten. He was as versatile and volatile as they, but whereas they had to concentrate on a career, their peer brother had no such restrictions. The straitened circumstances of his early life engendered a habit of meanness which he never threw off.

One of Lord Buchan's services to Edinburgh was to form, in 1780, the Antiquarian Society, though James Boswell even at the time thought him silly and affected;[2] then in 1791 he founded an annual festival commemorating the poet James Thomson. Buchan was widely read, had a good memory, and was a witty and lively dinner companion who did not monopolise the conversation. A regular career to channel his capacities would have made him a useful citizen.[3] But he dissipated his undoubted talents in foolery.

He was certainly quick in apprehension and could get the gist of a book, at least superficially, 'however abstruse'. He wrote essays, was a reasonable critic, and was a great book collector. But not the least of his distinct oddities was the sense of his own importance. For example, at the academic level he claimed that the secret of the young Brewster's distinguished paper on optics was his own revision of it. He was careful to present the university and other institutions with portraits of himself, a mild vanity compared with other self-indulgences.

At the absurd level, although he did not attend St George's Church, during services his mittens were regularly placed on the front gallery to gratify the congregation with the belief that he was there. As for the *Review*, he was so enraged by its opinions that one day on receiving the latest copy he laid it on his hall floor, ordered the footman to open the front door, and kicked the offending journal into George Street. He believed himself irresistible to women, and once told a handsome young lady as he was taking leave, 'Pray remember that Margaret, Countess of Buchan, is not immortal.'[4]

Yet he had many worthy friends and admirers, including Mrs Fletcher. On one morning call at her house he happened to coincide with the young Thomas Campbell, who knowing his reputation, rather stupidly amused himself by 'quizzing' him. The older man, keeping his temper, merely took up his hat and left. When he had gone, Mrs Fletcher lectured Thomas severely for so insulting an 'old' man (he was in his fifties), in a friend's house. Thomas was so mortified and even 'choked with rage' that he rang for a glass of water, swallowed it down and rushed from the house. For a whole week he kept out of Mrs Fletcher's way, but at last turned up again looking contrite; they shook hands, and all went on as before.[5]

The poet records that at the start of one university session (November 1808), when the usual crowd of students turned up to hear Dugald Stewart, Lord Buchan decided to 'take notice' of the famous professor by gracing the occasion with his presence. Arriving before Stewart he mounted the dais, looked round, 'put his hand to his lips, smiled graciously, and bowed to the audience. They shouted in an ecstacy of merriment; he bowed three times, they shouted as oft, and clapt their hands, till Dugald entered, and then he pointed to him, again smiling, as much as to say, "Mr Stewart has now a right and my leave, to your attention".'[6]

According to Robert Gillies, who met Lord Buchan at his uncle Dr Tytler's, at Dr Anderson's at Heriot Green, and later almost daily at Sir Brooke Boothby's, the peer 'never willingly sat still for even ten minutes together', fancied he knew everything on a subject after a few minutes' study, 'and could leap from one to another with admirable dexterity'. Gillies was sure he imagined himself infallible and believed his own exaggerated stories. 'If so, surely he was among the most remarkable and the happiest of all eccentric beings.' His misfortune was to mistake his 'buoyant spirits and quickness of superficial apprehension' for the inspiration of genius.

He even supposed his counsel to be of incomparable value to the King and Royal family, and that unless he favoured them with his advice, Britain's whole constitution would be endangered, so that he often sent them his personal advice. His letters were courteously acknowledged, usually by one of the princesses. Similarly he was convinced that the literary world, too, could not survive without his patronage.[7]

Lord Buchan, obsessional over his health, always rose at 6 and went to bed at 11 or 12 at night. Even on winter mornings he would be out before 7 and never neglected a visit to St Bernard's Well, whose water according to Gillies not only had an 'odious twang of hydrogen gas' but had no medicinal value. Lord Buchan would lecture anyone there within hearing on the value of early rising. Later, having taken offence at the well's guardian, he found 'a branch of the same detestable spring' nearby, built a shed over it and placed a bust of himself inside, with a copy of his own verses, of which Gillies insists that 'unluckily' he can recall only the first line: 'Ye beaux and ye belles, ye gay little tits!'

After taking breakfast, Lord Buchan sat down to write his letters, or essays which he intended for anonymous publication. Then followed his 'great work of the day': fondly supposing all Edinburgh's literary and scientific pundits and artists to be under his personal patronage, he reckoned it his duty to visit them daily with advice. If not received he used to leave his compliments and regrets that the householder had wasted the precious morning in sleep. 'Certain doors, it is true, were hermetically sealed against him . . . upon the whole he met with a very ungrateful world.' Hardly surprising since none of this loving care took the form of a sixpence of financial help, unless to clinch a bargain.[8]

Lord Buchan's own hospitality might be termed vicarious. One cold March morning Gillies's brother-in-law, Arthur Clifford, was invited to breakfast to meet George Dyer, Charles Lamb's poet friend. On their arrival the earl announced that they were to breakfast instead at Alexander Cunningham's, farther up George Street, 'in company with Burns' (his bust, that is). As a precaution he slipped a couple of eggs into his pocket. At Cunningham's he thundered on the door until a half-dressed maid-servant appeared and nervously admitted them to the parlour, where they found the remnants of a convivial night, punch-bowl still on the supper-table. Peggy reappeared with the master's compliments, but 'no' being vera well, he could not have the pleasure of seeing the gentlemen at that early hour'. Lord Buchan, with much emphasis on his own name, replied that 'if he's lying in bed at 9 he'll go to the devil'. Then, removing the holly wreath from Burns's bust, he placed it on Clifford's and Dyer's heads in turn, exhorting them to record this memorable day, when they were crowned *by him* with Burns's wreath. In silence the trio marched back to the Earl's own door, where he suddenly turned to face them and declaimed, while the helpless pair tried to stifle their laughter, 'Mr Clifford, the man who does not honour me in his heart for all that I have done – *is a fool!*'[9]

At a more notorious breakfast fiasco, which earned Buchan great ridicule, he presented himself as Apollo with nine aristocratic young ladies in costume as the Muses. Unfortunately Cupid, who entered with a tea-kettle, was naked, and the prudish young ladies ran off tittering and screeching. The peer, undeterred, would willingly have repeated the occasion with John Graham to paint it, but Graham prudently refused with the excuse that it would mean making ten portraits.[10]

His meanness was ingrained since the pinched economies of earlier life, and Susan Mein, who relates several stories of this 'most extraordinary, stingy, crabbed old man', observes that he always accepted any dinner invitations he received, but she never knew him give a summer party himself when he and his wife were at his country estate. Groups of ladies might come to see his gardens and the ruins of Dryburgh Abbey, where the fruit-trees, which he had barbarously nailed to the walls, were famed as the best in the county; he would personally conduct the visitors and invite them to admire, even feel – but never to taste. If his wife ever asked Lyon, the meek, incongruously named butler, to bring them peaches, Buchan would impatiently interrupt that they were not worth eating, 'you may as well eat a turnip'. His object in fact was to sell the produce in Edinburgh, and he was even known to demand a penny from village children for a handful of gooseberries.

The delightful Lady Buchan, daughter of William Fraser of Fraserfield, when at home spent much of her time spinning. When Susan Mein was in Edinburgh she would act as 'Matron' or chaperon at Edinburgh or Melrose balls, and the Earl would repay all the entertainment they received by a single winter ball in his 'Poets' Hall' at the Abbey, which everyone was sure to attend. On one of these evenings the Earl had a ludicrous accident. The Countess's maid used to warm her bed in winter with a large 'canteen' of hot water, which she would remove once she had helped her mistress to undress. On this evening the Earl left the ball in a huff over some trifle, and stumped off to bed without calling for his valet and without even a candle.

'Presently,' says Susan, 'a most dreadful roar or outcry was heard issuing from the bedroom.' The Duchess of Gordon, always in the forefront of any event, being near the ballroom door seized a candle and rushed upstairs with the others in tow. Writhing in agony on the floor was the Earl in his shirt, having jumped unsuspectingly into bed and scalded himself badly on the hot canteen. He was the more enraged at being surprised by the Duchess and her followers, and the angrier he became the more comic the guests thought it.

It was the Duchess who, according to Lockhart, when the Earl once boasted of his family's talents, asked with her usual cool insolence 'whether the wit had not come by the mother and been all settled on the younger sons'.[11]

On the bottom rung of the social ladder, yet not all that dissimilar to Lord Buchan in eccentricity, is a character described in one of the Rev. James Hall's picturesque anecdotes, probably embroidered in the telling but based on actual events. The story, 'a few years ago' (about 1800?), concerns a young merchant fallen on hard times, who on his customary walk down to Leith Docks had always given alms to a certain ragged old man. The beggar now accosted him to ask if he had suffered a misfortune, and whispered that if he called any evening at a house at the top of the Walk, and asked for David Black, he would 'hear something to his advantage'.

Sceptical but curious, the young man called, was admitted by 'a neat servant' to a well furnished parlour, and found the old beggar man and his wife sitting by a good fire, he in a decent brown suit and an elegant, if old-fashioned wig. His host rose and bowed in welcome; the wife retired, and then taking out a £200 note from a drawer, he pressed it on the visitor with a speech of gratitude. Listening to no refusal, he then invited him to supper, when he explained that he had no one to provide for, as his daughter, a fine girl of seventeen educated at Musselburgh boarding school, was taken care of. He had simply fallen into the begging habit despite entreaties to stop, and it had proved very lucrative. At one time he had made £4000 (sic) selling gingerbread in Parliament Close, until jostled out by a rival, but since then had done well on his present pitch.

The astounded young merchant pays another visit, finds the handsome daughter at home, and a classic romance ensues: the two marry, he retrieves his losses, and their happiness is tainted only by the kind old man's refusal to abandon the begging lay, wearing his tattered suit.[12]

Among those who hovered on the fringe of Edinburgh, seldom if ever visiting but always in touch with its leading characters, was Sir James Mackintosh, who combined the careers of politician, historian and philosopher. Born in 1765, after attending Aberdeen University and studying medicine at Edinburgh he moved to London in 1788.

He married a sister of Daniel Stuart, who from 1795 was proprietor and editor of the *Morning Post*,[13] and after her death married Josiah Wedgwood's sister-in-law. In 1795 he became a barrister at Lincoln's Inn and from 1804–11 held legal posts in India, then, returning to Britain, he sat as MP for Nairn (1813) and later Knaresborough.

A large man, Mackintosh had the disconcerting habit of talking incessantly without facially moving a muscle. Coleridge, who could not stand him, described his smooth, unlined and waxy face as '*hard*, motionless – a *flesh-mask*!'[14] Yet others expressed unqualified admiration. Thomas Campbell, for example, who met Mackintosh with other lions when living in London in 1801, said 'I know no man whose acuteness of intellect gave me a higher idea of human nature than Mackintosh.'[15] In his blatant satire the *Skeltoniad* Coleridge mentioned Mackintosh's unprepossessing blackened stump of a front tooth, 'waxy Face and a blabber lip'.[16]

Mackintosh admired Coleridge far more than the poet did him, apparently because *he* did not admire Wordsworth. This in spite of the fact that Mackintosh had encouraged Coleridge to write for the *Morning Post,* and generally acted in his interests. Coleridge consistently damned his views, swore his reputation as 'an Oracle' could not last, called him 'the great Dung-fly' and dismissed his Metaphysics lectures of 1801 as 'a wretched patch work of plagiarisms . . . of contradictions and blunders in matter of fact'.[17]

He somewhat modified his views later when Mackintosh stayed with him at Keswick for two days, finding him a fine conversationalist, 'very entertaining & pleasant' as they talked (of course) of everything under the sun). But he still thought him 'every inch the Being I had conceived him to be, weak in morals and cold in heart'.[18]

By 1807 Coleridge seems to have overcome his hostility, and now regarded Mackintosh with gratitude, even friendliness.[19] Meanwhile he was particularly admiring of Humphrey Davy, and when Davy fell dangerously ill that autumn Coleridge, expecting his death, suffered agonies of anxiety. 'Good heavens!' he wrote almost frantically to Southey, 'in the very spring tide of his honors – his? – his Country's! the World's!' Later he wrote to William Sotheby that Davy's achievements 'assuredly will place him by the side of Bacon & Newton – for his Inventions are Discoveries, and his Discoveries, grand general Principles . . .' [20]

Francis Horner, no mean judge, was another of Mackintosh's unqualified admirers. The two met in London early in 1804 before Mackintosh's departure for Bombay, when Horner wrote of him enthusiastically as his 'intellectual master', who widened his views in 'moral speculation, more than any other tutor I have ever had in the art of moral thinking; I cannot even except Dugald Stewart . . .' And to Lord Webb Seymour, Mackintosh was 'a *magnus Apollo* above all . . . His talents are of the highest kind, and of that kind perhaps the first in degree.' Stewart, though 'as bright a sun', was inclined to hide in eclipse, so that 'Mackintosh has dazzled me most'.[21]

What seems chiefly to have impressed contemporaries was his lightly-worn learning and brilliant conversational powers, for he was known as an intellectual dilettante, having dabbled in poetry, medicine, metaphysics, politics and journalism. He even studied for the bar, joining Lincoln's Inn in 1795, seriously enough to impress Edmund Burke. Much of his life was spent in travel, service in India, as an MP (1813) and later Privy Councillor. He was to contribute to the *Edinburgh Review* and publish histories of England and the French Revolution. Before his death in 1832 he had impressed everybody. To the Earl of Dudley 'He possesses a vast quantity of well-arranged knowledge, grace and facility of expression, and gentle and obliging manners'; while Francis Jeffrey remarked how, possessing that knowledge, it was something he could 'at all times so promptly and judiciously apply'.[22] He was perhaps, *par excellence*, the universal man of his time.

The famous Berry sisters also remain on the periphery, chiefly connected through their friendship with Playfair and Lord Webb Seymour. The latter they met when staying at Bothwell with Lord Douglas in August and September 1808. The gentle, intellectual devotee joined their expeditions and even one evening played ridiculous games and tricks. One they particularly enjoyed was 'false acting' – one person miming to the other's dialogue. 'In all this', records Miss Mary Berry, 'Lord Webb is as eager, as amusing, and as entirely occupied as he would be in the deepest discussion. He dances, he performs antics, and plays the fool with great vivacity, and at the same time with imperturbable gravity.' To Mrs Damer she praised his charm, combining 'perfect and elegant simplicity' with a lively mind 'upon all subjects'. If only, she added wistfully, 'he would not so doat upon disquisition upon mental *dissections*, and above all, upon accounting for everything which it is only necessary to feel . . .'[23]

At Minto in October, where Mary Berry stayed after leaving Bothwell, a large party of gentlemen included Playfair, Scott, Mr Eliot of Wells, 'The Castle Spectre', alias Monk Lewis, and 'three young Scotch lawyers and reviewers by name Erskine, Murray, and Thomson'. Murray was later the judge Lord Murray, and Thomson was by then Keeper of Records in Edinburgh. Mary Berry enjoyed their 'agreeable' table talk, 'Walter Scott, as usual, narrating, whilst Playfair and Lady Minto and I listened'.[24]

In November Lord Webb was soliciting Miss Berry's influence for Charles Bell, the eminent physiologist and surgeon in Edinburgh, for the chair of Anatomy at the Royal Academy on Sheldon's death. Bell, whom Lord Webb seems not to have known personally, had published *Anatomy of Expression in Painting* (1806) and was the discoverer of the distinct functions of the nerves, a subject on which he later wrote.[25]

The following summer Miss Berry again saw a good deal of Lord Webb in London, feeling the loss whenever he left town. 'He is rational and conversable, a lively fresh mind, and, in short, very unlike other people.' Playfair was another welcome friend, with whom when he was in London she visited the Cairo and Dublin panoramas. Playfair returned to Edinburgh in August (1809), and Lord Webb shortly rejoined the Berrys but set off for Scotland in mid-September after an affectionate leave-taking. 'How my heart thanks anybody for this sentiment, and how much more from one distinguished by his intelligence, and amiable simplicity of manners!'[26]

A phenomenal character to be seen in Edinburgh in 1803 was the 'Irish Giant', Patrick Cotter O'Brien, born in Kinsale in about 1761 and employed as a bricklayer. He had been accustomed to exhibit himself since 1779, yet hardly got over the sense of humiliation, and in later life was unsurprisingly thought to be captious and capricious. But financially he did well from his freakishness and invested in houses in Enfield, before dying at the Bristol Hotwells in 1806.

O'Brien was (according to Kay's *Portraits*) eight feet one inch tall and weighed half a ton. One witness said his hand was the size of a shoulder of mutton and his bones were abnormal – he had double knuckles, large lumps on his hips, and when he rose from sitting (usually on a table) 'his bones were distinctly heard as if crashing against one another'. Indeed he seems to have found it hard to balance upright, and would support his armpit on the top of a door.

When in Edinburgh he was shown at 'Salamander Land', a tenement opposite Royal Exchange, so called because it had escaped two great fires. Kay displays him as enduring a fitting for a greatcoat at Deacon Jollie's in Old Assembly Close.[27] According to Andrew Bigelow his skeleton, here claimed as eight-and-a-half feet, was exhibited in the anatomical museum.[28]

20
REVIEWERS AND RIVALS

'Conversation in this northern Athens is easy, animated, and indeed full of spirit and intelligence. Yet, though the feast of reason abounds, there is not much flow of soul . . . there are syllogisms and epigrams, and now and then pointed and brilliant sentences, and observations and reflections both acute and profound, but neither the heart nor imagination are much concerned . . . metaphysical subtilty . . . but little playfulness and less heart . . . People are too well bred, too well informed, and too well amused by the passing scene, to seek those resources in their imaginations . . .'

Mrs Grant of Laggan to Mrs Hook, *Memoir* . . ., 23 April 1810 [1.255–6]

Of the famous characters who continually hover round the Edinburgh scene, sometimes very briefly before a more permanent appearance, Thomas De Quincey was another of those physically tiny men who cut such a large figure in literary circles. He first appears not in Scotland but in the Wordsworth coterie, late in 1807: 'a remarkable and very interesting young man' (writes Dorothy Wordsworth); 'very diminutive in person . . . and so modest and so very shy, that even now I wonder how he had ever the courage to address himself to my brother by letter'.[1]

Earlier that year, the nineteen-year-old Byron was planning a Highland jaunt with a friend, travelling to Edinburgh by carriage and thence to Inveraray, where they proposed to buy shelties (Shetland ponies) on which to rise to 'places inaccessible' and eventually to the Hebrides – perhaps even to Iceland. It was not so long before Sir George Mackenzie made his expedition to the latter regions. Apparently Byron and friend never achieved the trip, perhaps not even to Edinburgh; but he had close Scottish connections, his mother a Scottish heiress and himself educated at Aberdeen Grammar School (1794–98). Then at Harrow he had been with two of the Erskine brothers, Henry and Thomas; and in adult life he maintained continually stormy relations with the *Edinburgh Review*.[2]

In February 1808 Byron was telling the Rev. John Becher how he had surely achieved great importance, as the *Review* was launching 'a most violent attack' on his *Hours of Idleness*. 'You know the system . . . is universal attack, they praise none, and neither the public nor the author expects praise from them'; on the other hand, they concentrated 'only on works requiring the public attention . . . They defeat their object by indiscriminate abuse', praising only Lord Holland's circle (Whigs); but those whom they damned were in good company, 'Southey, Moore, Lauderdale, Strangford and Payne Knight'. Years later he recalled how he had already heard, in advance, of its stringent criticism of himself and, on the day of its denunciation, 'dined & drank 3 bottles of claret . . . but, nevertheless, was not easy till I have vented my wrath and my rhyme, in the same pages against every thing and every body'.[3]

The review of *Hours of Idleness* in the January issue (1808) was (anonymously) by Brougham, though Byron supposed it to be Jeffrey's. 'I am cut to atoms . . . [It] has completely demolished my little fabric of fame, this is rather scurvy treatment from a Whig Review.'[4]

This was only months after Southey was scornfully turning down Jeffrey's invitation to write for the *Review*, an offer which Byron saw as a perfect subject for satire. His bitter comparisons in 'English Bards and Scotch Reviewers' (1809) were partly based on his belief (like Southey) that the 'Arch-fiend' spelt his name like Judge Jeffries, and he still supposed Jeffrey the author of the criticism. In 'English Bards' he also refers to 'paltry Pillans' and 'blundering Brougham'. From 1810, however, Byron was living abroad, and the course of his connection with the *Review* took a different turn.[5]

Coleridge had approved of Southey's cold reply to Jeffrey's offer (made through Scott), arguing their political differences; but he regretted Southey's 'joke . . . too like an Insult' in referring to the editor as 'Judge Jeffries', at odds with the rest.[6] Southey, meanwhile, had been astounded at Jeffrey's unaccountable hostility to Coleridge, 'a man whom he never saw', wondering at what seemed so unjustifiable an attack.

The *Review* had aroused such fury from the beginning that one reader cancelled his subscription after only the second issue, on reading its 'wanton and hard-hearted indecency' over 'a case of extra-uterine gestation', and an abominable allusion in the attack on Young. Southey indeed did praise highly Jeffrey's paper on Monnier opening the first issue, 'the best in the book'; whereas that on Kant he considered 'from beginning to end impudent babble, – perfect Scotch bold-faced impudence'.[7]

Coleridge had not seen more than a few issues, and that long ago. In May (1808) he was writing reproachfully to Jeffrey himself. 'What harm have I ever done you, alike in morality, politics, and – what is called – metaphysics?' But he assured Jeffrey that he admired his talents, sending 'every kind thought respecting your motives', balm to the editor in contrast to the usual vituperation from so many writers and poets. Coleridge presumably had an ulterior motive here, for he asked for, and got, the review of Clarkson's *History*

Left. The Ancient Assembly Rooms in the Old Town (from J. Skene, *Twelve Etchings of Views in Edinburgh*, 1816).
Crown Copyright: RCAHMS

Below. An early or mid eighteenth-century view of Edinburgh, showing the city before work began on the New Town.
Crown Copyright: RCAHMS

Top. The Old Town (from J.H. Shepherd, *Modern Athens*, 1829).
Crown Copyright: RCAHMS

Bottom. Calton Hill. J. Ewbank/W.H. Lizars, *c*.1790.
Crown Copyright: RCAHMS

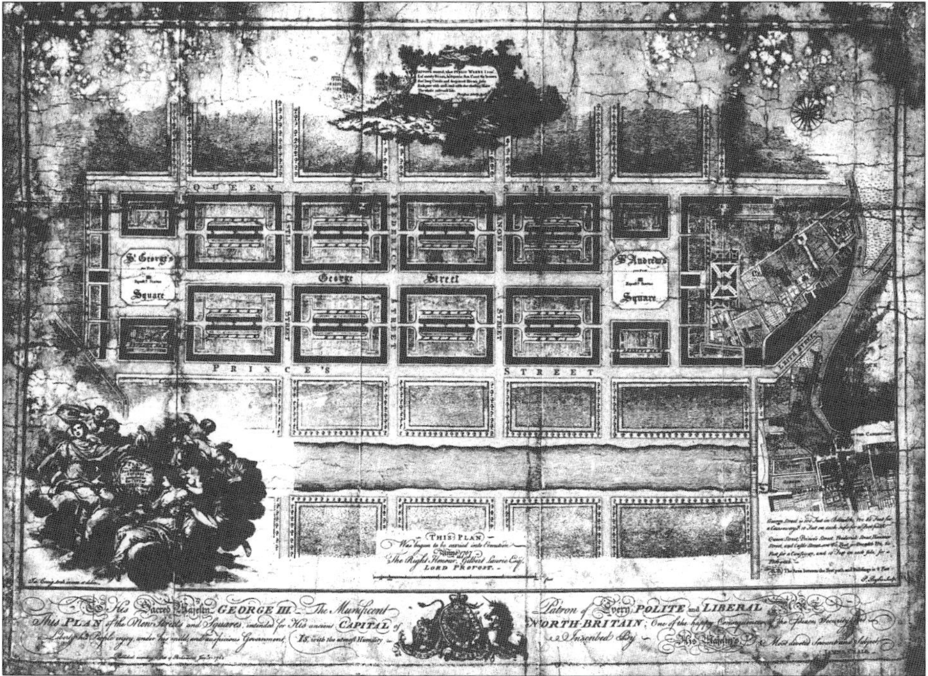

Top. Edinburgh Castle. J. Ewbank/W.H. Lizars. Crown Copyright: RCAHMS

Bottom. James Craig's winning plan for the layout of the streets and squares of the first New Town (1767).

Reproduced by permission of the Trustees of the National Library of Scotland

Top. St Anthony's Chapel. J.M.W. Turner. In the background is Holyrood Palace, and, beyond that, the Old and the New Town. Crown Copyright: RCAHMS

Bottom. Princes Street, looking east towards Calton Hill. A. Nasmyth, 1806. On the hill is shown a proposed monument to Lord Nelson. A different monument, designed by Robert Burn, was erected in 1816. Another interesting feature of this view is that it shows the east end of Princes Street before it was extended into Waterloo Place in 1815. Crown Copyright: RCAHMS

Top. Calton Hill. T.H. Shepherd/W. Tombleson, 1829. The east end of the Bridewell (House of Correction), designed by Robert Adam, is shown, with the Jail Governor's House in the background.

Bottom. North Bridge. T.H. Shepherd/E. Stalker, 1830. Beneath the bridge, where the railway now runs, can be seen the central fruit, vegetable and fish markets.

Right. Part of the floor plans of the Royal Infirmary, designed by William Adam, 1736–37 (from *Vitruvius Scoticus*).

Below. The exterior of the Royal Infirmary. J. & H.S. Storer, 1818.

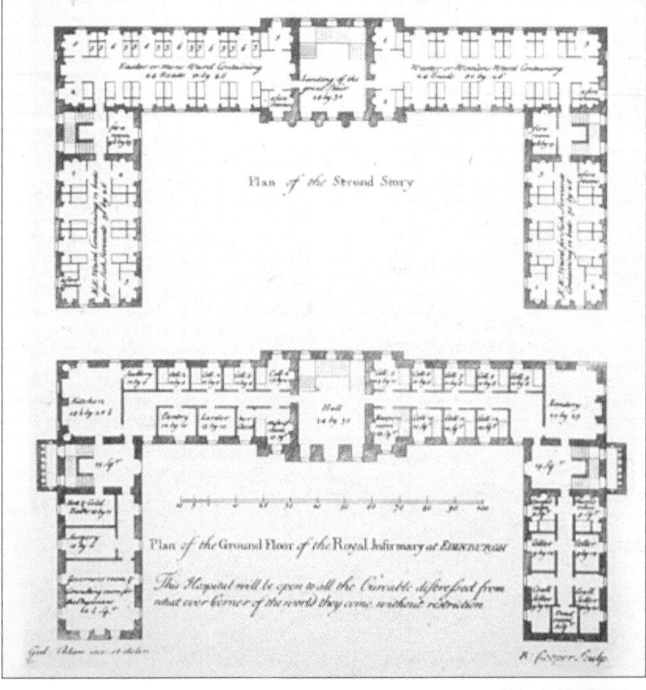

Top. The east end of George Street, showing St Andrew's Church and the monument to Lord Melville in St Andrew Square (from J.H. Shepherd, *Modern Athens*, 1829).

Bottom. The Assembly Rooms in George Street (from J.H. Shepherd, *Modern Athens*, 1829).

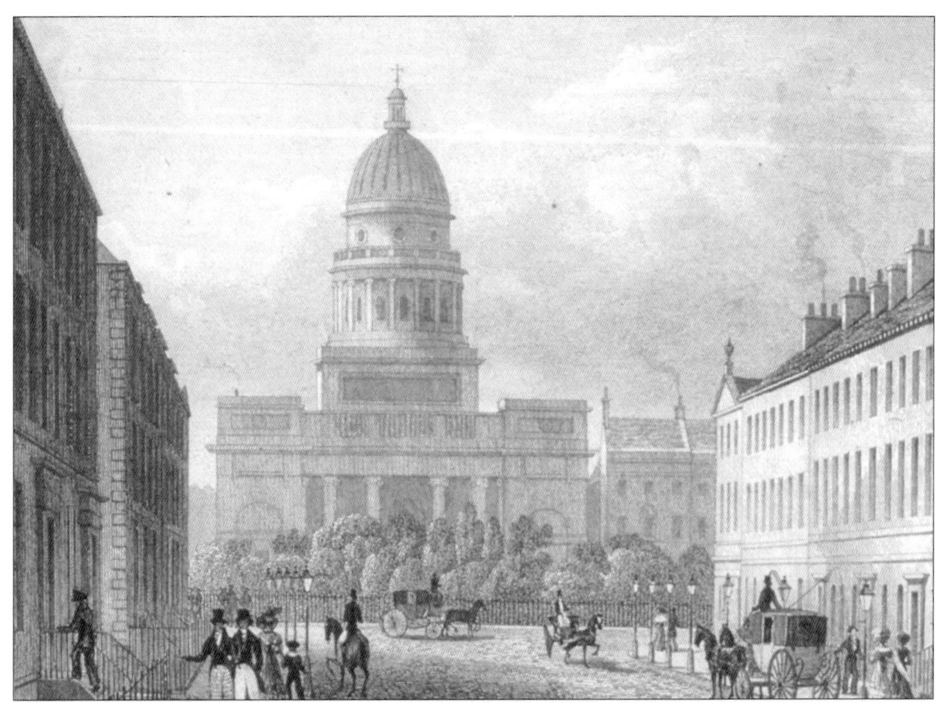

Top. St George's Church in Charlotte Square, viewed from the west end of George Street (from J.H. Shepherd, *Modern Athens*, 1829).

Bottom. St Andrew Square (from J.H. Shepherd, *Modern Athens*, 1829).

of the Abolition of the Slave Trade. Then, fearing he might have offended, he explained that he was in continued bad health; but when his review was published, he complained in a quite friendly spirit that while Jeffrey had not 'shamefully mutilated' it, as he was apt to do, two contradictory paragraphs had been added.[8]

He intended to follow this with a detailed argument against the *Review*'s current sneer, contrasting Humphrey Davy's 'indefatigable industry' with Isaac Newton's *genius,* but was persuaded not to send the letter. He described its contents to Davy, however, in December. He was inclined to blame public taste for encouraging the *Review* to indulge in 'sharp & often calumnious Personality', as the journal's large sales demonstrated, and admitted he was unworthily glad at the 'deadly stab' administered by 'XY's Essays in the Courier'.[9]

Jeffrey's mauling of the Clarkson review rankled with Coleridge, who even two years later cited it as the reason why he would no longer undertake reviewing, 'as I hold it utterly immoral'.[10]

Southey continued to write with customary vitriol of the *Review*'s 'vile placehunting politics . . . labouring to frighten the nation into a peace. They are equally wrong about the Catholic Question': if that Bill were carried, he foresaw that some Bonapartist Irish priest, under orders from the Pope, would get on board every ship in the Royal Navy![11]

German literature was then all but unknown in Scotland, though within a few years Goethe, Schiller, Lessing would take the literary world by storm. Walter Scott was a pioneer in being influenced by such poems as 'Lenore' and 'The Huntsman', which he translated, probably the only man in Scotland who could have done so, and Ballantyne launched them into print. The *Review* critics were suspicious and hostile over the innovation. There were still 'lingering effects of our obstinate conventionalism and *affectation*'.[12]

This appeared in the slow change of attitude to Wordsworth. 'We did flatter ourselves that, with the help of the *Edinburgh Review*, not only should we keep him down, but absolutely extinguish and annihilate him.' 'Irredeemably bad' was the Edinburgh verdict on *Lyrical Ballads* and the two volumes of *Poems*, and Thomas Chalmers during a visit pounced one evening on the poems lying on Gillies's table. Perplexity set in. 'Is the man crazy?' he muttered at one point, and he and Dr Black who then came in both laughed over 'Dog of Helvellyn' and the prosaic line 'What is the creature doing here?' All the same Chalmers struggled on, ending with the verdict, 'There is merit here', and feeling and sense too – 'if only the author had known how to express himself properly!'[13]

A major literary event of 1808 was the publication of Walter Scott's second long poem, *Marmion,* whose reception was mixed. His earlier success engendered 'a buzz of envy' and nit-picking, as Southey told Charles Danvers

(July 1808). In his view, though, Scott had taken a story suitable for a ballad and overloaded it with antiquarianism.[14]

The *Edinburgh Review* chose to attack with customary savagery. Gilbert Elliot complained to James Loch (15 May) that the piece was 'composed of all the bitterest ingredients in Mr Jeffrey's shop, indeed they say that it is rather a review of Walter Scott than his poem, and tho' I admire *Marmion* with all its faults, I shall not be sorry to see Scott smart a little for his sins both poetical and political'.[15] Alexander Murray wrote to Constable (27 June), 'It is in general unjust, hypercritical . . . Mr Jeffrey seems not to understand this kind of poetry', and while sometimes just, had mostly 'overshot the point'.[16]

A few weeks later Murray wrote that though it maintained its standards, *Review* authors were 'less independent and just than *of yore*' (surprising, in view of what enraged writers had said from the very beginning). The Whiggish *Review* was extending moral criticism to the beliefs of the dyed-in-the-wool Tory Scott, and Murray, like others, felt that his politics had been unjustly dragged in.[17]

Several readers thought *Marmion* inferior to the *Lay*. Cyrus Redding was delighted with a first reading, and with its 'happy abruptness in the termination'. A second reading did not please so much, 'and on the third [it] descended to what it really was, a versified story'. He was sure Scott was conscious of his poetic limitations, and that this was what later determined him to change his approach to literature; though he possessed certain qualities of the poet, he had not the poetic mind that could 'rise to real greatness, truth, and the better things of nature', and was therefore more suited as a novelist, dealing with 'earthly beings in antique dresses, and in times nearly forgotten'.[18]

Both the *Review* issue attacking *Marmion*, and the next, as Brougham told Loch in August, infuriated 'the ministerial folks here [London] . . . They storm beyond bounds, and as I am accused of it . . . I have the whole brunt of it to bear now.' (Perhaps if he had not been so eager to claim authorship in the earlier issues, he might not have been so frequently suspected now.) Brougham was still trying, rather equivocally, to argue that it was 'in the main quite impartial', and although anti-government 'I contend that it is above both sides and acts justly by each'.[19]

Young Robert Gillies, who counted Scott as one of his earliest friends, found himself 'riveted' less by the poem itself than by Scott's poetic epistles about nature which prefaced the six cantos. Scott sent his work to the printer piecemeal, when the rest was barely half-written, and Gillies thought he needed the spur of the printer's pressure – rather as Dickens was to do a generation or two later. The work had been delayed beyond the [Christmas] deadline, causing everybody to badger the publishers and pester Scott so much that he was probably influenced to use the secrecy he later maintained over the Waverley novels. He was, too, such a home-lover that he did not like involvement in controversy or being in the literary limelight: on Sundays and Mondays especially 'old John' and his coachman Peter were warned to keep visitors away, except for two or three old friends.[20]

The *Review* was usually in hot water about one thing or another. In January 1809 Lord Gower told Charles Kirkpatrick Sharpe that 200 copies of the last issue (No.26) had been 'countermanded' because of the indignation aroused by Brougham's 'democratical principles' expressed in his 'Don Cevallos on the usurpation of Spain'. As Gower put it, 'he was certainly rather indiscreet in throwing off the mask so suddenly, and 'tis just as well that he had let people see what sort of a fellow he is'.[21]

Having now reigned without a rival for half-a-dozen years, the *Review* was, too, now challenged by new publications. One was the *Quarterly Review*, to be published in London. Its editor William Gifford,[22] son of a Devon glazier and apprenticed in boyhood to a shoemaker, was an English example of talent spotted early and helped on its way, in this case to Exeter College, Oxford. From the 1790s he had published several works, and now late in 1808 was seeking 'promising young men' to contribute to a strictly literary, non-political rival to the *Edinburgh*. He had already garnered Samuel Rogers, Southey and Tom Moore, and others whose reputation Jeffrey had murdered, and 'who are rising to cry wo upon him'. This was Scott's verdict to Sharpe in December, when he had been asked to join in the recruiting. He lured Sharpe with the offer of reviewing anything he cared to write about, with no by-line but at ten guineas a sheet. He reckoned that could they only keep clear of the booksellers, whose 'influence' had 'ruined all the English Reviews', the new journal ought to succeed.[23]

In the event Gifford's first issue of the *Quarterly* in February 1809 had to hold over Sharpe's contribution through pressure of time, and Scott thought the paper showed signs of 'precipitate and hurried composition'. However, it did survive.[24]

Scott, who had been encouraged by Southey's attitude to cease contributing to the *Edinburgh*, expected that the rival journal would counteract 'the base and rascally politics of Jeffrey and that peace-mongering squad who would lay us at the foot of France'. Jeffrey and his Whig friends' new desire for peace found no sympathy among the Tories, who were determined to carry the war against Napoleon to however bitter a conclusion. There was a strong element of politicking in canvassing for the new *Quarterly*, which promised official news in contrast to what was regarded as the biased writings of Horner and Brougham – although Gifford agreed to this with some reluctance.

Cyrus Redding, looking back after half a century, saw the great virtue of the *Review* in its pioneering view on subjects that urgently needed reform – 'intense religious bigotry, the judicial bench little better than tool of the crown; the Test and Corporation Acts in full force, the press enslaved, illiberality and ignorance triumphant.' In advocating justice and free opinion, in time it 'had . . . the gratification of seeing the full realisation of the principles with which it set out', whereas the *Quarterly,* which specialised in prophesying the nation's ruin from free trade and free principles, was 'doomed to find its most cherished and reiterated opinions erroneous, and its averments falsified over and over'. 'In its classical articles, the Review has far outshone the Edinburgh as the Edinburgh outshone the Quarterly in the truth of its political predictions, and that advocacy of improvement and reform for which its reputation is imperishable'.[25]

Surveying the effect of the *Edinburgh Review* over almost a decade, and Edinburgh's literary situation in the previous generation, the French-American Louis Simond, having no axe to grind, took a balanced view. He recalled how, about 1770, the local literati produced *The Mirror,* 'to hold the mirror up to nature' and reflect the age; and later *The Lounger.* Since then knowledge had advanced so greatly that men of society, men of letters, *even women*, were alike versed in arts and sciences. At this point the *Edinburgh Review* entered the field, produced by a range of writers from satirist to 'scavant' and man of taste, with the object of covering all publications worthy of criticism. A century earlier London's *Spectator* had concentrated on literature, but there had been so many discoveries, new works of science and philosophy, that the world was more full of new ideas – studied and discussed by the reviewers.[26]

Their identities, though still not published, were now largely known, and they came from 'the liberal professions', lawyers, doctors, clergy, professors, MPs, not all of them living in Edinburgh. Whereas the new rival, the Tory *Quarterly,* was launched in London, the Edinburgh reviewers could claim that theirs had been a completely original venture, a model for the future.[27]

Having sold in America as well as Britain, it had in 1810 more than 12,000 subscribers, and was a little arrogant, a little flippant. (Thus Simond: there were those who had said so from the beginning.) And because everything here entered into politics, the reviewers were Whigs of the Fox school, their targets moderate reform, improved legislation, reduced Crown influence – anti-despotism, in fact. Their campaigns included Irish Catholic emancipation, abolition of the slave trade, ending of paper money, and settlement of a peace.

When the first *Quarterly* appeared, Southey as a contributor found himself 'in odd company, and not the most congenial', though undoubtedly more so than he had found the *Edinburgh* and its hateful politics – especially as he occasionally thought they might be right. But he blamed their changed attitude in becoming 'cowardly advocates for peace' after formerly defending 'the whole system of corruption against Cobbett' when the Whigs were in, and then praising 'Jacobinism' once they were out.[28]

At about the same time the Ballantyne brothers, James and John, were planning a new version of an annual English publication which had run for a considerable time in the last century: this time to be an *Edinburgh Annual Register*, or comprehensive survey of each previous year's events. Their project was in the offing for at least eighteen months, while they were commissioning such obvious contributors as Brougham, Allen and Horner. Constable's friend David Hunter, who learned of it in March 1807, thought it a strange and novel idea, though (as he told Constable) 'such a thing is much wanted'.[29] James Ballantyne, the editor, hoped that Charles Sharpe too, for a fee of £300,[30] would contribute a history of the year's events in 'a lively luminous picture' as by 'a man of genius'. In the event it was Southey who undertook the history, though the brothers had left the arrangement rather late, 'Sharpe having let them down'. In Southey's view he would have ruined it anyway.

He therefore took on the job with little time for preparation, but was able to arrange with Daniel Stuart to supply him with the current French and Spanish newspapers.[31]

Work on the *Register* kept Southey mainly occupied over the next two years. The 1809 issue was much bulkier than the opening volume of 1808, covering a very eventful year, and its length aroused much public complaint, but Southey was impervious.[32]

Southey's scorn for the *Edinburgh Review* never relaxed. In 1810, writing to Scott that Britain would prevail against Bonaparte provided they kept up their courage 'against such politicians as Whitbread and Brougham and Jeffrey', he was also advising Scott of his forthcoming *Quarterly* article on Methodism, 'which will appear to great advantage after Sydney Smith's shallow performances upon the same subject'. He added, 'I am not sorry to see the *Edinburgh* professing their belief in Malthus at the very time when I am making ready to come upon that philosophist, or philosophide, with a thunder clap.'[33]

In 1810 Walter Scott published his *Lady of the Lake*, earning scathing comments from Coleridge, who admitted to Wordsworth in October that his copy had lain unread on his table for weeks. He claimed that at least 'the first 98' pages proved his reluctance prophetic. 'Merciful Apollo! . . . between a sleeping Canter and a Marketwoman's trot – but it is endless . . . even Scott's warmest admirers must acknowledge & complain of the number of prosaic lines', and so forth. He reeled off a facetious 'Recipe for Poems of this sort . . . a vast string of patronymics, and names of Mountains, Rivers, &c . . . all the nomenclature of Gothic Architecture, of Heraldry, of Arms, of hunting, & Falconry . . . some pathetic moralizing on old times . . . with a *Bard* (that is absolutely necessary) and Songs of course'. Whatever might serve for Mrs

Radcliffe's romances would be equally acceptable to the public provided it were told in rhyme, '& the Ghost may be a Ghost, or may be explained'.[34]

Sadly, Coleridge then suffered a two-year estrangement from Wordsworth, through changing a decision to stay in Edinburgh under medical advice to overcome his opium habit, and instead taking up Basil Montague's proposal that he stay with him in London. Wordsworth wrote a rather strong warning to Montague on Coleridge's habits which made him out an 'absolute nuisance', such as his pothouse debts and his failings as a 'rotten drunkard'.[35]

As a contrast to all this savage literary skirmishing, in 1810 a much more restful, though no less acute, author came to live in Edinburgh. Mrs Anne Grant of Laggan (1755–1838), widow of a minister, was the daughter of Duncan McVicar of Craignish, who had been Barrack-Master of Fort Augustus, and as a young woman made with her father the first of her Highland travels which in 1806 resulted in her *Letters from the Mountains*. A prolonged stay in America led to *Memoirs of an American Lady* (1808), and by the time she moved to Edinburgh at the age of fifty-five her literary reputation was assured.

Mrs Grant had numerous children, who during her middle life died of various illnesses with depressing frequency, until by her own death only one son, John Peter, survived. In 1806 she had moved to Stirling and over the next four years visited Edinburgh several times. The first of her various Edinburgh homes was in the new Heriot Row, close to Henry Mackenzie.[36]

Mrs Grant, tall and at this time still slender despite her frequent child-bearing, was not particularly blessed with good looks. In 1808, on one of her visits to London when she stayed with Sir John and Lady Legarde at Sunbury, she was able to meet the celebrated Berry sisters, and Miss Mary Berry dispassionately records: 'Her figure and manners awkward, but not the least vulgarity in her manners or conversation.'[37] One wonders why the sisters should have expected any except that literary ladies were rather suspect.

She lived with one or other of her daughters and took in young ladies whose further education she supervised. There was plenty of room for them in Edinburgh, where her modern, up-to-date house was much larger than she had been used to, which made its furnishing 'a pretty serious affair'; but she arrived to find things already well organised, 'exceedingly good and pleasant'. A £100 royalty on her American book from a Boston admirer helped with the settling-in.

The lady pupils were limited to three or four; at present they included Lady Elizabeth Boyle, daughter of the Earl of Glasgow, and at Mrs Elizabeth Hamilton's instigation the 'docile and artless' daughter of Sir Hedworth Williamson, a County Durham baronet.

The house's situation opposite the new gardens rising uphill to Queen Street, and the view of the Forth at the back, was very agreeable, and there were many good friends close by. Already she was besieged by invitations and callers, including Scott and 'the formidable Jeffrey' – not, she guessed, because of her reputation as 'a scribbling female', but through mutual acquaintances. She had indeed been reluctant to move to Edinburgh, having found on her visits its society so alluring, conversation so delightful, and the fact that everybody knew everybody, that she feared the loss of her 'quiet habits'.[38]

Mrs Grant's descriptions of the notable figures she met are vivid and illuminating. Though gratifying, the attentions of so many celebrities threatened to be overwhelming – until, as she sagely forecast, her novelty wore off. (In fact it never greatly diminished, and apart from her lengthy literary discussions, much of her correspondence describes the exchange of such visits.)

When Jeffrey, one of her earliest Edinburgh callers, first paid his attentions Mrs Grant summed him up as looking 'the poet all over; – the ardent eye, the nervous agitation, the visibly quick perceptions', riveting one's attention on his 'flashes of the peculiar intelligence of genius . . . his conversation is in a high degree fluent and animated'.

One day that autumn she read to Jeffrey her friend Miss Fanshawe's critique of *The Lady of the Lake,* and he was so taken with it that he begged for an introduction when he next went to London. Mrs Grant found him generally unlike what she had expected: 'not the least ambitious of new or distinguished acquaintance' or fond of large parties and social show, but domestically inclined and wedded to 'the charities of home and kindred'. His sharp criticisms, as others had noticed, were quite at odds with his personal kindness. His conversation she thought had a kind of 'ungraceful impetuosity' (doubtless not helped by his bastardised accent), increased by his fiery expression. She adds the elegantly turned praise, 'He is lavish of thought, and gives a guinea where a sixpence might do as well; but then he has no change, and pays all in gold.'[39]

Before long Mrs Grant was confessing that despite her annoyance at his sharp literary strictures, 'I think I shall be forced to like the Arch Critic himself' who, 'though so petulant on paper', was so plainly affectionate and good-natured. He continued his calls, and as they moved in the same social circles they met often. She and her daughter went to the first dinner given by his very different brother John, now widowed and returned from America, living in a new house in George Street. 'Not at all literary or intellectual . . . rather friends and relations than savans', though they did have 'a little discussion on the Lady of the Lake'.[40]

During 1811 Mrs Grant fancied that Jeffrey had become cooler, for at parties he seemed to avoid her and 'looked askance'. Taking her courage in both hands she decided to invite him to a small party which she was reluctantly obliged to hold for some visitors, with the suggestion that if he *had* 'renounced' her he should boldly admit it, but if not, would he come to meet some people '*I knew he did like*'. It proved that, as with Southey some years earlier, Jeffrey had been embarrassed because he was about to publish a critical review, and he promised that he would indeed come provided a forthcoming 'little packet' did not change her mind. He explained that he always let friends know 'before they are led out to execution. When I take up my reviewing pen I consider myself as entering the temple of truth, and bound to say what I think.' She duly received the packet – presumably the review of her *Essays on Superstitions of the Highlands* – and replied diplomatically that she was satisfied he had done justice to the *subject*.

This misunderstanding being cleared up, soon after he called to ask her for introductions in the Highlands, as he and a couple of friends were about to visit Inverness-shire. She was amazed that he went, it being 'a region before untrod by critic or by tourist', and still more when he was delighted with the trip: 'I expected that, from the mere habit of carping, he would have criticised the mountains unmercifully.'[41]

Mrs Grant was less adulatory about her near neighbour Henry Mackenzie than were many contemporaries, who liked to call him 'the Scottish Addison': 'that is too high praise; for . . . he totally lacks humor or wit', essential to the life of a magazine. For example, 'one never takes up the Lounger but when one feels inclined to lounge', despite its distinguished and elegant sentiments. She admired Mrs Mackenzie, who, however, kept in the background looking after their large and accomplished family. 'Their house is the resort of the best society in one sense, that is, people of fashion with cultivated minds', and there one could meet such distinguished characters as Lord Webb Seymour, Lady Carnegie and Lady Minto.[42]

Mrs Grant had distantly corresponded with Walter Scott before she first met him during an Edinburgh visit in 1809. This was at the Duchess of Gordon's morning levée, when she had been pressed to stay until everyone had gone and then urged to come again on the Sunday evening when the Duchess would be alone, as then 'she never saw company, nor played cards, nor went out'. Mrs Grant duly turned up at 9 o'clock, and found half-a-dozen other visitors to whom no doubt the Duchess had said the same.[43]

The Duchess was a remorseless hostess. In 1801 Lord Calthorpe wrote with some shame to his cousin William Wilberforce of how after a Sunday at her house he felt 'I have not spent a Sunday with so much self-reproach since I came into Scotland'. 'There is something in the Duchess that pleases,' he confessed, 'although against the judgment . . . She seems to be on the same kind of terms with religion as she is with her Duke, that is, on terms of great nominal familiarity without ever meeting each other except in an hotel or in the streets of Edinburgh.'[44]

Mrs Grant thought Scott's appearance – as did most people – 'very unpromising and common-place', with 'no gleam of genius in his countenance'. That genius appeared entirely in his conversation, 'rich, various, easy, and animated', quite unlike the 'petulance', as she calls it, for which the legal profession were reproached.[45]

Louis Simond similarly commented on Scott's homely appearance. 'His countenance is not particularly poetical, – complexion fair, with a coarse skin, – little beard, [that is, a naturally hairless chin] – sandy hair, and light eyes and eyebrows, – the *tout ensemble* rather dull and heavy.' Yet as soon as he spoke, his eye would light up and his expression become animated. Tall and stoutly built, he was then (1810) nearly forty, and his lameness was very marked. He was very fond of telling after-dinner stories.[46]

Scott gave Mrs Grant a copy of the new edition of his *Border Ballads*. With that and *The Lady of the Lake* she enthusiastically determined 'What a fortunate minstrel is Walter Scott . . . to be the happy discoverer of so rich a mine of poetic material. Never was the harp of the North more exquisitely touched.' She was impatient with 'sturdy critics here' who denied his poetic status and dismissed his verse as 'jingle and jargon'.[47]

Scott's hankering after the role of Lowlands laird had meanwhile become a strong passion. In 1811 the lease of Ashestiel came to an end, and next year he purchased a small farm or cottage (as for some years he still termed it) which he at once set about enlarging and adding to its domain. Its local name Clarty Hole he changed to the more romantic, and territorially more appropriate, name of 'Abbotsford', and every moment that he could spare from his legal office in Edinburgh was spent at his new property, which he was begging friends to visit as soon as he had created more room, and news of its progress filled every letter he sent.[48] It was to be one of the most, if not *the* most, significant achievements of his life.

21
THE SOCIAL SURFACE

> *'Fine fellow* of 1805': 'less accomplished than those of 1763, without many of the vices of those of 1783 . . . He can drive a coach, full of ladies, equal to the most experienced coachman . . . can tell the good or bad qualities of a horse at first sight . . . can drink 3 bottles of wine, kick the waiter, and knock down watchmen with a good grace.'
>
> J. Stark, *Picture of Edinburgh,* Edinburgh, 1806, 419–20

> 'Internally very splendid, although their exterior has nothing to boast of in architecture'.
>
> (The George Street Assembly Rooms): Sir John Carr, *Caledonian Sketches,* Edinburgh, 1809, 196

> 'There are few countries, assuredly, where [the ladies] are more capable of conversing upon serious subjects. But it is not the fashion to talk politics before the ladies; from thence follows, that after dinner, the men remain a long time at table after the ladies have retired into the drawing-room. It must not be believed, as some foreigners have pretended, that this custom indicates an immoderate love of drinking . . . the generality of the Scots and English . . . seek to enjoy more rational and enlightened pleasures.'
>
> L. A. Necker de Saussure, *Travels in Scotland; descriptive of Manners, Literature, and Science*, London, 1821, 26

The season of 1808 was especially lively because the celebrated Duchess of Gordon was in Edinburgh. She was generally regarded as the leader of fashion, although her health was already beginning to suffer, and the death of her son Lord Alexander Gordon brought her great anxiety and sadness.

In June on her way north Charles Sharpe, who met her on a morning call, declared her to be 'perfectly *beautiful,* covered with lace veils and artificial roses, and surrounded by three ugly yellow London babes of the D^{SS}. of Manchester'.[1]

Some time later, commiserating with his shy sister over the lack of suitable society for her to meet, most of whom he dismissed as 'lamentable', he observed that 'as for the Duchess, she is, whatever [Mackenzie of Delvine] may say, the leading card both in Edin. and in London'. But he feared she might not trouble to be civil to their mother, as although she inclined to cultivate the accomplished she did not offer much in return.[2]

At this time all Edinburgh was laughing over a review by Mr Merriman of Sir John Sinclair's *Code of Health and Longevity.* Jeffrey, who realised that his journal's readability was best maintained by occasionally including light satirical reviews, had reckoned that Sinclair could take 'the whacks of Mr Merriman's baton'. It was a riot. The Duchess was completely caught out one day when, as she was reading it in fits of laughter, Sinclair himself walked in, and she had barely time to hide the magazine under a cushion.[3]

The Duchess, incidentally, did not wear well in old age. Ageing ladies had the dangerous habit of plastering their faces with white paint, which Cyrus Redding tells us was regularly used at least until 'the winter of 1805, not just rouge applied with a hare's-foot, but well caked white, which would fall off in scales'. Redding met her at a ball in Bath in 1806, when she was fifty-five or so, quite an age for those days, 'painted an inch thick, the paint crumbling off her neck'.[4]

Besides the literary ladies Edinburgh was graced by hostesses of great charm. Chief among them was the remarkable Mrs Fletcher, the Yorkshire girl who when very young had married the much older, forthright and worthy lawyer Archibald Fletcher. Mrs Grant of Laggan, on settling in Edinburgh, found that she made several delightful friends of English origin, and first among these she placed Mrs Fletcher. 'She is a very uncommon person . . . Her beauty is of a kind peculiar to herself: you have not seen such an ardent, soul-illumined countenance; you think of a Roman matron . . . There is so much energy about her' engrossed in work for others and in intellectual pursuits: 'she thinks less about herself than any one I know', and despite being for years 'the admiration of Edinburgh' for 'her personal graces and the charms of her enlightened animated, and unaffected conversation', she remained completely unspoiled. Mrs Grant, confirmed Tory, added innocently that they never discussed politics, which would be 'to no purpose', but that Mrs Fletcher generously allowed for her 'errors'.[5]

For some ten years Elizabeth Fletcher had been regarded as a 'ferocious Democrat', and her social circle was limited to Fletcher's professional colleagues and their families, with a few of wider interests such as Henry Erskine who was a leader of society as well as of the Whigs. But when Dr Anderson introduced the poet Thomas Campbell, with whom they became very friendly, Mrs Fletcher began to meet some of the literary circle through Mrs Elizabeth Hamilton (1805/6), thus cleansing her reputation among the Pitt/Dundas faction as a rabid radical.

The Fletchers already knew several of the *Review* contributors, who were mostly law-men. Comparing Edinburgh pre- and post-*Review*, Mrs Fletcher remarked on its 'electrical effects . . . on the public mind', and its beneficial political influence. One evening when Brougham was dining with them the party were (as was now usual for dinner-table guests throughout Edinburgh) discussing the probable authors. When Mr Fletcher, impressed by an article on Professor Black and Chemistry, remarked that 'the man who wrote that might do or be anything he pleased', Brougham significantly leaned forward to ask if he meant that literally. 'May he be Lord Chancellor?' 'Yes!' was the emphatic reply, more prophetic than he guessed. 'Lord Chancellor, or anything he desires.'[6]

Several discerning English families came to Edinburgh to educate their children, and to enjoy its brilliant society. Among these was Lady Williamson, widow of Sir Hedworth, of Whitburn, Co. Durham (and mother of one of Mrs Grant's pupils). The Williamsons lived a few doors from the Fletchers in Castle Street in a large Queen Street house, and the younger daughters went to classes with Mrs Fletcher's children. The families formed a strong friendship, partly through theatrical tastes: one winter Lady Williamson converted one of her drawing-rooms into a small theatre, where the two families rehearsed and acted to a degree that Sir Thomas Bertram would perhaps have deplored. They could entertain quite large audiences at their performances of the perennial *Douglas* and plays by Joanna Baillie.[7]

At the stream of Edinburgh dinners, balls and routs, Jeffrey always made a distinguished appearance. No one could fathom how he contrived to combine his literary and legal career with such a social programme, but he was not only always invited, he went. Like Scott, he spent the mornings at Parliament House; then he walked or rode, and in season had a daily calendar of dinners and suppers. More than one of the latter could be fitted into an evening, and Jeffrey walked from rout to rout, ending up wherever the supper-party would be the most congenial.

In his present unmarried state he was living in 'third-rate apartments' in a Queen Street tenement, whose bookshelves surprisingly contained – besides his necessary law-books and the latest publications needed for the *Review* – only a few worn-out monthly volumes. Robert Gillies always recalled the looking-glass above his chimney-piece, its tarnished frame crammed with 'a preposterous multitude of visiting cards and notes of invitation, which showered on him from all quarters'.[8]

While visiting families commonly rented whole houses, many visitors stayed in the increasing number of Edinburgh's new hotels. For example, Dumbreck's, which Louis Simond praised for its quietness and convenience. Furnished lodgings were also good: two large, well-furnished first-floor sitting-rooms and three bedrooms let at four guineas a week, and for about a further guinea per day the landlady's family would 'go to market' and do the cooking for her tenants. Hire of a manservant cost three-and-a-half guineas a month, presumably on board wages or fed by the household. Nor was it necessary to hire a carriage, New Town distances being so short – especially as the Second New Town was still only half built – and the sedan was still the easiest transport. An Edinburgh hackney coach, if required, was far superior to the broken-down old carriages for hire in London.[9]

Early in 1810 Edinburgh society was further enlivened by the arrival of Mrs Apreece, who had already taken London by storm and now proceeded to do the same in Edinburgh, having arrived with a clutch of introductions. She had been born Jane Kerr, daughter of Charles Kerr, of Kelso, and was the widow of Shuckburgh Ashby Apreece. Her parents-in-law, Sir Thomas and Lady Apreece, lived at Washingley, in Hampshire. When her 'mild and sincere' mother-in-law was widowed, subdued by sorrow but eager to please – having lived much in the world – she settled in Edinburgh in a house in Heriot Row next door to Mrs Grant.[10]

'Mrs Apreece and Mrs Waddington', writes Mrs Fletcher, 'divided the admiration of the Edinburgh circles between them, – the one attractive by the vivacity of her conversation, the other by her remarkable beauty and the grace of her manners.'[11] (Mrs Waddington's intelligent daughter Frances later married Baron Bunsen.)

Mrs Apreece had already caused a sensation in Ireland in 1808. When she called on the Edgeworths there had been so many stories about her that the family thought it must be a joke, but she proved to be real, stayed several days, and was 'very brilliant and agreeable'. It was to be the same in Edinburgh. Henry Holland, then a young doctor, reported how much she was admired; she also got on well with everybody. 'Mrs Hamilton and she like one another particularly', Miss Edgeworth had reported to Mrs Ruxton; 'they can never cross, for no two human beings are, body and mind, form and address, more unlike.'[12]

One summer evening when the Fletchers were staying at Frankfield, at the then rural Lasswade, as they sauntered about the banks of the Esk with some of their children discussing *Clarissa Harlowe,* which they had been reading and weeping over, who should turn up but Professor Playfair, his pupil, Lord John Russell, Henry Mackenzie's daughter Hannah – and Mrs Apreece. 'This very agreeable party returned with us to drink tea at Frankfield', relates Mrs Fletcher, and Richardson's creations were forgotten in 'the sparkling vivacity of Mrs Apreece, and the taste and refinement of her companions'.[13]

Mrs Apreece stayed most of the year in Edinburgh, returning south at the end of September 1810, 'greatly to our sorrow (to mine certainly very much)', confessed Playfair to Mary Berry, and this 'most amiable and charming woman' was eager to meet the famous sisters.[14]

Mrs Apreece had proved a great talking-point, and there was seldom a break between the occasions for gossip. The great scandal of the 1810/11 season was the exchange of matrimonial partners between Lord and Lady Paget, Lady Caroline Villiers and the Duke of Argyll. Since the Scottish divorce laws were much easier than in England and a husband's infidelity was accepted as legal grounds, Lord Paget obligingly came to Edinburgh to provide evidence of his adultery so that the Duke of Argyll could step in and in November 1810 marry his divorced wife, while Lord Paget was then able to marry Lady Caroline Villiers. The new Lord and Lady Paget between them had fourteen children by their former marriages. Argyll, 6th Duke and still unmarried at forty-two, had none, at least legitimate, and the new marriage produced no children. Simond noted that outside Scotland neither marriage would be regarded as legal.[15]

Another scandal was the marriage of the divorced wife of Lord Elgin, former Ambassador to the Porte, to her lover, who was happy to pay the injured husband £10,000 in damages. Simond attributed all this indulgence towards 'intrigue' to the idleness of the upper classes, probably no worse than in France; it was the newspapers' eagerness to publish it all that highlighted the affairs. Whereas in, say, the 1770s divorce was rare, it was now increasingly common – doubtless one of the effects of the loosening of morals and outlooks since the French Revolution.[16]

It was also in 1810 that James Hogg, the Ettrick Shepherd, came to Edinburgh and began publishing his periodical, *The Spy*, most of which he wrote himself. Once settled in Edinburgh, he was to became a noted, rugged literary figure.

The Spy, which ran for eighteen months, included satires on Edinburgh society supposedly contributed by visiting foreigners, who expressed themselves at a loss with its artificiality, which here sounds more descriptive of London than Edinburgh usually appears from the pens of actual foreign visitors.

Simond, for example, contrasts Edinburgh's social life with London and its later hours. While noting that assemblies were modelled on London style, with its much smaller population such evenings were more informal: one could sit and talk, play cards or even chess, and the tables would be scattered with the current pamphlets, rare books, prints and drawings, even toys with which some liked to amuse themselves. As for music, while a pretty girl might sit down to play and sing, and people gather round her, they would talk all through the performance. He admitted that her execution was probably rather indifferent.[17]

The Spy describes altogether more brittle affairs. One item tells how the author, a total stranger, after being courteously received at a huge party is abandoned by the hostess for other guests, while he is left ignored by all. (This does not sound like the usual fate of those who arrived armed with introductions.) He also comments on the lack of music or dancing, the sole entertainment being cards, at which one lady loses £500 in minutes with 'astonishing serenity', then gives up her place to a rich merchant's son who within half an hour loses 1000 guineas. Our stranger learns afterwards that the hostess, whose income is £3000 a year, has spent £500 on this evening alone.

After this 'insipid' evening he is himself 'robbed' at play (of 5 guineas) playing whist with the hostess's daughters in another group, and retires to a sofa to reflect gloomily on Edinburgh hospitality.

Hogg, as his alter ego, also exposes the hypocrisy of the 'Not at home' convention. To one caller it is explained that ladies are often too exhausted to receive on mornings after a night's dissipation. Another complains that although he has actually seen a lady through her dining-room window (who hastily retreats out of sight), she is gravely denied by her 'lying rascal' of a servant. Our author praises the literal approach of a Quaker in Nicolson Street, who adopts the simple expedient of a brass plate on the shop door stating 'Open at 12 o'clock'.

This gentleman too is lured to a party, starting at 11 when normally he would be in bed: 'small', with some 100 guests. Again knowing nobody, he is quickly fagged at being unable even to find room to sit down. Finds he must stay for the supper or offend his hostess, who has strained every nerve to be known as keeping Edinburgh's best table; she on her side amuses some, irritates others and displeases all in her endeavour to keep shifting them round as there are seats for barely half. Then in the carriage going home he learns from his niece that the lady is despised as a 'vulgar' woman trying to gain a reputation for taste.

Again, in the guise of a country gentleman correspondent, revisiting Edinburgh after many years, Hogg expresses the confusion in the city's fashionable streets. Impressed by the New Town and elegant buildings and shops, he is puzzled by pedestrians' habits. Who are these showy young women who fill the pavements? Making calls, shopping, taking a walk, he is told. Then why do they not walk somewhere pleasant like Calton Hill or the Meadows and not in these crowded streets? No, 'quite unfashionable'. Then he wonders at the groups of young men who swing along hanging on each other's arms. These turn out to be the students, much increased in numbers since his day. His spinster sister informs him that today's Edinburgh student is 'a worshipper at the shrine of fashion, rather than that of learning', and as the youths pass he is amused by the young ladies talking ostentatiously to attract their attention.[18]

To be a Whig in Edinburgh was to be one of an intellectual minority. Simond noted how the city, with no trade or finance and little industry was largely an obedient follower of the Tory Government. Such Whigs as there were would be found among the literati and younger lawyers, and only moderate at that. Few 'down-right reformers' existed in society, nor were there any in the working class. 'A jacobin tradesman is here a phenomenon . . . generally a man of bad private character.' One leading Whig informed him that all commoners were Tories, and 'among them *whiggism was rank democracy*'. [19]

Attitudes were changing, however. An annual dinner had long been held in the city in honour of Charles James Fox, to which when political tempers were high, few dared turn up as their names were noted at the door so that Dundas could be informed. As passions cooled and suspicions lessened, more attended, in 1810 150, in 1811 200. M. Simond was invited by Dr Thomson, Professor of Surgery. The Whigs were in good form and the occasion was one of good humour. The advocate Adam Gillies presided, and Henry Erskine assisted, making his after-dinner speech in a simple, conversational tone. Whiggish subjects were dealt with moderately and civilly: the need for a regency, hopes of the Prince of Wales's politics, parliamentary reform, Irish emancipation.

The numerous toasts were led off by one to Fox, each accompanied by a speech. One very young peer sneaked off for fear of having to speak when the Irish Catholics were toasted. When a toast was drunk to Lord Newton, the only judge present, Simond was surprised to see a monstrous figure heave itself to its feet, 'a true *porceau d'epicure*', with a raw bluish complexion, breathing hard with closed eyes, as if he might slip under the table in a stupor any moment: yet however faltering his delivery, he gave a short, sensible speech, and observed that he was the only judge appointed by Fox.

The evening advanced in conviviality though apparently not in drunkenness; several songs were sung, one 'by an old country gentleman set the table in a roar' in a dialect incomprehensible to Simond. Three professional singers named Elliot gave a skilled rendering of catches and glees. Alexander Nasmyth meanwhile was stuck in a corner, and in trying to leave had to jump over the table. Seeing this Henry Erskine called out one of his dreadful puns, 'Ah! Nasmyth, this is one of your land-skips!'

Port and madeira were served during dinner, and when the cloth was withdrawn, a bottle of claret was set before each gentleman, who could also order and pay for more. The cost of the dinner, 25 shillings, was not enough to cover the expenses.

Simond left at 1 a.m., while the hefty judge and a hard core of *bon vivants* sat on drinking until daybreak: next morning the judge (whose legal reputation was excellent) was seen on his way to court, apparently unaffected. A few days earlier Simond had heard him reproach a young man at a dinner party for his father's needless death: 'I told him he would kill himself; what! to reduce himself in his old age to a single bottle of wine at dinner – it was certain death!' [20]

The [illegible] [illegible] [illegible] [illegible] [illegible] [illegible] [illegible] [illegible] [illegible] [illegible] by an old country gentleman [illegible] [illegible] [illegible] [illegible] a dialect incomprehensible to Edmund. [illegible] Henry Erskine [illegible] [illegible] [illegible] [illegible] [illegible] [illegible] [illegible] [illegible] [illegible].

[illegible] [illegible] [illegible] the [illegible] apparently unaffected. A few days earlier Edmund had heard him [illegible] [illegible] [illegible] [illegible] [illegible] for his father's [illegible] death. 'I told him it would kill him [illegible] [illegible] [illegible] [illegible] [illegible] age [illegible] a single bottle of wine at dinner [illegible] [illegible] [illegible].'

22
FOUR MARRIAGES

> 'By the bye, I hear you are going to be married, but that I have heard so many times, that it produces no impression on me. Mackintosh says you are the cleverest man he ever met with.'
>
> Sydney Smith to Francis Jeffrey, 6 April 1813, *Letters of Sydney Smith*, 1953, I.236

In the summer of 1811 Percy Bysshe Shelley, nineteen years old and recently expelled from Oxford for atheistical views, spent some time in Wales persuading the seventeen-year-old Harriet Westbrook to elope with him. He succeeded. Towards the end of August they took the coach for Edinburgh, arriving about dawn on the 28th, and hired lodgings in George Street. By means of a false statement that he was legally qualified to marry, the young poet took his bride to the Rev. Joseph Robison, who married them next day. A day later again, the bridegroom was writing to his father asking for money, and explaining that they must stay until he received a reply, 'in consequence of having incurred a slight debt'.

Shelley observed in passing that at this season 'There is not a creature in Edinburgh, 'tis as dull as London in the dog days – there is however much worth seeing'. In spite of rain, he proposed to visit the main sights, Holyrood, Arthur's Seat, the Castle.

In his letter he followed this with a rather pompous justification of his conduct, and since his father intentionally did not reply, wrote slightly desperately on 27 September, 'No son can be so dutiful so respectful as me', and that his earlier remarks were only urged 'in case you act differently from the mild character which you have hitherto supported'.[1]

Meanwhile he had suggested to his friend Thomas Jefferson Hogg that he join them and make part of their honeymoon, as was customary, though usually it was a sister or friend of the bride rather than of the bridegroom. In his *Life of Shelley* Hogg recounts his uncomfortable journey north in some detail. Except for Northallerton all the inn meals were 'abominable', the long road was everlastingly dusty (he was travelling outside), Newcastle was 'smoky, dirty, half-savage but conceited', breakfast at Alnwick was 'filthy and utterly useless . . . at an odious little Inn', relieved only by a romantic view of the castle; but after the 'superlatively nasty' King's Head and 'impregnable' dinner at Berwick, Scotland's hills and vistas made up for what had gone before. Besides, he was young, all but impervious to the need for clean clothes, sleep or even food.[2]

Like many travellers of the time, Hogg made notes on the countryside and crops, the unenclosed fields, 'extensive moors', good corn and flourishing turnips, small windmills on the farms used for turning the winnowing and threshing machines, an improvement new to him. Dunbar was 'a dirty, stinking, fishing town', but a serious little middle-aged fellow-traveller began assuring his companions that Scotland was 'the finest, happiest, most refined and civilised country in the known world', and standing up behind the luggage he harangued Hogg on the excellence of the district, people and superior Lothian agriculture.

Edinburgh next came in for praise. 'A most remarkable city; and by far the most remarkable under the heavens . . . Yes, and it has a Review, as remarkable as itself!' Byron's quarrel with it was then recent, and controversy with Oxford University even then proceeding. Hogg, uncomfortably propped half round to hear his tireless interlocutor, had to accept that Oxford was 'silenced . . . totally annihilated . . . shoals of students would come flocking thence by thousands to Edinburgh, to Aberdeen, to St Andrews'; and while confessing he did not know him personally, he extolled the brilliance of that 'little man and a very clever man', Francis Jeffrey.

Tired out, at last he fell silent, and in time left the coach. It was Hogg's first experience of this kind of bore, and his panegyric seemed disproved when the coach entered the dark, narrow and mean-looking streets on Edinburgh's fringe. The wretched inn where they dismounted did not help, nor the fact that no one appeared to wait on him, nor his incomprehension of what anybody said. Finally shown into a squalid little bedroom, he slept soundly – perhaps not surprisingly after thirty hours in the open air and one hundred miles on top of the coach.

In the morning he was amazed by the contrast between the dingy inn and the sights around – castle, Calton Hill, and the buildings indicated by a grave passer-by, who conducted him to the Post Office to find Shelley's address, declaiming on Edinburgh's splendours the while. These included the sadly unfinished University, the bridge which spanned a valley with no water, and the Register House, 'the finest building on the habitable earth'. To all this Hogg kept a discreet silence.

George Street was a different matter. It was broad, noble, well-built – but deserted, and not yet fully inhabited. Shelley was staying in a handsome house on the south side, and received Hogg 'rapturously in a fine front parlour'. Here Hogg first met Shelley's bride Harriet, 'bright, blooming, radiant with youth, health, and beauty'. He must stay with them, insisted

Shelley, and the landlord showed him to a large and airy bedroom at the top of the house, an interminable if easy climb up a handsome stone stair, but with deafening echoes whenever a door in the house was shut.[3]

The lodging at 60 George Street was later turned into a shop, with internal alterations to ground and first floor, and an extra storey was added. The second floor was the 'top suite' in which Hogg stayed. The Rev. Joseph Robison, pastor of Leith Wynd Chapel, solemnised several illegal marriages until he was prosecuted in 1817 and banished from Scotland. A story that Shelley, doubting the legality of his marriage, as soon as he was of age remarried Harriet in an Edinburgh Episcopal chapel, is doubtful in view of their marrying in London in 1814. Peacock claims that, having asked the landlord to advance them money, he was obliged to treat him and friends to a wedding supper, and that when they were alone he knocked at their door saying that it was customary for guests to 'wash the bride with whisky'. The incensed Shelley caught up his pistols and aimed them, threatening to blow out his brains for impertinence, on which the fellow tumbled downstairs and locked the door.

This hardly fits with the rest of the story, or the account of their relations with the landlord, and is not mentioned by Hogg, who was not there, any more than was Peacock. Shelley might have told him an embroidered story as a joke, or out of bravado.[4]

The trio of friends now spent a happy time exploring Edinburgh, Harriet insisting on Holyrood first ('a beggarly palace, in truth') and delighted with the relics of Queen Mary and Rizzio. While Shelley left them to write letters – probably including another to his father – Hogg escorted Harriet to the top of Arthur's Seat, but as they turned to descend it was unexpectedly windy, and Harriet refused to stir, her chief concern apparently that it might reveal her ankles. Hogg, who had had no proper dinner for two days, unchivalrously abandoned her, climbing down slowly until she capitulated and had to run after him down the windswept hillside.

Their lodgings were good, including the wine, and the landlord's attendance at meals was excellent. His dirty servant Christie, however, rarely answered the bell and when she did assumed it was for 'the kittle' for endless cups of tea. Shelley, profoundly irritated by her talk, would retreat frantically to a corner while the others insisted on hearing about her dinner ('sengit head and bannocks').

The chief drawback for Hogg was his hard bed, but the landlord lectured him at breakfast on the absolute necessity of a straw mattress rather than a feather-bed. 'Health enjoins it. You cannot lie too hard.' Hogg gave up. 'I had got into the land of absolute wisdom, and I must make the best of it.'

Then there was the disappearance of his hat, which he had hung up in the hall. Nobody could have taken it, swore the landlord, his lodgers were 'high people – very high indeed'. Even Scotland's top grandees, thought Hogg, might not be 'above prigging a hat', which was hard, heavy and had cost him 35 shillings. The landlord changed his assurance that this was the safest place in Scotland to blaming Hogg for leaving it there. He offered to pay for the new one which Hogg bought in Princes Street, but was refused, and in future Hogg kept it with him in the sitting-room.

Shelley, usually notoriously careless about what he ate, indulged himself here in buying 'splendid plates of virgin honey' for breakfast on his way back from collecting his voluminous mail from the Post Office.[5]

Edinburgh was indeed 'empty', that is of all kinds of society and of the professions, though one day Hogg, finding the Parliament House open, witnessed a palsied old judge quavering out a judgment in broad Scots to a well-nigh empty house. Even the usher seemed hardly to know who he was. Meanwhile Shelley, constantly borrowing from the public library, seems to have spent much of his time reading, and both he and Harriet were busy translating works from the French. Hogg, not perhaps innocently, admired her pretty, bright and blooming neatness.

Unusually, the weather had become fine and hot, not a drop of rain fell and the nights were bright. It was the year of the comet, which in the evenings they viewed from Princes Street. They made few excursions as Harriet did not like energetic walks. Shelley would not leave Harriet and Hogg did not like to leave the two of them. But after studying until dinnertime they used to sally forth until dusk, return for tea, and listen to readings by Harriet. Hogg gratified his own curiosity by stealing out for a little sightseeing before breakfast.

The one problem of these halcyon days was Sunday. On their first Sabbath the landlord announced after breakfast, 'They are drawing nigh unto the kirk!', and his young lodgers looked out to watch the dismal perambulation of 'grave Presbyterians, with downcast looks, like conscience-stricken sinners'. On another Sunday when Hogg spoke of going for a walk, he was solemnly warned of the sinfulness of Sabbath promenading with intent, unless he were genuinely out by chance, which was innocent. So the little party fell into the habit of being 'casually' outside the house, and 'walked about a little, as we believed, innocently'. Even this had pitfalls. One Sunday, 'finding themselves' in Princes Street, Shelley laughed so immoderately at a remark of Hogg's that he was warned by 'an ill-looking, ill-conditioned fellow' that for laughing in the streets 'on the Christian Sabbath, you will be cast into prison and eventually banished from Scotland'.

One day they fell into the temptation of sampling a preacher recommended by 'a staid old gentlewoman' who praised the way he 'wrestled most powerfully with Satan, every Sabbath morn'. Hogg could not catch either name or church, but he and Shelley rashly chose to attend a service (Harriet said no, it would give her a headache).

The nearer they approached the church, 'plain, spacious, and gloomy', the thicker the crowds. Incautiously they allowed themselves to be led to a central bench, realising too late there was no escape. 'Loud, discordant, and protracted' singing followed, with extempore prayers and preaching. The sermon, threatening eternal punishment (said Hogg), was of 'prodigious length, repeating many times things that were not worthy to be said once . . . a stupid and preposterous absurdity', while Shelley, 'the picture of perfect wretchedness', uttered sighs 'that might seem those of conscience', but were in fact 'the anguish of his poetic temperament' thus so unpoetically trapped. After endless false hopes the preacher finally ceased, but even then the pair were pushed aside to make way for the provost and baillies making their exit. Harriet, to whom they recounted the woes of the past couple of hours, laughed heartlessly.

Even this did not prevent Shelley from attending a meeting at a large, dismal, church-like building to hear a Catechist whom Christie insisted that all 'children and domestics must attend'. Standing in a corner they watched while children and servants surrounded the sinister-looking, black-clad figure in the centre. All attended while he asked repeatedly, but to no purpose, 'Wha was Adam?' Dead silence from the listeners. When he continued angrily, 'Wha's the Deel?', 'Shelley burst into a shrieking laugh and rushed wildly out of doors', Hogg following slowly, amazed that they were not arrested by the elders.[6]

This strange existence continued for six weeks, until Hogg had to leave for a year's law studies in York. They hired a post-chaise for Harriet's sake and all set off together, Shelley laughing at Harriet, 'little Cockney', who couldn't tell a field of barley from a turnip crop. The fine spell had passed, showers of rain fell, and the journey was tiresome, Harriet's collection of useless indispensables had to be looked after, and Shelley kept disappearing in irritation.

In Edinburgh, the slight and delicate Harriet had attracted no particular attention in the street (where so many visitors had noticed that ladies could walk with propriety), whereas in York she caused much remark. Her tyrannical elder sister arrived to plague their lives, and the rest of them took off for the Lakes, where Shelley begged Hogg to join them; but in fact his peace of mind had been marred because Harriet revealed that in Edinburgh Hogg had made amorous advances. Hogg, of course, is silent about this, and the friends did not meet again for a year.

Shelley, exponent of 'free love', had no logical grounds for jealousy; it was Harriet who was less keen on the idea. They returned to Shelley's exasperated father in Sussex, stayed variously in England, Ireland and Wales, and in October 1813, still with money troubles, returned to Edinburgh.

Harriet claimed that, though she was still only eighteen, these had been the two happiest years of her life, and she was pleased to be back in Edinburgh: 'This city is, I think, much the best. The people here are not so intolerant as they are in London. Literature stands on a higher footing here than anywhere else . . .'[7]

Shelley was probably unique among Edinburgh's visitors in largely ignoring it except as a base for reading and study, as a dedicated Oxonian might regard the beauties of his alma mater second to his academic life. Yet a tantalising remark by Charles Kirkpatrick Sharpe shows that he could also indulge in socialising. In a letter to Mrs Balfour, tiresomely undated, Sharpe asks if he may bring to call Sir Timothy Shelley's son, with his friend – not Mr Hogg, nor Mr Peacock, but Mr Hutchinson. 'They are both very gentlemanly persons, and dance quadrilles eternally.' This sounds more like Sydney Smith's Michael than Shelley, and the lack of date renders it rather suspect. Elsewhere, Sharpe expressed himself about him fairly forcibly.[8]

This time they lodged at 36 Frederick Street, and had Thomas Love Peacock as a visitor. 'He is a very mild, agreeable man, and a good scholar. His enthusiasm is not very ardent, nor his views very comprehensive, but he is neither superstitious, ill-tempered, nor proud.' High praise, from the critical poet.[9]

Otherwise Shelley, still unreconciled to his father, was contracting debts. He ordered carriage repairs costing £13.18.6, for re-springing, new main plates, and new lamps, but made no attempt to pay. The coach-maker, John Dumbreck, had to apply to Sir Timothy after Shelley's death, plus £6.1.6 interest. Further, he ran up a debt of some £30 for their lodgings, tried to borrow from a friend in England, and eventually, after a stay of five or six weeks, had to leave the city precipitately for London.[10]

Shelley's and Harriet's adventures in Edinburgh were hardly typical, though at times the city must have been full of young couples who had escaped either to Gretna or to Edinburgh itself to contract a dubious marriage.

A few years later one whose marriage free-thinking Shelley would doubtless have approved was John Linnell, a descendant of the famous cabinet maker Linnell and son of a carver and gilder, and himself showing early talent for painting. In his late teens he was drawn to a Baptist sect and resolutely maintained an opposition to orthodox clergy. Betrothed to a girl named Mary Palmer, he long deferred marriage until he was satisfactorily settled, but doggedly already wedded to his principles he refused a church wedding, and elected to go to Scotland where they could contract a legal civil ceremony. In September 1817 the pair travelled by coach via Manchester, Lancaster and the Lakes – a journey itself unorthodox for an unmarried couple – and from Carlisle to Edinburgh by mail, arriving at 6 a.m. on Sunday, 21st.

He had letters of introduction to David (sic) Lizars, the engraver, and in the next two days called on him and other acquaintances, whose hospitality impressed him. Lizars enabled him to borrow Erskine's *Institutes* from the lending library, from which he was able to satisfy himself of the legality of his proposed marriage.

Even at this stage his friends urged him to a Kirk wedding, but he still staunchly refused. They married on 24 September with a simple declaration before the magistrate, James Gibson, with Lizars as witness. The unorthodox wedding was followed by a usual enough wedding tour, via Glasgow (where he painted a portrait) to the Highlands, and Linnell returned to a successful career as a portrait painter, often of Scotsmen, though he himself never revisited Scotland.[11]

Humphrey Davy's career was meteoric. In 1807 he was appointed Secretary of the Royal Society, and his publications were soon the subject of articles in the *Edinburgh Review.* His researches led him to the discovery of the bases of fixed alkalis, but also landed him in a dangerous illness, possibly from his visits to Newgate Gaol, seeking improvement of its sanitation and ventilation.

In 1810 he met the Edgeworths when he visited Ireland to lecture in November, where (Miss Edgeworth's stepmother wrote) he 'opened a new world of knowledge to ourselves and to our young people'. A year later he was visiting them, 'as usual full of entertainment and information of various kinds', 'mad about fishing' and sending them a trout – 'and a trout of Davy's catching is, I presume,' (wrote Maria to Margaret Ruxton), 'worth 10 trouts caught by vulgar mortals.'[12]

Meanwhile in 1810 the Sydney Smiths in Yorkshire had had a run of visitors, including Francis Horner, Jeffrey, and 'Mrs Apreece the learned lady', whom they all 'rather liked' and Smith hints that she was drawn to the flirtatious Playfair, 'circumvented by [his] diagrams . . . the first woman that . . . was geometrically led from the paths of virtue'. Replying later to a criticism of Jeffrey's, he wrote, 'she seems a friendly, good hearted, rational woman, and as much under the uterine dominion as is graceful, and pleasing', that is, not 'hermetically sealed in the lower regions'. Mrs Apreece and the Miss Berrys, whom Playfair had been eager to become friends when she removed to London, and who were now meeting frequently, claimed that 'upon the whole [Playfair] is the only man who can be called irresistible', despite his having grown 'thinner and older by some years' since Smith last saw him.[13]

At the end of the year Smith was writing to Mrs Apreece full of gallant compliments to her wit and charm, wishing she had come north. He begged her not to remarry, 'let him be whom he may: you will be annihilated, and instead of being an Alkali, or an acid, become a mere Neutral Salt'.[14]

A clear hint against Humphrey Davy. He was too late, however. Davy seems to have met her at Bulstrode late that August, and a few weeks later writes of her 'exalted' character and her influence on his own more untutored tastes. He was smitten, pined for her, was distracted, and early in 1812 declared his love. He (partly) confided his emotional distress to his brother John: 'I have been very miserable: the lady whom I love best of any human being, has been very ill.' Mercifully, she restored his happiness by recovering. To her he wrote, 'I have passed a night sleepless from excess of happiness. It seems to me as if I began to live only a few hours ago.'[15] A few weeks later, on 11 April, they were married. Mrs Apreece, having finally capitulated, had calculated her acceptance nicely. It was presumably hardly a coincidence that only three days earlier Davy had been knighted.

They travelled from London to the Highlands for their honeymoon, passing through Edinburgh, where Mrs Grant met them at an evening at Mrs Mackenzie's. She greatly admired Davy, 'the first chemist in Europe . . . very natural, and very amusing', and was not much surprised to find that 'she, like the generality of people who live much in and for the world, looks older than she is, and he much younger: they are, however, about the same age.' (Davy was thirty-four.)[16] This worldliness was what was, after not very long, to set them apart, Lady Davy's glamour overlaying a social frivolity hardly agreeing with Davy's sober and dedicated career.

'Sir Humphrey Davy the great', wrote Charles Kirkpatrick Sharpe, 'together with his lady the greater, are at present making a progress through Scotland. All our professors are paying court to the knight, who puffs around him that gas of paradise which he inhaled from the deceased Dr Beddoes, while Lady Davy charms every one with her radiant blue eyes and bluer stockings . . . she hath almost turned the brains of two natural philosophers.'[17]

On the news of Davy's marriage Maria Edgeworth wrote to Margaret Ruxton (20 July 1812), quoting Sir John Carr's *bon mot* that Davy, finishing his last lecture on the note that 'we were but in the Dawn of Science . . . probably did not expect to be so soon beknighted', and a piece of doggerel about the lady's earlier refusal of the suits of 'Church, Army, Bar, and Navy':

> Too many men have often seen their talents underrated,
> But Davy owns that his have been
> Duly *Appreeciated.*[18]

'I shall not envy kings, princes, or potentates', wrote the besotted Davy; '. . . I do not believe there exists another being possessed of such high intellectual powers, just views, and refined taste, as the object of my admiration.' She seems to have cast a spell over almost everybody, women as well as men. 'She has more heart, talents, quickness of parts and other excellent qualities', said Lady Holland – and from her this was praise indeed – 'than almost anybody. I really love her.'[19]

The sad truth was that, although in many ways Davy's extravagant praise was justified, the pair were too unalike to be happy for long. She had the gift of attracting people by her dazzling personality – small wonder that the academic Davy, brilliant in a completely different way, was so soon ensnared – but was too self-willed and independent, too much the socialite and not enough the loving and domestic partner, and her temper could be abrasive. Further, recurring bouts of illness made her often an irritable companion. Like many fashionable ladies she interested herself in work for the poor, had a lively mind, excellent taste, and a fascination based on more than a pretty face. Distinguished thinkers and writers, Playfair, Sismondi, Mrs Somerville, Mme de Staël, not to mention Jeffrey, Walter Scott (to whom she was distantly related), Sydney Smith and Henry Mackenzie, besides many of the aristocracy, were proud to be invited to her soirées. She was, rather, a creature to be admired more than loved.

Indeed, while fascinating all who met her, the new Lady Davy was a tiresome woman and unsuccessful as a wife. Letters between the couple reveal the disparity which soon showed through their mutual passion. Brilliant in society, she was not cut out for wedlock, but only in wedlock could a brilliant lady then fulfil her potential in society. She was not affectionate, not domestic, it was Davy who had to make the allowances. Revealingly they had no children (nor had she by her first husband).

Davy's bride had money, and his new release from the drudgery of earning by lecturing freed him for research and publication; on the other hand, he was tempted by the fashionable society life. He retained his Professorship of Chemistry at the Royal Institution, but spent more time in travel – the wedding tour to the Highlands that summer, partly with his brother John,[20] and much of the following two years in foreign travel. Meanwhile his experiments could be dangerous. In November 1812 an explosion of azote and chlorine nearly cost him an eye, for which he had 'the conjunctiva and cornea punctured', and suffered the effects for six months.

In 1815 after another Highlands tour Davy visited the mines in Newcastle to study firedamp and its possible remedy, with further experiments in the autumn. In 1817 he visited Orkney and later Edinburgh, but with Lord Gage, not at first with his wife, and in spring 1818 the pair went abroad for more than two years, returning only on the news of Sir Joseph Banks's fatal illness. (He died in June 1820.) By this time there had been several significant references to Lady Davy's health, to her 'constant attacks' of stomach upsets which suggest an amount of stress.[21]

In November 1816 Sydney Smith had written unsympathetically that 'The decomposition of Sr Humphry, and Lady Davy is entertaining enough. I wonder what they quarrelled about. He had a very ample allowance of crucible money at marriage.' Perhaps, he speculated, Davy had over-praised the 'secrets of chemistry', 'hence her disappointment, and fury'. To the non-scientist Davy might indeed be a bore, and they settled for independent social lives which only occasionally crossed.[22] Smith kept in touch with both, and in 1818 writes to Lady Davy of his gratification that, living in 'the most intellectual place in the world', she should keep up with him, a Yorkshire parson: 'certainly you do keep *one* of the most – perhaps the most agreeable house in London'. Sir Humphrey, meanwhile, was trying to drag her off for mineralogical research in the Augsburg Alps. Smith certainly found Davy a good companion, and on a Yorkshire visit in August 1822, 'really very agreeable, neither witty, eloquent, nor sublime, but reasonable and instructive'.[23]

Davy had by this time invented the safety lamp for use of miners, and in January 1819 was created a baronet. The increasingly ill-suited pair achieved no offspring to carry on his talents or title. On Banks's death in 1820 Davy was elected his successor as President of the Royal Society, and again unanimously for the next five years, resigning only in 1827 through his own ill-health.

He made numerous travels in Scotland, in 1822 missing the King's arrival by only a few days, dining with Scott, 'master of the royal revels', immediately before his departure north, and visited Scandinavia in 1824 – without his wife. Scott, whose relationship with Lady Davy increased their friendship, often met Sir Humphrey both in Edinburgh and London, and considered that he would have made a good poet, had he not preferred a life of science.[24]

About this time Francis Jeffrey's life completely changed. Since the partial healing of his acute sorrow at his wife's death, he had been a very eligible widower, successful, famous, brilliant, controversial, and still young. He had apparently not been entirely celibate, and in January 1809 Sydney Smith, writing to Lady Holland, hinted at one of his liaisons: 'great scandal about Jeffrey and the Duchess of Gordon. He is a very amorous little gentleman, and her disposition is not I fancy wholly dissimilar: it is probable therefore that they will build a nest.' He certainly did not mean a matrimonial nest, for (apart from her being more than twenty years older than Jeffrey), her husband the 4th Duke, though they had long lived apart, was very much alive. As it happened it was the lady who died, only two years later.[25]

Jeffrey's sister-in-law and her husband Robert Morehead had continued to be his great support, and he still made his almost daily calls on them in Hill Street in the half-hour between leaving his office and dressing for dinner, energetically discussing social, literary, personal and public events.

The French-American Louis Simond, who spent some fifteen months in Britain, of which from August 1810 to February 1811 were in Edinburgh, had emigrated to America during the French Revolution, and married the American-born Miss Wilkes, niece to the Radical John Wilkes. He was accompanied to Europe not only by his wife but by her own niece the seventeen-year-old Charlotte Wilkes. Although of course, such was the convention of the time, he names neither lady in his published account of his travels, they both, particularly the younger Charlotte, had a significant effect in Edinburgh.

Simond had earlier met Jeffrey's brother John, then living in America, who had returned to Scotland some time after the death of his own wife in 1807 and was living with Francis. Simond, arriving in the city in August, found 'everybody' away on their country estates, but notes that 'The two Messrs J' showed them round.[26] Francis, after his years of being essentially solitary, however superficially ebullient and social, now at last had the prospect of happiness with a lifelong companion. He fell in love with the lively Charlotte Wilkes.

The *Review* was continuing to cause him a headache, whether by criticism from readers or contributors' failure to deliver the goods. In a typical plaint to Horner he apologised for the journal's 'growing too factious', but added, 'but you judge rightly of my limited power, and of the overgrown privileges of some of my subjects . . . I am but a feudal monarch at best'.[27]

That was before he met Charlotte. In January 1811 he invited the Moreheads, the Fletchers, 'Mrs Erskine with her two sons and daughters, and Mr Holland' to dine. The occasion was highly intellectual, and Morehead noted feelingly: 'There was a good deal of scientific conversation', and even when they turned to 'general information' he found himself 'at a loss'. 'Meteoric stones – the four asteroids – the laws of the regularly increasing distances of the planets from each other – canals in France, in China – the great wall of China; all these and many other topics were considered.' Although Mrs Fletcher might not have been out of her element, no doubt most of these were discussed when the ladies had left for the drawing-room, as even Scottish ladies might have felt 'at a loss'.[28]

Near this time Jeffrey also invited Mrs Grant to meet the Americans, along with Henry Mackenzie and Mrs Elizabeth Hamilton. He must have been eager to know what Mrs Grant would think of them, and might well have been a little startled by what she eventually – though not until some two-and-a-half years after this meeting – wrote to her friend the poetess Catherine Fanshawe:

> One was a dark, gloomy-looking man, another his wife, the plainest, worst-dressed woman I had seen, and the third was a gay, fashionable-looking girl of 17, . . . Simond, though very unlike a Frenchman, being

> reserved, fastidious, and philosophic in the highest sense of the phrase, is a man of talent, great refinement, and agreeable conversation when he does converse. His wife is a person that, after the unfavourable impression of her unpromising exterior was got over, I liked exceedingly, – most candid, most disinterested, most benevolent, – with a cultivated mind, plain manners, and continual good humour.

According to Mrs Grant, Mme Simond had known Mrs Elizabeth Montagu and imbibed opinions from that quarter. The evening was a success, and during the following days they met again in Edinburgh, and several times attended Mrs Grant's 'little parties'. At the time, she noted, Jeffrey 'had not the leisure to fall in love with the fair American':[29] it was later that his fate struck when he met them again in London.

Jeffrey had earlier visited Sydney Smith at his Yorkshire home in Heslington in 1809, after he moved there to become rector of Foston. Now Smith tried to lure him again, full of admiration though often free with his comments on the *Review*. 'Do not be hurt by my critiques on your criticisms; you know . . . the love and respect I have for you . . . and also the very *high admiration*' – while expressing his reluctance to enquire about the paper's progress and always expecting to hear that it was 'dead or dying'.[30]

He was presumably exaggerating, and less than five months later Jeffrey had set off for America to marry Charlotte Wilkes.

Having proposed to her and been accepted, there had been the question of their immediate future. Charlotte's English father, long living in America, at one time thought of bringing his family back to Britain, where the wedding of Francis and Charlotte was first suggested. But finally she returned to America with the Simonds, and not until the spring of 1813 did Jeffrey arrange to follow and marry her there. This was a momentous decision, not only because few could hate a sea voyage more – but from 1812 England and her former American colonies had been at war.

During the summers of 1812 and 1813 the Jeffrey brothers and the Morehead family had moved out to Hatton, Lord Lauderdale's former seat, to spend happy vacations, returning occasionally for business to Edinburgh. In late June, when Francis had settled his Edinburgh affairs and arranged for Thomas Thomson to edit the *Review* in his absence, the brothers set off for Liverpool in order to embark for the States, Francis 'like a *preux chevalier*', commented Morehead, to bring his bride 'home in the midst of war'. 'This', he added more prosaically, 'will be a blank in our summer society.'[31]

Departure for the States proved not immediately possible, as Jeffrey wrote bitterly to John Murray on 20 June, and he feared they might even be delayed until the winter, as the Government were now threatening not to allow even Americans to sail until the question of British subjects' detention over there had been satisfactorily settled.

The enforced stay in Liverpool brought Jeffrey into contact with its leading characters, including the famous William Roscoe,[32] attorney, historian and banker – whom he did not care for. Nor did he like Liverpool, despite its famed lively social and literary activity, and its importance as the port where most Americans made their first acquaintance with England. 'All my recollections are Scottish', wrote Jeffrey, 'and consequently all my imaginations.' Indeed he realised here that he could not live out of Scotland.

He diluted the long wait by revisiting Edinburgh and Hatton for a month, returning to Liverpool in late August. While waiting for a ship he wrote exhorting Thomson to 'meditate *Review* both day and night, and to stimulate all the wise and good to lend their aid to that good cause for which I have lived and bled such extraordinary devotion'. With a hortatory 'Do not let the poor *Review* die till I come back, if any human exertion can keep her alive', he concluded, in a slightly melancholy contemplation of himself on the brink of this new step, 'My lot in this old world has been eminently happy, and chiefly in the kindness and excellence of the friends with whom I have lived. If I die now, I shall be to be envied.'[33]

On 28 August, on the eve of departure from Liverpool, Jeffrey was feeling ashamed at his sorrow over leaving, although sure he was doing right. He wished this momentous step 'had not been quite so wide and laborious', and was thinking affectionately of Hatton. On the 29th the brothers sailed in a cartel, the *Robert Burns*, 'full of visitors', he wrote, 'and a monstrous music of cheering mariners, squeaking pigs, and crying children'.[34]

His dislike of the sea proved justified. He was seasick, violent gales delayed their voyage, kept people from exercise and made him even fear being drowned. The cooking was 'horrid' and the passengers were 'crying children, chattering Frenchmen . . . and foolish women'. Even when they sighted land at last, on 4 October, they were not allowed ashore until the 7th, and the brothers then went straight to Charles Wilkes's house.[35]

Jeffrey's fame had of course preceded him, and he was invited to the White House. George Ticknor, a 22-year-old Bostonian who, educated for the law, had abandoned it for a literary career and was to be America's first cosmopolitan scholar and a student at Göttingen, was extremely impressed by him. Dining one evening at the White House he noted that the name of Jeffrey struck President Madison with a sudden silence; Ticknor therefore thought it prudent to refrain from mentioning the *Review*, or that he himself had already met Jeffrey. The following February, when the bridal pair had just returned to Scotland, he described the *Review* editor to his friend Charles Davis.

'A short, stout, little gentleman, about 5 and a half feet high, with a very red face, black hair, and black eyes.' This appearance must have been the effect of a decade of socialising and party-going. Gay, animated, restless, he made jerky movements almost like a puppet, the outward expressions of his 'impetuous and impatient character . . . I was very much delighted with Mr Jeffery.'[36]

The wedding was in November. Jeffrey visited several cities, met the Secretary, Munroe, and President Madison, with whom not surprisingly he got into an argument which lasted two hours.[37]

Jeffrey told Washington Irving at Craigcrook in 1817 that in America he experienced more comfort and even luxury than he had expected, but that he disliked the way they indulged in 'virulent political discussions at table'. As for the girls, he thought them 'flippant & ignorant and brought into company too early'. Presumably he did not think this of his Charlotte.[38]

Jeffrey at one time 'threatened' to write a book on female education, and just a year after his return to Scotland warned his father-in-law that 'of your free country among the most injudicious' practices was that 'American young ladies, who have not half as many tasks and restraints put upon them as young ladies everywhere else', showed visible marks of *ennui* in the misses just entered on their teens, 'who are allowed so prematurely to pass their whole mornings in parading in Broadway'.[39]

Despite some strictures, Jeffrey, like many of his contemporaties, was immensely struck by America's progress and prospects, and the vista of its new world.

While they were away came the news of the first real defeat by the Allies over Napoleon, as opposed to his moral and physical defeat in Russia. This was the battle of Leipzig in October, Napoleon's flight being on the anniversary of his flight from Moscow, and of his sea defeat in 1805 at Trafalgar. Like the Trafalgar victory, Leipzig was celebrated in Edinburgh as in other Allied cities with the usual salutes and illuminations.

The bridal couple and John Jeffrey sailed for Liverpool again on 22 January 1814, reaching it on 10 February, 'feverish with joy', and Jeffrey swore he would never part from his friends again.[40] (His later travels were all undertaken *with* friends.)

The disagreeable start to matrimony of two unpleasant voyages heralded thirty-four years of great happiness. Any pretence of retreating to a cottage was refuted by Jeffrey's still widening career in both his legal and literary capacities, and he lived devoted to his Charlotte and, before long, to their one daughter.

On their return to Edinburgh the couple lived at the small single house at 92 George Street to which Jeffrey had removed in May 1810 after his ten years on 'upper floors', and where they were to continue until 1827. They also had Hatton for another year, with its broken balustrades, choked fountains and 'half buried' urns. It was the following year that the happy tradition at Craigcrook began.[41]

23
EDINBURGH SHOPS

'The small number of shops in the New Town renders it dull; grass grows in most of the streets; and there is a want of that liveliness which, perhaps, would result from a more equal distribution of the different classes of society, throughout the two towns.'

John Stoddart, *Remarks on Local Scenery and Manners in Scotland during the years 1799 and 1800*, London, 1801, 1.79

'When I was staying in St John Street we spent our Saturday pennies . . . they reduced the price of a loaf to a shilling, and a halfpenny on moist also.'

A customer at Robert Shepherd, grocer's, in [Josiah Livingston], *Some Edinburgh Shops*, Edinburgh, 1894, 7

Scotland's economic poverty had long ago established a healthy respect for trade. In gentlemen's and even noble families, instead of limiting the careers for younger sons to the armed services and the church, Scotland was happy to enter them into trade, so that they had many noble clients. By the end of the eighteenth century Edinburgh, emerging as a centre for fashion, encouraged leading citizens to continue in a variety of trades: all kinds of fabrics, grocery and wines, meat brought in from the country, poultry and game, fish, cheese and other dairy produce, and raw materials and manufactured goods from England; not to mention imports from farther afield, Irish linen, luxury goods from France and the Mediterranean, Russian timber, iron and leather, to name but a few.[1] The Old Town shopping centre was between the West and Nether Bow: this especially applied to the cloth trade centred on the Lawnmarket, and in the Luckenbooths, partly surviving until their demolition in 1817.

At first the contrast between Old and New Towns was probably as stark as it would ever be, the former with its crowded medieval street pattern and dingy, largely seventeenth-century 'lands', the latter spacious with symmetrically built houses, in still gleamingly new stone blocks. Nowhere perhaps was the contrast more striking than in the Luckenbooths, the archaic stalls packed around St Giles' 'with their strange little ins and outs', as young

Thomas Carlyle saw them in 1809, 'and eager old women in miniature shops of combs, shoe-laces and trifles'.[2]

By 1807 shops were numerous and varied. There was Cunningham, the famous jeweller, Burns's friend who had inherited the bowl from which the poet drank while composing. Cunningham's speciality was Scottish 'pebbles' polished to be set as ornaments. There were, of course, the many and noted booksellers, especially Constable and Co., and these published several newspapers. Sir John Carr found Edinburgh tradesmen punctual, sober, courteous and industrious.[3]

Once the New Town was established, the shopping centre soon moved to Princes Street, which although designed as a residential street soon lost that status, and by the 1820s large houses had been converted into shops, and a decade later it was said to have 'the best stocked, highest rented and most handsome business premises and shops'.[4] Leith Street, and to some extent George Street, had by then also good shops.

For example, James Ritchie, starting as apprentice to Mr Howden, in May 1809 set up independently as a watch-maker in Leith Street, dealing not only with his own and other makers' watches but in cleaning and repairs, and selling watch-chains, thimbles and brooches on the side. Among his early customers were Walter Scott and Mme Tussaud. In 1819 Ritchie took over the 35-year-established Joseph Durward's business, in 1834 took on his son as partner, and the business continued under his grandson until 1953.[5]

In any town the most important shops are those selling food and drink, with clothes a close second. Edinburgh's largest grocer's was Robert Shepherd, at 83 South Bridge, 'next door but one to the arch at the south-west angle'.[6] He had many young assistants, and after making a good profit retired to Ettrick in 1812, but his approach to farming was unpractical, and he returned with reduced capital to start a shop opposite the University gates, run by his wife and pretty daughters. His new assistants were less good managers than the old, and because of his farming fiasco their employer tended to be laughed at as 'the Romantic Shepherd'.

Meanwhile his four original assistants had struck out on their own. Andrew Melrose took over the 'shop at the arch' and specialised in tea, making a lucrative business as Edinburgh's chief grocer.

A typical advertisement by Melrose, in September 1818, was for 'the Cheapest Teas in Scotland, at the old established Tea Shops', and 'arrival of their TEAS from the East India Company's September sale', besides their usual brands at 6s and 6/8d sold much lower than expected. The selected teas were Black Congo, 'very best blackish leaf', fine variants of Souchong, best Pekoe, and a Chinese mixture from 5/2d upwards.

In addition the range of groceries was extensive: besides green teas, coffee, chocolate and cocoa were sugar, spices, rice from different countries, vermicelli, arrowroot, tapioca, licorice, salt, saltpetre, salad oil, soda, yellow and white soap, and variants of starch – Prussian Blue, Mecklenburgh, Poland starch and Pearl Ashes. Not to mention such everyday foods as cheese, butter, bacon and hams, pickle, sauces, and imported wines and spirits. All this was obtainable at the shops at 83 South Bridge and 381 head of Canongate, and the wholesale warehouse at 12 Drummond Street.[7]

Foreseeing George Street as the centre for family business, Melrose bought a shop there which continued with the firm for well over a century, in time attracting all Old Town business. He employed about thirty staff including apprentices, all boarding with the firm, first in a house in West Nicolson Street and later the larger Chapel House at the top of Chapel Street. They kept good hours, were well looked after, and attended family worship on Sundays. For health reasons Melrose himself, who was thin and delicate, lived near Lasswade at Pittendreigh.

When the charter of the East India Company came to an end, so did their monopoly of the China and India trade.[8] Good quality tea, which had sold for 12 to 15 shillings a pound, fell in price to 8 to 10 shillings, and thenceforward about 32 million pounds a year were drunk. The prudent Melrose bought the George Street shop partly to develop his tea trade, sending a buyer to China as soon as their ports were opened in 1842.

Mossman & Co., at 11 Broughton Street and 11 Union Place, similarly advertised tea, wine and spirits, and a wide grocery range.[9]

Workers in the sugar trade needed to be tough, for sugar from Jamaica and Demerara arrived in hogsheads which the assistants had to dig out with a spade and mix by hand on the 'brod' with other varieties to blend colour and quality. James Richardson, another of Shepherd's first assistants, took a shop in Drummond Street and specialised in sugar. His partner, Muckle, proved too energetic a salesman and killed himself with overwork. As Richardson & Co. the firm moved to Catherine Street Court on Greenside and thence to a basement in Waterloo Place. Richardson himself later worked in Glasgow and Greenock, leaving the Edinburgh business to partners. He joined the Merchant Company's Widow Fund and died before he had subscribed a penny, but his widow qualified to become one of their first, and longest-lived, beneficiaries, who drew £12.10s (later £15) every half-year.

The third Shepherd assistant who prospered was John Christie, of the butter and oil department, who took a High Street shop opposite Knox's corner, and later a second, above Canongate Tolbooth, run by his younger brother Robert. Robert, however, saw better prospects in a New Town shop, and moved to North Hanover Street.

Though neat and tidy himself, Robert Christie evolved the eccentric idea of capitalising on an opposite reputation. Sure enough, 'Dirty Christie's' lured fashionable ladies, professors, Lords of Session – the ladies particularly charmed by graceful gifts of sweets and by his good tea. His shop windows, thick with mud, were crammed with tea-chests, and at night the counter was lit by candles stuck into beer-bottles, while nobility and gentry arrived in their carriages at the door. When one day the shop was newly painted, the news was said to spread through Edinburgh like some national sensation.

Coffee was now becoming a popular drink, thanks largely to Shepherd's youngest assistant, William Law, who became an expert and was known as 'Coffee Law'. Starting in the Canongate, like the others he moved to the New Town, with his younger brother George, trading as W. & G. Law, Grocers, at the north-east corner of St Andrew Square. Law went abroad to learn French coffee-making, for which he became famous in Britain, and invented his own coffee-roasting and grinding machine. He also opened a London shop, in Oxford Street, published pamphlets on local problems, and became Dean of Guild and finally Provost, when Edinburgh was at loggerheads over the water supply.

At the other end of the scale was the workaday grocer's where the fourteen-year-old William Chambers in 1814 applied for a job to help out his impoverished family.[10] Hearing of a vacancy, he trudged the two miles to Leith to offer himself as apprentice to a grocer in Tolbooth Wynd, whose chief recommendation was that he gave his apprentices board and lodging. It was an unprepossessing place.

> The windows exhibited quantities of raw sugar in different varieties of brownness, hovering over which were swarms of flies . . . Sticks of black liquorice leaned coaxingly on the second row of panes, flanked by tall glass jars of sweeties and peppermint drops; behind . . . there were observable yellow-painted barrels of whisky, rows of bottles of porter, piles of cheeses of varied complexions, firkins of salt butter, and boxes of soap. At the counter were a number of women and children buying articles, such as quarter-ounces of tea and ounces of sugar; and the floor was battered with dirt and debris.

William reluctantly goes in to present himself, and is at once written off as physically unfit to the job, whose 'chief qualification in demand was muscular vigour . . . to draw a truck loaded with several hundredweight of goods, to be delivered to customers, it might be miles distant', a job, in fact, better suited to a horse. The shopkeeper unflatteringly dismisses the applicant, but good comes of it, for on his return to the city he passes John Sutherland's, bookseller in Calton Street, opposite the Black Bull Hotel whence the London coaches start. Here an apprentice is needed and William proves eminently suitable.

As a bookseller's apprentice the duties seemed 'very easy. I would only have to light the fire, take off and put on the shutters, clean and prepare the oil-lamps, sweep and dust the shop, and go all the errands. When I had nothing else to do, I was to stand behind the counter, and help in any way that was wanted.' Besides being forbidden ever to sit down (a privilege never granted to shop assistants), the one thing he was never expected to do was to read the books.[11]

Mr Sutherland consoled the boy and his mother with the assurance that this was the way of all apprentices rising to be shopkeepers. The period of service was five years, the pay five shillings a week, and this was the inexorable rule.

Sutherland proved to be 'a stern disciplinarian', and his apprentices were treated as drudges. Besides his bookshop he kept a circulating library and was a State Lottery agent. As well as delivering parcels of books and stationery, William also had to deliver quantities of circular letters advertising the lottery, apparently to save postage. There might be up to three hundred such letters, parcelled up in bundles, and he had to walk miles through Edinburgh's thoroughfares and wynds. He determined to endure the harsh discipline and had at least the profit of learning a great deal about the city and its inhabitants.

Boots formed a major, and expensive, part of a gentleman's costume; country gentlemen in particular always wore top boots, such as Sir James Gibson Craig, renowned for his 'clean buff tops and spotless drab small clothes'. Most fashionable were the knee-length Hessians, finished with a silk tassel.

Forrest Alexander, born like many successful Scots into a poor family and having no education, taught himself good writing and book-keeping, studied the classics and became one of Edinburgh's most remarkable achievers. Starting very young in a Leith sail-maker's workshop, he was then apprenticed to a shoemaker, worked up to his own business and moved to a large shop in the then still little frequented Leith Street: the Black Bull Hotel opposite Nottingham Place was then the last building proper to Edinburgh. Alexander was another far-sighted business-man, foreseeing a busy highway and business centre as Leith's importance to the city increased.

He lived above the shop, started his own tannery and currying works in the Pleasance to supply himself with leather, became rich and soon bought the shop next door to accommodate a men's and women's department, and was Edinburgh's most fashionable stockist. Alexander's boots, made by his own staff, became famous. He also bought up the land on which Arthur Street and adjoining streets were built, and built himself a house called Oakfield.

As a businessman he was perspicacious. Private banks were then few, most commerce being in the rival control of the three chartered banks, Royal, Bank of Scotland and British Linen. Alexander and his friend Robert Cox, of Gorgie, who both dealt with the Royal Bank, had bills for discount returned as 'Not convenient' and were warned that they were 'doing too much business'. They determined to start their own bank with better regard for the customer, and opened the Commercial Bank at the corner of Picardy Place and Leith Walk. Alexander remained a director until his death.

Similarly, when the London Fire Insurance Company refused payment on a £600 fire loss when his policy had lapsed one day earlier, because his cashier forgot to renew the premium, the enraged Alexander decided to stop insuring from London and to form a Scottish company. This resulted in the Caledonian Insurance Company, which became one of the leading firms.

This forward-looking businessman appears to have been physically unimpressive, always walking with his gaze cast down to the pavement. On Saturdays he donned the red coat of the Burgess Club and played golf at Bruntsfield; on Sundays he always held family worship, as was frequent among such tycoons.

Another particularly opportunist merchant was William Fettes, son of a widow who sold tea in a tiny shop at the head of Baillie Fife's Close, opposite Fountain Well. A trapdoor and ladder led to their small house above. Fettes, educated at the High School, left (about 1765) to work for his mother as grocer, contractor, and underwriter of sea risks. Hard work paid off: in 1783 he was a merchant councillor, in 1785 Baillie, in 1788 he was one of the elite serving on the Deacon Brodie jury. In 1799 and 1804 he was elected Provost, and was created a baronet. In 1800 he also became a Director of the British Linen Bank, and took on two partners. The business, now Fettes, Tennant and Mylne, remained at 99 High Street until they moved to a large Clyde Street warehouse.

Fettes moved his house first to Princes Street, and later Charlotte Square, where he took care to entertain Corporation members and Government officials who might be useful to him. His public offices secured good contracts with the Government and services; he became Admiral of the Firth of Forth, and contractor for Naval Stores, by which he could evade duty on goods brought in – a practice more envied than criticised. He was one of many who engaged in the extensive local tobacco-smuggling racket, by which informers worked in collusion with the revenue officers, who then secured half the value as a reward.

Not surprisingly, Fettes died rich (in 1836), leaving many bequests to charity. He had had the intention of founding an updated version of Heriot's Hospital, but after his death his trustees instead opened a public school, Fettes College.

Edinburgh's market, on its terraced site down the north side of the High Street, supplied fish, meat, poultry and excellent vegetables. Sir John Carr in 1807 praised its quality, at least in summer (he did not experience it in winter). A staple for the poor was dulse, or edible seaweed, grown on the rocks on nearby coasts; it sold in pennyworths and was otherwise chiefly used for farm manure. Dulse, water and salt sellers, all women carrying creels, were common in the streets.

The fruit market was round the Tron. The famous summer strawberry supply, brought in by cart, was sold in baskets holding a Scottish pint, four times as big as the English pint; one hundred thousand were estimated as sold annually in the city and environs. The more luxurious wall-fruit and hothouse fruit were sold in pastry shops. Except for gooseberries, Carr regarded most Scottish fruit as inferior to English, and he thought that the markets' general appearance lacked the appealing neatness usual in an English market.[12]

As for wines, those drunk in the country and round the coast were considered purer and of better quality than in Edinburgh, where – as in London – it was usually diluted in the merchants' cellars. The mixture was created by 'a fellow standing in a hogshead of sugar' who shovelled it into a water vat, and stirred in 'alum water, corn brandy, and then a small proportion of real wine', which was then fermented, bottled and passed off as genuine. How widespread this practice was is not disclosed.[13]

As the nineteenth century advanced so did the New Town's sophisticated, luxury trade. Taken at random in November 1815 we find advertised Alexander Boyd, 'Ladies and Gentlemen's Fashionable Hair Cutter and Dresser, Manufacturer of Ornamental Hair, Perfumer, &c.' at 6 St Andrew's Street, specified as west side, second shop from Princes Street. He was cashing in on the popular music festival. 'Original Perfumery, Patent Heads of Hair, Perukes, Grecian Bandeaux, Glove, Cutlery, and Trinket Warehouse', ordered specially for the festival from the best London houses. Luxurious accommodation was guaranteed: 'Comfortable rooms are at all times ready for Dressing and Hair Cutting, at his warehouse, with proper attendance.'[14]

Or W. & P. Cunningham, at their silver plate manufactory at 77 Princes Street, had received a consignment from London of fashionable jewellery: 'rich Pearl Suits, Necklaces, Bracelets, Brooches, Lockets, Rings, &c, in coloured gold, and set with diamonds, Pearls, Rubies, Emeralds . . .'

They regularly dealt in silver, plate and plated goods, cutlery, and snuffboxes – having just secured some of these adorned with topical portraits of the Duke of Wellington, the Emperor Alexander and so on.[15]

At the mundane end of trade was coal. William Ross, late of Leith, in 1818 opened a large new coal yard at the west end of Princes Street 'in front of Kirkbraehead-house' (not, fortunately, when Mrs Grant was living there). For families who could not send a servant to collect, Ross diplomatically announced, he would pay for a porter.[16]

The swiss geologist Necker de Saussure, Professor at Geneva, who passed two winters in Edinburgh, gives a vivid picture of the city's prosperous shopping in about 1815:

> The North and South Bridge streets are ornamented by handsome shops of every description: these streets, animated by a continual passage of carriages, are furnished on each side by wide foot pavements . . . It is chiefly in the forenoon that the scene is most lively. At that time, students are seen returning home in numerous groups from their college, analysing, during their way, the learned instruction which they had just been receiving. Then, also, the fashionable world arrive from the New Town, to inspect the warehouses of the *Marchande des Modes*, the silk-mercer, and the elegant wares of the jeweller, rather for the purpose of complying with the laws of fashion, than of making any considerable purchases. The merchants . . . eagerly turn over their goods, and display their rich stuffs and precious jewellery, happy if the ladies, who occupy a great part of the morning in admiring these fine productions of the arts, reward them for all their trouble, in purchasing a modest ribbon . . . This amusement, much more general in Great Britain than on the Continent, is called *shopping*.[19]

24
AMONG THE POOR

'I have a tailor for my neighbour immediately below me – a cobbler – a tallow-chandler – a dancing-master – a grocer and a cow-feeder . . . and above, God knows what store of washerwomen – French teachers – auctioneers – midwives – seamstresses – and students of divinity.

(An Old Town lodging, once a Lord of Session's and formerly visited by all the ladies of quality in Edinburgh): 'Peter Morris' [John Lockhart], *Peter's Letters to his Kinsfolk,* 3rd edn, 1819, I.20

'Born probably of vicious and depraved parents, neglected in their education, placed among the most worthless as companions, encouraged to pilfer by cunning mid unprincipled resetters . . . they are brought to the gallows as mere victims of misfortune.'

'Amicus Juventutis' in *Edinburgh Weekly Journal,* 22 January 1823, on the death sentence passed on teenage boys for theft

In the streets visitors were still surprised to see neat, cleanly dressed women, even wearing gloves and perhaps carrying an umbrella, walking barefoot on the smooth – but often wet – pavements. Mingling with these were the fisherwives who walked miles to reach the fish market at daybreak, carrying the huge loads of the night's catch on their backs, secured by a strap across the breast. They looked strong and healthy, and sang cheerfully as they strode along; but strangers regularly remarked on their ugliness. The lower class woman was seen by none to possess any beauty.[1]

Some also remarked, early in the century, that there were few beggars on the streets, similar to Holland. The Scots were thought to look after the poor better than the English with their harsh poor laws. The Scottish law, dating from the time of William and Mary, though equally stringent was little applied. Instead, collections for the poor were taken on Sundays at the kirk door, and after service the schoolmaster or some other responsible person entered the amount in an account book. Beneficiaries of the distribution were announced from the pulpit, and the circumstances of those applying for aid were strictly investigated. Nor was there such misappropriation as the English habit of the funds' paying for expensive dinners for the overseers. Collections were also taken at funerals. If none of these sources sufficed, local land-owners were convened and assessed for an appropriate sum.[2]

The great gulf between the poor and the privileged life of, if not the rich, at least the leisured and professional classes, was unbridged. Savage penalties continued to be exacted for relatively modest crimes. Two men hanged for horse-stealing in January 1807 left pathetic accounts, presumably declaimed on the scaffold, of their background and failings. These pious plaints were most likely put into their mouths by the minister who attended their last hours.

John Smith, aged fifty, recounted how his 'respectable and honest parents' in England had given him 'an education suitable to their station . . . My youth was rather sober than otherwise.' Naïvely believing that it would take away sin he even took the sacrament 'in the English manner', then ran up a moral overdraft by 'plunging into all manner of villainy'. George Stevenson, who was thirty, was also English-born and had a limited education with little regard to moral or honest principles, but the result was the same: 'I easily fell prey to seduction without.'

Both men expressed realisation of their sins, and a due sense of gratitude to those who had attended them in prison. Or if they did not, the minister saw that they were recorded as so doing.[3]

The poet Thomas Campbell, when his own personal circumstances allowed, made a point of helping the less fortunate. One poor, friendless young fellow-poet, Andrew Stewart, had contributed verses to *The Scots Magazine*, including some in praise of Scott's *Lay*. At the age of twenty-three the unfortunate fellow was convicted of breaking into a glazier's shop and sentenced to death, but a couple of letters to Walter Scott brought about an appeal, and his sentence was commuted to transportation. The date was fixed for 22 February 1809. 'You will see my poems are of the humorous cast', he wrote. 'Alas! it is now the contrary . . . it was not the greed of money that made me commit the crime, but the extreme pressure of poverty and want.'

Stewart also wrote to Thomas Campbell while he was confined in the hulks awaiting transportation, who did his best to obtain further commutation to a fixed term of imprisonment. The transport sailed, and soon after, ironically, there appeared under Constable's imprint *Poems, chiefly in the Scottish Dialect*, 'by Andrew Stewart: printed for the benefit of the Author's Father . . .'

Stewart received little sympathy in Edinburgh, but he appeared 'reformed' (being scarcely a criminal in the first place), and corresponded with Campbell, who asked Mrs Fletcher to help the old father if still alive, and to send newspapers to Stewart. After numerous efforts by different people, Stewart was eventually freed.[4]

The Chambers family, having come down in the world, had had to move even from a West Nicolson Street tenement to the humbler Hamilton's Entry off Bristo Street. While not destitute, they were distinctly among the poorer members of Edinburgh's society. Normally, William relates, families of limited means from southern Scotland 'according to immemorial usage' settled in 'one of the second-rate streets in the southern suburbs', a colony 'sprinkled about in common stairs'. In the Nicolson Street tenement, below them at ground level was a poor widow huckster, above them a respectable family, the motherly widow of a clergyman with two grown-up daughters, and at the top, a cut-price tailor who worked sitting in his 'window-sole'. The Chambers's kitchen fireplace, back to back with the next-door tenement, admitted of the removal of a brick through which the respective servant girls could exchange Peebles-shire gossip.

Moving down in prosperity, in their Hamilton's Entry flat their neighbours were a poor scholar, Ebenezer Picken, reduced to teaching languages and trying without much success to sell volumes of poems, and his son Andrew who emigrated to America. The unbusiness-like Chambers senior tried to carry on his line as agent for the Glasgow cotton-traders, but was regularly cheated by workmen 'on the tramp', or untraceable in obscure courts in Fountainbridge or Back of the Canongate, who pawned the materials or obtained half-yearly advances through spinning hard-luck stories, making no effort to finish the job or repay the money.

Cheek by jowl with the family were others in a similar situation, shabby genteel widows or professionals come down in the world, with sons trying to get into a hospital for training, daughters to become governesses, run-down teachers on subsistence level, preachers who could not obtain a church and instead having to coach youths for their degrees. And young women reduced by becoming orphans, living 'by colouring maps, or by sewing fine needle-work for the Repository'.[5]

Such genteel poor families had brought to a fine art the evasion of taxes by ingeniously legal means, and while keeping 'square with the world', putting off the ubiquitous tax collector at the door with his 'portentous pocket-book' by a combination of wheedling, coaxing and positive promises to pay next time.[6]

At the very bottom of the pile, along with the thieves and pickpockets, was the beggar and hawker fraternity. One noted character was William Cameron, or 'Hawkie', described as 'Beggar, Street Orator & Wit', who was born about 1785 of poor parents in Stirlingshire, and ended his life after 1840 in the Glasgow poorhouse, where he compiled his autobiography.

Most of his account is unfortunately undatable, quoted dates being sparse and inconsistent, but he seems to have spent some years in Edinburgh. His career from 1815 was varied. Crippled early in life, he was apprenticed to a tailor, broke his indentures, and then lived by contrivance, in tailoring jobs, in hawking, as an itinerant amateur preacher, even in spite of his very rudimentary education, as a teacher. The high unemployment of the times made begging probably seem his safest bet, and he could provide useful information to fellow-beggars about the best streets for the 'pad' around Edinburgh.

> The Canonmills Road, as a 'pad', when I first started, was worth on an average, about 5s. and a few 'browns' [pence] daily. The Bonnington Road was pestered with pads, sometimes to the amount of 10 or 12. From Broughton Road – to Newhaven, from 10 in the morning till 6 at night, was worth from 1s.6d. to 2s.
>
> The King's Park to Piershill Barracks was not worth anything except on Sunday . . . before I left the city, there was such a number there, and their conduct was so bad, that one half could 'turn' it any day.[7]

Going back and forth over several years Hawkie was arrested only once, when 'calling books with a mob round me in Hanover Street, for which I got a severe reprimand'. Hawkie became an itinerant, and moved to Glasgow, to Paisley, even to England as far south as Whitby. Later he inherited £100 from an uncle, but having been easily persuaded to drink it all up, he then left Edinburgh for good.

PART III

1815–1822

'The town's rise during the war! . . . the streets and all the villages around glittering and resounding with troops, parades and reviews, admirals and fleets reaching and leaving the roads; useless offices multiplied . . . new streets rising every year; resident Peers, civic feats of municipal and national loyalty; the castle discharging its guns to hail victories; no Whigs with their teasing reforms, their vulgar appeals to the people . . . a triumphant Church, unbearded by railing Dissenters . . . a High Commissioner . . . every day with fresh splendour, and processing even on Sundays up the High Street . . . hailed all the way through an admiring crowd . . . a College so famous and so cheap, that the modern brood of insolent upstart rivals had not even been spawned . . . Courts which attracted above 600 practitioners to the Signet and above 400 to the Faculty of Advocates; everything excited and rose-coloured by the glorious waste under which the nation's and the city's debt grew; nobody thinking that a true balance sheet must one day be struck.'

Journal of Henry Cockburn 1831–1854, 2 April 1835, Edinburgh, 1874

'I went to Edinburgh, where I had not been for 10 years. I found a noble passage into the town, and, new since my time; two beautiful English chapels, two of the handsomest library-rooms in Great Britain, and a wonderful increase of shoes and stockings, streets and houses. When I lived there [from 1802], very few maids had shoes and stockings, but plodded about the house with feet as big as a family Bible, and legs as large as portmanteaus.'

Sydney Smith to Lady Mary Bennet, 20 December 1820, *Letters*, 370.

'With all its architectural attractions the New Town of Edinburgh is defective in two material points. It wants a fine church, and a noble square. The church of St George . . . is a dwarfish representation of St Paul's, if its dome be only considered. At hand, it shrinks into insignificance, and is flat and tame . . . The church of St Andrew . . . is an almost inconceivable failure . . . The Tower and spire are strait-laced to a degree, and the latter is absolutely wasting of an atrophy . . .

'Of the squares, only St Andrew's and Charlotte require notice.

'Charlotte is airy and cheerful . . . but the houses might have advantageously received, another story . . .

'St Andrew's Square is of comparatively limited dimensions, and is now almost entirely converted into public residences; such as hotels, banks, and places of meetings of public bodies.'

Rev. Thomas Dibdin, *A Bibliographical antiquarian and Picturesque Tour in the Northern Counties of England and in Scotland*, London, 1838, III.201

25
THE EXPANDING CITY

'We approached Edinburgh over the hill from whence Marmion saw the Scottish host encamped . . . I gazed in rapture on this truly romantic city, where Art has proved a true sister to Nature, both having combined to adorn this unrivalled capital.'

Frances Lady Shelley, *Diary 1787–1817*, London, 1912, II.54

'Came to Edingburgh by night – astonished at the city next morning – wild dream of a great Genius – finest city in Europe – may be in time the World.'

The Diary of Benjamin Robert Haydon, Willard Russell Pope (ed.) Cambridge, Mass., 1960–63, 26 Nov. 1820, 294

'Edinburgh is the finest city for situation in Europe. The two towns, old and new, are built on two ridges, which are joined by land bridges, like the towns of antiquity. Some streets run over the others . . . and afford beautiful combinations quite surprising. Towers, arches, houses, streets, bridges, rocks, castles, and craggy hills are tumbled together in a wildness and profusion of contrast and daring beauty . . . I never saw such a beautiful city, and if the inhabitants proceed with taste, they will make it the most beautiful place in modern times.'

B. R. Haydon to Miss Mitford, 5 Dec. 1820, *Correspondence and Table Talk*, 1876, I.67

'[From Calton Hill] you are placed between two towns, perfectly distinct, equally remarkable; to the left, the old town, black and severe, like the buildings of a fort in the days of chivalry; to the right, the new town, white and brilliant, like the enclosures of a palace. The houses are much higher than in Paris; the streets much broader than in London: almost all in a straight line, like those of Turin; and some are a mile in length. Most of the houses, moreover, are built of a white stone, sparkling with mica; and when the sun strikes on their spicular spangles, one would suppose that the buildings were inlaid with diamonds.'

Charles Nodier, *Promenade from Dieppe*, 1822, 77–8

Already at the turn of the century people had been congratulating themselves on Edinburgh's progress. Alexander Campbell, resident by his own admission for some thirty years at Logie Green, Canonmills, describes the city's appearance in 1800 and 1801. 'The lapse of 33 years has made a wonderful change, in every respect for the better in the appearance of the Scottish capital.' There was still less to describe of New Town than Old, but Campbell's account was completely up-to-date, even including stop-press footnotes.[1]

The chief lacunae, of course, continued to be the unfinished Register House, still uncompleted a quarter of a century after its beginning, and the new University building. Somewhat mortified by the hitch after the city's purchase of 'the late General Scott's elegant villa of Bellevue' with a view to extending the Second New Town, Campbell notes (24 February 1801) that, despite the plans submitted, including that by 'one of the first engineers of Scotland', none had been approved, and that it was now proposed to combine elements chosen from all four. The reason, he proudly observes, is their desire to build with an elegance suited to the 'charming spot thus so happily chosen, and to the taste of the times, now so much improved, since the commencement of that spirit of enterprise . . . more particularly in Edinburgh and its immediate vicinity, toward the close of the eighteenth century.'[2]

Nobody who visited the city, however, could fail to see that it was still very much in the making. Apart from those who limited their comments to admiration of the romantic old town, its picturesque surroundings, and the New Town's grandeur, nearly everybody exclaimed over the fine buildings, half-completed new streets, and the activities of masons.

When the youthful Elizabeth Grant received her first impressions of new Edinburgh in 1803, it was 'long enough for an abiding impression of that beautiful city to be made on a young mind. The width of the streets, the size of the houses, the brightness and the cleanliness' – in striking contrast to the grubby Old Town – impressed her, though still in its infancy. 'The new town was but in progress, the untidy appendages of building encumbered the half finished streets, and where afterwards the innumerable *gardens* spread . . . there were then only unsightly *greens* abandoned to the washerwomen.' The tradition of the washing/drying green lingers to this day, though long since tidily confined to the back grass of terraces. Spreading untidiness, piles of masons' tools and stones, and a half-finished air, were features of the New Town's different areas in turn for the next twenty years and more.[3]

Edinburgh, busy as long as the courts were sitting, and 'empty' between July and October, still was short of accommodation, as long as a great part of what is now known as the New Town had not yet been built, and hotels of acceptable standard were few. Robert Gillies noted in 1810–11 that no lodgings were available and the New Town was crowded with visitors, both from country estates and from abroad.[4]

Everywhere showed signs of building activity. In the very centre of the city, in the early years of the century the Parliament House was given a completely new exterior. Between 1807 and 1810 the architect Robert Reid converted the seventeenth-century building into a modern-seeming square, replacing its 1630s façade with a classical front. (Interestingly, in 1808 Reid adapted this eastern façade for the new court-house at Inveraray, in reverse, replacing the columned centre by a solid frontage of pilasters and Venetian window.) The Parliament House alterations, enclosing the old Outer and Inner Houses, contained a court room and Exchequer Offices. A western wing was completed in 1810, to form the long-proposed Advocates' and Signet Libraries.[5]

In the year that Reid began these alterations, a lottery was proposed to finance resumption of the long-dormant University building – but still it remained untouched. Similarly, the nearly completed Register House was to stand unfinished for years to come.

At much the same time there were plans for developing the area south of Edinburgh, proposed as early as 1795 with a feuing plan for Newington. This was the project not of architects but of James Reid, of the Exchequer Office, and the well-known surgeon Benjamin Bell, who was also a farmer with an eye to property development. The significant feature was an 'intended new road' as a main road to London, to run from the North Bridge to Nicolson Street and thence southwards to Newington via St Patrick's Square. In 1805 Benjamin Bell acquired the whole Newington estate, largely open fields with a few scattered houses, and for a decade from the first feuing in 1806 the area was built up, with the creation of Clerk Street in tenements, leading to villas set in gardens at both front and back which quickly became fashionable.[6]

At the city's east end there was a plan to develop the area round Calton Hill and land east of Leith Walk, for which in 1812 a competition was advertised, producing thirty-two entries. From these eight architects were invited to submit reports to be judged by Baron Clerk and the banker Gilbert Innes. That of William Stark, who died in October 1813 before finishing his report, was the most favoured, but not until 1818 was work begun on these lines, by Stark's pupil William Playfair.

The project, at an unfashionable end of Edinburgh and on an unwieldy site, was abortive, but it resulted in Royal Terrace, Edinburgh's longest, a single frontage of nearly a quarter of a mile and subdivided into colonnaded stretches, four Ionic, three Corinthian, along the north side of the hill; and Regent Terrace on the south side, with iron balconies at the first-floor windows, and Doric porches. Other terraces were built on the north side in and after 1820.[7]

North of the unfinished Second New Town, at the foot of the steep hill where, at the small industrial village of Stockbridge, a small stone bridge crossed the Water of Leith, much land had been owned since his marriage by the painter Henry Raeburn. His house Deanhaugh, slightly set back from the water-side, was a plain three-storeyed building near St Bernard's Well. In 1813, presumably unable to resist the opportunity of making a profit, Raeburn began to lay out a small building estate and to feu the ground. Here were built, first, Dean Street (1816–17, then named Mineral Street after the Well), Ann Street, begun 1815 but not completed for ten years, and the rest not until the 1820s, so that the feeling of countryside long persisted.[8]

The nearby Ross's Folly, or 'Antiquary's Tower' was unfortunately demolished in 1825 for the completion of Ann Street, though the old avenue of Deanhaugh and a rookery partly survived in St Bernard's Crescent (1820).[9]

Ann Street, in Ionic style, was unusual for Edinburgh in having front gardens, and in spite of its modest dimensions and still semi-rural site, its east side boasted an ambitious three-storeyed, pedimented central block, flanked by lower houses. The lower west side was adorned by Doric porticos, and gateway lanterns on cast-iron standards.

It was in this area that Thomas Carlyle, then a would-be writer for ever in search of a lodging sufficiently acceptable for cleanliness, quiet and good air, found himself (in 1821) constantly disturbed by the shouts and bangs of masons building the new streets surrounding Stockbridge village.[10]

Farther west, at the top of the steep glen of the Water of Leith and above the baxters' village of Dean, Lord Moray's estate, its house and parks bought by the 9th Earl in 1782, cut off the north-west corner of the New Town site: for some time this remained undeveloped.

Meanwhile, from 1813 new streets were being added to the Second New Town. The City, the landlords, the Heriot Trust, and a feuar, Maitland, agreed on a line for Shandwick Place as a western extension of Princes Street, first planned in 1801, and laid out by James Tait in 1809. This preceded a spate of building to the west. Immediately to the north was Easter Coates, an old estate with a complex history, and bought in 1813 by William Walker on behalf of his son, Sir Patrick Walker. In 1822–25 Robert Brown laid out a street plan for the Coates development: Coates Crescent, William and Walker Streets, Melville Street and Place, which continued to be built over the next thirty years or so.[11] The Heriot Trust, through their surveyor Thomas Bonnar, further developed Atholl Crescent and Place, as well as much of Torphichen Street (1824–31).

Gillespie Graham made an overall plan for the area, but seems not to have been involved in the actual building. On the other hand it was he who designed the splendid new, topographically odd estate for Lord Moray, son of the Earl who had bought the land in 1782, who feued its rural, pretty area for building in 1822.

The layout, a crescent, a circle and a much larger circle, with their linking roads, encompassed Randolph Crescent, Great Stuart Street, Ainslie Place and the grandiose Moray Place, with their connections to adjoining streets, Albyn Place, and Darnaway and Forres Streets, all running downhill. Such were the boundaries of the estate, cutting diagonally across the then corner of the New Town. On the north side it perched at the precipitous edge of the gulf of the Water of Leith. The effect is more unified and distinguishable than many of the new developments, which consist rather of grids of streets without a particularly noticeable overall plan. In detail the style is the Tuscan order, half-columns on the façades and pilasters at the corners. Begun in 1822, building went on, especially in the long-unfinished Moray Place, until the 1850s.[12]

To the east, development of the Second New Town north of Queen Street straggled on well after the Napoleonic Wars. Abercromby Place, Northumberland Street and Jamaica Street were completed only in 1819, Great King Street in 1823, and Royal Circus and India Street not even begun until 1819. In order to link the Circus and western part of the area with Stockbridge, the Heriot Trust commissioned an 'improved' plan from William Playfair, further widening both ends of the intended Circus to accommodate a road-line running diagonally downhill from Frederick Street to Stockbridge.

The solution of how to join the western streets to the new road far below proved ingenious and dramatic. The lofty houses at the bottom of India Street, six storeys with double basements in front, were at ground level behind because of the steep fall, towering above Circus Place at an acute angle, linked by a flight of steps in the space between them and the fortress-like retaining wall of the northernmost gardens, while the main road plunges steeply below.

The Frenchman Charles Nodier, who visited in 1822, writes admiringly of 'the projected place of the *Circus* . . . worthy of Athens herself', then expected to be finished in three months. In fact it was completed, to Playfair's design, only in 1823.[13]

Playfair's proposal for a church in the middle of one side of the Circus was not approved, and his St Stephen's Church was built only in 1827–28, on land below Howe Street acquired by the City in 1822. The Council's 1822 proposals for a church in Bellevue Crescent proved more popular, and the crescent's inhabitants also secured the unusual bonus of garden space in front.

Being a mason could often be hazardous. For example, two fatal accidents reported within a week in 1815, whose victims both died in the Infirmary, were caused by falls. One was in Great King Street when the stone being laid and pointed by a mason gave way beneath him and in his fall he was fatally bruised; another mason employed in building the new Methodist chapel in Nicolson Square fell three storeys and broke his back. Only a month later, when Dr Jamieson's old meeting house in Nicolson Street was being demolished, the whole roof crashed because the beams were not secured, and six men were injured, one of them dying soon after.[14]

Thus in the first two decades of the century residents, and visitors, saw plenty of evidence of new suburbs. There was a shortage of Church of Scotland churches, the only one yet building in the New Town being St George's in Charlotte Square (1811–14), but the Episcopalians built several, usually in the Gothic style, and of necessity situated on the town fringe. St George's Chapel in York Place had been designed in 1794 by James Adam in a strange octagonal style. In 1813 James Gillespie designed the city's first example of a gothic frontage, the Roman Catholic chapel in Broughton Street, which with the adjoining houses concealed a simple rectangle. Also in York Place was Archibald Elliot's St Paul's (1816–18), not unlike St John's at the west end of Princes Street by William Burn, also built in 1816–18.

There was also a scattering of dissenting chapels, including a Methodist in Nicolson Square (1815), classical with pilasters and rusticated arches; an Independent Chapel on a corner of Broughton Street, designed to match Albany Street and with a Palladian window with Ionic shafts (1816, by a builder, David Skae). Also in Broughton Place was Dr John Brown's Chapel, plain but for a Doric portico, designed by Archibald Elliot for the United Associate Synod in 1821; and in Nicolson Street, Dr Jamieson's, to Gillespie's designs in 1819 for the General Associate Synod. Most of these churches were considerably altered or added to in Victorian times.[15]

By far the most notable adornment of the city in this period was the creation of its imposing new eastern entrance. Already in 1813 an Act was passed for building a bridge (Regent Bridge) over the low Calton, enabling the creation of a new, level approach from that side. The road-line was designed by Robert Stevenson, the buildings were by Elliot. This ceremonial entry to Princes Street spanned the valley with a fifty-foot arch, which Elliot adorned on each side with an open screen flanking a high Corinthian arch. This bore a panel inscribed with the record of its building.

A hitherto unremarkable entrance to the New Town was thus now distinguished by Ionic porticos, with pilasters carrying entablatures along the flanking buildings, on the south side the Stamp Office, and east of the bridge, the Post Office, opposite the soon to be fashionable Waterloo Tavern and hotel.[16]

Entry into Edinburgh from the east became a magnificent experience.

At the same time the foundation stone was laid of a new gaol with the usual masonic and civic procession, and numerous spectators, with two thousand masons present, claimed to be the most brilliant ever. It was built on Calton Hill, the city to raise £12,000 of the cost. The gaol, also by Elliot, was so perched on the edge of a cliff, and so romantically castellated, that it was often mistaken for the castle. It was accompanied by a Governor's house, also with turrets and battlements. (It has since been demolished.[17])

With these additions, classical now supplemented by Gothic, new Edinburgh may be said to have graduated as a grand modern city. All it seriously lacked was completion of the Record Office and the grand college buildings.

Those who arrived at Edinburgh by sea were unimpressed by the dirty, narrow streets of Leith, but an important improvement to Edinburgh's port was its new docks, which although already enlarged required further modernisation. At low water the extensive sands had long proved inconvenient for shipping, and the costly stone pier, and wet and dry docks already built by the City, proved inadequate.

One of the new century's first ventures had been the inception in 1801 of the harbour (authorised in 1799), and at the same time, a new stone pier was begun west of the first. There was criticism over the site: Alexander Campbell reckoned that nearer the Black Rock would have been more accessible and have reclaimed more land, thus enlarging the harbour towards Musselburgh as far as the turnpike.

These, the first such docks to be built in Britain, covered five acres within high-water mark, later extended to include graving docks and slips. The first stage took exactly five years to complete, and merited another magistrates' procession, marching to the completed dock, and witnessed by many ladies and gentlemen. The first vessels to enter it were modest enough, the Fife packet and the *Buccleuch* fishing smack, accompanied by an artillery salute from the Fort and the naval ships anchored in the roads.[18]

About the same time the port town was beautified by offices for the Leith Banking Company (begun 1805), a handsome dome rising above four Ionic columns. There were new Assembly Rooms, equipped both for balls and winter concerts, and Leith was beginning to be noticed as a social rival to Edinburgh. A new Episcopal chapel was building in 1806, and houses on the east side were thought hardly inferior to the New Town. Merchants, bankers, and 'higher tradesmen' (claimed Sir John Carr) were genteel persons.[19]

Leith's trade had been hampered by the blockade of the North German ports, yet despite the absence of exportable manufactures, by 1807 trade was supported in the increase in ship-building, creating a demand for the new and flourishing local manufacture of ropes and cordage. The chief trades and imports were timber, tar and iron from the Baltic, flax and its seed from Holland. Then there were the iron foundries, distilleries and paper mills.[20] Edinburgh's paucity of manufactures was amply made up for by the industry of its port.

Such rapid expansion necessitated an overhaul of public services, especially the water supply, which from the late seventeenth century had been piped from a reservoir on Castle Hill, and also brought in by lead pipes from Comiston. In the 1780s a further supply was piped from Swanston on the edge of the Pentlands, with another pipe in 1790, and a second reservoir was created near Heriot's Hospital to supplement the old one on Castle Hill. The war years delayed further expansion though the city was still increasing in size, and in 1810 and 1814 annual shortages became serious. George Combe noted in October 1814 that water was selling 'at 6d per two stoup fulls – & from barrels'.[21]

By an Act of 1819 'a public-spirited few' formed the Edinburgh Joint Stock Water Company (capital £105,000, increased in 1826 to £223,000). For the size of their undertaking comparison with Roman achievements was proudly invoked. The new source was springs at Crawley and Glencorse, some nine miles from the city, brought by cast-iron seventeen-inch-diameter pipes, within a masonry arch 6 feet high and broad. The intervening ground was uneven and required laborious tunnelling, and even the open cuttings were up to 40 feet deep in places.

The Glencorse 'compensation' reservoir was intended to supply water to the surrounding mills, replacing the springs now appropriated for the piped Edinburgh supply. At the lower end of the valley a large dam about 80 feet high was built to contain winter flood-waters, nearly 500 feet thick at its base, paved with stone on the water side. The water was released when required through two large cast-iron pipes 'with astonishing velocity . . . a beautiful cascade'. The engineer James Jardine designed and executed the works, estimated to cost £120,000 and by 1823 nearly complete.

Hitherto piped water to houses had been possible only in the New Town, not without problems. Feuars were expected to pay the cost of the pipe outside their own building, but (for example) in 1821 Royal Circus residents complained that they were feued on the grounds of a supply from the Howe Street pipe, which had proved too small, and they demanded a second pipe to be laid alongside, with a £40 contribution from the Governors towards digging and laying.

The Old Town was still served by caddies, who tramped up and down tenement stairs lugging water at a penny a cask, drawn from the public wells in the streets. The new, assured supply from Crawley springs led in a few years to the disappearance of this time-honoured job.[22]

The other main service was lighting. An Act of 1812, aimed at introducing a more efficient police service, also empowered the Commissioners to regulate lighting and cleansing. From about 1815 a general move to replace the old train-oil standards with the new gas engendered rivalry between promoters of gas based on coal or oil, which was to come to a head in the 1820s.[23]

In March 1818 George Combe noted that the Gas-Light Company was laying pipes along Edinburgh's chief streets for lighting the following winter. A year later he was able to report that the theatre was now lit by gas, 'after the manner of Covent Garden, and most beautiful and brilliant it is'. Among the pieces it enhanced was the new operatic version of *Rob Roy*.[24]

Sydney Smith, incidentally, who after an absence of ten years paid Edinburgh a return visit in 1820, was rapturous about gas lighting which he experienced at Lambton Castle. 'What use of wealth so luxurious and delightful as to light your house with gas? What folly, to have a diamond necklace or a Correggio, and not to light your house with gas. The splendour and glory of Lambton Hall made all other houses mean . . .'[25] And Tom Moore saw gas in London in May 1822, at St Paul's with Lord and Lady Lansdowne, 'to see it lighted up with gas, for, I believe, the first time'.[26]

The matter of a canal to link Edinburgh and Glasgow, for the transport of coal and other minerals, had long been under discussion. A subscription had been opened and the engineer John Rennie had been consulted as early as 1798, when most canals were building or under discussion, but unfortunately the 'Union Canal' did not get off the ground during those boom years.

There was much discussion over the line of the route, and Rennie and Telford, who was later consulted, proposed different routes, while the Edinburgh magistrates were inclined to think it should be carried on to Leith rather than stop at the eastern fringe of Edinburgh. There was of course also the inevitable matter of land-owners whose property would or might be threatened by the building. In 1813 the new Lord Provost, Sir John Marjoribanks, had received the Union Canal Committee shortly after his election, Rennie was consulted, and the magistrates turned down the proposed line.

In March 1815 at the subscribers' request Telford arrived to examine the lines and ended by recommending what he considered 'the most perfect water communication that can be found', giving it decided preference.

After Telford reported to the House of Commons in London they debated on the second Reading of the Bill, but after much discussion the Telford line prevailed over the magistrates' view (who by a bare majority had voted for a terminus at Leith). The 2nd Reading was defeated, and despite the subscriptions raised, the canal was deferred for another three years.

The first spadeful of earth was dug only on 3 March 1818, at Fountainbridge, by the chairman of the canal company Mr Dowie of Appin, in front of many spectators. At the same time a start was made at several other places, such as Hamilton and Ratho. The engineer was again James Jardine and the estimated cost was £235,167. Parts were in use within a few months, but the whole was not completed until 1822, by which time the cost had inevitably risen to nearly £400,000.[27]

Thomas Carlyle made a curious though typically splenetic comment on an engineering discussion he witnessed in 1820 between Dr Brewster (for whom he always reserved much scorn) and Jardine. 'They set forth *how* canals were to be dug – bogs drained – coals found &c; and then went to communicate their speculations to the Royal Society of Physical Science in this "'ntellectual city".' This sounds reasonable enough, but Carlyle goes on, 'I am astonished to see this Doctor so flourishing a man. Except *activity* . . . he has few mental qualms that I can discover.' Carlyle's view was not shared by many.[28]

After the end of the Napoleonic Wars there was the question of what would be a suitable monument to the victory. In 1819 and 1820 Archibald Alison, among his other activities, was writing fine arts articles based on the idea of 'The Restoration of the Parthenon in the National Monument of Edinburgh', which he claimed was partly responsible for creation of the monument to be built on the Calton Hill.[29]

The site, within full view of all central Edinburgh, was eminently suitable; the subject at first met with resistance but it was generally accepted before long that Modern Athens merited a full re-creation of the Parthenon on its own acropolis, though some naturally complained that a 'modern' monument would be more suitable.

Whoever claimed credit for the initial idea, a meeting was held at the Assembly Rooms on 3 March 1819, chaired by the Duke of Atholl, on the subject of creating a National Monument commemorating the exploits of 'our gallant countrymen' throughout the world, as a Temple recording 'the efforts of genius and patriotism'. Lord Moray moved and Lord Belhaven seconded resolutions, adopted unanimously, that the victories 'in which the valour of Scotsmen was so conspicuously displayed in every quarter of the globe, justly deserve to be commemorated in the Metropolis of Scotland, by some appropriate Memorial of national gratitude'. It might suitably be a church, ornamented in a manner perpetuating naval and military achievements. Subscriptions of £1 and upwards were at once invited, those giving £25 or more having a right to a share in the church, though part should be kept free. A committee was appointed.[30]

The object of the memorial was much debated. One proposal was that the church or 'temple' should contain niches for monuments to the Scots who had fallen in battle. It was to be 'the finest restoration' of the then fashionable Greek in Britain, costing £60,000.

The basic drawings were made by C. R. Cockerell, from which Playfair made the final plans. The design at last approved, it was decided to lay the foundation stone during King George IV's visit in August 1822, and the contract, signed by Sir William Rae, Alison and Michael Linning, the

Secretarry, stipulated that every stone be cut to the dimensions of the original in Athens. The architects followed this with striking effect, some blocks weighing seven to eight tons, others in the entablature fifteen to eighteen, the huge blocks being cut from Craigleith quarry and dragged up by purpose-built carriages drawn by twelve horses and one hundred men.

Unfortunately the sum contributed remained obstinately below the target, which would have been exceeded anyway. The committee applied, unsuccessfully, to the General Assembly for permission to appeal to ministers. The whole project evidently did not appeal to the nation, and the fund never reached more than £15,000, for which barely a quarter of the whole could be built.

The Calton Hill, considered overloaded with the Nelson tower and the Observatory, had been nearly discarded as a site for the monument when in 1818 other alternatives were considered. 'G.A.', writing to the *Edinburgh Evening Courant* on 2 November, as part of a not infrequent complaint at the lack of height or of distinguished ornamental building in the New Town, suggested St Andrew Square as a site for a lofty column or obelisk. It would make a suitable termination to the fine street, and would 'tower above the square in simple majesty . . . admired by posterity as doing credit to our periodical taste' – in contrast to what he dismissed unflatteringly as 'Nelson's pastry shop'.[31]

This suggested site, and its eventual monument, proved more fortunate. The ground in the middle of the square had been enclosed, but remained unadorned until on 28 April 1821, the tenth anniversary of Lord Melville's death, the foundation was laid of the huge 126-foot fluted Tuscan column, based on Trajan's column in Rome, and intended to be crowned with his statue.

It was appropriately a naval affair: funded by Royal Navy subscriptions, its foundation laid by two admirals, Sir David Milne and Robert (later Sir Robert) Otway, C-in-C at Leith, and built by members of the Royal Navy and Marines.[32]

Local residents were uneasy at the height of such a monument near their houses, and the engineer Robert Stevenson was called to advise. The monument itself was designed by William Burn, and was complete in time for the royal visit. The 14-foot statue for the top, however, designed by Chantrey and made by Robert Forrest, was not erected until 1828.[33]

26
A NEW KIND OF NOVEL

'I hope you have read, or will read, Waverley. I am satisfied from internal evidence that Walter Scott, and no other, is the author of that true and chaste description of Scottish manners such as they existed at the time . . . He is not, however, just to the Highlanders.'

Mrs Grant of Laggan to Mrs Hook, 3 July 1814, *Memoirs of Mrs Grant of Laggan*, II.50

'He is, indeed, the lord of the ascendant, now in Edinburgh, and well deserves to be, for I look upon him to be quite as remarkable in intercourse and conversation, as he is in any of his writings, even in his novels.' (1819)

Life, Letters and Journal of George Ticknor, G.S. Hillard (ed.), Boston, 1909, I. 280

Early in July 1814 another literary bombshell struck Edinburgh, and after it – quite apart from its transformation of the author's life – the view of what novels could be like was to be radically changed. *Waverley* was set in Scotland; it was historical, concerned with the emotive period of the '45, it drew substantially on the peasantry and the vernacular as much as on the fashionable upper classes, and most characters were presented credibly in the round. Moreover, the modestly bound publication, in the usual three volumes, was published anonymously.

Walter Scott revealed in later years that he first thought of this novel in 1805, the year which started with his immensely successful publication of *The Lay* and continued with his entering into partnership with the Ballantynes. The few chapters he wrote barely set the scene of a not very inspiring young gentleman's visit to the Highlands, and William Erskine, to whom he showed the draft, was not much taken with it. Indeed there was not much to take as Scott had barely touched on his subject, namely the Jacobite rising. Scott put the spurned manuscript aside and even forgot where it was, so that any possible occasional yearnings to resume the story were defeated.

About 1808, the year of *Marmion*, his *Life of Dryden*, impending launch of the *Quarterly Review* and Scott's temporary rupture with Constable over the behaviour of the latter's hotheaded partner David Hunter, he was fired to take it up again for an odd reason. Having agreed to write the concluding chapters for an unfinished romance by the antiquary Joseph Strutt, a work too fanciful and probably too pedantically antiquated to succeed, Scott quite enjoyed the exercise, and the idea of a novel of his own, whether then or at some other time, took root.

Meanwhile, he embarked on the enlargement of Abbotsford and its land, and one day in 1813, looking out fishing tackle for a guest, behold, there in an attic was the forgotten, barely started, manuscript, shoved into an old desk drawer. Looking at its pages again, Scott thought the work worth rescuing. Quite quickly, without even working out a proper plot, he rattled off a complete romance and handed it over to John Ballantyne, who passed it to Constable, with whom the poet had recently been reconciled.[1]

Ballantyne, uncertain of the reception of this anonymous work, doubting if even one thousand copies might sell, took the precaution of also farming out a few copies for friends' opinions. One of these was Henry Mackenzie, now nearing seventy, his writing days over, and though of skeletal thinness, sociable and active as ever, undaunted by weather or circumstance. According to Robert Gillies, this 'patriarchal critic' was so delighted with the work that he hastened from his own house to Ballantyne's 'to express his conviction that this would turn out to be no ordinary novel . . . not the work of an ordinary man'.[2]

The work when published bore Scott's dedication to Mackenzie as 'our Scottish Addison'.

The book was completed by the end of June 1814, and Scott went off on a Highlands and islands voyage of some weeks with Robert Stevenson on a survey of lighthouses. On his return on 29 July he found that Constable, who had published his book on 7 July, had amazingly sold three thousand copies of this novel by an unknown author, and was ready for a third edition.[3]

That autumn Scott not only completed *Lord of the Isles,* which was published in January 1815 – a less successful poem than its predecessors, selling fewer copies and gaining only moderate praise – but in the flush of success over his venture into fiction, launched himself into a second novel. He had the bit between his teeth, and in the years to come he was galloping ahead, two and even three novels flowing from his pen each year.

Waverley, and in February 1815 *Guy Mannering,* were the talk of every dinner-table, the theme of almost every letter, every reader arrogating to him or herself the role of critic. Not least of the fun was the author's anonymity. He was not very heavily veiled, perhaps half of readers guessing who he was, but they were prepared to join in the sport.

Scott, famous for his poems, was enjoying a triumphant spring visit to London, where he was befriended by the Prince Regent, charmed by Lord Byron, and in August with three friends sailed for the Continent to visit Waterloo and Paris, resulting in two more productions, *The Field of Waterloo* – which for a change was generally damned – and *Paul's Letters to his Friends.*[4]

His manoeuvring between publishers had been largely due to their fragile financial situation. Debts were piling up, and on his return Scott sat down to write *The Antiquary,* completing it in four months and it was published in May 1816. It was his favourite so far and an immediate success, despite careless errors and occasional pomposities.[5]

As interesting to readers as the huge appeal of these novels was the extraordinary range of their possible authors. For anyone who knew Scott personally recognition was not difficult. They knew his tricks of phraseology and even some of the anecdotes, and many were quick to suspect his hand: for the legal knowledge, style of humour, turns of phrase, and descriptions they had heard him make. Among the discerning was Mrs Grant of Laggan, who was 'fixed in the opinion that it is Walter Scott's. I know his style of speaking, thinking, and observing so well'. Jeffrey, with whom she discussed *Waverley* when it was first published, agreed that he 'knows only one mind equal to this work, and his impress is on every page'. After *Guy Mannering* appeared, Jeffrey wrote to his father-in-law Charles Wilkes in America that he thought *Waverley* 'admirable; and another by the same author (who still wears his mask), not quite so powerful, but still a very extraordinary performance'.[6]

Later the rumour was started that the author was Scott's own brother Tom, who was living in Canada, and Scott doubtless thought this an acceptable supposition (if indeed he had not initiated it himself). Certainly Lord Glenbervie and his wife, who read *The Antiquary* while travelling in Italy, believed it. It was, he wrote in his journal, 'by the author of those two justly popular novels, *Waverley* and *Guy Mannering,* who is said to be a brother of Walter Scott's'.[7]

Six months later at home, when the author had *Tales of my Landlord* to his credit, Lord Glenbervie was again speculating. 'All the world seems agreed that the same author (or perhaps co-authors) wrote the Tales and the three other most successful novels' which were forecast to become classics, 'a sort of epoch in that species of writing'. The general view in Brooke's, White's, Murray's shop, the Royal Institution and elsewhere, was that it must be Scott's brother in Canada, or his wife, and that there were good reasons for the mystery. This conundrum, and speculation on why the Duke of Wellington had appeared in London for a couple of days, were, says Glenbervie, the main topics of gossip in the London world.[8]

Mrs Grant also mentioned the ludicrous theory that *Waverley* was the work of James Boswell's son Alexander, a minor writer and versifier and (Mrs Grant charitably observed) 'unquestionalbly a man of genius'. But not that sort of genius.

Another wildish theory was put to Washington Irving in Paris some years later by Lady Granard, 'to *mark her words* it would one day be known Scott only contributed the poetry & touched up the novels – written by another hand'. This was no discredit to Scott: far from it, 'His cause for fathering them was generous and would redound to his credit.'[9]

About the time of *Waverley*'s publication two cantos of the then unfinished *Lord of the Isles* were read out at a dinner party at Scott's old friend William Erskine's, whose guests included the Scotts, the Laird of Staffa and 'other chiefs'. A friend of Mrs Grant's who was present thought the verses 'worthy of the applause they received': applause which the poet could receive gracefully, without the feigned innocence which he often had to assume in the next few years when he heard his novels discussed.[10]

Frances Waddington did not read *Waverley* until 1815, when it induced a panegyric: 'gay fancy', she wrote to Professor Monk, 'sound reason; sterling humour . . . feeling, acute, profound . . . accuracy of observation', and so forth, while 'every part . . . impressed upon our minds the conviction that we owe it to Walter Scott'. At first they were told 'positively' it was his, then not, but, having read it, 'every perfection that shines forth in full splendour . . . is discernible in a degree to his conversation'.[11]

The gentle poet Crabbe was not alone in disapproval of Scott's cardboard heroes, lacking (he said) either gentleness or urbanity. (This view he expressed still more later over the eponymous *Quentin Durward* and *Nigel*.) Colonel Mannering he excused on grounds of mature age and odd situation, but in general Crabbe disliked 'fierceness and glorying'.[12]

Maria Edgeworth would have agreed. She wrote a long encomium on *Waverley* addressed to the author ('Aut Scotus, aut Diabolus!') on the lines of Miss Waddington's, while remarking to Mrs Ruxton that 'The Admiral' was critical as 'the hero . . . such a shuffling fellow'. But Miss Fanshawe loved it and Miss Edgeworth thought it genius. So carried away was she by the twists of the plot that it even seemed too real for her to accept the intrusion of 'occasional addresses from the author to the reader'.[13]

Among the few Scots who did not care for the sensational new novel were the Grants of Rothiemurchus, who received *Waverley* at Doune soon after its publication and just before they left for Edinburgh. They not surprisingly felt the opening chapters 'intolerably dull, so lengthy, and so prosy, and the persons introduced so uninteresting, the hero contemptible, the two heroines unnatural and disagreeable, and the whole idea given of the highlands so utterly at variance with the truth'. Damning enough on all counts, though the Grants were among the few airing their views who actually lived in the Highlands.

Guy Mannering, though it 'carried all the world before it', Elizabeth found little better – the material again second-hand, while she complained that the scenery was Galloway and the dialect Forfar.[14]

Sir Samuel Romilly's wife Anne wrote to Maria Edgeworth that despite the furore, 'we do not admire *Waverley* as much as it deserves . . . I did not like the hero, and thought the whole more a portraiture of individual than of general manners'; while recognising that Scots were naturally admiring – the *Edinburgh Review* must have praised it 'to your hearts content'. As for the author, first it was accepted that Scott, 'if he did not write it, certainly must have had a good deal to do with it', and a couple of months later they were in no doubt that he was its 'principal author', while in London 'the learned' did not suppose it by anyone else. As for his poems, in all Scott wrote 'one never can feel great interest for the Lover', and though Sir James Mackintosh thought *Lord of the Isles* the best thing he had written, 'he is puffer general particularly to Scotsmen'. The lady then scratched out this frank judgment and a few weeks later corrected it to say 'he said *worst* not best, but has since relented', and placed the poem 'low, though above Rokeby'.[15]

Tales of my Landlord she declared 'charming', however, again in no doubt of the mysterious author as Scott – or if not, 'it's marvellous' – and repeated the chestnut, this time offered by 'a gentleman back from America', about Scott's brother.[16]

Mrs Elizabeth Hamilton in Edinburgh and Lord Byron in England happened to read *Waverley* at the same time, soon after publication, with much the same reaction. Even after the first volume Mrs Hamilton was already 'so charmed by it, that I am all impatience for the remainder. It is quite Scottish, and gives such a picture of a state of society and manners now obsolete, as appears to me invaluable.' To Miss J.B. she observes cautiously that it is 'supposed to be from the pen of W.S.'

The following March there was *Guy Mannering* to discuss: 'are they not . . . excellent in their way'. She adds that 'though the name of Scott does not grace the title-page, it is seen in every other page of both performances'.[17]

Byron wrote enthusiastically to John Murray that it was 'the best & most interesting novel I have *redde* since – I don't know when'; and hater of blue-stockings, went on to disparage lady writers 'and all the feminine trash of the last four months'.[18]

He was to meet Scott on the latter's London visit in 1815, and the two took an instant liking to one another. Scott had sent him a Turkish dagger, and Byron responded with 'a large sepulchral vase of silver'.[19]

Sydney Smith's initial comment was almost an aside, to Jeffrey in December 1814. 'I think very highly of "Waverley"', and in a thinly disguised allusion to Scott, added that he was inclined to think the author was 'Miss Scott of Ancrum'.[20]

Mrs Brunton, the author of *Discipline*, on which she had been working when *Waverley* appeared, was dismayed that her modest work followed so hard on its heels, when she discovered that Scott was the author. 'What a competitor for poor little me!' She had been particularly impressed by the scenes at Carlisle towards the climax of the novel, 'absolutely matchless, for nature, character, originality, and pathos'.[21]

Another commentator, at least at second-hand, was the American John Quincy Adams, at this time a student traveller in England. At a star-studded dinner at Holland House in June 1816 he had for neighbour Sir James Mackintosh, who told him he had last year introduced Scott to a Mr Clay, 'the first of his admirers that he had ever seen from Kentucky'. The austere Adams seems to have been a sticky conversationalist but a good listener, and Mackintosh was playing the self-appointed critic. 'The construction of the stories . . . he said was good for nothing', though Scott produced 'admirable delineations of Scottish manners'; Adams objected but thought *The Antiquary* contained nothing not already seen in *Waverley* or *Guy Mannering*. Mackintosh enlarged on Scottish pedantry with the freedom of being a Scot himself (Adams had not been to Scotland), observing that whatever their other qualities, 'the palm of pedantry was universally awarded to his country'. At another large dinner, for the Duke of Sussex later that summer, the great punster Erskine repeated his *Morning Post*'s epigram on Scott falling flat at Waterloo, but 'he insists positively that Scott is not the author of Waverley', etc.[22]

Among the few serious critics were the Wordsworths. Dorothy drew attention to the glaring fact that one could 'care not a farthing for the hero', and except for the descriptions of 'Highland manners and customs' she was full of complaints that the Scottish characters were too 'outrageously masked by peculiarities' to please, that characters in general were poorly described, 'and as usual the love is sickening'. This perhaps tells us as much about Dorothy Wordsworth as about *Waverley*.[23]

Her brother, at this stage, was more interested in damning Scott's poems.

He did read Scott's novels, admitting 'considerable talent' and knowledge in *Guy Mannering* with which Scott was 'richly stored', but criticised it for ill-chosen adventures and uninteresting characters – except Meg Merrilees, and even she was described with 'that want of taste, which is universal among modern novels of the Radcliffe school'. He allowed that *Waverley* had raised Scott in his estimation and *Guy Mannering* had at least not lessened his standing. It was all damning with faint praise.[24] Thomas Moore, who met Wordsworth during his financial exile in Paris, was told that Wordsworth had never been in doubt of Scott's authorship, except (a good Wordsworthian touch this) for 'the infinite number of clumsy things in them; commonplace contrivances . . . and such bad vulgar English as no gentleman of education ought to have written'. When Moore mildly observed that the novels' number (this was in 1820) was perhaps too 'abundant' to be the work of one man, Wordsworth retorted that 'great fertility was the characteristic of all novelists and story-tellers', and Scott had been accustomed to legends and story-telling from childhood. He foresaw, accurately, that there was 'nothing to stop him as long as he can hold a pen'.[25]

Mrs Grant, incidentally, quoted a young lady's gaffe reported by Jeffrey, of *Guy Mannering,* that 'it was a great pity that such a clever book was not more genteel!' For this naiveté Jeffrey cruelly wrote her off as 'a Scotch cockney'.[26]

In spite of the success of his novels, Scott never gave up either poetry or non-fiction, but his next venture proved a resounding flop. *The Field of Waterloo,* the fruit of his Continental visit in 1815, was generally ridiculed. The Whiggish John Whishaw, considered cautious as a critic – that is, holding back until he heard others' opinions – expressed the general view of these unsuccessful European products, *Waterloo* and *Paul's Letters to his Kinsfolk,* in the waspish observation 'trifling commonplace work, written . . . for the sake of reimbursing the author, with some profit, the expenses of his continental journey'. No less withering was Lord Erskine's verse:

How vast the heaps of prostrate slain
On Waterloo's immortal plain;
Yet none by sabre or by shot
Fell half so flat as Walter Scott.[27]

'What a poem!' exclaimed John Wilson, 'such bald and nerveless language, mean imagery, commonplace sentiments, and clumsy versification. It is beneath criticism . . .'[28]

One could scarcely be more dismissive than that. 'The descent is indeed heavy from his Bannockburn to his Waterloo', wrote Lockhart later in his *Life of Scott.* But it was cheaply priced and had a wider circulation than Scott's earlier long poems.[29] Tommy Moore indeed wrote begging Lady Donegal to compose a rival poem on the subject. 'Do not let that pitiful, wretched performance of Scott's remain the only tribute that genius has paid to such glorious deeds . . . [You will] drive Walter Scott out of the field (at least that field) for ever.'[30] To Miss Godfrey he wrote, 'The battle murdered many, and *he* has murdered the battle; 'tis sad stuff . . .' He took particular exception to Scott's faulty rhymes (Hougoumont/long/strong), which implied a deplorable French pronunciation.[31] In comparison with the novels, *Waterloo* was a miserable failure.

There is always pleasure in picking holes in the successful. As early as 1809 Scott had written tolerantly to Charles Sharpe of a hostile review, 'When you have been as often and as bitterly reviewed as I have, you will have all the indifference of eels that are used to be flea'd, as the cook-wench says'.[32] Scott soon regained favour, though again behind his mask, with the succession of stories under the general title *Tales of my Landlord,* set in different parts of Scotland. First came *The Black Dwarf* and *Old Mortality.* His publishers thought the former bore marks of haste, and found the conclusion so disappointing that they asked him to rewrite the last chapters, a proposal which Scott, on his dignity as bestselling author, was quick to refuse.[33]

When these two appeared, Mrs Brunton noted that 'All Edinburgh was talking (till the Grand Duke Nicholas arrived to change the subject) . . . Beyond a doubt, they are from the same hand as Guy Mannering.'[34]

The title page attribution 'By the Author of Waverley' was abandoned for this series for the *nom-de-plume* Jedediah Cleishbotham. The usual people recognised Scott's hand, however, and he became a master of the equivocal reply, winding his comments in such a cocoon of vagueness as neither to confirm or deny.

Young Thomas Carlyle, surprisingly, was sure that neither *The Black Dwarf* nor *Old Mortality* could be Scott's. Indeed his friend Robert Mitchell in Annan had written of *Guy Mannering*, 'It is now understood to have no connection with Walter Scott'. Carlyle briskly told Mitchell that 'Certainly Waverly [sic.] and Mannering, and the Black Dwarf were never written by the same person.'[35]

Lord Byron, by then in Rome, thought the opposite – while his sister and his aunt were naïvely 'very positive' that *he* [Byron] had written them, based on the Dwarf's preoccupation with his own deformity, believing that everyone scorned him. When Byron read the book himself, all became clear.[36] Yet though he easily guessed the same hand in the novels, he had not yet realised it was Scott's.

John Whishaw, man of letters and friend of Francis Horner, Mackintosh and other Whigs, was convinced of Scott's authorship, 'and this is the clear and decided opinion of the most intelligent persons, and those who best know him in Edinburgh', especially as certain 'anecdotes and jokes were recognisably his'. He was sceptical of the Tom Scott theory (which Scott himself helped to put about), though agreeing that he might have 'had a hand'. *Old Mortality* and the rest were to Whishaw 'the most extraordinary productions', and 'In nice delineations of character, and freedom and vigour of colouring, it excels any of the avowed works of Scott in prose and verse.'[37]

Horner himself (who died in 1817) considered *The Antiquary* (May 1816) inferior in plot, 'but, indeed, they are all very indifferently executed in that respect . . .' Scott's plots, like some of his heroes, might often be weak, but his contemporaries were as ready metaphorically to tear to pieces books they admired as they were to criticise new buildings down to the last detail.[38] The recurring 'Meg Merrilees' characters already excited Horner's criticism, as they did later Sydney Smith's. *The Antiquary*, though for Whishaw 'extremely good' in subject, was in 'some respects unpleasing. The author writes with great powers, but with very little moral feeling, and delights too much in "battle, murder, and sudden death" . . .' This of Scott sounds strange indeed.[39]

Scott's own family, interestingly, were fairly mystified. The painter David Wilkie, who stayed at Abbotsford in August 1817, told his sister Helen that life there was 'nothing but amusement from morning till night; and if Mr Scott is really writing "Rob Roy" [how did Wilkie know it was *Rob Roy*?], it must be while we are sleeping. He is either out planting trees, superintending the masons, or erecting fences, the whole of the day. He goes frequently out hunting . . .'

Wilkie added, 'The family here are equally in the dark about whether Mr Scott is the author of the Novels . . . they hope he is the author, and would be greatly mortified if it were to turn out that he was not . . .' His daughters Anne and Sophia were especially provoked at being kept guessing. As Scott kept early hours both morning and night, he commonly wrote his stint in the hour or two after 6 a.m., without his writing labours, which he wore so lightly, cutting into the day.[40]

Rob Roy, published on the last day of 1817, did in fact cost Scott more trouble than usual. Throughout its creation he had been fighting against the first signs of what was at the time diagnosed as 'cramp in the stomach', and dulling his sensibilities with opium. Though Whishaw, who read the book at once, thought it less good than its predecessors, and not very successful, Mackintosh, Smith and many others disagreed, and it proved one of the most popular.

'It is more uniform,' wrote Henry Hallam, one of its critics, to Lord Webb Seymour, 'there are no such dull parts as in "Guy Mannering" or "The Antiquary", but on the other hand it never rises to the merit of either of these in their best passages. None of the characters are very good' – too similar to others in the novels.[41]

Whishaw, in London, commented that *Paul's Letters* were there thought 'a great failure; though it is evidently the work of a sensible man, and a practised writer', while apart from the account of Waterloo it was 'flat and insipid'. Odd, he thought, for the impact the battlefield must surely have made on a man never before on the Continent, and such a contrast to the liveliness of his 'supposed novels and in the "Tales of my Landlord".'[42]

The ambitious young advocate John Gibson Lockhart, who had not yet met Scott, approved of *Waverley* and *Old Mortality* for their familiar setting, but objected to the 'gross violations of historical truth' – a regular failing of Scott's. He remarks cautiously that the latest novels are 'supposed to be, like 'Waverley', by Walter Scott'.[43]

By the time Lockhart did meet the author in June 1818, he had to his own credit, or the opposite as the case may be, *Peter's Letters*, his contribution to the notorious 'Chaldee Manuscript', and his association with Blackwood's.

He must have known Scott by sight from attendance at the courts, and at large public functions; now they met at dinner at Home Drummond of Blair Drummond's. Scott, cordial as always, invited the talented young man to Abbotsford where (he told him) he himself was generally known as 'the Shirra'.[44]

One family impervious to *Waverley* was the solemn Somersets. The Duke admitted in February 1815 that he had not read it, 'but Charlotte [his wife] has and does not much like it. I conceive that the painting is too local to please much beyond the Tweed.'[45] This might be construed as typical English chauvinism, were it not that ever since *The Lady of the Lake* in 1810 the English had been swarming in increasing numbers to visit Highland scenery, and the Duke himself had toured Scotland in 1795.

The Duchess's brother-in-law Lord Webb was not surprised, observing with typical seriousness, 'she has scarcely seen enough, I imagine, of the middling and lower classes, to enter into the merit of a great deal of the painting', with the revealing comment, 'the enjoyment of the tale depends much upon a relish for broad humour, of which Charlotte is not susceptible'. He admitted that 'With many offensive errors in point of taste, it has considerable merit in its force of painting . . . it must be owned that two or three of the personages are gross caricatures'. He urged his brother to have a go, and said that provided he had patience to wade through 'the heavy chapters at the beginning', he would find much of it 'entertaining'.[46]

The Duke was unmoved. 'I can hardly prevail upon myself to become interested in a prose narrative of that kind. When I do read fiction, I like it in verse.'[47]

The publication of *The Heart of Midlothian* (1818), saw the start of the fullest and frankest, though not quite the first, of Sydney Smith's comments. He was at a disadvantage in reading it alongside the Holland House set, which deplored it, and Smith himself diplomatically tempered his approval. 'There is a great difference of opinion about Scott's new novel,' he told Lady Mary Bennet. 'At Holland House it is much run down . . . but it made me laugh and cry very often, and I was very sorry when it was over.' To Lord Grey he wrote on similar lines, adding, 'I think [it] excellent, quite as good as any of his novels except [*Old Mortality*] . . . He repeats his Characters but it seems they will bear repetition . . .' But he was cautious in opposing his view to Lord Holland and John Allen, 'such an assay or proof-house', and even admitted ironically to the overpowering Lady Holland, 'I am sorry we cannot agree about Walter Scott. My test of a book written to amuse is amusement; but I . . . ought not to say I am *amused* before I have enquired whether Sharp and Mackintosh are so . . .' Fortunately for his elaborate fence-sitting, at least the Lansdownes were 'for'.[48]

Richard Rush relates (at second-hand) how at a Holland House dinner Lady Holland proposed that they all write down their favourite Scott novel. 'Paper and pencil were passed, and a slip torn off as each wrote. Nine were handed to her, and each had the name of a different novel!'[49]

Tommy Moore thought *The Heart* an extravagant story, which indeed it was. Baroness Bunsen hated it.[50]

Rob Roy was the first of Scott's novels to be adapted for the theatre, played first not in Edinburgh but at Covent Garden (1819), and Nasmyth painted the scenery. It was followed by two more successes, *The Heart of Midlothian* and *Guy Mannering.*[51]

With what proved to be Scott's middle-period novels, Sydney Smith seemed inclined to fear deterioration. *The Bride of Lammermoor*, published in 1819 under Cleishbotham disguise, with *A Legend of Montrose* in the series *Tales of my Landlord*, earned Smith's praise; but at the end of the novel Scott announced that he was 'retiring from the field', presumably as much because he was known to be ill as that he feared he might be overtasking his imagination. Smith wrote to Constable, who had sent him a copy of *The Bride*, that 'as the author has left off writing, I shall not again be disturbed so much in my ordinary occupations. When I get hold of one of these novels, turnips, sermons, and justice business are all forgotten.' To Constable he was always noticeably diplomatic; yet the following month he was telling Lord Lansdowne that the book was 'laboured', an inferior version of Scott's true style, and 'more careless, with many repetitions of himself. Caleb is overdone . . . The catastrophe is shocking and disgusting.'[52]

Scott's amazingly prolific output, nine novels in six years, seemed to be fatally terminated with this production, when in the summer of 1818 he was seized with an excruciating and alarming illness which flattened him for many months. It proved to be gallstones, though not then so recognised.

According to Robert Gillies he had been in good form entertaining guests at home, when further guests arrived after dinner. During some music he felt a sudden cramp in his right side, so painful that he had to retire to his room – 'a violent spasmodic attack, attended with frightful pain'. This was so unlike Scott that everybody became alarmed, but he sent a message not to break up, and begging Mrs Henry Siddons to sing. The doctor arrived, and ordered complete rest. The pain and weakness continued for days, and after a week Scott was ordered to the country on a strict diet.[53] This was the first of the attacks to which he for the next year became liable.

The Americans Joseph Cogswell and George Ticknor saw him at Abbotsford in the spring, when he appeared at the point of death. They left him with great anxiety, Ticknor on the point of travelling south via the Lake District and Cogswell returning to Edinburgh. That same evening Cogswell was due at a party at Mrs Grant's, and also had the duty of delivering to Scott's wife in Castle Street a letter from Sophia explaining what had happened, when she 'had half a dozen hysteric fits . . . I never was more distressed in my life'. She was alone in the house, poor soul, apart from a servant boy and her son

Charles, who was himself 'in perfect agony'. In the following days Cogswell heard no further news, good or bad.[54]

Throughout the winter and spring of 1819 Scott's dreadful pain recurred at intervals. Towards the end of the legal session Gillies met him mounted on a Highland pony in Charlotte Square, evidently hating the exercise as taken merely for his health, and looking as ill as he was to look later in his last illness. He was wretchedly thin, could hardly sit upright, appeared 'threadbare and disordered and his complexion had deepened to dark olive brown'.

He told Gillies and his friend (who was sure he could not last more than weeks) that he could scarcely endure another such three months, and would follow whatever was prescribed. A few days later he seemed near death, and Gillies claims that a remedy he himself urged on Dr Dick, eventually tried at Abbotsford, brought about his recovery: 'a slow alternative course of medicine' – he of course does not reveal what – 'with very frequent use of the warm bath'. After the long, slow illness and an even worse bout that autumn, Scott's own dogged determination, and continued riding despite his pain, even though he had to be lifted on to his horse, saw him through.

Yet he seemed to find writing as therapeutic as exercise, and on his sickbed was mentally irrepressible. He was already dictating *The Bride of Lammermoor*, and later, *Ivanhoe* to his 'amanuensis' William Laidlaw, and John Ballantyne, often interrupted by convulsive spasms.[55]

27
SCOTT LIONISED

'How d'ye like Edinburgh?'
'It is the dream of a great genius', said I.
'Well done', said Sir Walter, 'when will ye dine with me?'

Autobiography & Journals of Benjamin Robert Haydon, Malcolm Elwin (ed.), London, 1950, 341–2

Poor Scott! Few contemporaries other than Mrs Siddons can have been so exposed to public view, and everyone felt justified – or impelled – to disparage his homely features. Disappointment was usually the initial reaction, that the great man should appear so ordinary, so rugged, even bourgeois, rather like a sturdy farmer. But then most, like Miss Edgeworth, at once modified their judgment by pleased admiration at the way his heavy expression lit up with animation the moment he began to talk.

Perhaps the most uncompromisingly disparaging account is by the young Frenchman Amédée Pichot, to whom Scott was pointed out in August 1822, swinging along Princes Street with a friend. It was almost Pichot's first day in Edinburgh, and the Consul, M. Duryer, drew his attention to one of three men approaching who, he said, was Walter Scott. His disappointment was almost ludicrous: a man of middle age, naturally tall and robust but, from his lame leg, '*condamné à se baisser gauchement sur une canne à chaque pas*'; his appearance '*très bourgeois . . . rustique même*', his dress unremarkable (perhaps having just returned from Abbotsford), in a green coat with '*basques écourtées, un pantalon large*'. Worst of all were his plain features, though by then healthy colour, grey eyes and '*saillans*' brows which gave him a rather hard expression, his forehead broad and at this moment from the walk slightly sweaty, his hair naturally curly but thin, '*cendrés et grisonnans*'.

Pichot lays on the disillusion thick, but charitably adds that perhaps this was '*un mauvais moment*', and that he could not at a single glance judge '*un de nos plus grands génies*'. (He dwells the more on his initial disappointment to point up his later visits to Scott and their long literary and general conversations, which he describes verbatim at great length.[1])

Scott had only to appear, to be accosted. In the vegetable market an old wife hailed him, addressing him as 'Abbotsford' and begging him to buy her fruit, but he laughed good-humouredly and gave her money instead. At the theatre he would appear unobtrusively in a box, purposely arriving late so as not to cause a stir.[2]

Scott's literary career was complicated by dealings with different publishers, financial arrangements, loans and speculations, tedious to unravel. Suffice to say that he over-spent, over-borrowed, and often exercised poor judgment (notably in his dealings with the Ballantynes, though he was early irritated by John Ballantyne's irresponsibility).

Scott was associated with Archibald Constable from 1804, with Longman's as his London outlet from 1805 and with the Ballantynes from the same year. At his suggestion James Ballantyne moved to Edinburgh and at once became a publishing success. But between rash speculations and lack of business acumen, by 1819 the pair were in financial difficulties. Besides, Scott was now deep in debt over the purchase and improvement of Abbotsford. He had quarrelled with Constable over the latter's partner Hunter's behaviour, and was offended by Jeffrey's harsh review of *Marmion* in the *Edinburgh* (1808), but with Hunter's death and the passage of time he was ready to enter into business with Constable again.[3]

Scott's chief the Duke of Buccleuch sometimes came to their rescue with loans and backings, but with the publication of *Waverley* money came rolling in, the first thousand printing followed immediately by a second and even a third and fourth edition in the same year (1814), rising to eight by 1817. From now on much of Scott's correspondence concerned royalties, bills, cash negotiation for publication, and connections with London firms. Scott felt ready to turn anything to good account – not always successfully, witness the *Waterloo* publications.

The Antiquary (1816) was published by Constable and, through Ballantyne's management, the first *Tales of my Landlord* by Murray. Ballantyne was becoming an embarrassment, but Scott could not shake him off, and Lockhart admits that the younger man was acting 'with cunning selfishness both by Scott and by Constable'. There were arguments about disposal of stock. Ballantyne, Scott claimed, was like a cat, and could 'tumble out of a 10-pair of stairs window and light on his feet'.[4] So he did, for several years.

When in September 1817 Scott invited Constable and his daughter to Abbotsford he had already been suffering 'cramps' for some months. He had hoped to have finished *Rob Roy*, but was so 'dreadfully broke up by company that he had not even a closet to be private in'. A November return of the cramps delayed completion further, but no sooner was it published, reprinting only three years later, than he was collecting tracts on the Porteous case. Then there was the finding of the Scottish Regalia in February 1818, and even this suggested a likely theme, but he abandoned the idea.[5]

Apart from the problem of Ballantyne and his 'tortuous', grasping methods – 'quite abominable', pronounced Constable, insisting on seeing each agreement every time a bill was renewed, Constable had family sorrows. A few months after he made a second marriage, his daughter by his first died. After the success of *The Heart of Midlothian* his partner Robert Cadell visited Scott at Abbotsford to discuss finance and their ambitious future programme. 'We have a prodigious stake in the great man', he wrote, but the financial problems continued. For the time being a large bequest from Scott's brother-in-law, Mr Carpenter, saved the day, and by Christmas 1818 Abbotsford was expected to be 'altogether habitable'.[6]

In January 1819 the whole of Scott's works, except *Marmion* which Murray insisted on keeping, were transferred by agreement to Constables, for £12,000, which seems never to have been fully paid off. Only a few weeks later came Scott's renewed agonising illness, 'with bleedings and blistetings' for hours, his arms 'sorely mangled with lancets'. He could scarcely speak for five minutes together for lack of breath, yet (as he said) 'while I had screamed and yelled for 8 hours', his pulse never rose from normal. It was his health that rose and fell: he was seriously ill on the publication of *The Bride of Lammermoor* and *A Legend of Montrose*, but again recovered. While he was dictating *Ivanhoe* to Ballantyne (himself ill and with a blistering plaster on his chest), he had to maintain great secrecy to maintain the doubt of his authorship.[7]

He could not afford to leave off, needing money for his son Walter's army commission, as well as still paying off land purchases. Yet Southey informed a friend that Scott had earned at least £80,000 that year, and on the death of his wife's brother he inherited for his children a further £70,000. But with his now precarious health (thought Southey) he might not live long to enjoy it.[8]

The Monastery was written in better health, and was no more trouble to him than the rest, though Scott agreed that it was not very interesting. Next he needed money for the expenses of the baronetcy conferred on him in March 1820, and he produced *The Abbot* jointly through Constable and Longman, while Ballantyne continued grasping as ever over loans and credit.[9]

Scott was now such a lion that he was sought out by other lions. Everybody who could get an introduction to him did so. With others, though they could meet only seldom, a connection was maintained at a distance. Scott and Lord Byron, who had a mutual admiration, had a further link over Coleridge, who accused Scott of plagiarising the substance of his unfinished poem 'Christabel'.

After their London spring meeting of 1815, Byron wrote to Coleridge relating how Scott had repeated to him much of the still unpublished poem, 'the wildest & finest I ever heard in that kind'; though admiration was tempered with his deploring the 'want of inclination & exertion' which was holding Coleridge back.[10]

Two years later Byron was delighted with the *Quarterly*'s glowing review, which at the time he did not know was by Scott, of *Childe Harold*. When he did discover it shortly after, he was even more pleased.[11]

He was distressed, however, to learn the *Edinburgh*'s attack on 'Christabel', and on himself for praising it; but in his extravagant attachment to Jeffrey, though he was sorry for Coleridge 'because, poor fellow, it will hurt him in mind and pocket', 'I shall never think less of [Jeffrey] for any thing he may say against me or mine in future', and could never forget his 'handsome' treatment of him in recent years. In fact 'I only wonder he did not begin before, as my domestic destruction was a fine opening for all the world . . .'[12] though he admitted that of those he knew, 'only Scott, Jeffrey or Leigh Hunt would have 'dared venture even an anonymous word in my favour just then'.

Meanwhile the 'news', or myth, which Scott was pleased to support, that Tom Scott was *'positively* [Murray says] the Author of *Waverley* &c.' had filtered through to him, with tidings of the latest, *Tales of my Landlord,* 'which is generally deemed even greatly *superior* to all the former . . .'[13]

Byron and Scott both praised Coleridge, Byron particularly distressed that a man of 'wonderful talent' and in financial trouble should be either reviled or ignored by the critics, and begging Moore in secret (because 'Jeffrey might not like it') to review him in the *Edinburgh*: 'It will be the making of him'. And to Coleridge himself urging him to get going and finish 'Christabel', quoting Scott's friendship and how his 'just appreciation of your capacity deplored to me the want of inclination and exertion which prevented you from giving full scope to your mind'.[14]

Scott was more kindly disposed to Coleridge than Coleridge to him, and 'Christabel' was a vexed subject, for Coleridge was convinced of Scott's plagiary; indeed to his annoyance Scott had quoted a fragment of a ballad, 'The Knight's Tomb' in *Ivanhoe* as 'lines from a contemporary poet, who has written but too little'. Scott liked the metre so much that he used them even a second time, towards the end of his life in *Castle Dangerous.*[15]

Scott pronounced himself horrified, and belatedly publicised his poetic obligations to Coleridge damned by the *Edinburgh's* 'infamous review' of September 1816. He affirmed that he had never even seen that review, let alone written it.

In 1820 Byron was writing from his Italian exile to beg William Bankes, John Murray and others for the latest Scott novels ('for surely they are Scott's'), with which he was increasingly 'delighted', preferring them even to the poems, and read his past novels 'at least once a day for an hour or so', though the latest seem 'too hurried – he forgets Ravenswood's name – '. 'Pray make him write at least 2 a year – I like no reading so well' and when

Scott received his baronetcy, Byron declared that in future he would think more highly of that title. 'By the way – he is the first poet titled for his talent – in Britain'.[16]

He was still awaiting *Ivanhoe* and *The Monastery*, had not written to Scott 'for I know he has a thousand things & I a thousand nothings to do', but wistfully hoped he might see him one day at Abbotsford. To his impatience *The Abbot* arrived before *The Monastery* (October), but Byron had a particular family interest in the former, 'being descended from Gordon of Gight', and recalling from his early childhood Loch Leven in 1798 and his mother's story of it. However, he sent a correction of some historical errors, and in writing to the artist Hoppner, confessed that *The Abbot* was 'not his best'.[17]

Murray would send him other books, but Byron declared that Scott's novels and the two periodicals *Edinburgh* and *Quarterly* were all he wanted: rudely dismissing 'Mrs Hewoman's' ('no more *modern* poetry'), or any protégé of 'Peter Turdsworth'. A year later he was complaining of Murray's sending 'trash'. 'Campbell is lecturing – Moore idling – Southey twaddling – Wordsworth drivelling – Coleridge muddling – Joanna Baillie piddling', and so on. At the beginning of that year he had claimed to have read all Scott 'at least 50 times', comparing him to the 'Scotch Fielding as well as great English poet – wonderful man! I long to get drunk with him'; and he praised his 'manly' character, fine conversation, and especially 'his good nature towards myself, personally'. He told Scott (January 1822) that 'nothing can or could ever persuade me since I was the first 10 minutes in your company, that you are not the Man'.[18]

To Stendhal in May 1823 he wrote praising Scott, as 'worthy of admiration . . . of all men he is the most open . . . the most *honourable*, the most *amiable*', and that although they differed in politics, 'he is perfectly sincere in them. Walter Scott is as nearly a thorough good man as man can be.'[19]

When passing through London in September 1815 one of those Scott had called on was the famous comedian Charles Mathews, to invite him to dine at Long's Hotel with him and Byron, only to find him out. He was doubly disappointed to learn from Mathew's wife that he was just setting off for Warwickshire – for Scott was keen to visit Kenilworth. On his entreaty, Mrs Mathews was able to persuade her husband to give up his coach seat in order to dine with Scott, so that the pair could set off together for Warwickshire that evening.

Scott chatted with her for half an hour over some engravings, and when 'this charming man' was about to leave she saw that it was raining hard and would have called a coach, or at least lent him an umbrella; but he expressed himself happy to walk in the rain, undaunted by weather.

'He was dressed oddly enough for London, in a dark green coatee, singlebreasted . . . something like a Squire's hunting-jacket. His nether garments were drab-coloured, with continuations down to his shoes.' In this countrified costume Scott set off for Bond Street, nonchalantly leaning on his stick, looking back along Leicester Place to nod at her standing in the window, 'with one of his fascinating smiles'.

Mathews, on his return, was equally charmed to learn of the invitation, having never met Byron. At dinner, when he also met a nephew of Scott's, 'Lord Byron was most fascinating', at what proved to be the last meeting between 'these two splendid men'. Byron (he said), 'handsomest man I ever saw', was 'the only man [to whom I] felt disposed to apply the word *beautiful*'. At dinner, as Scott said afterwards, he was 'full of gaiety and good humour', Mathews the comedian contributing a good share. Mathews and Scott then set off, to stay overnight at Stony Stratford. 'Delightful journey, – Scott delicious . . .!' wrote Mathews to his wife over breakfast.

By the time they reached Kenilworth and dined, they had added two more to their party and stopped at Warwick Castle on the way. Several of Scott's remarks Mathews recalled meeting again later in the novel, which would in themselves have been enough to establish the author's identity, had he not learned it already. Over a dinner with John Ballantyne, Constable and the actor Daniel Terry, Ballantyne, relaxed over the wine, had to their consternation let slip a reference to 'Scott's new novel'.[20]

Washington Irving, touring in Scotland in 1817, gathered that nobody now doubted Scott's authorship, while Jeffrey described Scott to him as 'Social, Joyous, full of anecdote, of irrepressible good spirits, picturesque & mimic' and – surprising perhaps to those who know him only from the novels – 'not over fastidious' in his anecdotes. 'Fond of a broad joke occasionally & quite a merry hearted man.'[21]

'You would be charmed with this fellow', wrote another American Joseph Cogswell, first meeting Scott between the bouts of his serious illness. 'There never was anybody like him for simplicity of manners, good humor, spirit in conversation, variety of learning, anecdotes, and all that constitutes a pleasant companion.'[22]

During February 1817 Mrs Grant, just back from the privilege of a breakfast with the Rev. Dr Chalmers, had a call from Scott, whom she had not seen for some time. He sat with her a while 'and was, as he always is, delightful: his good nature, good humour, and simplicity are truly charming . . . He, too, confirmed the maxim that true genius is ever modest and careless.' Her daughter Mary remarked on similarities with Chalmers: 'quiet unobtrusive humour, the same flow of rich original conversation, easy, careless, and visibly unpremeditated; the same indulgence for others, and readiness to give attention and interest'.[23]

One night in the beautiful summer of 1818 her son left her a copy of *The Heart of Midlothian*, and next morning at first light she started to read 'Walter the Wonderful'. 'My attention was so chained that I read on in bed, till I was summoned to breakfast; and now I am scribbling in all confusion and stupidity to overtake the post.'[24]

Scott's serious illness shook his friends as if an immortal had been threatened, 'a loss I cannot think of without fear and pain', Mrs Grant wrote. 'A life so spotless, a heart so kind, a temper so unclouded.' He called on her 'to take leave' for Abbotsford, observing that though he could not depart without shaking hands with her, he feared (she records) 'so much had he been shaken that I would scarce know him'.[25] In the autumn of 1820 she visited Scott during a holiday visit to Tweedside, finding him much better than feared and apparently quite restored, besides having with him 'that happy pair, the recently married Lockharts'.[26]

There was no getting round that plain and heavy appearance. Amelia Opie, who met Scott in London in 1815, at a breakfast party where Wordsworth was also present, was another who inevitably recorded how his expression in repose differed from his animated look. She had the opportunity to discuss with him their mutual writings, and he praised her *Father and Daughter.* At one point, she exclaims, 'never can I forget the fine expression of his lifted eye . . . The whole face became elevated in its character, and even the features acquired a dignity and grace from the power of genius.'

The next autumn she achieved a romantic ambition by visiting Scotland. After fulfilling a sixteen-year-old promise to Lord Buchan, she stayed with the eccentric earl at Dryburgh where she was kindly received; in Edinburgh she stayed nine days with Constable, and sat daily opposite Raeburn's portrait of Scott, though unfortunately its original was away from home. Rather to her chagrin, when she eagerly described her London encounter to Dr Thomas Brown (whom she had also met in London), Brown pooh-poohed her account of Scott's animated features and 'the fire of his blue grey eyes'. 'Nay, nay, Mrs Opie, do not go on with these flights of fancy, the face is nothing but a roast-beef and plum-pudding face, say what you will!'[27]

Most agreed with Amelia Opie, though Frances Lady Shelley in 1815 was even more critical of Scott's unprepossessing appearance: 'a club-foot, white eyelashes, and a clumsy figure'. She went on, however, 'He has not any expression on his face when in repose, but, upon an instant, some remark will lighten up his whole countenance, and you discover the man of genius. His conversation reminds me of his poems – the same ideas and images recurring – and often the same careless manner of expressing them.'[28]

Elizabeth Grant of Rothiemurchus was less susceptible to his charm, still less to his family's. The children she dismissed as ordinary: Walter 'a mere good-natured goose forced into a marriage he hated', Charles more talented but unfortunately dying when on his travels; Sophia 'awkward, very ignorant . . . not exactly plain yet scarcely otherwise, her husband did a great deal with her'. Anne was 'odious – very ugly and very pretending and very unpopular' from her irritable manner, though a good daughter. Walter had married Jane Jobson, written off by Elizabeth Grant as daughter of a 'fat, very vulgar' woman 'whose low husband had made his large fortune at Dundee by pickling herrings'.[29]

She particularly despised the whole family as 'inferior', which would perhaps account for 'the insipidity of his ideal gentlemen and ladies – he knew none better'. (For one thing this was not true; for another the Grants do not as a family seem to have been keen on books or reading; and in general Elizabeth, as her writings reveal, was quite a social snob.) Yet the Grants' own family, despite its impeccable pedigree, had some embarrassingly low connections, and thanks to the father's often unwise actions landed in plenty of trouble over the years.

During Lady Shelley's Scottish visit in 1819 Scott, his wife and daughter visited her at Newton Don and made no good impression. After dinner the gentlemen sat on until past 11, the evening ended only at 3 a.m. with whisky punch, and Scott seemed 'decidedly out of his element'. Meanwhile it was left to her to entertain his wife, 'a great bore', her English still all but unintelligible in spite of spending all her life in Britain since the age of five.

Next morning their breakfast meeting was more agreeable, and they were invited to Abbotsford. Here Scott, meeting them at Melrose in his favourite role of guide, transformed all they saw with his 'magic glass', poetically heightening beauties and concealing defects. He amused them with tales of Lord Buchan, who during Scott's late illness had busied himself with elaborate preparations for his funeral, and was quite disappointed when he recovered.[30]

At dinner Lady Shelley, still in innocence of Scott's authorship, criticised the insipidity of his heroes and heroines, especially the women. Scott suggested diplomatically that the author probably feared to be charged with immorality and made his central characters as blameless as possible. He did imply that Lady Shelley's skilled horsemanship – which he had witnessed in Paris – was 'the author's' inspiration for Di Vernon.

She found his voice irritating, a tiresome drawl, aggravated since his illness, giving it a monotony which 'provokes a yawn', even during his fascinating stories.[31]

When the couple went on to Edinburgh William Clerk, whom they met at Abbotsford, acted as an invaluable guide, and during a long talk on the Waverley novels convinced her that Scott was the author, with conclusive proofs together with reasons why he kept it a secret. He pointed out that, except for the wooden heroes and heroines, scarcely one of his characters was not a portrait of some acquaintance. Scott had the faculty of repeating verbatim whole conversations, even from years ago. As for the myth about Scott's brother, Tom Scott was not nearly clever enough.

Clerk recalled how in their early twenties both of them had attempted humorous verses on Captain Adam Fergusson, the Peninsular and Waterloo hero, but Scott's efforts had been such a failure that he said to his friend, 'Well, it is clear, Clerk, that neither you nor I were born poets.' Yet later, when he hit on the idea of the *Lay*, he was encouraged on showing friends the few lines he had written, and with few corrections went on from there. Clerk, like others, was impressed at how free Scott seemed to be with his time, apparently never occupied and always ready for social gatherings, riding or any 'literary diversion'. This would account for defects in his novels.[32]

Some of Lady Shelley's more jaundiced comments resemble Elizabeth Grant of Rothiemurchus on the whole family of Scotts. Scott and his wife between them received short shrift. By the publication of *The Antiquary* Elizabeth Grant remarks coldly on people's suspicions being aroused by his ability to spend so lavishly on Abbotsford, and his wife's setting up her own carriage, 'a Barouche landau built in London, and which from the time she got it she was seldom out of, appearing indeed to spend her life in driving about the streets all day'. To her, Abbotsford itself was 'that monument of vanity, human absurdity, or madness' of which even William Clerk (she claims) spoke as 'this melancholy act of folly almost with tears'.[33]

Elizabeth Grant's are not among the many contemporary accounts of Scott, being written many years after these events, and her indifference, verging on hostility, is unusual. She claims that when out in company, which was seldom, 'he was not agreeable, generally sitting very silent, looking dull and listless, unless an occasional flash lighted up his heavy countenance'. At home it was a different story, 'especially if he liked his guests'.

Elizabeth suspected that Lady Scott was the Marquess of Downshire's bastard daughter, a fairly fanciful theory as he was still an Eton schoolboy when she was born . . . though not totally impossible – and she reserved her special scorn for the unfortunate lady, who by the time they met 'had no remains of beauty, dressed fantastically, spoke the greatest nonsense in her broken English – and very frequently had taken too much wine'. She quoted an occasion at the Misses Pringles when her daughter Anne had to hurry her away under pretence of an attack of asthma. Few of the characters Elizabeth describes are treated with such disapproval as the Scotts.[34]

'Meg Merrilees appears afresh in every novel,' said Sydney Smith crossly when *The Abbot* appeared in 1820,[35] a complaint he repeated as novel followed novel.

'He has exhausted the subject of Scotland, and worn out the few characters that the early periods of Scotch history could supply him with.'[36]

'No more Meg Merrilees, and Dominie Sampsons!' he exclaimed on the appearance of *The Pirate* in December 1821, and to Jeffrey, 'It seems now that he can write nothing' without them.[37]

The Holland House circle pronounced *The Pirate* a success, once they had finished the first volume. 'We are much pleased with everything except an old Sybil, who is a mere copy of Meg Merrilees, and much less natural and probable.'[38] Scott already had his next novel, *Nigel,* in the press.

The Abbot, sequel to *The Monastery,* was 'now in hand' when Scott went to London to receive his baronetcy, shortly after King George III's death. For these two novels and *Ivanhoe* he was said to have been paid 9000 guineas, with a further 11,000 for the copyright of *Tales of my Landlord.*[39] *The Monastery* was generally thought a failure, especially for its ghostly appearances, though Whishaw considered that in spite of 'many defects' it had 'many passages which none but Scott could have written'.

He was there to attend the new King's coronation, when he made a surprising impression on a foreign visitor. Sitting near to him was M. de Montrond, a great admirer of his, though they had never met. When the trumpets sounded, the Frenchman 'saw a man in great ecstasies and half beside himself with delight and admiration at the show', and on asking someone '*Qui est cet imbécile*?', was told it was Scott. (Cam Hobhouse related this anecdote in 1827, the year before he himself met Scott, after which he ceased his malicious comments.[40])

Scott, 'now here enjoying his honours', seemed in good health and spirits. He was obliged to return to Scotland in April in order to marry his daughter to Lockhart. He explained to a friend that the wedding must avoid the Scottish superstition against a May marriage, as it 'would dwell on his daughter's imagination'.[41]

John Gibson Lockhart, son of a clergyman at Cambusnethan who the year after John's birth was translated to the College Kirk of Glasgow, was educated at Glasgow High School, did brilliantly at its University and then obtained a First at Balliol. Returning to Scotland in 1813 when still aged only nineteen, he had found himself lonely, poor, and at a disadvantage because of deafness from a childhood illness. Darkly handsome, almost Spanish-looking, he was proud and reserved, characteristics aggravated by his deafness, which made him appear more arrogant than he was. Like most deaf people he found it easier in society to talk to one person at a time.

In 1815 Lockhart moved to Edinburgh to read law. Sir William Hamilton, whom he had known at Oxford, brought him many Edinburgh introductions, and he became friendly with John Wilson, whom he described enthusiastically as 'a very warm, enthusiastic man, with most charming conversational talents, full of fiery imaginations, irresistible in eloquence, exquisite in humour when he talks (but too coarse in his humorous writing for the present age); he is a most fascinating fellow, and a most kind-hearted and generous friend.' On the dark side, he had 'a total inconsistency in his opinions concerning both men and things. And thus it is that he continually lauds and abuses the same person within the space of a day.' The sad fact was that Wilson still in 1819 had 'never applied himself to his own satisfaction in anything'.[42]

Lockhart describes meeting 'two violent Lakers' at dinner in 1815, one of them Wilson, the other Thomas De Quincey, 'a most strange creature' who having done brilliantly at Oxford in half his examinations had taken fright, fled to the Lakes, and become friendly with Wordsworth and his circle. He noted how De Quincey, after dinner, set two snuff-boxes on the table, one of which 'contained opium pills – of these he swallowed one every now and then, while we drank our half-bottle apiece'.[43] This was while Wilson was composing *The City of the Plague,* and he apparently set off with De Quincey on one of his walking-tours, to Staffa. Similarly in December he 'walked off to Cumberland . . . in the midst of the storm, in spite of his wife'.[44]

In December 1816 Lockhart passed advocate, earned a three-guinea fee in his first week, and in 1817 began to contribute to the new *Blackwood's Magazine.* After meeting Scott in 1818, he became engaged to Scott's daughter Sophia the following year.

Henry Fox, later 4th Lord Holland, was younger son of Henry, 3rd Lord. He was born with a slight hip deformity which made him lame, and was therefore educated by tutors, though in 1819 at the age of seventeen he went to Christ Church. Being who he was, he met everybody; being acute of perception he described them ably, and perhaps because of his disability his pithy comments were often spiked with acerbity. He met Ticknor at Holland House (before the American's Scottish tour) and found him 'sensible and well informed'; but a couple of weeks later at Woburn found he had 'offended the Duchess by his rudeness and want of manners, of which he gave us a good specimen the other night'.[45]

Henry attended Coleridge's lectures but thought little of them. 'His voice is bad, his subject trite, and his manner odious.' Meeting the pompous Somersets at Lansdowne House he recorded, 'The Duke looks like an idiot, she like a marine'; and in December 1820, again at Lady Holland's, 'Lady Davy so anxious and fidgety that she could hardly sit still or find a moment to scold Sir Humphry.'[46]

Poor nervous Miss Edgeworth, at Mrs Abercromby's, in conversation uttered 'exceeding flattery and praise of all connected with those she is speaking to, which she carried quite to a painful pitch'. And in January 1821, sitting by Thomas Campbell at dinner, Henry found the poet's voice 'sharp and querulous, his ideas vulgarly conceited', ready to praise or admire nothing and no-one that was mentioned 'except an idea of his own'. 'How odious all authors are, and how doubly so to each other!'[47] Henry might have been passing judgment on himself, but then he was only eighteen, and was not always so unkind.

In May 1822 he paid an extended visit to Scotland with the Hollands' faithful John Allen, spending several weeks in Edinburgh. A few months later, having fallen hopelessly in love with George Canning's daughter Harriet ('and becoming cross as poison, odious to myself and others'), at his parents' suggestion he went for a second time, with the Marquess of Lothian's son Lord Ancram, when they coincided with the King's visit.

During his first stay Henry attended the law courts, where, as he hoped, Jeffrey introduced him to Scott, 'what I have been most anxious for since I left London'. Daniel Sandford, an Oxford friend, son of the Bishop of Edinburgh, had found him Princes Street lodgings next door to his own, and plunged him into Edinburgh's Whig society.

From the courts Henry and Sandford went to Lady Morton's, and there was Scott again, looking over the Morton manuscripts, especially the Order in Council for Mary, Queen of Scots' imprisonment on Loch Leven, which he was taking great pains to decipher. Henry revelled in hearing his lively stories of old times – especially one which was revealingly like *Ivanhoe*. 'His head is full of expression, and his voice pleasant and engaging.'[48]

A fortnight later he was dining with the Scotts. 'Lady Scott is nearly an idiot, with great marks of her love for the bottle in her face', talking in her broken English and interested only in 'a horrid, ugly dog, that bites everyone but her'. The small party, including only one other couple and Charles Sharpe besides Anne Scott and a small nephew of Sir Walter's, was joined after dinner by Sophia, who sang 'wild Scotch melodies' in her deep voice, to a harp or unaccompanied. There were tunes on the pipes (he does not say who played), to Scott's evident enchantment, he joining in the choruses, relating family anecdotes, and showing Henry 'a pistol which Dundee wore at Killiecrankie'.[49]

Supper followed, with tales ranging from 'robbers, murders and banditry' to ghosts and visions, of which Scott told a number, including his own experience of a drunken evening with Captain Adam Fergusson (one of the evening's guests), when both were convinced that a third gentleman came and joined them. The subject of politics was avoided, except for Scott's own confessed Jacobitism, and the assertion that so strong was its tradition in Edinburgh that it would be unsafe for Prince Charles Edward's widow, Mme d'Albany, to make a visit.

As for Charles Sharpe, Henry found him clever but his voice tedious and his manner boring. He got home at 2 a.m.[50]

During this Edinburgh visit Henry became very fond of John Allen and admired his talents and knowledge, but was distressed by his bigoted opinions and intolerance of those of others. He had no gaiety or wit, and was inclined to repeat his patron Lady Holland's opinions as his own. On his second journey, Henry found young Lord Ancram 'agreable, good-natured and well-informed'.[51]

This time Lord Lauderdale had managed to fit Henry into his lodgings, when the whole city was in an uproar of excitement in the days leading up to the King's arrival. Poor Henry, miserably in love, desperately resolved to write a letter to Harriet proposing marriage, and was imprudent enough to confide in Sandford, who jeered at him for his pains. Henry joined in all the festivities, however, and on the fifth day called on Scott whom he found 'out of humour with the King', and himself out of favour for over-officiousness.

Meanwhile he was on tenterhooks over the effect of his letter of proposal, and at last after a sleepless night was really relieved to find out that it had never been delivered. A day or so later his full and detailed journal ceases abruptly for a couple of weeks, and in the months that followed he came to regret his rashness.[52]

The painter Benjamin Haydon, whose life was a series of struggles, few of them successful though his large historical and Biblical paintings had been hung at the Royal Academy since 1806, had a period of triumph in 1820. His large epic canvas, 'The Entry into Jerusalem' was first displayed in London in April,[53] when Scott was in London and learned of Haydon through his actor friend Daniel Terry. Haydon was invited to dinner with Scott by William Atkinson, Scott's architect at Abbotsford, when Scott was very complimentary and, having expressed a wish to see this famed painting, astonished Haydon by turning up even before the gallery was open and waiting, patiently sitting outside the door – a characteristic action which pleased Haydon immeasurably as 'a beautiful trait of the natural character of this great genius'. He was pleased to record that besides Scott, Wordsworth and Mrs Siddons also admired the work.[54]

In November he took his painting to exhibit in Edinburgh, a couple of months after Mary Hayman, his former love, who had married another but was now free, renewed their friendship and they planned to marry. When Haydon arrived in Edinburgh the city was 'in an uproar' over the triumphant acquittal of Queen Caroline, and Haydon, at Mrs Farquharson's lodgings in Princes Street, was woken from a heavy sleep by the smashing of her windows because they were not illuminated. His attempts to light any candles were frustrated by gusts of wind through the broken panes, which drew more showers of stones while he closed the shutters, 'and they battered till there was not a pane left'. After the same treatment of the neighbouring houses the mob roared on to the beat of drums into St Andrew Square, 'more ferocious' than a London crowd.[55]

He called on Scott in Castle Street 'and heard him stamping down. At the head of his first landing, he waved his stick, and cried: "Hurrah! Welcome to Scotland, Haydon." He then came down, squeezed, in fact gripped, my hand', and pressed him to come to dinner.

On this occasion, which besides Scott's wife, two daughters and Lockhart, included Haydon's old friend Sir William Allan, and Daniel Terry, Scott took wine with Haydon and said with his usual warmth, 'I say to you, as Hogg said to Wilkie, "I am happy to see you are so young a man"' (Haydon was thirty-four), and then made one of his not infrequent slips. Haydon told him he had climbed Salisbury Crags, and Scott said eagerly, 'Ah, when I was a youth I have often sat there thinking of my prospects in life. It is a glorious place.' This struck a chord with Haydon, who recognised it from one of the novels. Sure enough next morning he found it in *The Heart of Midlothian*.[56]

After meeting Scott in London, Haydon had written to Wordsworth of how delightful he found him, yet how puzzled he was by the surrounding mystery. 'You are aware he is suspected of being a concealed author', and while diplomatically trying to keep off, Haydon found he was 'continually alluding to the subject . . . I felt as if it were a species of quackery, and cannot but think all this has its effect in society.' It had certainly helped to increase his sales: could it have been intentional?[57] Earlier he had noted in his Journal that this 'kind, keen, prudent, deep man', with his strong feeling for nature, scenery, dogs and so on, must undoubtedly be the *Waverley* man because of his almost perverse way of 'giving you evident proofs . . . & then to chuckle at his conviction that good breeding forbid your saying so . . . the deepest [plan] to keep up an interest that ever occurred to any one'.[58]

Haydon had already met Lockhart, when out walking with Sir William Allan: a pleasure on his side, though he noted that Lockhart, who had attacked him as one of the 'Cockney school', was (not surprisingly) nervous, 'and he seemed surprised to find that I was human'. Studying his 'melancholy and Spanish head' with a painterly eye, Haydon saw 'genius and mischief' there. Any embarrassment was resolved by dining with Lockhart, who received him frankly and openly, and 'treated me then, and ever since, as if I was a man he had unwittingly injured'. Sophia, married to Lockhart six months earlier, reminded him of 'one of Shakespeare's women' – the only woman who did so apart from his own Mary Hayman.[59]

The exhibition was booked at Bruce's Rooms in Waterloo Place, where he held a private day, a novelty for Edinburgh. It was successful, though by

London standards the takings (between £4 and £14 a day), totalling about £500 for Edinburgh and £400 for Glasgow, seemed modest.

He was struck by the Scots' enthusiasm, approaching awe, for his painting, to the extent that one old man rebuked him for being there with his hat on. But disappointingly, as so often happened to Haydon, no authority rose to buying it for the benefit of the public, nor did praise in the Tory journals lead to any commissions or patronage.

He had, however, the satisfaction of disconcerting his hitherto hostile critics Wilson, Lockhart, Daniel Terry and even Scott, all of whom had taken his personal friendship with Leigh Hunt as a 'political and religious alliance', and those who had attacked him as 'one of the Cockney School of radicals and sceptics were astonished to find him a high tory and aristocrat, and a sound Christian . . . a very well read man and a good painter'. The tables were turned, and henceforward it was the 'liberal' press who attacked him.[60] Lockhart was now praising him in *Blackwood's* as 'already by far the greatest historical painter that England has as yet produced'.

He even got the better of the *Blackwood's* set, who ('fine dogs!'), still convinced of his Cockney-dom, challenged him to a gallop in the Pentlands, but the Devon-born Haydon riding on a borrowed mare outstripped them all in skill, speed and daring. 'Not a word about the cockney was heard for the remainder of my time in Auld Reekie.'[61]

Haydon noted people, hospitality and character in Edinburgh with approval. 'Their hospitality and heartiness were indisputable, their knowledge and literature were eminent; but their simplicity was the most striking.' What chiefly amused him was their conviction that London was the seat of Government only for its superior size, whereas in intelligence, enterprise and the rest it was markedly Edinburgh's inferior.

The still, clear wintry sunset in Princes Street, 'with the Castle and the Pentland Hills in radiant, glory, and the crowd illuminated by the setting sun, was a sight perfectly original'. It was illuminated not merely from nature:

> First you would see limping Sir Walter, talking as he walked with Lord Meadowbank; then tripped Jeffrey, keen, restless, and fidgety; you next met Wilson, or Lockhart, or Allan, or Thompson, or Raeburn, as if all had agreed to make their appearance at once . . . I wonder Allan never thought of it as a subject for a picture.[62]

Haydon's most striking experience of Scots hospitality was a dinner for thirty or so at the portrait and landscape painter Andrew Geddes'.[63] It included Sir Henry Raeburn ('a glorious fellow'), and George Thomson, who had set Burns's poems to music and sang some of them 'with great relish and taste' – when to Haydon's astonishment at the chorus of one he was left sitting while the whole party joined hands and jumped up, dancing round the table to the tune until they reached their seats again.[64]

After meeting Jeffrey as well as Scott, he noted the contrast: 'Jeffrey's expression piercing & bitter, the habit of 30 years' perpetual criticism [less than 20, to be accurate], Scott's genial, unaffected, beaming with humanity, the habits of a life of being alive to the beauties of Nature.' To Miss Mitford he wrote: 'Whatever you praise to Jeffrey, he directly chuckles out some error that you did not perceive. Whatever you praise to Scott, he joins heartily with yourself, and directs your attention to some additional beauty. Scott throws a light on life by the beaming geniality of his soul . . . while Jeffrey seems to revel in holding up his hand before the light in order that he may spy out its deformities.'[65]

John Wilson, whom Haydon met through an introductory letter, also invited him to a large party, and Haydon admired 'his light hair, deep sea-blue eyes, tall athletic figure, and hearty hand-grasp'. He thought he looked 'like a fine Sandwich islander who had been educated in the Highlands', and 'his eagerness in debate, his violent passions, great genius, and irregular habits, rendered him a formidable partisan, a furious enemy, and an ardent friend'. His famous enmity towards Keats 'marked him as the author of all those violent assaults on my poor friend in *Blackwood*'. Haydon described his adventure with the mob smashing the windows, and Wilson tried to catch him out by the mischievous comment, 'I suppose you took it to yourself?' Luckily Haydon spotted the trap and did not rise to it: such conceit would have been 'a glorious subject for the ridicule of *Blackwood*!'[66]

In triumph, though still in debt, still unable to get married, after 'I had dined, drank, talked, rode, and argued with the enemy in his camp', Haydon returned to London, and began to think about a vast painting of Lazarus.[67]

Poor Haydon. These had been happy months for him, not least his meeting with so many new celebrities. Some months later Scott, in London again, breakfasted with him along with Lamb, Brian Procter, and Wilkie, 'and a delightful morning we had', Haydon, the host declared. 'I never saw any man have such an effect on company as he; he operated on us like champagne and whisky mixed.' Haydon was so anxious not to lose the chance of getting Scott to his house that he had fetched him in a coach.[68]

In October Haydon married his Mary – but a month later was arrested for debt, and although bailed out, was imprisoned again the following May and his house stripped by creditors. Scott, to whom he wrote of his misfortunes, was among those who came to his help.[69]

Meanwhile the poor but ambitious young Chambers brothers, Robert and William, were laying the foundations of their successful career. With some trepidation, knowing his eccentric reputation and aristocratic manner, Robert called on Charles Kirkpatrick Sharpe with ideas about a work on Edinburgh. Sharpe received him kindly and told him that he and Scott had discussed making such a book, to be called 'Reekiana', but as Chambers had got in ahead of him, he would supply him with anecdotes. Hence the tales in *Traditions of Edinburgh* of Lady Eglintoun, Lord Alva (Lord Justice Clerk), and Kitty Duchess of Queensberry came from Sharpe.

In 1822 Chambers had an introduction to Scott from Constable, and was received in the Castle Street study with Scott's usual kindness and put at his ease. Learning that Chambers dealt in old books, he asked to be kept informed of rarities, and Chambers left 'astonished at the gentle and easy manners of a man whom I had been accustomed to regard as of a superior order of beings'.

Scott, as President of the Royal Society, put work in Chambers's way over the King's visit, sending him his own address on the Society's behalf to be transcribed with Chambers's calligraphic skill. Such hack work, however, was not for Chambers, and before long he was immersed in *Traditions of Edinburgh,* and Scott and Lockhart called on him to discuss the content.[70]

28
PERIODICAL WARFARE

'Readers in these kindlier days of criticism have no conception of the extent to which personal hostility allowed itself to be transported, in the periodicals of those times. Personal habits, appearances, connections, domesticities, nothing was safe from misrepresentations . . . carried to an excess which would have been ludicrous, had it not sometimes produced tragical consequences.'

Autobiography of Leigh Hunt (1784–1859), J. E. Morpurgo (ed.), London, 1949, 223

'If some being from another climate were to come to this and desire to know in what work the highest pitch of human intellect might be found he ought to be shown the *Edinburgh Review*.'

Mme de Staël, quoted by Lord Glenbervie in Francis Bickley (ed.), *The Diaries of Sylvester Douglas, Lord Glenbervie*, London, 1928, II.163

'I have great dependance on Wilson's powers, do not you see with what spirit the fellow writes whether it be to laud or blame or to mock? The worst fault about him is that he lets his imagination run away with him; if he leans to one side at all he leans too much, he either praises or blames in the extreme. Brougham is the same way. I don't like him. I would take Jeffrey for a model of all I ever read. He gives a cut now and then with much severity and at the same time with such perfect good nature . . .'

James Hogg to William Blackwood , 19 Oct. 1817: A. L. Strout, 'James Hogg's "Chaldee Manuscript"', in *Publications of the Modern Language Association of America*, Vol. LXV No.5, Sept. 1950, 703

'The diet of levity and sarcastic indifference, which had so long formed the stable nourishment of Scottish intellect, had by repetition lost, to not a few palates, the charming poignancy of its original flavour.'

[On the rise of *Blackwood's* v. *Edinburgh Review*], 'Peter Morris', *Peter's Letters to his Kinsfolk*, 3rd edn, 1819, II.204

As the century advanced, it was increasingly clear not only that Britain was in a golden age of literature and philosophy, but that this brilliance centred in Edinburgh and the North. Northern Britain was the home of the Lake Poets, Scotland and its Borders had given birth to Robert Burns and, later, Walter Scott and Thomas Campbell; Edinburgh University had produced leading historians and thinkers, David Hume, Adam Smith and in the next generation, Dugald Stewart and John Playfair; and the remarkable group of young wits, who also shortly made their mark in Parliament and in the law, had startled the country by the originality and provocativeness of their *Edinburgh Review.*

The *Review* and its contributors were uncompromisingly Whig. Edinburgh as a whole was immovably Tory. Francis Jeffrey and his colleagues had been bound to stir up opposition, indeed that was part of their intention, and after a few years it was not surprising that a political and literary rival must be launched.

With the continuing Napoleonic war, when the conqueror seemed to carry almost everything before him, a feeling spread among the Whigs that it was useless to resist and that peace under any terms should be sought. This view, to which Jeffrey subscribed, aroused much opposition among the Tories, especially in Edinburgh. The *Edinburgh Review,* its circulation now risen to some nine thousand, thus came in for much new criticism, one of the reasons which lay behind the production of the *Quarterly Review,* a vigorous rival produced as a counter-blast in London.

Its instigator was John Murray, as Tom Dibdin put it, among the first to treat authors 'with the respect due to gentlemen' and, like Archibald Constable in Edinburgh, a publisher whose London offices became a centre for leading literary characters. The first Edinburgh agent was John Ballantyne, of Scott's publishing firm, to be followed by the antiquarian bookseller William Blackwood; and instant contributors included Scott, Canning, Southey, George Ellis, translator of Middle English verse and one-time contributor to *The Anti-Jacobin*, Hookham Frere, MP, also a contributor to *The Anti-Jacobin,* and a collaborator with Ellis in his poetical collections, and John Wilson Croker, Tory MP and intemperate critic.[1]

The launch of the *Quarterly* in February 1809, at a high point of Jeffrey's success, marked the debut of the *Edinburgh Review*'s first and indeed sole serious rival, becoming a 'receptacle', as Cockburn put it, for the work of those who never, or no longer, wished to be associated with the Whiggish paper. That paper's trend towards opposition in deploring the war was seen by many as unpatriotic, and an article on Don Pedro Cevallo and French 'usurpation' in Spain provoked many cancelled subscriptions, when the *Review* was accused of Jacobinism.[2]

Scott himself was so offended that he would have no more to do with it, though Jeffrey, aware that they had overstepped the mark, promised him that 'no party politics should appear again', but the damage was done.[3] Jeffrey reckoned that Scott misunderstood what was merely a pledge to avoid violent opinions; indeed, he refused to take up his friends' urging him to refute this charge, on the grounds that he never had avoided politics, and would certainly not make such a promise now.

Scott was happy to transfer allegiance to a new periodical, but had no wish to become editor, although it stood for all that he most valued – orthodoxy, the Church, the monarchy. With this balancing production to the *Edinburgh Review,* literature and criticism were represented between the two for well over a century.[4] To the *Quarterly*'s first issues Byron, Moore, Crabbe, Coleridge, Southey were, needless to say, enthusiastic contributors.

William Gifford, the new journal's editor, was a glazier's son who had started life as a shoemaker apprentice, was assisted to go to Oxford, became a tutor and, after publishing two satires, *The Boviad* and *The Maeviad*, edited the *Anti-Jacobin* for George Canning. He was an unlikely editor for such a journal as the *Quarterly* and spent much of his energies attacking, or conniving at attacks on, major poets such as Wordsworth – notably his *Excursion* – and younger writers like Charles Lamb and Keats.[5]

Southey had already agreed to support the forthcoming *Quarterly,* Scott having withdrawn his *Edinburgh* subscription (the previous year Scott had been trying to persuade him to review for Jeffrey).

Southey, who morosely recalled 'the bleak Edinburgh winds' and his 'shivering antipathy to the long cheerless streets of your new town', explained in 1809 to H. C. Standert, a Taunton surgeon with literary leanings, how he had 'refused 10 guineas per sheet with the promise of a great advance for the Edinburgh upon the grounds of my total dissent from all its principles of morals and politics as well as taste'.[6]

De Quincey wrote to Dorothy Wordsworth a day or two after the *Quarterly* first appeared that externally, it was 'a thousand times more *tasty* (as the ladies say) than the Edinb.', and might well succeed through its novelty, combined with the pleasure of 'seeing the tables turned upon Mr Constable's authors' – an illusion, in the belief that the *Review* praised everything that Constable published; and that having now quarrelled with Longman's they would probably provoke Longman's authors too. As for enticing Jeffrey's readers away, 'the public may not fare much the better for exchanging one imbecile dictator for another; but . . . I cannot think [Gifford] so depraved a coxcomb as Mr Jeffrey', and, as an Englishman, Gifford was of course inclined to favour 'a set of rascally English-men opposed to a set of Rascally Scotchmen'. So De Quincey, for one, intended to subscribe to the new periodical, the more so as in his last issue Jeffrey had 'renewed his scurrilous trash about Mr Wordsworth'.

He added that as there was now also a *London Review*, 'the 3 rival powers make equal pretentions; all the way down Fleet Street and the Strand you see them lying side by side'. Whereas the *Edinburgh* in its arrogance used to announce itself by a single sentence, 'The Edinburgh Review is this day arrived', it was now rivalled by 'The Quarterly Review is this day published'.[7]

It was high time, in any case, that an opposite political view was stated in public, and a vehicle be provided for the many writers everlastingly seething with rage over Jeffrey and his colleagues. The political and literary monopoly was over.

In 1814, when Thomas Carlyle was on his first visit to Edinburgh, experiencing 'the fine Princes St tide of human life', the raw but ambitious youth from the west country shepherded about the capital by Campbell, an older and more sophisticated acquaintance, he caught a glimpse of another young man some ten years older than himself, who had made his mark in the Edinburgh literary world.

They were near Register House when Campbell nudged Thomas and murmured, as he glanced at a figure approaching them, '*Isle of Palms*; Wilson!' Thomas took meticulous note of this minor celebrity:

> a very tall strongly-built impetuous-looking man . . . with a profusion of blond hair, with large flashing countenance of the statuesque sort, flashing pair of blue eyes, which were fixed as if on something far off, was impetuously striding along, regarding nobody to right or left, and with large strides stepping along . . . His clothing was rough (I think some loose, whitish jacket of kersey-stuff), hat of broadish brim, on the big massive head, seemed to have known many showers in its time; but what struck me most was the glance of those big blue eyes, stern yet loving, pointing so authentically to something far away.

Long after he passed, unheeding of the crowd, Carlyle could see his tall figure head and shoulders above passers-by.[8]

Later, when living in Edinburgh, Carlyle would sometimes see him, but only in 1826, when he himself was becoming something of a celebrity, did they meet.

Wilson used to meet the Wordsworths in the Lake District when he stayed at his house at Elleray, and Dorothy, despite her fears for his at present idle disposition, approved of his 'good understanding, most affectionate heart, and very pleasing manners'.[9] Wilson's hour had not yet come, but a copy of the *Edinburgh Review* which she had seen at his house in spring 1809, in which an article on Burns contained a reference to her brother, brought forth an effusion of rage from the loyal sister: 'a compound of despicable falsehood, malevolence, and folly . . . It would be treating Mr Jeffrey with too much respect to notice any of his *criticisms* . . .'; but would be only right, she thought, to refute him publicly, hoping that De Quincey or some other friend might write to him care of the magazine and certain London papers. 'A private letter to himself would be of no use.'[10]

Attacks on Wordsworth were not allowed, but Scott was not exempt from sharp criticism from brother and sister, starting with *The Lady of the Lake* and continuing with his later poems. 'I love Scott much', wrote Wordsworth to Southey in January 1815, 'and greatly admire his various Tales etc; but it would be superfluous to say to *you* what I must think of the Lord of the Isles as a *Poem*.'[11] Part of this may have stemmed from his soreness at Jeffrey's (and the *Quarterly*'s) ruthless condemnation of his own *Excursion*.

In the *Quarterly*'s early days Jeffrey had written in gratitude to Horner for his promise to contribute to the *Edinburgh*, begging for copy 'as full, and long and popular as you can', and apologising for their having grown 'too factious'. He was inclined to divert part of the blame for this on to his contributors. 'You judge rightly of my limited power, and of the overgrown privileges of some of my subjects.' After words of praise for Crabbe, 'though the wretch has monstrous faults', and criticism of Dugald Stewart's latest work, for 'diffusiveness and want of doctrinal precision' and for its length, 'the sin of all modern writers', Jeffrey disconsolately added the perennial editor's complaint: 'Playfair is in Ireland, – Stewart at Kinneil, – Seymour on the Clyde, – Murray in Peebles-shire, – and Thomson in the Register House. I must be immediately in the printing-office, and anticipate 3 weeks of great discomfort.'[12]

The pattern never seemed to change. Seven years later, in September 1816 he wrote to his father-in-law Charles Wilkes that, in the midst of a *Review*, he was, 'as usual, in great perplexity and huge indignation at the perfidy of my associates. Playfair is in Italy, and so is Brougham. My excellent Horner is here, I am sorry to say, in a very distressed state of health . . . I do not know another individual so much to be lamented, on public and on private grounds', and when only a few months later Horner died in Italy, Jeffrey wrote, 'I have not known any death in my time which has occasioned so deep and so general a regret, nor . . . so warm and so honourable a testimony from men of all parties', for 'the pride and the ornament' of his circle. Horner's death was a great loss to the *Review* as well as to his many friends.[13]

Jeffrey's burden, heavy and unremitting, averaged writing one article a month for the paper besides slaving as its editor. In six years and twenty-six issues he had contributed seventy-nine articles, as Cockburn recorded, ranging through 'metaphysics, politics, biography, morals, poetry, travels, political economy, and some physical science'.[14] Part of his frantic activity had at first been doubtless to stave off distress and loneliness after his wife died, as was his constant social activity, at least before he met Charlotte Wilkes.

Those who took most against Jeffrey – besides offended poets and essayists – were strong, individual personalities who instinctively saw in him a rival. To Wilson, and hence to his wife, he was 'a horrid little man', to which she added revealingly, 'held in as high estimation here as the Bible'.[15]

In December 1809, urging Horner and the Whigs to 'do something popular and effective' in Parliament, Jeffrey advised him to abandon his 'aristocratical feelings' and side with the democrats. 'Do you not see that the whole nation is now divided into *two,* and only two, parties – the timid, sordid, selfish worshippers of power and adherents of the Court, and the dangerous, discontented, half noble, half mischievous advocates for reform and innovation? *Between* these stand the Whigs; without popularity, power, or consequence of any sort . . . utterly inefficient.'[16]

Before he could have received this letter Horner was writing to Murray (23 December) on his own anxiety that the *Review* was overstepping the mark in its political views, and regretting its indulgence in 'personal and merely party considerations', to the detriment of its own reputation. 'I am never afraid of any thing that Jeffrey does', he added, 'but I never open a new number without trembling for the possible indiscretions of his most able and most entertaining colleagues.'[17]

Horner was often able to set the record straight with Jeffrey's critics. 'Though Jeffrey often trifles with a subject expressly', he told John Murray in 1815, 'and often argues for exhibition, he never leaves me in doubt, when he means to do so, and when he is for the time in earnest.'[18]

Jeffrey's effect on people was vividly summed up by the American George Ticknor, when they met in Washington in 1814. He made an instant impression, as many small men do, entering a room 'looking self-satisfied, and with a light step', easily accosting strangers 'with a freedom and familiarity' which, while putting the young at ease, disconcerted those accustomed to a decorous society. On any subject introduced he would launch 'with a torrent of remarks', though this volubility was soon recognised as in tune with his ideas and not, like other impetuous speakers, gaining time by repetition. His fervent eloquence was 'as compact and logical as if he were contending for a victory in the schools', yet one quickly saw that this showed only a fraction of his potential.

Nor was he trying to show off his wit, 'his mind is full to overflowing, and conversation is his relief and pleasure'.[19]

On his return from America in 1814 Jeffrey had 'found the affairs of the *Review* in some degree of backwardness and confusion', and needed help to restore the situation. Regarding Tom Moore as of 'manly and noble independence' and with the likely skill at a 'classical, philosophical, poetical article, – such as a recent one in the *Quarterly* on Aristophanes', he was ready to offer more than the going rate of twenty guineas a (printed) sheet for 'contributions of the first order': thirty at least, probably more. Suspecting that an indirect approach might succeed best, he begged Samuel Rogers to make overtures to Moore.[20]

Louis Simond remarked in 1811 that the *Quarterly*, launched in opposition on almost every subject, could yet hardly rival the *Edinburgh*, which had 'founded a new school, destined to be the model for the critics of the nineteenth century'.[21]

Mrs Grant found the new magazine inferior 'in brilliancy and critical acumen to its antagonist'; but grieving to see 'wit and truth' on opposing sides while the first gained the instant advantage, it was 'easy to foretell what side will finally triumph', an idealistic prophecy not to be fulfilled. She adds shrewdly, 'Our metaphysicians are not the votaries of pleasure . . . they are *mischievously* orderly and moral, abstemious and decent; their whole end is the love of power'.[22] Mrs Grant, at that time still living in Stirling, had not yet met the literary lions who were to beat a path to her door in Edinburgh.

Scott had 'discovered' James Hogg, who came to Edinburgh in 1810, where after early struggles like *The Spy* he published the successful *Queen's Wake* in 1813. On its publication, like many new authors he tramped the city streets nervously peering into booksellers' windows, too scared to enter and ask its progress. But he began to meet the literary figures, partly through his friendship with the Rev. Robert Morehead of St Paul's Episcopal Chapel in York Place.

When Hogg's patron the Duke of Buccleuch, who in 1816 gave him a rent-free lease of Altrive, a farm near St Mary's Loch, died, Hogg lost a valuable backer, while thoughtless friends descended on him in the country and ate up his provisions, so that he fled back to Edinburgh to escape. He stayed for some months at Teviot Row, George Square with his hatter friend John Grieve, a man of literary discernment, and had the day-time run of house and books, and visiting with Robert Gillies – perhaps his happiest period. Gillies had begun working on German philosophers still unknown in Britain, including the poet Grillparzer (1817–20).[23]

Hogg had many influential admirers, who were amazed on meeting this poetic shepherd. There were Lord and Lady MacDonald, Sir John Trevelyan, John Kemble, and other Southerners who had never met such a man. A great friend in need was Mrs Brooke Richmond, hunter and horsewoman, an ebullient admirer.[24]

Hogg's literary progress was still chequered, however, with several changes of publisher. He was eager to meet John Wilson, who, he had been told, had 'hair like eagles' feathers, and nails like birds' claws: a red beard, and an uncommon degree of wildness in his looks' – a description not wholly exaggerated. At last he summoned courage to invite Wilson to dine one afternoon at his Gabriel's Road lodgings, with his encourager John Grieve. Wilson proved 'a man after my own heart', and they became almost inseparable.[25]

Quite early in his marriage, in 1812 John Wilson had published *The Isle of Palms*, a poem on which he had been working for some time. The somewhat over-blown and unlikely romance of a young couple wrecked on a South Sea island (including the birth of their child with apparently no trouble to either), which earned enough success in Edinburgh to bring him to literary notice. Scott was impressed, if with reservations: 'an excellent, warm-hearted, and enthusiastic young man' – 'something too much, perhaps, of the latter quality.'[26]

After a few years of his writing poetry in Edinburgh and Elleray, the family lost severely through the dishonesty of an uncle who had managed Wilson's late father's estate – perhaps a blessing in disguise. The couple moved to his mother's in Edinburgh, where her skilful management kept the family together, and Wilson was called to the bar. It was not long before he noticed a certain lack of vocation, and a great preference for walking in the Highlands. It was his wholly unorthodox taking of his wife on such an expedition that somewhat shocked Mrs Grant over his 'happy Bohemianism'.

She was distinctly so when in the summer of 1815 John Wilson carried off his wife for a Highlands walking tour. Even gentlemen were sometimes viewed askance by Highland farmers and crofters, let alone innkeepers, when they travelled without a carriage, a valet, and smart luggage; but to take a *lady* . . .!

'This gentle and rather elegant Englishwoman is to walk with her mate, who carries her wardrobe and his own . . . through all the odd bye-paths in the central Highlands, where they propose to sleep in such cottages as English eyes never saw before.' How were they to convince people that they were 'gentlefolk'?[27]

The following year she was describing Wilson as 'the most provoking creature imaginable . . . young, handsome, wealthy, witty', exuberant, learned, happy with wife and family and with no discernible vices. 'Yet his wonderful eccentricity would put any body but his wife wild' – she fortunately seemed 'made on purpose for him' and actually able to control him.[28]

His *City of the Plague,* published in 1816, was in total contrast to the fulsome *Palms*, 'the gloomiest and ghastliest of studies in the charnel-house style'. But a complete change now overtook him, and at a time when the periodicals had become highly political, he abandoned poetry for literary and political criticism.

Wilson had long talked of launching a rival to Constable's *Review* which must be 'bold, uncompromising, *out-spoken*' with 'originality, freedom, and freshness of style'. These qualities he evidently did not allot to either the *Edinburgh* or the *Quarterly*.

The perceptive publisher William Blackwood, meanwhile, saw a thriving future in Edinburgh's New Town, still generally visualised in these early decades as merely a suburb for the well-to-do upper classes. Even now legal, professional, academic and other business was still centred in the old city. There were the castle, University, courts, libraries, Royal Exchange, College of Surgeons, Heriot's Hospital, Watson's, the Royal Infirmary, churches, Assembly Hall, and Holyrood – not to mention the trade centres of culture, booksellers, printers and publishers. Blackwood, who saw beyond all this, in 1816 moved his shop and offices to a spacious suite at 17 Princes Street, till then a fashionable confectioner's. Amid forecasts of inevitable doom he opened his bookseller's shop and publishing offices.

He too was planning yet another rival to the *Review*, and on 1 April 1817, at the age of forty, he launched the *Edinburgh Monthly Magazine*. During the eight years of the *Quarterly* so far it had been noticeable that beside the *Edinburgh*'s lightness and wit it was heavy artillery, and it sold at a loss. With the warning of Hogg's short-lived *Spy* in 1810, a failed weekly grind, only the low-grade *Scots Magazine* still existed as a purely literary journal, and Blackwood thought a new monthly might succeed. The field seemed wide open to fire another salvo at the *Edinburgh* and the Whigs. Hogg joined Blackwood in this, as did Thomas Pringle, who had had a similar idea.[29]

Pringle, born in 1789 to a farming family near Kelso, was lame from a hip injury caused by a childhood accident, and generally used crutches, but he maintained a gentle, cheerful attitude, was devout and a lover of justice. At Edinburgh University, studious but not brilliant, he started writing poetry. He lived up to his idealism. On the opening night of Joanna Baillie's *Family Legend,* hearing that the 'Edinburgh Reviewers' were to turn out in order to damn it with catcalls, Pringle chivalrously gathered forty or fifty young men armed with clubs, who filled the pit and, the moment they heard a murmur of criticism from the audience, started to cheer, shout and clap, supplemented by the banging of Pringle's crutches.

Pringle had a dull job copying documents for the Commissioners of Public Records, and compensated by waking early to compose his poetry, which began to be published from 1809. He now joined Blackwood to edit the new journal with James Cleghorn, an actuary, editor of the *Farmer's Magazine.*[30]

Their opening number was decent but unexciting, although the list of contributors was respectable, including Lockhart, Wilson, Brewster and Hogg, who provided a story. There were verses and antiquarian articles, and Pringle produced a piece on gypsies, most of whose information he had gleaned from Scott. Gillies wrote a long review of Hogg's *Dramatic Tales.*

Unfortunately by the time they had produced only two issues the governing body fell out.[31] Pringle joined Cleghorn in abandoning Blackwood (who bought them out) for Archibald Constable, taking their subscribers' list with them.[32] Here they continued as *Constable's Edinburgh Magazine,* while in September 1817 Blackwood reissued himself under the reduced title *Blackwood's Magazine,* under which it was to flourish until 1980. Blackwood re-enlisted Hogg, Wilson, Lockhart and Gillies as well as Scott, and continued as editor for seventeen years until his death in 1834.

The rift which occurred when he had hardly started as a magazine publisher led to an enormous expansion of literary periodical writing in Edinburgh, largely because of the furore caused by an item in his very first issue, the 'Chaldee Manuscript'. The new *Blackwood*'s entered the world in a cacophony of controversy.

In its inception the 'manuscript' was the work of Hogg, a thinly disguised allegory mocking Pringle and Cleghorn and pillorying Constable and the Whigs. It was so grotesque that the victims might better have laughed at or ignored it, but many took serious offence.

Hogg had compiled his squib at Yarrow and forwarded it to Blackwood in Edinburgh, who did not care for it much, but showed it to Wilson and Lockhart who 'laughed till they were sick', ran up extensive additions and persuaded him in a rash moment to publish it in his first issue. It purported to be a newly discovered ancient manuscript and was intended as 'a sly history' of the 'great literary battle' with Pringle. The thinly disguised account of Edinburgh's literary characters hit the city like a storm, arousing rage, dismay, threats of libel action and accusations of blasphemy at its parody of the Bible.

It is tedious stuff, indigestible to the uninitiated: but most people in Edinburgh were in the know, and keenly felt the insult.

Taking fright at the reaction, Blackwood withdrew the 'Manuscript' after the first two hundred copies, and reprinted the issue minus the offending item, following up with an apology in the second issue. But the 'Manuscript' gave his new magazine a reputation for daring that it was now expected to keep up.[33]

Hogg had composed chapters 1, 2, parts of 3, and the last; most of the rest, in which the chief parodied characters appear, was by Wilson and Lockhart. The story, in (not very good) Biblical or *Pilgrim's Progress* prose, would be wholly incomprehensible without a key.

It ends with a great tumult, signifying the struggle between Blackwood-cum-Tories and Constable-cum-Whigs, whose outcome remains of course unrevealed.

A few characters remain unidentified; some are described flatteringly, some neutrally and some insultingly, notably Charles Kirkpatrick Sharpe. The object was doubtless, in a rather schoolboyish way, to offend as many as possible, and its success gave the new magazine a notoriety by which it went from strength to strength. Besides Wilson, Lockhart and Hogg, Blackwood garnered such distinguished writers and personalities as David Brewster, Barry Cornwall, Sir Thomas Dick Lauder and Professor George Dunbar. There were also Robert Gillies, Major Thomas Hamilton, who was to write *Cyril Thornton* and *Men and Manners in America;* and later, John Galt and David Moir, or 'Delta'.

In February 1818 Wilson's maternal uncle Robert Sym, WS, became a regular contributor under the name 'Timothy Tickler'. He was a grand Tory living in George Square, in Hogg's words 'an uncommonly fine-looking elderly gentleman, about seven feet high, and as straight as an arrow'. He was also a keen amateur violinist, an accomplishment Hogg found irresistible.[34]

Whereas the *Edinburgh* stirred up reaction, whether violently hostile or supportive, by deliberate intellectual provocation, *Blackwood's* quickly assumed a role of pinpricks and in-jokes. A few were ingenious, the most notable being Lockhart's fake review in February 1819 of a non-existent work called *Peter's Letters to his Kinsfolk,* of which he quoted copious extracts, all written by himself. It purported to be yet another critical view of Edinburgh society, thought, and leading characters, on the lines of the many already published from Edward Topham to Louis Simond, and it evoked such interest that people were soon clamouring for the book, and Lockhart found himself having to write it in full.

This gave rise to another spoof: when published, the book was labelled '2nd edition', the 'first' being the wholly imaginary work existing only in Lockhart's 'review'.

Lockhart occasionally gave an approving description or criticism, and a few characters named in *Peter's Letters* profited. One was Coleridge, roused by a favourable mention by 'Peter', together with the *Edinburgh*'s apparent intention of preventing sales of his work by its sheer hostility. Coleridge, therefore, in September 1820, rehashed some of his onslaughts in *Blackwood's.*[35] Another of whom 'Peter' gave a favourable account – he could hardly do otherwise – was John Wilson's younger brother James, by inclination a naturalist and keen Wernerian, but like so many of Edinburgh's gifted amateurs obliged to make his career in the law. He started to contribute to *Blackwood's* as nature-lover, poet, traveller and angler, and may also have written some of the humorous sketches. Among his essays were 'On the Kraken' followed by 'On the Sea Serpent' (March and April 1818), and in November, 'Zoological Inaccuracies of Poets'.[36]

One imaginary character was 'Ensign O'Doherty', based on Thomas

Hamilton's brother, 'a particularly handsome and gentlemanly young man in the army',[37] and created by a versatile Irish journalist named William Maginn (1793–1842), who had been a boy prodigy at Dublin University, graduating at the age of fourteen, and was at present living as a free-lance writer in London. He contributed to *Blackwood's*, from a distance from 1819, and in June 1820 came to Edinburgh to make himself known. It was a Sunday, Blackwood was in the country with his family, and finding his Newington house empty, Maginn was impressed that he was able to open the front gate and circle the house, looking in every window. In Ireland, he affirmed, 'no such temptations were allowed to prowlers'.

He therefore called at *Blackwood's* office next day, giving no name but asking for the publisher in an exaggerated Irish accent. Assuming he was an irate reader, Blackwood managed to avoid revealing the author's name in a long conversation at cross-purposes about 'O'Doherty', until Maginn in assumed rage confronted him with Blackwood's own letters. 'A cordial shake of the hand and a hearty laugh' soon followed and another friendship was launched. Maginn continued as a contributor until 1828, in 1825 became Paris correspondent of the shortlived *Representative,* and thence had a fairly mercurial career varying between fame and fortune and scanty earnings.[38]

One of the first issues of *Blackwood's* had also contained a slamming attack by Lockhart on the radical Leigh Hunt, representative of what he and Wilson termed 'The Cockney School of Poetry'. One of the sins for which the snobbish Lockhart could not forgive its members, who included Hazlitt and Keats, was their relatively humble background. They were criticised as circumscribed in views, metropolitan, sometimes almost trivial. 'Hampshire outvied Parnassus', says the journalist Cyrus Redding, dismissing them as 'an affected lackadaisical school . . . a sort of literary effeminacy'. Wilson also attacked them mercilessly in *Blackwood's,* as usual pushing his ridicule too far. At the same time he anonymously savaged Coleridge.[39]

Coleridge's reputation had gained little from his *Biographia Literaria* published that year. The *Edinburgh* had also been ruthless in attacking 'Christabel', as Coleridge comments in *Biographia Literaria,* 'with a malignity and a spirit of personal hatred' – and this from a man who 'has repeatedly pronounced it the first poem of its kind in the language'. He wrote bitterly to John Murray that the world ought to accept the views of Southey, Scott, Byron and others of his own 'Learning and Genius', rather than the 'wretched and . . . mystical Jargon of the Examiner and Edinburgh Review'. He was still more incensed by the 'outrageous' review in *Blackwood's* in October, generally held to be Wilson's work, particularly wounding as it revived a personal attack on Coleridge for having deserted his family. He would gladly have brought a legal action, but was advised against it by Crabb Robinson and Wordsworth.[40]

In March 1819 Coleridge met Blackwood personally and thrashed out his grievance, ending in agreement provided the magazine kept clear of 'private slander and personal malignity', and maintained opposite principles to the *Review*, 'moral, political and religious'.[41]

Wordsworth, who took criticism personally, and hard, fulminated as much about *Blackwood's* as he had about the *Review*. Early in 1819, when the magazine had existed about eighteen months, he wrote angrily to the Rev. Francis Wrangham, 'I know little of Blackwood's Magazine and wish to know less. I have seen in it articles so infamous that I do not chuse to let it enter my doors.' He had some time back refused it (civilly, he hastens to add) when personally sent him by the publishers. As it happened Wordsworth was not keen on periodicals, or even on new books, so was rather wasting his anger. He adds later that the articles which so 'disgusted' him were personal, 'referring to myself and acquaintances, especially Coleridge'.

Although the following year Wilson modified his criticism in 'Essays on the Lake School of Poetry', two articles at the start of 1819 entitled 'Letters from the Lakes, translated from the German of Philip Kempferhausen' actually reported conversations with Southey and Wordsworth, and it was these which so incensed the latter. Intrusion on personal life so prevalent in the early twenty-first century was then so frowned on that Wordsworth's reaction was perfectly normal. [42]

Wordsworth considered that the concurrent existence of two such reviews in Edinburgh had proved 'very injurious to free discussion', making it impossible for a writer not in public office to be heard, 'if his opinions should not suit either of those periodical publications'.[43]

Most *Blackwood* articles were of a high standard, but as vitriolic as the *Edinburgh*'s ever were; even clergy and philosophers like Drs Chalmers and Playfair came in for a slating. Wilson made hay with all this, and under his not inappropriate *nom de plume* 'The Leopard', stretched his claws.

There was plenty of other reaction to all these magazines. Walter Scott writes in August 1817 that Jeffrey again wants him to review for him (on the seventeenth-century Jacobitically inclined Scottish historian James Kirkton), and he would in fact have liked to do it, but is promised to the *Quarterly* and cannot do both. Charles Kirkpatrick Sharpe thought this a pity, as 'I believe the Whigs could get nobody but yourself capable of reviewing his period of Scottish history'. Scott was at this time already suffering 'spasms', early warnings of gall-bladder trouble, although at this stage he would endure agony for a night, and next day feel perfectly well.[44]

Thomas Carlyle, once settled (or rather, perennially unsettled) in Edinburgh, was accessible to both the *Edinburgh* and the *Quarterly*. In March

1817 he wrote to Robert Mitchell from Kirkcaldy that the latest *Quarterly* contained 'a great deal of foul & nauseating stuff', though it did at last give the Rev. Henry Duncan credit for his 'Parish Bank for the Savings of the Industrious'. A few months later he was writing to James Johnston there that the writers were dogmatic, displaying their learning 'to an unpleasant degree', were 'of that minute scholastic nature' (declaimed the 23-year-old Carlyle) 'which is eminently distinguished from knowledge' – and scared stiff by the thought of revolution. However, in its April number (XXXIII), the paper redeemed itself slightly by a measured criticism of Dugald Stewart's 'Dissertation' in the supplementary volume of the *Encyclopaedia Britannica* which Carlyle contrasted favourably with the *Edinburgh Review*'s lavish praise.[45]

Carlyle was characteristically not impressed by the spate of magazines flooding Edinburgh: Constable's new product the *Edinburgh Magazine,* a retitling of the former *Scots' Magazine* (August 1817), was a rival to *Blackwood's* own as *Blackwood's Edinburgh Magazine*; and the *Edinburgh Observer or Town & Country Magazine* appeared on 13 September by Peter Hill & Co. the booksellers and stationers, at 200 High Street. Carlyle observes caustically, 'I cannot pretend to say what this influx of magazines indicates or portends.'[46]

Indeed it had become an age of ambitious literary magazines. Soon afterwards came *The Metropolitan,* to which David Moir – 'Delta' of *Blackwood's* – James Hogg and Moore were all contributors.[47]

Of two other important publications at this time one was new, the other long established: the *Scotsman* weekly and the *Encyclopaedia Britannica.*

The *Scotsman*, first published in January 1817, was a joint product of two journalist brothers, John and William Ritchie (born in 1778 and 1781), and Charles Maclaren (born 1782), a Custom House clerk. William Ritchie had practised law for some years combined with writing for local papers, but when in 1816 an article exposing the shortcomings of the Edinburgh Infirmary was refused, he joined with Maclaren to publish their own paper, Maclaren editing the political items and Ritchie the legal and literary. From 1818 to 1820, while Ritchie was abroad, his place was filled by John Ramsay McCulloch (born 1789), a political economist. On Ritchie's return Maclaren gave up his Custom House post to take on the editorship, and until 1822, when McCulloch left the paper, it was a triple production. As an influential opposition paper it was, naturally, hated by the Tories.

McCulloch had studied mathematics under Professor Leslie, whom he admired, and Dr Thomas Brown, whose lectures thoroughly put him off metaphysics. Hazlitt found McCulloch (a view shared by Wilson) 'dry, plodding, husky, stiff' and of 'sublime dulness', though Henry Cockburn praised the dogged determination which had turned the ill-educated, unpromising youth from Kirkcudbright into an Edinburgh student with the passion of 'a lad who discovers in time what he has lost', succeeding in mathematics, general knowledge and political economy, the last of which occupied most of his career.[48]

Maclaren was secured by Archibald Constable to become also literary editor of the *Encyclopaedia Britannica.* This was started as a three-volume work edited by the printer William Smellie and published in numbers between 1768 and 1771, as a dictionary of arts and sciences for a 'society of Gentlemen in Scotland'. According to Constable it was launched by Colin McFarquhar, printer, in partnership with the leading engraver Andrew Bell. A second edition, extending to ten volumes, included history and biography (1777–84), and a third ran to fifteen (1788–97). All proved very successful, the third selling about thirteen thousand copies. The fourth edition in twenty volumes appeared in 1801–10.

Constable now became involved, and different editors, ownerships and trustees complicated the history until in 1812 Constable bought the whole copyright, and now planned to issue the sixth edition, to include Dugald Stewart's *Dissertation . . . Exhibiting a General View of the Progress of Metaphysical and Ethical Philosophy,* which was to prove so influential. Stewart's name and Humphrey Davy's (who in the event could not contribute) were a great draw to other writers. Stewart, paid £1600, was 'the great ornament of our book'. Playfair was next to agree, though offered considerably less, but died before the work was completed.[49]

After much discussion the editorship was accepted by Macvey Napier, who had studied at both Edinburgh and Glasgow Universities, and Constable allowed him to edit a new edition to include the supplement, in twenty-five volumes published in parts as the seventh edition. As literary editor Constable secured Charles Maclaren of the *Scotsman,* being a staunch Whig and sound historian well versed in science, and both Maclaren and Napier continued on the work, even after Constable had to sell out to the Blacks in 1826.[50]

Meanwhile *Blackwood's,* capitalising on the furore which had greeted the 'Chaldee Manuscript', continued to be a sell-out. Its vivacity and provocativeness made it a talking-point among the discerning, while the authors Wilson and Lockhart sheltered in anonymity behind Blackwood. These real perpetrators of 'Chaldee' seemed beyond suspicion, as they were employed elsewhere.

Both were extraordinarily prolific. Wilson, who compiled a list of imaginary subjects, claimed he could write a whole issue in two days, while Lockhart could produce a full printed sheet (thirty-two columns) in a day.[51]

On a personal level things were not always smooth. The waspish Lockhart and his witticisms were inclined to tread on toes. 'He was a mischievous Oxford puppy', declared Hogg, 'of whom I was terrified, dancing after the young ladies, and drawing caricatures of every one.' He found meeting him in company uncomfortable, and Lockhart liked to play tricks to confuse him, usually in a way difficult to quarrel with. The author of *The Scottish Man of Feeling* comments, 'Lockhart's dislike is prompted chiefly by politics, general snobbery, and the malicious pleasure of saying unpleasant things.'[52]

The next imaginary venture spun by Wilson and friends was a pretended shooting expedition to Deeside in August 1819 by the editor and his contributors, during which they recorded 'conversations', recklessly mingling real, disguised and invented characters: Wastle (De Quincey), Morris (Lockhart), the Ettrick Shepherd, Tickler, Kempferhausen (Gillies – because of his German inclinations), and so on. With typical insensitivity it included one harmless real character, Dr James Scott, a well-known dentist in Glasgow and Edinburgh nicknamed 'the Odontist', and ascribing to him non-existent works. It all savours rather of practical jokery of the Theodore Hook kind, which they and many readers thought funny.

This holiday fiction, written up as 'Christopher in the Tent', proved so popular that it was continued in the September issue, introducing new characters including Blackwood himself, Ballantyne, Pringle and Cleghorn, the Earl of Fife, the Duke and Duchess of Gordon and King Leopold of the Belgians. 'Christopher' was Wilson, still masquerading under the title of 'the veiled Editor', and somewhat on the lines of *Peter's Letters* they advertised another imaginary publication on his supposed adventures, entitled *Autobiography of Christopher North, Esq.*, Editor of *Blackwood's.* The author pretended to be sixty-eight or more years old.

Thenceforward 'Christopher North' was accepted as being editor of *Blackwood's*, and by that title John Wilson is better known to this day.

As for the so-called expedition's literary content, it was shot through with typical contemporary malice. The party is met by a fisherman and an Edinburgh caddy (apparently a real one, John Mackay of Frederick Street) with 'an old baggage-wagon, purchased at Jock's Lodge'. They conveniently find lying around a copy of *Transactions of the Royal Society,* and pretend surprise that page 372 has been 'riddled with shot'. It proves to be the first page of Macvey Napier's essay on Lord Bacon, which *Blackwood's* had ridiculed as impenetrable. Napier was a confirmed Whig, hence the scorn. Then they hark back to Byron's tirade of 1809 against critics, especially Jeffrey, in 'English Bards and Scotch Reviewers', and blame the *Edinburgh* for inciting it by contempt for Byron's poems. But 'What a moment of mortification' – a few years later when *Childe Harold* appears, behold a Jeffreyan volte-face: 'Down he goes on his knees, and worships the rising star. Puff! puff! puff!' (This comment smacks of Wilson.) And so forth.

The September issue also contained a lively account of Edinburgh's desolation during the summer or vacation months. 'Christopher' having returned to see the issue to the printer's, after surveying the abandoned streets and bought snuff from 'the fair Miss Fanny Forman', a tobacconist in Princes Street, thankfully goes back to the Tent.[53]

It was Lockhart who first suggested *Noctes Ambrosianae*, a feature which ran from March 1822 until February 1835. The first issue was supposedly by North and 'O'Doherty' – probably by Maginn, as was also the July issue in the name of Byron and O'Doherty. Wilson, however, was the master-mind, and of the seventy-one issues he composed more than half, assisted by Lockhart, Hogg and Maginn. It became the favourite article in the magazine, or 'Maga' as they regularly called it – especially in America.

While Blackwood continued as business director, gradually Wilson took over editorship. In November 1820 he became Professor of Moral Philosophy at the University (see Chapter 31), and perhaps his increased years and responsibility, along with Lockhart's move to London in December 1825 to edit the *Quarterly*, softened the sarcasm and his everlasting attacks on 'the Cockney School'. *Blackwood's* continued to attract such contributors as De Quincey, 'Delta', Allan Cunningham and even Mrs Hemans.[54]

Noctes Ambrosianae purported to be the critical dialogues of the clique, meeting regularly at Ambrose's Tavern in Gabriel's Road (about which Lockhart had written in *Peter's Letters)*. These too were largely imaginary and often much exaggerated. Read today, having lost their topicality, they seem tame enough, but in contemporary Edinburgh made an immediate appeal. Some exchanges still have pungency, such as an impassioned argument on the suitability of Calton Hill as the site for a National Monument.[55]

It took Mrs Grant little time to perceive the intellect behind the schoolboy malice of *Blackwood's*. However, although she had thought of sending copies to her friend Mrs Gorman, she decided that their content was too 'local' – too topical for outsiders' comprehension, and 'their abundant wit and humour' would need heavy annotation.[56] Later she observed to Mrs Hook how odd it was that 'all the wits (for wits they certainly are) . . . should be from the West of Scotland': starting with Lockhart, 'a handsome, gentlemanlike young man, in company reserved and silent, yet evidently a diligent observer', and the 'wit' behind Lauerwinkel. Sir William Hamilton's brother Thomas was author of *Memoirs of Ensign O'Doherty*, and John Wilson, admirer of Wordsworth, was 'a man of genius and talents, much goodness of heart, and considerable eccentricity'. (She could never get over that Highlands walking-tour with his wife.) His brother James she thought his equal 'in talent and judgment', with 'a sort of peculiar quiet humour, which is irresistible'; and finally, their uncle Robert Sym was author of the *Letters of Timothy Tickler* to Hogg and others.[57]

To Mrs Gorman in 1819 she described Edinburgh's magazine situation:

its two monthlies were 'the squires and precursors of those two formidable knights', the quarterlies *Edinburgh* and *London* (her name for the *Quarterly)*. The more recent *Blackwood's* 'abounds in attic salt' and personality. 'It is supported by a club of young wits' who 'certainly do not regard man', and this 'cruelly witty magazine' now sold four thousand a month in Edinburgh and as many again in London.[58]

In 1822 Josiah Wedgwood's wife wrote to her sister, Mme Sismondi, with some amusement that *Blackwood's* was 'always running at the E. Review and at all the authors with a malignity that I don't know how to account for. A number is regularly sent to Mackintosh at Brooks, he does not know from whom, and it generally contains some abuse of himself. It is astonishing the ill-will he excites, and I do believe it is nothing but his ill-manners.' It might have been equally jealousy at his remarkable 'cleverness', for politically he was moderate.[59]

The self-educated James Hogg, from his unprivileged background, had achieved literary success largely by his own efforts. Moving now in exalted circles, although never attempting to soften his rugged exterior he appeared (as the journalist Cyrus Redding put it) like one 'born in a higher grade of life'.[60]

Wilson, unfairly patronising, needled him too much, and when *Noctes Ambrosianae* became established Hogg complained that he 'made a show of him in Blackwood'. In the dialogues, 'Wilson is too bad, for he makes me say things I would not dream of uttering'. His manner was much quieter than the boisterous figure Wilson portrays, and he was too well informed to make many of the statements credited to him. According to Wilson, though good-humoured and basically shrewd, he was naïve and disarmingly vain, and his conversation had a quaint drollery.[61]

While at Altrive Hogg had married his sweetheart for ten years, Margaret Phillips of a large farming family in Annandale. She was nearly twenty years his junior and had had many admirers, but he was long her secret preference. They had five children. While Wilson's excessive caricature – 'Socrates-like wisdom and Falstaffian humour', writes Hogg's daughter in her life of her father, 'bombastic' – often offended Hogg, it offended his wife still more, and many people thought the ridicule overdone. Scott and Lockhart urged him to ignore it, and he never actually took legal action against Wilson, but it was enough at one time to engender a 'coolness'. Cyrus Redding gives a restrained judgment in his reminiscences of 'the frolics of Wilson . . . the mischief-making of Lockhart, the Toryism of Sym, and the Whiggism of O'Doherty', in which 'precept and practice were occasionally at war'.[62]

Julian Young records Hogg at his most boisterous on an evening described to him much later by Tom Moore. The occasion was a *Blackwood's* supper at Ambrose's, where Moore as a guest had met a mingled throng: not only Scott, Jeffrey and Lockhart but John Wilson, James Ballantyne, even a few ladies. Two of these were peeresses who had begged for an invitation on hearing that Moore was to be there, and turned up in full evening dress, 'in shoulders' as he put it. As they were unexpected, the others were in ordinary morning dress.

A place had been left vacant between the peeresses – not for Moore but for Hogg, who did not appear until halfway through supper, heralded by the reek of the cattle fair where he had spent the day. He was unconcerned, and quickly made himself at home with his fair neighbours, almost to excess. Once the cloth was withdrawn and the toddy appeared, a song was started, but with not enough zeal for the Shepherd, who clapped both ladies on their bare shoulders yelling like an Indian, 'Noo then, leddies, follow me! Heigh tutti tutt!! Heigh tutti tutti!'

In relating this unsophisticated anecdote, snobbish little Tom 'expressed himself horrified at Scott's want of refinement in giving his countenance to such people as Hogg, and taking part in such orgies as the Noctes Ambrosiane'. No comment.[63]

'I think Wilson the most powerful man in Edingburgh,' wrote Benjamin Haydon on leaving the city in December 1820, after Wilson's professorial election. He recorded how on first calling on Wilson he had found him out, and left his letter of introduction with the servant. 'He sent his man after me – wrenched my hand almost off by a manly grasp.' And he gives one of his perspicacious descriptions: 'Wilson, a wild ungovernable man of genius, without principle as much as a bull – fair complexion, straight nose, hanging brows, dark blue eyes, firm mouth, shaggy light hair – nervous, agitated, & vigorous in his expression, he gave one the idea of a wild child of the Mountains, not perfectly broken in by education . . .'

His impression of Lockhart was very different: 'full face, pale, broad forehead, black eyes, inarticulate utterance; don't like his laugh or look. He came up to me evidently affected, & welcomed me by taking both my hands . . . I like Wilson & suspect Lockhart'.[64]

Lockhart, looking back on his career in later years, admitted that in *Blackwood's* days he was still 'a raw boy': ten years younger than Wilson, he perversely inclined to attack men and institutions of which he knew nothing. He himself was too young in judgment and Wilson was 'a friend whose genius was perhaps the most unbalanced in the history of literature'.

He was, however, fulfilling a long-established ambition to become a writer. On his return from Oxford to Edinburgh in 1813 he had actually sat down to write a novel, but abandoned it as hopeless when *Waverley* captured the public. He was also considering the possibility of a periodical of his own when he met Blackwood, and on the strength of a fee generously advanced for a future German translation had gone off to Germany for the 1817 vacation, where a letter from Blackwood informed him of the rivalry with Constable and his own determination to start a new magazine. Lockhart promised to contribute.[65] By the time he returned from Germany Blackwood had already started his first unsuccessful venture.

When the great rows broke out between the papers the Whigs were irritated at *Blackwood's* new Tory rivalry, having 'considered persiflage their own fee-simple'; they singled out Wilson and Lockhart as scapegoats, Lockhart, though the youngest and least experienced of the Blackwood group, bearing most of the blame, 'Wilson passing for being a very eccentric fellow, and I for a cool one'. He had the buoyancy of youth, however, and in view of the all but crushing attacks, he needed it. Defending himself many years later to Haydon (1838), whom he had at first criticised for his Leigh Hunt connection, he claimed that in his inexperience he had been drawn in by Wilson to help with 'some squibberies', and had done so 'without malice', over Haydon or anyone else.

When he similarly attacked Hunt, Hazlitt and Shelley, he knew nothing of them, but wrote in general 'anti-Cockney' terms, aggravated by 'coolness, clearness of head, and logic'. It was not just that Lockhart was very young, he was as Lang puts it, 'constitutionally a mocker'. His incautious exuberance, however, damaged any hopes of a successful legal career, as long as a Tory government was in office, and his only prospects had to be literary.[66]

As *Blackwood's* progressed its critical attitude became unpredictable, with Coleridge and Haydon (for example) at first insulted, later praised, and even contributors coming in for attack; and when Wilson was angling to become a professor, of Moral Philosophy of all things, it became odder still. On the whole they went for the Whigs, the *Edinburgh*, the 'Cockneys', and Archibald Constable and his stable. A great deal of offence was regularly taken by a great number of people.

Lockhart had many positive qualities, or Scott would not have taken to him. Not that he did not deplore the company he had got into, and with Ballantyne as medium Scott offered him his own commission of writing the historical part of the *Annual Register*, for a fee of £300 a year. When in the autumn of 1818 he invited him to Abbotsford for a couple of days with Wilson, it was to meet (the second) Lord Melville. He was hoping to influence Lockhart to detach himself from the mischief-making Blackwood group.[67] Instead, Lockhart fell in love with Sophia, and Scott acquired him as son-in-law.

At the time of Wilson's professorial election, when the *Scotsman* was abusive to the point of libel, Scott wrote to Lockhart a letter intended to be seen by Wilson, who he hoped would not attempt retaliation. It would be 'like a gentleman fighting with a chimney sweeper – he . . . cannot avoid being smutted in the conflict'. He used the opportunity to warn Lockhart not to let himself go when in society, where there was always someone ready to store up the occasion for future attack. Indeed he should be more careful of his friends, and not join in Wilson's undignified skirmishes, particularly the 'Testimonium', a celebratory poem under the name of 'the Odontist' Dr James Scott, published in *Blackwood's* in July 1820. In this Wilson was at pains to ridicule his critic McCulloch, editor of the *Scotsman*. [68]

Mrs Somerville, who was distantly related to Lockhart, thought him 'too sarcastic to be quite agreeable'. Mrs Grant was becoming impatient with the lot of them. In 1819, before the accident which crippled her, she complained that 'The Blackwood has lost all shame. The last number is perfectly vindictive against the Whig observances in the bitterest satire and the keenest ridicule.' But they were selling 4000 copies, and evidently felt immune to criticism.

She was also disappointed with the latest *Edinburgh*, duller than any she could recall, and apart from 'justly praising Campbell and Samuel Rogers', confined to 'medical, surgical or Broughamical'. The *Quarterly* had strongly criticised Brougham's views on schools, and 'the hostility between these rival powers grows daily warmer', while Blackwood and Constable were also tilting in the lists.[69]

Lockhart's sneering attitude was the more disconcerting to observers as he cut such a handsome figure. Julian, son of the actor Charles Young who consulted Scott over his education when he was fifteen, closely studied the family while they stayed at Abbotsford in 1821, and was struck by Lockhart's 'beauty . . . in the prime of life . . . jet black curly locks' and 'the lustre of his splendid eye'.[70] And Maria Edgeworth, who met Lockhart there in 1823, was surprised to find him so handsome, 'quite unlike his picture in Peter's letters', his striking appearance enhanced by his aquiline, not to say saturnine dark good looks – hand in hand with those sharp, acidulous commentaries.[71]

Lockhart and his family now lived mostly at Chiefswood, on the Abbotsford estate. It was not a happy time for him, with his involvement in the long-drawn-out quarrel with John Scott, of the *London*, and he began to suffer from melancholia. In June 1821 John Ballantyne died, Walter Scott was writing *The Pirate,* and Lockhart himself set about a novel set in ancient Rome, *Valerius,* rather tedious and not very successful. There was an attempt to secure him a legal office but he did not appear enough in the courts to qualify, and in any case was not very good at public speaking. In 1822 he began a second novel, *Adam Blair,* rode to Inveraray to transact legal business, and returned to Edinburgh in July, in time for King George IV's visit.[72]

29
THE LITERATI IN THE FIELD

'You must consider that Edinburgh is a very grave place, and that you live with Philosophers – who are very intolerant of nonsense.'

Sydney Smith to Francis Jeffrey, 7 Aug. 1819, *Letters,* 1953, II.331

A surprising feature of the age is how many of the duels fought – and duels were not uncommon – were for literary reasons and by noted literary figures. Most had to do with libellous publications, and were the outcome of offences committed by the increasing number of magazines. Writers were as inclined to take up the sword, or rather the pistol, as the pen (except when as in the Blackwood/Douglas affair, they took up the whip).

The James Stuart/Alexander Boswell duel was as unfortunate as any, and perhaps the most discreditable. James Stuart, a WS, was a keen and public-spirited Whig, which made him unpopular with Tories among others, for example, when in December 1817 he made a speech at a public meeting – a novelty then just beginning to come into fashion – on the dangers of the city's proposed North Bridge Buildings and their threat to the Calton Hill view.[1]

In January 1821 a group of exasperated Tories launched yet another newspaper, the *Beacon*, editorially shrouded in obscurity though some of its contributors were supposedly of sound calibre, such as Wilson, Lockhart and James Boswell's eldest son Alexander, and surprisingly respectable clergy – and Walter Scott. Mrs Grant, who kept Joseph Cogswell plied with Edinburgh news after his return to America, described to him how the *Beacon* was 'abounding in coarse humor. It is the Scotch John Bull', and she recalled how things had changed over twenty years: formerly it was the Whigs who had 'the triumphs of intellect', but some were now dead and the rest were now 'grown worldly, dry and dull enough'; while the 'rising brood of young Tories sparkle with no common effulgence'.[2]

Cockburn condemns the *Beacon* as showing neither talent nor wit, and as an 'outlet for all anonymous slander' that a 'half defeated party' could heap on more successful rivals. In a celebrated literary brawl James Stuart set about Duncan Stevenson, the printer, in the street with a stick for a 'gross libel'.[3]

Alexander Boswell, then aged forty-six, was described by a neighbour, William Lennox, of Ayr, as six foot two inches tall, muscular, 'quite a model of a man . . . broad chest, head well set on his shoulders, a very noble carriage', and making a good appearance on horseback. Though his face was said to have no single good feature, when 'lighted up with his spirit and vivacity there was a fascination about it'. He was a dedicated Tory, 'well received at the Pavilion, and . . . made a Baronet at the Coronation' (writes John Whishaw).[4] But he fell into the error of making the most of a misguided talent for the lampoon and gibe. During 1821 he contributed frequently items that were often libellous, to *John Bull* in London and the *Beacon* in Edinburgh, and was heading inevitably for a duel. Both Lord Archibald Hamilton and Lord Duncan determined to challenge him, and the latter actually set out for Scotland to do so,[5] but was pre-empted by an earlier challenger. It was an especially unfortunate moment, as Boswell had just returned from the funeral of his brother James, who according to Southey was 'a thoroughly good-natured, inoffensive man, of considerable talents', and had recently published a second edition of Malone's Shakespeare, on which he had been working for years.[6]

The *Beacon's* next major insult was made to another Whig WS, James Gibson (later Sir James Gibson Craig), who, though used to such libels, determined this time to discover the author. He approached the Lord Advocate, Sir William Rae, believing him to be a partner, who after first denying it admitted that he and other public figures had subscribed a bond as sureties for any debt the *Beacon* might incur; so that they now controlled its funds and hence its content. Supporters included Sir William Arbuthnot, the Lord Provost, and the Solicitor General, James Wedderburn.

James Stuart personally demanded from the Lord Advocate a denial of any connection with articles attacking him, and eventually obtained it. Gibson's own enquiries seemed for a time to suggest that Walter Scott might be implicated, but on assurance that he had no such connection, friends intervened to urge an end to such calls, and demanded that the paper be suppressed. Although the bondsmen agreed to withdraw, their implication was now disgracefully revealed, and the *Beacon* disappeared after an existence of only about eight months 'a pitiable mass of blunders and imbecility' as Lockhart put it.[7]

These unsavoury proceedings were like a virus suppressed in one place only to appear in another form. Another rag similar to the *Beacon*, called the *Sentinel*, was next set up in Glasgow, and in this too James Stuart was libelled. Contributors were naturally anonymous; Alexander Boswell himself contributed under the name 'Ignotus'.

Its chief vulgarities were imputations of cowardice, and especially infuriating to Stuart was such doggerel as 'A New Whig Song'.

There's stot-feeder Stuart,
Kent for that fat cow—art,
How gregly he kicks ony ba', man . . .

Your knights o' the pen, man,
Are a' *gentlemen,* man,
Ilk *body's* a *limb* of the law, man;

Tacks, bonds, precognitions,
Bills, wills and petitions,
And *ought* but a *trigger* some draw, man . . .[8]

Stuart took out an action for damages.

Conflicting accounts of the unfolding events proliferated. One broadsheet claiming to set right erroneous accounts in the newspapers relates that, after Stuart had brought his action against the proprietors in March 1822, a stranger accosted him in the Parliament Hall who introduced himself as the editor Borthwick's agent, Borthwick being in prison for debt in Glasgow; and offered to produce all relevant papers, provided the action were dropped. In the event Stuart determined to go to Glasgow and examine the papers there, where they were brought to his hotel from the *Sentinel* offices.[9]

On looking through them he was appalled to find that the author of the most scurrilous was his own relative, almost friend, Alexander Boswell – although Boswell, evidently ashamed, wrote in a disguised hand.

It proved afterwards that Borthwick had no right to the papers, and much was made of this fact later, on the pretence that Stuart therefore had no right to them either, and the Lord Advocate actually indicted Borthwick for the theft.

Stuart returned to Edinburgh to await Boswell's return from London, which he did on Saturday, 23 March at 10 p.m., and according to one version, as he alighted from the mail coach a letter from Lord Rosslyn was put into his hand, which he read by the light of a street lamp. It requested an interview.

On the Monday morning Boswell met Lord Rosslyn at the Waterloo Tavern, who asked if he had composed the verses. Boswell refused to say, but could not deny it. Asked to apologise, which he might well have done, as for a tasteless joke, again he refused, and a duel was now inevitable. Boswell must have felt himself in too deep to withdraw, and in danger of being accused of the very cowardice and 'poltroonery' with which he had so readily larded Stuart; he had in fact anticipated a duel to the extent of asking a friend to act as second, and suggesting that (as he was a practised shot), should he prove victor they escape to the Rhine together to avoid the law.[10]

The affair seems to have been arranged in a very gentlemanly manner, including discussion over the venue, Lord Rosslyn's suggestion of abroad for greater safety being turned down, as 'he was as safe here as anywhere'. The

Hon. John Douglas (later Marquess of Queensberry), as Boswell's second, arranged the duel for a fortnight ahead to allow him to settle his affairs.

At the last minute the parties were bound over to keep the peace, and a hasty decision was made not to wait but to hold the duel next morning, in Fife, the nearest place to reach Lord Rosslyn. The latter even had to provide the pistols, as Sir Alexander had now no time to send for his and the shops were shut. Walter Scott says that Boswell dined with him shortly before the meeting, when he said nothing of it but seemed full of lively gaiety.[11]

The last arrangements were made, Dr George Wood was hastily called to stand by, and at 5 in the morning Boswell's party set off, stopping for breakfast at North Queensferry; they reached the rendezvous at Auchtertool on the coast a little before 10.

Stuart's carriage arrived about twenty minutes later, with the surgeon Robert Liston, who had not been told the purpose in advance, though it was not difficult to guess. Stuart wrote and Liston signed many papers. Douglas met Lord Rosslyn a little way outside the village, warning him not to come beyond the toll-bar in case he was recognised. He then fetched the others in his carriage to join the Earl.

They inspected the site; a 'hollow dell' which Rosslyn had pointed out from a hilltop, described as a beautiful spot in a field beside the road, was approved, and the parties assembled. In the usual last formality Douglas asked Lord Rosslyn if 'the matter could be accommodated' but was told, again as usual, that it could not.

By agreement, the two surgeons were to turn their backs on the duel until they heard the shots, and then hurry to the spot.[12] Douglas had told Boswell on the way that the best apology would be to fire in the air, but Boswell gave no hint of his intention. In placing him for the duel Douglas again instructed him, 'Make your fire in the air as distinct as possible', which he hoped would conclude the matter: he should aim at the bank, towards the seconds.

The distance of twelve paces was measured, the guns loaded. It was agreed that both contestants fire together, on a single word. Both fired, and Boswell fell, hit in the breast at the collarbone. Douglas and the surgeons ran forward, they probed the wound, which had fractured the right clavicle, and pronounced it mortal, but could not find the ball. There was no dressing material to hand – strange oversight – and Douglas borrowed Lord Rosslyn's horse and rode ahead to Lord Balmuto's house, where they prepared to receive the wounded man.

Three days later Sir Alexander died at the house, paralysed and in great pain, his wife having come to join him. The last fatal duel in Scotland had been that between Captain Macrae and Sir George Ramsay in 1790, more than thirty years earlier.

While Boswell had acted shabbily over the lampoons and, according to the code of honour, had only himself to blame, he was mourned as greatly loved by family and tenants. The unfortunate Stuart, manoeuvred into the situation by that same code, and probably fully expecting to fall himself, had shown no animosity throughout, and was agreed by all to have acted impeccably. On his victim's fall he took Lord Rosslyn's advice and left the scene at once, and also the country, leaving instructions where he was to be found. On 10 June he returned to Edinburgh when summoned to stand trial.

Six judges were present, presided over by the Hon. David Boyle, the Lord Justice Clerk, with the Lord Advocate as Counsel for the Crown and appearing for Stuart. Sitting alongside the judges on the Bench were several concerned friends and others (it was shortly before King George IV's visit to Edinburgh), including Prince Czartoriski, Lord Belhaven and the young Henry Fox. Stuart pleaded Not Guilty, and Cockburn opened in his defence, quoting from the indictment that he had acted 'wickedly and maliciously'. He pointed out that Boswell had had the 'fatal gift, when not combined with consummate prudence and the happiest temper', of 'great ironical powers' which he tended to use too recklessly.

In evidence Lord Rosslyn, John Douglas and the doctors minutely described the events of the duel, several witnesses testifying to Stuart's amiable temper, high reputation and honourable conduct. The trial lasted eighteen hours.

Henry Fox, sitting on the Bench between Lords Rosslyn and Belhaven, thought it very dull, partly because the outcome was assured, partly because the formality of 'proving the handwriting was dull'. He thought Jeffrey's speech less good than expected, while Cockburn's was admirable. Stuart himself was 'very much affected, and was two or three times in tears. His conduct has been admirable, and he has gained a great deal by the investigation'.[13] Sydney Smith wrote afterwards to Jeffrey that he 'read Cockburn's speech with great pleasure. I admire, in the strongest manner, the conduct of the many upright and patriotic lawyers now at the Scotch bar, and think it a great privilege to call many of them friends.'[14]

Jeffrey, summing up for the defence, felt it of interest to inform the jury that in France, in the short reign of Henri IV, four thousand men had been killed in duels, while during England's longest reign of George III, there had been only 170 duels involving 340 participants, only sixty or seventy of whom were killed. Only eighteen to twenty trials had followed, the jury in several cases making an instant acquittal.

In this case the jury withdrew for merely a few moments, and returned with a verdict of Not Guilty, 'received with strong marks of satisfaction by the audience'. It was nearly 5 a.m.

What Boswell's motive was in so unworthily attacking his kinsman remains conjectural. He can have had nothing personal against him, and his actions on the kindest interpretation were ill-advised. Political vindictiveness, at that time running high, must be the most likely reason.[15]

'This is the second fatal duel which has grown out of the license of the press', wrote Southey to the Rev. Herbert Hill. 'Neither party scruples at any slander which may injure or annoy its opponents' – 'a disgraceful system'.[16]

The judge in his summing up gave a sharp rebuke to the behaviour of the newspapers, 'which are now so perpetual in Scotland and have produced so much bloodshed and ill-will'.[17]

The antics of *Blackwood's* also led to some angry confrontations. Of the more notorious, one was farcical if brutal, another fatal. In the spring of 1818 a Mr Douglas of Glasgow took grave offence at a mention in *Blackwood's* under the name of Nicol Jarvie. Douglas, described as 'a disgusting, vulgar, conceited writer', came to Edinburgh armed with a horsewhip, followed Blackwood to his office and laid the whip across his shoulders. Before Blackwood had time to recover from his astonishment, the assailant walked off – leaving no address.

Once Blackwood had regained his wits he went out, bought a stick and, with Hogg in attendance, set off to look for Douglas. As luck would have it they found him about to step into the coach for Glasgow. Blackwood at once set about him with his stick, 'beat him as hard as he could, and then permitted him to take his place in the coach, and proceed home'. Blackwood's behaviour was approved as correct, 'the other man everybody thinks has acted like a fool'. That is the partisan version; there were probably faults on both sides.[18]

Less undignified though no less reprehensible was Lockhart's attack that same autumn on Professor Playfair, under the name of Lauerwinkel in the guise of a pretended translation from a German review. Here Playfair was accused of renouncing his early standards by joining 'unprincipled wits and insidious infidels', in such terms that indignant replies were made on the venerable professor's behalf. An anonymous critic, presumably a WS or advocate, published a pamphlet, *Hypocrisy unveiled and Calumny detected . . .* , accusing Wilson and Lockhart of 'conduct disgraceful to men of letters and gentlemen'. The defendants riposted with a challenge, which the pamphleteer published in the *Scotsman* (24 October 1818), but he did not reveal himself.

Wilson and Lockhart wrote separately in reply. Wilson, accusing him of cowardice: 'It is no part of a manly disposition to use insulting epithets to an unknown enemy.' Lockhart wrote on similar lines. The unknown person published these letters too in the *Scotsman*, with a string of reproaches, suggesting that Wilson was one of the 'principal vomitories of that calumnious and malignent abuse' spewed out in *Blackwood's* against Hazlitt and Coleridge, but pointing out that if he were not so involved it was not his concern, but if he were, 'you have lost every claim to the character of a gentleman' and could not claim a gentleman's redress.

At this point Lockhart lost interest, or courage, and his sole response was a caricature of the supposed author. The affair did him a lot of damage, including with Jeffrey, who deplored his attack on 'my excellent friend Mr Playfair'. 'If you still profess to take the same interest in that magazine', he wrote, 'I do not see that we can possibly co-operate in any other publication', with more to that effect, and reproaching him for trying to discredit religion. No reply, if there was one, has survived. The defendants evidently knew that there was nothing they could say.[19] At least one duel was thus avoided.

Similarly Robert Morehead, though a friend of Wilson's, could not refrain from reproaching him and Lockhart for these 'delinquencies', for if people of 'high and noble character' stooped so low, such 'torrents of abuse' were to be expected. He deplored the 'unhandsome personalities' and unjustifiable attribution of unworthy motives, otherwise 'there is not a piece of abomination . . . which will not be fathered upon one or other of you'.[20]

Although the mystery remained unsolved, Macvey Napier came under suspicion as the hidden attacker. Jeffrey flew to his defence, declaring Napier too great 'a gentleman and a man of education' to act so disgracefully. His friendship with Wilson was generally undermined.

This exchange of steaming vituperation took place within a few days. Jeffrey was particularly incensed that the *Edinburgh* should be accused, however implicitly, as a paper 'to discredit religion, or promote the cause of infidelity', as their fifteen years' record must prove. Levity or indecorum, yes, but never with deliberate intent to attack religion, nor did Playfair give credit to 'alleged infidel principles' through their columns.[21]

The matter ended here, Wilson evidently realising they had not a leg to stand on.

The Lockhart/John Scott affair was even less creditable. John Scott, born in 1783 two years before Wilson, had been at school with Byron. In 1820 he became founder editor of another, brilliant new magazine, the *London*, largely literary and with a similar range of subjects to *Blackwood's*, but omitting politics. He secured contributions from most leading writers, ranging from Wordsworth, De Quincey and Charles Lamb to the younger Tom Hood and Thomas Carlyle, and also gave room to the 'Cockney School' of Keats, Leigh Hunt and Hazlitt. Many of these writers were notably those viciously attacked by *Blackwood's*, and the two magazines were soon on the warpath.

In November John Scott went into action against *Blackwood's* 'fraud', of using invented and pseudonymous characters, like Wastle, Peter Morris the assumed author of Peter's Letters, and in particular the whole gang who peopled *Noctes Ambrosianae*. He claimed that these transparent pseudonyms were in fact deceptive, while *Peter's Letters*, pandering to 'paltry and nefarious curiosity', infringed 'the rules of decency and principles of honour'. He even attacked Walter Scott for supporting the magazine, and for backing Wilson's bid for the professorship, and actually implied that Scott might have written some of the recent articles. He also believed that Lockhart, not Wilson, was 'Christopher North' and editor of *Blackwood's*, and that it was he who was chiefly responsible for the attacks on Coleridge and others.

The quarrel stretched over some weeks. John Scott – whom Carlyle had encountered the previous Christmas in Glasgow 'amid dandy clerks and sparkling females', finding himself 'laughing sometimes even to soreness' at Scott's wit[22] – was already embroiled with Lockhart over a critical article on *Blackwood's* in the *London* in November. In January 1821, by which time two further attacks had been published, Lockhart was moved to a challenge, but not in his own name. Feeling that he could not leave his wife Sophia, who was pregnant and not well, he asked his friend John Christie, accompanied by Traill, a lawyer, to seek out the author and demand an apology, failing which he would meet 'the man' at York or elsewhere.

What followed next is again described in conflicting accounts. The opponents parleyed through their representatives, Scott demanding to know Lockhart's motives, Lockhart claiming that the articles were based on falsities. Obscure replies, misunderstandings, and general huffiness brought Lockhart to London ready to fight, claiming that John Scott was 'shuffling'. Horatio Smith (of *Rejected Addresses*), asked by Scott to act as second, refused, knowing nothing of duels, disapproving anyway, and recalling the ridiculous Jeffrey–Tom Moore affair years earlier. He did agree to act as mediator, but when the quarrel became too personal, withdrew.[23]

In the continuing quarrel Lockhart called Scott 'liar and scoundrel', and published a denial that he was editor of *Blackwood's*. He had now asked Peter Patmore, another young journalist and a friend of Lamb and Hazlitt, to be his second.

After further misunderstandings and a vitriolic correspondence, including over the wording of Lockhart's publication, and a last unsatisfactory meeting when Patmore and Christie could not agree over Scott's latest letter, on 15 February Christie unwillingly met Scott at Chalk Farm, with Traill as second. The day before, Sophia Lockhart in Edinburgh had borne a son, Hugh Littlejohn, rather delicate and slightly premature. This of course could not be known to any of the parties until after the duel.

Christie fired into the air, but Scott objected because he himself had taken aim. In self-preservation Christie was obliged to fire again, and this time to his horror hit Scott, who fell.

After initial hopes of his recovery of the wound, he died eleven days later,

Christie deeply distressed having done all he could, first to end the quarrel, then to conduct the duel without bloodshed. At friends' urging, although Wilson had offered to take him in, he took refuge in Boulogne. Fortunately for him and Traill, both were acquitted after an inquest (14 April).[24]

In principle it was Lockhart who ought to have taken up the challenge, and it might be thought that he sheltered behind Christie, who need not have fought on his behalf. On the other hand the quarrel was rather in the name of *Blackwood's* itself, and secondly, there were compassionate grounds because of Lockhart's young wife. On any view it was an unsavoury business, reflecting little credit on anybody. [25]

Mrs Grant reckoned that John Scott had brought it on himself by his unwarranted attacks, and that when Lockhart so unexpectedly appeared in London ready to give satisfaction, Scott had shrunk from it in a cowardly way; then, to save his reputation from such an imputation he rashly manoeuvred Christie into a meeting.[26]

30
LIFESTYLES

> 'I find living here very high. An hour ago, I paid my week's bill which tho' 15/2 was the smallest of the three which I have yet discharged . . . [for] the slender accommodation, mid the paltry ill-cooked morsel which is my daily pittance . . . [But] I was through about 50 rooms the other day – only one was offered cheaper and that greatly inferior.'
>
> Thomas Carlyle to his mother, 17 Dec. 1818, Charles Richard Saunders *et al.* (eds.), *Selected Letters of Thomas and Jane Welsh Carlyle*, North Carolina, 1970ff., I.152

City and country were still closely linked, the latter within easy walking distance, and every lawyer now owning a villa nearby – a modest version of the landed estates within a radius of about twenty miles. But the city itself was taking its modern shape. The main streets of the New Town were complete or at least planned if not already building, and a form of modern city life very unlike the old had become familiar.

'Here,' wrote Susan Ferrier of their George Street house in 1809, 'I contemplate the progress of the Arts in streets building, houses repairing, shops painting . . . I am regaled from morning till night with an enchanting variety from the majestic tumble of a Hackney coach to the elegant trot of a post-chaise', not to mention street cries such as 'Caller herrin'!', and Edinburgh's still surviving notorious 'olfactory delights'.[1]

George Street, central of the three spinal streets and the only one intended to be built on both sides, was its business centre, the other two being regarded as elegant promenades, although Princes Street had shops and Queen Street did not. In that same year Mrs Elizabeth Hamilton rented number 53 George Street from Mr French at one hundred guineas for four months, with the option of further extension at twenty-five guineas per month.[2]

The Ferriers had lived at number 25 since 1784 and in the autumn of 1815, when the house was a good thirty years old, they were doing it up. 'I'm not only painting and new furnishing the house from top to toe,' wrote Miss Susan, 'but . . . pulling it down and building it up again.' 'I've done nothing', she added, 'but run after masons, painters, and upholsterers . . . The upholstery is merely making up the drawing-room curtains anew, but . . . the workpeople here are so slow and so stupid there is no coming to an understanding or a finishing with them.' She may have been mentally comparing standards with work at Inveraray Castle, where a virtually resident work-force was on tap.[3]

The grandeur of a street did not necessarily make it agreeable, and Elizabeth Grant of Rothiemurchus greatly preferred George Street to the north-facing Queen Street, where in the autumn of 1815 on their usual return from the Highlands Mr Grant rented Lady Augusta Clavering's, 'the most disagreeable house possible; a large gloomy No.11 in Queen Street, on whose front the sun never shone, and which was so built against behind there was no free circulation of air through it'. The little service streets Rose, Thistle and Hill Street between the three main thoroughfares, and their still smaller 'lanes', effectively closed up their backs.

It was larger and more comfortable than Heriot Row, where they had lived the previous season, with 'four good rooms' to each floor, 'but they did not communicate. The drawing room was very large, four rooms along the side of it. There were, however, no convenient rooms for refreshments for evening parties, so during our stay in it nothing could be given but dinner . . . my little bedroom was to the sunny and quiet back of the house, and on the Drawing room floor.'[4]

Edinburgh still continued the old tradition of building in tenements or 'lands', but now alternating in batches with single houses, the usual style being a 'front door flat' leading to ground floor, basement and first floor, and a separate door, usually more modestly finished, opening on the common stair to the flats above. Francis Jeffrey also lived in Queen Street after his first wife's death, but far from grandly, 'third-rate apartments in a "land"', recalls Gillies, and surprisingly possessing no personal library, only a few 'tatterdemalion volumes' apart from his necessary law-books and the current periodicals. There was little comfort in his arrangements, and the most remarkable feature of his sitting-room was the looking-glass above the chimney-piece, round which were stuck 'a preposterous multitude of visiting cards and notes of invitation, which showered on him from all quarters'.[5]

Sir John Hay's George Street house, which the Grants rented for the winter of 1816–17, was 'infinitely more agreeable' than Lady Augusta's 'gloomy old barrack' – 'an excellent family house', said Elizabeth, 'warm, cheerful, aery, with abundant accomodation for a larger party than ours, but there was the same fault of but one drawing room and a small study off it'. This was a pity, for again there was no chance of giving a ball and, in this post-war period, Edinburgh was exceptionally gay and much fuller than formerly, though Party spirit was so rife that society was divided into distinct coteries.[6]

Princes Street, where Mrs Grant moved in the summer of 1815 from Heriot Row, had not only the advantage of open access – almost rural – but, unlike Queen Street it faced south and at Mrs Grant's western end it faced the castle.

'A very pleasant and convenient house . . . I look beyond it on green fields' (the site of Lothian Road). 'I have a little plot of ground behind, and I have 3 floors, with 3 good beds in each, over and above very neat attics, and below, a sunk story, with numberless conveniences . . .'

The Heriot Row house, though being her own property she was fond of it, had after all proved inconvenient, for lack of space with her bevy of young ladies sharing her home, and she leased it to tenants. She now had at least three girls, Miss Glassell, already with her four years, Miss Hamilton, and a new 'orphan heiress of considerable fortune'.[7]

Heriot Row, as chief street of the Second New Town, was at a slight remove from the very centre, and the steep slope separating it from Queen Street had not yet been 'improved'. Its number 4 was the first house which the other Grants had rented when for financial reasons John Peter found it expedient to move to Edinburgh and practise in the law (1814). It was engaged for them by the famous Miss Grace Baillie.

Having only one floor above drawing-room level it was ranked as modest, 'but', says Elizabeth, 'there were four rooms on each floor and they were all of a good size. The situation was pleasant, though not at all what it is now' (she was writing in about 1850). 'There were no prettily laid out gardens then between Heriot Row and Queen Street, only a long slope of unsightly grass, a green, fenced by an extremely untidy wall and abandoned to the use of the washerwomen. It was an ugly prospect . . . squares of bleaching linens and lines drying ditto were ever before our eyes' – except at weekends.

Mr Grant used the house also for his office, and their first sight on arrival was his large brass plate the size of a quarto sheet, engraved with 'Mr Grant, Advocate'. The tradition of a street of advocates had been early established.

The schoolboy William's rooms were on the same floor as the drawing-rooms, the latter linked by folding doors. Since the young family were all studying, Elizabeth's place had to be the drawing-room, away from the governess Miss Elphick and William in the schoolroom, spending an hour with each visiting master until the first callers came at 1 o'clock.[8]

Harriet Wynne and James Hamilton of Kames had settled there on their marriage late in 1809, 'remarkably pretty and fitted up with great taste', observed her sister Betsey Fremantle, visiting them early in June 1811; 'it has at the back a view of the sea and coast of Fife, in front it looks into Gardens, [sic] and is very chearful and airy'.

From here they walked to see their youngest sister Justine, married to Mr Finlay and having just bought a comfortable house in York Place: 'it is large, and in an excellent situation fitted up very neat and comfortable but not at all extravagantly'.

Altogether Betsey was 'much delighted with the situation of the Town of Edinburgh; the handsome appearance of the Houses and streets, all the

Buildings being of White Stone, high, and the windows large, the Streets are very wide, and most of them command an extensive view of the Sea'. Further, in a short evening's walk one could visit so rural a spot as St Bernard's Well, 'very romantic and wild scenery . . . so perfectly countrified that one could fancy oneself many miles from a Town'.[9]

The rural effect was only slightly changed when Raeburn started building on the land beyond the Water of Leith. John Wilson, who had long lived with his mother in Queen Street, in 1819 moved with his family, now five young children, to number 29 Ann Street, new, modest, quiet and out-of-town, 'small and somewhat inconvenient' (especially after the vast Queen Street).

At least Wilson's outlay was modest, a blessing for one who until not many years earlier had been well-to-do. To furnish his dining-room, sitting-room, nursery, servants' room and kitchen he paid a mere £195, his good-natured and prudent wife entering willingly into these economies. A squeeze for a family of seven and servants.

Although outwith Edinburgh's fashionable life, Ann Street yet had a respectable society of its own, among the artistic and literary set. It formed a kind of island, near to the dignified Sir Henry Raeburn's 'old mansion of St. Bernard's', itself a centre of hospitality and the ageing artist a picture of kind benevolence, 'his fine intellectual countenance lightened by eyes most expressive'. The Wilsons' next-door neighbours were Captain (later Admiral) Watson and his wife, the captain a relation of (Sir) John Watson Gordon, later President of the Royal Scottish Academy, but then a rising artist whose paintings Wilson bought, including a 'poetically conceived portrait' of his seven-year-old daughter Margaret (1820).[10]

Ann Street was but little removed from the humble village of Stockbridge, the small industrial hamlet now beginning to be built up as a residential suburb. George Combe, now a young lawyer, established himself at the newly built Hermitage Place, with a room for his brother Andrew, who had scarcely occupied it before his visit to Paris in the autumn of 1817. Badly placed, low-lying and ill-drained, the house yet had 'a beautiful and uninterrupted prospect of the country to the west', and was sheltered on the north-east.

Andrew's ground-floor room had no winter sun, and being long out of use during his absence was damp and unhealthy, yet from sheer ignorance they did not air the room properly before his return. The bedding was still damp, and poor shivering Andrew tried to warm himself merely by pulling these bedclothes closer to himself, with long-term serious effects. Years later he confessed that, had they only thought of it, sixpenny-worth of coals for a fire in the two days before his arrival might well have saved him from TB in later life.

Not long afterwards George removed their household to Brown Square, more central and better situated for his professional practice.[11]

James Hogg is quoted as lodging in Stockbridge in 1813, removed from his large High Street flat (for which he paid £26 a year), where his brother Robert had joined him while he attended the High School. It was from Stockbridge that he published *The Queen's Wake.*

'Stockbridge' in Hogg's case may have been liberally interpreted, as on 14 November 1813 he was writing gratefully to the literary-minded merchant Alexander Bald, of Alloa, from 10 Ann Street.[12]

Morningside was then not a suburb, but a country house, the summer country resort of James Ferrier and his family. Charlotte Clavering refers to it as 'rather an old-fashioned looking house with two stairs to go up to the door' – which she had believed to be a school. Here James Ferrier and his daughter retreated every spring from the smoke of Edinburgh.[13]

In the same area, also known as Canaan, John Wilson's brother James settled after his marriage to the accomplished Isabella Keith, who became interested in all that he himself was most concerned with. The young pair moved to Woodville, convenient not only for his church at New Greyfriars but for his uncle's at George Square, and 'scarcely a bowshot from the fine old Grange' of Sir Thomas Dick Lauder. It was a mere half-hour's walk from the college museum and the Royal Society's rooms (of great importance to Wilson), yet was set in a 'sylvan solitude' in two acres of ground, in which Wilson created an orchard, lawn, shrubbery and flower-garden, while in the 'groves' of Morningside even in winter it basked in sunshine, sheltered from wind and fog.

The front was more or less bounded by the windows of the two main rooms. In its hospitable interior Wilson's library was set up in the dining-room, his writing-table placed between fire and south window, his entomological cabinet at one end (a youthful purchase), and all available wall-space filled with his apparatus and the works of Cuvier, Lamarck, *British Birds*, and so forth. A portrait of Audubon above the fireplace flashed a fiery eye 'as the genius of the place', and in one corner were portraits of Wordsworth, Selby, Cuvier, Lucien Bonaparte and other admired characters.

Whereas Scott wrote his novels so secretly, early in the mornings before breakfast, that not even his nearest relatives could be sure when (or if) it was done, the shy James Wilson was gregarious within his own habitat. He preferred to work literally in the family circle, and would sit undisturbedly composing articles while one of the children was reading aloud to their mother. In this way, for example, he compiled his nineteen-page item on Angling for the *Encyclopaedia Britannica* of 1829, in the midst of general family conversation with a particularly lively visitor.[14]

George Combe, when by 1812 comfortably established at 11 Bank Street, had noted his happiness at being in a small household away from the 'bustle of a large Family', and as the months went on felt very satisfied, in good health, with good career prospects and good management by his sister. All the same, expenses proved higher than expected because of recent rises in the cost of provisions. 'Old wheat at 80, 84, 86/- a boll, oats and barley 50/-, quartern loaf 1/7, meal 3/5 a peck'. Despite an abundant harvest and continuing good weather, victual was so scarce that new wheat might fetch 70/- and at lowest was 60/- a boll, and potatoes 10d a peck. By the end of the year, though he was still content with his life, his ability to entertain friends and 'simple but good fare', provisions remained at much the same high price, bread at 1/6d a loaf and meal 2/3 a peck.[15]

In the autumn of 1814, with the Napoleonic wars apparently over, land prices and rents were down and wheat fell as low as 56/-. Meanwhile Edinburgh was suffering a water shortage, selling at 6d for two stoup-fulls and in the streets from barrels. The proposed Union Canal which would have helped solve the problem was under embargo, from opposition by the magistrates.[16]

Students lived a special life. Not all, by far, were under-privileged, though they tended to be frugal. Most lived in the Old Town because of proximity to the University, and Charles Darwin describes in October 1825 how he and his brother found comfortable lodgings at 11 Lothian Street near the college. The landlady, Mrs Mackay, was 'a nice clean old body – exceedingly civil and attentive', only four flights up and 'very moderate to some other lodgings that we were nearly taking'. The rent was £1.6s for two nice, light bedrooms and a sitting-room, lightness being unusual for the Old Town, which mostly had 'little holes in which there is neither air nor light'.[17]

The worm's-eye view, of how a poor and struggling student and would-be writer lived, is all too vividly exemplified in the chequered lodging experiences of the never-satisfied Thomas Carlyle, who lived in Edinburgh from autumn to late spring, returning to his parents in Dumfriesshire from May or June until about November.

Carlyle hated Edinburgh. He hated his own insecurity there and despised many of those with influence and authority, partly for what he considered their hypocrisy, artificiality or general stupidity, partly because except for his family he hated, or perhaps feared, most people. He hated the noise which kept him awake at night, the filth and above all the smoky atmosphere, which made it difficult for him to breathe. Much of his dyspeptic energy went into seeking acceptable lodgings, and surely few non-householders in Edinburgh changed their address as often as he.

The kind of lodging Carlyle needed was usually in, or in the precincts of, the Old Town. In 1814 he was lodging with Mr Jack Forrest, merchant, at 3 South Richmond Street, and already when he returned to the city in 1816 he was expressing disillusionment. Although he then implied that this might have been rather his fault than Edinburgh's, from then on that was approximately his attitude. Almost every autumn when he returned from his family he sought new lodgings, often changing several times during a season, and however satisfactory they might seem at first, there was soon enough for him to grouse about.

In November 1818, eking out a living by tutoring, he was again in South Richmond Street, this time number 5, a small room for which he paid 15/2d., complaining of the high cost of living in 'the slender accommodation, and the paltry ill-cooked morsel which is my daily pittance' (usually a 'dinner of fish or mutton & roots'). He also suffered from 'noisy brats' in the flat above, a schoolmaster's family where moreover they held a weekly musical evening at which Carlyle found the music maddening. But 'I was through about 50 rooms the other day – only *one* was offered cheaper and that greatly inferior'. Yet his health benefited from his mile pre-breakfast walk to one of his pupils, an amusing Guernsey gentleman named Saumarez who lived 'at the north end of the new town', and similarly to a young East India Company officer called Robertson, living with his mother 'much in the same quarter'. As for washing, his mother offered to take it, and although he did not want to burden her, he admitted that 'the clothes are ill washed here'.[18]

In mid-February he removed from 'Davies's Lodgings', having told the landlady to her great displeasure to hoist her 'ticket-board' announcing vacant rooms, because of the 'vermin of various sorts, which haunted the beds of that unfortunate woman, with sluttishness & a lying, thievish disposition'. His nearby old lodging at John Forrest's was booked, others were dirty, dear, or otherwise suspect, and at length he moved in with a cousin of Edward Irving's, Edward Hill, a law student from Dumfriesshire, at Mrs Scott's, 15 Carnegie Street. The inconvenience of sharing was offset by saving 3/6d. a week, besides cheaper meals, and 'neatness & comfort', with the concession of a fire in both their small rooms. Here the landlady did their washing and the two young men were reasonably provided with food from various sources. Carlyle stayed there until April (1819).[19]

Returning from his father's the following November he walked the whole wet journey, and resumed the search for lodgings. At last Mrs Thomson, a tailor's wife, offered a small back room at 8 Richmond Place, for 6/- including fire, a neat, clean room smoke-free and, she assured him, also free of 'most detested bugs'. Yet only a fortnight later he is writing, without explanation, from Mrs Duff's, 35 Bristo Street, 'a careful, decent kind of woman' and the best since he was in Kirkcaldy.[20]

His quiet, unstimulating life still continued with fulminations against current writers, 'Radical reformers', 'seditious orators', a killing frost, the misfortunes of farmers and the desperate plight of the poor. On the home front his complaint was of 'the stuff which they sell here under the name of butter', chiefly made up with sea-salt into 'a yellow sour-tasted substance' and with apparently little connection with milk. From the beginning of the year he was in bad health thanks to 'this smoky & most dusty town' which 'looks beautiful in the imagination'. He hardly knew which he hated more, Edinburgh's smoke and smells, the drivel of students or the shockingly 'unphilosophic' professors. Was it Edinburgh, or himself at fault he had the grace to ask.[21]

That winter of 1819/20, of national distress coupled with appalling weather, was reflected in Carlyle's never sanguine and now generally ill sentiments. 'Black inquietude, misery physical & moral, from one end of the island to the other, radical risings, and armed confederations of the higher classes', with the poor vainly trekking about the country in search of work.[22]

Another soaking return journey to the city in the autumn, this time by coach, launched him into the usual search when he found Mrs Duff's house was full, and the best available was at 16 Carnegie Street 'at the very outskirts of the town', with a good landlady, a Perthshire widow with two small daughters and one other lodger. She baked for him, and was at pains to make him comfortable in a 'clean, well-aired room'. The parlour was none too warm, but he had the advantage of a separate 'bed-closet'. Rooms were still dear, he complained, though his contemporary from Annan, fat stupid John Waugh (wrote Carlyle enviously), was living 'in a style as if Fortune smiled on him'. (She did not, in the event.) 'A fine room at 13/- per week, with all kinds of accommodation. . . .' Here Waugh entertained the weary Carlyle with 'large draughts of his indifferent tea'.

Within a fortnight the cold parlour drove Carlyle back on the prowl, despite the 'mighty good' Mrs Robertson. For a change he was recommended to the north side, 'far away – beyond the town . . . country air and warmth and good attendance for the same sum'. A frosty, bracing winter and enough teaching helped him through until Christmas, spent in Glasgow with Edward Irving, but still complaining of 'this vile smoky *mist* which is all the air we have to breathe here'.[23]

Again room-hunting proved unsuccessful. He was tempted by a house in Warriston Crescent where a preacher named Moon had lodged for some years, but finding that Moon was staying on he settled back with worthy Mrs Robertson, draughty room and all.

So he thought. By 25 January he was at 13 Arthur Street, and hoping to move after all to 30 Warriston Crescent, its strongly recommended landlady and the 'better air and better attentions out of town'. So allergic to weather was Carlyle that he was sure of its ill effects on his frail health. But Moon still stayed in Warriston, so he crept back to his friendly Carnegie Street lodgings, for nearby Arthur Street, though warmer, was otherwise no better, the mistress never appeared and he was attended only by 'a little tawdry affected *kimmiter* [weasel] . . . the air too was smoky as the moth of Vesvis, and the street was full of whores'.[24]

Better weather and better prospects improved his mercurial spirits, but by February he was complaining bitterly of sickness, hardly well since his return to 'this accursed, stinking, reeky mass of stones and lime and dung', and also sick of his friends. While a few days in Kirkcaldy set him up, the mere prospect of 'that old smoky city' across the Forth, where he must return for teaching, sickened him again. His present pupil was in Great King Street and every morning he was affected by the urge to return home, 'when I . . . penetrate the dense vapour that overhangs S. Bridge-street', cheered only by the brightening day.[25]

Spring and the prospect of bathing at Portobello evoked his first words of enthusiasm for the city in seven years, expressing pleasure in the pure air and the grand prospect from Arthur's Seat, the Fife hills, the crags and precipices immediately below, and Edinburgh's 'vapoury mantle' over 'the jagged, black, venerable masses of stone-work, that stretch far and wide and shew like a city of fairy-land'.[26] He even contemplated a suggestion by the provost of Kirkcaldy that he rent smart, spacious lodgings in order to take in 'two or three young' (squirelings), and supervise their education at the High School or College at 80 or 90 guineas apiece. Though nothing came of this, it was quite a positive idea.

It was that May that Carlyle, in company with Edward Irving, visited Mrs Welsh and her daughter Jane in Haddington. Though his eager suggestion that he supervise Jane's German studies met with a cool response from her mother, he was invited to call at 22 George Square, where she was about to spend a weekend.

Even in high summer Carlyle complained. 'This city is fast getting very unpleasant. The smell of it, or rather the hundred thousand smells are altogether pestilential . . . And then the dust, and, more than all together, the noise – of many animals, and many carts, and fishwives innumerable' – besides the watermen (Edinburgh was now perennially short of water) announcing their passing with 'long battered tin-horns', worse than 'an ass a hog and 50 magpies', and waking him every morning at 7 o'clock 'with a full-flowing screech'.[27]

Mrs Robertson, to whom Carlyle returned in early November, represented one of his most stable lodging periods, where he could enjoy seven hours' sleep until roused by the tin-horn man. But again he was wishing for quieter, airier surroundings.

So on 10 November kind Mrs Robertson was deserted for Mrs Simms of 9 Jamaica Street, a mile from the old centre and 'at the very north-west corner of the New Town', a 'neat little room and a bed-room' with a view of the Forth and the Fife hills, and 'a trim, little *brring* Northumbrian' landlady. Alas! A back room should have been peaceful, but here he was continually disturbed by builders at Royal Circus. 'There are about 50 masons chopping away at a new Circus on my right hand and on my left, by day; and when their rattling has ceased, various other noises take up their nightly tale.'

He was therefore receptive to the suggestion of Professor Swan, father of one of his pupils, that he move to the Union Street area to be near his boy, who lodged with his recently widowed aunt Mrs David Swan.

The aunt proved 'a most amiable little woman' whose unfortunate history he learned in 10 minutes, poor, with a little son, but cheery and with fortitude and he quickly felt at home.[28]

But despite his satisfaction with the 'poor little body of a landlady . . . very cleanly, and very attentive', he could no longer stand 'the noise of masons, dog-fights, cat-squallings, carpet-beatings', and being kept awake at night by a poor consumptive girl coughing in the flat below. Such a pity, for this was 'the best part of Edinburgh for air'.

In December Carlyle moved three times, to Mrs Sherlock's below at the same address (presumably found for him by kind Mrs Swan), to Mrs Cusine's at 5 College Street, and to Wilkie's lodging, 3 Moray Street off Leith Walk.

As he explained to his brother Alex on 4 December, 'The first room would not do, and was let to another, the second of the woman Swan's proved intolerably cold, and was let' – at 12/-, very dear. Mrs Swan tried for him for another week, and an hour before writing he was at last settled, again 'confoundedly dear' at 9/6d reduced from 12/- after much haggling. This room, 'in front and two stairs nearer the ground' than Simm's, 'looks warm and very clean and snug' – and of course, had good air.

Yet a week later he moved to 'the South', to College Street, hoping this would be the last. At Mrs Sherlock's he had proved to be only in the care of a servant, and besides it was as noisy as trying to sleep in a fulling mill, and she had the effrontery to ask him not to smoke, 'for it spoiled the room'. As an occasional cigar was one of Carlyle's few luxuries, this was unacceptable and he was happy enough to leave. His latest lodging, next door to the bookseller Smith's, was back among the smoke, and already, four days later, he was complaining of one of 'our worst days in the smoky city . . . a day like the shores of Acheron'.[29]

The odds are that Carlyle would never have found lodgings to his liking. There would either have been a draught, a barking dog, a coughing consumptive, the hammering of masons, or the city smoke. Indeed by 19 December he was complaining that College Street though 'open', in the centre of town, had less air, was '*enlivened* by the sound of 10 thousand carts and coaches', and was not particularly warm, though 'an elegant large apartment; and the people are very decent seemingly'. Mrs Cusines herself complained of being repeatedly fleeced by Irish students and others who took off without settling scores, and Carlyle was happy to agree to leave at Whitsun and return to Mrs Robertson, 'who purposes taking a *good* house, in some pleasant part of the city'.

He described his present daily life: breakfasting leisurely on 'a morsel of lukewarm tea' (preceded by an hour or two of writing), he would set off for his Great King Street pupils 'in the back of the New Town', then to the 'shrill and smooth-spoken' Captain Anderson, RN in George Street; dinner (beef-steak to-day), walking or reading, then another pupil, and from 6 onwards writing or reading, 'a laborious life, but such a one as suits me'. There was no clock in the house, and his chief lack was 'a Chronometer'.[30]

But alas! that very same night he was so disturbed that he fell ill again of his old nervous complaint: 'some drunken blackguard, trolling his obscene catch, as he staggers along the street'; not to mention 'the Stygian vapour in which all the Old Town of Edinburgh is almost constantly involved'.

So, on the march again. He found a back room at 5 Moray Street, the quietest yet. Besides, 'I have green fields beneath my very window, and nothing else between me and the forth', and the landlandy seemed cleanly and 'heartsome', in a well-ordered house, occupied only by her brother and her five-year-old son. The street was just below the Leith Walk toll-bar, and he could enjoy clear air, his usual pre-breakfast walk, and had plenty of work, which his situation made him now well enough to do.

So that on Christmas Day 1821 he told his mother that he was ready to start 'the book' which everybody – that is, chiefly Jane Welsh – was pressing him to write. Although he was fond of nobody in the city, there were now plenty whom he found pleasant to be with.[31]

Jane Welsh was in fact still pointing out the difficulty of her mother's disapproval and, worse, her own dislike of Carlyle's plaguing her, trying to extort promises. She wanted to see some of his written work before he turned up again.[32]

A more rackety experience of Edinburgh, in the 1820s, is given by Benson Earle Hill, an extrovert young army officer turned actor/author with a gift for verbose reportage. In *Playing About,* one of the works in which he deluged the world with a string of adventures recorded with dubiously verbatim dialogue, he describes joining the Scottish theatre in 1825, in company with his strait-laced sister Bell, who was easily shocked, and was supposed to be writing a play. Hidden among his tediously written anecdotes of Charles Mathews and others are a few nuggets of information.

They started off in temporary lodgings at Coulson's Hotel in Gabriel's Road, when Bell was horrified to find it was the site of the famous tutorial murder. They therefore moved to Mrs Wilson's at the St Andrew Square end of Rose Street, then to Mrs Ogilvie's on Greenside, where Benson falls into disgrace with the landlady by taking down her 'evangelical portraits', by 'humming tunes on the Lord's Day' and (finally given notice) by not getting up early – while the tiresome Isabel earns a caddy's scorn by not even being able to find the house.

Next they try Mrs Melville's in Dublin Street, are fed on Loch Leven trout in batter, Preston Pans herring, and finan haddie, but here too fall foul of the landlady who, admittedly in her cups, assails Bell. On to Mrs Millan's, in Clyde Street, a 'self-contained house' and respectable. But as some former lodgers return they move to a second-best suite at the Veitches, St Andrew Square, with a kind, clean landlady of unfathomable diction.

Hill, very English, sneers at such Scottish specialities as Lucky's oyster-house in Shakespeare Square, which indeed sounds dirty enough, and Bell shows ill-mannered unadaptability when dining with a respectable tradesman, where the starchy young lady refuses all drink, first their strong ale, then the wife's home-made (cowslip and parsley) wines, and finally the Scottish requirement of a glass of toddy before leaving the table. These constant changes of lodging begin to take on a significant tinge – not unlike Carlyle's a few years earlier.

The facetious young Benson suffered from a dishonest laundress, who spoiled their Christmas that year with a hard-luck story of how her old father woke to find his wife dead beside him in bed. Hill received her blessing by paying extra, but over Christmas and New Year the money must have gone on drink, for he heard no more of her, her father or his own laundry. At last 'I walked to that colony of laundresses, Duddistone', but could not find her. The locals told him she was 'a bad one', and had no parents anyway. The police tracked her down, money spent and clothes pawned. Hill eventually got these back at cost, but it wrecked their Christmas holiday.[33]

Hill is tiresomely unilluminating about the theatre, but we learn from the *Edinburgh Evening Courant* (25 February 1826) that at Mr Vandenhoff's benefit he sang a French song, but that Edinburgh audiences did not like things French.[34]

31
LITERARY FIGURES (1)

'A most brilliant contributor to the periodical literature of his day, a great inspirer of youth, and a standard and pattern to his countrymen of physical and Intellectual manhood.'

Sir George Douglas on John Wilson, *The 'Blackwood' Group*, London, 1897, 46

'It is odds if you ever sit down to dinner in a company of a dozen, without having to count three or four quarto makers in the circle. Poets are as plentiful as blackberries . . . And as for travellers – good Jehovah! . . . there have appeared at least 20 different lucubrations in that way concerning Paris alone within these last 18 months.'

Lockhart to James Christie, 29 Nov. 1815, Andrew Lang, *Life and Letters of John Gilbson Lockhart*, 2 vols, London, 1897, 95–6

One of Edinburgh's most remarkable visitors at this time, in this case eventually long-term, was Thomas De Quincey, who had first appeared there in 1814 when John Wilson introduced him to the up-and-coming writers. They had been at Oxford at the same time, though they met only later at Grasmere, through the Wordsworths.

De Quincey, son of a Manchester linen merchant, was born in 1785 and ran away from Manchester Grammar School to live a peripatetic life in Wales, then moved to London, went on to Worcester College, Oxford, met Wordsworth and Coleridge and moved to the Wordsworths' former cottage in Grasmere.

While at Oxford he had already begun to take opium, and from 1812 became an addict. He made a rather imprudent marriage to Margaret Simpson, a farmer's daughter,[1] and they had eight children. Having spent all his money, De Quincey took to journalism. By the time his most famous work, *Confessions of an English Opium Eater*, was published as a book in 1822 he had produced some remarkable journalistic feats in the way of pot-boilers, for example 'Murder considered as one of the Fine Arts'. Much of his later life was to be spent in and near Edinburgh.

Returning there in 1815, he impressed people by both his well-informed mind and his eccentricity, and though as yet he had published nothing he had 'scribbled' much. Robert Gillies thought he seemed as if he came from another world.[2] Lockhart, as we have seen, was impressed first by his taking opium at table and by his and Wilson's mutual admiration of *The Excursion* – and later, themselves setting off on one together, to Staffa.[3] (This may have been a misconception, or a change of plan; on 8 January Lockhart tells Christie how Wilson 'walked off to Cumberland a fortnight ago'.[4]) Wilson was rewarded by suffering a 'broken' head when the Carlisle coach overturned.

De Quincey, who was only five foot three inches in height, was one of the many little men – like Jeffrey, Thomas Campbell, Tom Moore – who made so great a mark on the literature of the time. 'Once seen, never to be forgotten', wrote John Ritchie Findlay, who met De Quincey many years later when, in his sixties, he seemed physically hardly changed. 'His features, though not regular, were aristocratically lined, and an air of delicate breeding pervaded the face. His forehead was unusually high, square and compact', his skin still smooth, but with a 'hectic glow' caused by the opium. His eyes, dark and strangely dim, had a 'dreamy look' presumably from short-sightedness. (James Hogg described them as 'fathomless'.) At the time of this description De Quincey was living at Mavisbank; he retained his old-world, courteous manners, free of ostentation, and like Charles Kirkpatrick Sharpe, stuck to the dress he had worn years ago, which by then hung loosely on his skeletal frame; he wore an ancient hat and often appeared *sans* shirt, collar or even shoes or stockings.[5]

John Wilson, when he became involved with *Blackwood's*, tried to persuade De Quincey to write for it too, but neither for the *Edinburgh* nor for *Blackwood's* was De Quincey capable of producing results, even with the lure of ten guineas a sheet (eight printed pages); he limited himself to borrowing money from Wilson. However, he did not remain entirely outwith the publication, as Wilson, unblushingly, repeatedly asked him for information to write his own articles.

This had gone on since Wilson's days as a law student, when, in the midst of intensive study to pass his civil law examinations, he undertook to open a Speculative Society debate ('Has the Peninsular War been glorious to the Spanish Nation?'), for which he felt totally unqualified; but as all his friends would be there, he had to cut a good figure. Could De Quincey supply the information? As if that were not enough, on the very same evening he was supposed to read an essay 'on some political or philosophical subject. I find I have not time, inclination, nor ability to write one.' Had De Quincey one such – or could he suggest one, 'not likely to be known here?' He was not even much concerned about the subject – perhaps literature? In this airy, cavalier way Wilson shamelessly milked his friend's brains, which were known to be of considerable extent. And by the way, it was fairly urgent, especially the talk on the Spanish war, as next week he was going to Glasgow.[6]

Early in 1820 Wilson was begging an item for *Blackwood's* since he had had to delay publication on its account. 'It becomes daily a more difficult task for Mr Lockhart and I to write almost the whole of the work', and Lockhart now about to be married, will have less time than before. He promises to publish 'whatever and whenever you send'. This from the man who a few years earlier was boasting how between them he and Lockhart could toss off a whole magazine in a few days.[7]

De Quincey's own incisive intellect appeared in his criticism of Dugald Stewart, of whom he was quoted as saying cruelly (in London in 1821) that he had 'no originality or grasp of mind' and 'constantly misunderstands and misquotes writers from taking their opinions at second-hand from others . . . All Dugald Stewart's disquisitions are little, and the subject of them of no moment, even if true.' He added his view that neither in Edinburgh nor on the Continent was Stewart thought much of.[8]

De Quincey joined Wilson's circle, standing out from the rest by the boyish looks which he retained until old age, and gentle voice, somehow, despite his unassuming manner, getting the last word. First he became their 'referee in knotty points of philosophy or scholarship . . . a paradox, a source of bewilderment'; then he was actually lionised. He was a night bird, or rather of the small hours, and for that reason Wilson gave parties late at night.[9]

It was after the Napoleonic Wars that Wilson's circle spread to its widest extent: his brother James, Captain John Mitchell, famed for military knowledge and much later author of the *Life of Wallenstein* (1837);[10] Captain Thomas Hamilton, Sir William's brother later known as 'Cyril Thornton' after his novel of that name; the painter (Sir) William Allan, later President of the Royal Scottish Academy; and Robert Gillies. The last (wrote De Quincey) had been in earlier days the host of 'gay saloons, resonant with music and festive laughter', with 'munificent hospitality', followed by thirty years of financial misfortune, 'of calamity, of sorrow, of malice, of detraction'.[11]

Whereas for eight years until 1812 De Quincey had used opium with little or no ill effects, when half starved in London in 1813 his frequent stomach upsets had caused him to increase the dosage. From 1817 the drug was affecting him badly. Its effects were in part to prevent him from finishing nearly anything he tried to write. He recovered for a time in Edinburgh, according to report after reading the economist David Ricardo (1819), and succeeded in writing *Prolegomena*, afterwards lapsing into hallucinations and drug-ridden gloom.[12]

During these years he was staying chiefly in the Lake District and in London writing for and then editing the *Westmorland Gazette* (1818–20), and he attempted to settle in Edinburgh again (December 1820), staying at 30 Northumberland Street. Through Sergeant Talfourd, whom he had met in

1808, he joined the Dissenting *London Magazine* from 1820, and was a friend of the Lambs. Always short of money, he claimed however to be now free of opium: he meant he had it under control. He borrowed money from Wilson (1821), who was indeed under heavy obligation to him for his pilfering of De Quincey's ideas, but wrote ungratefully, when the latter had drawn bills on him, that 'I have subjected myself by paying them to the greatest indignities and degradations', and hoped there would be no more. As for *Blackwood's*, 'if you could write for it, surely you would', unless there were some serious obstacle, and could then earn up to £150 a year.[13]

Meanwhile, in 1820 an unexpected change in career opened for Wilson when, on the death of Dr Thomas Brown in April, the chair of Moral Philosophy fell vacant, and a remarkable struggle ensued to appoint a successor. Wilson, surprisingly, was put up as a candidate. As the Edinburgh magistrates had the office of appointing University professors, the campaign for their patronage was political, similar to canvassing for an MP.

There was likely to be a great division, for the council were strongly Tory, and a leading candidate was the scholarly Sir William Hamilton, a Whig, and Wilson, despite his peculiarities, as a Tory would be acceptable. Two lesser, older candidates were the philosopher/barrister Sir James Mackintosh, now fifty-five, and the student of population Thomas Malthus, fifty-four. The contest really came down to the two friends Hamilton and Wilson, both former brilliant Oxonians but Hamilton a single-minded, reclusive scholar, and Wilson an eccentric of notorious career, not to mention his wild looks.

Hamilton was highly qualified for the post, and had influential friends. Wilson's association with *Blackwood's*, more especially the memory of the Chaldee Manuscript, and his attacks on Wordsworth and Coleridge, to say no more, seemed to all but Tory supporters to brand him as not even a respectable person, let alone one to lecture to the oncoming generation on Moral Philosophy. On top of it all Dugald Stewart, who had resigned in Brown's favour because of his health, could resume the chair if he wished.

Brown (1778–1820), philosopher, physician and poet, who had stood in for Stewart since his part retirement, had long been a close friend of Lord Webb Seymour. 'One of the best men I know', said Lord Webb, though in introducing him to his starchy brother the Duke of Somerset he feared Brown's unfortunate manner might not please. 'He is extremely sensitive, and there is an expression of soreness, irritability, and impatience, in his looks, the tones of his voice, and his gestures.' Though neither coarse nor ill-natured, he was sometimes too dogmatic for those who did not revel in intensive argument.[14]

The Duke graciously conceded that he might be 'a desirable acquaintance'. John Wilson, rather less graciously, wrote him off as a fool.[15]

It was not a lucrative post, professors' incomes depending on the number of their students, though Brown had earned £1000 a year.[16]

Walter Scott, rather surprisingly, supported Wilson, and he also received gratifying testimonials from Glasgow professors. His wife loyally thought he would fill the chair very well. 'All the principal men here on the *Government* side are most anxious for his success.' The Whigs were taking more part in the campaign than ever in Scottish politics. At one time it appeared that the contest was over as Stewart might indeed return, and Wilson took off for Peebles 'to recover his fatigue', but he was almost instantly recalled as Stewart after all resigned, and canvassing began in earnest.[17]

The campaign took a malignant turn, and after having attacked Wilson's mental powers and literary achievements the opposition turned to his morals: 'reveller', 'blasphemer', 'a bad husband and a bad father' (demonstrably untrue), altogether not a man to teach the young. Wilson had to seek evidence testifying to his blameless life from Mrs Grant of Laggan, to whom he wrote on his family's happiness: 'I am more at home than perhaps any other married man in Edinburgh', and felt deeply for 'the blessedness and sanctity of domestic life'. Could she send an appropriate letter? 'A hundred anonymous slanders will fall before the weight of your favourable opinion.'

Mrs Grant rose to the occasion, and obligingly wrote that she had known him from his childhood through friends, and personally since his marriage, in which he enjoyed 'no common portion of connubial felicity'. Indeed she waxed eloquent on his happy, devoted family life.[18]

Despite their differences, Wordsworth was another of the referees to whom Wilson wrote to request a 'certificate' of his suitability. In what Sara Hutchison thought a 'Jesuitical' reply, Wordsworth confessed that he had only a vague idea of the duties of the post and hence of anyone's fitness to hold it. He then put together a handsome bouquet, that if the job depended on 'pre-eminence of natural powers of mind, cultivated by excellent education', a comprehensive understanding of ethics and 'great energy of character with correspondent industry', then he had no hesitation in declaring that no one more eligible could be found.[19]

Scott wrote indignantly to the Lord Provost on 8 July that the attacks on Wilson were 'petty scandal', fabrications and distortions based on malice. He could vouch that Wilson was 'incapable either of composing parodies upon scripture', of supporting any association 'for forwarding infidelity or profaneness', or approving attacks on religion.[20]

In the four months before the election on 19 July Wilson had scarcely any rest, had become 'thin as a rat' (said his wife), and as for preparing for the university course, the canvass had left him no time. 'But for the detestable

Whigs the thing might have been settled 4 months ago.' They had longed for a holiday in Dunoon, but should he prove successful he would have to devote the next months to study.

Wilson was successful, gaining twenty-one of the thirty votes. Their servant Billy Balmer eagerly waited outside the offices until the voting was over, and 'came puffing down with a face of delight' to tell Mrs Wilson that 'Master was ahead a good deal'. She was overjoyed not only at the victory, but at his forbearance against the 'pertinacity of his enemies' and their 'meanness and wickedness'.[21]

He was not quite out of the wood. Deacon Paterson, determined to prevent his admission, swore to get the election rescinded on its statutory second reading a week later. He arrived with what he called 'a bagful of charges', but Wilson's friends rallied and would not allow him to open his green bag. During a long accusatory speech, he was repeatedly called to order even by Wilson's opponents, and at last his supporters won on a vote of censure, twenty-one to six. At this Paterson prudently offered an apology, and the censure was withdrawn. The opponents having let off steam, Wilson's election was confirmed, also twenty-one to six. 'So many slanderous accusations . . . proved unfounded', wrote Mrs Grant, 'that he was elected to clear his character, and mortify his enemies.'[22]

Now began an almost worse ordeal. Wilson, frankly, had very little idea about philosophy, and he had just four months to learn enough to keep ahead of his students. There was nothing for it but to go to ground and study, non-stop.

'I am perfectly appalled', wrote his long-suffering wife, 'when I go into the dining-room and see all the folios, quartos, and duodecimos with which it is literally filled, and the poor culprit himself sitting in the midst, with a beard as long and red as an adult carrot, for he has not shaved for a fortnight.'[23]

Wilson again turned urgently to De Quincey. First reminding him that his review of Malthus was urgently required for *Blackwood's,* he devoted most of his letter to complaining that he was 'quite at a stand', asking De Quincey for advice on reading, and ideas on Man as Moral Being, and on the senses. Would he also read and discuss with him his predecessor Brown's theory, so that he could even make sense of his ideas . . . and then on Greek philosophers, 'can you write me long letters about [them or their systems], or their philosophy?' By his detailed questions he tried to prise from his friend no less than letters long enough to pass off as his own lectures.

'What does', he asked plaintively, 'in your belief, constitute moral obligation? – and what ought to be my own doctrine on that subject?'[24]

It was as well to know what he was talking about before he started to talk.

Yet still De Quincey eluded him, and though heavily in debt, seemed incapable of writing suitable replies.

A great support was Wilson's friend Alexander Blair, with whom he corresponded on details of plans, completion of the book list, his opinion on theories and the arrangement of his lectures. He proposed to make a good opening impression with eight to ten popular, eloquent introductory lectures on the Greek moral system (this had Scott's approval). In the event he made these some of his chief lectures, especially on Socrates, a *tour de force* of eloquent pathos. Then there was the physical nature of man, the intellectual powers, taste and genius, a total of forty. On the problem of will, 'here I am in the dark'; moral nature or conscience, spiritual nature, final total fifty-eight. And at last, fifty on the duties of human beings. All this, he hoped, would produce 'something different from the common metaphysical lectures'.

'I am never out of the house, and may not be till winter', and as for his health . . .

Then he revised his approach: about eight lectures on 'Man's relations to God – Natural Theology'; twelve on 'his relations to man'; at least fifteen on the relations of Adoption and Institution, to include consideration of Government, Punishments, Poor Laws, thirty-three in all. Then 'Virtues and Vices, the different Schemes of moral approbation . . . little enough space'. They now totalled 108. He had notes of Stewart's lectures, 'feeble shadows of his published works, on which he bestowed incredible pains'. He cannot exclude metaphysics, or his enemies will claim he doesn't understand them and in order to shine over Stewart he wants to display 'a metaphysical power'.[25]

This plan he kept to throughout his teaching career, though later greatly modifying the content. All this filled a voluminous correspondence, including to Blair and to Professor George Jardine in Glasgow.

At last in November, after weeks of study closeted in his dining-room, at the start of the academic year the momentous opening day arrived.

It was a custom among the students to mob the opening lecture of a new professor, and whether because it was Wilson and there had been such scandal over his election, they turned out in droves. So many were there that the room could not hold them and they had to move to Dr Monro's anatomy lecture room. Wilson entered accompanied by Principal Baird, and Professors Home, Jameson and Hope, all in their gowns. 'Quite unusual', remarked the *Scotsman*: he had been alerted to the likelihood of disturbance – hence the backing – and guessed that because of the bitterness and partisanship a cabal would be lined up against him, 'such a collection of hard-browed, scowling Scotsmen', wrote one witness, 'muttering over their knobsticks, I never saw'.

When Wilson strode in, tall, broad-shouldered, with his florid complexion, wild fair hair and whiskered cheeks, they awaited the usual 'propitiatory introduction' on which to judge his performance. Instead, in thundering tones he launched right into the matter of his lecture, giving no opportunity for interruption, and without a pause kept up an unhesitating flow of rhetoric such as even his most distinguished predecessors had not achieved. 'Not a word, not a murmur, escaped his captivated, I ought to say his conquered, audience – until at the end they burst into riotous applause.'

Because of the change of rooms the lecture had started rather late, and towards the end of Wilson's 'elegant peroration' he was interrupted by Dr Monro, who swept in in his long white greatcoat, pulled out his watch and said uncompromisingly, 'Sir, it's long past one o'clock, and my students are at the door; you must conclude.' Keeping his self-possession with some difficulty, Wilson said a few more sentences and sat down.[26]

With this and a few more such lectures the critics were silenced. Wilson had found his metier: to instruct the young. Thenceforward his title was 'the Professor'. He had 150 lectures to give in that session, and succeeded magnificently. There were plenty to maintain that he was no more than 'a splendid declaimer', a poetry reciter, not a philosophy lecturer, and as he had feared, rightly ready to criticise him on metaphysics. But he now had the students on his side, his torrent of thought always heard in rapt silence, occasionally with noisy applause.

The youths noted how he would stride in, flourishing his scruffy roll of notes scribbled on the backs of old letters and letter-covers still with their seals, lay down his watch, look out of the window towards the spire of the Tron Kirk, then at once launch into his theme for the day in a hollow chant with a touch of the sepulchral.

He would draw out his sentences with continual pauses and interpolated sounds: 'Oo – the great goodness – uf – the – Knoights uf o – old!' Such fireworks in themselves would draw crowds in expectation, along with his odd phrases like 'The Philosophy of the Unconditioned', 'the Phenomenology of Cognition'. David Masson, a devotee, on first experiencing a lecture was nearly in fits at the sight of the wild, yellow-haired speaker and at his idiosyncratic delivery. He described Wilson's approach to Moral Philosophy as 'a rich poetico-philosophic medley' – chiefly speculative.[27]

As the years passed he still held his audience, eyes sparkling or darkening, 'tremulous upper lip curving with every wave of thought or hint of passion', and his long hair, turning from gold to grey, floating on his broad shoulders.

On Christmas Day when the first term had ended Wilson wrote to John Smith that, having now given thirty lectures he was approaching 'the moral division . . . my worst foes are dumb or sulky. The public, I believe, are satisfied. I need not say that my labour is intense.' But he could for the time being enjoy ten days of vacation, and need not start again until 2 January.[28]

Once settled in the post Wilson resumed writing for *Blackwood's,* and although never its editor became so identified by it that he gradually came to be known almost exclusively as 'Christopher North'. Sometimes he did produce almost the whole journal, and almost never less than two essays per issue. So fast did he compose that he fell into the habit of putting off until the last minute, so was always writing under compulsion. Copy covered the table, overflowing until the floor too was strewn with sheets.

According to his daughter, Wilson threw himself completely into the composition, polishing off breakfast at full speed before shutting himself in his study (never troubling with a fire even in winter), and allowing no one under any circumstances to interrupt him; he would then not stir from the writing table until he had completed perhaps most of a 'Noctes' item, or some other equally demanding paper. In later years at least he would have a dinner brought to him in his study as late as 9 o'clock, boiled fowl with potatoes, and a glass of water, no wine. He would then return to his writing until midnight, and even when he had got to bed might be roused in the early hours by a printer's boy.[29]

De Quincey, meanwhile, had sent him nothing in response to his plea, let alone his overdue magazine articles, despite being heavily in debt. In fact for six weeks he was very ill, almost to death, and thanks to this and the opium could produce no work. Furthermore, another son was born to him. Eventually in December 1820, drawing on Wilson for the coach fare, he came back to Edinburgh, where he was kindly received by friends who booked him lodgings and showered him with invitations in the hope of overcoming his writer's block. De Quincey stayed for six weeks, but produced only a single article.

He had his excuses. In an increasingly irritated correspondence he at length claimed that 'I see clearly that I must be [*Blackwood's*] Atlas . . . a more dreary collection of dulness and royal stupidity never did this world see gathered together than the December No. exhibits'; and asserting that he was hard at work to save it from a dismal fate. Blackwood was so offended that he cancelled their connection, and De Quincey returned to the Lakes, still drawing bills on Wilson until his refusal to pay further.[30]

This was the time of the *London Magazine's* attack on *Blackwood's*, and Lockhart's confrontation with John Scott. The duel with Christie took place on 17 February. That summer De Quincey went to London, and in September his *Confessions of an English Opium Eater* began to be published, to great acclaim, by the *London Magazine.* He did not return to Edinburgh until 1826.

A younger, more ambitious man at this time who also could not get his career started, was Thomas Carlyle, a total contrast to the privileged lawyer-writers and (usually less privileged) poets and their literary wrangling. As we know,

Carlyle never really liked Edinburgh, its 'foul air', noisy streets, and often unwelcome neighbours. Being poor, he walked nearly everywhere, even from home in Dumfriesshire or Annan, where he taught in 1815. But in February 1816 even he was joyful to see the city again after a three-day journey in snow and wind, only partly by coach.

Having completed his studies he wanted to write, was jealous of those who had succeeded in doing so, regarded most people he met as tiresome fools, and much of the time was suffering from dyspepsia.

He did praise Jeffrey and his achievements in the *Edinburgh*. 'He must be an extra-ordinary man', he wrote to Thomas Murray from Annan in 1814. 'No subject, however hackneyed, but he has the art of extracting some new thought out of it.' As for his critique on Byron, 'None but a man of keen penetration and deep research could have written such a thing . . .' But he ought not to narrow his field to politics.[31]

Whereas John Murray, having discerned that Scott must be the author of *Waverley,* criticised it for lack of humour, heaviness and excessive detail, Carlyle thought it 'the best novel that has been published these 30 years', and found much humour in it.[32]

When it came to metaphysics he was scathing of Dugald Stewart, whom southerners and the English admired despite disbelieving his principles. To Carlyle he seemed 'perpetually talking about analysing perceptions . . . & mighty improvements that we are to make – no one knows how', putting out 'disjointed notions & nondescript ideas'.[33]

For Carlyle the year was a long series of disappointments: even an ascent of Calton Hill in November to view the solar eclipse was thwarted in 'the unwholesome dews of morning . . . no man saw it nor woman either, the morning was cloudy – it even rained'.[34] And a meeting at the 'Philalethic Society' was disappointing too, with new members but no improvement, and what Carlyle considered as poor speakers. He did recognise that it must be largely he himself who had changed. 'When I quitted Edinr in 1814 – I felt as if I had been leaving the fountain head of knowledge and good humour and when I returned, its society seemed uninteresting, and their pursuits very stale and unprofitable!'[35]

Playfair next: Carlyle preferred his 'Dissertation Second' in the new *Encyclopaedia Britannica* supplement[36] to Stewart's, admitting 'It is distinguished for its elegance & Perspicuity', but 'I cannot admire this great philosopher, half as much as many critics do. He is so very stately – so transcendental – and withal so unintelligible . . .' He was patronisingly approving of the new weekly *Scotsman,* one of the several new periodicals, though 'a little violent in their Whiggism', and was sceptical about the new 'science' of phrenology.[37] To complete his distress an old acquaintance, William Irving, separated from his wife because of poverty, had first tried to commit suicide by taking laudanum, and when revived by an emetic, tied a string round his neck and – in the room where his children were asleep – opened the jugular vein. It seemed like some dreadful warning.[38]

This was the year of *Blackwood's* launch and re-launch and of the malicious Chaldee Manuscript. Carlyle could echo his own dissatisfactions in recounting the scandals and threats it evoked. The press was 'groaning with animadversions & replies'. There was also the public annoyance with the Council's determination to rebuild the shoddy St Anne's Buildings and wreck the view from Calton Hill (which Carlyle complained affected only a few feuars), and his irritation over Hogg's new tales which, he fumed, 'seemed to have been written under liquor'.[39]

At this time Carlyle was teaching at Kirkcaldy, and his splenetic visits to Edinburgh were sporadic. In 1818 he intended to enrol at the Divinity Hall, but was thwarted when the Rev. William Ritchie, Professor of Divinity and Minister of St Giles's, was too busy with management of the library, and when the committee drawing up the regulations submitted them, 'they gave much dissatisfaction to the Doctor', ending in 'great confusion, and several speeches vituperative and objurgatory'. Some fifty mutineers noisily removed to a classroom to draw up a list of grievances, which the Senatus Academicus investigated. The Divinity faculty in general was 'melancholy & unprofitable', and Carlyle dismissed the lot as 'dosing' and short on learning including Stewart's successor Dr Thomas Brown, and the professor of Oriental languages, the Rev. Alexander Brunton.[40]

He continued to damn the *Quarterly,* and wrote off Matthew Lewis's *The Monk* as 'the most stupid & villainous novel that I have read for a great while. Considerable portions of it are grossly indecent not to say brutish.' Poor Lewis scarcely earned a comment that was not condemnatory from anyone at all.[41]

Carlyle was usually happiest when at home with his parents. In October 1818 he gave notice to quit the Kirkcaldy job, having tried to discuss his future with Professor Christison in Edinburgh, but found him 'environed with a crowd of hungry schoolmasters', and all he heard was his exposition of 'the views of Messieurs Dufieff & Sanabbier, and . . . the merits of Sir James M'Intosh, the king, the late Ld Hopetoun, Dr Parr, the Calton-hill observatory, with 20 other things'. He was getting nowhere. Mitchell secured him some recommendations and he took lodgings in South Richmond Street, heard and criticised two lectures by Professor Robert Jameson ('he details a chaos of facts . . . in a manner as slovenly as he selects and arranges them . . . a total ignorance of dioptrics').[42] Living was expensive, and a box sent him by his family had been redirected, offloaded at the Grassmarket and stood for six weeks until not only had the shirts it contained become so mildewed that he could only use them as nightshirts, but he had to pay twice over for carriage (2s.10d.).

He was obliged to turn for a living to tutoring, and here he did obtain amusement from his various students. He also had introductions to Baillie Waugh, bookseller, who wanted him to write for yet another new review, but had so far limited himself to 'pleasant chat', and Dr Brewster who could offer him items for his *Encyclopaedia,* but though receiving him kindly, so far said nothing about writing. Waugh's *New Edinburgh Review* was predictably short-lived. Carlyle's spirits were mercurial,[43] so were his teaching commissions, sometimes four hours, sometimes only two or even nothing.

A friend explained the procedure of the famous 'letters of introduction'. 'You are received with a bow – the weather is discussed, and the merits of the last review – then you retire; some time after which you are invited to breakfast, and here the acquaintance terminates.' Carlyle, with more regard for truth and straight thinking than for social graces, was not one to adapt to this kind of convention.[44]

By February 1819 he was almost idle, unable to read or study; applying for books from the college library involved a long wait, only to find they were 'out'. He spent his time in solitary walks, and unwillingly associating with 'unfortunate persons'. Dr Brewster invited him to a Royal Society meeting in George Street, where Carlyle scornfully regarded the members as 'clean, well-dressed men' engaged in trivial discussion, Brewster being the most worthwhile member, whom he now began to consider more favourably. He tried mineralogy, but 'the wonderful lectures of the illustrious Werner's as illustrious disciple have completely destroyed all my enthusiasm'.[45] He re-started Italian, and kept moving lodgings.

Carlyle's regimen was to walk before breakfast, study German until 11, then stroll about the city with the pleasant, sensible John Fergusson, formerly Irving's assistant at Kirkcaldy, who also disliked teaching and was anxious to escape Edinburgh's 'sin & sea-coal'. One day they ran into Dr Brewster, who asked Carlyle to translate from the French a chemistry paper by Dr Berzelius – six long sheets of diffuse reasoning in a cramped hand. At least it was a job.[46]

Carlyle indignantly turned down the offer of teaching 'a stout, impudent-looking man with red whiskers' who haggled over 'two guineas a-month, for each hour'. The Berzelius paper looked not bad in print, and he moved lodgings again. He learned little geology from Jameson, but was improving his German.[47]

After the usual summer with his parents he returned in the autumn indolent and friendless. He decided after all to sign on for law under Professor Hume, the historian's nephew, whose lectures were nearly inaudible and who lacked his uncle's 'penetrating genius'; but he also attended other lectures, including Leslie's. In December 1819 his law books, especially Erskine's *Institutes*, weighed 'about 4 pounds avoirdupois; and you would [think] the very Goddess of dullness had inspired every sentence'.[48]

Radicalism and riots were much in the air, the 'Peterloo massacre' had taken place in Manchester in August, and although unrest was less serious in Scotland the poor were decidedly in bad straits. In December the volunteers turned out to support the soldiery, mounted guard in the castle, rode about valiantly while five thousand soldiers surrounded Glasgow, and the expected riot fizzled out. 'Radical Reformers – seditious orators – & warlike burghers are the humour of the day' (when people were not reading *Ivanhoe*).[49]

Again Carlyle maintained his frail health by walking twice a day between his studies, and at least found the law an intellectual challenge, but still his ambition to write beckoned from afar. Perhaps not so far after all, for that December, now living drearily in Bristo Street, he secretly worked on an unsolicited review of 'a late foolish M. Pictet . . . in Geneva', 'a mechanical *Theory of Gravitation*, elaborately worked out', and late in January delivered his parcel with a covering note to Jeffrey's valet, in George Street – with the same trepidation as nearly a generation later the young Dickens was to deliver his first journalistic piece, but with less success. He waited a fortnight with varying hopes, only to realise at last that he would hear nothing. Suppressing his chagrin, he decided to keep quiet about it, to everyone, let alone Jeffrey.[50]

Meanwhile Edward Irving paid Edinburgh a visit, basking in such popularity in Glasgow that his senior Dr Chalmers 'is thought to look with some anxiety at the pillars of his throne'.[51]

In December and January Edinburgh was plunged in deep frost, 'the capital of Greenland rather than of Caledonia', with 'ice & snow and bitter breezes', yielding at last to a thaw which gave Carlyle 'a filthy snivelling cold', while the poor's distress continued, though less than in the industrial areas. Even the farmers were suffering. The trainee idealists inspired Carlyle only with scorn, such as a volunteer he encountered 'with his buff-belts, his cartouche-box and weapons of war, obstructing the progress of his majesty's subjects along the streets'.[52]

Brewster, having lost Thomas Campbell's services, commissioned from Carlyle articles for the *Encyclopaedia Britannica*, and Carlyle took over a batch of 'Ms', each to consist of five or six pages: Montesquieu, Lady Mary Montagu . . . He dictated to young George Dalgliesh, 'a feeble but inquiring quasi-disciple of mine'. In London the Cato Street conspiracy was uncovered, and as spring approached Carlyle's health deteriorated while he felt increasingly conscious of solitude and the flight of precious time . . . his youth. Teaching and drudgery for the encyclopaedia barely sustained life, let alone spirit.

Now he had reached Sir John Moore and his father Dr Moore; then of 'Ns' only Necker and Nelson were still to write, and a review for Brewster's *Edinburgh Philosophical Journal*, on Magnetism of the Earth, which was published in January 1821. Brewster proved unexpectedly helpful, offered him more work, and hoped to arrange that he translate Mme Necker's *Life of Mme de Staël*. The money was little, but would keep him half a year.[53]

In May 1820 Carlyle left Edinburgh in another fit of disillusion over his law studies. David Hume had 'no spark of his uncle's genius', his lectures were 'the dullest piece of stuff I ever saw or heard of', and he finally abandoned them. Such writing as he had tried, other than 'the silly lives' for Brewster, came to nothing, and 'the last horrible winter' had further undermined his health.[54]

People were scouring the country in search of work, radicals were on the march, and Jeffrey produced 'two well-written articles' in the *Edinburgh*, on conditions in manufacturing, while in the *Quarterly* Southey was making 'delirious speculations' on radical reform.

In the summer the Wilson university election was looming, and although 'this is the age of philosophers', Carlyle admitted, 'the most astonishing of all sects – will be the *symposia* sect of moral philosophers reared under the wing of John Wilson Esq. In truth it was a clever thing to convert this man into a teacher of metaphysics.' He conceded that Wilson had genius.[55] In the new term he attended a couple of his lectures.

On his return in November there was another tiresome person to fulminate against: fat John Waugh, aged twenty-eight, son of an Annan shoemaker and convinced he was to become a successful doctor, who served Carlyle quarts of tea at his comfortable lodgings. Carlyle himself only found lodgings at a clean but chilly house in Carnegie Street, at the home of a schoolmaster's widow.[56]

Another review, projected by Brewster, like many others after a prolonged attempt came to nothing. But Carlyle now had access to the Advocates' Library and secured new temporary teaching. Thanks to frosty weather and the energetic walking to reach his pupils he was even feeling better, especially after he gave up eating porridge. He overcame the problem of his sedentary work by writing standing up, leaning against a chair at a desk placed on the table. In this way 'I wrote 7 hours without detriment.' He indulged in the occasional cigar with his tea.[57]

The bookseller Tait thought that Carlyle was 'one of the most hopeful youths of the part'. He spent Christmas in Glasgow with Irving, in wet weather; it proved disheartening among 'fat contented merchants – shovelling their beef over by the pound, and swilling their wine without measure, declaiming on politics and religion'. This was when he met 'the marvellous Dr John Scott'.[58]

Despite several disappointments, new prospects were dawning, and the next weeks are filled with hopes and prospects. Lodgings were as ever a problem, but Brewster invited him to dinner, when he met several men who seemed to him unworthy of the careers they had achieved, but at least he was meeting more people. 'I am not a genius', he said rather angrily to his mother, 'but a rather sharp youth, discontented and partly mismanaged, ready to work at aught but teaching.' Wrapping himself in the warm tartan roquelaure he had been given, he walked the cold night streets, alone but for the 'sons of Belial'. The Lockhart–John Scott quarrel, now raging, provided the chief gossip; the weather was improving, and Carlyle still juggled with idea after idea and lodging after lodging.[59]

In the lack of better employment he maintained his regimen of a morning cigar, the walk to his hour's teaching in Great King Street, return for breakfast (no porridge for health reasons), then a walk and reading at the Advocates' Library until dinner at 2 or 3 o'clock. Then came his amanuensis George Johnstone to write for him until 8 or 9, more reading, and after a late walk to Princes Street he would retire.

This fairly contented spell was succeeded by another bout of illness, melancholia and resentment against 'this accursed, stinking, reeky mass of stones and lime and dung', namely Edinburgh. Edinburgh alone was enough to make him ill, especially its famous smoke, turning him into 'a moping hypochondriac'. At least Brewster had kindly offered him a sixty-guinea commission of translating D'Aubuisson's work on geology (but this too fell through), and he tried St Bernard's Well spa water for his unruly guts.[60]

Two booksellers offered him work, Tait with translations, and Baillie Waugh, whom he despised as 'swaggering' and 'condescending', almost deferentially enlisted his help. 'I can have work, therefore, and good pay when I please.' But it was hack work.

'I write a very little, read some and walk some.' So it went on. He was heartened by going to hear Dr Thomas M'Crie, a Secession minister who had set up his own group and preached to the poor.[61]

While his health rocketed up and down with the weather, so did his hopes with the continual possibility and then collapse of commissions. The Scott duel in London caused a great sensation in Edinburgh, 'Scott having been a Whig and Lockhart the forlorn hope of our Tories. The latter has taken to bed, I hear, and well he may.'[62] And *Kenilworth* had been published.

When the sickly winter improved into spring, Carlyle could look forward to sea-bathing at Portobello. Waugh sent him Joanna Baillie's *Legend* to review, and John Wilson continued his 'volcanic lectures'.[63]

As summer approached Carlyle as usual found Edinburgh intolerable, stinking, pestilential, and now short of drinking water. His struggling career in these few years offers a disgruntled outsider's view of the city, never of high society but always of its literary fringe, and of the kind of lodgings the unprivileged might experience. But a new, unexpected horizon had now opened. Late in May he visited Haddington with Irving, who had come over for the General Assembly, and met Jane Welsh, from a noticeably higher stratum of society than himself, a pretty and bright young woman whose reactions to him were uncertain and her mother's only too much so. Although the impression was not mutually favourable, she took to learning German with him. At this stage much good it did either of them. But this, or something, stimulated Carlyle, and for five weeks he was 'writing day and night', mostly for the *Encyclopaedia*, now having reached the Netherlands and Newfoundland, before taking off for Mainhill for the summer.[64]

Early in 1822 Carlyle had the offer through Irving, now in London, of the tutorship of two boys of fifteen and thirteen, who were coming to the University for three months before their parents arrived, for £200 a year, with more permanent prospects if they suited. 'A round solid sum, for which a man would submit to much.'

The boys were Charles and Arthur, the sons of Charles Buller, a retired Indian judge. His wife, the daughter of Colonel William Kirkpatrick, had gone with her sister unenthusiastically to hear Irving preach at the Caledonian Chapel in Hatton Garden, and been fired with interest. Next day she sought Irving's advice on the education of her sons, and Carlyle was strongly recommended as a tutor.

The two boys arrived towards the end of January, and were to board for some months until their parents arrived with Dr Fleming, the minister at Lady Yester's church, at 26 George Square. Irving and Carlyle between them had spoken so strongly on the position and the emolument that (he told John), 'I need expect no supercilious or uncomfortable treatment there.'[65]

He was impressed by his young pupils, particularly Charles, the elder, who in turn used sometimes to accompany him almost back to his Moray Street lodgings in order to argue out some point. When Mr and Mrs Buller arrived Carlyle was at first equally impressed with them, at least with the husband. The elegant Mrs Buller was more stately and formal, but with Charles Buller senior, Carlyle enjoyed philosophical discussions.

They had taken a house in India Street, where the tutor and boys had use of a schoolroom and at 6 p.m. he took tea with the family. As the months went on his early, almost naïve reaction gave way to one more realistic but disenchanted.

This may have been aggravated by his returning bad health, his frustration at not yet writing, his lack of progress with Jane Welsh – and by six weeks of Siberian weather during the early weeks of 1823. His brother John was now lodging with him, whose jollier temperament helped to alleviate Thomas's black humours. He reacted cynically enough when a burglary took place in the India Street house and Mrs Buller, her husband being away, not knowing what to do, referred the matter to the tutor, who did know. The family then went to the Highlands for the summer.[66]

Carlyle ceased burning everything he wrote daily and got to work on a biography of Schiller, suffered disturbed nights from the neighbours, from the wind, in fact from anything, found his landlady in hysterics over distraint of her goods, and over-assumed his new progress with Jane Welsh, who abruptly snubbed his advances and told him he was a good friend, but 'Be your wife, never! never!' He went off home, and on other travels.[67]

William Hazlitt, son of a minister, had abandoned training for the church, first for painting and then for writing; having met Charles Lamb and through him other writers, he turned to a life in journalism and literary criticism.

As a staunchly liberal supporter of the French Revolution and then of Napoleon, he was generally concerned over social evils. He began to contribute to periodicals, notably the *Edinburgh Review*, from about 1812 when he was thirty-four, and published *Lectures on English Philosophy*, followed by *Characters in Shakespeare's Plays* (1817) and other works on drama and poetry. He also produced *Political Essays* (1819) on the state of the poor. Lockhart slated him in *Blackwood's*, slotting him into the 'Cockney School'. Jeffrey, who appears to have admired his work from at least 1814, in 1818 took his side over threatened litigation with *Blackwood's*. Since then they had continued to correspond.

In 1816 Hazlitt joined vigorously in the anti-Coleridge campaign, with articles in the *Edinburgh* and other reviews, not scrupling to attack the poet on personal grounds. It was the worse because he must have been suffering from guilt feelings over an early obligation, to not only Coleridge but Southey and Wordsworth, who some ten years back had admired his literary talent enough to help him escape the Bow Street Runners, and supplied him with money and even clothes when he was friendless and his parents had turned him out for 'unmanly vices'. Although his unworthy indulgences continued, to Coleridge's indignation Jeffrey cultivated Hazlitt for his very hostility.

When Coleridge's retaliation appeared in *Biographia Literaria*, Wilson slaughtered book and author in *Blackwood's* and Jeffrey, whom Coleridge had criticised for publishing Hazlitt's articles, riposted with a further attack by Hazlitt in the *Edinburgh*. The fact that he had earlier praised 'Christabel' made the present vendetta the more unworthy, pursued (as Coleridge said) with 'a malignity and a spirit of personal hatred'. One leading bookseller even told him that he dared not stock his work, as it would not sell because the *Edinburgh* damned it and the *Quarterly* ignored it.[68]

Hazlitt unsurprisingly excited conflicting reactions among those who knew him. Benjamin Haydon called him (in 1813) 'that interesting man, that singular mixture of friend and fiend, radical and critic, metaphysician, poet and painter, on whose word no one could rely, on whose heart no one could calculate'. A year later he was even more forthright. 'What a singular compound this man was of malice, candour, cowardice, genius, purity, vice, democracy and conceit.'[69]

He had little sympathy with Hazlitt's amorous follies with his 'lodging-house hussy', was scathing about the incongruity of his 'old, hard, weather-beaten saturnine, metaphysical face' (when Hazlitt was forty-four), 'absolutely twitching' in his emotion, and found his behaviour in general ridiculous.[70] Washington Irving limited his comments to observing that he always had dirty hands.

In 1818 Hazlitt considered giving a course of literary lectures in Edinburgh, but Jeffrey seriously warned him against it with some revealing comments. 'In general I think Edinburgh the worst place in the world for such experiments as you seem to meditate, both from the extreme dissipation of the fashionable part of its population, and from a sort of conceit and fastidiousness in all the middling classes, which, originating at least as much in a coldness of nature as in any extraordinary degree of intelligence, makes them very ready to find fault and decry.'

He explained that the only kind of lecture which did not fail in Edinburgh either 'pretended to reveal some wonderful secret, like Feinagle', or (less successfully) to offer short popular courses on subjects like Astronomy and Chemistry. Hazlitt might raise an audience of perhaps forty or fifty, 'not of the first rank or condition', and be condemned as a Jacobin by everyone else. 'We are quite provincial enough for that, I assure you, notwithstanding the allowance of liberality and sense that is to be found among us.'[71]

Hazlitt had agreed to contribute to Constable's *Edinburgh Magazine*, which in November 1817 had praised him and vindicated Leigh Hunt, whom *Blackwood's* had been attacking so savagely. *Blackwood's* turned on Hazlitt. 'It was indeed a fatal day for Mr Jeffrey, when he degraded both himself and his original coadjutors, by taking into pay such an unprincipled blunderer as Hazlitt. He is not a coadjutor, he is an accomplice . . .' Not surprisingly, Hazlitt took out a charge of libel, and Murray took up the cudgels, writing to Blackwood, 'I cannot perceive your object in literally running amuck of everyone.'[72]

It was in 1822 that Hazlitt's most curious connection with Edinburgh took place. In 1808 he had married Sarah Stoddart,[73] and they had a son now ten years old, but were evidently quite unsuited. After a few years Hazlitt plunged headlong into a would-be affair when, separated from his wife, he became besotted by Sarah Walker, the unremarkable, rather sluttish daughter of his landlady in Southampton Buildings (Chancery Lane). At first flattered, the girl was then scared by this passion and plainly did not care about him, but Hazlitt plagued not only her but his friends Sheridan Knowles and Peter Patmore with a series of intemperate letters which he was eventually unwise enough to publish under the title *Liber Amoris* (1823). The affair ended in emotional disaster, not to mention much uneasiness for the girl, and Hazlitt earned great moral disapproval.[74]

Meanwhile, having determined on a divorce, Hazlitt came to Edinburgh to qualify through the Scottish courts by a forty-day residence in the country. He stayed some time in Berwickshire at the Renton Inn, in order to write, and arrived in Edinburgh on 10 April, lodging at 10 George Street, almost opposite St Andrew's Church. He had arranged two lectures for May in Glasgow. Having not heard from his wife, he was even thinking of returning to London when on 21 April in Leith Walk, he accidentally met Adam Bell, who was to act as his legal representative, who told him that she had arrived at Leith that very day.[75]

This surprising woman, treated with some contempt by her husband's friends, kept a journal during her visit – partly as a record, partly to while away her solitary days – which shows her to have been sensible and down-to-earth. During the constant legal delays she went on almost daily expeditions, sometimes for several days, almost always on foot and walking her shoes to shreds.[76]

Sarah Hazlitt was in Edinburgh from 21 April to 18 July, arriving on the smack *Superb* from Tilbury. Her detailed journal, which ends as abruptly as it began, records the progress of the divorce suit and her numerous expeditions. For her first night she stayed at the *Blackwood's* coterie's haunt, the Black Bull in Catherine Street (where Hazlitt had also stayed), moving the next day to Mr Bracewell's at 6 South Union Place, for which she paid fourteen shillings with two shillings more for firing. She also subscribed to the nearby Sutherland's Library at 9 Calton Street, paying 4s. 6d. for a month, but does not record what she read, and bought a lottery ticket, which proved blank.

Most of her encounters were with Adam Bell, Hazlitt's dubious agent, and the *Scotsman* co-editor William Ritchie, also a friend of Hazlitt's. She was constantly under pressure not to hinder or oppose the action, and to start with she had to study the long Summons of Divorce, citing the facts of their marriage and of her husband's known 'cohabitation' in both London and Edinburgh. She learned that he was now frequently to be found at Mrs Knight's, the Anglo-Indian daughter of an officer, living in reduced circumstances at 21 James Street. How 'reduced' she learned later.

John Gray, the reliable solicitor of 10 Hanover Street, to whom the advocate George Cranstoun[77] recommended her, visited James Street and found it the haunt of 'a set of the lowest, abandoned blackguards', who refused even to speak to him until he loosened their tongues with liberal mulled port.

'The appearance of the house, people, and every thing about it, was more infamous than anything that he had before any idea existed in Edinburgh . . .' That, Sarah informed him with some disgust, was the kind of place and people, in London too, that her husband preferred to her company. One day she herself walked along the street and saw Mrs Knight in a window, 'a woman of colour with a white turban cap on', the houses gone down in the world and the surroundings squalid and depressing.

Much of her enforced leisure Sarah passed in long walks, first to the castle, Calton Hill and the observatory, then to Holyroodhouse and Arthur's Seat, and Newhaven, finding it a street of wretched fishermen's huts but with a few better houses now building, and a pretty, hedge-lined road back by Canonmills. It was eight days before she experienced anything like 'a summer day', which she employed in walking to the links, Restalrig and Leith Sands; but it was followed by more cold, hazy weather which did not enhance even a walk to the Old Town. Portobello she admired for its beach, 'gentlemen's houses and grounds', and fine views round the barracks on the return trip. Her comments were pithy and practical, though on more ambitious expeditions she evidently copied information from a guide-book.

From the beginning of May she suffered from a recurrent bowel complaint, probably aggravated by the tension and uncertainty, and several times had to stay in all day. On other days the weather was so bad, even once with hail and snow, that she could not go out, the wind so blustery one day in George Street that she had to return, and another time it broke two whalebone struts of her new parasol. A recurring worry was money shortage. As Hazlitt was in Edinburgh at the same time, she occasionally saw him, but he too was awaiting payment of fees, partly from the lectures he was giving in Glasgow.

Their recriminations increased, and he complained bitterly when, twice warned of long delays in the case, she took off on longer expeditions. One was an eight-day trip by steamboat from Newhaven to Stirling, and thence on foot to Doune, Callander, the Trossachs and Loch Lomond, catching a bad cold, and returning via Glasgow, the Falls of Clyde and New Lanark. She reached Edinburgh travel-stained and exhausted, apart from the stretches by boat having covered 170 miles on foot, glad to be back in her lodging 'and literally wash the dust off my feet', with the comfort of 'a thorough ablution' and clean clothes.

For reasons of economy she had moved to another apartment on the same stair, for only ten shillings, with Mrs Pillans, apparently a relative of the Rector of the High School. She now spent much time writing, and was stranded, money gone and Hazlitt back in London for a fortnight. The uncouth Bell enlightened her about her husband and Sarah Walker, and suggested she bring her son to school in Edinburgh while she set up as an instructor to young ladies. For this, she told him, she was not equipped. Meanwhile she was enduring Edinburgh's summer water shortage and had to drink bottled ale. She fell ill again, and the weather became so bad that she had to have a fire.

Her long walking expeditions continued, the Old Town, Stockbridge, St Bernard's Well with the gorge of the Water of Leith and its mill, and Mr Ross's tower built from ancient fragments and sculptures; and a seventeen-mile visit to Lasswade and Roslin. She also took another long 'jaunt' of five days, this time less tiring and therefore more enjoyable, taking the Burntisland ferry from Newhaven and then on foot as far as Perthshire, carrying her own basket of provisions, and needing only water from cottages. Returning via Stirling, she had covered 112 miles before taking the steamboat back to Newhaven.

Bell and his wife, who had just moved to 3 Pilrig Street off Leith Walk, she visited several times, once dining with his wife, when he came home drunk and started abusing her character, morals, appearance and everything else, then insisted on accompanying her home to continue his insults. She had some difficulty in preventing him from coming to her room, while his young son, whom Mrs Bell had sent to see him safely back, had to be protected from his blows. The encounter made her so ill that she had to wake the family in the night to send for Dr Graham, who prescribed dire remedies including laudanum, and Bell returned next day to make a further nuisance of himself under the pretext of apologising.

William Ritchie also called, and learning of Bell's behaviour warned her against his known character. He was himself exhausted after being in court until 5 a.m. on the Stuart/Boswell duel case. Next day Sarah was better, though drowsy from laudanum, and able to enjoy 'a nice roast chicken . . . with two glasses of port'.

Meanwhile Hazlitt had retreated again to the Renton Inn, hoping in vain to repeat his earlier writing spell. Bell was now putting the blame on him for malicious gossip about Sarah, both to himself and Mrs Bell, 'in a manner unfit for any modest woman's ear'. The date of taking the Oath was now fixed for 14 June, and she accompanied John Gray to the Parliament House for the tedious bureaucratic process with Mr Prentice, the Commissioner, 'a prodigious grave Ass in office', who insisted on putting them off for another week. The whole affair now seemed delayed for weeks. The Bells told her that Hazlitt had become violently enraged against her, and a meeting with him resulted only in arguments about money and their son. Nearly choked with anxiety, Sarah set off on yet another expedition, ten days in which she actually got to Ireland, and on her return on 29 June Hazlitt arrived with money and complained about her extravagance.

Still unwell, she resumed her local expeditions. One day, she accidentally encountered Hazlitt and his friend Henderson in a gig near Dalkeith Palace, and after their usual discussions she walked on to Newbattle, and the others passed her on the way back. Another time she walked to Gilmerton to see George Paterson's subterranean smithy, origin of Wayland's smithy in

Kenilworth, and her last pair of slippers (her shoes had long gone) was worn out, so that to walk was crippling. She could buy no more, and struggled painfully to Melville, Liberton, Barnbougle, Queensferry . . . twenty-four miles in a day.

She became friendly with a Mrs Banks or Bancks, who lent her *The Cottagers of Glenburnie* to read (she says nothing of reading anything else). She mended stockings, embroidered a handkerchief. She walked again to Newhaven to enquire about the boat to London, and thought the four-and-a-half guinea fare (without liquor) extortionate; and climbed Corstorphine Hill, admiring the country and the pretty villas round Slateford. Meetings with Hazlitt always ended in argument. Officially they were supposed not to meet, and of course could not travel back to London together. Hazlitt vilified her to Mrs Bell and others, claimed 'I was no maid when he married me', kept on about his passion for Sarah Walker and complained of being so long penned up in Edinburgh, unable to work.

At last she received a note for £50 through Ritchie, and learned that Hazlitt had boarded a boat the previous night, but she herself did not escape from Edinburgh before Bell had insulted her with obscene remarks and a veiled pass, calling her a fool to divorce and saying she ought to grab 'some old rich Scots lord' and settle here. The end of her stay was appropriately marked by heavy weather and a violent thunderstorm. After she went on board the *Favourite* on 18 July, we hear no more of her.

Hazlitt's own stay in Edinburgh, in spite of his complaints and shortage of money, had been more agreeable, or at least more social. He had Edinburgh friends, and had visited Roslin. More to the point, he had met Jeffrey.

'I have seen the great little man', he wrote to Patmore on 30 March, 'and he is very gracious to me – *Et sa femme aussi!* I tell him I am dull and out of spirits, and he says he cannot perceive it. He is a person of infinite vivacity.' He also told Hazlitt that his review of Byron's verse play *Sardanapalus,* intended for the February *Edinburgh,* would be published in the next issue. This was the first time they had actually met.[78]

On 17 April Hazlitt was invited to dine by William Ritchie, along with McCulloch, Thomas Hodgskin and George Combe, who left a description of the evening.

At this time McCulloch had only recently withdrawn from the *Scotsman.* At thirty-three he was the youngest of the guests. The modest and retiring Hodgskin, son of a naval storekeeper at Chatham, had gone to sea at twelve and retired at twenty-five as a half-pay officer. He wrote pamphlets and foregathered with Radicals in London, including Francis Place, who described him as rather gloomy, and 'singularly modest and unobtrusive, easily excited'. Since the war he had travelled in Europe, and when in Hanover had read an Edinburgh article by McCulloch, whose praise of Ricardo's new *Principles* greatly influenced him. He married a German girl, wrote up his travels, and with his wife gave German lessons, including to McCulloch. But he was unhappy in Edinburgh, and was considering returning to London to become a Parliamentary reporter.

George Combe had published his *Essay on Phrenology* in 1819, which had brought him Ritchie's friendship and interest and a favourable review in the *Scotsman* – good ammunition against the scepticism of Jeffrey and Sir William Hamilton. (Hazlitt was equally sceptical, though there is no suggestion that the subject was discussed that evening.)

Combe, recording the occasion, noted how Hazlitt not only drank no wine but consumed pints of tea, saying alcohol had only done him harm. He was shy among strangers, and sat fairly removed from the company, keeping his eyes down. In describing him ('short and of a moderate thickness'), Combe could not resist a detailed phrenological account of his head: 'Acquisitiveness, large . . . Individuality, lower large . . . Love of Comparison, large, very . . . Wit, rather large; Imitation, large . . . Love of Approbation seemed very large . . . The mouth speaks Combativeness and Destructiveness very strongly . . .' He also noted that Hazlitt had a courteous, well-bred manner, though his conversation was neither 'vehement' nor 'sparkling'. As for his ideas, they seemed more interesting on reflection than at the time, but covered 'a great range, literature, travel, art, politics, Tom Paine, Benjamin Haydon'. (Haydon's exhibition at Waterloo Place had closed only in February.[79])

When they parted, McCulloch went home to Buccleuch Place, and Hazlitt walked back with Hodgskin, who had lodgings at 11 Waterloo Place. Although Ritchie was supportive about the divorce, on which he had given Sarah Hazlitt sound advice, he may have felt either that Hazlitt was somewhat cavalier with his thanks, or have disapproved of his behaviour over the divorce; at all events the two seem not to have met again during Hazlitt's stay.[80]

In May Hazlitt gave his Glasgow lectures and then, back at the Renton Inn, wrote on 9 June that Jeffrey, with whom he had burdened at least part of the saga of his obsessional love, had kindly advanced him £100 'to give me time to recover'. He then set off on a Highland tour with Sheridan Knowles, during much of which he seems to have regaled Knowles too with his love affair.

After the third delay the divorce case was settled, and he was able to return to London.

He had made a tactical mistake during his visit in not making an overture to Constable or Wilson. Wilson relented enough to observe in the first *Noctes* 'O, Hazlitt's a real fellow in his small way', but in August 1823 he remarked that he 'shewed a great want of trap by not coming to sup with us during his late northern progress', while Hazlitt, less relenting, stated in *On the Scotch*

Character, 'Of all blackguards a Scotch blackguard is the worst'. Another lawsuit threatened, but was avoided.[81]

Recovering from his lapse into his emotional madness, and from arrest for debt, Hazlitt continued a prolific literary output, remarried in 1824 (apparently in Edinburgh), and travelled abroad, but three years later his second wife left him.[82]

32
LITERARY FIGURES (2)

'Pre-eminent . . . for that elegant simplicity and affecting interest, which powerfully awakens the finest sympathies of the heart . . . distinguished for his talents, his manners, and particularly excelling in the powers of conversation . . . a kind of patriarch in literature.'

Elizabeth Isabella Spence (on Henry Mackenzie), *Letters from the North Highlands during the Summer 1816*, London, 1817, 36

'There are few duller books, I think; how could it have got such reputation?'

Thomas Moore, *Journal*, II.256, 7 Jan. 1819, on *The Man of Feeling*

'Our critic is merciless to female genius, with the exception of Miss Edgeworth . . . Home's Douglas, Thomson's Sigismunda, and Miss Baillie's Tragedies . . . do not seem born to die.'

Mrs Grant of Laggan to Miss Catherine Fanshaw, 30 August 1815, *Memoirs of Mrs Grant of Laggan*, II.105

'I was much struck by his appearance. He was singularly gay . . . with an ease which was new to me then and which I have never seen equalled since. He was dressed in the height of fashion. What struck me most . . .was that he appeared so much older than he really was. He was singularly pale and old-looking.'

Thomas Hog younger on Patrick Fraser Tytler (1825), quoted in Rev. J. W. Burgon, *Memoirs of Patrick Fraser Tytler*, 1829, 182

While new figures were always appearing on the literary scene, of those who survived from two generations back the most distinguished was old Henry Mackenzie, hardy and sociable well into his seventies. When Robert Gillies met him at a dinner-party in 1810 he was sixty-five, then considered a great age, but though he had long ceased to write and appeared older than he was, he was a bundle of activity. 'No weather daunted him,' says Gillies, often out in wintry spells with his pointer, 'his attenuated form, wrapped in a long, dark *surtout*, which always seemed too wide, as if only a skeleton were under it, and his countenance, then worn away and sharpened, he was like a *revenant* from another epoch.' In company he was lively and unaffected, prone to quoting from Shakespeare.

On the whole, however, Mackenzie inclined to country life and field sports. Although his office as Comptroller of Taxes kept him much in Edinburgh – like the majority of its leading literary figures – up to the age of eighty he would take to the country during vacations with his gun and dogs.[1] When in Edinburgh, his frequent exercise often took him to look in at Ballantyne's, to be received with respect as 'the stedfast friend of Scott, and the patriatch of our northern literature'.[2]

Back in the 1700s Mackenzie had followed up his much admired novel of sentiment, *The Man of Feeling,* with *Julia de Roubigné, The Prince of Tunis* and other works, and in 1808 Constable published his complete opus in eight volumes. They remained good friends through life, apart from a misunderstanding over *Blackwood's* and the Chaldee Manuscript in 1818. Mackenzie, who had just arranged with John Home's nephew to preface an intended edition of the clergyman-playwright's works with his own memoir of Home, believed that Constable was connected with John Scott's attack on *Blackwood's,* which seemed to imply a breach of confidence over the 'Life of Home', and offended him the more as he had been disgusted not only by its scurrility but also by 'some late abominable articles' in *Blackwood's.* Furthermore, he found Lockhart's challenge to John Scott ridiculous. Constable (who was away at the time) assured him that he had nothing to do with Scott's pamphlet, and further that he too had been 'grossly attacked' in *Blackwood's* almost every month for the past year. Mackenzie made a full apology, and instead reproached *Blackwood's* as a 'most false and scandalous Journal'.[3]

Mackenzie was one of the celebrities whom the American scholar George Ticknor met in 1819, breakfasting at Lady Cumming's. 'He is now old, but a thin, active, lively little gentleman, talking fast and well upon all common subjects, and without the smallest indication of the "Man of Feeling" about him.'[4] Mackenzie, then in mid-seventies, was to live on until 1831 and the age of eighty-six.

Some of the young meteors of the 1790s were themselves now well into middle age. Thomas Campbell, whose *Gertrude of Wyoming* had earned such golden opinions in 1809, soon suffered a series of bereavements, first his younger son, then his mother who died of a stroke, and also his old friend James Grahame. He was living in London, where in 1811 he was preparing a series of lectures at the Royal Institute for 1812. Scott commented on his 'brogue', which he thought would not affect their success provided Campbell did not try to suppress it but 'read with fire and feeling'. Campbell in his turn was rather put out that Sydney Smith 'cautioned me against *joking* in my lectures! Was it not Satan reproving sin?' His friend and neighbour Lady

Charlotte Campbell attended the lectures (although Thomas would not allow his own wife), and the series was greeted with enthusiasm. There was even a threat that the Princess of Wales, whose lady-in-waiting Lady Charlotte was, might come to one of them, but she was dissuaded. There was discussion of repeating the lectures in Edinburgh. After a visit to Paris, the poet returned to Edinburgh in 1815 to settle a legacy, warmly received after his thirteen-year absence, and 'whirled about' from friend to friend.[5]

He paid his court to Mrs Fletcher, centre of the Whigs as Mrs Grant was of the Tories: 'the lady in Edinburgh by way of eminence, and her conversation is more sought than that of anybody there', wrote Ticknor in 1819, while Sir James Mackintosh and Henry Brougham both wished she lived in London, so that they could listen to her every day.[6]

Campbell in 1815 was astonished to find her now even 'improved in all points . . . her beauty, eloquence, wit, and warm-heartedness – all heightened by time', and she made her house available to him whenever he was not staying with his sisters.

He also for the first time met Mrs Grant 'who is even more than her writings bespeak'.[7] Mrs Grant on her side was pleased to see him 'cheerful, happy, and universally welcomed and caressed in his dear "Queen of the North", which he had had to leave 13 years ago in order to earn a living . . . He has visited me several times, and is so amusing and so original.'[8]

Seeing much of his friends the Alisons proved a little disconcerting, for he found the two sons already 'grave and sagacious young men, rising in professional eminence', while he himself with the Rev. Mr Alison 'better and fresher than when I left him', but still 'venerable', 'exhibit the contrast of two giggling old fellows'. (Campbell was thirty-eight.) The five-year-old daughter had become a handsome young woman, and as they all sat by the fire she would reminisce with Campbell over their days of 'alternate romping and quarrelling' when 'we used to be the mutual torment and delight of each other'.[9]

Other happy days were spent with the Stewarts at Kinneil, walking and reading with them and in 'most delightful conversations'. He read his lectures to the Professor, who applauded them as full of 'good poetry as well as in sound philosophy . . . nothing pleases him so much as listening for hours together to the most minute details of human character', especially the leading personalities of the time. As for his beloved hostess, she was charming as ever, and addressed him as her son.

Campbell went on to Glasgow by 'track-boat' to visit relations. While he was still in Scotland, the Battle of Waterloo was fought, and in honour of the victory he wrote his poem 'The British Grenadiers'.[10]

Scott would gladly have had Campbell settled in Edinburgh again, not just visiting for lectures, and in 1816 made a complicated proposal that he take on two sinecure university classes, on Rhetoric and History. The former was the more doubtful as the nominal teacher lived in Edinburgh and might not be keen to take a 'coadjutor'; the other gentleman, long retired to the north, received the £100 stipend but did not even pretend to give the lectures, and might well be shamed into accepting Campbell as 'colleague', if Scott could negotiate it. He wrote jubilantly that at present, the university's patrons the magistrates were 'rather well disposed towards literature (witness their giving me my freedom, with a huge silver tankard that would have done honour to justice Shallow)', while the Provost himself was 'really a great man, and a man of taste and reading'.[11]

Nothing came of this ingenious scheme, but by then Campbell was negotiating for lectures in the provinces. He was also distressed about his elder son, unhappy at school and in poor health, eventually diagnosed as melancholia, so that Campbell then kept him at home and taught him himself. The poor boy was eventually sent to a private asylum, but was discharged, uncured, a year later (October 1822).[12] Meanwhile Campbell, after a long-projected return visit to Germany, became editor of the *New Monthly Magazine* under a three-year contract.[13]

Tom Moore also had frequent difficulties, mainly financial, and in 1818 when his deputy for his sinecure post in Bermuda defaulted Moore became liable for £6000 and took refuge abroad. Jeffrey, ever generous, came to his rescue as he did with others. Moore's state was actually reported in the press, and Jeffrey, unable to discover the full particulars, asked Samuel Rogers to find out and deal with him diplomatically as go-between, keeping Jeffrey's identity secret.

Though not very flush himself, he could still spare £300, or even £500 on security, feeling he could not pass over this crisis since Moore was a family man.[14]

Joanna Baillie, having scored a great success in 1810 with her play *The Family Legend,* was living in Hampstead, receiving admirers and producing more plays and poems. Like ageing blue-stockings, head cooks and housekeepers, she liked to be addressed as 'Mrs'. Miss Berry, one of her acquaintances, read most of *The Family Legend,* which, she noted, 'had a vast effect upon Walter Scott, and one that was very pleasing, from the evident feeling of one poet for another'. The Berry sisters were also seeing a good deal of Playfair and Lord Webb Seymour, who were both in London in the summer of 1809. In 1811 Miss Berry spent a weekend with Miss Baillie in Hampstead, where she read her *Hope,* and they walked on the Heath, and read and discussed each other's work.[15]

Jeffrey, asked for his opinion of Miss Baillie's 'Tragedies' by Mrs Grant in 1815, 'speaks more favourably of them than he is wont to do where his opinion is asked' (she reported to her friend Mrs Rucker); but he says she tries to stick too closely to the Greek models, and that her tragedies are unplayable. 'Our critic is merciless to female genius', she remarks, 'with the exception of Miss Edgeworth.' She continues that no tragedy since the Union had kept its reputation except those of Caledonian origin: 'Home's Douglas, Thomson's Sigismunda, and Miss Baillie's Tragedies, which do not seem born to die.'[16]

Jeffrey's criticism of Joanna Baillie's plays had caused offence from as long ago as 1803 by its apparent flippancy, and for many years she refused to meet him. In autumn 1820, however, they met in Edinburgh – and inevitably ended by liking each other. Thereafter Jeffrey was her sincere friend, and whenever he went to London made a point of visiting her in Hampstead.[17]

Lady Charlotte Campbell later explained critics' 'mercilessness' to female writers. In her *Diary of a Lady in Waiting* (1838) she wrote, 'all women who meddle with literature, especially those in the higher ranks of life, place themselves in a pillory, at which every impertinent idler conceives he has a right to throw his rotten eggs'.[18]

In July 1816 Mrs Elizabeth Hamilton, never in good health, died, leaving a great gap in Mrs Grant's life. 'At her house a more selected circle met, where there really was little or no town gossip; the topics were literary or general', and a stranger received there at once met all Edinburgh's 'accredited company'.[19]

Elizabeth Spence, a bluish lady who visited Scotland in 1810 and wrote up her observations in letters to 'the Countess of Winterton', observed of Mrs Hamilton that she 'seems to be endowed with all the strength of the Scotch character; acute, judicious, philosophical, with a modesty which accompanies a real sound understanding, and much native benevolence'.[20]

Of Mrs Grant she said that her conversation was 'full of that native simplicity, original genius, elegant sentiment, and acute observation' as her *Letters from the Mountains* showed.[21]

Altogether, Miss Spence records with satisfaction, wherever she had been entertained 'the conversation is seldom frivolous. The women have more intellectual knowledge, and seldom speak or act without reflection.'[22]

The beautiful Mrs Fletcher, though not one of the literary set, was a leading hostess among intellectuals. Mrs Grant was gratified that her new house in Princes Street had 'brought me nearer her, which I consider as a great privilege', and she praised 'her beauty, talents, and benevolence'.[23]

'Learning of all kinds is now too common among ladies', wrote Mrs Brunton in 1818, 'to be any longer like Cain's mark . . . These hard times compel so many women to celibacy, that I should think it no bad speculation to educate a few for respectable old maids.' As an example of female distinction she quotes Mrs Somerville, who two years earlier had 'gained a mathematical prize, from Oxford I think, with perfect impunity; being still universally received as a very agreeable womanly sort of person'.[24] Mrs

Fletcher and Mrs Somerville were shining examples to their contemporaries that one need not be 'blue', but could be charming as well as brilliant.

Miss Edgeworth, who met Mrs Somerville in London in 1822, describes her as 'little, slightly made, fairish hair, pink colour; small gray round, intelligent, smiling eyes, very pleasing countenance, remarkably soft voice, strong, but well-bred Scotch accent, timid . . . naturally modest, yet with a degree of self-possession'.[25]

Although Maria Edgeworth did not come to Edinburgh until 1823, in 1813 she made a great sensation in London, where Miss Berry met her (with about seventy or eighty other people) at Lady Davy's. Miss Edgeworth, however, 'was my object. She is very small, with a countenance which promises nothing at first sight, or as one sees her in society. She has very winning manners', and received Miss Berry's praise warmly, reciprocating with many compliments over the latter's own productions.[26]

Many years earlier the visiting Swiss professor Marie-Auguste Pictet, who met Miss Edgeworth when she was thirty-five, had commented on her unremarkable appearance. 'A small figure, eyes nearly always lowered, a profoundly modest and reserved air, without expression in the features when not speaking . . . But when she spoke . . . nothing could have been better thought, and nothing better said, though always timidly expressed . . .'[27]

Her novels, though lacking in lightness and imagination, and too moral and didactic for many tastes, were remarkable for shrewdness and sharp observations of character.

A figure who constantly appears on the fringes, although in her later years she apparently seldom returned to Edinburgh, is Lady Charlotte Campbell, the beautiful younger daughter of the 5th Duke of Argyll. She was a kind of legend among admiring young men (and still when the same men looked back from middle age), and in her youth was mobbed in the streets of Glasgow for appearing in outrageously immodest clothes. Yet she made two surprisingly dull marriages, first to her kinsman Colonel John Campbell, by whom she had several children, and in 1818 to the Rev. Edward Bury. Her literary output included several novels, and she was also a friend and counsellor to Susan Ferrier. From 1809 she was lady-in-waiting to Caroline, Princess of Wales, living at Blackheath, and a friend of the Berry sisters and Monk Lewis.

Susan Ferrier, often compared to Jane Austen, was seven years younger than Lady Charlotte and youngest of the ten children of the 5th Duke's legal adviser James Ferrier, a gentleman who could be by turns unpredictably crusty or amiable and relaxed. They mostly lived at Morningside House, a couple of miles from Edinburgh, or when in town at 25 George Street. In his old age Ferrier's health was poor, 'an excuse', remarked his daughter, 'for wearing his old ragged duffel coat and not shaving his beard'. So that he cut 'rather a *picturesque* figure'.[28]

In youth Susan Ferrier several times visited the Argyll castle at Inveraray, whence she learned much about the habits of high life, later incorporated into her novels. At Inveraray she met Horace Walpole's friend the sculptress Mrs Damer, and became friendly with Lady Charlotte and especially with her namesake daughter, with whom she kept up a lively correspondence. With a native irony like her near-contemporary Miss Austen, she observed the characters she met, and late in 1810 read part of the manuscript of a novel she had compiled from them to Lady Charlotte, who fell about with laughter. The satire was unmistakable, and she declared it 'without the least exception the cleverest thing that ever was written'.[29]

Susan was then twenty-eight, an old maid, and too 'clever' not to remain one. She had then no serious thoughts of publication, but eventually Blackwood got to hear about it, and the result was *Marriage*, published anonymously in 1818, the first of her three novels spread over a number of years.

Marriage is not a particularly good novel, with a rambling, unstructured plot, and characters who rise and sink with not much planning; nor has it the lightness that infused Miss Austen's wittier novels. People are sharply, even cruelly, observed, with little concession to human kindness. The ridiculous Misses Edmonstone of Edinburgh were the originals of three spinster sisters, and other characters were not hard to recognise in this part *roman à clef.* But it was a springboard, and over the next few years Susan Ferrier improved her approach, so that *The Inheritance* in 1824 was better composed, and with a more satisfactory plot.

Walter Scott praised *Marriage* as a 'very lively work', in his conclusion to *Tales of my Landlord*, and for its description of Scottish characters. Starting with local fame, the book soon established itself outside Edinburgh. Some people in London actually thought it was by Scott, a fairly naïve assumption. It even ran to a French translation. Meanwhile Miss Ferrier, her sisters now married, continued to keep house for her father until his death in 1829.[30]

Susan Ferrier's limited experience of the aristocratic world occasionally shows. For example, having promised a grand ball to which the heroine is invited, she makes a craven retreat at the last minute, and instead the girl spends the evening virtuously visiting a worthy old lady – a let-down for the reader, doubtless because the author did not trust herself enough to write up such a grand occasion. Curiously, Lady Charlotte herself was once castigated by Charles Kirkpatrick Sharpe for socially unacceptable forms in her own satirical *Self-Indulgence* (1812), in which gentlemen address ladies as 'my lady' – 'surely not the mode of these times'. Sharpe hints that certain friends from whom she might have picked up the form were 'very low people'. 'She also insinuates', he added impatiently, 'that all gay young men begin life by becoming drunkards – an hypothesis which is now utterly false, both with regard to English and to Scots.' He was the more incensed because on the flimsiest grounds, 'Certain civil people in Edin. imputed it to me'.[31]

The poetess Carolina, Lady Nairne, was one of those ladies who would have considered it a disgrace both to her sex and class for her name to appear in print. Born Carolina Oliphant in 1766 to Lawrence, ADC to Prince Charles Edward, at the age of forty she married Major William Murray Nairne, a second cousin on her mother's side, who was heir to the dormant Nairne peerage, and was based at Edinburgh Castle.

They moved in 1808 to a new 'cottage' in Edinburgh's western suburbs on the slopes of Corstorphine Hill, where their only son William was born. He was a delicate boy, educated at home by tutors, including mathematics at 8 in the morning, by a student recommended by Dr Chalmers.

Mrs Nairne had an old friend in Mrs Campbell Colquhoun, Scott's early love, who had instead married the Lord Advocate. Near neighbours were the Alexander Keiths at Ravelston House, and in 1811 Mrs Nairne's younger sister Margaret married Keith, then aged about fifty, an old-fashioned character with an even older spinster sister. Their hospitality was also old-fashioned. The Nairnes were always among the party assembled there on summer Saturdays, expected to arrive 'early', play games on the lawn until 2, and when summoned by the tower bell, retire to prepare for dinner.

At 2.30 a Scottish luncheon, or dinner, was served with a menu of hodge-podge, cocky-leeky and haggis, and in good weather dessert was taken out of doors, under the trees. There would be a quaint sort of *conversazione* in the garden, not unlike that described in *Waverley* at Tullyveolan. There were always ladies in the party after tea or coffee, to which they were summoned by a gong, and everyone present was expected to sing, unaccompanied. No instruments were permitted. Mrs Nairne, who was also a talented artist, secretly compiled many songs, and adapted ancient lays.

The Nairnes were also friendly with the Misses Hume, Elizabeth and Agnes, the musical daughters of Baron David Hume, who used to entertain at their father's house and set the musical fashion in Edinburgh.[32] In 1821 the music publisher Robert Purdie consulted the Humes about issuing a collection of Scottish airs 'with words suited for refined circles' (says Lady Nairne's biographer the Rev. Charles Rogers). They in turn consulted Mrs Nairne, who had long wished to 'purify' Scottish song. They formed a ladies' committee with Mrs Nairne as president, but under strict secrecy, even using a pseudonym as Mrs Bogan of Bogan.

Scottish Minstrel, edited by Robert Archibald Smith, was published in six parts in 1824, but Mrs Nairne, terrified of discovery, even preferred to be assumed to be a man, lest the work was undervalued as 'a feminine production'. Most of her compositions were anonymous, and when she very occasionally met the publisher it was like Charlotte Brontë in reverse: seeing this lady simply attired 'in gentlewoman's dress' he never suspected that she was the wife of an officer at the Castle.

In their preface the editors expressed admiration for the (unattributed) verses of the composer of 'Land o' the Leal', not wishing to 'wound a delicacy, which shrinks from all observation'. Even twenty years later Purdie knew its author only as Mrs Bogan.

Besides 'Land o' the Leal', the poems included 'Caller Herring', set to an air by Neil Gow. It was apparently composed for the benefit of Gow's son Nathaniel, and sent to him by the one friend who knew Mrs Nairne's secret. The tune was based on the chime of the Tron Kirk. 'Land o' the Leal' was composed in honour of Mary Anne Erskine, who lived with her advocate brother William (later Lord Kinneder), to whom Scott dedicated Canto III of *Marmion*.[33]

It was Mary Anne with whom Scott fell so hopelessly in love in early youth. Too late, for she was already attached to Archibald Campbell Colquhoun of Killermont, Sheriff of Perthshire, whom she married in 1796, and had a daughter in 1797 whose death within a year left her inconsolable. Colquhoun became Lord Advocate in 1807, and in 1816 Lord Clerk Register.[34]

Mrs Nairne made her contribution to Edinburgh's era of literary mysteries, the period of *Waverley*, the Chaldee Manuscript and *Noctes Ambrosianae*, John Wilson as 'Christopher North', and Lockhart masquerading in *Peter's Letters to his Kinsfolk*.

In spite of the growing fashion for compositions in Scots, Mrs Nairne preferred to use English, which she considered 'so civilized', noting that 'everybody', even their servants, was trying not to speak the broad Scots tongue.

In 1822 during the King's Edinburgh visit, Major Nairne was presented by the Duke of Atholl at the Holyrood House levée, and on the King's return to England Scott submitted a memorial pleading for the restoration of forfeited estates. A Bill was passed in July 1824 and Nairne thus was restored to the title as 5th Baron Nairne, while their delicate son became Master of Nairne.[35]

During these years some of England's leading writers and essayists visited or revisited Edinburgh. Wordsworth made a return visit in the bitter winter of 1813/14 – 'the severest I have ever known', records Robert Gillies, who was mostly confined to his house in Heriot Row after a long illness, and seeing almost no one.[36] Meeting Wordsworth was the great event of his year, late in 1814 on the poet's arrival at the Wilsons'. As Gillies had already invited

Sharpe and another advocate to dinner, all three ended up going to meet Wordsworth. To Gillies's chagrin the (unnamed) third guest, observing that the poet said little during dinner, embarrassingly attempted to 'draw him out', blundering into subjects quite out of his depth, much to the barely concealed laughter of the rest – including Wordsworth himself.

Next day Gillies accompanied the Wordsworths, the poet's sister-in-law Miss Hutchinson and James Wilson on a walk up Corstorphine Hill, an expedition of three hours. During this time, he records, apparently without irony, the poet exposed all the fallacies of Gillies's own poetic beliefs, 'which were radically wrong', Wordsworth always being willing to enlighten the beginner while allowing any of his beliefs which he considered were true. They discussed poets, including Byron (allowed to have power and genius, but perverted and vicious), and Hogg.

Gillies was full of admiration of Wordsworth's 'lofty and buoyant spirit', for among convivial company 'no one could be more joyous' – thanks to an energetic constitution, strong moral principles and 'hydropathic' habits: he eschewed wine and spirits, and daily climbed his local mountains while he composed his poetry. The two remained friends for many years.

As for his reputation in Scotland, it was supposed that the *Edinburgh Review* had 'for ever demolished his pretensions'; but Wordsworth consistently treated such attacks with scorn.[37]

Mrs Grant had also been invited by Mrs Wilson to meet the Wordsworths at dinner, but the recent death of her daughter Anne, and other personal crises, prevented her. She reports dispassionately, 'Wordsworth, they say, talks incessantly, his conversation has the perpetual flow of a stream, – monotonous in sound and endless in duration . . . always speaking when he was not writing.'[38]

Mrs Grant herself was considerably embarrassed some years later when, during a call at Lady Charlotte's, 'a very handsome, fashionable young man asked if I was Mrs G. of Laggan. Hearing I was, he flew across the room, said I was one of the persons in Scotland he most wished to see, and kissed my hand rapturously, yes, rapturously.' As it was more than thirty years since anyone had paid her such a gesture, she wondered if it were due to 'folly or vanity'. 'I saw so much sanguine simplicity in his countenance, that I concluded it to be a boyish flight.' While this beautiful young man was holding forth on her poem 'The Highlanders', which had awoken his enthusiasm for Scotland, Mrs Grant learned from Lady Charlotte that he was none other than Captain d'Este, son of the Duke of Sussex and Lady Augusta Murray. When he left, Lady Charlotte and another visitor agreed that, while in anyone else such an 'act of homage' might appear ridiculous, in him his artless enthusiasm made it 'quite natural and excusable'.

Shortly afterwards Captain d'Este called on Mrs Grant, when she learned from him that his interest had been engendered from the age of twelve by a friend of his mother's, Miss Anne Grant, of Windsor. Mrs Grant then took the plunge and invited him to join a small party with Lady Charlotte and others, and she tantalisingly records that 'all passed off very agreeably'.[39]

Elizabeth Grant was less disconcerted by Captain d'Este than was her namesake. They had met him before, and now found him 'as natural as ever, asked himself to dinner, and talked of Ramsgate'. Although as a son of the Duke of Sussex he claimed royal status, he came in unannounced, and when her father went to lead him into the room and, at her mother's 'hint', the ladies all rose, he begged them to remain seated, bowed them out on their way to dinner and waited to escort her mother. Otherwise 'he conformed to common usage, let the servants wait on him', and ignored the absence of finger-bowls (a significant point for, as Elizabeth notes, 'nobody ever washed before royalty').

One unexpected non-event at the dinner was that Lord Abercromby, having accepted, sent a last-minute apology thanks to 'an unavoidable accident which happily would never be repeated'. The mystery was solved when they read in the papers next day that 'this grave elderly friend' had got married.[40]

Scott was far from being the only 'unknown'. Speculation on the author of the Waverley novels was indeed the stuff of dinner-tables, but in a quiet way the ladies also supplied interest. Mrs Grant was for a time sure that her friend Mrs Brunton, wife of the minister and authoress of improving works, had written *Inheritance*, and it was long enough before Susan Ferrier was known as its author. A fear of being classed among the blue-stockings may well have deterred many. Mrs Elizabeth Hamilton – and for that matter Miss Edgeworth – were well known, but though of respectable birth distinctly not fashionable, not upper class. Mrs Grant was *sui generis*. She was visited and sought after not only by the leading lights of Edinburgh and England, but by admirers from America, France, even the Middle East, as a luminary who, though she deprecated it, far outshone fellow ladies.

Walter Scott called her 'cerulean', Lockhart 'a shrewd and sly observer', and Wilson, 'Queen of the Blue stockings'. She found the term rather disconcerting.

Some lesser literary figures begin to emerge. There was Captain Basil Hall, son of Sir James, who inherited remarkable qualities from both parents, a talent for geology from his father, and the intelligence of his mother Lady Helen, daughter of the Earl of Selkirk. Going to sea at thirteen he developed a thirst for knowledge, powers of observation and acute perception, besides lively conversation. He acquired great admiration through the publication of a vivid description of his visit to Loo Choo (the Lin Kin archipelago, off Korea).

Hall's background was not entirely stable. His father Sir James, the Huttonian geologist, was according to Elizabeth Grant 'not actually crazy, but not far from it', and seemed to her a crackpot whose affairs were only saved by the management of his wife. A friend of both Hutton and Playfair, Sir James disproved the Wernerian theory by experiment, sat as MP for Mitchell in Cornwall from 1807 to 1812, and became President of the Royal Society of Edinburgh. A theory of his, that Gothic architecture evolved from reed wigwams, was expounded in his *Essay on the Origins, History and Principles of Gothic architecture*, published in 1813. Sir James and Lady Helen Hall had many children, for whom Elizabeth Grant expressed a kindly contempt, although the eldest son, whom she terms 'a fool merely', was actually an FRS.[41]

Basil Hall had a passionate temper, but was generous and bore no grudges. on the other hand although he was so obsessed with obtaining information, his conclusions were sometimes based on too little knowledge.[42] In July 1818, on his return from Loo Choo, he was at the peak of popularity, and next embarked on travels in Switzerland and Italy, along with Pringle of Yair and Archibald Alison, armed with introductions to Byron in Venice from the publisher John Murray.[43]

Then there was the lively young Patrick Fraser Tytler, a son of the judge Lord Woodhouselee, and on his mother's side related to Sir James Mackintosh. Lord Woodhouselee, in addition to his legal work, had been since 1786 Professor of History, though his lectures and academic research did not seem to interfere with his work at the bar. As well as history he was well versed in the classics, and published *Outlines of General History*, a standard educational work, *Essay on the Principles of Translation* (1791) and a life of Lord Kames (1809).

Patrick was the youngest of four sons of this gifted family, and similarly born into a gifted society studded with distinguished historians, philosophers and scientists. The family, noted for a sense of humour and of the ridiculous, were known collectively as 'the Woodlousehe, the Woodlouseshe, and the Woodlicethey'.

Patrick, born in 1791, started at the High School under Dr Adam and Mr Christison at the age of eight, not much of a scholar but with a marked talent for drawing, and more interested in joining in 'the bickers'. He was a fine mimic, used to advantage in repeating lively anecdotes, good at poetry and a great reader of romance and works of the imagination, the *Faery Queen,* the *Arabian Nights,* Percy's *Reliques.* His father's friends might deplore Patrick's lack of academic achievement, but the judge recognised his potential and was unperturbed. He employed tutors, the Rev. John Black and later, the

Rev. John Lee, to live with the family, whose learning was to direct Patrick's desultory reading.[44]

He was then sent to study, like a number of Scottish youths, under the Rev. Charles Jerram at Chobham in Surrey, where some of his educational shortcomings were rectified, notably his backwardness in the classics, in which he now began to excel. From here he returned in 1809 to study law, including two hours' daily tuition under the Rev. Mr Hogg with his friend Archibald Alison, in his father's Princes Street library.

In 1810 Patrick was instigator of a short-lived but brilliant new society, its thirty-odd members including Alison, Lockhart and John Wilson, intended to rival the now flagging Speculative Society, whose days of fame from a decade ago were sadly past. The newcomers assembled at the University on Tuesdays at 8 p.m., with the usual programme of essays and debates and the object of providing practice in public speaking. Patrick, no politician, preferred the essays to the debates, and showed well on the lighter side, with little hint of his historic potential.

Called to the bar in 1813 he was not particularly successful, as his father was now dead and he did not cultivate the legal pundits to establish connections. In 1816 the Lord Advocate, Alexander Maconochie of Meadowbank, secured him a minor post as junior crown counsel in the Exchequer, salary £150 a year, but for his income he relied chiefly on the family estate. Travelling with the two Alison brothers resulted in collaboration between the three to produce *Travels in France in 1814*, typical young men's product and typical subject for the time, but as the first published account of post-Napoleonic France it sold well.

Patrick then resumed a fairly hedonistic life, hunting, riding and shooting, staying with Sir James Hall at Dunglas, James Gibson Craig in Midlothian and on his brother's and cousin's estates, sampling life's pleasures before settling down. But he read extensively, especially in biography and religion, preferring a personal approach and concentrating on modern subjects.

His first solo published work, which occupied him two years, was *Life of the Admirable Crichton* (1819), exposing a number of myths about that character; and meanwhile with *Sir Thomas Craig of Riccarton*, published in parts, he established himself as a biographer.

Except for outdoor sports Tytler was not physically active, and excessive application to study undermined his constitution, so that even before he was thirty he looked careworn, hardly even young, his hair thin and already greying at the temples. After a voyage with the engineer George Stephenson and others to the Northern Isles and Norway (where he witnessed King Bernadotte's coronation), he returned to 'the legal Babel' with even greater reluctance in October 1818. In place of Edinburgh's 'crowded routs or noisy balls' he immersed himself in yet another new society, the Round

Robin, culled from twenty-four members of the Select Society and other highly-connected young men, who met fortnightly at Oman's Hotel in West Register Street, where Patrick exercised his poetic gift in writing songs which he recited for them impromptu.

'Tis a wearisome thing at the bar to stay,
To study by night and starve by day,
With never a fee for your wig to pay;
This life is wondrous plaguy.

During the popular disturbances between 1819 and 1821, provoked by the post-war social and economic distress, and aggravated by the trial of Queen Caroline over which the country was bitterly divided, Patrick was among the first recruits of a newly raised volunteer regiment, shortly transferring to a yeomanry corps which drilled three times a week on Portobello sands. Here his ebullient nature came into its own, continually composing songs on the day's activities which he sang after dinner, and popular for 'his delightful manner, juvenile spirits, and brilliant talents for jovial entertainment'. Lockhart and John Hope were members, and the commanders were the Earl of Wemyss and Henry Cockburn's brother Captain Cockburn. In 1820 they went to Glasgow when the Queen's trial and the general unrest provoked a rising in the West country, and in 1824 turned out to help extinguish the terrible fires in Edinburgh.

Meanwhile the social season no longer satisfied Patrick. Witty and apparently extrovert in society, in his journal he went in for serious self-examination. He composed his lively songs to well-known airs, like 'The Birth of the Robin' to 'The frog he would a-wooing go', and with Lord Craigie's nephew, Pringle of Yair, downed depression in punch at Oman's. But he felt torn between the law and literature.

He had become friendly with Scott, who, keen to see a full history of Scotland, with his seriously impaired health no longer felt capable of undertaking it himself. With Scott's encouragement, Patrick Fraser Tytler's career as a Scottish historian was now to begin.[45]

The dangers of a career in literature had been discussed by Mrs Grant in May 1816, on writers' tendency to detach themselves from everyday life. 'I think it is to the credit of my own country that except in colleges, there is scarcely such a thing in Scotland as a man making letters, or authorship I should say, his sole occupation.' Almost all had another profession, and in Scotland's middle and upper classes it was of course usually law.[46]

Mrs Grant was still disapproving of some aspects of the *Edinburgh*. Nearly a year earlier she had written to the same friend, 'You cannot more dislike the metaphysics and politics of this publication than I do: party brings together very heterogeneous matter, and there are papers . . . which nothing but the spirit of party would have made Jeffrey tolerate: the belles lettres are his peculiar province, and there indeed he is unequalled . . .' She noted that he had no time for 'pretension and exhibition' and the 'heartless fashionable intercourse, such as made up the brilliant society of France'; he praised 'the domestic affections and quiet home-born felicities of life'. If only, she thought, he could have published these separately.[47]

A few months later her daughter Mary heard a reading at the Moreheads' from Jeffrey's 'illegible Journal': 'a hand that only half a dozen people can read', but if they could, it was 'the quintessence of acute observation, clearly and happily though very concisely expressed. Take a sample: "Cambray – noted for its cambric, its league and its Fenelon."'[48]

Some time later Sydney Smith was complaining of the opposite. To Lady Holland he wrote in the summer of 1819 of an *Edinburgh* 'article of endless length *concerning,* and probably *by,* Brougham. The Scotch, whatever other talents they may have, can never condense; they always begin a few days before the flood, and come *gradually* down to the reign of George the third, forgetful of . . . the volatility of human attention.'[49]

He passed his complaint to Jeffrey: 'You must consider that Edinburgh is a very grave place, and that you live with Philosophers – who are very intolerant of nonsense . . . The complaint was loud and universal of the extreme dulness and *lengthiness* of the Edinburgh Review . . . I am a very ignorant, frivolous, half-inch person; but such as I am, I am sure I have done your Review good, and *contributed* to bring it into notice', that is, to more than 'the 8 or 10 grave Scotchmen with whom you live'.[50]

Smith underestimated himself, though there were also others willing to do it for him. Jefferson Hogg, while noting his 'more than clerical enjoyment of a good dinner', and appreciating his 'hearty, cordial genial laugh . . . and his incessant joking of jokes', at least in the provinces, complained that in London society he seemed a 'noisy, impudent, shallow, clerical jester', appropriating all the talk to himself. Piling on insult after vicious insult, Hogg wrote him off as 'the great diner-out', whom one could not avoid meeting at every dinner-party. He even belittled his sermons at his 'mean and small' Yorkshire church to the small congregation of farming families, in which incongruously 'his voice would have filled a cathedral . . . there was nothing remarkable or valuable in his discourse'.[51]

The external observers of the Edinburgh scene sometimes provide the most valuable insights into its leading figures. One of these was the American George Ticknor, of Boston, who had met Jeffrey in Portland in 1814 when Jeffrey was on his marriage visit. Ticknor sailed for England the following April, 1815, when he was aged twenty-three, in company with his father and four friends from Portsmouth, New Hampshire, and also with two sons of the diplomat John Quincy Adams on their way to join their father in St Petersburg. They arrived in Liverpool just at the time of the news of Napoleon's return to Paris from Elba.

Ticknor was delighted with England, the country and the hospitality he received, as well he might be: during his brief stay he was befriended by Lord Byron, who invited him to his Drury Lane box to see Edmund Kean, and Ticknor was surprised to learn that the 'very decent looking man' in the next box was 'Monk' Lewis, quite different from how he had imagined him.[52]

After three happy months the whole American party set off for the Continent, when George spent the next few years studying at Göttingen, a pioneer in the broadening of American academic learning.[53]

Early in 1819 he returned to London, met the Holland House circle, Sir James Mackintosh and Brougham, then travelled to Edinburgh. Here, he found, he experienced a feeling of buoyancy, 'a lighter heart and more confident expectations of enjoyment' than in any other capital; though unfortunately immediately damped by a letter from his father that his invalid mother had died, so that during his whole visit he was dogged by guilt about being there at all.[54]

His object, however, was to meet authors and discover their opinions, and learn about European books and writers, and with this in mind he called first on Mrs Grant of Laggan. From Walter Scott, Thomson and others he received kind help, learning to read Scottish poetry, and he was struck by the importance of the literary tradition: over here, thanks to 'the society of men of letters', it seemed a single question on the subject whose very fringes he was just beginning to touch, could bring 'an answer that is better than a volume', and such a society, he found, was strong in Edinburgh.

Edinburgh society, Ticknor thought, was excellent, 'in open-heartedness . . . almost unrivalled'; nor was it limited by class distinctions. The difficulty was to break through social conventions. He longed for serious talk, but with a group of people at a dinner, 'the conversation is rarely general; one person makes a speech, and then another, and finally it stops, nobody knows why'. He therefore had to tackle them singly. One pictures the earnest young man resolutely questioning one character after another, when as he said, 'if you insist on talking to him, it is most probable he will talk very well'. The exceptions to his strictures were Scott and Playfair, 'delightful men' under any circumstances.[55]

He was especially pleased with Mrs Grant, now in her seventies, in whose house 'an American . . . finds himself at home more easily than anywhere else in Edinburgh'. She was always happy to meet Americans, having lived in their country for so many years. In her, good nature and sense were allied with 'a natural talent, plain knowledge, and good taste, derived from English reading alone'. Despite her (by contemporary standards) great age, variable health and the sorrow of losing so many children, she never lost her interest in the world, and was full of tales of Highland life and history.

Having strangely observed that guests he met at her house were neither great nor remarkable, Ticknor goes on to mention Wilson ('a pretending young man, but with a great deal of talent'), and Hogg, 'vulgar as his name' and in conversation a complete contrast to his poems.[56]

Mrs Grant on her side was 'dazzled and delighted' by her American encounters that winter with a 'constellation of brilliant talents and polished manners', which greatly raised American reputation in the eyes of the literary.[57] Besides Ticknor, the most distinguished, there were Mr Campbell Preston of South Carolina and his friend Hugh S. Legaré, and Ralston of Philadelphia, 'handsome and high-bred', of a distinguished mind; yet Ticknor still outshone them all.[58]

Ticknor got to know Walter Scott and his family well, accompanying them to the newly dramatised version of *Rob Roy,* at which Scott (still 'Unknown') was unashamedly delighted, taking care to add with 'a comical Scotch expression of face', 'I wish that Jedediah Cleishbotham could be here to enjoy it!' He also met Scott at the courts, and was guided by him round the town – one of Scott's favourite pastimes with visitors – and shown the houses of famous men, with a tale for each and for every close and wynd.

Ticknor and Joseph Cogswell, invited to Abbotsford in March, were there when Scott was alarmingly taken violently ill. They left next day full of anxiety for their kind and celebrated host, and Ticknor went on to the Lake District, where he was rather dashed that Wordsworth 'seemed to despise Edinburgh, where, he said, you would not get so much knowledge at a lecture as you would in the same time at an English gentleman's dinner-table'. Wordsworth also spoke contemptuously, like most other people, of Monk Lewis, 'and, in short, seemed disposed to spare very little that came in his way'.[59]

Luckily Southey, whom he visited at Keswick, thoroughly approved of Ticknor – the third such visitor in a year, two of them 'by far the most accomplished and intelligent travellers whom I have ever fallen in with'.[60]

33
THE SOCIAL BACKGROUND

'I will leave Edinburgh with regret . . . altho . . . no richer of Cash than I have entered it so enormous are the expenses of this fashionable City where I really believe that as well as in America every person live perhaps rather above their income.'

J. J. Audubon to his wife, 24 March 1827, *Letters 1826–1840*, Boston, 1930, I.18

'Scotland will, in 20 years, perhaps much sooner, be revolutionised from head to foot; and then let England look to herself.'

Sir Walter Scott to J. G. Lockhart, 17 March 1826, Scott, *Letters*

'A literary set, including College professors, Authors, and others pleased thus to represent themselves. A clever set with Mrs Fletcher. The law set. Strangers, and inferiours. All shook up together they would have done very well. Even when partially mingled they were very agreeable. When primmed up . . . arrayed as if for battle, there was really some fear of a clash at times.'

Elizabeth Grant of Rothiemurchus, *Memoirs of a Highland Lady*, II.42

'What I miss most in London are the 4 or 5 houses [in Edinburgh] into which you can go at all hours, and the 7 or 8 women with whom you are quite familiar, and with whom you can go and sit and talk at your ease, dressed or undressed, morning or evening . . .

Francis Jeffrey to his American father-in-law Charles Wilkes, 13 April 1822, Cockburn's *Life of Jeffrey*, II.199

'Every night, some half a dozen ladies are *at home*, and every thing that is in the wheel of fashion, is carried round, and thrown out in due course at the door of each of them . . . the ladies of Scotland dance in common pretty much like our country lasses at a harvest home.'

'Peter Morris' [John Lockhart], *Peter's Letters to his Kinsfolk*, 3rd edn, 1819, I.220, 228

Elizabeth Grant, looking back in middle life on the Edinburgh society of her teens and early twenties, had a shrewdly observant eye for her contemporaries and a neat way of describing them. Comfortably at the top of the social scale (though her family was to prove far from comfortable in the financial sense), she could take a cool view without envy or defensiveness.

Henry Cockburn, describing the Edinburgh of 1811, when its population combined with Leith's had risen to 103,143, says that the New Town now consisted of nobility, gentry, and most of the rest in the law, the college, the church, and medicine – an aristocracy that shone 'undisturbed'. It was close-knit – though not inbred – thanks to the expense and difficulty of travel, and the lack, still at that point, of daily newspapers and even of books. [1]

Edinburgh society was not so constricted that literally 'everybody knew everybody'. The Grant of Rothiemurchus girls were, for example, much the same age as Helen Graham, daughter of General Graham, Governor of Stirling Castle, who for at least a couple of seasons spent their winters in Edinburgh, but they evidently moved in different circles, the former slightly grander. Helen – another shrewd observer – records a dinner in January 1825 at Alexander Rutherfurd's, then a young advocate, where the company consisted of 'sensible people', and here she met Jane Grant along with Jeffrey, Cockburn, Lord Eldin, the Dick Lauders and others. Her keen observation noted that 'Miss Grant seems a nice, pleasant, good-humoured creature, and as Sir William Fettes says has "a pair of eyes indeed", and makes good use of them too.' Often, however, Helen Graham's parties proved to be of superficial characters, and meeting the pundits was a matter of note. On their side, the Grant girls do not record meeting Helen or her circle at all.

Although Edinburgh people liked to ape London ways, keeping late hours and (as Scott put it) 'the strange precipitation with which we hurry from one place to another in search of the society which we never sit still to enjoy', it could never rival England's capital in size. To its advantage, Scott claimed, for London's new, immensely long streets merely separated people, three quarters of whose time was spent in covering the distance between friends.[2]

There was still no sign of the wars' coming to an end, and the situation at home was gloomy with poverty, unemployment and deep social unrest. The young men eagerly joined the Volunteers, and their exercises and camps were occasions of roistering enjoyment rather than military discipline.

Meanwhile fashionable life went on as if nothing else were happening. Elizabeth Grant, who came 'out' in Inverness in 1814, describes the form of the season in Edinburgh. It was their winter in Heriot Row, and all the young members of the family were still taking lessons, in French, Italian, the pianoforte and dancing. At this early stage of the season their engagements were dinners, 'the heads of the Bar, the judges, some of the professors, and a few others, all Whigs nearly' – in these days there was still little party intermingling in society. 'In January began the routs and balls; they were over by Easter, and then a few more sociable meetings were thinly spread over the remainder of the Spring.' It was a short season, but Elizabeth, not robust, found it exhausting. Her mother never noticed, though a family friend became sure she was suffering 'a galloping consumption'. What her mother did notice, to her great gratification, was Elizabeth's social success. 'I was high on the list of beauties, no ball could go on without me', and ladies giving dances begged introductions to her mother in order to be able to invite the daughter. 'Crowds of beaux surrounded us when we walked out, filled our drawing rooms when we staid within. It was very intoxicating', but it did not turn her head.[3]

Her father's friends included 'the cleverest of the Whigs', Lord Gillies and his wife, John Clerk and his sister, the Brewsters, the Jeffreys, John Murray, Thomas Thomson, William Clerk. Her mother, whose dinners were very popular, was more inter-party in her friends the ladies. She had the wisdom to give a ball at the beginning, before there was much competition. 'All the Beaux strove for tickets, because all the Belles of the season made their first appearance there. It was a decided hit', her mother proving a skilled and attentive hostess, and dancing went on until nearly dawn.

It was extravagant, of course, and finance was eventually to prove the family's undoing. Not only were their excellent dinners famed for the company, but Elizabeth sketches the expense of her mother's and her own costly gowns, made for them in London. She herself set the tone. 'I walked out like a hussar in a dark cloth pelisse trimmed with fur and braided like the coat of a staff officer, boots to match, and a fur cap set on one side . . . This equipment was copied by half the town, it was thought so exquisite.'

They ended the season with a large rout to pay off their social debts, which was interrupted by a shower of stones from the mob because John Peter Grant, who had recently taken his seat in the House, had supported the Protectionists.

In the uproar several ladies fainted, but Mrs Grant was advised that they were to have military protection, though this caused almost more confusion than the fury of the mob. Amid 'cheers, groans, hisses', a company of dragoons arrived, the rioters fled, and the guard, who stayed all night, ate up everything that the frightened party had left and a whole round of beef into the bargain. The family dined out on the adventure for a week.[4]

Among the Grants' circle was the noted Miss Grace Baillie, an extravagant dresser, switching from style to style as fancy took her. They had encountered her in the North that summer, dressed successively as a flower-girl, as Juno, as a queen, 'then Arcadian, then *corps de ballet* . . . stuck over with coloured glass ornaments'. At Kinrara there had been a great sensation when the lady inadvertently found her way into the wrong bedroom and surprised 'short, fat, black Mr Macklin in his tub!' Miss Baillie was too overcome with embarrassment to appear at dinner, trying to insist that he left at once, while he 'insisted on their swearing eternal friendship': the ladies were annoyed and the gentlemen overcome with laughter.

That winter Miss Baillie gave the last, and most splendid, party of the season in her ground-floor apartment, in 'an old fashioned corner house, in Queen Street, with 'small and ill furnished' rooms, which she dealt with by having all the doors removed, covering the walls with evergreens through whose leaves shone coloured lamps, festooned with paper flower garlands. Every room was pressed into service, filled with little surprises: a birdcage, 'a stuffed figure in a tower', a mossy stream trickling into a basin, and peopled with a shepherdess, a kilted 'highland laddie', a cupid, a gipsy, all offering sweets and delicacies, and ingeniously placed instruments provided unexpected music. It was so ridiculous that it was a brilliant success, inspiring the wits to verse, notably Alexander Boswell.[5]

This, Elizabeth's first season, was when she and a friend of her brother's fell in love. He was the son of a professor, and the pair innocently proceeded in a deepening friendship, they exchanged visits, and only when Elizabeth figured in the poem on Miss Baillie's party did the parents grasp the situation. The affair ended in sorrowful parting, for it proved the elders of the the two families were at feud, and Elizabeth was obliged to give up her lover. This blighting of her affection so distressed her that she grieved for months, and probably never entirely got over it.[6]

John Bell, according to Henry Cockburn 'the best surgeon that Scotland had then produced', was 'a morsel of a man married to a wife as small, and they lived in rooms proportioned to their size, in a flat in George Street'. The musical Bell gathered a group of players, himself playing a double bass larger than he was, on which his hands could barely meet, yet (says Elizabeth) 'produced sounds a giant only could have emulated'.

She describes a grand reception they once gave to return hospitality they had received, 'a Grace Baillie affair . . . their whole apartment thrown open, kitchen and bedroom and all, made to communicate not only by doors but by windows, oval windows cut in the walls, filled by book shelves at ordinary times and opened on this state occasion'. By thus giving the effect of mirrors, their tiny rooms appeared to be one large one, everywhere visible at once. Preparation and later restoration to normal caused total upheaval. Where could the couple sleep that night? wondered someone. 'In the case of the bass viol', gravely replied Jeffrey.

A young lady who also records tales of Miss Baillie was Lady Clementina Drummond, daughter of the Jacobite Lord Maurice Drummond.[7] Born at St

Germain and educated partly in England with Professor Playfair's sister, at a very early age she was carried off by her father to be company for himself, as her disapproving mother did not care for society, preferring to entertain at home. Clementina, barely fifteen, went with her father to visit the Comte d'Artois at Holyrood and even attended balls, including the exclusive Queen's Assembly on 18 January. She had (perhaps for this ball) a pink velvet dress brought for her from Paris by the Duchess of Gordon, who had indulged there in the latest extravagant fashions.

Lord Maurice in his youth had been enamoured, as were most young men of his generation, with such beauties as Lady Charlotte Campbell and Miss Robertson, and was eager to present his reluctant daughter to them. To her relieved surprise, Lady Charlotte was still beautiful, so was Miss Robertson, still unmarried and living to a great age.[8]

An era of eighteenth-century beauties ended with the death in April 1812 of the famous Duchess of Gordon, whose body, Sharpe gleefully related, was displayed at the hotel for a shilling a head. A panegyric on her life which appeared in the press was attributed to Professor Playfair, though Scott thought it too absurd to be his.[9]

Walter Scott, whose 'heavy-featured countenance' and broad Scots voice much impressed Clementina Drummond, taught her to play chess. They used to meet at Miss Baillie's, who despite her absurdly youthful dress and manner, was popular with young people and was always 'at home' in the afternoons, and as keen on a rubber of whist as on a ball.[10]

Her parties included Sir William Cumming Gordon, a lover of practical jokes, one of which resulted in tearing her juvenile beaded gown. In recompense he promised her one from France that would entirely outdo Edinburgh; but he insisted that her young lady friends be allowed to try it too. The packing case arrived, the young ladies and the gentlemen were summoned – including Walter Scott – and on the opening of the box it proved to contain all kinds of items of a rich 'Normandy costume': gold-embroidered blue petticoat, smart red jacket, fine lace neckerchief, and a lace-trimmed Normandy cap. Even the jewellery was not forgotten.

The girls excitedly tried on cap and jewels in turn, and when it came to Miss Mary Stuart, she looked so ravishing that Sir William fell on his knees and all but snatched a kiss, and Scott quoted a couplet from Pope. Tall, stout, fiftyish Miss Baillie had the good sense to realise that the dress would be quite wrong for her, and a few days later she raffled it at one of her famous fêtes, complete with little shepherdesses and a wizard to tell fortunes, while Miss Stuart, who conveniently won the raffle, adorned the splendid costume.[11]

This was only one of the extravagant entertainments, when 'private theatricals, balls, card parties, and picnics fast succeeded each other'. Lady Clementina was one of a morning visit with Miss Baillie and Sir William to St Bernard's Well, with its Harrogate-like waters. Also in the party were Lady Augusta Clavering and her daughter, 'a brilliant brunette', to whom Sir William paid great attention. When Miss Baillie mysteriously disappeared for some time, no-one knew where she was until she was seen some way off on top of a stile, frantically signalling while Sir William, 'laughing immoderately', was running off. They reached Miss Baillie to find her inarticulate with rage and unable to move: the deplorable Sir William had played one of his dreadful practical jokes. Having with elaborate politeness offered to help her over, once she had set her foot on the top bar and drawn her skirts after her, 'quick as lightning he knotted her ankles together with a pocket handkercheif, and ran off as fast as his legs would carry him', to resume his polite attentions to the Claverings and help them over stepping-stones.

It took a lot of persuading from Lady Augusta and others to talk Miss Baillie out of her fury, and she would not forgive Sir William until he had promised to buy twenty of her ubiquitous raffle tickets. Her brow finally cleared once they arrived for a luncheon at Mr James Erskine's near at hand, where Lord Maurice and Lord Buchan awaited them.[12]

Practical jokes were not confined to Scots – they were rather an indulgence of the age. The mercurial American Joseph Cogswell wrote to tell George Ticknor who was now in London that 'from a mere love of fun I have put 5 young men up to falling in love with the same lady, and once or twice, in a moment of great wickedness, I have thought of stepping in and attempting to supplant them all'.[13] This recalls the prank of a young officer who wagered successfully that he would make a certain lady the acknowledged belle, by persuading all his acquaintance to deluge her with poems and praises.[14]

Another time Cogswell and a friend, 'in the real spirit of mischief' supplanted the chair-bearers of two ladies they were escorting to a party, and went out of their way to reel clumsily and seek the roughest ground on purpose, bringing their charges at last 'in a breathless state of indignation and discomfort to their destination'. Hardly surprising.

Cogswell may be excused on the grounds of his melancholy on the brink of his leaving Edinburgh. He had tried to mitigate this by spending as much time as possible at Mrs Grant's and Mrs Fletcher's. He probably did not confess to either lady such antics with his contemporaries.[15]

Among favourite parties were those given by the officers of ships moored at Leith. Clementina describes one which brought a happy ending to a small drama. There had been a sailing party along the shore with about eleven people, including Clementina and her father, Miss Wharton-Duff and Mr Buller with his sister Lady Harriet Plunkett. 'Miss Wharton-Duff's vivacity was excessive', says Clementina with eloquent restraint, but the girl's reckless tomboyishness caused Buller many a trial. While the gentlemen were fishing, she climbed up a large rock to look at the view – rather adventurous for a young lady on her own – and was stuck on the way down. The party saw her in horror dangling by her hands, unable to find a foothold, and Buller, falling over one rock after another, rushed to her aid accompanied by peals of heartless laughter. In fact he so bruised himself that he had to be carried to a nearby cottage, and lay for three weeks unable to move, while Miss Wharton-Duff still laughed. When he recovered, she found his ardour rather cooled, while she kept up pretended gaiety.

Eventually the party were invited by Captain (later Sir) Francis Sykes on board his ship lying two miles off Leith – the nearest they could anchor. They were rowed over in small boats, and found a magnificent reception. At the ship's side each lady was raised in a throne-like chair, without damage to her gown, and was presented with a bouquet and tablets for the dances by the ship's officers. In a cabin specially fitted out as a dressing-room women servants were in attendance with needle and thread if required, while tables were 'piled up with gloves, fans, scents, shoes'. 'The quarter and main decks had been covered in and these, with the saloon, formed four large compartments', hung with flags and war trophies, tapestries, and exotic scarves, 'all shining with gold and silver embroidery'. Neil Gow accompanied the ship's band.

Miss Wharton-Duff alone was not enjoying herself, because she had a raging toothache. At last it became so unbearable that she courageously begged the ship's surgeon to extract the tooth there and then, and bore the operation with such fortitude that she was shortly back with the dancers, seeming livelier than ever – perhaps because she was dancing with Buller, and this gaiety enhanced her attractions. At the end of the evening her escort wrapped her carefully in her cloak and accompanied her to the boat. Shortly afterwards they were married.

Lady Clementina was pleased to relate that forty years later she saw the pair at Brighton, still happy, she as wayward and he as attentive to her whims as ever.[16]

Elizabeth Grant and her sister Jane – whose debut in society this was – in the spring of 1818 after a delightful season, enjoyed such a party when the Captain of a frigate then lying in Leith Roads 'invited all left of his winter acquaintance to a breakfast and a dance on board. We all drove down to the pier at Newhaven in large merry parties', and were rowed on board across the sparkling water by similarly 'merry sailors in their best suits'. Everything was perfect, including a beautiful day, 'such a gay little fleet', and an awning over the deck, with flags and 'a quadrille and a military Band all ready'.

All along the deck below a feast was laid out to which after the dancing on the upper decks they sat down at 4 in the afternoon. Jane was looking especially pretty and had been 'engaged by the little monkey of a Middy who had piloted us over'. After the 'collation' they danced again, until nearly midnight, continually plied with refreshments by their hosts. 'Sailors are so hearty, and every Officer of the ship seemed to feel he had the part of host to play. There never was a merrier *fete*.'

For this party the Grant sisters were dressed, as Elizabeth pointedly observes, 'like the best bred of the company, in half dress, white frocks made half high and with long sleeves . . . A few unhappy girls were in full dress, short sleeves, low necks, white shoes', whereas Miss Cochrane the Admiral's daughter, well used to such entertainments, was 'most properly dressed' of all, with 'a white well frilled petticoat, an open silk spenser, and a little Swiss hat' with a bunch of roses. 'She and the dress together conquered Captain Darling; they were married a few months later.'[17]

This enchanting day was equalled in splendour by one in 1819 which Charles Sharpe attended, though, as ever, he made the most of its deficiencies.

This was 'a superb party aboard the Vengeur', the guests driving down to Newhaven (he by hackney-coach) to arrive at 5.30 in the afternoon at the festively decorated ship. Curtains dividing the deck were drawn back to reveal the supper-tables, 'the prettyist spectacle' matching one he had seen at a Vauxhall fête, like a magnificent tent made of sails.

To the cynical Sharpe the rest did not match expectations – a play and a farce, with so great a crowd that 'after enduring suffocation, strangulation and many other *ations*' for half an hour, he scrambled through a convenient rent in the sail, 'almost losing my wig and shoes in the adventure'. The ball which followed was more agreeable, festivities went on until 6 in the morning, and all went well apart from a few ladies feeling sick; and Sir James Home, showing off to Miss Mary Hope and others as they disembarked, jumped from the ladder into the boat but fell into the sea with an undignified kicking of heels, amid the usual heartless glee.[18]

A simulated 'impromptu' party, ashore and not on board, was staged by Captain and Mrs Bingham. He was successor to Captain Dalling and commanded a frigate anchored in the Roads. During the winter they lodged in Edinburgh, and in summer took a small house at Newhaven. Late one winter an innocuously worded invitation was 'simply to spend the evening, tea . . . and a hearty Sailor's welcome'. Once tea was over the Captain apparently casually suggested, 'Couldn't we get up a dance, don't you think, for the young people?' – and quickly whistled up 'half a dozen smart young sailors in their best, who wheeled out the tables, lifted up the carpet, settled the seats round the room, and then ushered in a Band. It had all been prepared before' – but for the guests was a delightful surprise. Later the sailors brought in a supper, and entertained them with a hornpipe.

Among other less elaborate naval visits, which usually included a 'luncheon' of strawberries and cream, the guests would be rowed out for a 'little fête' on board a frigate for the 'collation', or instead of dancing would be rowed up the Forth for an hour or so.[19]

Formal dinners were still given, attended with mingled feelings. Elizabeth Grant praised her mother's arrangements over the seasons from about 1817 to 1820, who settled her social debts with 'five or six dinners, two small evening parties, and one large one, a regular rout . . . She understood the management of company so well, every assembly of whatever kind always went off admirably . . .' The niceties which contributed to success were brilliant lighting, 'plenty of refreshments, abundance of attendants, always a piece of matting spread from the carriage steps to the front door, and two dressing rooms with toilettes, good fires, hot water' – and a maid for the ladies ready with needle and thread. In Elizabeth's view, though everyone praised, few took the trouble to imitate.[20]

Although she did not care for the host, Elizabeth admired the dinners given by their then neighbour, John Clerk of Eldin, who lived with his unmarried sister Bessy, a former beauty, who kept house for him, and always invited at least one of the Grants. The guests were 'such pleasant people. All the law set of course, judges, barristers, and writers; some of the literary, some of the scientifick, and a great many country families.'[21]

There is no hint here of the complaint of formal dinners by certain others. Henry Cockburn detested them. Looking back from later years, he writes: 'Healths and toasts were special torments; oppressions which cannot now be conceived. Every glass during dinner required to be dedicated to the health of someone. It was thought sottish and rude to take wine without this.' A mere gesture was not nearly enough: the wine, which was not set on the table, had to be called for, the servant directed to the subject of the toast, and 'the caller was obliged to specify his partner aloud'. This could be agonising for the shy or the very young, and (says Cockburn) the timid took refuge in only drinking when they were invited. The host, or any other supposed great man, might polish off several, especially a group of ladies, at a time: 'he slew them by coveys'.[22]

All this made the passing of the grand dinner to a more informal way of entertaining a great relief to many people.

The days of heavy drinking were, however, far from past. All Cockburn's contemporaries were great drinkers. Wilson, Hogg, Lockhart, Scott, all died in their sixties, Wilson at sixty-eight but by then 'greatly changed in appearance', says Cyrus Redding, who goes on, 'Edinburgh in those days scorned thin potations . . . Wilson took port with his dinner, a custom peculiar to himself', and was famed for being able to polish off a bottle of whisky at a sitting. When, years later, visiting London Redding invited him to dine, they drank copiously. 'As usual, there was a wild earnestness about him that I don't recollect ever seeing in any other man. He never set about a thing with only half a heart' – certainly not about drinking.[23]

In a later generation Helen Graham, who occasionally met Cockburn on such ceremonial gatherings, disliked the formal dinner intensely. On at least one occasion she purposely took a substantial luncheon in order to eat little at the dinner – at Mr Binning-Munro's, brother to the surgeon Alexander Monro. 'Formal dinners are seldom pleasant, for the fumes from hot viands, rich sauces and the exertion of eating and drinking certainly cast a shade of stupidity over everybody . . . Everything that could please the eye and taste of the most refined epicure was not spared.' Any pleasure was further reduced by having to listen 'first to the gentleman on my right hand, and then on my left', both unusually garrulous for such an occasion.[24]

Like Benjamin Haydon, Helen Graham remarked on 'the usual absence of conversation at great dinners'.[25] The chief object appears to have been to impress the rest of society, do the right thing, spare no pains, and make a great show. Enjoyment on either side hardly entered into it.

Elizabeth Grant claims that 'all our set', mainly law-men and notably Jeffrey, was famed for keeping the best wines, the husband's province as catering was the wife's. By 1818 Scottish national dishes were served only in 'real old fashioned Scotch houses', like the Nairnes', and had largely given way to 'various abominations served up in corner dishes under French names'. Mrs Jeffrey, however, especially when entertaining at Craigcrook, would provide only what her cook was used to: 'her home fed fowl and home made bread, and fine cream and sweet butter, and juicy vegetables, all so good, served so well, the hot things *hot,* the fruits, creams, and butter so cold', and calculated to put everyone in a good humour.[26]

In winter, skating on Duddingston Loch was a favourite pastime, and the more severe the weather the more fashionable it was. The winter of 1813–14 (in which the Thames froze for the last time), was a record all over Britain. The severe weather, which lasted from the beginning of January until March, returned again after a brief thaw. When it finally broke Robert Christison measured the ice on the loch and found it eleven inches thick. It was 'daily frequented by crowds of skaters, curlers, and fashionable promenaders, and on Saturdays two military bands were in attendance'.

When snow fell it was overnight, and was 'regularly swept up in the morning into heaps scattered over the ice' which in time became high mounds, turning the loch into 'irregular streets and squares, among which it was no easy matter to find a party after being separated from them. Duddingston has never been so gay a scene.'[27]

By contrast 1826 had a summer of remarkable drought which extended from March for months and well into the autumn. Only a rare thunderstorm broke the spell, to be succeeded by even greater heat. In mid-July Christison measured 84 °F in the shade at 3 p.m. on three successive days.[28]

This was so un-Scottish as even to affect fixed sartorial habits. Young men abandoned neckcloths for 'a Byron collar and a narrow silk ribbon, with a gold ring run upon its ends'. Christison appeared in the Senate so dressed, to the 'high disapprobation' of the ever-correctly dressed Dr Hope. Nobody went out before sunset except on necessary business, after which the whole town was fashionably crowded. Sea-bathing became *de rigueur,* and the water at Trinity was unusually warm, inviting a long swim. At the Parliament House, the moment court business ended, the lawyers chartered every hackney coach available and set off in fours to Portobello, Leith, Newhaven, Trinity, Granton. One who refused was the 'tall, bony, rather elderly, censorious' Mr Forsyth, who would drive some miles in the stage-coach and walk back to town. When Professor Syme's brother David, invited to join in this heat-provoking exercise, refused because he was one of a four for Newhaven, Forsyth was shocked. 'What! are you one of the dirty beasts that need to wash themselves every day?'[29]

The idea of corporate responsibility was so little regarded at that time that when one December day in 1815 the watchman employed by the Lochend Skating Club found the ice on the loch unsafe and hung up warning boards at either end, several skaters on arrival questioned his right to interfere, some even with threats. A few, finding an apparently suitable spot at the Edinburgh end, insisted on skating on it, 'with great risk', while the watchman could do nothing but lay a 'saving rope'.

Word then came that a boy had fallen in, but at the Leith end, so watchmen and skaters ran along the bank dragging a ladder, but as soon as it was pushed out and a would-be life-saver crept out on it the ice, here only a quarter of an inch thick, gave way. A second man followed and also sank, and both had to be saved. The boy was 100 yards out, and Lieutenant John Gourlay, a naval officer from Gayfield Square, not long returned from war service, enterprisingly went in but sank before he reached the boy. Though ropes were thrown in, man and boy vanished, and before a boat could be brought round and with difficulty launched, half an hour had been lost. By the time the victims could be hauled out, by means of an ingenious 'searching rod' owned by Captain Manby and attached to the 'saving ladder', both were drowned.

The same 'insane disregard' for warnings, as the *Advertiser* put it, was displayed at Duddingston Loch when the watchman who plunged in after the skater, after sinking with him, was hauled out by the rope. After these disasters the public were urgently warned to heed the notices, and the Humane Society's instructions for reviving the apparently drowned were published.[30]

Besides the Argyll/Jersey affair there was the Mildmay elopement. Sir Harry Mildmay and Lord Rosebery had married two beautiful grand-daughters of the Earl of Radnor, Harriet and Charlotte Bouverie, very alike, on the same day. They made two happy couples, but Sir Harry's wife died in 1814 in her first childbed. Heartbroken, unable to respond to his friends' attempted consolation, he alternated between withdrawal and over-excitement, to the point of seeming unhinged. The beautiful Harriet Rosebery seemed similarly inconsolable for her sister's death, unable to overcome her melancholy even in society.

When Lord Maurice Drummond called on Mildmay one day at the Roseberys' and found Sir Harry alone, at once the widower burst into a confession that Lady Rosebery reminded him so unbearably of his wife that he must leave their house or he would go mad. Lord Maurice anxiously talked over the problem with Lord Rosebery, and between them they arranged a period of therapeutic travel for Sir Harry. But on the eve of his intended departure Sir Harry and his sister-in-law took off together.[31]

'Alas! . . . the miserable, abandoned Lady!' exclaimed Dr Sandford, 'nothing can be more shocking than this elopement.'[32]

They fled to Württemberg, where after the enraged husband had divorced Harriet, they were married (1815), and a few years later Lord Rosebery himself married again, to Admiral Lord Anson's daughter Anne.

A hardly less melodramatic contretemps was the courtship by the elegant, curly-haired Mr Beauclerk of Miss B——r, to whose exclusive circle he was introduced by Lord Fife. The match seemed eminently suitable, as the lady, who had a fortune of £4000 a year, was already about thirty years old. When her brother was ordered to Madras with his regiment, he left in full expectation of a wedding, the dresses were bought, the bridesmaids chosen – including Clementina Drummond – and the town was full of it.

One day when Clementina was visiting the betrothed pair, who were sitting happily on a sofa, a friend of the brother's named Bruce was announced. He seemed astonished to see them, and at last came out with, 'Why, Clark! what is the meaning of this?' The embarrassed Beauclerk, blushing with confusion, said nothing. Bruce left, but at once sent the lady a note explaining, with some reluctance, that Beauclerk was really a billiard-marker at a London club.

The agonised lady passed the note to her lover, who this time paled and rushed away and she, of course, fainted (Lady Clementina's local colour again?) Next day she retired to the country.

This joint disappearance raised speculation of another elopement, until one evening Lord Fife, who had been away, met Bruce and learned the story.

Fife reprehensibly greeted it with a laugh, saying what a pity Bruce had turned up 'just in time', and insisted that Clark was 'really a most agreeable fellow, and money was all that he wanted', so superior that in London he was regularly known as 'the Beau'. Lord Fife, in fact, was really sorry for the eleventh-hour disappointment – but was himself severely censured for his carefree attitude, not to mention for making the introduction in the first place.[33]

In the year following the peace, few large balls were given, only a few ladies retaining what now seemed a slightly old-fashioned event. The new fashion was for smaller parties, much preferred by the younger set as they suited the new dance, the quadrille. 'Old fashioned respectables' had strongly resisted it, as Elizabeth Grant tells us, and she too regretted the passing of 'the merry country dance', but she was among the first to make the quadrille fashionable and it became a craze. They all practised at home with Mr Finlay Dunn, who having learned it in Paris brought them the 'best' steps, and Elizabeth was one of a group of eight who 'burst upon the world' one evening at the Whyte Melvilles', the rest climbing on chairs for a better view. It was such a riotous success that they had to perform several times during the evening.

As the quadrille required more space than other dances, parties had to become smaller. Then, a band of not more than three sufficed, and the young preferred light 'refreshments' to suppers. All this so reduced the expense that a hostess could give several such parties during the season.[34]

During that season, 1816–17, Edinburgh was fuller of society, and therefore more lively. Elizabeth Grant notes, however, how that winter party hostility still prevailed, separating the upper classes into sets, in addition to the usual small coteries, each 'overvaluing itself and undervaluing its neighbours'.

According to her the 'fashionable set, headed by Lady Gray of Kinfauns', included 'regular party giving women who seemed to live for crowds at home and abroad', also 'unwillingly' including Lady Molesworth, a good wife and hostess since her marriage to the youth 'little beyond a fool'.[35] This was presumably the kind of trivial society earlier described by Hogg in *The Spy*.

The exclusive McLeod of McLeod set consisted of the Cumming Gordons, Shaw Steuarts, and Murrays of Ochtertyre. The card-playing set was led by 'old Mrs Oliphant of Rossie' and her daughters Mrs Grant of Kilgraston, Mrs Veitch and others, among them the Duchess of Gordon's cousin Miss Sinclair of Murkle, said to be 'the image of her'. The 'quiet country gentleman set' consisting of the Campbells, Lord and Lady Wemyss, Sir James and Lady Helen Hall, Sir John and Lady Steuart. In addition were the literary and academic set; Mrs Fletcher and the 'clever set'; the law set – and the outsiders. Sometimes they mingled, other times were 'ready for battle'.[36]

There were variations in private entertainment. A favourite informal port of call for the young was at old Lady Cumming's, who never went out but kept her shutters open when the family were at home in the evenings, as a sign to welcome passing friends for cards and music: 'Sophie Cumming played delightfully, Charles very well on the violincello', others sometimes joining in. Even her married daughter Mrs John Forbes, who had 'a houseful of children and an advocate's income', was persuaded to come and bring her 'work' – which might be seaming 'a pair of coarse sheets which she pulled by degrees from a large canvas bag', yet still (comments the strait-laced Elizabeth Grant with some surprise) 'did not look unladylike'. She adds the cautious rider, 'all the Cummings were queer'.[37]

Then there was the expedient adopted by McLeod of Harris who, having married 'poor, pretty little Richmond Inglis', was living with his bride's parents, and embarrassed by the number of invitations they received, responded by hiring the dancing master's 'academy', Smart's Rooms, contracted out for the supper, invited everyone they knew, and gave the best ball ever. It was then that the waltz was finally established in Edinburgh. So far its acceptance had been precarious for a season, but now, with two 'strong bands', resistance ended and 'the whole large room was one whirligig. The Laird of Harris and his brother were perhaps more graceful than any'. 'Ah!' said poor Richmond revealingly, 'If I had ever seen my husband dance, Mama would not have found it so difficult to get me to marry him.' (Being a good dancer proved not enough in the end, however, for having borne him seven children she eventually left him.[38])

According to Elizabeth, about 1818, apart from the occasional concert, public entertainment was very sparse. There were six Assemblies during the season, costing five shillings, of which she thought very little: 'ill attended, the small room never half full', and the large, which held 1200 people, was used only for the Caledonian Hunt Ball, for which tickets could only be presented by members. The private balls given at home were more popular even though 'inconvenient, troublesome and expensive', and always very crowded.[39]

The literary parties given by Mrs Grant and others in that field were of a very different kind. After her first year in Edinburgh in 1810 she had exclaimed ruefully how 'every cow of ours . . . has a calf': writing with 'the muddiest head' after two such evenings she explained how, although an intellectual party in Edinburgh must include a lavish cold collation, the guests were too interested in good talk to 'attend to vulgar gratifications'. Next evening, therefore, was for the unsophisticated to eat up the goodies, 'good, kind people, that dress finely, laugh heartily, and sing merrily' – sometimes well-born into the bargain – 'less fastidious, happier because less wise, and more benevolent because less witty . . . who could amply appreciate the value of a custard, a jelly, or a jest on its second appearance'.

'On these good people', she confessed, 'the lions and lionesses of literature would think their roaring very ill-bestowed', and 'would not for the world be caught eating blanc-mange while Mr Jeffrey and Dr Thomas Brown are brandishing wit and philosophy in each other's faces with electric speed and brilliance.'

All this Mrs Grant regarded with detached amusement: where would this 'reign of wit' end?[40] And where, then, would one allocate Mrs Siddons?

At Miss Hamilton's, a party which Mrs Grant and her daughter Mary attended in January 1819, the rooms were 'soon filled with all that is most gay and fashionable in Edinburgh, with so many thoughtless creatures dancing'. But the occasion was sadly marked for Mrs Grant because soon after they arrived she was told of the death of her former pupil Lady Elizabeth Boyle, who had been in poor health for some months: 'the time and place gave something like horror to the announcement', and she hurried Mary away lest she too should hear the news in these incongruous surroundings.[41]

For Mrs Grant that winter had been exceptionally social. 'I could tell you of such belles, such marriages, and such parties', that she had barely been able to spend half an hour with her old friend Mrs Henry Erskine a few doors off.

Not that Mrs Grant ever wholly wasted her time on mere socialising. 'If you did but know how many orphan girls I have had to seek employment and situations for! . . . and the necessary dining, the indispensable evening parties, the strangers that bring letters from friends.'[42]

After a few weeks she was almost thankful to catch a bad cold, 'which has procured me a week's admirable quiet'. But she could not get out of a dinner with the High School master Mr Pillans, particularly as she had never managed to accept his invitations before. The difficulty was that she was double-booked, having already invited friends for the evening. Pillans's dinner-company proved worthwhile, 'a very desirable society': Sir Harry Moncreiff and his daughter, the Rev. Andrew Thomson of St George's Church, his namesake the minister of Duddingston, the Rev. John Thomson (who was also a landscape painter), Francis Horner's parents and brother; and, 'besides two or three nameless youths', there was Campbell Preston, 'a most admirable American', whose company had already given Edinburgh great pleasure and who, she was sure, was bound to become 'an ornament to that great continent'. She was full of praise for his mind, good nature, native eloquence, and complete freedom from 'false decoration or false taste'.[43]

Mrs Grant had to hasten from this 'most desirable party' by 9 o'clock in order to attend her own. Guests had already assembled, and she had hardly the energy left to entertain them. Luckily, 'Music held the whole in perfect peace . . . O how often I say to myself in the evening, "Thus passes the day, deceitful, vain, and void."'[44]

Though one is tempted to picture Mrs Grant as homely and always stout, she was tall and, despite her many confinements, until 1820 even slender, and in good general health. In 1820, however, she had a serious accident which crippled her for life, leaving her able to walk only with crutches, and thereafter her figure filled out from the enforced lack of exercise.

Early that October, as she was leaving a shop in Princes Street, in descending the steps she tripped over the end of her trailing scarf and fell heavily to the pavement. In the fall she seems to have twisted round so that her temple violently struck the paving-stone, raising a large lump, and she was bruised all down one thigh and severely strained the sinews. There proved to be no broken bones, or in the then state of surgery she would never have walked again. As it was, a month later she could still scarcely put foot to ground, and her recovery continued slowly. She was then sixty-five years old.[45]

The philosophical lady reflected that her lameness gave her an excuse to stay at home over the winter, as her ever-widening circle of acquaintances had been proving such a time-waster, and further, because of Queen Caroline's trial political feelings were running so high that she was spared from hearing many violent opinions. By the end of the year she could stagger to her dining-room, and receive morning calls. She was then taking lessons in the use of crutches, and by January with their aid could walk round her room, but still slept badly from the pain at night. Still she persevered, with little complaint.

At the same time she was suffering from anxiety over her daughter Moore, a reserved young woman who had long been ailing, but was still able to 'drill' her with the crutches. By February, though free of pain, she was still unable to walk alone.

Her morning callers continued unabated, with sympathy over the accident. Edinburgh was at the height of the winter season, full of 'society', 'glowing with busy life, and gay with the flutter of all those human butterflies' – whose giddy course she was quite relieved at being unable to follow.[46]

It proved an anxious spring and summer. In May Moore burst a blood-vessel and for a week seemed unlikely to recover, and then improvement was slow. Looking back on last year's happy summer at Moffat when Moore was well, able to walk and ride, it was now an irrecoverable past, and the present was fraught with sorrow and anxiety, with deaths of old friends like Mr Smith of Jordanhill, whom she had known for forty years. An amiable, kindly man 'with so much delicacy', he died peacefully in a matter of minutes.

After four years of pain and recurring fever, borne with calm serenity, Moore died in 'tranquil repose' on 1 July 1821, in her twenty-fifth year. Her mother claimed that this serious girl had been already 'respectable and respected at 15', and she had endured illness throughout the best years of her youth.[47]

After her funeral Mrs Grant and her remaining daughters Isabella and Mary moved from the melancholy house in Princes Street to stay with the widowed Mrs Smith at Jordanhill, then in September to her friends the Misses Stewart, who having moved to Edinburgh from Albemarle Street, now had a charming cottage in fine grounds on the banks of the Clyde, opposite Holy Loch. Here her son joined them, before returning with Mary to reopen the desolate home they had left nearly four months earlier, an ordeal which she found even more painful than expected.

Mrs Grant was, however, resilient. Rheumatism had hampered her recovery, but with 'warm weather and sea-bathing' she hoped for improvement, and Isabella's active, cheerful company, giving up her own pleasures to take care of her mother and sister, was always a consolation. She could now walk with greater ease, though Isabella, who at ten had nearly died of measles, was now physically 'feeble', and a remaining anxiety was her son John Peter's career, he having set up that spring as advocate on his own account.

Meanwhile her general health was good, she had friends, the comfort of her remaining children, and she was resolved to conquer her disability because 'I daily see people who have surmounted this same misfortune'.[48]

An occasion which, in contrast to the lively entertainments of social life, partook more of Scottish solemnity than Scottish gaiety, was the wedding, ceremonious and serious. Charlotte Tait, daughter of Crawfurd Tait of Harvieston and Sir Ilay Campbell's daughter Susan, describes the wedding of her elder sister (also Susan) to young Sir George Sitwell which took place at their family house in June 1818. As Presbyterian usage allowed no such assembly in church, marriages normally took place in the bride's house. The old house was fuller than it could possibly hold', for the many guests who came from afar.

The family gathered in the drawing-room, the patriarchal and much beloved Sir Ilay in command of proceedings. He received the bride and bridesmaids on their entry, leading them to the centre of the room, where the pair took their vows and were joined by the old minister who had known the Tait family all their lives. According to custom, no ring was then given – that came afterwards, privately. There was a joining of hands, an extempore prayer, all standing, then the usual solemn address to the bridal couple.

Little in the way of celebration followed beyond cutting the cake, and the young pair departed in a shower of old shoes, bound for a Highland honeymoon with, as was customary, the bride's sister, Charlotte accompanying them as her supporter.[49]

Since Edinburgh society was so largely based on the law and the University, the long vacations especially in summer offered a chance of escape, and anybody who could afford it acquired a country property within easy travelling distance of the city, to which their families could retreat, joined at weekends and for the whole summer months by the husbands. Scott's

Abbotsford was a fairly long journey away, but Francis Jeffrey's Craigcrook was near enough to later become a part of the suburbs.

This small country mansion, on the eastern slope of the wooded Corstorphine Hill, had been occupied since about 1805 by Archibald Constable and his family, who had not attempted any alterations or additions. Besides Constable's six children his mother lived there, also his sister-in-law 'auntie Jan',[50] and often her father, Constable's old printer Willison. Already in Constable's time the place drew many visitors, starting the tradition of hospitality which was to last for many years.

Jeffrey's own first country venture was in 1812, during his widowhood, when he became tenant of Hatton, nine miles west of Edinburgh, joined there during the first two summers by his in-laws the Moreheads. This mansion, built by the Earls of Lauderdale, had a garden laid out as a fine landscape of lawns, avenues, terraces, fountains and sculptures, but long sadly neglected and overgrown.[51]

Francis Horner visited Jeffrey at Hatton in his first summer there, where he 'lives in a great house, and writes his reviews in a little gilded closet'. Looked after by the Moreheads and his brother John, 'he is perfectly comfortable, being strongly attached to them all'.[52] In the autumn of 1814, after returning from America with his bride Charlotte, Jeffrey gave up Hatton and rented from Constable Craigcrook, much nearer Edinburgh, with nearly fifteen acres, which cost him £1200. He held a fifteen-year lease in mortmain for a yearly rent of £32, but later extended it. 'An old keep', relates Cockburn, 'unmodernised and inconvenient, in an acre of poor kitchen garden, and in disorder'.[53] With a tower and turrets, it was really castle-like.

Jeffrey at once set about improving the house, removing some walls and growing ivy up others. He built a small addition on one side, and worked extensively on the garden – his wife's especial interest. Some years later he built a larger addition, but meanwhile Craigcrook was quite sufficient for entertaining.

In time, the house was bordered by a fine lawn on two sides, the fields sloping up to the woods were made into one by removing walls, and the land was extended to nearly forty acres. The chief drawback was the cutting off of the sunset by the hill on the west side. But the house and surroundings on low ground were thus agreeably secluded, and on the other sides the view was delightful to the Forth, Edinburgh and the surrounding hills, even as far as the hills of Perthshire and Stirling.

Jeffrey's first season at Craigcrook has echoes of Scott and Abbotsford. In May 1815 they were trying it out in advance of their first summer there: 'It will be all scramble and experiment this season, for my new buildings will not be habitable till next year, and the rubbish which they occasion will be increased by endless pulling down of walls, levelling and planting of shrubs, etc.'

He describes his acquisition: 'an old narrow high house, 18 feet wide and 50 long, with irregular projections of all sorts; 3 little staircases, turrets, and a large round tower at one end . . . with multitudes of windows of all shapes and sizes'. Near the door were some 'respectable trees', and the two old gardens were 'surrounded with massive and aged stone walls 15 feet high'. He was to turn the inner garden into grass and conceal the wall with shrubs, replacing other walls with sunk fences. On the north-west corner he was to build, in stone, a fine room of 28 by 18 feet for a laundry and store-rooms with above, 'two pretty bedchambers', the only rooms with a view towards the hill.

Meanwhile, as walls were still building, 'C. and I sleep in a little dark room, not 12 feet square, in the tower'. The new extension would cost him about £450, and the same again for a new roof and other improvements. The fields, by keeping them in grass, he could rent out for £60. He had found an 'excellent gardener', and would employ two labourers for a couple of weeks in spring.[54]

Horner, before he had even visited the place, approved of Jeffrey's keeping the old enclosing garden wall rather than opening the place up, and confessed that his own 'prejudice' was based on Bacon and Henry Temple, 'Much in favour of old garden enclosures near a house'. Indeed, writing from Lincoln's Inn, he envied Jeffrey's rural retreat, admitting that what he would have loved was 'to be in my own garden of Eden'. This, in his short life, he was not to achieve.[55]

Jeffrey's acquisition of Craigcrook affected the social life of many other people. Before the courts rose on 12 July they used to move there on a Friday evening or Saturday and return on Monday morning, then settled there for the rest of the summer. He was to spend thirty-four seasons there, to his great content. His wife loved working in the garden, and the estate was a mecca for his friends; only Abbotsford could outdo it for visitors in Scotland.

The Grant sisters Elizabeth and Jane used often to join them for a weekend or a day, sometimes the only other lady present being the clever if rather disagreeable Mrs George Russell. But there would always be a large group of male visitors, Henry Cockburn, Tommy Thomson, occasionally William Clerk, several young advocates before they married, and sometimes the Moreheads and Jeffrey's brother John, 'chance celebrities', and London friends at intervals. 'It was not a bigwig set at all', said Elizabeth. Her father, or Lord Gillies, would not have fitted into this 'riotous crew', whose free and easy antics the strait-laced Elizabeth rather shunned, preferring to be with the chatty, stoutish Mrs Jeffrey and her little girl Charlotte, and joining in their gardening. During the gentlemen's rumbustious games Jane, however, liked to stay with them as 'queen of the bowling green . . . admired by all those clever heads'.[56]

In July 1817 Jeffrey wrote to John Richardson urging him to visit: 'We have your old room for you here, and a new study in progress.' As a further lure, 'a whole wilderness of roses, and my shrubs are now so tall as not to be easily seen over. Moreover my whole lawn is green with potatoes', and a final irresistible touch: 'I have got 12 dozen of old claret in my old cellar, and am meditating upon an ice-house . . . Do come and be jolly for a week or two.'[57]

A month later Washington Irving, on his Edinburgh visit, was walked out to dine at Craigcrook by Jeffrey's brother, greatly admiring the views of Edinburgh along the road. The American found Jeffrey 'very pleasant and hospitable in his own house, & apparently very amiable & happy in his domestic character'.[58]

Saturday was the great day. Then the courts rose earlier, and legal and other friends hastened to be at Craigcrook by about 3 o'clock to enjoy bowling matches, walks round the garden and up the hill, and admiration of the wall with its beautiful cascade of yellow roses. A 'banquet' and generous potations were always provided. 'Mirth unrestrained,' says Cockburn, 'the talk always good, but never ambitious . . . What can efface those days?'[59]

Lockhart, in *Peter's Letters,* compiles a characteristic but in detail fictitious account of such a memorable afternoon. His description, much of it exaggerated, is obviously based on intimate knowledge of a place where he had been many times. First he gives a short description: 'old turreted mansion, much patched in the whole mass of its structure', as well as enlarged by Jeffrey, and a reference to the few trees immediately adjoining, offset by the view of the 'charming hill . . . wooded most luxuriantly to the very summit', and its garden and Jeffrey's pleasure in cultivating the fields. He next launches into a description of Jeffrey's dragging him 'over his ditches and hedges', discoursing knowledgeably of Swedish turnips and red-flowering potatoes: a full three-quarters of an hour of 'the great man' entirely on farming matters, no law or politics. Jeffrey is clad farmer-like in a short green jacket, grey worsted pantaloons, a black silk handkerchief and Hessian boots. 'How had Grub-street stared', reflects 'Peter', had they seen 'the prince of reviewers in such a garb!'

Playfair, Leslie and some young advocates now arrive, having walked over, followed by Robert Morehead and others 'of grave years'. He is surprised when these pundits propose a leaping contest, and as Playfair strips off (presumably coat and waistcoat), he and the rest feel obliged to follow. Apart from Professor Leslie the 'sinewy Caledonians' all excel, and considering his lack of inches Jeffrey was 'quite miraculous', while Playfair, also short, and aged at least seventy, could beat them all.

This fable, as much to flesh out his characters as to poke fun, leads on to a physical description of Playfair, with the minutiae beloved by contemporaries, not forgetting a glance at phrenology in describing his broad forehead across the temples, 'as, according to Spurzheim, all mathematical foreheads must be'. Leslie's brow was similarly broad, but though much younger than Playfair he was stout and heavy, and already turning grey. These descriptions go on in some detail.

The party are summoned to the drawing-room to meet Mrs Jeffrey and several ladies. Jeffrey does not change his dress, but remains in his farmer's garb through the evening. Dinner, notably 'a glorious turbot and oyster-sauce', is excellent, with plenty of champagne, Jeffrey's favourite, he guesses. 'The true reviewing diet is certainly Champaigne moussu, and devilled biscuit.' Literary table talk was markedly absent in favour of gastronomic discussion, and even at the dessert and claret (a superb Château Margaux) stage, topics were still light. Jeffrey, who spoke always as if spontaneously, threw off one idea after another without apparent effort, full of 'animal spirits' like his life, energetically combining writing and editing with his regular legal work, 'bubbling for ever upwards, and refusing to be exhausted'.[60]

Playfair, serene and venerable, by contrast spoke always after deep reflection, and with his unassuming profundity, always impressive. He was in fact just seventy-one, and died in the very year that *Peter's Letters* were published.

The temptation to present these distinguished men as it were in undress must have been irresistible to Lockhart, and however apocryphal the leaping-match anecdote, the character-sketches are shrewdly accurate.

Jeffrey's 'Sessional Saturnalia' became proverbial, mostly open to his legal friends.

In 1818 he was describing to his father-in-law Charles Wilkes his improvements to date: enlarging the domain by bringing in part of the wood, hiding the fence by ingenious means, and a generous planting of flowers. Nothing could lessen his pleasure – even 'a biting east wind' was counteracted by 'the sight of a clear spring babbling from a rock, and the smell of the budding pines and the common field daisies, and the cawing of my rooks, and the cooing of my cushats . . .' Alas, this was a swan-song for the season, when he must leave it for the courts and, until July, visit only at weekends. He was even impelled to add a lyrical postscript, about the larches, 'sycamores in full flush of rich, fresh foliage – the air as soft as new milk, and the sky so flecked with little pearly clouds full of larks'.[61]

The sad part of the idyll, of course, was the regular return to Edinburgh and the drudgery of the bar. And not all seasons were equally good. Although looking back on 'some idleness and tranquillity', he had to admit that weather-wise that spring had been poor, with perhaps seven fine days, mostly cold, then wet, and that he and Charley indulged their love for hills and woods by trudging out daily in mist and shower 'with scarcely a primrose to cheer us'. But bound though he is to town life, he takes great pleasure in his twelve acres laid out in grass, the hyacinths, auriculas, anemones in glory, the doves, sweet briar, wallflowers, gentians . . .' As for the *Edinburgh Review* he admits to being 'a sad defaulter' and farming out more articles.[62]

Henry Fox, who dined there twice during his second Edinburgh visit in 1822, enjoyed more delightful weather. The first time, in May, when he was with William Allen, Sandford and his elder brother, Henry left one of his more waspish descriptions. The party, which included Cockburn and John Murray, was 'very agreeable', and he allowed that Jeffrey 'would be a remarkably pleasant man, if he was less afraid of speaking Scotch and did not mince his words in such an absurd way. Mrs Jeffrey is a poor creature and not worth crossing the Atlantic for; she seems good-natured and inoffensive, but has St Vitus' dance and is very silly.'[63]

On 8 June he dined there again, with William Erskine, recently raised to judgeship as Lord Kinneder, Leonard Horner, Lady Davy, who was 'blooming', and Sir James Mackintosh, 'in great spirits at his success'.[64]

It was three days before James Stewart of Dunearn's trial, which Henry attended, though he was too anxious even to enjoy Jeffrey's 'beautiful speech' among the general dulness of the trial. The anxiety was over his friend Sandford's threatened duel with Hare, wanting Henry to be his second. But a couple of days later Sandford was persuaded to consult Jeffrey, and the pair then kept a very low profile while negotiations with Hare continued.[65]

Jeffrey's summers at Craigcrook continued after his career took him to London, as MP and later as judge, a period when he writes to his friends with nostalgia for the days of comparative youth gone by. Even Craigcrook could no longer relieve his settled melancholy.

34
THE CHURCH

'It is only necessary to attend the Scottish church for one month to become a fierce Episcopalian. It is impossible to bear the dulness and the repetition of the Scotch clergy while all the accompaniments to the service are wanting that can elevate the soul and supply the tone of feeling which is wanting in them.'

Journal of Miss Berry, 28 Aug 1814, 34–35

'All the wits and *philosophers of* Edinburgh bowed down to the power of his mighty genius, and heard from him, with reverence and admiration, truths which they would have sneered at from one less rich in the highest powers of intellect.'

Mrs Grant to Mrs Rucker, on the Rev. Thomas Chalmers, *Memoir and Correspondence of Mrs Grant of Lagan*, ed. by her son, 3 vols, London, 1844, 4 June 1815, II.137ff.

'Dr Chalmers and Lord Byron are at present the two wonders of the age, one for the exhaltation, and the other for the perversion of those high gifts that bring men nearest to superior intelligences.'

Mrs Grant to John Richardson, *Ibid.*, June 1815, II.137ff.

In the early nineteenth century the Church had been still influenced by the rather wishy-washy Moderatism which did not satisfy its more serious members, and in the General Assembly the Moderate/Evangelical struggle continued. Heading the Moderates was the stern, unbending Dr John Inglis (?1762–1834), free from what he considered fanatical precision, and independent and honest. He did not care for followers in the 'carnal policy', worldly ministers interested chiefly in stipends and glebes, but preached like a 'sound Calvinist'. Inglis had succeeded Principal Robertson as minister of Old Greyfriars in 1799, and in 1804 was Moderator of the General Assembly.[1]

Most active, efficient and also unscrupulous of the Moderate leaders was Dr George Cook (1772–1845), minister of Laurencekirk and son of a professor at St Andrews, where he studied and from 1829 was to become its Professor of Moral Philosophy. After twice failing to become Moderator, when he finally succeeded in 1829 he had to resign on securing the St Andrews professorship.

Of the leading Evangelicals, old Sir Henry Moncreiff of Wellwood was minister of St Cuthbert's, at the western end of Princes Street and then quite outside the New Town. Responsible, morally 'sound', and unswervingly loyal to the Gospel doctrines, he was yet longing for a new lead in the Church. Lockhart, in his assumed role in *Peter's Letters,* thought his eloquent prayer and sermon redolent of an un-English 'coarseness', illustrating 'bitter and dogmatic reprobations' of any differences of interpretation, yet melting to humanity. This he contrasted favourably with the 'puling and piping' of the Church of England. He declared himself disconcerted, incidentally, to see Moncreiff 'covered' as he entered the church and ascended the pulpit steps, maintaining the old Presbyterian fashion of entering with his hat on – the object being to repudiate any attribution of sanctity to the mere *place* of worship.[2]

The much younger Andrew Thomson, barely forty, fiercest and also the most fashionable, had been minister of New Greyfriars until 1814, when he moved to his 'new and magnificent place of worship in the finest square' (as 'Peter' phrased it), namely St George's. Until he arrived there from the Old Town, church-going had been quite out of fashion with New Town dwellers. Clear and practical as a preacher and devoted to the truth, he was a vigorous controversialist, with a sound grasp of the teachings of the Fathers. His secret was to expound important doctrinal questions clearly, in a direct and purposeful manner, thanks to his own worldly experience; hence after an initially cool reception he soon attracted a fashionable congregation. Henry Brougham, who had been his schoolfellow, called him the one man he would fear to meet in debate. His fine, muscular appearance was an obvious help, and though of homely features he had a bold mouth, strong forehead, 'chiselled' nose (always a favourite feature of the age), and sharp eyes.[3]

Apart from a couple of shining lights, neither based in Edinburgh, preachers of the first two decades of the century were pretty unremarkable. Beside the flashing genius of Chalmers and Irving other ministers seemed tame. Yet when the Free Church minister Dr Robert Gordon of Marischal College in Aberdeen came to Edinburgh in 1822, Mrs Grant considered it good fortune, and some even preferred his 'pious eloquence' to Chalmers. While Sir Harry, 'good, stern, sound Presbyterian', and the tough Andrew Thomson, sincere and able, were outstanding in their way, she regretted their political polemics. No other minister to her showed brilliance, and she reckoned the 'lump' of the Church needed leavening.[4]

Yet she noted new signs of devotion among the fashionable, more people turning openly Christian, so that no longer did the serious-minded retreat into corners in order to talk. Several zealous Presbyterians had even abandoned their churches for the Episcopalian Mr Craig – whom Mrs Grant considered not outstanding though sincere and doctrinally sound. 'Many fashionable young ladies resort there on the same principle that they go to hear Catalani.'[5]

Some of the clergy were academics (that is, pluralists), like Dr Alexander Brunton, widowed husband of the author of *Discipline* and other novels, who had died in 1818. His pale, delicate face with its resigned, 'melancholy sensibility' revealed his sad loss. As for the one sermon that 'Peter' heard, it was elegant (favourite term) and 'modestly impressive', a doubtless intentionally meaningless phrase.[6]

Christison describes him as 'strong, well-built, portly' with a flabby and 'not handsome' face. His courtly manner made him a favourite with the ladies and a success at the Tron Kirk. He was something of a 'clerical beau', clinging to the traditional tight black pantaloons and gaiters, 'a trying costume for human shanks', observes Christison dispassionately. As a 'double-dyed pluralist', minister, professor and Upper Librarian of the university, he obtained the only private house in the new University buildings, but for more than half the year lived six miles from Edinburgh at his 'pleasant villa' near Loanhead on a tributary of the Esk.[7]

In 1809 Brunton had been translated from New Greyfriars to the Tron Kirk. From 1813 he was Professor of Oriental Languages, mainly Hebrew, and later became Moderator of the General Assembly. Kindly and courteous, he would bow gracefully to his students in the street, and his smooth manner was perhaps meant to court popularity. 'As a teacher he was superficial', is the damning verdict of the Rev. Donald Sage (who had been one of his students), 'and as a preacher he was equally shallow and uninteresting'. This is presumably what is meant in *Peter's Letters.*[8]

Dr William Ritchie, whose rigid Calvinism appeared in his lectures and sermons – which he, like Sir Henry Moncreiff, read, in his case because otherwise he broke down entirely – was an 'extreme Moderate', meaning that he leaned towards Episcopacy. Influential Moderates in 1809 invited him to succeed Dr Hunter as Professor of Theology, and he was also a minister of Edinburgh's High Kirk of St Giles. When in Glasgow he had fallen foul of his elders for introducing an organ to his church. Though another 'elegant' speaker, well structured and serious, he was (says Sage) 'meagre and artificial'. He had only three forms of prayer, on which he rang the changes throughout the session. In 1827 he was to be succeeded as Professor by Dr Chalmers.[9]

Chief among the rest was Dr Thomas MacKnight, son of James, one of the Scottish 'true' theological writers, author of *The Harmony of the Gospels.* While he inherited his father's learning, he maintained a practical approach. In 1820 he was Moderator of the General Assembly.

A complete contrast was Dr Thomas McCrie, minister of a poor church in a humble district. Educated at Edinburgh University and ordained in 1796, he had been expelled as a Secessionist in 1809 and set up his own church in Davie Street, not far from Thomas Carlyle's one-time lodgings in Carnegie Street. Unlike Jamieson, he had a piercing voice and sometimes a wild shrillness, and spoke with a kind of haughty Puritanism. With his shrewd face and piercing eyes, Carlyle describes him as 'earnest-looking, lean, acute-minded, with much learning and thought, but no eloquence'; but he was impressed by the humble congregation, 'poor people with their clean faces, their attentive looks'.[10]

The mason Hugh Miller, when working at Niddrie House in 1823, had been urged by his two uncles in the north to hear McCrie, whom he recognised as having seen on an evening walk in 'the green lanes of Liberton'. He was 'singularly erect, spare, tall', pale-faced and with a melancholy expression, and 'an air of sedate power', an unusual combination of a clerical and military appearance. So striking was he that Hugh looked for some time after his retreating back, old-fashioned in a black suit, brown great-coat, 'the neck a good deal whitened by powder', as was the turned-up rim of his hat behind.

Attending his chapel next Sunday, Hugh discovered who this interesting character was. On that morning there was such a deal of coughing because of a change in the weather that the Doctor, rather annoyed, stopped suddenly in the middle of his argument. The coughing stopped, eyes turned in surprise, and there was dead silence for a whole minute. Suppressing a smile, McCrie said, 'I see, my friends, you can all be quiet when I am quiet.' For the rest of the day's services coughing was much reduced.

His discourses, neither flashy nor eloquent, were shrewd, but in Miller's view no other preacher produced such an effect. Had he been a Covenanter, he thought, McCrie would have made a general.[11]

In 1812 McCrie had obtained a doctorate, in 1816–18 was Professor of Divinity, and among his later historical works were histories of the Reformation in Italy (1827) and in Spain (1829).[12]

Dour devotion to Sabbath restrictions showed no remission, even over such a harmless activity as a walk. Crabb Robinson, visiting Edinburgh in 1821, and out early on the same Sunday that he heard Chalmers's warning against over-zealous Sabbatarianism, asked a passer-by what some handsome building might be. A grammar school, was the answer. 'But, sir,' added this stranger – possibly a journeyman weaver, he thought – 'I think it would become you better on the Lord's Day morning to be reading your Bible at home, than asking about public buildings.' Robinson, not to be worsted, accepted this as good advice, but offered some in exchange, so that 'we may both profit by our meeting. Beware of spiritual pride.' His answer was a scowl of 'Scotch surliness'.[13]

English people living in Edinburgh had had their own chapel since 1722, at the foot of Blackfriars Wynd. After the repeal of penal statutes inhibiting the Episcopal church in 1792 the Rev. Daniel Sandford, an English settler, formed a congregation which in 1797 built their own Charlotte Chapel in Rose Street,[14] and here they met until St John's Church (1816–18) was completed at the West End.

All other legal obstacles had been removed in 1804 when Episcopal bishops and clergy met at Laurencekirk and resolved to subscribe to the 39 Articles. Thereafter 'English Chapels' and Scottish Episcopal churches were enabled to merge. A month later Daniel Sandford formed a separate congregation which entered into communion, as did the Cowgate Chapel in February 1805, both retaining the English liturgy. Unity was achieved when in 1806 Sandford succeeded Dr Abernethy Drummond as Bishop of Edinburgh. During the 1811 General Assembly, the day after the ceremonial dinner, Robert Morehead addressed the Moderates expressing 'mutual esteem' between the two churches.[15]

Sandford, described in *Peter's Letters* as thin and pale, with an air of 'devout and melancholy [another frequently used word] abstraction, a deep yet tremulous voice', was Oxford educated, a good scholar, and preached eloquently without affectation. After weeks of listening to robust and energetic Presbyterians (says 'Peter'), his mild, gentle air seemed a relief. Sandford served as Bishop for twenty-four years until his death in 1830.[16]

The 1722 chapel meanwhile had been supplemented by two more small Old Town chapels, and in 1774 by a large 'United Episcopal Chapel' built by subscription in the Cowgate. When even this proved too small, the Gothic St Paul's Chapel in York Place was built for them by Archibald Elliot at the same time as St John's. The Cowgate building then became St Patrick's Roman Catholic Church.[17]

The Rev. Archibald Alison, minister of the Cowgate Chapel from 1800 until his death in 1839, whom Carlyle heard preach on an early visit to Edinburgh (1817), was a clear, elegant (as so frequently) speaker, but Carlyle thought his ideas 'distinct rather than profound'. Comparing him with Chalmers, one hearer described Alison as 'a glass of spruce beer – pure, refreshing & unsubstantial', whereas Chalmers was 'a draught of Johnnie Dowie's ale – muddy, thick & spirit-stirring'.[18]

Alison, whose chapel was larger than Sandford's, had a more popular approach. 'Peter' describes him as slightly pensive, with a noble serenity; large deep-set grey eyes, 'composed' lips and a high, pale forehead with 'a few thin, grey, monastic ringlets'. His voice, with a strong Scots accent, was clear and mellow, his reading impressive. Peter praises him as the only Scottish preacher who showed awareness of the natural world, and drew illustrations from it.[19]

In 1816 Robert Morehead, Jeffrey's brother-in-law, became chaplain to Princess Charlotte of Wales, and in 1818 was appointed Dean of Edinburgh, succeeding the Rev. James Walker, on the day when the new William Burn church of St John's at the West End was consecrated. Morehead habitually rose early and after his morning prayers would read from the classics, and from Italian, German and English literature. He was especially fond of poetry, and composed a 'poetical memorial' of his own life, paraphrases of the prophets, and translations from Latin works. From 1817, when he was elected an FRS of Edinburgh, until 1822 he contributed to reviews, such as the *Edinburgh Magazine*.[20]

His wife Margaret Wilson, daughter of the Professor of Church History at St Andrews was Jeffrey's cousin as well as being his first wife's sister.

The Episcopal Church was now flourishing, in spite of the suspect Jacobitism of most members, and in the Edinburgh area (though not in remoter districts) many of the landed gentry were members. They were funded by subscription and by support from England, the latter deplored by Peter who considered they ought to support their own poorly paid bishops.

Edinburgh had not a great many Catholics. Susan Ferrier sampled their chapel in 1816, 'with my spectacles on . . . and strange sights I saw as ever sour-faced Presbyterians looked upon, but the strangest part of the whole was the lecture or discourse, which was a red-hot exhortation to matrimony, and that from a Catholic I was not prepared for'.[21] She possibly overlooked the fact that Catholics who married would bring up their children in that church.

According to 'Peter', there were also numerous Protestant dissenting sects, mostly among the humbler classes: Tabernaclites, Haldanites, besides Wesleyan Methodists, several sorts of Independents, and a few Unitarians.

There were numerous dissensions in the General Assembly, heralding the Disruption of three decades later. As significant as these in the history of the Kirk was the emergence of one of its most notable ministers, the Rev. Thomas Chalmers, who in Assembly and pulpit had as great an impact as, in literature, had Francis Jeffrey or Walter Scott.

The hall in which the Assembly met had been unchanged for two centuries: it was part of St Giles', irregular in shape and ill lighted. On the east side was the canopied 'throne', an old carved oak chair of state. Here sat the Lord High Commissioner in his robes, officials and notabilities on either side, and richly liveried pages standing behind. These youths were usually younger sons of some of the oldest families.

Below the throne sat the Moderator, and in front at a railed-in table, the two Clerks of Assembly, the Procurator, and leading men of the Church, nominated by various burgh Presbyteries. Members sat in the body of the hall. At the west end opposite the throne was the bar. The hall was surrounded by public galleries. The building was long deemed inadequate for the purpose, and the Assembly later removed to a city church until eventually established in the New College and Assembly Hall, begun by William Playfair in 1846.

The Assembly was an affair of solemn ceremony. The Rev. Donald Sage, a Sutherland minister, describes in his *Memorabilia* the imposing opening which, according to tradition, followed a court held at Holyrood by the Commissioner as representative of the King. On the first day, 'a sermon was preached by the retiring Moderator, and the Commissioner, in a close carriage, escorted by a train of horse and a train of high civil dignitaries, proceeded in state from the palace, along the Canongate and High Street, to the High Church and then to the hall'.

After an opening prayer by the Moderator, the Commissioner formally addressed the Assembly as 'Right Reverend and Honourable', the Moderator replied, and addressed the Assembly in his turn. The debates then began.[22]

The whole performance strongly resembled House of Commons protocol, the Moderator taking the place of Speaker. Questions not settled in the lower church courts were referred here, and it was thus the forum at which talented preachers, sunk in obscure country parishes, had the chance to display their eloquence. When the subject was particularly contentious, the opposing parties could engage leading advocates to represent them.[23]

A seat in the public gallery was as much sought after as a theatre box for the most popular actor. In 1814, at Lady Williamson's request, Mrs Grant 'matronised' the Williamson girls, then her pupils, to witness 'the finest possible debate, the greatest possible crowd'. All seats were taken by 9 in the morning. This was the occasion when pluralities were vetoed, though at that stage to small effect. At the 1816 Assembly Mrs Grant was able to attend on only one day. 'The galleries of the church are filled with ladies and gentlemen of the first respectability, who go in the moment the doors open and sometimes remain 8 or 9 hours. There are spirited debates, and, what you would not expect in so grave an assembly, peals of laughter that make the house shake . . . nothing entertains so much.'[24]

Pluralities, the holding of a country living together with a professorship, though prohibited in 1814, were successfully defended the next year, and now in 1816 the question was raised afresh. All the strangers' places had been taken by 8 a.m., and by the time the debate started at 11 the crowd was so great that the lower galleries had to be cleared to make room for ministers. The debate lasted for twelve and a half hours, and one spectator claimed that he had stood in 'the window opposite the throne' throughout, and for an hour beforehand.

Chalmers, who spoke following the judge Lord Succoth, urged an end to all forms of plurality. His eloquence on the subject amazed even 'the fastidious Jeffrey', as Mrs Grant put it – who held the opposite opinion. Indeed that year Chalmers was 'the wonder of the age'. 'You would see, in the Edinburgh newspapers,' she wrote, 'what a sensation was produced by his sermon preached before the Commissioner on Sunday.'[25]

Jeffrey compared him afterwards to Demosthenes: 'There is something altogether remarkable about that man!' (At this time they had not met.[26]) The Edinburgh correspondent reported an audience transfixed and by the end reduced to tears.

The sermon was at the Lord High Commissioner's particular request. Once more, already by 9 in the morning the crowd far exceeded the High Church's capacity, long before the doors were opened. Then they poured into the building with such a rush that the Commissioner, judges and magistrates could scarcely push their way through to their own seats. Chalmers's text was Psalm VIII, 3,4, 'When I consider the heavens . . . what is man, that Thou art mindful of him?' One hearer noted that as he paused at the end of an argument 'a sort of sigh, as if for breath, was perceptible through the house'; and another, that at the end of possibly the same fine passage 'There ran through the congregation a suppressed but perfectly audible murmur of applause' – an unprecedented response. Similarly unprecedented was the applause which greeted the end of his sermon, which included accounts of the wonders and progress of science (noted by an advocate, John Marshall).[27]

Occasionally Chalmers went over the top. Once when he was arguing in a frenzy a member actually proposed an adjournment while he was so excited. Chalmers, nearly choked with indignation, shouted in his broad Fife accent, '*Exceeted,* sir! – *exceeted!* I am as cool, sir, as an algebraic problem!' – and indeed his intellect was always unimpaired by his emotion. From one of these furious tirades he could easily retreat to calmness.[28]

In 1820 fierce argument was provoked by the unworthy subject of the Royal marital quarrel. George IV, who had just succeeded his aged, blind and supposedly mad father, had attempted unsuccessfully to divorce his wife in 1814, when (with Henry Brougham's support) she was acquitted of the moral charges brought against her. There now arose the question of prayers for the Royal Family, and the Order in Council for the prayers in Scotland included the words, 'For his sacred Majesty King George, and all the Royal Family', omitting the name of Queen Caroline. Further, its extension to Scotland was considered 'unconstitutional and Erastian'. The Privy Council, however, had already in February requested the compliance of the previous year's Moderator, Dr MacFarlane.[29]

The Commissioner in 1820 was Lord Morton, an impoverished peer 'of open profanity and loose character' (says the Rev. Donald Sage), who had secured the office in order to mend his finances. The Moderator was Dr MacKnight. The Order in Council brought division between Moderates and Evangelicals to a head.[30]

Dr Thomson, opposing the Order, argued that constitutionally no civil authority might dictate to the Kirk, which according to the principle for which the Covenanters had fought had 'no spiritual head on earth'. He was opposed by the Solicitor-General, Dr John Hope, Dr George Cook, and Dr Francis Nicoll, Principal of St Andrews. The first descended to personalities, attacking Thomson for 'lofty presumption'. Dr Cook, while claiming that he supported the principle, saw here no infringement. Principal Nicoll expressed horror at a possible split between Church and State.

In the numerous speeches that followed, Lord Justice Clerk, David Boyle, a Moderate of great political influence, denied any establishment wish to infringe rights, but claimed that the Order prescribed not a prayer, but the persons to be prayed for. He moved that the Assembly should not adopt any declaration relating to an Order on prayers for the Royal Family. His motion was carried 126–53, but next day several members recorded dissent.[31]

The other vexed question long before the Assembly was lay patronage. By immemorial tradition the nomination of a minister had been by patron – a nobleman or laird – who would lay a deed of presentation on the Presbytery table requesting a trial of the nominee's qualifications. After his preaching in the church on a couple of Sundays, the Presbytery assembled to preside at the call. A formal announcement by the heritors, elders and so on was then made, stating their satisfaction with his qualifications and preaching, and requesting the Presbytery to concur in their appointment. After further trials they 'served the edict' on an appointed Sabbath, with a public request for any objections to be put forward. A further such opportunity was made on ordination day, and after the service the presentee was minutely questioned and must promise to perform the duties. (No allusion was made in this to the patron.) He was then received by prayer and the laying on of hands. The spiritual act of admission thus completed the title to the benefice, and the act of ordination was grounded on the people's acceptance.

This lay patronage, discontinued in 1690, had been restored in 1712 by a pro-Jacobite government, in the teeth of the General Assembly, and the system by which livings were disposed partly by private patrons and half by the crown and Town Councils, was then continued for the next century. Many clergy and Presbyterians objected, however, when obliged to ordain ministers in the teeth of popular resistance, and some so strongly that there were sometimes riots, or even the waylaying and removal of the minister, or leaving the presentee in an empty church. Sometimes the dragoons were even called in to ensure the ceremony went ahead. If all else failed, a recalcitrant congregation would simply ignore the new minister. Several small groups seceded from the church on this issue (including Thomas Carlyle's parents' congregation at Ecclefechan), and in half a century more than two hundred Secession chapels were thus formed.

Late in the eighteenth century leading clergy were opposing the indispensability of the people's concurrence, and the General Assembly gradually adopted the view that what mattered was the patron's presentation. The hallowed 'call' was not entirely dropped, but even a single signature was now held to suffice – thus keeping the form while losing the meaning. Even in 1782, when it had become an 'idle ceremony', the Assembly voted to retain the 'call' as 'immemorial and constitutional practice'.[32]

In the early nineteenth century, when Thomson in Edinburgh and Chalmers in Glasgow were inspiring the clergy by their zeal and drawing laymen to the church, minorities such as the opposers of plurality were increasing in the Assembly. Confrontation between the parties, however, was more over patronage and the appointment of ministers. The conservatively-minded Moderates argued that the church should keep within its strict legal limits, and were upheld by the Court of Session; while the Evangelicals held that the state had no right to interfere. It was this cleavage which eventually was to lead to the great Disruption of 1843, led by Chalmers and the Evangelicals.

There was also the matter of 'Burghers' and 'Anti-Burghers', who had split in 1747 over the Burgess Oath accepting the patronage system. Burghers accepted, Antis refused the oath, and they remained separate until in 1820 they merged to form the United Secession Church.

Meanwhile the Antis themselves had split into two sects, Old Light and New Light Anti-Burghers, both of which had influence in Edinburgh. The New Lights were headed by Dr John Jamieson (1759–1838), an antiquary friend of Scott and minister at Nicolson Street since 1797. He was editor of Scottish vernacular works and author in 1808 of an *Etymological Dictionary of the Scottish Language*. 'Peter' expressed amazement that such gifted men should support 'such pitiable sects of schismatics' in 'pettish and splenetic hatred'. He described Jamieson as 'sagacious-looking . . . with bright grey eyes, and a full round face', and preaching in a smooth, kindly tone.[33]

Thomas Carlyle, who attended their synod in May 1821, found himself at a loss. 'It was very unintelligible to me,' he told his mother. 'I could hear little and understand less. There was a medley of burghers and anti-burghers – all sitting promiscuously – some speaking, some listening, some not listening', but he was glad to see those few clergy he recognised laying down their differences and uniting in opinion.[34]

At the Assembly in 1821 and 1822 Chalmers spoke brilliantly in support of modifying ministers' theological education, to give them deeper and longer preparation for their calling. On this he was to suffer many defeats in succeeding years.

In 1821 a chief concern was the contest for the Moderatorship between Dr George Cook and Dr Mearns of King's College, both Moderates. The Evangelicals, led by Dr Thomson, were so anti-Mearns that they were willing even to support Cook (who was not, however, elected).[35]

The youthful Henry Fox, who had heard Chalmers preach a few days earlier, and who attended the Assembly with Sandford and Lady Morton, now heard him speak for a few minutes on the theological education debate, and was impressed not only by him but by the 'fluency and acuteness' of the many other clergy who spoke.[36]

As a preacher Chalmers was described as original, independent, enthusiastic, profound. Jeffrey was complimentary about him in the *Review*, and Dr Stuart of Dunure was not merely complimentary but (Chalmers admitted) 'very free, and, I believe, very just in his criticisms'. That year (1812) Chalmers, hitherto a confirmed bachelor, married Grace Pratt, and they settled at Kilmany in Fife, where he had built a new manse and improved its plantations. On the work side, he was busy 'improving' his sermons, whose fame already crowded his church with visitors.[37]

His *Encyclopaedia* article on 'Evidences of Christianity', published in 1813, which radically clarified his own beliefs, excited such interest in Edinburgh that he was urged to publish it as a separate work. Then his election to the Tron Kirk in Glasgow in November 1814, and his removal there 'in a blaze of unexampled popularity', gave further interest to his publications, and his appointment was greeted with as much pleasure in Edinburgh (where he continued to preach from time to time) as in Glasgow.[38]

Mrs Grant, a great admirer of his 'Evidences', heard him preach there during his first year, and in a typically judicious comment observed that, having for years 'employed his extraordinary abilities in displaying a lifeless form of religion', he was making up for it 'by preaching Christ only, and Him crucified . . . with what power, with what energy, what artless and unstudied eloquence'.[39]

Chalmers always wrote out his sermons, and read them from the pulpit to ensure their clarity. Unusual though this was for the Presbyterian Kirk, he found his mind so crowded with ideas that he did not trust extempore preaching; but because he wrote as he spoke, the read sermons had the merit of sounding impromptu. In the pulpit, unlike the unyielding Edward Irving, although he preached for at least an hour he would stop about halfway to read a hymn for the congregation to sing, while he took the opportunity to recoup his energies for the next bout of exhausting oratory.

He often composed while travelling, or when on a visit. In conversation his quiet, terse manner contrasted with the impassioned delivery and heartfelt speech which from the pulpit so affected listeners. From 1817 he began publishing his sermons, with such success that their sales kept pace with Scott's *Tales of my Landlord*.[40]

Mrs Grant accorded with the general opinion in praising his masculine energy and dignity which never descended to fashionable eloquence or hackneyed phrase, but used 'the first words that occur . . . sometimes homely enough', then rising to sublimity as he warmed to the subject, with the great gift of making Gospel doctrine acceptable to worldly listeners. She even coupled, or rather contrasted, him with Lord Byron, as 'the two wonders of the age – one for the exaltation, and the other for the perversion of those high gifts that bring man nearest to superior intelligence'. Byron, she witheringly pronounced, while possessing all worldly advantages, was 'regarded with disapprobation by all right thinking people', and Chalmers, without the advantage of 'birth, rank, polished manners, wealth or outward consequence', was venerated for the sanctity of his life and doctrines.

'Of all men he is the most modest, and speaks with undissembled gentleness and liberality of those who differ from him in opinion', she wrote in 1817. 'Every word he says has the stamp of genius', yet with his calm simplicity he seemed to radiate ordinariness. In February she enjoyed two hours of his company at a breakfast, 'a great intellectual feast . . . He was always powerful, always gentle, and always seemed quite unconscious of his own superiority.'

When Walter Scott, whom she had not seen for some time, joined the party an hour later, she began to notice similarities between the two: 'quiet unobtrusive humour, the same flow of rich original conversation . . . and readiness to give attention and interest'. 'The Divine' did have an edge on the novelist, however, by 'a more chastened dignity and occasional elevation'.[41]

Andrew Bigelow from Massachusetts, one of the Americans visiting Scotland that year, in his inevitable journal (published later in America) records first meeting Chalmers when he heard him preach at Lady Glenorchy's chapel. He happened to be sitting next to the phrenologist Dr Spurzheim, who was deeply absorbed, almost overwhelmed. 'It is too much, too much,' he murmured, passing his hand across his brow, 'my brain is on a fever by what I have been hearing.' This Bigelow thought remarkable from 'a cold and phlegmatic German'.[42]

Spurzheim was not attending Chalmers's sermon merely from curiosity. Chalmers was among those – Dr Abernethy was another – interested in his phrenological theories while others poured ridicule.[43] The Rev. David Welsh, another Edinburgh graduate and minister of Crossmichael, was a leading supporter, who ten years later was to become Professor of Church

History at Edinburgh and in the year of the Disruption was Moderator of the General Assembly, and following Chalmers's protest led him and the rest from the Hall.[44]

Bigelow later supped with Chalmers in Glasgow, also meeting his wife, 'a pleasing person and engaging manners', hostess that evening to several people including ladies. Without striving for effect, Chalmers appeared widely informed, quick and full of illustration. 'His colloquial powers are of a high order. Even in familiar conversation he is impressive and striking.'

Bigelow also heard him preach next day, on the eve of leaving for a three-month visit to London. Curiously, he comments that, while 'very vehement and impassioned', his style was marred by 'the profusion of his ornaments, the over-straining of his metaphors, the redundancy of his expressions' – rather the opposite of most critics' view. Like others, however, Bigelow noted Chalmers's lack of artifice and his style 'negligent and sometimes even coarse', along with entire absorption in his theme, and declared him undoubtedly the leading preacher of the age.[45]

This assessment has the great merit of clarity. Contemporaries fell over themselves in trying to define styles of preaching, often in such cloudy terms as to be almost meaningless.

Not everybody was equally pleased with Chalmers's preaching. John Whishaw, after spending three days in Edinburgh in 1820, heard him preach at Kirkcaldy, 'who did not satisfy my expectations. He has considerable powers, but is exaggerated in manner and matter. He preaches the high Calvinistic doctrines, and is, of course, deficient in good sense, and probably also in good faith. I greatly doubt his sincerity' – a singularly obtuse judgment. 'But he is an excellent parish priest at Glasgow . . . and he probably considers these violent doctrines as being most popular and efficient.'[46]

The physical aspects of famous clergy were also noted meticulously by those who met them or heard them preach (having usually a good hour to study them closely), and Chalmers came in for as dispassionately unflattering descriptions as did Walter Scott. Mrs Grant describes him as 'not merely plain, but vulgar' in appearance, with 'the worst Scotch accent', though these disadvantages were balanced by his 'manly simplicity'.[47]

Lockhart, in his assumed persona in *Peter's Letters,* describes him in minutest detail, not forgetting the fashionable phrenological diagnosis, noting his features, coarse at first sight, his pale complexion, half-closed lids, down-turned with 'drooping melancholy weight', and a deep cleft between nose and upper lip giving the lower face a 'leonine firmness'; marble-like, square cheeks, prominent cheekbones, light, dreamy and lustreless grey eyes which suddenly flashed with 'a watery glare' when enthusiasm carried him away. His forehead (phrenological interpretation here) was 'uniquely mathematical' – still broader across than either even Playfair's or Leslie's, and brows turned high at either end, characteristic, as Spurzheim had claimed, of all mathematical geniuses (such as Isaac Newton).

Indeed 'Peter' enlarges excessively on phrenological characteristics before remarking on Chalmers's 'dark crisp locks' that 'afford a fine relief to the death-like paleness of those massive temples'. He was of medium height and, though fairly slender, squarely built. Peter too remarks on his broad Scots accent and unmusical voice, cracked and strained at the start and not always even audible, but after his slow, drawling start, discourse bursting without warning into eloquence, while he sawed the air with gestures 'extremely rude and awkward'. In short, while he had heard more eloquent sermons, delivered with 'pulpit-enthusiasm', Peter had never heard any with such irresistible effect, the product of an original mind, talent for reasoning, and colourful argument. He admitted to feeling even 'my hardened nerves creep and vibrate, and my blood freeze and boil while he spoke'.[48]

In London in May 1817 Chalmers preached to congregations as enthusiastic as if he were a great theatrical star, attended at different services by Lord Elgin, Mackintosh, Wilberforce, Canning, Huskisson, Lord Binning and Lord Harrowby, and also by Sydney Smith's brother Bobus. George Canning was affected even to tears. On one occasion, at the Scotch Church in Swallow Street, Chalmers himself and a friend were almost unable to enter, as the crowd did not believe it was him. When William Wilberforce later arrived with a party of ladies including Lady Davy, they could not get in at all, until at last, as a small space was espied round the pulpit, someone pushed a plank through the window and rested it on the street railings, and while Lord Elgin waved to them encouragingly from inside, and Wilberforce hesitated, the undaunted Lady Davy ('no shrimp you must observe') boldly crossed the impromptu bridge.[49]

Outside the pulpit Chalmers did not invariably make an impression. In the same summer he visited the Lake District, and although he bore with him an introduction to Wordsworth from Crabb Robinson, the poet happened never to have heard of him and unfortunately 'by a most unlucky blunder' (as he admitted afterwards) addressed him as Dr Campbell. Chalmers, though far from vain, surely had every reason to expect to be known. However, Wordsworth was obliging enough to advise him on what best to see in the district in the time he had available.[50]

He had better luck with Jeffrey, whom he also first met in 1817, and who persuaded him to write for the *Review*. Chalmers's most important contributions were papers on his own particular subject, pauperism. The pair enjoyed friendship and mutual admiration, each appreciating the other's genius and virtues. Jeffrey regarded Chalmers as 'a great moral philosopher, an enthusiastic philanthropist, and the noblest orator of the age'.[51]

Later, in 1821, in a long discussion Chalmers urged Jeffrey no longer to veto articles on Christianity, and suggested that he admitted theology as a subject, for example by the Baptist minister John Foster, a confirmed Republican and critic of established Church institutions, who had published *Essays* in 1804 and contributed to various reviews. At Jeffrey's suggestion Chalmers personally wrote to Foster on the subject.[52]

Thomas Carlyle, then barely twenty-two, read Chalmers's 'boisterous treatise' on pauperism in the *Review* of February 1818, and was unimpressed. 'His reasoning (so they call it) is disjointed or absurd – & his language a barbarous jargon.' He had been more taken with the *Discourses* in 1817, which he considered 'abounds in that fiery, thoroughgoing style of writing for which the author is so remarkable' – and which showed him as a great fundamentalist.[53]

Chalmers served as minister at the Tron in Glasgow from 1815 until 1820, and then transferred to St John's Church there. During his eight years at these two churches he concentrated on work for the poor, setting up a poor relief system based on rigorous investigation, and trying all forms of aid before allowing anyone to be committed to pauperism. By means of church-door collections he reduced the cost to the parish by almost a sixth, prevented fraud, and limited parish relief to the wholly destitute.[54]

There had already been a move to translate Chalmers from the clerical to the academic field. One night in August 1819 when he was staying in Edinburgh, Sir George Mackenzie and Dr Brewster, backed by the urging of Dr Andrew Thomson, begged him to allow them to put him up for Playfair's chair of Natural Philosophy – which apart from any other advantage, would be very lucrative. The fact that Thomson's proposal appeared to expect him to accept disturbed Chalmers's Glasgow friends, who assumed that it was he who had taken the initiative. On the contrary Chalmers was canvassing for continued support for his Church projects. It took time to clear up this misunderstanding, before he could convince his parishioners that his devotion was unchanged and that he had no inkling of the proposal before he went to Edinburgh. He argued that, although an academic career would suit his taste, it might have dangerous implications because 'nothing . . . more effectually neutralizes a man's usefulness in this age of party violence and imputations, than the appearance of receiving anything from Government'.[55]

Meanwhile Chalmers came to preach in Edinburgh quite frequently, and his sermons were eagerly noted. Henry Fox, during his first Edinburgh visit in 1822, and the High School master Pillans, went to hear 'one of his high-flown sermons', on worldly love compared with love of the next. Like others Henry found the preacher's voice 'positively bad, his Scotch broad and vulgar', and unlike others, 'his doctrines absurd and sometimes odious; but yet it is impossible to let one's attention flag for one moment, or not to feel deeply interested and occasionally elevated . . . It lasted for a very long time, but I was not in the least tired, and, high as my expectations were raised, I was not the least disappointed.'

Far different was an evening service Fox attended the following Sunday at another church. The standard of preaching in Edinburgh was distinctly varied, and this time he 'heard a discourse about the Holy Ghost enough to make me hate him for life'.[56]

In 1821 Crabb Robinson heard Chalmers preach twice on the same day. 'In the forenoon it was a plain discourse to plain people, in a sort of school. In the afternoon it was a splendid discourse, in the Tron Church', against over-zealous Sabbath observance, which Chalmers called 'an expedient for pacifying the jealousies of a God of vengeance'. 'He represented the whole value of Sabbath observance to lie in its being a *free* and *willing* service – a foretaste of heaven', advice well aimed at the Scots. (Edward Irving later told him that 'the Deacons waited on the Doctor to remonstrate with him on the occasion of this sermon'.)[57]

Shortly before the King's visit in 1822, two sons of the 1st Baron Teignmouth, Charles Shore and his younger brother, on the morning after their arrival, heard Dr Alison preach at St Paul's Episcopal Chapel. Here was a minister whose voice was 'well modulated, his style chaste and elegant', but his treatment they thought superficial. Dr Chalmers, to whom Wilberforce had given them an introduction, was quite another matter.

'He wielded his mother tongue with a giant's force, and . . . if no vocabulary on either side of the Tweed could supply the word . . . he would unhesitatingly coin one for the purpose.' His energy was displayed with stamps and gesticulations almost, thought Charles, like some of the weavers in his audience.

Charles Shore remarks on Chalmers's breakfasts, crowded daily with foreign visitors and distinguished guests. He also describes his handwriting, 'like that of a retrograding crab, and the writing itself notoriously illegible: a defect not unfrequent in Scotchmen, and some of the most eminent.'[58]

Julian, son of the actor Charles Young, who started as a student at St Andrews in 1821 at the age of fifteen, contrived the following August to be in Edinburgh for the Royal visit before returning in September to the college, and during his visit inevitably heard Chalmers preach.

He too was disappointed in his physical appearance, seeing a man 'deficient in dignity and of homely aspect', not unlike Coleridge in build; but his face, 'pallid and pasty', seems to have repelled him most, with its commonplace features, apparently marked by smallpox, scanty hair 'roughed, as if his hands had been often passed through it', cold eyes, small, grey and 'fishy' which seemed peculiarly 'impassive, inexpressive'. Julian comments on the low though broad, well-developed brow, and in the fashionable phrenological jargon, saw in his skull 'great mathematical power', but deficiency in 'benevolence and veneration' – the qualities for which Chalmers was most noted. So much for phrenology.

But in the pulpit, carried away with 'the impetuosity of a torrent', even apparently transported by the sublimity of his ideas, left arm flailing like a windmill, he kept his congregation open-mouthed, scarcely even breathing . . . yet still his eyes were 'tame and lustreless' as if he were half asleep. Julian too thought it strange that he preached with the written sermon in front of him, not spontaneously, in the appropriately Presbyterian manner. How, he wondered, could Chalmers get away with it?

The minister's gifts were versatile: 'a profound mathematician, a great political economist, a far-seeing politician, a recondite scholar, a considerable theologian'. Receptive for a youth then only sixteen (but probably worked up in later years for publication).[59]

After witnessing the King's visit in August 1822, Chalmers took a tour in Dumfriesshire and then made a visit to England, chiefly in London. He met Dr Pye Smith of Homerton, at his suggestion preached there, and learned much about pauperism in London. There was also an unavoidable amount of socialising besides his preaching and discussions, which Chalmers felt guiltily 'to be a considerable interruption to my work'.

He also preached at Hackney, and a few days later in Hatton Garden at the then popular Irving's Caledonian Chapel. The place, designed to hold only six hundred, was crowded out. David Wilkie was there with another painter friend, Thomas Phillips, having come on with Sir Thomas Lawrence, who had first invited them to breakfast; they were lucky in finding excellent seats. Chalmers, arriving rather late, preached for an hour and five minutes, and Wilkie noted how, despite his unremarkable appearance and disagreeable voice and gestures, he commanded rapt attention with no need for eloquence. Afterwards the group met the preacher, Wilkie introduced his friend, and Lawrence repeatedly thanked Chalmers for the 'treat'. The minister in his turn was 'much gratified' to meet the distinguished President of the Royal Academy.[60]

While in England Chalmers made further studies of pauperism in East Anglia, and met with Lords Euston and Calthorpe and William Wilberforce, all interested in his work. He also visited a couple of London workhouses, and was entertained by Zachary Macaulay and other distinguished philanthropists. He was gratified to find that his *Review* articles had 'made a deeper impression throughout England than I was aware of'. He did have the embarrassment of meeting an outspoken rector of a parish near London, who said gruffly that 'he rejoiced to see a man from Scotland on the subject, for so much nonsense had come . . . through the *Edinburgh Review*'. Chalmers had to admit to being the author of this 'nonsense', but luckily having once cleared the air, the two parted on good terms.

After meeting Malthus at the East India College, being disappointed of a hoped-for meeting with Sir James Mackintosh, and making visits in the South Midlands, Chalmers returned to Glasgow after seven weeks away.[61]

His successes in Glasgow and Edinburgh continued, unlike his acolyte Irving whose popularity, after starting almost as high, began to wane. His pauperism articles also continued, comparing the approaches in Scotland and England. But the time was overshadowed by his father's illness, and in his own journal he records his sense of his own vanity, 'want of devotional feeling', mistrust of his reaction to praise, and his need for humility.

The idea of an academic career, meanwhile, had never disappeared from the horizon. When the chair of Moral Philosophy became available on the death of Dr Thomas Brown in 1820, Dr George Bell, with whom Chalmers had stayed that July at Merchiston Castle, assured him that he could have had the chair had he applied, whereas it had now gone to Wilson. But Chalmers was still too committed to parochial work for the poor, and his over-driven labours at the new St John's living had at that time been supported by his assistant the brilliant Irving. Meanwhile in 1816 Glasgow had created him a Doctor of Divinity.

The appointment to St John's involved Chalmers still further in philanthropic activities, so that in January 1822 when yet another professorial post was offered, because of the custom to offer only where acceptance was certain, the then Lord Provost and magistrates were careful to sound him out indirectly. But again he felt obliged to refuse, while admitting that he would have liked nothing better than to exchange the fatigues of his parish for 'the literature and intellectual society of our cultivated metropolis', and leisure for theological research. Yet he did not want to alienate the authorities, whose patronage he would appreciate.

In January 1823 the chair of Moral Philosophy at St Andrews fell vacant, and again having aired his doubts Chalmers eventually accepted, partly for health and personal reasons, partly because a new chapel of ease was planned for St John's, so that he could now leave with a clear conscience. Accordingly he removed to St Andrews in that November.[62]

What seems almost incredible today is the apparent insouciance with which famous men undertook philosophy professorships who were all but untrained for the job – as with John Wilson, who knew nothing of the subject, and who had for years been milking De Quincey's views to write his articles, and had to spend the summer in intensive reading before he could embark on the Moral Philosophy post in 1820. Thomas Brown did the same, also having a quiet summer to prepare; and now Chalmers had to study virtually from scratch before he was even free of his Glasgow commitments. He succeeded, and was thus launched on an academic career that lasted for twenty-three years until his death. When in 1827 the highest opening available to a churchman was offered him with the chair of Divinity in Edinburgh, Chalmers resigned the St Andrews post with acclaim.

The other preacher who flashed like a meteor across the scene, only to burn out a few years later in London, was Edward Irving. He was a near-contemporary and early friend of Thomas Carlyle, three years younger, their families living only a few miles apart in the Ecclefechan area, and belonging to the same Secessionist chapel. Irving's father, a tanner, had married slightly 'above' him, Miss Lowther, tall, black-eyed and handsome and presumably the source of his own good looks. They were a quiet, decent family, and thanks to her good management aspired to some gentility.

We first see Edward Irving at the age of sixteen, self-possessed for his years, courteous, well-dressed, dark and enviably handsome – as Thomas Carlyle, that uncouth young school-teacher, undoubtedly felt when the elegant youth turned up at his school. There was no getting over the sinister cast in Irving's eye, however, nor his odd diction: Thomas noted his pronunciation of 'circle' as 'circul'.[63] In the following years he heard of Irving's successes and his teaching at Haddington.

About Christmas-time 1815, when Carlyle was visiting Edinburgh, and spending an evening with his cousin Waugh, Irving came in with his friend the mathematics teacher Nichol. At this meeting they did not get on particularly well, Irving appearing sharp and slightly swaggering,[64] but when the following summer he led the worship at Adam Hope's house on Hope's wife's death, the two young men met in a more relaxed way, and later, when both were teaching at Kirkcaldy, became good friends.

They met more on visits to Edinburgh, however, when Irving was already licensed to preach, which he did rather bombastically with 'a trifle of unconscious playactorism', Carlyle thought. His early upbringing in Annan had left him with an 'Old-world stateliness of speech and manner' which imbued his preaching. When he first entered the church, he was not readily accepted by the Presbyterians because of his 'ower muckle grandeur'.[65]

Both Carlyle and Irving moved to Edinburgh in 1818, when Irving after a disappointing start did better than Carlyle in the teaching line, living in better rooms in Bristo Street, and giving 'breakfasts to intellectualities', whom Carlyle, who as yet had no pupils at all, thought stupid.[66]

In 1819 when Dr Chalmers needed an assistant in Glasgow, the Rev. Andrew Thomson recommended Irving, and lured Irving to preach at his fashionable St George's. (Carlyle, who at that time despised most people he met, thought Thomson 'a lean-minded, iracund, ignorant kind of man'.[67])

But he heard nothing. Details are confused over what happened next, but supposedly Irving, setting off to catch a boat to the West, boarded the wrong one and found himself in Ireland. Here he received a vague, belated message from Chalmers (we are not told how), and returned to Glasgow to take up the coveted position of Chalmers's assistant.[68]

Here at first, if respected, he was not understood, and one observer flatly 'took him for a cavalry officer', seeing him as 'the grandest-looking man in the town'. In time, however, he was greatly approved. At intervals he reappeared in Edinburgh looking prosperous, even more carefully and 'more clerically' dressed, in 'ample black frock, a little longer skirted than the secular sort, [and] hat of gravish breadth of brim'.[69]

In the post-war years of social unrest and radical riots, especially in Glasgow, Irving like Carlyle believed that the social order, a 'load of unveracities, impostures, and quietly inane formalities', would at length be overthrown, 'mutiny, revolt, being a light matter to the young'.[70] He joined in Dr Chalmers's work for the poor, and regularly visited among the poor Glasgow weavers.

Carlyle's own dispassionate view of Chalmers, whom he met there once or twice, dwelt on his narrow culture, lack of reading and ignorance of wider affairs, but he appreciated his 'natural dignity, ingenuity, honesty, and kind affection, as well as sound intellect and imagination . . . capable of impetuous activity and blazing audacity'. He generously observed, 'I suppose there will never again be such a preacher in any Christian church'.[71]

Irving's own preaching he thought 'opulent in ingenious thought', but lacking any clear direction. On Saturdays Irving shut himself up, saw and spoke to no one, and before bedtime would have his sermon (of at least an hour) ready and prepared.

Irving was not so perverse as to shun the King's Edinburgh visit in 1822, as did the disgruntled Carlyle. Shortly before this he took Carlyle off to Haddington, for those early unsuccessful visits to his past pupil Jane Welsh and her disapproving mother. In 1822, however, Irving had a call from the Caledonian Chapel in London, and left Chalmers and Glasgow for the South, living in Pentonville and enjoying a spell of extraordinary popularity, before his admirers (often even at second hearing) decided he was not after all so profound as they thought. Carlyle visited him there when tutoring the Buller boys, talked much with him and found him increasingly dissatisfied, visited by dozens of well-dressed middle-class people, whom Carlyle found mostly tiresome, ignorant 'or even silly and absurd'.[72]

When he began giving out his message, Irving rallied Scottish followers and, with them, the whole of London. It was Sir James Mackintosh who, coming to hear him and being greatly struck by his description of a family of orphans 'thrown upon the fatherhood of God', was led to impart news of this amazing new preacher to George Canning, who accompanied him to the church the following week. Canning then awakened general curiosity by his description of hearing a Scottish minister of a poorly endowed church, himself with no endowment at all, preaching the most eloquent sermon imaginable. Thenceforward Irving's pews were packed.[73]

Canning's visit brought Irving sudden fame and the dingy building was overflowing with celebrities. He was a powerful orator, 'a very demon of power', said De Quincey, with 'untamed energy'. William Hazlitt revealingly, finding him too theatrical, saw his success as 'the secret of attracting by repelling'.

According to Mrs Oliphant, Irving's genius was the same as his eventual undoing, that he believed not only in the divine origin of the Church but in 'his own divine commission', from which sprang his lofty manner of preaching. Any suggestion that he shorten his interminable, later two-and-a-half-hour-or-more sermons was greeted with indignation, so that even by the time he moved to London, fashionable crowds in Scotland had thinned and there were uncomfortable murmurings.[74]

Secretly Irving would have liked to marry Jane Welsh, but having an early sweetheart in Haddington, Isabella Martin, he was kept to the engagement by the girl's father. They married in 1823 and in 1827 removed from Pentonville to Judd Street in shabby Somers Town, his new church in Regent Square having been completed to represent the Scottish Church in London, its foundation laid by the Earl of Breadalbane. In time his over-lengthy sermons and tyrannical prayer meetings palled on congregations, and a passion for 'speaking in tongues' with groups of devoted ladies earned the disapproval of the Church.[75]

According to Julian Young, Irving, in about 1811 when he was nineteen years old, had had a passion for the stage, and joined Ryder's company then visiting Kirkcaldy. His appearance was wholly against him: odd accent, awkward gait, and worst of all, the sinister cast in his eye, merely earned him ridicule, and he had to forego that ambition.[76] Quite opposite was his effect in the pulpit, although he had not been an immediate success. When he first took a turn at preaching for Chalmers in Glasgow, some of the congregation left when he ascended the pulpit, muttering, 'It's no our Doctor.' Yet Julian Young is almost lyrical over his eloquence, as not only 'the very ideal of a Covenanter' but 'the most picturesque and imposing person I have ever seen': perfect profile, Grecian nose, 'beautifully chiselled' mouth, clear olive complexion and high brow. Not to mention his elegant, tall and broad-shouldered figure and raven hair, 'rich, and falling in heavy waving masses down to his very shoulder-blades'. This striking appearance was set off by the black frock-coat, knee-breeches and worsted stockings, and broad-brimmed hat. He did not wear clerical gaiters, possibly to make the most of his well-formed legs. In general, Irving's resembled the traditional doctors' dress. Julian, who once found himself following him on the road to Kentish Town, noted how not a soul who passed but stopped for a second look at this well-proportioned man in his quaint dress, walking abstractedly and ignoring the impudent stares of errand-boys.

Julian Young witnesssed both Irving's great days at Hatton Garden, when he was introduced to him, and on saying he was himself expecting to enter orders, receiving his blessing; and later at Newman Street, hearing the same sonorous utterances and Scottish intonation rolling out to empty benches. One of two ladies sitting there motionless uttered the unearthly sound which was part of the 'speaking in tongues' Irving had promoted. 'Very creepy,' Julian thought.

It was in his London churches that Irving made the most striking initial impression, and where his fall was the greatest. As Lord Eldon wrote to Lady Bankes, 'all the world' was 'running on Sundays to . . . where they hear a Presbyterian orator from Scotland preaching, as some ladies term it, *charming* matter, though downright nonsense'. The accent was off-putting, with his 'crucifeed', 'scorged', and 'high-sup' for 'hyssop'. Yet Mrs Williams Wynn, though highly irritated by many of his peculiarities, found herself listening for almost an hour and a half, riveted in spite of the crowd, the heat, and their distance from the pulpit. She concluded at the end, 'I never knew what eloquence was till I had heard Irving'.[77]

The trouble was, when the same crowds flocked back next time, the novelty had worn off and his extravagance jarred on them the more. While first impressions might linger, tediousness crept in. Even when meeting at someone else's house Irving received visitors like a maître d'hôtel and 'took the visit entirely to himself'.[78]

Cyrus Redding saw him one day walking on Hampstead Heath, at the height of his fame when he 'made the town crazy by denunciations and prophetic outpourings'. The journalist cynically concluded that those 'lank black locks and odd looks' were enough to put one off religion altogether, and once the extraordinary craze for the 'tongues' had worn off there seemed no real substance behind it: like listening to a Covenanter, he observed damningly.[79]

Even at his zenith not everyone was impressed. Miss Berry heard him preach in September 1823 at a farewell service at Hatton Garden when he was temporarily returning to Scotland. Although the weather was bad, long before the service began at 6.30 the chapel was completely full. 'He only spoke of himself,' she wrote disgustedly, 'of all he had done, and of all the miracles he had worked. His eloquence . . . seemed to me commonplace . . . We were not home till nearly half past 10 o'clock.'

Later on, when staying at Guy's Cliff, she heard Bertie Greathead reading Irving's sermons: 'very bombastic and high-flown; strong in words and weak in argument'.[80] The verdict came to be generally accepted.

35
COLLEGES AND SCHOOLS

[Before a lecture]: 'As the hour began to strike, there arose a simultaneous clamour of coughing and spitting, and blowing of noses . . . such was the infectiousness of their zeal, that I caught myself fidgeting upon my seat, and clearing out for action like the rest. At last, in came the professor . . . arrayed in a black Geneva cloak . . . He mounted his elbow-chair, and laid his papers on the desk before him, and in a moment all was still as the Tomb of the Capulets – every eye filled with earnestness, and every pen filled with ink.'

'Peter Morris' [John Lockhart], *Peter's Letters to his Kinsfolk,* 3rd edn, 1819, I.176–7

'Though one of the coarsest looking men I ever knew, he talked so much of polish and refinement that it tempted Mr William Clerk, of Eldin, to make a very clever model of his ungainly figure.'

Personal Recollections . . . of Mary Somerville, on Professor John Leslie, 1873, II.91

'Playfair is a most interesting man of 70. I would rather be like him, in general temper, manners, and disposition, than like anybody of that age I know. To say nothing of the amount of his culture and the elegance of his mind, which does not seem to grow dim with age . . . His conversation, was always without effort or pretension, and yet full of knowledge.'

G. S. Hillard (ed.), *Life, Letters, and Journals of George Ticknor,* Boston, 1909, I.279

'It is not easy to conceive a university where reading was more fashionable, where indolence and ignorance were more disreputable. Every mind was in a state of fermentation.'

Sir James Mackintosh, quoted in Spencer Walpole, *The Life of Lord John Russell,* London, 1889, II.45

Private schools might be as savage as the High School in its earlier days. James Nasmyth was removed from the tender teaching of his elder sister Jane to a top-storey school in George Street, run by Mr Knight. He was considered a leading teacher but was 'vicious and vindictive', driving home his lessons with a cuff on the head or a 'palmy' from a thick leather strap. James often went home 'with his back and fingers tingling and sometimes bleeding'. He was finally saved by a near-disaster.

After some grammatical failure the enraged Knight, grabbing him by the ears, beat his head so savagely against the wall that poor James fell with a violent nose-bleed, was carried home with a fearful headache, and kept his bed for more than a week. His father threatened court action, but finally accepted Knight's humble apology. Not surprisingly James never went back. 'I have ever since entertained a hatred against grammatical rules.'

From 1817–20 James had the usual spell at the High School, then still under Rector Pillans. Four under-masters occupied different rooms, of which the Latin class of nearly two hundred boys was taught by Mr Irvine, a limited and short-tempered man, sorely tried by the tricks of lower-form boys. At school they learned only the basics of language – by heart.[1]

Most of what James learned was in chemistry and mechanics, outside school. He left in 1820 with only a little classical knowledge, and continued with private classes – necessary antidote to the useless High School curriculum – in arithmetic and especially Euclid. His father naturally also encouraged him to practise drawing, especially exact copying, which proved invaluable in his later engineering career.[2]

In 1822 Charles Nodier observed that hardly anyone in Britain now knew Latin, even booksellers, which he explained by 'the fatal vogue of the deplorable methods of Bell and Lancaster, which have reduced all the inferior part of society to a superficial and coarse education, and have substituted a ridiculous mechanism in the place of the genius of teaching . . . You arrive in Scotland, you visit the nation in its most enlightened towns; and you find, not without astonishment, that almost every body has had the small-pox, and that hardly any body knows how to read.'[3]

In a typical middle-class street, Buccleuch Place, where Jeffrey had lived in his early married life, respectable though never fashionable, boys in the street-door flats attended the High School, and the many others in their younger years went to Mr Andrew's and Mr Lennie's where classes were very mixed but a good grounding was given. For writing and arithmetic they went to Moffatt's and Whitelaw's. Josiah Livingston, who lived there about the turn of the 1820s/1830s, records how William Maxwell Gunn, a young schoolmaster, set up a 'Southern Academy' at number 1, in an ambitious scheme to teach all the extra subjects under one roof. He himself taught classics and English composition. John Scott Russell, designer of the *Great Eastern,* taught arithmetic and mathematics, Mr Dalgleish writing, M. Monnard French, and later William Goold, 'a quite studious lad', son of a minister in the street, assisted in classics. Josiah, who started at Andrew's school, went on to the 'Academy', which by then had moved to number 22 and greatly expanded, with a certain amount of pretension. Gunn himself as rector had 'a desk like a pulpit', wore a gown (full of rents), started the day with prayers and added scripture to the syllabus, and only allowed the boys to approach him by written request. By then all the local boys attended his school, including many from Newington and other South Side districts. Teaching was of excellent standard, and had the advantage of smaller classes, with increased prestige over other schools.

The Academy kept good order, and allowed such freedoms as holding 'divisions' on the back green on hot days. Scott Russell on leaving was succeeded for arithmetic by Mr Johnston, 'the Sprug', who was much respected. The French master Monnard had to undergo plenty of tricks from the cruel boys (a common fate for Edinburgh's unfortunate French teachers), hiding his hat or putting shoemaker's resin on his chair. All including Josiah heartlessly joined in, though he did feel ashamed at poor 'Moosay's pained expression, but gentlemanly, uncomplaining spirit'. It seemed all too usual for poor unprivileged teachers, whether British or foreign.

The school kitchen, grandly known as 'the Hall', and surrounded by hat pegs, was where the boys gathered to eat their midday 'piece', with baps bought from the janitor Stuart, who lived in the back kitchen and sold them from an old iron deed-box.

One day a prize fight, supposed to be a great secret, was held there, crammed full by the boys, when two of them, Crawford Allan and Robert Blyth, put up a great show of feinting and blows, all simulated, which the others took as genuine. Someone went to warn Mr Gunn, who at once saw the whole thing was a hoax. The boys pretended they too had seen through the show.[4]

In the second decade of the century boys' entertainments were probably much as they had long been. Favourite were 'peeries', spinning tops, and 'young cannon'. James Nasmyth became famous at the High School for turning out tops on his father's foot-lathe, for which the boys would pay any price, centred so accurately that they could spin twice as long as a shop-bought toy, and without wavering at top speed in the highest achievement of 'sleeping'. James could also make small brass cannon, cast, bored and mounted on gun carriages, popular for the loud noise they made; and made kites and balloons of tissue-paper, which they flew on the Calton Hill.

The King's birthday on 4 June made an exuberant celebration with a salute by the castle guns at noon, to the number of years of his reign, by this time well into the fifties. The castle was soon enveloped in smoke, as reports echoed through the streets and hills. 'Coaches were hung with garlands, the shops were ornamented, the troops were reviewed on Bruntsfield Links, and the citizens drank the King's health at the Cross, throwing the glasses over their backs. The boys fired off gunpowder, or threw squibs of crackers from morning till night. It was one of the greatest schoolboy events of the year.' James's cannon were in great demand, and were fired until they overheated. The method was by flint and steel and a tinderbox, whose spark lit the hemp string match, soaked in saltpetre, and so the guns fired.[5]

Boys were encouraged to save their Saturday penny for some coveted item, a toy or paintbrush, saved in a 'penny pig' or thrift-box made of earthenware. The most these could hold was about 48 pence, and as they could not be opened, the money was gained by breaking the full pig with a hammer. The proceeds might be spent on a Saturday afternoon picnic, with an hour or so's walk to some attractive hill or ruined castle, where the boys lit a fire in the shelter of a dyke or hedge, or by a stream, with their flint and steel and tinder-box (no boy was without one), roasted potatoes, cooked herring on a gridiron, and finished off by blackberry picking.[6]

Josiah Livingstone also descrribes many a popular schoolboy's pastime, from shinty or a bicker, to the newly fashionable cricket. 'Bools' was very popular, played on landings on wet Saturdays, or on a wider stretch of pavement outside the mild and amiable minister's house, though his housekeeper Peggy was fierce enough at trying to scatter them. The nearby Meadows were less of a draw than might be expected, being 'a quagmire in summer', though in winter they proved a great resort for ice sliding. The area was fenced round with wooden posts and rails, covered with pitch, which the boys regularly climbed over to the detriment of their breeches. Along the centre ran 'the Stank', a deep, muddy ditch in which in summer they fished for sticklebacks with a stick and a worm on a thread. Or they would compete with each other, racing to leap over the broad Stank, but often fell in – especially when pursued by Roger, the Corporation employee supposed to collect rents for cattle-grazing and clothes-drying, but believed by the boys to be there with his dog for the sole purpose of keeping them off.

On Saturdays they would troop along to Portobello to swim, passing through Queen's Park and Duddingston through Abercorn Gate. Once on the beach, which was provided with 'bathing machines', as many boys as possible would crowd into a single one, jeering at anyone who showed reluctance to plunge into the water, and vying with one another to swim to 'the beacon'. They would round off the treat by buying 'a chittering chack' from Proudfoot, the baker at the top of Regent Street.

Playing ball against the gables of houses on either side was a favourite sport, and one May evening a newcomer, a handsome boy, appeared with an india-rubber ball, which none of them had seen before, so he was at once befriended, especially as he proved a good shinty player.

Great sport was made with even so simple a device as the lucifer, which outmoded the traditional flint and steel, by which the spark struck into a tinder-box and ignited a 'spunk' tipped with brimstone. One day Josiah and his cousin somehow obtained a shilling which they spent at Melrose's on the South Bridge on a box of the new matches, in which were two pieces of sandpaper through which to draw them. They passed a happy morning sitting on the common stair, taking turns to draw the matches through and watching them blaze into light.

The local boys were natural enemies with the 'keelies', who haunted the stables in a back lane, and there were fights and bickers often enough. Chief of their group was Walter Oliphant, a natural leader at Saturday excursions at shinty or a bicker, at which his side always won. They had no fear if Walter was in charge, broken teeth and heads or no, but felt they would beat the keelies even if their 'Sergeant White Breeks' was with them. On less rowdy trips they would troop out under Walter's directions to Blackford or Braid, especially in the glen by the Hermitage.[7]

Curiously enough it was an earlier Oliphant who inadvertently nearly caused a disaster for little Robert Christison, then about six or seven, very early in the century. The son of Oliphant of Condie, a boarder with Robert's father Professor Christison, went to practise arrow-shooting in the then large open park of the Pleasance near their home, and Robert who went with him was safely ensconced behind a whale-bone set up on the brow towards Dumbiedykes. Unfortunately, getting impatient, he peeped out just as Oliphant at last shot his arrow, which struck him on the corner of the mouth and cut out a small part. 'The bleeding was great; the terror greater – and the shooter was quite as much frightened as the shot. I do not think I ever saw him afterwards.'[8]

Edinburgh's society, with so many luminaries, was at its most brilliant, *pace* the surly comments of Southey: Dugald Stewart, Playfair, Jeffrey, Scott, Henry Mackenzie, Sir James Hall, Lord Webb Seymour, Henry Erskine, Murray, Alison, Dr Gregory, Thomas Brown, Professor Jameson, John Leslie, Dr Brewster . . . the list seems endless. Party rivalry, aggravated by the opinions of the *Edinburgh Review,* dominated society, the Church, the University, where metaphysics was still the most favoured subject.

Similarly the schism of the Huttonian–Wernerian controversy, between the uncompromising believers in fire or water as moulders of the earth's crust, preoccupied scientists, especially with the valuable evidence of Edinburgh's geological formation of basaltic and other rocks. A play expressing 'ardent Huttonian' views was heartily booed at the theatre by a claque of 'Neptunians', despite a prologue by Walter Scott and epilogue by Mackenzie.[9]

A gifted student would be certain to meet the leading thinkers and writers, whether from Scotland, England, Europe or America. Further, a student's-eye view of the various distinguished professors had a particular value. One such was Henry Holland, Cheshire-born and educated at Newcastle-upon-Tyne and Bristol, and later attending both Guy's and St Thomas's Hospitals in London; but it was his studies in Edinburgh from 1806 to 1811, from the age of eighteen, as the most highly reputed medical school in Europe, that laid the foundation of his career.

Holland, as a youth, had spent a vacation at Stoke Newington with Dr Aikin, brother of Mrs Barbauld, the lady philosopher and educationist, at whose house he met many writers. His first choice of a mercantile career, with two terms at Glasgow University and articled to a Liverpool firm, proved a mistake, and he was released to study medicine.

He made several Scottish travels, but his most spectacular venture was to join Sir George Mackenzie's exploratory voyage to Iceland in 1810, when he was a mere student, thanks to his having been at school with Sir George's partner Dr Richard Bright. After their eventful voyage, on their return in September the ship was so disabled that the party had to escape in a small brig, which itself was nearly wrecked before they arrived safely back via Orkney. Holland's association with this celebrated expedition assured his admission to all circles of Edinburgh society.

Holland formed friendships with Stewart, Playfair, Jeffrey and Dr Alison, and went on geological excursions with Playfair among the rocks near Edinburgh. He visited Dugald Stewart at Kinneil. He recalled one metaphysical discussion long after midnight in Playfair's room on Cause and Effect, when any sense of his own presumption was 'lost in the charm of arguing with one so genial and indulgent, and withal of such clear and upright thought'.

This subject had been angrily debated in the General Assembly on Leslie's appointment to the chair of Natural Philosophy in 1805, and 'the controversy dragged on both in books and debating societies', embittered by the connections with theology and 'the ambiguities of language' which together endeared them to the schools. Dr Thomas Brown's book on the subject was considered much the best, and at once raised his reputation, probably leading to his succession to Stewart as Professor of Moral Philosophy.[10]

As early as 1806 Stewart had added a supplementary course on political economy to his syllabus, a subject not before taught in a British university.

Professor Smyth also to some extent explained the subject in his lectures on modern history. The first real lecture series, however, was not until 1816 in Cambridge, when George Pryme, Fellow of Trinity College, specialised in the subject.[11]

On the eve of departure of the Iceland expedition, Professor Stewart ended his season's lectures with a review of his thirty-eight years' service at the University, now about to end – 'most pathetic and impressive'. Stewart's health necessitated his handing over to Dr Thomas Brown, but he returned in 1812. With metaphysics still paramount and Stewart at the height of his fame, he was dazzling students with magniloquence, combining liberal beliefs and 'moral grandeur' with intellectual distinction, investing the philosophy of mind with splendour. George Combe, a great admirer, studied his works, though he found little guidance about life there.[12]

Criticism of Stewart was usually on the limitation of his perception. Carlyle in 1815, discussing the *Quarterly Review*'s first article on Stewart's second volume of *Elements of the Philosophy of the Human Mind,* dismissed the reviewer's criticisms as 'prejudices natural to Englishmen', though he himself objected that Stewart was 'perpetually talking about analysing perceptions, & retiring within one's self, & mighty improvements that we are to make – no one knows how', which left the reader 'crowded with disjointed notions & nondescript ideas'.[13]

David Wilkie, returning to Edinburgh in 1817, making a visit to Kinneil by steamboat, found Stewart living 'retired, but in good circumstances, in the same kind of house that I should think Voltaire must have lived in when in Switzerland. His manner and also that of his family seems highly cultivated, but . . . you would never dream that he had written a book, and . . . he in no instance leads the conversation to his own particular studies. You never see him trying to say a good thing or a smart thing, but . . . never forget that you are in the presence of a judge, and of an uncommon man.'[14]

In 1818 Stewart, recovering from a fever, was disturbed that his memory seemed to be failing on events before and after, though his wife fancied such failures were normal. In other respects he seemed unchanged. With his (second) wife, daughter of George Cranston and sister of Lord Corehouse and Countess Purgstall, Stewart had a 'perfect union'. Professor Veitch, in his introduction to Stewart's correspondence (1858), described her as of 'high accomplishments and fascinating manners', with 'vivacity and humour, depth and tenderness of feeling'. At the height of his reputation she took on much of the responsibility as his aide and confidante, and he never considered his books complete until she had read them. A letter of introduction from her was the highest recommendation one could ask for in England or America. In youth handsome, indeed stately, she maintained a 'winning gentleness', and husband and wife together were the soul of hospitality.[15]

Years later Bulwer Lytton reflected that the great age of the philosophers, Adam Smith and Dugald Stewart, had since given way to one of transition, and that Stewart, of 'beautiful philosophising rather than philosophy', was 'the most exquisite critic upon the system of others that our language has produced . . .' By 1833, when Lytton was writing, like thinkers in every generation they were in 'an age of disquietude and doubt – of the removal of time-worn landmarks, and the breaking up of the hereditary elements of society and old opinions, feelings and ancestral customs and institutions are crumbling away'. Some saw it as a time of destruction, others as heralding a new millennium. This was well over a generation after the first French Revolution had threatened the established institutions.[16]

The Rev. Samuel Parr, who in 1819 also visited Stewart at Kinneil, reckoned that his work 'united the perspicuity of Dr Reid, the acuteness of Adam Smith, and the precision of David Hume'. But he found that he could not approve his 'system of mental philosophy', nor his 'contemptuous' references to Locke, and while admiring him as man of letters, he admired his views of science less.[17]

Lord John Russell, who as a student had lived at Professor Playfair's, attended Stewart's Ethics or Moral Philosophy class before his temporary retirement in the winter of 1810. On his return Russell was chosen to give the congratulatory address, composed by a committee of which he was chairman.

It was Playfair whom Russell found 'one of the most delightful of men, and . . . one of the most profound mathematicians of his age and country . . . one of the best and noblest, the most upright, the most benevolent, and the most liberal of all philosophers'.

Playfair combined the qualifications of philosopher, mathematician and creator of modern geology. As a writer he was distinguished by pure style and clear explanation, his works including *Elements of Geometry* and *Illustrations of the Huttonian Theory of the Earth.* Russell attended his lectures on Physics or Natural Philosophy in 1810–12, though he left without taking a degree.[18]

In March 1819, shortly before Playfair's death, George Ticknor wrote, 'I would rather be like him, in general temper, manners, and disposition, than like anybody of that age [seventy] that I know.' His culture and refinement of mind did not suffer with age: 'He has a childlike simplicity of manner, a modesty . . . and an open enthusiasm for all good knowledge as great as if he were beginning life instead of closing it . . . His conversation was always without effort or pretension, and yet full of knowledge, elegant, and producing a charming effect.'[19]

Carlyle as usual had something different to say. In 1817, commenting on his *Second Dissertation* in the *Encyclopaedia,* as 'distinguished for its elegance & perspicuity', he was almost alone in not admiring Playfair, who in his view did not reach the heart of a problem.[20]

John Leslie, one of the several remarkable men originally intended for the Church but turning instead to literature or science, had so hated Latin when at St Andrews University, aged barely thirteen, and was so keen on science, that he had to be persuaded into Latin by the offer of a ticket for the Natural Philosophy lectures as well. Later he mastered the language even to the extent of reading Lucretius for 'recreation'.[21]

On good terms with Archibald Constable for many years, he shared in many of his publications, contributed to the *Edinburgh Review*, and in 1814 agreed to bring out the first volume of the *Edinburgh Gazette* – subject to being paid 1000 guineas, not pounds. While planning the *Gazette* that autumn, like many other people he took the chance of visiting France, then reopened to foreigners. His advice on the *Edinburgh Encyclopaedia* was valuable; his own most important paper was a continuation of Playfair's contribution on 'The progress of Mathematical and Physical Science during the eighteenth Century'.

He did not neglect his professional interests. In December 1818 he was telling Constable that he had enrolled 112 students for his first class, sixty-three for his second, and found this more profitable than 'literary drudgery'. Could he only increase the numbers, he might have more leisure for 'some great work – probably Physical Geography'.[22]

The following year when the Natural Philosophy chair fell vacant on Playfair's death, again as in 1805 Leslie was called on as successor. Despite the Council's fear of a renewal of the violent clerical opposition which marred the last occasion, by 10 September Leslie was assured of success.

In 1822 a case was threatened against several clergy, including Principal Baird, and also Leslie, for deficient knowledge of Hebrew. The Council engaged John Hope on their side, but his being called to the House of Commons made an excuse to defer the trial until the winter. Leslie and his supporters, after strenuous efforts, succeeded in putting it forward to late July, when he successfully vindicated his own knowledge of Hebrew.[23]

Thomas Carlyle during one of his short early visits to Edinburgh (in March 1817) records hearing Leslie lecturing on heat. He 'displayed great ingenuity but his experiments did not succeed'. His *Philosophy of Arithmetic* was then shortly due out.[24]

On returning to Edinburgh in August next year he called on Leslie, 'who was very kind . . . & talked with me about two hours very frankly' and got him a book he required. He was then working on his Analysis, and Conic Sections. During the term Leslie passed him a difficult problem that he wanted to include in one of his books but had no time to work out, but after Carlyle spent a week on it without success, Leslie advised him to leave it alone and return to it later. 'This curious philosopher' even suggested that Carlyle ought to take up engineering and go to America: 'Great business there – Swiss gentleman went lately – making a large fortune – many bridges and canals.'[25]

In the autumn session of 1819 he heard Leslie once, apparently wanting to 'beat Chalmers on his own ground', and 'distinguished this season for the *piety* of his opening lectures'.

The blunt-mannered Leslie had moments of tenderness, usually in his vain amorous pursuits of unresponsive young ladies. William Wallace was even more blunt: bald with a strong Scots accent and 'a grim and intelligent countenance', said Carlyle, his manner was 'unaffected and patient'. At the age of fifty-one Wallace had just (1819) been appointed Professor of Mathematics and was the inventor of the eidograph, an instrument for copying drawings. He was said to be on the point of discarding Leslie's *Elements of Geometry* and 'curves of the second order' in favour of Playfair's 1795 translation of Euclid. 'Science, you see,' wrote Carlyle to Mitchell, after calling on Wallace, 'as well as Religion, is at times disturbed by the feuds of the professors.'[26]

Professor Robert Jameson, with whom Audubon was to have so much traffic in 1826, aroused frequent criticism. Joseph Cogswell, who arrived in Edinburgh in the early autumn of 1818, wrote after attending his lectures, 'Nothing ever cooled my ardour for mineralogy as much as hearing it taught by such a cobbler as Professor Jameson.'[27] Carlyle was similarly unimpressed by two lectures he heard. 'He is one of those persons whose understanding is overburthened by their memory. Destitute of accurate science, without comprehension of mind – he details a chaos of fact . . . in a manner as slovenly as he selects and arranges them', and his explanations suggested 'a total ignorance of dioptics'.[28]

In common with others he was equally scathing about David Hume younger, who 'owns no spark of his uncle's genius. His lectures on law are (still excepting Erskine's Institute) the dullest piece of stuff I ever saw or heard of. Long-winded, dry details about points not of the slightest importance to any but an attorney or notary public.' Carlyle attended less and less frequently and finally gave up, as doubtless did many fellow-students.[29]

The young Grants of Rothiemurchus numbered several professors among their friends or indeed admirers. The Professor of Chemistry, Dr Hope, having paid court to their aunt Mary, was 'still the flutterer round every new beauty that appeared', wrote Elizabeth, and he was more prepossessing, not to mention cleaner than Professor Leslie; yet Playfair, who was old and ugly, was voted 'charming'. He was not intimidating, he was fond of young people, and was glad enough to be diverted from mathematics to 'laugh over a tea table'.[30]

Playfair was one of the brilliant very little men, with a massive head, rugged features, and ill-shaped nose. However great his popularity, and it was considerable, it was not for his looks.

Another favourite with the Grants was the philosopher Dr David Brewster, a Tory but, like Jeffrey and John Clerk, a close friend of their father John Peter Grant.[31] He had studied at Edinburgh, was licensed as a preacher in 1804, then turned to law at St Andrews, and had some years of activity as an editor. His productions included the *Edinburgh Magazine* (later renamed the *Edinburgh Journal*), the *Edinburgh Journal of Science* and, notably, from 1807 to 1829 the *Edinburgh Encyclopaedia*. He made discoveries in the polarisation of light, invented the kaleidoscope, and as a result received several medals. In 1821 he was the first Director of the Royal Scottish Society of Arts, and ten years later joined in organising the British Association for Advancement in Science. He also became a Cambridge MA and a London MICE, and in 1832 was knighted.[32]

Dr Thomas Brown, Stewart's successor and considered as last of the Scottish metaphysicians, was sometimes not taken as seriously as he deserved. He affected dandyism and wrote bad poetry, which he read so beautifully at his lectures that students applauded – much to his irritation, for they never applauded the lectures. Ticknor viewed him as 'acute . . . but foolishly affecting a dapper sort of elegance', and his poetry as 'just above thread-paper' quality.[33] He had 'great fertility of mind, and delightful variety of intelligence and playfulness in his conversation'. He was also a devoted family man. He had published his lectures along with 'metaphysical' poems, and his *Wanderer of Norway*, published late in 1815, according to Mrs Grant was based on Mary Wollstonecraft's letters, heightened by her 'rich though gloomy imagination'.[34]

Amelia Opie met Brown in London, at a dinner where Spurzheim was being lionised, when Brown cut in on her listening to his theories. She knew of him as '*the* Dr Brown . . . the Edinburgh Reviewer, and the recondite reviewer of Mrs Opie in the first number of that celebrated work', but had been warned that he liked to '*faire le galant, vis-à-vis les dames*'. She was not surprised, therefore, to encounter 'a flattering Scotchman', and was angry with herself for feeling 'fluttered'. 'Mr Blair assured me he thought the philosopher quite conceited already.' On the other hand Brown was floored by having to listen to the sparkling flow of logic and philosophic knowledge from the blue-stocking Lady Mary Shepherd, for he detested literary ladies and (observed Mrs Opie) one who thus challenged him in his own field 'must have called forth all his reviewer bitterness'.[35]

The University's arts curriculum, or humanity and philosophy, comprised the following subjects: classics, rhetoric, logic, moral philosophy, mathematics, natural philosophy (physics), astronomy, and (later) political economy. Many intending medical students took an arts degree first, then for the degree of MD had to attend the classes at the Infirmary, submit a dissertation and pass examinations. Robert Christison, for example, studied all the arts subjects except astronomy. On payment of the class fee a ticket was issued entitling him to attend the lectures and demonstrations.

Many students lived Spartan lives, coming from poor country homes and existing on a diet of oatmeal, ham and cheese sent from their families by the carrier, to their humble lodgings in Edinburgh's high 'lands'. Academic supervision was minimal, and the extent of University provision was the library and classroom. The level of teaching, derided by Carlyle and others, was perforce fairly elementary as the boys had left school in their mid-teens and had still not acquired even basic principles.[36]

City control over University appointments led to many quasi-political machinations. On the death in 1812 of Dr Moodie, the Professor of Oriental Languages, their preferred candidate was the worthy but not exciting Dr Alexander Brunton (husband of Mrs Grant's authoress friend) but glowing testimonials were produced for Alexander Murray, for whom Constable's partner Cadell urgently canvassed Brougham, Wilberforce and Lord Castlereagh. The Provost, who of course opposed Murray, according to Dr Baird planned to keep these recommendations from the Council until Brunton's election was secured, and typical contemporary smears were circulated, denigrating Baird's motives and Murray's politics. 'I have been *accused* of being a writer (would you think it) in the Edinburgh Review', wrote Murray to Constable. Would his opponents (he asked Baird) think him less worthy because he had the esteem of Jeffrey and Scott, 'one the greatest poet and the other the greatest critic in the kingdom'?

He was equally amazed, at the election on 8 June, at the praise his eminent supporters lavished on him. Fifteen votes went to Murray, including those of Professors Christison, Leslie and Brown, giving him the victory by two votes, which he regarded (he told Constable) as 'victories over the old corrupt system of giving the Chairs . . . to middling unqualified men', and should serve as a 'check on the improper conduct of the Provost'.[37]

Brunton did eventually get the chair, in 1813, and in 1817 was one of the many scornfully written off by Carlyle as all 'dosing' and lacking in learning. To him the whole faculty was 'one of the most melancholy and unprofitable corporations' he could imagine, comprising Drs William Ritchie senior and James junior, Hugh Meiklejohn, Professor of Church History and Minister of Abercorn, the Rev. Alexander Brunton, and Dr Thomas Brown. On Carlyle's showing, the prospect seemed poor.[38]

The Rev. Samual Parr would not have agreed. Though he had criticised Scotland's lack of good grammar schools as preparation for the University, he admired Edinburgh High School's 'sound learning . . . so far as it extends', and appreciated the grammar book for young ladies published by Dr Pillans's second master, Carson. Admittedly, looking back to the great days of Hume, Smith, and Robertson, with their 'confounded strong heads' in the days of 'intense intellectual gratification', Parr also admired, in 1819, not merely the famous medical school but 'the many admirable lectures, delivered by a succession of the ablest professors, on the greatest subjects that can interest human curiosity, or exercise human understanding'.[39]

Sometimes the most illuminating views on the professors, and the course, come from the more articulate and observant of their students. Robert Christison younger was one of these, born the elder of twins in the same year as Andrew Combe, of Scandinavian descent in Forfarshire. Their father, Professor of Humanity at the University from 1806, was versed in philosophy and the physical sciences as well as the classics, and was a member of Edinburgh's literary, philosophical and scientific society. He was known for charitable gestures, even depriving himself of his own fees by handing out free course tickets to his classes.

One of Robert Christison's childhood recollections, and certainly his earliest medical experience, was of being treated with leeches after a rough street boy tipped him down an area in Drummond Street, and waking with some disgust to find four of these gorged creatures hanging from his temples.[40]

Educated with Mr Mylne in the Old Town, and then at the High School, Robert and his brother also had an elderly tutor for about three years, as their father in his last year as professor was too busy to supervise them himself. Arithmetic and writing were learned, as often with Edinburgh boys, at a private school.

In 1811 Robert went to the University, enjoying 'the abrupt cessation of corporal punishment, version "poemas", and the taking of places', and spent four years with the Faculty of Arts on the usual curriculum, adding botany and chemistry in 1814–15, and French with 'a great character', Louis Cauvin.

The classics classes included weekly lectures on philology, antiquities, and other interesting subjects. As for prizes, Robert's professorial father usually forbade his sons to compete. He was one of perhaps the few who profited from the unengaging Dr George Dunbar, harsh-voiced and unattractive in manner, stern features seldom relaxing to a smile, even when paying a student a formal Latin compliment. His lectures were so unrewarding that one boy claimed that he 'took some Greek with him to the College from the High School, but left it all in Dunbar's classroom'. To Christison, however, he was kind, probably because of respect for his father.

Christison senior, who had taken up mathematics at a late stage – as relaxation, becoming one of Scotland's most accomplished amateurs – was keen to encourage his son in the subject. Robert, therefore, worked through Newton's *Principia* at the age of eighteen. He was drawn to mathematics in spite of Professor Leslie's inability to communicate with beginners from his Olympian level, and his laboured, far-fetched style. This out-and-out mathematician, ending his account of Pythagoras, concluded, 'Thus died this illustrious philosopher at the advanced age of square of 9.'[41]

Physics under Playfair was a pleasure, 'a charming teacher, so simple, unaffected, and sincere in manner, so chaste in style, so clear in demonstration'. Although he read his lectures, he commanded attention by his simple, earnest delivery. Indeed he was unable to speak extempore. When as President he had to chair the public dinner of the Astronomical Institution after laying the foundation stone of the new Observatory, friends were anxious about his performance, but he got through by means of pithy toasts, including the toast of the day to the Observatory itself: 'May it be as stable as the rock on which it is built, and the science to which it is dedicated.'[42]

Playfair's dinner neighbour, the bluff Colonel Smith, who was one of his own ex-students, so heartily applauded this that he was misguidedly urged to propose Playfair's own health, and at once broke down. 'Professor Playfair, gentlemen, is a man – is a man – gentlemen, Professor Playfair . . . I say, gentlemen . . .' At last he brought out his point: 'By God, gentlemen, Professor Playfair is a man to go even to hell with.'

'Hell' was one of the unspeakable words, even in print except by an initial and a dash. A short shocked silence was followed by a huge peal of laughter and a hearty round of applause. Playfair was equal to the occasion. 'The gallant officer', he said, had surpassed all examples of the attachment of friends. 'I am not aware of any man, since the days of Pylades and Orestes, having been willing to accompany his friend – to the place he has mentioned.'[43]

The Rev. Dr David Ritchie, Professor of Logic and Metaphysics, and Dr Thomas Brown for Moral Philosophy, found Christison more an absentee than an attender. Ritchie was tall, big-boned and strong, his voice rough but powerful, and his delivery energetic but unpolished – 'more illustrious on the curling-pond'. As for Brown, though good in content, Christison found his 'affected feminine delivery' off-putting.

Rhetoric pleased him more, though the Rev. Dr Andrew Brown, like Ritchie an Edinburgh minister, was a 'prosy professor', but took an active interest in his students, which encouraged them to work. In this Christison did win a prize. Only Logic and Ethics did not draw him at all.

Having taken the full curriculum he was, under the current rule, entitled to an MA without examination. The general view was that 'nobody took it [the examination] but a dominie'.[44]

No modern languages were taught (nor even a couple of generations later), hence the invariable tutoring under some private French master. Christison's teacher Louis Cauvin, son of a Revolution refugee, was equally at home in France or Scotland, an accomplished member of a literary society. He was also a successful farmer near Duddingston, kept the profits from his products and thus became quite well off, and on his death in 1825 endowed a 'Hospital School' for twenty-six sons of decayed teachers, farmers and master-printers.[45] He taught for six hours a day, five days a week, and spent the rest of the time on his farm, galloping there on horseback; powerful and energetic, tallish, 'with a rubicund, pimpled face, and dark, restless, fiery eyes'.

He had a strong temper which he kept in check, except when his eccentricity encouraged students to practical jokes, which he suspected even when without proof. One day the school chimney caught fire and poured smoke into the room, and when the sweeps were called 'down came an old hat'. The enraged Cauvin bolted into the library, snatched up an elegantly bound book of engravings and rushed with it and the sooty hat into the anteroom, full of young ladies awaiting their class. Flinging down the hat he offered the book as reward to whoever would reveal '*le poltron qui m'a fait cette injure-là, – là – là*!' Nobody owned up.[46]

During Christison's university days, from 1811 to 1819, literary debating clubs were all the rage, the Literary Society having temporarily overtaken the old and once reputable Speculative Society, though its fashion passed like a comet. Some new debating club would start up almost annually by new students. One of these in Christison's time, a Juvenile Society, was enlarged from a club formed by the boys of the Rev. Dr Muckersy's academy in West Calder, four of them being young Muckersys. Dr Tweedie, who became a London physician, invited Christison to join, and others followed. One debate on the merits or demerits of gunpowder was wrecked when a speaker, well-dined and wined, unfortunately swayed backwards just as the Secretary rose to reach for a paper. 'Speaker, secretary and chair disappeared instantaneously, and were rolling on the floor. There was no longer any sober discussion that evening.' Future orators were always cheerfully cautioned if they approached too near the chair. Unsurprisingly, few amateur debaters gained more than interesting experience from these evenings, though the old Royal Medical Society founded in 1737 did turn out men of distinction.

Walter Scott's uncle Dr Daniel Rutherford, who occupied the Botany chair for thirty-four years from 1786, taught from 1813 at the Botanic Garden, by then in Leith Walk. He was a disappointed man, having started his career as an inventive chemist and discovered nitrogen gas, and had hoped for the chair of Chemistry. He died in 1819. Christison describes him as little and 'sluggish-looking' from frequent attacks of gout, with a reputation as gourmet. Appropriately he had 'a large placid face . . . heavy eyes, and a great mouth and jaw'. His accent was 'pure and scarcely Scotch', and his clear, well-styled lectures, 'full of condensed information', commanded attention in spite of starting at 8 in the morning. Though usually mild and kindly, he was subject to fits of temper, and would take it out on his highly qualified head gardener M'Nab, who acted as his demonstrator.[47]

Chemistry was Christison's favourite subject, a good field for the amateur since Sir Humphrey Davy's discovery of the composition of the alkalis (1814). Dr Charles Hope, whose father Dr John preceded Rutherford as Professor of Botany, would himself have preferred the Botany chair, but made a good career in chemistry. His lectures though pompous were clear and accompanied by good demonstrated experiments which, as in 1823 he had 575 students, had to be staged on a grand scale.

When Christison first attended in 1814 Hope had never had a disaster, but next year suffered an 'egregious' one. When he was demonstrating how snow melted by nitric acid produced extreme cold, the surface at once froze into a cake-like substance which he was to break up by a glass rod, but he was using a large inverted bell-jar instead of the usual 'strong-footed' one, and the rod suddenly plunged not only through the whole mass but through the foot of the jar as well. The luckily now diluted acid overflowed the table on to Dr Hope's fashionable tight black pantaloons, turning them instantly red, while the students shouted with laughter and Hope beat an embarrassed retreat.[48]

Though an ingenious analyst, who discovered strontium among other findings, he had given up chemical research for class experiments, but for these he employed only his assistant Dr Fyfe, so that the students had no practical study. The twin Christisons, Syme and a few others set up a Chemical Society and met weekly for experiments in Christison's attic in Argyle Square, later moving to a basement below Deuchar's shop, a druggist's opposite the College, taking it in turns to act as leader. There were some dramatic incidents. One day in the attic when Christison and Andrew Jackson were preparing the coke 'choffer', Jackson's cramming it with sticks to hurry it on created a stifling smoke, and though almost suffocated they dared not open the door as a family dinner-party was going on below. Instead, setting a box on a chair under the skylight, they climbed up and thrust their heads out to breathe, while the other youths arriving, who could not get into the locked room, saw the smoke and feared the worst.

A more serious accident was in Deuchar's cellar, when Christison and Syme were to demonstrate sulphuric ether but overheated the retort. Spirit and acid on being poured in frothed up in inflammable gas, and blew the stopper up to the ceiling. As the apparatus fizzed and thudded the group fled, leaving Christison and Syme to blow out the candles, and then try to hide under the table with room for only one. The whole thing blew up with a crash and a cascade of glass, then in a brief silence the rest of the society cautiously returned to view the damage. Aided by Deuchar with a Davy lamp, they found the retort blown twenty feet to the far corner, where Syme had taken refuge, bent double – shivered to fragments against the wall right beside his ear.

This did not discourage Syme, who experimented with solvents of india-rubber, and made a cheap solution distilled from coal-tar, which could render cloth waterproof. Although he published his findings in a short paper in Thomson's *Annals of Philosophy* (Vol. XII, 1818), he lost his chance when Charles Macintosh, a Glasgow manufacturer, patented his waterproof material in 1823, using caoutchouc dissolved in coal-tar naphtha.[49]

Syme, though still sufficiently interested in chemistry to build his own laboratory at home at Pitreavie, instead made a successful career in surgery and anatomy.

36
MEDICINE AND SURGERY

'Steep, well-like and sombre . . . In these dismal surroundings was performed much of the brilliant work of John Lizars, William Fergusson, Robert Liston and James Syme.'

Alexander Miles, *The Edinburgh School of Surgery before Lister*, London, 1918, 36

An Edinburgh medical degree was conferred after three years of medical lectures, and most students had also by then learned modern and ancient languages and general science. Sessions lasted six months, totalling eighteen months in the three years. The years 1800–1810, when Edinburgh's medical students averaged 739 a year, showed a rise of nearly 180 over the previous decade, and in the next decade they averaged 820, still rising and in some years exceeding 900.[1]

This was despite the disappointing Alexander Monro III, who after his father's retirement in the session 1808–09 continued as sole professor of Anatomy for a further thirty-eight years until the session 1848–49, the three Monro generations thus running the school for 126 years. This third Monro, though a voluminous if not distinguished author and a practising physician, and with the qualities of a good Latin scholar and a taste for painting, showed so little teaching talent that the University school of anatomy suffered a loss of reputation.

He had a deplorable indifference to his subject, and was so lazy that he was said (apocryphally) to be content to read his grandfather's lectures from notes made a century before, even to such careless oversights as 'when I was a student in Leyden in 1719', annually greeted by students with a shower of peas.[2] Monro's poor teaching drove students to attend John Bell's extramural lectures.[3] Extramural teachers kept professors up to the mark, and sometimes filled their vacancies. Moreover, being outwith University rules, they were able to develop such new specialities as mental disease, neurology, children's and tropical diseases, long before the University itself.

At first they taught in private buildings and in Surgeons' Hall, but with the increase in students and lectures, they extended into separate buildings such as those around Surgeons' Square, Brown Square, Minto House, between which rivalries sprang up.

When the Royal Infirmary was founded in 1729, and particularly after the new hospital opened in the 1740s, its managers admitted students for a small fee, thus providing unique clinical instruction on diseases under University professors or qualified physicians and surgeons. Students attended lectures and recorded daily reports. Clinical lectures were eventually given by all surgeons, not only the professor and senior surgeon. Surgeons wore white linen aprons, but in the surgical wards certain 'dressers', in blue checked aprons with sleeves and pockets, attended to help the 'visiting cupper' and to bleed patients, instructed by the surgeons in proper dressing of wounds.

The fame of the Extramural School spread until its importance was officially recognised, and by Town Council decree its teachers were authorised to hold classes for University students. The most famous of the early teachers were John Lizars, William Fergusson, Robert Liston and James Syme.[4]

John Bell and his brother Charles were talented grandsons of the Rev. John Bell, minister of Gladsmuir in Midlothian, who died young, and sons of the Rev. William Bell, Episcopal clergyman at Doune, Perthshire. Their mother was a granddaughter of Bishop White, and both parents were accomplished. Their other brothers, Robert and George, were distinguished in law.

Charles, thirteen years younger than John and trained by him personally, also studied in London. When almost a boy he helped his brother in the extramural anatomy class. He wrote an illustrated three-volume *System of Dissections* (1798–1803) when still a student, and three books of anatomical engravings of arteries, nerves and brain; he also wrote most of his *Anatomy of Expression* before leaving for London in 1804. It was in London that he largely made his reputation, and rather more in psychology than surgery. A fine draughtsman, he made the illustrations for John's *Anatomy of the Human Body* (1793–1802), and in particular the volume on the nervous system. Elected FRCS in 1799, as a surgeon he was skilled but squeamish, often seen to turn pale during operations.

In 1800, along with his brother and other younger surgeons he was debarred from the Royal Infirmary by their new regulation of exclusion. This led to bitter controversy, and as meanwhile James Gregory was pursuing his vendetta against John, in 1804 Charles went to London, while two new University chairs, Clinical Surgery (1803) and Military Surgery (1806) went to James Russell and the pathologist John Thomson.[5]

Much of Charles Bell's career was spent in teaching and writing in London. In 1825 he handed over most of his large museum collection to the Edinburgh College of Surgeons, along with water-colours he had made in Brussels after

Waterloo, as surgeon to British troops. In 1828, having disposed of his own school of anatomy at Windmill Street, he accepted the chair of Physiology at the new University of London, and in 1836 returned to the chair of Surgery in Edinburgh.

Edinburgh University's 'premier surgical chair', Clinical Surgery, set up by King George III in 1803 with a £50 stipend, preceded the chair of Systematic Surgery by twenty-eight years. The first professor, James Russell (1755–1836), whose forebears had also been surgeons, had in 1796 become President of the College of Surgeons. In 1800 he was one of the six Infirmary surgeons appointed by the managers under the new rules abrogating the 1738 agreement, and was thus unwillingly dragged into the controversy over appointments, when the Royal College viewed the new arrangement as 'breach of a solemn engagement', and debarred several of the more brilliant surgeons, notably the Bells.

There was an unseemly brawl on the day when Russell took over at the Infirmary, caused by the late appearance of his predecessor, Mr Flanagan. After waiting half an hour Russell decided to start the patients' round, but no sooner had he done so than not only Flanagan but the two Bells turned up with several other surgeons, and students, and Flanagan publicly berated him for discourtesy. As the argument became more heated the Infirmary management sent a message ordering the visitors to withdraw, leaving the consulting-room to Russell. In future members of the College of Surgeons guilty of 'such unwarrantable conduct' were barred access.

In fact Russell was a very courteous gentleman of the old school. Tall and thin, sporting a red wig, he dressed in the traditional black tail-coat, white neckcloth, Brummell-style choker and wide shirt-frill, with knee-breeches and silk stockings, unflattering to his spindly legs.[6]

Although the College had long agitated for a chair of Clinical Surgery, because its inauguration was made without prior consultation they felt the Crown had infringed on their privilege of teaching surgery, and lodged a protest with the Chief Baron (but got no further).

On transferring to the new chair in 1803 Russell had to relinquish his Infirmary status, becoming instead a 'permanent consulting surgeon' who might accompany the regular surgeons on rounds. He therefore had to base his lectures on cases of other surgeons, and also had no right to suggest Infirmary improvements.

Russell's lectures, held at 4 p.m. in a small room which opened off the consulting-room, drew many students. He spoke from a kind of pulpit, below which the benches tended to remain empty, as students too bashful to come forward, despite his invitation to take the empty seats, remained crowded at the back.

One student recalled his style as 'somnolent' – partly because of the class's late hour -and he had a habit of 'yawning while he spoke, and continuing to speak while he yawned'.[7]

Socially he appears to have been equally unstimulating. He was a friend of Scott's, who evidently did not think him over-lively company. 'Supped at Dr Russell's usual party', he wrote in his Journal on 5 December 1825, 'which shall serve for one while', and equally enigmatically, on 3 December 1827, 'We supped at Dr Russell's, where the conversation was as gay as usual.' At his town house at 30 Abercromby Place he held fortnightly gatherings during the session after the Royal Society meetings.[8]

Russell held the professorship for thirty years, establishing an appropriate place for the teaching of clinical surgery. He retired in 1833 at the age of eighty-one, and died three years later. Though not a profound thinker he was an accurate observer. Among his few publications were essays on necrosis (1794), diseases of the knee joint (1802), and late in his career, *Observations on the Testicles* – dedicated to the President and Fellows of the College of Surgeons.

The College of Surgeons in 1804 set up their own Lectureship on the Principles and Practice of Surgery, an annual course of the same length as the medical courses, available free to medical and surgical staff of the army and navy. The College's first Professor of Surgery was John Thomson (1765–1846), though the University naturally objected to such external rivalry.

The University's Regius professorship of Military Surgery was created in 1806, the result of a memorial addressed by John Bell to Earl Spencer, First Lord of the Admiralty and based on his own experience at Camperdown, urging creation of 'one great school of Military Surgery'. However, although he would have been the obvious candidate for the post, because of delay before it was established John Thomson was appointed instead, in addition to his chair of Surgery at the Royal College of Surgeons, where he had served two years.

Establishment of this latest University chair coincided with the Whigs taking office under Grenville, and Thomson was a confirmed Whig – but he had had no service in the field. Throughout the Peninsular War his sole war experience was a report on British Military Hospitals in Belgium after Waterloo, made with Dr Somerville, principal Medical Officer in Scotland and addressed to the Duke of York as C-in-C.

Thomson continued to hold both posts until 1819, when he was obliged from overwork to take on John William Turner as assistant at the College of Surgeons, and he finally resigned in Turner's favour in 1821. His object in the University post was to render the teaching of surgery more complete. On resigning the University chair in 1821, he failed to secure the Chair of Medicine, fallen vacant on Dr Gregory's death, and subsequently concentrated on pathological anatomy as an extramural lecturer.

In 1831, Thomson was appointed to a new University chair of Pathology – his third 'first', so that he was referred to as 'the old chair-maker', a tendency he passed on to his sons. Here he served eleven years, and made a valuable discovery in the promising James Young Simpson, who had produced a graduation thesis on 'Death from Inflammation' (1832) and whom he invited to be his assistant, encouraged to concentrate on obstetrics and launched on his career. Thomson retired in 1842 and died in 1846.[9]

In 1831, also, after 110 years of the three Monros, the Town Council recommended the Crown to establish a separate chair of Systematic Surgery, initially under Thomson's assistant Turner and from 1836 under Charles Bell.

Not everyone was satisfied with the training. Young Andrew Combe, completing his miserable apprenticeship with his master Johnson, towards the end did experience a little practice, attending Johnson on his rounds as medical officer at St Cuthbert's Workhouse.

In 1817 Andrew passed at Surgeons' Hall, but felt afterwards that this had merely begun his studies. Many years later (1838) he spoke to Sir James Clark of the damage young surgeons incurred by 'compulsory attendance on incapable and superannuated professors', who ought to have been made to resign when they became old. He reckoned that his real knowledge was acquired at the Hospital.[10]

At much the same time there was great dissatisfaction with the standards of the Infirmary, which was controlled by 'Ordinary Managers' who served for life, a closed system. 'Extraordinary Managers' voted only occasionally and were regarded (says Cockburn) as 'ornaments or encumbrances'. Public control was possible only at an annual contributors' meeting which, however, had become a matter of form.

Despite the monopoly of control the hospital appears to have been well managed until after the end of the Napoleonic wars, but in time strong criticism was made that the hospital was dirty, food was bad, the matron was insolent and the nurses were drunk. Managers and medical officers were at odds; but jealous of their monopoly, the managers refused to listen to complaints from the hospital clerks, and denied the alleged bad practices.

At a public meeting in January 1818 Jeffrey, John Wigham, a Quaker, and others after strong complaints obtained a proper committee, but it was formed in such a way that useful citizens were excluded – notably Leonard Horner, who had been a good manager – in favour of those who wanted to avoid a public enquiry, chief of them being the 'artful' Sheriff Rae. On investigation the findings proved so serious that certain 'idiot' members (Cockburn's word) persuaded the others to suppress them and issue a bland report, confined to recognition of 'a few defects' which would be removed.

Moreover, report and evidence were kept back until two days before the next meeting and the management and their supporters, led by David Hume and the Lord Advocate, Alexander Maconochie, praised the report and brushed aside criticism. The objectors, ill-prepared, mismanaged their attack and were easily defeated; but the managers were at least scared into taking heed, and conditions in the Infirmary gradually improved.[11]

The respected Dr John Barclay (1758–1826), who taught anatomy in Edinburgh for twenty-eight years from 1797 to 1825, had first studied for the Church. Son of a shrewd Perthshire farmer, he was taught by a good Latin scholar at the parish school, then studied arts and divinity at St Andrews, did well in the classics, mathematics and Hebrew, and was well liked for his kindness and good humour.

Although he became licensed as a preacher he worked more as a tutor, and in his twenty-ninth year, in the winter of 1789/90, he accompanied the two young sons of Sir James Campbell of Doune to Edinburgh to supervise their university studies. Here he attended medical and anatomy classes, gradually transferring his interest to medicine, took a doctor's degree in 1796 and dedicated his thesis *De Anime, seu Principio Vitali* to both Dr James Gregory and John Bell. Intending to concentrate on anatomy he attended Monro's lectures, studied with Bell and became his assistant, and after a time in London, set up as lecturer in 1797.

Barclay still maintained his theological interest, and sat in the General Assembly, whence he apparently derived a few pupils from among clerical friends.

With Sir James Campbell's help he equipped a small house in High School Yards for lecturing, adjoining Surgeon Square, and also set up a small museum with his own dissections, and with purchases. Not being a member of either Royal College he was officially unrecognised, and most of Edinburgh's hundreds of students were then under the care of the Bells and Alexander Monro. Diffident at the start, Barclay soon gained confidence and his students increased in number until he was able to buy a house in Surgeons' Square, where his lecture room became famous. The three-storey house, pillared and arched, had been built for Dr Andrew Duncan senior between the old Surgeons' Hall and Medical Society Hall, and had a theatre above, which Barclay enlarged to accommodate the still increasing numbers.

When in 1804 Charles Bell moved to London, the College of Surgeons officially recognised Barclay, giving him a Fellow's privileges, 'the highest honour that has ever been conferred on me' – probably in recognition of his *Anatomical Nomenclature* published in 1803. In 1806 he became FRCS (and Honorary Fellow 1821), and for the next twenty years had at least three hundred students a year. Throughout his career, until 1825, medical student numbers continued to be high.

Unlike Monro and Bell, who also ran medical practices, Barclay concentrated entirely on anatomical teaching and research, and on his museum. His highest income, from 1804, was £800 to £900 a year, charging an initial fee of four guineas, while second-year and 'perpetual' pupils paid less. In 1811 Barclay married one of Sir James Campbell's daughters, and at their house on the north side of Argyle Square they entertained many pupils.

Barclay lectured at 11 a.m. and repeated the same lecture at 6 p.m., for those who could not get in in the morning. At one time, when numbers were highest, he also lectured at noon. His lectures, clear and workmanlike, were somewhat marred by a rather snivelling delivery, the effect of snuff-taking, which he continued at frequent intervals during lectures without bothering to wipe his fingers. He was dedicated to his profession and passed all his time with the students and assistants, in lecture-room, museum or dissecting-room, considered one of the wits of Edinburgh and enlivening his lectures with humorous anecdotes. Sometimes he was so carried away that he continued talking after the bell, only to discover the students had all gone.

In his view, the true anatomists had been the early experts, who were 'sowers and reapers'; the two eighteenth-century Monros were the 'gleaners', and 'Last of all come the geese, who still contrive to pick up a few grains . . . Gentlemen, we are the geese.'[12]

Short but strong and well-made, with 'a large round head, bright eyes, humorous mouth' and eloquent facial expression, he was genial and good company, the life of any society. Further, he would always help a struggling student, offering free admission to lectures, even helping with fees to other professors. One story relates how, when an unscrupulous bookseller manoeuvred him into giving a poor student a free ticket, he picked out four guineas' worth of anatomy books from the shop shelves and made the protesting dealer present them to the young man. (A similar story is told of Professor Christison and the bookseller Laing.)[12]

Barclay's large museum collection included many skeletons, including an elephant's given by Sir George Ballingall, a former assistant. In a summer course on comparative anatomy he concentrated on the muscles, using a dead donkey which in warm weather became distinctly malodorous. For large classes he employed a demonstrator as well as the dissecting assistants: some of the former were youths whom he had helped to educate and had launched in the profession.[13]

As for human bodies, there was always a problem. Barclay covered all aspects of anatomy, with surgery and physiology, and at the end of the course showed operations. A dissection of 'soft parts', covered by a sheet, was also revealed at the end of the lecture. According to one anecdote his assistant, coming back at night to prepare the specimen for next day by the dim light of a candle, on raising the sheet was terrified to find it being pulled back again. It proved to be a dog.

Because of the expense and difficulty of finding dissection subjects, whose demand far outstripped local supply, items often had to be brought from London at some cost, to the irritation of London teachers; Liverpool and Ireland were also tried, Liverpool at one time supplying London, Edinburgh and Glasgow. Edinburgh with its many students never had enough, but Barclay was eventually found to have been acquiring bodies for a larger fee from the porter at St Thomas's in London. Moreover John Aitkin, as demonstrator, used to go out with the assistants and more adventurous pupils to maintain the supply of bodies, in ways unspecified. (After Barclay's death, Aitkin himself took up lecturing.)

The most notorious practice during this period and for some years afterwards was of course 'resurrectionism', vividly described by Robert Christison when he was employed at the Infirmary. He and colleagues enthusiastically connived, not without danger to the anatomy teachers' assistants, who were the chief actors, describing their methods of raiding town cemeteries.

The favourite time was a dark winter evening between 6 and 8 p.m., when darkness had fallen but the churchyard watch had not come on duty and city police night rounds had not started. The men were provided with wooden spades (to reduce noise), 'short, flat, dagger-shaped' iron hooks to raise the coffin lid, and a rope to haul it up. They spread a canvas sheet to catch the scattered earth, dug at the head end, and opened the coffin to break the lid enough to drag out the body, having heaped sacking over it to deaden the sound of the crack. They scrupulously stripped the body and reburied the grave-clothes, scraped back the surrounding earth to look as undisturbed as possible, and packed the now naked body in a sack. This was easily passed over the wall to be smuggled along the empty streets, and with relays of strong, fast diggers even a six-foot deep grave could be robbed in an hour.

Country churchyards had to be robbed later in the evening, and were studied beforehand for ease of approach. For these a gig was needed, and there was the added danger of passing toll-gates; yet though they had narrow escapes they were apparently never caught. One time they were spotted just as they had loaded the sack on to the gig. The driver whipped up and dashed away, while the team scattered. After three miles he threw off pursuit and dumped his prey, disappearing before the hue and cry reached the suburbs.

Both Monro III and Barclay were agreeable to this source of bodies since there was almost no other, and neither professor trespassed on the other's supply. It was after Barclay's death in 1826 that rivalry and dramatic confrontation started between opposing teams.[14]

An academic row blew up when Barclay's friends attempted to persuade the Town to found a chair of Comparative Anatomy for him in 1817. Some professors were in favour, and students eagerly joined in the fray, but Thomas Charles Hope (Chemistry), Robert Jameson (Natural History) and Monro III angrily opposed, as although neither ever taught anatomy, Jameson and Monro both claimed the subject as theirs. One of Kay's 'Portraits' showed Barclay mounted on his elephant skeleton riding through the college gates, with professors either supporting or opposing. Monro thrusts at him with a thigh-bone, and Jameson mounted on a walrus armed with a narwhal tusk, shouts 'Bar-clay? I know it not. Neither is it mentioned by the illustrious Werner!' Gregory encourages Barclay by pushing the elephant forward, and Hope pulls its forelegs back with a rope, which breaks and throws him down, with the over-optimistic title, 'Hope is lost, the rope gives way, and muscular motion wins the day.' But it was Barclay's supporters who lost, and the chair was not created.[15]

Barclay, who helped to establish a Veterinary School conducted by his own pupil William Dick, left a collection of important publications and his lecture notes. He also bequeathed to the College of Surgeons his museum collection of more than twenty-seven years, augmented by items from former pupils from all over the world, to be open to the public as well as students.

When in 1811 his students wished to present him with a piece of plate, he stopped their subscriptions and would accept only a much less expensive sign of appreciation, an address. Not long before his death in 1826 he agreed to their subscribing to a bust, which proved an excellent likeness and was placed in the museum.

Practice of Physic was under Dr James Gregory until his retirement in 1817. He retained his qualities into old age, bold and vivacious, of strong intellect, a fluent, clear lecturer and confident in treatments. He was a great draw for young students, a worthy successor to Dr William Cullen, teaching Theory for fourteen years and Practice for twenty-seven, and because of Edinburgh's high reputation his influence spread far and wide over a couple of generations, throughout the country and the colonies, where his tough methods were freely adopted over many years: 'free blood-letting, the cold affusion, brisk purging, frequent blisters, the nauseating action of tartar-emetic'.[16] Some of his treatments were ahead of their time, such as avoiding the universal blood-letting in fevers as not always suitable; and moving from 'a low diet' at the start of the frequent disease of 'consumption' to a generous meat diet in its later stages.

Gregory, who walked with a cane which never touched the ground but was carried over his shoulder or 'at the trail', also wore his hat during lectures, a habit for which he would bow and apologise at the start. Christison, who attended his class in 1817, recalls that on the last day, when the college bell rang at 10 a.m., he was in mid-sentence on the pathology of paralysis. 'The whole students at once sprang to their feet, according to custom, to rush to the Chemistry class. Gregory stood up too, raised his arm, and called out, "Stop! Stop, gentlemen! . . . one word at parting!" But no one stopping, he shouted. "Well, well! God bless you all!".' Such was his farewell to the class of 1817.'[17]

Gregory's death in 1821 was seen as an irreparable loss and, said Mrs Grant of Laggan, plunged Edinburgh into a 'universal shade of woe'. This 'noble specimen of genius and unblemished virtue' had been fifth in a line of distinguished forebears, and his mother had been daughter of the senior Baron of the Exchequer, Robert Ord.[18]

Mrs Grant also noted that 'His bounty amounted to munificence . . . he never took a fee from a clergyman's family, from a student, or from a subaltern. His wit was always ready, and he seemed quite unconscious that it was wit.' Also famed for the classical elegance of his writing, he could talk in Latin as easily as English.[19]

Among other lecturers were Dr John Gordon, who died aged only thirty-two after ten years of teaching anatomy; the demonstrator Andrew Fyfe, considerably older, who succeeded John Innes as dissector for the Monros; Alexander Walker; and Dr David Craigie.

Towards the close of Barclay's career Dr Cullen's great-nephew William started his teaching, and later still, Robert Knox became Barclay's successor.

Dr Gordon's death especially distressed the Grants of Rothiemurchus, who had been his particular friends since they met. He had a very full anatomy class, and in a social move upwards had left his old flat in Buccleuch Place for 'a nice house in Castle Street'. When all seemed rosy, he caught a fever, neglected it and, according to Elizabeth, stuck to 'too exclusive a meat diet' when he should have been living on slops. Gordon was among the first who tried 'high feeding' to counteract 'a consumptive tendency': so successfully that he tried it on himself, but (she thought) would have done better to study less and to exercise more. His widow, left not well off and with three children, had to move to Ayrshire.[20]

John Lizars, brother of the engraver William, was a 'draughtsman' anatomist, associated with Liston, Fergusson and John Bell, and as then usual in Edinburgh entered surgery via anatomy. In these great days of the private lecturers, when Monro Tertius' inadequate performance drove students to the Extramural School, they could choose between William Cullen on the use of the stethoscope, John Aitken on anatomy, surgery and physiology, and the great Robert Knox, whose expertise on morphology and his powerful lectures added to the popularity of anatomy.

With the lack of subjects for dissection, and the teachers' often dubious methods of obtaining bodies, illustrations and diagrams had to serve for providing information. The Monros, Bells and others produced fine engravings, but some, especially those of Lizars, were crudely gaudy. Lizars later became notorious for the contest with Syme for the College of Surgeons professorship in 1831, creating bitter enmity.

Robert Liston, a clergyman's son born in Linlithgowshire in 1794, studied anatomy with Dr Barclay, and surgery at the Infirmary and in London. Ambitious to become an operating surgeon, in 1818 he became a member of the Royal College of Surgeons both in Edinburgh and London.

He was one of the most brilliant demonstrators working with Barclay, until after a misunderstanding he set up on his own in the winter of 1818–19 as an anatomy/surgery lecturer with James Syme as his assistant, and sixty students.

They had the usual trouble over 'subjects', as Monro and Barclay secured what bodies there were, and several probably apocryphal stories were told of escapades, such as their once being driven off by Barclay's men with pistols.

To gain experience Liston worked at the Infirmary as surgeon's clerk under George Bell and Dr Gillespie, and when that job ended, he used to follow the operations, discussing them in the evenings with Syme, himself then a surgeon's clerk. This was not a time of high operating standards at the Infirmary. Liston, dexterous and bold in initiative, soon displayed operating skill, especially in cases refused or failed in by others, so that he became besieged by the sick poor, and had to operate in their homes or in special rented lodgings after he no longer had official admission to the hospital.

Senior surgeons suspected him of enticing patients away, and complained of his criticism of hospital practice and his 'interference' in the surgery department. In March 1822 the managers, without warning, prohibited him from entering the wards and especially the operating rooms, confirming the veto by the Court of Contributors, influenced by a strong and one-sided indictment from Jeffrey. Liston appealed unsuccessfully to the College of Surgeons, but as their President was himself an Infirmary surgeon he got little satisfaction. He then sent an open letter to the Lord Provost as Chairman of the Court of Contributors, but succeeded in being appointed to the Infirmary only in 1827.

During those five years he was operating privately, further increasing his fame by brief but significant publications. In one paper he gave to the Royal Medical Society on the fracture of the neck of the femur, he criticised surgeons' failure to immobilise and unite the fracture, as under good conditions was possible. In a series on aneurysms he described a sixteen-year-old boy, written off by the surgeons as incurable, for whom Liston, in a long and serious operation in a small, ill-lit room, removed the tumour, and although the boy nearly died in the process, he recovered (only to die, however, in a later recurrence).

Liston also introduced new surgical instruments, including bone pliers supplied by Mr Young, an ingenious cutler of College Street. Another extraordinary operation he described (1823) was removal of a huge tumour of the scrotum, bordering on elephantiasis, described in overpowering detail, the least repulsive being the insensible patient's revival by a pint of whisky.

One of Liston's gifts was his great speed in amputations, by a method more efficient than the tourniquet, compressing the arteries with one hand while he cut with the other. Cool and resourceful, he was vain enough of his skill and speed.

Liston made a powerful figure, six foot two and with a 'commanding expression', appearing dressed in a dark bottle-green coat with velvet collar, double-breasted 'shawl vest' and grey trousers tucked into Wellington boots. He would stand with one thumb stuck into his waistcoat armhole. Not a fluent speaker, he taught by example, and to students or indeed anyone but patients he was brusque, and had an unpredictable temper. Outside his job he was a keen sportsman, shooting, hunting and yachting.[21]

James Syme, five years younger and his distant cousin, had been urged by Liston into the profession, worked with him from the days with Barclay and then in their classes, then with Liston's encouragement himself continued with anatomy, and for a time they were in alliance.

Son of a land-owner of Pitreavie, Fife, Syme was born at 96 Princes Street (opposite where the Scott monument was later built), and attended Fulton and Knight's grammar school in George Street and then (1809) the High School, one of 130 boys under the kind Mr Gray and soon reaching twenty-fifth place. Though a careful student he was neither brilliant nor quick, but reserved and meditative. He and his brother also attended a private tutor, the Rev. Dr Simpson in York Place.

In 1815 his father John, through ill-judged land speculations, had been obliged to sell the family house at Lochore and rent Pitreavie Castle, near Dunfermline. James was still able to attend the University, starting in Latin under the elder Christison, then botany (his great love) for three years under Dr Rutherford, natural history under Professor Jameson, Mathematics with Professor Wallace and philosophy under Dr Thomas Brown.

From 1817–18 he was in Dr Hope's Chemistry class, which averaged four to five hundred students, but as at that time there was no practical study or even simple experiment, Syme and Robert Christison compensated by forming their venturesome private group. (Syme was also interested in the recent installation of gas.)

Though shy, he inherited his father's obstinacy and perseverance. Unlike Liston he was no sportsman, but enjoyed botanising with a few friends, and indulged his hobby of chemistry.

He was probably influenced towards medicine by Liston, and in 1817–18 Syme also joined Dr Barclay's anatomy class, then rising in reputation. At the start of the 1818–19 session, however, when Liston left Barclay after a disagreement and set up as an independent anatomy teacher, the still inexperienced Syme went with him as assistant and demonstrator. He rapidly acquired the skill, and sometimes did the lecturing. In 1820 he was appointed to the junior post of Medical Superintedant at the Fever Hospital at Queensberry House, a sought-after job but at that time hazardous, and he caught and nearly died of the fever.

In 1822 Syme studied in Paris at the Hotel Dieu, where bodies were easily obtained, and became a skilled dissector. He submitted papers to the Royal Medical Society, showing a sound grasp of principles, and was unsparing in terse criticism of contemporaries and instruments. In 1823, when he became an Edinburgh FRCS, he carried out Scotland's first successful amputation of the hip-joint, on a nineteen-year-old youth, Liston in this case acting as his assistant. With Syme's sound diagnostic skill and adaptability in emergency the whole operation took only a minute.

He was then offered the resident clerkship at the Royal Infirmary under William Newbigging, much of his work being the routine process of bleeding, of which he did not approve. The resident surgeon was then Robert Christison. On one occasion, ordered to bleed a boy weakened from a compound fracture, Syme instead fed him on steak and porter, which was angrily countermanded by his chief. Within two days the boy died.

Syme continued in partnership with Liston for the next five years until their estrangement; then on his own, still with no hospital appointment. Though a skilled operator he was neither fast nor 'elegant' and (wrote Dr Joseph Bell) 'entirely devoid of flourish and dash'; but he was devoted to the patient's case. In operations cool and silent, at other times his caustic language and occasional impatient obstinacy exacerbated arguments into out-and-out quarrels, and the inevitable paper war.[22]

From 1823, living at 12 Dundas Street, Syme was a fellow of the College of Surgeons, gave his inaugural dissertation on 'Necrosis', dedicated to Liston who was already a member, and continued teaching anatomy and surgery. Liston, retiring from Anatomy teaching, resigned his post to Syme.

At first they were mutually supportive, but after Syme's visit to Germany in 1824 for further study, rivalry and an increasing coolness grew up between them. As both were contentious and the field of surgery was tough and competitive, their relationship ended in acrimony, which was to have far-reaching effects in the profession.

Robert Christison would have chosen to be a civil engineer, but as his father could not afford to launch him he settled for medicine, and matriculated as a medical student in November 1815, joining Monro III's anatomy class, at first thoroughly put off by the sight of a corpse, and by his disgust at the theatre smell, which he never overcame.

Monro's careless indifference to his subject made him an unpopular lecturer. He could still give clear, precise lectures, but with passing years his classroom was 'the frequent scene of disturbance and uproar'. His 'prosector' Andrew Fyfe, one of Edinburgh's last to wear a pigtail, taught practical anatomy, every afternoon going over what the dissectors had done with their specimen, followed by entertaining anecdotes round the fire.

Next winter Christison studied under Dr Barclay, then moved on to Theory and Practice of Physic. The Theory, or Institutes of Medicine, was taught by old Dr Andrew Duncan (senior), benevolent, now somewhat senile and his teaching outdated, but liked for his kindliness and his boring weekly 'tea-and-talk parties'. Although in 1819, in the usual Edinburgh arrangement with ageing professors, his son Andrew Duncan junior was officially appointed successor and, meanwhile, conjunct professor, followed in 1821 by Dr Alison, the old man remained in office until he died in 1828 in his eighty-sixth year.

Materia Medica offered a winter morning lecture at 8 a.m., yet the popular Dr James Home drew so many students that at least twenty had to stand. Unusually for professors of the day, he would give an hour to examining any student who wanted a trial, and his lectures, if unexciting, were full of useful information. But when Dr James Gregory died in 1821 Home, then sixty-three, took over his chair of Practice of Physic, a misguided change on the Town Council's part, as he proved an instant failure and lost his students' respect and attention, vainly trying to conduct a class of rowdy and uncontrolled youngsters.

This appointment had caused another bitter struggle. While Home had had a reputation for success and popularity, his rival Dr John Thomson, Professor of Military Surgery, though skilled, was 'a combative, prominent Whig'. Better than either would have been Dr John Abercrombie, educated at both Aberdeen and Edinburgh, then at St George's Hospital in London, before becoming a successful Edinburgh practising physician where he greatly helped the poor. But his high reputation as physician cut no ice with the Council, who appointed on political grounds, and Home as a Tory was duly transferred to Gregory's vacant chair. While Home was doing so badly in his new appointment Abercrombie went on to further academic honours, became the King's physician in ordinary in Scotland (1824), and in 1836 was appointed Lord Rector of his old alma mater, Marischal College in Aberdeen.[23]

Christison, progressing meanwhile to the clinical side, now walked the wards for a year. He and others often dropped in on Dr Duncan's clinical visits, usually to the same old woman, Christian Jack. After listening to her mumbles for a minute or two he would straighten up and give out the same report. 'As yesterday . . . *Continuentur medicamenta.*' The other two physicians, Home and Rutherford, were more illuminating, though Rutherford firmly believed that all young girl patients were shamming, and always prescribed hourly 'a few drops of asafoetida', a strong-tasting, smelly gum resin, until the poor girls discharged themselves.

The Professor of Midwifery, the quarrelsome Dr James Hamilton, was stronger than his frail, unattractive appearance suggested, bewigged, stooping and always gazing at his feet, his harsh voice with a strong Scots accent. He was Scotland's chief obstetrical authority and his forcible delivery of apparently inexhaustible information went with inability to see opponents in an argument as anything but wrong. One notable quarrel was with the equally tough James Gregory, ending with a fight with their canes, a lawsuit and a £100 fine.

Yet Hamilton could show unexpected tolerance. In later years when Christison was his colleague, he was present during an examination when Hamilton passed a student who answered 'by rote', explaining that the youth had studied in Dublin, and had answered 'according to the nonsense he has been taught. I cannot punish him for remembering his lessons'. He added, however, 'I would not trust him with the delivery of a cat.'[24]

His three-month course, partly at the Lying-In Hospital for practical experience, was voluntary but always crowded, not least because of the attraction of his pugnacity.

The odd arrangement for Clinical Surgery was the teaching by James Russell, from 1803 when the chair was created for him until the age of eighty in 1833. As he was not an acting surgeon but 'permanent consulting surgeon', with no patients of his own, he could therefore lecture only on other people's cases, but not criticise. He dealt skilfully with this tricky situation, and despite the fact that his lectures were in the late afternoon and he was constantly yawning, they were well attended.

In the autumn of 1817 Christison entered the Infirmary as physician-assistant to Dr Thomas Spens, standing in for William Cameron, who had fallen ill with the epidemic fever then beginning to spread in Edinburgh. Christison was thrown in at the deep end, the start of two-and-a-half years of professional practical training. The title of the job was Physician's or Surgeon's Clerk (later renamed 'Resident Physician or Surgeon'), and these years were invaluable in putting him when so young with men some years his senior.

In spite of the danger of fever, which necessitated a reserve of deputies, this was a happy time for Christison, one of seven young residents. Benjamin Welsh, uncle of Thomas Carlyle's future wife, had been, first, assistant to

Dr James Hamilton senior (not the obstetrician) at the Infirmary, then Superintendant of the Queensberry House Fever Hospital – keen but fiery and 'one-sided', a wholehearted professional. In 1819 in his publication *The Edinburgh Fever*, Welsh claimed blood-letting as sole remedy. He later succeeded to his elder brother's Haddington practice, but died of tuberculosis before he could have seen his error through the change in fever treatment.

Christison's colleagues included Dr Somerville's son James Craig Somerville, a clever, talkative little gossip, inclined to stir up trouble but generally amusing, and William Cullen, then very handsome and a member of Edinburgh society, a linguist with a good memory and much energy. He was a thinker: not practical, and had little knowledge of either mathematics or the physical sciences. A witty and accomplished public speaker, he was too impetuous not to make enemies. One day meeting on the North Bridge Cullen amused Christison and his friend Charles Neaves with malicious witticisms at others' expense. When they parted, Neaves remarked that *they* would be the butt of his next encounter. Leaving the Infirmary in 1819 Cullen went on to St Bartholomew's in London, where Christison later joined him.

After a few weeks as Dr Spens's assistant Christison and a colleague were appointed to serve at Queensberry House, which had been turned into an emergency fever hospital under Dr Welsh, at the height of the epidemic then raging among the labouring classes. Dr Spens and Dr James Hamilton senior were visiting physicians, both admired by Christison, the former tall, slender, 'a thorough gentleman', resourceful and ready to consider new ideas, shy and so retiring as to be overshadowed by the more brilliant Gregory and Hamilton. Hamilton, old but vigorous and handsome, was a quiet humorist, full of jokes. He was committed to blood-letting, purging, and for syphilis, the mercury cure. Dr Hamilton was the last of Edinburgh's doctors to wear the traditional eighteenth century costume, including the buckled shoes and cocked hat, and in this dated costume already seemed quaintly picturesque.[25]

The fever of the years 1817–20 was Edinburgh's first notable epidemic, believed to have spread from the Continental garrison towns in 1814 (which was actually typhus). It visited all of Britain's larger towns except, supposedly, Birmingham. In Edinburgh it was aggravated by a bad harvest in 1816, and low employment and consequent malnutrition the following year, factors which also occurred elsewhere.

Christison describes the three forms of the disease, one of which, the 'relapsing fever' or synocha, ran to temperatures of 107 °F and after apparently subsiding, returned abruptly on the fourteenth day. Christison studied the disease for twenty-one months, during five of which he three times fell victim himself to the synocha type, which mostly left his mind clear so that he was able to make valuable observations. Most of his colleagues also suffered, and to keep the seven posts going a dozen reserves were needed. In two years these twelve suffered seventeen attacks, five having the fever twice and one three times.

Christison fell ill only three weeks after he entered the job, and endured the maximum temperature, almost expiring with heat though covered with only a sheet and lying in a through-draught between an open door and open window, in a cold March blowing hail-storms. On the sixth-day crisis he saw devils with tails thrusting their long noses through the bed-curtains, whom he assailed with a (totally imaginary) cudgel, shouting such nonsense that his attendants had to escape outside and laugh. Four hours of violent sweats brought down his temperature and pulse, so that he was 'in elysium'. Yet while he could see that Dr Spens and his aide George Bell were extremely anxious, he himself never doubted his recovery, in any of his three attacks.

Treatment at this time was Cullen's 'nauseating diaphoretic' tartar emetic, a sweetish, metallic-tasting poisonous crystalline salt used as an expectorant; but in this epidemic it had little effect. Dr Home tried his 'cold affusion', which in view of the violent heat caused by the fever seemed appropriate, but Christison found it unhelpful to himself or his patients, and it brought on a blinding headache. Blood-letting was still fashionable for fevers as well as for high blood-pressure. It proved to give at least temporary relief and even to 'break' the fever. Christison was bled to the maximum each time (thirty ounces in the first fever), all within eighteen months, without apparent serious after-effects.[26]

In less emergency-ridden days, the physician's assistant made his round after breakfast, making prescriptions in case of need. At noon he joined the physician's rounds, recorded his dictated notes, saw the treatment carried out, and visited again in the evenings. As an unofficial extra duty, any assistant who had been out at a late party was expected to make a night round and check that the night-nurses were awake.

At that time, 1817–20, Christison and his contemporaries noted abnormally high pulses in pneumonia, pleurisy, nephritis and rheumatism, 'acute local inflammations . . . attended with a violence of arterial action' which they treated by blood-letting: symptoms which they claimed disappeared in later years, though doctors who had not experienced them maintained that there had been no change. After about 1833 bloodletting was discredited and ceased to be used. In earlier days a man could lose between twenty and forty ounces before he became faint, whereas later, even a few ounces would cause faintness.[27]

By 1819 when Christison was preparing for final graduation, although he attended a grinder, he found his groundwork so sound that much swotting proved unnecessary. He even made a delightful walking expedition the weekend before his examination, though it proved almost disastrous, as one of his friends having drunk too much on the return trip, turned quarrelsome and got into a brawl at Liberton, only stopped by one of their ladies intervening. Christison, for one, was left with a black eye. He took the men to the Infirmary to clean up, and careful treatment and wet compresses reduced the evidence. But throughout the night he was rehearsing imaginary explanations of his condition to Dr Gregory, in the Latin in which the examinations were conducted. ('*Dic mihi, domine, unde venit hicce oculus caeruleus?*'[28])

For examinations the Medical Faculty met successively at each other's houses, the host of the day acting as chief examiner. This time it was Gregory, who put Christison through his paces for a good hour on anatomy, physiology and stomach diseases, a masterly scrutiny, fair and thorough. The other five doctors asked more perfunctory questions. The viva was followed by a written paper, a commentary on Hippocrates, a case consultation, and defence of a thesis. Most students got their grinder to write their thesis, but Christison wrote his own, straight into Latin (with a few paternal corrections) on the Edinburgh fever epidemic. One colleague crammed so many references into his thesis on gout, planning to use it as a handbook for future use, that Gregory merely said crushingly, '*Librum scripsisti, domine.*'[29]

After graduating Christison took a month's holiday, which ended in the fever, and on recovery he joined Newbigging's team of four as house surgeon, exchanging with Dr O'Brien. The consulting surgeon was Professor Russell.

Christison became very friendly with Newbigging, who, like a number of other Edinburgh surgeons, was also a general practitioner and family medical adviser. He thought Newbigging's acceptance of a knighthood in William IV's accession honours misguided. The post ended in April 1820, by which time Christison, still very shy with the ladies, had entered Edinburgh society, and fell in love with Harriet, a still adolescent daughter of David Brown, a St Petersburg merchant. After a prolonged and complex relationship they married six years later.

Meanwhile his father died, when Christison, travelling day and night to be with him, arrived only to see him unconscious and dying. He then studied for some time in Paris, returning in April 1821 to find a contest in progress for professorships, Gregory's death having caused a multiple shift between several rivals. Despite his youth (he was only twenty-four), Christison's name was put forward for the Chair of Medical Jurisprudence along with Professor Playfair's nephew James, an older student contemporary.

Months passed, and Christison began to think of lecturing in chemistry at the Extramural Medical School, and had even compiled a few lectures, when in January 1822 he learned that he had been appointed Professor of Medical Jurisprudence and his commission signed six weeks earlier.

The delay was due to a strange personal muddle. A glowing testimonial from Christison's Paris master Dr Robiquet had been referred to a junior Lord of the Admiralty, Sir George Warrender, whereas it was his chief Lord Melville, First Lord of the Admiralty, who controlled Crown patronage. But Warrender had recently offered to travel post to Scotland, at some inconvenience, to vote in a Haddingtonshire contest that turned on a single vote. His effort was successful, the seat was won, and Warrender could then decently pass on Dr Robiquet's letter and recommend Christison. So far so good, but as he was extremely dilatory over writing letters the recipient did not hear for weeks.[30]

On 23 February Christison was inducted as Professor. His duties began on 1 May starting at once on his lectures. He served in the post until 1832, then moved to the chair of Materia Medica, where he continued until 1877.

37
TWO SIDES OF THE LAW

'All the people attached to the law, which indeed are the people of Edinburgh, are obliged, with their families, to stay in town till the court of Session rises in July; then every creature is seized with the rural mania; and this town, with all the green delights of groves and grassy hills . . . is as much forsaken as if the Roman malaria had taken possession of it. You saw it at the lowest ebb . . . I could wish you saw it again, glowing with busy life, and gay with the flutter of all those human butterflies.'

Mrs Grant of Laggan to Miss Catherine Gorman, *Memoir*, 29 April 1821, II.287–8

Although Edinburgh was swarming with men of the law – writers to the signet, advocates, judges – it swarmed even more with men who were fully qualified in the law but never practised. Some never attempted it, some did so half-heartedly, like Patrick Fraser Tytler, who kept travelling abroad, riding to hounds, staying with friends on their estates. Some, like Archibald Alison, might inherit a good law practice from their fathers' reputation, but Patrick did not, his father being now dead; but then, he made a career instead as a historian.

A young man on passing as advocate paid a total of £100 in fees, plus a gratuity of £2.15 to the Parliament house door-keeper.[1] Then began the grind of attending daily at Parliament House, hanging around hoping for a cause, until 2 o'clock in the afternoon. This was followed by writing up papers running to fifty or sixty pages, for which they might earn only two or three guineas, or else preparing a debate, or looking up some cause. Alison, who was himself keen to get on with his study of population, extravagantly claims that he still managed to send at least one thousand pages a week to the agents, first written by himself, then copied out by his unfortunate clerk.

But lawyers did have the seven-month vacation: from mid-July to mid-November, then almost a month over Christmas, and two months from mid-March to mid-May.[2]

Mrs Grant, having invited to dinner Mr Crawford of Auchinames who had arrived with a letter of introduction, was amused by his surprise at the relaxed familiarity of the courts, judges and advocates alike unconstrained.

After all, she explained, they had all been at the High School and the College, had played golf together, discussed literature since boyhood. Although 'we have not, nor ever had, authors by profession', when advocates turned author it was not regarded as a slur on their legal profession.[3]

In the first decade or so of the century one of the most noted, or rather notorious, of the advocates, whose career was still expanding, was John Clerk of Eldin, advocate in 1785, Solicitor-General under the Whig Government (1805–6), and he ran a large practice before he became a judge in 1823.

Accounts of Clerk in the law are equally positive and negative, as if he had two natures. Cockburn allows that he was independent, learned – especially in the arts and literature – 'honest, warm-hearted, generous, and simple . . . a steady friend'. This was counteracted by self-admiration for his own achievements (which were not always actual) – from conviction, not vanity. Impatient of contradiction, he would enlarge on his virtues and insist on his beliefs, and when, as often, he was challenged, sure of his infallibility he became fierce. 'Pugnacity was his line.' Sure of his superior legal knowledge, he often insulted opposing counsel and even the judge.

He was popular, however, for his humour and originality, provided he were not roused to scorn. Except for Lord Buchan, few men can have had so many stories told of them. Even in the midst of a vehement argument he might suddenly pause, lift his eyeglass to his brow, and with a warning smile utter some 'diverting piece of Clerkism' – and while everyone was still laughing, cap it with another. He and Jeffrey were good complements, and Jeffrey could manage him better than most, excelling in retort when Clerk was at his most provocative.[4]

His waywardness made him an unpredictable supporter in spite of his 'muscular' mind. Instead of following the usual Scottish practice of wading through the huge quarto volumes of written arguments, he left the writing of papers to 'author bodies and sic like', and did not use the *viva voce* pleadings which lawyers prepared, often treating them very rudely. 'He was regarded as one of the wickedly wise (or wisely wicked) among Scotch Whigs', says Robert Gillies, and earned the highest fees of any at the bar, hence his lavish expenditure on pictures.

Gillies, like other young advocates, spending much of his day either gossiping in the court or listening to cases, found that Clerk's speeches 'beguiled' many a dull hour. 'His broad Scotch dialect, which he cherished for its power of expression, the breadth and lucidity . . . his often recurring fits of disdainful and immitigable wrath, his merciless and withering sarcasm were altogether admirable.' One peer was said to have arranged with the doorkeeper always to call him when Clerk was to plead an appeal, so that he could be sure to be there.

Clerk had blue eyes with extremely bushy eyebrows, 'coarse grizzly hair, always in disorder, and firm, projecting features', giving him the look of a 'thorough-bred shaggy terrier'. He was also very lame from a boyhood accident, with one leg at least two inches shorter than the other.[5]

He was the near neighbour of the Grants of Rothiemurchus when they were living in Picardy Place, and – largely because of his endearing sister Bessy – Elizabeth, Jane and William Grant 'half lived in their house'. The Clerks always invited one of them to make up their dinner-parties when anyone dropped out, and the company was always good: 'All the Law set of course, judges, barristers, and Writers; some of the literary, some of the scientifick, and a great many county families', in their surroundings, richly adorned with paintings and curiosities.

Elizabeth heartily disliked him, partly for his known and discreditable private life, his severity and cynicism, partly for his 'truly hideous' appearance, harsh enough when at rest, but 'demoniack when illumined by the mocking smile that sometimes relaxed it. I always thought him the personification of the devil on two sticks.' When entertaining he hardly spoke to his guests unless to make some crushing comment, though his remarks, when applicable, were generally prized, and if carried away by a subject he was 'really luminous, masterly'. Yet while he terrified all the young men, he was always kindly with the playful young ladies.[6]

Robert Blair, a man of great probity and understanding, learned (except in science) and dignified, cared so little for office that he twice refused the post of Lord Advocate, until in 1808 he agreed to accept the highest office of all, the Lord Presidentship. Portly in figure, taciturn in manner, he was a learned and principled lawyer with a clear, forceful and racy style, but tended to be lazy – perhaps, Cockburn thinks, because he was inclined to get excited and to combat this, retreated to quiet. 'It is rare to find a fiery disposition and a strong love of ease combined.' As a speaker his great merit was in 'luminous exposition of legal views'.[7]

Blair was widely read and devoted to literature, the classics, and some languages. Robert Gillies suspected that his naturally impatient disposition might have contributed to the stroke from which he died in 1811 – only days before Lord Melville, who had come to attend his funeral.[8]

Charles Hope, who succeeded Robert Dundas of Arniston as Lord Advocate in 1801, and became Lord Justice Clerk in 1804 and Lord President on Blair's death, was tall and majestic in bearing, with a fine, full and deep voice, so distinct that even a whisper could be heard. Cockburn calls him 'the tongue of the party, and in the van of all its battles' – a great gift for public speaking but marred by a lack of tact, and his great weapon, declamation, was not always used at the best moments.

Hope was Cockburn's first professional 'patron', and used to take him on circuit, despite Cockburn's Whiggism always proving a kind friend.[9]

His son John, called to the bar in 1816, was Solicitor-General from 1822, on the death of James Wedderburn, to 1830, when he became Dean of Faculty, and later served as Lord Justice Clerk and became a Privy Councillor.

Tall and thin, with a forbidding appearance and stiffly formal manner, 'No young man could have had less personal attraction', says Cockburn, 'measured without dignity – grave without weight and cold, if not sour'. John also exhibited an off-putting over-confidence.

But then he had started very young, in 1811 when he was only sixteen, with a pamphlet denouncing the *Edinburgh Review*'s 'political guilt'. In 1816, when he became advocate, and the Whigs were holding the best posts, he was pushed to prominence by his keen fellow-Tories in a very few years, unfortunately drawn into the acrimonious political scene.[10]

George Cranstoun, a friend of Scott's, though a fund of classical knowledge was so profoundly versed in the law that he wrote about almost nothing else. His speeches, elegant and precise, built up arguments 'stone by stone' until he had neatly demolished his opponent. But he was too deliberate and artificial in presentation to move his hearers. He kept his decided views to himself and close friends, so that to many he seemed 'indifferent to common distractions'.

Cranstoun, one of whose sisters had married Dugald Stewart and the other had become Countess Purgstall and lived chiefly in Germany, led a retired life, appearing in court only on the most important issues. With a gentlemanlike, formal manner, he had a classical profile, yet his face seemed almost featureless. In 1823 Cranstoun became Dean of the Faculty, and in 1826 was raised to the Bench as Lord Corehouse.[11]

One of the more unprepossessing members of the faculty was Alan Maconochie (1748–1816), who had been Professor of Public Law at the University until 1796, when he became a judge as Lord Meadowbank. He published works on agriculture as well as on the law.

Meadowbank was an uncouth figure, with short, thin thighs, inward-turning feet, and head bent forward on an immensely long neck. He was said to look like a baboon, while he had a long, awkward face and a voice that was harsh and shrill. Boswell's father had compared it to 'a cracked hautboy', another judge to 'an obstreperous hen'. He was rather undeservedly laughed at, for though an able, intellectual advocate he would spoil a case by expressing eccentric views with an air of pretension, full of 'metaphysical phraseology'.[12]

Edinburgh's most popular advocate Henry Erskine had retired in 1812 to his small estate of Amondell near Edinburgh, adjoining his brother Lord Buchan's property which in time he would inherit. Despite his ability and wit his career was eventually rather disappointing, but he was imaginative and high-spirited and had a happy, congenial marriage with his talented, generous wife Erskine Munro. An accomplished speaker, he was strong in argument, expressive though not affected, fluent though not verbose and, for wit, renowned almost to excess, as rather than take him seriously people expected him to amuse. Brougham observes approvingly of his speaking voice that it lacked 'accent or provincialisms'.[13]

The Rothiemurchus Grants spent a day with them at the Amondell villa – really an enlarged cottage – he had himself designed and where he was now busied with improvements. Having left politics and now on a reduced income, he was inclined to become bored, so he and his wife used to give 'early dinners' which, being such good company, were a treat for visitors. This was a second marriage: from the first he had 'two sons no way worthy of him', says Elizabeth Grant, and two married daughters. His second wife, a widow, daughter of a failed Glasgow merchant, had lived in youth in reduced circumstances in Ayrshire, and then married a Mr Turnbull. Her sister had married more grandly; one of her brothers was Sir Thomas Munro, and the other, Alexander, married a Miss Brown, the handsome sister of the notable lady who had contrived to marry herself to Sir Arscott Molesworth. Erskine, who retained his physical and intellectual powers to what was then old age, died in 1817 at the age of seventy-one.[14]

Another of Scott's close friends, William Erskine, educated at Glasgow and an advocate since 1790, was one of the few who knew the secret of *Waverley*. He had been Sheriff Depute of Orkney, was amiable, talented, interested in German literature, and wrote Scottish songs. Cockburn claims he was of 'feeble habits', perhaps a polite way of referring to what appear to be unfounded accusations of 'immorality', which undermined his health. In 1822 he was raised to the Bench as Lord Kinedder, but died only a few months later on 14 August, and was succeeded by the aged writer Henry Mackenzie's son, also Henry, an able lawyer.[15]

Two other characters formerly associated with Edinburgh had long had their careers in London. Henry Erskine's brother Thomas (1750–1823), created Lord Chancellor in 1806 with the title 1st Baron Erskine, subsequently spent much of his career in England, defending causes of liberty against oppression, including (most recently) opposing the bill against Queen Caroline, protesting against the Six Acts, and working for negro emancipation.[16]

He returned to Edinburgh in 1820 after an absence of almost fifty years, when a public dinner was given in his honour. He was also to attend the annual Fox dinner and at the last minute presided as well, when the Duke of Hamilton who was to have chaired it was taken ill.

Erskine, with 'sparkling anecdotes', paid eloquent tribute to Fox, and reminded the other guests that he in Edinburgh was born within three days of Fox in England, and thought himself fortunate to have known and worked with him. On the strength of this gathering, Erskine's praise rang for days.

His own dinner, planned for early February and temporarily postponed when the news arrived of the King's death, was finally held on the 21st. Although the illness of Lord Rosslyn's sister and the Duke of Hamilton's wife called both of these peers to London, and many other would-be guests were caught up in the impending general election, more than three hundred nobility and gentry attended.

The occasion was convivial, and with the usual toasts, speeches, and glees, the dinner was excellent. As it also commemorated Henry Erskine, a large transparency adorned the end of the room, showing a pillar carrying an urn, suitably inscribed to both brothers.

At the dinner Erskine revealed how, when he disembarked from the packet at Leith, he could scarcely recognise even Arthur's Seat, and on reaching Edinburgh itself realised that 'not one stone . . . stood upon another when I left old Edinburgh'.[17]

Lord Erskine was a great lion in London, where people fell over themselves to meet him, sometimes disconcerted to find him a non-heroic figure. Lady Morgan (Sydney Owenson), versifier and author of *The Wild Irish Girl* (1806), admits that she was 'in love with the idea of Lord Erskine', and on meeting was at first disappointed to find 'a thin, middle-aged gentleman', who wore a brown bob-wig and 'spoke like other persons'. But they got on well, and later met frequently. 'He was always delightful, always amusing, frequently incoherent, and, I thought sometimes affectedly wild . . .' A true sibling of Henry and Lord Buchan.[18]

The successful lady writer Amelia Opie, who was in London in 1814 during the visits of the foreign emperors and kings, met almost everybody, including one evening Lord Erskine, Sir John Sinclair and Dr Thomas Brown together at a dinner. The first, by his 'very agreeable though incessant egotism, and tales of himself' distracted her from the philosopher, whom she already knew: 'Embarras de richesses. Any one of these three lions would have been enough at once.'

And Benjamin Rush's son Richard, now minister to London from the United States (1817–25), was impressed by Erskine in 1818 at a party at the Duchess of Cumberland's at St James's Palace – the man of whom he had most heard and most wished to know, recalling how Erskine's brother Lord Buchan had corresponded with his father. Erskine, then nearly seventy, retained his youthful personality. 'It was a treat to see so much genius with so much playfulness' – 'Such a social flow from one whose powered eloquence . . . helped to change, on some fundamental points, the English law.'[19]

And finally there was the irrepressible Henry Brougham, who since he had been called to the bar in London in 1808, had continued to write for the *Edinburgh Review,* joined Wilberforce in the anti-slavery movement, was twice an MP, campaigned for popular education, enquired into various abuses and, notably, championed Queen Caroline before and during her trial. This did not make him a less controversial figure.

Cockburn did not care for him, any more than had poor Lord Eskgrove, regularly tormented by Brougham, whom he called 'the Evil'. 'Cool, impudent and resolute', said Cockburn. His talent, energy and eloquence were offset by a lack of true care for his fellow-men, and he was jealous of possible rivals – such as the gifted and upright Francis Horner. As a brilliant, very young man, he had produced his work on Colonial Policy and was capable of combining work or study for up to fourteen hours a day with the habits of an undergraduatish boon companion.

But Broughan had as many admirers as enemies. Sir George Mackintosh meeting Richard Rush at dinner at the Marquess of Lansdowne's, in talking of the House of Commons, in 'few and significant words' summed up Brougham as the first 'for various and universal information on political subjects'. This (Rush thought) should be taken seriously, for Mackintosh himself, without a harsh word on anyone, was a 'deep and calm observer of men and things'; 'profound master in speculative thought . . . the modern Burke'.[20]

These were gentlemen on the right side of the law. There were a few hundred men, and quite a lot of women, in Edinburgh's increasing number of prisons. The old Tolbooth survived until 1817, but the old Canongate gaol was still used for debtors, and there was also the Bridewell, designed by Robert Adam and built in 1791–95, and the new, advanced replacement for the Tolbooth designed by Archibald Elliot built between 1815 and 1817.[21] Charles Nodier commented on it in 1822: 'The present prison is new, but in the ancient taste, like almost all the buildings that are erected in Great Britain.'[22]

The Quaker philanthropist and prison reformer Elizabeth Fry and her brother John Gurney in 1818 paid a visit to Scotland in which they visited prisons in every town between Doncaster and Aberdeen. Mrs Fry had been interested in workhouse and then prison conditions in London since 1806, and had caused a sensation by braving the appalling conditions in Newgate to visit the inmates, who soon became her devoted admirers.

The brother and sister were usually accompanied on their northern prison visits by the Provost and other influential gentlemen. On their return south they stopped to see the Edinburgh gaols, and on 5 September with Provost Mackenzie and others visited and noted in detail the extensive new Gaol, which in plan resembled London's Horsemonger Lane. The castellated, dramatically sited building on the side of Calton Hill, with its Governor's house so placed on the overhanging hill above as to allow a good view of all the prison yards, was to replace the antiquated Tolbooth in the Old Town.

On the ground floor were separate day-rooms for women, untried men, debtors, men convicts, and the infirmary. Above were airy night cells opening on to long galleries, with good bedding and each with a bible. Condemned prisoners were in separate cells, chained to an iron bar – a needless safeguard also used elsewhere mistakenly, the Quakers thought, especially in Scotland where six weeks passed between trial and execution.

The infirmary was regularly visited by the surgeon. The kitchen, though much too small, seemed to provide 'excellent' food (by prison standards). In mornings and evenings it was porridge, with half a pint of beer in the morning. Dinner was ox-head broth with barley and 'garden-stuff'. The only prison clothes supplied were a weekly clean shirt, and shoes and stockings. Blankets were cleaned every month and the prison whitewashed yearly. Prisoners were given 3d a day for firing.

Mrs Fry and her brother approved of the conditions, except for the shackling, but felt that juveniles ought to be housed separately. Further, as the women's night cells were thought too close to the men's, they were now instead kept all night in the day-room – a serious evil which, however, was soon changed.

The Bridewell, close by, was a working prison, but then under repair, so the prisoners instead of being at work were shut in their cells. Its layout by Adam was to become famous, semi-circular with a central watch-tower to allow for overall inspection. It had four storeys, with thirteen cells on each floor, opening towards the tower, and the infirmary on the attic floor. The inspector stayed on the second floor, in a semi-circular room with long narrow windows which allowed him to see without being seen. In the courtyard a pulpit facing the front cells served as a chapel, which could be seen from all cells.

The working cells on the other side were surrounded by a vaulted passage which ran the whole semi-circle on each floor, separating them from the night cells, which looked to the outside. Prisoners, unless they already had a trade, were put to weaving linen, cotton and wool. The skilled men worked as carpenters, painters, shoemakers, whitewashers, and the women were made to cook and launder. They also cultivated the garden, and made all the clothes and bedding. Earnings went towards their maintenance, but any surplus could be saved, while part was held back for six or twelve months until a good-conduct certificate was earned.

Surgeon and chaplain came regularly, services were held twice a week, with catechism on Sundays, and the illiterate were given two hours' daily teaching. They were considered well clothed, fed and cleaned – with even a weekly bath, and the visitors thought the bedding even too comfortable:

straw mattress, sheet, pillow and two double blankets, probably better than many of them had ever known.

This working system, although considered admirable compared with 'idle' prisoners, had disadvantages. The curious layout allowed prisoners to see into other cells, an 'improper and dangerous conversation' to be guarded against. And night cells were so designed that every two had doors and windows close enough to allow prisoners to talk at night. Worse, the prison was too small. It was designed to hold 144 people, with fifty-two work-rooms, but the number far exceeded that, cells were overcrowded and 'evil communication' too often interrupted work. Both prison governors were, however, praised for 'assiduity and humanity'.

The two Quakers recommended that another prison for men be built, keeping Bridewell for women only. They also felt that 'a committee of benevolent and independent persons' to provide instruction and employment should make regular visits in order to restore the inmates to virtue and respectability.

The old Canongate debtors' prison, which was about to be superseded by a new one then building east of Bridewell, though clean, orderly, and visited weekly by a minister, was also overcrowded, especially as everyone was kept indoors because it had no yard. The new prison was to have room for them to follow craft trades.

Finally, there was a recently-built lock-up for vagrants, for those not yet committed, or unable to find bail, and for criminals awaiting execution, which again – in spite of being new – deplorably kept these last in chains. Again the bedding was good, and prisoners had an allowance of 6d a day.

Edinburgh, interestingly, compared very favourably with Glasgow's Bridewell, which 'teems with mischief', had small dark cells and no exercise yard, the prisoners poorly clothed and seeming both hardened and riotous. On the other hand it actually had water-closets adjoining the day-rooms, which seemed a credit to the architect (John Paterson, 1795). They did not mention sanitary arrangements in Edinburgh, and presumably there were none, save for doubtless evil privies. Most other places merely kept 'tubs for filth'.

Of the Scottish prisons visited, Edinburgh ranked medium good, partly because of the religious and teaching facilities. Its chief evil was the two-to-a-cell at Bridewell and the Canongate; and the worthy Quakers were doubtful about the luxury of sheets and pillows, 'a provision which amounts to unnecessary and perhaps injurious indulgence'.

While Glasgow, Haddington and Aberdeen were undoubtedly the worst, in general the northern prisons showed a spirit of awareness – presumably influenced by John Howard's reforming attitude – and of benevolence shown by magistrates. The visitors recognised that most prisons led to increase, not decrease of crime, the bars and chains caused needless suffering, and prisons were altogether too often 'the very seminaries of crime'.[23] Apart from an improvement in cleanliness, much of what they reported might almost have been said today.

Demolition of the fifteenth-century Tolbooth in 1817, much to the disgust of Walter Scott and Charles Kirkpatrick Sharpe, was part of the magistrates' desire to 'improve' the Old Town which as usual consisted of sweeping away as many antiquities as could be replaced by something else. Sharpe, urging conservation or restoration on historic or romantic grounds, received short shrift from the Provost.[24]

It was 'sold two days ago for the sum of 200 and some odd pounds', wrote Sharpe to Scott in October 1817, 'to my huge regret; for as to beautifying the old town of Edin., the idea is ridiculous. Every invasion of this nature destroys its character . . . I would not move one stone of it.' His and Scott's attitude was to remain unfashionable (except among unheeded romantics) for decades. Scott contrived to salvage the doorcase and its surround, which he installed at Abbotsford, and Charles said disgustedly that though he would have liked the stone where the pike displaying traitors' heads was fixed, he was too late. He did not know, he added ironically, 'whether the Town Guard' – a notoriously outdated institution – 'was knocked down with the Tolbooth', and wished he could have afforded to commission Raeburn to paint them full-length for display in a gallery in the manner of the imaginary row of Scottish kings at Holyrood.[25]

Like it or no, the Tolbooth, and the Luckenbooths, went for good.

Probably the most interesting account of the prison in its later days was provided by William Chambers who, when he was apprenticed to his grinding bookseller master, had to call at various prisons to sell lottery tickets. Chambers gives us a description not only of the Tolbooth but of its inmates, something the Gurneys did not think of doing.

William visited often during the last three years of the Tolbooth's existence, and in addition he had to canvass the Holyrood sanctuary and the other gaols. The most generous, he found, were Holyrood debtors, mostly 'third-rate shopkeepers' who having struggled with rents, taxes and debts for years had finally given up the struggle and found Holyrood an almost restful haven.

The Tolbooth he described from the entrance upwards. The door which Scott acquired was the single entry, the very one attacked by the Porteous mob in 1736, at the foot of the south-east turret, and was opened by the turnkey from a small vaulted room just inside. The Town Guard occupied the whole ground floor, which faced north – supposedly ready for emergencies. At the top of some fifty steps the outer turnkey rang a bell at an inner door, admitting to the large hall, with a south-facing stanchioned window, seats ranged along the sides, and a sanded stone floor. From this concourse separate departments for criminals and debtors were reached, criminals to the east, debtors to the west. Of the latter, some were awaiting trial, and during the day were free to move between Hall and upper storeys, just like a lodging-house. Crossing the hall to the west gable, on the flat roof of a lower building one could look on the place of execution.

Without the boards of management and inspectors later introduced to prisons, life within walls was fairly free, nominally supervised by the magistrates. The 'Captain' whom they appointed was usually 'some old citizen who stood well with the corporation'. Debtors, living more or less as under house arrest, could receive visits at any time, and buy food and drink at 'a cosy little apartment, half-tavern, half-kitchen', run by the stout Lucky Laing, whence one could note 'the pleasant sounds of broiling beef-steaks, and the drawings of corks from bottles of ale and porter'.

The then Governor, Captain Sibbald, benevolent and twinkling-eyed, in his 'sober pepper-and-salt-coloured suit', was paid only £150, but would put himself out to help a young prisoner to a new life, or underwrite a debt to save a debtor from being parted from his family.

The other side of this was the regular inflow of criminals awaiting hanging, but these too Sibbald would help. He intervened to alleviate the barbarous regimen of a bread-and-water diet for the whole six weeks between conviction and execution, in spite of the Lord Advocate's objections; he made sure that the poor man was 'comfortably shaved' on the morning of his hanging (presuming that he cared); gave women a last glass of wine as they were led through the Hall – and once even paid for a dentist to draw a tooth for an agonised prisoner.

Peter, the bald, one-eyed Hall-keeper, padding about the floor in carpet slippers and in a woollen cap, was aided by a curious, self-appointed volunteer known as Davie, who was simply there for the free accommodation. He made himself useful in several ways, surreptitiously shared a prisoner's bed at night and lived on crusts and leftovers. Davie could do anything, carry letters and messages, do shopping, order a dinner from Mrs Ferguson, a near-by taverner. He could even conjure up a bottle of forbidden spirits. Always jolly, singing, ready for a hand at whist, he was often rewarded by a small tip when a debtor was released.

The two rooms at the west end had windows only on the north and south, but by hanging a mirror outside the stanchions of the west window above the entrance, it was possible to see anyone entering, and even beyond. In this way prisoners were able to watch the victorious 42nd Regiment, or what was left of it, marching back to the castle after Waterloo. More ghoulishly, this was where the gallows beam was slid out for an execution, by means of a slit at the gable-end, normally kept covered; its other end extended for a couple of feet into the debtors' room. Here Davie had his shared bed, and one day after an execution, while the victim was still suspended from one end, William Chambers came upon Davie and a debtor 'jocularly seated' on the other.

This job gave William in his teens a view 'down into the depths of society . . . among the shifty sub-middle classes'.[26]

Other people who had the run of the prison were failed hangers-on in the professions, trying to scratch a living from jobs for any down-and-out prisoner – such as a doctor, who having wrecked his career through drink, patrolled the place in case some sick debtor wanted a certificate to allow him home.

There were plenty of people sad to see the passing of the old building. On the day of its destruction Alexander Nasmyth, along with his nine-year-old son James, and a young artist named John Linnell, were there among a large crowd, where they were joined by Walter Scott. The real 'Heart of Midlothian' was a nine-feet-square oak and ironbound cell, closed by an iron door. The workmen hacking away at the building got so far and could not pull it down. 'After stripping it of its masonry, they endeavoured by strong levers to tumble it down into the street. At last with a "Yo! heave ho!" it fell down with a mighty crash.'

Only the door, its bolts and bars burst off, still held the 'iron chest' together. Everyone, including the young artist, rushed forward to look into this innermost fastness, and to forage for fragments. Gradually, as the dust settled, in the space underneath could be seen many mummified skeletons of rats, one of which Linnell picked up and wrapped in newspaper as a souvenir.[27]

Many years later Julian Young, on a nostalgic return visit to Edinburgh with his family, could not refrain from 'a harsh word or two' on the vandalism of its destruction. However, when he stood on its site, he had to admit that its removal was not entirely a loss.[28]

At the opposite end of the scale was the life of debtors at Holyrood. During the French royal family's residence there Lord Maurice Drummond used to take his daughter Clementina to wait on the Comte d'Artois, whom he had known in former days at Versailles. While the Prince, though saddened by the death of Mme de Polastron, was still handsome, some of his courtiers had worn less well. The Comte de Coigny, still with fine features, had become so fat and gouty that he was almost unrecognisable.[29]

In 1814 when the war appeared to have ended, the party left Holyrood and Lord Maurice and his wife and daughter left soon afterwards to live on the Continent, with Lady Campbell (sic) and her son and daughter, de Coigny, the Chevalier de Rebourguille, and the Comte de Bêranger, who was nephew to Clementina's grandmother the Duchesse de Melfort. Their lively eight-day voyage to London was a festive event, and was also cheered by dances and games of whist.

D'Artois used to walk the streets of Edinburgh on Sundays, when it was permissible, 'exceedingly struck with the decorous behaviour of the people, and their regular attendance at public worship'. This seemed to him to imply a heavenly reward, and he felt he ought to emulate the virtuous behaviour by forbidding his court to play tennis. They then fell back on backgammon, but he forbade that too. Inconsolable, they protested strongly. It might not be part of their own religion, replied the inexorable Prince, but 'it is a respect which we owe to their hospitality . . . to give up a trifling gratification that is incompatible with their ideas of sanctity and decorum'.

When he left for France some of his courtiers, too frail, or too poor, to accompany him, were kept supplied by the local gentry with fruit, game and other delicacies. Before some of them set off, Edinburgh made an illumination for the battle of Leipzig, and they lit their windows with a transparency inscribed 'Eternal Gratitude for Generous Hospitality'.[30]

The prolonged stay of the French left a lasting impression, and their vacated rooms were regularly shown to visitors. Charles Nodier in 1822 was much affected, not least because of the simplicity of their accommodation. 'What a subject for historical meditation – the Bourbons taking refuge in the tragical palace of the Stuarts!' The first sight to greet Louis XVI's brother on awaking would have been the portrait of Charles I's family after his execution.[31]

The sanctuary continued to house unfortunate fugitives from creditors. William Chambers, on his lottery ticket rounds, visited this 'cluster of decayed buildings in front and on both sides of the palace, and would nearly always find there distinguished but impoverished Englishmen, 'some of them gaunt, oldish gentlemen, seemingly broken-down men of fashion, wearing big gold spectacles'. Possibly down-and-out gamblers? He used to bring them books from Sutherland's circulating library, and be given 6d for his pains.[32]

When the improvident Tom Moore had to flee his creditors, Samuel Rogers did his best to persuade him to take refuge in Holyrood. 'There he could have lived cheaply and comfortably, with permission to walk about unmolested every Sunday' – and besides, on Sundays he could have dined with Walter Scott, or Jeffrey! He was most put out that Moore '*would* go to Paris', which cost him about £1000 a year and was socially a great loss to his friends.[33]

In 1816 Patrick Fraser Tytler, as an idealistic young advocate, after campaigning for three months won a case to secure 'aliment' for an unfortunate debtor, whose 'obstinate and uncharitable' creditor had forced him into sanctuary in the first place, refusing him even the 'common support' allowed to felons. Until he achieved this victory the poor man actually had to be kept by the charity of his fellow-prisoners.[34]

The sanctuary also appears in fiction. Mrs Johnstone in her rambling *The Saxon and the Gael* (1814) is ready to pack off her extravagant young heir Lord Macallan after he has dissipated his capital in London . . . except that he saves himself by fraud. And the anonymous author of the satire *Edinburgh* (1820) cruelly describes, without disguise, Lady Mary Home and her sister, the amorous unmarried daughters of Captain Francis Douglas. They are descendants of an unsuccessful claimant to the earldom of Marchmont, the 3rd Earl having died in 1794 without male heirs, and had long occupied a Holyrood garret. The author, spitefully describing their immediate family, expresses disgust at their living in such shabby lodgings, 'dishonoring an old and noble name', while their brothers are serving their country. He describes Lady Mary as pretty but her sister as 'dark, coarse, and vulgar looking, with more of a gentleman-like than a lady-like appearance', and neither of them fastidious either in company or morals: 'not difficult of access . . . being equally amorous'. The purpose of this vicious exposé is apparently to shame the decadent ladies into repentance.[35]

Holyrood, while officially providing apartments for the oldest-established Scottish peers, was also the periodical scene of a peers' election. In July 1818 Mrs Grant chaperoned her young ladies to such an occasion, which she observed with her customary needle-like sharpness.

> There was something impressive in seeing the body of Scottish nobles assembled in that long resounding gallery, where the shadows of so many monarchs seem looking on to witness their proceedings. To hear them announced, and see them enter in succession, was something; and the Abjuration oath . . . was what really amused me, – such a barrier against the poor dead Pretender and half-alive Pope. The voting was very tedious, and this great room excessively hot and crowded.

She concluded, 'for me . . . there was only a general notion that I never saw so many plain, ill-dressed lords, or so many beautiful and well-dressed ladies'.[36]

There was one other set of prisoners whose lot, though dismal, was mercifully finite. These were French prisoners of war incarcerated in Edinburgh Castle.

All the while the war was going on in distant countries, people at home were made aware of it by companies of troops and bands parading the streets, the drilling of recruits, who were then packed off overseas, and every now and then the booming of the castle guns roused anxiety until news of some victory was announced in the *Gazette*. A military air pervaded the city as friends and neighbours joined the volunteers. James Nasmyth used to be surprised to see familiar faces 'metamorphosed into soldiers' and drilling on Bruntsfield links – demonstrating their loyalty as well as patriotism. Troops would march past, headed by bands, and windows be thrown up for residents to watch, with 'crowds of boys . . . as usual, hand to hand in front of the drums and fifes', and then 'the pioneers in front, with their leather aprons, their axes and saws, and their big hairy caps and beards'.[37]

When victories were announced, there would be an influx of French prisoners, many of them sent to the castle, where their quarters were a row of low, temporary sheds behind a palisaded yard, separating them from the free world but enabling them to talk to visitors, rather like animals in the recreation part of a zoo.

Charles Dibdin, visiting in 1800, was one who, in the manner of those who went to see lunatics, saw the Frenchmen in their compound. 'The French prisoners . . . performed for us a grand ballet in a capital style . . . I found these prisoners what I never ceased to find Frenchmen, full of design, impudence, and adulation . . . We bought their baubles, saw their show, paid them handsomely, and came away.'[38]

For a time the prisoners were in the charge of handsome Charles Wake, with the Northamptonshire Militia; and the Tait children – one of whom, Charlotte, he was to marry in 1822 – often used to visit. The men had a pathetic appearance, 'more like sickly old-looking boys than men', noted Charlotte, and they relieved their monotonous hours and days in handiwork. They had an apparently generous supply of food which they used to prepare in the enclosed yard, 'potage, ragout, bouilli . . . out of the simplest materials'. Of their rations they kept every meat bone, cleaned, washed and polished to an ivory-like surface, and from these they produced 'marvels of ingenuity: Ladies' workboxes, card-cases, fruit-knives', brooches and other carved work and little figures of women at spinning-wheels. Visitors snapped up the pretty objects with enthusiasm, for a pittance, though not haggling as they felt sorry for the men.

The prisoners were sometimes heard singing, but the sound was dismal in the extreme. When they were repatriated, many actually never returned to their homes.[39]

When the war was thought to have ended in 1814, there occurred 'an extraordinary scene' when they were mustered outside the castle and marched down to the transports at Leith which were to take them home. It was night and the procession was by torchlight. Everyone turned out to watch. The freed prisoners marched through the main streets singing the revolutionary 'Ça ira' and the Marseillaise, even more haggard by torchlight and cheered along by dense crowds lining the streets and hanging from windows, an unforgettable scene.

It was not long before Napoleon was on the loose again, and next summer James Nasmyth, thoroughly impressed by the prisoners' procession, witnessed a different assembly as local citizens gathered in Charlotte Square to see off the garrison of officers and troops. 'It was a fine summer evening . . . The bands were playing at their last performance, "Go where glory waits thee!" The air brought tears to many eyes . . . After many a handshaking the troops marched to the Castle, previous to . . . early embarkation for the Low Countries on the following morning.'[40]

Then came Waterloo. Again the castle guns were fired and anxious crowds gathered, having read of the casualties in the *Gazette.* It was not long before the 42nd Regiment, the Black Watch, returned, having lost two flank companies cut to pieces at Quatre Bras, and the rest having suffered heavily. It was a remnant that had returned to the main battlefield and rallied for victory. Early in 1816 they came back to Edinburgh, marching to the city centre cheered by crowds lining the streets from Musselburgh onwards. By Piershill the throng was so dense that the two miles to the castle took two hours. James Nasmyth, eight years old, was with his parents and sisters, watching from a balcony at the top end of the High Street and listening for the distant cheers that heralded their approach.

> The High Street was wedged with people excited and anxious. There seemed scarcely room for a regiment to march through them. The house-tops and windows were crowded with spectators . . . The high-gabled houses reaching as far as the eye could see, the crown of St Giles', the Tron, the picturesque lands.
>
> At last the head of the gallant band appeared. The red coats gradually wedged their way through the crowd, amidst the ringing of bells and the cheers of the spectators . . . every house-top was in a fever of excitement. As the red line passed our balcony, with Colonel Dick at its head . . . the red-and-white plumes, the tattered colours riddled with bullets, the glittering bayonets, were seen amidst the crowd that thronged round the gallant heroes, amidst tears and cheers and hand-shakings and shouts of excitement . . . the soldiers being almost hidden amongst the crowd. At last they passed, the pipers and drums playing a Highland march; and the 42nd slowly entered the Castle.

This, to James who remembered it, was always one of Edinburgh's most extraordinary scenes.[41]

It was one which may even have been witnessed by some of the more privileged prisoners in the Tolbooth.

38
ARTISTS AND MUSICIANS

[Turner sketching during the King's visit:] 'The gaiety and clamour, the firing of guns . . . the bonnets and kilts, . . . and the universal excitement of a national holiday . . . The admiral's barge, the men-of-war – he even stops to sketch a porter reading a newspaper.'

W. Thornbury, *The Life of J. M. W. Turner, RA*, London, 1862, I.368

'A general love of the arts has increased, is increasing, and cannot be diminished.'

Edinburgh Annual Register, 1819, 252

When David Roberts returned to Edinburgh from his Scone assignment at the beginning of 1816 (see Part Two, p. 247), a friend suggested that he might find work as a painter at the Circus building. At this time it was doing well under the 'very gentlemanly' proprietor Mr John Bannister, who expanded its shows to plays and pantomimes. The bashful David, faint with anxiety, climbed the stair of 5 Nicolson Street with his drawings, and when arrived, hardly dared ring the bell. Bannister received him kindly, however, approved his drawings, and commissioned him to paint 'a set of wings for a palace'. David bought canvas, laid it on his dining-room floor, ground his colours and set to work. Thus he had achieved the height of his current ambition – to be a scene painter.

All he knew of the art was from watching with delight from the Theatre Royal's shilling gallery such shows as *Aladdin* and *The Forty Thieves*, of which he used to make sketches as soon as he got home. His work was approved, Bannister was kind, and at the end of the season employed him for a year, so that he travelled to England with the company for 25 shillings a week and his travelling expenses. To his parents' well-founded distress he set off with the rest in a caravan – but luckily for him on the very first night the landlady urged him to leave the party, as the life was held in such low esteem. From then on David travelled separately. After a season at Carlisle, Newcastle and in Yorkshire he returned to Edinburgh in January 1817.[1]

Bannister now entered into partnership with Corri and the house reopened as the Pantheon, equipped with a stage as well as a ring for equestrian shows. But it soon failed, and in May they closed. The luckless Bannister took his company to Portugal, failed there as well, and he died ruined.[2]

David then reluctantly returned to house-painting, working with Gillespie Graham at Abercairny, and later at Condie on the River Earn. At his parents' wish he again returned to Edinburgh in January 1818, and signed on with a well-known decorative painter, John Jackson, 'a sincere lover and patron of art'. First he worked at Lord Lauderdale's, Dunbar House, then at Craigcrook for Francis Jeffrey, and his imitation of woods and marbles earned him praise. 'I painted the library of Jeffrey imitation of dark old oak, to match some carvings that he had purchased belonging to Stirling Castle.'

Meanwhile he improved his leisure time by drawing scenes and buildings, which the kind Jackson approved – but fretted all the time at not being a scene-painter. But a London company had now taken the Pantheon and brought their own artists, and only when they left in July, and Corri wanted the house re-decorated, was David re-engaged at a salary of 25 shillings. Once free from Jackson's job he was, with great glee and excitement, to work exclusively for the Corri brothers at the start of the winter season.

He was now working with Corri's chief painter Mr Dearlove, an ingenious creator of paper helmets, banners and other useful props of the sort used in shows, but not much of an artist in the true sense. As the building had no painting room, they had to work on the stage at night, for rehearsals were going on most of the day and shows in the evening. David, who could sleep in the early evenings, was able to turn up fresh for work, but Dearlove was usually exhausted after daily rehearsals and acting as well as painting, and after telling David what to do he would collapse. Then he would come back and spoil the job with 'finishing touches'. One day David managed to pack him off to sleep at home, and once on his own, painted and rolled up a scene of Rome, with a speed and skill that astonished everyone when it was lowered for the performance. His friend Monro, the stage-manager, learning that when the theatre closed he would have no choice but to return yet again to housepainting, promised to recommend him to the Glasgow Theatre. David sceptically went back to Jackson – but only six weeks later received an offer from Monro for a job at Glasgow for 30 shillings.

A week earlier, David had been given permission to study in the Trustees' Academy under Andrew Wilson, and had copied four heads. He was proud of his outline drawing, and told Wilson so – to receive the salutary reply, 'Ah! in nature there are no outlines.'

Once in Glasgow he unfortunately fell ill, ran out of money and had to be helped by his mother and Monro; then things began to go right. Most of the Glasgow scenery was by Nasmyth, which David carefully studied, and his own work so benefited that when William Murray and Mrs Henry Siddons came to act for two nights, Murray was so impressed with his scenery that he borrowed him to paint two scenes for *The Heart of Midlothian,* which were much approved.

It was now 1820: David married and sent his new wife to stay with his parents, and secured a painting contract from Murray at the Theatre Royal, £2 a week 'but find your own colour-boy'. He completed a tour with the Glasgow company, in spite of rather shabby treatment by the manager, Mason. Owed several weeks' salary, he had to set out on foot from Dumfries to Edinburgh, carrying his simple 'traps', and covered more than seventy miles in a day and a half. His new Edinburgh job started in October.[3]

In the summer of 1821 Roberts painted scenery for *Henry IV, Part II*, which ambitiously introduced a painting of the recent coronation of George IV. Meanwhile he became friendly with the painter Clarkson Stanfield,[4] who had arrived with 'a very powerful company' under William Barrymore at the reopened Pantheon, and brought a letter of introduction to David from his father James Field Stanfield, an actor and author at the Glasgow Theatre.

Stanfield, whose fine Pantheon scenery was much admired, was very helpful to David, especially as he had London experience. Paintings which he exhibited at Edinburgh that summer were much talked of, and he encouraged David to submit too, but he was rejected. However he persevered and the following year he submitted three, all of them shown and two selling for 50 shillings each, to Baron Clark Rattray and James Stewart of Dunearn. For this he had worked hard enough, painting by candle-light after finishing at the theatre.

He was now earning 37/6d. nett at the theatre (the other half-crown going to the colour-boy), and was set up in 'a snug little house' in the Canongate. Occasionally he could sell a picture, or 'a transparent window-blind', and when, after painting scenery for the Christmas pantomime which Barrymore produced for William Murray, he was urged to try his luck in London, he felt that he was better off working in Edinburgh.

He had another, secret, assignment for Alexander, the actor whose parts included Rashleigh in *The Heart of Midlothian*, who having quarrelled with Murray (a not infrequent event with his company), took on 'the minor theatre' in Glasgow. David painted the scenery at night, some of it at home, packed it on long barrels or rollers, and Alexander and his brother carried it on their shoulders across the Calton Hill to the 'Convening Room' at the Pantheon, and thence transported it to Glasgow. For this job Alexander deferred payment as he was low in funds, offering a few pounds on account, and David generously let him leave the debt until times were better. Alexander did well at the Glasgow theatre, but never paid him.

In the late summer of 1822, when Murray laid off Roberts for a few months, he seized the chance of approaching Barrymore, who was now at the Royal Coburg Theatre in London, was given an offer, and in August sailed on the Leith smack. In the autumn he returned to fulfil his engagement with Murray at £3 a week, then packed everything and moved with his wife to London, much to his parents' sorrow. This voyage took three tedious weeks and they arrived so late that David lost a promised job with the actor Robert Elliston at Drury Lane.

But he was now established in London, had plenty of theatre work, and before long was exhibiting at the Royal Academy.[5]

Alexander Nasmyth was really a man of parts. Having started with portraits but fallen foul of Henry Dundas, 'King' of Scotland, for Whiggish sympathies, attending the Fox dinners and befriending reformers, he found commissions fell off. Nasmyth then turned to landscape painting, for which, fairly standardised though his compositions were, he became known as 'the Father of landscape painting in Scotland'.

He was also commissioned for 'improving' landscapes, siting mansions and romanticising old ones. In his enthusiasm for preserving old trees for more than their timber value he was ahead of his time, and he made judicious use of them in planning a landscape.

Nasmyth, who was a kind encourager of younger artists, set up an art class at his house at 47 York Place, in a spacious top-floor studio, with a fine view extending from Stirling to the Bass Rock, and he designed a belvedere on the roof, and a separate workroom equipped with tools for his ingenious devices.

One way and another, as painter, architect, mechanical designer of gadgets, in addition to his success in theatrical design, he worked from morning till night.

During the theatre's more adventurous phase after Henry Siddons's death in 1815, Nasmyth was much in demand for scenery. In 1810 he had painted new scenery for *The Winter's Tale,* in which Mrs Siddons appeared, and in 1814 for *Aladdin*, with Mr Whitmore from Covent Garden. He now had a series of the Waverley novels to paint for, as adaptation followed adaptation – though now painting landscapes rather more than for the theatre. His last major such commission was sixteen scenes for *The Heart of Midlothian* in 1819, which opened in late February 1820: six of the scenes were twenty-four feet long. Nasmyth respected the medium and felt no snobbery for it, apparently much enjoying his commissions.[6]

Always deeply interested in Edinburgh's architectural development, he was professionally consulted over the layout. His son James (one of eleven children) records how he used to 'stroll about, wherever building was in progress, or new roads were being laid out', to watch with an enthusiasm inherited from his own father, who had begun many of the buildings. Here his artist's eye was unerring.

'His admirable knack of modelling the contour of the natural surface of the ground, and applying it to proposed new roads or new buildings, was striking and characteristic' and he would discuss it with the architects and builders. This especially applied to the downhill extension from Queen Street as the Second New Town progressed, and according to James Nasmyth the grateful magistrates actually granted him £200 along with a complimentary letter, addressed to him as 'Alexander Nasmyth, Architect' (1815).[7]

Nasmyth's sole surviving plan of a town garden was for his proposals for the Dean estate (Sir John Nisbet's), the area north of the Water of Leith, with an asymmetrical Gothic towered house, also with a prospect tower. He designed irregular tree patterns, a spiral walk from house to road, and perhaps a flower garden. At Nesbit's request for an extension linking his estate with the edge of Edinburgh, he created access by a new Dean Bridge and approach roads. There is no record of this, though James Nasmyth claims that the bridge was built under James Jardine's superintendence, and that Telford later merely widened it and added parapets.

Finally in Edinburgh, Nasmyth made a proposal for the Mound, linking Old and New Towns, adapting the old tenements and designing 'twin-domed palaces flanking a grand city gate' – recalling the twin churches of the Piazza del Popolo in Rome, and built on existing bases. According to Walter Scott, this would have been 'the most superb thing in Europe', but prohibitively expensive.[8]

Nasmyth's friends included Sir James Hall of Dunglass, the amateur geologist, whom he had met in Italy, and who in winter lived with his family in George Street. Sir James, a keen student of art and science, was among those who painted in Nasmyth's studio, and Nasmyth helped him with his essay, *On the origin of Gothic Architecture,* and made most of its illustrations (1813).

After Nelson's death, Nasmyth offered a design for the proposed monument on Calton Hill. It was approved, and subscriptions were soon secured, but when the estimate was found slightly to exceed the funds, 'a nominally cheaper design was privately adopted. It was literally a job' – dismissed by his son James as a 'vulgar, churn-like monument . . . inverted spy-glass', whose cost in fact exceeded that of Nasmyth's proposal.[9]

Hugh ('Grecian') Williams (1773–1829), a friend of Professor Playfair's son the architect William Playfair, who owned a number of his paintings made in Athens, had travelled extensively in Italy and Greece until 1818.

In February 1822 he held an exhibition of his own works, watercolours of Greek ruins and scenery, each accompanied by a classical quotation chosen by Professor Pillans. 'A most beautiful display of art and of taste', wrote Henry Cockburn, and should easily cover the £200 or so expenses and make him a profit. 'It is becoming a fashionable lounge', he wrote, and Williams needed only 'some poor blind, snuffy old, card-playing haridan of a Dowager to take him up'. The opening ('glorious . . . God-like') was celebrated by a dinner for twelve, 'being the 9 muses and 3 graces': Jeffrey, John Murray, Rutherford, Pillans, Joseph Bell, Cunningham, Williams, Leonard Horner, Cockburn and a few others. 'Surrounded by Greek scenes . . . nobody but ourselves in the house – had we not a night of it? . . . and had you but seen the two professors, Pillans and Bell [appointed that day Hume's successor as Professor of Scottish Law], engaged, with Jeff piping as a little Pan, with a Pyrrhic dance!'[10]

On return from Athens Williams had charmed Mrs Grant of Laggan by bringing her from his travels a wreath of ivy from Virgil's tomb, and a chaplet of Attic olive from Delphi, both presented through the medium of 'an enthusiastic friend'.[11]

Early orphaned, Williams had been brought up by his grandmother and her second husband, Louis Ruffini, who lived at Cragside, an old house adjoining the King's Park (long demolished), supposedly the seat of the laird of Dumbiedykes in *The Heart of Midlothian*.

In 1820 Williams published a two-volume account of his travels in the form of letters to the talented minor artist, the Rev. John Thomson of Duddingston. According to his friend Henry Cockburn, he was 'by far the most beautiful painter in watercolours that Scotland has yet produced'. Williams died in 1829, 'the severest loss' to the Arts in Scotland, according to Cockburn.[12]

In the contemporary passion for drawing such parallels, the clergyman Thomson was known as 'the Scottish Ruysdael'. He painted quietly in his manse, landscapes, of all the surrounding places, and in summer the Highlands, quite unconcerned with sales or prices, though he was so admired for his strength and originality that high prices were sometimes offered.[13]

The three artists Andrew Geddes, David Wilkie and William Collins were born within five years of each other and, after starting in Edinburgh, studied at the Royal Academy in London, where they became friends. Geddes was the son of an Auditor of Excise, a man of taste and a collector but strict and forbidding as a father. He acquired rare prints through the dealer Thomas Phillips, and was a friend of the distinguished collector Colin Macfarquhar, so that Andrew from boyhood knew the fascination of the arrival of portfolios of rare books and prints from London, and the thrill of their unpacking. He used to accompany his father to sales and sometimes himself spent all his savings (a shilling or two) on some not very good copy. The auctioneer, Martin, took a fancy to the eager boy, and might even start the bidding with a price within his range, nodding in his direction – or alternatively warning him if it were too expensive.

At nine Andrew went to the High School, and became a favourite of the masters in spite of drawing caricatures of them. Oddly enough, his father disapproved of art, or artists, as a profession, so Andrew practised drawing and painting secretly, in his bedroom from first light on summer mornings. He met and was befriended by the advocate John Clerk, who also saw his talent and let him in any time to study his collection, lending him paintings to copy, to his father's astonishment – even Old Master drawings when Andrew was only twelve or thirteen; and so good were his copies that some were later taken for originals.

After leaving the University Andrew entered his father's office, much against his own wishes, but having no choice. But as the office closed at 3 o'clock, he was free from the early afternoon. For nearly five years he worked there conscientiously, so much in awe of his parent that he never dared ask for his salary, nominally £50, but got by on his pocket-money.

He made a visit to London with his father's friend Anthony Stewart, a miniature painter, and when his father's death in 1809 left him entirely free at the age of twenty-six, following the advice of Clerk and others he threw up the job and went to study at the Royal Academy in London. Here he met Benjamin Haydon and was fortunate enough from the start to have a seat beside David Wilkie, with whom he became lifelong friends. And he was now able to indulge his passion for Old Masters, especially Rembrandt, going to the sales and visiting all the collections.

After a few years he returned to Edinburgh, where John Clerk assisted in his progress, even commissioning him to buy paintings. He set up as a professional painter, especially of portraits of any size, building up a large practice. Between 1810 and 1814 his commissions included Lord Hermand, Lord Buchan, Sit John Dick of Prestonfield and his wife, and William Allan, who had long been travelling in Russia and returned in 1814. Allan elected to be painted in Caucasian dress.[14]

Geddes set up his own printing-press and for years produced etchings, returning to London from time to time for the sales, where he kept an apartment for some years in Conduit Street. When in Edinburgh he still lived with his mother and sisters.

Geddes's portrait of Wilkie was considered the only true likeness of his fellow-painter; among other celebrities he painted were Dr Chalmers, Henry Mackenzie and Francis Jeffrey – all later engraved. On the strength of all this he applied to become an RA, and was so hurt at being ignored that for ten years he could not be persuaded to try again.

The discovery of the Scottish regalia in 1818 induced Geddes to commemorate that momentous event, and his painting which introduced portraits of many leading men, including of course Scott, was exhibited in both Edinburgh and London. As, however, it found no takers, Geddes cut it up and sold it as separate portraits.

At the height of his success, rather to friends' disapproval, Geddes moved to London. In 1819 he was invited to accompany George Oswald, Rector of Glasgow University and now an invalid, on foreign travels, but when all was planned, to his great grief Oswald's health seriously deteriorated and he died, losing Geddes an unparalleled opportunity.[15]

John Lockhart's alter ego 'Peter' describes in detail William Allan's studio, several flights up in Parliament Close, 'the most picturesque painting-room, I fancy, in Europe'. Allan had brought many trophies back from his eastern travels, now adorning his studio. 'The wainscoat is completely covered with rich clusters of military accoutrements, Turkish scimitars, Circassian bows and quivers, hauberks of twisted mail from Caucasus, daggers, dirks, javelins, and all manner of long unwieldy fowling-pieces – Georgian, Armenian, and Tartar . . . in circles, having shields and targets of bone, brass, and leather for their centres. Helmets, of all kinds and sizes, are hung from the roof . . . with most gorgeous draperies of shawls, turbans, and saddle-cloths', like some barbarian palace. Allan himself harmonised with his setting in 'a dark Circassian vest, the breast of which was loaded with innumerable quilted lurking-places now occupied with the harmless shafts of hair-pencils' and in his hand the stalk of a Turkish pipe which he used as a 'pallet-guard'. In appearance he was black-haired and swarthy, his hair tufted, his brows shaggy and eyes large and sparkling, 'speaking witnesses of the life of roaming and romantic adventure'.

His most famous painting then in the studio, was the 'Sale of Circassian Captives to a Turkish Bashaw' (later sold to the Earl of Wemyss and March), and most of his work was in exotic mode – ravishing women, 'dark and savage men . . . Skies of burning blue . . . Cities of flat-roofed houses . . . huge white domes and gilded cupolas'.[16]

At this time there were many meetings between Scots visiting London, Scottish painters working there, and English who later visited Edinburgh. The 'anecdotal' painter Charles Leslie, who had been born of American parents in London in 1794 and lived in America from the age of five, had returned to London in 1811 when still under seventeen, to study at the Royal Academy. In 1821 he became an ARA – in 1826 an RA.[17]

Leslie met Walter Scott in London in 1820, at breakfast at Washington Irving's, and again in 1821. Scott called on him to look at his painting 'May Day', which he praised, and was 'particularly kind and friendly', making suggestions about the painting, such as that Leslie add some archers. 'His hearty kindness of manner is particularly delightful', he told his sister Betsey (20 April). In 1820 Scott had been sitting to Sir Thomas Lawrence, just knighted and having just succeeded Benjamin West as President of the Royal

Academy. So (wrote Leslie to Washington Irving on 2 April), 'we shall now have a more intellectual portrait of him than any of the others'.

Turner, who was engaged on his contribution to *Provincial Antiquities of Scotland*, a set of views of Scottish castles by different artists, came to Edinburgh in October 1818, from where he sketched Roslin, Borthwick and Dunbar, but at this stage Walter Scott, who was to write the text, was the only person to see them. At first Scott did not care for the painter, considering his fingers as 'itchy' as they were 'ingenious', but he was later persuaded to allow him to illustrate his works.[18]

Altogether Turner did not make a good personal impression. The Edinburgh Schetkys invited him to breakfast, and he was certainly 'very gracious' about both Alick's and Jane's work, but they were put off by his cold manner.

'We intended to have had a joyous evening on his account, but finding him such a stick, we did not think the pleasure of showing him to our friends would be adequate to the trouble and expense.' Worse, he accepted a dinner invitation from the portraitist William Nicolson, 'and after preparing a feast and having 10 fine fellows to make merry with him, Turner never made his appearance'.[19]

'Alick', Schetky's brother, was a doctor and amateur marine painter, and was working in Rochester. He offered Turner a loan of his sketch of the *Fighting Temeraire.*[20]

The Rev. John Thomson of Duddingston contributed eleven plates to Scott's *Provincial Antiquities and Picturesque Scenery of Scotland,* eventually published in 1826 by John and Arthur Arch, Quaker booksellers in Cornhill. Turner supplied twelve plates, Schetky, Nasmyth and others the rest.

The work had been published in parts, and did not sell well, but there was evidently something to be got for a painter in Scotland. In 1819 Turner sent Robert Stevenson at Baxter's Place his drawing of the Bell Rock Lighthouse (early July) by the smack *Swift*, a difficult subject on which he would welcome Stevenson's advice. He valued it at 30 guineas.[21] The drawing was used as the frontispiece to Stevenson's *Account of the Bell Rock Lighthouse* in 1824, engraved not by George Cooke, who was too busy, but by J. Horsbrugh.

The prospect of work during the royal visit was a tempting one. Turner enjoyed recording national events, and had now met a number of Scottish artists both in London and Edinburgh, ranging from Nasmyth and William Allan to Wilkie, Collins and Geddes. Sailing up the coast, Turner in Edinburgh arrived in advance of the royal visit, on or about 7 August, and was accordingly there on the quayside when the Royal Squadron docked on 14 August, standing alongside Scott's friend James Skene, the amateur topographical painter, and other artists sketching the landing on Custom House Quay.[22]

Francis Chantrey, though neither living in Edinburgh nor much visiting – he was born in Sheffield in 1781 and at sixteen persuaded his family to apprentice him to a Sheffield wood carver named Ramsay – became well known through the statues he made for Edinburgh.

At twenty-one Chantrey had bought out of his indentures and, through a local artist Raphael Smith, took up painting while still making his living as a carver. A fever caught in Ireland lost him his hair – like Robertson and Thomas Campbell.

He began to succeed as a portrait painter, exhibited at the Royal Academy in 1804, but then turned chiefly to sculpture. He married a cousin in 1811, and through meetings with well-known radical activists like Horne Tooke and Sir Francis Burdett, and connections made through them, built up a successful practice in portrait busts. Friendship with Lord Meadowbank (Allan Maconochie) brought the commission of a bust of President Blair, of the committee on which Lord Meadowbank was chairman. He also created the statue of Lord Melville for the column in St Andrew Square. In February 1818 he was elected an FRS, and that autumn visited Edinburgh. In 1819 he travelled to Italy.

When George Street became punctuated with statuary it was Chantrey who designed the figures, including Lord Chief Baron Robert Dundas, the bronze statue of William Pitt and later King George IV.[23]

Among Chantrey's friends were Scott, Southey, Samuel Rogers and many academics and churchmen. His work was generally praised by the nobility of either party. Some wrote him off as an 'imitator', and indeed he did imitate, but his personal insight into his sitters and the naturalism and simplicity of his work made him extremely popular, especially for his figures of children.

In 1821 the foundation stone of the monument to Lord Melville was laid in St Andrew Square, eleven years after his death, with subscriptions from the Navy (in view of his last public office as Treasurer to the Navy). The ceremony was witnessed by a number of people. As residents of the square were alarmed at the prospect of a high column in this hitherto enclosed space so near their houses, the designer William Burn was advised by the engineer Robert Stevenson on how to secure the foundation. The work was newly completed when the King arrived on his visit in August 1822.

The 136-foot-high Doric column was a simplified version of Trajan's column in Rome, fluting taking the place of the original's sculpture. Chantrey modelled the figure of Melville which eventually surmounted the top, carved by Robert Forrest and not set up until 1828.[24]

Tom Moore, who visited Chantrey's studio in London in 1821, noted 'his *atelier* full of mind; never saw such a set of thinking *heads* as his busts: Walter Scott's very remarkable from the length of the head. The eyes, Chantrey says, 'are usually taken as a centre . . . but in Scott's head the upper part is even longer than the lower'.[25]

Everybody of course knew David Wilkie. He and Chantrey were complete opposites, and some believed they disliked each other: but in the many times they met they were never known to disparage one another. Chantrey much admired Wilkie's grouping, expressions, way of conveying a story, and his chiaroscuro; as for the two men's personalities, the solemn Wilkie was a great contrast to the jolly bonhomous Chantrey, keen fisherman and sportsman. So far were they from mutual hostility that Wilkie appointed Chantrey one of his executors.

Wilkie, 'argumentative, unclassical, prudent, poor and simple' in Benjamin Haydon's view, was now known in London as 'the Scottish Teniers'. Archibald Constable's friend David Hunter when visiting in 1807 had called at his studio 'and found a number of people there waiting to *see anything of him*' for he was established above others – rather unfairly to Benjamin West, thought Hunter, who had just met the President. Wilkie stayed for months together with his patron, Lord Mulgrave. He was still only twenty-two, 'red-haired – a good-natured, unaffected, modest, unconceited, simple, agreeable young lad', wrote Hunter as if he felt this the highest praise.[26]

He made less impression on Cyrus Redding, who met both him and Haydon in Plymouth in 1810 at the King's Jubilee, when they were staying with Haydon's father, a printer-bookseller. 'Wilkie disappointed me. Perfectly self-possessed, he was destitute of life and energy, pale almost to delicacy . . . Not bashful or exactly clownish in manners, but simply awkward. His Scotch accent was decided.' He spoke only on commonplace subjects, did not seem to want to talk about art and was inclined to 'coarse after-dinner allusion' – a Scottish trait, observes Redding censoriously; and with that grave expression of his, the effect was 'rather like a Quakeress singing licentious songs'.

Haydon, on the other hand, 'energetic, fiercely ambitious, full of grand ideas and romantic hopes', Redding found overflowing with talk on art, views, the Elgin marbles. There were ludicrous scenes as he tried to teach the awkward Wilkie to swim. Full of energy, he worked thirteen or fourteen hours a day, while Wilkie, devoted to art, seemed oblivious to scenery, and in painting most interested in humble cottage scenes.[27]

Wilkie went to Paris with Haydon, along with half the world, in the summer of 1814 – and thought the Luxembourg Gardens 'much finer' than Vauxhall, and the less magnificent Tivoli Gardens superior in such amusements as rope-dancing and fireworks. In 1816 he visited Holland with the engraver Abraham Raimbach, and did not return to Scotland until 1817.

Now thoroughly sought-after, he was 'quite hurried about', visited Roslin with Joseph Lister and his family, and with William Allan went to Holyrood. The painter-minister Rev. John Thomson of Duddingston was suggested as a good fellow-traveller to the Highlands, but when he called Wilkie found he had gone away, or would probably have joined him – his wife too, 'also a great enthusiast'. He therefore travelled alone, stopping on the way at Kinneil to call on Dugald Stewart, who received him very kindly; and visited Glasgow which, he wrote to his sister, was 'really a magnificent place'. 'There are some of the streets here that would make a street in the city of London look like mere trumpery.' While there he saw a good deal of Dr Chalmers, who accompanied him to Lanark.

Wilkie had already written to Scott, who recommended places to visit in Argyll, and invited him to stay at Abbotsford on his return, via the Blucher coach, which ran three times weekly to within a mile of Abbotsford, tickets from the Black Bull in Leith Walk.

Wilkie returned from his Highland tour in October.[28]

At Abbotsford he met James Hogg, the Duke and Duchess of Buccleuch, Adam Fergusson and others. It was then that he noted how physically impossible it seemed for Scott to find a moment to write novels, and that even his family seemed in the dark as to whether the Great Unknown were he.

In 1820 and 1821 he saw Scott in London, first at the sculptor Francis Chantrey's, then bringing him to see his painting. Another time, after a dinner Scott told him stories 'of the marvellous kind, connected with popular superstitions', a subject dear to the novelist's heart. On Scott's 1821 visit, coming to look at Wilkie's 'The Pensioners', he seemed pleased with the group portrait of himself and family, but suggested that on Wilkie's next time in Scotland he might try for a better likeness of Lady Scott. Wilkie's next time, as it happened, was during the royal visit with his fellow-artist William Collins, which kept him fully occupied and on which he made detailed notes.[29]

William Collins, Wilkie's junior by five years, was born in London to a poor Irish father, and by his talent was able to study at the Royal Academy. In 1812, when he was twenty-four, his father died. Collins's work was encouraged by several connoisseurs, Sir George Beaumont, Sir Thomas Heathcote and others. In 1818 he met Wordsworth and Southey on a visit to the Lakes, and went on to Edinburgh with Francis Chantrey and his wife in August. Here he heard 'excellent discourses', from Dr Alison in the morning and Dr Brunton on the same afternoon, sketched with the Chantreys at Leith but they were driven off by the rain, breakfasted at Roslin and then walked along the river to Lasswade, and next evening was again wet through when climbing Arthur's Seat. He visited Queen Mary's apartments at Holyrood, dined with the Raeburns, sketched the castle, and having thoroughly done justice by Edinburgh left by the 2 o'clock coach for Keswick to revisit the Beaumonts and the Wordsworths.

Friendly though he was with Wilkie, Collins was well aware of his natural formality and reserve, which often misled strangers into thinking him haughty. Wilkie indeed could not mix easily with company, and only relaxed into his true warmth and gaiety when with fellow-artists and close friends. Then, 'as if by magic' he became playful, animated in voice and with a ready laugh. He was full of anecdotes and humour. He had an odd habit of saying 'Relly!' to almost everything, and one day when he and Chantrey were dining with Collins, Chantrey ventured to draw his attention to it. 'Now, for instance, suppose I was giving you an account of any interesting matter, you would constantly say, "Relly!"'

'Relly!' exclaimed an astonished Wilkie.

Collins had for several years been attached to Harriet Geddes, whose sister Mrs Carpenter was a portrait-painter. They had met in 1814 at a ball given by artist friends, but Collins's uncertain prospects and present poverty kept him long from 'declaring' himself. They met for some time in society, and only in 1821, meeting in London by chance and both still single, Collins dared to speak out. His prospects had considerably improved, and he risked an engagement. His mother, who in principle approved, urged further caution, and even withheld her consent for a year. (Collins was now thirty-three.) England was restricted by a 'vexatious Marriage Act, requiring various oaths and attestations from parents and guardians', and Scotland, with its lax marriage laws, seemed to beckon as a welcome haven. Collins was thinking seriously about this when he, Wilkie and Andrew Geddes joined in a hilarious coach-journey to Scotland in August 1822 with the prospect of making paintings of King George's visit.[30]

Two other artists make a contrast: one, a Scot, by his social diffidence which seems to have hampered his progress in England, the other an Englishman who, unusually, does little but complain about his Scottish sitters.

John Henning, who was to make a career in England in portrait sculpture, maintained an Edinburgh link through correspondence with Mrs Grant. Born in Renfrewshire in 1771, he started as a cabinet-maker, turned to portrait busts, and was first invited to work in Edinburgh, where his simplicity and native candour, combined with his creative power, made him a favourite. But Edinburgh was a small society, and by 1811 he had modelled everyone available. He was esteemed by Dugald Stewart, Scott, Jeffrey, Mrs Fletcher; all took 'delight in his artless conversation' and admired his genius.

On advice he then tried his luck in London, the better to maintain his young family, but few of those to whom he was recommended were still there, and at first only the Marquess of Stafford employed him. Mrs Grant, who took an almost maternal interest in him, begged Sir Walter Farquhar to commission a head, or Henning's insecurity might be 'too much even for his cheerful and buoyant spirit'. She also promised to introduce Henning to Charles Grant, of the India Office, and Francis Horner appears to have helped him.

Over the next few years Mrs Grant wrote to Henning encouragingly and not always tactfully with exhortations and advice, while he was achieving introductions to the Princess of Wales, Princess Charlotte and the Marquess of Lansdowne. She sympathised with his afflictions, calmed his frustrated feelings. 'Mrs Fletcher took the deepest interest in your letter . . . a fair and lively transcript of a mind softened by feeling, lighted up by genius.' Unwittingly patronising, she continued to load this man of humble background with uplifting advice. She warned him not to be too easily wounded or resent intended civilities from 'the Tragic Queen' – Mrs Siddons, who in Edinburgh had spoken of him with nothing but kindness. His real difficulties, she explained, were more likely to arise less from his humble status than from the jealousy of other artists, one of whom (naming no names) might be the means of his losing Princess Charlotte's commission.

On 20 June 1812 Mrs Grant was advising how Henning should address the Princess, and again unintentionally condescending, explained, 'The conversation of one who is so entirely a man of nature as yourself, and the plain and harmless sincerity in all you say and do, must be to her an amusing novelty.' She warned him, however, to put his views 'merely as opinions, not as dogmas', and consoled him that 'your native benevolence and general good feeling will . . . stand you in the stead of polish'. A month later she was again cheering his solitary gloom.

The Princesses were pleased with Henning, and in May 1813 Mrs Grant was reporting to a New England friend that the Princess of Wales had indeed taken a fancy to his conversation, so he was in fashion.

Mrs Grant had meanwhile been overseeing the care of his children, who lived in Edinburgh with an aunt, and early that May she packed them off to join their father in London. She also lent him money, and in April 1814, still cheering, insisted that they cancel the debt and not think of repayment; besides, she was seeking a subsidy from another source. Again she exhorted him to regard his rustic manners as more an asset than a liability.

He continued to rail over his perhaps largely imaginary miseries, however, until by December Mrs Grant became quite impatient, repeating her intention of the £50 as a gift, not a loan, and of his manners as asset, not obstacle.[31]

This seems to be the end of her well-meant exhortations. It was probably hard for anyone in her social situation to understand the doubts and insecurities of a presumably timid man of Henning's background, catapulted by his talents and career ambitions into a milieu in which he felt totally unequipped. Once his portrait busts became fashionable, he had rich clients and a successful career.

The rather carping Englishman who unwillingly set up in Edinburgh was Thomas Uwins, born in Pentonville in 1782 and at fifteen apprenticed to Benjamin Smith of Judd Place, a not very talented engraver. Uwins learned more from the chief apprentice, William Holl, but he disliked engraving and after his working hours from 9 till 7 he would draw in overtime, and at tea would even sketch the tea-things. One of Smith's neighbours was the actor Barrymore, who generously handed out theatre tickets to the youths.

Uwins studied at the Royal Academy in Sir Charles Bell's anatomy class, specialised in miniatures, became a member of the Water-Colour Society in 1810 and was its secretary several times. In 1815 he went to the Lake District with introductions to Wordsworth and Southey, in 1817 went to France, and in 1818–19 was in financial difficulties. He made illustrations of Scott's works, which proved useful as gifts when he was abroad, and corresponded with him.[32]

The sculptor Samuel Joseph introduced Uwins to the Wilsons of Highbury, and on an accidental meeting urged him to try his luck in Edinburgh, where he himself was now established and doing well with good connections. Similarly the enterprising Finsbury bookseller James Lackington commissioned him to undertake orders for him in Edinburgh, for which he would get up to £100.

In the autumn of 1821, therefore, Uwins went to Scotland to seek portrait commissions. He was not very satisfied. In Dunkeld, where he seems to have gone first, all were friendly, but elsewhere the Scots seemed rude and haughty. He was offended with the 'vulgarity and insolence of the people of Edinburgh'. Even in the country meanness showed: everything was enclosed, and they charged large fees (in the Perth area) to travellers for looking at the scenery.[33]

Waiting for the execution of Lackington's commissions, he was tempted to take on portraits, and thus raise himself from his small, ill-paid London jobs which only damaged his sight, provided he could succeed with 'the cautious, suspicious, calculating Scot' in a land where artists 'are something thicker than three in a bed' and not much in demand.

Although Uwins was in Edinburgh during the King's visit, he got nothing out of it except a few transparencies. For a year after he settled there he had nothing but difficulty. The chief commission which had tempted him here was abandoned, and it would have kept him while he was canvassing for jobs. His first success was with Mrs Fry's sister Miss Gurney, who became a friend, and also knew many of his own friends; but when he started on two small portraits of her his long-suffering eyes gave out. He therefore had to give up trying small jobs and must stick to 'life'.[34]

That summer, however, he heard the Genevese minister the Rev. Caesar Malan, preaching in French. Uwins liked the Swiss, and the minister appealed to him, so that he used to follow him around trying to take a sketch under great difficulty, in rooms full of people, as Malan's time was short and he was much sought after. Uwins's success led to subsequent 'connections', especially with Lady Carnegie, 'a sort of Lady Huntingdon here', and also to Lord Leven's family, with the opportunity to visit Melville Castle which he loved for its 'heavenly calm'. He also engraved and published a small head of Malan, for the benefit of his school in Geneva.

In the spring of 1823 with the sitting of the General Assembly he reckoned that he would be unlikely to persuade any kirk members to sit for him, and in any case all normal business was suspended, so he made a short trip to London. But he soon returned because he was at last getting 'connection and popularity' starting with cheap chalk portraits at five guineas, which he had raised to seven in January and was now about to raise to ten – a move which always led to a 'momentary suspension' of business. It was almost a pity that everyone so liked his chalk heads that nobody wanted an oil portrait for 10 guineas, which would be less laborious to turn out.

But there were plenty of rivals for oil painting, none for chalk. 'Making old women young and ugly women handsome is now my daily occupation', wrote the still disgruntled artist to his brother. 'To keep it up is no easy matter, I can assure you.'[35]

George Combe visited his studio, and, seeing an unfinished portrait of the artist's brother Dr David (a stranger to him), gave him such an accurate description that Uwins warmly took up the science of phrenology. Combe noted that in Uwins's own face 'imitation and secrecy', both necessary to an artist, were 'large'.

Uwins had a premonition of his mother's death, and returned to London in the winter of 1823–24, though his intuition was slightly warped: she actually died on 25 August 1824, which proved to be the same date as his own death in 1857. Uwins then went to Italy, where he remained until 1831.[36]

As for amateur painters, every young lady either attended drawing classes or had a master come to the house. The Grant sisters were taught drawing by Mr Wilson, head of the Academy of Painting, who was strongly recommended by John Clerk. Elizabeth attended his painting studio twice a week with other young ladies. She was especially present when he gave a lecture on some particular drawing or print, which proved helpful to their own work. It was, she said, 'like opening another eye' to the natural beauties round Edinburgh.

In the winter of 1819 a collection of fine paintings was shown every morning at an empty house in York Place, hired for the occasion, heated and lighted, and with enough seats for everybody 'the most agreeable of assemblies', always something good to see and discuss. All owners of good paintings contributed works, and liked to stand around studying their own with an 'air of triumph'. This too showed the value of Wilson's lectures, when he took his young students there to talk to them on the spot – though Elizabeth found she did not always agree with his views.[37]

Probably the best-known collector was John Clerk of Eldin (1757–1832), the advocate, who became a judge in 1823. His four drawing-rooms in Picardy Place were (says Elizabeth Grant) 'just a picture gallery, hung with paintings by the "ancient masters", some of them genuine! There were besides portfolios of prints, clever caricatures, and original sketches . . . a thousand curiosities were spread about.' In his buying, 'the enjoyment was in the acquisition, not in the intrinsick merit', his latest purchase always being his favourite, for example 'a hideous daub called a Rubens . . . it must have been a mere sketch, and never finished'. At the sale after his death, she was told, many were written off as 'trash'.[38]

Clerk, himself a talented artist, would say, 'If any one wants gude picters, let him gang to Tours, for Sir John Dalrymple has been there and picket oot a' the bad yuns.'[39] Though a clear-sighted lawyer who could detect fallacies and falsehoods at a glance, over pictures it was said he could be 'cheated as meekly as a lamb'. He once paid £700 for two pictures which the vendor had bought for £38. By degrees he assembled a large collection, and besides the drawings and paintings covering his walls, he had volumes of bound sketches, such as Captain William Elliot the marine painter's who exhibited at the Royal Academy in 1784. Others, unbound, lay scattered about the tables. Everyone who called on business was diverted by the appearance of his consulting room, bookcases full of books, floor spread with 'little ill-placed tables' adorned with precious china, 'strange boxes, bits of sculpture, curious screens and chairs, cats and dogs (his special favourites), and all manner of trash, dead and living, and all in confusion'.[40]

Clerk kept one large picture on an easel which no one was allowed to see, and although he never managed to finish it, fondly supposed that one day it would prove his *magnum opus.* His personal relaxations were 'modelling, painting, training of cats and dogs'.[41] He also kept teapots, saying, 'I weary of mysel', I weary of a' things, I weary of my sister, I weary of my cats, but I *never weary* of my ten teapots.' As for the cats, one was called Aminadab, another Rebecca, and he kept a 'class' for them, with the standard Scottish places of 'Dux' and 'Booby'. Once a terrific cats' concert took place behind his house . . . he threw up the window and read the Riot Act.'[42]

Clerk did not resemble the beauty of his collection, but in the eyes of Mrs General Graham was 'like a satyr, or a picture of Pan . . . most uncouth, both in manners and appearance'. Her observant daughter Helen at a dinner party there thought that while the occasion took them 'quite amongst the *bel esprits*', Lord Eldin himself was 'not *bel viso*, or *bel corps:* he grows uglier and uglier'.[43]

When he stood upright his lame leg hung in the air. At home he might be found 'in a red worsted nightcap, his crippled limb resting horizontally on a tripod stool, and many pairs of spectacles and antique snuff boxes on a small table at his right hand'.[44]

His more agreeable sister Bessy was also talented, 'painted a little, modelled in clay beautifully, sometimes finishing her small groups in ivory and her busts in stone or marble'.[45] She died in 1821, 'whom I saw but a few weeks ago', wrote Susan Ferrier, 'in her own house apparently in perfect health and surrounded with all the eye could desire to look upon of fine pictures, costly furniture, and all that was rich and rare'.[46]

It was not a particularly distinguished time for music in Edinburgh. The ending of the Music Society reduced St Cecilia's Hall in importance, and it lost its fashionable clientele. Most concerts tended to be at Corri's Rooms, whose changes of role were frequent, and recitals were sporadic.

But in 1814 a grand music festival was planned for the following year, the most important of its kind to be held in Edinburgh to date. George Hogarth (who was to become Charles Dickens's father-in-law) was then a young WS, and a friend of Scott and Lockhart among others. He was a keen amateur musician, composed music and played the cello, and the festival was largely possible because of his enthusiastic support. It was for the benefit of public charities, under the Presidency of the Duke of Buccleuch.

It began on 31 October 1815, and people poured into the city for weeks beforehand. 'There is nothing seen, heard, or felt here', wrote Henry Cockburn to Thomas Dick-Lauder, 'except the approaching festival and Saddlers balloon.'[47] Susan Ferrier, distracted by the extensive alterations and renovations they were making at their George Street house, was anxious to have it ready for them to move back in time for 'the Festival and the preachings'. Even the morning concerts, held in the outer hall of Parliament House, were expected to be crowded. 'Everybody agrees that it will be the grandest thing that ever was seen or heard throughout the kingdom.'[48] In the evenings the concerts were held at Corri's Rooms.

Henry Cockburn, who admitted to being tone-deaf and 'did not comprehend' the music, was told that it was good, though 'it sprang more from charity than from love of harmony . . . We have become an infinitely more harmonious nation since then [he was writing in the 1820s]. Indeed none of our advances is more decided than our musical one.'[49]

Leading singers and instrumentalists were engaged for the morning Parliament House concerts (selections of sacred music by Handel, Haydn, Mozart, Beethoven and others, including Haydn's *Creation* and Handel's *Messiah*), and in the evenings at Corri's full works by 'the most esteemed composers'. Edinburgh's chief artists were also joined by singers from outside such as the virtuoso Domenico Dragonetti, his recital partner the cellist Robert Lindley, the tenor John Braham of course, the organist John Camidge, and many lesser performers. The conductor was Charles Ashley.[50]

The festival went on for a week. Although morning concerts started at 11, the doors were open at 9 and a fashionable crowd already assembled by 7, four hours ahead. The *Messiah*, which drew a huge 'genteel company', was a great squeeze, the house full by 10 in the morning to the disappointment of several hundred people.

Elaborate arrangements were made for carriages to set down and pick up at both venues: for example at Corri's they must go down York Place single file, leave by Catherine Street, and afterwards pick up with the horses' heads towards York Place, 'assembling at the head of Leith Walk in front of Crichton's coach work'. Servants (on whom the responsibility fell) were to be instructed in the arrangements, which the police were to enforce. Other special arrangements were made by the Provost and magistrates, such as ordering hackney coaches to be available on their stands from 8.30 p.m., and not to charge extra fares.

Six transferable tickets were obtainable for three guineas, singles at fifteen shillings, from Oman's Tavern, and the leading music shops such as Manners and Millers. Such was the demand that an extra morning concert was held, with favourite items from the *Messiah* and other works, on the morning of Sadler's balloon ascent, to accommodate which the concert started an hour earlier.

Braham's singing was praised as with great feeling, Mrs Salmon's with sweetness and power, and other inevitably meaningless terms. The whole occasion, surpassing all earlier attempts, excited great interest eliciting more than two columns of newspaper description, not least because of the crowds, exceeding any since the Caledonian hunt balls held at Holyrood, or when the crowds were drawn to the races. The profit was £1549.11.3½, of which £1500 was given to the trustees, namely the Lord Provost, Lord Justice Clerk and Lord Chief Baron, supposedly to be handed to public charities.

At the end, a fashionable ball was held at the Assembly Rooms, with the Countess of Moray as Lady Directress. Two days later came Wyndham Sadler's adequate if not very dramatic balloon ascent, and the week ended with a 'grand military promenade and ball' at Corri's Rooms on the Saturday, with Neil Gow conducting.[51]

One of the festival's objects was to promote musical taste, and hence 'moral habits' of 'innocent recreation'. Certainly the public performance of music in Edinburgh now became less of a rarity, and a second and third festival were held in October of 1819 and 1824.

A much appreciated addition to Edinburgh's scanty musical entertainment was provided by a small opera company brought by John Loder (1788–1846), who combined music publishing with playing the violin. They presented excerpts and scenes from favourite operas, 'very well got up' says Elizabeth Grant. Giuseppe de Begnis, a bass, and his recently married wife Giusepina Roazi, a soprano, sang scenes especially from *Figaro*, and *Don Giovanni*. Elizabeth and Jane saw on the counter of a music shop a new arrangement for piano duets from *Don Giovanni* – the first successful attempt to bring such music to 'the family circle', and she and Jane practised together and then sprang Leporello's opening aria on their astonished father, waking him from his afternoon nap.[52]

At Corri's Rooms, in November 1818 Jane Schetky informs her brother in London that their next 'institution' concert is to be on 4 December, for which *The Creation* is in rehearsal: Mrs Salmon would sing, and Finlay Dun play a violin solo.[53]

St Cecilia's had descended somewhat in the social scale, its audience now largely composed of the middle classes, minor legal, literary and commercial families. The satirical 'novel' *Edinburgh* in 1820 describes an evening there led by 'the merry-faced Italian' leading at the harpsichord, his fat wife near by (though he 'runs after every servant girl'), and 'his languishing affected niece, with her dejected eyes, hung-down head, and infantine air', a moderately good orchestra, and George Burnet, natural son of Innes of Stow, 'looking over the orchestra with spectacles on nose'.

The author describes the concert as indifferent in spite of their pains, largely because so little encouragement is given by the nobility, the gentry are parsimonious, and they have no musical taste except for reels and ballads.[54]

St Cecilia's was not entirely wasted. The Forum debating society, to which George Combe belonged, met there, at least in February 1814. Combe describes the 'most splendid and elegant place, capable of containing 800 persons', and on this occasion soon filled with a 'genteel' audience. The subject, incidentally, was 'whether the lower orders are benefited by civilisation', and the motion was carried, but 'the speakers were overawed by the increased splendor of the house and increased numbers of their audience, and the debate was languid and bad'.[55]

More music was probably performed in drawing-rooms than in public halls. Every young lady was of course expected to be able to sing and play as well as to draw, so that like other centres of population Edinburgh had a generous supply of drawing and music masters. The Grant girls had a harp master, M. Elouis, so expensive that on their mother's suggestion several families joined to form three classes a week, paid quarterly. With eight pupils for two hours at a time, 'he made quite a fortune'. The girls played concert pieces, doubling the parts, and soon 'the fame of our achievement spread over the town', people begging to climb the common stair to Elouis' garret 'to listen to such a number of harps played by such handsome girls'. Some of their mothers deprecated such an exhibition, but the Grants' tiresome governess Miss Elphick insisted on chaperoning them.

There was an etiquette crisis when a party of young men 'just happened' to be passing as the girls came out of the class, some of whom were their regular dancing partners, 'so that there were bows and speeches and attendance home'. Miss Elphick tried holding back until the next class arrived 'but the Beaux waited too'. Then she whisked them away early, but, when that did not work, she fairly took Elouis to task and reviled the 'Edinburgh gentlemen' as well.

One day Elouis quite overstepped the mark, when a handsome, moustached, 'braided and belted' army officer entered and was offered a seat. 'Every harp was silent.' M. Elouis in polished terms introduced his 'musical amateur' friend and begged them to continue. The enraged Miss Elphick rose to her feet, commanded the girls to collect their music and put on their shawls and bonnets, and swept the lot of them downstairs before Elouis could even make his apologies. Neither the Grants nor the Hunters returned to his classes, and having lost so many pupils, he soon had to give up.

Singing-mistresses similarly sometimes took two or three pupils together. Elizabeth's voice noticeably improved with lessons from Mrs Bianchi Lacey, who gave some delightful concerts with her husband and Miss Simmons in the small Assembly Room. She was neither young nor powerful of voice, but her neat performance and fine expression were a revelation to Elizabeth. Mrs Lacey liked her enough to give extra long lessons, taking pains over such details as position of head and chest, 'the smile with which the mouth was to be opened', clear enunciation, and general technique.

At Mrs Lacey's first concert they were much amused when old Sir John Hay, one of the Assembly directors, squired her about, bringing 'negus, a shawl, a chair', anything, while young William Grant was assiduous with the (greatly inferior) second singer Miss Simmons. Mr Grant was so impressed that he offered Elizabeth a dozen lessons, though their stay in Edinburgh that season allowed for only ten; but they went to the Laceys' concerts, twice had them to dinner, 'sang as much as we liked', and Mrs Grant gave an evening party for them when 'their singing enchanted every body'.[56]

39
A NEW START IN THE THEATRE

'The whole light [gas] proceeds from the centre of the roof, where one large sun of crystal hangs in a blazing atmosphere . . . all blended and glowing into one huge orbe of intolerable splendour . . . every face in the audience, from the gallery to the orchestra, is seen as distinctly as if all were seated in the open light of noon-day.'

'Peter Morris' [John Lockhart], *Peter's Letters to his Kinsfolk,* 3rd edn, 1819, I.315

'They had been crushing, singing, and swaying for nearly five hours; and every now and then a man was rolled out from the front over the heads of the mass . . . seething, dishevelled, exhausted, and fainting. When at last the door opened the screams in front were quite alarming.'

The Life of Sir Robert Christison, Bart, ed. by his sons, Edinburgh, 1886, 314–5 (before the performance of *Rob Roy* during King George's visit, August 1822)

'There is no describing the sensation [Mrs Siddons] has excited. The sweet spring of Miss O'Neill seemed not to attract more admiration than *her* rich and mellow autumn.'

Mrs Grant to Mrs Gorman, 19 December 1815, *Memoirs of Mrs Grant of Laggan,* II.116

'The attentions of Murray and Mrs Henry Siddons, the comforts of the theatre, my dressing-room, altogether make this the only town, out of London, where I like my profession.'

Charles Mathews to his wife, 19 Jan. 1818, Mrs Anne Mathews, *Memoirs of Charles Mathews, Comedian,* London 1838, 431

On Henry Siddons's death in 1815 the theatre was closed for several days. Sadly missed though he was, they had to carry on, his widow continuing as manager, and at her request her brother William Murray, a competent accountant, acting as their stage manager, maintained the standard of the company and visiting players, and helped sort out their tangled finances. To the cost of conversion of Corri's Rooms, plus the annual rental of £800 on a three-year lease, was added re-leasing of the 'old' theatre at 2000 guineas a year for twenty-one years dating from 1809, the year of the renewed patent. Further, Siddons had incurred £1500 expenses for restoring the old theatre, and £500 for converting Corri's back to a concert hall. Six years' rent for the old theatre at £12,500 brought the total debt to £21,000.

To deal with this Murray realised all his own assets and his paternal inheritance, borrowed £1000, and for the time being owed a year's rent. Siddons, a less shrewd manager than his brother-in-law, might never have succeeded in freeing the theatre from its financial problems, and its real success dates from Murray's managership. In publishing the gloomy figures, Murray appealed for public support, diffidently requested a shilling increase in box charges, and alerted them to the difficulties. At Mrs Henry's benefit on 1 May – the night originally intended for Siddons's own – they raised the largest sum ever, £420 from a packed house, and on the closing night on 20 May, Murray gave a stylish address to the audience, which was to become a regular feature.[1]

Mrs Siddons senior's successor as leading tragedienne, the beautiful Miss Eliza O'Neill, made her first appearance in August, as Belvidera in *Venice Preserv'd,* which led to scenes reminding old stagers of Mrs Siddons's own Edinburgh debut: Highland porters camping out for seats and sometimes coming to blows over places, while fashionable families left their breakfast tables to watch the skirmishes.[2]

Mrs Grant noted that the excitement over Miss O'Neill exceeded that over the defeat of Napoleon, with 'a violent contest about seats . . . People came flocking from the country in large numbers to behold this paragon'.[3]

A great curiosity late in September, curiously ignored by the various theatre historians, was the appearance of a group of 'American Indian Warriers', fresh from thirty successful nights at Covent Garden, who excited great interest in Edinburgh. For a few nights they displayed their 'manners and habits' in 'grand historical ballet', *La Perouse, or The Desert Island.*

They were introduced on 28 September with the inducement for locals of seeing *the real thing,* with 'appropriate Music, Scenery, Machinery, Dresses, and Decorations'; Davy and the late Morehead supplied music, Pyett the scenery, Ronaldson the 'machinery'. All this comprised 'Storm, and Shipwreck, Romantic Grotto, View on the Island, Inside of Perouse's Hut, Exterior of ditto, and concluding scene of the Astrolabe [the ship] at anchor'. In true pantomime style, a full three-dimensional staging would alternate with drop-scenes (View on the Island, Exterior of hut).

Much was made of the fact that only three 'Europeans' appeared in the show, the 'Navigator' La Perouse (with his wife and child). There were

'Natives of a neighbouring Island', William Murray playing the suitor to Umba in order to provide romance, with a black servant and a chimpanzee played by a boy, Master Anderson. The rest were authentically Indian, including the chief Senung-gis (Long Horns), Ue-tan-goh (Black Squirrel), and so on in the local spelling. The entertainment included their ceremonies and 'peculiar customs', and a full rendering of 'North American Indian War Song, March and Dance; an Indian Combat, with bows and Arrows; Clubs and Tomahawks; Indian Sports, shooting at a mark with Bows and Arrows, with the Dance of Peace'.

To combat a rumour that at least some of them were English in disguise, on 3 October they left the stage to appear in the stage boxes, for anyone who wished to take a closer look.

The performance was somehow grafted on to other plays, such as *Captain Cook,* and *Robinson Crusoe.* On 5 October, 'to increase interest the chief will issue his orders and receive answer in their native language', and would keep the prizes competed for in the last act. Their last appearance was on Saturday, 10 October, but in an odd extension to their performance, that day they were invited to compete against the Royal Archers. Odder still, they seem not to have put up a very good show against the Scots.

The competitors assembled in the field of butts where the Archers shot at 'rovers'. The Indians were not accustomed to long-distance shooting, so that comparison was not altogether fair, but to the Scots their 'accoutrements', though capable of great precision over short distances, seemed 'coarse and awkward'. At the end, to their great pleasure, they were presented with arrows and bowstrings, and the chief made a long speech of appreciation, admitting their surprise at finding 'brother archers' in Edinburgh, especially at the distance and accuracy of their shots.

That evening, as their last, was their benefit night, and in compliment to them, members of the Archers attended the show.[4]

As this presentation completed the season, at the end William Murray gave his address to enlighten the audience of the current situation. They had been successful, he said, but were still dependent on public support, and he pointed out how many improvements had been made to the building: repainted boxes, gas-lighting as at Covent Garden. He was several times interrupted with applause, especially when he scotched a rumour that Mrs Siddons was leaving for a London engagement: she was going only temporarily, for health reasons. The *Courant* writer on the 15th indulged in judicious praise for their productions and good wishes for a better future.[5]

They were able to reopen in November with a debt of £3100, with a season lasting only thirty weeks in the year. The new box prices aroused no opposition. Mrs Siddons senior, her powers scarcely diminished at sixty-two, returned on 18 November 1815 for the first of occasional benefit nights in aid of the family. Neither Mrs Grant nor her family attempted to see the celebrity, 'but all our friends have been constant in their attendance on this declining luminary, and declare that her setting brightness equals any thing they have seen formerly . . . there is no describing the sensation she has excited. The sweet spring of Miss O'Neill seemed not to attract more admiration than *her* rich and mellow autumn.'[6]

Not only was Mrs Siddons's energy unchanged, but in her retirement she had managed to lose weight. Opening with Terry as Lady Macbeth, she then played in *Douglas*, and ended with her benefit and positively last appearance on 30 November, in *The Gamester*.

Amelia Opie, who had met Mrs Siddons in London in 1814, recorded that her sister returned home after the visit 'raving all the way, saying she was the most beautiful, delightful, agreeable, and I believe, even the *youngest* woman she ever saw'.[7]

Miss O'Neill followed with her other roles including Mrs Haller in *The Stranger*, again to great applause and the theatre crowded every night, the doors besieged for hours beforehand by the servants impatiently awaiting the first chance to buy tickets.[8]

The comedian Charles Mathews made a return visit in 1816. He had already played in Edinburgh in 1812, when his joyful ebullience was the most startling contrast to Mrs Jordan's reactions that can be imagined. He wrote to his wife from Port Patrick on his way to Ireland that April, 'after 33 hours bumping over scotch roads . . . Edr turned out as delightful as Glasgow was horrible . . . and the warmest reception I ever yet met with, because I have considered an Edr audience so difficult to please . . . Harry [Siddons] says I am the greatest card he ever had. Hundreds turned away at my benefit. I reckon Edr an annuity to me for the future.'[9]

His 1816 visit was not so happy. It was April again, and he caught a chill on the way from York, on arrival in Edinburgh trying to struggle on but too hoarse to act. Dr Bell warned him that if he did not rest he would damage his voice. The theatre was accordingly closed, but after a few days he felt much improved, 'thanks to Bell, water-gruel, no wine, broths, &c.'; the symptoms had gone, and now he had four days to rest until Wednesday, and having cancelled his Dublin booking would make up with a couple of extra nights in Edinburgh. Further, on Bell's advice he was to stay until the Monday at Constable's house with 'every comfort'.

He blamed the weather for his illness, 'so dreadful, that even the natives cannot stand it . . . Half the theatre are sick . . . the sun has not peeped forth', rain and snow were unceasing, with an east wind and enveloping fog. By 16 April he was quite recovered, had played again the previous night and was 'as strong as ever'. So after all he would go on to Dublin, being 'in vigour again': he dare not lose his profits. For his benefit next day he hoped to net £300.

Still the snow continued, yesterday had four hours of it, 'as deep . . . as ever I saw at Christmas', so that he thought the house would be engulfed.[10]

Mathew's speciality was a series of one-man sketches which he called 'At Homes', using his gift for mimicry and skill in adopting different accents, which always brought the house down.

Mrs Henry Siddons resumed acting that January (1816), as Viola, her first stage appearance since her husband's death. At first she seemed understandably emotional, but the enthusiasm of the audience was a great support. In March, John Kemble reappeared for three weeks, Mrs Kemble started the summer season in July, and Miss O'Neill played for almost three weeks in August, and while as popular as before, was inevitably compared unfavourably with the great Mrs Siddons.[11]

The real sensation of the year was the first appearance in Edinburgh of Edmund Kean, who opened on 7 October as Richard III. His unusual style excited some criticism (Coleridge described it as 'like reading Shakespeare by flashes of lightning'), but it 'electrified the playgoers . . . with his vivid action and extraordinary originality'. Another critic said his acting 'pleases less than it astonishes'. Among the parts he played were Shylock (with Mrs Henry as Portia), Othello, and on his last, benefit night on 12 October, Hamlet.[12]

Kean was so popular in Edinburgh that the Highland Society presented him with a magnificent sword in honour of his Macbeth, and he was invited to a meeting chaired by its President, Henry Mackenzie, then in his eighties, presumably also including Scott, Wilson and many critics and philosophers. When John Pillans questioned him about his eloquence, Kean answered that he had no 'rhetorician's laws' because Shakespeare was his own interpreter and if he himself were judged highly (he thought), it was because of his devotion to and deep study of Shakespeare. Further, 'I forgot the affections of art, and relied upon the emotions of the soul', and 'thought more of intonation than of gesticulation', and of expressing feeling than of observing rhetorical rules.[13]

Miss Spence thought Edinburgh showed greater appreciation of such talents than did London, perhaps (she suggested) because the theatre was not attended by 'the lower classes', and in this 'intellectual city' actors could display their skill to an audience of the gentry and aristocracy, so conscious of their etiquette that they would think it 'extremely inelegant to interrupt the illusion or emotion of the actor by applause', hence not over-lavish with praise. 'They fervently greeted Kean, with no ingredient of the mob.' He was much admired as Sir Giles Overreach in *A New Way to Pay Old Debts* and in his Shakespearean parts Richard III, Othello and Hamlet.[14]

In 1817 the first dramatisation of one of the Waverley novels, *Guy Mannering*, adapted by Daniel Terry, was staged while it was still playing at Covent Garden, with a medley overture which continued in use for at least seventy years. People remarked that Murray had been slow enough in presenting it, but apart from Mrs Henry as Meg Merrilees it had a weak cast and at first ran for only twelve nights. The next production brought great improvements. Mackay, an exellent comic, did well as Dominie Sampson.[15]

The problems attached to running what was effectively a provincial theatre were hard to overcome, as put forward by the *Scotsman* in January that year. A city with so small a population could not be expected to keep top players for long, however well supported. The writer partly blamed the public, who, he said, were getting what they asked for, namely 'puerile' productions of pantomime and melodrama, at which Murray was successful: he ought rather to instruct, and encourage good plays as well as good performers, not just 'the painter and mechanics'. Mrs Henry came in for praise for her 'distinguished chasteness and purity of manners, attitude and feelings', especially in 'serious comedy', and the writer went on to analyse the good and bad qualities of the company: Mrs Nicol's continuing success in her amusing 'aged department', Russell a good comic, even outshining Mathews in taste, Murray was incapable of parts needing 'pathos or emotion', and so on.[16]

All the same they lured some celebrities that year: John Philip Kemble in March, in the first of twelve farewell performances prior to retirement, almost all Shakespeare.

Scott saw his *Coriolanus* on 22 March, analysing his performance at some length. 'You know what a complete model he is of the Roman Patrician', and his gift for seizing on some particular weakness or passion of a character, but more 'natural' and 'delicate' traits escaped him. Scott spoke approvingly of his reformed habits, having 'given up wine, which he used to swallow in pailfuls, and renewed his youth like the eagles'.

Kemble had begged Scott to write some valedictory lines and the time he spent 'criticizing and correcting; till he got them quite to his mind' was as tiring for Scott as for the actor, for he insisted on editing the content to his own satisfaction to such an extent that he 'dragd me into the land of metaphysics and rythmical harmony where I am not at present very equal to follow'. Kemble's final performance was as Macbeth on 29 March, when he spoke Scott's envoi in costume.

> As the war-horse, at the trumpet's sound,
> Erects his mane, and neighs, and paws the ground.[17]

On that evening he had a heavy cold, but its severity gave way to his own energy, as he said before the curtain rose that he was 'determined to leave behind him the most perfect specimen of his art he had ever seen'.[18]

Kemble was dignified in manner with a 'slow, measured enuciation'. He disliked meeting strangers, who found his formal, taciturn manner off-putting, though it disguised his simple and domestically-minded nature. On acting days he would dine at 2, rest until 5 or 6 when his wife would wake him for coffee, then dressed and was driven to the theatre wrapped in a cloak. As an actor he was type-cast, particularly excelling in Shakespeare, to whom he was devoted, especially as Lear or Coriolanus.

He retired at the height of his powers, but was a sick man. He gave up his lodgings and took 'a good family house' in Heriot Row, where he lived for six months with a 'hydropathic regimen' before going abroad, where he died at Lausanne in 1823.[19]

Robert Gillies, who knew Kemble quite well, sometimes had them to dinner, with his neighbour the great Edinburgh host Alexander Gordon, owner of the city's best picture collection acquired from the Colonna Palace in Rome. Kemble and Gordon sometimes called on one another, Kemble merely to help himself to books, and Gordon equally briefly, as he was often busy giving French lessons.

Two nights after Kemble's last appearance the celebrated 'low comedian' John Liston made his first Edinburgh appearance, an unqualified suceess in *The Chapter of Accidents*, the audience flocking to see him and the press full of praise. Two nights later again he played Dominie Sampson, ending on 5 April – and on 7 April Kean reappeared for a week. Widely different from Kemble, he often received equivalent applause for the same parts. He had not Kemble's heroic grandeur, or 'chivalrous and princely' bearing; his attitudes were ungraceful, his voice husky, figure tiny, and accent odd, with its drawn-out rs – gurr-ave, urr-reverend. Yet his unusual genius was shown from the moment he appeared.

Then during the summer season Joey Grimaldi, the darling of Sadler's Wells, first appeared in some of his favourite characters, sang his speciality song 'Tippity Witchit', and one day appeared with his son.[20]

That year Charles Mathews was in France, but in 1818 he returned to Edinburgh, this time in January, just as unlucky with the weather, snow, hurricanes, chimneys blown down, £1000-worth of damage to a newly built chapel . . . The only walking he dared try was between his lodging and the theatre, which indeed he feared might be wrecked.

He made a great hit with *An Actor of All Work*, in which to start with, he made the mistake of turning the Scotsman into an Irishman for fear of insult, until he was warned it was quite the other way: the change would be taken as 'a bad compliment to their sense'. So he played as a Scot, made a tremendous hit and 'they roared at every line'. By a happy chance, with Murray playing the manager, Mathews had a line, 'I'm told you-a set up a show i' this toon', which brought a positive 'screech'.

The play was a sell-out, with box-office queues almost every night.

'They are the only real theatrical audience in the 3 kingdoms', said the jubilant Mathews – they even got the point of lines the Haymarket audience missed. On the Saturday his intonation for one sentence was so just – 'Fie mon! hoo, hoo con I recount aw the perteeclers o' his insanity?' that for that line alone he had several rounds of applause. How different from the tetchy Mrs Jordan was Mathews, who so enjoyed life: he had 'a delightful day' on the Sunday with Terry and his wife at the Scotts. 'The attentions of Murray and Mrs Henry Siddons, the comforts of the theatre, my dressing-room, altogether make this the only theatre, out of London, where I like my profession.' This was despite an apparent difference with Murray over the size of his offer.

Mathews' talents made him an instant celebrity. He attended the courts when William Erskine was in the middle of a speech. Happening to glance his way, the advocate 'stopped, laughed, and shook his fist at me', which caused everyone to turn to look. Charles says he 'blushed up to the eyes' (rather unlikely), while Erskine, the moment he sat down again, scribbled a note to the judge, Lord Gillies, who in turn craned over to look. 'What the devil brings you here, mon,' exclaimed Erskine as they all left the court. 'You spoilt my speech! – I canna afford to be taken off.' He explained that his note to the judge was a warning to be on his guard, 'or we should both be upon the stage before supper to-night'.[21]

Blackwood, who had engaged Peter Patmore to write on the theatre, was pleased with his first articles (paid at 10 guineas a sheet). 'In you I have found a most valuable correspondent', he told him, and asked if he could produce something on Mathews while he was here. 'We are all very much behindhand in this city in theatrical knowledge, and the more criticism on living actors you can interweave . . . the better for Scotch readers.'[22]

Frederick Yates, a new actor who had been educated at Charterhouse and then served in the Peninsula, made his first stage appearance in Edinburgh in March 1818 as Shylock and as Richard III, the start of a successful London career. Kean reappeared in April with Edinburgh's first production of *Richard II*, and his own first Edinburgh Romeo. Indeed there were several 'firsts', too tedious to recount.

Yet the season had been less successful than the previous year, and the *Scotsman* journalist noted that, while the company was now 'considered the best out of London', the theatre was not at present very popular. Yet it had been so improved that it was lighter and more comfortable than London theatres, and one sat 'comparatively in a drawing-room'. Why was it not more frequented?

'If the people of Edinburgh were as intellectual as they are fond of being thought', why were they so 'chary of committing themselves' to their feelings? He recalled only one occasion of expressing their true emotions, and that had been Mrs Siddons's first farewell, in *Henry VIII*. 'It was shortly after the prince Regent had quarrelled with the Whigs', and at Henry Siddons's lines,

'Oh how wretched/Is that poor man that hangs on princes' favours!', 'the whole audience seemed electrified'.

The *Scotsman* relented at the end of the year, after the autumn closure had brought further improvements, including a complete repainting of the interior and, more interestingly, installing gas lighting on the model of London theatres. There were other touches: a police officer was in attendance, and at the end, an attendant would come to inform occupants of boxes when their carriages had arrived. The gas had a brilliant effect. 'Superb – magnifique!' declared the *Scotsman,* and the directors inspected the interior to their satisfaction. Should the lighting fail, they were able to revert to the old oil lighting, and this was shortly demonstrated when (it was claimed), because of 'the immense extent of pipe within the walls', and gas's tendency to rise, the supply was turned off the chandelier burnt for nearly ten minutes, allowing time for the oil system to be re-lit.[23] George Combe praised the effect of the new gas lighting 'after the manner of Covent Garden, and most beautiful and brilliant it is'.[24]

According to Elizabeth Grant 'old Mrs Siddons' returned in May and June for a twelve-night benefit for her grandchildren and to settle the theatre's 'pressing debts', though this is mentioned neither by Dibdin nor by Chambers. Still she seemed little changed, certainly not in appearance or voice, and the chief sign of age was her moving more slowly from increasing stiffness. Elizabeth recorded with awe her last appearance, as Queen Catherine, notably in the trial scene: 'the scorn of her attitude, and the outraged dignity of the voice . . . We were breathless.' As for her Lady Macbeth, Volumnia, Constance in *King John*, 'ah, no such acting since, for she was nature, on stilts in her private life'. She quotes the anecdote of her simple order to a waiter, 'blank verse and a tragick tone being her daily wear': 'Bring me some beer, boy, and another plate.'[25]

One evening Mrs Siddons younger offered Elizabeth a seat in her own box to see John Liston, the highest paid comic actor of his day, as 'Lubin Log' *in Love, Law and Physic.* His odd countenance used to send people 'into convulsions' without a word, and coming in as it were from the coach laden with parcels, as he asked for 'a numbrella' and his ''at', he threw up at the box his famous 'look . . . never could be such another grotesque expression of fun', 'a sly twinkle of one squinting eye, or the buck tooth interrupting a smile . . . We were ill with laughing. He played that whole farce to us, to Mrs Harry and me . . . every one agreed he had surpassed himself.'[26]

Mrs Grant went in July to see Miss O'Neill act Mrs Haller, 'admirably', in a crowded house, with 'the Arch-Critic' sitting behind her in the box. 'I never saw such an all-alive creature, or one whose feelings are so youthfully keen . . . She is admirable on the stage, and most respectable at all times: the intelligent composure and elegant simplicity of her manners please me exceedingly.' So respectable was this actress that she had known Mrs Grant's daughter Mary, and as she was lodging near them, she called on them with her brother and sister.[27] Only the next year Miss O'Neill married Becher, an MP, who became a baronet, and thus left the stage.[28]

Yet apart from the appearance of such stars as the Kembles, Young and Mathews, and the redeeming Mrs Henry Siddons, Edinburgh theatregoers had to put up with 'our own poor third rates'.

The great event of 1819 was the production of an opera based on *Rob Roy*, adapted by John Pocock, which had been a success at Covent Garden the previous season. No expense was spared on the scenery, by Pyett, Grieve and William Grieve, and this 'most memorable and important piece' opened on Monday, 15 February, and ran for an unprecedented forty-one nights. It was to be repeated every season during Murray's regime, and for decades remained 'a trump card', known as the 'Managerial Sheet Anchor'. George Combe told his brother, when it had already played for thirty nights, that it was 'acted to perfection', Charles Mackay played Bailie Nicol Jarvie 'to the Life' and Scott was delighted with his realisation of the character.

Hamerton played Rob Roy and Alexander, Frank Rashleigh. Thunderous applause greeted the piece from the packed house, starting with Scott's arrival with family at his box (as it always did), though he himself was a bundle of anxiety.

The elaborate scenery included scenes of a view of Glasgow Bridge, the Clachan of Aberfoyle, and a moonlit loch. The *Courant*, in a carping review, wrote oddly that the dialogue being mostly borrowed from the novel showed 'the dearth of dramatic talent' in this age of exceptional literary men. The music, based on Scottish airs, was well sung and the actors mostly received a share of displeasure. The *Scotsman* on the other hand was full of praise, except for the musical finale, '*mal apropos*, absurd and ridiculous', complaining otherwise only that the music interrupted the plot, and would be better sung between acts – an unusual criticism of an opera.[29]

Even hundreds of people who had never been to a theatre were overcome with admiration. After the twenty-fourth performance the house was fuller than ever. Scott wrote to Terry (18 April) that Murray had already made more than £3000. He also wrote to Mackay in the character of Jedediah Cleishbotham, praising his performance and pretending he had visited the gallery incognito.

The production helped to put the theatre on its feet, after mediocre seasons and low funds. One important outcome of its success was the establishment of an Edinburgh Theatrical Fund to relieve 'decayed performers' which was launched at the theatre on 26 February. A committee of actors was formed, and the fund was set up in April under the patronage of the Duke of York, with numerous noble supporters, the Dukes of Argyll, Gordon and Queensberry, the Earls of Buchan and Moray and others, along with numerous baronets, the Lord Provost, Lord President and Lord Advocate, William Erskine, and of course Walter Scott. Annual directors were appointed, and a benefit night for the Fund was fixed for 5 June, with a performance of *Rob Roy* itself.[30]

The most important appearance during the year was a return of Edmund Kean, but he was out of favour over rather shabby behaviour in a Drury lane production of *Switzerland*, a tragedy by Miss Jane Porter which had been a complete failure. Edinburgh audiences were therefore this time less ecstatic (April).

Macready had an unsuccessful appearance in July, when he barely covered his expenses, claiming in his *Reminiscences* that he was consoled by an unprecedented 'warmth and approbation', and by the presence in the audience of old Henry Mackenzie. His regrets on leaving 'that beautiful and interesting city' were increased by his inability to visit Scott, who was laid low with a second attack of serious illness.[31]

The theatre was now well re-established. In August Prince Leopold of the Belgians visited the city, and 'Edinburgh was all alive', recorded Southey sourly when about to set off on a Highlands tour with Telford. 'He went to the theatre, and the whole family of Tag, Rag, and Bobtail (more numerous than any of the Macs and all the Campbells) were swarming in Princes Street till midnight.' Southey spoke more favourably of the new buildings than of the populace.[32]

There was a recital in October by the celebrated singer and actress Catherine Stephens which was attended by Lady Shelley and her husband. Returning after a beautiful sunny day, followed by the inevitable haze, passing the theatre on the way from Calton Hill they saw the concert notice and on an impulse went in. The theatre was so empty that they got front seats, and enjoyed a beautiful recital of Scottish ballads well suited to the small theatre; 'Auld Robin Gray', sung with 'a degree of pathos difficult to describe', was rapturously encored.

Discussing the thin house afterwards, they decided that Edinburgh's characteristic was 'sobriety in the search for entertainment'. Lady Shelley cites in evidence Catalini's concert a few years back, so successful (and lucrative) that she had decided on a return visit the next year. 'No one who had heard her before went again . . . they had heard her. There was no satire in this, for the same thing happened with Miss O'Neill. I saw her play, literally to empty benches' – again in the front row, whereas on her first visit 'the pressure was so great that people were fainting. All the boxes had been taken previous to her arrival in Edinburgh.'[33]

Miss Stephens coincided in Edinburgh with another Charles Mathews appearance, successful as ever. He was 'going on famously', making a great hit with his *Trip to Paris*, more than he had expected, 'the greatest hit I ever made any where in that part', twice repeated and certain favourite lines earning the usual tumultuous applause. For his benefit night all boxes were taken, and meanwhile 'All the world are here. 'Tis the Musical Festival', and he was lucky enough to hear a delightful concert at the theatre, with not only Miss Stephens but Braham, Ambrogetti and good instrumentalists. This time Mathews ended with a week spent at Dupplin as the guest of Lord Kinnoull, before continuing on his tour, first stop Glasgow.[34]

On the death of King George III in January, by order of the Lord Chamberlain all theatres were closed from 1–17 February, and on 19 February Mrs Henry recited a 'monody' in his memory.

Only four days later Tom Dibdin's adaptation of *The Heart of Midlothian* was advertised. He had adapted the novel the previous year for Covent Garden, and then at the 'Royal' in Edinburgh and the Pantheon. (These might well have been not Dibdin's but another version.) Dibdin's own was at 'the minor theatre' and drew audiences 'almost beyond precedent'. Mrs Siddons, who had been in London had seen it at the Surrey Theatre, asked for a copy, and once back in Edinburgh produced it at the Royal under Dibdin's name, and in spite of the earlier production at 'the Caledonian Circus', and the Covent Garden version at the Royal, it had a triumphant season.

The version at the Royal ran for twenty-eight consecutive nights, the second for only eight. Nasmyth painted views of Edinburgh for the first version, and Mrs Siddons played Jeanie Deans, Mrs Murray Effie.

Almost as successful as *Rob Roy,* it continued a 'stock piece' as long as the resident company survived. Scott, appearing in the lower boxes, and Lord Erskine, recognised in the second row, were both cheered.[35]

Various Scott novels were presented, sometimes only for a night by a visiting actor such as Liston, as Dominie Sampson in March. Otherwise apart from a visit by Kean in July, ending in his benefit on the 29th as a farewell before he left for America, the season was uneventful.

In December the fourth Waverley adaptation was staged, Terry and Pocock's version of *The Antiquary,* with additions, and the inevitable songs. This too had a successful run (twenty-two nights), and was renewed a dozen times in the season.[36]

Robert Chambers recalled the decade which followed as one of excellent management, and the players of his youth as masterly. 'Genteel, wiry Mr Jones, for Mercurio and Charles Surface, – Mr Vandenhoff for tragic parts . . . Denham, with his bulky figure and thick voice, in King James and Dandy Dinmont . . . Mr Murray himself, not allowed to be a jot below the Listons . . . Mrs Henry Siddons, beautiful, graceful, with a voice which seemed to penetrate the audience', and so on. David Roberts was painting the scenery for a time, Mr T. Fraser played the hautboy 'which had witched the soul and flooded the eyes of Burns'. Then there were the visiting actors,

Charles Kemble, Kean, Liston, Mathews, Terry. 'Verily it was worth while for a play-goer to live in those days.'[37]

The year 1821 was marked by a row between Murray and Alexander, who was appointed manager of the Carlisle Theatre, a summer establishment. His weekly salary was £2.10s.0d., and he asked Murray for a ten-shilling rise, but Murray refused.

This caused misunderstanding and ill feeling, actually culminating in an open row on the stage, and Murray refused Alexander's annual benefit. The actor then engaged the Pantheon and held his benefit there, after which he left Edinburgh, and embarked on a long managership in 'the west'.[38]

The company had gained an ex-army officer, who came to Edinburgh from Newcastle in 1819, acted Iago to Kean's Othello, and took leading parts for several years before moving to Dublin, where he became manager. After some poor seasons he retired and became Kean's secretary. His real name was Cole, but he called himself Calcraft, a name of some distinction.[39]

Melodramas and unmemorable productions gave way in August to a season of English operas, ending in 'a magnificent spectacle' of the coronation in *Henry IV* Part II, which ran for the rest of the season and was staged again on reopening in October. *Monsieur Tonson*, 'a poor farce', in November was graced with scenery by David Roberts and ran for forty performances during the season.

Early in 1822 Pocock adapted *The Legend of Montrose*, with the usual music from old Scottish melodies and scenery by Roberts (who with permission copied Nasmyth's views of Inveraray Castle and Loch Lochy). This, the fifth Waverley adaptation, was less successful, and on first production ran to only eleven nights. On 1 April, Charles Kemble, John's senior by two years, appeared for the first time for many years. Calcraft, for his own benefit, produced his own adaptation of *The Bride of Lammermoor*, especially licensed for Edinburgh. He himself played Edgar, Mrs Siddons Lucy Ashton, and after a single first showing it too became popular. A different version of *Guy Mannering*, renamed *The Witch of Duncleuch*, in May was followed by a three-week closing, and then yet another Scott, Dibdin's *Kenilworth*, with Calcraft as Leicester and Amy Robsart by Mrs Siddons, Murray as Blount, but it ran for only six nights.[40]

Everything now was geared to preparations for the King's visit in August, and the theatre was done over at least twice, before and after, with elaborate additions to receive the King.

The complications of the rival theatre under its various names and roles continued after Henry Siddons's abortive attempt to run it. In 1815 Edinburgh's

Musical Festival concerts were held here, and in 1817 Corri advertised in the *Courant* that the New Pantheon would open on 12 February under Bannister's management, with a specially written introduction by Mr Amherst and equestrian performances by the whole company. There would also be a new French ballet produced by Simpson of Covent Garden, more horsemen, tightrope performers, clowns, and 'To conclude with a pantomime'.

A proper circus ring was built, together with a stage, with the evident intention of future theatrical shows. The interior, described as 'elegant', was supposedly designed by no other than William Burn.[41]

The first season was limited to circus and ballet, with the usual admission charges of 3s, 2s and a shilling. In November Corri illegally introduced burlettas and operas, for which he was not licensed, and his success encouraged him to progress to melodrama. In 1818 an extraordinary venture called *Old and Young*, 'an entire new spectacle founded on a popular novel, with new scenes, dresses, combats, &c', and including a ballet with leading dancers, turned out to be *Rob Roy*, a version that preceded Pocock's Covent Garden version by two months. The *Courant* gamely praised it as 'ingeniously contrived', but although the opening was well filled and Lady Menzies and other fashionable ladies 'graced the boxes', it was not a hit and was soon withdrawn.

Murray and Mrs Siddons reacted to this theatrical solecism by presenting a bill of suspension and interdict to the Court of Session. Corri, in answer, admitted the patentee's exclusive right to all entertainments licensed by the Lord Chamberlain – but claimed exemption because his productions were not licensed! He succeeded to the extent that the Court did not grant the interdict, but Lord Hermand passed the bill for trial, in which case he would probably have lost. But as before then Corri had become bankrupt, the action was quashed.[42] However, he continued as manager, or lessee, of melodramas and other productions at the Pantheon.

Next year (1819) he started up with *Rob Roy*, with rope dancing, ballets, *Cherokee*, 'with the celebrated dog Carlo, from the Surrey and Coburg theatres', all apparently under the umbrella of dramatised novel. An actor called Rattlin later gave a 'comic lecture' imitating Mathews. The plagiarism continued. Next came a version of *The Heart of Midlothian* by Montague and Jervis, followed by a pedestrian occupying 'the ring', then an exhibition of 'artificial animation', and a 'mechanical and optical museum'.

The autumn was filled with Italian operas, with Corri at the piano, and Miss Corri with Signors Begrez and Ambrogetti as singers, followed by Tom Dibdin's version of *The Heart*, not to mention equestrian shows, burlettas and ballets, while the new year 1820 opened with a fancy ball, tickets 7s, gallery 3s and music by Neil Gow.[43]

So it continued. The programme was nothing if not varied. Numerous adaptations of Scott filled the bill, and in 1822 Charles Mathews, having fallen into dispute with Murray and the Theatre Royal, appeared at the Pantheon instead, with his popular 'at home' entertainment, top tickets five shillings.

Mathews's performance was preceded by an impostor's attempt to cash in on his success. This man hired a room and circulated handbills advertising one of the famous sketches, 'Mathews at Home', shortly before the real actor's arrival. His show was deplorable, caused a row, and he was chased by a mob to the police office, where he had to seek sanctuary for the night. In the morning he was brought before a magistrate, but his pursuers had melted away, and as no charge was brought he was simply dismissed.

When the real Charles arrived and opened on 5 February, there were some doubts that Edinburgh had now got 'the real Simon Pure'. More complicated still was his disagreement with Murray and transfer to the Pantheon. 'I have got a horrid place to act in', he told his wife, 'across a ride; it is a circus.' The doubts over his identity on the 'Irish Mathews' hoax caused a fall in box office receipts to only £80 on the first night, but once the public were sure 'I *was* I' they flocked in and they took £132 – quite an achievement, as the Theatre Royal was open, and the circus boxes were worth only £5.

Meanwhile it was 'Mathews weather' – four changes since his arrival. He tried retreating to 'private walks' on the Calton Hill to study his act, but the weather was so wet and boisterous that this proved impossible. Terry told him that he was blown right into the street, fell against a stranger and the two had to cling to each other to keep upright.

Mathews was much gratified when Scott brought his family to the show, especially as they had met and dined in London a year or two back, with Byron and Terry. Now, coming out of the Pantheon after his show, he saw Scott in the lobby, and went up quietly to shake his hand. Polite remarks were exchanged – and Scott plainly did not recognise him – and asked him how he enjoyed the show. There was much laughter when Charles admitted who he was. Scott invited him to visit next day, a gesture he much appreciated, from a man he held second only to Shakespeare. Accordingly he, Terry and Mrs Terry had 'a most delightful' Sunday with them.[44] That September Mathews went to America until the following year.[45]

Apart from a few circuses, this seems to have ended the existence of the upstart Pantheon. The interior was again remodelled, and Corri now being dead, it reopened as the Caledonian Theatre under new management.

40
ADVENTURES AND CURIOSITIES

'She stands nearly 7 FEET HIGH, is remarkably Stout, and well-proportioned, possesses a pleasing and interesting Countenance, and is allowed by all visitors to be The Tallest, Largest, and Strongest Woman in the World.'

Mrs Cook, The Giantess, poster in *Broadsides 1819–31* (British Library, 1825, b.30 (37))

A curious find at Bellevue in August 1807 was linked with the strange story of an unsolved murder committed almost a year earlier. A journeyman mason, walking through the grounds with two companions, came across a parcel of banknotes hidden in a hole, 'in a stone enclosure by the side of a hedge' (as Chambers tells us).[1] They decided to take the weather-stained packet to Mr Clark Rattray, the sheriff, who found it to contain about £3000 in notes from several banks.

These proved to form the bulk of more than £4000 stolen from William Begbie, a bank porter with four children, whose body had been discovered the previous November in the Old Town, stabbed to the heart with a sharp bread-knife. The unfortunate finder was a little girl, on her way kettle in hand from her mother's in Tweeddale Close off the High Street, to fetch water from the well for tea. The dead man had been on his way with the money from the British Linen Bank's Leith branch for their head office, which then occupied the former town mansion of the Marquesses of Tweeddale.

Begbie's murderer was never found, in spite of many enquiries and the offer of a £500 bank reward, with a further Government promise of a free pardon to any accomplice with information leading to the killer. All that the sheriff and his officers could discover was that Begbie's journey had been shadowed by a man whom children had also seen about the supposed time of the murder, running from the close and down Leith Wynd off the Netherbow. The weapon was identified as bought that same day and 'ground upon a grinding-stone, and smoothed to a hone'. A Perth and Edinburgh carrier was arrested on strong suspicion, but proved to be innocent, and the case was left open.

For a time public suspicion then rested on a Leith doctor, 'a dissolute man and a gambler', who shortly committed suicide. Discovery of the notes at Bellevue, for which the bank awarded the finders with £200, did not help to a solution. But long after, a paper published in 1822 by Mr Denovan, a Bow Street officer, may well have established the murderer's identity.

In *The Life and Trial of James Mackoull,* Denovan described the recollections of a teacher in Leith, who as a boy of fourteen had apparently witnessed the circumstances of 1806. The boy, who was serving on a ship just returned to Leith from Lisbon, had brought presents for his mother and sister living in the Netherbow opposite Tweeddale Close, and he set off that afternoon with them hidden under his jacket, as the gifts were 'contraband'. On his way up Leith Walk he was alarmed by the sight of 'a tall man carrying a yellow-coloured parcel under his arm and a genteel well dressed man in a black coat, dogging him', who was cautiously keeping to the opposite side. He supposed that the man with the parcel was a smuggler and his follower a customs official, and terrified of himself being accosted the boy kept a close watch on the supposed officer, whose face he never saw.

At the head of Leith Street the 'smuggler' went by the North Bridge and his follower kept on by the Register Office. 'I hove to, and watched him', but the man followed his prey up the North Bridge. After a moment the boy slowly followed, but seeing no more of either of them he shortly turned off towards the safety of his mother's house.

Just as he reached Tweeddale Close 'I saw the custom-house officer come running out of it, with something under his coat', and hurry down the street. Now thoroughly alarmed, fearing he had been spotted, he quickly dropped his own parcel at his mother's and returned at once to Leith.

Relating his 'narrow escape' to the mate, he was roundly told off for going ashore without leave. Next day, learning of Begbie's murder, he did not doubt he had seen the assassin; yet it never occurred to the boy to report it to the magistrates. A few days later his ship sailed, was by ill luck captured by a French privateer, and he spent the next years in a French prison until rescued by the peace.

The story now shifts to James Mackoull, 'a London rogue, of unparalleled effrontery and dexterity', a gambler and pickpocket.

He had haunted Scotland for some years, and in 1805 and 1806 had been in Edinburgh, frequenting a laigh coffee-house in the Ship Tavern and living in 'a mean lodging at the bottom of New Street in the Canongate', near the scene of Begbie's murder. He passed as a Hamburg merchant turned out by the French and now practising as a skin-dyer. Suspicion never fell on him for the deed, and he left the country for some years until in 1820 he was arrested for a bank robbery in Glasgow, brought to Edinburgh for trial, and condemned to be executed.

Denovan, who had evidently learned the former sailor's story, based his certainty of Mackoull's guilt of the Begbie murder on a conversation he had with him in the Edinburgh condemned cell, in the presence of the Governor Captain Sibbald. By agreement with Sibbald he disarmed Mackoull's suspicions by harmless pleasantries, and then gave the Governor a signal, putting his hand to his chin as he asked the prisoner, 'By the way, Mackoull, if I am correct, you resided at the foot of New Street, Canongate, in November 1806 – did you not?'

At this Mackoull stared, rolled his eyes, and fell back on his bed as if in a fit. At last he started up, exclaiming wildly, 'No! I was then in the East Indies – in the West Indies. What do you mean?' He then hastily agreed that he had gone to Dublin, claiming he had won £10,000 by gambling there, and wished he had stayed. 'He now seemed to rave, and lose all temper,' and Denovan left, fairly convinced by this circumstantial evidence of Mackoull's guilt.

Mackoull escaped hanging for either crime, for while still under reprieve for the Glasgow robbery he died in gaol. It was another two years before Denovan published his paper containing the story of the evidence of the boy sailor.[2]

The world then as now loved curiosities and phenomena. In 1813 Edinburgh witnessed a remarkable example of both in the person of the nine-year-old Zerah Colburn, the American 'mathematical boy', one of those youthful prodigies born with an extraordinary memory for mental arithmetic. In no time he had learned the multiplication tables up to 100, knew all the prime numbers and factors, and was able to memorise and learn the rules of square and cube roots. Unlike many such prodigies, he was also intelligent.

Zerah was born to a poor middle-aged farmer in Vermont, who like several fathers of boy geniuses, once he realised his son's quality decided to exploit it, and exhibited him in New England. In 1812 he abandoned his debt-ridden farm in order to bring the boy to England.

Abiah Colburn was armed with letters of introduction, and fame had preceded them. In London at Spring Gardens Zerah was visited by, among many others, royal dukes, the sixteen-year-old Princess Charlotte of Wales, several of the nobility, Sir James Mackintosh and Sir Humphrey Davy, yet expenses swallowed up their profits.

When in London Zerah took tea with the Quaker philanthropist William Allen, of Stoke Newington (November 1812), who also tested the 'calculating powers' of 'the extraordinary lad from America'. 'They are truly prodigious, – he almost instantly gave the cube-root of any 9 figures proposed.'

Though with no formal education Zerah had learned to read and, in London, to write. In order to finance his schooling Mackintosh, Davy and others started a subscription list for a memoir, and in an attempt to widen this list, visits to Ireland and Scotland were arranged.

Father and son arrived in Edinburgh from Dublin and Belfast in November 1813, and the prodigy was visited by Dugald Stewart, John Playfair, Dr Brewster, Dr Macknight and other academics, though the one thing they did not achieve was much increase in the subscription list.[3]

Harriet Elliot wrote to her brother Viscount Melgund, who had seen 'the calculating boy' in London, that she had now seen him twice and was 'extremely amused . . . not only from the wonders the boy performed, but from the contrast in the manners of my three companions' – Lord Webb Seymour, Playfair, and Thomas Thomson. The unworldly Lord Webb made a hash of the arrangements, having proposed an 11 o'clock visit 'because nobody else went so early', and then not appearing at their house until nearly one. He then, after some time chatting to Lady Minto, retired to a window with his memo book to 'prepare some questions for the boy'. This took him an hour and by the time they at last saw Zerah he had just three questions, 'which the boy answered in about a minute – & then poor Ld Webb had to begin again to his task'.

Playfair, meanwhile, 'showed off the boy *till an admiration*', treating him 'just as an old nurse wd a favorite child, & seemed full as *proud of him* – and quite delighted when he found out Mr Playfair in a mistake'. Zerah was quite at ease; while Thomson 'sat *knawing* the top of his walking stick, chuckling at Lord Webbs vain efforts to puzzle the boy, & admiring Mr Playfair'.

Harriet described the hopeless inability of 'the wise men of Edinburgh' to understand Zerah's 'method'. His phenomenally quick answers on square and cube roots made Dugald Stewart imagine he must memorise them from a table; but other responses he could not attribute to memory. Though Abiah Colburn intended to write up an account of his son 'in which he promises to explain his method as far as he knows it himself', Harriet was sceptical, 'but as the Brown-toasters all thought it worth while to subscribe, I let them put down your name [her brother's] too'.[4]

Zerah was not infallible. The Rev. Daniel Sandford, writing to his name-sake son in late December of 'the wonderful American boy', of whom he was content to hear from the accounts of others, stated that 'Leslie puzzled him, and so have other persons; and it is generally observed, that he discovers a question and answers it at once, or not at all. Like a tiger, if he misses his first spring, he does not try another.'[5]

'The arithmetical boy has left us', wrote Lord Webb enigmatically to his ducal brother, 'after affording the philosophers here a very interesting object of investigation.'[6]

Zerah's remaining ten years in Europe saw many disappointments, largely financial, though punctuated with successes. At the peace of 1814 he went to Paris, accompanied by Professor Leslie; and with the help of Washington Irving whom he met there, and later of the temporarily restored Emperor Napoleon, he attended the lycée. Money difficulties dictated his return to England (February 1816). Here Lord Bristol placed him at Westminster School and in two-and-a-quarter years he learned what took other boys four or five.

Further complications in their affairs caused Zerah to leave school and take to the stage, still aged only fifteen (May 1819), playing Norval in *Douglas* – doubtless an attempt to rival Master Betty. Next they tried Scotland and Ireland again, travelling steerage to Leith in a five-day steamboat voyage. Much of the time they seem to have been destitute, relying on the help of friends, including the kind Dugald Stewart whom they visited at Kinneil.

Neither Scotland nor Ireland offered hope for the theatre, and in July 1820 they returned to London in some privation, where Zerah tried teaching, first as an assistant at Highgate school, then in January 1822 in his own small establishment. His father failed to raise another subscription, and Zerah returned with his prospectus unsuccessfully to Edinburgh, Glasgow and Belfast. In Edinburgh he had the mortification of learning of a boy with similar gifts to his own, George Bidder, under the patronage of 'a Scottish nobleman'.

George Combe made a (third) cast of his head for study purposes, but cannot have found any faculty for making money.

Zerah's last years in England are soon told. His father's health failed and he died in February 1824 after more than a decade of increasing disappointment.[7] With Lord Bristol's help Zerah settled his father's debts and returned to America, sailing from Liverpool in May to rejoin his still impoverished family. He resumed teaching, turned to religion and entered the Methodist ministry. His mathematical ability, though impaired in time, never left him. In 1829 he married, had three daughters, and in 1833 published a rather pompous memoir, with reflections on the English, Scots and French, and many religious comments. Zerah died of TB in 1836, aged only thirty-five.

This was the disillusioning career of a one-time boy genius.[8]

George Bidder (1806–78), three years older than Zerah, had a more successful life. He too was early exhibited by his father as a 'calculating phenomenon'; he was educated in Edinburgh. The *Annual Register* in 1819 described how he had impressed a group of 'scientific gentlemen at the age of 13, for example, in two minutes he calculated the cube root of 122615,327,232'. His process was entirely mental, and he memorised the numbers, given to him orally, by repeating them to himself. He did not work by the usual mental arithmetic rules; for example, in calculating products he got the highest numbers first. He too reckoned that he could communicate the process, 'by an apparent species of intuition'.

Bidder appears to have been assisted by the canal engineer James Jardine, for later in life he formed a 'Jardine' scholarship to help gifted boys. He himself became an engineer, was associated with Robert Stephenson on the London and Birmingham Railway, and worked on London's Victoria Docks.[9]

Some 'curiosities' were of merely physical abnormality. At the beginning of January 1822 a young 'giantess' of twenty-one known as Mrs Cook was exhibited on the Earthen Mound, after a spell in London where in 1818 she had been shown at the Earl of Yarmouth's, and seen by members of the royal family including the Prince Regent, and various noblemen. 'She stands nearly 7 FEET HIGH,' ran the Mound poster, 'is remarkably Stout and well-proportioned, possesses a pleasing and interesting Countenance, and is allowed by all visitors to be The Tallest, Largest, and Strongest Woman in the World.'

At the same time was displayed James Henry Lambier, 'the American Giant', just arrived from the United States and claimed as the largest man in the world. He was a 28-year-old Bostonian, eight feet high and weighing more than 30 stone, but well-proportioned and of prepossessing appearance. In total contrast was 'the Yorkshire Little Man', Joseph Lee from near Ferrybridge, barely ninteen and almost a Tom Thumb, thirty inches high, weighing twenty-two pounds and also well-proportioned. He was plausibly claimed as the smallest man.

To view these freaks adults paid a shilling, children and servants 3d.[10]

A rather pathetic story with an unknown end was of Helen Oliver, a young woman who ran away from home in Saltcoats early in 1818 after a period as a farm servant in West Kilbride, where she was said to have had 'a peculiar intimacy' with a ploughman – who proved to be a woman. This affair evidently affected her later career, for she now donned her brother's clothes and, calling herself John Thomson, went to work as a plasterer in Glasgow, Paisley, Lanark and Edinburgh. After she was 'discovered' by a Glasgow acquaintance she confessed to her employer and moved to Aberdeen, but in about 1820 was working in Edinburgh on the new Moray estate, lodging with a washerwoman adjoining the canal basin.

Nobody suspected her sex, remarking only that she appeared 'delicate' and perhaps consumptive, her ruddy complexion belied by slenderness. After about six weeks on the job she fell off a scaffold on the site one morning and knocked herself out on a hod, covering herself with lime spilt from the hod 'hawk'. Her neighbouring worker trying to clean off the lime from neck and breast thus discovered her, but said nothing until the dinner-hour when he told his mates. In the afternoon they ragged the girl by talking at her about 'John Oliver' (sic), 'the female plasterer' thought to be not far off.

Not surprisingly she soon had enough, slipped away on a pretext, and so vanished. Later a labourer met her on the road to Musselburgh, bundle on arm, and guessed she might be off to Haddington. So end the recorded facts.[11]

This and the seamier end of society were recorded in broadsides selling for a penny or so as sensational matter for those who could read, and published in Edinburgh and Glasgow. One of these listed, in doggerel verse, 'all the Bonny Ladies . . . assembled in Edinburgh during the Race Week', with their fees.

> To Edinburgh Races, we understand,
> There has arrived a sporting band
> Of playful Girls, from every land,
> In Venus' wars to lend a hand.

First comes the smartly dressed McRae from Glasgow, fair-haired seventeen-year-old Meg from Aberdeen, 'always seen' in Shakespeare Square, and a list of girls from Crieff, Inverness, Paisley, all lodging in the equally insalubrious St James' Square. Silvery-haired, blue-eyed Margaret Reid stayed on the South Bridge, others in the Old Town. Their charges varied 'from half-a-guinea to a crown', but, the broadside cynically notes, plenty of cheap stuff might be found for as little as a penny in the Canongate and Blackfriars Wynd, while at the top end of the scale was Sue from London, set up in private lodgings and suggestively joined by a Parisian protector.[12]

Sadler's balloon ascent vied with the 1815 music festival in drawing crowds. After Vincent Lunardi's ascent in 1784 no further balloon attempts were made in Edinburgh until Wyndham Sadler, a young engineer made his in 1815, coinciding doubtless for publicity's sake with the great music festival. 'Mr Saddler Junior' (he was only nineteen at the time) had worked for the Liverpool Gas Company but left in order to become an aeronaut. He had also been a member of the Board of Naval Works, and Inspector of Chemistry to the Army and Navy.

He was not very lucky. First taking off in Glasgow on 19 October, he struck a very wet day and was airborne (not very high) only as far as Milngavie. However, on landing he was hospitably entertained by Mr M'Nayr, returned to Glasgow in a chaise and four, and appeared at the theatre to a cheering throng.

His balloon of seventy-four foot diameter was of fine silk over a strengthened framework, and was designed when inflated to resemble a Corinthian temple whose colonnade was adorned with full-length figures. It also had an elegantly appointed car, whose magnificence had been intended for a display in Paris at Louis XVIII's coronation. It was oval, borne on eagles at each end, lined with purple and gold, and on its railing were the arms of England and the Orders of Saints Patrick and Andrew. Burnished ropes attached it to the balloon, with a purple silk canopy painted with signs of the zodiac and other decorations, surmounted by a coronet.

The *Edinburgh Advertiser* claimed this as Sadler's forty-ninth ascent, apparently confusing him with his father. Tickets at five shillings were bookable in advance, and take-off was on Friday, 3 November from the courtyard of the College. Every step in its progress, even preceding its inflation at noon, was marked by the firing of a castle gun, until the ascent in the afternoon. (As usual, the various descriptions of the affair differ in points of detail.) The start was delayed by shortage of water to dilute the acid, which had to be brought up in buckets. Meanwhile the crowd was kept in order by troops from Piershill. The press made the most of the achievement, the solemn farewell between Sadler and his father and friends, crowds of fashionable spectators, and (luckily) the fine weather.

The crowd was even larger than expected, both round the College and on the surrounding heights. The fine day was marred by a hazy atmosphere, likely to obscure sight of land or the ships stationed for possible rescue. And unfortunately Sadler had left his chart behind.[13]

Every slope or point of vantage was filled with eager spectators, said to be unprecedented, and extravagantly claimed at more than 100,000. 'The appearance of Arthur's Seat, Salisbury Crags, the Calton Hill, Nelson's Monument, Castle Hill and the steeples, was truly grand and picturesque.' The *Scotsman* reporter does not make it clear whether this remarkable spectacle was the crowds, or the view enjoyed by the privileged balloonist.[14]

Because of the haze Sadler, floating eastwards over Salisbury Crags in a westerly wind, could not look out for the coast of Fife. He reached a maximum height of three-quarters of a mile, but after only eight minutes (one account says seven) he opened a valve and descended in a field between the post road and the sea. He had only reached Portobello.

The crowd did not mind. Sadler, exhausted, was surrounded and carried shoulder-high to the village, while the crowd so mobbed the balloon that it was broken to pieces, and could only be packed up for its return with difficulty, followed by a gang of boys and 'idle persons' who for some reason pelted people on the road with potatoes. The destruction was quite accidental, with eager throngs treading on the precious silk. Back at the College, Lord Elibank and other gentlemen awaited his return and congratulated his achievement, while the weather turned dull and overcast.

Edinburgh was very full for the music festival, and crowds of spectators on the Calton Hill, the Crags and round Nelson's column, generously estimated,

Above. The façade of the University, now called Old College, South Bridge (from J.H. Shepherd, *Modern Athens*, 1829).

Left. The Library, Old College, photographed c.1900. Scottish Colorfoto Collection.

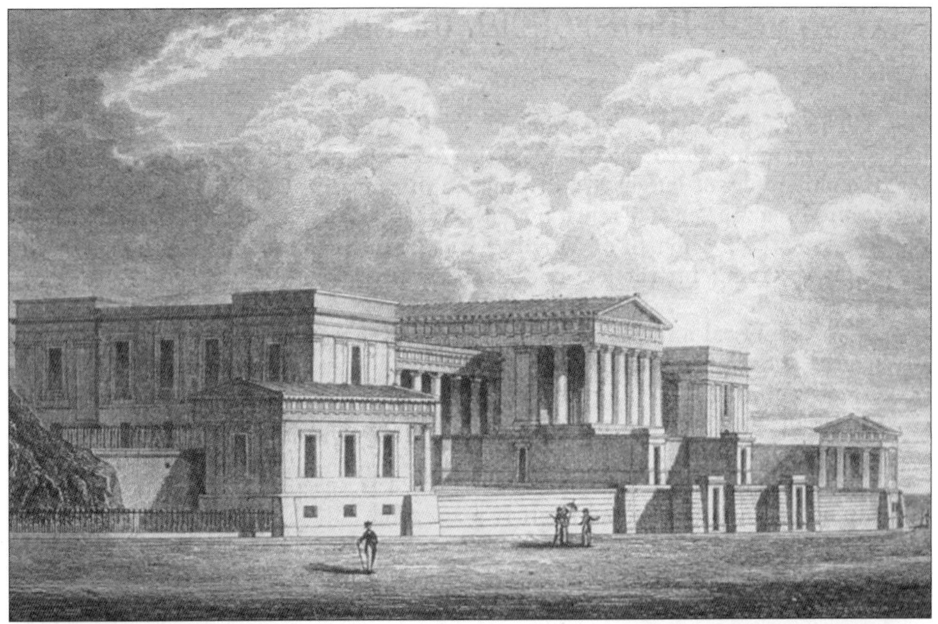

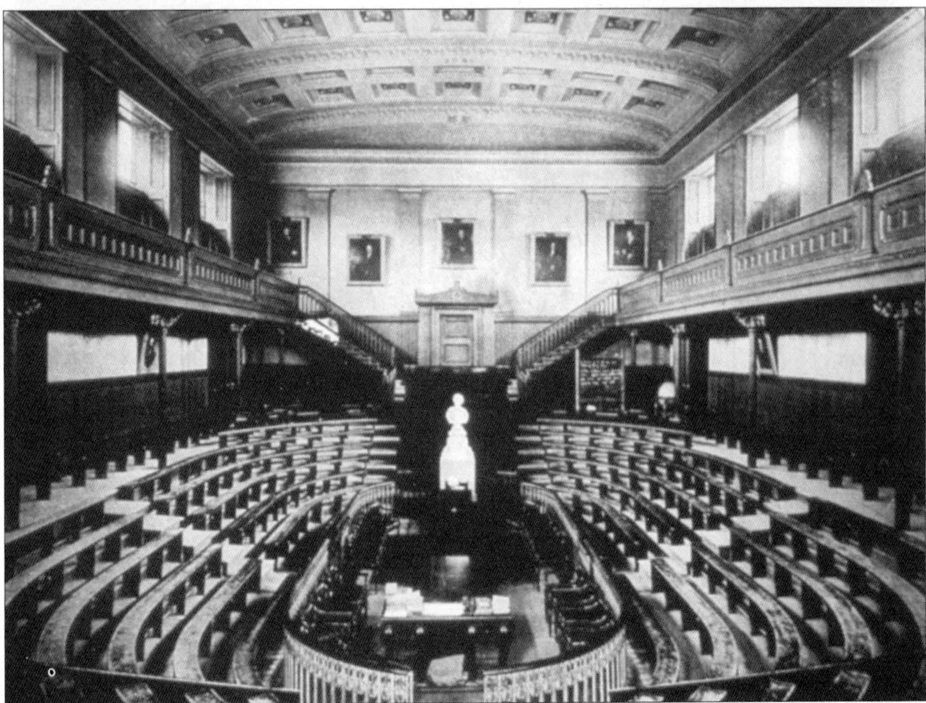

Top. The Royal High School. Crown Copyright: RCAHMS

Bottom. The Assembly Hall of the Royal High School, photographed c.1910.
Crown Copyright: RCAHMS

Top. The Edinburgh Academy, *c.*1830. Crown Copyright: RCAHMS

Bottom. The Advocates' Library (from J.H. Shepherd, *Modern Athens*, 1829). Crown Copyright: RCAHMS

Top. The Theatre Royal (from J.H. Shepherd, *Modern Athens*, 1829).

Bottom. Physicians' Hall. J.H. Shepherd/J. Henshall, 1829.

Top and bottom. Moray Place (above) and Royal Circus (below), both constructed in the second phase of the development of the New Town (from J.H. Shepherd, *Modern Athens*, 1829).

Top. Tanfield Hall was erected as an oil gas-works in 1825, and was later used as the Assembly Hall for the Free Church of Scotland.

Bottom. Holyrood Palace and Abbey. J. Ewbank/W.H. Lizars, c.1850.

Top. The Custom House, Leith (from J.H. Shepherd, *Modern Athens*, 1829).

Bottom. The Orphans' Hospital, designed by William Adam, 1734 (from *Vitruvius Scoticus*).

Above. The Orphans' Hospital being demolished to make way for the railway station. Calotype, D.O. Hill and R. Adamson, *c.*1845.
National Galleries of Scotland

Right. The Scott Monument under construction. Calotype, D.O. Hill and R. Adamson, *c.*1843.
National Galleries of Scotland

was the largest seen until the King's visit some years later. 'Nothing can be more awful than the immediate ascent,' was the pronouncement, 'the most anxious and most interesting moment.'

Sadler later made more successful flights, including a crossing of St George's Channel from Dublin to Holyhead in 1817; but in 1824, when only 28 years old, he made a crash landing and died of his injuries.

In March 1822 another flight was advertised by Signor Spirelli, with posters at every corner, that on Monday at 2 p.m. he would exhibit his 'Newly Invented Apparatus for Flying', and attempt a flight from 'the Pinnacle of Arthur's Seat to Salisbury Crags', a most ambitious effort.[15]

There were some even more ambitious. John Howell, printer and editor, who later went in for restoring paintings and porcelain, is said for good measure to have built and tried out a flying-machine from 'an elevated point at the foot of the west side of the Mound near the old tannery'. Unfortunately he quickly crashed on a pile of stones, lucky only to break his leg. In another mechanical attempt he and his brother tried out a submarine he had designed, in the Water of Leith. It instantly capsized. It was quickly dragged to the bank and John Howell, nearly drowned, was rescued.[16]

'Old Dr Syntax', or William Combe (1741–1823) – no relation to the phrenologists – was a miscellaneous writer of travels, novels and pamphlets. His three fictitious accounts of the 'Doctor's' journeys, in 1812, 1820 and 1821, and his adventures on his old horse, parodies of the travel books of writers on the Picturesque such as William Gilpin, were illustrated by Thomas Rowlandson. Having been born about 1741, he was by contemporary standards pretty old, and when in Edinburgh was guyed by other writers. According to John Wilson's daughter, he dressed like his creation, and strode very fast along Princes Street, portfolio under arm, 'as if full of important business'. Some wag might offer him a 'preposterous decoration' such as a turban, a 'Yeoman's helmet', or whatever, which he would don and stand about in ostentatious display, especially if the street were crowded.

He also made a nuisance of himself at University lectures, taking a conspicuous seat, and opening his portfolio to take notes or to sketch the lecturer. 'If it grew dark, he would solemnly draw from his pocket a small taper and strike a light', whose small illuminated disc, lighting up his solemn, cadaverous features, distracted the audience. 'The Professor of Civil Law was particularly plagued in this way, but all the lecturers suffered except Wilson, of whom he had a wholesome dread.'[17]

Another curious tale was of a ghost, claimed to have been seen by a gentleman's servant in 1815. He was summoned to the police court for putting out this story about a house in Jamaica Street, which prevented its being let by the owner. The servant 'positively avowed' to having seen the ghost several times and even talked with it. Becoming a little wilder, he asserted that 'it was of a copper colour, dressed in a red nightcap', but claimed that he was enjoined to secrecy and refused to say what they spoke of.

The police bound him over for a year under a £5 penalty, but before leaving the court he begged leave to ask the magistrate if he might speak to the ghost in future, 'as he had promised to see him again, and to partake of his hospitality'. This was reported in the *Courant*, but unfortunately, as with many newspaper stories, that is all we ever hear of it.[18]

If Lord Buchan had been merely the fool that some liked to picture him, he would never have attracted the attention of the many distinguished people who sought his acquaintance.

He had American connections, and on the female side was related to George Washington. When Benjamin Rush was studying in Edinburgh they had become friendly and subsequently corresponded for nearly fifty years, and when Rush's son also came to study in Edinburgh, he too was anxious to meet the Earl.

There was talk of a box made from the oak tree in which William Wallace hid after the battle of Falkirk, which Lord Buchan had presented to George Washington. The latter in his will restored it to Buchan, who then sent it to Benjamin Rush – but having reached America it was unfortunately robbed on the coach to Philadelphia, and never recovered.[19]

In 1817 James Watt, then in his eighty-second year and only two years before his death, came to Edinburgh from Glasgow and was given an enthusiastic welcome by scientists and literary men alike. Lord Buchan gave a dinner at his George Street house for this 'cheerful old man' of such wide knowledge. Among the guests, besides the obvious Scott and Jeffrey, were Sir James Hall, President of the Royal Society, and Alexander Nasmyth, whose son saw him next day and records Watt's 'benevolent countenance and his tall but bent figure'.[20]

At the opposite end of the spectrum was Buchan's undoubtedly odd behaviour. When the Grants of Rothiemurchus lived in George Street in 1816 they were his near neighbours, and Lord Buchan, who among them cared only for Elizabeth, used to appear at their house to give her lessons in etiquette. Wearing a shepherd's plaid, and with his long white hair loose over his shoulders, he ticked her off for biting her nails, rapping her fingers if he saw she had, and sometimes gave her some odd small curiosity: a supposed tooth of Queen Mary, or a bone of King James V. 'How many flighty people there were in Scotland', observed Elizabeth tolerantly: 'neither of his extraordinary brothers quite escaped the taint'.[21]

Then there was his former housekeeper Mrs Farquharson, who let rooms in Princes Street where Benjamin Haydon stayed on his visit in 1820. She had been supplied with cast-off furniture to equip her house, though in view of Buchan's noted meanness how she achieved this is hard to explain. For example, the old chairs were much too heavy to lift, so that instead of offering one to a guest, he had to be directed to it.[22]

The long-suffering Lady Buchan died in May 1819, having borne her spouse no children. In her heyday she had acted as the royal representative at the Queen's Assembly, which no one could attend without a voucher, the equivalent of a Lord Chamberlain's ticket. In 1810, for example, when the very young – too young – Lady Clementina Drummond was entering society and Lord Buchan, a close friend of her father's, had suggested she might go, Lord Maurice was willing, but Lady Buchan and Clementina's mother disapproved – in the end she was allowed.[23]

The Buchans had been married for nearly fifty years. Lord Buchan, 'that compound of wit and folly', as Mrs Grant termed him, 'buried her with honest undissembled glee, and in two days made his proposals – at seventy-four, you observe – to a very fair young lady, his neighbour in the country, which she absolutely, nay scornfully, rejected'.[24]

Only a month later he was in London, and dining in Upper Brook Street with various Erskine relatives and Richard Rush as fellow-guests.

Mrs Fletcher describes how, in 1820, Buchan's younger brother Lord Erskine, agreeable and entertaining – though less engaging, she thought, than his late brother Henry, and with a plainer, less courteous manner betraying signs of his stressful life – called on them with an interesting account of the state trials on which he had formerly worked. Another time he called with Lord Buchan, and pleased them with a 'fund of amusing political anecdote'.

It was on this occasion that Erskine told them a piece of royal scandal in which he had been concerned and to which, he claimed (perhaps even with some pride), 'many of the disastrous measures of the Regency are owing'. The story was that some years back Mrs Fitzherbert had been embarrassed by Lady Hugh Seymour's leaving her the guardianship of her daughter, which she as a Catholic opposed on political as well as religious grounds. The Prince sent for Lord Erskine and warned him that 'it would kill her and the child if they were separated', and Erskine suggested that he ask Lady Hertford to intercede with her husband, who was the girl's uncle. 'He did so, and from this accidental acquaintance has arisen the influence Lady Hertford has obtained . . . a curious piece of secret Court history'. The 'disaster' claimed by Lord Erskine was because 'she governs the King with despotic sway'.[25] To this incident Lord Erskine attributed the then Regent's change of policy, continuation of the war with France, and all the disasters of the Regency period!

The anonymous author of the satirical novel *Edinburgh* in 1820, a *roman à clef*, if so disjointed a work could be dignified by the name, describes among numerous other events the arrival and experiences of a student visitor from Gothenburg – a crude popular device. He is invited to a party of 'literati' who include Lord Buchan under the psedonym 'Lord Urbane', who himself invites our traveller to a party at his house.

Lord Buchan is fairly accurately described: he enters 'with a quick and irregular step', looking about for 'approvers' and raising his spectacles to smile and look 'consequential', while the circle of professors opens to receive him. ('The Scotch have a vast respect for a lord.') He is described as having 'a good heart, much reading but greater eccentricity, and some confusion of mind'. Every sentiment he utters is greeted by 'Admirable!' – 'Just so!' – 'Vara true, indeed, my lord!' To their joint dismay a young Oxonian learnedly caps a pronouncement, but is saved by Lord Urbane's inviting him to his wife's party, upon which the conceited youth is praised for his genius by the sycophantic crew.

Our traveller is later enlightened about the peer: renowned despite his eccentricity for justice, patriotism and kindness, besides his exertions for Scottish literature – patronage of Tytler, Burns and others, and an annual commemoration of Thomson etc. – and especially for high-mindedly insisting, when he succeeded to the peerage, that the Government no longer send him a pre-arranged list of peers for his vote.

Lord Urbane's party is an opportunity for the author to revile one Edinburgh personality after another. A 'temporary saloon' has been set up in the George Street house, and a lavish entertainment is staged, with Lord Urbane in flesh-coloured costume to suggest nudity (but too baggy), surrounded by virgins of all ages, mostly peers' daughters (he is said to value title above talent), also partly nude. This event may have been exaggerated, and at this point a tedious fictitious plot gradually emerges but with endless reversion to descriptions of thinly disguised characters, all maliciously presented, and not all identifiable.[26]

Travel to Edinburgh, if one did not have one's own transport, took three forms, stage coach, steamer up the east coast to Leith, and walking. The last was by no means uncommon in any part of Britain for many decades, as any novel by Charles Dickens reveals. People thought nothing of walking twenty or thirty miles in a day, like Sarah Hazlitt during her prolonged wait for a divorce; or the two Alison brothers who, elated by news of the victory of the Pyrenees (September 1813), set off from Edinburgh at 8 in the morning and walked twenty-one miles 'without drawing breath or halting for a second'. A five-minute breather and they completed the whole thirty-five miles to Rochsoles in nine hours, blistered and thirsty, 'but in the highest spirits'.[27]

In his old age James Ferrier, WS, related how as a boy he had walked the sixteen miles to Linlithgow to see his grandmother – though the kernel of the story was not the walk, but that on arrival she laid a pigeon pie before him, and as in delight he stuck in his knife he not unnaturally said he could make a dinner of it. 'Will ye so?' exclaimed the old lady, snatching it from him, and the starving boy saw it no more.[28]

Coach travel had nothing romantic about it, especially for an outside passenger. Serjeant Robert Butler, who worked first as a boy servant, then trained as a weaver, but in time of shortage and unemployment joined the army, describes his return on furlough from Belfast with another youth. This was in 7 August 1806, on top of the coach, a 'dreadful day of thunder, lightning, and rain' which caused widespread damage.

Once they reached Saltcoats they were the only two outside, and the insiders kindly offered to make room – but Butler piously refused, on the grounds that he had joined up to endure everything that was going.[29]

Thomas Carlyle, who regularly travelled between Ayrshire and Edinburgh, graphically describes his sufferings in letters to his family. Ending his second Edinburgh visit in 1815 with departure one Sunday 'in the gayest humour in the world', after enduring only a few miles on the outside in 'biting breezes', despite his greatcoat he had to retreat inside. Just under a year later he returned to the city, a fearsome three-day journey, partly on foot. 'I never was more happy at seeing Edinburgh' – in view of his hatred of the place praise indeed.

In late August 1818 he walked the eighty-one miles from Ecclefechan, dry and windy after a day's rain, and arrived at Edinburgh at 5 p.m., after a presumably very early start. In November 1819, on foot again, 'the roads were very bad & the weather very wet'. In 1820, however, when he came by coach, for those on the roof 'it rained upon us heavily' all the way from their approach to the top of Ericstane, where the three counties of Dumfries, Peebles and Lanark meet, 'till we had arrived within 20 miles of Edinr . . . the storm was so rough as soon to soak the lower part of my back . . .', and so forth.[30]

In 1822, when his brother John was coming to Edinburgh to study, this experienced traveller warned him to sit inside the coach if the weather were at all damp: 'you have no Idea what a task it is to sit all day motionless on the coach roof in the month of October'.[31]

A London voyage was theoretically more economical than road travel, which required at least two nights' lodging as well as meals on the way, whereas by sea, food and lodging were included in the steamer fare, and the voyage was hardly longer than coach travel up the Great North Road. But because of the weather there was always uncertainty over the time of arrival, when besides sea-sickness, passengers might easily be delayed for a day or more.

Sea travel was perhaps more comfortable, with sailings from Leith down the coast and up the Thames. Steamboat voyages from about 1813, taking approximately three days, were recorded by Scott, the actor-manager John Kemble and many others, while the King himself arrived by water in August 1822. But it was not without hazards, and even more exposed to the elements than the luckless coach passenger in snow and on muddy roads. Serjeant Butler, who for some years was courier for bullion for a large army contractor and linen manufacturer in the early 1820s, regularly sailed with the Leith Shipping Company on the *James Watt.* One day, lured by publicity, Butler tried the luxurious new *United Kingdom* steamship, equipped with such comforts as chairs and even looking-glasses, instead of the usual bleak fixed benches; but the captain's unpracticality and lack of common precautions were proved after a few hours, when the wind got up increasingly, by dinner-time violent enough to smash dishes and bottles on the newly-laid tables, and there were no sandbags to hold things in position.

By night, says Butler drily, sobbing ladies were padding barefoot and dishevelled from their cabins in 'a perfect hurricane', only to see their distress embarrassingly reflected in the elegant wall-mirrors. In one bizarre touch, to everyone's terror the head of a black-faced sheep, part of the meat cargo in the stern, was dislodged from its meat-hook and swept up against a saloon window. The luggage in the ship's waist, which seems to have had no protective tarpaulins, was flooded and spoiled, as storm and rain pounded on for two whole days and nights.

All this time the galley was out of action and no food could be cooked, though anyway most passengers were too sick to eat. The captain, who should have been engaged for familiarity with the route, was new to it, his pilot was drunk and incapable, and when the fury at last began to abate, the ship drifted on to the Union Sandbank.

Either passengers or crew then persuaded the captain of a man-o'-war, who happened to be a passenger, to take over, and this gentleman soon put things to rights. First directing the 120 people to assemble aft to help raise the bows from the sand, he backed the engines and successfully brought them off. A distress signal was fired, and a shore boat with a pilot came to their aid.

The dreadful voyage ended at last when they limped up the Thames next afternoon, 30 hours late . . . and for his return voyage to Edinburgh Serjeant Butler was careful to book a passage with the old *James Watt.*[32]

During the wars sea travel was rendered hazardous by possible – indeed likely – enemy action. Before the days of steam Daniel Carless Webb, who sailed from Portsmouth in 1811 under what might have been supposed to be armed protection in the *Gorgon*, converted for prisoners of war and carrying forty-four guns, was nearly murdered by an act of gross treachery.

On board was M. Hypolyte de Creuze, a gentlemanly officer in the Italian navy, bound with other Frenchmen to a new purpose-built prison at Penicuik. Webb, attracted by his manners and his plight, even invited him to the officers' cabin to help translate a petition to the Transport Board for de Creuze to obtain an exchange. This unscrupulous officer used the opportunity to locate the arms depot in the cabin, and overnight perfected an elaborate plot with a companion, Pierre le Marchand, to overpower the sentinels with a band of picked men, seize the ship and, at breakfast, murder all the officers.

During the dark hours the conspirators started to cut away the planking round the fore hatchway, but unfortunately for them the plot had been overheard by a couple of French-American prisoners, who took the story to the captain. The hatch party was surprised, the conspirators overpowered and de Creuze and his fellow le Marchand put in irons for the rest of the voyage.

The prisoners were kept on board until the weather improved, but meanwhile Daniel Webb spent a week or two enjoying Edinburgh's social whirl, and the usual jaunts to Roslin and Dalkeith. He returned to Leith to rejoin the *Gorgon* as the prisoners were being disembarked, to be taken under guard to Penicuik, and ironically 'made a parting bow' to the slippery gentleman whom he had courteously assisted and who had so nearly succeeded in murdering them all.

Webb's adventures were still not over, and his return voyage was almost more colourful. After a fast sail with the tide down the coast, arriving at the Downs an enemy ship was sighted, and they had to haul off towards France, but then spotted three privateers standing from Boulogne, hoping to intercept stragglers.

Luckily the *Plover* sloop, firing her guns, hove into view to defend the *Gorgon*, and she was able to make for the Thames. This last mishap had lengthened the unusually fast voyage to almost a week.

Such were, should one elect to go by sea, the unpredictable hazards of a simple trip to Edinburgh in wartime.[33]

Incidentally, transports of prisoners of war were usually shipped to Edinburgh from the south of England, disembarking at Leith and being marched from there to the Castle. On the muddy, rutted and frozen road many lost their shoes. One such transport of three to four hundred men, mostly sailors, whom Louis Simond visited in February 1811 through the introduction of Colonel Maghee, formed part of a total of some 50,000.[34]

A gruesome and disgraceful event illustrating a near-inhuman attitude to the unfortunate and the malefactor occurred in 1818. A gentleman calling himself

'Eye Witness', obviously in the law, published a pamphlet addressed to the magistrates on the gross mishandling of the hanging of Robert Johnson, condemned for highway robbery with violence.

The writer, who had gone to the Signet Library to collect a book, while he was waiting saw a crowd gathering to witness an execution. He and others went out to have a look, but were ordered off by the printer Alexander Smellie and 'a little bustling officious creature', who told all who were not Writers to the Signet to leave. But when the policeman guarding the temporary gate erected at the end of the church opened it by chance, pressure from the crowd forced them inside the enclosure. They were thus trapped in the unpaved area where the old gaol had stood, railed off for a space to approach the gibbet, between the Signet Library, the County Hall ('a wretched caricature of an Athenian Temple'), and the irregular gables of St Giles'. The gibbet had been erected opposite the church's large west window.

The condemned man approached steadily and ascended the scaffold. Only when prayers and other 'devotional exercises' were done did he seem to falter, and once he reached the drop his composure was gone; he stood convulsively clasping and unclasping his hands, involuntarily reached to his neck, and flushed and turned pale in turn, still trying to keep calm as he was prepared for the noose. The cap was pulled over his face and he was partly bound, and with some relief the involuntary watcher turned away.

The next few minutes were grim in the extreme. Someone shouted, 'Good God! the man's feet are not off the scaffold!' Slowly strangled by the rope, he was standing in agony, vainly trying to assist in his own hanging by convulsive jerks, while the magistrates stood by, doing nothing.

A city officer, Alexander Campbell, was the first to shout for carpenters to cut away the support, but when they did come they hacked for some ten minutes without shifting the 'machinery', while the wretched victim still hung there convulsed.

The crowd, having grasped what was happening, burst into an indignant roar and pelted the scene with a shower of stones. The magistrates fled for cover into the church, abandoning the unfortunate officials and still more unfortunate Johnson. Suddenly a gentleman sprang forward and cut the man down. 'No rescue', shouted the mob, and the wretch lay panting on the scaffold until some officers carried him into the Police Office, where they left him to recover. The magistrates made out that the rope was too long, the hangman was new and unfamiliar, and they were trying to find out who cut the man down. Of course they did not find him, and having themselves deserted the scene were not in a position to charge anyone with the crime of cutting down a victim within the statutory half-hour.[35]

During the next half-hour a surgeon tried to bleed Johnson, who did not bleed but showed other signs of life. The reserve police cleared the streets, and a magistrate ordered up a party of soldiers from the Castle. The most gruesome part of the episode now followed, with an actual repetition of the execution on the re-erected 'apparatus'.

Blame was cast on the mob (as so often), for had they not given way to their rage, official efforts to complete the hanging would have succeeded in a few minutes. Bad enough, indeed.

The site of the gibbet was unusual. Traditionally, hangings took place in the Grassmarket and only in recent years had it been set up near St Giles's, because of the proximity of the old gaol. With the gaol's demolition the spot, more cramped, and more frequented than the Grassmarket, lost any suitability it once had. Further, claimed 'Vindex', being now right outside the church instead of adjoining the gaol, it was a profanation.

The *Scotsman* described how some of the mob boarded the scaffold and cut down the victim, actually succeeded in restoring him to consciousness, and had even carried him some way down the street before the police tardily returned to their posts and attacked them with bludgeons to recover the body. The next phase was reminiscent of the French Revolution: Johnson, who by now had lost his shirt and some other clothing, was lying partly naked in the middle of the street outside the Police Office. After quite a long pause, the police dragged him some twenty paces into their 'den' adjoining the church, where bled by a surgeon he was partly restored, but unable to speak.[36]

While this was going on the soldiers arrived from the castle, and were ordered by the magistrates to load. At 13 minutes to 4, an hour and a quarter after poor Johnson should have expired, he was brought out again, his clothes so roughly thrown about him that when they raised his body they fell off so that 'decency would have been shocked'.

What followed was most disgraceful of all. A kind of makeshift table only eighteen inches high had been set up on a 'solid platform', only three or four feet from the ground. With his clothes now 'adjusted', the rope was again fastened round his neck, and held up by this he 'was left vibrating' with his feet on the table. 'At last, the table was removed from beneath him, when, to the indescribable horror of every spectator, he was seen suspended with his face uncovered, and one of his hands broke loose from the cords . . . his fingers convulsively twisting in the noose. Dreadful cries were then heard from every quarter.' A chair was brought up which the executioner climbed to force his hand away, but did not cover his face, 'a spectacle which no human eye should ever be compelled to behold'. At last someone threw a napkin over it.

The short northern day had now darkened, street lamps had been lit and soon stars were visible in the sky. Not until 23 minutes past 4 was this second 'butchery' finally ended. As soon as Johnson gave the signal the table should have instantly dropped to the level of the scaffold, but as it was so low and ill-constructed, instead of the usual sudden drop, by which his body should have fallen with a jerk, shortening his suffering by dislocating his neck, they could not remove it for nearly a minute after the signal. The fall was then so short that he ended 'half-standing, half-suspended and struggling in the most dreadful manner'.

The magistrates' excuse, trying to blame the crowd, was pitiful, as the hanging was bungled from the start. The general comment was that the hangman should have examined the 'machinery' so closely as to see that the drop was too short. The magistrates admitted the 'state of torture' in which Johnson was left, that he was alive when cut down, that the officers had eventually seized and carried him to their office, opened his veins, then strung him up again while still alive. Why had they not applied for guidance at once from the Lord Advocate, or Solicitor-General?

Legally it might be argued that the second hanging was homicide, if not murder, departing from the legal warrant under Scottish law by which a hanging must take place between 2 and 4 p.m., and to render death certain a body was left hanging for an hour after sentence was carried out. As Johnson was re-hung only a few minutes before 4, his death must have taken place after the hour, and the law had been outraged.

Henry Cockburn's notes on his copy of one of the pamphlets commented on the mob's righteous anger on witnessing such shameful mismanagement, all too visible from Johnson's being so near the ground and just in front of the church window. There were so many stones around as to 'make a *bicker*, and a rescue, irresistible'. He added that the gentleman who cut him down was never identified.

The magistrates sacked the superintendent of works and ordered a new, high, moveable apparatus to be made, never to be erected in front of a large window. This reform slightly appeased the public and shifted some of the blame from the authorities.

There were of course excuses. 'Amicus Ventatis' in an 'Address to the Inhabitants of Edinburgh' vindicated both police and authorities, claiming that Johnson died within five minutes of his second hanging, which was 'a disagreeable duty' once the 'humane' attempt to resuscitate him had succeeded. Further, the drop had been tested six times, its failure being the fault of the executioner's too-long rope. Nor had the magistrates wasted time – they were prevented by the mob.

As for hiding in the church – were they to stand by and be lynched? Altogether, he wrote off the 'blustering pamphlet' as 'malicious and glaring falsehood', and the *Scotsman* account as 'half-false, half-true reports'.

'Civils' made an indignant reply to the 'Eye Witness' pamphlet, 'thrust upon me in a book-seller's shop', as a 'weak, cowardly, passionate, malicious, and false' attack on the magistrates, 'production of an ignorant and insolent mind'. He accused the author, plainly a WS, of skulking under anonymity, and went on to intemperate railing at 'his manners as a gentleman, his talents as a writer . . . his character as a man'. There was no kind of insult that 'Civils' did not load on 'Eye Witness', merely for telling the truth, and maintained that cutting Johnson down was likely to cause a riot, and even prolonged the man's suffering. (But how would that anonymous, would-be saviour be expected to guess how the authorities would finally handle the deplorable affair?[37])

41
PHRENOLOGY

'A calm, excellent man, with a clear natural style of didactic speaking and very benevolent objects. Some wise people call him a quack, but I am satisfied that he really believes in that folly.'

Journal of Henry Cockburn, 1831–1854, 29 October 1834, on George Combe, Edinburgh, 1874

One great curiosity of the early decades of the century was the doctrine of phrenology, first introduced in Vienna by Dr Franz Joseph Gall, who claimed that the shape of the skull determined, or at least demonstrated, mental and emotional characteristics. Areas such as intellect, religion, criminal disposition, poetic gifts, mathematical ability, all were to be discerned, and meticulously charted. Gall's disciple Dr Johann Kaspar Spurzheim (1776–1832) spread the message by writing and lectures, and visited Edinburgh to lecture at least in 1816 and 1822. (By this time the imperial Austrian regime had long banned such lectures in Vienna, suspecting a tendency towards determinism.[1])

In Edinburgh the great exponent of phrenology was George Combe, and later to some degree his brother Andrew, who from 1817 to 1819 was studying medicine and surgery in Paris, including under Spurzheim. Sir George Mackenzie of Coull, back from his Icelandic exploration, who was a keen literary and philosophical dilettante, impulsive where George was practical, investigated this alluring subject with him.

In April 1818 George contributed a paper on phrenology for the second issue of another new Edinburgh quarterly, the *Literary and Statistical*. Writing to tell Andrew this news, which he hoped his brother would pass on to Spurzheim, he also described a natural genius he had met in the person of a Linlithgow shoemaker. Among several ingenious machines he had invented was one for perpetual motion, a mystery which long fascinated scientists and amateurs. It had worked in the previous October; unfortunately the machine failed once it was out of the man's reach. In view of this, Combe was particularly interested in the inventor's ill-developed 'organ of Constructiveness', and a close examination of his head revealed a highly developed imagination.[2]

Combe shortly decided to spread the word on phrenology by publishing collected essays, accompanied by a lecture series on its philosophy with anatomical back-up from Andrew. He was careful to avoid the subject in conversation as likely to excite argument, unless someone was seriously interested. New disciples, however, were coming into the fold.

In 1819 Combe, who by now had a large legal practice, removed to a house at Hermitage Place in Stockbridge, bordering on the country to the west. He was providing for Andrew, who returned home in December that year, frail in health and needing to set himself up in a medical practice; but the following May they removed to Brown Square as a better situation. Andrew's health was so poor, however, that he shortly went abroad again, this time to Italy. Their older sister Jean was still their housekeeper, until her death in 1831. William took over the family brewery management. Another brother, James, died aged barely twenty-one from a chill caught during an expedition down the Forth in a boat fitted with machinery and paddles. Curiosity of the talented amateur seems to have been a characteristic of all the brothers. Abram was influenced by Robert Owen, whose experimental mill was now operating in New Lanark, and George accompanied him there on an exploratory visit, but suspected the attempt would eventually fail.

The brewery had been hit, like most businesses, by the war and its aftermath, but with two of the brothers managing the firm, even at a loss, they were spared the bankruptcy that overtook many, and in time their fortunes recovered.

George rehearsed his phrenology lectures at home before a few friends – their sister Jean among his converts. Progress was interrupted by the unexpected death of their mother, and he therefore deferred the course, but went ahead with publishing. He was undeterred by ridicule, convinced that attackers' arguments were unsound. He published the work at his own expense, £120 for 750 copies, partly backed by his brother Abram, aware it would make a loss as 'works on philosophy by an obscure author never sell'.[3]

Combe's own arguments, which affected the attitude even of his sceptical friend William Waddell, were as follows: As dissection cannot reveal the functions of an organ, how could anatomists claim Gall and Spurzheim were wrong? Reflection on consciousness cannot reveal the organs, therefore metaphysicians themselves were ignorant. He corresponded with Dr P. M. Roget in London, who had (he claimed) given false data in the 'Craniology' article in the *Encyclopaedia Supplement*.

Once his book was printed by Bell and Bradfute, he could persuade only one bookseller to stock it, so the printers were obliged to sell it themselves. Sales were fair. It was reviewed in the quarterlies, Dr Thomas Brown bought a copy, and by degrees more booksellers agreed to stock it. Dr Hibbert, while attacking the science in an address to the Edinburgh Medical School, agreed that it was well defended by Combe, and Macvey Napier, editor of the *Britannia Supplement*, 'a metaphysician of the old school', took a cautious stand. At Principal Baird's request he attended a demonstration, to ensure the subject was tested by proper investigation, when even the sceptics Dr Monro (III) and Professors Wallace and Jameson were persuaded to attend. Through his *Essays* George met and became friendly with the *Scotsman* editors William Ritchie and Charles Maclaren, and became a contributor.

In February 1820 Combe, with the Rev. David Welsh, Brownlee, an advocate, the solicitor Waddell, and Lindsay Mackersey, an accountant, a Phrenological Society was launched, which by 1821 had attracted thirty-three members, and in December 1823 they launched the *Phrenological Journal.*

By 1821 even former sceptics had joined the society. Dr Baird, admitting it was a valid scientific investigation, was still open-minded. Dr Chalmers, who came to look at George's casts of heads, found himself staying a hour longer than he intended. It was George's persistent support that saved both Spurzheim and Gall from extinction by ridicule. Ministers were denouncing the science from the pulpit, arguing that it led to materialism, and Glasgow University, though admitting Sir George Mackenzie's work, banned the *Essays* from its library. But before long the phrenologists had to rent a small shop in which to display the casts, as visitors were becoming so many.

A member of the Edinburgh Medical Society read a paper on the subject which drew such crowds that Combe himself could not get in, and the debate went on until 2 a.m. Much of it displayed such ignorance that Combe agreed to speak himself on the first available occasion, and had to denounce malicious rumours, such as that Spurzheim and Gall had themselves abandoned the subject and were laughing at the 'gullible Scots'.

In April 1821 a couple of scoffers tried to catch him out with a clumsy hoax. A doctor cousin of Dr Gordon, author of the *Edinburgh* article, with the help of a painter friend, modelled a head from a large turnip, and sent a cast of it to Combe, pretending it was of Dr Tornhippsen, 'an uncommon character' from Sweden. Needless to say Combe at once spotted the deception, and got his brother Abram to write a verse parody. The perpetrator called next day to assure him that no offence was meant, but the authors of *Noctes* could not resist a malicious pretence that the false head had been diagnosed in good faith as constructive, philoprogenitive and so forth. The half-forgotten incident was thus dragged up again until Combe published an answer in the *Phrenological Journal* arguing that had the imitation only been good, a perfectly valid interpretation might have been made as if of a real skull, but 'the imitation was execrably bad, and the cast smelt so strongly of turnip that a cow could have discovered its origin'.

He now kept his collection at his Brown's Square house, where he demonstrated twice a week, and would meet visiting eminent scientists or philosophers. He fitted up the room for lectures, even borrowing his own drawing-room chairs when the crowd was too great. Sometimes when it proved too much for his energies, his sister Jean took over the demonstration.

Combe was overworking, to the detriment of his health, but managed to keep going by a strict diet and limiting his drinking. He learned to dissect the brain, and gave a lecture series from May to July (1821), completing nine of the sixteen at the rate of one a week. It was soon after this that he met Hazlitt on his Edinburgh visit, on the occasion of the supper at Ritchie's, and analysed his appearance and manners from a phrenological point of view.

For his first lecture on 14 May he expected an audience of twenty or thirty: about seventy turned up, though Barclay and Baird, both invited, were unable to attend. About sixty-five came to the next, then the numbers dwindled to thirty or forty. Andrew, now returned from foreign travels, helped with the dissection of first animal, then human, brains. As Edinburgh was now showing more interest, Combe was encouraged to start a winter course in November, but disappointingly only nineteen attended.

The Society now moved to premises Combe bought in Clyde Street, including the hall where Spurzheim had lectured in 1816. The casts, set up in the hall, were displayed to the public on Saturdays. Audiences consisted of 'respectable professionals', though few of them cared to acknowledge the doctrine for fear of jeopardising their careers.

Of Combe's rare errors one of the more unfortunate was his diagnosis of David Haggart, a nineteen-year-old pickpocket who regularly escaped from prison, and was finally executed for murdering a turnkey with a stone concealed in a bag when caught trying to escape from Dumfries Gaol. Combe, who visited him when he was imprisoned in Edinburgh, reported that his skull showed developed Conscientiousness and Secretiveness, but a deficiency in 'Love of Approbation'. While in gaol Haggart wrote a sketch of his life, claimed repentance, and maintained that the murder was unpremeditated. After his execution Combe examined a cast of his skull and found 'Conscientiousness' small after all. He was magnanimous enough to publish his error, but to his mortification opponents ridiculed him in *Blackwood's* and in the *Literary Gazette*.

Despite this he amassed a corpus of respectable supporters, such as Dr Chalmers, and Dr Abernethy who published a pamphlet on the subject, and the Society's members increased to more than eighty. Intending members were expected to have their heads 'examined' when they joined. The membership fee was a guinea, essay sales rose, and Combe had a copy of it bound interleaved with space for notes and corrections.

Combe would examine heads on request, seldom mistaken in his estimation. In September 1822 a *Blackwood's* writer, the Rev. George Croly, arrived as a scoffer: Combe diagnosed in his head a large Love of Approbation,

Secretiveness, and Combativeness, which between them 'play the deuce with him. He affects smartness, and a contempt for seriousness, all I believe from false notions of Greatness.' One might suggest that this deduction stemmed as much from Combe's own perceptiveness, intuition, call it what you will, as from the study of the shape of heads. However, to avoid criticism over possible error, Combe determined in future to avoid 'drawing character from developments not taken by himself'.

One leading supporter, the Rev. David Welsh (1793–1845), minister of Crossmichael, and from 1827 of St David's, Glasgow, made an influential defence of phrenology against the charge of materialism. Other noted believers were Dr Richard Pool, editor of the *New Edinburgh Review,* and of course Sir George Mackenzie and George's own brother Andrew. Furthermore, they were gaining supporters in Europe, and in the USA.

There was a brisk trade in phrenological casts. In 1823 Luke O'Neil and Son, Statuaries, of 125 Canongate, were advertising themselves as 'Artists to the Phrenological Society', with a large collection of casts available at their workships, presented by Sir George Mackenzie, including Dr Gall, Pitt, Hume, Napoleon, James Thomson (the poet), some executed murderers and two 'idiots'.

Their own casts of face masks included many celebrities, Newton, Cromwell, Haydn, Voltaire, Wilkes, King George III and the Duke of Sussex, Shakespeare, Johnson, Reynolds, Mrs Siddons, Prince Charles Edward, several 'mental calculating boys' including Zerah Colburn, to name but a few.

They also had casts of skulls including mummies (obtained from Spurzheim), American Indians and other Asiatic and African characters; also including murderers.

Masks could be taken on order, single casts could be boxed and sent for two to four shillings, and – showing how they must have expanded their business to include this fashionable craze – what was possibly their original line of products, reliefs and vases for chimney-pieces and gardens.[4]

Combe was now living a prosperous life, employing two clerks and an apprentice, and cultivated a grave demeanour, seldom laughed or showed emotion. By 1824, when easier circumstances allowed him more relaxation, though still only thirty-six, he had white hair and appeared well into middle age. His friendships took long to develop but were lasting and deep. By the time he launched his third course in May 1823, he enrolled twenty or so in the audience, all new, including two clergymen. He was working on publication of his own *Transactions,* thirteen essays with his own introduction, chiefly from papers already read. Publication was deferred until the autumn, and the cost of nearly £200 was borne by the bookseller John Anderson. A hundred copies were sent to London, all of which sold, and more were ordered. Feeling that his campaign was now getting across to the public, Combe ventured on a quarterly.

Andrew, who in 1823 embarked on a medical practice, which he continued for nine years until illness interrupted, contributed two papers to the 1824 *Transactions,* and in 1827 became President of the Society, serving two years. He continued to live at his brother's, until 1832 when George married Mrs Henry Siddons's daughter – but himself 'scrupulously refrained from matrimony' from fear of hereditary transmission of disease. Gentle and kind, he would always help others, when at home indulged in a jocular humour, and was fond of children, though knowing he would have none of his own.[5]

Phrenology was always a natural subject for typical spoofs and jokes. In 1816 Southey had compiled a satire aimed at his enemy Jeffrey ('the Prophet Jehephary'), imitating the style of the Chaldee Manuscript. He pictures the editor as suicidal over political events, dismissing pistols (a dig at the Tom Moore duel), and hanging, and finally lulled to sleep by the reading aloud of a *Review* paper, by 'Surjawi'. In his dream or nightmare the physician refers him to Spurzheim, who waxes excited over his huge 'organ of party', occupying the space where patriotism, and part of veracity, ought to be, the rest being excluded by the organ of malice. Nor has there ever been so vast an organ of assurance. In place of taste is a depression, but he has a large organ of vanity, sore from the blows of 'Sahothy the Chief Poet' and others. Among other remedies 'Archy the Constable' suggests oil of flattery. The whole piece is compounded of the malice which seems to have formed journalists' major weapon of the time.

Another who indulged in scoring off phrenology was Robert Gillies, who at Lasswade was a near neighbour of Sir William Hamilton and John Campbell Colquhoun[6] with whom he would take long walks discussing medieval literature, religion, and aesthetics. Hamilton, amused by the doctrine of phrenology, went to great trouble to disprove it by experiment. One morning he closely examined Gillies's head, to compare it with the published account of Voltaire's, and 'proved' that his 'bump of wit' was far more pronounced than that philosopher's.[7]

42
THE SCOTTISH REGALIA

'. . . the Crown Room and the old chest therein were opened on the 4th inst in presence of the Commissioners, and that the Crown, Sceptre, arid Sword of State were found in perfect order and preservation. The Crown is said to be particularly fine . . .'

John Wilson Croker to Sir Benjamin Bloomfield, 7 February 1818, A. Aspinall (ed.), *The letters of King George IV, 1812–1830*, Cambridge, 1938, II.245

'. . . the whole Regalia were found exactly in the state described in an official document made out in the year 1707 at the time of their deposition'.

Alexander Maconochie, Lord Advocate, to Lord Sidmouth, 7 Feruary 1818, *op. cit.*, II.246

A great drama early in 1818 was the official search for the Scottish Regalia. Crown and Sceptre had not been seen since 1707, when at the time of the Union they had been locked away in the castle with a guarantee that they should never be taken to England. King James VI had been eager enough to leave them behind when he departed to assume the joint crown in 1603, and they had been deposited at Dunnottar Castle. Here they seemed threatened with danger during the Cromwellian war, when the Protector seemed likely to invade the whole of Scotland, and they were uplifted for safe keeping by the Earl Marischal, until delivered to Lord Glasgow as Lord Treasurer in 1701.

They had evidently been at least on view during James Duke of York's visit in 1685, for in that year the Crown's old purple velvet bonnet was replaced by a crimson velvet cap, richly adorned, with further jewels and an ermine edge. However, since their locking away in 1707, along with the Sword of State and a written Act of 'Depositation', nothing had been seen of them. Had they been illegally spirited away? Were they after all in England? In 1794 a Commission was actually appointed to open the Crown Room to search for records, but they found nothing except a large oblong oak chest, secured by two strong locks for which they had no keys, and a thick coating of dust to show that it had lain for years undisturbed. They felt that their commission did not authorise its opening, and the room was again sealed.

Hugo Arnot, in his history of Edinburgh in 1788, was extremely sceptical of their continued existence in Scotland. 'Whether they be there still is very problematical. If they be, nothing at least can be more absurd than the way in which they have been kept . . . No mortal has been known to have seen them . . . it seems probable that the regalia have been privately removed by a secret order from the Court . . .'[1]

Walter Scott, for one, would dearly like to prove him wrong. During his visit to London in 1815, when he waited on the Prince Regent at Carlton House, he raised the subject, got the Prince's interest, and secured permission for a commission of officers of state (he of course being one) to investigate the mystery once more, this time with authority to open the chest. If, of course, it was there. Scott himself had doubts, and in January confided them to his chief the Duke of Buccleuch, a fellow-Commissioner. He had, indeed, seen what was claimed to be the Crown of Scotland at the Tower of London, which did not augur much for his hopes.[2]

In the event the Duke was ill and could not attend the opening of the room, but a party of ten attended on 4 February 1818, headed by Charles Hope the Lord President, the Lord Justice Clerk David Boyle, Kincaid Mackenzie the Lord Provost and various legal officers.[3] Considerable public interest had been aroused, and a crowd gathered on Castle Hill, eager to learn the outcome, and their national pride was excited.

The party met at the Governor's house, received by the guard with a military band, listened to the reading of the Royal Commission and other official documents, and went with the King's Smith to the Crown Room, which proved to be closed by two doors, the outer of oak, the inner of iron grates. There was indeed nothing in the room except the locked chest, but this they were now authorised to open.

Forcing the locks proved a lengthy and difficult task, but at last it was opened. 'It would be very difficult to describe the intense eagerness with which we watched the rising of the lid of the chest', wrote Scott to his friend J. W. Croker, 'and the progress of the workmen in breaking it open . . . It seemed very hollow . . . and I began to lean to your faction of the Little Faiths.'[4]

Inside this dusty receptacle there really were the Crown and Sceptre of Scotland, and the Sword of State; nothing else but the Act of 'Depositation', but these precious objects exactly answered to the historic descriptions.

The jubilant Commissioners ordered the royal standard to be raised, 'and the soldiers cheered a salute, which was heartily echoed from the Castle Hill, where a numerous crowd had assembled, anxious to learn the event of the search'.

No time was lost in passing on the information. The Lord Advocate, Alexander Maconochie, wrote to Viscount Sidmouth while the Commissioners were still in the room (though not posted for three days), that all was found exactly as described in the document of 1707, 'in high preservation', while the Crown was 'sufficiently splendid to satisfy not only national but even Jacobitical vanity'. The same day John Wilson Croker informed Sir Benjamin Bloomfield that he had just heard from Scott of the find, 'in perfect order and preservation . . .'[5] Not only the find, when scepticism had become general, but the marvellous condition of the treasures, must have seemed like the realisation of some magic spell.

The crown of pure gold, with two circles or fillets, was studded with precious stones, 'topazes, amethysts, garnets, emeralds, rubies and hyacinths . . . and with curious enamellings'. The upper band alternated diamonds and sapphires, its points tipped with 'as many great pearls, as in barons' coronets', and with ten 'crosses fleury' each with a great diamond between four great pearls in the cross. A few pearls were missing. The crosses fleury alternated with ten fleurs-de-lys.

This was the difference between the Scottish and other royal styles: only the Scottish crown was 'heightened' with these alternating symbols; the English alternated crosses patée with fleurs-de-lys, the French had all fleurs-de-lys. After the union of the Crowns, heralds, engravers and others 'ignorantly' represented the Scottish Crown as like the English.

The arched top of the Crown appears to date from James V's time, and its workmanship was thought inferior to the rest. The overall dimensions were: diameter nine inches, from under-circle to top of the cross patée, six-and-a-half inches, circumference twenty-seven inches.

The Sceptre was silver double-gilt with a hexagonal stem divided into three, part engraved, with on top of the stem on one side the Virgin with the letter J, on the second St James and letter R, and on the third, St Andrew and figure five. The full length was thirty-four inches.

The five-foot-long Sword of State was in a contrasting style. It had been presented to James IV in 1507 by Pope Julius II and was a fine Renaissance Italian piece, its handle and round pommel silver over gilt, with Julius II indented with gold on the blade, and above the cartouche, the Papal symbols, the ensign of two keys with tassels, and the triple tiara.[6]

Three days after this triumphant discovery the Commissioners revisited the Crown Room to witness the taking of accurate drawings and information, after which the chest and room were again locked and a sentinel, in honour and as precaution, was stationed below the window. A week later William Adam, the Lord Chief Commissioner, wrote to Lord Melville recommending Scott's friend Captain Adam Fergusson to be in charge of the regalia, a man 'very indifferently provided for', who could be given an apartment near the

Crown Room and admit members of the public when required, to see the treasures at a small fee.

'I have never been more pleased since the battle of Waterloo', wrote Scott to William Dundas, 'than with this discovery . . . I think I should have had my full share of blame had the research been unsuccessful.'[7]

The Crown Room was fitted up for exhibition and opened on 26 May 1819, attended by Yeomen Keepers in the costume of the Bodyguard of the King of Scotland, scarlet, faced with black.

In December 1830 King William IV had four more items of Stuart importance deposited, which had been bequeathed to him by the late Henry Cardinal York, younger brother of Prince Charles Edward. These were a golden collar of the Garter, presented to James VI by Queen Elizabeth; a badge of the Order of St George, the St Andrew, with a miniature of James VI's Queen, Anne of Denmark, and King Charles I's sapphire and diamond Coronation ring.[8]

Among eager visitors to the Regalia under its early display arrnagements was John James Audobon, for whom it proved a slight anticlimax. After greatly admiring the view from the castle parapet, he and his escort the Rev. William Newbold paid their shillings and were admitted to a small dark room, whose large padlock was unfastened by 'a red-faced, bulky personage dressed in a fanciful scarlet cloth . . like mouldering tapestry'. The Regalia, spread on a table also covered by a scarlet cloth, was reflected on the face of this attendant 'so that he looked like a large tomato', as he declaimed a long description of the objects. Audobon felt disappointed. 'It had not one thousandth part of the beauties I had seen from the parapet.'[9]

Fanny Kemble, who during her time at Edinburgh's theatre in 1830 was shown Jacobite relics, and offended her host by referring to 'the Pretender's sword' ('Wha' did ye say, madam! it was the *prince's* sword!'), relates a story told her by Sir Walter. After the discovery, when official decision as to the disposal of the Regalia was still under discussion, he was urgently requested for a sight of it from 'an old lady of the Maxwell family', who being nearly ninety years old feared she might not live to see them displayed.

He escorted the lady to the Crown Room, and watched, greatly moved, while she tottered from his arm, 'fell on her knees before the crown, and, clasping and wringing her wrinkled hands, wailed over it as a mother over her dead child'.[10]

43
ACCOLADE

'You should have been in Edinburgh to see the King's reception, which had something very wild and chivalrous about it, resembling more what we read in Oliver or Froissart, than anything I ever saw.'

Sir Walter Scott to Benjamin Haydon, n.d., 1822, Haydon, *Correspondence and Table Talk*, 1.356

'It seemed to me that I had been walking through some enchanted country under ground . . . Every spotlight as noon-day, each house illuminated with splendour, but empty and deserted. Then the thick crowd through which we edged our way . . . The admirable behaviour of the people. Not a drunken nor an uncivil man among them. With their clean best clothes, the common people seem to have put on their politest manners . . . The greatest crowd was in Prince's-street, the Waterloo Buildings and on the Bridges . . .'

Jane Grant, Friday, 16 August 1822, in *Letters from Jane and Mary Grant* on Edinburgh visit, August 1822, Dublin, n.d.

'The town is in a state of deathlike repose after its late excitement . . . I went with the Fletchers one day to see Holyrood . . . such gawks as to go and look at a bare room and an old, empty throne. The *presence chamber* is just decent and no more.'

Susan Ferrier to Mrs Connell, Sept 1822, 163

The high emotions raised by finding the Scottish Regalia also roused patriotic thoughts about Scotland's past. In 1820, William Mackenzie and Colonel David Stuart founded a Celtic Society, a combination of club, militia and preservation society, and encouraging the wearing of Highland dress.

On his 1820 visit to London, Walter Scott was created a baronet. He had had thoughts of making a novel about the Regalia, but thought better of it and wrote *Kenilworth* instead, a novel with a distinctly royal flavour, making much of Queen Elizabeth's royal progress. In the same year (1821) he attended George IV's coronation. Arrangements were made for the new King to visit, first Ireland that same year, and the next year Scotland. Scott indeed thought the two events might follow on one another's heels.

On setting off for the London steamboat he had left a message for James Hogg, via Lockhart, that the King would certainly visit soon, on his return from Ireland. 'There must be a "King's Wake" for certain, and you must clear forthwith your brawest pipes for the nonce.' He himself had to return soon after the Coronation to discuss arrangements with the Lord Advocate. Meanwhile, although he had made arrangements for Hogg to attend the coronation dinner, and urged him to come to London and stay with Lockhart, to his disappointment Hogg, in money difficulty over his farm, refused. He did, however, compose a drama, *The Royal Jubilee*, for the visit, which was presented to the King, and Scott received a gracious acknowledgment through Robert Peel.[1]

Charles Kirkpatrick Sharpe, expressing his gratification at the thought of seeing the King at Holyrood, had earlier slyly suggested that the royalty they would really like to see would have been the (then) Princess of Wales. 'We were threatened, you know, with a visit when she was to be sent to Holyrood Abbey.' Writing at a time of 'Siberian' weather plunging everyone into 'torpor and dulness . . . I, for one, should be vastly delighted at her arrival . . . I think she is excellent fun'. That would have been memorable indeed.[2]

The summer of 1822 therefore saw great preparations and mounting excitement. Mrs Grant, who was thrilled by the prospect, had written pretending a casual attitude to her friend Mrs Colonel White, then staying in George Street. 'By leaving Edinburgh before the King's visit you will escape the prevalent mania on the subject, which is very strong at present, and with none stronger than with those who affect a dislike of royalty.'[3]

Scott, very much directing the proceedings, saw to it that a truly Scottish impression, in spite of Jacobite undertones, was made by summoning the clans. Humphrey Davy, who had been staying in Edinburgh, saw them assembling in the Highlands early in August ready for 'marching bag and bagpipe (not baggage) to Edinburgh, with as strong expressions of loyalty as if they had never been Jacobites, and Scotland is all in commotion'. Dining with Scott, 'master of the royal revels', before setting out, he had been 'amused to see the deep interest he took in tailors, plumassiers, and show dress-makers, who are preparing this grand display of Scotch costume.'[4] Baron de Staël, whom the Grants of Rothiemurchus family met at Blair on their way to Edinburgh, observed that Scott was 'quite childish about the pageant he is preparing for the King'.[5]

Scott, who had met the Rev. George Crabbe in London in 1821, had begged the poet to visit Abbotsford. It was in a way unfortunate that Crabbe and the King then hit on the same month for a visit, especially as Scott was to be continuously involved with the ceremonies, so that he had to stay at Castle Street and not Abbotsford. Crabbe arrived some days before, but during the royal visit Scott was dining daily at the King's table, so that many of his hostly duties, including sightseeing, devolved on Lockhart.[6]

Hundreds of people descended on the city as visitors, or returning from their estates. Not everybody would, or could, be there. The French visitor Charles Nodier, in Edinburgh only weeks before but missing the visit itself, enlarges on the 'lucky chance' which had brought there 'ten or a dozen chiefs of clans in all the pomp of their admirable costume'; and he waxes lyrical over the sight of a chief 'with his poniard and pistols, like a buccaneer, his *cacique* cap, his cloak resembling Grecian drapery . . . his club of laburnum bent back as the sign of his command, his savage demi-nudity, and with all that, his noble and gentle mien'.[7]

Charles Shore and his brother, sons of Lord Teignmouth, also left the city shortly before the visit, having seen it all the previous year in Ireland. Once was evidently enough. Robert Gillies, not long back from Germany and short of money, elected to stay with his wife in their Lasswade cottage, which they illuminated a couple of times in the King's honour, until their neighbours begged them to give it up for fear of firing the thatch.[8]

Thomas Carlyle took care to be away.

The situation was strange enough. No English monarch had visited Edinburgh for 170 years, since James II and VII as Duke of York stayed with his daughters at Holyrood; and he was a Stuart. Much embarrassing verse was penned for this new visit. A young Collector of Poor Rates, Robert Gillfillan, composed some anticipatory lines to the tune of 'Johnny Cope':

Come hame baith marquis, duke an' peer,
Ower seldom do we see you here;
Auld Reekie's in an unco steer
Ye'll surely come that morning . . .

Waes me! it's lang an' mony a day
Sin' Holyrood wi' kings was gay;
O! wad he only 'mang us stay,
When he comes down that morning.

This poem had the great merit of stating unequivocally what was in many people's minds.[9]

Henry Fox, who had earlier left Edinburgh for a few weeks but then been persuaded by his parents to return with Lord Ancram, arrived on 10 August, a few days before the King, to find the city 'in a state of wild confusion'. Lord Lauderdale[10] had kindly found him temporary accommodation in his own lodgings. Next day Henry and his friend Sandford, visiting Craigcrook, found Jeffrey 'in a state of alarm lest the Kg should knight him. Mrs Jeffrey is half distracted at the notion.' They need not have worried.

They also called on Lady Breadalbane at Holyrood, into whose apartments Henry moved next day, and on the 14th, when the King had arrived at Leith, dined with the family there. He also found the Duke of Hamilton 'in a flannel dressing-gown, much agitated about his dress and his dignities, having received no specific commands'. Charles Sharpe called, to discuss at great length a gauntlet that had arrived: 'whether it ought to be so long or not, whether it was to be sewed with gold thread, &c. &c. &c.'[11]

The ladies were even more agitated. The budding young French writer Amédée Pichot, who deferred his departure for the Highlands just long enough to witness the King's arrival, admitted he would have preferred to see Edinburgh in its normal state. Call on any of the professors, hoping to discuss a scientific question, you would find him studying the wig he is to wear at the levée, or rehearsing the speech he is to make before the King. Or call on a 'bourgeois' and his wife – who had a sense of order and economy to shame 'nos coquettes de Paris' – and find her practising the management of her train before a glass, having been honoured by an invitation to the Drawing-room.[12]

The business of the train was no joke. Lady Scott had told Pichot about ladies' anxiety over their presentation, a general preoccupation for as court dresses had to have a train, which many, perhaps most, were not used to, much practice was required before a cheval glass. The Grant sisters Jane and Mary spent hours of instruction with the kind and patient Mrs Henry Siddons in the art of its management. At the Drawing-room, Lady Scott explained to Pichot, one's train would be carried by the Gentleman Usher until one reached the King, who after the lady's low curtsey would raise her and kiss her on the cheek. ('*Est-ce de rigueur?*' asked the amazed Pichot, too young to have known about the etiquette of the French *ancien* royal or even the Napoleonic court.) The lady then retired backwards to the fringe of the circle, a difficult maneouvre unassisted, without much preliminary practice. In the old days of stiff paniers the gown itself had been some support, but the slim lines of contemporary fashion gave no such help.[13]

It seemed as if the monarch was rapidly becoming a sort of puppet, an occasion for which Edinburgh society could indulge its wildest romantic fantasies.

There was plenty of profiteering. Pichot and his unnamed companion had had to try house after house, and were offered a room at the Black Bull for two guineas a night. Eventually 'une bonne dame' in the town gave them the same service for two guineas a week.[14] And this was even before the King had arrived.

The painters David Wilkie and William Collins arrived on the 10th, Collins in a new coat for the occasion, but Wilkie promised to outdo him once his own of sky-blue arrived. Wilkie already had a commission to make a painting of John Knox for Lord Liverpool, but for his own purposes he planned a work that was to embody the whole royal visit, based on either the High Kirk, the Castle or Holyrood. Both men had letters of introduction, and the Lord Chief Commissioner, William Adam, courteously took them to see the elaborate preparations at the palace, and then to Leith as the scene of the landing – the part that more interested Collins. Scott's friend and contemporary Captain Adam Fergusson, who was now Keeper of the Regalia, whom they met at Holyrood, was 'in great glee', arranged Wilkie's admission for the arrival, and told him that Scott was expecting him (whom he met, kind as ever).[15]

Another harbinger was the new Home Secretary, Robert Peel, with his wife Julia, who only three months earlier had borne their first son Robert. Accompanied by Peel's private secretary Sydney Streatfeild, they went straight to Melville Castle where they were to stay. Having preceded his monarch, Peel also had to outstay him until 29 August.[16]

Meanwhile at the Theatre Royal, whose season had had only a modest start, William Murray was making grand preparations, building a 'handsome portico' over the royal entrance, and a platform covered with crimson cloth from which folding doors opened on to the former box office, now transformed into 'a handsome apartment, brilliant with lamps . . . reflected in immense pier glasses'.[17]

And the crowds were converging on Edinburgh, on foot, on horse and by carriage. So congested were the roads that carriages were lined up waiting for the ferry across the Forth, and one or two people laid on impromptu horse-races along the dusty high-road to while away the time, which country people stopped their work to watch agape.[18]

The King was voyaging in his personal yacht the *Royal George,* less elaborate and more comfortable than his father's the *Royal Sovereign,* which always accompanied his voyages. Among the King's suite was Sir William Knighton, recently appointed Keeper of the Privy Purse, who had already attended him on the Irish state visit. An elaborate programme had been worked out for different ceremonies or festivities every day, but it proved difficult even to get this started. As it was August, the northern weather was even more unpredictable than usual, and the planned disembarkation at Leith Roads on Tuesday, 12th, had to be deferred because of a deluge, for not one day but two. The night was 'wet, stormy, and uncomfortable', recorded Knighton.[19]

In the morning Amédée Pichot breakfasted with the Scotts in Castle Street, finding Scott already in his uniform as Deputy Lieutenant of a county, military fashion in a blue coat with red facings and sword at his side. After breakfast he climbed into his carriage and drove to Leith to greet the King on board. '*Ici disparait le poète et commence le rôle de courtisan*,' commented the slightly shocked Pichot, '*qui a quelque chose de dégradant ou de ridicule pour le génie*.' If the King did not create Scott a peer, he felt, he would be unworthy of his homage.[20]

On being told that Scott had arrived alongside, the King exclaimed, 'The man in Scotland I most wish to see! Let him come up.' Scott, apologising profusely for the Scottish climate, and quoting a Highland innkeeper's apology once made to himself, 'In the name of my countrymen I'm just ashamed o' the weather!', made a suitable speech in the name of the ladies, who had made a St Andrew's Cross which he then presented to the King.[21]

The King, of course, had met Scott a number of times, but Sir William Knighton had not, and like most people was at first taken aback by his appearance. 'He has no trace in his countenance of such superior genius and softness of mind as the beauty of his writings displays . . .' That is (again as usual) until he spoke.[22]

The King offered Scott a glass of cherry brandy, which having drunk, Scott begged and was given the King's glass as an honoured souvenir; and promptly sat on it on reaching home.[23]

The weather still made the King decide to delay his landing for a further day, a sound decision as it proved, as the next day (14th) was a blaze of sunshine.

On the evening before his landing there were fireworks over the city, and though Pichot claimed he had seen better at the Tivoli, he admired the way they turned Arthur's Seat into an erupting volcano. The further delay had made people restless, and in still heavy cloud they had pressed forward towards the already crowded Calton Hill to get a sight of the squadron off Leith, through various kinds of optical instruments, until an evening storm dispersed them.[24]

The city was further illuminated with the inevitable candles and lamps in every window, sometimes every pane, along with colourful transparencies, allegorical, burlesque or just naïve.

There had been misgivings over how the people, who for years had been overlooked by royalty, would receive the Hanoverian King, and further, many were full of indignation over this particular monarch's recent treatment of his Queen. But whether from instinctive loyalty, to a Hanoverian or no, a sense of the honour of the occasion, or even from mere curiosity, the turnout was enormous. Thousands had come to Edinburgh from all over the country, every hat and bonnet was adorned with heather – a plant not noticeably part of Edinburgh's own flora – and those who could not find accommodation (and they were many), or could not afford it, had camped on Calton Hill or Arthur's Seat in order to get a continuous view of every procession and all the illuminations.

'There were many more heads in the town than there were roofs to cover them', recorded Julian Young, who had arrived the previous day on his way back to Aberdeen University. Many locals rented out 'the rudest accommodation on the common stairs'. Some country people were rumoured to have sold their own beds to find money for the journey.[25]

Pichot had already met Sir Walter Scott and his family in the excited throng, and after parting with them followed them for an hour, noting that wherever Scott was recognised, people made way for him. He then climbed the Calton Hill, from which the illuminated scene was like a vast fire, in which Old and New Towns, the public buildings, domes, columns, towers, all sparkled with flame, enveloping the whole of Edinburgh in its mantle.[26]

Neither Elizabeth Grant of Rothiemurchus nor her mother had felt well enough to attend the grand visit, but the two younger girls Jane and Mary (brother William was already in Edinburgh) were squired by their father for the whole occasion, even though because of their reduced circumstances it 'was with lace, feathers, pearls, the old landau, the old horses, and the old liveries'. For the girls it was entirely delightful, and between them in journals and letters to their mother they recorded a blow-by-blow account of almost every minute of every day, whom they met and what they did and felt. They were staying with their cousins the Ironsides in Great King Street, with a constant coming and going with the Gibsons at 12 Picardy Place, and Mrs Siddons, whose charming house was at its very end. There was constant tension and anxiety about getting, or not getting, tickets for the Peers' Ball and/or the Caledonian or Hunt Ball, with hopes and promises from peeresses and parents, until almost the last minute.[27]

On Thursday, the weather having at last improved, the King's entry to Edinburgh could be staged. The Royal Squadron, anchored in Leith Roads, was dressed overall, the *Royal George* surrounded by other royal yachts and three frigates, with, on the fringe, the steam yacht *James Watt*, which had escorted the squadron from Greenwich in case the wind should fail. The King was rowed ashore by sixteen sailors in the royal barge, dressed in admiral's uniform with a thistle in his hat and the new St Andrew's Cross on his breast. With him were the Marquess Conyngham (husband of his current lady friend), Lord Graves, and Sir Charles Paget the Commodore; following were barges of the captains of the accompanying ships.

As they passed the pierhead a group of three young gentlemen, sons of Leith notabilities, struck up Scottish airs on the pipes, to shouts and cheers from the crowds. The flattered King bowed constantly. Then at the Custom House, the burgh of Canongate band struck up the National Anthem, and Canongate magistrates, deacons and trades representatives advanced and lowered their standards, while from the balcony children cheered and waved handkerchiefs. More bows from the King. As he approached the landing place, sailors in the smacks flanking the bridge gave three well-drilled cheers, supported by more from the shore. At last he stepped ashore to be greeted by the waiting grandees. The whole arrival had taken twenty minutes.[28]

The King descended by a temporary stair on to a platform,[29] while the sailors stood at the salute, and was received by the Marquess of Lothian – Lord Lieutenant of the county – with William Dundas, Lord Clerk Register, the senior Leith Magistrate Baillie John McFie,[30] the officers of state, the Leith magistrates – and Sir Walter Scott. Drawn up on the quayside were the Royal Midlothian Yeomanry, the Royal Regiment of Infantry, the King's Bodyguard, the Royal Company of Archers, the High Constable of Leith, and the Royal Dragoon Guards. The obligatory speeches of welcome were made.[30]

On the quayside was William Collins, who had secured a pass from the Leith baillies and had seen the boat anchor a mile and a half offshore the previous day, at the point when people had feared that the uncertain weather might have caused the King to land at Dunbar and finish the journey by carriage. He had chosen the landing as the subject of his commemorative painting, but although he had a good view of this and the other ceremonies, and on the King's departure even accompanied the royal yacht down the Forth, all he achieved was a few preliminary sketches. Once the first excitement wore off he realised this was not his forte – he should stick to nature and landscapes. In any case these days were so filled that even his sketches were 'few and slight', and he had no opportunity to make finished drawings even of the Leith arrival.[31]

Among the watchers were also Dr Chalmers and his wife and daughter Anne, who had been on a quayside platform from the beginning, and witnessed every detail from the moment the disembarkation was signalled by a gun fired from the royal squadron. Though disappointed that the King was not to visit the radical city of Glasgow, Chalmers made a point of being in Edinburgh for the occasion. 'It is a sight', he told his wife beforehand, 'that will leave an indelible impression upon young people.'

He was beside himself with loyal enthusiasm. 'The bells of Leith have struck up a merry peal. Leith Fort and the vessels of war in the Roads are thundering away; Edinburgh Castle and every gun on the surrounding heights responding . . . The people on the pier are with difficulty persuaded to keep their seats . . . The King is off the end of the pier in his barge with the royal flag flying, with 16 rowers. He is now advanced half-way along the pier. The air rings with acclamations . . .'

One bystander noted how Chalmers hailed his monarch with a 'Well done – honest fellow – God bless him!' And he turned to his neighbours to say, 'Is not monarchy congenial to our nature?'[32]

The King boarded his open carriage and the procession to the city moved off, preceded by the Lord Lyon and other heralds (costumed as described in *Marmion*, noted Pichot, awaiting them in Picardy Place), their mantles sweeping the ground, with gold ornaments and embroidered boots. Then the more soberly uniformed regiments, including the Scots Greys, the 'terribles *chevaliers gris*' of Waterloo, and the Midlothian yeomanry detachments of the Celtic Society's Highlanders, and the picturesque real Highlanders. The King's carriage was surrounded by Archers and Glengarry's suite (who had insisted on the honour). Carriages of the nobility, and then the magistrates, followed. The Baillie of Glasgow excited some mirth when a spectator hailed him as 'Bailie Nicol Jarvie', a cry taken up with ironic applause – signifying Edinburgh's superior attitude to commercial Glasgow.[33]

Instead of the National Anthem the Highlanders were playing 'The Campbells are Coming'. Julian Young, in the crowd, was amazed by their 'towering indifference', some of them 'hardly deigning to cast a look' at the King, who on his side seemed astonished at the 'huge hill of human life' on Arthur's Seat, and when they reached Princes Street, at 'the sea of men and women surging from one end of it to the other. He rose – threw up his hands and arms; then sank back in his carriage, and burst into tears.' Thus Julian.[34]

Along the whole approach from Leith to Edinburgh was 'one running cheer', records Robert Mudie, which seemed to move the King, for he raised his hat and bowed repeatedly, looking attentively at the crowd. He may have been a little taken aback by the contrast with his arrival in Dublin the previous year, where the reception arrangements fell into confusion.

Everywhere was sparkling with colour and gay costumes, like some lively Continental city at carnival time. Arthur's Seat looked almost as if some besieging army were investing the city, and the road round Salisbury Crags, usually empty, was crowded with scarlet-clad soldiers. Banners floated from the castle, and everybody was dressed in their best, with well-dressed strangers, many of them English, green-clad Archers, tartaned Highlanders in plaids and plumes, never before away from their mountains – sober Scotland was reeling under the dramatic impact.[35]

The studied indifference maintained by many Highlanders was partly from clannish pride, and still more the influence of the leading chief, Alexander Macdonell of Glengarry (whose train included relatives of Robert Gillies). Glengarry, proudest, vainest, most would-be militant of the chiefs, was more at home in the mountains than at a grand urban ceremony. Intensely tenacious of his rights, he insisted on being attended by his 'tail' of suitably clad clansmen, armed from head to heel and swaggering about ready to stir up trouble.[36]

This ostentation disgusted Henry Cockburn. 'The affectation of Celticism was absurd and nauseous' – probably Scott's idea – though Edinburgh's burghers had never been less than poles apart from rude Highlanders. For the chiefs to appear in full rig might have been acceptable. However, they not only arrived with 'tails' but (he claimed) the tails were not even Highlanders but 'base Lowlanders' hired and dressed for the occasion – it was a matter for ridicule. Worse, in Cockburn's view, was the vulgarity of how 'hundreds who had never seen Heather had the folly to array themselves in tartan'. Yet worse still was to come.[37]

Pichot made a similar comment. At his first sight of a Highlander in the street, fully clad and armed, he was enchanted, *'un de ces enfans libres des montagnes'*, he enthused, *'pleine de noblesse et d'aisance.'* Then the man turned round. *'Le charme fut rompu.'* He was wearing spectacles. He was probably just a member of the Edinburgh Celtic Society.[38]

The Royal Company of Archers was also much in evidence in uniforms so archaic, almost medieval, that it was supposed that Scott must have had a hand in this too.[39]

Scaffolds had been erected in front of many, or most, houses along the route. On the previous day these had been a melancholy sight in the rain, when on a false alarm, the gun having signalled the squadron's arrival, many people had hurried out to take their places and been driven back by the pouring rain, while those unfortunates who were in the street were drenched, white gowns and white trousers splashed with mud, smartly clad yeomanry muddied, their horses' cockades drooping and servants' new liveries tarnished with wet. And indoors, the elaborate refreshments were likely to be wasted when word came that the landing would be put off till the morrow.

Much cleaning, drying and polishing must have gone on overnight, for now, the sun brightly shining, the sky clear, cockades were gleaming, harness brightly glistening, the pavements crammed behind the yeomanry-lined centre space, and every house with benches and windows filled with spectators. Even the roofs were covered with people hanging on to the tall chimney-stacks and elegant young ladies were waving their handkerchiefs while the air rang with the military bands, cheers and Scots airs on the pipes. Those who did not live there rented places at three shillings apiece.

At Picardy Place, where a kind of triumphal arch had been set up, the street was lined by constables of Edinburgh and Midlothian Yeomanry, and the Lord Provost and Town Council in their robes waited to present the King with the keys of the city. Here Mrs Siddons's party in the first house, and the Gibson Craigs in the next, had a ring-side view. The procession then passed round the foot of Calton Hill by the 'new road' connecting Princes Street with Abbeyhill, below a dense crowd of spectators, probably the most thickly gathered of all, giving the best and most comprehensive view.[40]

Mrs Fletcher, no lover of kings at any time, was watching with her three daughters from a window above Trotter's shop in Princes Street, with a view of the cavalcade and military escort approaching down St Andrew Street, then crossing towards Holyrood below the Calton Hill. She was more involved than perhaps she might have liked, for both her sons had been pressed into donning military uniform for the occasion. Imposing though the procession was, she was less affected by 'the gilded coach or the fat gentleman within it' than by 'the vast multitude assembled – some said 100,000 people – animated by one feeling of pride and pleasure'. The King could not have been better received, she drily observed, had he been the best of Kings.

Mrs Grant of Laggan sat with the Fletchers. A great royalist, though she habitually wore widow's black, she had donned a spendid gown of salmon-coloured satin, and enthusiastically waved her handkerchief with the rest as the King passed.

Mr Archibald Fletcher, then very frail, had insisted on being present, taking a place on the Bar platform. The contrast between loyalist Mrs Grant, and the more radically inclined Mrs Fletcher, might have been remarkable, but instead (Mrs Fletcher writes), 'They all had a good laugh at my expense, who, somewhat notorious for being no lover of Kings, was actually detected shedding tears and waving my handkerchief "like the lave", as the pageant passed.' She made the excuse of being carried away by the emotion of the crowd.[41]

Roderick Murchison, geologist, was there on the thronged Calton Hill, and chiefly noted Walter Scott's 'beaming face and white hair'.[42] James Nasmyth was there, seeing with enthusiasm how every street, window, housetop and surrounding hill was crammed. Pichot too hurried to climb the Calton Hill to watch the last part of the procession towards Holyrood, while the cannon placed on hilltops repeatedly fired and echoed one another, and the distant Forth, gilded with the blessed sun, was itself crowded with all the boats that had surrounded the flotilla.

He then descended to sample Princes Street, where amid shouts of joy everyone was looking proud. But near David Hume's tomb he passed a sad sight. A poor blind piper in shabby, torn plaid, and with tattered faded ribbons to his pipes, stood on the pavement, starting up a pibroch, a reel or a lament, to which passers-by might stop for a moment to listen, but shrank from his shabby clothes, while others hurried past never noticing. An equally shabby dog, his master's cup in his mouth, sat head down as if ashamed. Pichot, equally ashamed of his own 'sterile' pity, slipped a shilling into the empty cup.[43]

Like many other strangers, Pichot was impressed by the orderliness of the crowds, combined with respect without servility. The French, blasé with spectacle and the regular arrival and departure of emperors and kings, were further oppressed by an armed gendarmerie. Not here the hedges of bristling bayonets, merely a thin line of police. [44]

Awaiting the procession at Holyrood as it descended Abbeyhill were companies of the regiments stationed in Edinburgh Castle, the Sutherland Highlanders and, inside the entrance, Celtic Highlanders. The whole gathering saluted the King as he arrived, and the bands struck up the National Anthem. His entrance to the palace was regarded as so symbolic that the moment he set foot in the porch, 'a deafening shout of triumph ascended from the multitude' (writes Mudie), answered by a royal salute from the castle and Salisbury Crags guns.[45]

Here the king was received by the Duke of Hamilton as Keeper of the Palace, who presented him with the keys, with the Duke of Montrose and Lord Melville. He was escorted to the Throne Room and there formally received from the Knight Marischal the Regalia or Honours of Scotland, namely Crown, Sceptre and Sword of State, then returning them to their holders. He then held a brief Court.[46]

David Wilkie's chosen spot for the King's arrival was here – inside not out. Nobody was admitted except in Court dress, which Wilkie evidently hired, and he and the Edinburgh sculptor Samuel Joseph (with whom Collins was staying), by arrangement with the Chamberlain's officers, were allowed to change their clothes in an attic. The homely Wilkie was quite transformed, 'with hair-powder and all the et-ceteras . . . really splendid'.[47] Busy sketching away, he made several versions of the occasion, all slightly different.

At 3.30 the king boarded his carriage again to be driven, doubtless with some relief, to Dalkeith Palace, where he was to stay for the nights with the Duke of Buccleuch.

Henry Fox, with a rare display of complete enthusiasm, thought that 'The procession was brilliant; the day fine; the people enchanted.' His rooms at Holyrood were actually next door to the Royal suite, and he was able to see from his own windows the King boarding his private carriage as he set off.[48]

Inevitable sneers came from Thomas Uwins, though he did admit that the grand processional arrival was 'truly magnificent', Calton Hill 'thick with people, rising above their heads', and the mountains looming above. 'Sawney is now in all his glory. Princes Street and the North Bridge are as much crowded as Cornhill and High Change', while the King appeared visibly affected, and the Scots touched by his gentlemanly, graceful manner. But Uwins hastened to inform his brother that the Scots did not excel in graceful gestures. Many had not risen from their comfortable seats, 'hats were but tardily taken off, and coolly held about an inch above their heads'. He carefully noted such comments from the crowd as 'He's nae sae ill-fa'red though, for a' they said aboot him', and 'I looked to see a muckle fat faggot, but the chield's a decent-like body.' Complimentary, really.[49]

Uwins naturally complained bitterly of the Highlanders' and Glengarry's attempt to revive 'feudal tyranny' – a complete masquerade as the days went by, the chiefs with their 'lounging, idle clansmen'. 'Their carriages are never seen in the streets without 6 or 8 of these fellows running on each side, at equal distances, breathless in their attempt to rival the speed of the horses.'[50]

The Home Secretary, who attended the King with the Duke of Montrose and Lord Melville, was able to report to London how well everything had begun. He was suffering from eye trouble and generally not well, and on returning to Melville Castle for the night, found that disturbing news had arrived. Lord Londonderry, the Foreign Secretary, from over-anxiety and overwork had committed suicide. In great distress, Peel at once drove to Dalkeith Palace to inform the King. The news cast a damp over the proceedings, but was generally kept in the background so as not to interfere with the festivities.[51]

Sir William Knighton was at Dalkeith Palace, with the King's suite. 'I am such a close prisoner here', he wrote, and not able to attend the various events – 'and this place is six miles from Edinburgh'. But the palace boasted several paintings by Reynolds, and one of its rooms was where General Monk had signed the treaty restoring King Charles II. That King's portrait hung beside Knighton's bed, in his 'magnificent room' close to the King's. And he saw a dozen hares together on the lawn.[52]

In the evening everyone was out seeing the illuminations, which spread even to the suburbs, and parties like the Grants which set out in groups, or rather pairs with gentlemen escorting ladies (Jane, to her pleasure, with Mr Jeffrey), easily became separated. Many decorations were limited to a candle in each window, or at each pane, some designed in 'figures'. Of the public buildings the grandest was the Lord Provost's in Charlotte Square, whose normally dark front was brightened by many lamps. The more ambitious sightseers tottered home exhausted.

'Never shall I forget the happiness, the delirium of that evening', claimed Jane, '. . . You never saw a small room so crowded the night of a great Rout, as were all the broad, long streets of this magnificent town that evening.' All the same, on arriving back at Jeffrey's she was lame and ready to faint, and did full justice to a generous glass of wine. After that, scarcely able to take another step, she was carried off to a late party in a chair.[53]

There was as much etiquette about dressing for the processions as if one were going to court. Ladies were expected to wear caps, white and gaily decorated, for the arrival, and for the grand procession to the castle the following week, white hats with pearl-coloured feathers. When the court dresses arrived from London, complete with 'four pairs of silk stockings, satin slips and a packet of gloves', they were accompanied by elaborate instructions from the dressmaker for the hairstyle with bows and feathers, and how to fix the train over the stays once the dress was on, to hang over the left arm. The same dress, without train or lappets (headdress streamers) but keeping the feathers, was to be worn for the ball.

There were calls, parties, invitations, dinners, the theatre – which was packed every evening. The Grant girls were delighted to see as much as possible of the Jeffreys and to visit them at Craigcrook. Invitations came so thick and fast that there was continual debate over whether one could fit in so many junketings in one evening ('return from Craig Crook, walk all over the illuminated Town, go to Mrs Gillies and the Assembly . . .') It was complicated by the necessity, sometimes perforce ignored, to change one's dress in between.[54]

County families were all sending gifts of game for the King's table, so John Peter Grant sent back an order to Rothiemurchus for thirty brace of ptarmigan, with instructions on when they were to be shot and when put on the coach. He also, to Elizabeth's annoyance, sent for their treasured Glenlivet whisky, for 'the King drank nothing else' – 'long in wood, long in uncorked bottles, mild as milk', she thought sadly. But their loss proved a gain in the long run, for the whisky, along with the ptarmigan all shot by one man in a day (the King did not get them all, some were distributed to friends), were made much of at the Palace, and in 1827 a judicious reminder of the gift when the Grant family were in straitened circumstances, 'at a proper moment by the gentlemanly Chamberlain', led to their father's being given a knighthood and sent as puisne judge to Bombay.[55]

Throughout the King's stay, Henry Fox was enjoying (so far as his lovesick state allowed) a glittering social life among the leading aristocracy, attending the theatre, visiting Roslin, climbing Calton Hill ('I never saw anything prettier') and an unending round of parties. On the day after the King's arrival he also 'walked all over the town to see the beautiful illuminations – quite like fairy-land'.[56]

The Rev. Mr Crabbe had been having a more sober time, though with plenty of the usual kind of socialising. He managed only a single walk with the over-pressed Scott, to St Anthony's Chapel, as figuring in *The Heart of*

Midlothian. Otherwise his fortnight was spent partly with Lockhart, partly with Henry Mackenzie, who between them enlightened him on tartans and clans, and he walked about the city a great deal by himself, received with respect by all who encountered him. He settled with the Scotts as if one of the family, with his unsophisticated, kindly manner, the odd pithy maxim thrown in. Lockhart was impressed by his 'noble forehead, his bright beaming eye, without any thing of old age about it, his sweet, and, I would say, innocent smile, and the calm mellow tones of his voice'.[57]

Crabbe and Mrs Fletcher eagerly renewed their old friendship, for they had met many years earlier at her father's when he was about thirty years old – he was now sixty-eight, white-haired, and (*pace* Lockhart) seeming old for his age, and was one of the most popular men of the day. He dined with them several times, including one day with Mrs Somerville, the distinguished lady astronomer, and Mrs Fletcher's good friend Mrs Wolfe Tone Wilson with her son William Wolfe Tone, who had come over from America.[58]

One morning while Tone was sitting with the Fletchers a scene rather like Mrs Grant and the Chevalier d'Este was enacted. Mr Crabbe was announced, and had scarcely seated himself when Tone rushed over to him, sank to one knee and kissed his hand. He then silently resumed his seat. After he left they explained to the astonished Crabbe, who was half wondering if 'the young gentleman was not out of his mind', that the gesture sprang from 'his Irish blood and French education'.[59]

This was not the first embarrassing encounter the poet-clergyman had had. On his very first morning at Scott's, arriving for breakfast before his host, he found in the breakfast parlour two or three exotically garbed gentlemen, talking to each other in some unintelligible language. Foreigners, of course. Crabbe himself, in his old-fashioned clerical dress, breeches and buckled shoes, appeared equally odd to the strangers, who took him for 'some learned Abbé'. Their joint French was execrable, but between them they managed to drum up an awkard exchange, until Scott arrived and with a cheery 'Good morning!' ended the confusion in laughter as the exotic visitors proved to be Highland chiefs.[60]

There was one extremely colourful evening at Scott's, when Collins and Wilkie, who were among the guests, saw him in a new role. Once the table was cleared for drinking, the exuberant Scott proposed singing 'Carle now the King's come' while the company joined in the chorus. Scott himself, regardless of either lameness or dignity, jumped up calling on all to join hands and dance round the table to the tune. The illustrious gathering eagerly let themselves go (said Collins afterwards) in a way 'to have brought back to earth the apparition of John Knox himself'.

This was presumably the occasion, attended by the chiefs, described by Crabbe. The Macleod, The Frazer, The Ferguson and Lord Erroll were in their splendour, 'all gentlemen', noted the slightly surprised Crabbe, 'but remote from our society'. Most notable, as usual, was the great Glengarry, who flatteringly took notice of the old poet. He was also able to talk to Lady Glengarry, his neighbour at dinner, 'and Sir Walter was the life and soul of the whole. It was a splendid festivity', he concluded, 'and I felt I knew not how much younger.'[61]

One day Crabbe joined Lockhart with two of the other *Noctes* authors, Wilson and Hogg. To the gently reared Crabbe, Hogg's ordering of a can of ale, rather than the expected claret or champagne, was a matter of amusement. He also managed to meet the 'chiefs of the opposite clan': Jeffrey, John Murray, Professor Leslie and others. Unfortunately of neither meeting did he leave any account.[62]

Henry Fox was dining at grander and more decorous gatherings, one at Sir George Warrender's, among whose guests was Mme de Noailles, 'who is staying with Sir George, and he is in love with her. She laughs at him, and is not very susceptible herself.'[63]

The day following the King's arrival was quiet, so far as royal events were concerned, but the city was again illuminated at night, while at intervals the castle cannon fired, answered by salutes from the Calton Hill and Salisbury Crags.

The Grants, staying at their cousins the Ironsides' handsome house in Great King Street, were spending much time with kind Mrs Siddons at her pretty Picardy Place house, with much heartburning over their various attempts to secure tickets for the two grand balls. They were rather shocked at the cavalier way in which Lord Tweeddale's family had descended on the Gibsons at 12 Picardy Place, where were already staying the whole Lauderdale family with their daughters, who had just arrived when the Tweeddales, who had continually put them off with conflicting messages, finally turned up. There were, 'besides their own enormous party, 3 Ladys' maids, a valet, a footman, and a coachman, besides the 2 children and their nurse'. Even the large New Town house was stretched, and the younger Gibson had to give up his room for the ladies' maids and his father even had to put the valet into lodgings and send the two girls to a friend's.[64]

The next royal excitement was the gentlemen's dressing for the Saturday's Levée, Mr Ironside himself curling all his relatives' hair with the tongs as the hairdresser, Mr Urquhart, did not turn up, while in the next room the girls were instructing other friends with what they had learned from Mrs Siddons about trains and curtseys for the Drawing-room.[65]

Carriages started to arrive along the 'new London road' by 10 a.m., and by noon had formed a long line back towards Waterloo Place and Regent Bridge, as far as Hanover Street, eventually almost to the far end of Princes Street.

Henry Fox, presented by Lord Lauderdale, found the King gracious and fairly talkative. 'Hot and full. I never saw such ridiculous figures', says Henry, who was as snobbish as the next person: 'grocers, tailors and haberdashers were among them'.[66]

The most ridiculous figure was perhaps the King, who appeared in Highland costume in the Stewart tartan, showing 'his manly and graceful figure to great advantage', as one charitable account had it. 'I had some doubts on this point', writes Peel, 'but I dare say it greatly pleased the Highlanders.'[67]

Henry Cockburn was disgusted. 'King George IV held a Levée without breeches!' The sixty-year-old King 'exhibited himself publicly in a kilt!! . . . bare or trousered the knees were undoubtedly philabegged'. There was a famous repartee by a lady – Cockburn says Lady Jane Dalrymple of Bargeny, Elizabeth Grant (who of course was not there) says Lady Saltoun – to one complainant, apparently 'a Southron Scott' , 'so large a man, whose nudities were no longer attractive'. – 'Nay,' was her reply, 'we should take it very kind of him, since his stay will be so short, the more we see of him the better!'[68]

Sir William Curtis's similar garb was the cause of a different kind of embarrassment, for as he too was fat, and was standing near the King, several people naturally mistook the two. John Hamilton Dundas saw his mistake as he was actually kneeling to kiss the hand, and with great aplomb 'called out, "Wrong, by Jove", and rising, moved on undaunted to the larger presence'.[69]

It was the presentation of William Murray Nairne that enabled Scott later to appeal successfully to the King for the restoration of the forfeited peerage.

Another who attended was the ageing Crabbe, gratifyingly recognised by the King, who 'received him with attention'. Of this occasion too Crabbe unfortunately left no description, but composed verses on the subject.[70]

David Wilkie, who had kept his court dress, was there too, for Scott let him use his name on the 'presentation card'. Once again he changed in the attic, then joined the crowd in the Long Gallery. When he was presented, and Lord Glenlyon read his name from the card, Wilkie approached his monarch (as previously instructed), 'half kneeling on my right knee'. He held the extended hand close to his lips, then rose and bowed. The King at first seemed not to recognise him, but on hearing his name read out he looked again, smiled suddenly and said 'How d'ye do?' At this mark of favour Wilkie bowed even lower, and passed on with the rest.

He was indeed honoured, for usually the King spoke, even so little, to only a few of the chief guests. Passing round to the grand entrance, he was led by the Under Chamberlain back to the Presence Chamber by another door and was able to watch the proceedings, noticing how particularly gracious the King was to the Scott family.[71]

There was a story of a late arrival – in Julian Young's version an old laird 'of no mean estate', in another a young nobleman – who was flustered by finding people already coming away. Reaching the antechamber and anxiously asking what he was supposed to do, he received the casual instruction simply to make a low bow and pass on. Following this vague information he was almost in the Presence before Lord Erroll, standing by, saw his confusion and hissed at him, 'Kiss hands! kiss hands!'

'On which', Julian Young tells us, 'to the delectation of the King, and the dismay of all around him, the poor startled man faced about, and then retreating backwards, kissed both his hands to the King.'[72]

After the levée, which closed at 3.15, the King held a Privy Council, and left at about 4.15 for Dalkeith, where the Duke of Argyll and the Earl of Fife dined with him.[73]

Returning home when the ceremony was over, Walter Scott was ringing at his own Castle Street door when Mr Glassford passed by. 'Well, Sir Walter,' he asked, 'what does the King say of the good town of Edinburgh?' – 'Say!' exclaimed Scott, '"I always heard the Scotch were a proud people; and they may well be proud, for they are a nation of gentlemen, and they live in a city of palaces."'[74]

It was not the first or last time a southerner had been astonished at Edinburgh's magnificence, and even if Scott exaggerated, the King, whatever his many faults, had the gift of gracious compliment. However, the euphoria soon began to wear off.

The disgruntled Thomas Uwins recorded that 2000 were received at the Levée, 'as many as could afford to buy or hire a sword or a bag-wig', and later at the Drawing-room 2500 ladies were presented, many of whom (he claims) had let their houses in order to afford 'a white satin dress and a plume of feathers'.[75]

After this first ceremonial, few people mention the first Sabbath's events, though some of the Grants' party went to the Rev. Mr Alison's Episcopal 'chapel' and were rather disgusted by his gushing address. 'Every word "The King", and with shaming references to this barren country and sunless climate in a land which was nothing until its Union with a "BRAVER *Nation*"!' This while (it so happened) the sun beat down and people were nearly overcome with the heat.[76]

The King spent a relatively quiet day at Dalkeith Palace. Next day, at Holyrood, he received the formal addresses of numerous institutions, including the four universities (Jeffrey represented St Andrews).[77]

Scott, as President of the Royal Society, had been able to put work in the way of the struggling Robert Chambers, sending him his address on the society's behalf to be copied in his best calligraphy. It took Chambers two days and he received a fee of five guineas. As a result of this achievement the Wernerian, Medical and Caledonian Horticultural Societies all brought him their addresses to be copied, 'and I cleared about 18 pounds in little more than a week', reported Chambers triumphantly. All were presented to the King who, examining them at leisure at Dalkeith Palace, remarked on their 'curious neatness'.[78]

Other addresses presented to the King included the Faculty of Procurators, Edinburgh Chamber of Commerce and the County of Forfar.

By the 19th, when Henry Fox called on Scott, he noted a kind of reaction. The novelist was out of humour with the King, and had himself been snubbed for his over-officiousness. But they were only halfway through the festivities.[79]

Thomas Uwins – who remarked, not altogether charitably, that Scott's attempt to throw an 'air of romance' about the visit received a rude blow at the sight of placards in the street, 'court dresses lent or hired' – was pleased to record the rumour that he was before long less in favour than expected. Surely (he says), 'Royal Geordie' had no time for romantic views, and knew that such occasions must be business-like.[80]

Henry's round of parties continued, including one the day after the Drawing-room, a large star-studded dinner at Sir George's, when another crisis had been announced. News came in the morning from Dunrobin that Lord Stafford had suffered a stroke and was 'alarmingly ill'. Lord Francis Leveson-Gower set off at once in one of the royal steamboats. He was twenty-two, and had married only that June Charlotte Greville, who had been reluctant to marry him or anyone, and now there was some gossip because in this crisis she continued to go out in society. 'After all one cannot expect her to care', sagely observed the worldly-wise Henry Fox, 'and though I think it would be better taste to stay at home, it does not much signify, for as Ly Gwydyr *justly* and *Scotchly* remarks, all the property is entailed.'

Henry had attended the Drawing-room on the 20th, accompanying Lady Elphinstone. 'The display of beauty very transcendent, the dresses pretty, and the suite of rooms much the best in any English palace. The K^{g} was civil to me and spoke.' Henry, still desperate over his love, imprudently wrote his proposal to Harriet and now must await her answer.[81]

David Wilkie, again present in a semi-official capacity, thought it 'a very unfair sample of our Scottish ladies', though the King graciously declared himself impressed, and privately said he had never seen so few diamonds and so little dirt – a comment on both the Scottish and the English court. There were about five hundred of them, of 'the most distinguished rank, fashion and beauty', mostly wearing white satin with spangled under-dress and white feather plumes. Only one or two wore tartan – perhaps those who could not afford to commission a special dress for the occasion.[82]

Susan Ferrier, not one of those honoured with an invitation, went with Mrs Graham 'to see the Duchess of A[rgyll] dressed . . . She was very splendid in French white satin and tulle, embroidered with silver and diamonds . . . but I thought I had seen her more beautiful when less gorgeous'. The Duchess (who had invited Miss Ferrier to her own At Home, 'but keep me from such things!') told her afterwards that 'never was anything seen like the awkwardness and uncouthness of the novices' on the occasion. 'The peeresses mobbed his Majesty – at least, crowded him so much that he could not stand it.'[83]

For the Grant sisters it was both ordeal and triumph. Tutored by Mrs Siddons in the management of curtsey and train, they had been preparing since early morning. They had had to endure the ministrations of a different hairdresser, an obstinate little Frenchman who was at the front door before they were even dressed, and left them with plumes stuck out at the back of their heads like funeral horses. In this style they went for breakfast to Mrs Siddons (who had had their court dresses overnight), and with her help fixed their head-dresses over again, to (everyone thought) delightful effect, and all agreed that the girls looked perfectly at home in their finery.

All this preparation and anxiety for a ceremony that lasted literally a moment.

Jane carried off the occasion with aplomb, but poor Mary was so nervous that at first she forgot what to do with the train, was helped by the Lord in Waiting and, hardly able to put one foot before the other, scarcely even saw the King, aware only of 'a pair of thick lips, and . . . a most immense man, much, much above me'. It was all over before she was fully conscious of where she was.

Meanwhile kind Mrs Siddons had been fidgeting at home, cold supper on the table, wine, hartshorn in hand, worrying about every possible disaster large or small that might have become them. When they did come back safe and sound, she had to go off and rehearse Portia, and then act at night.[84]

She was acting with Edmund Kean, whose day, it was generally agreed, was past. Crowded though the playhouse was night after night that week, Kean got little or no applause. 'He rants abominably', John Wilson had written of his appearance at Glasgow, even several years earlier, 'and on the whole is no actor at all.'[85]

Traffic control for both Levée and Drawing-room was at least in theory meticulous. For the latter, carriages were instructed to fall in line in Waterloo Place, proceed along the new road and set down at the principal entrance to the Palace, then continue along the South side to King's Park and line up until called for on the North side of the King's private road, pick up in the same order, and drive off along the Canongate. Sedan chairs had to approach via Canongate, set down by the principal door and wait by the north wall of Palace Yard. Only those with entry tickets were allowed to enter the Yard.

For the Levée, as we have seen, nervous guests started to line up in their carriages up to four hours before the allotted time, and when the near-mile-long queue moved forward it was at first too fast, so that on a sudden halt one or two carriages had their back panels pierced by the poles of those behind – to the danger of the footmen perched on the back.[86]

For Wednesday the only royal arrangement was a private dinner party given by the King, followed in the evening by a concert, at which Neil Gow and his company played Scottish airs.[87]

The King's evenings tended to be informal and spent at Dalkeith. He also went one morning for breakfast at Melville, where the rusticated Gillies and his wife walked down from their Lasswade cottage, and from the lane saw him 'pass in a very brisk trot, *more suo*, to and from his carriage'. On the lawn Gillies met James Hogg, with the Rev. Dr George Croly to whom he had been introduced at Blackwood's, and somehow he managed to get the recipe for the Carlton House punch from Sir Carnaby Haggerstone – but lost it.[88]

A relatively informal day was followed on Thursday (22nd) by what for most people was the highlight of the whole visit: the grand procession from Holyrood to the castle, marred once more by typically disappointing Edinburgh weather.

It was calculated that the King sat for four hours on the route there and back, simply in order to be stared at and cheered by innumerable subjects and hailed by cannon and military bands – but said that he would not do such a thing again.[89]

The Scottish Regalia was at Holyrood between 12 and 24 August, under constant guard of Highlanders of the Celtic Society, especially those in the train of the MacGregor of MacGregor. It had been ceremonially uplifted from the Castle's Crown Room by the Knight Marischal, the Duke of Hamilton, Sir Walter Scott, the Lord Provost and others, and escorted by the Clan Gregor and the Midlothian Yeomanry, with the band of the 77th Regiment. It was now to make its first official royal appearance in procession since 1707.[90]

One piece of demolition in the interests of traffic, i.e. the procession, which the conservationist Henry Cockburn considered vandalism was the magistrates having ordered the removal of an obstruction of the remains of the two hundred-year-old Weigh House at the junction of Lawnmarket, the West Bow and Castle Hill. As its spire had had long been demolished it had become 'an ugly lump', but for its antiquity alone it should have been left.

Cockburn salvaged features from it at the removal: the City arms, and the 'Pack and tun', for his house at Bonaly.[91]

Stands had been built along the castle esplanade for the county gentry, and along the Royal Mile the streets were lined by the city guilds and other bodies.

The procession, headed by the state trumpeters, was followed by detachments of the Yeomanry and Scots Greys, with Celtic Highlanders. Then came the heralds: Marchmont, Knight Marischal, Usher of the White Rod, and Lord Lyon. They preceded the 'Honours', carried by their custodians: Earl of Morton with the Sword, the Hon. John Stuart, in tartan, with the Sceptre; he was the Earl of Moray's second son, and represented the Earl of Sutherland. Finally the Crown on its cushion, carried by the Duke of Hamilton as premier peer of Scotland. They were flanked by elaborately costumed pages. The Earl of Erroll, as Lord High Constable, an office conferred on his family in 1321, accompanied the procession in his ceremonial robes.

This occasion was the grandest of all, and in spite of the dismal weather, all eyes were fixed on the Crown.

All the same, rain and dirty streets did literally cast a damp air. Susan Ferrier was one of those who thought the entry to the city had been more effective. 'It was really grievous to see the rain pouring upon white satin cloaks, and pages wading through the mire in satin shoes.' Further, the King's carriage – there were no others on this occasion – 'was by no means so splendid, and he himself invisible to mortal eye'.[92]

However, those able to watch from windows were better off. The Fletchers had been offered a place in the High Street by a former servant, now living with her family there. The loyal soul who could easily have let her windows for £5 or even £10 each, insisted that they were to be for the Fletchers, free, or for nobody. By a sad stroke of fate, while the crowds outside were cheering the passing procession, the poor woman indoors was watching by the deathbed of her daughter.

Julian Young, who unlike Henry Fox had to be content to witness only these public occasions, had stood for an hour in the crowd near the castle, noting 'the fussy self-importance of sundry provosts and baillies and deacons', who were making the most of their temporary power, and bewildered councillors who had not read the programme beforehand. Henry, nearby at Sir George Warrender's, was not necessarily better off, as the pressure of guests in the house was so dense. Wilkie and Collins had a good view from a seat on the scaffolding, and, in spite of the rain, for Collins this was the best day.[93]

After fears that the lowering day would end in cancellation of the procession, the Grant girls dressed in their new white silk spencers and the obligatory hats and went in the carriage as far as the top of the Mound, from where they walked up to where the stands for the Lords Lieutenants and county friends were erected. 'It was a very good way of showing off the aristocracy of the country to his Majesty.' The high stands, hung with scarlet cloth, were protected above with supposedly rain-proof awnings. Alas, the protection was a myth. The occupants sat for what seemed a very long time with rain pouring all round them, until by degrees it penetrated between the awnings, while the luckless onlookers put up umbrellas and parasols regardless of those behind. Mary Grant was just out of the rain, Jane was in the midst.

The trumpets announced the cortège, and many celebrities passed unnoticed while all craned their heads for the King. Arriving at last, he seemed oblivious to the weather.

'Good God! what a fine sight,' he was reported as saying. 'I had no conception there was such a scene in the world.' And, 'Rain! I feel no rain.' In view of his recent reputation it must have been a rare treat to experience what seemed such whole-hearted enthusiasm.

The Duke of Hamilton, carrying the Crown, 'looked very well indeed', thought Henry. 'He, or the regalia was loudly applauded – which, I did not make out.'

At the castle gate there was a ceremonial presentation of the keys by the Governor, Sir Alexander Pope, followed by the King's disappearance inside and an uncertain pause. The crowds hesitated. Where was he now? Should they go home? 'We'll see his sonsie face nae mair, be sure! He'll gang hame to Dalkeith anither way.'

Then, with 'electrifying' suddenness, the Arthur's Seat cannon roar, the castle guns answer, and in the clearing smoke they see the King waving from one of the embrasures of the half-moon battery and bowing. It made an impressive sight.

'Rather absurd and useless,' thought Henry. 'It was, on the whole, a failure.' He might have appreciated it more had he felt less squashed.

Dr Chalmers, who was cheering from the side, believed some of the crowd felt the same, and reproved bystanders who sounded too muted. 'Why, sir,' he cried to one, 'you are not half vociferous enough!' His monarchical loyalty was orthodoxy itself.[94]

Robert Peel, much of whose time had been spent in dealing with the loyal addresses presented to the King, feeling unwell and distressed by Lord Londonderry's death, had largely kept in the background, and even watched the procession – with Scott, with whom he was getting on well – from the pavement. He had also excused himself from the public dinner on health grounds.[95]

The King had doffed his hat despite the rain, and for about ten minutes stood bowing gracefully to his subjects. No-one could do such things better. Umbrella-less, and drenched, he was determined to acknowledge this wild and welcome enthusiasm.

He was then received at the Governor's house, and presumably dried off, before the procession on its four-hour round trip returned to Holyrood by the Mound, Princes Street and Abbeyhill.[96]

The aftermath was less euphoric. The road underfoot was filthy, ladies were soaked to the knees, feathers drooping to their waists, and Jane Grant, drenched through the awning but 'an immense Kingite' ever since her presentation, was among the worst sufferers.[97]

At least three parties were held that same evening, the Grants at Lady Keith's finding themselves at one 'horridly stupid; the men and girls vulgar looking. We knew hardly anybody', the heat overpowering and only the supper a redeeming feature. But at least they were by now delighted to have achieved one ticket for the Peers' Ball and two for the Caledonian.[98]

The Procession had been the grand climax for the populace; later events were less formal, and with less pomp the King seemed closer to his subjects.

Henry, indeed, was better pleased with the Review next day on Portobello sands. He went with Lady Gwydyr, 'a clever, long-headed woman', so good-natured that she seemed 'a great flatterer', and rather obsessed with trifles. 'The review was beautiful. The K. rode a white horse he bought here. It went admirably.' Henry was in a state of nervous gaiety, calculating that Harriet must now have received his letter of proposal.[99]

After the Procession washout, the Review had a bright sunny day, and 'equipages' and people in their best clothes flocked down to the waterside, past the Calton Hill and Salisbury Crags still covered with gaily bedecked tents. Scarlet-clad officers on brightly caparisoned horses, landaus filled with smartly dressed ladies, 'barouches, barouchettes, curricles, gigs, open chariots, one-horse chaises, carts full of hearty farmers and their rosy families, stage coaches . . . [were] all bound to the same place for the same purpose'.[100]

On the shore were stands crowded with onlookers, booths displaying rare shows, odd-looking characters careering about on horses, grand carriages, on the sands seen to perfection in the brilliant sunshine, against the glittering sea.

The King, bowing and regularly touching his hat, rode between the regiments to the cheering of the throng; then the regiments passed before him in review, and even the scattering of the soldiery and the huge crowd at the end was a spectacular sight.

The parade of cavalry and yeomanry amounted to almost three thousand troops, stretching nearly a mile along the shore. Their commander, Major General Sir Thomas Bradford, followed the King and his escort of the

Greys with his staff.[101] The Celtic Society Highlanders, who were also on parade, were nearly kept out by the mistaken withdrawal of the cavalry piquet supposed to keep the ground clear.

The Duke of Argyll (who throughout the visit had worn Highland dress) here commanded a battalion of eight hundred Highlanders, in which the Celtic Society marched with clansmen of the Sutherlands, MacGregors, Campbells and Drummonds. While the King was praising the 'brave highlanders of steady and soldier-like appearance', one of them was carrying the sword used by his father at Culloden.

Then came the grand ball at the Assembly Rooms.

Only Mary of the Grant sisters had been able to get a ticket, after all the promises and maneouvrings, and was miserable, knowing no one. But she was greatly impressed with the appearance of the Assembly Rooms, the first saloon hung with glazed blue and yellow calico, resembling silk, its pillars wreathed with flowers, and its magnificent chandelier glistening. The largest, finest room was splendidly decorated with a raised dais, crimson-covered, with fine velvet chairs, and in the middle above the chair of state a canopy of crimson velvet bordered with gold, lit by huge candelabra and the splendid chandeliers. The supper room tables were decorated with elaborate confections. The landing at the top of the stairs, by which the King would arrive, was guarded by beefeaters.[102]

Henry, who had been dining in a small party with Lady Francis, went on to the ball at 9 o'clock. The King arrived at 10, stayed for an hour and was received by a committee of peers including the Duke of Atholl.

He shook hands with the Chief Commissioner Adam, and mingled with the dancers, who were so crammed that many could not even set eyes on him.

'I never saw so striking a sight,' said Henry. 'All ladies in plumes, and everybody in full dress. Dss of Argyll looked magnificent. Two Miss Maitlands were the beauties, and Ly Glenorchy [wife of the Earl of Breadalbane's heir] looked well . . . Reels were danced for H.M. who was pleased.'

Henry stayed with Lady Francis, whom he liked in spite of her provokingly 'total indifference to everything about her and no care for what she does or says', but he was also lumbered with Lady Elphinstone, 'amiable, but tedious and sticks like a leech'. Lord Erroll, whom he met and liked, in spite of his magnificent appearance in the Procession had had to leave his wife at home because 'poverty prevented her coming. He is beautiful.'[103]

The King, who took up a position almost in the middle of the room, seemed delighted with the Scottish music, often looking approvingly at the band and snapping his fingers to the rhythm.[104]

Although the Rothiemurchus Grants mixed with the 'best' society, Mary had not been out in Edinburgh, and though she recognised many people, knew only a few families. However, she was rescued by Gabriel Hamilton, who knew everyone, hailed the most aristocratic of them in a familiar way, and kindly saw her to supper, so that she was able to pass judgment on the greatest. The Duke of Hamilton, in Highland dress like the other grandees, was 'like a dancing master and an Italian greyhound. He stood on my toe', bowing and grimacing in apology. 'The Duke of Athole is a great pig; the Duke of Montrose, ugly; the Duke of Argyle, very interesting.' So much for Scotland's leading aristocracy. 'The Duchess of Argyle is beautiful, and looked lovely in a kind of Highland bonnet, done with gold . . .'

The King, though much crowded and overheated in the press, took no refreshments, in field marshal's uniform as usual but wearing boots – for 'a would-be Celt' at the Review had awkwardly lamed him by dropping his pistol on his big toe.

With a gracious farewell to the Duchess of Argyll the King left at 11. After he left quadrilles were danced in the inner room, but it was either too hot or too crowded for many to join in. Parties tended to stick together, because if one moved away it was impossible to find anyone again.

The supper room, built out in a temporary back extension, was made up like a tent with fluted sides in pink and white calico, and lighted with chandeliers, 'like some fairy palace', thought Mary. All the same, she found the evening more impressive than enjoyable.

When her party left at 1 a.m. there was fearful confusion, carriages drawing up and being waved on while their owners were still struggling on the stairs, or at best, ladies being shoved down and bundled in. Outside was an even worse scrum. 'Soldiers, menacing with their bayonets; the mob hissing and groaning, footmen hallooing, and Highland porters flinging about their arms.'[105]

The ball had been managed by William Murray of the theatre, who had, besides, advised on the procession, fitted up Holyrood and the Parliament House for Saturday's banquet, and acted every night into the bargain. At 4.30 that afternoon he had arrived to check the Assembly Room arrangements, to find Lord Leven in great distress about some 'disgraceful' piece of decoration, and without ceremony tore it down. At 6.30, leaving everything in good order, he went on to the theatre to act at 7.[106]

On Saturday the Lord Provost William Arbuthnot, magistrates and town council gave a civic banquet in the Parliament House for the King and about 250 guests. The room, elaborately decorated, was fitted up with a dais for the King's table on the south side, under the great window. Left of it, the two niches in which the Lords of the Court of Session normally sat in court, were occupied by Nathaniel Gow's orchestra and a choir. The royal table was horseshoe-shaped, to hold a select party of about thirty, and was under a canopy. The Lord Provost sat on the King's right hand. Again Court dress was *de rigueur*, and because of the limited numbers the only invitations went to high officials or those closely connected with the King.

The new Advocates' Library served as his withdrawing-room, and the rest of the party was received in the Signet Library immediately below. There was, unfortunately for ladies, no gallery to which they could be invited to view this masculine occasion.[107]

After a traditional Scottish menu, including haggis, sheep's head and hotch potch, forty-seven toasts were drunk. Following the dessert William Howison Crawford held a silver basin for the King's hands, a traditional duty, or honour, enjoined for his estates at Braehead.

As the whole visit (apart from the items delegated to, or arrogated by, Sir Walter Scott) had been the responsibility of the Lord Provost, the King announced at the banquet that he was to create him a baronet.

The next day was the second Sabbath of the royal visit, and this time the King made an official appearance at St Giles'. Great was the contrast. Official handbills had been distributed, warning people how they should act and where they should be, and instructing that there should be no cheers that day. Later (on 2 September), *The Times* remarked caustically on the too well-drilled programme, which 'displayed none of the symptoms of glowing enthusiasm'.[108]

As a result, everybody remarked on the sober, reverent behaviour of people in the streets. There was neither noise, cheering nor thundering cannon as on the previous days. As the King drove up to St Giles', anyone who was on the streets was silent and with bared head. Silence reigned, and the Rev. George Crabbe fancied the streets were deserted. 'A total stagnation – a quiet that is in itself devout', which assorted well with the polite respectability he had noted in his walks about the city.[109]

Collins, Wilkie, Turner and William Allan were all at St Giles', where Wilkie hoped to make a sketch of the giving of the King's alms. This hope proved abortive, as an 'officious official', who thought the action of alms-giving would appear unseemly, removed the King's Plate so that His Majesty could not leave the money – 100 guineas – and it had to be sent afterwards.

Wilkie had asked Dr Chalmers if Dr Blair was to be the preacher, and Blair was inclined to weep with emotion in the pulpit; the Doctor replied drily, 'Why, if he does, it will be George Blair to George Rex, greeting!'[110]

It proved to be not Blair, however, but Dr Lamont, the Moderator, 'a sharpish, common-place body, very proud of himself', says Cockburn. He had been at pains to compose a high-flown sermon, but luckily Sir Harry Moncreiff, who heard of it, warned him that an 'ordinary' sermon would be more appropriate: 'and if there be anything particularly fine, even in that, cut it out!'[111]

While the King was making his state appearance at church ('which will do more than any other thing to make him popular'), the Grants and friends went to view the Royal Squadron, which had been on view daily to the public. Despite a 'provoking shower' as they set off, counteracted with boat cloaks and umbrellas, they enjoyed a lively and interesting visit, the sea crowded with pleasure boats sailing to and fro, the yachts filled with officers in full uniform, doing the honours of their ships to the elegant visitors.

While on Captain Adams's ship they were entertained to a delicious 'collation' in the officers' cabin, with the Lord President's son Mr Hope, first Lieutenant, at the head of the table and the captain walking round them to ensure good service.

The Grants were continually astonished at the capacity of Mrs Siddons's two sons, particularly Henry, who could happily put away two large dinners or suppers in succession. 'Eating too much never does me any harm', Henry declaimed, 'but eating too little does not agree with me!' To which his little brother rejoined casually, 'If you were to reverse *one* word you would speak very good sense.'[112]

Next evening was the Caledonian Hunt Ball for which both Grant sisters had achieved tickets which materialised at a late hour. They went first to a dinner party, already dressed in their court dresses and plumes, which had also been the rule for the Peers' Ball.

They arrived at the Assembly Rooms at 8.30, but it proved less crowded and not quite so 'restricted to high people'. They had a fine view of the King, who arrived at 9, received ceremonially by the Caledonian lords in waiting, in livery of blue coats with red collar and cuffs, smothered in gold lace, and the members of the hunt. Their costume after a great fuss had been settled as scarlet coat and green collar (their usual dress) but in court style, with white cloth waistcoats and breeches, and silk stockings with buckled shoes. They carried white wands.

The King stayed for two hours, during which reels were continually danced before the throne near which he stood, beating time to the music and talking attentively to the Duchess of Argyll and Mrs General Balfour. He also moved about the room, where were other reels (and after he left, quadrilles and country dances in the small room). As for the elegant tent-like supper room, this time provided with seats, he merely looked in and moved away.

Afterwards Jane danced a reel, getting into difficulties with a loose ribbon which caught in her foot, and could neither be pinned up nor torn off. At last a kilted Macleod chieftain produced his knife for another gallant to cut it off. 'Who shall say hereafter that the Highland dress may not be of use in a drawing-room?'[113]

Susan Ferrier's 'Cousin Mag', widow of her Uncle Walter Ferrier, who had failed to see the King during the Procession and could not get a Peers' Ball ticket, attended the Caledonian Ball and came afterwards to spend the day with Susan, 'brimful of delight, having been at the Hunt Ball, patronised by Lady Rollo and squired by my Lord, and standing within two feet of the King'.[114]

Henry Fox, during intervals between royal events, had walked with George, Lord Morpeth, to look at Nelson's Monument, and dined at the Royal Hotel with Lady Francis, followed by seeing two acts of Edmund Kean as Macbeth. (These partial attendances at the theatre, which one would have thought tantalising, were far from uncommon, and an accepted way of helping to fill an evening.) He turned up to the Hunt Ball, 'the counterpart of the Peers' Ball', but says little about it. Lord Gower arrived in Edinburgh on his way to Dunrobin, to attend the sick Lord Stafford, but set off next morning 'without saying a word', leaving Lady Francis with no-one to escort her there. Henry passed time with her playing écarté, and a few hours later she too set off.

On Monday morning (26th), after a sleepless night Henry learned with some relief that Howard had after all never delivered his proposal to Harriet. Tantalisingly, there is no more of his account of the royal visit, of his lovesick anguish, or of the gilded aristocracy among whom he moved. Resuming his journal some weeks later, he drops hints that he regretted 'his rashness and absurdity at Holland House', without further explanation.[115]

The Grant sisters' letters and diaries end as abruptly as Henry Fox's journal. There was probably no time for them to write more, and the rest had to await a personal account when the girls arrived home after their memorable week.

The visit was drawing to a close. On Monday morning a ceremony of a very different kind, which the King – to the disappointment of many – did not attend, took place on the Calton Hill.

This was the laying of the foundation stone of the much heralded 'National Monument' which, under discussion at least since 1817, was to crystallise, as it were, the idea of Edinburgh as the Modern Athens, a restoration of the Parthenon, appropriately on its hill or acropolis above the city.

An appeal had been launched in January for £42,000 for its realisation. Signatories of the appeal had included, of course, Sir Walter Scott, besides Jeffrey and Cockburn, though so far only a few thousand pounds had come in.

For the foundation ceremony, which was in traditional masonic style, the King was represented by a whole committee of peers. There were also, of course, the Lord Provost and magistrates, a committee of contributors, and most numerous, the brethren of the Masonic lodges, assembled in the Parliament Square at noon, while the Grand Lodge gathered in the Signet Hall.

The Duke of Hamilton was sworn in as Grand Master Mason, and at 2 o'clock the procession, headed by him with former and provincial Grand Masters, moved off, approaching round the south side of Calton Hill.

Here they took their places, the band played the National Anthem, addresses were made, and sealed bottles containing the obligatory coins, newspapers and so on were placed in the cavity. A crane then raised and placed the stone.

This was claimed to be the grandest, most splendid such ceremony so far seen in Edinburgh – even though many spectators had hoped for even better, to see the King.[116] Hopes for a completed National Monument were to be equally disappointed.

David Roberts made a special curtain for the Theatre in honour of this event, showing 'A View of the Parthenon'. This was particularly appropriate since that night had been chosen for the King's ceremonial theatrical visit, for which he had diplomatically chosen *Rob Roy,* adapted from the novel by John Pocock.

Edmund Kean was chagrined that the piece chosen was one in which there could be no part for him. The piece had been 'made' by Charles Mackay, who had identified himself as Bailie Nicol Jarvie and was probably largely responsible for the play's success with the public. The theatre had had a modest season so far, and that evening was to improve their fortunes.[117]

Once again Edinburgh suffered a steady downpour. The doors did not open until 6, but in spite of this and the weather, crowds had gathered round the pit and gallery entrance by noon, and by 2 o'clock were dense. People became so soaked that a cloud of steam rose above the mob. When the doors did at last open, those who had waited longest were swept up by the pressure in 'a great moving, whirling mass', last-comers being mostly first in, and those in front pushed out. Although the Full House board was soon displayed, still they milled around, and some, led by 'a stout athletic Gael', climbed over the heads of the rest and got through the top section of the door. Once inside, despite the unpleasant smell of soaked, steaming garments, the good-humoured crowd sang Scottish songs to pass the time. At 7.30 Edinburgh society, in the shape of the box occupants, arrived.

The King arrived at ten minutes past eight and was greeted by the Lord Chamberlain and William Murray, each holding a silver candlestick, and was ushered through the grand new portico. The audience cheered enthusiastically as he entered the box, and when this subsided the curtain rose on the whole company, who sang 'God Save the King' while the audience stood to join in.

Each actor, on entrance, bowed deeply to the King, who plainly enjoyed the play, laughing loudly at several incidents including the Bailie's 'None o' your Lunnon tricks here!' Besides Mackay, Denham played Rashleigh, Calcraft Rob Roy, and the King afterwards expressed his especial pleasure to Murray at seeing Mrs Henry Siddons, for this one night playing Di Vernon.

At the end amid wild enthusiasm there was another rendering of the national anthem. The *Scotsman* noted, apparently not without some glee, that Scott's arrival had been cheered, 'though not enthusiastically or very generally'.[118]

Next day the very last ceremony was performed, at Hopetoun House. General the Earl of Hopetoun had served with distinction in the Peninsular War, and that year was Captain General of the Royal Company of Archers, and Gold Stick for Scotland. To-day he entertained the King and his train to luncheon, together with the Archers, Yeomanry and his own tenants, numbering more than a thousand.

The King's party, escorted by the Scots Greys, drove through Edinburgh by the usual route, by this time evoking far less response from the people as he passed. At Hopetoun, the house was filled with privileged visitors, who while awaiting the King's arrival at noon were enjoying a cold collation.

On arrival the King entered the saloon accompanied by Lord Hopetoun and his brother Sir Alexander Hope (Lieutenant Governor of the Castle), each bearing a sword. Henry Raeburn was then called and was knighted by the King, and then Adam Fergusson, through Scott's influence, Keeper of the Regalia since its re-discovery.

Chief Commissioner Adam, who had been first to shake the King's hand on his arrival at Leith, was also the last before he embarked on his yacht at Port Edgar. He had invited Collins and Wilkie to breakfast on board the *Royal George* – for Collins was (vainly) hoping to make a companion piece to the arrival for the departure.

Collins, greatly impressed by the whole visit, both by the King's apparent delight and the way in which he had been received by the Scots, 'from the lord to the meanest peasant', noted that 'The regularity and dignity of a Scotch mob is really surprising.' He accompanied the royal yacht down the Forth, but was nearly carried out to sea, having great difficulty in persuading the Master not to take him on but to put him off at Leith.[119]

The newly knighted Raeburn had invited his artist friends to dine at his house at Stockbridge for a 'jollification', along with the Chief Commissioner, John Clerk and many others. Fergusson (Wilkie told his sister) 'blushed even more than usual', and Mrs Raeburn refused to be addressed by her new title. After dinner there was of course a bumper to the new knights, Sir

Henry modestly acknowledging the favour, and Sir Adam opting for a song instead of a speech – 'The Laird of Cockpen', with 'The Turnemspike' as encore. Wilkie and Collins had been invited to go on to visit Blair Adam by Commissioner Adam, from where they continued with their planned Highlands tour.[120]

Wilkie had spent some time during the visit with the Lord Provost, discussing King Charles II's statue in Parliament Square, which the magistrates were proposing to remove along with so much of Edinburgh's past; but Wilkie's persistence persuaded them into a restoration. Similarly, under Mrs Coutts's pressure it was now proposed to restore the old Edinburgh Cross.[121]

Of his four choices for subject for paintings, Wilkie would have preferred the scene at the Kirk on Sunday, but the King, supposedly captivated by Highland splendour, instead chose the scene on his arrival at Holyrood, with the Chiefs on either side. He also insisted on a change of his own pose as he received the key, from one of 'easy grace!' to an appropriately martial stance.[122]

The sculptor Samuel Joseph, 'merely from seeing him at the shows here', had contrived to make a bust of the King, which was so successful that the pleased monarch gave him a personal sitting.[123]

'This is a vile day,' wrote Scott to Sir William Knighton on 29 August, 'but it is right Scotland should weep when parting with her good King.' He was certain of lasting good effect from the visit, sincerely believing that everything had been so admirably managed that no 'single whisper or misrepresentation' could arise. As for the affair of the kilt, he went to great pains in defence.

In his district, where there had been a rumour of the King's gross appearance, he claimed people were delighted to see, instead, 'a portly handsome man looking and moving every inch a King . . . In short it is a great stake played for and won and the King himself showed his pleasure in the visit.'[124]

Robert Peel, who had to stay on until the 29th, got on so well with Scott that the latter was emboldened to put to him that Mons Meg might be returned to Scotland, and the following September Peel raised this with the Duke of Wellington.[125]

Lord Melville wrote to the King on the 29th that although, on first announcing the visit, he had not doubted the Scots' feeling of duty, he had not anticipated the deep-rooted royalist feeling, 'which evidently pervaded the great body of the people', and he was convinced the visit would bring 'important public benefit'. He could hardly say anything else.[126]

Cockburn took a very different view. Writing admittedly some quarter-century after the event, he considered that the visit's effect was nil. The King was too genuinely unpopular to reconcile criticism, and the people were merely gazing at a spectacle, as of 'a Chinese Emperor and his gongs, elephants and Mandarins'. The Scottish temperament was naturally restrained, and only rational loyalty had been shown.

Of the results, Raeburn's knighthood indeed made 'a useful compliment to Scottish art'. The (proxy) foundation laying of the National Monument was hoped to stimulate production of funds – which in the event were not forthcoming. A subscription was also started for a statue of the King, which was later executed by Chantrey. This over the years became 'one of the black men' in George Street.

'On the whole', said Cockburn, 'after his Majesty had sailed down the Forth again, his visit left no more trace on our land than his vessel did on the waters.'[127]

The Times was at pains to point out that by the end of the visit the people of Edinburgh seemed 'quite tired of the royal ceremony', which had thrown them out of their regular habits, and on his last drive through the streets on the way to Hopetoun there was little observation of his passing.[128] There seem to be echoes of this today at the fag-end of the Edinburgh Festival.

PART IV

1823–1832

'The first view was more splendid and imposing than any spectacle I have ever witnessed. Dublin and London . . . furnish nothing which can be compared with the *coup d'oeil* from the brow of Calton Hill. However critics in architecture may cavil at the construction or uniformity of the buildings, when taken in detail and examined closely, it is impossible for any one not to be forcibly struck with the magnificence and splendour of the whole, which at the first approach appears like an immense castle or palace . . . it is in external appearance the most beautiful city I have ever seen, or ever expect to see, should my travels extend the world over. Nothing can surpass it in grandeur and beauty.' (1825)

Nathaniel Carter, *Letters from Europe*, 1827, 1.240

INTRODUCTION

From about the mid-1820s we become aware of a new atmosphere in Edinburgh, more in tune with our own times. There has been a slump, there is much unemployment and unrest among the poor, there are riots, more in Glasgow and the West than in Edinburgh. Firms go into liquidation, notably Constable, and the consequent ruin of Sir Walter Scott overshadows the later part of the decade.

The city settles after the visit of King George, and in 1824 suffers a rude shock with the worst ever of its many fires, damaging much of the centre of the Old Town. There are new services, gas, an improved water supply, there is talk of railroads.

Literary magazines abound, or rather rise and fall, now disseminated among more of the population. The Chambers brothers contribute to popular culture by their widely circulated periodicals. The *Edinburgh Review* acquires a new editor, when Jeffrey's advancement in a legal and political career prevents his continuing.

Those who were leaders early in the century find they have become (by standards of the time) old: new faces now appear. Jeffrey goes from strength to strength, as Lord Advocate, as MP, as a judge, but more and more melancholy.

Wild John Wilson seems wilder, though older. Meanwhile new literary figures take over: Thomas De Quincey, Thomas Carlyle, suddenly to his own astonishment almost lionised. Religious dissension in the General Assembly throws into prominence the gifted preacher Dr Thomas Chalmers, and there is greater, if grudging, tolerance for Dissenters, notably Roman Catholics.

Tourism increases, and the modern gaols and numerous new charitable institutions, orphanages, schools for the deaf and dumb, are added to visitors' programmes.

All this while Scott in his effort to pay off his huge debt, is conscientiously turning out novel after novel, work after work, and planning reissues of multiple volumes. He would have succeeded, had his now unpredictable health not let him down.

There are medical scandals such as the body-snatching of Burke and Hare, there is a typhoid and later the cholera epidemic. And there is a constant background of rumbling discontent, latent fears of revolution (some thought it inevitable), and clamour for change. The end of the Twenties and start of the Thirties are full of Whig/Tory hostility and the gradually looming prospect of Parliamentary Reform, a prolonged struggle whose success, and the consequent lurch towards bourgeois society, predate by a few months Scott's return from abroad to die. His death brings an age to an end, when Edinburgh's own pre-eminence in literature, philosophy, the sciences, dwindles with the departure – by rail – of new MPs to a modified Parliament in London. The age of the Athens of the North fades away.

44
A RASH OF NEW BUILDING

'What I never tired of admiring was the *ensemble* of this majestic town, the streets of which rivalling each other in extent and beauty, would however at length oppress the imagination with the monotony of their symmetrical grandeur, if this impression were not suspended . . . by the view of some conspicuous building, or some verdant, umbrageous *square*, which separated them from each other.'

Charles Nodier, *Promenade from Dieppe*, 1822, 80

'I never preconceived a place better than Edinburg. It is exactly what I fancied it, and certainly is the most beautiful town in the world – you can scarcely call it a city – at least it has little of the roar of millions, and at this [season] is of course very empty.'

Benjamin Disraeli to John Murray, 17 Sept. 1825, J. A. W. Gunn (ed.), *Benjamin Disraeli Letters: 1815–1834*, Univ. of Toronto Press, 1982, 34

'Edinburgh must be the handsomest city in the world.'

J. J. Audubon to his wife, 21 Dec. 1826, *Letters*, I.II

'The only city in the World where the Parthenon might be erected with something of its ancient splendour.'

B. R. Haydon, 26 Nov. 1820, Willard Russell Pope (ed.), *The Diary of Benjamin Robert Haydon*, Cambridge, Mass., 1960–63, II. 294–5

'No greater contrast can be imagined than between the filthy cramped conditions of the coarse black dwellings, and the poverty of their occupants, and the magnificence, elegance and airiness of the new streets.'

Karl Friedrich Schinkel, *The English Journey*, David Bindman (ed.), *Journal of a Visit to France and Britain in 1826*, Yale UP, 1993, 150

'The remarkable change which has taken place during the last 60 years, both in the appearance of the city and in the state of society, is not perhaps to be equalled in the history of any city in the world.'

J. & R. Burford, *Description of a View of the City of Edinburgh, and Surrounding Country now exhibiting in the Panorama, Leicester Square . . .* London, 1826

'I suppose, and it is generally supposed, that the whole world does not contain any thing of the size more grand and imposing than the new entrance over the Calton-hill.' (1819)

Rev. William Carus (ed.), *Memoirs of the Rev. Charles Simeon, MA*, 3rd edn, London, 1848

'We passed the Parthenon of Mr Playfair, in other words, the *Museum* and *Academy of Painting* – a stone building of remarkable brilliancy and component parts – encrusted with exterior ornaments, almost with the profusion of gothic art. It should not be at the bottom, but at the top of a hill.

'A huge pile of earth, called *the Mound* . . . than which nothing more ugly or more bungling can be conceived, brought us to the upper part of the High Street.'

Rev. Thomas Frognall Dibdin, *A Bibliographical antiquarian and Picturesque Tour in the Northern Counties of England and Scotland*, London, 1838, II.485

The grand new entrance to Edinburgh from the London Road, and the ceremonial Waterloo Place, had given a great boost to the city's architectural status, and with the 1820s at last seeing completion of the Register House and the University, and the libraries adjoining Parliament House, the New Town may be said to have taken its permanent shape.

There was more to its development than that however, for the numerous private estates round the perimeter of the city were now being handed over to builders, so that from about 1823 the decade sees the laying out of an enormous number of new streets. Yet the chief building achievement was in the many charitable and cultural institutions, and the public services.

Invaluable information was recorded by two interested persons, the anonymous author of *Improvements in Edinburgh during the Year 1823*, an exhaustive documentation published early in 1824, and the also anonymous diary and commentary of building achievements between 1823 and 1833.[1]

Progress on Adam's Register House at last began in February 1823, at such speed that by December it was roofed, and completion began of its more than one hundred rooms. To date it had cost nearly £40,000, and thanks to the efforts of the Lord Register Lord Frederick Campbell, and his deputy Thomas Thomson, almost as much again – £30,000 – had been voted by Parliament.

Next in importance, and begun a few months later, was what came to be known as the Royal Institution. This was the idea of the Board of Trustees for the Manufacturers, to be a joint establishment for the Royal Society of Edinburgh, the Society of Scottish Antiquaries and their Museum, the Royal Academy, and the Institution for the Encouragement of the Fine Arts in Scotland. Further, it was to be an answer to the perennial Mound question – and as might have been expected, soon created further problems. Designed by the architect William Playfair, it contained libraries, museums, meeting rooms for its occupants, an octagonal room for exhibiting water-colours and a sculpture gallery. It was opened in 13 February 1826 with a public dinner. In May there was a movement to form a Royal Scottish Academy here, which held its first exhibition in 1827. It was expected to cost £56,000, though before long Playfair was called back to make considerable enlargements.[2]

Playfair's first problem was to create a sure foundation on the mass of 'travelled earth' and rubbish which constituted the Mound, which he solved by building 1800 five-foot piles in five parallel rows, machine-driven to within a short distance of the top. These extended under three of the sides, with a greater number under the intended portico and entrance front. The tops of the piles were joined by wooden bars, and the space between filled with masonry. The building was to rest on a level timber floor laid across this foundation.

Building proper began in July 1823. Playfair's pure Grecian style was greatly admired, with its eight-column Doric portico towards Hanover Street, and thirty-two columns along the other fronts.

Hardly less important was the new boys' school, the Edinburgh Academy. The famous old High School in Infirmary Street, close to the Infirmary building, now seemed inadequate for the growing city's needs, and this new establishment was a rival. Designed by William Burn, and begun in August 1823 at the foot of Howe Street, it formed an impressive vista at the foot of the steep hill. This was then totally obscured in 1828 by the building of Playfair's St Stephen's Church. Among the directors were the Lord President Robert Dundas of Arniston, Sir Walter Scott, Henry Cockburn and Leonard Horner.

The site was part of the old Distillery Park in Canonmills, on land feued from the Governors of Heriot's Hospital. On the south or main side of the long, low building was a six-column Doric porch, behind which was the oval assembly hall, seventy by fifty feet. The school, accommodating 600 boys, had eight major and eight smaller classrooms to be heated with warm air.

The building was set in a large three-acre playground, partly covered in for bad weather. It was due to open that October and estimated to cost £12,000; but parts were still building in 1836 – long after it had lost its vista to Playfair's church. The *Edinburgh Journal* author had been sceptical of the school's success, for 'its Situation is too far out of the way even for the patrician part of Edinburgh'.[3]

Not far off, in Henderson Row, also in the Distillery Park, was built James Gillespie Graham's Deaf and Dumb Asylum, on nearly three acres of land also feued from the Governors of Heriot's, and intended for 120 children. Begun in May, it was built in little over a year and cost £5600. Its function inevitably dictated a simple 'charity' design, four storeys and attics, behind a plain pedimented front. It was extended in 1893.

Of six new churches, three were intended as chapels of ease for St Cuthbert's. One was needed for the rapidly growing south side. Here Robert Brown's Hope Park Chapel (now Newington and St Leonard's) with a Greek pilastered front and small steeple, was a landmark in an area which had few such. It took only nine months to build (April 1823 to 2 January 1824), and held a congregation of 1800. The author of *Improvements* expressed violent disapproval of a lack of taste in choice of site, which prevented the building's being seen except from immediately in front, 'so *thrust* upon the street (being in a direct line with the house)'. He also asserted that at 73 feet it was too narrow and in design too tame to inspire respect: it would have been seen to best advantage a few yards away, forming an ornamental closure to Montague Street. (Perhaps the anonymous author lived so near at hand as to feel personally concerned.)

Of the other chapels begun that year for St Cuthbert's, the Claremont Street chapel (later renamed St Bernard's), by James Milne, adjoined Saxe-Coburg Place. For this the author reserved still greater spleen. Its orthodox Palladian façade with paired Ionic pilasters, and central pediment headed by a three-tier steeple with a cupola, was condemned as the Kirk Session's indulgence in 'their own *peculiarly classic* propensities', which they imposed on the architect, strictly adhering to 'an order of architecture peculiar to themselves'. In fact, too many such chapels were trying to echo St Cuthbert's style.

There was also Edinburgh's first Unitarian Chapel, in Young Street, one of the service lanes off Charlotte Square. Built within six months in 1823, though hardly distinguishable from the neighbouring houses in the modest street, it was actually equipped with an organ. It was demolished in 1970.

In the north-east quarter, Bellevue Church by Thomas Brown, city superintendent of public works, was sited in the middle of Bellevue Crescent, designed by Thomas Bonnar, his predecessor in the post, who was dismissed in 1818. The crescent, begun in 1819, was not finished for several decades, and the church was founded on 15 August 1823, anniversary of the King's visit the previous year. With a Corinthian portico and tall spire, in a popular mingling of classical and Gothic that purists might deplore, it was estimated at £11,000.[4]

A building which invited lengthy description and unbounded admiration was the 'British Hotel' at the west end of Queen Street, designed by Mr Alison, architect, of London Road, on a spot which even eighteen months earlier had ended in country, but was now incorporated into Edinburgh by the building of the Moray estate. It consisted of two houses thrown together and enlarged by additional storeys, an entrance portico and balconies to the upper floors. The chief items for praise were its separate units, distinguished for convenience (and a certain class distinction) by doors of different woods: on the principal stair rosewood, the second oak, the third mahogany, the fourth wainscot and the top (servants') painted white. Apartment numbers were engraved on the door handles and keys, rather than being 'blazoned' as usual on the door, and to reduce noise the well-furnished bedrooms had double doors. There were also 'rooms for Bachelors' – that is, singles.

One great innovation was speaking tubes connecting flats with the servants' quarters, and (also apparently still unknown in Edinburgh hotels) a rear service stair to remove the sight and 'bustle' of servants from the guests, just as they would be at home. The architect's 'scientific knowledge', combined with his client Morley's 'ingenuity and refinement of taste' over fittings, produced an hotel which was quickly patronised by the aristocratic classes. The whole account reads suspiciously like a crypto-advertisement.[5]

New monuments included the equestrian king's statue, commemorating his visit and designed by Chantrey by royal command. At £10,000 it cost as much and more than some of the new churches. There was much discussion over its eventual site. The artist ambitiously suggested a position in front of Holyrood, to be created by pulling down old houses and planting a vast lawn, enclosed by a wall and railing, with for good measure a handsome new crescent opposite the palace communicating with Regent Road and Piershill. A grand entry would be created by a 'superb gateway' or triumphal arch opposite the new crescent, crowned by the statue. The toll income would cover the demolition costs.

The unstated implication was that there would be future royal visits, thus fittingly provided for, while the neglected palace became once more a favourite haunt.

Meanwhile £2000 had been collected, largely from patriotic Scots in India, for Flaxman's bronze statue of Burns to complete the Burns monument. The model showed the poet in his native costume contemplating 'the mountain daisy', subject of one of his favourite poems, and holding a scroll engraved with another favourite, 'The Cottar's Saturday Night'.[6]

Among the chief landscaping embellishments was improvement of the long-neglected Queen Street gardens, extended by an Act of 1822 from their original limit east of Hanover and Dundas Streets. Throughout 1823 labourers were stocking the whole steep open space between Queen Street and the terraces of Heriot Row and Abercromby Place with shrubs and plants. Next season they were to rail the western part and remove the boundary wall with Lord Wemyss's ground, in the hope that he would prove neighbourly enough to dispose of his gardens, or else lay them out in keeping. The improvements were due to 'the laudable exertions of Mr William Bell of Queen Street'.

Since 1820 work had been progressing for the University on twelve acres of Inverleith as a new site for the Royal Botanic Gardens, opened in 1824. Within a high stone enclosure wall, by 1823 most plants had already been transferred from the Leith Walk grounds. Classrooms for the professors had been designed by Robert Reid, together with greenhouses with ornamental cast-iron roofs, and nearly four hundred feet of stoves. No expense was spared, and the new gardens were hailed as 'excelled by none in Britain'.

The building of a proliferation of new streets went on with bewildering rapidity. To mention only a few, estates were being laid out by Robert Brown, including the completion of the 'third new town' extending north from Princes Street, bordering Tait's Shandwick Place of 1809: Melville Crescent and Street, and Walker Street, for the Walker Trust (1822–25); the streets bordering Leith Walk, Haddington Place, Annandale Street and Hopetoun Crescent, for Major John Hope in 1825–27; and the northern extension of the Second New Town including St Stephen Street, NW Circus Place and Henderson Row, for James Peddie (1829–36). On the south side, Brown laid out Clerk Street in 1823.[7]

Newington on the south, and Stockbridge on the north, were now joined to the city. The architects or builders of Newington remain anonymous, with Rankeillor Street, St Patrick's Square and, more interestingly, its pretty villas.[8]

At the foot of the hill beyond the Second New Town, James Milne's picturesque Saxe-Coburg Street and its church, Danube Street, Dean Street and St Bernard's Crescent, were built between 1822 and 1824. Of these the most striking, if not most beautiful, was St Bernard's Crescent. It has an 'alarmingly Grecian façade', as Ian Lindsay describes it, not designed until 1824, apparently suggested to Raeburn by David Wilkie during the King's visit, with its out-of-scale centre of vast Doric columns rising two storeys flush with the façade, the main rooms behind set back and darkened.[9]

The author of *Improvements* meticulously lists every new street, even counting their houses, noting how new suburbs had been created from Newington and Stockbridge and the new building in Leith and Newhaven. All this indicated, he proudly pointed out, 'continued prosperity and rapid expansion', and when numbered with the churches and public buildings, was the greatest progress in the New Town to date.

The author of the *Edinburgh Journal* more cautiously observed that although eight hundred new houses were being added yearly to the housing stock *(Improvements* says only 350), they 'seem not to lower rents', standing at anything between £15 and £150. New houses were quickly occupied, and the vacated older houses were as quickly taken up.

Thomas Hog, Patrick Fraser Tytler's brother-in-law, writes of the housing style, describing Patrick's own Melville Street house in detail: 'Most of the Edinburgh houses are constructed on one plan. On the ground floor there is commonly a dining-room in front, lobby, butler's pantry, &c. and behind, a handsome square room, reserved as occasion may serve for business, a sleeping-room, or otherwise.' In Fraser Tytler's house this was used as a study.

'It was fitted up with glazed book-cases, a few choice prints, a bit of sculpture and one or two pieces of china and antiquity. His library table was always covered with choice and favourite books for daily use arranged in rows . . .' The prints were also favourites and the statues included 'one or two of Campbell's earlier models, some designs for the Hopetoun monument, and two little cupids . . . A vase or two in imitation of china' (painted by Rachel), and on the chimney-piece, 'a first attempt in oils of Campbell the sculptor', Tytler's protégé. Then there was his 'standing-desk': he always wrote standing.[10]

John James Audoubon, the American bird painter, pleased with his lodging at Mrs Dickie's, 2 George Street, soon after his arrival in October 1826 allowed his eyes to rove round his well furnished sitting-room:

> the pair of stuffed pheasants on the large buffet . . . the sweetly scented geraniums opposite them, at the black hair sofa, the arm chairs, the little studying cherubs on the mantle piece, the painted landscape on my right, the print exhibiting Charity well appropriated by Free Masons, and at last my own face in the mirror.[11]

Such detailed descriptions are usually the work of visitors from abroad, and most likely of Americans, they being among the keenest observers over here. Edmund Griffin from Pennsylvania, grandson of a Revolutionary officer, was twenty-five years old, of a literary, poetic bent, and ordained in the episcopal church in 1826. In Edinburgh in November 1829, he admired the houses as better suited to receive company than those of New England, though so much space was given over to entertaining that he was perplexed to know how families had room to sleep. The drawing-room on the first floor (in Griffin's terminology the second), covered the whole width of the house, with a small parlour behind separated by a folding door, often left open to make a single large room. 'The dining-room is always below, and the library beside it. The furniture is much plainer than ours, but far more tasteful. No flaring mirrors or gilt pier-tables are to be seen; the most striking objects are an ottoman in the middle of the room, and a chandelier above it. As few as possible . . . chairs are admitted; their place is occupied by sofas, and in some instances by cushioned benches placed along the recesses of the windows. The dining-room is always very plain.' Griffin also noted the simple costume of ladies, compared with American women's garish dress.[12]

Some indication of the furnishings of different houses may be gleaned from sale advertisements, for example in the *Edinburgh Advertiser* in 1815, from Mrs Marshall Gardiner's at 39 Northumberland Street, quoted as 'elegant': from the dining and drawing rooms, 'grey moreen window curtains, Grecian chairs and couches, mirrors, an 8-day clock, rich cut crystal', and from the kitchen, china and stoneware. In 1818 the *Courant* advertises what would have been a more old-fashioned style, from the late Countess of Hyndford's at 9 St John Street, including 'a set Mahogany Dining Tables and Sideboard', large mirrors, 'an Indian Cabinet, in excellent preservation, a very extensive assortment of rich coloured Indian China; a few dozens very old Wine Glasses; a Mahogany Wardrobe and Bookcase; a Housekeeper's Press, with grocery drawers; several chests mahogany Drawers, and Bookcases, with mirror fronts, an excellent 8-day Clock'; from the kitchen, 'Jack and Tackle', copper kitchen ware and from the bedrooms, 'capital Down Beds, with Bedding'. This, like the last, was sold by Dalgleish & Forrest, of 65 Potterrow.

A few days later comes what is announced as 'Modern Household Furniture', from Mr Caird's, 30 James's Square (though not a fashionable address): 'Mahogany and Rosewood Dining, Tea, and Card Tables; Chests of Drawers; 12 Dressing Glasses; Mahogany and painted Chairs; Carpets; Registration, Steel and Brass mounted Grates and Fire-Irons; Sideboards; Drawing-room Furniture and Curtains; Sofa Bed complete; Tent Beds; Down and Goose Feather Beds; English and Scots Blankets; Hair Mattresses'; and the usual china, 'a new Jack, complete', costing 7 guineas – and even 13 dozen empty bottles.[13]

By the 1820s some of the magic of New Town elegance seems to be wearing off, and visitors complained of its bleak isolation. In 1825 Isabel, the young actor Benson Hill's stuffy sister, rather unexpectedly preferred Old Town bustle to New Town grandeur, where walking on her own she often 'saw no one moving', unless it were a figure seemingly out of the vanished past: old Dr Hamilton 'in old-fashioned full-dress black, with powder, bag, cocked-hat, and gold-headed cane'; or it might be Lord Glenlee, Europe's oldest judge (Sir William Miller, b.1755), the last to walk in Edinburgh in his judge's wig.[14]

Amédée Pichot, who arrived just before the King's visit in 1822, defied anyone to visit the city twice '*sans être désenchanté*': a '*triste*' silence reigned in the streets away from Princes Street, whereas life and movement were in the Old Town, where each floor of a huge building housed a family – a rather curious harking back to the old after a half-century of visitors grovelling in admiration of the classic lines of the New. Pichot noted how students, advocates, men of affairs daily deserted the 'immenses rues' of the New Town and hastened to the other side of the Nor' Loch and the Old. '*Les riches d'Edimbourg se son construit une vast solitude.*'

Indeed, while admitting that those '*comme il faut*' all lived in the new squares, circuses and semi-circles '*toutes tirées au cordeau, de temples grecs ou gothiques, de maisons à peristyles, d'édifices publiques, de colonnes*', in these grandiose spots barely forty years old, he was surprised to see architecture he thought so lacking in grace, '*tant d'hôtels regulièrement mal construits, tant de croisées sans entablement, une église qu'on peut comparer à une marmite* [cooking pot] *renversée, et autres preuves de mauvais goût dans tout ce qui est détail*'.[15]

Similarly the Prussian neo-classicist architect Karl Friedrich Schinkel, visiting Edinburgh in 1826 after experiencing London and the industrial Midlands, expressed an equivocal response, though his comments are disappointingly sparse. Though disgusted at the 'pockets of squalor' in the Old Town, he was impressed by its new streets cut through the poorer quarters, and praised the city's setting 'like an isolated Jewel' and the magnificent stone and its skilful cutting. He briefly summarised the new buildings: Nelson's monument, the Observatory, the 'Pantheon' as he calls it though not a quarter built, the Adam workhouse, the picturesque Gothic Bridewell 'like a castle . . . with various battlements, turrets and gates, etc.', and the fine new road constructed along the rocks of Calton Hill.

But he affirms with some disapproval that 'My system is frequently in evidence here, but often with mistakes'. Plans he intended for an architectural sketchbook show wall construction methods closely resembling those of the University. 'There is much use of pilasters, and detail derived from Greek monuments, but lacking a feeling for proportion and its practical application. Everything seems more of an experiment than well-organised endeavour.'

Interestingly, Schinkel's warmest admiration was reserved for Tanfield Gas Works, 'an excellent plant' to which he and his friend Beuth were taken by Thomas Thomson. Though he mistakenly believed that Walter Scott had a hand in the layout, he praised William Burn for its 'most sophisticated construction', accompanying his own notes with roughly captioned sketches on the works.[16]

A lasting testimony to Schinkel's visit is the elegant Arthur Lodge at

60 Dalkeith Road, begun in 1827, then at the edge of the country and with an uninterrupted view of Arthur's Seat. Built as 'Salisbury Cottage' for a jeweller named Cunningham, it is attributed on stylistic grounds to Thomas Hamilton.[17] Half concealed behind its precinct wall, with its spare, clean angles and Greek detail, the debt to Schinkel is obvious.

In his tour of the city Schinkel noted 'new churches with unfortunate towers', a point contradicted some years earlier in Lockhart's *Peter's Letters*, which praise the dome of the recently completed St George's Church, and commented on by Robert Southey on the eve of his Scottish tour in 1819: a 'dome of some pretensions'. Being Southey, he qualified this already equivocal noun. 'In the near view I should like the building without it, but it appears well in the distance.' He thought it worth comment that people in Edinburgh were 'beginning to have a taste for ornamental churches', and a frequent complaint about a monotonous skyline was being counteracted.[18]

In mid-decade came new market buildings, first at Stockbridge (architect Archibald Scott), in St Stephen Place in 1825, based on market buildings in Liverpool; only its Greek Doric entrance survives. The city's own central market for fish and poultry, claimed to be the best in the country, opened in 1826.[19]

Audubon explored these markets early in his stay in Edinburgh, crossing from New Town to Old over the bridge before breakfast, and descending the many flights of steps until he was 'positively under the bridge'. The vegetable markets, fruits and meats were he thought well arranged, 'but the low situation and narrow kind of booths in which the whole is exhibited is not agreeable, and compared with the famous new market of Liverpool it is nothing'.[20]

Between 1825 and 1828 William Burn's long, two-storeyed John Watson's Hospital, an orphanage, with a central Greek Doric portico, was built at Bell's Mills in what is now Belford Road, whose immediate surroundings still give a rural illusion. Money for its foundation had been left in trust for charity.

Far more striking was Thomas Hamilton's building on the far end of Calton Hill, away from the town, of a new Royal High School, finished in 1829. The usual masonic honours attended its foundation, the boys marching in procession. The estimated cost was £17,000, but ended at £24,200 after the original contractors went broke.[21] Also in Greek Doric, it is distinguished by advance and recession of planes, with a temple-like central portico and lower wings, whose colonnades end in temple blocks, the porticos facing the central feature.

Newspapers in 1828 proudly listed such Edinburgh achievements and possessions as including a royal palace, a college, a riding school, military academy, royal exchange, and seventy churches, eleven courts of justice, seven libraries, two theatres, fort-two insurance offices, thirteen public hospitals, sixty charitable institutions, eighty public houses, five bridges, and 850 streets and lanes.[22] The mind boggles.

Several Improvement Acts were either passed or rejected during these years, and most contained a clause on that perennially vexed subject the Earthen Mound. In 1819 of several proposals Playfair's was considered the best, reducing the level towards the south end to form a horizontal terrace for a row of one-storey shops, with a central arcade. The object of low-rise building was not to interfere with views of either castle or Salisbury Crags. By this plan for the 'huge deformity', 'a great eyesore would be removed, an unoccupied mass of earth and rubbish covered with ornamental buildings'.[23] Today, after more than a century and a half of two monumental classical buildings on the lower part of the site, it is hard to imagine the frustrated fury the Mound aroused in Edinburgh for more than thirty years, and how disagreeable must have been the daily sight of this solid, formless pile of rubbish, with no foreseeable purpose or future.

There was also a renewed threat that the south side of Princes Street might yet be built on, and now that the street was largely turned over to shops there were fewer private residents to object. The Faculty of Advocates instead took a hand, objecting to amendments proposed in the Improvements Bill of 1825, and a new Bill in 1827 specifically secured the gardens east of the Mound as 'a pleasure ground'.

Among the most ambitious schemes for the Mound was that of Alexander Trotter in 1829, who, regretting the recent conversion of residential property to shops and warehouses, had in 1821 dreamed up a plan for a 'Grand Gallery' linking Old and New Towns by 'a large warehouse' (that is, multiple shops) on ground level and 'commodious dwelling apartments' on the upper floors. As building of the Royal Institution rendered this impracticable, he then put forward an elaborately detailed plan for an arcade, which in order to avoid public expenditure could be financed by a 'cess'. The proposals included lowering the ground at the Hanover Street end, layout of streets, and re-use of dug-out earth. There was even a proposal for an art exhibition gallery.

Because his plan drew public attention, Trotter published a set of drawings by George Bell, a sixteen-year-old student at the Royal Institution's Academy, of the palace front and pedestrian arcade, and a model was exhibited at Mr Hatton's, a carver and gilder at 98 Princes Street. The elaborate proposals included coffee rooms, reading rooms, insurance offices and so forth, even a scheme for a form of central heating.

Trotter called a meeting on 5 May 1829, chaired by Sir Robert Liston and including Sir John Hope, Drummond of Hawthornden, Gibson Craig and others, besides the architect Archibald Elliot younger (the elder Elliot had died in 1823).

Unfortunately several drawbacks were shown up by a report by Thomas Hamilton in 1830, that the layout departed from the connection via Bank Street, and that it would enter the High Street opposite St Giles's and spoil the surroundings.[24]

Further suggestions by Hamilton and, in 1831, by Playfair, ran into difficulties with Tod's Trustees, landowners to the top of the site. No agreement was made until in 1834–5 the question was partly resolved by certain modifications, establishing the zigzag shape of the road between New and Old Towns. No building was allowed other than Playfair's National Gallery of 1845 and his uncharacteristic departure into Gothic with the Secessionists' 'New College', begun in 1846. The open space between Old and New Towns was saved.

Further changes authorised by an Improvement Act in 1827 included a new western entrance to the city, an improved northern approach with George IV Bridge, and modifications to the West Bow. On 15 August a ceremonial foundation-laying of bridges took place, one over King's Stables Road, one over the Cowgate.

The former was part of the complex reorganisation of the approach to the High Street from west of the castle, involving destruction of the Combe family's brewery in the insalubrious Livingston's Yards where George and Andrew had spent their restricted, unhealthy childhood. The brothers had been trustees of the property since 1814, and demolition about 1827 of this and adjoining properties finally did away with the unlamented area of brackish, smelly pools and generally unappetising atmosphere. The result, after negotiations which dragged on for years, was a new western approach from the newly developing suburbs beyond Heriot's Hospital and the West Bow, linking with Bread Street and Port Hopetoun on the canal, and included the new King's Bridge, a mound, and lowering the level of the High Street (which greatly incensed Charles Sharpe).[25]

The Town Council was set upon 'improvement', sometimes carried to what local opinion felt were excessive lengths, especially in the view of such romantics as Scott and Charles Kirkpatrick Sharpe. Some they managed to avoid or modify, others not.

'Not contented with making the old town of Edin. a new Athens', the Council now threatened historic buildings. The old gaol at Leith, dating from the time of Queen Mary of Guise, wife of King James V and mother of Mary, Queen of Scots, was redundant since the foundation of the new gaol, laid in August 1823 – a 'new barbarity' designed by James Gillespie Graham;

so the old 'most beautiful morsel' had to go. Provost Henderson, said to be keen on preserving antiquities and therefore 'a very jewel of a provost', was approached by both Scott and Sharpe to keep at least the outer wall, 'the last thing of this kind left in this part of the world'.[26]

Learning that demolition was imminent Sharpe, ill though he was, took a hackney to St John's Street to plead with the Lord Provost. 'I found him very stately, but condescending . . . He seemed a little struck with his own stupidity', and was evidently impressed at mention of Scott's name, 'at which all Hell trembles'.[27]

The building, also known as 'the Queen Regent's house' was in fact finally demolished only in 1846. Meanwhile Sharpe managed to salvage some of the woodwork. The difficulty was to deal with the many landlords involved. For example, when he discovered an interesting carving 'in a mean house in Leith', brought from the citadel 'from the room called Oliver Cromwell's', there were so many owners that he could get no consensus. 'Meanwhile the handle of the jack fell down, and broke off the foot of one of the figures.'[28]

This was but a small part of the many threats to the past. Quarrying had been going on round Salisbury Crags since 1818, in order to build a public road, and at the same time give employment to out-of-work weavers come to Edinburgh from the west. The rocks there, incidentally, were far from safe, and more than one amateur mineralogist had narrowly escaped injury when large chunks falling barely missed them. Professor Christison senior had witnessed such a fall from afar one morning while shaving at his house in Bruntsfield.

In January 1826, on top of the ruination of bankers, booksellers and Sir Walter Scott, came a series of 'improvements' crises caused by 'the sad spectacle of Salisbury Crags laid in ruins by ill taste and avarice', namely the opening of a new quarry which Sharpe saw when returning from skating on Duddingston Loch, under Holyrood's very windows.

Further, by the 'new infliction of a new taste' a vandalistic 'restoration' was going on at Holyrood itself, against the King's wishes, by 'a sort of cornice' projecting over the roof slates above the back wall, destroying the Carolean resemblance to a French château.[29]

Sharpe appealed to anyone who might have influence, including Lord Gower, Henry Dundas, Lady Stafford and Lady Gwydyr, who secured the King's intervention over Holyrood, and was, as she admitted, boring everyone she met on the subject. Lady Stafford, in an advanced minority view for the time, wrote, 'I lament as you do the innovations and repairs, if they are carried further than to prop up and support the memorials of former times. When lost, nothing can replace them, and it is an active stupidity to think that by making a Glasgow of Edinburgh the latter will gain.'[30]

Sharpe, apparently on Lord Gower's advice, wrote an attack for the *Edinburgh Advertiser* (1826) in answer to one of theirs, that 'city *improvements*' were encroachments 'little short of downright Vandalism'. Now it was a plan to spoil the castle's picturesque effect by lowering one side of the surrounding wall. In forty years he had seen 'the rage for *improvement*', the disaster of the fire, the 'irretrievable' injury of Salisbury Crags and destruction of Calton Hill – but never expected an attack on the castle. To 'throw it open' for better public view was misguided: castles were built not for views but for defence.[31]

Sharpe followed this with a facetious draft of an 'Act for embellishing and improving the town of Edinburgh', proposing among other things to paint the entire castle white to reflect the sun, bore a tunnel between Grassmarket and New Town to facilitate sale of turnips and cabbages from the new Nor' Loch garden, and cut rock niches for busts of Provost and Baillies to demonstrate 'the excellent taste of the present dynasty of Edinburgh', with other even wilder suggestions. That 'striking beauty' the Mound should be extended on both sides, 'fairly filling up the uncouth valley' and thus saving on regular problems such as drunks falling in and hats blowing off.[32]

He was urged to apply to Scott as 'all-powerful in everything regarding Scotland', but at this stage Scott could be of little assistance or support, having quickly set about selling his Castle Street house and disposing of its contents before leaving the city for a few months.

'The danger of our Castle spoils my sleep,' Sharpe told him. 'I am sure that a word from you to a certain hero would fix the affair as it should be.' Scott obliged by appealing to the Provost, 'but I fear the rabid disposition to demolish whatever looks ancient is a passion too strongly planted in the breast of all corporate bodies to be combated by any argument of mine'.[33]

As years and decades passed, Edinburgh continued in the hands of the 'improvers'. An improvement that never succeeded was completion of the National Monument on Calton Hill, started with such high hopes, and with a contract stipulating that every stone must be of the same dimension as the Parthenon.[34]

To criticisms that the monument ought to have had a modern design, Archibald Alison replied in an article in the *Edinburgh Review*, that the object was to form public taste by re-creating 'the most perfect models in existence'.[35]

It could well have been 'the finest restoration' of Greek architecture in modern times, had the funds amounted to more than a quarter of the total required. Like the Register House and the new College, the monument stood year after year an unfinished shell. Unlike them, so it remained, a magnificent monumental folly. Occasionally a misguided attempt might be made to complete it but would mercifully come to nothing, and one could read many a moral lesson into its splendidly sited shell. Or not, as the case may be.

45
SCOTT IN THE HEIGHTS

'[*The Monastery*] was written with as much care *as the others* – that is, with no care at all.'

Walter Scott to James Ballantyne, 28 March 1820, in Thomas Constable, *Archibald Constable and his Literary Correspondents,* Edinburgh, 1873, III.134–5

'People in the country hardly believe that another work can be so soon after Peverill.'

Archibald Constable to Sir Walter Scott, 23 May 1823, *op. cit.*, III.267

'We may gorge the public.'

Robert Cadell to John Ballantyne, 18 June, 1823, *loc. cit.*

The year 1821 had seen not only *Kenilworth* and, in December, *The Pirate*, but the death of John Ballantyne, whose health had been failing. Constable too fell ill, and went south for his health.

Although the snobbish Lockhart had corresponded with Constable since December 1814 about an eventually unwritten novel of his own, the two men did not meet until the summer of 1818, when Constable was struck by the young man's handsome appearance, while Lockhart remarked to Scott that he had been unprepared to find a bookseller 'of such gentlemanlike and even distinguished bearing'. 'Ay,' said Scott with a smile, 'Constable is indeed a grand-looking chield', and reminded him of Fielding's description of Joseph Andrews: 'an air which to those who had not seen many noblemen would give an idea of nobility'. Visiting him later, often with Scott, Lockhart found Constable established without show or ostentation in 'a respectable country gentleman's seat'. Julian Young observed in his *Recollections* that the publisher was floridly handsome, with 'a presence that would have become a Duke'. His chief weaknesses were vanity, and an overbearing temper.[1]

Scott was distressed at the party feeling in Edinburgh, whose violence he was certain would end in bloodshed – as so it proved. '*The Scotsman* and

Review have much to answer for. I have kept Lockhart out of the scrape, in which some of the young men are knee-deep.'[2]

In the autumn of 1821, before going to London, he made an agreement renewing the anonymity clause, accepting 5000 guineas for his last four novels, which had already earned him at least £10,000 in little more than a year. Sales had in fact fallen slightly, and there was some talk that Scott ought to lay off production; but in his anxiety to cover his too-high outlay on Abbotsford he committed himself to four more novels in the next two years, *Peveril of the Peak, Quentin Durward*, *St Ronan's Well* and *Redgauntlet.*[3] It was becoming rather like the over-investment in the South Sea Bubble.

Certainly Sydney Smith thought Scott was over-stretched, and in some respects – or characters – repetitive. *Kenilworth* he had thought 'very good indeed; there cannot and will not be 2 opinions upon it. The dialogues are a little too long. Pray let us have no more Dominie Sampsons – good but stale . . .' However, 'the author has completely recovered himself, and the novel is excellent . . . Flibbertigibbet is very good and very new'. Yet to Lady Grey he admitted,'Very good, and entertaining, though far inferior to those novels where the scene is laid in Scotland.'[4]

With *The Pirate,* however, Smith expressed doubts. Even Scott's genius 'has its limits, and is exhaustible. I am afraid this novel will depend upon the former reputation of the author . . . I do not blame him for writing himself out, if he knows he is doing so, and has done his *best*, and his *all* . . . pray (wherever the scene is laid) no more *Meg Merrilees* and *Dominie Sampson* – very good the first and second time, but now quite worn out, and always recurring.'

To Jeffrey Smith expressed much the same view, that it was one of Scott's 'least fortunate', in which he seemed unable to rid himself of those two recurring characters. 'One other such novel, and there's an end; but who can last for ever; who ever lasted so long?'[5]

In June 1822 he thought *The Fortunes of Nigel* better than *The Pirate*, if not of the highest order, and while at least there was no Meg there was 'a Dominie Sampson in the horologer'. The first volume, he conceded, was 'admirable. Nothing can be better than the apprentices, the shop of old Heriot, the state of the city'. On the other hand, 'the story is execrable' and – a not uncommon failing with Scott – 'the gentlemanlike light witty conversation always . . . very bad. Horrors or humour are his forte.'[6]

During Arctic weather in January 1823 Smith was reading *Peveril of the Peak*, good, but 'not good enough for such a writer. The next must be better or it will be the last. There is I see Flibbertigibbet over again . . . There is one comfort, however, in reading Scott's novels, that his worst are better than what are called the successful productions of other persons.' To Lady Grey he confided that for Scott it was 'a middling production'.[7]

Meanwhile Scott was making the best of his family's prospects, praising

William Allan's portrait of the younger Walter, now serving with his regiment with the Duke of Cumberland in Berlin: 'one of the finest pictures of the young lieutenant you ever saw', and he also had great faith in a brilliant future for his son-in-law Lockhart. Although still building at Abbotsford, he was feeling more confident as his family was now provided for, 'And – now I have got my legs again, I have no fear of a speedy failure' – though that year and the next, heavier legal commitments hampered his writing.[8]

In May 1822 when Scott published *The Fortunes of Nigel,* he wrote *Halidon Hill* in two days and was paid £1000. Constable, after absence in England for more than a year, returned to Edinburgh in August in time for the King's visit, for which Scott had spent much of the summer heavily involved in its preparation.[9]

The year 1823 opened with snowstorms violent enough to be historic – particularly as in recent years snow in Edinburgh had been comparatively rare.[10] They endured it in Yorkshire by the end of January, '3 feet of Snow on the ground and all communication with Christendom utterly cut off', wrote Sydney Smith from Foston. Unexpectedly, up drove Sir James Mackintosh, unheralded, with his family and seventy-two books in a chaise and four, proposing to stay. 'His letter of communication arrived the following Morning.'[11]

By 2 February the storms reached Edinburgh. Sir Walter Scott wrote to Sir William Knighton a follow-up letter, whose predecessor 'I dare say . . . is sticking fast in the snow, or lost altogether; for such a storm has not been known since the memory of man, and several mail-bags have burst open as they transported them on horseback, and many letters have miscarried . . . We are keeping ourselves as warm here as cold weather will permit.'[12]

'The country is one grand white winding-sheet', wrote the Rev. Robert Morehead on 4 February. Four days later it was as bad, 'the roads are blocked up; no mail from London has arrived for a week', and even by 11 February not all the mails had come in as not all roads were yet clear.[13]

'Certainly', wrote Thomas Carlyle to Jane Welsh, 'since the retreat from Moscow, there has been no weather like this: it would do credit to the northernmost point of Nova Zembla', and he gave a graphic account of 'portly Burghers' shrunk with cold, slithering to the ground 'ankle-deep in melting ice'. On 10 February coaches were still stopped, and Jane wrote from Haddington that the snow, 'rising higher and higher', had killed her passion tree, but luckily by now 'is beginning to tumble off the houses', and roads must surely be open soon.[14]

It was a month before the temperature really began to improve. 'There never was such weather in my time as these 6 weeks about new years day,' Carlyle wrote on 8 March, 'you could not go out of doors without getting your fingers frostbitten and your face cracked by the pinching blast' and 'continual dampness by the snow . . .' But at last 'The atmosphere has cleared up, I see the bright Fife hills out of the window, and feel the kindly breath of the west . . .' By late March it was 'clear spring skies', and by mid-April 'this long anxious winter' had become 'a dreary dream' and given way to spring sunshine.[15]

Having shown the King how wet it could be, Edinburgh was now reminding its inhabitants how severe could be its winters. In London, meanwhile, the King was still talking admiringly of the Scottish reels he had seen in August, and Lady Stafford was planning 'to set a Caledonian Ball agoing for the Scottish Hospital'. This, the new orphanage for children of London Scots, was then being built just outside London.[16]

Nor was summer particularly pleasant. 'Here is base rainy weather', wrote Scott to Sharpe from Abbotsford on 27 July, 'one day always following worse than its predecessor, and within are 4 idle boys and twice 4 busy carpenters, the idleness of the former decidedly the more noisy than the industry of the others.'[17]

By then Scott had been visited in Edinburgh by Maria Edgeworth, a meeting both found memorable. Miss Edgeworth, travelling with her sisters Harriet and Sophy, after staying with the Dugald Stewarts at Kinneil, from which they visited New Lanark and Linlithgow, drove into Edinburgh to take up lodgings engaged for them at 32 Abercromby Place.

'By this approach to Edinburgh there are no suburbs; you drive at once through magnificent broad streets and fine squares. All the houses are of stone . . . and of a kind that is little injured by weather or time.' Their street was 'finely built, with hanging shrubbery garden, and the house as delightful as the situation'. After unpacking their bags they paid a short call on the Alisons, with whom it had been arranged they should dine on their first day; 'but on our return home we found a note from Sir Walter', explaining unavoidable changes of his own plans.

In a post-postscript Scott suggested, as an afterthought, they call at Castle Street at once, as the laird of Staffa was coming that evening with a clansman who was to sing 'Highland boat-songs and the like'. Would they look in 'without ceremony' to hear 'what is perhaps more curious than mellifluous' – no party, just family, 'no dressing to be thought of'.

It was 10 o'clock, they were tired, 'not fit to be seen', but Miss Edgeworth thought it right to accept, called a hackney coach, and they went just as they were.

Sir Walter's hall was lighted, and as the door opened they heard 'the Joyous sounds of loud singing'. Servants announced their arrival, and from the anteroom she heard Scott's voice for the first time, 'The Miss Edgeworths *come*.'

Upstairs, in the light of a single globe lamp a circle of people sat singing and beating time, who stopped at once as they came in, and Scott cordially stepped forward to receive them.

They had never met. Her first impression of Scott was the usual: not as large or heavy as expected, and more lame, but in his moment of welcome, 'his countenance, even by the uncertain light . . . pleased me much, benevolent, and full of genius without the slightest effort at expression; delightfully natural . . .'

He introduced his wife, son, daughters and son-in-law, with his friends Charles Sharpe and 'Mr Clark', and when she begged not to interrupt them, he at once called on Staffa 'to bid his boatman strike up again'. Handing the ladies the end of a silk handkerchief he made them join the circle, stamping feet and joining the chorus of a Gaelic song, 'roared out' by the boatman who, eyes nearly starting from his head, rapturously stamped to the incomprehensible words, while the rest followed. It was like a dream.

They had supper seated at a round table, informal and relaxed. Scott, 'one of the best-bred men I ever saw . . . from good and quick sense and feeling', put them at their ease. He sat beside her at supper and 'I could not believe he was a stranger, and forgot he was a great man'. Lady Scott too was as she had heard described, 'French dark large eyes' and evidently once very handsome; 'civil and good-natured'. Sadly, there was never much more to say about Lady Scott.

Next day they called for the author at Parliament House, 'who came out of the Courts with joyous face', bent on his favourite pastime of showing friends the sights of Edinburgh, full of information and anecdotes in 'the most magnificent as well as the most romantic of cities'.

That day, dining at the Alisons', they met Mr and Mrs Skene, John Hope the Solicitor-General, Dr Brewster, and Lord Meadowbank and his wife Mrs Maconochie. 'Mr Alison wanted me to sit beside everybody . . .'

Next day they heard Alison preach, 'his fine voice but little altered. To me he appears the best preacher I have ever heard.' Then they dined at Scott's, again only family, with the Skenes and Sir Henry Stewart, and again she sat by Scott, charmed with his stories, scraps of poetry, remarks on national character, with the power 'which cannot be given by the polish of the London world and by the habit of literary conversation'.

Scott's authorship was still an open secret, and Mrs Skene joked about the 'barefaced' way in which a copy of *Quentin Durward* was lying on the table. Next day he accompanied the Edgeworths to Roslin, and like so many others, Miss Edgeworth wondered how he could find time to write all he did, when 'he appears to have nothing to think of but to be amusing, and he never tires'.

Lockhart, whom she thought handsomer than his portrait, though silent and reserved, 'appears to have much sensibility'; the slight, elegant Sophia was natural and pleasing with a 'graceful simplicity', and the mutual affection between father and daughter was noticeable.[18]

Mrs Fletcher, who had earlier entertained the Edgeworth brothers as students, met the three sisters at the Alisons'. Nobody could call Miss Edgeworth attractive, but Mrs Fletcher noted that she was vivacious, good-humoured, and a clever conversationalist, if 'more sprightly and brilliant than refined'. Her racy Irish humour had too much blarney, or over-compliment, for the discerning Mrs Fletcher's taste, who felt she could not quite take her seriously. Dining with them later with the ex-ambassador Liston and his wife at Milburn Tower, she found the authoress's repartee appear to greater advantage.[19]

Lockhart, meeting her again at Abbotsford, described her as 'little, dark, bearded, sharp, withered, active, laughing, talking, impudent, fearless, outspoken, honest, Whiggish, unchristian . . .' the list was endless. 'I like her one day, and damn her to perdition the next.' With characteristic uncharitableness he continued that 'She, Sir Adam Fergusson, and the Great Unknown are too much for any company', but he invited James Hogg to meet her, as she had a great desire to meet *him*, 'the Bore'.[20]

The sisters' memorable visit continued with travels to Loch Katrine and Callender, back in Edinburgh visiting other friends, and a happy fortnight at Abbotsford. They left on 10 August via Glasgow to sail home to Ireland, where two years later Scott was in turn to visit them.

At this late stage there was still some small controversy over Scott's authorship. Constable, when staying in London, according to Tom Moore several times forgot himself when breakfasting with Rogers by speaking of Scott as the author. Tom, from his debtor's exile in Paris in February 1822, wrote that Scott's friend Stewart Rose told him 'he has no doubt of his being the author of all the novels'. John Adolphus, a young English lawyer, son of a barrister, had the previous year published critiques of the Waverley novels in which he insisted that they could only be Scott's. A fine book, thought Mrs Grant, who read it in 1823, based on reading and reflection, and demonstrating that the novels could not be written by 'any one but the author of Waverley'.[21]

Even after he had become 'the Great Well-Known' Scott indulged in fanciful small deceptions over his authorship. At the theatre one day he turned to a guest with a laugh saying how he wished old Jedediah Cleishbotham could have witnessed the play. On the death of his old friend Lord Kinedder (William Erskine), a family friend – a lady, of course – misguidedly decided in the interests of good taste to destroy Scott's letters which would have revealed to the world his authorship beyond doubt.[22]

It needed no revelation to establish his fame. Benjamin Haydon, on his return visit to Edinburgh in November 1821, when he found 'only' William Allan in town, was much amused to see in a coffee-room a coaching bill advertising the 'Sir Walter Scott, light post coach', plying three times a week between Edinburgh and Carlisle. 'This is true fame, is it not?' he wrote to Miss Mitford. 'No one would think of attracting passengers by calling a post coach "The Wilkie".'[23]

Miss Mitford quoted a story of a tiresome fellow who having secured an introduction to Scott, stayed a week. This was a not unlikely hazard, but in a possibly apocryphal corollary two young gentlemen were said to have retreated to a window to laugh about him, when Scott hobbled over to say, 'Come, come, young gentlemen, be more respectful. I assure you it requires no small talents to be a *decided bore*!'[24]

The cross-grained, bitterly anti-British novelist Fenimore Cooper, as ready if not readier to give offence as to take it, trod on everyone's toes. Mrs Somerville recalled that when Sir James Mackintosh presented him to Scott in England, Mackintosh had inadvertently offended him (it was almost impossible not to) by a graceful compliment to Scott as 'your great forefather in the art of fiction'.

'Sir,' said Cooper rudely, 'I have no forefather.'

He was no more popular with the British than they were with him. Yet when Mrs Somerville met him again in Paris she found him infinitely less touchy, 'perfectly liberal' and while his manners were still 'rough' he was now ready to admit his own country's faults.[25]

Another American, Nathaniel Willis, learned from Tom Moore of Scott's fondness for whisky at dinner: never in excess, but 'his constitution was Herculean . . . he denied himself nothing'. Moore himself recalled an evening at which Scott was present: 'We had hardly entered the room when we were set down to a hot supper of roast chickens, salmon, punch, &c, and Sir Walter ate immensely of everything' – the sadder in retrospect when compared with his last, dying passage through London.[26]

St Ronan's Well, partly based on the Boswell/Stuart duel, with a modern setting, was a new departure for Scott, and in Mrs Grant's view not a successful one: 'hangs very ill together'; 'an obvious intentional satire . . . we do not so readily follow him in this new and thorny walk'. To Sydney Smith, however, it was 'by far the best' for some time. Despite some cases of 'mistaken and overcharged humour', he agreed with Mrs Grant on its well described characters, even if Clara's vulgarity (in his view) exemplified Scott's inability to depict 'well bred men and women, – and yet, who has seen more of both'.[27]

Tom Moore observes how Scott, keeping up a lifestyle conducive to his writing, in spite of crowded days with mornings at the courts, his hospitality and his obsession with Abbotsford, gave the illusion of being almost idle, available to everyone. He would formally dine at home *en famille*, and write in the evenings or early morning. Writing was so neessary to him that even when he was ill he dictated for up to four hours together.[28]

Nor was he ever afraid of labour. When editing the *Annual Register* he had the use of several books on which, theoretically, he could do a scissors-and-paste collating job. Rather than cut up books, however, he laboriously spent hours transcribing the relevant information, so that he could keep them for his library.

Despite his learning and wide reading, there were great gaps in Scott's culture. He was oblivious to paintings – at the Louvre it was said he would not go out of his way to see the 'Transfiguration of Christ'; nor, apart from his beloved Scottish ballads, did he care for music.[29]

By the early 1820s Scott seemed certainly to have regained the prolific exuberance he had shown before his crippling illness. In spite of the suggestion that he lay off in case of over-production his output was undiminished. A Scott Shakespeare was discussed, as well as an annotated edition of the novels, not to mention a publication devoted to their poetry. *Nigel* sold well in London, but *Quentin Durward*'s sales were disappointing, and even Scott began belatedly to wonder if people might be reluctant to buy so often. He agreed to complete only those he was contracted for, the last being *Redgauntlet*, begun in June 1824, and, lest the fiction vein be worked out, try his hand at biography, for example, Napoleon.

With *Redgauntlet* 'Walter is himself again', writes Mrs Grant; 'who says that his forte is low characters?' The same year, 1824, produced Susan Ferrier's *Inheritance,* following a long time after her first novel *Marriage.* In some people's view – inappropriately, Mrs Grant thought – it was praised as even 'excelling the invisible charmer'.[30]

It was not only Scott who was over-producing. The plentiful money supply over the last few years, and the demand for publications, had launched many projects and not only in publishing. Gas, mines, future railways, all spawned joint stock companies in confident enthusiasm, new streets were forging ahead, and demand for books increased with the spread of literacy among the middle and manufacturing classes. But by April 1825 the money supply was beginning to dry up. Constable's ambitious project for a 25-volume issue of British novelists, and his plan to launch an Encyclopaedia for Youth, to which he expected Scott, Sydney Smith and Miss Edgeworth to contribute – not to mention a proposed Miscellany in seventy-six volumes – were running up against a shortage of money among London bankers.[31]

Too many bills were coming in, Scott owed £27,000 to be paid the following year and, like other writers, he suffered from publishers paying not in cash but in deferred bills. This still illusory money was in turn spent on Abbotsford.

There were domestic sorrows. Scott's brother Tom died in March 1823; his son Walter came home ill, and Constable's younger daughter died of TB.[32]

Among works with which Scott was, though indirectly, concerned was the young Robert Chambers's proposed *Traditions of Edinburgh*, for which he called extensively on the joint knowledge of Scott and Charles Kirkpatrick Sharpe. Scott's 'homely kindliness', from Robert's first timid call in 1822, not only put the fertile, still inexperienced young man at his ease, but opened to him exciting avenues of research.

During the following year Scott and Lockhart in turn called on Chambers to discuss *Traditions*, though Scott mistakenly ascribed to Sharpe material which Chambers had supplied. The book appeared in 1825, though after 1824 circumstances prevented Scott and Chambers from seeing much of one another.[33]

Sharpe himself saw little of Scott during this time, because of the former's variety of ills, especially eye trouble and later tooth trouble, which kept him a regular invalid, but on Raeburn's death in 1823 Scott, rather incongruously, was all for putting up Sharpe as his successor as King's Painter (a post worth only £100 or £150), and wrote proposing him to Sir William Knighton. Lord Melville meanwhile had already recommended Wilkie to Pitt, who not surprisingly preferred him. Sharpe was grateful for the failed attempt, though Scott, who had also enlisted other supporters, was greatly put out.[34]

A social glimpse of the Scott family a few months after the Edgeworths' visit is given by Helen Graham, whose family was evidently at the outer ring of his social activity, possibly an annual or seasonal invitation in which a number of families would be included. Scott was apparently not well known to the Grahams.

At this dinner, in January 1824, a 'most agreeable' evening which included Henry Mackenzie and Commissioner William Adam, she notes their host's 'unpleasant expression' in repose, and the way he lit up as soon as he began to talk. Describing his head, as so many inevitably did, she noted the 'peculiarity' of its shape, 'I should think the phrenologists would make something of it', chiefly because of 'a projection on the crown' which he called his 'attic storey . . . he has an additional one, from whence issue these novels I suppose, for that they are his is surely the case'. Light hair and eyes, clumsy lameness, were all forgotten in 'the charm of his conversation'.

Lady Scott, a complete contrast, was 'a funny looking little bodie and very fond of showy dress, and completely foreign both in manner and appearance'. Her manner was said to be 'variable', but that evening she was kind and hospitable. As for Anne Scott, her satirical attitude showed that in her own eyes she was clever, but she was too censorious and spoke slightingly of every girl in Edinburgh.[35]

Among anecdotes Scott related that evening was one to illustrate the ill effect of cheap whisky on the poor. A woman who was refused credit offered her bible as a deposit, and when that too was refused exclaimed indignantly, 'What kind o' a bodie, maun, ye be, whan ye'll no tak the word o' God or more?'

There was also a conversation about the reliance contemporary people placed on their servants, which Sir Walter deplored. 'I like to be my own man', he said, and related the story of the fall of the Castle of Ibris in Fife. 'Every man's man had a man, and that was the way the castle was ta'en.'[36]

Anne Scott did not appear to advantage. At a dinner shortly after, Helen noted how having made spiteful remarks about Mrs Anstruther's singing, when it was over she effusively praised it to her face. At the Scotts' dinner mother and daughter, in the drawing-room before the gentlemen reappeared, had both torn to pieces a pretentiously bad Irish would-be novelist, Miss Crump, who had forced her novel on Scott for his opinion and then, having published it, had the effrontery to pretend in the preface that he had approved it. Worse, she pursued Walter the younger with unwanted attentions.

Miss Crump was seen the next month at the 'grand ball, rout and supper' of Mrs Douglas of Tillwhilly, where the percipient Helen noticed a difference between female and male reactions. A lady pointed out the would-be novelist as 'that affected-looking creature, just like a parrot'. Later she overheard a gentleman describing her as 'that handsome fashionable-looking woman in black satin and feathers'.[37]

Although Helen Graham did not often encounter the Scotts, a year later she met them all at a ball (Mrs Munro's), when there was 'none handsomer to my taste' than Lockhart, 'one of the finest countenances I ever beheld, like a beautiful picture'.[38]

It was at this time that both Scott and Sharpe were enlisting help to stem the continuing erosion of old Edinburgh by the Council, starting with the threat to the old gaol at Leith. Sharpe was much hampered by his health. Suffering such miseries from his eyes that he was hardly able to see, he was still able to discuss material for *Traditions of Edinburgh* with Robert Chambers, the murder in Gabriel's Road, the early eighteenth-century shooting by Mrs Macfarlane of Captain Cayley for attempted rape, and the murder of Sir George Lockhart of Carnwath, the seventeenth-century Lord President, whose close was 'pulled down when those odious new buildings were erected in the jail'.[39]

Chambers, eternally grateful for this mine of information from 'the greatest man and the greatest antiquary I know', presented Sharpe with his first volume of *Traditions,* 'very absurd and very inaccurate', for which he apologised being still only twenty years old.

'Oh Mr Sharpe,' he wrote in October, when plying him with more questions, 'why did you not write the "Traditions of Edinburgh" yourself? Why did you leave that task to a plodding, compiling, industrious pack-horse like me?'[40]

Sharpe's chronic bad health continued, 'very sick with the drugs doctor gives', keeping much to his room, and next suffering from 'my very ears swelling up like a donkey's' and all turning 'black and purple'. He was practically flayed by treatment with 'scalding water', and surprisingly recovered, 'a good deal shaken'. Almost worse than his physical agony, by this means he lost the chance to acquire a stone chimneypiece, dated 1412, from a house being pulled down in the Cowgate, which was broken up and used to build into a new wall.[41]

Chambers did not always have an easy passage. He fell foul of one of the old Miss Edmonstones of Duntreath, who called on him personally to attack him for an unsympathetic item on her great-aunt Lady Lovat, who, she claimed, was 'a perfect paragon'. He ruefully quoted Scott's advice, that 'these old Scotch ladies had a very bitter rind, which repelled strangers, whereas their *kernels* were tolerable enough, and that was what their friends tasted of them'. Chambers recalled his own grandmother who, 'though practically kind', and always giving him presents, had been 'so sour and ill-natured in speech and to appearance . . . that all I got was accompanied with a scolding or a box on the ear'.[42]

46
CARLYLE RISES

> 'I ask myself often what I am doing in this accursed place, [Edinburgh] which for many years has been to me the scene of woes, greater than the heart of man has formed an image of. The answer is, I am printing a book . . . but when that is done – Quick, March! is the word.'
>
> Letter from Thomas Carlyle to his brother Alexander, *The Collected Letters of Thomas and Jane Welsh Carlyle*, 21 February 1824, III.34

The mid-1820s were to see a complete transformation in Thomas Carlyle's fortunes, but 1823 had him at a very low ebb. Much of this he put down to his bad health, aggravated by the mercury treatment prescribed by Dr Bell, but conversely, much of his bad health may be explained by his frustration at not being able to write, despising nearly all the people he met, and probably most of all, his uncertainty about Jane Welsh.

On New Year's Eve 1823, having just passed his twenty-eighth birthday, he felt suicidal and depressed. 'I want health, health, health . . . I am becoming quite furious . . . If I do not soon recover I am miserable for ever and ever.' The drugs had a lowering effect, draining him of ambition and leaving sleep the only desirable state. He was engaged to translate Wilhelm Meister, and was trying to write up Schiller, but was 'scribbling not writing . . . my mind will not catch hold of it.' He abandoned even his notebook for two and a half years.[1]

Yet only a month earlier he had been writing to his father of his 'contented' state and 'blythe' talks with his employer Buller (while admitting to distaste for the high-born manners of the lady). His correspondence with Jane Welsh was warm, his quiet life, knowing few people and sharing lodgings with his brother John pleasant enough. They were 'getting into Kirks gradually'; he wrote all the morning, then burnt all he wrote, and did not enter the town more than once a fortnight.[2]

To David Hope in Glasgow he was more open, largely with the usual grouse about Edinburgh. 'Two thousand dull heads set a-working in the university, twenty times as many hard hands in the various workshops . . . manufacturing shawls and instruments and furnishings and all the apparatus of luxury; politicians wrangling; the "mob of gentlemen" talking insipidities and giving dinners.' And even more he hated its atmosphere 'compounded of coal-smoke and more gases and odours than ever chemist or perfumer dreamed of'.[3]

Matters hardly improved when the year opened with six weeks of frost, snow, ice and biting winds. But in February he was invited to visit Haddington; the visit was a success, and his subsequent letters to his love were addressed 'My dear Jane', subscribed 'most affectionately yours'. Irving thought he could get Carlyle a *London Magazine* series on literary men, starting with Schiller; and in March the weather at last began to improve. Meanwhile John's 'jolly presence' soothed his brother's black humours.[4]

His personal programme was made uncertain by the Bullers' inability to settle theirs. With the spring vacation he was again invited to breakfast regularly with them, as had been the custom before the college term. Colonel Buller took young Reginald to school in Surrey, and Mrs Buller, quite at a loss when a box of valuable ornaments was stolen that night, was obliged to rely on Carlyle to handle calling in the thief-takers and so on. The box, missing some items, was recovered. Meanwhile at night he was regularly woken by either noisy neighbours or the equally noisy weather, but at last he was making a start on Schiller for the *London Magazine*.[5]

But in another crisis his landlady was turned out when 'trustees' descended and sold her furniture, so that she had to move out. Carlyle was reduced to eating at a steak shop and himself had to move to the Bullers'. Here it was painters and decorators who moved in while the Bullers went to the Highlands. Carlyle was left in temporary charge, and in dudgeon went off to Mainhill, frustrated that though meeting Jane four times when she came to Corstorphine, it was hardly at all to themselves.[6]

He then had to join the Bullers near Dunkeld, decreasingly charmed by them, corresponding faithfully with Jane, until his rash assumption that they would marry elicited her shocked rebuff.

In February 1824 Schiller was complete and he was back in Edinburgh, met by Jack and resuming the grumbling search for rooms. His health was no better. 'I ask myself often what I am doing in this accursed place, which for many years has been to me the scene of woes . . . The answer is, I am printing a book . . . but when that is done – Quick, March! is the word.' Finding that Dr Bell believed he was 'quite well', he wrote him off as 'a consummate ass'. Yet in the next breath he admitted to being reasonably happy, and Jane was now addressing him as 'My dearest friend'.[7]

Otherwise nothing was right. 'The creatures' were too busy printing law papers to give time to his, unless he 'went to bully them every second day', and he was at odds with the 'base earthy Bloodsuckers the booksellers' over payment and copyright. 'Nothing but write and walk, walk and write from morn till midnight', a real treadmill – and he could not even get a seat in a church, 'nor are their parsons of the kind I like to hear'. At this stage he was hating everybody, perhaps himself more than any. 'I have called on no man since I came within the walls of . . . this heartless and conceited place.'[8] Just as well, perhaps.

In the spring he went back to Mainhill and returned briefly on business in mid-May, remarking again that in Edinburgh 'I have not one single friend, not even an acquaintance that I value'. Publishing matters went better, and he was ordering eight author's copies of the book for Edward Irving and two for Jane's mother Mrs Welsh, the remaining ten he would keep. He did contrive to meet Jane for a farewell before leaving to rejoin the Bullers in London, was further thwarted because his steamboat did not sail, and rather than wait four more days he booked on a smack sailing overnight.[9]

The week on board infuriated him with his few fellow-passengers, Sir David Innes, polite and harmless but 'most ugly and most stupid of the sons of men', who snored all night, two ladies who spent the voyage sick in bed, and a young man who constantly took snuff. He hated the lot of them, including the captain.

London he disliked almost as much. He was disenchanted with the Bullers, especially the wife's living for fashion and show, and he was sour about everyone he met except Mrs Montagu's nephew Barry Cornwall, and Irving, who he thought had mellowed.[10]

He was particularly venomous towards Thomas Campbell, 'heartless as a little Edinburgh Advocate', smirking like a shopman, worldly and conceited, and dandified with his literary-looking bow tie, blue frock coat and trousers, and dapper black beard – 'shallow, sneering, pragmatical'. He did not bother to accept Campbell's invitation to his next 'Literary déjeuner' – of hacks.[11]

Coleridge, whom Carlyle also met, fared little better at his hands: fat, flabby, 'watery mouth', 'snuffy nose', earnest brown eyes, high brow and bushy grey hair. Yet he admitted the poet was kind, religious, poetic and had 'a forest of thoughts', but seemed to have no resolution to work, and 'he preaches, or rather soliloquises'.

He did later express admiration for the well-to-do and charitable merchants supporting Bible Societies, in places like Walthamstow.[12]

To crown all, his un-admired employer Mrs Buller decided to discharge him, so instead of accompanying the family to France, he moved to Irving's at Pentonville, and in mid-July travelled to Birmingham to try a cure with John Badams, a medical adviser.

Carlyle's further thumbnail sketches of the literati he had met were mostly to their detriment. Only Barry Cornwall was allowed to be 'a kind little fellow'; Campbell again was a 'whisking antithetical little Editor', Coleridge, incessantly talking, 'round fat oily yet impatient', his mind 'totally beyond his own controul', and for good measure Charles Lamb, who came in for especial venom, rickety, sprawling, seemingly always part-drunk with ale and laudanum; and finally Hazlitt, fleeing the bailiffs, who 'takes his punch and oysters and rackets and whores at regular intervals'. Carlyle admits that he had not actually met Hazlitt (who that spring had married Mrs Bridgwater).[13]

Meanwhile Jane's letters were verging on flirtatious – with other men, whose wooing she took a rather perverse pleasure in dangling before Carlyle, interrupting one letter to ask pettishly, 'Have you got rid of that infamous accent of yours? . . . Why do you speak Annandale?'[14]

Badams's treatment – including soft-boiled eggs, tea, a glass of wine before dinner – and his personality, pleased better, and in September Carlyle returned to London and joined Irving, his wife and baby for a holiday in Dover – with an unexpected short trip to Paris with Mrs Buller's sister Mrs Strachey and family, returning to Pentonville lodgings near Irving in November.[15]

While his work on Schiller was at the printers, and he chased after them and corrected proofs, he admitted to his brother John that he was happier now that he felt in control of events; and meanwhile he was treated in a friendly manner by Mrs Montagu, the Stracheys, Procter (Barry Cornwall), and Allan Cunningham. Irving's status had stabilised, no longer as a fashionable preacher but for the present accepted by earlier sceptics, and to Carlyle he seemed 'among the best fellows in London'.[16]

Carlyle even found he got on better with Thomas Campbell, admitting him clever, and enjoying a reasonably pleasant conversation, but still thinking him vain, 'dry in heart', and cold. His judgment became more kindly on learning of Campbell's early difficulties in London, on 'a penny-worth of milk and a penny roll a day' – but now descended to taking refuge in 'sneering and selfishness'.[17]

Deciding that London was 'not the place for one like me', he determined to return to Edinburgh, and made a formal proposal of marriage to Jane, claiming that each would be fulfilled in the other. Jane quickly replied that she was not in love, and had 'unalterable' objections, but (with her mother's approval) she would at least marry nobody else. On further reflection she admitted that, though months ago she would never have contemplated the idea, 'at present I consider this the most *probable* destiny for me'. Both were in torment . . . but must never part. With this Carlyle expressed himself content.[18]

After last-minute arrangements about Schiller, and the offer to write a life of Voltaire, he spent a week at Irving's, had a final meeting with Coleridge (now 'an inspired man'), and left London on 27 February 1825, stopping for some days in Birmingham on the way to 'icy Edinburgh . . . my true but hard and forbidding fatherland'. He vowed never to stay, however, if his 'former state of frightful solitude' were to recur.[19]

Re-established in Edinburgh in mid-April at 18 Salisbury Street, Carlyle was offered a share in a literary journal by Brewster, to divide Belles Lettres with Lockhart, Brewster taking scientific subjects, 'and together we shall beat the world'. Although he (rightly) felt no confidence in this plan, he admitted the friendliness of the gesture, and confided in Jane, 'I am already twice as happy in you as I was', and he was able to visit her at Haddington. Further, he was invited to make translations from leading German novelists. But his health quickly deteriorated, and he fled again to his parents to recover.[20]

He was now being recognised as a writer of consequence, was introduced to Sir William Hamilton ('among the best men I have ever met in Edinburgh') and to Dr Nicholas Julius, scholar and philanthropist, from Hamburg, 'who almost embraced me as a father, because I had written a Life of Schiller and translated a novel of Goethe's'.[21]

Summer with his parents, who moved to Hoddam Hill that May, was happy enough except for the separation from Jane. She wrote him what amounted to a real love letter in July, and after numerous delays was able to visit him there for a week in September. Yet her mother, possibly now that a permanent relationship actually seemed to be looming, was becoming suddenly hostile.

However, Carlyle was cheered by Jeffrey's review of *Wilhelm Meister* in the August *Review* (no. LXXX), earning him Carlyle's approval as 'an honest and clever man, and by far the best of them all' – although he treated the book only as 'a heap of beautiful fragments'.[22]

John, in Edinburgh, kept him informed of literary news – Lockhart's appointment as editor of the *Quarterly* in London at a salary of £1500, and that the hitherto unknown young Thomas Macaulay had written the Milton article and was 'a favourite or protégé of Brougham'. At the end of the year Thomas and Jane appeared to be more or less officially engaged, and he prepared to return to Edinburgh because he was running out of books.[23]

John found them both comfortable Salisbury Street lodgings, at number 21 at its very verge, and in sight of Salisbury Crags: two bedrooms and a parlour, a respectable-seeming landlady, sixteen shillings a week including parlour fire. He was kept busy supervising the printing of his *German Romance* by the bookseller Tait, and found himself sought after by Brewster – whose magazine project did fall through – and even Professor Leslie. But it was a problem time, with Constable's failure and Scott's consequent ruin. Before long Carlyle resumed the familiar grouse about 'the smoke and bustle and icy coldness of Edinr – prosaic, money-making' (as even Jane now called it).[24]

After some disappointments his parents succeeded in buying another farm, at Scotsbrig. John sought a house in Edinburgh, and Thomas instantly proposed marriage again – suggesting Jane live with his parents for a year at Scotsbrig and then perhaps move to Edinburgh. Her mother consented; there were confusions and delays over the property and over finding an Edinburgh house, where he found that prices for even humble cottages had risen to at least £30, plus taxes.

He was seeking books from Dr Julius, now back in Germany, and from Crabb Robinson in London; he suffered his usual bad health and she her headaches, but at last in May (1826) Mrs Welsh secured them a modest house on the edge of Edinburgh, at 21 Comely Bank, 'quiet and light and dry', a pretty flower-garden and a tree before the door, and a back view over fields (rent £32), and the Welshes let their Haddington house, for they too needed money.[25]

Carlyle was now struggling to write a life of Hoffmann. Mrs Montagu wrote from London that his work was being advertised in advance; and that Irving was now becoming merely a voice – 'more fervent, more zealous, more mystical and more prophetical every day'.[26] Thomas Murray was proposing that they take over the *Scots Magazine,* which Constable could no longer keep on; after much discussion this too came to nothing. The summer over all south Scotland was oppressively hot for several months, there was delay on the Comely Bank house, and Jane reminded Thomas that they had known each other for five years, and that for seventeen months, since the previous January, she had 'held myself your affianced wife'. But they had not met since her visit to Templand the previous September.[27]

The book was off his hands in late July, to be published late in November, and Carlyle expressed his 'vehement purpose' now to write 'something out of my own heart and head'.[28]

They were ready to move, last wedding preparations were made, and mutual anguish was expressed at the purgatorial prospect, though Carlyle, relieved at completion of his work, declared an end to his 'black and bitter' period.

He and John went to Templand together for the wedding, on 17 October, and the newly married couple returned straight to Edinburgh that same evening to find 'a blazing fire and covered table . . . a perfect model of a house . . .' Carlyle did not mention Jane's feelings, but he himself was jittery, bilious, sleepless (Jane had thoughtfully arranged him a separate room in case of need), and in his notebook, resumed on 3 December after a second long gap, he made a cryptic entry. 'Comley Bank. Married! Married! – *Aber still davon!* – and of a thousand other things. I am for business.'[29]

47
JEFFREY'S PROGRESS

'A short, stout, little gentleman, about 5 and a half feet high, with a very red face, black hair, and black eyes. You are to suppose him to possess a very gay and animated countenance, and . . . all the restlessness of a will-o'-the wisp, and . . . fitful irregularity in his movements – the natural indications of the impetuous and impatient character which a further acquaintance develops.'

G. S. Hillard (ed.), *Life, Letters and Journals of George Ticknor*, Boston, 1909, I.44–5 (on Jeffrey in America)

'Those who know Mr Jeffrey at a distance admire him; those who are better acquainted with him love and respect him.'

William Hazlitt, June 1829, Howe's *Hazlitt*

In the summer of 1823 Jeffrey achieved a long-planned Continental tour with his family, his father-in-law Charles Wilkes, Henry Cockburn and John Richardson, a Parliamentary Solicitor friend. It was the usual round, Low Countries, Rhine, Switzerland, Venice, Milan, Paris. 'We have agreed very well,' he wrote, 'Cockburn being despotic and the rest of us dutifully obedient.' According to Cockburn, their harmony was marred only by Jeffrey's 'inveterate abhorrence of early rising', so that they always had to travel in the heat of the day.[1]

Before leaving, Jeffrey had got out 'a nice number' of the *Review* (no. LXXII), in which his own contribution had been an item on Byron with 'a little cruel medicine'. Since the war the *Review* had reverted to its original literary themes, and Jeffrey's own articles had been limited to these. Despite his gloom at the country's political and social future – as expressed when in London in April 1822 on an appeal, he prophesied (to Charles Wilkes) that popular unrest, and the lack of union in Parliamentary opposition, ensured that 'we are tending to a revolution', even if 'so slowly, that it may not come for 50 years yet' – in his writings he usually avoided politics. For five years following the war he had contributed scarcely anything on the subject. There was a paper in October 1819 (no.64), 'short but excellent' as Cockburn said, blaming the parties equally for most of the country's ills, in what he considered its worst period since 1793. He also wrote on Mme De Staël's *French Revolution* (September 1818), and on the 'jealousies' between America and Britain – an attempt to minimise the mutual hostility between the two, a subject close to his heart, as one knowing more about America than the majority of his countrymen.[2]

In person he continued outspoken on politics, though without actively pushing for reform, a subject viewed with alarm by Establishment-centred Edinburgh, where 'emancipation' was treated with such hostility. He was chief speaker at a meeting held at the Pantheon in December 1820 and presided over by Sir Harry Moncreiff's son James, a two-party demonstration to petition the Crown to dismiss Lord Liverpool's Government. It was the first such meeting of a 'respectable' public for some quarter of a century and, held at the time of the Queen's trial, when feelings were high on either side, was greeted with hostility even before it met. However, Jeffrey's opening speech was so moderate in tone that fears vanished, extravagant views were avoided, and in the event several positive resolutions were carried and 17,000 signed the petition. Only 2000 opposed.[3]

Jeffrey had been installed shortly before as Rector of Glasgow College for the year, a position second only to the Chancellor, and usually chosen by the professors from local gentry. No-one had been elected for academic qualities since Adam Smith more than thirty years earlier, but in recent years the electors had been the students, divided into four 'nations'. Jeffrey's being an ex-Glasgow student might have had some influence on them, but he was elected chiefly for his public and literary fame. The following November, 1821, he was re-elected, and on his retirement in 1822 he founded a prize.

The 1822 candidates were Scott and Mackintosh, between whom the 'nations' were divided two and two, but on an individual count Mackintosh was ahead. Jeffrey, who had the casting vote, was himself divided between emotional preference for Scott, and reason, which favoured Mackintosh. Eventually he decided for the latter.[4]

So anti-party politics was Jeffrey that in 1821 he refused the suggestion that he enter Parliament, 'from taste as well as prudence', he told Wilkes, having no ambition for public life. When eventually he was thrown into it, it was with reluctance and with many regrets. When forced to be in London he always hankered after Edinburgh and especially Craigcrook, in both of which his roots were so deep. His London visits were usually on Scottish appeals, for example a case which he argued in 1824 before Lord Chancellor Eldon, hating to appear before a court totally ignorant of Scottish affairs, not to mention his dislike for formal legal dress, especially the wig, which in Scotland he wore as little as possible.[5]

Still continuing his busy legal practice, which occupied him for up to ten or even twelve hours a day during the eight-month session, Jeffrey further combined active, lively social life with *Review* contributions: in the six years from 1819 to 1825 he produced thirty-six articles on literature, biography and history.[6] In November 1822 he again deeply offended Wordsworth by his provocative review of the poet's *Memorials of a Tour on the Continent,* a 'Tirade of abuse' as Wordsworth termed it, beginning with the statement, 'The Lake School of Poetry, we think, is now pretty nearly extinct'. He eloquently dismissed Wordsworth's 'emphatic insanity' and 'singular barrenness and feebleness of thought, disguised under a sententious and assuming manner and a style beyond example verbose and obscure'. Small wonder at his victim's fury. But 'This is as it should be', wrote Wordsworth to Lord Lonsdale. 'Attachment to the institutions and Religion of our Country is enough to make a man odious with the Whigs, as they call themselves, who are indeed running a desperate course.'[7]

By the mid-Twenties, however, Jeffrey became more preoccupied with politics, attending the numerous Whig public dinners whose influence was greater than might appear, supported as they were by leading characters. They were organised by Leonard Horner, who in 1821 had founded the Edinburgh School of Arts.

The annual dinners on or near Charles James Fox's birthday were now held in an atmosphere more relaxed than in former days, when police spies took note of everyone attending. Jeffrey was a regular speaker, still avoiding party and keeping to general liberal principles. At the dinners in January 1825 and 1826 he acted as president – in 1826 again urging respect and tolerance for the United States.

Also in 1825, at a dinner in November for Joseph Hume, he spoke twice, on behalf of Spanish and Italian exiles in Britain, and on 'combination' laws and the dangers he saw in strikes and unions. Published as a pamphlet, this quickly sold more than 8000 copies.[8]

He did take rural holidays. Apart from the extended Continental tour of 1823, in the summer Jeffrey regularly took his family to Loch Lomond, and from 1822 was offered the use of Stuckgowan, a Gothick villa on its shores, regularly until his daughter's marriage in 1838. His father-in-law Charles Wilkes with his own two other daughters, Jeffrey's sisters-in-law, also visited them at Craigcrook and Edinburgh.[9]

Despite an ebullient social life Jeffrey was, rather, home-loving, devoted to his wife and daughter, and Ticknor, who, after first encountering him in America, had met him in Edinburgh in 1819, noted that in his own country he was 'a much more domestic, quiet sort of person'. Yet he was to be met 'everywhere, in all parties, dances, and routs, and yet found time for his great business and was, on the whole, rather pleasant in his own house'.[10]

In general, Jeffrey did not appear to find society's demands irksome, unlike Tommy Moore, who dined out almost nightly, beset with invitations and, discovering one day in 1823 that having mistaken a dinner date he was unexpectedly 'free', declared he felt temporarily released from 'servitude' 'as if chains had fallen off me'. (Though one wonders what Moore would have felt had he not been 'carried along so inevitably' by daily dinners.[11])

During the 1820s the young Carlyle used eagerly to look out for Jeffrey, whom he had not personally met, in the courts. His appearance fascinated him: 'a delicate, attractive, dainty little figure, as he merely walked about, much more if he were speaking; uncommonly bright black eyes, instinct with vivacity, intelligence and kindly fire; roundish brow, delicate oval face full of rapid expression; figure light, nimble, pretty, though so small, perhaps hardly five feet four in height'. Below short, wig-less black hair his puckered brow was lightened by an 'arch' look when he brought off some clever remark. His voice, so irritating to many, Carlyle described as slightly metallic, 'almost plangent', clear but never shrill, with a small almost sniggering laugh. The Scots accent which in early youth he had worked so hard to shed was on occasion ostentatiously brought out especially when he wanted to imitate old Lord Braxfield.[12]

Others reacted differently. Cam Hobhouse, not the most charitable of critics, first meeting 'Jeffrey the Great' at a London party in 1821, saw 'a little, black-eyed, smart, ill-tempered mannered man', observing that he was 'not attentive' to people, and one gentleman he actually cut. Mrs Jeffrey he described with equal lack of enthusiasm: 'dark, with St Vitus dance in her nose and chin'.[13]

Helen Graham, who met Jeffrey early in 1825, among 'the great' at the young advocate Alexander Rutherfurd's, did not find him agreeable, suspecting that he usually felt 'bound to perform as a "lion" to the company'. However, as he was sitting near her mother, some way off, she could not hear much of their talk; and some six weeks later again at Rutherfurd's, she conceded that the occasion was 'an intellectual feast, where I gobbled up all my intellects listening to Jeffrey'. He was then 'in a delightful humour', and she was pleasantly surprised that when the party took time out to visit the puppet theatre he enjoyed it like a child, 'the best satire upon human nature he had ever seen'.[14]

The *Review* meanwhile was producing the travels of Charles Waterton, and the new contributor, young Thomas Babington Macaulay, wrote on the infant London University, 'very spirited and able, but violent and exaggerated, and little calculated to serve the cause it espouses'.[15]

Constable had in 1823 urged Tom Moore to settle in Edinburgh, telling him in confidence that the *Review* was 'sinking' as Jeffrey had not time to run it as he wished, and would be glad to hand over to Moore. The salary was

£700, plus £2800 received from contributors. Moore pointed out in reply that the job was also too demanding for his own time, and anyway he would not settle for less than £1000.

Both Constable and his partner Cadell considered Moore the best replacement should Jeffrey stand down, one who would revive its reputation and make it 'more literary and more regular'. First, however, even supposing this were true, they needed to get Moore to Edinburgh, and in this they did not succeed.[16]

In 1826, when the Phrenology craze was at its height, Jeffrey asked Sydney Smith to review Combe's *System of Phrenology,* now in a second edition, but on reflection Smith declined, and eventually it was Jeffrey who wrote a good long (too long, Smith thought) review of 'the Bumpists, which destroys them'. Combe, who saw through the anonymity, wrote reproachfully to Jeffrey, who replied in the next issue.[17]

That summer he stayed with the Smiths in Yorkshire, and Smith, though dreading the expense of the journey, hoped to visit him in Edinburgh the following spring. Eventually through domestic problems he had to delay the trip twice. In November 1827 Jeffrey visited Foston again, when Smith noted that his throat had begun to give him trouble: 'So much wine goes down it, so many million words leap over it, how can it rest'. 'Pray make him a judge,' he begged Lady Holland, 'he is a truely great man and is very heedless of his own interests.'[18] As it turned out, Jeffrey might well have preferred never to have become a judge, so little true happiness did his later career bring.

Carlyle, after his years of admiration at a distance, and his abortive attempt to interest Jeffrey in a review of Pictet's *Theory of Gravitation*, which he handed to Jeffrey's manservant but was ignored – a slight which the hyper-sensitive Carlyle kept to himself – at last met the great man. In the spring of 1827 Barry Cornwall, whom he had met in London, offered to introduce the struggling would-be author, and Carlyle, recently married, his professional life still tenuous, strode along George Street with the necessary letter.

He found Jeffrey in his ground-floor study, 'a roomy not over-neat apartment . . . with a big baize-covered table, loaded with book rows and paper bundles; on one or perhaps two of the walls were book-shelves, likewise well filled, but with books in tattery ill-bound or unbound condition.' (So little had Jeffrey's 'library' changed in a quarter of a century.) The room was cheerful with a fire and a pair of lighted candles.

'My famous little gentleman laid aside his work', and having offered Carlyle a seat started a lively conversation that lasted for some twenty minutes, discussing Carlyle's work and his recent translations from the German, and the younger man was soon at ease, able to speak frankly. When he left the house he felt cheered and full of gratitude.

On a formal return call Jeffrey proposed Carlyle's writing on German literature for the *Review,* thus opening a door which Carlyle had been fearing would remain ever closed. In the next issue he contributed a piece on *Jean Paul,* and in June an elaborate paper on German literature. Both aroused a good deal of interest.

This launched him in the literary world at last, and he was soon offered more work for Jeffrey and also for other journals. Jeffrey was also much taken with Jane Carlyle. An accomplished flirt, he would daintily kiss hands, especially with pretty women, and delighted them by 'pretty and witty speeches'.[19]

In this way what seemed to be a long-term friendship was also launched. The two men often walked together, that is to say, Jeffrey accompanying Carlyle home on horseback, gently ambling while Carlyle walked alongside, discussing literary and 'theoretic' subjects, Jeffrey trying to wean Carlyle from 'German mysticism' back to the more literary field, while Carlyle dismissed 'dead Edinburgh Whiggism, Scepticism, and Materialism'. They talked for hours at Craigcrook, long after everyone else had gone to bed, or walking in the woods there, and Jeffrey would escort Carlyle part of the three-mile walk back to Edinburgh; or they met in the street, or at Parliament House for 'a cheerful bit of talk'. In May 1828, when the Carlyles moved to Craigenputtock Jeffrey promised to visit, and more than once took his family there to stay.

Even so, Carlyle in piercing judgment felt that he could hold his own with the famous editor-critic, whom he assessed as not 'deep', but 'I found him infinitely witty, ingenious, sharp of offence', while Jeffrey on his side, thin-skinned though he was, was kind enough to accept the gibes. On many subjects they were not really in tune, though at this stage it did not much matter. Carlyle also got on well with Jeffrey's wife, appreciating her sincerity and 'clear natural insight often sarcastically turned'. Her round-featured face, he thought, if not pretty, was at least 'comely'.[20]

Carlyle, now thirty-two, had waited long enough for full recognition of his potential. Jeffrey, at fifty, though at the height of his powers, was suffering the effects of tracheitis picked up on one of his circuit journeys. He was never to be completely well again.

48
A CALAMITY

> 'As for the voracious fire, – it still lives in its ashes, still smokes in spite of two days' constant rain, and still haunts my imagination, and still a voice of woe seems to proclaim that the glory of old Edinburgh is departed . . . What we have lost, that can never be restored.'
>
> Mrs Grant to Mrs Hook, 22 November 1824, *Memoir*, II.70

The Old Town of Edinburgh continued to be very vulnerable to fire, and 1824 proved an exceptional year, when they averaged one a month. Among the worst were destruction of Hay & Gall's, a large printing-house in Niddry Street, and soon afterwards, a building on the North Bridge. At midsummer, in the worst fire since 1700, a 'low tippling-house' at the head of Royal Bank Close fell in burning and 'devastated half the east side of Parliament Square'. Chambers tells us it was still in flames the next afternoon, a town officer was killed, and the engines played on its smoking ruins for three days. It was a historic building, the last which still retained a piazza of the kind once a feature of old Edinburgh, and at one time Boswell's father Lord Auchinleck, had lived in the fourth flat. A huge gap was left in the lofty, close-set tenements of the High Street and East Parliament Square.[1]

Nobody could have foreseen, however, the extent of the disaster which struck in November.

Late on the evening of 15 November, Robert Morehead was quietly at home reading Hebrew and Latin, Mrs Grant of Laggan was visiting friends far on the west side of Edinburgh, and the Fraser Tytler ladies were working and reading in their Princes Street drawing-room. At about 10 o'clock, an alarm of fire was started in one of the tall lands of the High Street: Chambers says at Kirkwood & Sons, copperplate printers. Others claim it started in a flat in one of the highest tenements. At all events by 11 o'clock it was quite destroyed. The fire-engines were called, but for some reason no water could be supplied immediately, the flames spread and a high wind – 'a perfect hurricane', says Fraser Tytler – at first caused it to envelop the whole building and then blew the flames eastward. 'Fire was spouting out of every window, while the wind, with a roar louder than the loudest thunder was pelting against the doomed edifice.'[2]

At the Fraser Tytlers' when Archy Alison rushed in to tell them the news, Patrick's first thought was that, from the direction of the wind, the Advocates' Library would be in danger. In a few minutes they were out of the house, and quickly joined by more young advocates, the brothers Basil and James Hall, Alexander Pringle and others, and members of the yeomanry. The ladies, for whom going to view such a spectacle on the spot would have been unthinkable, hurried upstairs to look from upper windows.[3]

Mrs Grant, returning from her friends, found her street deserted – everybody had gone to see the fire. Alexander Nasmyth and his sixteen-year-old son James were among those who saw it all.

The wind carried burning embers to nearby empty houses, which themselves burst into flames. The puny efforts of the fire engines, summoned from all over the city and from neighbouring towns, could not quench the flames. Soldiers were called from the castle to line the street against crowds, and the Lord Provost, Sheriff, baillies and other officials turned up, but no-one seemed to take charge.[4] The yeomanry were there to help with the engines and also to hold back the crowds.

'Whole ranges of lofty old houses were roaring with fire', says James Nasmyth, and in two or three hours several acres of the highest, densest houses in the High Street were blazing, some of thirteen storeys. Floors crashed and threw out embers, walls of the narrow buildings acted like a huge funnel as the wind blew through the windows. Even walls melted in the intense heat into 'a sort of glass'.[5]

Almost worse, sparks blowing eastwards ignited the Tron steeple, which was far too high for the engines' jets to reach, and it raged unchecked. 'The flames curling up the pinnacles . . . tossed about in wild eddies by a high wind at its summit, and shaking their burning wreaths over the illuminated city', reminded Alison of the English bombardment of Copenhagen in 1807.[6]

The large Tron bell was melted, and (says Mrs Grant) 'the volumes of smoke and glowing skies wore all the appearance of a volcano'. At last the whole steeple crashed.

Nasmyth got permission to climb the tower of St Giles', from whose parapet they could view the whole, and found up there already a party of privileged people, including Walter Scott.

'At the very time this was going on', says Mrs Grant, 'a house in the Parliament Square took fire in the garret . . . the eighth story, and was not overcome until a great part of the square was reduced to ashes.'[7]

Meanwhile the *Edinburgh Courant* office, a tall narrow land better built than the rest, was in danger, and its clerks were busy collecting books and papers from it until its top flat took fire. Some enterprising men hurried to the next tenement shouting to the firemen below to direct a pipe on to the *Courant*, but not only did this take an hour, but no sooner had they got the pipe up than it broke, and it was too late, anyway.

Among the showers of sparks and burning flakes, some falling on the crowd like snow and burning their clothes, rain began to fall, not enough to quench the fires, and about 5 in the morning the pinnacle and top of the *Courant*'s front wall collapsed. Flames burst out to the street, and one after another the adjoining buildings went, including the Old Assembly Hall, one of the Old Town's most massive buildings, which was then occupied by the bookseller Bell and Bradfute.[8]

Patrick Tytler and Alison were trying to help the engines in their vain task. Quantities of water were pumped up, but a huge pillar of fire arose, visible 30 miles away at Melrose. The fire-fighters were up all night, while troops still patrolled the street to maintain calm and order. The Tytlers' manservant was sent back and forth for news, and once was able to bring back a scribbled message, and another time Alex Pringle ran down to reassure the ladies, now in their nightcaps and wrappers.[9] Lockhart was also seen on duty, wet to the skin and, naked sword in hand, 'the very picture of a distressed hero in a strolling party's tragedy'.[10]

Apart from its elements of melodrama, the scene was of horror and devastation, yet it was to be outdone by the inferno of the next night. They had thought the fire was under control. Patrick, like the other volunteers, had returned in the early morning, but was no sooner in bed than he was ordered out with the yeomanry, as the soldiers had been on duty for thirty-six hours. His family did not see him again until 5 o'clock, when his descriptions terrified them. He had seen 'the gable of one of those high houses vibrating in the wind, as if it had been the branch of a tree, for two hours, before it fell in with a tremendous crash'.[11]

Then at 9 o'clock the fire-drum beat again and crowds and volunteers again rushed to the scene. In Parliament Square they found 'a prodigious and evidently unconquerable fire raging in the lofty buildings' of the courtyard's east side. Beyond was the huge tenement, Edinburgh's tallest, only six storeys on this side but fourteen at the back because of the fall in ground level. By midnight a bright light was seen in one of its skylight windows, and the fire spread so fast that the vast building was soon ablaze in 'a tempestuous gale from the south-west'. In the wind flames rose to a great height and were (says Alison) 'whirled about as the blast veered, in a frightful manner in the dark abyss of air far above the highest buildings in the city. The roar of the conflagration drowned even the howling of the autumnal tempest.'[12]

Descriptions become conflicting and the order of destruction confused. By the morning of the 18th the fire seemed extinguished. Patrick Tytler, following orders, reported at 2 a.m. to the riding school, but was at once ordered by Colonel Cockburn to go home to bed. The rest of the troops were still on duty guarding piles of salvaged furniture in the streets.

Twenty-four hours later Patrick was sent for again, by the Solicitor-General, when the men working the engines were completely worn out and hardly able to continue. The Solicitor sent to Leith to order up sailors from his brother's man-o'-war in the roads, and both he and Patrick helped them work the engines until 8 in the morning, along with Basil Hall. Patrick, always calm in the crisis, suggested covering the Advocates' Library roof with wet blankets to safeguard the books, and helped a party of men to do it. Hall told the ladies afterwards that during all the pandemonium his brother James sat quietly sketching the ruins, and completed eight drawings which were afterwards published to raise money for the victims.[13]

Hundreds of poor people had lost their homes and most of their possessions. Hugh Miller, who with fellow-masons at Niddrie House had learned of the fire by a countryman on his way home (who told them with some satisfaction that they would all have jobs next winter rebuilding the city), went up in the evening after their work finished.

By then the Tron steeple was burnt out, and only the skeletal masonry outline survived that had supported the wooden broach, from which Fergusson's bell donated by George Drummond had fallen 'in a molten shower'. Upper storeys were now all consumed, and only on the lower floors were fires still burning, gleaming fitfully on the tall dragoons with their bright drawn swords, riding up and down the middle of the street between groups of miserable homeless – or 'ruffian men' suspiciously eyeing the piles of salvaged goods.

Hugh witnessed the incongruous sight of a brightly gas-lit barber's shop whose owner was undisturbedly shaving a customer, even though fire-engines were at that moment playing on his gable wall, while the forehead and cheeks of his immensely fat old customer were streaming with perspiration from the 'oven-like heat' as he sat like a grotesque gargoyle, open-mouthed.

Far sadder were the glimpses of distressed refugees. From a lane came a poor man staggering under the weight of 'his favourite piece of furniture, a glass-fronted press or cupboard', all he had managed to rescue, followed by his wife. But he tripped over some obstacle, 'tottered against a projecting corner, and the glazed door was driven in with a crash'. 'O ruin! ruin! *It's* lost too!' wailed the wife in despair, and the husband answered hopelessly, 'Ay ay, puir lassie, it's a' at an end noo.' This speedily reduced Hugh's excitement to distress. Elsewhere he saw shivering groups gathered round the broken remains of their possessions. Nearly two hundred families were already homeless.

Passing a common stair leading towards Canongate from Parliament Close, through an old eleven-storey building, he noticed 'a smouldering oppressive vapour', but thought little of it at the time. Less than an hour later the whole place was engulfed in flames from ground floor to more than 100 feet above its tallest chimneys, and its tenants, about sixty families, quickly joined the homeless in the streets.[14]

Light flickered on the roof and window tracery of St Giles', which glowed in an extraordinary crimson and amber.

By 5 o'clock on the second morning when the fires were so violent that it seemed that the Old Town would be entirely consumed, the whole city was enveloped in the lurid glare, and it was visible as far as Tweedside and the Fife hills. At this point the fire reached a vacant site, the remains of the earlier fire, and here it halted. At 6 o'clock the walls of the burning buildings fell in with a crash, and a dense black cloud arose from the ruined masonry and timber.

Jane Welsh, who was visiting in George Square, wrote to Carlyle (who was then staying with Edward Irving in Pentonville) of their 'continued agitation' throughout for the safety of their friend Bradfute's property, which was destroyed by the new fire which started up on the second morning. 'I verily believe,' she wrote, ' another night of it would have killed me.'[15]

There was of course a strong element of voyeurism, besides a kind of shrugging off by those not personally endangered. Josiah Livingston, reminiscing years later over his boyhood, recalls that when Tommy Kerr, a South Bridge glover, was told by a friend that Parliament House was on fire, and that they should go and watch, said airily, 'Fegs, no, oull seed all in the Courant the morn.' When the much nearer Tron Kirk caught fire, Tommy still did not move, for he 'saw it all for naething frae his ain shop door, and he got an awful fright'.[16]

The Graham family, who had been in Stirling for some weeks, returned to Edinburgh just at the time the fire was raging. On the morning of 19 November they visited James Ferrier and Susan, the latter waiting to go with Mrs Miles Fletcher to see the ruins.

'The town is in a doited state from this calamity, I suppose', wrote Helen Graham, 'and nothing else is talked of.' They drove through part of the Cowgate, from which the ruins 'looked very fine', but the most striking sight was the high gable, still standing, of Edinburgh's fourteen-storey tenement, the 'Head Laund', 'which used to be shown to strangers as the highest house in Edinburgh', and was to be removed that night. 'Nothing remained of it but this gable, a complete shell and seeming to threaten destruction to all around it.' When they passed among the crumbled wrecks of tenements, which no doubt some of them had never seen at such close quarters, Helen thought sadly, 'What abodes of wretchedness and filth and all that is disgusting are there', though her aunt assured her that they were far from Edinburgh's worst. It was a relief to emerge from these 'dark and loathsome and pestiferous' dens to the comparatively fresh air of the Grassmarket.[17]

Between three and four hundred people were made homeless. By the time the fire burnt itself out at 8 o'clock on the morning of the 18th, the only old building surviving in Parliament Square was the land adjoining Exchequer Buildings, which had also escaped a fire in 1700. Walls were still crashing down and causing injury; a cloud of dust darkened the day, and burning fragments fell as far off as Easter Road toll-bar, a mile and a half away. Several people were injured by falling masonry and walls, and throughout the day more alarms were started in different places, chiefly from chimneys fired by burning embers. Towards the evening a heavy shower helped to extinguish housetops, on which the magistrates had ordered a watch to be kept.

Chambers enumerates the lost buildings: in the High Street, four six-storey lands and their base storeys, up to half a dozen more in each of several closes. Nearly as far as the Cowgate were heaps of fallen ruins still threatened by walls tottering above. Along the front of Parliament Square, four 'double' lands each of seven to eleven storeys were lost. As many as six or seven families might have been crammed on each floor. A boy was trapped and killed by falling rubbish in the *Courant* building while two others escaped, one injured. Some injured were carried to the Infirmary. Some of the towering, dangerous walls were brought down by mines laid by sappers, commanded by Captain Head. The most spectacular was the fall, in several portions, of the leaning wall of the huge building on the south-east angle of the square, without injuring anyone, to the admiring shouts of the watchers.[18]

The unfortunate families who had lost homes and possesions were lodged by order of the magistrates in the old Queensberry House off the Canongate, and clothes and food poured in from all sides, together with nearly £5000 the sympathising public subscribed for their benefit. 'In short,' observed Mrs Grant, 'all that class will probably be better off than they were before this calamity.'[19] Where they would live in the long term was another matter. It was months before the site could be cleared, and as usually happened with houseless poor at that time, many of them probably had to double up in already overcrowded tenements with existing tenants.

A poor Irishman who had emerged from a wretched garret wringing his hands and declaring he had lost everything, excited near-mirth when some of the crowd ran up to try to help, and found nothing but a heap of straw and a rickety chair; but the poor fellow called piteously, 'Gentlemen! is it not my all?' And some of the reactions were that the fire was a judgment, because of Edinburgh's recent Music Festival, regarded as a godless affair.[20]

It was the irreparable loss to Edinburgh itself that distressed Mrs Grant and certain others even more. 'I hardly think there was any one that lamented more than myself the destruction of the venerable buildings of the Old Town.' The loss oppressed her spirits for a long time. 'My ideas have been so completely ignited by the recent calamity', she wrote more than a month later, 'that . . . I should talk of nought but fire, if I once touched on that terrific subject.'[21]

49
A CRISIS

> 'With cold, stolid, iron visages, Modern Athenians witnessed that profanation; with prefect nonchalance they took possession of his old-accustomed abode, which he was never more to enter.'
>
> Robert Gillies, *Memoirs of a Literary Veteran*, 1851, III.138

In 1825, the last complete year of his prosperity, Sir Walter Scott was already aware of rumblings of financial anxiety. Like other activities the book trade had been expanding, with an eye to the new market among the industrious artisan, bent on self-improvement.

Scott's reckless extravagance on Abbotsford and its lands, and his simple but ever-generous hospitality, had become a byword. Although it did not appear in his outward behaviour, he recognised the dangers and in his boundless energy and confidence relied on fertile output and continued royalty and capital payments. He and others knew they were pushing too hard, and *Quentin Durward* following on the heels of *Peveril of the Peak* so took readers by surprise as to be 'too quick for the pocket'. 'We may gorge the public', admitted Cadell to James Ballantyne, when they agreed to limit production to the works now contracted for. But when in 1824 Scott finished *St Ronan's Well* (his best for some time, claimed Sydney Smith; 'a complete failure', said Cam Hobhouse) and at once started on *Redgauntlet,* then worked on a second edition of Swift, he had to meet Constable to try to put his affairs on a sounder footing.[1]

Proposals were lavish enough on Constable's side: his projected *Encyclopaedia of Youth* and his seventy-six volume *Miscellany* filled the horizon, and relations between publisher and author seemed cordial. 'This is the cleverest thing that ever came into that cleverest of all bibliophile heads', wrote Lockhart to Constable in May 1825, and Scott was equally enthusiastic. It would be a revolution in bookselling (they all agreed over the claret), working towards Constable's ambition for 'a good library in every decent house in Britain', selling by tens of thousands, 'ay, by millions!'[2]

This was the more desirable, as Scott was warning Constable that 'the vein of fiction was nearly worked out' (a wrong prediction, as it proved). In the summer he and Lockhart visited Ireland, where Miss Edgeworth was favourable to Constable's plans, and on their return the weekly *Miscellany*, dedicated to the King, selling at half a crown or so a month, was planned to start in the New Year with Basil Hall's *Voyage to Loo-Choo*. But in November Constable, in London, was hearing of business failures and commercial gloom.[3]

Scott's Irish tour, and Tommy Moore's stay at Abbotsford in November and the comedian Charles Mathews with his son over Christmas, were to prove his last, outwardly unclouded, visits of pleasure. In July Moore had acknowledged Scott's kind, half-joking intimation of mortality the previous year that 'if I did not come & see you, before you died, you would appear to me afterwards . . . I shall take care & have the start of you'. At this stage, to Moore's regret, they had met only once.[4] The meeting was achieved in November, when a brisk bout of illness kept Moore longer than expected in Edinburgh and enabled him to meet friends a few more times.

Scott delighted Moore with his recollections and revelations. 'He had passed the early part of his life with a set of clever, rattling drinking fellows', says Moore, and though fond of old ballads had never thought of poetry: it had been Monk Lewis who first set him on that path. And to Moore's pleased surprise he talked freely of his novels without attempted concealment, admitting that while out shooting or walking, now when he was rising fifty-seven, ideas came to him less easily. A possible straw in the wind . . . Moore, like others, was mildly surprised at Scott's total lack of interest in the arts and the classics.

'I would not have lost this visit to Scotland for any consideration', he wrote to Owen Rees. 'Great as Scott is to the world, one must see him closely and at home to appreciate him properly', and he would have gone round the world to hear his parting words: 'My dear Moore, we are now friends for life.' What with his happy stay with Jeffrey in addition, it was 'the most gratifying fortnight I ever spent' and sent him home with 'a sunshine on my spirits'.[5] Unfortunately this did not last, as he caught a bad cold when crossing Shap Fell – but when recovered on return home, he was soon raving about Yarrow, Scottish songs and other delights.

Scott's financial ruin followed so soon on this happy visit that having visited Abbotsford even increased Moore's distress, and after doubting for some weeks whether it would be proper to send condolences he did so in February, knowing how bitter was the loss and having experienced Scott's worth at first hand.[6]

His annoyance at the *Quarterly*'s review of his own life of Sheridan was the more painful, suspecting that it was the work of Lockhart, 'that "infidus scurra"'. 'What a pity', he wrote to Jeffrey, 'that Scott should have such a dark spot on his disk as this fellow is.'[7]

Charles Mathews, visiting Abbotsford at the year's end, ebullient over the success of his theatrical tour, was not least gratified at the social success of his son Charles the younger, who came with him. First, young Charles made a good impression on Jeffrey at dinner, 'no small boast'; then, at dinner at James Ballantyne's, their host placed Charles next to 'the Great Well-known', and the youth, 'all hopes, all fears', was cheered by Scott's unstinting praise of his manners and later, his singing. 'He's a very nice lad, that, and exceedingly clever,' affirmed Scott, inviting the pair to Abbotsford. ('Scott never flatters,' Cadell assured them next day. 'His praise is indeed worth having.') Next, the architect Playfair invited young Charles to see his drawings. 'In short,' wrote the glowing father, 'I look upon this trip as one of the most fortunate and important events in his life.'

At Christmas father and son dined and slept at Constables' near Roslin, who for the first time to them threw off 'the veil of mystery' about Scott, and described how he had one day come across him alternately writing a piece of *Woodstock* and a chunk of *Napoleon*, together before him on the table, alternating 'dry history' with imaginative work as refreshment. [8]

Only a month before, Scott for the first time in his life started to keep a journal, much regretting (as also posterity must) that he had not done so long ago. He probably saw it as an aid to working out his finances and his future.

'I here register my purpose to practise economics,' he entered on 25 November.

'No more building;

'No purchases of land till times are quite safe . . .;

'Clearing off encumbrances, with the returns of this year's labour . . .'[9]

It was already too late, even before the fateful year 1826 had dawned. 'My extremity is come', he recorded, when Ballantyne called on him on 18 December.[10] Catastrophe was precipitated because of the intertwining of the several publishing firms involved, Hurst and Robinson the London printers, Constable, and the Ballantynes, with whom 'I must go for company'. He continued to weave plans for earnings from various sources, and believed he could weather the crisis. In a month he was – not exactly undeceived, but faced with the stark facts. His debts amounted to over £40,000. Even then, after the first dreadful shock, his positive, resourceful nature began to work on how to overcome them.[11]

The minutiae of the joint ruin of Scott, Constable and the Ballantynes are complex and, especially to today's reader, tedious; what to us is more interesting is how they dealt with it. Constable was criticised for not going to London sooner or after Christmas to negotiate; the stoppage of cash was blamed on further borrowing or discounts and the refusal of their bills, because the banks themselves were at a stand.

Constable was ill, Scott too was in poor health. Pandemonium spread with the failure of more firms, but Scott digested the calamity and set about a rehabilitation programme. He had his modest legal salary. He must sell his Castle Street house and retire to Abbotsford, and when in Edinburgh stay in lodgings. To boost morale, he announced the publication of *Woodstock,* and must use to the full his sole remaining asset, his books existing or yet to be written. By completing a volume of *Napoleon* he could raise more. To his relief, the creditors agreed to a private trust by which he could keep Abbotsford; but he was disillusioned by Constable's unrealistic confidence and his 'last mad proposal' for Scott to guarantee £20,000. From then on the two hardly met, and on 21 July 1827 Constable died at his home.[12]

Before that time Lady Scott's health, too, had failed since the disaster, and while their possessions at Castle Street were being auctioned off, she was dying at Abbotsford. The end came on 16 May, before Scott could reach her side, and about ten days later he returned to Edinburgh and his job. Robert Gillies, who for some years had been in Germany, was himself in serious financial trouble, was repeatedly put to the horn for his large debts, and was urged by Scott to mend his fortunes by setting up a journal on foreign literature. Things seldom went right for Gillies, but he had reflections to spare on Scott.

'If only his ambition had been prudent' and stopped with Abbotsford, he declared. If only friends had started a subscription to save his Edinburgh house – which Scott could never bear to set eyes on again, always making a detour rather than pass it. Gillies visited him in 'a third-rate lodging, in North St David's Street', one of several in which Scott passed melancholy nights when he could not be at Abbotsford. He was pushing himself to write, his former three-hour minimum daily output forced up to as much as ten or even twelve hours a day, and in Gillies's opinion the forced pace showed in his work.

Yet Scott had sympathy to spare for his old friend, even suggesting he stay at Chiefswood. Gillies declined, with gratitude, and after a last Abbotsford visit, whose company was now limited to close family, though with Scott apparently in reasonably good form, he sailed for London in September, for twenty years scarcely to see Edinburgh again.[13]

Most people had something to say on the catastrophe, not always with unmixed implications. Miss Mitford wrote to Haydon of how hard Scott must feel it to be 'deposed, at his time of life' from his literary, indeed world pinnacle, 'the more especially as the great falling-off in the late works rendered it desirable for his fame that he should cease writing' (4 May 1826); and later, learning that the debt had been contained at £40,000, remarked even more plainly that she was 'one of those who think he has had his reward both in fame and money'. Learning that *Woodstock* had earned him 8000 guineas, without maintaining that he was overpaid (though indeed she did), she was saying 'Simply that he is well paid'. Several writers, rival or otherwise, could not help a certain self-satisfaction at this come-uppance.

Miss Mitford drove home the point in praising *The Last of the Mohicans,* by the insufferable Fenimore Cooper, at the expense of Scott – except for the latter's first three novels and *The Heart of Midlothian.* America, she thought, would in time outstrip Britain 'as Rome did Athens'. Interpret this as we may.[14]

Some sprang to the barricades. 'When I think of the wretched Trash', wrote Coleridge, 'that the Lust of Gain induced [Scott] to publish for the last 3 or 4 years, which must have been *manufactured,* for the greater part, even my feelings assist in hardening me . . . Heaven knows! I have enough to feel for without wasting my Sympathy on a Scotchman suffering the Penalty of his Scotchery.' The vultures, held off for years, were closing in.

Coleridge was even more mordant over the revelation, so-called, of Scott's authorship. While defending Scott's silence, he criticised his allowing the suggestion that the author was his brother, who had left the country for debt in 1813. 'Precious morality, Master Walter! if this were true – and so you contrive to have the whole world believe a falsehood in order to defraud your Brother's Creditor's!'[15]

It is hard not to read into all this a widespread jealousy of Scott's phenomenal earnings.

Yet in 1829 Coleridge was expressing appreciation of Blackwood's continuing to send him his magazine, only criticising the space it gave to party politics and political economy: 'Blackwood and Sir Walter's novels have been my comforters in many a sleepless night.'[16]

However, friends and strangers alike were impressed by Scott's philosophical response to the catastrophe, still more so by his resilience. In no time he was planning the programme of further writing, new editions, and stop-gaps to make interim payments to his creditors.

'The Minstrel is too great a man ever to be lessened by adverse circumstances', wrote Mrs Grant soon after (February 1826). For Constable she had small sympathy, except for his ten children by two marriages; but lamented 'the kind-hearted, talented, and liberal-minded James Ballantyne'.

Looking back on Scott's career to date, she exclaimed, 'What do we not owe to this highly gifted being . . . for purifying and refining our taste, and sweeping the paltry trash of inglorious novels, like cobwebs, from the palace of invention', setting a chivalrous and courteous example to young men. Though his hospitality had been so generous, by Edinburgh standards it was not lavish; yet (said Mrs Grant) his conversation 'drew so many to his table, that the literal roast and boiled feast was perpetual . . . from the Continent, from America, from the uttermost parts of the earth' – not to mention poor writers, whom he liberally helped. Abbotsford was his undeniable weakness and part of his undoing, 'neither tower, bower, nor castle, but a fanciful mixture of all three, so embowered and be-pinnacled'.[17]

At the beginning of 1827 she was writing to an American friend that 'through the softened shade of adversity, [he] appears to me greater than ever'. He and Anne were now sharing a small house, 'seeing no company, and devoted to his literary labours; but when he is seen, placid, cheerful, and unaltered'. And in September, praising 'Walter the wonderful's' venture into biography with the completion of *Napoleon,* 'I glory in his equanimity', bearing everything with 'calm fortitude', and because the Whigs 'cavilled' at the new work, this devoted Tory admirer felt 'much inclined to cavil at the Whigs'.[18]

Cam Hobhouse, more waspish if more scholarly, recorded that the Comte de Flahault, dining at Lord Tavistock's, had told him that for the Napoleon biography Scott had consulted scarcely any original documents, and proceeding from the literary to the personaal, the Count added that 'associates' said 'they never heard him, in company or elsewhere, indulge in a single generous sentiment; he rather sneered at all efforts of individuals for the public good'. This sounds so unlike Scott as to be a malicious fabrication.[19] At this stage Hobhouse had never met him.

In the following year John Murray introduced them in London, and Hobhouse's view changed with almost comical abruptness. 'Nothing can exceed the simplicity of his look and manner.' The two talked of Byron, a happy subject with both, and Hobhouse ended, 'I hope to improve my acquaintance with this extraordinary man, certainly one of the most extraordinary that our country has ever produced.'[20]

Scott had gone to Paris in October to consult authorities for the Napoleon biography, and friends met him when he passed through London. Mrs Arbuthnot saw him several times in November, including at a large dinner-party the Duke of Wellington held in his honour. 'He is grown thin & *full* 5 years older', noted the lady, 'since I last saw him, which was at the Coronation' – though as that was anyway five years earlier it was hardly surprising. Despite his misfortunes 'he is in great spirits & talks a good deal of his "Life of Bonaparte"'. She was much put out on one occasion by the 'bad taste' of a Mr Bankes, who 'hogged the conversation', and his loud voice drowned Scott.[21]

During this visit Scott was sitting for his bust for Chantrey, and would often call on Frances Lady Shelley, who was living in a small Chester Street house during a long convalescence. One day after one of her breakfasts, 'while the great man was intent on his conversation', her daughter Fanny stole up behind him and surreptitiously cut off a lock of his greying, sandy hair. Another time, an evening when Wellington and Mrs Arbuthnot, both frequent visitors, were there, Scott 'told ghost stories until we were afraid to separate', with his gift for making the most unlikely tales seem real. Lady Shelley herself visited Abbotsford the following summer.[22]

On his return from Paris Scott took furnished rooms in the new Edinburgh area of Coates Crescent, where Gillies had found him in good spirits, but as he was now spending even more hours in writing, getting up even earlier, his penmanship had become small and cramped. At home he still received only close friends, but *Napoleon,* in nine volumes, had sold for £11,000, well above the expected profit, and he was now in a position to start paying his debts.[23]

By this time Scott had felt it advisable to admit his authorship, which he did at a public dinner of the Theatrical Fund on 23 February 1827, though it surprised almost nobody. Yet even then some people had still believed in the myth about his brother. It was 'in order to prove his right to the MSS', as Mrs Arbuthnot observed.[24]

His admission revived remarks about Scott's solemn denial of his authorship to the King, which (Haydon noted) 'does not seem popular. *On dit*, that it is ostentatious', for the sake of his puffing *Napoleon*. 'How like the world!' he commented, first they damn him for not confessing, now suggest a paltry meaning when he does. But he ought not to have given his 'word of honour'.[25]

'There was something about Sir Walter Scott – foxy,' adds Haydon on another occasion. 'Amiable, dear, delightful man as he was, he yet had something of a look as if he had been "playing fox".'[26]

Dorothy Wordsworth wrote of the revelation 'when the great Unknown was revealed to all Eyes', that despite her great fondness for Scott, she 'could not but grieve at such display'.[27]

Sir James Mackintosh had told John Merivale in 1824 that he considered that Scott could never admit authorship because of his being 'unhandsomely pressed by the King', which 'he denied somewhat too stoutly'.[28]

There are various versions of this famous misjudgment of Scott's, which at best must be considered a gaffe. Haydon's is third-hand: at a dinner in March 1827 Hook was reported as saying that Croker had said he was there when Scott was dining with the King, and the King said, 'Let us drink to the health of the author of the "Waverley novels"'. Scott, without being asked, responded, 'I assure your Majesty upon my honour and word, I am not the author.' The King said afterwards he knew he was lying, and hoped he would never acknowledge it.[29]

Haydon, who in contrast to Scott's reaction was 'suffering the tortures of the inferno' over his own financial disasters, may be forgiven for observing that Scott's 'distresses' were cushioned by what Haydon took Scott's word as being 'a handsome competence'. When Scott was reaping the profits from *Napoleon*, he remarked with slight irritation that 'These dreadful times have done no harm to these "nouveaux riches". It has taught them they smell of mortality.'[30]

In 1828, when Scott again visited London, staying with the Lockharts, he was still in fairly good form. To that painter's pleasure he sat for 'his fine head' early in May to Haydon, who was almost as much gratified by Scott's kissing his boy Frank. Scott sat for him after a breakfast with Sergeant Talfourd, Charles Eastlake and a young surgeon, 'and a delightful sitting it was'. But despite his reunion with his favourite daughter Sophia he seemed depressed, and it was hard to forget that since they last met Haydon had been in prison for debt, and Scott had lost over £40,000 'and is ageing'. He did, in his usual fashion, relate 'some wonderful tales', including of that favourite subject the supernatural, but was quieter than formerly. But he retained his 'penetrating look' which Haydon recalled as a characteristic.

A few days later Haydon called on him with Chauncey Hare Townsend, who was 'in agony' to meet him, and though Scott talked in his usual pleasant manner he showed a habitual 'musing, heavy sadness' Haydon had not seen in him before the John Scott duel and death.[31] An additional anxiety was that his son-in-law Lockhart seemed now not to be as well received as Scott would have liked. His little grandson, the Lockharts' boy John, ailing and deformed, was a sadness to them all, suffering as he appears to have done with spina bifida.

By contrast Mrs Arbuthnot, meeting Scott again at Lord Bathurst's dinner for him on 5 May, found him 'in high health and spirits'. It was probably a reaction to lively company.[32]

William and Dorothy Wordsworth, whatever their attitude to Scott's ruin, authorship, secrecy and so on, admitted to spending 'a charming day' with him at Hampton Court, and to being delighted at meeting Sophia, 'as everybody is, who knows her'.[33]

Back in Edinburgh this time Scott settled in Shandwick Place. At Abbotsford the following year he still seemed in good health, though living at a lower pitch. He continued his labours in his modified life between Abbotsford and Edinburgh lodgings.[34]

In 1829 Scott began publication of a collected edition of the Waverley novels, with notes, and meanwhile had completed two further novels, *The Fair Maid of Perth* in 1828 and *Anne of Geierstein* in 1829.

In the autumn of 1830 Scott resigned his post as Clerk of Session, refusing to accept the full salary as pension. By that time, however, his health was beginning to fail. Unlike his usual self, he was becoming peevish and irritable. Late in that year he was lodging at 124 Princes Street.[35]

These domestic changes were not the result, like Carlyle's, of restless failure to settle, but of his various travels and removals to Abbotsford. At the beginning of that year, when still at 6 Shandwick Place, he had had an alarming intimation of mortality. One day in February Mrs Young, of Hawick, called while he was writing as usual, about a manuscript memoir of her father, and to their joint anxiety, after he gave her some kind of confused reply he found he could not even speak.

After a period of their 'mutual astonishment' he managed to ring the bell, and make a sign to his servant which caused the latter to alert his daughter Anne while he hurried to the doctor. After about a quarter of an hour Scott recovered a little, was put to bed and bled by the surgeon – but from this preliminary stroke warning he never fully recovered, his legs remained weak and his hands were affected so that his writing was full of blots and smudges. He found it necessary to give up alcohol, and keep to a simple diet, but his natural 'hilarity' had deserted him, leaving him heavy and dull.[36]

This was the man who for the next couple of years was still to struggle on against his continuing financial burden. He was so near to reaching success.

50
STAGES OF FRIENDSHIP: WILSON, JEFFREY, CARLYLE

'I found the literary men of [Edinburgh] still active in their vocation, and to me undeservedly kind and courteous; nevertheless, the general tone of their speculation was such as to make me revisit my solitude, when the time came, with little regret. The whole bent of British endeavour, both intellectual and practical, at this time, is towards Utility . . . now fast rising into its full maturity.'

Carlyle to Goethe, *The Collected Letters of Thomas and Jane Welsh Carlyle*, 22 December 1829, V.50

'never at bottom a superlative esteem for him, tho' I recognised with admiration his great and singular gifts, liked him really well, and . . . could well have desired more talk and intercourse'.

Carlyle speaking of Wilson in 'Christopher North', in *19th Century and After*, LXXXVII, January 1920, 103ff.

'Certanly Jeffrey is by much the most loveable of all the literary men I have seen; and he seemed ready nay desirous to cultivate a farther intimacy.'

Carlyle to his brother John, *Collected Letters*, IV.229, 4 June 1827

'People come on foot, on horseback, and even in wheeled carraiges to see us; most of whom Jane receives upstairs . . . We receive invitations to dinner also . . . Only to some 3 or 4 chosen people we give notice that on Wednesday nights, we shall *always* be at home.'

Carlyle to his brother Alick, *op. cit.*, IV.185, 3 February 1827

'I am in fact becoming a sort of Literary Man, like my neighbour, and the people wonder at me more than enough.'

Carlyle to Alick, *op. cit.*, IV.285, 26 November 1827

[Of Macvey Napier:] 'Without absolute learning or talent in the higher senses, he was intelligent and sensible, well read in morals and metaphysics, very industrious, and he had a good, plain clear style of composition . . . [but] a hard air and manner, and a foolish notion of his own importance.'

Journal of Henry Cockburn 1831–1834, Edinburgh 1874, 14 February 1847 (?)

John Wilson, as Tory journalist and now as professor of philosophy, was probably equal in fame to Jeffrey. Carlyle – who after the success of his first publications and his relatively mellowed state since marriage, was giving little weekly tea-parties hosted by Jane, and beginning to meet and accept the literati – while well-nigh falling in love with Jeffrey during their first years of acquaintanceship, had no such success with Wilson. He notes that while he and Jane might now have met everyone worth knowing, Jeffrey was the only one who seemed to either of them 'a valuable acquisition'. 'Wilson, a far *bigger* man, I could have loved, or fancied I could; but he would not let me try', and he believed perhaps arrogantly that Wilson might have been suspicious or even jealous – 'apprehensive I might think less of him the better I knew him'.[1]

Late in 1826, posting Dr Julius with Edinburgh's literary data, he mentioned *The Lights and Shadows of a Scottish Life*, a sentimental novel published in 1822, as by Wilson, 'a wild exuberant genius . . . believed in secret to be the great mainspring of *Blackwood's Magazine*'[2] – suggesting that Carlyle was as yet far from any inner ring of Edinburgh writers. Wilson and Lockhart had contributed to a notable failure, *Janus,* or *The Edinburgh Literary Almanack,* intended by Oliver and Boyd as an annual, but after a single issue in November 1825 it folded ignominiously.[3]

It was six months after this letter to Julius before Carlyle in early July 1827, after much abortive planning, actually met Wilson at the lodging of John Gordon, a visiting friend from Kirkcudbright[4] who used to speak of Wilson to him. He was prepared to be greatly impressed.

> A man of the most fervid temperament, fond of all stimulating things, from tragic poetry down to whisky punch. He snuffed and smoked cigars and drank liquors, and talked in the most indescribable style . . . Daylight came on us before we parted; indeed it was towards 3 o'clock as the Professor and I walked home, smoking as we went. I had scarcely either eaten or drunk . . . merely enjoyed the strange volcanic emotion of our poet's convivial genius.
>
> He is a broad sincere man of 6 feet, with long dishevelled flax-coloured hair, and 2 blue eyes keen as an eagle's. Now and then he sank into a brown study, and seemed dead in the eye of law. About 2 o'clock he was sitting in this state smoking languidly, his nose begrimed with snuff, his face hazy and inert; when all at once flashing into existence' – he suddenly put a question to his host: 'I hope, Mr Gordon, you don't believe in universal damnation!' It was wicked, but all hands burst into inextinguishable laughter.'

Wilson promised to call on the Carlyles, and Thomas hoped to know him better, making the characteristically spiked comment that 'Geniuses of any sort, especially of so kindly a sort, are so very rare in this world.'

They never did know each other better, as Carlyle observed many years later in his essay intended for his *Reminiscences.* He admits to having 'never at bottom a superlative esteem for him, tho' I recognised with admiration his great and singular gifts, liked him really well, and . . . could well have desired more talk and intercourse . . .' It was Wilson who proved wary, keeping him at arm's length.

After this 'enviable honour of a mouthful of speech with the great Professor', Wilson and Carlyle, when they saw each other in the street, used to exchange a few words – 'if it suited both parties', as Carlyle drily observed. Even this was memorable. 'His conversation, never so casual, in such brief meetings, had generally something piquant in it unlike that of other men; a spicing of wild satire, caricature, or off-hand quiz, wild not cruel . . . And he loved to *dramatize* any fact of doctrine to you by an example that might come to hand.'[5]

During such pavement talks Wilson probably inflicted on Carlyle an individual trick he had, on reaching the nub of an argument, of suddenly stopping and facing about to block the way as he delivered his point, looking the other full in the face. Then he would step back and walk on – and probably soon repeat the process. This and his characteristic costume of broad-brimmed hat, long flowing hair, and close-buttoned black coat, made him a memorable figure in the street.[6]

After about a year of such meetings the two had grown no more intimate, and Carlyle guessed they never would. Only once or twice did they visit one another's house, especially when Carlyle left Wilson the Goethe letter and medal which he had hoped to deliver personally to Scott, when Wilson assured him he would visit them at Craigenputtock, 'but you must write specially to ask me'. This was in October 1827. Carlyle did, but knew Wilson would not answer. He reckoned that in Wilson he saw 'the making of a great man . . . but not quite *all*'.[7]

'I suspect he feels a sort of division from me,' he confided in John, 'for . . . he has in a great measure renounced [striving after the *idea*] and between Blackwood and the Scotch Kirk-Session, has almost degenerated into Fichte's "Mongrel".'[8]

In his November summary to Mrs Montagu of his new acquaintances (he was cautious in applying the word 'friend' except unhesitatingly to Jeffrey). Carlyle admitted to liking Wilson, and 'could almost love him, were not the Devil in him! He is a man of genius, of a noble glowing heart – but – he has sold himself to the world; and Satan (in the shape of Blackwood) pays him the price monthly.'[9] It was selling himself to the world that Carlyle was eventually to blame on Jeffrey, not allowing that if he had, Jeffrey was the first to regret it.

Wilson was an animal-lover. He once confronted a brutal coal carter beating his broken-down horse in Moray Place, unfastened the cart and tipped its load into the street, then led off the miserable horse to find it a kinder home.[10] His own home was open house for dogs, often those of visiting friends. Chief among them was Tory, brother to Fang, one of Wilson's and both sired by Blackwood's dog Tickler, 'a long-backed yellow terrier', turned-out front paws and a mild expression. Tickler visited and stayed at will, was friendly to all, but particularly fond of Wilson, impartially treating his and Blackwood's house as home. He never turned up at church but was known as 'a dog about town' – would wait even for hours at the theatre or the Assembly Room door, though sometimes attaching himself to preferred strangers and even accompanying them home.

Wilson's own favourite was Bronte, a black Newfoundland he had as a puppy from 1826, who would escort him to the college every day; until one day at the height of the Burke and Hare trial in 1827 he was found dead, probably poisoned, a victim of one of Dr Knox's Anatomy class who took offence at Wilson's comments on the case in *Noctes Ambrosianae.*[11]

Early in March 1825 Wilson had written to Robert Findlay of Easter Hill, 'I am building a house in Gloucester Place, a small street leading from the Circus into Lord Moray's grounds. This I am doing because I am poor, and money yielding no interest.' If circumstances permitted he planned to take in '2 or 3 young gentlemen' as lodgers, and hoped this would be bruited around to provide him with candidates.

Gloucester Place, on the new Moray estate, resembled its neighbour India Street in being divided between houses and tenements, the former, as with Wilson, personally financed by single householders. Wilson's, number 8, was ready the following year, and here he was to live for the rest of his life. No 'young gentlemen', however, were taken on.

In home habits Wilson remained Spartan, never having a fire in his room, however Arctic the weather, nor admitting gas-light (after once accidentally blowing it out and nearly gassing everyone), but he used a tallow candle in a common tin candlestick. Every morning the servant was expected to place candlestick, snuffer and inkstand on his desk, the last being an earthenware figure of Arion on the dolphin which his wife had bought in a Stockbridge shop in 1820. The shop was kept by a young man as yet unknown – Robert Chambers.[12]

Wilson continued his contributions to *Blackwood's* at undiminished rate. In 1830, for example, they were never less than one a month, and in January two, February, four and March, three – a total of 1200 columns in the year.[13]

Carlyle, however much he longed for it, could never make Wilson be wholly serious, and he would shift from the speculative to the sentimental, or 'into the realm of quiz'. Always awakening laughter in others, he himself, to Carlyle's recollection, did not laugh at all.[14]

In May 1830 Wilson was reviewing, in mixed terms, the first book of poems by a new poet, Alfred Tennyson. In winding up he commented that he might to start with have 'exaggerated Mr Tennyson's not unfrequent silliness, for . . . in our humourous moods, many things wear a queer look to our aged eyes which fill young pupils with tears; but . . . we have not exaggerated his strength, and . . . have done no more than justice to his fine faculties'. Wilson was then fifty-five, Tennyson just twenty-one.

The poet was not amused. In his poems of 1833 he replied to the ambiguous criticism:

> You did late review my lays
> Crusty Christopher;
> You did mingle blame with praise,
> Rusty Christopher:
> When I learned from whom it came,
> I forgave you all the blame,
> Musty Christopher;
> I could *not* forgive the praise,
> Fusty Christopher.

(In later editions, however, Tennyson did drop or modify the poems criticised.[15])

In July 1830 the Rev. John McVickar, from New York, breakfasted alone with Wilson, and 'had much talk'. His view of the professor was dispassionate. 'He is a strong-minded, unpolished man, but not of the kind one expects to see in the chair of morals', and notes that his election had been supported by Scott and Lockhart, while Jeffrey had been opposed. A Royal Commission was now considering 'the relative powers of professors, patrons, visitors, etc.', whereas under the old system 'each professor governs his own class', and the whole body ruled the college with little outside interference.

Wilson told McVickar that he would study or write for up to fifteen hours at a time, '6 am to 9 pm without moving or eating, which fits of intellectual labour were succeeded by equally immovable fits of indolence . . .'[16]

Much later the acidulous Sir Henry Taylor, in Edinburgh in 1835, wrote with hostility particularly of Jeffrey but approved of Wilson, whom he esteemed 'the most gifted of the many men who have put their talents into the pig-trough in these times'. He thought his appearance matched expectation: 'a jovial, fair-haired ruffian, full of fire and talent, big and burly, and at the same time wild and animated', with 'one of the most lively and capacious-looking foreheads' ever seen, and with the oddity of 'a flashing eye under a light-coloured and almost bald eyebrow'. Remarkable to look at, with conversation to match. Wilson urged Taylor to dine whenever he should be free: he dined twice and had supper once, thinking he had 'seldom met with any person more striking in his way'.

He also wanted Taylor to meet De Quincey, except that he hardly dared to venture out because of debts, and related the story of De Quincey's coming to him for a day and staying nine months, during which he was hardly seen.

Wilson seemed to Taylor like one of Robin Hood's men – or even Robin himself, 'jovial, but fierce . . . full of fire and animal energy, and of wit and sarcasm . . . a man who has always been the king of his company'. He concluded that 'moral philosophy was never taught by a wilder or more fiery Professor, and he was certainly by far the most considerable man I met with in Edinburgh'. In writing to Lady Hislop he noted that he had met numerous judges and professors, 'great and small, . . . and chiefly Professor Wilson (of the great) and Lord Jeffrey (of the small)'. A preference as revealing of Taylor himself as it is about the two men.[17]

At the time of the Reform Bill Wilson was of course a hot opponent. An impassioned 'oration' which he delivered at the Tory meeting on 29 November [1831] was a powerful apologia for his convictions, repudiating the criticism that Tories were 'enemies of education, and have no love for the lower orders'. For himself, he was at pains to record with some satisfaction that not only had he had 'no patronage beyond what my own honourable character gave me', but 'I have sat by the cottar's ingle on the Saturday night, and seen the grey-haired patriarch with pleasure unfold the sacred page . . . and it is said I belong to that class who hate and despise the people . . .' His wife was loyally behind him. 'I hope you are as much disgusted as we all are with the passing of this accursed Bill,' she wrote to her sister. 'I never look into a newspaper now, but we shall see what they make of it by and by.'[18]

The University students were as divided over the Bill as the rest of the city, and the more liberal now viewed their old favourite *Blackwood's* as an enemy. Friendships broke up, threats were passed. Crowds attended the 'Reform' meetings until at last the Tories determined, late in the day, to hold one themselves. (The style of regular political meetings, party by party, had not then evolved.) The liberals debated whether to break in and outvote them. A younger friend of Wilson's experimentally spoke in favour of such an invasion, at which Wilson drew himself up to his considerable height and warned that if anyone he knew 'meddled', 'I hope I may be the first – (pause) to kick him out into the street.'[19]

In later years Wilson mellowed towards the Whigs, after his daughter Mary (author of his biography) married the Whig J. T. Gordon who became Sheriff of Midlothian. The pair lived with the widowed Wilson for eleven years. By degrees he became friendly with leading Whigs, Jeffrey, Cockburn, Rutherford.[20]

Carlyle, returning from the west in August 1827, found Jeffrey away for a week, and planned to settle for 'my *large* Article for his Review' on the state of German literature, then to return to his neglected book. Jeffrey wrote gratifyingly, 'I feel at once that You are a man of Genius – and of original character and right heart – and shall be proud and happy to know more of you.'[21]

He wanted Carlyle's work by mid-September, and sent him a draft for twenty guineas for the Richter article – which he had not yet started. They met briefly at Craigcrook, 'the little fellow friendlier than ever', and Jeffrey promised to call at Comely Bank. This friendship proved a boon to Carlyle, still drifting on the fringe of literature. Jane was thoroughly approving. 'He is quite a little jewel of a man, and seems to love my Husband truly, who in return as truly loves him.'[22]

Meanwhile their bijou home proved a peaceful haven. It was the time when anybody who was anybody, including Carlyle, was applying for, being put up for, or being urged to apply for, a chair of Rhetoric at the new London University, though in the end even Dr Chalmers did not get a post. Leonard Horner had been appointed its first Warden. Jeffrey was urging on Carlyle, though doubting his success in view of his sectarianism and perhaps even heresy. Carlyle replied typically that he was 'merely more open to light than others of his Craft', whereupon Jeffrey gave him a letter to Horner and offered to recommend him all round.[23] Carlyle accordingly called indefatigably on Horner, who lived on the other side of the Old Town in Lauriston Lane, taking time off to finish his precious review – twice finding him out and 'after the most fatiguing perseverance' reaching him the third time, only to find that London would as yet have no Professor of Rhetoric at all.

This brought him to a stand until he found that, as Chalmers had not after all got the Moral Philosophy chair, this was a possible alternative, and he renewed his canvassing for the support of Irving, Jeffrey, and Rev. Dr Duncan. Brougham, a potentially influential ally, had gone to London, and Carlyle accordingly sent him a copy of his latest *Review* article. Jeffrey suspected the post might be kept open for years. So Carlyle continued, with increasing renown, producing for the *Edinburgh Review* and for London's new *Foreign Review.*

'It is surprising to see how much stir these bits of writing cause here in Edinburgh,' he told his mother. 'The people' (he meant Jeffrey) 'seem to think that I am a genius perhaps, but of what sort only Heaven knows.'[24]

By late October they knew that London would not be his; that the post had been offered to Thomas Campbell, who refused, and it did indeed for the time being remain unfilled. During that wet month Carlyle had produced 'The State of German Literature', having hovered between a stand as idealist and realist. His brother John had come and gone, to Munich, and they were expecting their sister Jean, persuading her that Edinburgh was not 'half so grand' as she feared.[25]

It proved that Brougham fought shy of Carlyle, and the authorities were 'alarmed at my German predilection'. Jeffrey also found that Dugald Stewart had recommended 'some *Frenchman* or other', namely the philosopher Victor Cousin. Meanwhile the German literature paper was ready to appear in the next *Review* (which was late). Carlyle followed his exertions by a spell of idleness, reading trash, digging his garden and mentally relaxing. He was finding he quite liked Edinburgh – chiefly because of the friendship with Jeffrey.[26]

In November, still on these honeymoon terms, Carlyle wrote of his gratitude to Barry Cornwall for his introduction to this 'kind and truly delightful acquaintance', whose sole fault at this stage of their friendship was indeed 'a thumper': that he was in the law. 'Truly a rare phenomenon, and amongst the best of that rather unhappy race, Men of Letters now extant.'[27]

Since Dr Chalmers was now appointed to the Divinity chair in Edinburgh (as from 1828), there was next a suggestion that Carlyle might replace him in Moral Philosophy at St Andrews. Jeffrey and others thought he had a good chance, and he applied to Goethe for a testimonial, but warned that these appointments were usually decided 'by very *unfair* principles'. As he told Procter, to whom he also applied, Jeffrey, Wilson, Leslie and Brewster were all backing him.[28]

Carlyle's head was still spinning with his enthusiastic reception by critics and fellow-writers. 'I am in fact becoming a sort of Literary Man, like my neighbours [a change indeed], and the people wonder at me more than enough', and reported to John that his *Edinburgh* paper had been 'received with considerable surprise and approbation by the universe'. De Quincey had praised him in the *Saturday Post*, Sir William Hamilton had said it was '*cap'tal*', and Wilson told John Gordon that it had 'done me a *deal* of good'. He followed it up with a long essay on Zacharias Werner and sent it to the eager James Fraser in London. After taking the week off, he started on Tasso.[29]

By the turn of the year he had as much work as he could produce, and was further negotiating with booksellers for a reissue of *Schiller*, since its first edition had never been advertised, reviewed, or even displayed and was now praised in Constable's *Miscellany*.[30]

He was still rapturous over Jeffrey: 'an intellectual Ariel, with a light ethereal-ness of spirit which the weight of whole Courts of Session resting on it for quarter-centuries has not been able to suppress. There is a glance in the eyes of the man, which almost prompts you to take him in your arms.'[31]

The professorial application went in at the end of January (1828), and Jeffrey's own testimonial had been so glowing that it 'might of itself bring me any Professorship in the island'. Jane said she could kiss him for it. Only Goethe's testimonial did not arrive, but he was sending two portrait medals which Carlyle could distribute to his friends. As for the post, they suspected it had been filled even before he applied.[32]

To balance their failure to hear news of his application, Carlyle's fame in London was growing, and rather to his surprise – though neither he nor Jane were in good health – 'This Edinburgh is getting more agreable to me, growing more and more a sort of home.'[33]

Among the minor literary figures Carlyle was now meeting was George Moir, who visited them at Comely Bank, author of *Wallenstein* and *The 30 Years' War* (1827 and 1828), 'a small clear man; but very modest and will learn much, being honest and open'. They met again at Sir William Hamilton's, and grew closer, 'a kind, lively, very ingenious *Small*'.[34]

Quincey was there, under the weather from worries and opium, and Hamilton's brother the Captain, or 'Cyril Thornton', original of *Blackwood's* 'Ensign O'Doherty', 'an exceedingly gentle and wholesome man', with a stammer. The rest of the party Carlyle wrote off as 'German Tourists, and Editorial gentlemen; and babes and sucklings . . .'

The party continued to the small hours, and Carlyle, always on a restricted diet, and 'Thornton' between them 'drank half a glass of claret and supped on one potatoe each'. He concludes rather patronisingly that the endless talk was mostly 'of the smallest', but 'innocent to a degree', and that 'on the whole the literary society of Edinburgh may be about as good as any other literary society' – of which at this stage Carlyle had actually experienced very little.[35]

Jeffrey's overtaxed life prevented them from meeting more than once a month, while Wilson seemed to shrink from everyone, and besides had been ill for some weeks and was contemplating a trip to Switzerland with De Quincey. The latter, on whom Carlyle had just called, was predictably still in bed, his 'dirty very wicked looking' landlady pointing out that he never got up until 5 in the afternoon.[36]

The Goethe medals, two of them intended for Scott, at last arrived in April, on which Carlyle wrote Scott a suitable adulatory letter begging that he might deliver them to his 'native sovereign' in person. He had no reply. Another of them he hoped to present to Lockhart. He wrote to Goethe at some length recording the growing popularity in Britain for German literature and its reviews in the various journals – notably one by himself and one by Jeffrey, and others by Scott and George Moir.[37]

In April the 28-year-old barrister Thomas Babington Macaulay met Jeffrey during a visit to Edinburgh, and was soon adding his own assessment of him. After his first *Review* article in 1825 he had soon become one of its chief props.

Curiously enough he describes Jeffrey rather as many people described Scott: 'He has 20 faces . . . infinitely more unlike to each other than those of near relatives often are', and like Scott, in repose showed nothing of his power. 'But as soon as he is interested, and opens his eyes upon you, the change is like magic. There is a flash in his glance, a violent contortion in his frown, an exquisite horror in his sneer, a sweetness and brilliancy in his smile . . . The mere outline of his face is insignificant. The expression is everything.' Similarly his voice, chameleon-like in mimicry and imitative ability, could vary between broad Scots, the 'snappish and quick', or 'rotundity and mellowness'.

Macaulay was impressed by Jeffrey's family affection, his way of every few minutes dropping a caress or a loving word on wife or daughter. Both accompanied him on his travels, and just as he was full of tenderness to them, they in turn idolised him. As for his work habits, he would get up only when he had to, and go to bed when he could no longer keep awake. He would settle to work anywhere, as much in the drawing-room or his wife's 'boudoir' as in his own study, whether working on briefs or his *Review* articles.

This varied habit was of a piece with his range of conversation, from (Macaulay noted) the flat to whimsical brilliance and strong prejudice. Among these prejudices were blue-stockings, coteries, ladies' albums filled with flattery, and 'all the other nauseous tricks of the Sewards, Hayleys, and Sothebys'. And although he often complained of ill-health, Macaulay was almost deceived into suspecting hypochondria, for 'I really think that he is, on the whole, the youngest looking man of 50 [actually 55] that I know, at least when he is animated.' In this, appearances were deceptive.[38]

In 1827 Jeffrey and his family had moved from George Street to 24 Moray Place, to live there for the rest of his life. The magnificent house on the new Moray estate was part of the still unfinished circus-like octagon which was not completed until the 1840s, and in Macaulay's eyes was equal in grandeur to Grosvenor Square in London.

It was a happy time; a time before changes set in. Henry Cockburn records Jeffrey's contentment at Craigcrook, dozing on the sofa, reading novels and poetry beside a cheerful log fire, long, lounging breakfasts with no 'feverish anticipations of to-morrow's battles'; Charley in her early teens growing and blooming, already as tall as her diminutive father, a pet thrush and a parrot to look after, and Charlotte herself losing her awkwardness enough to enjoy entertaining more than formerly. Meanwhile Jeffrey's practice was flourishing, and even the unavoidable London legal visits could be lightened by reunions with friends.[39]

But the changes were in the air. Tracheitis was now a constant problem for Jeffrey,[40] and the *Edinburgh Review* was becoming another. Already at the start of 1825 Jeffrey was finding that he needed to reduce *Review* work so as not to affect his legal commitments, and was asking John Allen to look out for clever young writers in London. 'The original supporters of the work are getting old, and either too busy, or too stupid, to go on comfortably, and here the young men are mostly Tories.'[41]

The Carlyles were now planning removal to Craigenputtock, with all that that entailed. It was completed at Whitsun 1828. Jeffrey, calling before their departure, 'looking cheery as ever' and being presented with one of the Goethe medals, promised to visit, though strongly disapproving of their leaving Edinburgh. They spent their last two nights with him, 'surely one of the kindest little men', and Carlyle owed him articles on Tasso and Lockhart's *Life of Burns*, but couldn't get down to them. He concealed his disappointment over Scott's silence with the excuse that he might be 'a busy or uncourteous man'.[42]

The Jeffreys first visited them in October, 'a fairy time', despite their initial trepidation, and despite rain and mud. According to Jane, Jeffrey amused himself 'in the simplest manner: he talked – talked from morning till night, nay till morning again'.[43]

On another visit, one night, 'what with mimicry of speakers, what with other cleverness and sprightliness, he was the most brilliantly amusing creature I have ever chanced to see'. It was almost the last time they were to meet in this state of unalloyed admiration.[44]

Apart from brief Edinburgh visits they remained at Craigenputtock until Carlyle removed to London in 1831. In this way they missed the Burke and Hare sensation and the typhus epidemic. They were concerned over the 'Catholic Question', and Carlyle was one of only three in their parish who refused to sign the petition against emancipation. They also missed the death of King George IV in June 1830, an event ignored in Carlyle's correspondence (though the following year he did by chance, when in London, happen to be by for the Coronation Procession of William IV). Relations with Jeffrey were harmonious, except for Carlyle's annoyance at Jeffrey's slashing of his Burns article.

But he was in an intellectual desert; he needed books – the *Quarterly*, the *Westminster*, either series of *Tales of a Grandfather*, begged from a neighbour visiting Edinburgh. In August 1829 they met the Jeffreys in Dumfries on their way to London, and promised to visit them on the return to Edinburgh in a few weeks.[45]

On this visit, in October, which left them weary with 'racketting and rioting', they were treated almost like lions, and Jane confessed that she liked it as much as she had at sixteen, 'and I cried as much at leaving it', happy though they were to be home again. Carlyle wrote to Wilson inviting him for Christmas, *as promised*, luring him with the ease of transport; but he did not come.[46]

With the new Wellington Government in April 1828, Jeffrey's English friends, including Smith, were urging him to seek a judgeship, though he confessed half-jokingly to Cockburn that he hankered rather after the 'dignified ease of a Baron of Exchequer', a profitable sinecure. The role of editor was to some extent as Lockhart also viewed it – a social stigma, which Jeffrey, although he always dealt with 'gentlemen' and avoided any 'tradesman-like' taint, suspected stood more in the way of so high a legal honour than did his politics.[47]

In 1829 the offer of advancement came, when the Dean of Faculty Sir James Wellwood Moncreiff, son of Sir Henry (who had died in 1827), became a judge as Lord Moncreiff. The Deanship, Scotland's highest legal honorary post, was theoretically a one-year office, but as a Dean was rarely superseded it often proved to be for life. To take it on would mean resigning the *Review* editorship, which despite anxieties over its current state Jeffrey was naturally reluctant to do; but the only competitor was the Solicitor-General, John Hope, who magnanimously withdrew, leaving the field open. On 2 July Jeffrey was unanimously elected Dean, with a kind speech in his favour from Hope, seconded by Cockburn.

It was to their credit that the Faculty elected this rampant Whig who was all but identified with the *Edinburgh Review,* and his election was patently a result of his popularity and his literary and professional distinction. It 'showed the improvement of public opinion', Cockburn approvingly observed, 'and the softening of party hatred'.[48]

Jeffrey's last issue of the *Review* was accordingly for June 1829, briefly pre-dating his election; and it was almost his last as contributor, for he subsequently produced only three or four papers. In the twenty-seven years since 1802 he had written 201 essays, many unsigned but easily recognisable, embracing almost every imaginable subject. Over those years the journal's attitude had scarcely budged, so that in the view of his enemies its 'errors' were still entrenched. Almost never did Jeffrey deign to reply in a later issue to the stream of enraged letters and pamphlets that poured from the pens of its critics.

He had always set out to find new authors, suggested subjects and given them useful advice on how to satisfy public taste, occasionally rejecting or, to their greater chagrin, editing their work or modifying extremes. Indeed, except during his time in America, he revised and edited every issue. His was always the strongest influence on the paper, and it was never to scale the same heights again.

Further, during the more than quarter-century of its existence the *Edinburgh Review* had substantially influenced public opinion, and helped to mitigate intolerance. When the talented young group had first started, the Government's 'dread of the people' since the French Revolution was still strong, change or possible improvement was strongly resisted, religious intolerance was rife and all Dissenters were crippled in career and even lifestyle. Ignorance among the lower orders was preferred by the authorities to the supposed dangers of education; criminals and lunatics were barbarously treated; learning was almost static; and new subjects like geology and political economy were in their infancy.

In little over a generation all these attitudes had been modified or even changed; religious toleration was taking over, the slave trade was ended, education of the masses was actively considered, other learning was widening horizons, and even electoral reform was no longer universally seen as the precursor of revolution. For much of this new and more liberal approach, the invigorating air that blew from the *Edinburgh Review* may be thanked.[49]

Jeffrey's successor as editor, fifty-three years younger than himself, was Macvey Napier,[50] who had studied at both Edinburgh and Glasgow Universities, had known Archibald Constable since 1798, become librarian to the Writers to the Signet in 1805 and between 1814 and 1824 edited the supplement to the *Encyclopaedia's* sixth edition. In 1827 he had begun editing its seventh edition, and since 1824 had been Edinburgh's first Professor of Conveyancing. His qualifications seemed indeed impeccable. All that was lacking was the personality which could in any way rival Jeffrey.

If Jeffrey fancied that release from the *Review*'s quarterly burden would free him for a more restful life, he was to be undeceived. In December 1830 under a new Whig Government he was appointed Lord Advocate, Scotland's most powerful office, and his next step voluntarily or involuntarily, was made towards the demands of public life.

51
STAGES OF FRIENDSHIP: JEFFREY, CARLYLE

'Jeffrey has been here with his adjectives, who always travel with him.'

Sydney Smith to Lady Holland, 6 Nov. 1827, Nowell C. Smith (ed.), *The Letters of Sydney Smith*, 2 vols, Oxford, 1953, II.472

'But for the restraint of the Whigs . . . revolution would unquestionably have broken out . . . [on Lord Grey's resignation] the immediate presence of a great popular crisis . . . terrible silence – nothing but grave looks and orderly public proceedings, unconquerable resolution . . . the lurid and sulphury feeling of a coming storm.'

Journal of Henry Cockburn 1831–1834, 22 May 1832, Edinburgh, 1874, 29

'The regeneration of Scotland is now secured! . . . The Tory party, as such, is extinguished . . . In a few years the Whigs will be the Tories, and the Radicals the Whigs.'

Ibid., 6 Aug. 1832

'The victory which it celebrated was not one of blood . . . the victory of truth and morality gained over corruption and misrule . . . a permanent and instructive lesson to futurity.'

W. Millar (ed.), *An Account of the Edinburgh Reform Jubilee*, celebrated 10 August 1832, Edinburgh, 1832

Carlyle's affection for Jeffrey seemed as warm as ever. Throughout the winter of 1829–30 they corresponded, for example, discussing the new *Review* under Napier, which included Hamilton's piece on Victor Cousin, though as Carlyle wrote to Napier, despite its considerable 'metaphysical reading and meditation' it would prove unintelligible to many 'English minds' – 'full of subtle schoolman logic'.[1]

Jeffrey was begging him to return to Edinburgh and not despise his 'fellow scribblers'. Carlyle in turn said he wanted to earn £100 from his writing, and Jeffrey countered by offering it out of his own income. To this Carlyle's reply, dictated by pride, was that under 'Republican Equality' each man must live on his own resources.[2] But he felt due gratitude.

John Carlyle was now back from Europe and settled in London, at Judd Place off the New Road, and Thomas passed on Jeffrey's request that, when he came to London at the end of April, John call and introduce himself. 'One of the daintiest, kindliest, best little men you ever set eyes on,' Carlyle wrote to his brother, 'a perfect jewel of a man.'[3] As it turned out Jeffrey forestalled him by getting his address from Procter, and John was invited to visit. He in turn liked both Jeffrey and his wife, and was given a letter to the surgeon and neurologist Charles Bell, who was now at the London University.

Carlyle was working on a four-volume anthology of German authors, but his proposal for a collection of pieces for the *Edinburgh* and the *Foreign Review* was turned down by both. The Jeffreys were promised for another Craigenputtock visit, and turned up at short notice in September. As Dean of Faculty Jeffrey seemed neither well nor happy, but 'we all like him even better than we did. He is the most sparkling pleasant little fellow I ever saw in life' – and here Carlyle makes a comparison with Goldoni, 'or Southern Comic Minstrel', ultimately seen as more criticism than praise.[4]

He told his mother (28 September) that he was 'more than usually friendly and interesting', and they all parted with 'real regret', though hoping that next year Jeffrey would come on his own, 'a much more commodious method'. He added, 'I reckon him one of the best persons that I have ever seen; also that he is growing "sadder and wiser" as he increases in years.'[5]

A later return visit to Craigcrook by the Carlyles proved to last '*at least* a week too long': Jeffrey's health was beginning to fail, he slept badly and stayed up till all hours, and every evening the two men fell into 'sharp fencing-bouts', for the first time openly showing their 'radical incompatibility' over most subjects. 'You are so dreadfully in earnest!' Jeffrey would tell the humourless Carlyle, and Carlyle penitently admitted later to being, on his side, 'far too frank . . . about moral matters'. He knew he could not disagree diplomatically, or without risking offence.

According to Carlyle Jeffrey at last realised that 'I *could* not be "converted", and that I was of thoughtlessly rugged rustic ways, and faultily irreverent', while Carlyle saw Jeffrey as lacking true insight into literature, or any other serious subject: 'most gifted, prompt, ingenious . . . essentially a *Dramatic* Genius' but 'never a deeply serious man'. To Jeffrey it became clear that Carlyle was in sympathy with the *Blackwood's* opposition style, 'against the old excessive Edinburgh Hero-worship'. Carlyle partly blamed Jeffrey's legal career – always speaking as if having to convince a jury – and his eventual entry into politics, though never entering deeply into Jeffrey's own disturbance at the change. Meanwhile 'stormy sittings', as Mrs Jeffrey called them, were more frequent, with Carlyle increasingly 'obstinate and rugged'.[6]

But they still kept up a busy correspondence, and Jeffrey three times offered Carlyle a £100 annuity, which Carlyle, with his inflexible rule of 'Republican Equality', declined handsomely but conclusively. Yet Jeffrey was not rich. He was generous. (Carlyle did once borrow £100, but paid it back in weeks.[7])

Jeffrey took Carlyle's work with him to offer to Longman's via Moir, as a riposte to Moir's publishing 'a long, unasked, abusive and almost ill-bred criticism'. After Carlyle had overcome his first fury, he reflected on Moir's real kindness, 'sufferings and even miseries', and decided it had been written 'only in a sad fit of depression'; so he sent a friendly letter and endeavoured to be kind. He also recalled that Moir had perhaps not one true friend.[8]

Napier had co-opted Carlyle anew for the *Review*, and vexed him by asking for an article on the heretic fifteenth-century priest William Taylor, 'a wretched Atheist and Philistine'; he begged to be given an English subject for the future. No matter what, however, he still found 'no Periodical so steady . . . the salary fair, the Politics respectable'. Fraser's, by contrast, paid worst of all. He suggested to Napier that his brother John might also contribute.[9]

As legal adviser to the Crown the Lord Advocate was Scotland's leading legal officer, and as there was no Scottish Secretary, and Scottish affairs were little understood at Westminster, he had to undertake its general business. Francis Horner had long ago complained that, what with having to manage elections, General Assemblies, town councils and so on, and manage criminal business and prosecutions, the Lord Advocate was 'no better than a sub-clerk in the Treasury'; he was further responsible to the parties as well as to the Government, responsible for measures whether supported or opposed, and whether or not he was familiar with the subjects.[10] In the generation since Horner's dictum (1804) Scottish business had greatly increased, yet the fifty-three MPs found their requests and complaints largely ignored, and the Government, which had no desire (or knowledge) to take over the work, should at least have increased the authority of the Lord Advocate. Much later, in August 1832, Lord Grey did agree to relieve Jeffrey of his political duties and limit the job to legal matters. He did not do so.[11]

Although in power and influence equivalent to England's Attorney-General, the Lord Advocate was poorly paid, at most £3000 a year, and with no possible further rise in the scale except to a judgeship. Furthermore, the office required a seat in Parliament, and this, in the period from his appointment in December 1830 to May 1832 with the passing of the Reform Bill, cost Jeffrey £10,000; it also required his living so much in London that his legal practice began to be affected. A year after taking office Jeffrey, believing that no-one ought to serve as Dean of Faculty-cum-Solicitor General-cum Lord Advocate, in December 1831 resigned the Deanship to Charles Hope.[12]

Leaving his beloved Edinburgh and especially Craigcrook was to Jeffrey a sad blow, particularly during the summer when he had to stay in London initiating policy and undertaking affairs of which he had no previous experience. Only his sense of duty prevailed, and he saw little compensation in the trappings, 'glorious in a flounced silk gown, and long cravat . . . every day in a wig, and most days with buckles on my shoes!' He did reflect that his father, who had predicted a disastrous career for him because of his Whig leanings, would surely have been proud.[13]

The tangled events leading up to the passing of the Parliamentary Reform Bill were now being set in motion. The accession of the new King William IV having necessitated a General Election, the Prime Minister, the Duke of Wellington, who had succeeded Lord Goderich in 1828, made an irrevocable statement of admiration of the British Constitution. This led to a final split in the Tory party by the Canningites, who were inclined towards reform. Meanwhile, now that the issue of Catholic Emancipation was won, the Whigs were able to concentrate on other reforms, and to crown all the July Revolution in France, which finally overthrew Charles X and established a thoroughly bourgeois monarchy by constitutional means, seemed a significant precedent for change in Britain.

In December 1830 at the General Election the Duke lost office, and three days later Lord Grey formed a joint Whig/Tory Reform ministry, which included not only Brougham – who was given a peerage – but three Canningite peers, Lords Melbourne, Palmerston and Stanley. A committee was appointed to draft a Reform Bill.

Henry Cockburn expressed himself overcome by the latest appointments, the taking over of Lord Grey as Prime Minister and all the events of these miraculous days.

> Jeffrey . . . who all the powers of the bar and bench conspired to prevent being made *Collector of Decisions*, Lord Advocate of Scotland! Brougham, long the horror of the respectable, Chancellor of England! both by their genius and principles alone! Grey . . . realising, in power, all the splendid visions of his youth! Toryism, with its narrowness and abuses, prostrate. Whigism no longer the watch word of a faction but expanded into the public creed! Government by patronage superseded . . . The last links of the Scotch feudal chain dropping off . . .[14]

It was Lord Grey who appointed Jeffrey Lord Advocate, thus handing over Tory-ruled Scotland to the Whigs. In January 1831 – one of the most severe Januarys on record, in which the driver and guard of the Edinburgh coach both died of exposure in the snow – Jeffrey stood for Parliament for the Forfar burghs. This proved a riotous affair, whose sole reason for violence was that the mob supported his rival candidate Captain Ogilvy, shouting 'There's Jeffrey – murder him – kill him!', and he was generally hustled. The rumour that they tore his clothes proved to apply to the Provost of Perth.[15]

Sydney Smith, now a Prebend at Bristol, and spending his annual statutory residence there, was jubilant over the irony of seeing 'all the Edinburgh Reviewers in office', and equally excited at the drama of the diminutive Jeffrey's election. 'They say he fought like a Lyon, and would have been killed had he been more visible, but that several people struck at him who could see nothing and so battered infinite space instead of the Advocate.'[16]

In the end there proved to be a legal hitch, the Dundee vote was declared invalid, and Jeffrey was at once unseated, though allowed to take his place pending judgment. He was instead elected for Malton in Yorkshire, surrendered to him by Lord Fitzwilliam (April 1831), having first been persuaded reluctantly and unsuccessfully to stand for Edinburgh. Here his opponent was the sitting member William Dundas, son of Lord Arniston the younger, who had the Council's support though all public bodies petitioned for Jeffrey. On 3 May Edinburgh Council elected Dundas by seventeen votes to fourteen, 'the last general election', says Cockburn, 'at which any Scotch town-council had it in its power to perform the elective farce'.[17]

This election provoked mobs and riots, when Professor Robert Christison, who seemed to get his fingers into many a pie, served as a captain of a company of special constables, of whom three hundred 'active, able-bodied, young' men were raised – armed only with sticks.[18]

Jeffrey, filled with melancholy, had to leave behind his beloved wife and daughter. And then, after only weeks, the new Parliament was dissolved.

Once having reached London from his Malton constituency, Jeffrey, pale and thin, was joined by his family. Mrs Montagu, having heard so much about him, now meeting him for the first time was greatly surprised. 'Instead of sharp flashing eyes, I found mild and reflecting ones, and a neatness and composure of person, with a business air, which reminded me more of professional habits, than of literature.' She saw in him an 'unpretending goodness, and natural warmth', which kept him from the dangers of success. She liked Mrs Jeffrey too, perhaps in time more than her husband. In some ways Mrs Montagu, because not emotionally involved, was more discerning about Jeffrey than Carlyle, for all his razor-sharp perception, was to prove.[19]

During the freezing January weather Carlyle, kept indoors, appropriately redrafted some 'Thoughts on Clothes' – what was to become *Sartor Resartus.*

In August, when he had to go to London to negotiate its publication he lost no time in leaving a card at Jeffrey's house. A few days later he breakfasted with them, 'all very kind', and Jeffrey came in wearing a yellow nightgown, 'greyish face, clear roguish eyes', and said to his daughter, 'Why Charly I've got cholera I believe'. He had not, luckily, though plenty of people had already.[20]

Before leaving for London Carlyle had drafted and been a co-signatory to a letter sent to Goethe for his birthday and signed by '15 English friends', including John Carlyle, Maginn, George Moir, Wilson, Scott, Lockhart, Southey, Wordsworth and Bryan Procter. While in the metropolis Carlyle consulted Jeffrey about his latest, *Teufelsdreck*, and its problems. Jeffrey feared that the best likely offer would be a small edition by Longman.[21] But meetings, apart from the occasional breakfast, were limited to brief chats.

Jeffrey was naturally immersed in the business of the Bill. He had sent the Carlyles a copy of his hour-and-three-quarter-long speech on the First Reading in March. They had been much concerned over 'what he would say', fearing that because of his light voice and now poor health he might not cut much of a figure in the House. Cam Hobhouse reckoned that 'his fluency and argumentative powers were admirable; but he was too quick and too close for a popular assembly such as our House of Commons'. John Allen thought it 'logical in reasoning and happy in illustration', but not well heard because of his weak voice; also it 'had at times too much the appearance of a lecturer, and too little of the sharpness of the debater'.[22]

During the Reform agitation Alexander Somerville, garden labourer at Dickson's Nurseries at Inverleith, and three fellow-workers, would combine to buy a tri-weekly Whig paper the *Caledonian Mercury* – half-price, a day late. In a packed bothy Somerville read aloud Lord John Russell's 'great speech' of 1 March to the other gardeners, who keenly followed the ups and downs of the debate, receiving the King's dissolution of Parliament with great enthusiasm.[23]

The Bill was roundly rejected and another election followed. Edinburgh's thirty-three members of the Town Council chose Dundas in the teeth of a petition for Jeffrey by most of the city's adult population (Somerville among them). 'Terrible riots ensued.'

The passing of the Bill's second Reading, by a majority of one, was greeted with a combination of illuminations, riots, broken window-glass, and bell-ringing. The Lord Provost and anti-Reform corporation held out against the request to illuminate until the atmosphere became threatening, too late to publicise their capitulation: his house in Abercromby Place was attacked by mobs rioting through Queen Street, Moray Place and the squares. Later they threatened to throw him over North Bridge – a popular form of revenge – and he had to take refuge in a Leith Street shop.

Once the Whigs were re-elected with an increased majority, the Reform Bill was re-introduced, passing safely through the Lower House. Jeffrey was seriously concerned at the prospect of revolution – as he saw it – should the Lords overturn it. 'There will be rick-burning I imagine as last winter . . .'[24]

Sydney Smith, who could not rest until he saw Jeffrey made a judge, had been singing his praises to Lady Grey for at least two years. Before they had met him he was urging his merits as 'a man of rare talent and unbending integrity, who has been honest even in Scotland', and having exhorted him to speak on the Bill in Parliament he commended him further to the lady: 'Pray perceive his worth and talents piercing through his bad manner.'[25]

Carlyle seems to have been almost impervious to the demands the campaign made on Jeffrey. As he had half suspected, Longmans turned down his 'Literary History', and he thought Jeffrey's reactions disappointing. 'He really has no leisure to think of anything but his politics, so that I never get the smallest private talk with him. Indeed, how can he help me?'[26] The least reflection would have shown that Jeffrey could no longer help any literary friend as he had when he was his own man. His own man he no longer was, and few regretted it more than himself.

John Carlyle was doing rather better, now appointed 'Travelling Physician' to the Countess of Clare, a great invalid who was bound for Italy, with a salary of 300 guineas, all found, to start on 1 October.[27]

At the end of August 1831 (shortly after meeting Charles Lamb, for whom he always professed profound disgust and contempt) Carlyle managed a brief talk with 'the Duke of Craigcrook', as he liked to call Jeffrey. 'The poor little dear is so hurried that he cannot help it', but he promised to look carefully at his manuscript. This was another disappointment, disillusionment even, though so far not openly expressed. He and John did visit the House to see 'the poor little Darling, with a grey wig on it, and queer costie with bugles or buttons on the cuffs' – in a foreign country and speaking to complete strangers.[28]

In writing to Jane, Carlyle confessed a shamefaced criticism of Jeffrey as guilty of 'frivolous Gigmanity' (a rather tiresome personal term of abuse), having now realised that their ways could not lie together. Jeffrey was seen as to blame for no longer being able to devote time to furthering Carlyle's career . . . yet he could see that he was in danger of becoming too censorious. It was that he could not forgive Jeffrey for falling into politics, being unable to see that politics had grabbed him, not vice versa. 'Surely there is no magnetism in the Duke; but only an Electricity for collecting *Straws*; his environment here is as stupid fully as it was in Edinr.'[29]

But he was rightly concerned to find Jeffrey ill with anal fistula, an old complaint for which in October he had to be operated on – and admitted that his was 'a villanous life'. Yet the day after Carlyle's visit (24 September) Jeffrey was speaking on the Reform Bill in the House. A few days later Carlyle was joined in London by Jane.[30]

October was a cruel month, Jeffrey ill and in great pain, Jane ill after her travels, and Carlyle's father slowly dying, though he survived until January

(Carlyle received his last letter from him late in September). In Edinburgh people were dying of typhus, and in London the spread of cholera was a serious threat. And to popular fury the Lords rejected the Reform Bill.

After serious riots throughout the country, a fresh Bill was introduced early in 1832, which this time the Lords intended to defeat by means of wrecking amendments. Faced with the alternative choice of flooding the Lords with new supporting peers, Lord Grey offered his resignation, the King accepted, and sent for Wellington.

Popular outrage was now so violent that civil war was feared, Wellington warned the King that in this situation the country was ungovernable, Grey and Brougham were called but refused office unless the King agreed to create peers, and the Lords gave way.

At the height of the campaign there were frequent demonstrations of the popular will, accompanied by prophecies of doom from the Tory old stagers. Charles Kirkpatrick Sharpe reported to Scott on 9 April on 'a shameful scene . . . the folly, or roguery, of the provost was at the bottom of all. The mob consisted of imps remote from manhood and young jades from the back of the middens and the Cowgate. Their shrill screams denoted their age. For two hours the whole town was at the mercy of these monsters', and for the first time that he could recall there was 'not a single dragoon at Piershill', nor would the provost have called them out. Houses were illuminated in the usual way, to which by degrees Sharpe's mother capitulated. 'For my own part,' he rages, 'had the fortress been mine, every pane of glass should have perished.'[31]

A few days later huge crowds gathered outside the General Newspaper and Advertising Office in St Andrew Square to await the express bringing the result of the Second Reading division. At 7 o'clock a shout went up to clear the way as a chariot drove up, which gathered more crowds as it crossed the bridges, bearing an Extraordinary Express from the proprietors of *The Sun* in London. It had by 'unparalleled exertion' completed the journey in just thirty-six hours, the House having risen only at 7 the previous morning. The majority vote was announced to the crowd, and a great cheer went up.

An hour and a half later an express from the *True Sun* arrived at Mr Somerville's office in Clyde Street with the account of the debate.[32]

The next anxiety was whether the Lords would again defeat the Bill. Edinburgh's Reform Committee called a public meeting for Tuesday, 24 April in the King's Park to discuss resolutions and a petition to the Lords, and a memorial on the subject to Lord Grey.

This became a grand turn-out by the Trades, who decided to march in procession with banners, emblems and bands when they had them. Mostly young and neatly dressed, they assembled in the Meadows at noon, and as the long procession wound its way through the High Street and Canongate some 50,000 people in holiday clothes had turned out to watch.

At the hustings they were met by Sir John Dalrymple (who had convened the gathering), Sir James Gibson Craig, Sir Thomas Dick Lauder and other liberal-minded gentlemen. Sir Thomas led off by proposing a cheer 'to our friends of the working classes'; John Archibald Murray, a 'staunch reformer', was appointed chairman, begging them not to remove their hats to him, and raising another cheer by disclaiming that Scottish public meetings always ended in riots and bloodshed. Long speeches ended in the desired resolutions, the crowd drew Dick Lauder's carriage back to Princes Street, and an orderly procession of the Trades marched to the Lord Provost's in Moray Place to thank him for consent to the meeting. With more cheers as they passed the Lord Advocate's, they continued up the Mound to disperse at the North Bridge.[33]

That was the official newspaper account. Charles Sharpe gave a more jaundiced description. 'After some of our sourest Whigs had ranted their souls out to all the rubbish which loads the earth in the King's Park, a Sir Something, in the first place, was hauled along the street in a rusty open carriage, standing bolt-upright and bareheaded, bowing to the mob and to the mail-coaches as they passed . . . In the coach with him were three fat vulgar-looking women, dressed like the Cowgate roupwives at a christening.' Sometimes he fell over with the jolting of the coach.

'After this came a long procession of the trades, as they are called, of Athens, with every sort of banner and wild beast imaginable – beavers on the end of poles, reform, Adam and Eve, and a huge pair of horns high above the rest' – which apparently offended the prudery of some. The accompanying music was 'borrowed from the caravan of wild beasts', 'our new lawgivers' all got drunk, and Sharpe even blamed three new cholera cases of the day on the procession.[34]

Public opinion now prevailed, the Lords did not oppose, and the Bill finally passed in June 1832.

'The Whig Ministry is all out and gone to the Devil, Reform Bill and all . . . For us here it is little more than a matter of amusement,' wrote Carlyle rather inaccurately to John, now in Naples. He adds casually that they have been in touch with Jeffrey only once, briefly. 'For him I rejoice in this revolution of the wheel.'[35]

'What oceans of absurdity and nonsense will the new liberties of Scotland disclose!' wrote Sydney Smith. 'Yet this is better than the old infamous jobbing, and the foolocracy under which it has so long laboured . . . Pray take care that Jeffrey is the first judge. I have that much at heart.'[36] This further step did not happen until 1834.

Jeffrey himself was not in rejoicing mood. The Act once passed, he felt depressed, with 'a sense of the littleness and vanity even of those great contentions'. Longing to go home, he was kept in London to move a request to appoint an interim Sheriff of Selkirk in place of Sir Walter Scott, who was now too ill – indeed on the point of death – to serve under the Act or to appoint a substitute.

Once Parliament adjourned, in mid-August, he was free to be in Scotland until it met again the following February. But he had to be re-elected for the reformed Parliament. He was nominated for Edinburgh and shortly afterwards elected in December, he and his fellow-member the banker James Abercromby securing nearly 8000 votes between them. 'All men are disappointed in him a little,' pronounced Carlyle glibly, 'but remember his *past* services.'[37]

Meanwhile Wilson, who had been 'loud in the political way', was cruising along the south coast on his way to Cork, joined apparently by chance by Basil Hall.[38]

Jeffrey returned to London in a better frame of mind, knowing he had many friends there and now having fewer official problems. With him were his wife and daughter, servants, his pet parrot in a large cage, and a small dog named Witch in a soft travelling basket. Jeffrey's fondness for domestic pets was the source of much friendly banter and complaints that 'the hearth-rug and the sofa were seldom free'.

But he wrote to Cockburn when his entourage had got as far as Stevenage, 'I left you all more sadly this time . . . partly because I could not but feel how fast the tide of life is ebbing away from us.'[39] His tide had years to ebb yet, but it was now never free from ill-health. On arrival in London he was ill with apparent debility and tracheitis trouble for more than two months, 'nearly voiceless'.[40]

Carlyle meanwhile had started a paper on Luther for the *Review*, was still struggling with another, 'Characteristics', and had several commissions on the go. He met Lamb again, more disgusted than ever, and also met James Hogg, now being somewhat lionised in London. Leigh Hunt he met and liked. In March he and Jane left London, by coach for Liverpool, and thence by steamer to Dumfriesshire, where Carlyle received a letter telling of Goethe's death a few days earlier.[41]

He had to write on Byron, whom he dismissed as theatrical, insincere, morally bad, 'a huge sulky dandy . . . I love him not, I owe him nothing . . .' except a grudging pity.[42]

Back at Craigenputtock, they were not to return to Edinburgh until early January (1833). They were now able to keep a couple of horses and go riding together. Edward Irving had been expelled from his church by the General Assembly that May, and had taken to preaching in the fields bordering London. They hardly heard from Jeffrey. In the summer Scott, brought back dying from Italy, had been struck down in London by his final illness, was unconscious, and at that time hardly expected to reach Scotland.

Scott's death passed unrecorded by Carlyle, who probably felt sore and refused Fraser's offer to write on him, disliking 'obituary kind of work'. He was more concerned over the cooling off with Jeffrey, with whom his relationship had 'long been visibly to me, a rather fruitless one. His world is not our world; he dwells in the glitter of saloon chandeliers, walking in the vain show of Parliamentaring and Gigmanity, which also he feels to be vain.' Carlyle did express sympathy over this, though not enough, and he sensed, if rather over-stating it, that Jeffrey was 'declining in the world's grace, and knows as well as the world that his Political career has proved a nonentity'.[43]

52

DE QUINCEY AND SOME LESSER LUMINARIES

'I am an acquaintance almost a friend of – The Opium Eater's! Poor Dequincey! He is essentially a gentle and genial little soul, and only . . . the Iety [egotism] is strong and both together sometimes overset his balance.'

Thomas Carlyle to Mrs Montagu, *The Collected Letters of Thomas and Jane Welsh Carlyle*, IV.280, 20 November 1827

'[Basil Hall], that curious fellow, who takes charge of everyone's business without neglecting his own . . .'

Sir Walter Scott on Basil Hall, quoted in *Archibald Constable and his Literary Correspondents*, II.471

'[Lockhart] was a mischievous Oxford puppy, for whom I was terrified, dancing after the young ladies, and drawing caricatures of every one.'

Douglas S. Mack (ed.), James Hogg, *Memoir of the Author's Life*, Edinburgh, 1972, 75–6

'[William Dunlop, 'my countryman', castigates Hogg] for pestering us with fourpenny papers, an' daft shilly shally songs, an' bletherin' an' speaking in the Forum, an' yet had stuff in you to produce a thing like this' *[The Queen's Wake]*

Memorials of James Hogg, the Ettrick Shepherd, edited by his daughter Mrs Garden, 2nd edn, 1887, 57–8

'A city of palaces, as it is now sometimes called . . . But all these splendid buildings are of trivial import compared with the mass of intellect and science which had . . . grown up to such a height as to rival, and perhaps to outstrip, every other city in the world.' (1823)

Montague Weekley (ed.), *A Memoir of Thomas Bewick, written by himself*, London, Cresset Press, 1961, 182

Thomas De Quincey, since his attempt to settle in Edinburgh in 1820, had limped from article to article and magazine to magazine, claiming he was now opium-free (under control, to be exact), but he was never creditor-free. By 1825 he was also being pursued by Wilson, now settled in his new Gloucester Place house and urging De Quincey to send 'a due contribution, which must be at the London publishers' by the New Year, luring him with the offer 'till Doomsday' of 50 guineas a year for 100 pages, 'easily written'. Soon his urging is desperate, as the press is stopped on De Quincey's account. And incidentally, Wilson needs his advice for his own review for the first *Quarterly* issue.[1]

De Quincey actually produced a series for *Blackwood's* on German writers, and continued it for two years – along with his 'Murder considered as one of the Fine Arts' late in 1827. This brought him to Edinburgh again in 1826, where at first he lived in the 'wretched lodgings' where Carlyle saw him.

One day when he visited Wilson at Gloucester Place, the weather being stormy, he stayed on. And on. Wilson invited him to stay over, a room was made up – and De Quincey became a fixture for nearly a year.

In one way he gave the household little trouble, rarely appearing at family meals and preferring to eat very simply in his room, but at some odd hour, sleeping late, or in a drug-induced stupor, and turning night into day. His eating habits, however, were a burden on Betty, the servant who prepared his meals.

She reported to him daily and received his courtly instructions as if he were addressing a duchess. 'Owing to dyspepsia affecting my system, and the possibility of any additional disarrangement of the stomach taking place, consequences incalculably distressing would arise . . . if you do not remember to cut the mutton in a diagonal rather than in a longitudinal form.' (So Wilson's daughter records a speech at which she could hardly have been present.)

His diet was invariable, the slice of mutton cut from the loin, boiled rice, coffee and milk. 'The bodie has an awfu' sicht of words,' Betty complained: her master would have ordered a whole dinner with a mere wave of consent, but 'here's a' this claver aboot a bit mutton nae bigger than a prin'. She was sure De Quincey, whom she regarded as a genius, would make a fine preacher, 'though I'm thinkin' a hantle o' the folk wouldna ken what he was driving at'.[2]

The ounce of laudanum which De Quincey daily swallowed left him prostrated in the mornings, when he might be found lying senseless in front of the (doubtless now dead) fire with his head on a book, arms crossed on his breast. He was accordingly scintillating late at night and into the small hours, and Wilson from time to time arranged supper parties to coincide with his guest's time of greatest brilliance and eloquent charm.[3]

One who often met De Quincey at Wilson's was Thomas Tod Stoddart, son of a distinguished naval officer and born and educated in Edinburgh. He was a minor writer who met many other writers, and as a youth had been much encouraged by Wilson, his friend for nearly fifty years. He described De Quincey as 'the most fluent conversationalist and subtlest logician of his day'. Already he seemed 'aged-looking' (contrary to what others thought who met him when he actually was old), and Stoddart was surprised that, considering his eccentric way of life and diet he outlived the Lake Poets and survived to old age. Attempts to give up opium proving vain, he ended on more than 3000 drops of laudanum daily, yet retained a lucid, fertile mind to the end.

His handwriting, incidentally, Stoddart compared with Chalmers's, in two styles, one for ordinary use, another very flowery, used for entries in scrap-books and albums.[4] Carlyle encountered his work soon after his own marriage, when, though his health seemed no better, he was gradually beginning to relax into Edinburgh society and cease his incessant railing against city, literati, weather and his fellow-men generally. He read De Quincey's *Confessions of an Opium Eater*, which when published in 1821 (as Carlyle noted in writing to Dr Julius) had been 'highly popular', and its author, 'ruined by Opium as he says', was 'a man of real talent'.[5]

Next year he was to meet De Quincey in person. The first time was 'half accidentally' at Gordon's, when because of his criticism of Carlyle in the *Edinburgh Review*, the little man 'grew pale as ashes at my entrance'; but Carlyle actually took the trouble to 'recover him' and then kept him in talk until late. A week later De Quincey called at Comely Bank, bringing the two of his children now living with him, and stayed until midnight.

Carlyle, in his new and kindlier mood, said of him, 'He is one of the smallest men you ever in your life beheld; but with a most gentle and sensible face, only that the teeth are destroyed by opium, and the little bit of an under-lip projects like a shelf . . . A slow, sad and soft voice, in the *politest* manner . . . with great gracefulness and sense', except that he was 'given to prosing'. Carlyle sympathised with his being reduced to undesirable lodgings and living by 'writing all day for the King of Donkies' – the proprietor of the *Saturday Post*. Why did he not earn a little by translating Jean Paul's biography for *Blackwood's*? Established as he was himself beginning to be, Carlyle found some of the milk of human kindness brimming up towards other unfortunates.[6]

The little man was too hooked on the opium habit to profit, and in the following April (1828) Carlyle reported him 'very low'.

Over the next few years De Quincey was in various lodgings, Great King Street, Forres Street, 12 Duncan Street, at one time at Duddingston, another at Lasswade. Sometimes he stayed at Wilson's when Wilson and his family were at Elleray.

He did turn out important contributions for *Blackwood's*, such as 'Dr Parr and his Contemporaries, or, Whiggism in its Relations to Literature' (1829). In spite of its politics he also later wrote for the Whig/Liberal *Tait's Magazine*, launched by William Tait in 1832 in opposition to the Tory *Blackwood's*, and including such contributors as Cobden, Bright and John Stuart Mill.

Some of his contributions were brilliant. His 'Last Days of Immanuel Kant' in February 1827, straight-faced and funny, and his black comedy on murder, which posed as a lecture to a 'Society of Connoisseurs in Murder', earned him the reputation of eccentric genius.

These were fairly prolific years, with De Quincey's profitable connection with *Tait's Magazine*, which in spite of its politics made room for literary essays, and for this, over the next fifteen years he produced some of his best work.

Late in 1828, temporarily at Wilson's, he was writing the bulk of his articles for the *Edinburgh Literary Gazette*, made a new contract with Blackwood, and brought his elder children William and Margaret to Edinburgh for their education, moving for a time to Captain Hamilton's.[7]

The summer of 1828 he had spent at Rydal, after which things began to go wrong. Some of his *Blackwood's* articles were not used, only 'The Toilette of the Hebrew Lady' appearing; the Carlyles were away in Dumfriesshire, trying to raise money on a mortgage of Thomas's grandparents' farm. In 1829 De Quincey produced almost nothing – except another son; and Wilson's proddings were vain.

In 1830 he planned and negotiated for another novel, never wrote it, also planned a history of the Crusades, stayed with Wilson desperate for money, and struggled to produce more for *Blackwood's*. His wife, left behind in Penrith lodgings, struck and brought the other children to Edinburgh, where they were never again parted until her death; moving from lodging to lodging, sometimes good, sometimes squalid. A move to 7 Great King Street, 'somewhat above the necessities of a needy man of letters', was on the pretext of taking lodgers, but he did not take any. His wife was often ill, leaving him to run the house and look after the children. Captain Hamilton used to press him to dine and let Margaret stay, 'Never mind her dress, Annette will supply her.' The younger girl Florence, who cried at night, would be rescued to sit up as a treat with her Papa as he worked.

Renting the large Great King Street house was part of a mistaken idea that here he would be stimulated to write, especially as it was near his friends Captain Hamilton ('Cyril Thornton') and his brother Sir William, both of whose libraries he was able to use. But as he could not manage his own affairs the creditors were often after him, and in 1831, despite his writings, they were foreclosing. A bookseller sued him for a £37.16.6 debt, the water company threatened to cut him off, and Wilson's brother made him a loan; but they had to move to a smaller house at 1 Forres Street (£80 a year, but he paid only £15).

In August he had to slip out at 5 a.m. to avoid arrest, was 'put to the horn' and declared 'a rebel'. As he could meet only half the debt he was sent to the Tolbooth, but got out by means of a 'sick bill' declaring physical unfitness. During the next nine years he was put to the horn nine times.[8]

Between 1832 and 1834 *Blackwood's* published De Quincey's series on the Caesars, and other articles, and following this his autobiographical sketches. De Quincey was easily lured by the prospect of higher fees, but not only was his output always sporadic, but fastidious care over his own work kept him repeatedly re-writing.

Klosterheim, a sort of German Gothic novel set in the seventeenth century, he produced in a lonely fit, finished it in March 1832 and succeeded in publishing it in May, hoping it might save him from 'an abyss of evil into which very few have ever descended'. He was now able to canvass several magazines for work, but could get little satisfaction from Blackwood, who was ill, dying in fact (he died in 1834). De Quincey in desperation sold books, borrowed, wrote 'like a fiend' and for two years was hardly to be seen.

So it went on. Now with eight children, though one died, and owing more than £600, he moved to a cottage in Duddingston. He narrowly escaped when creditors spotted him at the child's funeral. Late in 1833 he was registered in Holyrood as a debtor, where Major Miller of Dalswinton and his family were kind to him. One Sunday, enjoying the debtor's customary weekly freedom, after an agreeable evening at Ambrose's with *Noctes* companions, De Quincey missed the statutory midnight clocking-in and had to stay hidden at Ambrose's for a week – while his Holyrood landlady was out of her wits with anxiety.[9]

Charles MacFarlane, traveller and minor novelist, writing of De Quincey (who, incidentally, he said had added the 'De' to his name), described him as 'strange and more than half-crazed, and led by his own bizarre imagination to believe in the stories he related of himself'. He thought he could have made a good income from *Blackwood's* had he only worked consistently, but even Wilson had to drop him eventually because of his haphazard living. MacFarlane claimed that working for *Tait's Magazine,* 'ultra-Liberal Whig Radical', was in despite of his 'aristocratic' pretensions, and in it 'he vented a good deal of spite, malice and calumny', especially on Wordsworth and Coleridge.[10]

Sir Henry Taylor, who when in Edinburgh in 1835 spent much of his time fulminating against Jeffrey and praising Wilson, was unable to meet De Quincey as Wilson had hoped because of his fear of venturing out of doors in case of arrest. Taylor recounts his prolonged stay at Wilson's and his habit of going upstairs to bed with his candle as Wilson was coming down at 7 in the morning. 'A Gentle, courteous creature', Wilson called him; the waspish

Taylor commented that he seemed to be 'one of those gentle creatures who don't care what they do to you behind your back'.[11]

James Hogg, who had followed his extraordinary, indeed unique story, *Confessions of a Justified Sinner* in 1824 with *Queen Hinde* (1825) and *The Shepherd's Calendar* and *Songs* in 1829, at the age of sixty-one in 1831 made a visit to London to enjoy a late but welcome accolade, with a public dinner at Freemasons' Hall on his birthday on 25 January (1832), which by good fortune coincided with Burns's.[12]

The object of the visit was to negotiate publication of his *Altrive Tales,* but the project failed when the publisher went broke.

As for his impressions of London, Hogg was surprised to find that, compared with Edinburgh, there seemed to be 'no deep drinking', and for six weeks, night and day, he swore that he had not seen a single drunk.[13]

His voyage in the *Edinburgh Castle* gave no foretaste of the 'triumphal' visit he was to enjoy in London, but suggests the quiet tenor of his domestic life. There were no other cabin passengers and the trip was tedious: 'ate and drank, played at cards, and whistled on his flageolet, took his nap after dinner, and his toddy at night, the same as at home'. They were delayed for three days at Holy Island, and again off Norwich and the mouth of the Thames.[14]

Once in London Hogg was lionised, meeting 'everyone', usually on the assurance that it would not be a party, and always arriving to find the drawing-room crammed. He heard Edward Irving preach and thought him touched with 'enthusiastic madness', met the Lockharts, met Carlyle, met Cam Hobhouse at the Beefsteak Club.[15]

Hogg caused some amusement by walking through the streets of London in his grey shepherd's plaid, 'the vain goose', as Carlyle put it. He was living in style but (according to Carlyle) exciting as much laughter as respect. Carlyle might have reflected that anything not in accordance with their daily experience could arouse Londoners' derision, and that the unsophisticated Hogg might be merely exercising normal habits by wearing his traditional garb. 'Utterly a singing *Goose,* whom also I pitied and loved', comments Carlyle patronisingly.

The two met at the same dinner where Carlyle first met Lockhart, and his sketch of Hogg was Carlylean in perception. 'A little red-skinned, stiff, sack of a body, with quite the common air of an Ettrick shepherd; except that he has a highish tho' sloping brow (among his yellow-grizzled hair) and two clear little beads of blue or grey eyes, that sparkle if not with thought yet with animation. Behaves himself quite easily and well. Speaks Scotch, and mostly narrative absurdity (or even obscenity) therewith. Appears in the mingled character of Zany and raree-show.' Carlyle added censoriously that 'the conversation was about the basest I ever assisted in.'[16]

It was significant that, while everyone wanted to make a joke of Hogg, Lockhart did so most, 'Hogg walking thro' it, as if unconscious, or almost flattered.' He had been put through a gruelling training with Wilson's mockery in *Noctes Ambrosianae*. 'His vanity seems to be immense', continued Carlyle, 'but also his good nature . . . chearful, mirthful and musical . . . His poetic talent is authentic, yet his intellect seems of the weakest' (pretty damning in Carlyle's eyes). His charm was that 'he is a real product of nature, and able to speak *naturally* – which not one in a thousand is'.[17]

Cam Hobhouse's impression was of 'a good-natured, broad, and sandy-faced man', who 'sang his own songs, and made excellent whisky-punch'. He seemed 'a simple, funny fellow'.[18]

Susan Ferrier, a writer whose lifestyle could hardly have been more different from Hogg's, in 1824 after a silence of six years published a second novel, *Inheritance*. It had been written at Morningside House during summer sojourns, a place too small for secrecy from her family, and she was annoyed that her sister Helen leaked the secret to a few people, as the publication was again intended to be anonymous.[19]

Inheritance is better composed than *Marriage*, and again with well-drawn characters. The plot, based partly on the famous 'Douglas Cause', introduced her father in the guise of the 'cross-grained, misanthropic' Adam Ramsay.[20] Her cruder first novel had been the tentative bud from which opened this 'finished and masterly' work – enhanced by some half-dozen more years of life and experience of its author. John Murray told Miss Ferrier that Jeffrey was 'particularly pleased with the Nabob and Spouse, the letter from the Lakes, and the P.S. to it'. Sir George Douglas in *The "Blackwood" Group* points out the book's more acid tone than Jane Austen's, 'downright to the verge of cruelty',[21] especially in exposing the 'rawness and self-sufficiency' of the Scottish character.

The novel was a great success. A suggestion of dramatising it was unfortunately pre-empted by the minor playwright Edward Fitzball, who had recently adapted both *Waverley* and *Peveril* (1823 and 1824), but his work on *Inheritance* was clumsy and the play was a failure. The book itself, however, was so popular that it was soon 'in every house in Edinburgh, and the author as well known as if her name were prefixed to it'.[22]

Miss Ferrier continued to keep house for her tyrannical old father, whom her two sisters had escaped by marrying, and lived an unavoidably quiet, though busy, life until he died in 1829. She was then free to visit Abbotsford in the October, and also removed to number 7, and later number 10, Albany Street.

She suffered from eye trouble for some years, and in 1830 made an unsuccessful consultation with a London oculist, after which she had to keep to a darkened room; but she and her family all escaped the widespread influenza epidemic in 1832.

We get a glimpse of her still at Morningside one spring day in 1825 when her niece Helen Graham and her brother Henry walked out to visit, in company with the garrulous Miss Dalmeny Edmonstone, and wishing to be spared enduring such a walk ever again: the old lady 'with a tongue as long as George Street and as loud as St Andrew's Bell' – 'like the continual dripping of water . . . question after question, but never requiring or waiting for an answer'. Aunt Susan's company at Morningside was a relief, enjoying her time in the country, and the brother and sister were escorted home by their uncle 'Nabob Connell' who squired 'Miss Day' in front, 'the *beau* and *belle* of the last century'.[23] Miss Dalmeny was one of the three weird sisters caricatured in *Marriage*.

In 1831 Miss Ferrier published a third novel, *Destiny*, begun in 1827, much of which she wrote at Stirling Castle while visiting Helen's father General Graham and family. Again characters were drawn from life, but the construction was less satisfactory, unsuccessfully blending two separate but parallel plots with artificial dialogue and rather trite comments.

For her first two novels she earned only £150 and £1000 from Blackwood; the third book was dedicated to Scott, who secured £1700 for her from Cadell.

As the years passed Miss Ferrier lived a restricted life, able to receive her friends only at tea, and was said to have become more formidable and difficult. *Destiny* was her last venture into fiction, and she lived on, still unmarried, until 1854.[24]

Captain Basil Hall (1788–1844), son of Sir James Hall the Huttonian geologist, had a varied career, serving in the Navy, accompanying Lord Amherst's mission to China, interviewing Napoleon on Saint Helena in 1816, travelling in the Far East and Korea, an expedition he published as *An Account of a Voyage of Discovery to . . . the great Loo Choo*, and from 1827–28 in America. His friends were at first unenthusiastic about his writing up his travels, lest it brought him 'the title of a book maker' when 'it is not customary for officers so to do'. Fortunately he was reassured, and his works were a success. Margaret, daughter of the diplomat Sir John Hunter, who began by laughing at his foibles, ended by marrying him (1825).

In 1824 he became concerned with the intended 'Encyclopaedia for Youth and for Mechanics', and in 1825 with Constable's *Miscellany,* to feature his travels in Loo Choo and South America. A proposed cookery book did not materialise, but a *Miscellany* of his own culled from about twenty volumes was eventually published after Constable's failure.[25]

Mrs Grant, who met Hall in 1824, expressed herself 'never more surprised. I looked for a bold weather-beaten tar, but I found a gentleman, with a soft voice and soft manners, pouring out small-talk in half-whispers to ladies.' She conceded that he was considered 'very estimable'.[26]

Hall, a man of 'acute and wakeful intellect', culture and wide experience, claimed some ten years before his death to have 'enjoyed to the full each successive period of my life . . . as a middy, I was happy – as a lieutenant, happier – as a captain, happiest'.[27]

He was in touch with Constable first in 1819 over the second edition of his account of Loo Choo, whose sales were increased by advertising it on the covers of journals, especially the *Review*, a novel idea which Hall regarded as a 'princely' move. His *Travels in North America* also pleased Mrs Grant, who dutifully ploughed through its three volumes in 1829. She had of course a personal interest in the subject, but her American friends had led her to expect 'an over-grown lampoon'. Instead she found it stimulating, with polished style and a 'manly candour' (always one of her words of praise), and a gratifying 'indulgence and benevolence' towards the Americans, who were neurotically sensitive over perceived criticism, especially from the British. As the lady shrewdly comments, 'The national pride and vanity of the Americans about their country far exceeds Nebuchadnezzar's; but . . . they will learn by experience that pride goeth before a fall.'

Warning a friend in the United States not to be shocked that she herself was not shocked, she pointed out that though 'jealous for the honour of America', it would not be enhanced by 'that voracious greed of praise which seems to expect applause, unbounded, and unceasing, for all that exists, or that is done and doing, in America'.[28]

This was borne out when the American Mrs John Farrar, who met Hall after he had been in the States, did so with some prejudice as 'the traducer of the Americans', and complained that 'His manners were as rude and eccentric in his own country as they had been in the United States.'[29]

In later years Hall's mind unfortunately gave way, and he spent the last two years of his life in a mental asylum, dying in Haslar Hospital in 1844.

Thomas Babington Macaulay, a luminary of the younger generation, born in 1800 in London, became a Fellow of Trinity College, Cambridge in 1822. In

1824 he made quite a sensation at the Freemasons' Hall in London by a speech described in the *Edinburgh Review* as of remarkable eloquence. He was then invited to contribute to the journal, and his first article, in August 1825 on Milton, was also highly praised. This was the badge of success, as it was to be with Carlyle.

An article on the London University was also much talked of, 'very spirited and able', wrote Whishaw, 'but violent and exaggerated, and little calculated to serve the cause it espouses'.[30]

Macaulay was controversial, like other leading writers of the *Review*, and incurred Wilson's wrath, for one, for attacking Southey. 'Intellectual juvenility', Wilson declaimed, who in a *Noctes* dialogue observed scathingly, 'Only think of a clever lad o' three-score-and-ten, on his death bed, who can look back on nae greater achievement than haeing since . . . abused Mr Southey in the Embro' Review.'[31]

In early days Macaulay was a protege of Brougham, who admired his articles, considering him 'the most rising man of the time'. But Brougham later complained to Jeffrey that he 'took up too much of the *Review*', was angry that Jeffrey published his essay on John Stuart Mill, and preferred to ignore him. Jeffrey, when trying to ease himself out of the editorship, offered the post to Macaulay, but Brougham was so hostile that he dropped the idea: as Macaulay put it, 'he felt that his power over the *Review* diminished as mine increased'. He countered by trying to monopolise the articles, and snatched one on the 1830 Revolution from under Macaulay's very nose. When he entered Parliament, after he took the oaths Brougham cut him dead.[32]

In spring 1828 Carlyle, learning from Jeffrey that 'the rising sun' was coming to Edinburgh, commented without much enthusiasm of Macaulay's recent article on Dryden, that he had 'no glimpse or forecast of *true* Poetry'. Admitting that Macaulay was 'the young man of most force at present before the world', he likened him to an ironmaster, whose talent was vigorous for such business but nothing higher. 'The limits of his worth are discernible enough. Great things are not in him.' This proved one of Carlyle's more pigheaded judgments.[33]

Macaulay sat in Parliament from 1830 as a Whig, first for Calne, then Leeds, and took an active part in the Reform debate. Carlyle, who saw him in the House in 1832, again found plenty to criticise: 'a short squat thickset man of vulgar but resolute energetic appearance. Fair-complexioned, keen gray eyes, a large cylindrical head set close down between two strong round shoulders; the brow broad and fast-receding, the crown flat – perhaps it was baldish. Inclines already to corpulence, tho' I suppose he is not five and thirty' (he was actually thirty-two). 'The globular will one day be his shape, if he continue.'[34]

Crabb Robinson had earlier noted him as the most promising of his generation, lacking delicacy or sensibility, but strong, eloquent and overflowing with talk, cheerful, well informed, generous with help. (1826)

Macaulay, at first slovenly in dress, with an ill-tied neckcloth and usually standing with one hand in his waistcoat pocket, later became more dandyish, with embroidered waistcoats – but still hand in pocket.

He was also so clumsy with his hands that he could scarcely pull on his gloves, and distinctly lacked all the accomplishments prized by young gentlemen, unable to swim, row, drive, skate or shoot, and he even hated riding. His main activity in fact was walking, though often with his eyes glued to a book.[35]

Two notable older figures were more remotely connected with Edinburgh. Although Thomas Campbell had spent so much of his youth there he had lived in London since 1804, with a crown pension granted in 1805. In the 1820s he was concerned in the founding of the new London University. As he grew older he became more crotchety, largely because of an unsatisfactory marriage and the problem of his son's health. Cam Hobhouse, meeting him in the street one day in 1830, thought he had 'a half-crazy look and air', particularly as he remarked that Christianity was 'getting into general disrepute, much more so than the monarchy'. (George IV had recently died.[36])

The Rev. John McVickar, shortly before returning from London to New York in October 1830, met Campbell at Miss Harriet Douglas's, where he had been invited to 'drop in' one evening and perhaps designedly left his call until 11 p.m. 'Of inferior interest to the other great poets we have met', he noted tersely.[37]

Cam Hobhouse, however, despite some adverse comments, considered that as a poet Campbell was 'in the very first line', though 'Byron is incomparably the greater'. He also claimed that he knew Campbell better than most and, after his death in 1842 (when he complained that the funeral was ill-managed), he discounted the various 'eulogies' on his character. 'He was vain, captious, uncertain, exceedingly suspicious, and had nothing in his general conversation either amusing or instructive.'[38] But he explained this by the poet's always remaining poor. Campbell's later life was certainly not over-happy.

The other celebrity who maintained links, however distant, with Edinburgh was the admired polymath Sir James Mackintosh. In 1828 Macvey Napier, then still editing the *Encyclopaedia*, asked Mackintosh to complete Dugald Stewart's history of eighteenth-century Metaphysical Philosophy, Stewart then being so ill that he guessed they would never meet again. 'There is no man alive so capable of doing it justice.' Mackintosh haggled over the fee, the length, his own health, and finally on the work involved to bring it up to date, for (he argued) including 'German systems' would more than double the labour. He succeeded in completing it by June.[39]

Tom Moore, who often met Mackintosh at dinner, his own or others', found him, as did many others, always 'delightful; his range of knowledge and memory so extensive . . . from Voltaire's verses to Sylvia up to the most voluminous details of the Council of Trent'. Another time it was early advocates of religious liberty, French poetry, college reputations, dangers of mathematics . . .[40] Mackintosh was the classic Universal Man, and was blessed with a phenomenal memory, was a philosopher, and above all a great conversationalist. At first defending the French Revolution, he later changed his view and agreed with Burke. After serving in Bombay from 1804 to 1811 he sat as an MP from 1813 and became Professor of Law and General Politics at Haileybury from 1818 to 1824. He published works on philosophy and, more importantly, history, but his projected *History of England* took years to produce. Samuel Rogers, in one of his more caustic moods, told Moore one day in 1829 of John Allen's complaint of the 'difficulty of getting him to write his *history*, while he does any number of articles' – 'he was like your profligate fellows, who will go after any one but their wives, being always ready and willing to write anything but his book'.[41]

In 1830 Moore received proofs of the *History*, and professed himself 'on the whole, not disappointed', considering 'the expectation with which one must always approach any thing of Mackintosh's'.[42]

A curious trait of Mackintosh's, which George Grenville related to Moore one day as they returned from Holland House, he thought indicated a self-mistrust in the great conversationalist which 'prevents his great acquirements from telling in society as they ought': a habit of 'advancing 3 or 4 steps forward while he is conversing, then, as if suddenly recollecting himself, retiring again'.[43]

The Rev. John McVickar, who met Mackintosh in 1830, considered him 'the ablest man I have yet met with, – his conversation strongly marked and not a little Johnsonian'. Later, when McVickar was visiting at Craigcrook, Jeffrey told him that Mackintosh was indeed the ablest man of his time, full of learning, with a wonderful memory, and never ponderous.[44] With all this, the inescapable fact is that Mackintosh achieved relatively little beyond being so highly regarded as being remarkable.

Carlyle, who met him at Jeffrey's London house, also thought him the best of the current Whig philosophers and politicians, if not without 'a due spicing of hypocrisy and something of Pedantry'. In appearance he was grey-haired, of middle height, 'broadish', well-dressed, courteous though not extravagantly so; in his grey eyes, 'intelligent (unhealthy yellow-white)', Carlyle saw 'a dash of *cautious vivacity*'; 'triangular unmeaning nose; business mouth and chin', sensible and 'official' looking.[45]

Mackintosh was then not long for this world. He died in May 1832, four months before Sir Walter Scott, still working on a history of the French Revolution. Moore, dining soon after tête-à-tête with Rogers, quotes his host as saying that 'he had sacrificed himself to conversation; that he read for it, thought for it, and gave up future fame for it'.[46]

This might almost be a variant of a view of Sydney Smith, another in whom Moore always took delight: Smith 'never minds what nonsense he talks, which is one of the great reasons of his saying so much that is comical'. And 'as a conversational wit, beats all the men I have ever met'.[47]

Smith was another who was seldom able to return to Edinburgh in later life. The expense of a journey prevented all but the rarest visits, and he relied on friends visiting him and his family at Foston.

Macaulay encountered him at York in 1826 when on the Northern Circuit, impressed by 'the queer contrast between his black coat and his snow-white head . . . the clerical amplitude of his person, and the most unclerical wit, whim, and petulance of his eye', summing him up as 'one of the wittiest and most original writers of our times'. Another time he noted his 'rapid loud, laughing utterance, and his rector-like amplitude and rubicundity'; and that he 'talks from the impulse of the moment, and his fun is quite inexhaustible'.[48]

Lord Brougham, who seemed to some observers to become wilder and more eccentric with passing years, even with rumours of temporary insanity, was often known to speak under the influence of 'deep potations', as for example during the Reform Bill debates, after drinking deeply of mulled port.

He lost office in 1834 with the fall of Lord Melbourne's Government, when his behaviour was held to be extremely undignified. In the course of another three decades of his extremely active career, he never held Government office again.[49]

53
OLD PERIODICALS AND NEW VENTURES

> 'The change that has gradually taken place during the last 30 or 40 years in the numbers and circumstances of the reading public, and the unlimited desire of knowledge that now pervades every class of society . . . The general diffusion of education and of wealth, has occasioned a vast increase in the number of readers, and in the works which daily issue from the press.'
>
> Basil Hall, *Voyage to Loo-Choo, and other places in the Eastern Seas, in the year 1816 . . .*, Edinburgh, 1826, Preface

During the 1820s periodicals underwent several vicissitudes. In 1823 Carlyle reported to his friend James Johnston that *Blackwood's* was 'said to be going down; the sale is lessening, I hear, and certainly the contents are growing more and more insipid. I hope yet to see it dead; it is a disgrace to the age and country. Talent joined with moral baseness is at all times painful to contemplate.'[1] In fact *Blackwood's* survived until 1980.

Many people were indeed tiring of the stream of invective that issued from that paper, and by 1825 Lockhart was sufficiently eager to try something else. He and Scott discussed Constable's scheme for cheap literature for the people. Scott having tried unsuccessfully to obtain for him the Deputy Advocateship, Lockhart embarked on joint editorship with Scott of the works of Shakespeare. More significant for his career was his agreeing to take on the editorship of the *Quarterly*, whose future was then uncertain. His farewell dinner in December, with some fifty guests, was held under the cloud of rumour about Constable's financial difficulties and the extent of Scott's involvement.[2]

With the Solicitor-General acting as preses and Dundas of Arniston as 'croupier', much wine was drunk, and there were songs and speeches in honour of 'Don Giovanni, who fell asleep in his chair, about one in the morning', as Scott related to his son Walter.[3] Lockhart and his family left for London, in anxiety over the health of their son Johnny. Their problems were aggravated when his disability proved to be a spinal disease, and this and the premature birth of their second son, Walter, in April, were all at the height of the drama of Scott's ruin and Lady Scott's failing health. Meanwhile Constable was also in London, attempting to explain the financial situation and to raise money, if possible by selling copyright, besides his 'mad proposal' to Scott to raise £20,000 in Edinburgh.[4]

In Edinburgh itself in 1825 Robert Morehead, long a contributor to the *Scots Magazine* and for some years its editor, had proposed a penny weekly to Constable, as an improving magazine aimed at 'the peculiar circumstances of the lower orders', encouraging them on equal terms to liberal studies and with a religious touch. He felt sure of contributions from both Scott and Maria Edgeworth. This was one of the projects that sank with Constable's bankruptcy, but Morehead was one who stood by the ruined publisher (like Basil Hall, though both unable to help financially), having always appreciated Constable's liberal treatment of authors, and what 'the literature of Scotland owes to you'. He supported the *Miscellany*, which was able to continue. Constable, his fertility undiminished, also produced his money-making scheme for cheap popular works by well-known authors.[5]

In 1829 Jeffrey had to leave for England before his last issue of the *Edinburgh Review* was ready, and hand over to Napier when it was already late. The delay was Brougham's, who had not sent his paper on Locke, and Jeffrey warned they could wait no longer 'unless he is very peremptory'. 'Pity the last agonies of an expiring editor.'[6]

In its most glorious days the *Review* had published articles extending to fifteen and even twenty pages, but of late years this had been reduced to an average of ten. Macvey Napier, as new broom, suspecting that readers on the whole did not care for long articles, wanted to limit their length so as to widen the scope by including 'new, or profound, or interesting or amusing subjects'.

He feared that change of editorship might cause a shortage of contributions, but on the contrary found himself bombarded with offers from eager authors, and had diplomatically to turn away many reproachful would-be contributors. Jeffrey warned him that an *embarras* was worse than a shortage, when 'the difficulty of putting off those you have solicited is increasing'. He suspected that Brougham had been holding off to see how Napier's first issue was received. Long afterwards Sydney Smith told Ticknor (then on a return visit to England), with Hallam and Fraser Tytler, that in the *Review*'s early days they had at first been unwilling to give Brougham any direct influence, 'because he was so violent and unmanageable'.[7]

Between them Brougham and Macaulay were in rivalry like a pair of prima donnas. Many contributors could be temperamental. Jeffrey warned Napier early in 1832 that Carlyle 'will not do' unless he, as editor, took 'the liberties and pains with him that I did, by striking out freely and writing in occasionally'. By now, however, Carlyle was finding his feet and not amenable to editorial interference. 'The misfortune is', said Jeffrey, 'that he is very obstinate and, I am afraid, conceited, and unluckily in a place like this [London], he finds people enough to abet and applaud him . . . It is a great pity, for he is a man of genius and industry . . .'[8]

In spite of the brilliant figures, old and new – Brougham, Macaulay, Carlyle – still contributing to the *Review*, the general feeling was that under Macvey Napier some of the spark had gone out of it.

The brothers Robert and William Chambers, though starting with a very modest outlay and with expansive ideas, seized any opportunity, and created others. William, recommended to a Cheapside publisher's agent selling cut-price out-of-copyright editions of popular works, helped with a trade sale at the Lord Nelson Hotel in Adam Square. The sale, first of its kind, was a success, and when helping to pack up the remainder William admitted to the agent that he planned to set up his own business but had no money – otherwise he would have bought some of the discounted books. Praising his frankness, the agent offered him £10-worth of samples on credit.

'That was a turning-point in my life.' Much elated, William packed his prizes in a tea-chest and wheeled them in the borrowed hotel truck to his Leith Walk shop. Following the example of the notable Lackington of Finsbury Square, he set up a street stall, its shop furniture made by himself with deals from a local wood-yard.

Hard work and increasing sales helped pay off the loan, and frugal living and ploughing profits into stock helped him to expand. To save the expense of buying bound books William learned how to bind, bought the books in sheets and bound them himself. In spite of poor sales on wet days, the stall proved an inviting place to buy, and the long straight pavements, thirty to forty feet wide, allowed plenty of space. William and Robert shared the shady side with two other stalls. Various experiments paid off, such as selling books which he had created in his fine, carefully learned calligraphy, which earned little but brought useful contacts.[9]

The two also met some of the poor, obscure poets who 'hung about the outskirts of society', including Robert Gilfillan, the grocer's apprentice of Leith, who wrote popular Scottish songs, and the romantic John Denovan, a former tea-dealer's porter at the foot of Leith Street. The latter's life was a long struggle: mad about poetry, then about politics, and editing *The Patriot*, a radical weekly. Scott used to call at Denovan's Leith Wynd lodging, where he subsisted by roasting coffee. He died in 1827.[10]

William was able to enlarge his shop and to live in a small, uncarpeted back room; he secured a primitive printing press for £3 and went in for letterpress printing. Self-taught in this too, he printed the essayists and poets whose work he spent his small leisure-time reading, limited to eight pages at a time, and printing 750 copies which required 20,000 pulls. He could buy only a few quires of paper at once, and worked on profitless wet days or late at night. He discovered a versatile old weaver's reed-maker in Paisley who illustrated his songbook, which he sold at a shilling and cleared £9, with which he bought new type and went in for poster printing. He also secured commissions such as printing toll-tickets and pawn tickets, and started writing himself.[11]

The two brothers now attempted their own periodical, Robert as author and editor, William as printer and publisher. Called *Kaleidoscope* after Sir David Brewster's 'optical toy' invention and published fortnightly, sixteen pages at 3d, their first issue was on Saturday, 6 October 1821.

Producing this on the antiquated press was a heavy job, their younger brother James laying on the ink and William printing in two halves and stitching together, working to deadlines up to sixteen hours a day with the briefest of breaks, and incurring 'dreadful headaches'. Their only free time was on Sundays, for a walk on the links. The paper barely made its way, lasting little more than three months (to 12 January 1822).[12]

All these trials and privations, however, equipped each of them with capital of about £200, and about this time Robert came to Scott's notice over his calligraphic transcript of *The Lady of the Lake*, presented to him via Constable. He also produced some talented sketches, and his *Illustrations of the Author of Waverley*, speculating on the origins of characters and episodes of the novels (printed by William), sold well. Robert moved to India Place as 'intermediate to something better', and in the following spring (1823) William moved to Broughton.

It was now that Robert embarked on writing down his early explorations of old Edinburgh, describing odd characters and incidents, and recording stories told him by old inhabitants, some of whom could recall life in the early days of George III. He feared this would be of 'very limited interest', with little popular appeal, and would scarcely cover its outlay.

The ebullient Constable had more confidence in the idea, Robert secured the interest of Scott and Sharpe, and in 1824 the first part of *Traditions of Edinburgh* was issued, later published in two volumes. As Constable expected, it proved 'astonishingly' popular, and in a year had made an expected profit of £450 – though meanwhile stretching the cash-flow.[13]

The success of *Traditions* led Robert to follow up in 1825 with *Walks in Edinburgh*, which further added to his reputation. In 1826 he published *Popular Rhymes of Scotland*, with contributions from Scott, which ran into three editions.

By these means Robert had been introduced to many of Edinburgh's leading men and, still only twenty-two, was well advanced in his career. He now moved to Hanover Street, with their brother James, worked as hard as ever and, also in 1826, produced a two-volume *Picture of Scotland,* garnered from 'toilsome peregrinations' collecting historical items throughout the country. He also contributed to Constable's *Miscellany* in 1827, the publisher's attempt to re-establish himself after the crash. A history of the '45 included information provided by several families (1828), and expanded material from *The Lyon in Mourning,* collected more than half a century before. Robert heard of and acquired these manuscript volumes, which he published as *Jacobite Memoirs of the Rebellion of 1745*.

He also wrote and published verses, provided material to Lockhart for the biography of Burns, contributed to *The Picture of Stirling* (1830), and published a collection of *Scottish Jests and Stories* (1831), running into two editions. This was a novel idea as many people were convinced that the Scots, apart from their caustic humour, were incapable of wit.[14]

In 1829 Robert married Anne Kirkwood, daughter of John Kirkwood of the Glasgow Custom House. For some half-dozen years the brothers had striven to graduate from the tough, constricted present to a happier future, but before they achieved this they had been involved in an imprudent lawsuit brought by their father. This was an attempt to retrieve for the family a worthless old house now in other hands, and when he lost the suit his sons had to foot the bill. Their father, who never got over the loss, died in 1824 during the week of the great fire.

William gave up his old press and himself turned to literary work, produced *The Book of Scotland,* on Scottish institutions, then joined Robert in a *Gazetteer* of Scotland, collecting material and living very cheaply as he travelled about the country, writing the work at night and in between ordinary business, while Robert acted as final editor. This brought them £100.[15]

In the 1820s, by means of various new institutions, education and a taste for literature spread among the poorer classes. First was the Edinburgh School of Arts in 1821, followed in London and Glasgow in 1823 by Dr Birkbeck's Mechanics' Institutions. Also in London, such influential men as Lords Auckland and Althorp, Lord John Russell, Brougham, Mackintosh and Captain Basil Hall were responsible for the Society for the Diffusion of Useful Knowledge (1825), publishing cheaply works on the sciences and general knowledge. Their first publication was in 1827, the year when Constable's first *Miscellany* appeared, starting a vogue for similar popular, low-priced works of information.[16]

Cheap periodicals now spread, particularly with the popular feeling aroused by the Reform agitation, many of them rubbish which did not endure, consisting largely of unauthorised extracts lifted from books, and repetition of old stories. Nor were they reliable in production date. William Chambers now took a hand with a journal of more worthy content, and on 4 February 1832 he and Robert, with no other assistance, launched their weekly *Chambers's Edinburgh Journal*, for three-halfpence. Its intention was announced in an opening address as providing the labouring classes with instruction and worthwhile entertainment – but avoiding politics.

It became an instant success, selling 50,000 copies in the first few days – exceeding any other sales in Scotland; and shortly copies became available in London too, by its third number selling 80,000. This drove out the bad in Edinburgh, whose other cheap papers collapsed. Nor did new rivals succeed in London, except Charles Knight's *Penny Magazine,* supported by Brougham, which ran until 1845.

Robert at first produced the whole *Journal.* Their lifestyle instantly improved, they moved to larger premises, and after the fourteenth issue Robert gave up other works and became joint editor and partner in their new firm, W. & R. Chambers.[17]

There were of course changes and difficulties. Their younger brother James died in 1833, and for the next twenty-one years the two brothers continued without needing any written contract. Robert wrote successful leading articles in the form of improving essays, and William, more popular instruction aimed at the young, all of high moral tone. Their old hand-presses, heavily labour-intensive, had to give way to more modern equipment, and to produce such thousands of copies new steam-driven machines were introduced, and stereo type plates were used, of which a set was sent to London for the English copies. The original folio size was reduced to quarto, then octavo.[18]

Robert had continued on good terms with Scott, by now through letters, when Scott was confined to Abbotsford by illness. Scott's last letter to him, on 2 August 1831, was written when he found speech difficult and was trying to keep up exercise by riding, 'or rather crawling about my plantations in the morning'. Indebted for his many kindnesses, on Scott's death Robert felt his loss keenly, and at once started on a memoir, which he issued in popular format in October and sold 80,000 copies.[19]

54
THE SOCIAL SCENE: FEASTS

'I remember my secret surprise, knowing the men to be of first-rate talent, at hearing how much of their conversation was generally devoted to the discussion of wines and other material subjects.' (1817)

Reminiscences of Charlotte, Lady Wake, 68

'A sumptuous breakfast soon is spread
Composed of tea, of eggs, and bread,
Rich marmalade, hung beef, and butter.
Said Doctor, 'nothing could be fitter . . .
With Doctor Johnson I agree
What time he says a man should be,
A guest of Scotia's breakfast-table
As often so he may be able'

William Combe, *The Tour of Dr Prosody, in search of the Antique and the Picturesque* . . . London, 1821, 72–3

As each generation tends to maintain that the last was better, so ageing spinsters of the 1820s mourned the social habits of their youth. The old Miss Campbells of Newfield compared Edinburgh in 1824 unfavourably with the days when they met 'dukes, marquesses, earls, barons, baronets, and knights . . . at every party', ladies would look only at generals, and 'pretty girls got handsome partners'. Where were these now, they asked Helen Graham, for Edinburgh's 'bonnie lassies'? Long ago, added Miss Emily, they were 'a' so grand-looking, tall and finely dressed, no wee shilpit puirbit-like things as they are noo, wi' their waists drawn in till ye might span them, and their heads frizzed out like wild beasts'. It was these youths' fathers who had seemed so alluring. The comment has a tinge of the regular dissatisfaction over latter-day fashions.[1]

Even the younger generation might affect dissatisfaction. In the winter of 1825 Miss Louisa Macdonald claimed to be quite tired of Edinburgh, complaining (said Helen) of 'the constant dressing and undressing; waste of time being obliged to walk the streets for exercise, there being no other promenade' (the ornamental gardens off Queen Street and Princes Street had not been developed); 'and meeting the same people over and over again'. As for parties, Louisa 'determined to retire from them altogether': hosts did not care whether they saw one, and one became tired, 'unfit for the next day's labour'. *'La vie qu'on mène à Edinbourg de nos jours,'* she went on, affecting international fashion, *'est singulièrement monotone. On va se promener toutes les après-midi, sur le pavé de George Street, et le soir l'on se demande les uns aux autres si l'on y a été.'* No wonder she was bored.

Only a month later old Miss Steuart, praising young Jemina Buchanan and her sister as they left their house, admired these 'two merry, natural creatures. How seldom are such to be met with nowadays. The young misses and masters are all so fine.'[2]

A generation later again it was the same story. Charles Ainslie (Sir Philip's grandson), who first appeared in Edinburgh society, delicate and shy, about 1823, between 'the detestable Charterhouse' and going to Sandhurst in 1825, looked back from a later time when the picture had entirely changed. 'I don't know whether London has been the gainer, but Edinburgh has greatly lost by this desertion of her aristocracy, and its winters retain nothing of those better times but their frost, snow, and piercing winds. At the balls, dinners, and evening parties there still lingered knee-breeches and buckled shoes . . . and elegant Macdonald of Clanranald still appeared in the morning in tight pantaloons and Hessian boots.'[3]

In the 1820s the young certainly enjoyed the vogue for fancy dress balls which then swept society. Helen Graham was not fortunate enough to be invited to the famed 'Bachelors' Ball' for which all Edinburgh dressed up, but in March 1825 she and her father, in company with Mrs Fletcher and her party, attended the Fancy Ball which equally drew 'everyone', and costumes were extravagant and bizarre. One which did not quite succeed was Mr Hay of Spott's 'Modern Greek in the peasant costume', for 'so unacquainted were the natives of this modern Athens with the dress of the Greeks that he was regarded as a very laughable object'.[4]

There were certainly fashionable fads, and just as in the previous century the famous Campbell sisters, daughters of the Duke of Argyll, were mobbed when they walked out (admittedly for their outrageous dress), now the beautiful Miss McLane, regarded as Scotland's most outstanding, was 'followed by the mob in the street, until she was obliged to take refuge in a shop . . . and gave up going to the theatre because the pit thrice rose up, and taking off their hats to show it was done in respect, called upon her to come to the front of the box . . . that they might see her'. This was during Ticknor's visit in 1819 – who himself did not particularly admire her. Though he admitted that she had 'an open, radiant kind of beauty, an exquisite complexion, brilliant black eyes and hair, and a very graceful figure and manner'. And she was quite unaffected, without conceit although with 'a perfect consciousness of her own beauty'. With all that, 'she had half the titles of Scotland at her feet'.[5]

Perhaps Ticknor, perhaps the old Miss Campbells, might have admitted that gilded society was not always intellectually stimulating. Charlotte, Lady Wake, recalling her girlhood days as Miss Tait, a member of leading Whig society, when invited to their cousin John Murray's, was struck by the circumscribed conversation – of Jeffrey, Horner, Lockhart and other Whig notables. 'I remember my secret surprise, knowing the men to be of first-rate talent, at hearing how much of their conversation was generally devoted to discussion of wines and other material subjects.'[6]

The ladies themselves may have contributed more intellectual content. Mrs Grant of Laggan, dining in February 1823 at the house of James Smith of Jordanhill (son of her old friend Mrs Smith) and his wife – 'a dinner of authors and artists' including Raeburn, Wilson, and Dr Brewster – enjoyed 'much good and lively talk', and good music in the evening. To her old friend she wrote approvingly that she 'never saw a dinner better arranged, or a company better assorted. This last is by far the most difficult part of the business.' Everything depended upon it.[7]

Smith's wife soon afterwards took the now crippled Mrs Grant on 'a delightful airing' to Inverleith House and Newhaven's curious chain pier, through bustling Leith, its harbour crammed with ships. She was then left to her own thoughts on the South Bridge while the other ladies went shopping; but Mrs Grant, who never went near a shop window, was well amused by the unfamiliar sight of the lively street in the sunshine.[8]

From the following New Year Mrs Grant's life was even more restricted after another fall. Fearing that the wound would aggravate the erysipelas from which she suffered, the doctor proscribed reading, writing, even company.[9]

Helen Graham was having a livelier time, though apparently no nearer finding a husband and, now well into her twenties, in danger of becoming left on the shelf. Life seemed to be a round of dinners and parties, not always to her pleasure, any more than they were to Henry Cockburn.

'Formal dinners are seldom pleasant', she observed, 'for the fumes from hot viands, rich sauces and the exertion of eating and drinking certainly cast a shade of stupidity over everyone. Everything that could please the eye and taste of the most refined epicure was not spared.' The occasion was Mr Binning-Munro's, brother of the doctor, Alexander. Helen had taken the precaution of making 'an ample luncheon beforehand' so as not to fall into the trap of over-indulgence, but, perhaps as a result, had no defence against the boredom of 'listening first to the gentleman on my right hand and then on my left'.[10]

At old Lord Eldin's one day in February 1824, while there were not many guests, Helen found plenty to amuse her: the walls covered with his beautiful drawings and Old Master paintings, and a huge book of sketches to be examined, by the marine painter Captain William Elliot, who had exhibited at the Royal Academy in the 1780s. Yet Helen felt uneasy. 'There is a sort of indefinite feeling of gloominess and blackness about the Whigs, certainly not congenial to a Tory, even the wives and daughters have it.' Miss Clerk, who always acted as hostess, was the very caricature of an old maid, 'very prim, correct, demure and stiff'. Lord Eldin conducted Helen's parents, the General and his wife, through the rooms to describe his pictures and drawings, while Helen, left with Miss Gibson Craig, found she could hardly extract a word from the girl, and escaped to examine the priceless possessions at leisure, 'as the inanimate objects in the room took my fancy much more than the animate'.[11]

Detailed descriptions of social habits are, obviously, not written by the people to whom they are familiar; we again rely on the accounts of visiting Americans, to whom they were strange, and the later reminisences of the old. The French-American bird painter Audubon, as sensitive as a jellyfish, revelled in the simple dinners at his friends the Lizars', but finding himself a celebrity endured many a grand dinner. Often they proved less intimidating than he feared. He particularly liked Captain Basil Hall and his wife, where although his first dinner with them was sumptuous, he was relieved to be spared the ordeal of having to propose wine with another guest, 'a completely foppish act that I cannot bear'.[12]

One who minutely described the arrangement of a dinner-party, probably in the 1830s, was Mrs Janet Story, a minor lady authoress in Edwardian times, who lovingly recalled her childhood life at the then newish 37 Melville Street. As her father had served in India, Indian dishes always figured on the menu, but otherwise their dinners conformed to the regular Edinburgh style.

The party might be as many as twenty-two, so that the fine mahogany dinner-tables (from Whytock and Co.) were brought out and fitted with their leaves, and the entire household polished them, 'first rubbing them hard with a small square piece of cork, and then finishing with dry rubbing, with a piece of flannel or even an ordinary duster'. The Highland porters, Robertson and Davidson, who guarded the end of the street, would be called in by local households for such tasks as messages, carrying luggage, beating carpets – and especially rubbing tables, which their strength qualified them to do better than the women servants. Further, as no protective mats or cloths were laid on the table when hot dishes and wines were placed on it, after the dinner the whole process had to be repeated.

A chef for the day, usually Mrs Clerihew, must be engaged to supervise the large party, and a head waiter to arrange the table service, usher in the company and generally superintend. This family preferred to employ the sober and dignified Kemp, head janitor of the Academy, 'for many years at the head of the Edinburgh staff of waiters'. Then there was disposal of the children, who, dressed in their best, were allowed in the drawing-room until dinner was announced, petted or ignored as the case might be. They reappeared at the dessert stage, to be stuffed with goodies by thoughtless guests, for them the great treat of the evening.

In this household, where the husband insisted on the best of everything, no trouble or expense was spared. Dinner started with two soups in handsome silver tureens, and two large dishes of fish, at head and foot of the table respectively, the husband serving one, the wife the other. Following these came 'four massive *entrée* dishes, placed heavily on the table', first to be seen, then handed to the guests: in this house they always included a curry.

This was only the beginning. On removal of the silver *entrée* dishes a huge joint was placed opposite the host, either of beef or mutton, and at the opposite end an enormous roast or boiled turkey. The latter was carved by the male guest of honour, the former by the host. Colonel Gore-Browne, a frequent guest, used to boast that he could adequately serve all the guests from one side of the breast, so that the family was haunted by 'visions of cold sliced turkey' for the next couple of days. Halfway down the table another large dish might contain a pair of ducks, a ham or tongue, or a beefsteak pie.

For dessert, oddly some guests preferred a macaroni cheese, which would be placed at the foot of the table. 'At the other end towered a magnificent erection of spun sugar and pastry, filled with luscious preserves.' There were also side dishes, one perhaps 'a simple pudding', and replacing the *entrée* dishes, 'four handsome cut crystal dishes . . . containing a white vanilla and a pink raspberry cream, a pale wine jelly, and one tinted crimson with drops of cochineal'. It was at this point that the children were admitted to revel in tempting morsels.

Such a dinner was at the very top end of the scale, and it was small wonder that people like Henry Cockburn and Helen Graham deplored their over-richness and formality.[13]

Such excessive entertainments were only for conspicuous consumption, and many a dinner was given at equivalent social levels with much simpler menus. The American Nathaniel Carter, invited for 10 o'clock in 1825 to a supper by Robert Jameson, Professor of Natural History, in Royal Circus, found two of the assembled ladies and gentlemen were playing Scottish songs at the piano. He was generally impressed by the ladies' handsome appearance, intelligence and social charm, with 'less fondness for show, and more simplicity of manners', than the English.

Some of the guests were from distant parts of Scotland, including from the Orkneys, not to mention the Mathematics Professor who was being importuned by a group of young ladies to arrange an evening when they might take a look at Venus or the moon through his telescope. Supper was not announced until midnight, when the party, placed 'promiscuously' round different tables, enjoyed cold dishes with wine and punch, the whisky, water and sugar being sent round separately to be mixed at will. The menu ended with various fruits. Carter felt himself 'highly gratified with the generous hospitality'.[14]

He also accepted an invitation to dine *en famille* with Jeffrey at Craigcrook, which although at the now fashionable late hour of 6 o'clock was 'a series of genuine Scotch dishes, from barley broth to the bannock . . . Two species of fish from the Forth, a dessert of native fruits, half a dozen kinds of wine, one of which was old Madeira from his friends in the United States, and a round of whiskey, the usual finale of a Scotch dinner.'[15] The liquid part was evidently of greater importance to Jeffrey than the rest.

Menus for strong stomachs are recorded by the boon companions of *Noctes Ambrosianae.* Supper for six in 1829 was similarly geared to the liquid aspect, the meal starting with hodge-podge and turtle soup. The table was adorned with 'punch à la Trongate' in the centre, sherry and madeira at Hogg's end, 'Vin de Grave, and Johannisberg, both thoroughly cooled', beside Tickler, and whisky on the sideboard. The remove, or second course, was 'a salmon frae aboon Peebles and . . . a turbot from off Fastcastle', and the second remove, 'a sheep's head frae Yarrow, thanks to our Shepherd', and a boar's head, attributed mysteriously to Goethe, whose health is then drunk 'three times three'. A green goose is casually mentioned, with peas, then a Stilton cheese; and when serious drinking starts, it is Glenlivet, Cockburn's '48 sherry, Brougham's Madeira, port and claret. Serious hangovers doubtless followed.[16]

Next spring they record a dinner at 6 p.m. by gaslight, for All Fools' Day, all wearing court dress, starting with several soups: mulligatawny, Scotch broth, cocky leeky, giblet soup, potato soup. Round the sides, oxtail, white and 'Peas' soup, hodge-podge, carrot, brown and oyster soups, and turtle soup. ('What a misty evening!' – 'nae wonder – wi' 13 soups a' steamin' up to the skies!')

An hour occupies each course, accompanied by the usual facetious chat; then comes a fish course, turbot, Bo'ness bass, Windermere char; haddock, sole, whiting, halibut, cod's head 'and shoulders', eel, mackerel, Loch Leven trout, pike and salmon, disposed round the four sides.

The third or meat course starts in the centre with beef-steak pie, haunch of venison, rump; pâtés and fillet of veal round the side. Also ham, round of beef, sweetbreads, saddle of mutton, 'palates', sirloin. At one point, Ambrose exchanges the four main dishes, saddle with fillet, sirloin with round, by which means, says Hogg, each member got adequate access to carve his own round.

Finally a course of 'fowl': 'cock of the wood', flanked by plover and ptarmigan in the centre, round the sides pigeons, chickens, pheasant, ducks, turkey, partridges, 'How Towdies', grouse, wild duck, goose.

This being April Fools' Day, there is a strong suspicion that the impossible feast represents more a Scottish gourmet – rather gourmand – fantasy than a real menu. Rather more realistic is a reference to a 'shilling ordinary' in 1826: 'beef, bread and beer, with some vegetables'.[17]

Another *Noctes*, apparently peripatetic – and probably again apocryphal, especially the first item – recorded in 1825 ran thus: 'at North's [i.e. Wilson's], 500 oysters, at Dr Mullion's, three-score kidneys, at O'Doherty's "ham, turkey, and one dish"; at the next, "daw"; at Hogg's, steaks and onions, at Tickler's a dozen lobsters.' Mullion asked admiringly, 'What would Barry Cornwall say to such a sight?' – O'Doherty: 'Nothing. He'd faint on the spot.'[18]

Incidentally it was at fashionable houses that the unwary were likely to meet modish kickshaws. Robert Gillies, who introduced James Hogg to many of Edinburgh's society families, records how at Lady Williamson's (Sir Hedworth's widow), where Hogg first encountered ice-cream, he supposed it to be 'a fine het sweet puddin''. Innocently taking a generous spoonful, he was so overcome that tears sprang to his eyes and the butler had to revive him with a glass of whisky.[19]

Tea, which followed dinner after an interval of an hour or so, is rarely described, but Patrick Fraser Tytler lovingly recalls the large round table in the drawing-room of the Princes Street house, which when they left Edinburgh in the 1830s he and his sisters reproduced as nearly as possible: that table where had sat Scott, Dugald Stewart, Playfair, Henry Mackenzie. 'Glorious tea-drinkings . . . with pyramids of cakes, saucers of strawberry-jam, and tea and wit of the purest flavour . . .'[20] The marvel is, given the size of dinners, that anyone could accommodate pyramids and saucers full of anything.

In general Scottish society seemed to please. 'The society here is certainly excellent', wrote the American Ticknor in 1819. Their sincerity, rather than their pretensions to fashion, impressed him. 'In open-heartedness I imagine it is almost unrivalled.' Nor was Scotland bound, as in England, by artificial distinctions.[21]

Visitors especially appreciated evening parties with 'Belles, Beaux, Advocates, Savans, and Craniologists . . . Of the Savans, Leslie and Brewster are the most distinguished . . . The two philosophers hate each other most cordially.'[22]

One active socialiser was Thomas Moore, who in 1825 visited Abbotsford and Craigcrook, and stayed with William Murray of the Theatre. He met 'everybody', including Henry Mackenzie, James Ballantyne, and Wilson, at whose house he attended a supper and thought the guests an odd lot. This included Hogg, who yelled out songs (Moore's own singing was usually a vital part of these entertainments), and invited him to visit his farm. It was at the end of this Edinburgh visit that Moore was unfortunately taken ill, was dosed with laudanum by Comte Flahault, and had to delay his departure. As a result he was in Edinburgh to attend the opening of the courts and see Scott and Jeffrey again, and to visit the theatre in order to see its new lighting and redecoration, as well as attending a performance.[23]

Dinners of a masculine variety are also described by Lord Frederick Lennox, whose detailed reminiscences are, like those of *Noctes*, probably exaggerated, during a rackety month in Edinburgh in 1832. Patrick (later Lord) Robertson, a leading advocate, entertained his friends at his Drummond Street house, Patrick Maconochie, another advocate, at his Princes Street flat, and the rest of the gang returned their hospitality at Gibbs's Hotel or some other good inn. On Mondays they used to meet, up six flights, at a house near the Flesh Market renowned for haggis, tender rump steaks, strong whisky punch and a beautiful 'waiteress'.

One December evening Robertson invited the group to Drummond Street for 6.30 (London's fashionable hours were creeping in), all famished, Lennox and George Russell after skating on Duddingston Loch, the others including the surgeon Liston having ended their 'studies' with a long walk.

Dinner over and the cloth removed, 'toasts were proposed, speeches made, and songs sung'. When 11 struck, Lennox decided to leave, having drunk liberally, but one of the party had already discovered that they were victims to 'the old Irish fashion of locking the street door, and putting away the great coats and hats'. Lennox, with a feeble excuse of checking the barometer, slipped out with a napkin and the green baize cloth used for the small table where dishes were placed when brought in. Twisting one into a turban and throwing the other over his shoulders as a cloak, he sneaked downstairs and bribed a kitchenmaid to let him out the back way. In this odd costume he hurried through the bitter night air to Gibbs's Hotel and explained his situation to the landlord.

He sent Robertson a note on exchanging the borrowed gear for his own clothes, and received a reply of execrable puns, 'We return your Gibus hat, but don't *gibe us* . . . the loss was scarcely *felt* . . . keep the table cover as . . . you richly merit to be crowned with *green bays*'.[24]

This was certainly not the kind of junketing with which, say, Mrs Grant was familiar. At the other end of the scale would be the meals taken by Thomas and Jane Carlyle, extremely simple so as not to disagree with his tender stomach. They normally dined on a mutton chop at the now unfashionable 4 o' clock, and in the evening, when most families drank tea, they took coffee. Carlyle regularly complained of Edinburgh eggs, and his mother usually supplied eggs and butter from Annandale, but soon after they were married Jane found a country supply of eggs, and Thomas had one every day.

'Good ham and cheese and even good eggs are to be had here in Edinburgh,' she told her mother-in-law, 'good butter too perhaps, if one knew where to seek' – but Annandale butter had a better flavour.[25]

Traditional Scottish dishes like hodge-podge and sheep's head were often enjoyed by visitors, rather to their surprise. John James Audubon, domiciled in Edinburgh in 1826, much enjoyed sheep's head at his kind friends Mr and Mrs Lizars', who regularly entertained him at 2 St James's Square.[26] He was also impressed by the menu at a dinner with the Antiquarians in November, at the Waterloo Hotel, Lord Elgin presiding. They dined at 6, and with Lizars on one side and 'my good friend P. Neill' on the other, 'I was helped to a sumptuous dinner indeed'. The first course was entirely old-style Scottish, 'such as marrow bones, cod fish heads stuffed with oat meal and garlic, black puddings, sheep's heads, tracheas of the same, and I do not know what all'.

The 'second dinner', a great contrast, was 'quite *a l'anglais*. I finished with a nice bit of grouse.' (At the end, much to his alarm, Audubon was called on to make a speech, and sweating with fright but summoning resolution, 'for the first time in my life addressed a large assembly'. In three short sentences he wished the society well, and to relieve his distress Lizars poured him a large glass of wine and presented it with a 'Bravo, take this!'[27])

Audubon was so regularly *not* in that when he dined at home he records the menu: 'herrings, mutton chops, cabbage and fritters' (27 November), 'fried oysters and vinegar, and stewed Scotch herrings' (17 December), while not surprisingly, when he told Mrs Dickie he would be out, she would have nothing ready for him. One day he and the Lizars brothers had a luncheon at home, 'some fried oysters, some drink and some cake', while packing up a parcel to send his wife (27 December), and 'oysters, cooked and raw' appear again when supping at Barry's Hotel with Sir William Jardine and his uncle Mr Mole, and John Lizars (22 December).[28]

The literary breakfast, a social phenomenon sadly extinct since the 1930s, was then usually greatly enjoyed, and recorded with pleasure by guests. Though Cam Hobhouse, admittedly in London, complained in 1832 how in Chelsea he 'walked about at what is called a breakfast: the dullest of all our dull English amusements', and a dozen years later dismisses 'the most tiresome of all amusements – a breakfast'.[29]

It was not so in Edinburgh in the 1820s. 'We often went out to breakfast, and always found the tables covered with beefsteaks, ham and eggs, divers varieties of salt fish, marmalade, jellies &c &c.' So wrote the Rev. Adam Sedgwick in 1825, even if his order of presentation sounds daunting. 'In a corner of the table you might indeed see a tea-urn and a coffee-pot; but these things are non-essential in a Caledonian fast-breaking.'[30]

Not long after, it was the young Benjamin Disraeli who was lyricising on the subject. 'I revel in the various beauties of a Scotch breakfast – cold grouse and marmalade find me however constant.'[31] These were of course culinary, rather than literary delights. Usually it is the latter that contemporaries praise, perhaps taking the menu for granted.

Audubon breakfasted 'most heartily' at George Combe's, 'on mutton ham and good coffee', before the ordeal of having his head cast for phrenology.[32]

'Peter' eloquently describes a breakfast at Abbotsford, *'a la fourchette'*: 'in which tea, coffee, chocolate, toast, and sweetmeats officiated as little better than ornamental out-works to more solid and imposing fortifications of mutton, ham, hung-beef, and salmon killed over-night . . . spear and torch-light method'.[33]

The American Nathaniel Willis and a friend, arriving in Scotland by steamer in 1834, joined in 'a Scotch breakfast' next morning at 9 a.m., 'cold grouse, salmon, cold beef, marmalade, jellies, honey, five kinds of bread, oatmeal cakes, coffee, tea, and toast; and I am by no means sure that this is all'.[34]

This was not necessarily the daily fare of many, especially children. Catherine Sinclair, in her children's novel *Holiday House,* written probably in the late 1820s, mentions the 8-o'clock breakfast of a group of children on porridge and buttermilk, a thoroughly health-giving menu. This was perhaps outweighed by these children's feasting for the rest of the day, first at 10 with their hostess on 'tea, muffins, and sweetmeats', and later a luncheon, a dinner, tea and 'a supper of poached eggs'.[35]

As for meal-time conversation, the Rev. Edmund Griffin noted to his shame that here it was 'far more literary' than among Americans, being neither 'blue' nor pedantic, but 'sensible and instructive', and 'manages to get over the mud of scandal, and the dust of frivolity without soiling a shoe'.[36] First, of course, one had to enter the house. There would be a fine engraved door-plate, 'a well polished and well brightened piece of brass 8 by 5', as Audubon admired at Dr Thompson's at 80 George Street.[37]

By American standards the formality of a visit had advantages. 'A servant receives your name at the door', noted Griffin, 'and transmits it through an ascending file of some half-dozen of his fellows, to the entrance of the drawing room; there it is audibly pronounced, attracting at once the attention of the master and the mistress of the house.' Before one could address anyone present a formal introduction was still needed, but 'to a stranger it saves the awkwardness of a long search for his inviters, whom perhaps he may not even personally know'.[38]

This was providing one could brave whoever answered the door. There were plenty of unkind jokes about callers put down by arrogant servants. An uppish Edinburgh footman was a different proposition from one in London. One young midshipman whose ship, on a mission to scour the North Sea for smugglers, had put in at Leith and who was invited to dine at a gentleman's house in Edinburgh, was much embarrassed when the glaring boy in buttons who answered the knocker mistook his midshipman's full rig (minus dirk) for a servant's livery. 'Whar did ye git yer mainers? Wha's flunkie may ye be, if I may make sae bauld . . . gang round to the back door an' I'll tak yer message.' It took some time for the mortified youth to convince power-hungry Buttons of his identity.[39]

Continental visitors were intrigued by the difference between households in, say, Berlin and in London or Edinburgh. Instead of housing many lodgers with easy access for visitors to both men and women residents, in England where each house might contain a single family, and in Edinburgh's New Town where many 'single' houses had been built, 'the door is constantly shut' (writes Frederick von Raumer); 'every knock, every one who goes out or comes in, is heard, and the master or mistress exercise a strict supervision'. As for the servants, 'a maid servant who is discovered in equivocal proceedings immediately loses her place, and finds it difficult to get another. The race of cooks and housemaids is therefore certainly more chaste and decorous than in Berlin.'[40]

On the other hand, a servant who had thus lost her character was probably driven to the streets.

The August races at Musselburgh were an unfailing attraction. Catherine Sinclair takes her young people in *Holiday House* to watch, driven by their hostess aunt in her phaeton. Miss Sinclair spares a moment to compare the spirited horses with the 'long row of cart-horses with galled sides, shrivelled skins, broken knees, and emaciated bodies' driven by carters and work-people, 'dragging their weary load along'.

The colourful scene at Musselburgh has 'piemen ringing their bells – blind fiddlers playing out of tune – boys calling lists of the horses – drums beating at the starting post – ballad-singers squalling at the full pitch of their voices – horses' galloping – grooms quarrelling – dogs barking – and children crying'. Once parked behind a chariot fairly bursting with ladies, two of the boys sitting in the rumble spread a cloth on the carriage roof and stuff themselves with oysters, sandwiches, and tumblers of porter.

The crowds delight the children: 'jockeys riding about in liveries as gay as tulips – officers in scarlet uniform – red flags fluttering in the breeze – caravans exhibiting pictures of the wildest-looking beasts in the world – bands of music – recruiting parties – fire-eaters, who dined on red-hot pokers. The scene was unforgettable to those of any age.'[41]

55
THE SOCIAL SCENE: PERSONALITIES

'Surely you have heard of Mrs Fletcher – of her beauty, talent, and benevolence.'

Mrs Grant of Laggan to Mrs Hook, 1 Oct. 1816, *Memoirs of Mrs Grant of Laggan*, II.151

'[Mrs Fletcher] is the Mrs Montague of Edinburgh, her house being the centre of all that is literary, amiable, and distinguished, and is herself no less characterized by intellect, than by virtue, by wit, than by taste, softened by a captivation of manner rarely equalled.'

Elizabeth Isabella Spence, *Letters from the North Highlands, during the Summer 1816*, London, 1817, 36–7

'[Mrs Grant] is an old lady of such great good-nature and such strong good sense, mingled with a natural talent, plain knowledge, and good taste, derived from English reading alone, that when she chooses to be pleasant she can be so to a high degree.'

G. S. Hillard (ed.), *Life, Letters and journals of George Ticknor*, Boston, 1909, I.278

'In general, the Scotch are a tall and admirably formed race, full of bone and muscle – men and women – without even a spark of beauty; with no humor, but extraordinary sagacity; very civil in their way, and extremely obliging; far superior, in general, to the English in understanding and intelligence; and, in all their habits, prejudices, and, above all, their religious notions, apparently made of cast iron, which will break, but never bend.'

Rev. Henry Colman, *European Life and Manners*, Boston & London, 1849, II.388

'Nobody would believe in England, what an immense expenditure of strength and animal spirits goes on, on these occasions [a ball]. Young men and children, old men and maidens, all jumping, whirling, and toiling alike. . . . the oldest and gravest in the land cutting capers, snapping fingers . . . brandishing their arms, shaking their legs, clapping hands, whooping, yelling, and screaming . . . The older they get, the more mad do the gentlemen become; but the truth is the dance is of their day, and they like to show it.'

Charles Eastlake Smith (ed.), *Journal and Correspondence of Lady Eastlake*, London, 1895; I.57

'This beautiful and delightful city . . . I think little of its streets and its rows of fine houses, though all built of stone, and though everything in London and Bath is beggary to these; . . . I think a great deal of the fine and well-ordered streets of shops; of the regularity . . . in the management of business . . . here all is civility; you do not meet with rudeness, or even the want of a disposition to oblige, even in persons in the lowest state of life.'

William Cobbett, *Tour in Scotland . . . in the autumn of the year 1832* (14 October 1832), London, 1833

A minor character who made herself much felt in Edinburgh in 1827 was the American lion-hunter Miss Harriet Douglas, whose father George Douglas had settled in New York in the 1770s and was cousin to Sir George Shaw, a later Lord Mayor of London and a descendant of Covenanters. Miss Douglas's father died when she was ten. She was now thirty-seven and, like many a contemporary lady of that age, fairly desperate to find a husband. She came over in order to settle an uncle's will, with two brothers who remained in London while she stayed with a cousin.

Edinburgh and the Scots appeared kindlier than London, and the lady lost no time in enjoying its social pleasures. Her cousin Elizabeth, who had married Robert (later Sir Robert) Abercromby of Forglen, took her on visits every afternoon in the chariot, to dinner parties and balls, to the theatre to see Charles Kemble, to French lessons, and lectures on electricity and geometry, 'which I did not understand'.

She also stayed with Mrs Grant of Laggan, whom she had met in America, presumably when very young. Here her dilatory appearances at breakfast exasperated her hostess, who after Harriet's thwarted attempts to start a conversation, broke her silence to say frostily,

If I make a remark,
It will be of the lark.

In general she was seen as a very tiresome lady, and it was reported that in New York her family was equally so, laughed at for their pretensions. Edinburgh society not unnaturally took Miss Douglas to be characteristic of New Yorkers, but after visiting the States Mrs Basil Hall wrote that 'the whole family are quizzed here and thought quite as strange as we could think them.

They are by no means popular and are most prodigiously vulgar', though very rich, and assiduous at entertaining.[1]

Edinburgh efforts were concentrated on trying to meet Sir Walter Scott, first through a letter from his sister-in-law, next by meeting Anne Scott at a party and again later, but she was chagrined when Anne did not even call. At an exhibition 'Sir Walter came in late and bowed to me from the earnestness of my gaze'; but shortly afterwards she was disconcerted to learn that he had taken a party of friends back to Abbotsford – *she* surely might have been one! Either Anne or Sir Walter had evidently overlooked it, for later he wrote to Maria Edgeworth (who had also written to him about her), that he had heard she was in Edinburgh, and that Anne, who apparently bungled it, '*could should would* or *might* have called upon her', but he was uncertain of the precise state of affairs.[2] At this time he was seldom in Edinburgh, and exchanged visits only with a few old friends. It was more than a year before Miss Douglas attained her wish.

She did, however, become friendly enough with Sir John and Lady Sinclair and their daughters to visit them frequently at their fashionable George Street house, met (and danced with) a son of Mungo Park, called with her brothers at Grecian Williams's studio and saw him often – he had travelled in Italy with their cousin William – and with Mrs Grant visited the eighty-two-year-old Henry Mackenzie. She even dared to discuss with Jeffrey his review of Thomas Campbell's *British Poets,* and 'enjoyed seeing him inspired to great eloquence about poetry'; and at the same time met Sydney Smith, whom she told effusively that a sermon of his on the text 'There is but a step between me and death' had done her more good 'than any one I ever heard'. This inspired him to invite her to visit Foston on her way back to London.

Miss Douglas was at best plain, if not ugly; she gushed, she overdid her praise. Yet she did have suitors, shilly-shallied about both, and about another in New York, and asked Mrs Grant's advice. Mrs Grant, while frank in pointing out her shortcomings, was also kind enough to give encouragement, and Harriet appreciated this enough to call her mentor 'one of the most genuine creatures in the world'. Mrs Grant on her side was strangely flattered by her regard, 'at her time of life unexpected'.[3]

Another who liked this American was the cranky John James Audubon, whom she met at Professor Jameson's and then visited in his rooms, surprised to find him not in wolfskins and with flowing locks, but with hair cut and in an orthodox coat. He confided that he had felt miserable at the party, at which her own artless conversation had given him his only pleasure. He even assured her that 'She should be the happiest woman in Edinburgh, because everybody liked her.'[4]

The Basil Halls had reason to be grateful to her, as they were also to Audubon, for on the eve of their departure for America with their month-old baby she, like him, was able to give them many useful tips, not to mention introductions to her mother, sister and friends.[5]

On Miss Douglas's return to London in spring 1827, having been in Edinburgh since January, she then travelled in Ireland and Wales. Amazingly, though perhaps because of her fortune, she received several proposals, including one from Prince Pückler-Muskau, who writes scathingly of her in his memoirs. She sailed back to Edinburgh to take expert advice – and even more amazingly, received a proposal from Mrs Grant's son. Still unable to decide between these tempting offers, she departed for the Highlands with her brother and their Abercromby cousins – but not without first having achieved dinner with Sir Walter Scott.

'A professd lion-huntress', he wrote on 1 July, 'who travels the country to rouse the peaceful beasts out of their lair . . . She is very plain, besides frightfully red-haired . . . An awful visitation . . . this poor woman has the bad taste to think direct flattery is the way to make her advances to friendship and intimacy.' He relented slightly next day, when she again dined with them, and he did 'that was civil'.[6] Indeed, the two later became quite friendly.

In the process of time so did others, including Wordsworth and Miss Edgeworth, when her artless enthusiasm, naïve curiosity and genuine admiration for intellect were seen to balance her uneducated flattery. As for Scott, she had no qualms about telling him that meeting him was 'the proudest day of my life', and when he dined with them he was in the middle of relating anecdotes (which prevented him from eating his dinner) when his carriage came for him at the height of their enjoyment. He said, sincerely no doubt, that 'he was truly sorry to part with us'. After a tour of Scotland so thorough as to take her to John o' Groats, Miss Douglas visited Abbotsford on her return in September, was made as welcome as everyone always was, and Scott was cordial, if not exactly admiring.[7]

Mrs Grant recorded of Miss Douglas in July 1828 that she was 'quite a character . . . Her faults are too obvious; she never concealed any thing in her life, nor indeed had much to conceal; but her good qualities are sincerity, candour, a perfect sunshine of good humour, and . . . a sweet and even temper.' She was charitable, religious, and simple as a child, had 'a profound admiration of talent, and, like all other Americans, loves title; but she is the humblest creature I know, and bears reproof with the greatest meekness'.[8]

Among the celebrities Miss Douglas met were the Listons at Milburn Tower, where Lady Liston kindly invited her to breakfast, accompanied by Mrs Grant. This was quite a success as Miss Douglas was able to give them 'anecdotes of their mutual American friends', and they spent two hours in the Listons' beautiful gardens. At Miss Douglas's wish they also called on Henry Mackenzie at Old Hailes, three miles west of Edinburgh, 'a fine old gentlemanlike place'. Mrs Mackenzie and their family lived a retired life, 'yet always receiving the best company', and their 'slight evening refreshments, where crowds never come', were regarded as a great privilege.[9]

Sir Robert Liston had enjoyed a remarkable career. His mother was a farmer, and he was born in 1742 in a humble cottage which, in the days of his fame, he preserved alongside the grander house he now inhabited. Brought up to farming, a ploughman at the age of fifteen, he had been 'discovered' and taken up by the Elliots of Minto, educated at Edinburgh University and taken abroad as tutor-companion to Sir Gilbert's son. Lord Bute later secured him an embassy post abroad.

In his time Liston was envoy-extraordinary and ambassador-extraordinary in Stockholm, Washington, Constantinople, although he did not marry until he was fifty (to Henrietta Marchant); he then had more than thirty happy years of married life until his wife's death in 1828. The deep attachment between Liston and his wife made friends fear that her death would shortly be followed by his, but he resigned himself to his loss, recovered his energies and travelled to Italy, where he was so struck by a classical tomb he saw there that he made a copy of it and had it set up as a memorial to his wife in a wild landscape opposite to Milburn, 'near an old church in a romantic and beautiful spot'.

On a small hill sloping towards the temple was a typically slovenly Scots village, which formed such a contrast to the classical tomb that Liston was inspired to improve it, making a proper road, a pretty schoolhouse and neat cottages, and a green. The locals, lazy rather than poor, were taken by the idea, and themselves started to plant shrubs.[10]

Liston, now rejuvenated, was much sought after by parties of visitors – including Mrs Hemans and her sons, and he frequently dined in Edinburgh and went on to parties elsewhere. When the Rev. John McVickar visited him in 1830 he was eighty-six, and still in the midst of his restorations. The McVickar family called on their way to Craigcrook, when for some reason the ladies remained in the carriage while the clergyman paid his call. Liston received him courteously in his 'beautifully castellated mansion', in 'a splendid Gothic drawing-room, panelled with cedar', and later invited the party to breakfast.[11]

In his ninetieth year Sir Robert went to London to dine with the King and 'fellow knights'. He lived until 1836, the admiration of contemporaries.

When history repeated itself and Charles X, King of France, and his suite again established themselves as exiles at Holyrood in 1830, few people were surprised. The Carolinan Henry Legaré, in Paris in 1823 shortly before

Louis XVIII died, when the deceptively soft-seeming but really 'clever-and bold-spirited' Duchesse de Berri had cast a spell over the old King and family, foresaw that if another revolution ousted the Bourbons it would be in favour of the Duc d'Orléans rather than the young Napoleon.[12]

Thomas Carlyle's Paris visit in 1824 was after Louis XVIII had died, whom he saw lying in state. He also saw the newly succeeded Charles X walking in the street, 'a swart, slightish, insipid-looking man, but with much the air of a gentleman, insipidly endeavouring to smile and be popular as he walked past'.[13]

Yet even Charles X had a distinct air. Years later the Duke of Wellington told Frances Gascoyne-Cecil that 'in the drawing-room' there was no comparison between him and George IV, the former 'so infinitely superior as a gentleman'; yet at the head of his troops on horseback he showed as 'a mere *péquin*'.[14]

'If some change does not take place soon, there will be a revolution', wrote Sydney Smith to his wife in 1826. 'The Bourbons are too foolish and too absurd', he declared, disgusted with the King's excesses after witnessing an extravagant religious procession. 'Nothing can keep them on the throne.' He also noted how old, indeed unrecognisable, the King had become since he had dined with him at the Duke of Buccleuch's in 1814.[15]

King Charles was accompanied at Holyrood by his son, the Duc d'Angoulême, and his duchess, who was Louis XVI's daughter, and the Duchesse de Berri with her daughter and son, besides his heir, the twelve-year-old Duc de Bordeaux. Frances Williams Wynn had seen the Duchesse d'Angoulême in England in 1814 and described her 'sour, ill-tempered, vulgar countenance', 'blear-eyed'.[16]

Mrs Grant, on the other hand, revered the Duchesse for piety and filial affection, and declared a 'passion' to see her, while admitting that the Whigs, who glorified the revolution, said she had 'an unpleasant expression . . . quite a scowl'. Mrs Grant told them it was 'virtuous indignation'. Her sympathy with the 'forlorn royalties' effaced her strong 'anti-Gallican prejudices'. She could even admire the Catholicism shown by the King and the pious, 'long-suffering Dauphiness'.[17]

Charles was certainly agreeable in society – merely unfit to be a king. A member of Mr Gibson-Craig's family met him shooting near Riccarton, and went up to show him the best grounds, finding him 'an agreeable old gentleman'. Sir Robert Liston, who at Milburn Tower was near at hand, called on the Duc de Bordeaux's tutor, whom he had formerly known, and on returning his call the tutor brought the boy with him – 'intelligent-looking', he reported to the Rev. Robert Morehead.[18]

Boys living in Buccleuch Place, behind Holyrood, also used to see the King out shooting, with the Archers, and thought the young prince 'a podgy little youth', wondering that such deference was paid him. But they were curious to see these figures, part of history, perhaps part of the future as well.[19]

Many a story was told of these casual encounters with foreign royalty. Charles Kirkpatrick Sharpe recalled that during the former stay, Mme de Polistron lived in 'a small white-washed house, on the left of the Chapel, looking into the Park', while her son by the King, Louis Polistron, 'a very handsome youth' who died young, had attended Mme Rossignol's dancing school. Now, it was rumoured, the King was to marry Mme de Gontaut, 'who rules the roast already. Here is a new Mme de Maintenon, full as clever, but not quite so pretty.'[20]

He also reported how 'the Dss de Berry is foolish enough to make people stand up in her presence, which is a great blunder in madame. I saw her one day in the street, attended by three blackguard-looking men, and very meanly dressed.' As for Mme de Gontaut, he had seen her long ago, 'and a very curious person she was. I hear she hath become quite an old woman. She was clever, but such a dirty thing in her person.'[21]

There was also the difference between the *ancien régime* and the *arriviste* aristocracy. Tom Moore was told by a French lady he met how her father had once met the Comte d'Artois, as he then was, with Lord Hastings and the Duc de Bracas, and was 'much struck, not only with the high-bred deportment of all three, but with the great resemblance they all bore in their manners to each other'.[22]

Yet Charles Sharpe got a very different impression in 1831 when de Bracas, whose title was a Restoration creation, called with an introduction by Sir John Sinclair's son George. 'I have no great *gout* for such people now . . . I felt confident from his manner that he was *new* . . . He may know much about coins, of which I know very little, but I am sure he is very ignorant as to pictures . . . and how he lingered – I thought him anything but civil.'[23]

The King's retinue walked about the streets, 'and lounge in a certain bookseller's shop . . . a favourite, the king having known him 30 years since'.[24] This was Robert Miller, who told Mrs Grant of an interview with the royal family's 'clerical retinue'. He had known the King's confessor during their former stay, but except that he was now Archbishop of Rheims did not know any of his 'added dignities'. Calling at Holyrood he found ' a whole conclave of the priesthood', and the Archbiship, who was seated, received him kindly and presented him to the three confessors of the Angoulêmes and of the Duchesse de Berri – who were all standing before him until he told them to sit.

Miller was not sure how to address the Archbishop, and listened carefully until he heard one of them ask 'His Eminence' if he wanted some air, and was then careful to use the title.

This was the first Cardinal, he notes with interest, who had set foot in Scotland since Cardinal Beaton.

'It is now rumoured that the Ex-Dey of Algiers is coming to Edinburgh,' commented Mrs Grant. 'One grows dizzy in looking at this whirl of alteration.'[25]

Her inbuilt respect for royalty gave the party a special interest for her, and when three beautiful white ptarmigan were sent her from the Highlands, this naturally frugal lady did not enjoy the gift herself, but sent it with her compliments to the Dauphiness, for which next day she received 'a polite acknowledgement'.

A year or so later she expressed her amusement over conjectures about the authorship of anonymous 'Lines sent to the young Duc de Bordeaux'. The odds are that the author was herself.[26]

This second Bourbon residence was in a somewhat lower key than the first, and made less impact on Edinburgh society. For one thing, the chief character was now so old, and can have retained few illusions. He eventually withdrew with his court to Prague, where he died in 1836.

Like Sir Robert Liston, Mrs Grant might have been forgiven for believing that she had outlived her friends, but her sound constitution saw her through until 1838.

The Rev. John McVickar, whose forebears had emigrated from within a mile or two of Inveraray in Argyll, was the son of a leading New York merchant. Travelling for his health, with his wife and two eldest daughters, on arriving in Edinburgh he first visited Dr Chalmers, next dined with Jeffrey, called on Liston, heard Dr Andrew Thomson preach, breakfasted with Wilson, visited the Botanic Garden with Thomas Erskine, and at Liston's instigation called one morning on Mrs Grant. He was heralded on horseback by 'Mr Fletcher, a young artist', presumably a son of Mrs Fletcher's.

McVickar, whose descriptions of his encounters are vivid and discerning, describes how they found Mrs Grant, who was then seventy-five, in her 'very large house, in very comfortable style' – Brae House opposite St Cuthbert's, then on Edinburgh's western outskirts. 'We were ushered into an empty but not unfurnished, literary-looking drawing-room' – an interesting diagnosis. 'She came in supported by crutches, and aided by a servant, looking old and broken by years, but still with much dignity. The moment she sat down, however, she was full of life and interest.'

Mrs Grant explained to McVickar in some detail about his family's distinguished West Highland ancestors, urged him to visit his clan chief, Lord Glasgow, and wrote in his daughter Anna's album.[27]

Henry Mackenzie, always a friend and a frequent visitor, in 1823 begged Mrs Grant to translate some legendary Gaelic poems, which she found a much more difficult assignment than the modern Gaelic, and her memory was rusty; but she was anxious to oblige 'the old Evergreen', kind and delightful as ever, and she had a high opinion of him, 'more animated, more correctly informed and pleasant, than any young person I know'.[28]

In 1825 a petition was drawn up by Sir Walter Scott, attested in his own hand, to solicit the King for a pension for Mrs Grant. It was signed by many friends, including Sir Robert Liston, and was to be presented to Robert Peel, the Home Secretary, by Sir William Grant, former Master of the Rolls. Until then Mrs Grant had no suspicion of this move, and her son was briefed to break the news to her just before he left Edinburgh for London.[29]

That same year she had a miraculous escape, after a prolonged tour in the north Highlands taken for the sake of her daughter Mary's health. She might easily have, but did not, sail back from Inverness to Greenock on the *Comet* steamboat, which sank with the loss of nearly all passengers. On her return to Edinburgh, everybody she knew came to call on her: as she wryly comented, she 'became quite the fashion because I was not drowned'.[30]

Among her congratulations was, of course, one from her old admirer Mackenzie, now turned eighty, and still a regular attender at Royal Society meetings, at which he read out spirited memoirs. Recently, in discussing the mind's activity in dreams, he had told her that once last summer in his sleep he translated a French epigram, which on waking he wrote down and sent to Professor Dugald Stewart. Mrs Grant capped this with an experience she had had as a girl, during the voyage back from America, when she dreamed a ballad, though she never wrote it down. To her surprise Mackenzie quoted this experience at a later Society meeting, and sent her a ticket to attend.[31]

It was in June 1826 that she had moved to Brae House, beyond the west end of Princes Street, which 'I had long coveted without even a hope of possessing it . . . A garden, rich in fruit-trees, and on my arrival beautiful with loads of blossom, and affording shelter to swarms of little birds, as well as blackbirds and thrushes, is at the end; there is a most luxuriant bush of white roses at the window, where I sit . . . I have a handsome drawing-room, with 3 windows looking to different quarters; a large, airy bed-room, commanding fine prospects, on the same floor, and behind that, my son's business room . . . We pay for the whole only half the rent of the house in Princes Street.'[32]

In 1827, established in this haven, and seemingly indestructible though continually battered, she endured further distresses. Since Isabella's death her last surviving daughter Mary had drooped and required care, and her son, almost 'sunk' under the blow, was only gradually reviving his spirits. Mary died on 16 November, leaving her mother feeling unnaturally apathetic. She now had two companions, sensible, kind Mary Maccoll, a good influence, and the meeker Margaret Steven. They were then joined by Miss Fulford from Devon, 'quite a curiosity, & so ardent, so talented'.[33]

Friends too were dying. Early in 1828 Dr Hook, Dean of Worcester and husband of her great friend in Moseley, died; while her one-time pupil Miss Glassell, whose marriage to Lord John Campbell had started so happily, since the previous year had sickened and died only two months after her friend Mary Grant, leaving a young family. And other deaths were to follow.

Mrs Grant started her morning with 'serious reading', including precious last letters from Mary to her gifted friend Miss Fletcher – for during the day she was constantly interrupted, and by evening quite worn out.

Though full of visitors, she described the day in 1830 as 'very monotonous', meaning unchanging. She could rarely go out to visit: 'indeed I cannot afford it; sedan-chairs, my usual conveyance, would soon find their way to the bottom of my little charity purse'. In summer she woke early and read 'something not too interesting' until 6 or 7 a.m., then would sleep for another hour. By 9 she was dressed and at the breakfast table, 'to accommodate my son', who had to leave for work. 'We read the Bible only before breakfast; afterwards I have a sacred half-hour. Then I begin a letter, or write 2 or 3 pages in a manuscript which I shall leave behind me. Afterwards come dependants . . . [who] want a letter to someone, or advice, or a governess' place, &c, and my protegees have turned out so well that I have constant applications for such persons.'

Household concerns were taken care of by young Miss Maccoll, so she was free to receive visitors at the appropriate social hour. Many came on sunny days, many too on non-sunny days, for personal reasons. In between she would contrive to write at least part of a letter, and to read. On good days she could sit for an hour in her garden, where visitors would join her on 'a long seat'.

A little after 5 her son came back from his office, when they dined. Between then and tea 'I can never apply to any thing', and would surely slumber off had she not taught Mary chess. Then came tea, 'my only nectar and never fails to refresh and invigorate me'. In the evening she knitted, she and Mary read to one another and made comments. Her son returned to his office, and a few friends might join her for tea or coffee. 'This is a sketch of the routine of our lives.'[34]

She went to hear Edward Irving preach at Moncreiff's – nothing smaller would hold the crowds – and thought he had 'little coherence'. There was the egregious New Yorker Miss Douglas, artlessly keen to meet all celebrities, and there were Mrs Grant's many kind friends, almost too kind and overwhelming. Some were her 'young ladies' from former years; some were families begging her to spend the summer with them. In September 1828, she accepted to visit old Miss Trotter of Mortonhall, at Blackford House, a lady of 'stately form and firm, energetic and high-principled character', who despite her great age took an active care of her. Miss Trotter had old, aristocratic connections, and 'usually asks 2 or 3 ladies to meet me, – always people of intellect, for she "canna be fashed" with any other', and as soon as one lady left she would summon another. Her table was simple but sufficient, 'fruit, poultry, every thing growing on her own farm, well dressed, and excellent of their kind'.[35]

There was also a gratifying visit from two more American friends, Professor and Mrs Norton from Harvard, he handsome and 'in the prime of life, animated and imaginative', with no American foibles beyond a 'slight intonation', she 'beautiful and graceful', with 'relaxed, elegant manners and good taste'. 'I have rarely seen so fine a couple.'[36]

In 1829 Mrs Grant as usual spent a pleasant summer with Mrs Smith, who with her sister Mrs Brown was the sole survivor of her early friends. Her domestic arrangements were always agreeable. The Princes Street house had had the advantage of the castle view, 'the rude grandeur of the rock, and its military music, that seemed to descend from the clouds'. Brae House, though equally near the view of the castle, was more frontal.[37] But friends continued to die off, General Stewart of Garth, her old friend Mrs Hall, the talented Miss Bannerman at Portobello, and Mrs Hook's brother Sir Robert Townshend Farquhar. She could no longer write at night because of her poor sight, and in the mornings was always 'oppressed with visitors'.

In August 1830, however, she had a 'ludicrous experience', on one of the few occasions when she was induced to accompany Mary and some young friends to Hopetoun House for an exhibition of fruit and flowers. The beautiful rooms, attractive with many floral arrangements, looked at their best. Mrs Grant, bonnetless and in cap and shawl, descended from her sedan chair and, as she entered, was surprised to see a lady in similar garb, taking her place in an equally splendid adjoining room. She had a clear view of the stranger, sitting apparently a little behind, and from time to time turned her head with interest to view this fellow-cripple, 'this withered flower', whose eyes met hers with what seemed to be equal sympathy.' She seemed somewhat familiar, and was of similarly 'ample' figure, though Mrs Grant thought with some complacency 'that I had a better face, hers being almost ugly'. All the same, she thought, she would like to be introduced when the exhibition was over. On leaving, both ladies rose at the same time, but the stranger vanished from her sight.

'Think of my mortification at having the laugh of the whole house against me on coming home. There was no such room, and no such lady.' She had been viewing her own self through a pair of looking-glass doors.

The others had thought her expressed wish to meet the stranger was meant as a joke, and her self-deception, which in anyone else would have seemed extraordinary, was natural to Mrs Grant: she had not seen her reflection in a glass for at least two years.[38]

Well-meaning friends sometimes over-stepped the mark. In November she received an eight-page anonymous letter, exhorting her to live less 'in and for the world' – surely one of the last people to whom such a homily should have been addressed. Her reading of improving works was undiminished, and one of her few worldly wishes, expressed to Mrs Smith, was that should she live long enough, 'I might go by the railroad to breakfast with you, and return here to dinner.' No chance of realising this daring vision was to materialise until the next decade.[39]

As time passed, while Mrs Grant's letters became fewer because of the diminution of surviving friends, they became proportionately longer; and of necessity more full of reflection than of information. The return of the exiled French royal family to Holyrood prompted her strong monarchist feelings and even effaced her 'anti-Gallican prejudices', expressing some scorn for Whig inconsistency that Catholicism was appropriate in Ireland (where she considered it a disaster), excellent in England, 'where the light of the Reformation shines', yet 'odious' in France – where it was the national religion, and professed by Charles X and the pious and 'long-suffering Dauphiness', whom Mrs Grant admired for the qualities which the French detested in her.

Mrs Fletcher, always greatly admired, and a legend even years later after she had left Edinburgh, sometimes proved almost too overpowering to the shy. The mature George Ticknor, who met her again in 1838, nearly twenty years after his first Edinburgh visit, recalls how in those early days 'Brougham, Jeffrey, and all that clique' gathered round her, and now in her old age her 'talents still command their admiration and regard'.[40]

Helen Graham found her more formidable. Like Mrs Grant's sickly daughter Mary she was a friend of Margaret, wife to Mrs Fletcher's son Miles, and the Graham family frequently joined the Fletchers at parties and other junketings. At one not very enjoyable evening at the Edmonstones' in March 1825, besides 'that lion of lions' Grecian Williams there were not only Mary Fletcher and Miles and his wife, but 'old Mrs Fletcher with her piercing eyes, which seem really to search into the inmost recesses of one's soul'.[41]

This disconcerting effect was even more powerful with John James Audubon, who had been given an introduction to her as to a dozen other celebrities; but while he rapidly became charmed with many he met, and liked Mrs Fletcher's daughter who first called on him, he was then put out because a promised call by her and her 'young ladies' did not materialise, and he had to cancel a sitting for his portrait with John Syme. Then, only a few days later, having endured such a sitting, 'durance vile' for two and a half hours, he was about to sit down exhausted to his dinner when he received what almost amounted to a summons from her, and felt obliged to attend her house at once.

Mrs Fletcher was renowned for her beauty, even to old age, but Audubon saw 'a woman not handsome but good looking, more characterful in her features than women are generally . . . I was struck with the strength of all she said, although nothing seemed to be studied . . . the fruit of a long, well fed round of general information. She, of course, praised my work but I scarce thought her candid. Her eyes reached my very soul . . . at one glance she had discovered my great inferiority.' Her children he thought '*gentil* looking' but not 'subordinate'.

'Lucy, I feared her probably too much to like her . . . She positively riveted me to my blushes, and never before have I felt so stupid. I was glad I had met with her, and yet still better pleased that I was at liberty to go.'[42] The poor fellow, though he knew the worth of his own work, was so unconvinced of its value in the eyes of others, and on the other hand so convinced of his supposed lack of education and intellect, that with people like the unique Mrs Fletcher his jellyfish timidity came into play.

Patrick Fraser Tytler and Pringle of Whytbank were one night in August 1824 riding to Whytbank from Abbotsford when, after fording the Tweed at Birdside, Tytler told Pringle that during the evening Scott had taken him aside to propose his writing the history of Scotland, which he himself no longer felt fit enough to undertake, because of the research it would require into Scotland's little-studied archives. He offered help and advice in obtaining access to documents, and Tytler agreed to the suggestion. This was a turning-point in his life, and much to his own taste. It was to establish his fame as a historian – after the four years which it took him to complete the first volume.

In spring 1825 he became acquainted with the Hogs of Newliston, a well-to-do, old-established family, and the following January he became engaged to the daughter Rachel, 'of uncommon beauty and elegance, with a charming disposition' but delicate. They married at the end of March.[43]

As a member of the Midlothian Volunteer Yeoman Cavalry, Tytler was among the 'most conspicuous', and stood out for his pleasing manners and 'exuberant flow of spirits' and wit – not to mention his extempore songs, later published as *Songs of the Edinburgh Troop*.

One afternoon in 1825 he stole off duty from Portobello sands to spend a quiet afternoon with his brother at Woodhouselee. Unfortunately he was soon missed, and it was easy to guess where he was. 'A corporal's troop, with a led horse and a mock warrant for seizure' were despatched to apprehend and bring back the deserter.

Escaping through a back door, Patrick hid in the glen till he thought they had left, but his colleagues, who knew him too well, caught him 'at the very threshold by the ambush which waited his return, deprived of his arms, mounted on the led horse, and carried off in triumph' back to Musselburgh camp. He was so delighted by this charade that by the same evening he had composed a song which he sang to riotous applause next day at the mess table, a rollicking affair once one grasped the rhythm and vowel-sounds.

Private Tytler, forgetting quite, sir,
That truth, the soul of discipline
Most undutifully, in the month of July,
Set out for Woodhouselee to dine.

The adventure continues with his discomfort while in hiding:

The cold damp ground it wet his rear,
And Pat would have sold, sir, ere he was an hour older,
His prospects for a pot of beer . . .
On the swift brook's margent he was seized by the Sergeant,
Who strapped the traitor to his saddle seat . . .
I'm told by Sergeant Scott, that the villain's to be shot,
As a warning to every Carabineer . . . [44]

Rachel's fortune, added to his own, proved of great value, giving Tytler the independence to live in London, where most of the necessary documents were to be found. In all, the *History of Scotland* took him twenty years. It was heavy labour, copying out the manuscripts by hand and having to write much of the work twice over.

The first two volumes, published in November 1828, taking the story to the establishment of the first Stewart kings, were highly acclaimed. Tait, the Princes Street bookseller, printed only 500 copies, so quickly sold that before the next two volumes were published he ran off another 750, and a third edition followed. For volumes III and IV, in 1829, there was a much larger printing. Scott wrote long reviews, dispassionate and fair, in the *Quarterly*, expressing any disagreement with respect and courtesy.[45]

With this encouragement Tytler, who moved to one of the large new Melville Street houses, carried on for a further five years, probably the happiest time of his life. He and his wife had a son and two daughters, but her health was failing. He also needed to be more in London for research, and meanwhile with the fall of Wellington's Government in 1830 he lost his post as Junior Counsel in the Court of Exchequer, along with his friend Sir William Rae, Lord Advocate.

He hoped to succeed Dr John Gillies as Historiographer Royal of Scotland, but in the event Gillies lived to 1836, and the first vacancy thus occurred only under a Whig Government. The Reform Bill riots in April 1831 also prejudiced the prospects of any ambitious Tory.

Tytler had meanwhile formed a distinguished circle of friends and acquaintances in London, thanks to his reputation, which brought him to the notice of Lord Melville, Lord Teignmouth, the *Quarterly* editor John Murray, and Lord Holland. At Murray's suggestion he embarked on a four-volume series of *Scottish Worthies* (1831–33), as part of a 'Family Library' on the lines of Constable's successful *Miscellany*. Reform Bill disturbances delayed the project, and meanwhile Tytler continued with his History, and at Oliver & Boyd's request wrote a *Life of Raleigh*, which also sold well in America.

His wife's health was sadly now so fragile that she was ordered south, and they settled in Torquay, where he completed *Scottish Worthies* and worked on volume V of the *History*, but her illness was now serious, and she died in April 1835.[46]

In January 1831 came the sad loss of one who was deemed well-nigh immortal, Henry Mackenzie, in his eighty-fifth year. Mrs Grant herself was now something of a curiosity, and had for some time realised with dismay that in her old age – she was seventy-five - she had endured frequent bereavements and numerous accidents, but was carried through by her strong constitution – 'People come, not to see, but actually to look at me'.[47]

Eye trouble kept her from writing for some time, or from taking in young ladies, but returning spring, and the domestic virtues of her 'unwearied son' brought renewed enjoyment. Yet from her windows she could see the graves of four daughters, Mary, Isabella, Anne and Moore, all buried in the West Kirk opposite. In moments of nervous depression 'I feel as if I had survived every body and every thing worth living for, and were nearly alone in a changed world.'[48]

She was happy in Brae House, however, 'a rural oasis' protected from the 'stone and mortar' which was Edinburgh's version of London's 'bricks and mortar', a term of reproach on the post-war rash of building; but events were to dictate yet another move before long.

She also now took on a new young lady, Miss St Paul, daughter of Sir Horace St Paul, in Northumberland. Her sedentary life condemned her to reflective comments on the outside world, and on books. There was Tom Moore's new *Life of Byron*, by which she was 'by turns amused, disgusted, and delighted. What sound sense, what a sparkle of wit, with what detestable profligacy, and what lamentable misery of mind . . .' A far more balanced comment than from many who were ready to condemn Byron out of hand.

A confirmed Tory, she declared on the subject of the Reform struggle that 'nothing can equal the horrors of mob government . . . if the aristocracy desert themselves, they deserve the worst that can happen to them'.[49]

Failure of eyesight and memory, and a severe influenza epidemic that summer, prevented correspondence until the autumn. She herself was despaired of, but again her iron constitution saw her through. When the doctor recommended country air, her son discovered Blawlowan, a sheltered spot near Stirling, where she and her young cousin stayed for some six weeks in idyllic surroundings. But meanwhile more friends, or friends' relatives, were dropping off, while one, 'Mrs L', had fallen into the 'absurd belief in modern miracles and prophecies' of the Row heresy. Meanwhile the exhortation to Mrs Grant to think less on the world had rankled, and she reflected that her devotion to family and friends had ended in the loss of them all.

Another warning came when she suffered a serious fall in December 1831, when on leaving her room one morning, her crutch became entangled and, 'in a kind of reverie', she fell full length. Fearing for her brittle bones, she really thought her time had come, but wonders were achieved by the doctor's prescription of hot salt fomentations. Towards the end of January she confessed to Mrs Hook that her 'odd, elastic frame . . . which always rises from a crush like trodden camomile' was now restored.[50]

Now there was cholera, seemingly a salutary divine warning – and the Reform Bill again raising its head. 'I was always angry at Jeffrey's politics', she said, 'yet I know so much good of his private character, that I am sorry for his own sake to see him launching forth firebrands and arrows, and saying, "Am I not in sport?" He is no money-lover, and is kind-hearted, and a most generous relation; and moreover his talents, though in some respects misapplied, help to keep up our national credit for genius.' Jeffrey was now Lord Advocate, and later MP.[51]

Demands on Mrs Grant's time still did not lessen. Mornings 'evaporated . . . in the hearing requests, and giving very painful, because unsatisfactory, answers to people not in the least interesting, who give me credit for influence I never pretended to have'.[52]

'Of late so many of our stars have set, none others rising to supply their place, that the sky seems darkened.' Another friend of half a century, Mrs Brown, died in the spring, and consolation was found in Mrs Hemans's 'Poet's Dying Hymn'. 'Sir Walter Scott and she', she confessed, 'have been to me the fabled fountain of youth: I drink and feel renovated.'[53]

A personal upheaval now loomed. Her devoted son John Peter was getting married, to none other than shy Margaret Steven, now about twenty-three, whom they had known since childhood, affectionate and now maturing as a personality. John Peter was buying a house for himself, and she must move with them. Though fully expecting to end her days at Brae House, with its trees, flowers and distinguished view, she must now join them in a humdrum new house in a new street, 10 Coates Crescent, where they moved in May.

'You cannot imagine what the divorce has cost me', she told Mrs Hook – but Brae House was 'too like myself, too old and unfashionable'. Coates Crescent was larger, finer and fashionable; she only wished that in time she would feel at home.[54]

In the summer of 1832 her son took off for the Continent, urging his mother to go to the shore. The place he recommended was taken, so she and Mary Maccoll set off without preamble for Innerleithen, which having two springs was becoming increasingly popular as a watering-place, in 'a quiet vale in a pastoral county'. Accompanied by a maid and a 'travelling library', the ladies dined at a good inn, after which Mary shopped around and found good lodgings in a new house with Mrs Boyd, 'a very pretty lady-like person', and here for some two months Mrs Grant spent a happy retreat, 'sequestered in a kind of Patmos that was much to my taste'.[55] It was certainly like being in a foreign village, for in Edinburgh she was besieged by her many friends, acquaintances and kinsfolk.

Here is a time to leave Mrs Grant. While she was away Sir Walter Scott died, already half out of this world. James Ballantyne, saddened by the death of his wife, died soon afterwards. The year 1832 was like a list of famous obituaries, including Sir James Mackintosh, and old Rev. George Crabbe. Meanwhile her son, married in London in March 1833, was on the point of entering on a new life with his young wife.

Mrs Grant lived until late in the year 1838, but we may leave her history almost co-terminous with the life of Scott.

56
THE CHURCH: GREAT PREACHERS AND DIVIDED ISSUES

'We arrived at Edinburgh on a Sunday, that is to say, on one of those days of strict observance, when every house is closed, every shop is impenetrable, and all the world is at prayers. The solitude was immense, absolute; and the first feeling we had of Edinburgh was, that this prodigious city had been anciently built up by a race of giants who had long since disappeared from the earth.'

Charles Nodier, *Promenade from Dieppe* . . ., 1822, 78

'The Scotch are fond of ceremonials and solemnities and commemorations, partly owing to their nationality, and partly perhaps in opposition to the spirit of the Kirk which is austere and forbidding. Then there is to recommend them the intoxication of speechifying . . .'

Wordsworth to Crabb Robinson, *The Correspondence of Henry Crabb Robinson and the Wordsworth Circle (1808–1886)*, Oxford, 1927, II, 565, 9 February 1844

'. . . the Scotch Church – an immense quantity of verbiage in their preaching, touching the feelings but seldom outliving the preacher'.

John Wilson, 26 Nov. 1843, quoted in *Journal and correspondence of Lady Eastlake*, I.107

'Immortal happiness was his sole ultimate aim . . . Everybody loved the quaint, picturesque oddity of his look, figure, and manner; his self-coined diction and thick articulation; his taste for cumbrous jokes, and the merry twinkle of the eye.'

Journal of Henry Cockburn, 1831–1834, 13 June 1847, on Dr Chalmers's death, Edinburgh 1874

In the 1820s, when the General Assembly was seriously divided between Moderates and Evangelicals over the issues of patronage, pluralities and Dissenters' disabilities, the church was still under the spell of the brilliant Chalmers and – in this case not officially approved – Edward Irving.

Chalmers, having finally overcome his scruples at deserting the pulpit for academia, partly for health reasons, partly because a chapel of ease was now planned for Glasgow, in 1823 accepted the chair of Moral Philosophy at St Andrews, and he embarked on what was to become his career for the rest of his life.

In 1824 he was again nominated to the General Assembly as Elder for Anstruther Easter, and hoped he might be so annually. Although Sir Harry Moncreiff warned him that 'some of the more violent' might question his commission, in the event such an objection was thought 'too glaring'.[1]

This was the first Assembly appearance of the Rev. Donald Sage, minister at Regolis and a fervent Evangelical. He was not blind to his party's shortcomings throughout their opposition to the Moderates, and considered their 'fundamental error' was having too much of the party spirit and too little of the Gospel, wrangling too much and using weapons as sophisticated as those of the worldly Moderates.

Sage described in detail both protocol and proceedings, and several of the representatives. Dr John Inglis, head of the Moderates, Principal Robertson's successor at Old Greyfriars Church, 'a tall, hard-featured personage considerably in the decline of life', had a voice like the rusty creak of a prison door, 'in every respect the reverse of melodious'. Though neither elegant nor eloquent as a speaker, to use the two favourite descriptions, he was vigorous in mind and shrewd in argument.

Dr George Cook, almost equally able but far more eloquent, was similarly disadvantaged in delivery and tone, usually wearing 'a sardonic sneer', and with a 'sort of whine or howl peculiar to the natives of the south of Scotland'.

So far not very agreeable listening. Then there was Dr Francis Nicol, Principal of St Salvator's and St Leonard's, a fluent party man who had secured his position through landownership and wealth, though in ability he could be matched by any 'plodding, well-fed, active farmer'. Principal George Husband Baird, organiser of the Assembly's education scheme, who had spent a summer travelling to promote education in the North and the Orkneys, was prudent and efficient but not particularly ambitious as a leader.

Up in a side gallery taking notes sat Dr Andrew Thomson of St George's, 'the instinctive dread of the whole Moderate party', at whom even the boldest spirits cast nervous glances while arguing 'their creedless and Erastian dogmas'.[2]

Chalmers was much in consultation with Sir Harry, at his house discussing tactics with Andrew Thomson and Dr McGill, and later with Cockburn. Chalmers, despite his apprehensions, spoke well on the Pluralities debate, which took up a whole afternoon and evening, and attracted so great an audience that the police had to be called to clear the galleries. 'All the gentlemen behoved to be turned out', many of whom had been squatting on the floor, and when made to stand by the policemen, 'all dusted from head to foot', 'raised the most tremendous peals of laughter'. Dr Haldane, though not one of the squatters, had also somehow attracted a lot of dust, to the audience's great amusement.

Chalmers, 'most shockingly squeezed', did not speak until 8 in the evening, even though speakers were limited to three on each side. Cockburn gave one of his finest speeches and Dr Stevenson McGill, Professor of Theology at Glasgow, spoke for two hours. Chalmers left after his own speech, as next day he was to speak on pauperism.

In this he supported a motion to petition against a Bill to abolish the existing poor rates, then before Parliament, which he considered too sweeping. In his opinion the Poor Laws merely increased the evils, whereas change ought to be permissive.

He was equally vocal on other matters, and carried a petition for a new Gaelic chapel in Glasgow against the opposition of the ruling party of Inglis, Nicoll and others, who argued that there were plenty with unlet sittings. Chalmers, who had eight years' experience of 'the spiritual necessity of thousands' in Glasgow, pointed out that the Highlanders, even with a new chapel, would still be under-provided. The petition was carried 99 to 71.[3]

He ran into trouble, however, over his 'overture' made three years earlier on the length of divinity students' studies. In 1823 the Assembly had insisted on limiting attendance at Divinity Hall to one year, but the question was dropped through lack of interest. Chalmers, who considered that his overture should not be thus set aside, fell foul of Dr Inglis, who objected to his speaking more than twice on the subject. Chalmers therefore sat down, but on being appealed to rose again and claimed that Inglis had high-handedly 'borne him down'. This caused an uproar; Inglis objected to such language, Chalmers argued that house orders were being 'overbearingly enforced', the students' gallery applauded with 'a tremendous ruff', and the House was soon in 'a whirlpool of confusion', Inglis and others vainly starting up to address them while others shouted angrily to clear the gallery.

After a deafening interval order was restored, the students on Dr Brunton's advice left before they were turned out, and lively debate resumed. Chalmers's good humour at length prevailed over murmurs of dissent, and a heartening majority voted to re-transmit the overture.[4]

The Evangelicals, after being long in the shade, were beginning to be in the ascendant and able to challenge the Moderates, largely because Dr Andrew Thomson was so vigorous an exponent of their doctrines. At the 1825 Assembly the parties were again in collision.

Thomson and Chalmers united in the debates, the former combining sound sense and genial personality with quick repartee and anecdote; unusually he was equally good at extempore and prepared speeches. They 'did gloriously' in opposing the Crown presentation of a non-Gaelic-speaking minister to Little Dunkeld, and its rejection, moved by Thomson and seconded by Chalmers, was comfortably carried.[5]

The pluralities debate on Wednesday, 25 May lasted until midnight. A pamphlet of Chalmers of twenty years earlier in which he approved of pluralities was quoted in his teeth, but in a vigorous refutation he pointed out that it was written when he was applying for Professor Playfair's chair of Mathematics, Playfair having insisted to the magistrates that the clergy could produce no competent candidate. Chalmers had indignantly defended the clergy, claiming that the cloth was not incompatible with teaching mathematics. 'Alas! Sir,' he now declared, 'so I thought in my ignorance and pride . . . I penned what was outrageously wrong . . . I recklessly thought not of the greatness of eternity.' With this 'sublimity' he quenched every sound in the House, and was greeted by 'a death-like stillness'!

They narrowly lost the pluralities debate, the custom of a double appointment to a pulpit and a professorship having now been established for some years (despite Playfair's objections). The opposition's nominal victory was achieved by packing the debate with elders, though most of the clergy voted with Chalmers, and church and public alike now seemed to oppose pluralism.[6]

As for students' attendance at divinity school, forty Presbyteries were required to support the conversion of the 'overture' to law, and they were now still short of three. Chalmers was convinced that by next year three more would have been converted.

He spoke seven times. 'This has been a glorious and very hopeful Assembly', he declared jubilantly, 'the most bustling' for ages. Meanwhile the week left him exhausted.

At the end of the last day, arriving at Dalry House, he went to bed at 7 o'clock and slept for ten hours, having had little sleep during the whole Assembly.[7]

That year George Sinclair of Ulbster, an established scholar, was elected an elder. He was a voluminous writer of pamphlets, including on the problems of the Kirk, and the emancipation of slaves.[8]

In 1826 Chalmers's efforts to improve theological education achieved part success, in that it was confirmed that all students must attend a full year at Divinity Hall. This was also his last opportunity to argue against the 'corruption' of combined church and academic offices, but again he was defeated. A few months later a Royal Commission on the Scottish Universities was appointed with power to remedy evils, and the General Assembly deferred further debate until it should report.[9]

While the Moderate party was still at the height of influence, the strongly resistent Evangelicals attempted by adopting an ecumenical policy to resolve their own members' differences, though not until 1833 did their numbers outstrip the Moderates. At this and subsequent Assemblies their aim was unity, a spiritual union known as 'The Conference', its sole object being the good of the church.

During Assemblies Chalmers was always in demand to give sermons, for example on 5 March 1826 he preached at the High Church on cruelty to animals, on which he had worked for six weeks. On 7 May, at the opening of the Assembly, he officiated in taking the sacrament at Hope Park Chapel.[10]

The previous summer on a return preaching visit to Glasgow, he had visited Mrs Grant's friend Mrs Smith of Jordanhill, now at Meadowside, where he met Mrs Grant herself, though on the whole he was meeting other clergy. In September 1827 Mrs Grant, returning from another such visit, was invited by a lady 'to meet her confessor, Dr Chalmers, a person whose genius and whose piety I respect highly, though there are certain points on which I differ much from him'. Apart from their theological differences, he earned her respect by the 'perfect artlessness and originality about his conversation', and the fact that he appeared modest and unspoilt. 'He and the great Well-known', she told Mrs Hook, 'are the only persons I see whose manners are perfectly simple.'[11]

During the 1827 Assembly Dr Nicoll suffered a stroke, but was able to attend the meetings. Chalmers, who as usual attended with Moncreiff, was chiefly concerned with the case of a recalcitrant divine, the Rev. Roderick M'Leod. This minister, appointed to Bracadale in 1823, had consistently refused to carry out baptisms, until out of fifty-seven children only seven had been baptised, and he refused the Presbytery order, which was repeated in 1824, when a representative was sent to his parish to see that baptisms were carried out: M'Leod himself still refused the office and in May 1826 was suspended for two months. An appeal was made on his behalf, and the 1826 Assembly, supporting the Presbytery, offered to restore M'Leod if he complied. Still he would not consent. The Presbytery's proposal to depose him was considered too harsh, as he was acting according to conscience.

Chalmers and Cockburn both spoke on his behalf in the Assembly, and the case lasted until 7 at night. Not surprisingly M'Leod was 'a little dour and impracticable', but Cockburn spoke admirably and Chalmers, though he thought his own speech his worst ever, was acclaimed as at his best.

It was a knotty case. The Solicitor-General appointed a committee of Drs Cook, Taylor and Chalmers to deal with the obstinate character, a thankless job. After they discussed the matter with him continuously for a couple of days, at last M'Leod acknowledged himself wrong in an acceptable form of words, an admission which 'carried him most triumphantly through the Assembly. The Moderates rejoiced over him as a stray sheep.'[12]

A lighter side of Chalmers is shown on the occasion of the General Assembly supper, held at the Waterloo Hotel on the Friday, 25 May. The festivity, prolonged by toasts and speeches, continued until 2 a.m. Professor Wilson was among the many guests; Dr Baird presided, and Lord Glenorchy, acting as what was incongruously known as 'croupier' or assistant chairman, sat at the bottom end of the centre table with the McLeod of McLeod as his own croupier on one side, Dr Chalmers on the other. Chalmers, called on to make a speech, complained that Dr Baird had put two toasts into his hand just as he sat down at table, 'the more especially, said I, that I had ever since given my whole time and attention to the carving of an immense turkey and other duties of a most weighty croupiership'. This, he adds artlessly, 'produced a laugh'.[13]

During this year Chalmers was offered the chair of Moral Philosophy at the new London University, another temptation which had Brougham's support, but he felt unable to give a definite answer. He was also invited by Edward Irving, now in London, to open his new Regent Square church, and accordingly Chalmers went by sea, voyages in which in both directions the passengers pressed him to preach on the Sunday. More than one hundred attended.[14]

At Irving's service two young ladies, Charlotte Wedgwood and Fanny Mackintosh, heard Chalmers preach and Irving pray. There was a huge crowd, people still trying to force their way in when the church was full, causing a near-riot. The two ministers aroused a varying response. Chalmers 'has a very bad voice', reported Charlotte, 'but is certainly a very fine preacher. If he had but Mr Irving's beautiful voice he would be perfect. Mr Irving gave a prayer of an hour's length, which is, I think, more than twice too long. Moreover his praying is so theatrical as to be disagreeable – a much worse fault in praying than in preaching.'[15]

In that year, 1827, Sir Henry Moncreiff died, having served at St Cuthbert's for more than fifty years. Another death was of George Fergusson, Lord Hermand, who had married an aunt of Henry Cockburn's wife. 'My dearest Jeffrey,' wrote Cockburn on 15 August, 'the world does not seem to me to be the world without Hermand and Sir Harry. After a few more of the aged go and leave us in the front rank, I shall begin to feel I must feel old.' He added that his own mother, his brother-in-law Dr Davidson, thirty-seven years his senior, and Richardson's wife, were also hourly expecting death.[16] Dr Chalmers's mother had also died that year, in Anstruther, when he stayed with her to the end.

Chalmers took up the post of Professor of Divinity at Edinburgh in the year 1828. He now left the fine old house he and his family had occupied and moved into 11 Argyle Square in Edinburgh. He and his wife brought their daughters' governess from St Andrews until they had settled after the 'amazing bustle' of their first weeks, and whereas in St Andrews Chalmers had had to deal with perhaps a dozen letters a week, he was now bombarded with more than fifty. He was also besieged by visitors, and was reduced to posting up a notice in the lobby to be shown by the servant to casual callers, begging them as politely as possible to leave.[17]

Now that he was wholly back in Edinburgh, Chalmers held the university post until the Disruption in 1843. He already had a reputation as a thoroughly illuminating lecturer and projecting his subject into the listener's mind. One of his students at St Andrews recorded that 'in a few emphatic and impassioned sentences' he 'set before us the whole philosophy of a subject and . . . *lodged for life in our minds*'.[18]

Beside Chalmers other preachers pale into insignificance: the Episcopalian Dr Alison was, according to Ticknor, 'dignified, mild, and gentlemanly';[19] old Sir Harry Moncreiff at St Cuthbert's, 'the simple church', was 'stern and venerable', his church being a stone's-throw from Mrs Grant's then house. In its immediate vicinity was 'the beautiful chapel of St John . . . where Bishop Sandford, more gently venerable, breathes the milder spirit of Episcopacy'.[20] At St Andrew's, where perhaps revealingly 'quarters' or unallocated seats were always available, Helen Graham attended with her aunt Susan Ferrier before the family fixed on a regular church, to hear the Moderator Dr Grant. Helen was warned in advance to cough 'pretty loud' in case Aunt Susan nodded off.

In December 1827 Mrs Carlyle senior, having arrived in Edinburgh with Jane to stay at Comely Bank, went to hear the Rev. Andrew Thomson, 'not much to her satisfaction', records Carlyle, since he 'had to light 4 candles before ever he could strike'.[21]

On the whole a church service, under many preachers, had become an ordeal, yet it was one seldom shirked. 'The singing was succeeded by prayers,' writes Frederick von Raumer. 'The clergyman made such a lamentable hippocratic face, as if he were near to death, or to martyrdom, and . . . began such a drawling, monotonous, lamenting, sighing and groaning, that I felt quite wretched, uncomfortable and . . . could scarcely remain . . . The sermon was at least twice as long as a German sermon but with a double portion of repetitions and tautologies.'[22]

The year 1828 was marked by the 'Apocrypha controversy' between two Evangelicals formerly friends, the Rev. Andrew Thomson, whom Jeffrey called 'the sledge-hammer of divines', and the Rev. Henry Grey, then at the New North Church. Thomson's attack on the British and Foreign Bible

Society's publishing a Bible incorporating the Apocrypha led to a pamphlet war, and caricatures showing the two ministers as fighting dogs.[23]

Edward Irving, meanwhile, who had been taking London congregations by storm – to start with – in 1828 was obliged to return to Edinburgh to defend himself before the General Assembly.

In 1827 a small group of Primitive Methodists arrived in Edinburgh from the 'Sunderland Circuit' to establish a mission, though they early clashed between themselves over which of them should undertake the preaching. John Bowes, a twenty-three-year-old preacher from a Yorkshire farming family, came with his wife Sarah, who was in late pregnancy and after only a month in Edinburgh gave birth to a still-born daughter.

They arrived in July and preached in the Grassmarket, at Leith, Newhaven and elsewhere, conducting prayers and classes. On 22 July Bowes claimed to have had one thousand listeners on Leith Links, and on 29th much the same number in the Grassmarket. He disapproved of his colleague Thomas Oliver, 'made of mysticism, insanity and perverseness', and was in dispute with the Sunderland committee because he 'would not make a division and oppose N[athaniel] West'. The committee dismissed him; Oliver and Tillotson, another preacher, tried to take over their chapel at Heriot's Bridge, and Tillotson left the group.

There was inevitable hostility from some Edinburgh quarters. Bowes, who visited the sick and families, on 6 August notes that these were 'principally professed Roman Catholics; but so much ignorance and bigotry I have not witnessed before. Some of them would neither read our tracts, nor permit me to come away without abuse; others did both.'

He did notch up some successes. At their 'Quarterly Love-feast' on 27 August, which lasted for three hours, many were 'wounded by the spirit' and remained to pray. 'Many cried aloud and wept for mercy, and many shouted aloud for joy.'

They also met at a 'floating chapel' held by the sailors at Leith, opened an unoccupied church, started meetings in a Stockbridge schoolroom, another at the Water of Leith, and then one at Richmond Court, so crowded that people could not get in. At other times Bowes preached in the open air at Leith Citadel, or Portobello. He and his wife moved into a house, partly furnished by supporters.

One woman they converted was a brothel-keeper, who dismissed her 'poor girls' and freed her house from its 'evil practices'. In 1828 Bowes's wife gave birth to a girl, and he went down to Sunderland to discuss his differences with the committee, but the fellow-ministers fell out among themselves. Some left, other preachers joined.

In 1830 Bowes took a spell in Dundee, and later undertook Missions in Kirkcaldy, Perth and elsewhere; in 1831, still only twenty-seven years old, he settled in Dundee. The progress of Methodism in South Scotland was far from smooth.[24]

It may well have been Methodist street preachers who rudely disturbed Frederick von Raumer's meditations in 1835, while enjoying the spiritual beauty of the Forth from 'the end of the long dyke' at Leith. His enjoyment was interrupted by a loud noise, at which he turned to see a large crowd surrounding a man 'with a round hat, immense whiskers, a Bible in one hand, and his gloves in the other'. The gist of his harangue was that religion was 'to teach you, not to live, but to die; not to enjoy, but to endure privation', the world being the despicable prey of Satan, and man should 'prepare only for the wrath to come'. Leaving this gloom to walk back to the city in the gathering dark, he came upon another such crowd at the corner of Princes Street, surrounding another prophet of 'sin, vengeance, punishment, death, damnation'. These two, following on a dismal sermon in the morning, 'were surely enough to crush a stone!'[25]

In 1828 Chalmers put up a creditable argument for a congratulatory address as part of the Address to the Throne on the emancipation of Dissenters which had attacked 'the ramparts of Toryism' by the repeal of the Test and Corporation Acts. Such addresses were usually prepared by the 'Old Moderates', but in this case none would move it as it would favour Dissenters too much. Chalmers therefore took it upon himself. He achieved a respectable minority vote of 77 to 123, in spite of the whole party massing against him – including Edward Irving, who sat opposite and was 'wild upon the other side . . . as if his eye and looks, seen through the railing, were stationed there for my disquietude'.

Irving was there to answer his own critics who declared his views heretical. One violent sectarian denounced him as an enemy to Christ's gospel. 'The colloquy that ensued was highly characteristic. Mr Irving's part of it began with – "Who art thou, O man that smitest me with thy tongue?"'[26]

Irving was now such a controversial figure that, having no church in Scotland, his status as elder was challenged, but in spite of Dr Andrew Thomson's opposition the Moderator allowed him to sit. The Lord High Commissioner even invited him to dinner when Sir Walter Scott was placed opposite him, and thought him unctuous and his squint 'diabolical'.[27]

Outside the Assembly Irving was drawing crowds in lecturing on Prophecy. The venue had been intended as St Andrew's, but it proved too small for the hundreds that flocked to hear him preach. Chalmers and friends tried to force their way in on the Friday, but in vain. They had better luck on the Monday when Irving had moved to the West Church (St Cuthbert's). This was at 6 o'clock in the morning. 'It is quite awful,' recorded Chalmers. 'There is power and richness, and gleams of exquisite beauty, but withal a mysticism and extreme allegorization which I am sure must be pernicious.'

Later in Irving's visit, when he was speaking at Kirkcaldy, so great was the crush that the gallery collapsed, killing thirty-five people before he even left the vestry, and Dr Dickson made this an excuse for not allowing him to preach the following year. Chalmers had attended a course of Irving's there, but scarcely understood a word.[28]

In 1829 Chalmers again pleaded for relief for the Catholics, which he had advocated from his youth in the face of prevailing hostility. The argument was induced by the King's speech in February on the removal of Catholic civil disabilities, when Mackintosh wrote urging Chalmers, because of his known views, to support by means of an appropriate sermon. Chalmers had agreed, though pointing out that public statements were unusual in Edinburgh unless provoked by an 'anti' demonstration. He did make two public statements on the subject, one of them at Irving's church, which was printed.

Before the Assembly started there was a meeting in mid-March at the Assembly Rooms in support of the Bill: seldom 'such a spectacle . . . an extraordinary assemblage', the speakers including Jeffrey and Sir James Moncreiff besides Chalmers, who argued that such disabilities were a 'dead weight' about Protestantism. Such was the applause that he could hardly continue, and at the end all stood waving their hats in the air for minutes on end.[29]

The crowd was immense, thousands of all ages pressing round the entrance for more than an hour, passing the time in intelligent discussion, regardless of a raw morning haar. Most were Whigs 'from their shops and offices in the High Street and the Bridges', delighted at the shake-up of old Scottish Toryism. At last when the doors opened and they tumbled in, to cries of 'Shame!' they found the hall already packed with people – many of them ladies.

Young James Dodds, who was later to write Chalmers's biography, was pushed under the gallery by heavyweights, and like them had to climb and perch uncomfortably on two seats, kept from falling only by the crush. He was pressed from behind by the whole weight of a fat old man at least eighteen stone, and encumbered by the hat of another who unheedingly placed it on Dodds's head. In this position he endured some three or four hours, crushed, blinded, stretched and suffocated, hearing the shouts and cheers as speakers arrived, along with the stamping and clapping of applause, 'There's Jeffrey! – There's Chalmers!' All around him rose on tiptoe, and poor Dodds, almost in a stupor, could see nothing at all.

At least he could hear. Jeffrey, fluent and persuasive, spoke in his 'high, sharp, penetrating accent' with its noted affectations. Sir James Moncreiff, harsh and 'masculine', made 'a vigorous forensic argument'. Cockburn, 'bland, homely', with his simple eloquence sometimes raised a laugh.

Then the struggling Dodds became aware of a new emotion: first a hush, then the audience was rising with a triumphal shout, 'Chalmers! Chalmers!' and he forgot his pains.

Now he was carried away by 'flashing antitheses . . . bold images, forceful argument', until at the close suddenly, by a movement of the crowd, he got a clear view of Chalmers, grasping the staff which at one moment he had hurled to the ground as a symbol, declaiming, 'With this mighty engine I will overthrow the tyranny of Antichrist, and establish the fair and original form of Christianity on its ruins.' As he ended, the huge audience rose, shouting acclaim for several minutes.

'Never had eloquence produced a greater effect upon a popular assembly,' exclaimed Jeffrey, though such a statement might have been made many a time in the preacher's career.[30] All this was achieved despite Chalmers's unimpressive, high-pitched voice, which proved an equal disadvantage now that he was a university lecturer.

This year Chalmers was distressed by the death of his brother Alex at Kirkcaldy in April, when he tried to get to his deathbed but arrived after he had died.

In 1830 was the 'Row Heresy', the doctrinal errors uttered by the ardent young Rev. Mr Campbell of Row near Gairloch, who preached with 'slender theological discrimination' on the atonement, arguing that men's sins were already pardoned, and personal salvation was 'of the very essence of saving faith'. A spate of sermons, pamphlets and reviews was poured forth in reply. Chalmers, though he maintained a mild interest in Campbell, kept out of this, as he did from Irving's speculations on Christ's human nature.[31]

Like Irving, Campbell believed in the return of the miraculous gifts conferred on the early Church. Chalmers kept an open mind on the gift of tongues supposedly descending on Mary Campbell, a dying woman, and later on a man at a Glasgow prayer meeting – phenomena which convinced Irving. Experts who examined Mary Campbell's writings were baffled, as they appeared to be in no known language.

The Row heresy caused dissension within families, with the pretence to work miracles based on spiritual pride. The sect expected the Millennium within fourteen years. They even attracted 'the gayest of the gay' to become converts to their ascetic views.[32]

Mrs Grant of Laggan, who expected fairly gentle treatment by the Assembly of 'the clerical culprits from the west country', complained that 'in taste, morals, and I fear to say religion, there seems to be no fixed standard' – 'So many books . . . that the old sound divines and the English classics are neglected and forgotten.' Later she was much distressed at the succumbing of her friend 'Mrs L' to 'that absurd belief in modern miracles and prophecies'.[33]

Chalmers made two visits to London that year, thus missing the General Assembly, to give evidence to a Committee on the Poor Law for Ireland, when he expressed his own liberal views. He was much lionised, and met Mackintosh, Lord Lansdowne, Leonard Horner, Brougham, Coleridge, Elizabeth Fry and the Buxtons and Gurneys, Joanna Baillie and other philanthropists. He was also nominated to take part in a deputation from the General Assembly with a congratulatory address to the new King William IV. In July he was appointed a King's chaplain in ordinary in Scotland. He received a congratulatory letter from Peel. He was also able to meet Irving in what proved to be their last meeting, but failed to shake his fanatical belief in the restoration of miraculous gifts.[34]

All this was happening against the background of the July French Revolution, which roused a demand for Parliamentary reform in Britain, and at the same time the movement in the Scottish church that led eventually to the Disruption; and an uprising against the Established Church in England. Chalmers was at the head of a move to revive Scotland's national parochial system and to abolish patronage. From this emerged a wider campaign for spiritual independence, which in time absorbed the others, with Chalmers as champion.[35]

1830 also saw Robert Morehead's publication of his *Dialogues on Natural and Revealed Religion*, drawing a connection between religion and philosophy, on which he had been engaged for some years; and the biography of Bishop Daniel Sandford, who died earlier that year. 'A truly spiritual-minded person,' thought Mrs Grant on meeting him, 'a finished gentleman, both in manners and feeling, and . . . profound scholar, quite in the Oxford manner.' His happy disposition had seen him through a life dogged by illness, and the two 'took much to each other, often met'.[36]

In February 1831 the Church lost another leading light when the Rev. Andrew Thomson collapsed and died after a Presbytery meeting. On leaving the hall, he happened to meet a friend in the street, and the two had walked together as far as his own front door in Melville Street when Thomson, turning quickly round, fell suddenly insensible on the pavement. The news 'passed like lighting': Chalmers hurried to the house, but it was in vain, Thomson could not be revived.

Chalmers, who declared himself 'unhinged' by the death, next day cut his college class short in order to pay tribute to Thomson. The funeral on 15 February, attended by some two thousand gentlemen, included magistrates, ministers, professors and members of many institutions. All shops were shut in the streets through which the cortège passed, and an estimated ten thousand people were watching from pavements, windows, even housetops. As usual, this was claimed as unprecedented – never before had there been such a funeral, or such a spontaneous show of appreciation.

On the Sunday Chalmers preached a funeral sermon at St George's, describing Thomson, among many other praises, as 'a joyous, hearty, gallant, honourable and out-and-out most trusty friend', with 'a dauntless and direct, and right-forward honesty . . . impatient of aught like dissimulation'.[37]

In June another death which had serious consequences was of Dr Meiklejohn, Professor of Church History, which opened up the question of a possible plurality. Jeffrey, who was at the time Lord Advocate, reassured Chalmers that the post would not be joined to a living, but in fact the salary was so small that it was never held separately. The Rev. David Aitken of Minto, approved by the Tory Town Council and the Senate, was offered the post but refused,[38] and Dr David Welsh who had had a Glasgow living since 1827 was appointed, Jeffrey assuring Chalmers that it was his recommendation that guided Lord Melbourne's choice.

The Rev. John McVickar, having heard the polemics of the two most celebrated – or notorious – preachers of the day, which could be exhausting even to the devotee, confessed that he longed for 'the solemn, quiet services' of his own church in America, 'after being excited by the eloquent vehemence of Dr Chalmers, and disgusted by the rant and grotesque acting of the once celebrated Edward Irving', full of 'folly and insanity'. He did, however, find Chalmers, now back from London, 'a real treat'. In Edinburgh he walked one morning to Chalmers's house for breakfast, to be received by his wife, 'a very lovely and intelligent woman, 3 silent daughters, and the doctor, with characteristic frankness and simplicity'. Their hospitality was also extended to 'some half dozen students or licentiates'. First they listened to a chapter from the Bible, followed (on their knees) by family prayers. 'Three hours passed away quickly and pleasantly at and around the table', after which the visitors all left together, and agreed to meet again. Chalmers gave McVickar notes of introduction to professors and literati (apart from Jeffrey, from whom he had already heard).

McVickar also went to hear Thomson, 'the most powerful reasoner and the most eloquent speaker I have yet heard. He is a little-big man, with broad shoulders, a coarse face, and an enormous head.' He read his sermon, but 'with freedom and earnestness'. McVickar indeed heard no extempore preacher but the Baptist Robert Hall. He noted that Chalmers, having written a sermon, memorised it for delivery. Jeffrey explained that he was diffident of his extempore ability, and while preparing the sermon had to be sure of no interruptions.[39]

Meanwhile Chalmers himself had been offered the living at Greenock West Church, but declined, preferring to stay with his Divinity chair. At the beginning of the year he had objected to a motion before the Edinburgh Presbytery for a day of public humiliation and confession, considering that individual 'congregational fasts' were best and that the country was too divided to impose a general compulsion.[40] A year later, when cholera was a nation-wide threat and the outbreak had reached Haddington, Edinburgh did announce a fast day. This seemed to be pre-empted by the Government's announcing a National day, and there was therefore a call to suspend the Edinburgh day, but a number of people including Chalmers resisted this, as cholera was now rife in 'the pauper haunts' of the Old Town and the Water of Leith, and the fast was locally observed.[41] The national day was not held until October.

The 1831 General Assembly's main issue was Edward Irving's 'false doctrine', which appeared the more serious because two ministers under his influence now believed that Jesus having become human had taken on man's 'fallen' nature. The two were deprived of their licence to preach, the Assembly condemned Irving's doctrines, and any Presbyteries where he attempted to preach were ordered to call him to the bar. Irving did not attend the Assembly, but was expelled in his absence, and was similarly condemned by the London Presbytery. Thereafter he had to retire from his Regent Square church in London and instead took to open-air preaching or 'field days' round Islington. His cause was far from lost, and although he died prematurely in 1834 his followers carried on with his doctrines and founded the Catholic Apostolic Church.[42]

The other minister who continued to fall foul of the Church was the Rev. Mr Campbell who, in an unprecedentedly long sederunt, from 11 in the morning until 6.15 in the evening, was condemned by a solemn deposition for his belief in 'the doctrines of universal atonement and pardon'. Campbell was also driven from the Establishment. This Chalmers did not attend, reckoning it would take a month to read all the material and form a judgment.[43]

The Establishment itself was now under attack, and Andrew Thomson before he died helped form an Edinburgh society aimed at limiting patronage which later, after the Reform Bill, petitioned for its abolition. Another society, the Voluntary Church Association, aimed to get rid of all Established religion in the belief that compulsory religious institutions were 'inconsistent with the nature of religion, the spirit of the Gospel, the express appointment of Jesus Christ, and the civil rights of man', a threat which rallied the Church.[44]

In 1832 Chalmers was appointed Moderator, and was therefore debarred from joining in the debates. He opened the meetings with a daily prayer, and closed the last meeting with a sermon. He also left his mark on Assembly protocol. Traditionally the Moderator held daily public breakfasts, and the Commissioner held daily public dinners, including on the two Sundays. Chalmers disapproved of both, and dropped the breakfast, but could hardly refuse the Sunday dinners. He therefore begged the Commissioner, Lord Belhaven, for a dispensation, and by agreement the Sabbath dinners and breakfasts were dropped altogether.[45]

The current agitation for Parliamentary reform, which was only one major aspect of the general social unrest and questioning of traditional systems, stimulated Chalmers to clarify his own ideas on political economy, influenced by Malthusian warnings. These ideas he shortly published along with his lectures, which he had already started to revise and edit for publication: and launched a mission to educate the labouring classes for their improvement and the betterment of their miserable lot.[46]

The debate on patronage continued in subsequent years, as did agitation about the Establishment, culminating a decade later in Chalmers leading the Disruption of the Church.

57
THE EDUCATIONAL SCENE: SCHOOLS

'This is the only country in civilized Europe . . . wherein attainments of that kind [the classics] are regarded with a very slender degree of admiration . . . for these 200 years Scotland has produced no man of high reputation, whose fame . . . rests upon what we call classical learning.'

'Peter Morris' [John Lockhart], *Peter's Letters to his Kinsfolk*, 3rd edn, 1819, 1.154

'Even philosophy has fallen; intellectual science now prates of phrenology, chimeras of politics, education &c. And natural science of gas, steam, &c. &c.

'Alas, Edina! all your streets and schools
Have brought you wealth, but all a wealth of fools.'

City Scribes and Country Readers – A Satire, Edinburgh, 1825 (NLS LC 137)

The early to mid-1820s saw important advances in education in Edinburgh, two for schoolboys, the third for unprivileged adults. The new schools had a contentious origin. In 1822 an independent, subscriber-supported new 'seminary' was proposed, but its subscribers were persuaded into settling instead for a school on the same lines as the High School, and therefore Council-backed. A site was agreed on beside Canonmills, north of the New Town, with William Burn as architect. But the estimates proved much higher than the £12,000 expected, and further, Councillor Blackwood objected on two grounds: that Edinburgh could muster only a thousand boys suitable to learn Latin, too few to merit a second school; and that the intended two-guinea entrance fee would exclude poor boys, counter to the principles of Scottish education.

In the resulting delay, Councillors began to think that the existing High School in the Old Town was both cramped and inconvenient, as so many pupils now lived in the New Town. On the other hand, a new school near

Canonmills would prove just as inconvenient for other districts, and besides, as a competitor it would eventually drive the old High School out of business (even though the latter had huge classes of up to two hundred boys).[1]

The Nor' Loch (drained, of course) was actually suggested as a site; or alternatively Sir Laurence Dundas's former house in St Andrew Square, now used as the Excise Office. The subscribers rejected the Nor' Loch as encroaching on Princes Street, and insisted on the Canonmills site. The Excise Office proposal did not materialise and the Council agreed on a new building, but reckoned that by this time Edinburgh had no suitable space left except beyond the east end, on Calton Hill. They invited Thomas Hamilton, who worked in the Greek Revival style, to produce a plan costing a maximum of £20,000, of which they offered up to £2000, the rest to be raised by subscription.

Cockburn, Scott and the other original backers refused this proposal and instead went ahead with the William Burn building at Canonmills, at the foot of Howe Street. The Edinburgh Academy, though its building was not complete until 1836, opened as a school in 1824.[2]

The Councillors' new school on Calton Hill was begun in 1826, but the contractor first ran out of funds, then early in 1828 sacked his workmen, then died. In spite of this the school was finished in 1829 at little over £4000 more than the intended maximum, barely £4300 of which came from public subscription.[3] It certainly ended with a more commanding site than the Academy (whose effect as a vista-closer was spoilt in 1828 by William Playfair's St Stephen's Church), and its temple-like structure and commanding hilltop position, even though it was out of sight of the city, made an impressive exit on the London side. The High School moved to these magnificent new quarters in 1828, when the old building was sold to the adjoining Infirmary as an extension of the surgical hospital.[4]

The new Academy confounded the fears that Edinburgh could not support two schools of such standard. As a proprietary day school, it was intended to raise the quality and reputation of higher education for boys of all classes. Its supporters were impeccable: Jeffrey was among the original proprietors and was later a director; the school was opened in the presence of, among others, Sir Walter Scott, Henry Mackenzie and Sir Harry Moncreiff; and the first headmaster, the Rev. John ('Taffy') Williams, son of a Cardigan schoolmaster, was acclaimed as one of the greatest scholars Wales ever produced. He had been educated at Balliol, and until his appointment to the Edinburgh rectorship was vicar and also master of the school at Lampeter.[5]

Williams, who was Rector until 1827 and again from 1829 to 1847, was admired for his 'lively and instructive conversation on Welsh history and antiquities', which suggested to Scott the plot of *The Betrothed.* Under him the school was soon regarded as Edinburgh's best, and inspired others.

The course lasted seven years, and more of its pupils went on to Oxford or Cambridge than from all others after its founding.[6]

Though a day school like most in Scotland, the Academy ranked as a public school, and all leading families sent their sons there. Archibald, eldest of the Tait brothers (who in 1869 was to become Archbishop of Canterbury), moved there from the High School, which none of the brothers had liked except that it was near enough for them to be much at their home and garden at 2 Park Place.[7]

The annual examination was regularly attended by the fashionable world, its prize-giving being regarded as of great importance. In 1827 when Henry Cockburn presented the prizes, having examined the boys in turn, he called pale, delicate Archie Tait to the front before the large crowd of spectators to present him with no less than six chief prizes, including two medals for Greek and the head boy's gold medal. He then called out the even more embarrassed lowest boy in the class, to present a backhanded compliment: 'If this manner of youth be the booby, what must the dux be?'[8]

In 1830, when Jeffrey presided and gave the prizes, the Rev. John McVickar, visiting with Thomas Erskine with a letter of introduction to the Rector, was astonished at the brilliancy of unseen translations from Livy, especially one by a fifteen-year-old boy. He declared the school 'a rival, though not so acknowledged, to the High School', and 'more aristocratic and more upon the English system', in contrast to the Latin-dominated High School, teaching also Greek and mathematics.[9]

Catherine Sinclair's children's novel *Holiday House* describes such a school prize-giving, probably at the new Academy, where Frank (of course) is dux, and Harry and Laura are taken to see the ceremony. 'A hundred and forty boys, all dressed in white trousers and yellow gloves' sit 'in rows, opposite to six grave learned-looking gentlemen, who seemed as if they would condemn all the scholars to death!' The long speech by their Principal is given in Latin and Greek.

The children's uncle Major Graham remarks on the good fortune of Scottish boys in not being sent away, like the English, to boarding school.[10]

There were also specialised schools providing for the disadvantaged, which in these enlightened days were moving to more modern premises. The Merchants Maiden or Trades Maiden School had in 1818 removed from Bristo Street to 'an elegant new building in a fine park at Laurieston'.[11] John Watson's school for destitute children, founded in 1759 by a Writer to the Signet, moved – again in 1828 – to a presumably intentionally plain and workmanlike building by William Burn on the skirts of Edinburgh at Belford Road. The Asylum for the Industrious Blind in Nicolson Street, when holding its anniversary service in October 1818, took the opportunity of publicising its teaching of the making of 'Hair, Wool, and Straw Mattresses; Basket Work of all kinds, making of Twine, Cord, and Pack Thread, Door-mats; teazing of Hair and Wool', all for no profit except payment for the children's labour.[12]

Meanwhile the many private schools continued their services. In April 1815, for example, the *Edinburgh Evening Courant* advertised that Miss Duncan's boarding school would remove at Whitsun from 5 Picardy Place to number 7 adjoining, where 'the access will be much easier, and she will be able to accommodate a greater number of BOARDERS and DAY SCHOLARS'. In October 1818 Mr Thomas Ewing's school advertised to start on 10 November at 41 North Hanover Street, for ladies and gentlemen, boarding available for pupils under fourteen, and teaching elocution, grammar, geography and history.[13]

A new departure in 1821 was the opening of Scotland's first School of Arts, a college of science for working men and women, initiated by a distinguished committee, besides the Lord Provost and members of the Council including Horner, Jeffrey, Cockburn, John Murray of Henderland, James Milne and others. One of the first students was the thirteen-year-old James Nasmyth, who remained until 1826.

At its annual general meeting in 1824, held on 1 June, a day after the General Assembly rose, at Leonard Horner's earnest request Dr Chalmers was present, when Horner read the report and Chalmers moved its adoption. It was considered an important achievement (wrote Horner on 28 June) 'when so many new institutions of the sort are in agitation', and when 'mechanics' were 'throwing off the assistance of the better educated classes, from a most mistaken idea of independence', rejecting the valuable opportunity of bringing them together. He and Chalmers had discussed the report at supper on the eve of the meeting, and Chalmers in his speech praised the institute for raising the status of 'this class of persons generally, made them more intelligent and moral, more rational and orderly . . . better members of society', to general benefit. Scott seconded his motion: it was their sole meeting on a platform representing the same cause.[14]

For obvious reasons the lectures were held in the evenings, and covered a comprehensive range from elementary principles to top level, with special attention to the quality of the instructors. It was organised on university lines, with sessions from October to May, lectures, and examinations. It was in fact the first technical college, and the curriculum of the later Mechanics' Institutes seemed superficial by comparison.

The staff included Dr Andrew Fyfe for Chemistry, clear in exposition and providing useful experiments for a crowded class, with great competition for front seats. Dr Lees and Mr Buchanan lectured on 'Mechanical Philosophy'; Mathematics and Geometry were rather less popular. Once the library was provided, crowds regularly formed at the door before opening hours, almost like queuing for a favourite theatre performance.

The school took over the old St Cecilia's concert hall, its orchestra space converted into a rostrum, with space for apparatus, and with surrounding seats in concentric circles it became a pattern for others in Scotland, for which James Nasmyth was able to construct illustrative models. Half of the profits from this he gave to his father, using the rest to pay for tickets for university classes, Dr Hope's on Chemistry, Professor Wallace on Geometry and Mathematics, and his 'valued friend and patron' Professor Leslie on Natural Philosophy.[15]

It was to further the work of this institute that Archibald Constable in 1824 proposed to publish his comprehensive eight-volume *Encyclopaedia for Mechanics*, considering that the works so far published to satisfy the new thirst for knowledge were inferior, whereas the one he planned would be 'entirely devoted to manufactures and the mechanical arts', extending to such relevant subjects as topography, statistics and biography. While he was haggling with Leslie over fees and scope, they were overtaken by the financial crash, and the project never materialised.[16]

An early version of socialism which approximated to a form of education was the campaign of the philanthropic Robert Owen, who had a considerable influence on George Combe and his brothers Abram and William. Owen (1771–1858), a Welshman widely read and as widely experienced, notably in the cotton trade and managing cotton mills, in 1799 bought up David Dale's New Lanark mills, in 1814 formed a new company and set about realising his idealistic visions of improving the human lot. In 1817 at a meeting at the City of London Tavern he expounded his ideas for 'villages of unity and co-operation'.[17]

George Combe, who was impressed by his theories, by October 1823 was evolving educational theories of his own. His brother Abram, a tanner whose works adjoined the family's brewery, had meanwhile visited New Lanark in 1820 at the age of thirty-five, and had met Owen. After his typical Combe-style upbringing, 'dreary and joyless' with its oppressive Sabbaths, he had lived for two years in London before setting up in business and starting a family in Edinburgh. Abram was soon converted to Owen's theories – even to firmly believing that Edinburgh's grand newly built Royal Circus might be destroyed within five years to give way to an Owenite Community building. He spent the rest of his short life as a kind of missionary for the new ideal system.

First, in 1821 Abram started a 'Practical Society' to carry out Owen's communistic principles, launching a New Lanark-style school for some 130 children and involving five or six hundred families, opening a co-operative society, and holding evening instruction, enlivened by dancing and social meetings. Unruly hooligans were converted into zealous, affectionate children, while their parents and elders abstained from drink, tobacco and swearing. Abram himself became a vegetarian. But as so often happened, after a year or so the initial enthusiasm waned, members dropped off and left to work elsewhere.

Abram, not yet daunted, built dormitories and kitchens in his tanyard and started a small community, intending to share profits, but unfortunately this soon collapsed. Between 1820 and 1825 he published books and pamphlets on the crusade, and in 1825, joined by Hamilton of Dalzell and other well-to-do supporters of Owen, bought the 299-acre estate of Orbiston east of Glasgow on the river Calder. Here they started to build on an ambitious scale for their community. Only one wing was completed, though by March 1827 even this held more than three hundred. But it was ill-thought-out and badly managed, and outsiders complained of the occupants' lazy and dirty habits. At first Combe in his idealism relied on automatic self-government and refused to intervene. In time the community overcame its teething troubles and was sufficiently organised to start an iron foundry, a dairy and a weaving company, a gardeners' group, and for a time it went well. In August 1827 when Abram Combe died of a chill, he could look back with some satisfaction on his crusade.

The community continued under his brother William, but ran into financial problems, he lost all his property, and finally the building was destroyed. Robert Owen, who in 1825 had gone to America to start New Harmony, returned in 1829 poor but undiscouraged, and the idealistic movement continued for some years despite debts at Orbiston and waning of the founders' enthusiasm.[18]

58

THE EDUCATIONAL SCENE: UNIVERSITY AND MEDICAL SCHOOL

'The fashionable place here now is the College; where Dr Thomas Charles Hope lectures to ladies on chemistry. He receives 300 of them by a back window, which he has converted into a door. Each of them brings a beau, and the ladies declare that there never was anything so delightful as these chemical flirtations. The Doctor is in absolute extacy with his audience of veils and feathers.'

Cockburn to Kennedy, 27 February 1826, *Letters Chiefly Connected with the Affairs of Scotland, from Cockburn to Thomas Francis Kennedy, MP*, London, 1874, 138

'They dine alone or together, just as it suits them . . . the whole course and tenour of their existence is unacademical.'

'Peter Morris' [John Lockhart], *Peter's Letters to his Kinsfolk*, 3rd edn, 1819, 1.151

'A very recent and contracted institution . . . [lacking] public or corporate splendour . . . Any young man who can afford to wear a decent coat, and live in a garret upon porridge or herring, may come to Edinburgh and pass through his academic career, just as creditably as is required or expected.'

Morris, *op.cit.*, 1.195–6

'A beating of feet and clapping of hands took place, that quite shocked me . . . The Doctor came in and all was hushed as if silence had been the principal study of all present.'

John James Audubon, 4 December 1826, Alice Ford (ed.), *The 1826 Journal of John James Audubon*, University of Oklahoma Press, 1967, 273

'It may pounce upon you in an instant.'

[On the cholera]: *Chambers's Edinburgh Journal*, 1st issue, 4 Feb. 1832, 7

At the University, the early neglect of Political Economy gave way by the mid-1820s to its establishment as the leading 'practical moral science', and an attempt was made to set up a professorship. John McCulloch (1789–1864), an Edinburgh graduate, had devoted himself to the subject, contributed articles on it to the *Scotsman* since 1817, of which he was also editor in 1818–20, and from 1818 to the *Edinburgh Review*. In 1824 he lectured in London, and next year when he published his *Principles of Political Economy*, there was much discussion in Edinburgh over the proposed founding of a Regius Professorship to be offered to him. On the recommendation of William Huskisson, then President of the Board of Trade, a memorial was signed by a number of supporters offering to endow the chair should the Crown create it. This was drawn up by Jeffrey, and the thirty or forty who signed it included five judges and twelve professors.[1]

In spite of Huskisson's and Canning's support, McCulloch was certain they would not succeed. 'It is the curse of Scotland that the ruling faction there are as base as possible, and that their master here [Lord Melville] is as bad as they are.' He proved right, that Melville would insist on following the opinion of the Scottish authorities, then 'the whole thing will be at an end'. The pretext was that Dugald Stewart was already giving his own small courses on the subject. McCulloch was instead appointed to a chair in London, and not until 1871 did Edinburgh get one.[2]

Dr Chalmers's opening lecture as Professor of Divinity was given at 11 o'clock on Monday, 10 November 1828, an unpropitious day of snow and hail showers, despite which from 9 o'clock onwards a huge crowd, barely restrained by police, gathered in front of the lecture-room doors, while the more privileged got in by the private entrance. Like John Wilson eight years earlier Chalmers, who arrived with an abstracted air, launched at once, on this occasion, into an opening prayer which silenced his audience, and then quickly roused them to rapturous applause.

The room was just inside the college portico on the right, reached by a narrow stone stair, leading to a gallery overlooking the quadrangle. The students, mostly young Scots studying for the church, aged between eighteen and twenty-five, would gather round here, joined by a number of Irish Presbyterians, and even retired officers.

Chalmers regularly turned up punctually, always looking hurried and absent, vanished into his small anteroom, where he did not like eager strangers to pursue him, and put on his gown and bands. He kept these on a side-table, in 'an odd brown-covered old volume of Leibnitz'.

In the lecture-room, more like a chapel than a classroom, dingy and badly laid out and darkened by the gallery raised on iron pillars, with a raised pulpit opposite, the audience was usually between 100 and 130. The gallery was occupied by the army veterans and distinguished visitors, the main hall by the students. Chalmers, still with his absent air, came in from his private door, mounted the pulpit and read the short opening prayer. Then, on starting the lecture he often found he had forgotten something; and once had to beat a hasty retreat, mumbling from behind his hand, 'My artificial teeth have gone wrong.'

David Masson, a regular attender, describes his performance (when he did start) as unique, 'every lecture a revelation'. He usually lectured sitting, reading from a book or manuscript, then, with growing excitement, might leap up, 'catching off his spectacles so that they hung from his little finger', flushed, stamping, gesticulating, and with some sudden extempore interpolation. His oratory always included some 'nervous shock' which might draw applause, though he usually insisted on silence.

The subjects, Natural Theology and Evidences of Christianity, were familiar, and Chalmers was quickly established as 'king of theological science'.

For this key academic post he was paid £200 a year. Besides his students his lectures attracted other clergy, professors, lawyers and numerous other gentlemen, and at the end of the first session Robert Morehead sent him a doubtless very welcome donation, on behalf of the many outsiders in his audience.[3]

Chalmers combined his academic career with his annual work for the General Assembly, now even more demanding because of the Kirk's increasing internal dissension, and in 1843 it was Chalmers who pioneered the movement leading to disruption and the setting up of the Free Kirk. He then left his University post to become Principal and Divinity Professor of the new Free Church College (1843–7), and this he occupied until his death.

Edinburgh professors enjoyed surprising longevity. Admittedly Professor Chalmers died at 67, but Dr Christison, years later analysing in his memoirs the careers of the seventy-eight members of the Senate who had died since 1820, found that 66½ was their *average* age, and that for those who entered the job early a long life seemed secured. Of the ten who entered between 25 and 30, survival was on average seven years longer than might be expected, and of eight starting below 25, ten years; while those entering in their 30s did best of all, with an average of eleven years.

Principals did better still, Dr Robertson dying aged 72 after thirty-one years' service, Dr Baird at 79 after forty-six years, Dr Lee at 79 after thirty-one years, and Sir David Brewster, who was 77 when he took over, survived nine more years and died at 86.[4]

George Husband Baird, who had been appointed Principal in 1793 on the death of the distinguished historian William Robertson, continued in office until 1840. His appointment was pure nepotism. Barely a year after he married Lord Provost Thomas Elder's daughter he had become a DD, minister of New Greyfriars church, Professor of Hebrew, and Principal of the University. The joke ran that his chief claim to office was his middle name.[5]

Provost Elder had himself shown much ability in fending off seditious movements during the French Revolution; but his son-in-law on appointment was still young and inexperienced. Baird, however, though lacking determination in conflicts, proved generally able. A High Church minister and a good scholar, portly and of middle height, he was round-featured, benign, cheerful and of polished manners.

Baird also, incongruously, had a magnificently commanding bass voice, which boomed out in an eloquence that touched on the bathetic. For example, on the death of Lord President Blair, in giving the funeral sermon he slipped somehow from the President's death to that of his own son, recently thought to be killed in a hunting accident. On this catastrophe, 'having gone forth into the fields to meditate . . . I looked, and beheld a man coming from afar . . . I saw that his countenance betokened woe. And I said unto him, Friend, thy countenance betokeneth woe. And he answered and said: "The Lord President Blair is dead."'[6] This brings to mind nothing so much as the deliberately biblical grandiosity of the Chaldee Manuscript.

In 1822 the Senatus Academicus numbered twenty-eight professors. The Divinity Faculty, headed by Principal Baird, Primarius Professor of Theology, had three other professors. Arts had seven, Law four, Medicine six. There were also other professors not then formally incorporated in the curriculum, such as Midwiferey (Professor James Hamilton), while another subject, Astronomy in the Faculty of Arts (Professor Robert Blair), was not taught at all.[7]

Charles Darwin and his elder brother Erasmus both experienced the variety of subjects required for a medical degree, though neither seriously intended ever to become doctors, and their father, learning of Charles's lack of enthusiasm, decided to take him away from Edinburgh after two years. The following year he went to Cambridge.

Charles, born in 1809, had at school appeared of only ordinary ability, and was removed early by his father who feared he cared only for shooting and dogs. When Charles entered the University in 1825, still under seventeen, Erasmus was completing his studies with only one year to go. Matriculating for introductory lectures Charles started a few days later, after paying their fees and entering their names in a book. Until the session of 1826–27, presentation of a class ticket was sufficient to admit a student, but in that session the college started a register, though not until 1828 was evidence of attendance required. To obtain library access a ticket from a professor was necessary. Charles had to seek confirmation that he would be only seventeen on his next birthday, as he would be unable to take a degree before he was twenty-one, and must therefore spend an interim year abroad. However, in the event this contingency did not arise.

Except for Dr Hope's Chemistry classes Charles found the lectures, which constituted the whole teaching system, 'intolerably dull', and the subjects distasteful. Materia Medica with Dr Duncan at 8 in the morning in winter was 'something fearful to remember', while Monro made Anatomy 'as dull as he was himself, and the subject disgusted me'. He believed that he might have overcome his disgust had he been obliged to practise dissection, and he missed what would have been a valuable experience. Attending the clinical wards proved distressing, and the two hospital operations he attended were both 'very bad . . . one on a child, but I rushed away before they were complete', and could never be persuaded to attend another. With no form of anaesthetic 'the two cases fairly haunted me for many a long year'.[8]

John James Audubon, the following year, suffered to much the same degree, as must many a young student. He attended Dr Knox's anatomy lecture, then visited Mr Bell's 'disagreeable' museum and, shocked by its venereal subjects, was glad to return to the salubrious streets of 'fair Edina'. Dr John Lizars, at his own anatomy lecture, operated on 'a beautiful dead body of a female, quite fresh. But afterward I went to the dissecting rooms where such horrible stench existed that I thought I would suffocate.'[9]

Another favourite subject with Darwin was marine zoology, and with Robert Grant he used to collect specimens to dissect from tidal pools, amateurishly enough and without a microscope, but he read a paper on an interesting discovery to one of the numerous student societies, the Plinian (possibly founded by Professor Robert Jameson, who certainly encouraged it), which met for papers on natural science in an underground room at the college. In this Darwin showed that the 'so-called ova of Flustra' were actually larvae which had independent movement through cilia. Though these papers were not printed, Grant noted Darwin's discovery in his own memoir on Flustra. Grant, considerably older, 'dry and formal in manner, with much enthusiasm beneath this outer crust', published in the *Edinburgh Philosophical Journal* (1825–26). In 1827 he became Professor of Comparative Anatomy and Zoology at London University.[10]

The dissertations of the Royal Medical Society – a student debating society – too confined in scope to please, Charles considered mostly rubbish. He derived more interest from going with Grant to the Wernerian Society to hear papers on natural history, including Audubon in 'interesting discourses on the habits of N. American birds, sneering somewhat unjustly at Waterton'. Interestingly he met a black man, now living in Edinburgh, who had travelled with Waterton and stuffed birds for a living. Darwin took lessons from him and found him 'a very pleasant and intelligent man'.

He also once accompanied Horner to the Royal Society, where Scott was in the chair as President, apologising as 'not feeling fitted for such a position'. Darwin, who 'looked at him with awe and reverence', had little idea at the time that he himself would become an honorary member of both this and the Royal Medical Society.

In his second year he found the Geology and Zoology professor 'incredibly dull', enough to put him off the subject altogether, especially on hearing him declaim ridiculous theories as fact on Salisbury Crags.[11]

Charles does not name this professor, but one suspects he was Robert Jameson, Professor of Natural History, who at different times included Meteorology, Hydrography, Mineralogy and Geology. Christison describes Jameson as a popular lecturer who conducted studies in the field, in the local quarries of sandstone, limestone and greenstone, and round Arthur's Seat, Salisbury Crags and Corstorphine and other surrounding hills. Christison, who in his first summer at the University attended this wiry, well-proportioned and upright enthusiast, accompanied him on taxing expeditions. Jameson had often outwalked his father and the Rev. Dr McKnight on Highlands visits, loaded with anything up to sixty pounds of stones and specimens. On one occasion a party of 150 foregathered at Glencorse Bridge, seven miles out of Edinburgh, walked up the valley (not then flooded for the reservoirs) to Habbie's Howe, then over the hills to Currie, and home via Bruntsfield Links and the Meadows. On their return Professor Jameson was fresh as when they started, but of the 150 young students, only Christison (as he recalled with pride) and one friend had lasted the course.[12]

Apart from dull or off-putting lectures, Charles Darwin enjoyed his time at Edinburgh, its surprising landscapes, and his absorbing expeditions. In January 1826 he wrote scathingly to his sister of a 'long stupid lecture' on Materia Medica just endured from Duncan, for which he could find no word 'expressive of its stupidity'. Duncan was 'so very learned that his wisdom has left no room for his senses'. Hope, at 10 o'clock, was some compensation. Erasmus joined Charles for these, then went on to hear Lizars on Anatomy, 'a charming lecturer', while Charles attended the hospital at noon and then heard Anatomy from Monro: 'I dislike him and his lectures so much, that I cannot speak with decency about them.' He did thoroughly appreciate the thrice-weekly clinical lectures on sick persons at the hospital.

Tantalisingly, Darwin's revealing comments on the lecturers end here, and no more letters on this period seem to have survived.[13]

In the late 1820s attendance at the College of Surgeons was high and rising, in 1826/27 anatomy lectures drew 470 and 558 respectively, and practical anatomy

262 and 296. In 1828 the two courses offered at least five lectures a week for the five-month extent of the session. In 1829 the Practical Anatomy course was raised from three to six months, and in 1838 to twelve.[14] In 1830 the total of matriculated students at the University was 2500, Chemistry, the largest class, having about 500, while Moral Philosophy had only 150. During the seven-month long vacations most students found it necessary to take some job, as teachers or tutors, or writing for the journals.[15]

The period after Dr Barclay's retirement in 1826 was the most important for the medical faculty, when all students were obliged to attend its lectures. Long before Monro retired in 1846, numbers had fallen (1836) to less than 700 and eventually to only 330, partly because of his inadequacy, partly through new competition from other medical schools. Yet the Edinburgh school still supplied professors of Anatomy to all Scottish universities, and anatomists and surgeons to the London schools.

The sixteen years from 1826 were the time of Robert Knox (1791–1862), Barclay's successor as extramural Anatomy lecturer. He formed a large museum and within four or five years had attracted unprecedented numbers. Lecturers had very different approaches: Knox was a 'morphological anatomist', explaining human by comparative anatomy. He often unfairly ridiculed his contemporaries, but his command of the subject, and his eloquence, stimulated the many students who themselves became famous.

Knox was therefore soon Edinburgh's most popular Anatomy lecturer. A born orator and inspiring teacher, he soon had 500 pupils including besides students, aristocrats, lawyers, artists and writers. Educated at the High School, he had taken his MD at the University in 1814, served from 1815 as an assistant army surgeon and attended the wounded at Waterloo. From 1817 to 1820 he carried out scientific research at the Cape, and between 1825 and 1831 was conservator of the College of Surgeon's museum of comparative anatomy and pathology, a post he gained through his papers on anthropological and natural history research, having led the campaign to buy Charles Bell's collection. When already famous, he became notorious over the celebrated Burke and Hare trials of 1828–29.[16]

Meanwhile Robert Christison embarked on his first lectures as Professor of Medical Jurisprudence, on 1 May 1822, with material from medical case histories, treatises and French works. He also studied German to widen his field, and after three years his original series had been transformed to a more topical basis, and his initial sprinkling of students had increased to ninety when, by his eleventh session, he moved on to Materia Medica.

His 'medico-legal' experience was increased by acting as reporter and witness in court cases, and on the advice of the Solicitor-General John Hope, he set up as an unofficial Government 'standing medical counsel', discussing cases with his brother at their lodgings.

Certain doctors in the extramural school gave medical testimony a bad name by appearing in opposition to witnesses, one even boasting how often Cockburn as counsel had engaged him because he was known to 'say anything you like'. Once, employed to confuse the professional evidence in an arsenic poisoning case, his evidence was so vague that it became contradictory. First insisting that he had observed only symptoms of natural causes in the dead woman, when pinned down for a straight answer by the Lord Advocate, he admitted that she had died of arsenic. 'Then what the devil brought you here?' audibly muttered his lordship.[17]

Christison's minute observations and deductions often enabled him to show proof of innocence, or inconclusive evidence, having grasped many surgeons' gross ignorance on certain points, and their slapdash official examination of bodies. They mistook pseudo-morbid symptoms which appeared after death for actual symptoms of disease, and overlooked potentially vital details. Once a violent brothel-keeper, accused of stabbing a lawyer's clerk with a carving knife, swore that the victim and his drunken friends had been so offensive that she had snatched the knife in defence, and he fell on it. One of his friends swore she had raised the knife and struck. As the body, examined at the Infirmary, showed an unmistakeable gash, the surgeons would have had it sewn up again when Christison, a mere onlooker, suggested they establish the direction of the wound. Sure enough, it was found to penetrate downwards, and the accused was therefore found guilty.

Christison included such examples in his lectures, illustrating that the size and direction of a wound, foreign bodies, and the organs affected, could all provide clues to the weapon, force of the blow and other points.

Poisoning cases always led to legal battles and contradictory witnesses, yet many surgeons were quite ignorant of toxicology, though taught since 1814 – a promising field for Christison. The apparent insufficiency of evidence usually opened the way to a 'not proven' verdict. Two favourite poisons were arsenic and the oxalic acid used to polish brass and the yellow tops of fashionable boots. By studying these with a colleague he introduced a more scientific examination, which the Lord Advocate then officially adopted.[18]

Following in Dr Thomas Charles Hope's footsteps, Christison used experimental demonstrations, first testing them in private – especially after he discovered how widespread was adulteration of drugs. His published report, confirmed by enquiries in London by Dr Jonathan Pereira at St Bartholomew's and by the new Pharmaceutical Society, helped to end this dangerous practice. In 1829 Christison published his collected studies as *A Treatise on Poisons,* including a survey of the medico-legal aspects.

Study of a number of 'nuisances' in manufacture followed on from an interesting investigation made with Dr Edward Turner in 1827 on the action of poisons on plants. A market gardener consulted them who brought an action against a manufacturing chemist at Bonnington Bridge (Newhaven). The two experimented by keeping young trees and plants for twenty-four hours in controlled conditions under a bell-jar, some with hydrochloric, others with sulphuric and nitric acid. The plants recovered when restored to the air, as their stems were unharmed though exposed leaves died. Sulphuretted hydrogen or carbonic oxide, on the other hand, attacked the 'internal organs', and these plants died.[19]

Despite the increasing importance of dissection in the study of Anatomy, the supply of bodies was still officially limited to executed criminals until the Anatomy Act of 1832 allowed a controlled supply of unclaimed bodies from hospitals and workhouses. But dramatic events were to precede this change, and in 1826–27 the shortage was at its worst.

A curious case reported in the *Edinburgh Evening Courant* in January 1826 illustrates the divided opinion on this subject. A coach proprietor in Newcastle named Loftus, who suspected that bodies were being taken by mail-coach to Edinburgh, stopped the next doubtful 'packet' passing through on the 'Telegraph' from Leeds, which weighed more than sixteen stone. Police were called, and indeed found inside the still undecayed body of a man in his forties, six feet tall and heavily built. The parcel was addressed to Mr Simpson of 61 Princes Street, Edinburgh. A coroner's inquest could establish no signs of violence, an unknown cause of death was recorded, and the body was buried.

The *Courant* perhaps unexpectedly (unless the report was written by a surgeon) adopted a censorious attitude to this 'meddling', which deprived the profession of a body vital to research. The surgeons must now order another – and another grave would be disturbed. Who was the better for this discovery? they thundered, aware that this stand was against public opinion: but people must realise that surgeons needed subjects, obtained with the least possible 'shock to the feelings of the community'. How could that be done if such officious seizures were made by 'busybodies'? The practice was acceptable, it was implied, provided the public did not know.[20]

If this diatribe had any effect, it was long-term.

In 1828, when the scandal was at its height, Dr Knox drafted a report to Peel (which appears never to have been sent) on similar situations which had arisen. There had been interceptions of body packets at Liverpool, Greenock and Carlisle, which were seized although the authorities well knew of their destination.

In the Carlisle case a jury was called and a bland verdict accepted that 'they knew not' how the body came there. Anatomists (Knox said) were naturally anxious to avoid such incidents, and to pick only bodies of persons known to have no relatives. There could be 'alarming reprisals' in graveyards where such seizures were made. He also quoted an unsavoury occasion when rivalry between teachers led to two cases on board a steam packet in Dublin Harbour being seized by a rival's assistant armed with a warrant, and – as he claimed – largely to aggravate public ill-feeling and to intercept the supply, 'their contents were left exposed on the quay' for two days.[21]

Many unscrupulous characters were involved in the business, or the hospitals and lecture-rooms could not have been supplied at all. In 1828 four fellows of the College of Surgeons were lecturing on Practical Anatomy, besides the Professor. Of the estimated total of 900 medical students, 380 were said to have attended the extramural classes. In the previous winter about 150 bodies had been used, costing on average £9 or £10 to the lecturers, but supply had not kept pace with demand. If 300 students annually attended practical anatomy classes, a body supply of at least one per student was required, ideally priced at £5 each, Obtaining them from London not only cost more, but reduced the number available to London teachers, leading to fierce arguments between teachers and snatchers and between the men themselves. When even the London supply was drying up, Ireland was an alternative, where the public was less outraged by the trade.

It was the Burke and Hare revelation that brought matters to a head in 1828, seriously implicating Dr Knox. William Burke, a navvy aged about thirty-five, and William Hare were Knox's chief suppliers, taking care to provide bodies which showed no apparent marks of violence. Burke lodged with Hare and his wife, and throughout the winter of 1827–28 they perfected a method of supply, striking up acquaintance with apparently solitary men, lodgers and possibly strangers to Edinburgh, Burke's mistress and Hare's wife acting as decoys. The victims were plied with drink until at a planned moment one of the murderers would give 'a friendly embrace', or perhaps stumble, throwing the man on his back and pinning him down, one pressing his chin upwards to close his mouth and covering his nostrils, while the other held down his limbs until after a few minutes he stopped breathing, with no signs of foul play. They then, doubling his limbs and forcing his head down, bundled his body into a small box, and carried it under cover of darkness to Knox's dissecting rooms in Surgeon Square.

According to Burke, who might have been boasting, sixteen unfortunates lost their lives in this way. Eventually a visitor to his lodgings saw a body under his bed, and went to the police. By early morning when the body had been taken to Knox the alarm had been raised, the body was traced by the police and was reclaimed that same day.

Newbigging and Christison were appointed to the medico-legal inspection. This victim was a woman, middle-aged, 'well nourished and without a trace of disease', dead of asphyxia. They concluded that bruises had been made before death, from blows or possibly a fall; there was also a post-death cervical spine injury to the body when still warm, and death was probably by smothering rather than strangling, though of this there was no proof. Suspicious though it was, it was not a basis for a murder charge, but luckily Hare and his wife were inclined to turn King's evidence, naturally much encouraged by the authorities. The indictment was for three murders, Newbigging's and Christison's views coinciding with the accused's confession.

Knox came in for strong criticism, regarded by the mob as 'art and part' of the crime, and was hanged in effigy from a tree outside his house in Arniston Place, the house attacked and windows smashed, and only the arrival of the police prevented its being sacked. For fear of his life Knox could go out only after dark, and by back roads – though he was 'strong, agile, and resolute' with a short and stocky body, and carried pistols. A committee headed by the Marquess of Queensberry which enquired into his complicity found no proof. According to Christison, Queensberry may have deliberately ignored suspicious incidents because of Knox's popularity as a leading lecturer, because of his 300 students, and because of the known shortage of bodies.

Christison, who spoke to Knox early in the proceedings, pointed out that the body found by the police must have been warm and 'flexible' on delivery, and had obviously never been buried. Knox passed this off with the claim that he had received at least ten bodies in a similar state, acquired through his spies who kept watch at low lodging-houses in the Cowgate, Grassmarket and West Port areas, who would buy a corpse from a landlord before anyone had claimed it for burial. An unlikely story, Christison felt, for any death in such surroundings would bring a queue of visitors to look at the corpse, and a string of 'orgies' until it was taken for burial, leaving no interval possible for removal. Indeed James Syme had told him that he himself had tried this method when teaching anatomy, without success. Christison considered the gifted Knox as notably deficient 'in principle and in heart' and likely to close his eyes to any suspicion as to the cause of death.

At the trial Burke's mistress escaped with a 'Not proven' verdict, being *in loco conjugis* and subject to his orders, and although she knew all about it she had 'fled into the lobby to escape seeing it'.

Hare himself, as King's evidence, was not put on trial, as he could not now legally be charged, and he was released from the Tolbooth and 'spirited away' to avoid lynching. He was being taken to Dumfries by night on the stage-coach, and much was the indignation of an unsuspecting sheriff fellow-passenger, on finding in the morning with whom he had been travelling. He moved at once to a cold outside seat. Burke, tried on 24 December, was convicted, condemned, and hanged on 28 January 1829. His body was publicly dissected by Knox's rival, Alexander Monro, in the University.

Eventually the scandal put paid to Knox's career. His dignity at the trial, and his well-thought-out replies to accusers won the day, and he continued his teaching. His skill as lecturer kept his classes full for some years, until thanks to his heterodoxy numbers fell off and he left Edinburgh. He published a number of medical works, was made a fellow of the London Ethnological Society in 1860 and in 1862 honorary curator of its museum, but in the same year he died, according to Christison near-destitute.[22]

'Take care you are not killed for dissection,' wrote Sydney Smith to a friend in January 1829. 'If I see a fat man and a thin man together I feel sure that it is a surgeon and his suffocator, and I run for it. There are men out after Rogers to my certain knowledge.'[23]

Charles Kirkpatrick Sharpe was offered a share of a window to watch Burke's execution. 'Mr Stevenson, the bookseller', wrote Mr Robert Seton, 'wished one window for Sir Walter Scott and yourself, but on account of the number that has applied, that will be out of my power. But I shall be happy to accommodate Sir Walter and yourself with a share of one.' [24]

An Anatomy Bill was introduced in Parliament in spring 1829, but proved so unsatisfactory in detail, and dealt with such an unpopular a subject, that it was withdrawn. In 1831 a modified version was brought up, after a Burke-and-Hare attempt had been made in London, and this time was passed, ending most of the difficulties of body supply.[25]

James Syme took over the Anatomy course from Robert Liston in 1823, soon after which their good relations cooled to the level of feud. Indeed medical feuds seemed the order of the day. Syme therefore set up a separate School of Medicine with Dr Mackintosh at Brown Square, equipped with classrooms, anatomy and lecture rooms and museum. Syme taught Anatomy and Practical Anatomy, and Surgery; Mackintosh, Medicine and Midwifery; and Dr John Fletcher, Physiology. They became an instant success, attracting many students, though their application for a charter as an extra-academic school of medicine was refused by the pompous Lord Advocate, Andrew Rutherfurd.

Syme moved over entirely to Surgery, partly because of his now bad relations with Liston, partly because of the scandals raised by body supplies and graveyard raids.[26] Syme now left the Brown Square school and started his own surgery class, which by the session of 1828–29 had become Edinburgh's largest with 250 students. He contributed papers to the *Edinburgh Medical and Surgical Journal*, and courageously undertook a risky operation refused by others, removal of a large tumour on the jaw which he rightly diagnosed as benign (1827). But he failed in 1829 to obtain a post at the Infirmary, whose managers were afraid to appoint him because of the feud with Liston;

therefore he opened his own independent surgical hospital, with a ten-year lease on Minto House, near Brown Square in Chambers Street.[27]

The house, being not in but adjoining the Old Town, was on a relatively healthy site, in private ground on the slope halfway between North College Street and the Cowgate. It had fifteen rooms, the usual closets and pantries, even a good water supply and WCs on each floor. The largest and most elegant room, eighteen feet high, was well suited for conversion to an operating theatre and lecture room. Syme acquired two house surgeons through advertising, raised a public subscription, supplementing the capital from his own funds, and opened his hospital on 8 May 1829. In three months 380 would-be patients applied, of whom he admitted seventy, and he performed thirty operations, with only two deaths. In the next quarter, 553 applied and he admitted sixty-four, demand always depressingly far exceeding supply.

Instead of giving general lectures on a group of cases, Syme adopted the more up-to-date teaching system, bringing in patients for students to examine personally, and to describe and treat cases.

Syme lived successively at 12 Dundas Street, Forres Street and eventually Charlotte Square. Now well-known, he married the daughter of a Leith merchant and sister of a former school friend, and – although it meant borrowing – set up the carriage which had become very necessary for him to meet his many commitments.[28]

In 1831 two new Edinburgh chairs were instituted: Pathology, for John Thomson, and Surgery, for John William Turner, his successor as Professor of Surgery at the Royal College of Surgeons. Syme applied for the resulting College of Surgeons vacancy, but was opposed by John Lizars, who was appointed by a single vote majority. Syme thereafter concentrated his energies on Minto House. By summer 1832, 2500 had applied for admission; 340 were admitted, and he built a new lecture-room.[29]

On Professor John Russell's retiring after thirty years at the age of eighty-one, Liston applied for his University chair of Clinical Surgery, but retreated when Russell demanded a compensatory life annuity of £300. After some negotiation, Syme agreed to take the post on those terms, and succeeded to the chair in 1833. When in August the Royal Infirmary offered to place three wards under his care, he decided to close Minto Hospital, which he had maintained by advancing £1775 of his own. Its patients then totalled 1094, averaging 337 a year, despite having only twenty-four beds available – probably a larger number for its size than any other hospital. The hospital was then taken over and run under altered circumstances for another fifteen years.[30]

Violent quarrels and feuds between leading medics were almost a norm in Edinburgh at this time. The pugnacious, litigious Dr James Hamilton, who succeeded his father Dr Alexander Hamilton as Professor of Midwifery, conducted continuous lawsuits, including against Dr Andrew Duncan senior and Dr James Gregory (ending in blows and a successful claim for assault, when Gregory asserted he would pay twice over for another go at Hamilton), to name but two.[31]

Short, plain, fair-complexioned and stooping, eyes fixed on his toes, Hamilton was (says Christison) 'little in figure in all respects'. One pamphlet of his provoked Thomas Charles Hope to an unwise accusation of lying; Hamilton sued him for defamation, and again won, but with a farthing damages and shared costs. Professor Hope was showered not only with congratulations but also with farthings, one of which he was said to have ceremoniously sent to Hamilton with a request for a receipt.[32]

The 1820s were altogether a time of contention in the Edinburgh academic world, surgeons against physicians or against each other, and the Senatus Academicus against the Town Council, with repeated clashes over their relative administrative power, not resolved until 1858.

Though of great significance, the minutiae are complex and tedious. The professors, although personally left in control of their own classes, were still appointed by the Town Council; surgeons were until 1778 in the status of the other 'trades' (that is, crafts), headed by a Deacon rather than a President. In 1825 the Senatus made proposals for sweeping changes to the medical course, including extending it from three years to four, requiring a hospital year following the medical degree and insisting on inclusion of certain compulsory courses. This led to an open clash at a high level (Councillors robed, academics gowned) and a lawsuit referred to the Court of Session. The latter found the Council to be still the governing body, disregarding the changes of the past century and reverting to the ambiguous terms of the original royal grant. The Senatus appealed to Peel as Home Secretary and a Royal Commission on the University was set up under Lord Rosebery.

This did not report until 1831, and although it recommended transfer of power to the Senatus, Town Council patronage was left alone, so that of twenty-six professors, fifteen were still Council appointees. Few of the changes were thought acceptable and many misunderstandings were left unresolved. The root of the problem was always political, and even the new Government of 1831 was inclined to pander to Town Councils and especially feared to offend Edinburgh.[33]

Von Raumer noted the phenomenon of Scottish universities not being ecclesiastical bodies, and thus less dependent on their own Presbyterian Church than were Oxford and Cambridge on the English Church. Until the 1831 Royal Commission, 'no examination and change of the statutes had taken place in Scotland for one hundred and thirty years', hence the commissioners inevitably found aspects to criticise.

At this time professors' income varied from £113 to £2213, mostly derived from their class fees, the highest being the Professor of Chemistry, while – a sign of the times – a Professor of History was actually considered superfluous. Raumer saw many parallels with the defects of German universities: the total effect of instruction was inadequate, students were indifferent to 'certain branches of science', certificates of attendance were valueless, and 'degrees are too precipitately conferred'.[34]

After Burgh reform in 1832 it was affirmed that 'the charge of a great University was not a suitable duty for a municipal body', but this seemed to remain a pious platitude. The Senatus, having failed to assert its status as an independent body, turned apathetic and student numbers began to fall. A meeting held in 1857, when they had fallen from 2300 (1823) to 1550, ended in a bill to institute a complete change in the University constitution, introducing new freedoms and passed as the Scottish Universities Act in 1858.[35]

The other most serious events of the end of the decade were the epidemics of typhus fever in 1827 and of the cholera in 1831–32.

One who was faced with dealing with the typhus was Robert Christison, who in 1827 was appointed a Physician to the Royal Infirmary and was in addition busy with his work on poisons, and joint editorship with Dr Craigie of the *Edinburgh Medical and Surgical Journal.* Since the end of the 1818–19 outbreak, thought not to be true typhus, annual fever cases had fallen back from 2064 to 100 but suddenly in 1827 3900 cases were admitted, and the following year 770.

Queensberry House, which provided 150 beds, was reopened as the fever hospital and the usual emergency arrangements made. Like the previous epidemic, it came at a time of high unemployment, and was largely confined to the poor and the working classes, the better-off hardly being affected. The worst areas were in the Old Town: Fountainbridge, the West Port and Grassmarket closes, the Cowgate, and the High Street and Canongate wynds (many of which were ruthlessly demolished in later decades). As no attempt was made to keep affected households in quarantine, whole districts were soon endangered.[36]

Carlyle remarked on the 'unhealthy winter' and the epidemic early in the year. 'The Hospital has been found too narrow to accommodate the poor people, and a temporary receptacle fitted up for them is also almost full.' Students and doctors working at the Infirmary became infected, and one of their friends was cavalierly sent out to lodgings to be 'lying among strangers', without the hospital troubling to be sure exactly where. (Carlyle's own health, by contrast, seemed better, and happier for personal reasons, not least because he had actually begun to write a book.[37])

There was also an 'intermittent fever', common at the end of the eighteenth century, but which finally disappeared in Scotland by 1863. Further, in the autumn of 1828 epidemic dysentery appeared, again chiefly among the poor, and in Edinburgh less severe than in Glasgow; its cause was never established. The hospital admitted only the most violent cases, and more were treated at home. A number died. Christison, who describes symptoms and treatment of the various outbreaks, treated the dysentery with opium. After 1828 few such cases recurred.[38]

Christison continued at the Infirmary until 1832, when he was appointed Professor of Materia Medica.

The final fright was the cholera which, appearing from the east, spread across Britain in 1831, and towards the end of 1831 was daily expected in Edinburgh. Everyone was scanning the tri-weekly *Courant*, and the bi-weekly *Scotsman*, for news of its dreaded approach from London. It finally arrived along the coast, from Sunderland, and reached Haddington about the turn of the year, finally fetching up in Edinburgh in Fisherrow.

People rubbed their bodies with camphor, supposed to be a protection, and burned tar barrels in the street to ward off infection. Josiah Livingston records the alarm when a case was reported in the next street to Buccleuch Place, which housed 'a somewhat lower or poorer class'; then little David Somerville in their own street fell ill. Their doctor, who was puzzled by the symptoms, consulted Dr Abercrombie, and the local boys, anxiously waiting outside the house, on their emergence saw Abercrombie saying something which made their doctor 'look aghast'. David died the same day, then the doctor was taken ill, and in a few hours was dead. As soon as Abercrombie had enlightened him on the diagnosis he was convinced he too must be infected – as indeed he was. Poor gentle little man, accustomed mostly to dealing with confinements, or the occasional measles or whooping-cough. Ironically, as Livingston remarks, their district did not suffer from typhoid or diphtheria, because their houses had no internal drains.[39]

Another irony was that many people were so alarmed at the prospect of the Reform Bill that they hardly knew which evil to fear more. Charles Kirkpatrick Sharpe, whose health these days was usually very poor, expressed himself disturbed by both. 'The Whigs or the cholera will very soon cure all . . . everybody is in a consternation, and so am I – for people past 50 must, it seems, go off in spite of drams and mustard-poultices . . . What a strange disease this new pest seems to be! . . . so superior in destruction to the plague, which did in days what this contrives in hours.'[40]

In January Mrs Grant, filling in her friend Mrs Hook on Edinburgh news, dismissed the cholera in a few words and insisted that Reform was by far the worse evil. A month later, however, she was willing to see cholera as 'a salutary warning of divine wrath' (over the Reform Bill, no doubt), and was thankful that attacks locally had been relatively few and not all fatal. Others too, she thought, considered it a judgment, when she saw people wearing an air of 'quiet solemnity'.[41]

Many people in London fearing the outbreak were at the same time anxious about its progress in Edinburgh. Carlyle was inclined to play down the danger, largely to avoid alarming his mother, though admitting that it was 'sudden, and the people have heard so much about it; scarcely a year but there is a *typhus fever* in Glasgow or Edinburgh that kills *far more* than the Cholera does'. Indeed, Samuel Dickenson, a promising medical student friend of his and John's, had taken the fever and died in the autumn when on duty as House Surgeon at the Infirmary. When it did reach Edinburgh, Carlyle again observed that 'a Fever, much more fatal in its character', was already current, but 'being only a *common* death, little heed is paid it'.[42]

Even in London the epidemic kept its distance, and when it did arrive it was not in Carlyle's area. Jeffrey, back in town and exhausted by the Parliamentary session leading up to the Reform Bill, reported that, though here more severe, 'it excites very little sensation, and scarcely any alarm' – presumably because, again, the ravages were mostly confined to the lower classes.[43]

Robert Chambers discussed the crisis thoroughly in the first issue of his *Edinburgh Journal* in February, including a history of bubonic plague and its distinction from cholera. While the latter affected 'the dissolute and famished', he reassured his respectable readership that 'those of regular habits who enjoy good food and raiment usually escape'; and that it was curable, and only half of cases were mortal. Unlike the plague, it was useless to avoid it by fleeing to the country; the best prevention was personal cleanliness, removal of 'filth', ventilated rooms, temperance and avoidance of such 'indigestible' foods as raw fruit.

He describes the symptoms: 'languor, coldness, giddiness, and slight bowel complaint. It usually comes on with purging, vomiting, and cramp'. A faint pulse, cold skin, contracted features, sunken eyes were all precursors of the attack. Recommended treatment was to keep warm, preferably in bed wrapped in hot blankets maintained by hot bran bags, or hot water in 'stone bottles or tin canisters'. As for remedies, two teaspoonfuls of flour of mustard seed in half a tumbler of warm water 'to excite full vomiting', followed by a wine-glassful of brandy or whisky and hot water. If the attack continued, twenty to forty drops of laudanum, with two teaspoonfuls of magnesia in peppermint water, with a mustard poultice over the stomach to relieve the pain. The whole experience sounds eminently disagreeable.[44]

Three weeks later David Moir, the Musselburgh physician who wrote under the name 'Delta', warned that the disease was 'virulently contagious' and that a district or street should be isolated as soon as it appeared. He poured scorn on the theory of its 'whimsical wanderings' (in which Chambers obstinately believed), and urged not only strict isolation but cleaning the houses of the poor besides feeding and clothing them.[45]

So little was known of the disease, and indeed so little was learned of it from this first of the several outbreaks in the century, that when the artist Turner in December had completed his first contributions for illustrations to Scott's *Poetical Works*, he was at a loss what to do with them. Advising Robert Cadell not to come to London for safety's sake and suggesting he send the pictures by mail, he actually asked for any available information in Edinburgh on cholera treatment, since London not only seemed to know of none but had no cholera hospitals, and some doctors even diagnosed the epidemic as typhus.[46]

Fanny Kemble, whose cousin had alerted her that 'the plague is certainly within 6 miles of them', even found it hard to believe despite her distress at its effect in 'that beautiful, noble city . . . where the purifying currents of keen air sweep through every thoroughfare and eddy round every corner . . . a freer, finer atmosphere than all the world beside!'[47] Even its fine and bracing air, alas (not the air that Carlyle had so detested), proved no safeguard.

Some curiously insensitive comments were made on the epidemic. Lady Harriet Leveson Gower, on the way north in July expecting rumours of it on the journey, only met a denial in Ferry Bridge and then in Dunbar; but in Edinburgh found it still lingering in the Old Town, whence, she remarks coolly, 'the people of the new seem very sensibly to abstain, but it is a privation to travellers'. At her hotel on that account 'they wash in the house', meaning presumably laundering, which she praises as an example of good sense.[48]

Nor was cholera the last of Edinburgh's ills. Later in the year there was also an influenza epidemic, which continued into the following year, and few households entirely escaped. In February 1833, when the weather was exceptionally stormy, most houses had their invalids.[49]

The controversial and ultimately unprovable 'science' of phrenology continued its chequered progress. In 1824, when George Combe visited London, he found public interest evaporating and the subject in difficulties through disagreements among supporters. At his request, Spurzheim came over to the rescue.

Back in Edinburgh the prospect was brighter: two courses proved a great success, and Combe also lectured in Glasgow. Just before Christmas the Phrenological Society held a dinner at Oman's Hotel, at which the evening's chairman James Simpson, an advocate, presented him with a large silver goblet 'as a mark of respect and gratitude'. Combe was the first to admit ladies to his lectures, for which they too, in gratitude, made him a presentation, a pair of silver calipers.[50]

Next year he gave further successful lectures, while in London Spurzheim was reviving interest. Societies started up elsewhere in England and also in America, all making Combe an honorary member; some eminent scientists joined. At the dinner for Brougham in 1825, in summarising the speeches – apart from Jeffrey's (except that he 'preached it'), Cockburn's and Brougham's own, 'miserably bad' – he noted that Brougham's head was 'decidedly above an average in size, and very high'.[51]

About this time one of Combe's long-established clerks was proved to have robbed him of the considerable sum of £500 over a period of years, but this was not an example of Combe's being caught out. He had long ago diagnosed a lack of conscientiousness, and neither prosecuted nor even dismissed the clerk, who had a family, for in his view the law would be useless, being not corrective but punitive. He reproached the culprit for such behaviour after 'the benefits heaped on him', and warned that he could no longer expect to be trusted.[52]

Phrenology temporarily acquired more respectability when the second edition of *Combe's System of Phrenology*, published in October 1825, was reviewed by Jeffrey (September 1826), pushing up its sales. It was a thoughtful though condemnatory review, describing the theory as 'absurd' and 'fantastical' but accepting Combe's talent and acute observation. A ding-dong of answers and answers to answers ensued over the next five months. Combe's first, an eighty-one-page defence, was also a reply to *Review* attacks of earlier years, accusing phrenologists of 'dogmatism and arrogance'. 'The folly had lasted rather too long' – twenty-one years, to be exact.

Combe revealed that Spurzheim had told him that after the attack in 1815 (no. XLIX) sales of the book had entirely dropped off for four years, but then picked up again. He pointed out that in London and Paris phrenology was now flourishing, contrary to Jeffrey's claim, and that further study increased its adherents.

He also referred to the turnip hoax, which he had 'instantly detected', though *Blackwood's* had still tried to maintain it was a real deception. Indeed, Jeffrey's assumption that this and similar fabrications were true accused phrenologists of 'flagrant and ridiculous blunders'.[53]

Combe was now developing a controversial religious theory based on his early doubts and attempts to reconcile Divine Grace with man's condition – then considered wildly heterodox, especially since the threat to religion by the French Revolution. His ideas, expressed in two papers, 'Human Responsibility as affected by Phrenology' (1826) and 'Constitution of Man' (1827), appeared to bewildered and indignant readers as an attack on Christianity. Though still a church-goer, and accepting the moral teachings of religion, Combe was evolving his own doctrine of human responsibility, which he put into his latest lecture series, and was seen by listeners as much a threat as a benefit to society. He therefore printed only a few copies for private circulation.[54]

Sir William Hamilton now entered the field with two addresses refuting the phrenology theory, given to the Royal Society of Edinburgh in 1826 and 1827. No debate was admitted after these lectures, nor would he agree to publish them, which could have started another pamphlet war. Phrenology lost another opportunity when in April 1827 Hamilton lectured at the University 'for the benefit of the distressed operatives', when although he agreed that Combe might either make a reply, or give a follow-up lecture in a college classroom, the Senatus Academicus refused, as he was not a member of the University.

Instead, Combe gave a lecture at the Assembly Rooms, at the request of the Committee for Relief of the Distressed Operatives themselves. It went on for three hours, with demonstrations of many skulls, and brought in a large sum to the Operatives' Fund. A prolonged controversy followed, ending in arbitration, an objectionable move in Combe's view: Hamilton was represented by Dr Christison, as Professor of Medical Jurisprudence, Combe by Dr John Scott, and they co-opted James Syme as Lecturer on Anatomy and Surgery. Combe requested that the arbiters should examine Spurzheim, who was to visit Edinburgh with his wife (January 1828), but Hamilton, who was compiling a long letter of refutation of Spurzheim for the *Caledonian Mercury*, again refused, a curiously ungenerous reaction.

Over the ensuing argument, conducted by letter, Hamilton sometimes lost his temper while Combe and Spurzheim kept theirs. Spurzheim had to deliver a long-booked lecture in Glasgow, which his opponents seized on as a pretence that he had fled. In vain did Combe urge Hamilton not to stir up prejudice by what he regarded as mispresentation, and the controversy continued.[55]

Laymen who had a brush with phrenology were alternately impressed and sceptical. In 1823 Combe had visited the painter Thomas Uwins, where he saw an unfinished portrait of the latter's brother Dr David, whom he had never met. On studying it Combe gave so accurate a description of his character that Uwins was encouraged to become a disciple. Combe remarked that in Uwins's own head the 'imitation and secrecy' necessary to an artist figured largely, a judgement hard to question.[56]

Carlyle wasted no time on the subject. In noting the publication of the new

Phrenological Journal and Miscellany, started that year, he quickly wrote it off as 'a journal of Spurzheim's scull doctrine!', adding for good measure, 'Error and stupidity are infinite in their varieties, eternal in duration.'[57]

In the Christmas vacation of 1824 two distinguished Cambridge scholars, Adam Sedgwick, a Fellow of Trinity College and Woodwardian Professor of Geology, and William Whewell, scientist and mineralogist, stayed some weeks in Edinburgh, when (writes Whewell) 'we fell in with the phrenologists, who . . . have taken my head for one of their examples'. He confessed to being not much impressed. He thought they hardly 'showed much discrimination in their remarks upon it'.[58]

While in Edinburgh they met everybody: 'Belles, Beaux, Advocates, Savans, and Craniologists'. These last Professor Sedgwick described as providing the most amusement. 'They are perfectly sincere in their faith, tho' I confess I could only regard them as a set of crazy humourists.'[59]

Humour was what Tom Moore saw in them too, who delighted in poking fun at them, particularly a practitioner named Deville, who overjoyed the sceptics by his missing the point and failure to see the obvious. For example, he deduced that Moore's friend Lord Lansdowne 'gave his opinions without deliberation', and as for Sydney Smith, his chief characteristic was diagnosed as 'a fondness for natural history, and for making collections of the same. Altogether [writes Moore] 'this was the worst exhibition I have seen him make, though very amusing from Sydney Smith's inextinguishable and contagious laughter, which I joined in even to tears.'[60]

This was in London. In Edinburgh, on the other hand, a few months later Combe not surprisingly became interested in the painter John James Audubon and his eccentric appearance. Visiting him in November 1826 he 'spoke much of the illustrating powers exhibited about my poor skull' (Audubon relates), 'of the truth of his theory, begged that I would suffer a cast . . . &c., &c.', and sent him a card for his winter lectures.[61]

On the 27th he was invited to Brown Square for supper, escorted by the kind William Lizars. 'I entered the dwelling of phrenology!' Not only that, but Combe had invited leading colleagues and phrenologists, including Mr Scott, president of the Society, Dugald Stewart, William Ritchie, and a German composer, Charles Weiss. There were also Miss Scott and Miss Combe, 'neither of them', says Audubon dispassionately, 'by any means handsome'.

At Combe's entreaty, on his arrival President Scott was allowed to examine the heads of the visiting celebrities, and Combe made an introductory speech. 'I have here two men of great talents. Will you please tell us what their natural powers consist in?'

The president, with a bow, affirmed that Weiss had musical faculties. Then, looking at Audubon's forehead, he said, 'There cannot exist a moment of doubt that this gentleman is a great painter, compositor, colorist, and I would add a very amiable man, but he might take this as a compliment!' 'The company', says Audubon, whose self-esteem was rising daily, 'was highly gratified.'

After supper Weiss played the flute 'most sweetly', Miss Scott sang, and 'at 1 o'clock Music and painting, locked arm in arm, together left the company'. Weiss gave Aubudon a card for his concert and they parted at the corner of Rose Street.[62]

Three weeks later, when Audubon was feeling less self-conscious and very appreciative of the relaxed, hospitable way in which he was everywhere received, he dined again at Combe's (18 December). This, at 5 o'clock, was of course a more formal occasion. He does not name his fellow-guests, but again they were evidently phrenologists, as that was the subject of conversation, and he found Combe 'an extremely agreeable companion and host'. (He had to leave at 7, to accompany Lizars to the Royal Scottish Academy meeting.)

Two days later Audubon, after a hearty breakfast at Combe's on 'mutton ham and good coffee', underwent the promised phrenological examination, and it was from here that he went on armed with a note from Combe to the advocate, John Simpson, whose clerk led him to the Courts to seek Jeffrey . . . a first attempt which failed as Jeffrey did not appear.

The very next day Simpson invited Audubon and the naturalist Prideaux Selby for 'a phrenological supper' at 8.45 at 33 Northumberland Street. Nothing but phrenology was talked of. Simpson compared the two visitors' heads. 'I had more colouring, he said', but over the prolonged supper the others argued with him on 'the formation of colors', and although very sleepy he fiercely demonstrated his knowledge of 'prismatic composition'. He walked home with Selby in some relief at midnight in 'the rarified, pure air'.[63]

The process of sitting for the cast had proved not altogether pleasurable. Taken up to Combe's '*sancto sanctorum*', he was shown the instruments in a beautiful silver box, 'a neat present from the ladies who have attended his lectures these last two years'. With Andrew Combe acting as secretary, George probed with his fingers, meticulously measured the skull, and 'with most exquisite sense of touch' found and noted the significant protuberances.

Next the victim had to sit with closed eyes for an hour, 'my face and hair oiled over, and plaster of Paris poured over my nose to form a mold of the whole, then a bust will be made, and there . . . only "simple and intelligent Audubon", as your good son Richard was pleased to call me', he wrote to Mrs Rathbone in Liverpool.

The results were both startling and gratifying. 'I was astonished when they both said that . . . I had great veneration for high, talented men, that I would have made a brave general, that music was not to be compared with painting in me, that I was extraordinarily generous, &c. Now', he continues modestly, 'I know all to be facts, and how they discover them to be so is quite a puzzle to me.' He was given a copy of the findings, signed another for the brothers to keep, and agreed that George might use the material in his next lecture.

In writing to Mrs Rathbone on the experience in detail, he added Combe's comment that his skull was a better proof of the 'system' than had been those of Napoleon, Molière, or Garrick.[64]

In August 1827 Combe's elder brother Abram died of tuberculosis and, while another brother, William, tried to carry on his work, the Owenite project was disintegrating, probably because, as George warned him, no 'ideal' community could succeed unless it consisted of 'enlightened and moralised' people.[65]

These vicissitudes were paralleled in phrenology, now achieving prominence again in Edinburgh under George Combe's personal guidance, failing in Glasgow, and full of dissension in London, while in some small towns new societies were forming.

Spurzheim and his wife spent several months in Edinburgh, made a tour to the Trossachs with Combe and friends, and the pundit's two lectures were 'fashionably attended', one drawing some eighty students. Spurzheim was widely entertained in society, esteemed for his learned attainments and 'unassuming gentlemanly manners'. In August they had the sad news of the death of Dr Gall near Paris. He and Spurzheim had been estranged for some time, and Gall was by then too ill to see him.[66]

In June 1828 Combe's essay, 'The Constitution of Man', was reprinted in both Edinburgh and London, and though he had suppressed the section on human responsibility it greatly offended the Evangelicals, who now regarded him openly as a 'dangerous infidel'.

They embarked on a new philanthropical crusade when in September George and Andrew, on a steamboat excursion, met Samuel Wilderspin, who was a great advocate of infant schools. The brothers invited him to promote their founding in Edinburgh.[67]

He came in November, given free use of the Clyde Street hall, and Combe introduced him to William Ritchie and Charles Maclaren, the *Scotsman* editors. The Evangelicals warned that if Combe, author of an 'infidel' book, were known to be involved, the crusade would be wrecked. They were worsted in the ensuing campaign, however, George was co-opted to the schools committee, and at a public meeting the opening of a school was agreed. An attempt to reject Ritchie as a director was also defeated. The project went on, and Combe's book sales actually increased, despite a continuing smear campaign condemning the schools as 'an infidel and phrenological job'.[68]

In 1829 a lecture tour in Ireland evoked yet another new phrenological society, and Combe had now so many supporters that controversy seemed hardly to trouble him. There was a long correspondence on his 'Constitution of Man' with the American Unitarian clergyman Dr William Ellery Channing and others, and a newspaper battle between the *Caledonian Mercury* and the *Scotsman* ended in Ritchie's challenging the *Mercury* proprietor, Thomas Allan. Combe was unable to prevent this duel; the authorities got to hear of it and bound them over, but the combatants merely changed duellists, Maclaren replacing Ritchie and Allan handing over to his editor Dr James Brown.

Combe joined principals and seconds at a Hanover Street coffee house (11 November) to arrange the meeting, and early the following morning the combatants met in a field on the Ravelston road. Luckily both missed, agreed that no more should be said, with no demands or concessions, Maclaren and Brown exchanged bows, and parted. Allan appealed for damages, but ended with a compromise.[69]

In 1830, William Combe having emigrated to America, Livingston's Yards was commandeered for the building of the road between Castle Terrace and the High Street, and the family brewery, which had become expensive to run, was closed, the compensation payment of nearly £10,000 being divided between the surviving family.[70]

There were some sad family losses. Andrew, who suffered a serious lung complaint, went to the Continent with their niece Marion Cox, and was feared dying, but recovered and resumed his medical practice. Their sister Jean died in January 1831 and William Ritchie in February. Andrew's 'Observations on Mental Derangement' was refused for the *Review* by Jeffrey's successor Macvey Napier, who would admit no phrenology.

A third edition of the *System* published in 1830, with modifications to the names of certain organs, had a small steady sale, but many were leaving the society because of Evangelical hostility, lecture attendance fell, and debts mounted. In the following year the course sold few tickets, the audience dwindled to the twenties, and next winter Combe was obliged to abandon it, though outside Edinburgh the movement still flourished. Dr David Welsh resigned as president, unable to accept Combe's moral system, and Combe's contribution in the *Journal* on man's capability for improvement started another long controversial correspondence.[71]

George campaigned for several philanthropic movements – shorter hours for working men, abolition of Sunday work, evening lectures for the 'industrial classes' on science and philosophy, though the School of Arts refused his offered course on these subjects. Things looked up in April 1832 when he gave six lectures on Insanity to students of Dr McIntosh, and lectured on Theory and Practice of Medicine to two hundred students and more than twenty gentlemen. In May a further course at the request of the 'Mechanics, shopkeepers and clerks' again drew more than two hundred, eighty-four of whom took the opportunity to examine the casts and skulls at the Phrenological Society's Clyde Street hall.

As a result, an eclectic programme of lecture courses for the working classes was arranged on chemistry, natural history, phrenology, physiology, and later, botany, astronomy and moral philosophy.[72]

A new character now briefly took a hand, William Ramsay Henderson, son of Alexander, a banker, of Eildon Hall and Warriston. The younger Henderson, who lived in Gayfield Place, did not marry, hated business, and indulged in foreign travel, landscape painting and poetry. His father, who died in July 1828, set up a trust for his estate, allowing him £500 a year. Henderson was interested in phrenology and, but for a speech impediment, would have liked to run his own lecture course for working men in Leith. In compensation he willed his property in May 1829 to trustees, including George and Andrew Combe, for cultivation of phrenology. This enabled them to sell the 'Constitution of Man' to students for a mere 1s. 6d instead of six shillings. Henderson himself lived only until 1832.[73]

In June 1832 Spurzheim went to America on a lecture tour, but caught a chill and, vulnerable from overwork, died in November. Combe, who had been invited to follow him, deferred the journey. Meanwhile he had been writing extensively for the *Scotsman,* and that summer stood in as editor for a couple of weeks in Maclaren's absence.[74]

The Combe brothers had become good friends of Mrs Henry Siddons. Her cousin Fanny Kemble, in her Edinburgh visits in 1828 and 1832, became very attached to them both, perhaps more to the gentle, amiable Andrew who lacked George's 'angular rigidity of person and harshness of nature'. Andrew's own works on hygiene and physical education advocated such common-sense advice as on the value of fresh air and cold baths.

During her first visit Fanny, still in her teens, sat for a portrait bust to the Combes' friend Lawrence Macdonald, who had trained at the Trustees' Academy and had already been in Rome, where he helped to found the British Academy of Arts (1823). He was back in Edinburgh in 1827 and exhibited in the Royal Scottish Academy; from 1829 to 1838 he was a member.

While Fanny was sitting, George Combe stood by to look on, when her aunt came in with a little bag of some of her favourite confections, raspberry puffs. Seeing the bag Fanny jumped from the model's throne and seized them. 'There now, Macdonald, I told you so!' exclaimed Combe, and mouth full of tart she heard them laugh as they explained that Combe had impressed on Madonald her developed 'organ of alimentativeness', namely, greed.[75]

During her visit in 1832 Combe took Fanny to see his museum, where she spent two hours listening to a description of the anatomy of the brain. Though diffident on hearing Combe's 'account of the numbers who attend his lectures and of the improvement of their bodily and mental conditions', she could not help feeling doubtful of 'the reforming power of their system'; while, feeling like Hamlet, she sat on the floor with a lapful of skulls. Among these Raphael's was considered one of the best – though later she learned that it was a wrong attribution, and was thought instead to be his friend Marcantonio's.[76]

Combe's personal life had now completely changed. In youth, because of a scrofulous complaint, aggravated by the damp situation and bad air of Livingston's Yards, he had been too timid to think of marrying. In his changed and mature circumstances, in 1831 at the Siddonses' house he met Henry Siddons's spinster sister Cecilia, who with her aunt Miss Graham of Duntroon, her sister Elizabeth and other ladies, was a keen student of his afternoon lectures. (The evening lectures were reserved for 'shopkeepers, clerks and students'.) Cecilia now became a frequent guest at his house in Northumberland Street. Andrew stayed there in the winter of 1832 and in spring 1833 went to Paris. Cecilia painted three portraits of him, then painted George.

In April 1833 Cecilia and George became engaged, but could not marry until November; she was thirty-nine, he forty-five. For their wedding tour in November they went on extensive Scottish travels, then moved to 12 Charlotte Square, while Andrew, with Marion Cox as housekeeper, remained in Northumberland Street – an excellent arrangement for all.[77]

George, who continued to publish phrenological pamphlets, lectured in America in 1838–40 and in Germany in 1842, and died aged seventy in 1858. Andrew, always of a more sickly constitution, had become an MD in Edinburgh in 1825 and continued in practice until 1840, producing popular treatises on health. He died unmarried in 1847, aged only fifty.[78]

Throughout their careers the brothers suffered hostile judgments on their 'science', which ultimately proved unsustainable. If phrenology might be regarded as Combe's King Charles's head, colouring all that he wrote, his humanitarian feelings and principled moral philosophy also pervaded what he wrote and believed, though he was convinced that phrenology would be the answer to all problems.

A short answer to that lies in a shrewd comment made by Fanny Kemble. She felt amused that Cecilia 'had quite as much trouble with her household, her lady's-maids were quite as inefficient, her housemaids quite as careless, and her cooks quite as fiery-tempered and unsober . . . in spite of Mr Combe's observation and manipulation of their bumps previous to engaging them'.[79]

59
ARTISTS AND MUSICIANS

'A large and highly Interesting Collection of BIRD, PLANTS, and other subjects of NATURAL HISTORY of North America, by Mr Audubon, of Louisiana, collected during the last 20 years and upwards, in some of the most unfrequented parts of that Continent.'

Edinburgh Evening Courant, 18 November 1826

Sir Henry Raeburn died in 1823, and his office as Limner to the King was handed on to David Wilkie, who owing to illness had been making slow progress on his work on the King's entrance to Holyrood. Wilkie, like the other promising young Edinburgh artist David Roberts, was now working in London, but both returned to Scotland from time to time, while the noted English artists Turner and Haydon also made return visits.

Roberts, doing well in London in theatrical as well as more orthodox painting, revisited Edinburgh in the vacation of 1824, where he also painted theatre scenery. His next years were successful and included travel in France and Ireland, and the Rhine, a journey cut short by the 1830 revolution in France.

That same year in July he exhibited his 'Departure of the Israelites from Egypt' at the Scottish Academy. He also painted a new drop-scene for Edinburgh's Theatre Royal, 'a Gothic foreground with Edinburgh in the distance', which was greeted with loud applause. In London Roberts was elected President of the Society of British Artists in Suffolk Street, and persuaded fellow-Scots to submit their work. And in 1831 when Patrick Nasmyth, Alexander's son, known as the 'English Hobbema', died in Lambeth aged only forty-four, Roberts joined with eleven other Scottish painters in London to erect a memorial in the churchyard, which elicited an appreciative letter from Alexander.[1]

Meanwhile Edinburgh's Board of Trustees for the Manufacturers having launched its Institution for the Encouragement of the Fine Arts in Scotland in 1819, in 1823 founded a gallery, designed for the foot of the Mound by William Playfair, to house also the Royal Society and the Society of Antiquaries. Unfortunately the board of directors included no artists, and although some were proposed in 1824, they were not offered voting powers or any financial control, and Raeburn, who had urged founding an Academy on the lines of London's, died before any action could be taken.[2]

The Royal Institution paved the way in February 1826 with an exhibition of 'modern paintings', established, new or amateur. It was unprecedented in Edinburgh, and claimed as unrivalled, while perhaps exciting as much interest from its venue as its content. The *Edinburgh Evening Courant* reporter, devoting a long column to it on 11 February, contrived to do so without naming a single painter, while showering vague praise on the occasion and the works.

Among the chief paintings exhibited (which the reporter got around to mentioning several days later) was William Allan's 'John Knox admonishing Queen Mary', which drew the greatest crowds; the Rev. John Thomson's 'View in Ireland', the largest sea piece – almost too large for the room – was also praised. Others mentioned included Scrope's scene in Calabria. Less attention, however, was devoted to the paintings than to the occasion.

Playfair was especially praised for rendering the room 'completely comfortable', supplementing its elegant roof-lit galleries, hung with crimson cloth with gilt moulding on top, and black and gold Italian marble chimney-pieces, with under-floor stoves as well as the open fires. Further, those attending the private view were gratified at 5 o'clock as the light began to fade, by the occasion turning into a feast when visitors were (as he oddly phrased it) 'electrified by the sudden blaze of gas light' from the handsome ceiling lustres, and tables spread with cold food were suddenly supplemented by hot soup and other comforting dishes, supplied by Ross of the Royal Hotel. In a sophisticated touch, instead of bustling to find seats, they found their places identified. Peers, judges, notables and some 120 gentlemen, artists, amateurs and patrons of the arts, heard Lord Elgin describing the objects of the Institution. Maintaining that it would be 'fruitless to attempt to establish a Royal Academy in so limited a sphere as Scotland', they were therefore following in the footsteps of London's British Institution, established some twenty years earlier, in bringing great works of art to the view of students.

Henry Mackenzie recalled the days of his youth when Scotland had barely encouraged the arts, gratified by the visible progress made since then. As for the artists, even here not one was named unless they spoke at the dinner, as James Skene, Nasmyth, and Scrope, or were toasted, as Hugh Williams, William Allan and Wilkie.[3]

Charles Kirkpatrick Sharpe, always a great traditionalist, was unimpressed in March by the modern portraits. 'It reminds me of the description of a witch in the old song:

Her hair it curled all like snakes,
Her mouth stood all awry,
And where you thought to find a nose,
Alas! there stared an eye!'[4]

Sydney Smith, visiting Edinburgh with his family in 1827, went to an exhibition of Scottish portraits, but was also not impressed. 'High Cheek Bones are not favourable to the fine arts,' he complained to Lady Grey.[5]

Not until 1827 did artists shake free to form a Royal Scottish Academy of Painting, Sculpture and Architecture, with the backing of the then Home Secretary Robert Peel and Sir Thomas Lawrence. The Academy's first home was at Waterloo Place, with William Nicholson as its first secretary; David Roberts was urged to exhibit there and contributed liberally to the funds. The first Academy dinner on 14 April made quite an impression, Nicholson referring to artists' 'severe struggle for the independence of their profession', and with the lessening of prejudice and such backers as Lord Hopetoun, 'the artists who clung to the Institution are at last ashamed of the connection, and have thrown off their allegiance'.[6]

'The differences between the Institution and the Scottish Academy have reached their maximum,' reported Wilkie to Andrew Wilson in September 1829. 'The Institution has one principle of durability – wealth. The Academy, to make up for this, have had recourse to speculation.'[7]

Wilkie had spent much time in Edinburgh in 1824, along with his one-time fellow-student William Allan, who had made a name in Russia and returned to set up in Edinburgh. In September Wilkie was honoured by a public dinner, given for him at the British Hotel by seventeen fellow-artists, headed by Nasmyth. He also visited Lord Leven at Melville Castle, who wanted a portrait of the Earl of Kellie, and worked for some weeks on his Holyrood drawings, a portrait of the Knight Marischal, details of the Regalia, a drawing of Lord Morton, and a chalk drawing of Dugald Stewart, now old and paralysed, who wanted a portrait for his wife by someone who had known him 'in better days'.

Wilkie also made efforts to persuade the Lord Provost not to remove the statue of Charles I from Parliament Square, and discussed the prospect of restoring Edinburgh Cross. In November he went on to Abbotsford to embark on a portrait of Scott.[8]

In the next few years Wilkie suffered many family troubles, with sickness, financial problems of relatives, and the death of his brother in India; but he was able to travel abroad, returning in 1828 with his health improved.[9] He re-started his 'Entry to Holyrood', and in December Scott asked him to illustrate the Waverley Novels. Accordingly in September 1829 he revisited Edinburgh, where he spent time with among others the painter-minister the Rev. John Thomson of Duddingston and visited Sir Robert Liston at

Milburn Tower, who secured him a visit to Hopetoun. Susan Ferrier met him in October on a brief visit to Abbotsford, surprised to find him 'very unlike his own works, being a tall, sickly, grave, stiffish person' (he was still under forty-five).[10]

Wilkie's appearance was indeed not prepossessing. Cam Hobhouse, dining with his sister next year in London, 'sat next to a gaunt, coarse-looking, middle-aged man, who hardly spoke a word all dinner-time, although sitting next to Mrs Lockhart, Sir Walter Scott's most pleasing daughter. I felt vexed when I heard I had been sitting next to Wilkie, the great artist, without having an opportunity of hearing a word from him.' He does not account for himself not troubling to speak to Wilkie.[11]

Lady Salisbury, meeting Wilkie in 1833, when he had been commissioned to make sketches from the Waverley novels to accompany a spectacular performance at Hatfield of Tableaux Vivants, though finding him 'totally unformed', felt that he 'pleases from the utter absence of all affectation'. This was a not untypical aristocratic reaction. Despite his awkward manner and 'looks of a clown', she discerned 'a good deal of sense and observation concealed beneath his oddities'.[12]

The art world suffered a loss that year in the death of the President of the Royal Academy, Sir Thomas Lawrence, who had also been Painter in Ordinary to the King. This proved a disappointment for Wilkie, whom George IV nominated as Lawrence's successor, hoping it would enable him to be elected to the Presidency, but the office was instead voted to Martin Archer Shee. Wilkie at last submitted his King's Entry to Holyrood to the Royal Academy that year, with a large royal portrait.[13] On the King's death he was continued as Painter In Ordinary by his successor William IV, and the portrait of George IV, intended for Holyrood, was sent up by sea and shown at the Royal Institution (prevented from showing at Holyrood by the exiled French King's return there).

Turner, in 1826, contributed twelve plates to Sir Walter Scott's *Provincial Antiquities and Picturesque Scenery of Scotland,* published by the Quaker booksellers John and Arthur Arch, of Cornhill. The Rev. John Thomson, to whom Turner sent a bank bill for his share of £80, contributed eleven, and Schetky, Nasmyth and others the rest.

Later Scott asked Turner for twenty-four plates to illustrate his poetical works, for which Turner charged 25 guineas apiece. In 1831 he revisited Scotland on this account, taking in the Lakes on the way, and with an invitation to Abbotsford. Being a poor rider he was worried about travel in the Highlands, and anxiously asked Scott if the new steamboats might solve the problem.[14] Scott now went off to Malta in the forlorn hope of improving his health, Turner made his tour, expenses paid by Cadell, and his first proofs of the engravings were expected by New Year 1832. By February, when cholera was rife in London, he was anxious about sending drawings and vignettes by the mail.[15]

Scott's death that September was followed immediately by the appointment of a committee to decide on an appropriate monument, on which both Turner and Wilkie were invited to serve, the latter emotionally greatly affected at the first meeting called to discuss it.[16]

In 1829 Hugh 'Grecian' Williams, who was an associate of Edinburgh's Royal Institution, died, presumably of cancer, his face and figure 'fatally altered' according to Henry Cockburn, but in 'astonishing cheerfulness' although well aware of his approaching death. 'Another excellent friend' gone, Cockburn sadly reflected, in a year of many famous losses.[17]

Among other figures in the art world was a sculptor, a second Thomas Campbell (1790–1858), one of those gifted youths of humble background discovered and helped to a career. Patrick Fraser Tytler had encountered him as an apprentice, a 'mere boy in a marble-cutter's shop', thought him clever and intelligent and was impressed by his 'rude attempts at modelling'. He gave up his own time to teach the youth French and Italian in his room in the mornings, before going to Parliament House, and in 1818, after Thomas had studied in London, as he himself had no funds to send him to Rome, he and friends persuaded Innes of Stow to advance the money, which Campbell eventually was able to repay. In this way a successful career was launched.

In 1824 at Tytler's encouragement Campbell submitted a model for the intended equestrian monument to Lord Hopetoun, expected to cost £6000, and on the day when the models were judged invited Campbell to dine with him, hoping to be able to drink his health in success. They were not disappointed. A note came from Tytler at Oman's to say, 'Campbell has been victorious . . . The horse is chosen.' From 1827 to within a year of his death, Campbell exhibited at the Royal Academy.[18]

A young Irish portrait and travel painter, William Bewick, arrived in Edinburgh in March 1825 seeking commissions from celebrities. 'The great Well-known, the Arch-Critic, and many others sat to him', records Mrs Grant, and she was amused that, after having exhausted 'all more worthy subjects' he called to show her some of his work, including of Charles Maturin and Lady Morgan, and asked if he might do a head of her too.[19]

Charles Sharpe told Scott that Bewick had also called on him, when he was in bed, but had left a picture which he thought 'very well done'. 'But the people here never think of having pictures copied, and all flock to be daubed by Mr Watson.' The rival George Watson (1767–1837) had been a pupil of Nasmyth's and in the 1780s of Sir Joshua Reynolds, settled in Edinburgh and in 1826 became first president of the Royal Scottish Academy.[20]

Another, much younger, painter, who was also an actor, Montague Stanley, was born in 1809 to a naval officer who died when he was three. The family moved to Halifax, Nova Scotia, and while he showed an early talent for acting and took to the stage, Stanley was also gifted at drawing. Back in Britain, he acted in York in 1824 under the name of Manby; then in Edinburgh under his own name, from 1828 successful in romantic parts; but with more fondness for sketching, especially scenery, he began to paint for Edinburgh's Annual Exhibition.

Though acting in Dublin and London, Stanley was principally based in Edinburgh at the height of popularity until 1838, when he left the stage, was elected ARSA in 1839, reluctantly converted to religion by his brother-in-law, and turned to teaching art and elocution. He also had a talent for versifying.[21]

There were now many recitals and concerts, at the George Street Assembly Rooms and at the Pantheon. One remarkable appearance in 1826 was that of the pianist George Aspull, a boy prodigy now twelve, who had been performing since he was under eight years old, taught by his father, a failed Manchester merchant who had turned to music teaching. He had made rapid progress, was heard by Kalkbrenner and in London by Clementi, played before King George IV at Windsor and was soon all the rage. He gave the first rendering in England (at Brighton) of Weber's Konzertstück, went to Paris, was admired by Hummel and Rossini and for the last ten years of his short life was touring almost continuously in Britain.

In Edinburgh he gave four concerts at the Assembly Rooms, hailed as 'the wonderful boy Master Aspull', and at the last, on 4 March, was presented with a medal by Sir John Sinclair. He also had a good voice, and his concerts were supported by William, one of his nine brothers, and Miss Eliza Paton as singers. His performance was described as expressive and 'impassioned'.[22]

George had another six years to be famous. In 1832 he caught a cold at Clementi's funeral which turned to a fever and led to his death in November.

In spite of the visits of famous singers and of celebrities like 'Master Aspull', and the grand music festivals of 1815, 1817 and 1824, Edinburgh seems not to have taken music to heart. The St Cecilia concert hall had been tried and failed, the celebrities at first took audiences by storm, but there was as yet no permanent effect. This had an obvious influence on standards, as Elizabeth Rigby experienced at a grand concert in 1842, whose singers included Miss Novello, Miss Hawes and others. 'Knowing that the Edinburgh public don't hear much good music, they took great liberties and sang atrociously.'[23]

By far the most colourful and most documented artist who appeared in Edinburgh at this time was John James Audubon, the French-born painter of birds and animals living in America, who came to England and then Edinburgh in 1826. Born in France in 1785, the illegitimate son of a French naval officer, he early showed a talent for drawing birds, and at the age of eighteen was sent to America to take up business. In this he was not very successful, and having married Miss Lucy Bakewell in 1808, by 1820 was quite ready to concentrate on painting. Studying birds in the backwoods, he lived a hunter's life, supplementing his interest by teaching drawing and painting portraits, and having amassed a number of works, in 1826 he brought them over to seek patrons in Britain.[24]

Audubon's journals and correspondence for this visit, which survive *in extenso*, form an admirable record of the artist's daily life and are worth attention for his fresh eye on society.

They reveal him as shy and nervous, at first reacting with some resentment to fancied snubs from various professors to whom he had introductions, but soon responding with warmth and affection to the many who showed interest. He was under a triple disadvantage, first as being illegitimate, then as a foreigner in America, and doubly so as a French American in Britain. Furthermore, he cut a picturesque figure, rather on the lines of John Wilson, with long flowing hair, sometimes wearing his hunter's dress, and with the natural, unaffected manner of his unsophisticated background.[25]

Audubon spent time in Liverpool and Manchester before travelling to Edinburgh, where he arrived on 25 October. Obliging fellow-travellers, the family of Dr Grenville Pattison, saw him to good lodgings next day, 'the second door in George Street, (perhaps the most beautiful street here)', at Mrs Dickie's, 'a fine bedroom and a fine, well-furnished sitting-room' for only one guinea a week.

After initial disappointment at finding contacts either out or away from Edinburgh, he was able to meet two distinguished scientists, Dr Robert Knox the anatomist and Professor Robert Jameson, founder of the Wernerian Society and of *Edinburgh New Philosophical Journal*, whom at first he found intimidating. He was further disappointed to learn that Sir Walter Scott was now a recluse and also busy at work writing *Napoleon.* Feeling acutely lonely he opened his portfolio of bird drawings, wondered if he could ever publish them, and could scarcely eat his dinner for tears.

Audubon was somewhat consoled by the appearance – and experience – of Edinburgh itself, walking and admiring 'the streets, their good pavement and foot ways, the beautiful uniformity of the buildings, their natural grey coloring and wonderful cleanliness of the [whole]'. This was partly from its contrast with 'dirty Manchester', 'but the picturesque *tout ensemble* here is wonderful'. The castle, the bridge over 'a second city below', the mountains, the public grounds and monuments delighted him.

The friendly Pattisons, his earliest admirers, brought a fair-faced Miss Ewart to call, who, they told him, could draw 'uncommonly beautifully'. Pattison praised Audubon's work, and Miss Ewart 'said with a smile that it seemed America would certainly surpass all other countries in point of arts and sciences in less than another century'. She thought the works he showed her 'exquisitely beautiful', sure that they would delight Sir Walter. Audubon begged them to notify friends that he would display his work here daily between 10 o'clock and noon.

Much encouraged, Audubon made more calls to leave cards, met and liked Patrick Neill, printer, naturalist and Wernerian, and returned to refresh his lunch with 'a tumbler of Scotch grog'.

He walked to Leith, saw *Rob Roy* at the theatre and was careful to leave purse, watch, pocket-book and even pocket handkerchief at his lodgings, and to arm himself with a sword-cane.

Next morning the Pattisons brought in twelve ladies, besides Thomas and John Todd, to see the drawings, and during their two-hour visit Professor Duncan, whom he had been trying to contact, appeared. Several people promised introductions to Scott, and later he called on Jeffrey, who was out, so Audubon left his card. 'What a mess of books, papers, letters, portfolios and dirt, beautiful paintings, engravings, and casts, with such parcels of unopened packets . . . Why, Lucy . . . what have I done compared with what this man has and has to do! I much long to see that famous critic . . .'

Next day arrived Dr Knox with a friend, 'who pronounced my drawings the finest in the world', promised to introduce him to the Wernerian Society, and 'talked very scientifically indeed – quite too much so for the poor man of the woods . . . It is really amusing and distressing at the same time to see how inimical to each other men of science are, and why are they so?'

Patrick Neill introduced Audubon to the engraver William Home Lizars, in St James' Square, who having shared his umbrella back to the lodgings, the moment he entered the room and saw the contents of the portfolio ceased his chat about Prideaux Selby's ornithological work[26] and exclaimed in astonishment, 'My God! I never saw anything like this before!' The amazed engraver at once wrote urging Selby and James Heath to visit. From then on Audubon was to be almost continuously overwhelmed by visitors, admirers and praise.

He became particularly attached to the kind Lizars and his warm and hospitable wife, whom he termed the 'first lady'. Had it not been for the distressing lack of letters from his wife, he was beginning to feel very satisfied.

Professor Jameson, who proved not alarming but cordial and friendly, entertained him to breakfast – 'quite the man for me now'. When he walked about people stared and whispered. 'That's a German physician, I know' ('Fudge!' *sotto voce* from Audubon). 'That's a French nobleman' ('Bah!'). Lizars presents him with a book of Edinburgh views, with an admiring inscription. He buys chalks, crayons and sable hair. An exhibition is proposed. Professor Jameson, seeing his many letters of recommendation, says, 'Mr Audubon, the people here don't know who you are at all. But depend on it, they shall know!' John Wilson's brother James, the naturalist, visits, 'an agreeable man who invited me to dine at his cottage next week'.

Visits include to Neill's pretty little 'hermitage', he meets familiar and new acquaintances, is asked to sit for his portrait to John Syme, RSA, a pupil of Raeburn, and Lizars promises to engrave the result. His room is besieged by nobility, gentry, ladies; the Lizars give him a sumptuous supper party and he is thwarted in trying to get on with painting wild turkeys for a show by the crowds turning up in his room from 10 o'clock onwards, including the ladylike actress Miss Stephens and her brother. He becomes so distracted that he walks out to dine with his near neighbour David Bridges still in slippers. The modest though proud backwoods huntsman is overcome at being on such terms with grandees, but between dining at grand houses, where be is always warmly received, he can always relax for an evening with the delightful Lizars.

Lizars offers to publish the first number of his *Birds of America*. 'I felt quite dazzled with uncertainties of hope and of fear.' He meets Mrs Fletcher's daughter (who was later to marry the naturalist Sir John Richardson), many other young ladies call, and in mid-November he opens his exhibition at the Royal Institution where he is shortly invited to show free of charge.

He paints at home, and sits for his own portrait. The seventy-five invitations which he sends to the opening are to people who have been kind, people whose help he needs, and *'all the artists of Edinburgh!'*

George Combe calls and begs to make a cast of his skull, which he says displays such 'illustrating powers'; Professor Wilson praises *Birds of America,* and is 'quite kind' . . . 'How proud I felt that in Edinburgh, the very vitals of science, learning and solidity of judgment, thy husband was liked, well thought of . . .' He plans to stay until the new work's first number is out, then take proofs to Liverpool to canvass for subscribers, and send copies to every distinguished American, from John Quincy Adams downwards.

Finishing the Wild Turkeys painting, he spends hours writing a commentary for the exhibition, so immersed that he takes it to Wilson 'still undressed', unshaven and in slippers, but Wilson is never one to heed such trifles.

He paints assiduously, this time Wood Pigeons. He endures the ordeal of a grand dinner at Professor Robert Graham's, 62 Great King Street, embarrassed to hear his 'outlandish name' announced by the footman, but solaced by meeting many beautiful ladies, and perfect politeness from everyone; though to such sumptuousness he would still prefer 'adventurous dinners of turtle eggs on Thompson Creek'. He has to pay 12 shillings for a carriage to dine at Craiglockhart, two and a half miles off, then another shilling for a toll. 'A dear dinner, this.'

Winter sets in and early afternoons. He is impressed by the snow, having seen none for at least five years. Snow lies on the hills about 'this enchanted city', and one day to his astonishment the gas lamps are 'let loose' by 3 p.m., so he has to stop work earlier. It turns cold, and he suffers even though 'wrapped up in flannel shirts and drawers'. It is scarcely light at 7.30 in the morning. He continues to sit, stand rather, for his portrait, wearing his wolf-skin coat, 'sick enough of it'.

Lizars accompanies him to 'the dwelling of phrenology', George Combe's in Brown's Square, to meet many of the fraternity. On return home his kind landlady Mrs Dickie is waiting up with a letter from America – but it is not from Lucy but from Governor Clinton and has taken thirty days . . . 'I am quite mad of disappointment.'

At a tedious portrait sitting he learns that Scott is at the Royal Institution, hastens there breathlessly, but finds he has gone up to preside at a meeting. He writes to Wilson begging an introduction to 'the great, Scotch, Well Known'. This longed-for meeting is not to come about until 22 January 1827.

By the end of November the portrait is done, a good work though a less good likeness. The exhibition is still well attended, but he is reluctant to go often, as 'to be gazed at by a crowd is of all things the most detestable to me'. His portrait is displayed there instead, rather it be stared at than the original.

At the Antiquaries' Dinner, Innes of Stow presents him to the President, Lord Elgin, and he is relieved there are so many people he knows. Sweating with fear, he has to reply to a toast, and Lizars revives him with wine. The ordeal over, he is glad to have been there, especially as Lord Elgin is very complimentary, and they meet again at the Institution next day.

Audubon's stay continues on the same eventful lines, meeting and in general liking, celebrities. He is even invited to dinner by a complete stranger he mistakes in the street for another. Sir James Hall and his brother Basil call, Basil wanting information on American travel. Calling on them later, he is impressed by Basil's wife's appearance and youth, by their evident happiness, and by Hall's polite kindness, 'far differing from the usual on such slight acquaintance'.

Wilson writes him up in *Blackwood's*, and Audubon begs a dozen copies to send to America. He paints the Otter in just thirteen hours, proud that he could not have done it better in thirteen weeks. He attends Dr Knox's anatomy lecture, disconcerted on entering the room when 150 students stamp their feet and clap their hands, 'that quite shocked me'. But then everyone who enters gets the same treatment – except Dr Knox himself: 'all was hushed as if silence had been the principal study'. He reaches a point where one day, he cannot recall where he is invited, and rather like Tommy Moore is glad to spend a quiet evening instead with the Lizars, usually being kept up until 1 and 2, then up again to start painting at 6 a.m.

At dinner at Ritchie's, in George Street, he notes the social custom of inviting more guests after dinner for tea and music – all waiting to hail '*The Great Unknown of America!*' Lizars' proofs are ready. The painter William Allan calls, after his Academy of Arts lesson, 'an extremely agreeable man, full of gaiety, wit and good sense', and a great traveller in eastern Europe and the Levant. He is again taken aback when an exhibition visitor passes a false sovereign, and another attempts to steal a drawing from the Institution. Enquiries are set on, and the terrified thief drops the rolled-up drawing outside Audubon's door. The saddest aspect of this is his finding that the young suspect was deaf and dumb, an illegitimate son of Sir Henry Raeburn's and a ward of Basil Hall's. Thoroughly shaken, Audubon stops the warrant for his arrest.

All this while there is no letter from his wife, and by 10 December he is fearing some terrible accident has happened. But two from her arrive the very next day, and his world is transformed. He is excited about ordering a new coat, though three tailors are consulted before he is satisfied; and he dines with Lucy's cousin the Rev. William Bakewell and his family. He takes a paper he has written on the carrion crow to Dr Brewster, and reads it with a nervous breathlessness that only his wife would understand. 'A man who never looked into an English grammar . . . who has always felt awkward and very shy in the presence of a stranger, one habituated to ramble alone with his thoughts', now reading his 'puny efforts' to such a learned man! He perspires still more than at the Antiquarians' dinner . . . but a large Newfoundland dog who comes in to caress Brewster relieves his tension. Brewster's wife puts him at ease, as (he reminds Lucy) well-bred people here, especially ladies, always do.

The ornithologist Selby, with Sir William Jardine, expected for some time, eventually reached Edinburgh, and Audubon met him with pleasure and interest on 13 December, again impressed that Selby was a gentleman as well as a genius.

His carrion crow paper was now in proof, but Brewster warned him that only thirty foreigners might become Royal Academicians, and their quota was already exceeded. On the other hand, he learned that Scott was anxious to meet him.

Lizars' brother got a couple of cats for him to paint. He contrasted the informal dinner with the Lizars' – not a day passed without his seeing them – with the formal evenings at the Halls', which he attended resplendent in 'beautiful new pantaloons, new splendid Lafayette coat, and . . . my own face to embellish the whole'.

He met Dr Stokoe, a former Government physician, employed as Napoleon's physician on St Helena but dismissed for not kowtowing to 'barbarous government'. Stokoe had news of Napoleon's nephew Charles Bonaparte, arrived from America to Liverpool, and before starting work Audubon wrote to him.

He then bought and killed a tame pigeon, packed his mounting equipment and went to demonstrate to the Wernerian Society. 'What a name it has in America! The room is a plain oblong square, and two tables, one chimney, many long seats, and a chair for the President.' On the table was a stuffed swordfish, the day's examination subject. He met several acquaintances, and the members were impressed by his ingenious wiring of a specimen for drawing. Professor Jameson spoke in praise of his work, and to stamps and claps he was unanimously accepted a member. Audubon agreed to read a paper on the alligator at the next meeting.

Invitations still poured in, including another from George Combe. At Lady Hunter's, where he dined in his new finery, though most of the guests were titled he no longer felt 'so uncomfortable', they were so uncommonly kind, affable, and truly well-bred. In the rainy Sunday small hours he returned home, and helped by Mrs Dickie's son, 'committed *Murder*' on Daniel Lizars's unfortunate cats, hung them up and arranged them in 'fighting attitudes'[27] 'like two devils for a dead squirrel'.

For lack of daylight the cat painting took longer than he would have liked. He finished it in two days, working 'like a journeyman carpenter'. It was raining again, so he carried the painting to show Mrs Lizars, dined at Combe's, 'an extremely agreeable companion', then went on with Lizars to the Royal Academy meeting.

Two of his bird plates were on display. The committee retired to discuss Brewster's proposal that the society subscribe to the work, Selby and Jardine arriving just before the meeting. Audubon had to listen to some professor's 'long, tedious, laboured lecture' on the formation of languages, 'a very poor mess'. To his great regret Scott had sent his apologies. He and Lizars left before the committee's decision, being invited for supper at Dr Russell's in Abercromby Place; but he was surprised that many distinguished members 'knew nothing of America beyond her laws or the situation of her principal cities'. He was tired out; everything was magnificent, but he missed Lucy, had been working since 6 in the morning, and 'supping at this house I felt quite sick of the whole'. Again he did not leave until 12.30.

He was breakfasting next morning with Jardine and Selby, 'dressed smart', at their base at Barry's Hotel in Princes Street. It was then that he met the barefoot beggar child for whom he parcelled up his spare linen. His hosts presented him with ducks and hawks 'to draw after my fashion'; they accompanied him home to witness his method, and in no time he had them drawing a small squirrel, feeling like a dream to be teaching 'men so much my superiors'. He then read them his now published carrion crow paper, shocked to find it so edited by Brewster to improve his style that he 'destroyed the matter'.

After a 'blustery' military dinner he was thankful to go on to the Lizars' and find the ladies alone, like 'a pleasant bath after a day's march'. Lizars came in with Jardine and Selby to say he had been 'elected by acclamation' to the Society of Arts. 'Thus I possess one title in foreign lands!'

Next day Combe (after a hearty breakfast) examined his skull, his findings proving a surprise. Combe gave him a note to an advocate who, he hoped, would lead him to Jeffrey, but although they found 'a hundred other advocates strutting with their raven gowns and powdered, curled wigs', Jeffrey himself was not in court.

Selby sent him three fine pheasants, which he would paint as if attacked by a fox, for his London exhibition in March.[28] Lord Morton sent a polite invitation asking him to come to Dalmahoy for a day and a night. He set up a male pheasant, which his two new pupils joined him in drawing. Meanwhile the Lizars ladies are stitching his new shirts, 'for I am frequently obliged to dress twice a day, the greatest bore imaginable'. He lost a precious day awaiting a canvas, 'a vast deal in a man's life glass', wrote letters instead, then with Selby visited the advocate Simpson at 33 Northumberland Street, where nothing is talked of but phrenology.

He still politely received his numerous daily visitors, painted as much as possible before it turned dark at 3, even when twenty-five times disturbed; yet found he quite enjoyed the attention. If he had to grind his own colours it made him fretful and had a bad effect on the painting. Meanwhile, though the exhibition continued popular, the weather affected numbers, and expenses were high even with free use of the hall, swelled by payments to door keepers, 'card bearers', and street sweepers.

On 24 December the exhibition closed, and the drawings and painting were taken down. Audubon diplomatically presented 'Wild Turkeys' to the Royal Institution in gratitude for their help, although he could have sold it for 100 guineas.

He was greatly homesick for his wife and weary from reaction. Next evening, when 'The gas lights were dimly shining through the thick, warm, moist fog', he derived comfort relaxing in a large, well-stuffed, black armchair, while Mrs Lizars and her sister cut out his linen. After supper there, he went to bed early and fell asleep exhausted.

On 27 December Lord Morton's carriage drove him to Dalmahoy. He was kindly received by the frail, aged Earl, and intrigued to find a bathing closet adjoining his room, 'large porcelain table, jars of water, drying linens' (which he did not use, thinking himself clean enough), and a WC. In the morning the two young women cleaning the drawing-room vanish the moment he appears; at breakfast and luncheon no servants are seen. He gives a drawing-lesson to the good-looking (not beautiful) Lady Morton, is invited to return to Dalmahoy next week and is dropped back in Edinburgh in time to dine with the Halls.

Here his portfolio is available for inspection by an after-dinner crowd, but he is so exhausted that he takes an early leave. He sees 'a curious notice' on himself in *Blackwood's*, evidently by Wilson. Next day, having had two letters from Lucy, he paints happily, and dines again at Hall's, now his most assiduous suitor, in order to meet Jeffrey.

This wished-for climax proves a surprising disappointment. Jeffrey appears to Audubon 'a small (not to say little) being with a woman under one arm and his hat in the other. He bowed very seriously indeed . . . I conceived the personage to be full aware of his weight in Society. His looks were shrewd, but I thought much cunning resides over the eyes cast about. And the man talked so abundantly that I did not like him at all.'

The American wife, with her nervous twitch and an 'uncommon share of *plainliness* (for I never called a woman ugly in my whole life)', he found not interesting. He and Jeffrey seemed shy of one another, and Audubon records a feeling of cavalier treatment. 'If *he* was Jeffrey, *I* was Audubon, very much his equal.' Audubon had travelled far in two months.

Having taken umbrage, he was impervious to anything Jeffrey said or did, would not reciprocate thanks for what he had done, 'for he had done nothing for me', and despite his fame 'I thought he wanted a little of the polish and finished manner of *simpler men*'. In fact, he could not forgive Jeffrey for being too clever, and conversely, liked the Halls more and more.

Curiously, during the evening little was said of America, and he came to the conclusion that they carefully avoided the subject and that neither of the Jeffreys 'knew much about it besides their reading'. Strange conclusion.

With this unsatisfactory encounter Audubon concludes his 1826 journal.

For his last months in Edinburgh we are dependent on the less accurate and often paraphrased publication of his diaries by his daughter.[29] It was during these months that he had the adventure with the sedan chair (see Part II, p. 192), and also visited the Scottish Regalia. He also had a meeting with the nineteen-year-old Joseph Kidd, 'a promising young artist in landscape' (5 March), who was later to paint backgrounds to some of Audubon's works;

an evening at the sculptor Samuel Joseph's, when he acquitted himself well on the dance-floor; and the departure for London of Basil Hall, who had proved a good friend.

He also described the heavy snowstorms in early March which stopped the mails, when 'people are waddling along through it in the streets, and giving a lively representation of Lapland winter'. The same day he was deeply impressed by a sermon of Sydney Smith's. 'Oh! What a soul there must be in the body of that famous man . . . He made me smile, and he made me think more deeply perhaps than I had ever before in my life.'

He also had his famous hair cut, and drew up a framed epitaph, 'the will of God usurped by the wishes of Man', reminding him of the shearing of those about to be guillotined.

Audubon also at last achieved his wished-for but dreaded meeting with Sir Walter Scott on whom he called on 22 January.[30] Scott was in a quilted morning gown of purple silk; he rose from his labours on Napoleon to greet him cordially and records how he was struck by Audubon's 'simplicity of manners and behaviour', and his still long, 'not yet tinged' hair. Audubon in turn was impressed by Scott's 'long, loose, silvery hair' – 'he looked like Franklin at his best'. Fascinated, he regarded him closely like 'a celestial being' struck by the 'long heavy white eyebrows'. 'His little room was tidy, though it partook a good deal of the character of a laboratory', and he noted Scott's closely written lines sloping from the left to the right, with 'an immense deal on very little paper'. Scott sent for his daughter Anne, 'black-haired and black-dressed, not handsome but said to be accomplished'. They had much talk, Audubon chiefly a listener.

At the opening of his exhibition at the Royal Institution (13 February), Scott came up to talk to him, warmly pressing his hand, but Audubon's perverse diffidence overcame him, and he not only excused himself from joining Scott in a glass of wine but was too scared to partake of the many delicacies provided.

He painted a great deal, copied his drawings, attended many meetings, remaining as shy as ever in company, and visited Rosslyn Chapel. On his last night in Edinburgh, at the Royal Society, he heard Sir William Hamilton lecturing '*against* phrenology, which would seem to quite destroy the theory of Mr Combe'.

Lizars, who had started engraving Audubon's works in November, completed aquatints of the first set of ten by the following spring.[31] In April Audubon went to London to canvass subscribers, but two of Lizars's workers struck, and had to be replaced by the two Robert Havells, father and son, to complete the work. The 435th and last hand-coloured aquatint was engraved in June, 1828, and about 175 copies of this remarkable book were completed. In 1828 Audubon went on to Paris, and until 1839 divided his time between Europe and America, seeking material and subscriptions, and completing illustrations.

A tragic epilogue to the history of Lord Eldin's famous collection of paintings occurred when they were sold after his death at his house at 16 Picardy Place.

The sale had attracted such attention that his executors ordered that nobody might be admitted without a card from either them or the auctioneer, Winstanley.

On Wednesday 13 March 1833 the two first-floor drawing-rooms were cleared and the pictures removed ready for the sale, to be held in the front or smaller room, starting next day at 1 p.m. A wooden barrier was made across the room to keep the public from the porters carrying the paintings, and the folding doors were left open. In the front room a makeshift 'easel' was rigged up with a chest of drawers standing on a packing-case, covered with green cloth, with the auctioneer's and clerk's tables on the other side of the fireplace. Five rows of benches were placed for the public. Providentially at the suggestion of Lord Eldin's neighbour James Gibson Craig, the carpet, which was old, was left in place.

A vivid account was compiled by none other than John Howell the Thistle Street 'polyartist', who had been put in charge of the library which contained the china.

The first day, Thursday, was a regular crush, people arriving early and crowding the stair as well as the two rooms; Friday was less crowded, so was Saturday, though there were about 150 of them, including about a dozen ladies, and people were pushing more towards the 'easel'.

At about half-past two, when the sale was in full swing, there was a sound like a form giving way, and the easel toppled forward. John Howell rushed to straighten it, but the grinding and tearing continued, and as he turned he saw the floor giving way beneath him.

He fell through to the library below, bruised though not seriously hurt, but was quickly buried under falling bodies, suffocated with lime and dust, and it turned as dark as midnight. The sound of breaking glass made him fear the whole house was collapsing, but it proved to be Mr Grant smashing windows to let in air, while rescuers were forcing the library door (the key was in Howell's pocket).

Howell, sure he was going to die, partly protected himself under a beam, but was surrounded by groans and painful movement, the sound of victims being carried out. In the now faint light he could see his fellow-sufferers, clothes in shreds and coated with white dust, their voices hoarse and choked, while he himself was heavily bruised and strained. It took about a quarter of an hour to rescue them all, he being one of the last.

He then fetched water from the kitchen for the victims while rescuers

Top left. John James Audubon (1785–1851), ornithologist and artist. By John Syme.

US National Archives and Records Administration

Top right. Henry Peter Brougham, First Baron Brougham and Vaux (1778–1868), jurist, politician and co-founder of the *Edinburgh Review*. By Andrew Morton.

Scottish National Portrait Gallery

Left. Lady Charlotte Campbell By J.W. Tischbein.

National Galleries of Scotland

Top left. The Rev. Thomas Chalmers (1780–1847), theologian and reformer. By Thomas Duncan.
Scottish National Portrait Gallery

Top right. Bobert Dundas, Lord Arniston (1713–1787), Solicitor General for Scotland, Lord Advocate, Lord President of the Court of Session. By Andrea Soldi.
In the collection of Arniston House

Right. Henry Erskine (1746–1817), jurist. Attributed to William Yellowlees, after Sir Henry Raeburn.
Scottish National Portrait Gallery

Top left. George Drummond (1687–1766), Lord Provost of Edinburgh, civic improver. By Sir George Chalmers.
Scottish National Portrait Gallery

Top right. Thomas Carlyle (1795–1881), historian and essayist. By Charles Linnell.
National Galleries of Scotland

Left. Susan Edmonstone Ferrier (1782–1854), novelist. By Augustin Edouart.
Scottish National Portrait Gallery

Top left. Mrs James Grant of Laggan (née Anne MacVicar, (1755–1838), poet and essayist. By James Tannock.
Scottish National Portrait Gallery

Top right. James Hogg (1770–1835), novelist. By Sir John Watson Gordon.
Scottish National Portrait Gallery

Right. Francis Horner, politician. By Sir Henry Raeburn.
Scottish National Portrait Gallery

Top left. Francis Jeffrey, Lord Jeffrey (1773–1850), judge. By Colvin Smith.
Scottish National Portrait Gallery

Top right. Henry Mackenzie (1745–1831), writer. By Colvin Smith.
Scottish National Portrait Gallery

Left. Sir Walter Scott (1771–1832), novelist and poet. By William Nicolson.
National Galleries of Scotland

Above. John Gibson Lockhart (1794–1845), novelist and critic, with his wife, Charlotte Sophia Scott. By Robert Scott Lauder.

Scottish National Portrait Gallery

Right. Henry Dundas, Viscount Melville (1742–1811), jurist and politician. By Sir Henry Raeburn.

Courtesy of the Governor and Company of the Bank of Scotland

Above. Harriet Murray,
Mrs Henry Siddons. By John Wood.
Scottish National Portrait Gallery

Left. John Wilson
(pseudonym, Christopher North)
(1785–1854), critic and essayist.
By Sir Henry Raeburn.
Scottish National Portrait Gallery

Right. The Rev.
Sydney Smith (1771–1845),
cleric, essayist and wit.
By John Henning.
Scottish National
Portrait Gallery

Below left.
Andrew Combe,
phrenologist.
By John Hutchison.
Scottish National
Portrait Gallery

Below right.
The Rev.
Edward Irving
(1792–1834),
preacher and mystic.
By Hamilton W. MacCarthy.
Scottish National
Portrait Gallery

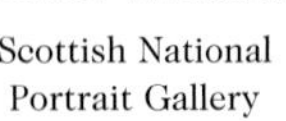

hurried about collecting smashed wood and items of value, while he shouted to them to avoid breaking the china.

They had fallen sixteen feet, dragging the carpet with them, which saved worse injury as they slipped rather than tumbled: the injuries were caused by the falling forms and piling bodies.

On the Monday when he went back, the library was cleared of timber but was a scene of desolation. Two-thirds of the floor was strewn with trampled hats, torn catalogues, shoes, gloves, umbrellas and walking sticks. Lord Eldin's china was surprisingly intact, except for one large teapot and two parcels of the ten dozen plates.

The disaster was blamed on the 'criminal stupidity' of using coarse timber for the joists, and particularly the beams supporting the floor, which was 26 by 18 feet and supported only by two 6-by-12-inch beams. The builders had evidently tried to strengthen it by bolting on two lengths of old ship's oak, but the bolt had passed through a knot-hole and the floor gave way where the lengths had met in the middle. It was reckoned that the floor had been gradually collapsing under the pressure from the crowds, since the beginning of the week.

The auctioneer Winstanley fell the farthest, from his table raised above the floor, which precipitated him on to the others, grabbing at but missing the chimneypiece and falling on a library bookcase and thence down. He and others, much bruised, got out through a window. George Ashton, his clerk, managed to cling to the grate and scramble into the chimney, from which even the victims had to smile on seeing his legs and coat-tails protruding when the dust cleared.

When the collapse happened two chairmen were carrying a picture between the rooms; one fell and was injured, the other was safely still in the back room where people escaped. Thirteen doctors turned up to help, others were already there, while Gibson Craig found and passed round some wine.

One man was killed, Alexander Smith, a banker, found under a chest with severe contusions. Among the thirty-six most heavily bruised or injured were several artists, J. B. Kidd of Dundas Street, J. F. Williams of Princes Street, with broken ribs, and the Glasgow engraver Haldane, also with a broken rib. Henry Jack, a carver and gilder of Jamaica Street, who was severely injured in the face by a splinter, died a fortnight later leaving a wife and five children, for whom a subscription was raised.

People in the street had first been warned of the disaster by the sight of bloody-faced, dust-covered men rushing from the house, while clouds of dust from the windows made it look like a fire. A crowd soon collected and broke into the room as a rescue party. In the drawing-room above, where a few standing had escaped, only eight or ten feet of floor still remained by the window.[32]

60
CRAFTSMEN AND LABOURERS

> [Greenside, Calton Hill:] '. . . coppersmiths, tinsmiths, brassfounders, gold-beaters, and blacksmiths . . . Little boys looked in and saw the men at work amids the blaze of fires and the beating of hammers . . . their dexterous use of the hammer, the chisel, and the file.'
>
> Samuel Smiles (ed.), *James Nasmyth, An Autobiography*, Edinburgh, 1883, 73

Hugh Miller, who came to Edinburgh from Cromarty to work as a mason in the summer of 1824, when the building mania was at its height before the bubble burst, gives a remarkable insight into the habits, attitudes and morals of skilled masons of the time. He had been introduced to a master builder by Thomas Veitch, the Town Clerk, who helped advise him on an albatross of a building he had been unfortunate enough to inherit in Leith, and he was taken on as a hewer at Niddrie House.

This mansion outside Edinburgh had been built for Andrew Wauchope in the 1730s, and William Adam had added a pavilion, offices and a burial-place in the grounds. A century later William Burn made a castellated addition for Colonel William, the current Wauchope.[1] Sixteen masons were employed, with labourers. All were skilled stone-cutters, especially in mouldings: 'far above the average of the masons of the north country', thought Hugh, who was nervous of his status with them as he had no experience of the 'old English style' of 'mullions, and transoms, and labels'. His diligence, however, paid off, and when the first pay-night came round the foreman, who had been watching him, rated his pay to be level with the rest. In time, too, he was entrusted with difficult tasks.[2]

His relationship with his fellow-masons, however, remained uneasy for some time, as some of them were jealous of this northerner, 'a Highlander newly come to Scotland', pretended they could not lay the stones he had worked, and the hewers refused to help him carry the heavy ones. He was backed by the foreman, a pious and worthy man, who promised that if he stuck it out the others would in time come round.

Hugh's crime was that he was not a drinker, and therefore would neither join them nor treat them, and as during this building boom 'the men were masters and more', even the foreman could not support him too openly. The grateful Hugh felt indignant at 'the mean fellows who could take such odds against an inoffensive stranger'. He spent his solitary leisure time exploring the district and the woods, pursuing amateur geology in the quarries and nearby coal-pits, and striking up an acquaintance with the local colliers. His own lodging was in the cottage of an old farm-servant and his wife, with not even a partition between their bed and his, but that was the pattern in the village. He was even joined after a few weeks by a second lodger, a Seceder like the foreman, who had lived in a 'turbulent' household until he could bear it no more.

This man, John Wilson, was only a labourer and earned half the wages of a skilled mason, but on weekdays no mason was better dressed, or on Sundays wore a better suit. 'A decent man', he was a great reader, mainly of religious and theological works. Two of the masons were also Seceders, but 'more polemical and less devout', and convinced of 'the positive worthlessness of Establishments'. In 1824, eight years before the Reform Bill and its aftermath let loose 'many a pent-up opinion', agitation was already boiling up among intelligent Dissenters.

Only these Seceders had any religious feeling. The general run of masons were 'really wild fellows, most of whom never entered a church'. The reaction which had already begun against the 'cold, elegant, unpopular Moderatism' of Blair and Robertson was mostly among the educated and upper classes. On the other hand most of the working population had abandoned the church during the past generation or so, and working men in the Edinburgh area were, if not actually Seceders, not religious.

The conscientious and sensible Wilson, well-informed though not at all intellectual, was blind in one eye from a gunpowder explosion at a quarry, but maintained a contented air and was pleasant if homely in features. His job was to mix mortar and carry building materials with a fellow-labourer of totally opposite character and appearance. John Lindsay, grey-haired and whiskered, handsome and aristocratic-looking, was almost pathologically miserable. He was the bastard of an Earl of Crawford, as Hugh Miller put it with only a marriage certificate between him and the title. He never contested it, however, and carried on as a mason's labourer. The others used to call to him, 'John, Yearl Crawford, bring us anither hod of lime!'[3]

The devout Miller noted the marked difference between these southerners and northern Scots. Among them here religion of any kind was barely tolerated: as for example one man patronisingly observed that he 'aye liked to be in a kirk, for the sake of decency, once a twelvemonth'. Wilson, keeping his own belief a secret, used to make an excuse at night to retire outside to say his prayers, until Miller taxed him with it. After that, he arranged evening prayers in their cottage, Peggy agreeing and taciturn old William, who had never been to a church, affirming that he 'wasna for that'. Wilson's prayers were so long that William sometimes fell asleep on his knees. During all of Hugh's stay, however, 'I saw neither minister nor missionary'.

The skilled men formed a kind of unenlightened gang. They were well paid, fortnightly on Saturday nights, but by the time the first weekend was past barely half a dozen of them had not poured out most of their generous wages, about £6 a head, on 'drinking and debauchery'. He had rarely seen time so mis-spent, Hugh observes, as in these days of well-paid, regular employment. Groups of three and four would set off at once for Edinburgh, not to be seen again until the Monday or Tuesday evening, when they dropped in with 'the horrors', as they called it, 'pale, dirty, disconsolate-looking'. For a couple of days they still suffered hangovers, and would brag of the weekend's exploits once they recovered.

Their hero was the raffish, 23-year-old Charles, or 'Cha', a natural leader, tough, dark and six feet tall. He was among the more intelligent, and of some strength of character despite his wildness. Though a spendthrift and unprincipled he was generous, and could (Hugh felt) have been 'noble'. He was one of the few who had not joined in persecuting Hugh, and had once even helped him single-handed when the others deliberately left him to man-handle a huge block; he would actually talk to him now and then, not unrewardingly, for he was not only a skilled artisan but had some knowledge of architecture. He was even interested in books, and had an eye for nature. Cha's history was sad enough: in earlier youth he had got into a fight and seriously injured a work-mate, fled but was captured, and served three months in prison, 'in the worst company in the world', and on release he became more reckless than ever. Nor did he save a penny from his earnings, so that after the crash following the mid-1820s 'mania' he, like thousands of others, lost his job, in desperation enlisted in a regiment bound for the colonies – and was heard of by colleagues no more.

Most of the men's free time was spent in taverns, sometimes in unsavoury areas like the West Port. They had some lively adventures. One weekend Cha and two others took their whole fortnight's wages on a Saturday evening, spent the night in a brothel, and hiring a coach next morning took three women of the town on 'a jaunt of pleasure' to Roslin. They then spent a similar night in Edinburgh and returned to their work at Niddrie without a farthing. The total outlay was £6.12s: £2.4s each on a fortnight's pay, a high figure for the time. They received admiring praise from their mates, who for days afterwards went on exchanging similar stories.

Then there was the tale of an Edinburgh mason who on receiving a legacy of £80 on the death of a relative, at once took home his tool chest and put it away, bought smart clothes, hired a hackney coach by the week to go to all the fashionable events, and every day drove in his carriage to visit his former colleagues. Within six weeks the money was all gone, and he philosophically fetched out the tool chest and went back to his job. Despite Hugh's disapproval of such wasteful extravagance, the men probably did not see it that way, and very likely thought the taste of high life well worthwhile.

The men were certainly capable of kindly acts. One time Cha and three others rescued a country youth in a High Street den who had fallen into the hands of a gang of women who first robbed him, then when he threatened them with calling the watch, tied him up, pulling an apron so tightly round his face that when the masons freed him he had all but choked.

By autumn the men had grown tired of tormenting Hugh, and the work itself was more pleasant. Hewing large stones under the fine trees of the park was an agreeable change from struggling with outsize blocks. The men objected to the winter rates introduced after Hallowe'en, and instead of a sixty-hour week the pay was reduced to 15 shillings for forty-two hours. Having got into the way of over-spending, they talked of a strike. Master builders regularly cut back in winter, but the feckless masons had never thought of laying money aside. A couple of weeks after the pay reduction, the men gathered together to announce a district strike, though the more provident Hugh warned them they could not last beyond the next weekend. Charles suggested they indulge in a day's 'fun', that is, joining a large meeting on Bruntsfield links as a country masons' deputation, with a speech on their rights and duties.

Some sixteen of them marched into Edinburgh in a body, in their aprons and working clothes, stained red from the distinctive local stone, and the crowd gave them a cheer. There was a gathering of about eight hundred, with 'a few crack orators', so in spite of his mates' urging Cha did not make his speech. But as no-one was in charge of the gathering, the only thing agreed after a lot of sometimes rubbishy verbiage was to adjourn, agreeing to meet in some hall in the evening.

Out of curiosity Hugh joined Cha and the gang at the inevitable pub, a low tavern in a half-ruinous Canongate tenement. It was windowless, lit by a dim gas jet, thick with tobacco fumes and the smell of spirits. From a trapdoor in the floor came confused sounds, a yelping dog and rough voices, proving that it was one of the low dram-shops that kept cramped boxes of badgers, to be baited by the dogs their customers brought with them. The masons, who had brought a repulsive wall-eyed dog of their own, were told that they must wait an hour or so for the present bout to end.

After spending this in hard drinking they climbed down a ladder to a dark, dank and smelly vault, and enjoyed the brutal sight of the already blood-stained badger fighting off a new attack; then climbed up again for more drink. The older men whose 'debauchery' had told on their constitution were more drunk than their vigorous younger colleagues, conversation became louder, incoherent and full of oaths, and eventually Cha himself became so embarrassed at Hugh's witnessing this that the two put down their share of the payment and left together. Hugh spent the rest of the evening with his geologist's hammer in the King's Park.

The famous workers' meeting had resumed with greatly depleted numbers, as many, like Charles and the rest, had just drunk out the evening and never returned. The protest petered out, and by degrees the masons accepted the masters' terms.

The masons' poor dog came to a sad end. There was a story of sheep-worrying at a local farm and that the shepherd was coming along with a law-officer. The dog vanished as if by instinct, but on his return his owner tied a rope round his neck, dragged him off to a water-logged old coalpit nearby, and drowned him.

William Ross, a former friend whom Miller had met again in Edinburgh, was a keen supporter of strikes and hitherto illegal combinations, confident that the working-man would eventually benefit, and acting as clerk for a society of house-painters. The start of the building mania coincided with the first of the major strikes. The more sober-minded Hugh, while seeing good in the 'combinations', considered strikes pointless: 'It is the wilder spirits that dictate the conditions . . . They are the tyrants to their fellows.' William was not persuaded by his dictum.

Ross also had other interests, however. He had done some painting from life, and now turned to ornamental painting, in which he became a master. Miller does not unfortunately reveal the client or place for which he painted a ceiling in oils, 'in bold relief some of the ornately sculptured foliage of the architect', which so impressed his client, himself an amateur painter and son-in-law to a distinguished artist, that he exclaimed in astonishment to his wife at the excellence of this 'mere mechanic'. Will was later summoned from Glasgow to Ireland, where he completed a richly painted ceiling for a bishop.

In November 1824 Hugh and his mates witnessed the great fire in Edinburgh; he attended the great preacher Dr M'Crie's services, went to the theatre, which he thought very poor, and managed to set up a work-table and book-shelf in his humble cottage.

His working conditions were now much easier, the men now accepted him, the busy season started and wages even overtook the previous year's. But now there was a new hazard. Masons were severely affected by the stone dust, and Edinburgh stone-cutters were known to suffer lung trouble by the time they were forty. Few lived to be more than forty-five. Hugh began to suffer so severely that he was obliged to leave the job and take the boat back to Inverness, knowing that in half a year many fellow-workmen might be dead.

There was a curious corollary to the latter part of his Edinburgh job. Hugh, proud but all too conscious of his status as a stone-cutter, had refrained from presenting himself with an introductory letter to a cousin – another William – who had become a senior clerk and manager in Edinburgh, and then as times were booming, set up his own business. Since he was only a 'working man' and not in a profession, Hugh feared his cousin might be ashamed of the connection. But Will, hearing he was in Edinburgh, was trying to trace him, and when eventually Hugh found the courage to call at his rooms in Ambrose's Lodgings, Will welcomed him warmly, chiding him for not coming sooner.

He was persuaded to stay on and meet visiting friends, who proved to be chiefly medical and divinity students. Hugh, to his relieved surprise, found he could meet them conversationally on equal terms.

An odd coincidence was that Will's lodgings were immediately above the rendezvous of the *Blackwood's* coterie, and one of their meetings was going on below them at that moment. It would be pleasant to record that Hugh was able to set eyes on the group, even briefly – especially as several times he had hung about in Castle Street hoping in vain by some lucky chance to see Sir Walter Scott. But neither was to be.

William Ross escorted Hugh to Leith to catch the boat, and at the last moment his cousin Will unexpectedly appeared, having taken time off his work to say farewell. As they shook hands Hugh felt shame at his own pride, and regret for lost opportunities.

It would also be pleasant to record that his cousin Will prospered, but he was among the many who lost his business in the crash of 1825–26, struggled on for some years in London, and finally secured a judicial appointment in the West Indies, where however, thanks to the climate, he died when aged about fifty.

An interesting comment on the fate of unemployed masons is made by the beggar 'Hawkie', who pursued his adventures as far as Whitby at what must have been about the time of the financial crash and building slump of 1826. 'At that time the builders in Edinburgh made a stop which cast thousands of people over the country in starvation; they were all over England . . . There were masons and wrights coming to the lodging-houses begging for a night's lodgings without a morsel of supper or breakfast' – while professional beggars, 'making money like "slate-stanes"', would never offer them a scrap.[4]

Edinburgh masons may have been more dissolute and open to temptation than other Lowlands or north country craftsmen. At all events Hugh Miller was left for life with a poor opinion of working men in general: 'selfish and wilful as spoiled children, brutishly sensual, flippantly because ignorantly infidel, habitually profane'. Even their abundant work and high wages did not prevent a mean, narrow jealousy of himself as an outsider. Cha was the best of them, but heedless and thoughtlessly spendthrift as the rest.

Hugh had eventually gained the men's respect by resolutely holding his own, besides, he excelled in swimming, jumping and running. But he never got over his distrust and contempt for their feckless way of living for the moment, and through that, for workmen in general.

Nor was he impressed by the proto-unions' efforts to better their lot, arguing with William Ross that while such men might gain petty office within the union, they would never gain real power; even the 'fluent gabbers' could do no more than express the semi-articulate sentiments of the masses, unless they acquired more wisdom. In fact, at that time the class system, despite the upper classes' fear of revolution, was too strong. One thing he could not foresee was the effect of mass publication and of the movement for self-education and self-improvement which shortly increased.

Miller himself, though fearing his lung infection was irreversible, recovered after returning to the north, thanks to rest and his own sound constitution. He set about improving his own education, wrote and published, contributed to a newspaper in Inverness, and met Principal Baird, who persuaded him to write his autobiography.[5]

Another progressive thinker who, like Hugh Miller, started off in the mason's trade was Alexander Somerville, a carpenter's son who also later published an autobiography. He worked as a mason's labourer at Cove, in Berwickshire, where his attempts to interest his fellows in campaigning for better work and pay conditions earned him only sneering laughter, and indeed threats.

In February 1831 at the age of twenty he moved to a job in Edinburgh where since the 1825 crash building had been at a standstill, with streets left half-built, and completed houses still uninhabited. It was, in fact, over-built, and there was little work for masons. Instead Somerville had a job at a nursery gardener's, James Dickson & Sons in Inverleith Row. For this he was paid six shillings a week, plus his lodging in the bothy. Others had varying wages: of six gardeners lodged here, only one earned as much as seven shillings, while some twenty to thirty other young men who found their own lodging received eight shillings, and a few master gardeners nine. These last either hoped to move to some better situations or had come down on their luck.

Somerville noted that although they were well educated, having studied botany and served apprenticeships, they were now working for a scavenger's pay. The system for such employment was similar to England's, the nobility and gentry seeking their own master gardeners from just such nurserymen, and master gardeners themselves seeking their journeymen and foremen. Only in Scotland, however, were they reduced to half-pay while awaiting such opportunities.

As for conditions, in the bothy Somerville had to share with five others, his own lot being 'a narrow space within a recess in the kitchen compartment . . . hardly wide enough to have held two coffins': it was unpleasantly overheated, only two feet from the fire, and separated from the greenhouse stove-pipes by a thin wall, with no ventilation. 'Outside the bothy', he relates, 'all was flowery, green, and ornamental', inside 'odiously unhealthy'.

The living was meagre, weak porridge with rank buttermilk or 'sour dook', peculiar to Edinburgh; for dinner salted potatoes and an occasional herring, for supper oatmeal. Never meat, rarely bread. Somerville lived half-starved on at most four shillings a week, for he spent the rest of his pittance on 'books, stationery, newspapers and postage'. Never had he for so long 'suffered so much from hunger and philosophy', studying at night or in summer from day-break.

At that time of year his work included trenching and digging beds for sowing, and wheeling manure through narrow alleys. In the spring he volunteered to flag and cover the open drains they had dug in the winter. Unlike many of the the others, Somerville was favoured by his employers – for his industry and willingness. When he left the job, unusually he received a good testimonial.

Somerville took a keen interest in the Reform Bill agitation, which he and his colleagues eagerly followed. In September, he gave his notice at the nursery, and finding no masons' jobs available, nearly starved. Eventually he joined the Scots Greys.[6]

Hugh Miller, besides his disillusioned observation of the lifestyle of masons, had gained an insight into the lives of colliers in the Edinburgh area. It was part of the Midlothian coal basin, and had at the time several pit villages which subsequently died out. One near him was Niddrie Mill, 'a wretched assemblage of dingy, low-roofed, tile-covered hovels', homes to 'a rude and ignorant race of men', who until quite recent years had been literally slaves. Of all the many poor and unendowed in and round Edinburgh, the colliers and their families, and their fellow-villagers of whatever job, were perhaps the lowest and most wretched.

It was barely four miles from the city, yet all the older men had been born in servitude, as had their forebears for generations. None might move or change their job without the laird's permission. The Act which freed them had been passed as recently as 1775 – several years after the founding of the New Town of Edinburgh which was to propel that city into a modern age. Even then under certain provisos some were actually kept in bondage until a further Act of 1799, which admitted that many were still so. When after another quarter-century Hugh Miller witnessed the pit village, its men of fifty and over would have been born to slavery.

Nobody in the village showed much intelligence, whether the colliers or the slightly more privileged farm-servants, labourers, carters or low-grade 'mechanics'. Had they had either intelligence or initiative they could have found jobs in Edinburgh.

The women's jobs were as physically demanding as the men's, if not more so. It was their task to lug the coal from the mine to the surface, up a long wooden turnpike stair in the shaft. It had been estimated that their average day's labour was the equivalent of carrying a hundredweight from sea-level to the top of Ben Lomond.

These women Miller found repulsive to look at, like 'the lowest and most degraded savages in voyagers' accounts, with a shape of mouth which over several generations disappeared: wide, open, thick-lipped, projecting equally above and below' – perhaps because of the exhaustion with which they dragged their burdens up, crying like infants – and then having discharged them, immediately returning singing gaily with their empty creels.

The cottages, of which that where he found lodging was one, were all identical, 'equally dingy, dirty, naked, and uncomfortable'. His own landlord and wife were between them almost without an idea in their heads, and thanks to their age, ignorance and degraded status, seemed scarcely aware of the barely decent arrangements by which Miller, and later also John Wilson, slept at one end of the small hovel and they at the other.[7]

Another side of industry is illuminated by the early life of Alexander Nasmyth's son James. Edinburgh did boast some iron foundries, of which the largest was Paterson's, 'admirably conducted' according to James, who had good reason to be appreciative. Its intelligent overseers were usually promoted from the labourers.

One of these, William Watson, 'a skilful designer and draughtsman and an excellent pattern-maker', was in charge of construction and repair of steam-engines, water-wheels and other mill-work. He made drawings on deal boards as a guide to the mechanics. His son Jemmy kindly took thirteen-year-old Jamie Nasmyth to see the foundry, how iron castings were made, and how mills and steam-engines produced their power – 'an instructive school of practical mechanics'. He was even able to lend a hand, especially on Saturday afternoons, in humble tasks such as holding the straight edge for Watson, and Watson as he made his mechanical drawings explained the details, especially the use of Euclidean principles. His two sons, who were both mill-wrights, worked from his wooden templates from which the foundry-men or moulders reproduced in cast iron, and the smiths in wrought iron.

Lewis, another foreman, of 'great taste and artistic feeling', made architectural and ornamental iron castings. Most original of all was Johnie Syme, a man of sly humour with a twinkling eye, in charge of the old Boulton and Watt steam-engine powering the works. This 'produced the blast for the cupolas, in which the pig and cast iron scrap was daily melted and cast' for the various products. Johnie was a jack-of-all-trades, 'a complete incarnation of technical knowledge' and a wizard at mechanical problems. He was also in charge of Paterson's noted boring machines, for 'the boring of a steam-engine cylinder was considered high art *in excelsis*'. From Syme Jamie Nasmyth learned about hardening and tempering steel – by which red-hot steel was hardened instantly on plunging into cold water, then tempered by adjusting the heat.

Another industry from which James learned was Smith's, a large Portobello colour manufactory producing white and red lead and many colours. The entrepreneur, a shrewd, genial Yorkshireman, was a Leith merchant with a taste for chemistry, and his son Tom took after his skills. Tom was a schoolmate of Jamie's, and used to signal to him by hoisting a white flag in their garden at the foot of Leith Walk, for which Jamie a mile off kept a lookout with a spyglass, and hurried down to join him.

Smith's house was 'like a museum' of cabinets of 'interesting objects in natural history, geology, mineralogy, and metallurgy', many of them specimens brought by sea-captains who had taken his colour manufactures for sale overseas. Smith encouraged the boys to experiment in making their own acids, which after initial bafflement they achieved.[8]

In 1823, on a visit to Stirling with his father, James visited Devon Ironworks, and shortly met the mining engineer Robert Reid, a helpful expert versed also in literature and science. He was interested in young people, would call on James in his workroom to advise him on tools, brought other experts to visit, and took James on business trips, for example to Bannockburn colliery area, and Carron.

By the age of seventeen James had thus gained practical knowledge of mechanical tools, and made working models of steam engines, and even an engine to grind his father Alexander's oil-colours. He was commissioned to make small workshop engines, and models for Mechanics' Institutes. One sectional model of a condensing steam-engine 'of the beam and parallel motion construction' for mechanics was made for the Edinburgh School of Arts; another he made for Professor Leslie's Natural Philosophy lectures, completing a unique set of apparatus, which so pleased Leslie that he gave James a ticket for his classes – and would expound his 'original and masterly views' on fundamental principles, especially Dynamics and Philosophy of Mechanics, vividly illustrated in lectures.

The School of Arts, in the former St Cecilia's Music Room, had converted the old orchestra space into a lecture table, with space for apparatus, surrounded by concentric seats. Jeffrey, Horner, Murray and others, all directors, often sat in an alcove to hear the evening lectures. When a library was added it was besieged by a crowd on open nights, and many supporters and organisers presented books. James Nasmyth attended the lectures from 1821 to 1826.

He turned his own bedroom into a brass foundry, bricking up the fireplace and taking up the carpet, and installing a furnace fuelled by gas coke and kitchen cinders. With this he could raise a white heat which would melt several pounds of brass in a crucible. He collected old scraps of brass from his father's workshop, and by adding tin or copper created a strong alloy, 'the true bronze or gun metal'. Although this room was above his father's bedroom, once he had taken out the cooled metal and rearranged the furniture, no-one would have guessed its recent use. He was not supposed to work at night, but would do so secretly, deadening the noise of ramming the sand into the moulds by laying a carpet underneath. His mother, fearing the effect of over-work, would come in saying, 'Ye'll kill yourself, laddie, working so hard and so late.'

Despite his parents' fear for his health in this intensive foundry work, and university classes at his tender age, besides a bad attack of typhus during the 1828 epidemic, James's strong constitution saw him through.

His models were mostly made in his father's workroom with a foot-lathe and stove, and the large smithing was done by his friend George Douglas, five minutes' walk away, who had started as a jobbing smith and now had a smithy and foundry on which he could make steam engines.

The pair were mutually supportive. James made George a better steam-engine which could drive large lathe machinery and speed production, nearly doubling output. George then acquired another foundry, and with more sophisticated tools made so many steam engines for agriculture that they became a common sight in the Lothians.

James, still only nineteen, experimented with a road steam carriage, a form of transport much under optimistic discussion about 1827. He exhibited a working model to the Society of Arts, who were enough impressed to order a machine able to carry five or six passengers, for which the members raised £60 in contributions.

The heavy parts were made by Anderson's foundry in Leith. Manufacture took four months, and then during three months there were successful trials along several miles of the Queensferry Road, carrying eight passengers on benches four feet above ground. James created a draught with the waste steam, 'discharging it into the short chimney of the boiler at its lowest part' – not knowing that George Stephenson had done the same – a use which later succeeded with locomotive engines.

The society saw this carriage as only an interesting experiment with no commercial future. James therefore broke it up and sold its two high-pressure engines and their boiler for £67. This sum would, ironically, have covered the expense of making and keeping the carriage on the road.

He also sketched the steam engines used by breweries and distilleries in the area, made by different engineers and showing different 'peculiarities'.

To further his knowledge he sailed to London and worked for Henry Maudsley at his Lambeth machine shop, where he not only impressed Maudsley but met Brougham, Wilkie, David Roberts and other Edinburgh notables, and Brougham introduced him to Michael Faraday. Less than two years later, however, Maudsley died of a chill. James continued for a few months with the partner, Field, and then, deciding to set up for himself, returned to Edinburgh with a stock of castings, rented a plot behind Douglas's foundry at Old Broughton, a few minutes from his home, and built a temporary workshop.

With varieties of lathe, and boring and drilling machines he soon needed assistance, to handle plane and saw, chisel and file, and a hearty young millwright called Archie Torry from Shotts Iron Company's Edinburgh factory offered his services at 15 shillings a week. This was the start of twenty years' employment for James, who also took on an apprentice.

After an ill-advised attempt to make a rotary steam-engine at Robert Steen's urging, which (as he had foreseen) proved no better than others, James decided to move from Edinburgh. Eventually he decided on Manchester, and in 1834 left Scotland, taking Torry with him.[9]

'I heard this evening that a very unpleasant feeling was rising amongst the working-classes, and that the shopkeepers in the Metropolis were so much alarmed that they talked of arming themselves.'

Cam Hobhouse, *Recollections*, IV.57 (4 Nov. 1830)

'Wretched dwellings round the market-place, inhabited by riff-raff, the Castle presiding over it all, appalling contrast with the new town and its elegance . . . We walked along dreadful streets with strange black stone hovels, into the better parts of the town behind Heriot's foundation.'

Karl Friedrich Schinkel, 5 July 1826, in *The English Journey*, London, 1993

Dr Chalmers, living in Forres Street in 1833, would walk by Edinburgh's 'latest wonder', the Dean Bridge spanning the ravine of the Water of Leith. The village far below, though only hundreds of yards from the centre of Edinburgh, was almost cut off, 'antiquated and decayed; cooped within steep narrow precipices; with tall gaunt chimneys, untenanted and crumbling granaries, rough dirty streets, miserable hovels . . . with scarce any sign of life or action, except two or three lounging figures, the noise and froth of mill-wheels, the grunting of pigs, and the squalling of children without childhood'. In the cholera epidemic it became notorious for its 'extreme ignorance and violence'. Yet in contrast to the New Town's 'encroaching pomp', so near and yet so distant, it had a quaint charm, and its old masonry, foaming pools, steep banks and unrestrained growth appealed to artists.[10]

There was little to charm in the poorest quarters of the Old Town. The American Rev. Henry Colman, walking round the Grassmarket, Cowgate and Canongate areas the morning after his arrival in 1843, was shocked by its degradation. 'The filth, the nastiness, the nakedness, the drunkenness, the horrible condition of the streets, and yards, the narrow wynds, the dark closes'; not to mention the towering lands, each floor crammed with families, lacking yards, 'common conveniences', stair windows and even street doors. Passage and stair were all too visible. The streets were crowded with bare-headed, barefoot people, 'thousands of miserable, starving, drunken, ignorant, dissolute, poor, forlorn, wretched beings, in the midst of what is called a Christian community'.[11]

Colman visited the 'Hospital or Almshouse', which relieved all who applied during the night, and learned that on the Saturday there had been eighty-one – though often there were more. Yet even this was not as bad as Dundee, where the linen factories worked a fourteen-hour day (including an hour and a half for meals) for 4 shillings a week, most of it spent on lodging, and for diet nothing but porridge.[12]

There had been poverty and distress, unemployment, and the spread of radical clubs since the ending of the war. John James Audubon, walking home on New Year's Eve 1826 at 10 o'clock, kept a brisk pace, for 'in Edinburgh it is rather a dangerous thing to be late in the streets, for vagabonds are wont to commit many errors at this time. Murders and other sinful acts take place. To prevent these, the watch is doubled, and [more than] usual quantity of gas lights afforded.'[13]

Audubon, with his innocent but observant eye, noted, as had many other strangers, the unattractive appearance of the poor. The women reminded him of squaws. 'Their walk is precisely the same', as was how they carried burdens, with 'a leather strap passed over and poised on the forehead attached to large baskets without covers, and waddle through the streets with toes inward, just as the Shawanees for instance. Their complexion, if fair, is beyond rosy, partaking indeed of purple, cold and disagreeable. If dark they are dark indeed. Many of the men wear long whiskers and beards, are extremely uncouth of manners, and still more so of language.'[14]

Not that the less unprivileged classes were always an improvement. Frances Lady Shelley complained in 1819 how she had been 'much struck by the absence of beauty among the middle classes in Scotland . . . during the whole time I was in Edinburgh I never saw one [pretty girl]. The good looks of the peasantry are completely destroyed by exposure to weather, which, as they wear no bonnet, has a tendency to contract the forehead and to give them a peculiar *grin*.'[15]

Women who always attracted attention were the fishwives in Fisherrow, carrying willow baskets on their backs the six miles from Leith harbour to Edinburgh loaded with up to two hundredweight of fish, their masculine manner matching masculine strength. Grant Thorburn, yet another American, in Edinburgh early in 1834, observed that the roles of the sexes were here reversed, the men often kept at home by bad weather and looking after the children, the wife out earning their keep in the city. Any woman incapable of this job was scorned by her peers. 'Her! What wad she do wi' a man, that canna win a man's bread!'

The dress of these 'singular amazons' was elaborate. Their heads were bare as across their forehead stretched the broad belt supporting the basket, the two coming off together. Their dress was 'a voluminous and truly Flemish quantity of petticoats' of different weights and colours, some hanging free and others bunched up giving them a bulky look; 'a blue cloth jerkin, and several fine napkins' over neck and breast. By this time they seem to have progressed beyond others in wearing strong black leather shoes and white worsted knitted stockings, apparently changed every day. No class seemed to have improved more in forty years, attributed to the introduction of Sunday schools and no longer spending all the pay on drink.[16]

Prostitutes were not greatly in evidence. Audubon, again walking home at 10, found Edinburgh 'much clearer of those servile wretches that infest both Liverpool and Manchester at those hours'. He did, however, have an encounter early in his visit during his naïver days, accosted by a well dressed woman who 'with good language and a soft voice told me that she was very poor and much in need, offered to do anything for me for a little money. I thought this a stranger way of craving charity than anything I had seen yet.' On his excusing himself as a foreigner, with no change, she 'damned him', and he hurried off and 'knew well what sort of a woman this wretch was'.[17]

A more heartrending experience occurred one morning in December as he set off to breakfast with Jardine and Selby, revelling in the day and shaken from his reverie by a barefoot, ragged and starving child. Aubudon gave him a shilling, but the poor child 'complained so of want' that, had he dared, he would have taken him to his rich friends for breakfast. Instead he took the child home with him and made up a parcel of all his spare linen, which he gave him with five more shillings and his blessing. 'I felt – oh, my Lucy, I felt such pleasure – I felt as if God smiled on me.'[18]

One man who was deliberately poor was the miser Joseph McWilliam, a former gentleman's servant, who lived in Rose Street and was laughed at by fellow-servants for his 'penurious habits' and mean clothes. For fifteen years he lived in a damp cellar below Mr Cowie, a hairdresser, with neither bed, chair nor table, and always in the same clothes.

The unfortunate wretch was accidentally burnt to death in June 1826, when more than £3000, acquired by unknown means, was found among his miserable possessions, in banker's receipts and property title-deeds. A pile of rubbish might have been expected into the bargain, but he 'absolutely denied himself every comfort and convenience of life', and turned everything he had into money.[19]

Others were characters well known at least to certain inhabitants. There was the carrier whom the Carlyles called 'Waffler', who 'stuttered intensely, drank much whisky, and had sunk in the world (pitied, laughed at, almost loved) down to "Bobby" (B-b-bobby) and the road-car Bobby drew'.[20]

And there was Mrs Dempster, a poor blind itinerant violinist, very talented, and well known locally for her Scottish tunes, which she used to play regularly outside certain houses. Robert Gillies, returning to Edinburgh to pack up his King Street possessions in 1827, heard her outside the house, at her usual place and time – between 6 and 7 o'clock – yet his butler told him she had not been round since Gillies left. He went to the door and asked her, rather emotionally, if she knew he had moved. Indeed yes, she countered, 'against your will, to a vile, wicked place, but something told me you would come again this day. Indeed, I heard your voice in the night.'[21]

Many who subsisted on that frequent refuge of the poor, selling matches in winter for lighting fires, contributed in summer to the decoration of fire-grates by selling 'gaudy paper hangings'.[22]

There was the usual proportion of rogues and exploitation of the poor. Catherine Sinclair's fictitious Harry, in *Holiday House,* is warned by his uncle Major Graham that a boy he would have given money to might beg or steal for drink, and that most money given them 'goes straight to the gin-shop'. He quotes a gang of twelve- to fourteen-year-olds seen drunk at a Portobello alehouse. The trick of maiming or disfiguring a child and turning him out to excite pity was not uncommon (at least so many adults believed).[23]

There were those who made it their business to minister to the poor. Mrs Fry, who had visited Edinburgh gaol in 1818, returned in 1834 and 'had very solemn religious times in the Gaol and large Refuge, also shorter ones in the Bridewell and another Refuge . . . entire strangers ministered to my wants, and upheld my hands'.[24]

Dr Chalmers, who worked tirelessly for the poor in Glasgow, tried to improve the Dean Village by means of a similar 'Territorial System'. With a population of 1356, it boasted only 143 sittings for any church; a meeting-house near the village was attended by only five locals, while the rest of the congregation came from outside.

Chalmers launched his campaign in 1833 by sending a missionary door-to-door, to befriend the people and urge them to come to his meetings. Once started, they gradually moved to larger halls, eventually to an old malt granary which could squeeze in 400. They then subscribed to build a church, which opened in May 1836, and before long the locals had taken up 700 of its 1000 sittings. This action at last stirred the Kirk to action, and at the 1834 General Assembly a Church Extension Committee, with Chalmers as Convener, was appointed.[25]

The Rev. Robert Morehead attacked the problem from a different angle, with his plan for a weekly paper to encourage study in the poor and induce nobler thoughts, but eventually dropped the idea as too ambitious, and as pre-empted by Constable's *Miscellany*. But in 1828 at Corstorphine, where he lived in a small villa, his wife noted how girls were 'rough and neglected', taught neither 'morals nor manners, nor sewing nor knitting', and that the parish schools had no women teachers. By means of raising funds and subscriptions, helped by the minister, she was able to employ a mistress and start a small school.[26]

Mrs Fletcher, after the death of her daughter Grace in 1817, largely retired from society, and spent much time in charitable work, especially for the Beggars' Society. In 1822 and 1823 she also tried to interest her friends in the reform of delinquents, and for seventeen years a small house in Dalry Lane was run as a refuge for boys from the prison and Bridewell. One hundred and sixteen boys were admitted during that time, most of whom could be claimed as 'reformed'.[27]

There were philanthropic attempts to deal with the great distress suffered by the labouring poor in the 1820s, when all manufacturing towns had high unemployment and weavers and factory workers were thrown out of work. In February 1826 the Glasgow cotton mills were down to half-time, and by the end of the month two large steam-loom works had been forced to close.[28] The unemployed formed Radical clubs and sought political solutions. The Glasgow weavers prepared for reform by force, and started drilling in the evenings, while many starving weavers came to Edinburgh.

A committee was set up and subscriptions were taken to find them temporary work, and it was thus that the roads and walks round Calton Hill and Salisbury Crags were made, including the fine panoramic walk below the crags. But it was a hard, uncongenial task for weavers with delicately trained fingers, used to handling threads, but now with no choice turning to rough labour with 'mattock, shovel, and handbarrow'. The road they built was called 'the Radical Road'.[29]

New houses were now not uncommonly built with gas already installed, and there were some inevitable disasters. In Shandwick Place (built in 1809 by James Tait), in 1825 the footboy, Colin Mackenzie, in his employers' absence tried a favourite dodge among the local boys – removing the burner from the gas-pipe in a front cellar. The escaping gas had no exit, and 'the unhappy urchin instead of calling in proper assistance came with a lighted candle to examine the mischief he had done'. There was of course a terrible explosion, which killed the boy and injured a maid-servant, alarmed the neighbours, and rendered the butler speechless with fright. Scott, relating the catastrophe to his daughter-in-law Jane, remarked with regret that this would 'check for a time the use of gas which was becoming generally popular'.[30]

A few days later he observed to Henry Mackenzie that a gas inspector was sent for after the explosion, which as he explained to these novices was inevitable if someone came in with a naked light, by 'the long previous escaping of gas into a very confined place without vent either at door or window'. On this disaster gas stock naturally fell, 'as furiously Nervous people will be *timbersome*', said Scott, but it soon rose again four per cent.[31]

There was great rivalry between oil and coal gas. An Oil Gas Company, discussed in 1823, was incorporated by Act of Parliament in 1824, with offices at 34 St Andrew Square. The Chairman and Vice Chairman were Scott and James Dundas of Dundas, both of whom had lit their houses by oil gas, with Roderick Mackenzie, WS, of 2 Queen Street, as Secretary, and twenty-two directors. These included James Gibson Craig of Riccarton, the advocate Miles Angus Fletcher, John Robison, Secretary to the Royal Society, and several other advocates, WSs and merchants.

The promoters argued the superiority of oil gas, based on papers written by Ricardo: it contained no 'sulphuretted hydrogen' and could not corrode the pipes and cause leaks, and not being dependent on heavy coal consumption, it generated less heat and moisture. Its 'superior brilliancy' (claimed the prospectus) made it both admirable for shops and convenient for houses, and 'it bids fair to supersede every other mode of lighting'. As for the Coal Gas Company, 'There is scope enough for both in this large City'. *Meters* (a new word) for measurement of its use were supplied to consumers.

Lyrically the prospectus pictured freedom from smell, corrosion and tarnish, and eminent suitabililty for 'Public Offices, Writing Chambers, Shops, and Manufactories', while since lustres and chandeliers could be adapted, orders were being taken 'for lighting the best houses in town'. The charges were 4 shillings per 1000 cubic feet, plus 8 shillings for meter hire. As for efficiency, an argand lamp equivalent to six candles was reckoned to consume a foot of gas per hour, and 'a single jet-burner consumes one-fourth of this quantity'.

Comparatively, for four hours' use per day, 300 days per year, a large argand burner with oil gas would cost £3.12s, tallow candles (at 9d a pound) £10.2s.6d, wax candles at 3s.6d £52.10s, and argand burners with 'a French-shaped chimney' would allow more light for the same combustion of gas.[32]

These and other claims naturally brought forth answers from the Gas Light Company, in July 1824, in the shape of a summary of Professor Leslie's reasons for preferring coal gas, based on 'philosophical experiments conducted by persons of scientific eminence': namely Dr Edward Turner the chemistry lecturer, Dr Robert Christison, now Professor of Medical Jurisprudence, and Dr Brewster of the *Encyclopaedia*. In reply, the Oil Gas Company argued that Leslie's calculation was based on an unsuitable measuring instrument, the plutometer, which was more affected by heat than light, while their own conclusions were based on findings of Faraday, Ricardo and others. Pointing out that their price was no higher than coal gas, they appealed to public experience.[33]

The following January (1825) a third party took a hand, a 'Portable Gas Company' founded in London and now to be established in Edinburgh and Glasgow, whose prospectus advertised a newer, safer and cleaner portable gas, using compressed oil gas. The London Portable Gas Company were prepared to introduce the 'Portable Patent Gas Lamp' developed by their engineer David Gordon, the patentee, no threat to piped gas supplies and harmless to 'metallic goods, pictures, elegant binding of books, or gilded furniture', safe from explosion, and usable anywhere. A separate Edinburgh Company, with offices at 26 Clyde Street, were issuing £5000 capital in £1 shares, of which the London company would take up half, and invited inspection of a portable lamp at the Waterloo Hotel.[34]

At the same time railways were much under discussion, and here too Sir Walter Scott was a pioneer, appointed to a committee to build a railway from Kelso, twenty miles off, 'which would accommodate a valuable track of country with coal and lime'. In March 1825 they met local lairds and the engineer at Abbotsford. A few days later Scott turned this to good account in getting rid of a bore. In the middle of writing to his new daughter-in-law Jane, now in Ireland, he was interrupted by Henry Cranstoun, a noted pretentious old would-be dandy. As the lesser of two evils Scott proposed a long walk, and hit on the device of out-boring him about 'railroads', full of detail about passes, cuttings and crossings, until at a parting of the ways he was able to make a formal offer of dinner in the safe knowledge that Cranstoun would hastily take his leave.[35]

61

THIEVES, CONFIDENCE TRICKSTERS AND BEGGARS

[Leith Walk:] 'Odd looking dependents on public charity . . . old blind fiddlers seated by the wayside; sailors deficient in a leg or an arm, with long queues hanging down their backs, who were always singing ballads about sea-fights; and cripples of various sorts, who contrived to move along in wooden bowls, or in low wheeled vehicles drawn by dogs.'

William Chambers, *Memoir of Robert Chambers with Autobiographic Reminiscences of William Chambers*, Edinburgh, 1872, 135

The business of a hanging was marked with an oppressive ceremony, such as the condemned would never have encountered except at their trials. Naval executions were carried out on a platform erected on Leith sands within the floodmark. In January 1822 two seamen of the schooner *Jane*, of Gibraltar, Heaman, aged about thirty-six, the thin and swarthy ship's mate, a native of Shields, and the stout French cook Gautiez, were convicted of piracy and murder, having seized the schooner on her way to Brazil with a cargo of specie, and murdered her captain and another seaman.

The two were picked up from the New Gaol at 9.30 in the morning on 9 January, and in the usual manner dragged on a horse-drawn hurdle across Regent Bridge and down Leith Walk, accompanied by an intimidating escort of magistrates, dragoon guards, police and city officers attended by halberdiers, white-gloved baillies bearing staves, gentlemen attending the magistrates, and clergy – the last in carriages. The platform had been erected on the sands at the foot of Constitution Street, near the Naval Yard, where the Leith officials and magistrates awaited the cortège, besides spectators lavishly estimated at 40,000. The bell of South Leith tolled throughout the process of the execution, and the wretched men's bodies were afterwards escorted by the dragoons to Dr Monro's classroom for dissection, for the benefit of his students.[1]

While people were overwhelmed by the spectacle, they were not inhumane, and a subscription was quickly collected for Heaman's French wife and her four children, then living in Edinburgh in distress.

Executions were always reported in newspapers or broadsheets with maximum detail of the crime, criminals' background and appearance, and their reactions, whether affecting or hardened.

Sometimes the accused were mere boys, probably living street lives and with little chance to grow up responsible citizens. Two such were Thomas Black, about seventeen or eighteen, and John Reid, only fifteen, who in June 1823 broke into Alexander White's, a Leith merchant with a house at Summerfield, and the exhaustive list of their theft included much silver flatware – toddy ladles, dessert and teaspoons, plated ware including a wine funnel, and a quantity of clothing – 'a blue coat, an olive surtout, two black pairs of Silk stockings, 3 shirts, 3 silk handkerchiefs, a night cap', and a musical snuffbox, besides items belonging to a lodger. It was reported that people in the house had seen the boys a few days earlier hanging around, when they evidently spotted a possible entry by climbing a paling to an upper window.

Arrested at a friend's house with some of the booty, they were not tried until November, when they were reported as 'habit and repute thieves' and behaved with studied indifference, Thomas even keeping his hat on. The Lord Justice Clerk having solemnly exhorted them, sentenced both to death, but a month later John's youth gained him a reprieve.

Thomas Black was executed at the usual spot at the head of Liberton's Wynd in the Lawnmarket, attended by several clergy including Dr Grant of St Andrew's Church. Despite the flaunting of his hat at the trial, Black was said to be less 'hardened' than his younger colleague, dressed himself in black, and appeared both mild and intelligent. Given the traditional chance of haranguing the crowd, he exhorted them against Sabbath-breaking as the cause of every evil.

Thomas had obviously been affected by the reality of his situation, and he asked for a separate cell so that he could reflect in peace on his life and fate, though despondent and refusing food for a couple of days after Reid's reprieve. He then recovered to calm resignation, and on removal to the Lock-up the day before his execution, he joined fervently in the prayers, and on 16 December on the scaffold appeared devout and attentive.[2]

A poor man working in the Post Office as a letter stamper was found guilty of stealing banknotes over a period between December 1827 and March 1828. He was suffering from home problems, and on arrest 'became quite deranged' and had to be taken to the asylum. In spite of this the Lord Justice Clerk all but directed the jury to find him guilty, merely because he had so pleaded. He too was harangued at great length at his execution, but remained calm. The broadsheet account includes a long poem, apparently his own though very little to the purpose.[3]

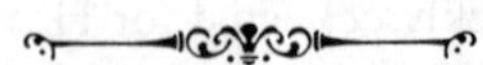

One case reported at great length, and with a curious sequel, was that of William Watt, a confidence trickster from Forfar in his twenties. He was outlawed in 1827 for embezzlement from his respectable clerical job with an Edinburgh lawyer, escaped to London and resumed his tricks at a City haberdasher's, Todd, Morrison & Co., where his talent and industry had gained him a job. When discovery was threatened, after hiding in London he made off and returned to Edinburgh.

The main interest of this case was the method adopted by the Bow Street Runner Daniel Forrester, City officer of Mansion House area, who was on his track and followed him to Edinburgh. Watt, disguised by long bushy hair, whiskers and mustachios, arrived penniless at Leith, adopting the name 'Captain Williams', and wrote to his mistress in London to come up by the next Leith smack, and pick up a letter of instructions at the Post Office directed to 'Mrs Williams'.

Forrester, who got wind of this, boarded the smack at the wharf, pretending to book a place for Leith but actually taking note of any 'ladies' on board, when he particularly noted Mrs Williams and her luggage. He left the ship, however, and travelled to Edinburgh by mail, arriving two days later in time to await the ship's arrival in harbour. He then tracked the young woman to lodgings in the dubious Shakespeare Square area, where she parked her luggage and went to the Post Office for the letter.

She had been warned of the risks, because she took a circuitous route to a tenement in Calton Street, where Forrester's spies passed by the house. At length she was traced onwards to 121 Rose Street, which she entered after cautiously looking round, as Forrester's men kept a strict but discreet watch.

Forrester then went to her Shakespeare Square lodging, pretending to enquire for accommodation, somehow contrived to enter her room and took note of her luggage. Later he learned that she had been spotted in Princes Street, arm in arm with a young man in Hussar officer's uniform. He too now went after them, and having kept them under surveillance finally pounced, claiming Watt as his prisoner.

'A violent struggle ensued; a clumsy attempt was made to trip the officer, when the latter . . . knocked the heels from below his opponent; they fell, the officer uppermost. A crowd gathered; a police officer came and threatened the assailant, who, while he held his opponent down with his knees and one hand, with the other shewed his baton of office, and demanded the assistance of all present . . .'

Watt was then taken to the Police Office, and on him was found the letter to his lady friend, with its instructions for her circuitous progress, and £700 was later said to be found in his trunk.

On the Monday Forrester set off by the mail to London with his prisoner. Next day, handcuffed together, they boarded the Highflyer at Newcastle, and after they had dined at the King's Head at Northallerton in a private room, Watt made a bid to escape. He took to his heels in the inn yard as they came out to board the coach, but the hostler in one of the stables, hearing a cry of

'Thief!' dashed out to tackle him. Again handcuffed together, the two set off in the coach.

Examined in London at the Guildhall by Mr Alderman Ward, among many similar charges it was revealed that Watt had fraudulently converted a bill of exchange for £228 from a Birmingham linen-draper. His trial was at the Old Bailey in May 1829, when he was sentenced to fourteen years' transportation to New South Wales.

The sequel to these escapades, so far as recorded, was that Watt, assigned to a settlement two hundred miles from Sydney, contrived to 'insinuate' himself with the Scottish superintendent and was allowed to return to Sydney. His intelligence and industry recommended him, and eventually he worked at Archdeacon William Broughton's.[4] He now began publishing articles in the local papers, and became manager of the *Sydney Gazette*, getting its dissipated ex-convict editor under his influence. He had a child by a local woman. So plausible was he that Government officials were conniving at his activities, but the Governor was warned of his character and Watt was transferred to Fort Macquarie. Here he was allowed to marry the former *Gazette* proprietor's widow (having all but squandered the man's property), got in with the police magistrate, and raised such dissension between him and the harbour-master that a court of inquiry was appointed, following which both officials were dismissed and Watt's ticket-of-leave was cancelled.

But somehow he absconded, and the last we hear of him, in the summer of 1836, is that he was caught and sentenced to be flogged as a runaway. Whatever his final fate, Watt had had a good run for his – or rather other people's – money.

Some of the saddest tales of beggars are related by Chambers, including one who had started as a prosperous New Town seedsman, whose name he prudently withholds. Having invented a contrivance for cutting fruit from the tops of tall trees – 'a curious tall engine' with a kind of scissors at the top – he had one of his boys parade this affair up and down Princes Street, now and then pulling the string to snap the scissors shut. This was usually done in the sight of suitable-looking country gentlemen, 'broad-skirted men with top boots', who would be certain to ask what it was and be presented with the maker's card.

The end is sad because Mr —— used to indulge heavily in drink, starting with a morning tumbler of spirits and water, fetched by his boy from the tavern opposite and hidden under his apron. He was so enraged one day to see the boy advancing with the damning object clearly in view that he struck him 'insensible' into a corner among the seed-bags, and this was evidently the beginning of the downward slope. Chambers relates seeing him a few years later buttoned into a very outdated coat, a hat 'the most woe-begone', face inflamed and manner crazed-looking. Later on he seemed to be employed by a delivery agency, but relapsed into destitution and near-madness, lying in rags in a heap in the Cowgate uttering 'a maniac curse as I stumbled over him'. A cautionary tale of the evils of drink.[5]

The age is advancing towards Victorian sentimentality. Shortly afterwards Chambers quotes a touching tale published 'some years back' of a poor Italian boy, who as his sole means of income used to display a white mouse in a cage. One day of heavy snowfall, the boy was seen devastated, fondling the mouse which had died of cold, vainly trying to warm it back to life. At last recognising failure, he laid it on his knee, contemplating a hard and sorrowful future. The tale is doubly disturbing as, like Schubert's poor old hurdy-gurdy player, no hint is dropped on whether the narrator thought of giving any help.[6]

Another unhappy saga was probably all too recurrent in those days. 'About a year ago' a poor old white-haired man regularly stood in some New Town street. A lady who often passed had paid little attention until one day hearing a sigh, she stopped, but in reply to her question he merely held out his battered hat in silence. Embarrassed, she confessed to having 'not a farthing' on her – but promised a penny next time. But seeing him again next week she had to confess the same. The poor man burst into tears.

When pressed he told her his sadly not unusual story. His father had been in the East India Company service; his mother he had never known, and after being educated at a 'seminary' twenty miles from Edinburgh and then at St Andrews University, receiving regular remittances through an agent, he was summoned to join his father in India. Here he learned, as he had half suspected, that he was illegitimate. The father left the boy in India to sail to England on a visit, but died on the voyage, and a nephew who came out claimed his entire property, heartlessly leaving the son penniless. Forty years of hardship followed and the son eventually returned to Scotland, in poor health and without friends or relations, scraping a living by publishing travel sketches and articles, but now in old age reduced to destitution.

The conscience-stricken lady gave him her card, had him to her house and for a couple of months regularly helped him, until suddenly he ceased to appear. It was the time of the cholera, and as she feared, she read in a newspaper one day of an old man reduced so low that he had deliberately incurred the disease by visiting an infected house, hoping to be taken into care. Unfortunately he succeeded all too well, acquired the symptoms next day, and after twelve hours of 'intense suffering' died in the hospital.[7]

Such tales of hardship were legion, and depended on the charity or neglect of the better-off, not always to be relied on so long as there was no regular care for the poor or sick.

Slightly less dismal, if still harrowing, was the tale of an old soldier who plied the knife-grinder's trade, uttering his unintelligible cry as he trundled a battered machine around the streets, a ruinous affair patched together with iron clasps, bits of rope and even rags. At last, as he was sharpening a boy's penknife one day in George Street, the whole thing gave up the ghost, the treadle ceased to operate and it fell in a pathetic heap of pieces as the poor fellow stood in 'that lordly street', a picture of woe.

Here comes the *deus ex machina,* in the person of Sir William Maxwell of Monreith, himself a former soldier, who having witnessed the tragedy from his window opposite, at once came out of the house and gave the knife-grinder an order for some 15 shillings, enabling him to buy a new machine.[8]

Chambers's anecdotes offer some small insight into the common sufferings of the poor, before, during and after the Napoleonic Wars.

62
THE THEATRE

'The Theatre is so small that it is altogether out of proportion with the grandeur of the City. But as the drama is very little cultivated in Edinburgh it has not been found necessary to construct a new theatre. Society in Edinburgh presents so many resources, that the inhabitants do not feel the want of theatrical amusements.'

L. A. Necker de Saussure, *Travels in Scotland, descriptive of Manners, Literature, and Science*, London, 1821, 20

'It is quite possible to observe the minutest workings of an actor's face from the remotest part of the pit or the boxes . . . [newly lighted] in a most brilliant manner with gas . . . every face in the audience, from the gallery to the orchestra, is seen as distinctly as if all were seated in the open light of noon-day . . . the redoubtable Edinburgh audience [young law-men in the pit], all set free from their 3-legged stools and fustian-sleeves early every Saturday evening . . . and a few quiet comfortable citizens . . . like sheep among foxes.'

'Peter Morris' [John Lockhart], *Peter's Letters to his Kinsfolk*, 3rd edn, 1819, 1.313–6

The stage had now acquired some respectability as a profession. Many a young gentleman like Benson Earle Hill indulged an urge to act for a few years if not longer, and a number of professional actors were sufficiently regarded as gentlemen to be invited guests of the upper classes – for example Scott's friends Daniel Terry and Charles Mathews. As for the ladies, many were not only of impeccable virtue but ended up marrying peers.

Jane Welsh had been at school with Marianne, or Mary Ann Paton, who became a singer and in June 1824 was performing at the Playhouse in Edinburgh. Jane, who went to the theatre on horseback, found her in her green-room, 'the same but infinitely lovelier' than in her schooldays, graceful and dignified. At seventeen the two girls had vowed 'always to love one another', and this 'heavenly creature' was now a talented performer, and just as affectionate. She had been married only weeks earlier and received Jane with her new husband, Lord William Pitt Lennox . . . but later divorced him, and remarried in 1831. When in Edinburgh she sang Rosina in *The Barber*, and Susanna in *Figaro,* among other parts; by 1826 she was considered a leading soprano.[1]

Miss Stephens, another indubitable lady, was habitually escorted by her brother, admired by Scott, Audubon, by everybody. Charles Darwin, not yet seventeen, on coming to Edinburgh University in 1825 in his first term, was thoroughly enjoying himself. 'We spend all our mornings promenading about the town, and in the evenings we go to the play to hear Miss Stephens, which is quite delightful; she is very popular here, being encored to such a degree, that she can hardly get on with the play.'[2]

Tom Moore that November found that he himself had become a show. Having arrived from Abbotsford to Craigcrook, he was walking about the Courts with Jeffrey, seeing Scott on duty at his table, 'being myself the greatest show of the place and followed by crowds from court to court'. He begged Jeffrey to dine early so that he could see the theatre. Scott agreed to join him with Thomson – though Moore found him here 'a different man' from at Abbotsford, 'a good deal more inert, and . . . not near so engaging or amusing'.

But Scott was well aware of the reception Moore would have. 'We went into the front boxes, and the moment we appeared, the whole pit rose, turned towards us, and applauded vehemently. Scott said "It is you, it is you; you must rise and make your acknowledgement."' Moore hesitated, but the crowd started to shout his name so 'I rose and bowed my best for two or three minutes' – and had to go through it all again after the next two acts, while the orchestra played 'Irish Melodies'.

He and Scott were in the second row; Jeffrey and ladies soon arrived and sat in front of them, Jeffrey 'highly pleased with the way I was received', saying repeatedly 'This is quite right!' People in the gallery were protesting because they could not see Moore well.

In a neighbouring box sat the Duke of St Albans, with Mrs Coutts whom he later married, and Moore had to 'renew my acquaintance' with the lady before they left, which was not until 10, 'very tired with my glory', and having to pack before leaving in the morning.

This visit was a piece of good luck, for having been suddenly taken ill at a party, and having to prolong his stay in the north, Moore had this unexpected opportunity to see the newly appointed and lighted theatre, not to mention the opening of the Courts.[3]

John James Audubon visited the theatre very soon after his arrival in Edinburgh, when he was lonely: before long he would not have time. Finding it opened at 6.30, he whiled away the hour in a print-shop and presented himself promptly at the pit door. 'It was crowded by gentlemen and ladies . . . ladies of the second class go to the pit, the superior class to the boxes, and those of neither . . . way above.' The house, though small, was well lit, and 'ornamented' by 'many handsome females' (for whom Audubon, though virtue itself, always had a special admiration). Being American, he noted particularly how at 'God Save the King' everyone rose and removed their hats.

As for the play, which was *Rob Roy*, he found the characters natural, the scenery well represented and 'the dress, manners and language quite true . . . I would, were it possible, always see "Rob Roy" in Edinburgh', for as staged in America it is 'quite a burlesque' – in Kentucky, for example, they did not know how to wear the costumes, blow the bugle, or present proper scenery, bagpipes and so on. Here the leading actress was again Jane Stephens, who seemed to him affected, though she acted quite well, 'by no means equal to Miss Foote'. The evening left him well pleased.

About a week later he was to meet her in person when she and her brother called to see his paintings. 'She was called such a *delicious* actress so frequently by my learned friends that I will . . . suspend [my judgment] until I see more of *hers*.'[4]

Charles Mathews reappeared in Edinburgh in January 1826, when he was delighted with a visit to Abbotsford, nearly cancelled at the last minute as Scott was taken ill, but he was assured that Scott had written asking Scrope to give him a lift on the Monday, 'and here we are, enchantment . . . a castle fit for the magician of the north to inhabit'. He was particularly pleased that Scott was so taken with his son Charles the younger, and very melancholy when the party finally broke up. Scott, who had business in Edinburgh – sad business too – took young Charles in his chaise to meet the mail at Selkirk, while Mathews senior was 'trundled into a cold post-chaise' on a lonely, icy journey to join the Newcastle post-road at Kelso.

A return engagement in March 1828 was delayed when he fell ill at York, but after two postponements and loss of bookings he was able to continue. He suffered typical Mathews weather. 'The snow arrived on the same day with myself . . . The weather was delicious all the time *I was in bed.*' On arrival he consulted Liston, and shortly recovered. Similar weather greeted his return in January 1830, 'the first snow in Edinburgh the day I arrived, the day I acted, and none since'.[5]

Mathews long seemed to have a charmed life, surviving a series of near-fatal or bizarre adventures, and lame from a hip injury caused by a fall from a tilbury in 1814. In 1824 he lost heavily through rash investment, and in 1833 he had to give up his Kentish Town cottage and move to Bloomsbury.[6]

In January 1830 Mathews attended the Edinburgh Theatrical Fund anniversary dinner, when the Lord Provost proposed his health. In responding Mathews observed that it was 'well asked' by the *Edinburgh Review* 'why the best men refused to write for the theatre': in ancient Athens, by contrast, protection of public amusements had appeared more important than running the war. 'Modern Athens', therefore, ought to set a similar example by supporting the arts, namely by funding distressed actors. Vice and immorality on the stage, he pointed out, were calumnies. 'Indeed, if there had not been females present, he would have said the green-room was the worst place for an intrigue in the world.'

Mathews was gloomy over the future of the profession. 'As the theatrical families die off there are no successors to take their places; and in 10 years, they will all be preached out of amusements. Fanatics have no such power elsewhere.'[7] As things turned out, he need not have worried.

Charles Mathews never complained of his reception in Edinburgh, whereas Macready, who played there in April 1833 and thought he handled *The Stranger* 'pretty well', had '*particular* evidence of the comparatively phlegmatic temper of this audience' in the applause expected in Act IV.[8]

Fanny Kemble, then in her late teens, first visited Edinburgh for a long stay with her cousin Mrs Henry Siddons, 'the happiest [year] of my life'. She became a devoted admirer, as indeed 'men, women, and children not only loved her, but inevitably *fell in love* with her'. Though not conventionally handsome, Mrs Henry's face was 'sweet and most engaging', her figure pretty, 'her voice exquisite, and her whole manner, air, and deportment graceful, attentive, and charming', with 'a touch of demure playfulness' yet suggesting self-control, 'moral force and determination'.

She needed all those qualities, widowed young as she had been with four children, as joint proprietor with her brother William Murray and regularly appearing on stage. Fanny makes much of the fact that the combination of her widowhood, attractiveness and 'shining conduct' earned her a special position, and 'our Mrs Siddons' could outlast any famous visiting star. She was not a particularly good actress, lacking the 'natural versatility of power of assumption' that could portray a character totally unlike her own. She was especially good in parts like Viola or Rosalind, not so in tragic parts. Her striking likeness to her brother William made her especially suitable in *Twelfth Night*.

William Murray himself, who did not shine as a manager, Fanny thought 'one of the most perfect actors I have ever seen on any stage' – so accomplished, indeed, that she wondered what he was truly like. He had expressive though not handsome features, habitually depressed-looking, and though a lively conversationalist and could be very animated, was 'a very melancholy man, with a tendency to moody morbidness of mind'. He was married to the sister-in-law of Tom Moore, but kept up such a regular flirtatiousness that he could not address any woman (says Fanny) without an air of 'sentimental courtesy and tender chivalrous devotion'.

The Siddonses were cousins to the Combe brothers George and Andrew, with whom Fanny spent many happy hours, though sceptical of their phrenological fixation. Her particular fondness for the younger Andrew, who had more charm and humour and used to take her long drives in his gig, alarmed her mother on her return home, lest she was thoughtlessly falling in love after this 'gigging'. How old was he? 'Oh, ever so old!' laughed Fanny. To her he was, though still well under forty.[9]

William Murray, like other managers, was not above a certain chicanery when it came to plays and playwrights. In 1828 when James R. Planché's drama *Charles XII* had been produced with great success at Drury Lane, it was spared pirating by other managers as it was not yet printed. Murray wrote to ask the performance fee, thought the modest request for £10 quite acceptable, but felt obliged to refuse, for 'since the introduction of half-price in the provinces' the expense of producing 'after-pieces' was not worth the fee. Yet having refused, Murray went on to procure a copy secretly, and produced the play without permission, 'at whole price' (1829).

To prevent such piracy in future, Planché called together dramatists, managers and other theatrical friends to discuss the problem over a dinner, when they determined to seek immediate protection by Act of Parliament. After a first attempt by the Hon. George Lamb failed to pass 3rd Reading, Edward Lytton Bulwer took up the charge and got a Bill through both Houses, receiving the Royal Assent in June 1833. Though not foolproof, it greatly improved the protection of dramatists, and subsequently 'managers have to thank the unworthy conduct of one, who was considered amongst the most respectable of their fraternity, for the first Dramatic Authors Act'.[10]

In 1829 Fanny Kemble, now twenty, embarked on her stage career and was at once a brilliant success. In 1830 she and her father went on tour after their London season, reaching Edinburgh in June for a two-week engagement.

Her chief impression, like Macready's, was the unresponsiveness of Edinburgh audiences. 'The death-like stillness . . . distressed me a good deal.' She had been forewarned, not least by her cousin Mrs Henry, who told her how the great Mrs Siddons, after a grand outburst of passion which elicited not a scrap of emotion, would mutter, 'Stupid people!' – yet their natural undemonstrativeness would suddenly give way to an enthusiasm equally extreme. Once Mrs Siddons's sleepwalking scene had been 'so vehemently encored' that she was 'literally obliged to go over it a second time'.

The newspapers too were critical, in this case of Fanny's 'diminutive stature and defective features', though Sir Walter Scott partly made up for this by his own glowing tributes. Jeffrey called one morning, and like others 'complains piteously that I am not prettier. Indeed . . . I heartily wish I were; but I did not think him handsome either, and I wonder why he is not handsomer.'[11]

The boon companions of *Blackwood's*, enthusiastically drinking a bumper to 'the promising young niece of glorious old Sarah', argued at length on whether she had 'genius' or was merely 'clever', though Christopher North rhapsodised inordinately. 'Has she not, in tragedy, *genius*? – her attitudes, her whole personal demeanour – are beautiful. They are uniformly appropriate to the character and to the situation . . .', and so on about her silvery voice and the brilliant 'attitudes'.[12]

There was little time for socialising in between 'rehearsals, riding, sitting for my bust, and acting', apart from hurried meetings with friends; but she was delighted to meet Scott, whom she and her father encountered walking down Princes Street while they were on horseback. Scott begged to be introduced, cordially invited them to visit, but the only invitation they had time for was a breakfast, when Scott, in the 'Border burr' which delighted her, congratulated Fanny on her horsemanship, 'a great merit in the eyes of an old Border-man'. She also liked the contrasting Sir Adam Fergusson, quick and bustling; but was most impressed by Scott's 'almost affectionate manner', which made her forget 'all awful sense of his celebrity'.

There was unfortunately no chance to visit Abbotsford, which she was to see only after Scott's death, on a parroted housekeeper's tour.

They went on to Glasgow, where audiences received her far more warmly. Fanny threw herself so entirely into her parts – Juliet, Belvidera in *Venice Preserved,* Portia, Mrs Beverley – that she sometimes was still carried away by emotion after leaving the stage; indeed, at one point she developed a 'side-ache' which brought on an attack of erysipelas.

Fanny retained a strong affection for Edinburgh, if not its audiences: 'I believe I love the very east wind that blows over the streets of Edinburgh.'

But her father was continually facing financial ruin, and in desperation they determined on a two-year trip to America, starting with a short season in Edinburgh at the end of June 1832, after a miserable departure from London when they even feared creditors might hinder their leaving.

Their houses were fair, and she was mostly pleased with her own acting, 'but of all the comfortless people to act to, commend me to our Edinburgh audiences. Their undemonstrativeness, too, is something more than mere critical difficulty to be pleased; there is a want of kindliness in the cold, discourteous way in which they allow a stranger to appear without . . . the slightest token of their readiness to accept the efforts made to please them', as happened to several of her fellow actors, Didear, and John Mason, in spite of his ranting and pulling her about in the last scene of *Romeo and Juliet.*

Her mother, who was with them, had to leave, and after a miserable parting Fanny sat listening to her father's stifled sobs, and looking from their windows in York Place at the steamer still docked at Newhaven. Suddenly her father exclaimed aloud, they saw the ship moving off, and arrival of her carriage for the theatre called her to a sorrowful departure.

Her own play *Francis I* was produced, though she did not like her part in it. Mornings were spent in rehearsal and she was acting every night. She saw George Combe, William Allan the painter, and the son of Sir Robert Liston, with some of whom she went riding. This was the time when Scott, just returning from his last travels, stopped briefly in Edinburgh before being taken to Abbotsford to die. Fanny had some happy encounters with friends, but Sir Walter's dying state cast further gloom on their forthcoming farewell to Edinburgh, to friends, to home.

On her last day, 14 July, Fanny, Murray, Allan and Byrne rode out towards Habbie's How, 'having obtained half an hour's grace off dinner-time', and as they left the 'enchanting spot' of Woodhouselee 'a cloud fell over all our spirits'. Allan, who could not bear formal farewells, took his leave as they dismounted, 'as if we were to ride with him to-morrow . . . And I never saw him again.'

Her benefit that night was *The Provoked Husband*. The house was appreciative and at the end clamoured for her father, who came out to make his farewells. In the dressing-room were Mrs Harry and her daughter Lizzie, silently weeping, her father came in and embraced them with a broken 'God bless you!', and they had to leave. 'It is the terrible distance . . . it is that dreadful America.'

They sailed from Liverpool, where the cholera was raging; with her father and aunt 'Dall' Fanny sorrowfully embarked, an unwelcome voyage on an unwelcome assignment, leaving the rest of their family behind. They had expected to return after two years, but Aunt Dall died after an accident, and after all Fanny stayed, unexpectedly and unhappily to marry Pierce Butler.[13]

The Panorama on the Mound still drew crowds, and one of the most vivid descriptions of it was given by the mason Hugh Miller, who visited it probably in 1824. It was a site for all kinds of shows, 'from the smoking baboon to the giant of 7 feet and a half', and was housed in the circular wooden building in which all the panoramic scenery painted or brought to Edinburgh was shown.

Miller left his work at Niddrie an hour early and, with no idea what to expect, went to the display with William Ross, to see the Battle of Trafalgar and scenes from the later part of Napoleon's career.

In a darkened gallery, hung with green cloth, the Panorama was seen through a 30-foot opening in which was vividly represented the limitless ocean, the British fleet bearing down on the enemy, pennant flying, vessels heaving on the swell and bustling activity on board – seamen at the guns, officers giving orders, others scanning the enemy through their glasses. Its naturalness exceeded even a camera obscura, and Miller fancied himself truly on the spot.

A second scene showed the battle in action, and the *Victory* just as Nelson was fatally wounded, sword falling from his hand, features distorted in pain, and his officers attending, while all around the guns were firing. The third scene showed the battle at its close, the French ship *Redoubtable* on fire as its crew jumped overboard or clung on desperately, while around were dismasted, wrecked vessels with a few unfortunates still clinging to the rigging.

The impression was so overpowering that Miller said afterwards that the scenes far outstripped the stage and scenery of a theatre.[14]

In later years the apathy of Edinburgh audiences did not improve. William Macready, returning for a season in 1846, found them no more to his liking than before. His performances were mostly of Shakespeare, and the response was sometimes better, sometimes worse. *Lear* was attended by 'a very middling house (they will not come to see me here) which was cold in the extreme . . . it is slaughterhouse work to act these characters to these audiences'. For *Othello* a poor house seemed enthusiastic; *Werner* was warmly received. With *Macbeth* he found his own inspiration lacking, and he was upset by 'contretemps', such as his 'drunk and impertinent' hairdresser.[15]

Elizabeth Rigby met Macready with Benjamin Haydon at Jeffrey's, and thought that because of his bad complexion he presented 'a very ugly face at first', but showed 'much character and expression'.[16] At the end, 17 March, he reckoned he had done less well than twenty-one years earlier when the terms had been less and the weather worse. 'I was then abused and attractive. I am now admitted, at last, to be a great artist, yet *regardez l'epreuve*.'[17]

63

LAWYERS AND LAW-BREAKERS

'[Lord Glenlee] was the last man who will ever walk the street in his judicial wig . . . Till he got so feeble latterly as to require a sedan chair, his practice was to walk to Court in his wig and long cravat, his silk stockings and silver buckles, and his cocked hat in his hand – a gentlemanly figure. Presidents Campbell and Blair proceeded in the same way, and they all lived in the southern quarter of the city – Glenlee in Brown Square, Campbell in Park Place, and Blair in George Square. The people were so accustomed to the sight that they scarcely noticed it.'

Journal of Henry Cockburn 1831–1834, 11 Jan. 1840 (on death of Lord Glenlee), Edinburgh, 1874

[Advocates:] 'Well-educated and accomplished gentlemen, who not only keep each other in Countenance with the rest of the world, but . . . render this mode of life highly agreeable in itself. These persons constitute the chief community of loungers and talkers in Edinburgh.'

'Peter Morris' [John Lockhart], *Peter's Letters to his Kinsfolk*, 3rd edn, 1819, I.214

'The advocates are a very agreeable set of men, not half so much the slaves of their profession, and on that account infinitely better informed on subjects of general interest, than our lawyers.'

Rev. Adam Sedgwick, 1825, in Willis Clark and McKenny Hughes, *Life and Letters of the Rev. John Sedgewick*, Cambridge, 1980, I.265

Edinburgh's courts in session were imposing and the costume elaborate. In the outer courts six Lords sat singly, and to save time and expense usually without juries. If the judge did not decide on the spot the case was referred to the inner courts.

Of these there were two, each with four judges, from whom the sole appeal was to the House of Lords. The remaining fifteenth judge sat separately. These were jury courts, over which six Lords presided on Mondays. It was in the first division of the inner court that Sir Walter Scott was daily to be seen.

Judges' robes were blue with loose sleeves, with crimson knots of ribbon, and crimson velvet capes. From the chin hung a long band like a single cravat. Their powdered wigs were small, 'frizzled in front, but curled formally behind . . . with a pair of dependent queues'. Advocates' wigs were similar, their gowns of plain black silk, crêpe or bombazine, with loose three-quarter-length sleeves. The young American clergyman Edward Griffin, who gave a detailed description of courts and occupants in 1829, remarked on the unfortunate back view of their wigs, for to save their coats they did not powder the back curls, and there was a ludicrous sight of 'the queues dancing up and down as they argued'.

Otherwise Griffin, as an American, approved the gravity of the costume as a bulwark against the 'outrageous spirit of democracy' which in the USA, he considered, diminished dignity by breaking down distinctions.

This was when Jeffrey had been appointed Dean of Faculty and thus head of the bar, which had lost him some £1500 a year by his resignation from the *Review* editorship. Griffin was greatly impressed by his appearance and personality. 'He is a gentleman of the old school, and possesses a cordial courtesy of manners, which puts one at one's ease with him . . .'[1]

The architect Karl Friedrich Schinkel in July 1826 was struck by witnessing 'the Lord Chief Justice hearing a case amidst the noise of the public wandering round the room, secretaries etc. sitting around' – unexpected informality on so grave an occasion.[2]

The first step up the ladder for an advocate was to become one of the three Advocate Deputes whose rather onerous duties were to weigh up the evidence in all cases and decide whether they should be tried, to draw up indictments, and conduct trials. When Archibald Alison, called to the bar in 1814, was promoted to this office early in 1823 – ahead of both Lockhart and Menzies – more than 2,500 cases were on the go. A further duty was to consider cases referred from the Sheriff Courts, in which the Lord Advocate and Solicitor General rarely took part. Thus between them the three Deputes administered all Scottish criminal law, and even a week's absence would build up a backlog of cases.[3]

In 1824, on the Solicitor General's persuasion, Alison composed a paper comparing Scottish and English criminal law administration, with a view to introducing the popular English system of grand juries and unpaid JPs. Alison's own experience inclined him to the opposite, considering Scottish officials to be better at administering justice, professional public prosecutors more efficient than private counsel, and further, Scotland's own Habeas Corpus Act, dating from 1701, a better protection for the individual. His pamphlet caused quite a stir, drawing only a tepid reply in the *Edinburgh Review* (January 1825); the idea of introducing the English system was dropped.[4]

Alison's marriage in 1825 to Elizabeth, youngest daughter of Colonel Tytler and niece of Lord Woodhouselee, together with his arduous legal duties put paid to his early indulgence in travel, and thereafter he resumed work on his population studies, completed on 22 December 1828 after years of research. 'It was at 11 at night sitting in the drawing-room in St Colme Street beside Mrs Alison.'[5]

Almost immediately, in January 1829, on the wise urging of his wife, he transferred his energies to a *History of Europe during the French Revolution*. Its object was to illustrate the danger of revolutions, and he expected to run to four or five volumes to be completed in a couple of years or so. In fact it was to be published over nine years, from 1833–42.

For all this research he soon found even the Advocates' Library inadequate, and began to amass his own for the house he had himself designed in St Colme Street. He eventually invested £4000 on books.

Although like many contemporaries Alison foresaw radical change and even revolution in Britain, he considered mankind 'neither so good nor so bad as they are generally supposed to be', a view he demonstrated as prosecuting counsel at William Burke's trial in December 1828. Even in him he found redeeming traits, for when after a twenty-four-hour trial his mistress Mary was acquitted, Burke flung his arms round her and exclaimed, 'Thank God, Mary, you are safe!'[6]

One of Alison's colleagues on circuit (on which his wife used to accompany him) was old Adam Gillies (1760–1842), who had become a judge as Lord Gillies in 1811, from 1812 was a Lord of Justiciary and in 1816 a Lord Commissioner of the Jury Court. This eminence he achieved by his own talents and originality, having no influential family or friends to back him. His quick apprehension and forceful arguments in pleading and in charging juries on tricky cases gave him the edge over other advocates. He was impartial in approach, and in private life courteous and unassuming.

Henry Cockburn Alison regarded as too indolent except when stirred to effort; in private life he was hospitable, 'simplicity and *bonhomie* itself', keeping open house at Bonaly to colleagues and young friends. While less intellectual than the formidable John Clerk of Eldin, he was a better orator, and outshone everyone at moving his hearers, so proving a great influence on juries, whom he could sway to a 'Not Proven' verdict.[7]

Tom Moore, on meeting Cockburn at Craigcrook in November 1825, found him 'very reserved and silent; but full, as I understand, of excellent fun and mimicry when he chooses'. (As for the Advocates' Library, which he visited a few days later, Moore thought it 'rather too gay and ornamented; fitter for ladies than lawyers'.[8])

Cockburn, when he became Solicitor General in 1830, wrote of himself that in his official capacity he was grave and solemn, but that (referring to the annual Habbie's How expeditions) 'there's a fellow very like him, who traverses the Pentlands in a dirty grey jacket, white hat, with a long pole. That's not the Solicitor General, that's Cocky – a frivolous dog . . . use all freedom with him.'[9]

Andrew, Lord Rutherfurd, who lived a few doors from Alison, lacked both Cockburn's power to move feelings and Jeffrey's exuberance, but had an acute legal mind and was a fine Classical and Italian scholar. His expensive tastes were funded by a large income, and having bought Lauriston Castle west of Edinburgh he built a magnificent room on to it to house his large library of fine editions. 'My dear Alison,' he exclaimed one day, 'do you buy books to *read*?' He was a friend of Jeffrey, and adopted a similarly affected manner which some found irritating.[10]

As for the alarming Lord Eldin, 'acknowledged head' of the bar when Alison was called, until he became a judge in 1822, though a careless writer, infrequent reader and lacking in eloquence, he was acute in mind and forceful in argument, which only Gillies could withstand. 'Strong argument, caustic expression, and occasional happy antithesis,' says Alison. One recorded repartee was to Lord Chancellor Eldon:

'In plain English, my lord –,' begins Clerk.

'In plain Scotch, you mean, Mr Clerk.'

'In plain common-sense, my lord, if you understand that.'[11]

Eldin's off-putting appearance was rendered more so by his heavy limp and countenance. He was inevitably sometimes mistaken for his near namesake the Lord Chancellor, on which he punned, 'It's all my "i".' This was doubly appropriate, for one eye (said Helen Graham) looked 'as if it was in pursuit of the other; that is a most hideous squint of a different species from any I ever saw before'.[12]

In 1830 a number of economies were introduced by the abolition of nineteen legal offices, saving £23,000. Sir William Adam, appointed Lord Chief Commissioner of the Jury Court in 1815 when it was first instituted, was among those who thus had to retire, leading to a curious situation in which, should he make a valedictory statement, an official reply must be made. The circumstance was unusual, for until then no head of office had actually retired, except when the unpopular old Sir Ilay Campbell was turned out in 1784.[13]

In the same year Alison had his first two cases before the House of Lords, with Brougham as his leading counsel and Jeffrey in opposition. Brougham, though in Alison's view did not match Clerk or Cranstoun, was unrivalled in 'sarcastic power'. That autumn Alison went on his last, Northern circuit with his wife.

In November the Duke of Wellington resigned on the issue of the Reform

Bill, and Sir William Rae and the rest of the Scottish Crown counsel accordingly had to resign with him. Like them, Alison was now out of a job. On the very same day two writers' firms with which he was associated failed, and overnight his income dropped by £1000. This was the more untimely as he and his brother had recently bought the charming Woodville near Colinton, at the foot of the Pentlands; and Alison seemed faced with ruin almost commensurate with Scott's.[14]

However, by tailoring his ambitions, he too now concentrated on literary output, contracted with Blackwood to produce two folio volumes of *Principles and Practice of Criminal Law* for 200 guineas, and started to write within a week of his leaving office in November. In nine months he completed volume I of a book which became a valuable work of reference.

He was also pushing on with volume II of his *History,* the more eagerly because of the current 'popular ferment'. Blackwood, while praising the work, complained it was didactic and 'Gibbonish', and if only it were livened up he could use it in his magazine. Alison profited by the suggestion, and started an alternative career writing political papers, the first, 'On the French Revolution', appearing on 1 January 1831. In April when Lord John Russell introduced his Reform Bill, a further paper, 'On Parliamentary Reform and the French Revolution', was noticed in the London press. Several of Alison's predictions were to be fulfilled, for example that the Reform Bill would vest power in the 'trading class'.

Alison continued to produce a monthly paper for *Blackwood's,* completed the first volume of a book on criminal law in October in ten months, dedicating it to Rae, and at night worked on his *History.* 1833 saw both Volume II of *Criminal Law* (March) and the two-volume history in April, 1000 copies printed for 250 guineas, a generous fee for an author still unknown. Eventually the *Edinburgh* gave it a fair review, the *Quarterly* ignored it.

These Alison claimed as the happiest years of his life. In 1834 he was made Sheriff of Lanark, and at the same time turned down the offer to be Solicitor General. In 1835 he and his family moved to Possil, leaving Edinburgh with regret.[15]

Executions never ceased to exert their fascination for the populace. On 16 April 1828 was the hanging, after the failure of two appeals, of Mary McKinnon, the brothel-keeper convicted of knifing the young lawyer whose evidence by Professor Christison helped to convict. 'A stout fine looking woman, rather lusty', she was only twenty-eight. She was the daughter of an army quartermaster and at the age of fifteen had been seduced, disowned by her father and cast off by the seducer, and had lived on the South Bridge in Edinburgh for some years. She was certainly a tough character, but had had to fight against the odds all her life.

The Rev. Andrew Thomson, who broke the news to her of her doom, found her 'resigned', though when sentenced in court she had fainted away for some minutes. Since then she had behaved 'becomingly' in Calton Gaol, receiving almost nobody except clergymen and a few pious gentlemen. Early on Monday, 16 April the scaffold was erected at the usual spot at the head of Liberton's Wynd near the Lock-up, where McKinnon had been taken for the night, and the usual crowds had gathered by 3 a.m. The condemned woman was brought out attended by the Revs Porteous and Thomson, and by the magistrates. Her behaviour was thought 'very becoming', and the execution just before 9 took place before a larger crowd than had attended for years.[16]

There were some tough decisions. In September 1829 William Adams, a young slater believed to have a wife and family, encountering Michael Pirnie, a mason, in the Pleasance, followed him to the Vennel in Cowgate with a story that he wanted to sell his coat to his grandmother. As they were going up the stair he knocked Pirnie down and robbed him of a snuff-box and what money he had. Quickly found guilty, Adams was recommended to mercy because of his youth and his supposed family, but the Lord Justice Clerk sentenced him to death on the grounds that the manner of the crime, in the very centre of Edinburgh, demanded an example for public safety. No reprieve was expected, as robbery with violence was seldom commuted.

Several friends attended the execution on 6 January 1830, which excited some sympathy because Adams was an Edinburgh native, who lived with his grandmother and was known by her name (Reid). After a psalm and some impressive prayers, he addressed the spectators. 'I am a young man brought to an untimely fate by my crimes. I trust all who witness my situation will take warning . . . pray to God for their own souls – read the Bible, and keep the Sabbath . . .' One wonders how much of these speeches was framed by the attending clergy, and what spiritual inducement (or coercion) was given to the sufferer.[17]

Such crimes and their sentences illustrate the deprived lives and squalid thefts of (usually) the poor. On New Year's morning 1831 a 'horrid murder' was committed on a common stair in Dunbar Street, near the Canal Basin at Fountainbridge. Mrs Calderwood, forty years old with five children, wife of a respectable potato dealer who hawked his wares round the town, had sat up as usual to receive visitors on New Year's Eve, when two young brothers, canal labourers, were among the callers. They stayed drinking in 'mirth and jollity' until about 3 o'clock in the morning, when she showed them downstairs with a candle.

Some time afterwards her husband found her lying dead on the stairs with cuts and bruises to her forehead and a ten-inch wound running up from her lower abdomen. 'Delicacy forbids us to be more explicit', which suggests that she was more or less disembowelled.

At the trial it appeared that there was some grudge between her and one of the men, whom she had met on the stair during the First Footing, and that high words were followed by blows and kicks, during which she was thrown down to the lower floor. This accounted for the bruised forehead, but nobody ever admitted to the stab wound.[18]

These broadsides in their dozens were a form of Penny Dreadful to excite sensation, and covered anything from murders, brawls, multiple thefts with assault, and scuffles between passengers and hackney coach drivers. At the very least they make depressing reading.

64
THE LAST YEARS OF SCOTT

'Dear Sir Walter! I love that Man, though I can scarcely be said to have lived with him at all, but I have known him for nearly 30 years.'

William Wordsworth to Samuel Rogers, 30 July 1831, *Letters*, V.310

'Blackwood and Sir Walter's novels have been my comforters in many a sleepless night when I should but for them have been comfortless.'

S. T. Coleridge to Wm Blackwood, 20 Oct. 1829, *Letters*, VI.82

'He sent me a message the other day, saying, that if I did not come and see him soon, it would be too late; and I know that he speaks in this tone before his family.'

Robert Southey to Mrs Bray, *Selections from the Letters*, 1856, IV.234, 13 August 1831

'He was the reverse of every thing haughty, austere, or forbidding – was frank in his address – easy of access, and entered readily and familiarly in to casual conversation with all he met . . . He was, strictly speaking, a gentleman.'

Edinburgh Evening Courant, 24 Sept. 1832

'The death of this great writer came upon the world like an electric shock.'

Cyrus Redding, *Recollections*, III.216

'Dear Scott! . . . I see him in the Court, and on the street, in company, and by the Tweed. The plain dress, the guttural burred voice, the lame walk, the thoughtful heavy face with its mantling smile, the honest hearty manner, the joyous laugh, the sing-song feeling recitation, the graphic story – they are all before me a hundred times a day.'

Journal of Henry Cockburn, 1831–1854 (6 May 1838), Edinburgh, 1874

A happy picture of Scott at Christmas 1826 is given by Jane Schetky, the painter's sister, when the Edinburgh members of their family dined at Lockhart's to meet Scott and Sophia, an unexpectedly small but pleasant, quiet family party. 'He is really a dear old man', she wrote, 'for his hair is grey, and he looks old. We sat round him great part of the evening, hearing him relate anecdotes, and conversing with him upon pictures, people, and things. We had not much music, as he is not very musical', only a couple of duets in German, which he liked. Next day Scott left for Abbotsford, where they later paid a morning call.[1]

Since the sale of Castle Street Scott had moved to the series of dismal lettings, such as the 'third-rate lodging in St David's Street' where Gillies found him busy writing after dinner, and after his visit to Paris and the publication of his *Napoleon,* the furnished house in Coates Crescent where again Gillies called on him, still over-taxing himself, in December 1827.[2]

In 1828 with a new edition of the novels, he was still writing, living partly with Lockhart in London, and when in Edinburgh at Shandwick Place (where he had the disagreeable experience of the partial stroke, from which he recovered but to a lower pitch).

Scott wrote to Charles Sharpe from Abbotsford on the day after his sixtieth birthday in August 1830 of his planned retirement from the Court of Session post, 'if the economy of the ministers will leave me enough to live on', as he reckoned that over the years 'I have been pretty hard worked'. But 'one of the greatest losses I shall have is not seeing you.'[3]

After this retirement, Scott was still persuaded by the Royal Society to continue as their president, even though he was too ill to officiate. But now his health really began to decay and his temper became uncharacteristically peevish and morbid. The struggle for the Reform Bill worried him intensely, as one of the many who was convinced it would be the ruin of the country.

In 1829 the twenty-year-old Felix Mendelssohn came to Scotland with his friend Karl Klingemann, equally bewildered and enthralled by the torrent of rhapsodic experiences that burst on them. The romantic Felix, affectionate and spontaneous, sent his family ecstatic letters about the beauty of Edinburgh and the splendour of the places they visited. On their Highland tour, he composed his 'Fingal's Cave' overture (sketched out, to be exact, before they even got there), but meanwhile at the end of July when they visited Holyrood, the room of Rizzio's murder and the now roofless chapel where Queen Mary was crowned, 'I believe I found today in that old chapel the beginning of my Scotch symphony.'

'How kind the people are in Edinburgh, and how generous is the good God.' The ebullient youth, who had an introduction to Sir Walter from a London friend, was determined to make an effort to see him, 'to escape a scolding from you, dear Mother, if I return without having seen the *lion*'.

It did not work out quite as he hoped. On 31 July they got to Abbotsford, somewhat out of their way, and Klingemann obligingly penned a lyrical, wholly mendacious account of Scott's calling on him at Melrose, hailing him as a fellow writer and putting up the pair of them in a 'strange old-fashioned apartment'. In actual fact, when they drove up (unheralded), it was only to find Scott on the point of departure, 'stared at him like fools, drove 80 miles and lost a day for the sake of at best one half-hour of superficial conversation'.

But at least they saw him. And the irrepressible Mendelssohn continued, 'Today, however, was glorious. We have forgotten the ills of yesterday, and can laugh over them.'[4]

In the same autumn Edmund Griffin, aged twenty-six, grandson of a Revolutionary officer and friend and protégé of the Rev. John McVickar, came to Europe from Pennsylvania on showing signs of TB and being advised to travel for his health. He had been ordained, and was a keen, articulate observer, but arriving in England from the Continent he was lonely, homesick and suffering a feeling of anticlimax until he was befriended by a kind and hospitable family. At the beginning of 1830, after several tours in England, he spent three months in Edinburgh.

Here he met Mrs Grant, Mackenzie, Dr Chalmers, Jeffrey, all of whom impressed him enormously. He visited the courts, which he described in detail, and 'in the first division of the inner court' was gratified to see 'no less a person than Sir Walter Scott'. Griffin, uniquely, noted that 'his shoulders are remarkably sloping, giving an appearance of great longitude to his neck'; and in walking his bad leg caused one knee to 'bend and turn inwards', in a slow progress painful to watch. 'His head, bald upon the crown, is considered a wonder by phrenologists. It is certainly the highest above the ears I have ever seen.' Griffin evidently watched Scott closely on several visits, carefully noting every detail, and in court fancied that Scott seemed almost asleep, or at least far withdrawn. He too was startled by Scott's sudden brightening in conversation so that 'you forget what you lately thought his torpid and unmeaning features'.

Griffin preceded the Rev. John McVickar to Europe by some months, and McVickar had hoped he could take over his post in the Columbia department of Rhetoric and Belles Lettres during his absence, but Griffin died before arrangements could be completed.[5]

The end of the McVickar family's Scottish visit was passed at Abbotsford, arriving at Melrose after visiting Roslin to find a message from Lockhart inviting them to dine that same evening. Having contrived to change and get there in half an hour, they found a small party, and McVickar was at first disappointed by Scott's contributing so little to the conversation, but he soon revised his impression.

Next morning after he attended church in Sir Walter's pew, Scott asked him how he liked the preacher the Rev. George Thomson. He couldn't hear a word, McVickar confessed. 'You must not complain,' said Scott. 'You have heard as much as any of his hearers for 10 years past.' He also explained that he was 'the father of the original Dominie Sampson'.

The next day, Monday, 26 July, McVickar recorded as a red-letter day, when Scott, having written for two hours before breakfast and two after (9 to 11 a.m.), exerted his full spell on the party, proving as usual better in small groups than in general society. He drove the ladies through the plantations, and all were much taken with his dog.

They stayed for three days, Sir Walter detaining them once more, and before they left he wrote a few lines in the twenty-year-old Anna's 'book'.

Unlike Edward Griffin, McVickar left Britain with great regret, and the feeling that the Continent would prove a change for the worse.[6]

Coleridge could never quite get over his resentment about Scott and *Christabel.* When Alaric Watts asked him for a 'critique' he agreed on condition that it would 'not be deemed an attack on Sir Walter Scott, tho' I have little reason to hold myself obliged to him – and yet I should be most unwilling to give a pretext for the rumour that I want to detract from his merits'. But in a couple of years he was acknowledging the 'comfort' he derived from reading Scott's novels.[7]

Even at this stage of his career and in this state of health Scott's output was nothing if not varied. In 1830 it was *Letters on Witchcraft and Demonology*, of which a London bookseller sent Mrs Grant a copy, though she detested 'witch-finders' and found the story of cruelty and folly revolting. She related to her friend Mrs Smith how in early days she had known of a later case than the last that Scott quoted, having met the grand-daughter of 'a reputed witch' who had been burnt at Inverness: she had boasted of her powers, threatened the popular, good-natured Provost Macintosh, who fell ill and was found to have images stuck with pins, and she was duly burnt. 'Little room for incredulity or compassion here', commented Mrs Grant severely – for the woman had intended evil. She was amused, however, at how Scott kept off second sight, suspecting that like her – like all imaginative people – he secretly believed in it.[8]

Scott followed *Anne of Geierstein* of 1829 with two more of the series *Tales of my Landlord*: *Count Robert of Paris* and *Castle Dangerous* (1831). Cam Hobhouse, ready to admire since he had met the novelist in 1828, read them with disappointment, 'incredibly inferior to almost all his other performances, and smelling of apoplexy. Nevertheless, no one else perhaps could produce so good and lively an historical fiction as either of these tales.'[9]

A reputation for accuracy was not Scott's chief merit. One day at Longman's after his death Tom Moore records that, talking of his 'rapid and careless manner of writing', Lardner mentioned that when Scott sent him the MS of his *History of Scotland*, 'he begged that he would be so kind as to "throw in a few dates and authorities"'.[10]

On the other hand Scott's composition was neat and unaltered: like Shakespeare he seems never to have blotted a line. Elizabeth Rigby, shown his manuscripts at Cadell's in 1843, remarked how there was 'no pause, no idle tracings with the pen in moments of doubting thought – page after page had the appearance of being copied from some work before him . . . The paper was large common writing-paper, not foolscap.' Three pages of manuscript represented fifteen pages of print, approximately a day's work. Miss Rigby says of *The Heart of Midlothian*, especially of Jeanie Deans, that it is the novel 'most fitted to please and edify a woman'.[11]

Wordsworth, who was hoping to visit Scott in 1830, was obliged to defer the expedition until the next year. Meanwhile he had met the Deemster of the Isle of Man, John Christian of Unerigg, to whose niece his son became engaged. Christian begged him to make a diplomatic approach to Scott about amending historical inaccuracies in *Peveril of the Peak* (1822), and this, to Wordsworth's gratitude, Scott gladly did.

Soon afterwards Scott had another 'seizure', when he had been planning a London visit, but one evening he did not wake from his after-dinner sleep, and when Anne finally roused him, for several minutes he could not speak. 'A violent affection of the nerves', a warning he could hardly ignore. The Lockharts hastened to come and be with him.

Rogers wrote warning Wordsworth of his small stroke, and Wordsworth in his reply reported a similar 'dangerous attack' Coleridge had had a few weeks earlier; and that Sir Humphrey Davy was 'gone' (he died in Geneva on 28 May). 'Surely,' he reflected, 'these are men of power, not to be replaced should they disappear.'[12]

James Skene, Scott's friend of many years, records that Scott's last conscious visit to Edinburgh was during heavy snow in February 1831, when he stayed a week with Skene and Cadell to wind up formalities, especially over the disposal of Abbotsford to his children, and settled a new edition of one of the novels. Although the snow made it difficult for him to get about, he enjoyed small parties at friends' houses, and was optimistic about bringing his financial affairs to a happy conclusion as the new publication would bring in another £10,000 towards his debt.[13]

Scott was suffering headaches if he tried to be over-active, and sometimes could not write for long at a time. Friends were now urging him to try a foreign tour, especially as David Wilkie, in poor health for some time, had come back from abroad much restored. But although his finances were sufficiently improved to allow Scott to travel, his health was such that he could neither enjoy it nor stay at home.

In March, in a last public appearance, at a Roxburgh county dinner to register a strong protest against the Reform Bill, it was unfortunate that, so high were political feelings, this genuinely loved character was hissed by some of those present.[14]

Wordsworth achieved the planned Scottish tour in September, which was chiefly to see Scott while yet he could, relieved that he proved well enough to receive him and his daughter. Scott indeed warned him, in 'an affectionate message' sent via Sir Henry Tayler, that he was all too aware that he was dying, but he was now about to go abroad. 'I am therefore anxious to go and fulfill an engagement of many years standing.'

After a series of delays, including a serious eye complaint, Wordsworth and Dora set off in mid-September, Dora driving her father in 'a little four-wheeled Phaeton' with a young horse of limited speed, so making short journeys and taking six days to reach Abbotsford. Dora's cousin Charles, a student at Christ Church, joined them from Newcastle by coach and on foot, 'a fine, cheerful fellow . . . glad of the opportunity of seeing a person of so much importance as Sir Walter'.

Wordsworth's eye trouble caused them to halt at Ullswater for a couple of days; but 'I was determined however to see you and yours, and to give my daughter the same pleasure at all hazards'. They found Scott, during their three-day visit, delighted to see them but 'much broken', though by all accounts better than even a few weeks back. Though 'shattered' by the series of mild strokes which mostly left him with impaired speech he was as active in mind as ever, and (would only his physicians allow him) would write for eight hours in the day, 'the worst thing he can do', agreed Wordsworth. The planned foreign tour was rather to distract him from trying to work than from any expectation of real benefit.[15] The visitors hoped that the break from his obsessional sedentary habits (that is, writing) would do the trick. Wordsworth was sanguine over the prospects, especially as another friend who visited the next month had recovered from a much worse stroke. It was a forlorn hope.[16]

This was to be Scott's last chance to entertain guests – who included the Lockharts – for immediately afterwards he left on his travels to Malta and Naples, cheered on his way from Abbotsford by a farewell sonnet that Wordsworth wrote for him at Callander after they left. Wordsworth wrote six altogether, and their Highland tour, idyllic in scenery and season, was like a timeless dream. They returned by the Trossachs, leaving the unfortunate horse exhausted at Bonawe, and having to hire horses for the rest. [17] Lines which Scott had written in Dora's 'little green book' – in which Mrs Hemans' was the first entry – were the more prized as 'an affecting testimony of his regard' at a time when his health and even mental powers were so impaired.

There was no doubt that Scott was rapidly breaking up. 'Whatever the newspapers may say, his health and his spirits are broken', Southey had already written to Mrs Bray on 13 August 1831. 'He sent me a message the other day, saying, that if I did not come and see him, soon, it would be too late; and I know that he speaks in this tone before his family' – in spite of having every intention of continuing to write as long as his strength held out.[18]

The author and traveller Charles MacFarlane recounts how at Smyrna in 1827 he met George Douglas, son of Scott's neighbour and friend Dr Douglas of Galashiels, who told him that his father had long anticipated Scott's ruin because of his extravagance, huge expenses and purchases of land, and his constant entertaining at Abbotsford, and had seen how 'the poet's hilarity was on the decline, that his brow was not unfrequently clouded'. He used to say that Scott had been 'a happier man before he set up for a great laird'.

Back in London from Turkey in September 1831, Douglas accompanied MacFarlane to the British Museum and was shown the library. Here they found Scott, 'in an inner, private room, seated at a table with an open black-letter volume before him', and the astonished Douglas, with a start and a blush, exclaimed, 'Sir Walter!'

Scott, rising, recognised him and grasped his hand with a hearty 'Georgie, my man, is it really you . . .', and exchanged eager questions and news. On Douglas introducing MacFarlane, Scott courteously said how glad he was to meet him 'as he liked some of my doings etc.' (MacFarlane, though he had seen Scott in Edinburgh as a youth, had never actually met him.) They sat together for a good hour until interrupted by the Chief Librarian, Sir Henry Ellis, bringing in 'a dingy lady in black' – presumably a *bas bleu* – to meet him. 'He is sadly altered,' said Douglas on leaving. 'Did you observe how lame he is, and how feeble? His voice and his laugh are lowered, quite altered.'

Next day MacFarlane met Scott again at John Murray's 'much-frequented drawingroom' in Albemarle Street, when Scott told him in melancholy tones that he was off to Malta for his health, and asked about his Italian travels. He politely declined – doubtless because of exhaustion – Murray's eager invitation to dine and meet Washington Irving and others.[19]

Among those who saw Scott in London on the eve of his last travels was the late King's Keeper of the Privy Purse, Sir William Knighton, who again was shocked at the change in him, 'considerably thinner; his countenance expressed doubt and dejection . . . a consciousness of his decay of intellect . . . accompanied by a mistrust of his own powers even in conversational intercourse. When he laughed it was excessive; I cannot say whether this was his natural habit.'

On this occasion, early in October, Scott talked much of King George, of whom he had been very fond, and recalled his kindness in preventing him from kneeling at the Edinburgh Levée. He also mentioned how he had there been followed by a peer who had some address, but by contrast was received with 'kingly contempt' – His Majesty 'drawn up quite erect'.[20]

Benjamin Haydon, who called on 'dear Sir Walter' in mid-October, 'was affected at his alteration, though much heartier than I expected'. It was a distressing encounter. 'His mind seemed shaken. He said he feared he had done occasionally too much at a time, as we all do . . . a touch of the old humour.' After half an hour when Haydon got up to leave, Scott rose too, 'took his stick, with that sidelong look, and then burst forth that beautiful smile, of heart and feeling, geniality of soul, manly courage and tenderness of mien, which neither Painter nor Sculptor has ever touched! Perhaps it may be [the] last time I may ever see him . . . if it be, I shall rejoice that this was the last impression.'[21]

Except for Haydon's visionary sight of Scott's corpse the following September, it was indeed.

In the spring Charles Kirkpatrick Sharpe had been in almost as poor shape as was Scott, who would have begged him to visit Abbotsford, but 'I see it is in vain, though you have infirmities enough to condole with at home', and he could offer 'a little open carriage to drive about with, and all appliances and means to make you happy at home'. Sharpe, though he confessed he felt better, did not go, as he was now kept in Edinburgh on tiresome legal business.

In London in September Scott wrote what proved to be his last letter to Sharpe, in what he rightly guessed was 'a long, perhaps an eternal, farewell'.[22]

In October Tom Moore met Scott at Lockhart's, rather shocked at his appearance and especially his difficult speech. It was mostly a family party, but included Murray, and Sir William Rae and his wife. Scott rarely joined in the conversation, and Moore could only understand him with difficulty. Afterwards upstairs there was a large Scottish gathering of Macleods, Ruthvens, Lady Louisa Stuart, Lady Belhaven and others. Moore was again painfully struck by Scott's vacant look, and reflected on the dreadfulness of his living to survive his 'mighty mind'. 'It seems hardly right to assemble company round him in this state.' Yet in 'the sad wreck' of his life his good temper and kindness were unimpaired.

Next day Moore picked up his son Tom at Charterhouse and took him to call on Scott, 'determined that the little dog should have to say in future days that he had seen this great man'. Scott was, as was his nature, kind to the boy. Moore asked him to sign a copy of his *Demonology* for his wife Bessy, and Scott told him he would have been glad to have given the book as well.

Next day again he was invited to dine with Scott at Lockhart's. 'Had it been in better times, I should have had many a lively tale to enrich these pages with, but he spoke little.' One exchange he did recall, when Lockhart said that no matter how bad a book, if it had a story Scott would read every word. 'To this Sir Walter pleaded guilty very amusingly.'[23]

He was not to see Scott again.

If friends had thought Scott would allow his mind as well as his body to rest while abroad they were disappointed. Even in Malta he insisted on writing, and drafted out a new novel based on the Turkish siege of 1565. His last letter to James Skene, dated from Naples on 5 March 1832, though speaking indeed of two new novels, and on an improvement in his finances, was almost illegible and broke off in mid-sentence.[24]

One of the many who met him in Italy was the Hon. Frances Mackenzie, a descendant of Lord Seaforth. 'Just now we have Sir W. Scott who is a very amiable *sick Lion* & has I believe been much annoyed by being *lionized* at Naples – poor man it is sad to see him so changed as his memory fails, & he is very feeble & variable, occasionally with somewhat of his former spirit.'[25]

Another was Frances, Baroness Bunsen, grand-daughter to Mrs Delany's beloved ward Georgina Port, married since 1821 to the Chevalier Bunsen and living in Italy. She had been a great reader of the Waverley novels since the beginning. In the spring of 1832 they saw much of Scott in Rome and invited him to dine, though 'the first time of seeing him was quite a shock to me', not having realised how difficult he now found it to speak. 'But . . . his conversation is much of the same sort as formerly, and his expression of goodness and benevolence really venerable, in the midst of physical decay.'[26]

Lockhart's and Sophia's son, never robust, had died on 15 December after a long illness, and in answering Wordsworth's letter of condolence he was able to give apparently cheering news of Scott in Malta.

'Poor Scott!' wrote Southey to Landor in late June. 'When he arrived in London he was incapable of recognising any one; but on the following day, his senses were so far recovered that he knew Lockhart and his daughter. The case is utterly hopeless, and, very possibly, may by this time be over.' Sir George Mackintosh, 'believing and hoping', had already died.[27]

Forecasts of doom were correct; Scott's condition was of general deterioration, and he was brought back to London on 13 June a dying man. When he could be moved on, the painful journey to Scotland was undertaken, and almost miraculously he reached Abbotsford still alive. Scott's constitution still just carried him on, only half conscious and in a painfully humiliating dependent state. Southey reckoned that he would die still £16,000 in debt, though his current writings would suffice to reduce this considerably.

That was on 16 August. Just a month later he heard from Lockhart that 'there had been mortification for eight days, broadening and deepening hourly . . . every night was expected to be the last, and yet he lingers on'. What was happening was gangrene; and while Scott was daily, hourly dying, it was also the time when thousands were daily dying of cholera.[28]

During his last weeks he had been rarely conscious, could hardly speak, but was able to understand what was said to him, and uncharacteristically was inclined to complain. Though reduced to total physical dependence on others, like an infant, during the days he was up in a bath-chair and even outside on the grass, until gangrene finally set in. His Edinburgh physician Dr Ross, who was visiting his own brother at Gattonside, attended him in the last week of his life until he died, at 1 p.m. on 21 September.

In London Benjamin Haydon, nearly a year after he had last seen Scott, at 5.30 in the morning of 22 September dreamed vividly that he saw Scott's house shut up, 'except his bedroom windows, which were a little open. In it he was dead and lying a corpse.'

Haydon was so distressed by this presumably telepathic vision that he decided to write to Lockhart for confirmation. He had not yet done so, however, before on 24 September he received a letter informing him of Scott's death.[29]

Sir Walter Scott's funeral was held five days after his death on Friday, 26 September. Carriages arrived from Edinburgh and from all over the Borders, and the whole neighbourhood was in mourning, hung in drapery and crêpe as cottagers silently watched the cortège pass, as did all Melrose. After refreshments were served at Abbotsford at 1 o'clock, Principal Baird said a prayer and the procession moved off to Dryburgh Abbey via Darnick and Melrose. The most moving moment was possibly when the funeral carriage reached 'Scott's View', and here, because they had always done so for Scott to admire the sweep of landscape and hills, the horses instinctively stopped.

Among the huge number attending were Lord Melville, Sir Thomas Dick Lauder, Sir John Pringle, Sir David Erskine, Macvey Napier, Thomas Thomson, William Clerk, the architect Robert Reid and many others.

Scott's death almost literally shook the world. 'The death of this great writer came upon the world like an electric shock', writes Cyrus Redding (who had personally met him only once in London, in 1823). 'It seemed as if a fibre of the great human heart had snapped asunder.'[30]

Yet the news was inevitably greeted with a certain relief. Julian Young on hearing it, aware that Scott's physical decay had prepared friends for the event, admitted that that and 'the dilapidation of his fortunes . . . almost reconcile one to it'.[31]

Tom Moore, in a warm letter of sympathy to Lockhart acknowledged the undoubted release from suffering Scott's death represented, when 'the thoughts of the pain *he* was suffering haunted me day & night'.[32]

'No individual perhaps, in any age or country', said the *Edinburgh Evening Courant* on 24 September, 'ever attained, merely by his literary efforts, a higher degree of celebrity than the Author of Waverley', whose name, blazoned over the civilised world, was synonymous with genius and equally with moral worth.[33]

On a more personal level Mrs Grant observed that one had to meet Scott to appreciate 'the charm of his simplicity of manners, his ever good humour, and that sound sense . . . unostentatious yet ever-waking benevolence'. In conversation 'he never dazzled, but always delighted you; it was always original yet . . . He seemed always more disposed to please and amuse than to shine', and always put people at their ease.[34]

Already before Scott's funeral a meeting had been called, to which all were invited, at the Assembly Rooms for 4 October to discuss an appropriate monument. Again crowds attended the meeting, which was really like a memorial gathering. They included the Duke of Buccleuch, the Marquess of Lothian, the Earl of Rosebery, the Lord Advocate, Lord Meadowbank, the Lord Provost, Sir Thomas Dick Lauder, Sir James Gibson Craig, the Professors John Wilson and James Pillans, and Trotter of Dreghorn. Buccleuch, Duke Hamilton, Lothian and Melville were the highest ranking of the huge committee appointed to discuss the monument, a debate which went on for years.[35]

About a month after Scott's death a different committee was formed to raise a fund to buy Abbotsford for his family. Luckily Scott's settlement of the property on Sophia was legally valid, as her fortune of £60,000 had been advanced as guarantee, and her claim took precedence of creditors. Tom Moore was one of the committee; but he was less tempted by requests for them to merge and subscribe to a monument. 'As if the most solid monument', he wrote, 'and the most welcome to the spirit of Scott himself, would not be the gift to his family of the place which will be for ever connected with his name.'[36]

EPILOGUE: AFTERWARDS

'Of late so many of our stars have set, none others rising to supply their place, that the sky seems darkened.'

Mrs Grant to Mrs Hook, *Memoir and Correspondence of Mrs Grant of Laggan*, edited by her son, London, 1844, 26 January 1832, III.224

'As for the people, they are now as formerly, all of *one sort;* meet 20 of them in a day, they are all most probably talking of the same subject; and that mostly an insignificant one, and handled in an insignificant way.'

Thomas Carlyle to his mother, 13 Feb.1833, *Letters*, VI.324

'. . . talking of the general spread of information and of a certain degree of artificial cleverness that is now in progress, which will ultimately raise the whole of society to the same level, and render distinction a rare phenomenon'.

Thomas Moore, 15 Oct.1833, *Diary*, VI.344

'The New Town from its noble position, the unity of its plan, the elegance as well as the solidity of its public and private buildings, its improved sewerage, its handsome squares and public gardens, its shops, its Princes Street, its George Street, its Ainslie Place, its Moray Place, etc. etc. may challenge competition with any city in Europe, as an eligible residence, with one exception, and that is – *climate.*'

Julian Young, *Last Leaves from the Journal of Julian Charles Young, AM* (Rector of Lymington, Warks), Edinburgh, 1875, 140

'In variety of interesting objects, I know of no place equal to it, not even Naples . . . it would be something to clap Edinburgh on the shore of the Adriatic or Mediterranean, per Bacco! professors and all, with their political economy and all other economies. The poor Italian would stand no chance with so acute and prudent a people.'

William Wordsworth to John James Masquerier, 19 Oct. 1833, *Diary etc. of Henry Crabb Robinson*, II.141

'Disliking this city as much as I can suffer myself to dislike any place, I cannot be blind to its extraordinarily grand and beautiful appearance; it is more like a metropolis in the *coup d'oeil* it offers than any British city.'

William Charles Macready, *Diaries*, 1.22

'Edinburgh looks gloriously beautiful, but there is a want of civilisation about it still, and it is infinitely more like a foreign than an English town.'

Harriet Leveson Gower (Lady Gower), 26 July 1832, in Mildred Lady Leconfield (ed.), *Three Howard Sisters,* London, 1955, 236

'. . . the wonted, meretricious frippery of modern architecture'.

Charles Kirkpatrick Sharpe, Remarks on the Disfigurement of Edinburgh (1827), in *Letters of Sir Walter Scott & Charles Kirkpatrick Sharpe to Robert Chambers, 1821–45*, Edinburgh, 1904, 55

'A kind of wholly grand and half-deserted city, which has been built too ambitiously for its population.'

Nathaniel Willis, *Pencillings by the Way* (September 1834), London, 1942

'Trade, except in one or two branches, has left Leith, our Port; its docks are bankrupt, our college has not a shilling.'

Journal of Henry Cockburn, 1831–1854 (2 April 1835), Edinburgh, 1874

'The whole of that beautiful ground [site of the Nor' Loch] will be given up to railways, with their yards, depots, counting-houses and other abominations . . . which will ruin the peculiarity of the valley between the old and new towns, and . . . possibly lead to building on the south side of Princes Street . . .; the apathy of the (unexcited) public is astonishing. The majority, indeed, would sacrifice the beauty of Edinburgh to its trade.'

Ibid., 9 Jan. 1837

The passing of the Reform Act, ushering in a period whose climate of change seemed to many to hold the implied threat of revolution, ended the days of backward-looking, mainly Tory Government. The death of Sir Walter Scott drew a line under that passing age, and there is no doubt that he did not belong to the coming decade.

But the new age had been signalled well before that. The years following Scott's financial ruin in 1826 were already marked by great change, not least by Jeffrey's retirement as editor of the *Edinburgh Review* and absorption into the law and politics as Dean of the Faculty in 1829, then as Lord Advocate, afterwards obliged to enter Parliament and finally becoming a judge. With this, and the change in the *Review* under Macvey Napier, Jeffrey's literary influence vanished. Jeffrey had initiated the *Review*'s fashion of questioning everything and everybody by criticism and pinpricks, but its oracular status and international fame now diminished. An era of twenty-seven years had come to an end.

Walter Scott was of that era, and his years of struggle to repay his debts in increasingly bad health curtailed his time in Edinburgh (and London) society; in future much of his entertaining was through Lockhart. Although after the publication of *Napoleon* his financial situation improved, with the series of strokes from late 1828 Scott had to be more of a passenger in social gatherings, when those who met him so increasingly remarked on his frailty. Similarly Jeffrey, to his own regret drawn into politics and life in London, while suffering unceasing nostalgia for Edinburgh and for old friends, was catapulted into a life that he did not relish.

Besides, very soon there were the railways. Between reformed politics and rail travel, leading families and members of society were drawn from Edinburgh to London. Edinburgh of the mid-1830s and 1840s, while much of its physical appearance remained unaltered, became noticeably different.

In 1825 James Abercromby had given Tom Moore at Bowood a clear explanation of the then Scottish voting system: 'There is no popular election whatever in Scotland, it is as if the lords of the manor in England were to elect themselves; for it does not even depend upon property, but upon a sort of right, like that of the manorial right, which may be held independent of the property.'[1]

Later that autumn, Moore noted that 'one of the Scotch colleges' appositely interpreted Edinburgh's city motto, '*Nisi Dominus Frustra*', 'Unless you are a lord you cannot get on here.'[2]

Hitherto in burgh elections, each of four or five burghs elected a delegate who between them elected the MP. From 1832 MPs were elected not by councillors or delegates but by householders who paid £10 rates. In the counties, where voters had been limited to those holding land from the Crown, again £10 householders or landowners were now qualified. As in England, the basis of voting became bourgeois, and this had a similar effect on the MPs.

The Reform Act not only increased Scotland's MPs from forty-five to fifty-three, giving Edinburgh and Glasgow two each, but under it several county constituencies were merged, and the remaining twenty-two returned one each.

Carlyle, who returned to Edinburgh for a time in January 1833, fed up with Craigenputtock, was even ready to tolerate the city, especially as Stockbridge where they now lodged was still a quiet, clean village. But after London the city itself seemed village-like, stagnant and small. His impression was of course affected by having lived for nearly two years in London; but now, particularly after the Reform Act, this parochialism was to characterise Edinburgh in years to come.[3]

Scott's friend James Skene's wife Jane, recalling in later years the life of their youth, with its intimate small parties, which regularly included any distinguished visitors, wrote regretfully of the passing of 'the best society', such as later could never be assembled because of the marked changes it had undergone. It no longer had either the most important literary magazine, nor leaders of society to preside over gatherings – as had her own father, Sir William Forbes of Pitsligo, and later, Jeffrey, and Scott. Now, the chief families travelled by rail to London for the winter, drawn by the reformed Parliament and the increased ease of travel.[4]

The year 1832 was a bad one for celebrated deaths, with the loss of Sir James Mackintosh, the Rev. George Crabbe and Sir William Grant, besides Walter Scott. Soon after Scott James Ballantyne died, already depressed by the loss of his wife. Of Scott's contemporaries surviving into later decades Jeffrey was still pre-eminent, despite his removal from Edinburgh for much of the year.

Sir Henry Taylor's view of Jeffrey was, to say the least, ungenerous; but then, he liked Wilson – and Wordsworth, whom he met in London in 1831. The two of them had met Jeffrey at Mackintosh's, who at Jeffrey's request introduced them. Lockhart, who witnessed the 'ceremony', told Taylor that 'Wordsworth played the part of a man of the world to perfection, much better than the smaller man, and did not appear to be conscious of anything having taken place between them before.' A wise attitude.

Southey, another unforgiving anti-Jeffreyan, told Taylor in March 1833 that his own supposed 'arrogance and intolerance' stemmed originally from the *Edinburgh Review,* later from Lord Byron, and finally was 'confirmed by the frequency with which ill-natured papers in the "Quarterly Review" written by other persons have been ascribed to me'. He reveals that Jeffrey 'once spoke of the arrogant manner in which I brought my pretensions forward'.[5]

Taylor, visiting Edinburgh in 1835, after some ill-natured comments about the Calton Hill, met Wilson, Jeffrey and Pillans. The first he thought gifted, lively and good company. Jeffrey, with whom he dined, he regarded with scorn, 'neither agreeable nor otherwise, but ran on cleverly enough in a small way', showing 'levity without gaiety. One only wonders that he could ever have been considerable enough to be a curse to the literature of his times, and one only learns that the mischief which men may do bears no proportion to their means of doing anything else.' Admittedly by the 1830s Jeffrey was at times in the way of melancholy decline, but so mean an assessment seems hardly fair to the Jeffrey we know and love.

Taylor saw almost as much of him as he did of Wilson, and again he told Southey (who must have been gratified) that Jeffrey was 'worth seeing in order to understand by what small springs mankind may be moved from time to time', and that he produced 'with a sort of dribbling fluency, the very mincemeat of small talk, with just such a seasoning of cleverness as might serve to give it an air of pretension'. This guestly view of his host was followed by the grudging admission that 'the little fellow has his merits; I believe him to be good-natured, and, in his shallow way, kind-hearted'. His products in literature he regarded as 'the result of vanity and ambition' rather than malice, thinking it 'a fine thing to be a clever man of the world'; but marvels how for twenty years he could 'keep the sunshine from the cottage door of a man of genius' – Wordsworth? Southey? – 'one cannot but wonder how so small a man could cast so large a shadow'. After this overflow, Taylor adds patronisingly that Jeffrey's wife 'seemed to be a good-natured, unaffected and intelligent woman'.

Taylor passed mornings in Edinburgh reading, writing and walking on the hills. He met numerous judges and professors at several dinners, but spent 'most of my evenings in solitude at my inn'. Had the hosts known the comments their guest would make on them, his evenings might have been even more solitary.[6]

Jeffrey's relations with Carlyle ended on a sour note. On their return to Edinburgh in 1833 they renewed correspondence, usually through Jane, but when later in the year Carlyle applied to Jeffrey to support his application for the remodelled Edinburgh Observatory, Jeffrey sent him a sharp, 'scolding' reply, and thus their intimacy ended. Jeffrey undoubtedly soon regretted this, and when, as he was giving up the Lord Advocateship, they met again in London, he resumed his former habit of calling on them. But, says Carlyle, cruelly unforgiving, he had then 'practically become little or nothing to us'.[7] In his later years the rift must have been painful to Jeffrey.

Jeffrey was almost overwhelmed by correspondence, committee meetings, even the number of friends to dine with, and during the run-up to the post-Reform Act elections had 'such meetings and speechifyings to electors' that he could not escape even at Craigcrook, with fifteen more electoral meetings to attend, one for every Edinburgh ward, usually in churches where he had to give 'discourses'. Desperately though he loved Edinburgh, he almost regretted London.[8]

Once back there, he called on Haydon, who also began to see in him certain limitations. 'He amused me delightfully, & talked incessantly; but there is a sharp, critical discovery of what is defective in Nature which is not agreeable . . . He sees nothing in Nature but what is a subject of criticism.' Ten days later Haydon returned his call, met his wife 'who seemed bitterly afflicted with a nervous disorder since I saw her', and found Charlie now a young lady. And next time Jeffrey called, on 9 March, he insisted on talking '*his* way': 'You must not take the lead, or my Lord looks at his watch.'

But soon Jeffrey was sitting to Haydon for his portrait, 'and a delightful sitting it was. I hit him powerfully, with his keen eye, & his sarcastic mouth. He talked delightfully – on Poetry, Phrenology, Painting . . . I was very sorry to part with him.' Again his wife and daughter were with him, and he was in 'amiable humour'.[9]

In 1846 it was Benjamin Haydon who made a return visit to Edinburgh, where he gave a lecture, and attended Jeffrey's 'soirée', who innocently congratulated him on looking so 'fat and well, the sure signs of prosperity': did he but know, Haydon was on the verge of suicide. Jeffrey himself was 'looking very old, feeble, and the piercing expression of his face softening evidently with a submissive quiescence . . .'

It made Haydon recall what Jeffrey had once said to him of William Hazlitt, 'He always reminds me of the tired ass in the desert, without occupation, profession, or pursuit.'[10]

In 1835 George Ticknor, now a distinguished cosmopolitan scholar, and author of a classic history of Spanish literature which established America's literary profession in high standing, returned to Europe after sixteen years, at the age of forty-three with a wife and two small girls. After travels on the Continent in 1838 he met Jeffrey in London at a dinner party, and found him now more agreeable.

'The superciliousness he showed when he was in America, and the quiet coldness I used to witness in him sometimes in Edinburgh . . . were not at all perceptible to-day. He was very lively, yet showed more sense than wit', and recalling the great days of the *Review*, he compared Edinburgh's 'present state of society' as 'much less brilliant than it was when I was there formerly'.

A couple of days later, breakfasting with Sydney Smith, he learned more about the origin of the *Review* and its first editors, including the admission that 'they were originally unwilling to give Brougham any direct influence over it, because he was so violent and unmanageable'.[11]

Charles Dickens first visited Edinburgh in June 1841, with his wife, for a dinner in his honour at the Waterloo Rooms. Jeffrey, who wanted them to stay with him, was in such poor health, and the occasion proved so inconvenient, that at first they stayed at the Royal Hotel, 'perfectly besieged' by admirers. They managed a visit to Jeffrey at Craigcrook for a couple of days, but found him 'very unwell'.[12]

Elizabeth Rigby, who later became Lady Eastlake, moved to Edinburgh with her mother and two sisters in 1842. She was not much under six feet tall and thirty-three years old, a good conversationalist and keen observer. Her summary of Jeffrey, of whom she saw a good deal, was perceptive. 'A small, dapper man, with splendid eyes, of which he well knows the use, and great play of face; but otherwise with that insignificance of appearance which is perfectly indifferent to the wearer of it . . . A felicity of expression and playfulness of illustration, which show how ready are the weapons of speech. He says of himself: "It is only bad wine that gets sour with keeping."' Later she called him 'the soul of good company' combined with 'the neatest little person in the world', if 'rather finikin' in his way of talking – 'with incessant French words not too well pronounced'. Calling on them one morning he appeared 'as sharp as a needle, and as fresh as a rose; the youngest man of 70 I ever saw . . . the greatest artist of conversation I ever met with, but the art too apparent'.[13]

In 1845, back in Edinburgh after living in London and a visit to Russia, she renewed their acquaintance. 'There is a picturesque precision in all he says . . . Like Turner, he makes the common things graceful; he has still both the fire and delicacy of youth.'[14]

Henry Cockburn summed up Jeffrey in similarly warm terms: interested in everything, his charm lying in his well-stocked mind, generous heart and lively spirit. Yet he seldom laughed, and 'his voice was distinct and silvery; so clear and precise that, when in good order, it was heard above a world of discordant sounds'. He spoke too fast – on entering Parliament he took a warning against this so seriously that he sometimes went to the opposite extreme. Francis Horner had once said that if he 'could only speak slow, and add a cubit to his stature, and be a little dull, nobody could oppose him'.

Cockburn hailed him as 'the founder of a new system of criticism . . . a higher one than had ever existed. As an editor, and as a writer, he did as much to improve his country and the world, as can almost ever be done by discussion, by a single man.' As early as 1812 Sir James Mackintosh on first meeting him said that he was 'more lively, fertile – and brilliant – than any Scotchman of letters'. A generation later this was still as true.[15]

On Jeffrey's death in 1850, Professor Christison wrote that his mind 'continued vigorous to the last . . . his love of conversation constant, so that he had always the better share of the dialogue even with his physicians; his diction copious, terse, and poetical'. He had the ability, on closing his eyes, of being able to summon before him some book or newspaper, a political article in *The Times,* a review in the *Quarterly* – and (though Christison does not explain how he could know this) 'This was his occupation within a few minutes of his death'. If true, it was a fitting parting after a life of one who changed the face of journalism and gladdened the hearts of his contemporaries, to mention only two of the achievements of this acerbic, lovable man.[16]

Many years later Carlyle, who in 1838 had cynically written him off as 'an amiable old fribble, very cheerful, very heartless, very forgettable and tolerable', defined his deficiencies more thoughtfully and with some regret. 'He was not deep enough, pious or reverent enough, to have been great in Literature; but he was a man intrinsically of veracity; said nothing without meaning it in some considerable degree; had the quickest perceptions.' There was something in him, he fancied, of a 'potential' or 'Scotch Voltaire'. He adds with evident sorrow, 'A beautiful little man . . . and a bright island to me.'[17]

If Jeffrey – who in 1841 was caught weeping over the death of Little Nell in *The Old Curiosity Shop*, and whom Moore had once when singing spotted shedding tears over certain of his songs – increasingly hid softness and regret under an outward shell, John Wilson as years advanced seemed to some to become more coarsened.

Ticknor, who met him on his 1838 Edinburgh visit, when Wilson had added editorship of *Blackwood's* to his academic post, made a characteristically shrewd assessment: 'He answered much to the idea given of him among the roisterers of the "Noctes Ambrosianae". He is a stout, coarse, red-faced person, with a great deal of red, bushy hair flying about his face and shoulders, taking snuff freely, and careless in his dress, talking brilliantly, sometimes petulantly, and once or twice savagely.'[18]

Carlyle had long given up caring (or seeming to care) for Wilson, and after his temporary return to Edinburgh in 1833 they scarcely met. 'I rather fancy he dislikes my Radicalism, worse than I do his Toryism.' He was said to have become quieter, and 'Lion as he is, cannot look at me . . . with *free* regard, but eyes me from behind veils, doubtful from some mischance from me, political or other'. There was probably an element of jealousy in Wilson's suspicious wariness.[19]

Julian Young later recalled encountering Wilson in Blackwood's shop, when he thought he 'had the head and locks of a Jupiter Tonans. He was the most dashing and athletic of sportsmen, the most uncompromising of Tories, and the most playful and benevolent of companions.'[20]

Charles Dickens encountered Wilson in the Parliament Hall during his visit in June 1841. Wilson, then fifty-six, had just had an attack of paralysis in his right arm; but he made a tremendous impression on Dickens, who guessed at once it was he. 'A tall, burly, handsome man . . . the bluest eyes you can imagine, and long hair . . . falling down in a wild way under the broad brim of his hat. He had on a surtout coat, a blue checked shirt; the collar standing up, and kept in its place with a wisp of black neckerchief; no waistcoat; and a large pocket-handkerchief thrust into his breast, which was all broad and open.' Followed by a shaggy terrier he rolled on at a fast pace, head in air, eyes wide open. 'A bright, clear-complexioned, mountain-looking fellow, he looks as though he had just come down from the Highlands, and had never in his life taken pen in hand . . . He is a great fellow to look at, and to talk to, and, if you could divest your mind of the actual Scott, is just the figure you would put in his place.'[21]

Wilson excited either extravagant praise or violent hostility. Elizabeth Rigby was another who in 1842 came (almost) into the former category. Meeting him at dinner, she found him 'a most remarkable-looking man, and would be venerable if his hair were within bounds'. Long hair, unless on an artist, was fairly suspect. 'He is good and religious', she added, 'as well as witty and poetical.' But then she knew that Wilson had 'loved and knew [Scott] as a brother', a sure way to her heart.

Calling on him some time later, she took note of the 'four broad-brimmed hats . . . and as many snuff-coloured coats' hanging in the hall, and found him 'rocking in a chair, and taking snuff, looking like a wild man, and talking the most polished, excellent man'. She hastened to add, 'He is very charming . . . He has a very handsome face, such a splendid complexion: water-drinking does not disagree with him.'

He was as taken with her as she with him. He 'announces to the world that he is very much in love with me . . . He sends me the most absurd messages by his married daughters' (she was thirty-three, he a widower of fifty-seven); and some time later, dining at his house, 'There never was a more living personification of genius: never knowing apparently what is the next word he is to say, and yet always saying the best.' 'Drollery more than wit', she amplified some days later, adding cautiously, 'He is as slovenly and disorderly as such a genius, but nobody else, may be.'

Late the following year the magic had not faded. 'He is splendid, unlike other men in mind and person – more character in both than any hundred could have.'[22]

In 1846, dining at Sir William Allan's, 'most choice' (company, not food), Wilson appeared outstanding. 'Everything he says, whimsical as it may be, bears the impress of sincerity: he takes nothing ready-made . . . He seems to delight in speaking kindly of his fellow-creatures, and, as he always speaks the truth, his censure is awful.'[23]

Flirtatious or no, Wilson did not seriously tempt Elizabeth Rigby, who in 1849 at the age of forty married Charles Eastlake, himself fifty-six, who the following year became President of the Royal Academy and in 1851 received a knighthood.

By the early 1840s Carlyle was famed for a number of things, including his dyspepsia, and was described as '*sui generis* . . . after no fashion known among the moderns' with 'his domineering ascendancy in talk, his sarcastic humour, and his general grimness and contradictoriness'. David Masson, at Cheyne Row in 1843, noted his powerful features, thick hair still untouched with grey, 'strong bilious-ruddy' complexion, overhanging brows and deeply sunk eyes. He had not yet grown a beard to obscure the fine lines of his mouth, and with his erect figure, nearly six feet tall, 'apart from the fire of genius in his eyes' he resembled a tough Scottish farmer. His 'purest and most stately English' with its strong Annandale accent, emphasised each syllable in the Scottish manner, no monotonous pulpit tone but 'a distinct lyrical chaunt', which Jane Carlyle herself had caught from him.[24]

That characteristic voice haunted others. Meeting husband and wife in London in 1844 (she 'a more refined half'), Elizabeth Rigby compared Carlyle's appearance with Burns's, 'the head of a thinker, the eye of a lover, the mouth of a peasant. His colours, too, seem to have been painted on his high cheek-bones at the plough's tail.' With his Scots accent he had an intonation 'measured and musical'. A few days later she added that he was 'perfect in his way; that is, a wayward genius, now kindly, now fretful; the best laugh I ever heard.'[25] When he was back in Edinburgh next year after travels, Jeffrey compared his writing to 'reading history by flashes of lightning'.

We may leave him with a glimpse in 1850 by the almost equally disgruntled Macready, when during a morning call by the couple 'Carlyle inveighed against railroads, Sunday restrictions, almost everything, Ireland – he was quite in one of his exceptious moods.'[26]

Lady Salisbury, on meeting Lockhart in 1833, thought him 'very agreeable, not the less so for his bitterness – a Tory Rogers'. Two days later she thought him 'of the despairing order of politicians – with too much reason, I fear'. Sophia seemed 'simple and natural with plenty of Scotch shrewdness; her manner is totally unformed but pleases from the utter absence of all affectation'.[27]

When Lockhart published the first volumes of his *Life of Scott* in 1837 Crabb Robinson poured on it, or rather on Sir Walter Scott, the vials of his scorn. 'The book is intolerable, and must injure both the subject and the writer. It is a memoir of the trade of book-making and exhibits the poet in the very lowest point of view imaginable.' Next he spilt still more venom on the page, 'worse and worse as it goes on. I am glad to find the opinion of the world at large agrees with mine.'

This was at Volume III. Robinson plodded on, and next spring when he finished reading the sixth volume noted, seemingly without irony, that it had 'raised him [Scott] greatly in my estimation. His conduct after the calamity was exemplary.' In fact he dismissed Scott in the years of his success as a mercenary book-maker, and in the time of his misfortunes was ready to sympathise.[28]

A less tolerant view was expressed in review by Macaulay, that while Scott was free of the usual literary men's petty jealousies, from the *Life* other faults appeared: of 'a man greedy of gain – profuse and ostentatious in expense' and acting like a gambler. Indeed he did not think Scott a principled man, and felt that Jeffrey would have been a better choice as the work's reviewer, because of his love for Scott.[29]

Miss Rigby wrote of Lockhart in 1844:

> Mr Lockhart is a man whom few can judge; his known satire and his apparent coldness make him feared and mistrusted . . . But with the most chilling reserve, he has the most genuine openness . . . No man can see the real from the unreal so accurately; no one estimates real goodness so highly, or holds false greatness so cheaply . . . It is seldom one sees so genuine a literary character . . . There never was a face with so little of the animal in it; the features, too, spiritualised . . . excessive sourness and ineffable sweetness . . . A man sought by everybody, pleasing few, and caring for fewer.[30]

To Lady Eastlake (as by then she was) news of Lockhart's death in 1854 was a great blow, 'one of the most interesting men I have ever known', and to her always kind: her whole literary life, she claimed, was 'formed by him'.[31]

Wilson's death preceded Lockhart's by less than eight months. When Lockhart died Julian Young remarked succinctly of his unpopularity in Scotland 'in spite of personal beauty and a winning address', because of 'the sarcastic propensity of his mind, the hauteur of his bearing, and his social exclusiveness'. Like many such men he was an affectionate husband, and besides, an indulgent father and a devoted son-in-law.[32]

The shadow of Scott still stretched across the horizon, and his novels were as much read and discussed as ever. After all, there were twenty-nine of them (according to how you count them). There were interesting comments and criticisms. Cam Hobhouse, in 1834 visiting several great houses in turn, at Oxenfoord was told by Sir John Dalrymple, who showed him a letter on the story of the *Bride of Lammermoor* sent him by a relative, how he was 'indignant at the liberty taken with facts . . . and thought the honour of the Dalrymple family compromised'.[33]

Baroness Bunsen, who had met Scott in Italy on his dying trip, in 1836 out of curiosity over his later novels read *The Heart of Midlothian,* and thought that it proved the stupidity of the 'multitude' who thought it his best. 'To my feelings it is the very worst I have ever read', its sole merit being its basis on a historical event. The element of 'sensationalism' displeased her, and in general she now came to despise Scott's achievements as a writer and his reprehensible commercial attitude to authorship. She probably barely grasped the seriousness of his financial insecurity – and if she had, might simply have disapproved.[34]

Macvey Napier had moved into Scott's old house in Castle Street, where in 1838 George Ticknor called on him, with a hint of disapproval. 'I was received upstairs in Mrs Scott's drawing-room, fitted up for a bachelor and man of letters, but lighted as if to receive a party – a fancy in which, I believe, Napier indulges himself every night.' [35]

Other celebrated figures claim a last notice. Miss Rigby met Thomas De Quincey in Edinburgh in 1845, 'small, shrewd, sour, with acute eyes and wonderful breadth of brow'. She was struck by a glimpse of him in the dingy, crowded Old Town streets when returning from a drive: among the crowds of working people, 'a small man, old, yet with a fire in his eye and freshness in his step, small and delicate; it is De Quincey, with thoughts in him belonging to no one else – that brilliant eye and refined face never to be forgotten'.[36]

De Quincey produced more journalistic pieces, and in 1853 began supervising a collected edition of his works. He died in 1859.

The warm friends of the early decades of the century were now showing their age. The American Nathaniel Willis describes Tom Moore in detail in 1834, when he was fifty-five, sad to see how his hair, 'which curled once all over . . . in long tendrils, unlike anybody else's in the world . . . is diminished now to a few curls sprinkled with grey, and scattered in a single ring above his ears'. Wrinkled forehead and cheeks of 'wintry red' were offset by 'a most prominent development of the organ of gaiety', and eyes still sparkling 'like a champagne bubble'.[37]

'Organ of gaiety' – it was hard for any contemporary to escape the influence of phrenology jargon, whether they believed in it or not. Elizabeth Rigby remarks on how pervasive it was and often applied unconsciously. She met George Combe in 1842 and confessed that 'I should think that I pleased him as little as he pleased me': 'a tall, puritanical, dissenter-looking person, with a good forehead in attestation of his intellect, and a hard face in betrayal of his morals'.[38]

Fanny Kemble, who also returned to Edinburgh in 1842 and always felt a warmer affection and admiration for Andrew than for the thornier George, was shocked at how emaciated the former appeared, conscious that the 'point of his knee-bone, through his trousers . . . looked so terribly and sharply articulated that it seemed as if it were coming through the cloth'. In face and expression, however, Andrew Combe was bright and benevolent as ever.[39]

Thomas Campbell, mostly in London, became a trial to his acquaintances and friends long before he died. 'His head is a shop, not a manufactory,' wrote Carlyle, 'and for his heart, it is as dry as a Greenock kipper.'[40]

On reading of his death in 1844, Macready, who was acting in Montreal at the time, wrote, 'He outlived his acceptability, and was latterly intolerable in society; but what a charming poet.' The more charitable Mrs Fletcher, aware of his better qualities, was certain that 'if he had been more happily married he would have been a different man'.[41]

But then Carlyle was also wholly unenchanted by the sparkling gaiety of Sydney Smith, dismissing him as 'a mass of fat and muscularity, with massive Roman nose, piercing hazel eyes, huge cheeks, shrewdness and fun, not humour or even wit, seemingly without soul altogether'.[42] Sometimes the sage could be remarkably obtuse.

Lord Brougham had lost office in 1834 along with Lord Melbourne, when his behaviour was said to be extremely undignified. With passing years he seemed to some observers to become wilder and more eccentric. In the course of another three decades of his extremely active career, he never held Government office again.[43]

Frances, wife of the 2nd Marquess of Salisbury, who met him in 1838, felt that the 'oddity of his face, and gestures, his Scotch accent, and affected freedom of manner in speaking to everybody' did not detract from his being 'one of the most agreeable men I ever saw, and the more so as his conversation . . . appears to be only the overflowing of his spirits and a mind stored with ideas'.[44]

There was quite a sensation that October on the report of his sudden death 'by the breaking of a carriage – killed on the spot!' Crabb Robinson, deeply shocked, noted that he 'never remarked a more general sentiment of terror. Such power extinguished at once!'

'Oh, what a lamentable waste of sensibility!' he wrote angrily next day. 'It was a hoax!'[45]

A final glimpse of a colourful much younger personality, is Fanny Kemble's of Thomas Macaulay at Bowood in 1841, impressed by his 'speech-power', full and sonorous voice at full volume. He was always to be found declaiming on the drawing-room hearth-rug, 'always talking, always answering everybody's questions about everything, always pouring forth eloquent knowledge'.[46]

Three of Edinburgh's four leading ladies lived to a great age, and a fourth to a respectable seventy-two, and even when mostly living elsewhere they never ceased to draw admirers to their side.

In 1838 the gifted Mrs Dugald Stewart died, aged seventy-two and having survived her husband by ten years. She was distinguished both for her active benevolence and her intellectual distinction, always partner to her husband's studies and always reading what he had written. If not always conversant with his more abstract points, she was of great value to his work by 'illustrating it by a play of fancy and of feeling, which could come only from a woman's mind'.

She was herself a competent versifier, with 'quiet perception of human, and playful wit'; and was a friend of Scott, Henry Mackenzie, the Gregorys, and the Rev. Archibald Alison. Handsome, even stately in youth, in her old age she made people aware of 'a certain benignant expression in her eyes', 'a winning gentleness of manner, – a meekness by which she had exercised greater influence . . . than others could do by an assumption of dignity'.[47]

Mrs Grant, who also died in 1838, at the age of eighty-three, had been visited that April by George Ticknor on his return visit. He found her 'in comfortable quarters, and cheerful . . . but from age and its infirmities she is a fixture, unable to leave her chair without help. But she was as cheerful as she used to be . . . She is certainly a remarkable person.'[48]

In 1834 the New Yorker Grant Thorburn had called on 'this venerable lady', to be told by the servant at 11 in the morning that she never received before 2 o'clock. Bearing in mind the gentry's hours he had encountered – bed at dawn, rising at sunset and dinner at 9 p.m. – he was wise enough to ask if the lady were actually up and dressed, and hearing that she was, presented his card with a request, as a New Yorker, to see her as a great favour. The servant returned at once and ushered him upstairs. Mrs Grant would always receive an American.

'In the middle of an elegant parlour sat the old lady, her back to the fire, and before her a desk covered with books and writing materials. "Be so good, Sir", said she, "as to hand yourself a chair, and sit down by me. I am not so able now to wait upon my friends as I was 60 or 70 years ago! Then, raising his card, she added, "*This* is a passport to me at any hour."'

They talked for hours, seeming like minutes, on her father's service eighty years earlier at Niagara, on changes in American cities, and on early Dutch settler families.[49]

Thorburn, Scottish-born near Dalkeith and at first working in his father's trade as nail-maker, had been suspect as a 'Friend of the People' and emigrated in 1794 on what proved to be a career of struggles and successes. He was the original of John Galt's character, Lawrie Todd.

When Mrs Somerville visited Cambridge in 1832 William Whewell, then Professor of Mineralogy, was impressed not only by 'one of the best mathematicians in England', and her recent *The Mechanism of the Heavens* (1831) as 'one of the most profound works' to date on the Newtonian theory, but like all who met her, by the work which came from 'the pen of a lady' that would do credit to any mathematician. Like them, too, he was equally struck by her personality, so unexpectedly 'a very feminine, gentle, lively person, with no kind of pretence to superiority in her manners or conversation', and also as accomplished as ladies were expected to be in 'music, drawing, and various languages', and engaged in educating her own daughters.[50]

Mrs Somerville on her side, revisiting Edinburgh in 1844 when she and her husband were living in Italy, stayed with Jeffrey, recording that 'no one who had seen his gentle kindness in domestic life, and the warmth of his attachment to his friends, could have supposed he possessed that power of ridicule and severity which made him the terror of authors'.[51]

When living in Rome Mrs Somerville formed a friendship with Fanny Kemble's sister, and Fanny visited her there in 1845, 'the admirable woman whose acquaintance I had coveted for her and for myself . . . her successful devotion to the highest scientific studies enhanced the charm of her domestic virtues, her tender womanly character, and perfect modesty and simplicity of manner'. Nearly thirty years later the then very old Duke of Somerset said of her in Naples, '*Elle est si bonne, si savante, et si charmante, que la mort n'ose point la toucher.*'[52]

Mrs Somerville, who lived until 1872 to the age of ninety-two, had little connection with Edinburgh in her mature years. Mrs Fletcher, who reached eighty-eight and died in 1858, similarly lived in the north of England in later life, but was ever in the thoughts of her Edinburgh contemporaries.

The most formidable of these ladies, she still in old age drew admirers almost to her feet. Henry Crabb Robinson called on her in 1846 in the Lake District where she was living only three miles from Wordsworth, and would visit to 'talk at our ease on topics not gladly listened to at Rydal Mount'. 'She retains all her free opinions', he noted, ' . . . she is excellent in conversation – unusually so for a woman of 76'.[53]

Two years later Henry Cockburn was pleased, even envious of his daughter's meeting Mrs Fletcher. 'That's a woman for you! go to her once again . . . say, "Oh, dear Mrs Fletcher, give me some of your talent – more of your enthusiasm – and most of that glowing and boundless benevolence which makes your aged face and grey hairs more beautiful than all the charms of even your beautiful youth . . ."'[54] He was the more insistent because his daughter's engagement to Thomas Cleghorn was not to his liking.

In 1849 Baroness Bunsen, visiting the Lakes and calling on Wordsworth, now in his eightieth year, at dinner 'saw an old lady whom I had seen forty years before at Edinburgh, – then a beautiful woman, and now at eighty so preserved in mind and body that I should have known her anywhere. Her name is Mrs Fletcher.'[55]

The division in the Church at last came to a head in 1843, thereafter known as the year of the great Secession. The courts having ruled that the patron who held the right of presentation was at liberty to appoint the minister of his choice, and that with a few exceptions, 'for life, literature, or learning' the church could not object, ministers in defiance claimed the right to reject without appeal to the presbytery. The Government was adamant, whereupon led by Professor Chalmers, four hundred ministers resigned from their livings in a single day, leaving the established churches empty. In this 'great division' (says the Rev. Henry Colman, a visiting Bostonlan Unitarian and agricultural expert), 'women are apt to [go] with the anti-government party'.[56]

A secession meant new churches, and while they were building secessionists worshipped in halls, schoolrooms, even factories, or out of doors. A spate of meeting-houses sprang up across the country, and Colman was repelled by their style. 'The Presbyterians seem to have had a particular spite against everything ornamental, and the seceding churches which they are now putting up all over Scotland, the most awkward and ugly erections you can think of, show that in this respect they have made no advances.' Covenanters of old, and Presbyterians in the 1840s, 'seem to abjure all taste', in contrast to the 'exquisite embellishments' of the Catholics and Episcopalians.[57]

Having been appalled at the poverty and squalor in the streets of Edinburgh and Glasgow, Colman was more than a little shocked at what appeared as hypocrisy in church. Congregations were 'full of rancour' against those who did not conform to their views, and spent their time arguing about church government. What a commentary, he thought: they lavished money on heathen missions, and neglected their wretched brethren at home.[58]

During his visit to Britain he would spend the whole of his Sundays at 'meeting', 'no small affair to sit through a Scotch service . . . the prayer was more than three-fourths of an hour long, and the sermon two hours'. Returning to Edinburgh, 'this beautiful, I may say splendid city', in September 1844 after visiting England and Ireland, on his next Sunday he attended morning service at Dr Candlish's, 'who passes for a Dr Channing' (the American divine), and the afternoon at Dr Ritchie's, ' a canny and hearty Scotchman, a learned and very acute man, whose sermon was quite too long though practical and excellent'.[59] And this was the style for decades to come.

'The modern part surpasses, in my opinion, almost everything of the kind I have seen elsewhere . . . the houses display a greater variety [than in London], and are built, not of brick, but of a very beautiful real stone. The public buildings, churches, libraries, &c manifest great taste and architectural judgment; we nowhere see such unharmonious buildings as those at Charing Cross [or]

Buckingham Palace . . . The Edinburgh architects excel those of London, and the enthusiasm of the public authorities for the embellishment of their native city is deserving of great praise . . . It is to be hoped that Calton Hill will be transformed more and more into an Athenian acropolis . . .'

Frederick von Raumer, *England in 1835*, III.165–6

'How beautiful are the lights of Edinburgh . . . the splendid sweep from Canon Mills up Dundas Street, two graceful serpents of light, with the two fainter lights at George IV's statue like their two meeting eyes. The height and depth of parts of the town are most fully seen thus: lights small and dull glimmer below your feet, and windows large and brilliant shine above your head, receding in higher and higher tiers.'

Journal & Correspondence of Lady Eastlake, I.110

In 1831 the population of Edinburgh was 138,000, and only a year later had risen to 162,000, yet this was the lowest increase of eight cities quoted. It had suddenly been outstripped by Liverpool with a 44 per cent increase (from 131,000 to 189,000).[60] With the growth of new centres of industry, of which Edinburgh had been an exemplar, and the influence of Parliamentary reform and the new railways in drawing people to the south, the city was almost becoming a backwater.

The visual changes witnessed by returning visitors were largely infilling and Gothicising. 'Edinburgh has extended to St Leonard's, and the home of Jeanie Deans is now the commencement of the railway!' recorded Nathaniel Willis in 1834, 'How sadly is romance ridden over by the march of intellect.'[61] This was Edinburgh's first line, known as the 'Innocent Railway', completed in 1831 by the engineer James Jardine to carry coal between Newton, near the Dalkeith area's mines, and St Leonard's goods yard. As the owners, the Edinburgh and Dalkeith Railway, established in 1826, had no engines, the wagons were horse-drawn.

The railway was a success, later serving both passengers and freight, and branch lines were extended as far as Dalkeith, and in Edinburgh to Fisherrow and Leith. Railway expeditions became popular, the open wagons holding up to forty people, Newhaven fishwives being carried separately. About 200 yards along the line was a tunnel where wagons were coupled together to enter the down section, contrived by counterbalancing with an up-train and controlled by a stationary engine at the top of the tunnel.

By the 1840s the railway boom was in full swing and in 1844 the new North British railway was formed, which in 1845 took over the Dalkeith company, replacing the narrow gauge with broad, and upgrading to steam power.[62]

In 1847 the main railway line to London came to stay, and to Fanny Kemble as to many people then and since, the cutting of the railway through the still new gardens below the Castle and Princes Street 'cruelly spoiled them', although from Princes Street itself the line was not then visible. But 'the Gardens themselves are ruined by it'.[63]

The railway ran below another bone of contention, the huge new monument to Sir Walter Scott. When in 1840 Macvey Napier was invited to subscribe, he admitted that he would have willingly done so 'if I were satisfied that it would be a real ornament to the City, but we have already so many public monuments that I am not disposed to add to the number. Having the honour of representing the most beautiful town in the empire, I am not willing to be art and part of spoiling it.'[64]

The design of the monument was thrown open to competition in 1836, and third prize was won by George Meikle Kemp (1795–1844), a shepherd's son who, after starting as a carpenter's apprentice and later a millwright at Galashiels, became interested in architecture, self-taught though for a time (1831) working as a draughtsman in William Burn's office. On the competition being reopened, Kemp was the winner with his extravagantly Gothic, openwork design like this pinnacle of a vast submerged cathederal. The monument was built between 1840 and 1844, in which year Kemp, now on the brink of a successful career, was drowned when he accidentally fell into the Union Canal. The statue of Scott, by Sir John Steele, was added in 1846.

In 1843, when the principal storey had been built, additional funds were needed to complete it, a situation in which nothing changes over the decades, even centuries. 'As such things are usually managed,' writes the Rev. Henry Colman, 'they began with insufficient means, and they extended their plan, and rendered it much more expensive than they had originally designed; and so they have got completely aground.'[65]

Fanny Kemble did not admire the result, so totally at odds with anything in Edinburgh, though it was claimed to be an exact copy in stone of the carved wooden Episcopal Throne in Exeter Cathedral. She found ugly the white and grey contrast of monument and statue, and wished they had been in the same stone. Before many years were out both were blackish anyway, and remained so for decades to come.[66]

Colman was more impressed. While he admired the monuments to Lord Melville, Pitt and King George IV, in his view Scott's far surpassed those he had seen on the Calton Hill. Nelson's was 'in bad taste', Thomas Hamilton's Grecian temple to Burns required a fee for entrance to view Flaxman's statue, and Dugald Stewart's monument by Playfair (1832) 'has no beauty'. By now Gothic was the favoured style, so that eventually Scott's monument would be 'a great ornament to a city, in its new parts, pronounced by those competent to judge, among the most beautiful and splendid in Europe'.[67]

Calton Hill seemed destined to be a repository for monuments. One that was avoided was in 1842 when Sir William Drysdale, 'a staunch Tory and a dear old soul', as Miss Rigby put it, the only Tory on the Radically-inclined Council, succeeded in defeating a proposal for 'a monument to some wretches who were convicted of sedition towards the end of the last century and banished to Botany Bay, but who are now, according to the present enlightened notions, lauded as martyrs'.[68] Politics had defeated art.

A heavy early Victorianising suffused such newly built-up areas as Drumsheugh, site of yet another old estate. Later travellers, while remarking on Edinburgh's increased grandeur, bemoaned the changing atmosphere. The ever-unfortunate Robert Gillies, constantly fending off financial ruin, on return in 1847 after twenty years writes feelingly, 'The whole town appeared to me more cold and sombre, and (except for the railroad whistle) more silent than heretofore. No *cadies* with numberless sedan-chairs appeared at the street corners, at night no brilliantly-lighted houses indicated, as of yore, the hospitality of rout-suppers and balls.'[69]

Mrs Somerville, also in the 1840s, was less disturbed. 'I found Edinburgh . . . picturesque and beautiful as ever, but enormously increased both to the north and to the south. Queen Street, which in my youth was open to the north and commanded a view of the Forth and the mountains beyond, was now in the middle of the new town . . . a new generation had sprung up, living in all the luxury of modern times.'[70]

Yet many houses showed a 'To Let' board, and a proportion in the formerly most fashionable streets had become lodgings. Apart from the many professional men, residents except in the newer developments tended to be retired gentlemen. Anyone expecting trade and commerce was, like the Rev. Henry Colman, surprised to find almost none, and even Leith Harbour, apart from the 'magnificent improvements' financed by the Duke of Buccleuch, seemed relatively inconsiderable. Colman, as an agricultural expert from Boston, was in Britain and Europe for three years studying agricultural conditions. The New Town still impressed him with its elegant and striking monuments. 'This city has not quite met my expectations, and yet I can hardly say why', he wrote; but on the credit side, 'scarcely in London have I seen so many and so well-filled bookcases'.[71]

The old city he found 'perfectly odious and detestable', probably increasingly so since former days. Crowded hotel accommodation obliged him to fall back on lodgings, outside which at night two respectably dressed women broke into a fight by moonlight, 'with fists, scratching faces, pulling hair, and plenty of oaths thrown in', watched by a crowd of 'wretched class', and ignored by the police, despite the calls of Colman and friends.[72]

Elizabeth Rigby found more to admire in the Old Town's rugged aspect, its High Street 'certainly the most wonderful street in Europe', 'rude, time-worn dwellings . . . old, squalid, begrimed, but never tumble-down; unbending as the national spirit, and rough as the national manners'. Yet opening off it would be some 'wretched, filthy, arched wynd . . . framework to the loveliest distance of the Forth'.[73]

In the half-century following the 1830s Edinburgh changed more, including in its services, than it had since the New Town was built, with the installation of piped water, soil pipes, gas, and the attendant 'subsidiary appliances and luxuries'. Josiah Livingston, writing in the 90s, added 'cabs, omnibuses, railways, and tramways', cheap postage, and the wide dissemination of literature and science.[74] Much of this was not very visible until the 1850s.

Julian Young, returning in 1872, remarked on former open spaces ('barren wastes') now built over. Modern buildings had replaced many of the ancient thirteen-storey Old Town lands, including Playfair's Gothic College begun in 1846 for the Secessionists, and the National Security Savings Bank. His list of new works included the two classical museums, the handsome Calton Hill monuments, the 'vigorous statues of John Wilson and Allan Ramsay', new Post Office, two railway termini, lodging houses, Donaldson's Hospital, also by Playfair of 1842–54, the Calton Hill terraces, Regent, Calton and Royal, all begun since his last visit, the Maitland streets at the West End and new churches. Looming over all was the vast, overpoweringly Gothic Scott monument, so unlike the cool classical Edinburgh of former days. Young also expressed sorrow, as had Scott himself, at the loss half a century earlier of the old Tolbooth.[75] (Sir George Gilbert Scott's St Mary's Cathedral (1879) at the west end had not yet been built.)

Among early improved hotel accommodation were the Hopetoun New Rooms at the British Hotel at 72 Queen Street – the same hotel admired in *Improvements in Edinburgh* of 1823. The rooms were designed by Thomas Hamilton and opened in January 1826. 'A more splendid hall can scarcely be imagined,' said the *Edinburgh Evening Courant*: 'it is nearly a hundred feet long, and very lofty, with a fine orchestra in the centre', and could be subdivided into smaller rooms by means of external machinery. Centre and wings were lit by 'splendid lanterns', and adorned by columns and pilasters.[76]

The accommodation now being offered was indeed becoming luxurious. In 1841 the Royal Hotel, immediately opposite the castle, provided Charles Dickens and his wife with 'a handsome sitting-room, another next to it . . . a spacious bed-room, and large dressing-room adjoining . . . There was a supper ready last night which would have been a dinner anywhere.'[77]

Simpler lodgings could also be satisfactory in the centre of the town. In 1843 the Rev. Henry Colman, after two hours' search, found Princes Street lodgings at nine shillings a week, 'excellent quarters' after finding he would be charged a guinea a day at some 'fashionable hotel', and where he could order what he liked and enjoy his customary 'simple dinner . . . much better for it'.[78]

As for Abbotsford, it had gone the way of tourist attractions. William Macready, who was able to visit it in 1846, was greatly disillusioned. 'The most disagreeable exhibition I have almost ever seen, itself the suicidal instrument of [Scott's] fate, and monument of his vanity and indiscretion . . . Everything seems as if he had died last week, and in the worst possible taste, they show the clothes he last wore.'[79]

Elsewhere in Scotland Burnsiana and Scottish baronial, a half-remembered echo of Scott's medieval romanticism, influenced by Queen Victoria's sudden and enduring love affair with Scotland, laid a heavy hand on city and country for the best part of a century. To quite a number of people Edinburgh's magnificent classical splendour was rendered almost invisible by the myth. Added to which was the increasing ignorance of both Edinburgh and Scotland itself by southern England, hardly to be rediscovered with the renewed appreciation of New Town Edinburgh from the 1950s.

But it survived, in spite of becoming from the second half of the next century, for three and more frantic weeks in the year, the victim of its own increasingly multi-Festival. In a still greater change, it was at last to see the return of its own Parliament – though not, alas, to the original Parliament House, not even to the High School on Calton Hill, but to Holyrood.

Floreat!

SELECT LIST OF LEGAL AND CIVIC OFFICERS DURING THE PERIOD 1764–1836

Lord High Commissioners

1764–72	David Earl of Glasgow
1773–6	Charles Shaw, Lord Cathcart (2nd time)
1777–82	George Earl of Dalhousie
1783–1801	David, Earl of Leven & Melville
1802–16	Francis Lord Napier
1817–19	William Earl of Erroll
1820–24	George, Earl of Morton
1825–30	James, Lord Forbes
1831–41	Robert Montgomery, Lord Belhaven (who serves 3 times)

Moderators

1801	William Ritchie
1802	James Finlayson
1803	Gilbert Gerard
1804	John Inglis
1805	George Hamilton
1806	William Taylor
1807	James Sheriffs
1808	Andrew Grant,
1809	Francis Nicol
1810	Hugh Meiklejohn
1811	Alexander Rankine
1812	William McMorine
1813	Andrew Brown
1814	David Ritchie
1815	Lewis Gordon
1816	John Cook
1817	Gavin Gibb
1818	John Campbell
1819	Duncan Macfarlane
1820	Thomas MacKnight
1821	D. Mearns

1822	David Lamont
1823	Alexander Brunton
1824	Andrew Duncan
1825	George Cook
1826	Thomas Taylor
1827	Robert Haldane
1828	Stevenson Macgill
1829	Patrick Forbes
1830	William Singer
1831	James Wallace
1832	Thomas Chalmers

Lord Provosts (*Book of Dignities*, ed. Joseph Haydn & Horace Ockerry; London, 1890)

1760–1	George Lind
1762–3	George Drummond
1764–5	James Stewart, and 1768–9
1766–7	Gilbert Laurie, and 1772–3
1770–1	John Dalrymple, and 1777
1774–5	James Stoddart
1776	Alexander Kincaid, d. in office
1778–9	Walter Hamilton
1780–1	David Steuart
1782–3	John Grieve, and 1786–7
1784–5	James Hunter Blair
1788–9	Thomas Elder, and 1792–3, 1796–7
1790–1	[Sir] James Stirling, and Sir, 1794–5, 1798–9
1800–1	[Sir] William Fettes, and Sir, 1804–5
1802–3	Neil MacVicar
1806–7	Donald Smith
1808–9	William Coulter, d. April 1809
1809–10	William Calder
1811–12	William Creech
1813–14	[Sir] James Marjoribanks
1815–16	[Sir] William Arbuthnot, and 1821–2
1817–18	Kincaid Mackenzie
1819–20	John Manderston
1823–4	Alexander Henderson
1825–6	William Trotter
1827–8	Walter Brown
1829–30	William Allan
1831–2	John Learmonth
1833–6	[Sir] James Spittal

Lord Advocates (*Book of Dignities*)

1766	James (later Sir) Montgomery
1775	Henry Dundas [Visct Melville]
1783	Hon. Henry Erskine, and 1806
1784*	Ilay Campbell of Succoth (later Bt)

1789	Robert Dundas of Arniston (3rd time)
1801	Charles Hope of Granton
1804	Sir James Montgomery (2nd time)
1806	Hon. Henry Erskine
1807	Archibald Colquhoun
1816*	Alexander Maconochie
1819	Sir William Rae
1830*	Francis Jeffrey
1834	John Archibald Murray (later Sir)

* later judge (from Jeffrey onwards invariably become judges)

Lord Clerk Register

1767	Lord Frederick Campbell
1777	Do., appointed for life (d. 1816)
1821	William Dundas

Solicitors-General (*Book of Dignities*)

(next in rank to Ld Advocate; Crown Counsel)

*1775	Alexander Murray of Henderland
*1783 +	Ilay Campbell of Succoth (afterwards Bart)
1784	Robert Dundas
1789	Robert Blair of Avonton
*1806	John Clerk of Eldin
*1807	David Boyle of Shewalton
*1811	David Monypenny of Pitmill
*1813 +	Alexander Maconochie of Meadowbank
1816	James Wedderburn
*1825	John Hope
*1830	Henry Cockburn
1834	Andrew Skene
* +	Duncan M'Neill

* later judge
+ later Ld Advocate

Dean of Faculty

1801	Robert Blair of Avonton
1808	Matthew Ross
1823	George Cranstoun
1826	Sir James Moncreiff, bt
1829	Francis Jeffrey
1830	John Hope

GLOSSARY OF SCOTTISH TERMS

art and part – (a legal term) indirect participation in a crime (by instigation, advice or assistance to the perpetrator)
bicker – a noisy team fight
boll – unit of measurement equivalent to 140 lb
decreet arbitral – sentence following submission to arbitration
feu – land tenure for a fixed annual payment: originally a feudal tenure, where the vessel paid in kind or cash in lieu of military service
greet – to weep
laigh – low: basement level
land – tenements under one roof with a common entry
lum – chimney
policies – pleasure-grounds of a mansion
put to the horn – charge of a debtor to pay on pain of arrest, originally to blasts of a horn
royalty – limits of a Royal Burgh
stickit (minister) – a licentiate never attaining a pastoral charge
tawse – leather strap for chastisement
wynd – a narrow alley

LEGAL OFFICERS

Advocate – member of the Bar, corresponding to English barrister
Baron of the Exchequer – a judge of the Court of Exchequer
Court of Session – supreme civil court of Scotland
Lord Advocate – chief officer of the Crown and public prosecutor
Lord Justice Clerk – judge next in rank to Lord Justice General (Lord President)
Lord of Session – judge of the Court of Session
Lord President of the Court of Session – highest criminal judge of Scotland
Lord Provost – chief magistrate of the city, similar to English Lord Mayor
Procurator Fiscal – presiding officer in criminal cases in inferior courts
Writer – a legal practitioner
Writer to the signet – member of society of solicitors, with exclusive rights to prepare summonses etc. to court of justice

NOTES

Part I

Chapter 1: A Daring Concept

1 Joseph Taylor, late of Inner Temple, Esq., *A Journey to Edenborough in Scotland in . . . 1705*, Edinburgh, 1903, pp. 94–5. This remarkable account of Scotland on the brink of the Union of the Parliaments is very revealing, not only of the state of the country but of its total foreign-ness to southern English at the time. The others in the party, probably also young Templars, were 'Mr Harrison' and 'Mr Sloman'. The writer goes on, 'We were now got into a very desolate Country . . . I concluded I was going into the most barb'rous Country in the world. Every one reckon'd our Journy extremely dangerous, and told us 'twould be difficult to escape with our lives.'

2 Dr Thomas Somerville, *My Own Life and Times, 1741–1814*, Edinburgh, 1961, pp. 47–8.

3 Hugo Arnot, *The History of Edinburgh from the Earliest Accounts to the Present Time*, Edinburgh, 1788, p. 328; Sir Daniel Wilson, *Memorials of Edinburgh in the Olden Time*, 2nd edn, 2 vols, Edinburgh, 1891, vol. II, pp. 182–3.

4 W.T. Fyfe, *Edinburgh under Sir Walter Scott*, London, 1906, p. 3.

5 [Nicolson Street] Somerville, *Life and Times*, p. 49; Arnot, *History of Edinburgh*, pp. 326–7.

6 Arnot, *History of Edinburgh*, p. 324.

7 Henry Mackenzie, *Anecdotes and Egotisms, 1745–1831*, ed. Harold William Thompson, Oxford, 1927, pp. 43–4.

8 James Boswell to John Johnston, 15 Feb. 1763, in *The Correspondence of James Boswell and John Johnston of Grange*, ed. Ralph S. Walker, London, 1966, p. 49.

9 Mrs Piozzi, Thrale MSS 1789, in Rylands Library, Ryl.Eng.MS 623, f.8.

10 Mackenzie, *Anecdotes and Egotisms*, p. 44.

11 A.J. Youngson, *The Making of Classical Edinburgh 1750–1840*, Edinburgh University Press, 1966, pp. 60ff.

12 Richard Pococke (Bishop of Neath), *Tours in Scotland, 1747, 1750, 1760*, ed. Daniel William Kemp, Edinburgh, 1887 (17 & 18 Sept. 1760), pp. 307, 308.

13 *Edinburgh Evening Courant* (*EEC*), 5 Aug. 1769; Youngson, *Classical Edinburgh*, pp. 65, 301, n.27; Arnot, *History of Edinburgh*, p. 313.

14 Mackenzie, *Anecdotes and Egotisms*, p. 220.

15 William Cowan, 'The Buildings at the East End of Princes Street and the Corner of North Bridge', *Book of the Old Edinburgh Club* [*OEC*], vol. I, 1908, pp. 137–54.

16 Youngson, *Classical Edinburgh*, pp. 86, 91; Cowan, *loc. cit.*; Arnot, *History of Edinburgh*, p. 317.

17 Cowan, *loc. cit.*, p. 150.

18 Youngson, *Classical Edinburgh*, p. 302, n.17; Ian G. Lindsay, *Georgian Edinburgh*, revised by David Walker, Edinburgh, 1973, p. 47.

19 Youngson, *Classical Edinburgh*, p. 84.

20 Arnot, *History of Edinburgh*, p. 318; *Letters of David Hume*, ed. J.Y.T. Greig, 2 vols, Oxford, 1932, vol. II, 208, 232ff.

21 J. Bennett Nolan, *Benjamin Franklin in Scotland and Ireland, 1759 and 1771*, Phila-

delphia, 1938, pp. 138, 170; Benjamin Franklin to William Strahan, 27 Oct. 1771, in *The Papers of Benjamin Franklin*, ed. William B. Willcox, Yale UP, Vo.18, 1974, p. 236.

22 Franklin to Strahan, 17 Nov. 1771, *Franklin Papers*, vol. 18, 250–1; see also Nolan, *Franklin in Scotland*, pp. 171ff.

23 Mackenzie, *Anecdotes and Egotisms*, pp. 169ff.

24 Nolan, *Franklin in Scotland*, pp. 201–2; *Franklin Papers*, vol. 19, 1975, p. 50 & n.

25 *Letters of David Hume*, vol. II, p. 30, f.n.; Francis Watt, *The Book of Edinburgh Anecdote*, Edinburgh, 1913, p. 140.

26 Youngson, *Classical Edinburgh*, p. 88. N and NE of St James' Square was 'Clelland's Feu', on which the NE side was erected about 1786 by a builder, Robert Wemyss. At number 15, end of the block numbers 6 to 15, from May 1796 John James Ruskin, who was to become John Ruskin's father, took a modest sixth (attic) floor tenement, for which the residents' rates in 1802 were recorded as £20, compared with £30 to £60 for most others. (Until 1856, when City taxes were first levied, residents levied their own.)

The square never became fashionable, during the nineteenth century declined in status and respectability, and in 1969 was demolished for the building of St James Centre. [Youngson, p. 98; *The Ruskin Family Letters*, ed. Van Akin Burd, vol. I, 1801–1837, Cornell University Press, 1973, 3n.–4n.]

27 Arnot, *History of Edinburgh*, pp. 313, 324ff.; *A New History of the City of Edinburgh*, 4th edn, 1800, p. 46.

28 Thomas Pennant, *A Tour of Scotland, MDCCLXIX*, Warrington, 1774, vol. I, p. 58.

29 Robert Chambers, *Sketch of the History of the Edinburgh Theatre-Royal, prepared for the Evening of its Final Closing*, 25 May 1859, Edinburgh, 1859.

30 Rev. L. Tyerman, *The Life of the Rev. George Whitefield, B.A., of Pembroke College, Oxford*, 2 vols, 2nd edn, London, 1890, vol. II, pp. 196–8.

31 Mackenzie, *Letters to Elizabeth Rose of Kilravock*, ed. Horst W. Brescher, Edinburgh, 1967, pp. 30ff. and *passim.*

32 Joseph Farington, *Tour in England*, 1792, transcript in Edinburgh Public Library, qYDA 1861, 792, 9 Sept. 1792; Robert Chambers, *Traditions of Edinburgh*, Edinburgh, 1825, vol. I, 76.

33 Edward Topham, *Letters from Edinburgh; Written in the Years 1774 and 1775 . . . during a 6 Months Residence in Edinburgh*, London, 1776, pp. 270–4 (25 April 1775).

34 Arnot, *History of Edinburgh*, p. 318. Charles Kirkpatrick Sharpe remarks of Arnot (1749–86), without noticeable affection, that he was 'so thin, that he resembled a clothed skeleton. He married his cook-maid, whom he had imbued with his irreligious principles.' Sharpe adds that his daughter 'drowned herself for the love of some soldier, at the Black Rocks at Portobello – a sad sample of the fruits of her father's doctrine'. This was presumably after her father's death, as Arnot was only thirty-six when he died, having published his *History of Edinburgh* in 1788 when he was thirty, and *Criminal Trials in Scotland* the years before his death. (*Letters of Sir Walter Scott and Charles Kirkpatrick Sharpe to Robert Chambers*, 1821–45, Edinburgh, 1904, p. 30, Memoranda, 1824.)

35 *The Life of Sir Robert Christison, Bart.*, ed. by his sons, 2 vols, Edinburgh, 1886, vol. II, p. 414.

36 Topham, *Letters from Edinburgh*, p. 13.

37 Arnot, *History of Edinburgh*, p. 320.

38 *Boswell for the Defence, 1769–1774*, ed. William K. Wimsatt and Frederick A. Pottle, Heinemann, 1960, p. 227.

39 Youngson, *Classical Edinburgh*, p. 95.

40 *Ibid.*, p. 105.

41 Elizabeth Grant of Rothiemurchus, *Memoirs of a Highland Lady*, 2 vols, Edinburgh, Canongate, 1988, vol. I, pp. 6, 7–8.

42 RCAHMS, *The City of Edinburgh*, Edinburgh, 1951, p. 207; Youngson, *Classical Edinburgh*, pp. 95–6.
43 *Boswell in Extremis, 1776–1778*, ed. Charles McC. Webb, Yale edn, Heinemann, 1971, pp. 61, 62–3, 89.
44 Philo-Scotus [Philip Barrington Ainslie]. *Reminiscences of a Scottish Gentleman*, London, 1861, pp. 62f.
45 The name Gabriel's Road arose from a murder that took place in 1717, when Robert Irvine, a tutor, sometimes called Gabriel, was caught out by his two charges, sons of Gordon of Ellon, when making free with their mother's maid, and in revenge he stabbed the boys to death in this lonely place. But the killing was observed from Castle Hill, and in no time Gabriel was arrested, condemned by the baron of Broughton in whose jurisdiction it was, and hanged, with the barbarous addition of the hacking off of his hands with the same dagger he had used for the murder. (Robert Chambers, *Traditions of Edinburgh*, new edn, London and Edinburgh, 1868, pp. 385–6.)

Chapter 2: The Old Town and High Street Living

1 Mackenzie, *Anecdotes and Egotisms*, p. 43.
2 Charles Kirkpatrick Sharpe, Memoranda, 1824 or 1825, in *Scott and Sharpe Letters to Chambers*, p. 40.
3 Somerville, *Life and Times*, pp. 334ff.; Rev. Charles Rogers, *Scotland Social and Domestic*, Grampian Club I, London, 1869, pp. 97f., 107–8.
4 Somerville, *Life and Times*, pp. 327ff.; Topham, *Letters from Edinburgh*, pp. 195ff.; Rogers, *loc. cit.*, pp. 103ff.
5 [*The Life and Travels of John Macdonald*], *Memoirs of an 18th Century Footman*, introd. John Beresford, London, 1927, p. 236.
6 [Mrs Mary Anne Hanway], *A Journey to the Highlands of Scotland, with occasional remarks on Dr Johnson's Tour*: By a Lady, p.p., London [?1775], pp. 8, 10.
7 See, for example, *Guy Mannering*, chapter XXXVI.
8 Somerville, *Life and Times*, pp. 11, 23. See *The Autobiography of Benjamin Rush*, ed. George W. Corner, Princeton U.P. (for American Philosophical Society, vol. 25), 1948.
9 Somerville, *Life and Times*, pp. 368, 369. Certain charitable institutions were, however, founded at the turn of the century, the Blind Asylum in 1795, the Magdalen Asylum in 1797; and in 1810, the Deaf and Dumb Institution.
10 Topham, *Letters from Edinburgh*, p. 87.
11 Henry Cockburn, *Memorials of his Time*, Edinburgh, 1874, p. 375.
12 *Letters of Benjamin Rush*, ed. L.H. Butterfield, 2 vols, Princeton UP (American Philosophical Society, vol. 30), 1951, pp. 31–2 (20 Dec. 1766).
13 Topham, *Letters from Edinburgh*, p15.
14 Mrs Hanway, *Journey to the Highlands*, pp. 16, 17 (10 Aug. 1775).
15 Topham, *Letters from Edinburgh*, pp. 48f. Edward Topham served in the Life Guards to the rank of major, and in about 1790 ran a paper called *The World* in partnership with a Jewish barrister called Samuel. When Topham retired to 'the Wolds', he used to call on his former co-editor when in London, who was then editing *The Pilot*. The journalist Cyrus Redding, then an occasional contributor, who used to see him there in about 1808, describes him as of medium height, 'stout, full-faced, ruddy-complexioned' and grey-whiskered, with gentlemanly manners and 'much openness of disposition'. For a long time Topham maintained what Redding thought 'a singular attachment' on marital terms with Mrs Wells, a rather second-rate actress, and they had three daughters, whom their father had educated to become 'elegant and accomplished Women' and who made good

marriages. Mrs Wells unfortunately took to drink, developed 'an ungovernable temper', and left home for London, where she consorted with other partners and converted to become in turn a Jew and a Roman Catholic. Samuel always refused to see her, but would help her financially. Meanwhile Topham published plays and other works, including a life of the miser Elwes. He died in 1820. (Cyrus Redding, *50 Years Recollections, Literary and Personal, with Observations on Men and Things*, 3 vols, London, 1858, vol. I, pp. 85–7. And see *The London Stage*, 1600–1800, ed. William Van Lennep, 11 vols and Index, S. Illinois University Press 1965–8; index B.R. Schneider, Jr, *Ibid.*, 1979.

16 Mackenzie, *Anecdotes and Egotisms*, pp. 15–16.
17 Boswell, *The Great Biographer, 1789–1795*, ed. Marlies K. Danziger and Frank Brady, Heinemann, 1989, pp. 235–6. Boswell was so explicit on this subject that he realised that even if he were to apply for a Scottish judgeship, it would be unlikely to be offered him.
18 Topham, *Letters from Edinburgh*, pp. 82f., 278–9.
19 *Ibid.*, pp. 340–44.
20 Mackenzie, *Anecdotes and Egotisms*, p. 74.
21 Topham, *Letters from Edinburgh*, pp. 349–53.
22 *Ibid.*, pp. 372–9.
23 S.F.L. Schetky, *Ninety Years of Work and Play: Sketches from the Public and Private Career of John Christian Schetky, by his daughter*, Edinburgh & London, 1877, p. 3.
24 Mackenzie, *Anecdotes and Egotisms*, pp. 75ff.
25 Topham, *Letters from Edinburgh*, pp. 127ff.
26 Rev. John Sinclair, *Memorials of the Life and Works of the late Rt Hon. Sir John Sinclair, Bart*, 2 vols, Edinburgh, 1837, vol. I, p. 41.
27 C.K. Sharpe, Memoranda, in *Scott and Sharpe Letters to Chambers*, p. 44.
28 Topham, *Letters from Edinburgh*, pp. 154ff.
29 Mackenzie, *Anecdotes and Egotisms*, p. 57–8.
30 Topham, *Letters from Edinburgh*, p. 160.
31 *Ibid.*, pp. 227ff.
32 Mackenzie, *Anecdotes and Egotisms*, p. 59.
33 Somerville, *Life and Times*, p. 335.
34 Mackenzie, *Anecdotes and Egotisms*, pp. 59–60, 82.
35 Simon Gray [Sir Alexander Boswell], 'Old Town tea parties', in *Edinburgh, or, The Ancient Royalty;* A sketch of Former Manners, Edinburgh, 1810.
36 William Creech, in *The Statistical Account of Scotland*, vol. II, *The Lothians*, ed. Sir John Sinclair, Edinburgh, 1794, pp. 26f. and 47f.
37 *Parties and Pleasures*, the diaries of Helen Graham 1823–1826, ed. James Irvine, [Edinburgh], 1957, pp. 18, 33, 242, n.21; *Memoir and Correspondence of Mrs Grant of Laggan*, ed. by her son, J.P. Grant, 3 vols, London, 1844, vol. III, p. 108 (Mrs Grant to Mrs Fletcher, 14 Dec. 1826).
38 Princess Dashkoff returned to Russia in 1782, directed the St Petersburg Academy of Arts and Sciences and became first president of the Russian Academy. Under Catherine the Great's successors, however, she was exiled to the provinces. (See entry in *Encyclopaedia Britannica*.)
39 Notes by Scott for Chambers's *Traditions of Edinburgh*, in Scott and Sharpe, *Letters to Chambers*, p. 67. See also Chambers's *Traditions*, 1825 edn, vol. II, p. 48.

Chapter 3 The Fabric of Edinburgh Society

I The Church

1 Rush, *Autobiography*, p. 52.
2 Somerville, *Life and Times*, pp. 62f.

3 See Rosalind Mitchison, *A History of Scotland*, Methuen, 1970, pp. 354, 355; T.C. Smout, *A History of the Scottish People 1560–1830*, London, Collins, 1969, pp. 233–6. Mackenzie, *Anecdotes and Egotisms*, pp. 97–8.
4 J.H. & S. Storer, *A Graphic and Historical Description of the City of Edinburgh*, London, 1818, pp. 89–91; *A New History . . .*, pp. 31ff.
5 Somerville, *Life and Times*, p. 56; Francis Watt, *A Book of Edinburgh Anecdote*, Edinburgh, 1913, p. 46.
6 Somerville, *Life and Times*, pp. 60, 61, 57.
7 *Ibid.*, p. 61. Robert Dick (1722–82), DD Edinburgh 1759, was transferred to Trinity (a former collegiate church) in 1753. Robert Walker (1716–85) was transferred to the High Kirk in 1754. In 1771 he was Moderator of the General Assembly. (*Fasti Ecclesiasti Scoticanae* vol. I., pp. 134, 60)
8 The Old Kirk was the south transept of St Giles'. Dr James McKnight (1721–86), minister there from 1778 and before that at Lady Yester's Church, though not an eloquent preacher was a good translator, and spent nearly thirty years on a careful translation of two Pauline epistles. He also published a number of other works. It was he who baptised (1811) Archibald Tait, who succeeded Dr Arnold as headmaster of Rugby, became Bishop of London and in 1869 Archbishop of Canterbury. (*DNB*)
9 Cockburn, *Memorials*, pp. 200–01.
10 *Ibid.*, pp. 36–7. *Personal Recollections, from early life to old age, of Mary Somerville, with selections from her Correspondence*, by her daughter, Martha Somerville, London, 1873, pp. 91–2. On Moncrieff's death in 1827 Cockburn wrote to Jeffrey, 'The world does not seem to me to be the world without . . . Sir Henry' (15 August 1827), *Some Letters of Lord Cockburn, with pages omitted from the Memorials of his Time*, ed. Harry A. Cockburn, Edinburgh, 1932, p. 22.
11 *Remains of the late Rt Reverend Daniel Sandford, D.D., Oxon, Bishop of Edinburgh in the Scottish Episcopal Church*, with a memoir, by the Rev. John Sandford, 2 vols, Edinburgh, 1830, vol. I, pp. 24f.
12 Farington, *Tour in England*, 6 July 1788.
13 R.L. Willis, *Journal of a Tour from London to Elgin made about 1790 in company with Mr Brodie, Younger, Brother of Brodie of Brodie*; printed from the Original MS, Edinburgh, 1897, p. 52 (14 July). The evidence points to the year being actually 1793, when the younger Brodie married Miss Wemyss.
14 *The Early Married Life of Maria Josepha Lady Stanley, with extracts from Sir John Stanley's 'Praeterita',* ed. Jane H. Adeane, London, 1899, p. 145 (Maria Stanley to her sister Louisa, 26 Oct. 1797).
15 *Memoirs of the Rev. Charles Simeon, MA, with a selections from his writings and correspondence*, ed. Rev. William Carus, 3rd edn, London, 1848, p. 97.
16 Topham, *Letters from Edinburgh*, pp. 280–83; Somerville, *Life and Times*, p. 367.

II The Law

1 Topham, *Letters from Edinburgh*, 299f.; Somerville, *Life and Times*, p. 107.
2 Peter Halkerston, LLD, *A Digest of the Law of Scotland, relating to Marriage*, Edinburgh, 1827, pp. 64, 67. See also Topham, pp. 318ff. Halkerston quotes the case of Margaret Aitken in 1782, where 'it was found, that verbal declaration, on several occasions, by an Englishman, to a Scotswoman, in Scotland, constituted marriage'. The apparently unwilling spouse was in fact a Mr Topham, and if this is our English visitor of the 1770s, it provides unexpected information about this gentleman, of whom so tantalisingly little is known.
3 Students destined for the law usually took several courses; but in 1777 Lord Kinnoull, with whom Lord Alva's son John Erskine stayed while at college, warned his father the judge that his studies so far were only preliminaries. 'The

Learned Languages are mere Toolls,' he argued, whereas John needed 'the art of Reasoning . . . the principles of moral Philosophy, which is the Ground work of Legislation', and also the essential Rhetoric. Lord Alva wanted the boy to go on to a foreign university, perhaps with the Earl of Breadalbane's son, but, said Lord Kinnoull, 'I well know . . . that *Nothing* can be learnt at any foreign University, except the living Languages & bodily Exercises, such as Riding, Fencing, & Dancing.' This might be suitable for a peer's son, but for a youth like John who had to qualify for a profession it would only cause an interruption. (Erskine Murray MSS, NLS 5084/6–8)

4 Scott's Autobiography, in J.G. Lockhart, *The Life of Sir Walter Scott, Bart*, 10 vols, Edinburgh, 1902, vol. I, p. 61–2.

5 Robert J. Mackintosh, *Memoirs of the Life of the Rt Hon. Sir James Mackintosh*, 2 vols, London, (1835 &) 1836, vol. I, p. 22.

6 Cockburn, *Memorials*, pp. 98–9.

7 Chambers's *Edinburgh Journal*, vol. I, 1832, p. 100.

8 *Some Letters of Lord Cockburn*, p. 86.

9 Cockburn, *Memorials*, p. 100.

10 *Ibid.*, pp. 104f.

11 Watt, *Edinburgh Anecdote*, p. 21.

12 Cockburn, *Memorials*, pp. 97–8.

13 Watt, E*dinburgh Anecdote*, pp. 8ff.

14 Alexander Fergusson, *The Hon. Henry Erskine, Lord Advocate for Scotland*, Edinburgh, 1882, pp. 241–2.

III Schools

1 Charles Gibbon, *The Life of George Combe*, 2 vols, London, 1878, vol. I, pp. 6–7.

2 Cockburn, *Memorials*, p. 11.

3 Scott's Autobiography, in Lockhart, *Life of Scott*, vol. I, p. 28.

4 *The Life and Times of Henry Lord Brougham, written by himself*, 3 vols, Edinburgh, 1871, vol. I, p. 3. In Scott's time the dux was always James Buchan, later a distinguished doctor in Egypt, and third in the class was Henry Dundas.

5 Gibbon, *George Combe*, vol. I, pp. 17ff.

6 Cockburn, *Memorials*, vol. 1, pp. 3–5.

7 Lockhart, *Life of Scott*, vol. I, pp. 32–33.

8 Schetky, *Ninety Years*, p. 15; Fyfe, *Edinburgh Under Scott*, pp. 19f.

9 Gibbon, *George Combe*, vol. I, pp. 23f.

10 Mary Somerville, *Recollections*, p. 22.

11 *Ibid.*, pp. 23ff., 59. Dr Hugh Blair, minister of the High Kirk and Professor of Belles Lettres, was one who encouraged young Mary Fairfax in her painting. Hearing of the girl's talent, he asked her mother if he might see her pictures, and to her great delight sent a long and generally admiring commentary. He hung the works in his drawing room in Argyll Square and showed them off to connoisseurs including a number of ladies, all of whom praised them. (*Ibid.*, p. 57)

12 Topham, *Letters from Edinburgh*, pp. 355ff., also 87.

13 Mary Somerville, *Recollections*, pp. 62–3.

14 *Letters written for the post, and not for the Press*, London, 1820, p. 12.

15 *Autobiography of Mrs Fletcher*, with letters and other family memorials, ed. [Mary Richardson], 3rd edn, Edinburgh, 1876, p. 92.

16 *Ibid.*, pp. 81, 91.

17 Rev. John W. Burgon, *Memoirs of Patrick Fraser Tytler*, London, 1859, p. 20.

18 Mrs Fletcher, *Autobiography*, p. 103.

19 Lockhart, *Life of Scott*, vol. I., pp. 107–10; Burgon, *Patrick Fraser Tytler*, pp. 18ff.

20 Mary Somerville, *Recollections*, p. 15; Burgon, *loc. cit.*

21 Alexander Campbell, *A Journey from Edinburgh through Parts of North Britain*, 2 vols, London, 1802, vol. II, pp. 156–7 and n.

IV Edinburgh Societies

1 Cockburn, *Memorials*, p. 23.
2 Lockhart, *Life of Scott*, vol. I, p. 199.
3 Cockburn, *Memorials*, pp. 23–4.
4 Lockhart, *Life of Scott*, vol. I, p. 199–200.
5 Cockburn, *Memorials*, pp. 64–6.
6 Brougham, *Life and Times*, vol. I, pp. 89–90.
7 *Ibid.*, Appendix X.
8 *Ibid.*, vol. I, p. 91 and Appendix XI. Robert Heron (1764–1807), a weaver's son from Kirkcudbright, was a prolific writer. He had edited Thomson's *Seasons* (1789, 1793), was arrested for debt in 1794 but used his time in prison to write part of a history of Scotland, later edited London papers including *The Globe* and published several other works. He was an elder for his own district of New Galloway. (*DNB*)
9 Brougham, *Life and Times*, vol. I, p. 67.
10 James Hutton, *Theory of the Earth*, 2 vols, 1795. An unfinished third volume was published posthumously, in 1799. Hutton (1726–97), educated in Edinburgh, Paris and Leyden, originated his view of the formation of the earth's crust and the uniformation theory of geology, which initiated the fierce controversy with the 'Wernerians'. His supporters were known variously as Huttonians, Plutonists and Vulcanists.

Abraham Werner (1750–1817), born in east Germany, founded the 'Neptunian' school claiming rocks to be of aqueous origin, and vigorously opposed those who believed, like Hutton, that geological evolution had been continuous and uniform. (*Ency. Britannica*)
11 Mackintosh, *Memoirs*, vol. I, pp. 25f.
12 *Ibid.*, vol. I, pp. 29, 37.

V University

1 The Scottish University Act, 1858.
2 Brougham, *Life and Times*, vol. I, p. 78.
3 Frederick Augustus Wendeborn, *A View of England towards the Close of the 18th Century*, trans. from the German, 2 vols, London, 1791, vol. II, pp. 172ff.; Topham, *Letters from Edinburgh*, p. 205.
4 Somerville, *Life and Times*, pp. 11–23.
5 The Hon. Evelyn Ashley, *The Life and Correspondence of Henry Temple, Viscount Palmerston*, 4 vols, London, 1879, vol. I, p. 8.
6 Sir Alexander Dick of Prestonfield (1703–85), born a Cunyngham and inheriting his mother's name Dick with her estate, was a physician who studied at both Edinburgh and Leyden, was President of Edinburgh's College of Physicians (1736–63), and promoted the Medical School in the University. Dr Johnson visited him at Prestonfield during his Scottish visit.
7 The Hon. Mrs Atholl Forbes (Mrs Margaret Forbes), ed., *Curiosities of a Scots Charta Chest*, Edinburgh, 1897, pp. 188–9.
8 Topham, *loc. cit.*
9 *Ibid.*, p. 219.
10 Wendeborn, *View of England*, vol. II, p. 172.
11 Bartholomew Faujas de St Fond, *Travels in England, Scotland, and the Hebrides*, 2 vols, London, 1799, vol. II, pp. 224ff.; Benjamin Rush, *Autobiography*, American Philosophy Society vol. 25, p. 50.

12 Mackintosh, *Memoirs*, vol. I, p. 22; Fyfe, *Edinburgh Under Sir Walter Scott*, pp. 60f.; Somerville, *Life and Times*, p. 61; John Kay, *A Series of Original Portraits and Caricature Etchings*, new edn, ed. H. Paton, 2 vols, Edinburgh, 1877, vol. I, nos XLI, XLII.
13 Brougham, *Life and Times*, vol. I, pp. 74–5.
14 Cockburn, *Memorials*, p. 44.
15 *The Correspondence and Public Papers of John Jay*, ed. Henry P. Johnston, 4 vols, New York and London, 1890–93, vol. III, pp. 71–2.
16 [Col. M.D. Stewart], *Memoir of the Late Dugald Stewart, Author of the Philosophy of the Human Mind*, p.p., Edinburgh, 1838; *Encyclopaedia Britannica.*
17 *Memoirs of the Life and Writings of Thomas Chalmers, DD, LLD*, by his son-in-law, the Rev. William Hanna, LLD, 5 vols, Edinburgh, 1849, vol. I, pp. 42–3; Sir Archibald Alison, *Some Account of my Life and Writings*, ed. by his daughter-in-law, Lady [Jane] Alison, 2 vols, London, 1883, vol. I, p. 41; *Memoirs and Correspondence of Francis Horner, MP*, ed. Leonard Horner, 2 vols, with additions, Boston and London, 1853, (Francis Horner, Journal, 17 Dec. 1800), p. 131; Fyfe, *Edinburgh Under Scott*, pp. 28f. *The Wit and Wisdom of the Rev. Sydney Smith.* A selection of the most memorable passages . . ., Longman, 1860, p. 219.
18 *Life and Letters of Thomas Campbell*, ed. William Beattie, 3 vols, London, 1850, pp. 241, 381–2.
19 Brougham, *Life and Times*, vol. I, p. 66; Alison, *Some Account*, vol. I, p. 41; Chalmers, *Life*, vol. I, p. 91.
20 Horner, *Memoirs*, Journal, 22 May 1799, vol. I, pp. 84–5; Mary Somerville, *Recollections*, p. 90.
21 *Edinburgh Magazine*, August 1805; Alison, *Some Account*, vol. I, p. 41; *Edinburgh Annual Register*, 1819, pp. 316–24.
22 Rosamond Brunel Gotch, *Maria, Lady Callcott. The Creator of Little Arthur*, London, 1937, pp. 75, 78–80.
23 H.M. Colvin, *A Biographical Dictionary of British Architects, 1600–1840*, 3rd edn, London, John Murray, p. 763.
24 Gotch, *Lady Callcott*, p. 80.
25 Cosmo Innes, 'Memoir of Professor Dalzell', in Dalzell's *History of the University of Edinburgh*, Edinburgh, 1862, vol. I, *passim*. See also Philo-Scotus, *Reminiscences*, pp. 62f.

VI Medicine and Surgery

The following works of reference have been consulted for this chapter, and for Part III, Chapter 10 and Part IV, Chapter 13:

John D. Comrie, *History of Scottish Medicine*, 2nd edn, 2 vols, London, 1937
Clarendon Hyde Cresswell, *The Royal College of Surgeons of Edinburgh 1505–1905*, Edinburgh, 1926
Harold R. Fletcher & William H. Brown, *The Royal Botanic Garden, Edinburgh, 1670–1970*, Edinburgh, 1970
Sir Alexander Grant, *History of the University of Edinburgh*, 2 vols, Edinburgh, 1884
Douglas Guthrie, *A History of Medicine*, London & Edinburgh, 1945
A. Logan Turner, *Story of a Great Hospital: The Royal Infirmary of Edinburgh, 1729–1929*, Edinburgh, 1937
Alexander Miles, *The Edinburgh School of Surgery Before Lister*, London, 1918
John Struthers, *Historical Sketch Of the Edinburgh Anatomical School*, Edinburgh, 1867

1 Craig, *Royal College of Physicians*, chs 2 & 3.
2 In his will Dr Pitcairne left a jereboam to be drunk on the restoration of the

Stewart kings. In 1800 Dr James Gregory's successor in Physiology, Professor Andrew Duncan, and others agreed by a somewhat elastic interpretation that the terms would be satisfied provided Pitcairne's tomb were restored. The jereboam was then broached. Guthrie, *History of Medicine*, p. 226.

3 Fletcher & Brown, *Royal Botanic Garden*. See also Elizabeth Berry, *The Writing on the Walls*, Edinburgh, Cockburn Association & others, 1990, p. 85. The site is now covered by Waverley Station. Watt, *Book of Edinburgh Anecdote*, p. 74

4 Struthers, Edinburgh Anatomical School, p. 17ff.

5 Grant, *History of the University*, vol. 1, pp. 293–317.

6 Thomas Somerville, Life and Times, pp. 11–23.

7 Logan Turner, *Story of a Great Hospital.*

8 Struthers, *Edinburgh Anatomical School*, p. 28ff; Logan Turner, *Story of a Great Hospital.*

9 'From Overseas. Letters of a Colonial Student in Medicine in Edinburgh to his Parents in S. Carolina, 1746–1749' [John Moultrie], in *University of Edinburgh Journal*, vol. IV, 1930–31, pp. 270–4.

10 R.E Wright Sinclair, *Doctors Monro: A Medical Saga*, London, 1964, p. 77; Struthers, *Edinburgh Anatomical School*, p. 17ff; Guthrie, *History of Medicine*, p. 229.

11 Alvin R. Riggs, 'The Colonial American Medical Student at Edinburgh', in *University of Edinburgh Journal*, vol. IV, 1930–31, pp. 270–4.

12 Benjamin Rush to Jonathan Bayard Smith, 30 April 1767, in *Letters of Benjamin Rush*, vol. 1, pp. 41, 58.

13 Benjamin Franklin to Dr Thomas Bond, 6 July 1771, in *Franklin Papers*, vol. 18. 1974, p. 165. Franklin and Bond were later co-founders of Pennsylvania Hospital.

14 Do. to Do., 5 Feb. 1772; *Ibid.*, vol. 19. 1975, p. 65

15 Topham, *Letters from Edinburgh*, pp. 212f.

16 Thomas Ismay, Student of Medicine at Edinburgh, 1771, to his father, *University of Edinburgh Journal*, vol. VIII, 1936–7, pp. 57ff.

17 Benjamin Rush to John Morgan, 20 Jan. 1768, in *Letters of Benjamin Rush.*

18 John Moultrie to his parents, 29 Sept. 1746, in 'Letters from a Colonial Student', *loc. cit.*

19 Innes, 'Memoir of Professor Dalzell', *loc. cit.*, p. 5.

20 Benjamin Rush to Trustees of Dickinson College, Philadelphia, 21 Oct., 1786 in *Letters of Benjamin Rush*, vol. 1, p. 397; Riggs, 'Colonial American Students', *loc. cit.*

21 Alexander Miles, *The Edinburgh School of Surgery before Lister*, pp. 79–80.

22 [John Bell], Answer for the Junior Members of the Royal College of Surgeons of Edinburgh, to the Memorial of Dr James Gregory, Edinburgh, 1800, pp. 10ff.

23 *Ibid.*, p. 38

24 *Ibid.*

25 Miles, *School of Surgery*, pp. 48f. *Kay's Portraits: A Series of original Portraits and Caricature Etchings* . . . new edition, Edinburgh, 1877, 2 vols, vol. II, p. 45 (No. CLXXXVI).

26 Miles, *School of Surgery*, pp. 48f.; Lord Byron, *Childe Harold*; Andrew Duncan, *Poems*, 1818. Andrew Duncan the elder (1744–1828), friend and contemporary of Thomas Erskine, a St Andrews MD (1769), studied medicine at Edinburgh from 1762 under Drs Cullen, Gregory and Monro II. He was five times President of the Royal Medical Society, a Licentiate of the Edinburgh College of Physicians, and for a time worked as a surgeon in China. In the 1770s he launched a medical quarterly. He first proposed a public lunatic asylum, not achieved until 1807 (in Morningside). In 1790 he succeeded Gregory as Professor of the Theory or Institutes of Medicine (Physiology), in which he became Physician to the King in Scotland on Gregory's death, and was also President of the new Edinburgh Medico-Chirurgical Society. His published works include many poems. (*DNB*)

27 Miles, *School of Surgery*, p. 44.
28 *The Autobiography of Benjamin Rush*, vol. 25, p. 44; Boswell, *The Applause of the Jury*, ed. Irma S. Lustig and Frederick A. Pottle, Heinemann, 1982, p. 55 and n.; Mackintosh, *Memoirs*, p. 23.
29 Sruthers, Edinburgh Anatomical School, p. 39f. ; Miles, *School of Surgery*, p. 60f. John Bell's anatomical school was later attached to the Infirmary and known as the Lock Hospital.
30 See n. 21.
31 Dr Gregory was of a quarrelsome disposition, and a wrangle with his equally irritable colleague James Hamilton, successor to his own father as Professor of Midwifery, ended in a blows and a court case. Although Hamilton was awarded £100 damages, Gregory maintained the satisfaction of beating him up was worth the money. (Hamilton, incidentally, was the last physician to visit his patients in a sedan hair, in 1830.) (Guthrie, *History of Medicine*, p. 231).
32 Struthers, *Edinburgh Anatomical School*, pp. 40–4; Miles, School of Surgery, pp. 60–75.

VII Tories and Revolutionaries

1 Quoted in David Masson, *Edinburgh Sketches and Memories*, London, 1892, pp. 153ff.
2 Cyril Matheson, *The Life of Henry Dundas, 1st Viscount Melville, 1742–1811*, London, 1933.
3 Cockburn, *Memorials*, p. 77.
4 Masson, *Edinburgh Sketches*, p. 153.
5 Cockburn, *Memorials*, p. 82.
6 Mrs Fletcher, *Autobiography*, p. 64.
7 *Scots Magazine*, 1792.
8 Philo-Scotus, *Reminiscences*, pp. 24ff.
9 *Ibid.*, pp. 27–8.
10 Rosalind Mitchison, *History of Scotland*, pp. 364–5.
11 Alan Wharam, *The Treason Trials 1794*, Leicester UP, 1992, pp. 47ff. *The Traveller's Companion through the City of Edinburgh and Suburbs . . .*, Edinburgh, 1794, pp. 63–5.
12 Margaret Forbes, *Beattie and his Friends*, Westminster, 1904, p. 282.
13 Walter Scott to Miss Rutherford, 5 Sept., 1794; *The Letters of Sir Walter Scott*, ed. H.J.C. Grierson, London, 1932, vol. I, pp. 34f.
14 [John Pease], 'Journal of a Traveller in Scotland, 1795–1796', ed. Peter Barber, in *Scottish Historical Review*, vol. 36, 1957, pp. 25–31.
15 Lockhart, *Life of Scott*, vol. I, pp. 257–8, 261.
16 *Ibid.*, vol. I, pp. 273–4.
17 *Ibid.*, vol. I., pp. 297–8.
18 *Ibid.*, vol. I, pp. 302, 303n.
19 Cockburn, *Memorials*, p. 118.
20 Scott had met Margaret Stuart one wet Sunday afternoon in Greyfriars churchyard, and offered her the shelter of his umbrella on the walk home. He was greatly in love with her for several years, but eventually she married Sir William Forbes of Pitsligo.
21 *James Plumptre's Britain. The Journal of a Tourist in the 1780s*, ed. Ian Ousby, Hutchinson, 1992. Plumptre, a Cambridge graduate who passed much of his youth in walking tours of Britain, remarks on the disfiguring effect of the new barracks (1799), 'built in a heavy formal manner' which 'far out-top the other parts of the castle' (5 June).

22 Gibbon, *George Combe*, pp. 32–34.
23 Thomas Campbell, *Life and Letters*, vol. I, pp. 87–9.
24 *Ibid.*, vol. I, *passim*.

VIII Theatrical Progress

1 *The Correspondence of James Boswell with David Garrick, Edmund Burke, and Edmond Malone*. Private Papers of James Boswell, vol. 4, Heinemann, 1986, pp. 31–2 and n.
2 Topham, *Letters from Edinburgh*, pp. 110ff.; Boswell, *The Ominous Years, 1774–1776*, ed. Charles Ryskamp, Heinemann, 1963, p. 74 (7 March, 1775).
3 Mackenzie, *Anecdotes and Egotisms*, pp. 194f.; Boswell, *The Ominous Years*, pp. 71, 74 (25 February, 7 March, 1775).
4 *Scots Magazine*, March 1775, pp. 165–6.
5 Topham, *Letters from Edinburgh*, p. 244; *Edinburgh Evening Courant*, 4 & 11 March 1775.
6 Mackenzie, *Letters to Elizabeth Rose*, pp. 43, 97.
7 *Boswell in Extremis*, pp. 17–18 (30 July 1776); *The Applause of the Jury*, pp. 57, n., 280; *The English Experiment*, 1785–1789, ed. Irma S. Lustig & Frederick A. Pottle, Heinemann, 1986, (11 February 1789). Vincent Lunardi, *An Account of 5 Aerial Voyages in Scotland*, London, 1786. The story of Lunardi's ascent early in October 1785 is one of accidents and frustrations, over the site (eventually from Heriot's Hospital grounds), the balloon's late arrival by wagon from Liverpool, delay in supply of cisterns for the 'vitriolic acid' needed for its power, even authorisation of a cannon salute to mark the flight. All was endured with alternate despair and elation by the mercurial balloonist (who, if the portrait frontispiece to his account does not flatter, was extremely handsome). He was ecstatic over Edinburgh's romantic setting and Scotland's female beauties, three of whom begged to accompany him, to his regretful refusal. Wind and weather finally defeated his flight.

   Lunardi dedicated his account to the Buccleuchs, who were great fans on the occasion.
8 Arnot, *History of Edinburgh*, p. 383.
9 Robert Chambers, *History of the Edinburgh Theatre*, 1859; James C. Dibdin, *Annals of the Edinburgh Stage*, Edinburgh, 1888, pp. 181ff.
10 John Wilson once observed that this laugh proved that Edinburgh had at least exhibited *some* kind of civilised advance – else he would have concluded they lacked taste and feeling altogether.
11 Chambers, *ad loc.*
12 Col. Thomas Thornton, *A Sporting Tour through the Northern Parts of England and Great Part of the Highlands of Scotland* (first published 1804), London, 1896, pp. 21–22 (15 & 16 June 1784). A mob had gathered intent on destroying Haig's Distillery at Canonmills.
13 Chambers, *ad loc.*
14 Duchess of Buccleuch to Lady Louisa Stuart, 3 August, 1784, in Lady Louisa Stuart, *Gleanings from an Old Portfolio*, ed. Mrs Godfrey Clark, 3 vols, p.p., Edinburgh, 1895, p. 266.
15 Col. Thornton, *loc. cit.*
16 Margaret Forbes, *Beattie and his Friends*, p. 202 (Beattie to Miss Valentine, 28 May, 1784).
17 *Life and Letters of Sir Gilbert Elliot, 1st Earl of Minto, from 1751 to 1806*, ed. by his great-niece the Countess of Minto, 3 vols, London, 1874, p. 152 (Elliot to his wife, 12 April 1787 (and NLS 11046/142)).
18 Faujas de Saint-Fond, *Travels in England*, vol. II, pp. 245f. French visitors usually admitted to suffering excruciating torments when listening to the pipes, including

in the 1820s the French Consul M. Hugo, who warned Amédée Pichot not to indulge his curiosity in that direction. Hugo related how he had confessed to his host that he missed variety in the music, as all the airs appeared to be dirges. '*Comment, ces airs mélancoliques?*' exclaimed the Scot, '*ce sont des airs de mariage!*' Pichot persisted, however, and for some time felt the same monotony, but was at least prepared to put himself if possible in the place of Scottish listeners, as the pipers in their 'antique costume' advanced with a pride reminiscent of the piper of old who was among a chief's leading officers. Also, by following the judges' motions and expressions, Pichot was able to distinguish between pibroch, variations, marches, coronachs and reels. (Amédée Pichot, *Voyage Historique et Littéraire en Angleterre et Ecosse*, 3 vols, Paris, 1825, vol. III, pp. 230–4.)

19 Lady Louisa Stuart, *Gleanings*, vol. II, p. 149 (Duchess of Buccleuch to Lady Louisa, July 1789).

20 P.W. Clayden, *Early Life of Samuel Rogers*, London, 1887 (20 July 1789).

21 Charles A. Malcolm, 'Diary of George Sandy, Apprentice W.S., 1788', *Old Edinburgh Club*, vol. XXIV, 1943, p. 54 (9 July 1788).

22 Boswell, *Laird of Auchinleck 1778–1782*, ed. Joseph W. Reed and F.A. Pottle, New York, McGraw Hill, 1977, p. 304 (1 April 1781); *The English Experiment*, p. 71 (14 June 1786).

23 J.C.B. Cooksey, *Alexander Nasmyth HRSA, 1758–1840*, Paul Harris, 1991, p. 64; *The Intimate Letters of Hester Piozzi and Penelope Pennington 1788–1821*, ed. Oswald G. Knapp, London, 1914, pp. 125–6. Although Mrs Esten secured a court decree against plays acting at the rival theatre, it remained a competitor for some years.

24 Robert Heron, *Observations made in a Journey through the Western Counties of Scotland in the Autumn of MDCCXCII*, 2 vols, Edinburgh, 1793, vol. II, p. 507.

25 Philo-Scotus, *Reminiscences*, pp. 31f.

26 Forbes, *Scots Charta Chest*, p. 286 (Sir Alexander Dick, Occasional Memoranda Book, June 1781); Lady Louisa Stuart, *Gleanings*, p. 142 (Lady Carlow to her sister Lady Louisa, 23 July 1781).

27 Another daughter, Susan, married Crawfurd Tait, and their son Archibald became Bishop of London.

28 Philo-Scotus, *Reminiscences*, pp. 72–74.

29 [R.L. Willis], *Journal of a Tour*, p. 50.

30 Philo-Scotus, *Reminiscences*, p. 46; Fyfe, *Edinburgh under Sir Walter Scott*, p. 128; Chambers, *Edinburgh Theatre*.

31 Mrs Somerville, *Personal Recollections*, p. 45.

32 Mrs Somerville, *Personal Recollections*, p. 51.

33 *James Plumptre's Britain*, p. 130 (11 July 1799).

34 *The Letters of Sydney Smith*, ed. Nowell C. Smith, 2 vols, Oxford, Clarendon Press, 1953, vol. I, p. 38 (Smith to Mrs Beach, 18 March 1799).

35 Chambers, *Edinburgh Theatre*.

36 *Brougham and his Early Friends. Letters to James Loch 1798–1809*, ed. R.H.M. Buddle Atkinson and G.A. Jackson, 3 vols, London, 1908, vol. I, p. 219 (Andrew Clephane to James Loch, 25 Dec. 1800).

37 Chambers, *Edinburgh Theatre*; James C. Dibdin, *Annals of the Edinburgh Stage*, pp. 334–5.

Chapter 4: Building a New Town

1 Youngson, p. 84; Town Council Minutes, 7 March 1781; Chambers, *Traditions*, 1825, p. 62.

2 Youngson, pp. 82–85; Lindsay, *Georgian Edinburgh*, p. 30. The parish of St Andrew, the New Town's first church, was taken from St Cuthbert's. A chime of

bells, cast in Whitechapel by William and Thomas Mears, was installed in 1789; the only other church in Edinburgh with a peal was St Giles'. St Andrew's first minister was the Rev. William Greenfield. (*Notes on the History of St Andrew's Church, Edinburgh*, Edinburgh, 1884.)

3 Alexander Campbell, *A Journey from Edinburgh*, vol. II, p. 180.
4 Innes, *Professor Dalzell*, vol. I, p. 47 (Dalzell to Robert Liston, 6 Dec. 1784).
5 Lindsay, *Georgian Edinburgh*, pp. 46–8; Youngson, pp. 81–2, 91ff.
6 Innes, *Professor Dalzell, loc. cit.*
7 Thomas Newte, *Prospects and Observations*, p. 308.
8 The eight-year-old Henry Cockburn, on his first terror-stricken journey to school in October 1787, was momentarily diverted by traversing the planks temporarily thrown across its unfinished arches. (*Memorials*, p. 3)
9 Cockburn, *Memorials*, p. 6; *The Traveller's Companion*, 1794, p. 57.
10 Chambers, *Traditions*, 1825, pp. 49–50n.
11 *Ibid.*, p. 52.
12 J. De Lancy Ferguson, *The Letters of Robert Burns*, 2nd edn, ed. G. Ross Roy, vol. I, 1780–1789, Oxford, 1985, p. 228 (Burns to John Richmond, 7 Feb. 1788).
13 Innes, *Professor Dalzell*, vol. I, p. 73 (Dalzell to Liston, 25 Jan. 1787).
14 [Mound] See, e.g., J. Stark, *Picture of Edinburgh; containing a History and Description of the City*, Edinburgh, 1806, p. 72. A picturesque version of Boyd's Brig is illustrated in Kay's *Portraits* (no. CLXXII), 'The Lawnmarket Coach, or a journey along the Mound', popularly known as 'the Mud Brig'. The alternative story is that people in the Lawnmarket, inconvenienced by the lack of communication with Princes Street, about 1783 opened a subscription for a thoroughfare, and a foundation of whins and furze was laid. Convener Jamieson, who opened a quarry opposite Hanover Street (the then limit of Princes Street building), obtained the magistrates' permission to fill it with excavation rubble, and the work was carried on.

Kay's picture shows a planned pioneer drive across the ridge (as preliminary to a dinner), the Committee of Burgh Reformers walking in front, and their wives and others in a coach and six behind. As the treasurer went bankrupt and made off with what funds were left, the intended 'expedition' could not take place.

15 Stark, *Picture of Edinburgh*, pp. 72–74. James Maitland, 8th Earl of Lauderdale (1759–1839), who succeeded to the title in 1789, was educated at Edinburgh, Oxford and Glasgow, admitted advocate 1780, MP 1780–89, a Scottish representative peer 1790, created a peer of Great Britain 1806, briefly a Privy Councillor 1806. A strong opponent of William Pitt, but from 1821 became a Tory.
16 Thomas Newte, *Prospects and Observations*, pp. 320–1.
17 Stebbing Shaw, *A Tour, in 1787, from London, to the Western Highlands of Scotland*, London [1788], p. 186.
18 Innes of Stow, 7 Dec. 1787, SRO MS GD113/5/75b.
19 John Stoddart, *Remarks on Local Scenery and Manners in Scotland during the Years 1799 and 1800*, 2 vols, London, 1801, vol. I, p. 80.
20 Philo-Scotus, *Reminiscences*, p. 146.
21 The Lang Gate had been the route taken in 1689 by Claverhouse when retreating with his dragoons, whom he halted here while he climbed the rock to the castle sally-port to see its Governor, the Duke of Gordon. (Philo-Scotus, *Reminiscences*, p. 13)
22 In this rural area in the winter of 1761 General Scott's *chef de cuisine*, a keen gambler, was found at a small gate into the grounds, stabbed to death and robbed, presumably of a large sum won at his favourite tavern in Gabriel's Road nearby. (Philo-Scotus, *Reminiscences*, p. 152)
23 *Scots Magazine*, September 1786.
24 Robert Chambers, *Notices of the most Remarkable Fires in Edinburgh, from 1785*

to 1824, including an account of the Great Fire of November 1824, Edinburgh, 1824, pp. 40ff.

25 Boswell, *The Applause of the Jury*, p. 204 (10 April 1784); *The Correspondence of Edmund Burke*, vol. IV, ed. John A. Woods, Cambridge, 1963, pp. 43ff.

26 Innes, *Professor Dalzell*, pp. 42–3 (Dalzell to Liston, 20 April 1784). Hatton, a late seventeenth-century mansion built by the 1st Earl of Lauderdale, incorporated a fifteenth-century tower house. It was subsequently sold to the Earl of Morton, later declined in status, and was demolished in 1955.

27 Burke, *Correspondence*, vol. V, ed. Holden Furber, Cambridge, 1965, p. 221 (Dr William Robertson to Burke, 26 August 1785), pp. 222, 229; *The Diary of the Rt Hon. William Windham, 1784 to 1810*, ed. Mrs Henry Baring, London, 1866, pp. 59ff.

28 *Cookery and Pastry, As taught and practised by Mrs MacIver, Teacher of those Arts in Edinburgh*, 2nd edn, Edinburgh, 1787, pp. 251, 257ff.

29 Mrs Frazer, *The Practice of Cookery, Pastry, Pickling, Preserving, &c.*, Edinburgh, 1791, *passim*.

30 R.P. Gillies, *Recollections of Sir Walter Scott*, London, 1837, p. 29; Mackintosh, *Memoirs*, vol. I, pp. 21–2.

31 *Letters of Scott and Sharpe to Chambers*, p. 39 (Sharpe, Memoranda, May 1826).

32 Henry Skrine, *Travels in the Eastern Counties, and Northern Highlands of Scotland . . .*, London, 1813, pp. 159, 93.

33 *Ibid.*, p. 159.

34 Rev. Daniel Sandford, *Remains*, vol. I, pp. 24ff.

35 Joseph Farington, *Tours in Scotland*, 9 Sept. 1792.

36 Thrale MSS 1789, Ryl.Eng.MS 623/9v.

37 *Ibid.*, 11v.

38 Clayden, Early Life of Samuel Rogers (*Edinburgh Journal*, July 1789), pp. 91f.; see also *Reminiscences and Table Talk of Samuel Rogers*, ed. G.H. Powell, 1903, pp. 22ff.

39 Kay, *Portraits*, vol. IV, pp. 399–400.

40 Maria Lady Stanley, *Early Married Life*, p. 56.

41 Sydney Smith, *Letters*, vol. I, p. 52, Smith to Michael Hicks-Beach, Dec. 1799.

42 A. Campbell, *A Journey from Edinburgh*, vol. II, p. 190.

43 Philo-Scotus, *Reminiscences*, p. 78.

44 Charles Dibdin, elder, *Observations on a Tour, through almost the whole of England, and a considerable part of Scotland . . .*, 2 vols, London, [1802], p. 208 (1800).

45 Gibbon, *George Combe*, vol. I, pp. 22, 29.

46 Philo-Scotus, *Reminiscences*, pp. 89–92. In due course all the prisoners were freed through an exchange with the enemy.

47 Kay illustrates a cockfight in 1785, held in the Assembly Rooms' kitchen, between Lanarkshire and Haddingtonshire, described as a great levelling between the nobility and the roughs, and claiming its popularity in Scotland. There was a cockpit on Leith Links and another in Edinburgh. (Kay, *Portraits*, vol. I, no. XLIV.)

48 *The Statistical Account of Scotland*, 21 vols, Edinburgh, 791–9, vol. II, *The Lothians*, 1794, ed. Sir John Sinclair (letter from William Creech), pp. 21ff.

49 *OEC*, vol. XXV, pp. 30–33; Cockburn, *Memorials*, p. 152; Colvin, *Dictionary of British Architects*, p. 181. It became the Royal Blind Asylum, enlarged by McGibbon and Ross in 1883–84 and 1892, and was demolished in 1978.

50 Sir John Carr, *Caledonian Sketches, or A Tour through Scotland in 1807*, London, 1809, p. 197; Stark, *Picture of Edinburgh*, p. 330; *The Correspondence of George, Prince of Wales*, ed. A. Aspinall, 8 vols, Cassell, 1963–1971, vol. V, p. 235 (Lady Moira to Col. McMahon, 12 July 1805).

51 Carr, *Caledonian Sketches*, p. 74.

52 *Statistical Account, loc. cit.*
53 Philo-Scotus, *Reminiscences*, pp. 146f.
54 A 1790 visitor noted that Lord Moray's villa, Drumsheugh, was still on the edge of town, 'a delightful house and garden . . . commanding a noble view down a wood bank of Leith Water'. Although 'the new buildings begin to elbow his lordship', his grounds kept them at bay: 'This is literally run in urbe.' (R.I. Willis, *Journal of a Tour*, p. 50.)
55 Philo-Scotus, *Reminiscences*, p. 67.

Chapter 5: The French Exiles

1 *Memoirs of the Duchesse de Gontaut*, trans. Mrs J.W. Davis, 2 vols, London, 1894, vol. I, pp. 84ff; A. Francis Steuart, *The Exiled Bourbons in Scotland*, Edinburgh, 1898, pp. 12ff. For the Comte 'Artois, see Kay's *Portraits*, vol. I, p. 214, no. LXXXIX. Holyrood, thanks to its Abbey, had been an ecclesiastical sanctuary since the time of King David I, and subsequently a royal sanctuary. When in 1646 the Duke of Hamilton was appointed hereditary Keeper of the palace, his jurisdiction included the sanctuary. As a refuge for debtors it gradually dropped out of use until legally ceasing under the Bankruptcy Act (Scotland) 1913. See Hugh Hannah, 'The Sanctuary of Holyrood', in *Old Edinburgh Club*, vol. XV, 1922, p. 55.
2 A. Campbell, *A Journey from Edinburgh*, vol. II, p. 140.
3 Steuart, *Exiled Bourbons*, ch.II; see also *Gentleman's* and *Scots Magazines*, *ad loc.*
4 Lady Louisa Stuart, *Gleanings*, vol. III, p. 99.
5 *Memoirs of Louis Philippe, Comte de Ségur*, ed. Eveline Cruickshanks, London, Folio Society, 1960, p. 184.
6 *Life of Sir Robert Christison*, vol. I, p. 7.
7 Steuart, *Exiled Bourbons*. Ch.3.
8 *Memoirs of the Comtesse de Boigne*, ed. Charles Nicollaud, 3 vols, London, 1907–8, vol. I, pp. 126–7.
9 A Campbell, *A Journey from Edinburgh*, vol. II, p. 140.
10 John Henry Manners, 5th Duke of Rutland, *Journal of a Tour to the Northern Parts of Great Britain*, 3 vols, London, 1813, vol. I, p. 178 (31 August 1796). The Duke of Rutland was somewhat ridiculed for his publicised travels. Eight years later, when he was expected at Castle Howard with his brother-in-law Mr Norman, Lady Harriet Cavendish wrote to her grandmother Countess Spencer, that he would probably make his undistinguished visit 'formidable in publishing it in his next tour and giving us some share of the ridicule of appearing in print, whether one was hungry at dinner or tired at supper etc'. (*Hary-O, The Letters of Harriet Cavendish 1796–1809*, ed. Ld Granville Leveson-Gower, London, 1940, p. 99.)

The following autumn Rutland and King dined with the Fremantles at Englefield Green, who thought him 'a good-looking young man, Mr King a horror but very clever'. (Betsey Wynne Fremantle in *The Wynne Diaries*, ed. Anne Fremantle, Oxford, 1952, p. 290.)

11 Mackenzie, *Anecdotes and Egotisms*, p. 226. The Prince, who had been courtly, fashionable, and very handsome – as Henry Mackenzie well remembered seeing him in Paris, splendidly accoutred at a military review – by the time he appeared at Holyrood was to be seen 'wrapped in an old surtout', and Mackenzie 'almost wept' to see him, accompanied only by 'his favourite' M. de Puysegur, 'in a little dirty close in the Canongate where they had been looking at . . . the old Theatre'. (*Ibid.*, p. 223.)
12 *Ibid.*, pp. 225–7.
13 Duchesse de Gontaut, *Memoirs*; Francis Steuart, *Exiled Bourbons*, p. 247; Comtesse de Boigne, *Memoirs*, pp. 133–4.

14 J. Lucas-Dubreton, *Le Comte d'Artois, Charles X*, Paris, 1927, p. 69; Francis Steuart, *Exiled Bourbons*, p. 55 (29 August 1798).
15 A.J. Mackenzie Stuart, 'A Royal Debtor at Holyrood', *Stair Miscellany*, vol. I, 1971, pp. 193–201.
16 Comtesse de Boigne, *Memoirs*, p. 134.
17 Duchesse de Gontaut, *Memoirs*, p. 125; Francis Steuart, *Exiled Bourbons*, pp. 61ff. Monsieur was noted for that gift of Princes, kindness to their servants. One day when back in Paris he saw his former Edinburgh hairdresser in the street, who had come to France to study fashion; and stopping his carriage he called him over, talked to him kindly for some time, and invited him to call at the palace next morning, when he cordially asked after all those who had been generous to him in exile. (Mackenzie, *Anecdotes and Egotisms*, p. 223.)
18 *Private Correspondence of G. Leveson-Gower, 1781–1821*, 2 vols, London, 1916, vol. II, pp. 322–3 (Lady Bessborough to G. Leveson-Gower, 26 August 1808).
19 Louis Simond, *Journal of a Tour and Residence in Great Britain, during the years 1810 and 1811*, 1st edn, 2 vols, Edinburgh, 1815, vol. I, pp. 271–2.
20 Charles Nodier, *Promenade from Dieppe to the Mountains of Scotland*, translated from the French, Edinburgh & London, 1822, p. 85. A number of contemporaries mention the Bourbon sojourn at Holyrood, either at the time or on subsequent visits to the palace. See, e.g., The Hon. Mrs Sarah Murray, *A Companion and Useful Guide to the Beauties of Scotland and the Lakes*, 2 vols, p.p., 1799, vol. I, pp. 121–2.

Chapter 6: Interregnum

1 *A New History of the City of Edinburgh*, p. 47.
2 Sir Gilbert Elliot, *Life and Letters*, vol. III, pp. 235–6 (Lady Minto to Lord Minto, 21 February 1802).

PART II

Introduction

1 This was occasioned by Hope's statement in a debate that of the original Scottish law lords, 'The Lord High Chancellor is no longer in existence. The Lord Privy Seal exists merely for the purpose of appending the Seal of Scotland. The Lord Justice General is the mere nominal head of a Court at which he never presides. By a special Act of Parliament the Lord Justice Clerk can have no seat in the House, and is wholly confined to his own Court.' The whole duties of these departments therefore devolved upon the Lord Advocate. (*Parliamentary Debates* vol. II, p. 802, (1804); quoted in Fyfe, *Edinburgh Under Sir Walter Scott*, p. 171).
2 W.M. Gilbert, *Edinburgh in the 19th Century*, Edinburgh, 1901, under 1800, 1801, 1802.

Chapter 7: The Young Whigs and the Edinburgh Review

1 Jeffrey (1773–1850), who went to the High school in 1781 expecting a tartar, was surprised to find Luke Fraser 'a plump, jolly, heavy-looking man, rather foolish-like than otherwise'. He spent four years near the top of the class, tearful if he lost a place, 'a little, clever, anxious boy'. (Henry Cockburn, *Life of Lord Jeffrey*, 2 vols, Edinburgh, 1852, vol. I, p. 6.) In some respects the same adjectives would apply to the temperament which he suffered all his life.

2 Cockburn, *Life of Lord Jeffrey*, vol. I, p. 34.
3 Jeffrey to his brother, Dec. 1792, *Ibid.*, vol. I, p. 52.
4 Do. to Do., 4 Nov. 1793 and 1 June 1794, *Ibid.*, vol. I, pp. 58, 61.
5 Do. to Do., 3 Aug. 1800, *Ibid.*, vol. I, p. 116.
6 Alison, *Some Account*, vol. I, p. 34.
7 Horner, *Memoirs*, vol. I, pp. 5ff., 70ff.
8 *Wit and Wisdom of Sydney Smith*, pp. 463f.
9 Smith to Leonard Horner, in *Wit and Wisdom*, pp. 102, 463f.
10 M. Lyell, *Francis Horner and Leonard Horner*, Edinburgh, p.p., [1890s].
11 Francis Horner, Journal, 7 March 1802, in *Memoirs*, vol. I, p. 177; Lady Guendolen Ramsden, *Correspondence of Two Brothers: Edward Adolphus, 11th Duke of Somerset, and his Brother, Lord Webb Seymour . . .*, London, 1906, pp. 13–16.
12 Horner, Journal, 21 Feb. 1799, *Memoirs*, vol. I, p. 72.
13 Maria Stanley to her aunt Serena, Sept. 1800, *Early Married Life*, p. 203.
14 Lord Webb Seymour, Diary, 12 June 1800, *Correspondence of Two Brothers*, p. 18.
15 Sydney Smith to Michael Hicks-Beach, 30 June 1798, *Letters*, vol. I, p. 20.
16 Do. to Mrs Hicks-Beach, 15 July 1798, *Letters*, vol. I, pp. 21–22.
17 Do., letters to Mrs Hicks-Beach, Aug. 1798–March 1799, *Letters*, vol. I, pp. 22–38.
18 Do. to Do., May 1799–3 March 1800, *Letters*, vol. I, pp. 39–55.
19 Do. to Do., 5 Nov. 1800 and n.d., *Letters*, vol. I, pp. 62–3.
20 Do. to Francis Jeffrey [1 August 1801], *Letters*, vol. I, p. 65.
21 Do. to Mrs Beach, March 1802, 13 Dec. 1801, *Letters*, vol. I, pp. 68, 67. Alexander Gordon's father was grandfather to the mid-Victorian statesman, the 4th Earl.
22 Do. to Do., March 1802, *Letters*, vol. I, p. 68.
23 Do. to the Hon. Caroline Fox, sister of Lord Holland, 14 June 1802, *Letters*, vol. I, p. 69.
24 *Ibid., loc. cit.*, and to Mrs Beach, July 1802, *Letters*, vol. I, p. 70.
25 Do. to Hon. Caroline Fox, *loc. cit.*
26 Cockburn, *Life of Jeffrey*, vol. I, p. 125.
27 There are discrepancies over the occasion. Henry Brougham does not appear to have been there, but he describes the stormy night when 'Sydney Smith first announced to me [sic] his idea of establishing a critical periodical', adding the characteristic and revealing comment, 'I believe he had already mentioned this to Jeffrey and Horner'. At all events, according to Brougham that night was the first occasion of serious discussion by those three together. Brougham, *Life and Times*, p. 251.
28 Jeffrey to Robert Morehead, 24 May 1802, Cockburn, *Life of Jeffrey*, vol. II, p. 61.
29 Cockburn, *Life of Jeffrey*, vol. I, p. 120.
30 *Ibid.*, vol. I, p. 136.
31 Jeffrey to Horner, 9 April 1802, *Memoirs of Francis Horner*, vol. I. p. 186.
32 Cockburn, *Life of Jeffrey*, vol. I, p. 131. According to Brougham's calculation, noticeably generous to himself, in the first four issues, each of 26 or 27 articles, Smith wrote 18, Jeffrey 16, Horner 7 and Brougham himself 21. The eight original contributors soon increased to 11, who included Walter Scott, and after the twentieth issue increased again. In the first 20 issues, Jeffrey wrote 75, Smith 23, Horner 14 and Brougham (according to himself) 80. (Brougham, *Life and Times*, vol. I, p. 255.) The numbers have since been calculated slightly differently for the first issue, scoring Horner 3, Jeffrey 6, and including 4 by Brougham (*The Wellesley Index to Victorian Periodicals 1824–1900*, ed. Walter E. Houghton, University of Toronto Press, 1966, vol. I, pp. 430ff. For the first four issues the *Wellesley Index* gives Smith 20 or 22, Jeffrey 16 (one of them with Horner), Horner 13 and Brougham 20 or 19, based on his claim in *Brougham and his Early Friends.*
33 Cockburn, *Life of Jeffrey*, vol. I, p. 131.

34 Edward Lytton Bulwer, *England and the English*, 2 vols, London, 1833, vol. I, pp. 64–5.
35 Lockhart, *Life of Scott*, vol. II, pp. 198ff.; Fyfe, *Edinburgh Under Sir Walter Scott*, p. 181; Edgar Johnson, *Sir Walter Scott. The Great Unknown*, 2 vols, Hamish Hamilton, 1970, I.197.
36 Brougham to Loch, 20 Aug. 1802, *Brougham and his Early Friends*, vol. I, p. 344.
37 Horner, Journal, 20 Sept. 1802, *Memoirs of Francis Horner*, vol. I, p. 209.
38 Horner, Journal, 20 Nov. 1802, *Ibid.*, vol. I, p. 211.
39 Horner to James Loch, 24 Jan. 1803, *Ibid.*, vol. I, p. 221.
40 Jeffrey to Horner, 3 Sept. 1804, Cockburn, *Life of Jeffrey*, vol. II, pp. 91–2.
41 Alexander Murray to Archibald Constable, 15 March 1803, Thomas Constable, *Archibald Constable and his Literary Correspondents*, 3 vols, Edinburgh, 1873, vol. I, p. 229.
42 Thomas Thomson to Horner, 24 Dec. 1803, Cosmo Innes, *Memoir of Thomas Thomson*, Edinburgh, Bannatyne Club, 1854, p. 52. According to the *Wellesley Index to Victorian Periodicals*, the review of Bentham is attributed to Jeffrey (April 1804), while Thomson wrote on Dr A. Geddes (Jan. 1804).
43 Lady Stanley to her aunt Serena, 1804, *Early Married Life*, p. 268.
44 Brougham to Loch, 7 Nov. 1802, *Brougham and his Early Friends*, vol. I, p. 363.
45 Do. to Do., 28 Jan. 1803, *Ibid.*, vol. II, p. 32.
46 Cockburn, *Life of Jeffrey*, vol. I, p. 137.
47 Jeffrey to his brother John, 2 July 1803, *Ibid.*, vol. II, pp. 73–4. Alexander Hamilton (1762–1824), an orientalist, when a prisoner in France during the Napoleonic Wars compiled a catalogue of Sanskrit MSS for the Paris Library, and taught the language to Schlegel. He became Professor of Sanskrit and Hindu Literature at Haileybury. (*DNB*)
48 Jeffrey to Horner, 5 Jan. 1804, Cockburn, *Life of Jeffrey*, vol. II, p. 142.
49 Do. to Do., 19 Nov. 1804, *Memoirs of Francis Horner*, vol. I, p. 296.
50 Do. to Do., 20 Jan. 1805, Cockburn, *Life of Jeffrey*, vol. II, p. 96; Cockburn, *Life of Jeffrey*, vol. II, p. 163.
51 Jeffrey to his brother John, 2 July 1803, *Ibid.*, vol. II, p. 75.
52 *Ibid.*, vol. I, pp. 161–2.
53 *Life and Writings of the Rev. Robert Morehead, DD*, edited by his son, Charles Morehead, Edinburgh, 1875, p. 151n.
54 Jeffrey to John, 15 Aug. 1805, to Horner, 12 Oct., Cockburn, *Life of Jeffrey*, vol. I, pp. 164–8.

Chapter 8: The Second New Town

1 Much of the material in this chapter is based on Connie Byrom's paper in *The Book of the Old Edinburgh Club*: NS vol. 3, 1994, pp. 37–61, 'The Development of Edinburgh's Second New Town'. See also Youngson, *The Making of Classical Edinburgh*, pp. 206–7, etc.
2 Byrom, n.6.
3 Sibbald held this post until his death in 1809; he also designed a manse for St Cuthbert's in 1793, Lady Yester's Church in 1803, and Portobello Old and Windsor Place parish church in 1809. (Byrom, pp. 43–4.)
4 *Edinburgh Evening Courant*, 11 June 1800.
5 See Henry Cockburn, *Memorials*, pp. 151–2: '. . . the mere beauty of the town was no more thought of at that time by anybody than electric telegraphs and railways; and perpendicular trees never find favour in the sight of any Scotch mason . . . The axes, as usual, triumphed . . . the whole spot was made as bare and as dull as if the designer of the New Town himself had presided over the operation.'

6 Among the Elliot brothers' most famous commissions were Taymouth for the Earl of Breadalbane (1806–10) and Stobo in Peeblesshire, for Sir James Montgomery (1805–11).
7 See also *James Nasmyth, Engineer, An Autobiography*, ed. Samuel Smiles, London, 1883, pp. 42–3.
8 Byrom, p. 50.
9 George Winton, James Nisbet, Thomas Morison. Heriot Row and Abercromby Place were to be two storeys and basement (the many dormer windows now spoiling the line of the former were a later modification), rising to a maximum of 33 feet for the main row and 51 for the projecting end-houses. No houses in the cross streets must rise above their level, and houses on the lower parallels were similarly strictly limited in height. 'Storm windows' (attic dormers) or 'raised Breaks . . . in addition of French roofs' were allowed only in the main cross streets Dundas/Pitt and the minor Cumberland, Nelson, Jamaica and others.
10 The grander streets were to be of broached ashlar, or 'rock work' in the base storeys, the others of 'polished, droved or broached ashlar', with 15-inch blocking courses, with a maximum projection of 3 inches. All must have sunk front areas and good iron railings. Even pavement widths were dictated. Water closets were allowed, to project a maximum of 5 feet from the back wall and 6 feet above the 'parlour floor', and where ground was allotted for stables, only coach-houses and washing-houses must be built there. Sewers were to be planned and supervised by Sibbald, and built and maintained to the satisfaction of the Dean of Guild.
11 The City's bankruptcy in the 1830s further allowed slowed completion, and parts of the east end of Royal Crescent and north end of Bellevue Crescent were not finished until as late as the 1880s, Edinburgh by then having a surfeit of housing, and newer areas like the Moray estate having become more fashionable.
12 John Gerrard, Colin McWilliam, David Walker, *The Buildings of Scotland: Edinburgh*, London, Penguin Books, 1984, p. 335.
13 Byrom, p. 55.
14 William Park, 'Extracts from the Journal of Jessy Allan, wife of John Harden, 1801–11, in *The Book of the Old Edinburgh Club*, vol. XXX, Edinburgh, 1959, p. 83 (summer 1803).
15 Andrew Clephane to James Loch, 14 March 1803, *Brougham and his Early Friends*, vol. II, p. 50.

Chapter 9: A Mecca for Visitors

1 Andrew Clephane to Loch, 14 March 1803, *Brougham and his Early Friends*, vol. II, pp. 49–50.
2 Elizabeth Grant of Rothiemurchus, *Memoirs of a Highland Lady*, vol. I, ch.1. Her father, [Sir] John Peter Grant, a Speyside landowner, gifted but unpractical, was later to practise in Edinburgh as an advocate and to sit at Westminster as an MP.
In 1903 5 Charlotte Square was acquired by the Marquess of Bute, and is now owned by the National Trust for Scotland.
3 *Edinburgh Review*, No.1, October 1802.
4 S.T. Coleridge to Robert Southey, 13 Sept. 1803, *Collected Letters of Samuel Taylor Coleridge*, ed. Earl Leslie Griggs, 6 vols, Oxford, 1956–71, vol. II, pp. 98–9; William Wordsworth to Southey, 16 Oct. 1803, *The Letters of William and Dorothy Wordsworth*, ed. Ernest de Selincourt, 2nd edn, revised by Charles L. Shaver, Oxford, 1967, vol. I, pp. 414, 413.
5 Dorothy Wordsworth to Lady Beaumont, 4 May 1803, *Ibid.*, vol. I, p. 561.
6 Dorothy Wordsworth, *Recollections of a Tour made in Scotland in 1803*, Edinburgh, 1894, pp. 244–5.

7 Coleridge to Southey, 13 Sept. 1803, *loc. cit.*
8 *Edinburgh Review*, April 1803.
9 Cockburn, *Life of Jeffrey*, vol. I, pp. 154–5.
10 John Thelwall, *A Letter to Francis Jeffrey, Esq., on certain calumnies . . . in the Edinburgh Review*, Edinburgh, 1804; and *Mr Thelwall's Replies to the Calumnies . . .*, Glasgow, 1804.
11 Wordsworth to Thelwall, Jan. 1804, *Wordsworth Letters*, vol. I, p. 431n.
12 Do. to Do., *loc. cit.*, vol. I, pp. 432–3.
13 Southey to Coleridge, 14 March 1803, *The Life and Correspondence of the late Robert Southey*, ed. by his son the Rev. Charles Cuthbert Southey, 6 vols, London, 1849–50, vol. II, p. 203.
14 Southey to Williams Wynn MP, 20 Oct. 1805, *Selections from the Letters of Robert Southey*, ed. by his son-in-law John Wood Warter, 4 vols, London, 1896, vol. I, pp. 341–2.
15 *Ibid., loc. cit.*
16 *Ibid.*; Southey to John Rickman, 27 Oct. 1805, *New Letters of Robert Southey*, ed. Kenneth Curry, 2 vols, Columbia UP, 1965, vol. I, p. 406; to Charles Danvers, 7 Nov. 1805, *Selections from Letters*, vol. I, p. 345–6.
17 Southey to Danvers, *Selections from Letters, loc. cit.*
18 Do. to Do., 25 May 1807, *New Letters*, vol. I, p. 452.
19 Do. to Richard Duppa, 22 Nov. 1805, *Ibid.*, vol. I, p. 408.
20 Do. to James Grahame, 4 Jan. 1808, *Ibid.*, vol. I, p. 469.
21 Do. to Walter Scott, 8 Dec. 1807, *Life and Correspondence of Southey*, vol. III, pp. 124–5.
22 *Life and Letters of Thomas Campbell*, vol. I, p. 364.
23 Gibbon, *Life of George Combe*, vol. I, p. 54.
24 *Life of Thomas Campbell*, vol. I, pp. 375, 381.
25 *Ibid.*, vol. I, p. 392.
26 *Ibid.*, vol.II, p. 85n.
27 *Ibid.*, vol. I, p. 405n.
28 *Ibid.*, vol. I, p. 433. George Ellis (1753–1815), FRS, RSA, prolific author and poet, travelled with Lord and Lady Malmesbury, knew Pitt and Canning and founded the *Anti-Jacobin*. Scott addressed the 5th Canto of *Marmion* to him, and on visits to London used to stay with him at Sunninghill, Ascot. In May 1811 Ellis reviewed *The Lady of the Lake* in the *Quarterly*. He married the daughter of Admiral Sir Peter Parker, but died without issue. (*DNB*)

Thomas Young (1773–1829), a brilliant physicist, Egyptologist and master of ancient and modern languages, born to a Somerset Quaker family, early showed his gifts when at 14 he became a tutor in the Gurney family. He studied medicine in London and from 1794 at Edinburgh, under Gregory, Andrew Duncan and Joseph Black. In 1795, touring the Highlands, he visited the Dukes of Argyll and Gordon. After further study in Germany and at Cambridge, he practised as a physician and lectured widely in London, from 1801–3 was Professor of Natural Philosophy at the Royal Institution and from 1802 Secretary of the Royal Society. Among various posts he was distinguished for his work and publications on optics. (*DNB*)

29 *Life of Thomas Campbell*, vol. I, pp. 437–8, vol. II, pp. 15, 68.
30 *Memoirs of Horner*, vol. I, p. 368.
31 Horner went to Italy for his health, but died in Pisa on 8 February 1817. He had a distinguished parliamentary career, serving later as MP for Wendover and then St Mawes; was chairman of the Bullion Committee (1810), when he recommended resumption of cash payments, again advocating it in 1816; and spoke energetically in Corn Laws debates and against slavery. He also published certain works. He never married.

32 Dr Thomas Percival to William Wilberforce, 24 June 1803, *The Correspondence of William Wilberforce*, ed. R.I. Wilberforce and Samuel Wilberforce, 2 vols, London, 1840, vol. I, pp. 267–8.
33 William Wilberforce to William Pitt, 25 Oct. 1805, *Correspondence*, vol. II, p. 51.
34 Mary Gordon, *'Christopher North'. A Memoir of John Wilson*, 2 vols, Edinburgh, 1862, vol. I, pp. 29f.
35 *Ibid.*, vol. I, pp. 28–34, 40ff.
36 *Ibid.*, vol. I, pp. 70f.; John Kay, *A Series of Original Prints and Caricature Etchings*, new edn, 2 vols, Edinburgh, 1877, no. XLIV.
37 *Ibid.*, Kay, *Portraits*, vol. I, no. XLIV.
38 *Christopher North*, vol. I, p. 161.
39 Dorothy Wordsworth to Lady Beaumont, 28 Dec. 1809, *Wordsworth Letters*, vol. II, pp. 178–9.
40 The Edgeworth family also met Davy in Clifton, where Maria Edgeworth's sister Frances was married to Davy's chief, Dr Beddoes, and where the first of her six children was born. Dr Beddoes unfortunately died in 1808. (Augustus J.C. Hare, *The Life and Letters of Maria Edgeworth*, 2 vols, London, 1894, vol. I, p. 141.)
41 Elliot, *Life and Letters*, vol. III, p. 237; Horner, Journal, *Memoirs*, 31 March 1802, vol. II, p. 182.
42 *The Autobiography & Journals of Benjamin Robert Haydon*, ed. Malcolm Elwin, London, 1950, p. 50.
43 *The Collected Writings of Thomas De Quincey*, new and enlarged edition, ed. David Masson, Edinburgh, 1890 (14 vols), vol. III, pp. 13, 14.
44 [Sir] James Hall to Dr Marcet, 25 July 1804, NLS MS 3813/39/40. Phillips later published *Elementary Introduction to the Knowledge of Mineralogy* (1816) and, with William Conybeare, *Outlines of the Geology of England and Wales* (1822). He was the elder brother of Richard Phillips (1778–1851), the chemist who also worked on mineralogy and was to become President of the Chemical Society (1849–50). (*DNB*)
45 Do. to Do., 18 March and 14 May 1805, *Ibid.*, pp. 45–6. NLS 3813/43 & 4; to Dr Marcet, 25 July and 18 Sept. 1804; NLS 3813/39/40. William Cary (1759–1825), philosopher, was an instrument maker from 1790. (*DNB*)
46 Hall's sons were Basil, the noted traveller and author, and James, a gifted amateur painter and friend of David Wilkie, who exhibited Scottish landscapes at the Royal Academy. (*DNB*)
47 Lady Stanley to Louisa, 22 May and 6 June 1809, *Early Married Life*, p. 317.
48 Brian Connell, *Portrait of a Whig Peer*, London, 1957, p. 426.
49 *The Letters of the Third Viscount Palmerston to Laurence and Elizabeth Sulivan, 1804–1863*, ed. Kenneth Bourne, Camden 4th Ser., vol. 23, London, Royal Hist. Soc. 1979, pp. 5ff.
50 Southey. New *Letters*, vol. I, pp. 342,369,372.
51 Elliot, *Life and Letters*, vol. III, pp. 230ff.
52 Gotch, *Maria, Lady Callcott*, p. 80.
53 Lord Minto to Lady Palmerston, 10 Jan. 1802, Elliot, *Life and Letters*, vol. III, p. 234; Lady Minto to Lord Minto, vol. III, p. 231.
54 Lady Minto to Lord Minto, 2 April 1802, *Ibid.*, vol. III. p. 245.
55 *Life of Thomas Campbell*, vol. I, pp. 396f.
56 Thomas Campbell to Dr Currie, 4 Sept. 1802, *Ibid.*, vol. I, pp. 453–4.
57 A. Campbell, *A Journey from Edinburgh*, vol. II, pp. 250f.
58 *Ibid.*, vol. II, p. 254.
59 Rev. James Hall, *Travels in Scotland, by an Unusual Route . . .*, 2 vols, London, 1807, vol. II, p. 580.
50 Simond, *Journal of a Tour*, vol. I, p. 374.

Chapter 10: Political and Social Change

1 Elliot, *Life and Letters*, Lady Minto to Lord Minto, 30 May 1806, vol. III, p. 383.
2 Do. to Do., 22 June 1806, *Ibid.*, vol. III, p. 385.
3 Do. to Do., 6 July, Dugald Stewart to Lady Minto, [?28 June] 1806, *Ibid.*, vol. III, p. 386. Lockhart strongly denies any suggestion that Scott himself sang the song, which he claims was sung by James Ballantyne (Lockhart, *Life of Scott*, vol. I, p. 187n.)
4 Lady Minto to Lord Minto, 5 June, 6 July 1806, *Ibid.*, vol. III, pp. 384, 386.
5 Mitchison, *History of Scotland*, p. 366.
6 Hare, *Maria Edgeworth*, Maria Edgeworth to her aunt Mrs Richard Ruxton, 30 March 1803, vol. I, pp. 135–6.
7 *Memoirs of the late Mrs Elizabeth Hamilton*, by Miss Benger, 2 vols, London, 1818, vol. I, pp. 21ff., 110, 151ff.
8 Elizabeth Hamilton to a young friend, 1803, *Ibid.*, vol. I, p. 163.
9 *Ibid.*, vol. I, pp. 174, 176.
10 Hector McNeill (1746–1818), poet, born near Roslin, then living and educated in Stirlingshire. His life was punctuated by time in the West Indies and service at sea and in India. About 1776 he inherited his father's small estate, later married and settled near Stirling, where though he had written poems since boyhood he did not yet succeed as a writer and spent time in Jamaica, which he again visited when his health failed after a spell of writing productively in Scotland. Again home with health restored, he became well known as a poet in Edinburgh. In 1801 he published two books of poems, with later editions, and is remembered chiefly for his Scottish songs and ballads. His portrait was painted by Mrs Grant's protégé John Henning.
11 *Memoirs of Mrs Hamilton*, vol. I, pp. 163ff.
12 R.P. Gillies, *Recollections of Sir Walter Scott*, London, 1837, pp. 157f. The 'stout coachman' was Peter Mathieson.
13 Sir John Carr, *Caledonian Sketches, or A Tour through Scotland in 1807*, London, 1809, pp. 203–4. Carr (1772–1832), a barrister, knighted in 1806, travelled extensively in Europe and published his experiences.
14 Jeffrey to Horner, 15 June 1803, Cockburn, *Life of Jeffrey*, vol. I, p. 147.
15 Do. to Do., 8 Aug. 1803, *Ibid.*, vol. I, pp. 148–50.
16 Harold William Thompson, *A Scottish Man of Feeling*, Oxford, 1931, p. 379.
17 Cockburn, *Life of Jeffrey*, vol. I, pp. 150–2.
18 Carr, *Caledonian Sketches*, p. 196; A. Campbell, *A Journey from Edinburgh*, vol. II, p. 181.
19 *The Memoirs of Susan Sibbald (1783–1812)*, edited by her great-grandson Francis Paget Hett, London, 1926, pp. 210–11.
20 Rev. James Hall, *Travels in Scotland*, vol. II, pp. 603, 605.
21 Sibbald, *Memoirs*, p. 205.
22 *Memoirs and Correspondence of Susan Ferrier, 1782–1854*, ed. John A. Doyle, London, 1929, Susan Ferrier to her sister Mrs [Janet] Connell, 17 Jan. 1802, p. 36.
23 Sibbald, *Memoirs*, p. 170.
24 *Ibid.*, pp. 111–2; Joseph Mawman, *An Excursion to the Highlands of Scotland and the English Lakes*, London, 1805, p. 93.
25 Sibbald, *Memoirs*, pp. 111–2, 125–6, 132. In 1807 at the age of twenty-four, Susan Mein married the considerably older Colonel Sibbald, had eleven children, and eventually settled in Canada.
26 *Ibid.*, pp. 206–7. *The Scots Peerage*, ed. Sir Balfour Paul, vol. VIII. Miss Jackie Gordon, a fairly meddlesome lady, in the summer of 1808 brought a case against a peruke-maker in the Small Debt Court, claiming that he had made her a wig deficient in hair; she won the case. Her matrimonial case she took to the English

courts and won that. 'So do you keep out of her way,' Alexander Robertson warned his friend Charles Kirkpatrick Sharpe, 'and never let her catch you at the golf-house.' (*Letters from and to C.K. Sharpe*, vol. I, pp. 369, 473.)

27 Rev. James Hall, *Travels in Scotland*, vol. II, pp. 583–5.

28 *Correspondence of Sarah Spencer, Lady Lyttelton, 1787–1879,* ed. by her great-granddaughter Mrs Hugh Wyndham, London, 1912, pp. 67–8. Sir Arscott Ouvry Molesworth, 7th Baronet, 1789–1823, married Mary, daughter of Patrick Brown, on 7 July 1809, and they had two sons, of whom the elder, William (1810–55), became the 8th Baronet, and two daughters. Lady Molesworth long outlived her husband and died only in 1871.

29 Elizabeth Grant, *Highland Lady*, vol. II, pp. 41–2.

30 Carr, *Caledonian Sketches*, p. 203.

31 Sibbald, *Memoirs*, pp. 207ff. After Cunningham's death, Burns's widow presented the punch-bowl to Archibald Hastie, who in 1858 bequeathed it to the British Museum, where it is now displayed in Gallery 47, Case 7 (Medieval and later Antiquities, Accn no. 1858, 4–12, 1).

32 Gotch, *Maria, Lady Callcott*, pp. 71ff.

33 *Ibid.*, pp. 74–76, 84–86. In 1809 Maria Dundas went to India with her father, sister and a mentally retarded brother; here she became betrothed to Captain Thomas Graham, RN, was married to him for some years, and after his death married Sir Augustus Callcot), living mostly abroad. As Mrs Graham she had great success with her improving work which earned an almost notorious fame, *Little Arthur's History of England* (1835). She had several children, and died in 1842, having dictated a remarkably frank autobiography of her early years.

35 Carr, *Caledonian Sketches*, pp. 200, 202.

36 *Autobiography of Mrs Fletcher*, pp. 102–3.

37 Rev. R. Morehead, Journal, 12 Jan. 1811, *Life and Writings*, p. 150; Carr, *Caledonian Sketches*, p. 204.

38 James Hogg, *The Spy*, Edinburgh, 1810–11, no. XV, 8 Dec. 1810.

39 Mrs Dunlop to her son John, 23 Oct. 1800, *The Dunlop Papers*, vol. III, *Letters and Journals*, ed. J.G. Dunlop, p.p., Frome/London, 1953, p. 123.

40 Simond, *Journal of a Tour*, 18 Aug. 1810, vol. I, p. 274.

41 *Ibid.*

42 Carr, *Caledonian Sketches*, p. 118.

43 Simond, *Journal of a Tour*, vol. I, p. 269.

44 Carr, *Caledonian Sketches*, pp. 119, 116.

45 Sibbald, *Memoirs*, p. 226.

46 Helen Graham, Diary, 25 March 1825, *Parties and Pleasures*, p. 128.

47 John James Audubon, Journal, 4 March 1827, *The Life and Adventures of J.J. Audubon, the Naturalist*, ed. Robert Buchanan, London, 1869 (2nd edn).

48 Lady Georgina Peel, *Recollections*, London, 1920, pp. 149–50.

49 Carr, *Caledonian Sketches*, p. 168.

50 [James Livingston], *Some Edinburgh Shops*, Edinburgh, 1894, pp. 33–37.

51 Charles Kirkpatrick Sharpe to his mother, 14 June 1808, *Letters*, vol. I, p. 339.

52 Livingston, *Some Edinburgh Shops*, *loc. cit.*

53 Carr, *Caledonian Sketches*, p. 169.

54 Hall, *Travels in Scotland*, vol. I, p. 581; Simond, *Journal of a Tour*, vol. II, p. 51.

55 *Svedenstierna's Tour, Great Britain, 1802–3*. The Travel Diary of an Industrial Spy, trans. E.L. Dellow; David & Charles, 1973, pp. 124f.

56 Mawman, *An Excursion to the Highlands*, p. 96.

57 A. Campbell, *A Journey from Edinburgh*, vol. II, pp. 204–5.

58 Carr, *Caledonian Sketches*, pp. 108–9.

59 *Edinburgh in the 19th Century*, entry for 1801.

60 Simond, *Journal of a Tour*, vol. I, p. 269.

61 *Ibid.*, vol. I, p. 268; *Statistical Account of Scotland, 1791–1799*, ed. Sir John Sinclair, vol. II, p. 33.
62 Carr, *Caledonian Sketches*, pp. 115–6.
63 Simond, *Journal of a Tour* (20 Feb. 1811) vol. II, p. 62.

Chapter 11: A City in a Landscape

1 Coleridge to Southey, 13 Sept. 1803, *Collected Letters*, vol. II, p. 989.
2 E. Grant, *Memoirs of a Highland Lady*, vol. I, p. 23. The gardens referred to would be Queen Street. Blackwood's Hotel was at the Princes Street corner of North Bridge.
3 Simond, *Journal of a Tour*, vol. I, p. 267.
4 A. Campbell, *A Journey from Edinburgh*, vol. II, pp. 192–3; Watt, *Book of Edinburgh Anecdote*, pp. 257, 269. Francis Garden, advocate, 1744, Sheriff of Kincardineshire 1748, joint Solicitor-General 1760, in 1765 was employed in the Douglas Cause; he was a Lord of Session as Lord Gardenstone 1764 until his death, and Lord of Justiciary 1776–87. He published writings on his travels, and was the founder of Laurencekirk in Kincardineshire.
5 A. Campbell, *A Journey from Edinburgh*, vol. II, p. 205.
6 Hall, *Travels in Scotland*, vol. I, p. 580.
7 A. Campbell, *A Journey from Edinburgh*, vol. I, pp. 4–5; Dr Margaret Wood, 'Survey of the Development of Edinburgh', *Old Edinburgh Club*, vol. XXXIV, p. 42 (1974).
8 A. Campbell, *A Journey from Edinburgh*, vol. II, pp. 115–6.
9 Stark, *Picture of Edinburgh*, pp. 86–9.
10 J. Mawman, *An Excursion to the Highlands*, p. 104.
11 *Svedenstierna's Tour*, pp. 121–3.
12 Carr, *Caledonian Sketches*, pp. 56, 78.
13 A. Campbell, *A Journey from Edinburgh*, vol. II, pp. 190–1.
14 Simond, *Journal of a Tour*, vol. I, p. 267.
15 A. Campbell, *A Journey from Edinburgh*, vol. I, pp. 3–4, vol. II, pp. 222n.; Stark, *Picture of Edinburgh*, p. 72.
16 *Ibid.*, p. 181; Carr, *Caledonian Sketches*, p. 77.
17 Simond, *Journal of a Tour*, vol. I, p. 269.

Chapter 12: Literary Revenges

1 Thomas Moore (1779–1852), with a grounding at Trinity College, Dublin, and the Middle Temple, took to writing poetry in his twenties as a prolific composer of ballads and verses, many of them popular in drawing-rooms. His many publications and collections included *Poems by the late Thomas Little* (1801), and *Odes and Epistles* (1806). He also published lampoons. He had earlier held a government office in Bermuda, after which he had temporarily to take to the Continent to avoid prosecution for his deputy's debts. He later became a friend of Byron and Leigh Hunt; he was entrusted by Byron with his memoirs, which he unfortunately destroyed, partially compensating in 1830 by writing Byron's biography. In later years Moore survived on two government pensions.
2 *The Letters of Thomas Moore*, ed. Wilfred S. Dowden, 2 vols, Oxford, 1964, vol. I, p. 102n.; *Edinburgh Review*, July 1806.
3 *Memoirs, Journal, and Correspondence of Thomas Moore*, ed. Lord John Russell, 8 vols, London, 1851, vol. I, pp. 199f.
4 *Reminiscences and Table Talk of Samuel Rogers*, ed. C.H. Powell, London, 1903, pp. 219–21.

5 *Letters of Thomas Moore*, *loc. cit.*
6 Rogers, *loc. cit.*
7 The full account of the non-duel is in *Memoirs, Journal* etc. of Moore, vol. I, pp. 199f. George Murray, Lord Fincastle, in 1809 succeeded his father as 5th Earl of Dunmore.
8 Rogers, *loc. cit.*
9 Moore, *Memoirs, Journal* etc., *loc. cit.*
10 Lord Byron, *English Bards and Scotch Reviewers*, London, [1809], p. 25.
11 Moore to Byron, 1 Jan. 1810, Moore, *Letters*, vol. I, pp. 134–5.
12 Byron to Moore, 27 Oct. 1811, *Ibid.*, vol. I, pp. 161ff.; *Byron's Letters and Journals*, ed. Leslie A. Marquand, 11 vols, John Murray, 1973ff, vol. II, pp. 118ff.

Chapter 13: The Literary Scene

1 Mrs Anne Grant (1755–1838), daughter of Duncan McVicar of Craignish, who was appointed Barrack-Master of Fort Augustus in 1773, already showed a talent for observation and criticism during a visit that year with her parents to Inveraray. She married the minister of Laggan, Inverness-shire, lived for some time in America and, in her long widowhood with a large family, made a name as authoress with *Letters from the Mountains* (1806), incorporating her Inveraray letters, *Memoirs of an American Lady* (1808) and, after her removal from Stirlingshire to Edinburgh, *Essays on the Superstitions of the Highlands* (1811). She was honoured and befriended by all the celebrities, was granted a Government pension in recognition of her works, and her voluminous literary correspondence was later edited and published by her one surviving son, John Peter Grant (1844).
2 George Paston [Emily Morse Symonds], *Little Memoirs of the 18th Century*, 1906, p. 285; *Dublin University Magazine*, pp. 37, 529.
3 *Memoirs of Mrs Elizabeth Hamilton*, Elizabeth Hamilton to Miss J— B—, 21 June 1809, vol. I, pp. 91–94. The recipient was perhaps the daughter of her sister, Mrs Blake.
4 Do. to Dr H[amilton?], 12 Dec. 1811, *Ibid.*, vol. I, p. 145.
5 Hare, *Life of Maria Edgeworth*, vol. I, p. 165.
6 Maria Edgeworth to Mrs Ruxton, Feb. 1809 and 9 Aug. 1813, *Ibid.*, vol. I, pp. 165, 218–9.
7 Charles K. Sharpe to his mother, 14 June 1808, *Letters*, vol. I, p. 341.
8 Elizabeth Hamilton to Miss J— B—, 9 July 1814, *Memoirs of Mrs Elizabeth Hamilton*, vol. I, pp. 178–81.
9 Do. to Do., *Ibid.*, 2 Oct. 1815, *Ibid.*, vol. I, pp. 187–8.
10 Sharpe to his mother, 23 [July 1803], *Letters*, vol. I, pp. 177–8.
11 Do. to R.H. Inglis, 17 May 1805, *Ibid.*, vol. I, p. 228.
12 Scott to Sharpe, [Jan.] 1808, *Ibid.*, vol. I, p. 321.
13 Do. to Do., 30 Dec. 1808, *Ibid.*, vol. I, p. 350.
14 *Scotsman*, March 1851. See also *Gentleman's Magazine*, May 1857, pp. 557–9.
15 *Scotsman*, quoted in Sharpe *Letters* (Memoir by Rev. W.K.R. Bedford), vol. I, pp. 65f.
16 *Life and Letters of Thomas Campbell*, vol. II, p. 158.
17 *Ibid.*, vol. I, p. 243.
18 Thomas Constable, *Archibald Constable and his Literary Correspondents*, 2 vols, Edinburgh, 1873, vol. I, p. 219.
19 *Ibid.*, vol. II, p. 171–80.
20 James Hogg, *Familiar Anecdotes of Sir Walter Scott*, ed. Douglas S, Mack, Edinburgh, Scottish Academic Press, 1972, p. 109.

Chapter 14: The Law and the Offices

1 Thomas Carlyle, *Reminiscences*, ed. J.A. Froude, 2 vols, London, 1881, vol. II, pp. 3–5.
2 Lockhart, *Life of Scott*, vol. II, pp. 274–5.
3 R.P. Gillies, *Recollections of Scott*, pp. 157f. Sir Brooke Boothby (1744–1824), baronet, was a poet and author of works on political matters. He was a friend of the Edgeworths.
4 This was Hope's sole speech in Parliament, when MP for Edinburgh (1804), in a debate on his censure of a Banffshire farmer who dismissed his servant for becoming a volunteer.
5 Brougham, *Life and Times*, vol. I, pp. 229f.
6 Thomas Erskine (1750–1823) was the counsel who obtained a Not Guilty verdict for Lord George Gordon in 1781, and in 1792 defended Thomas Paine, for which he lost his office of Attorney General to the Prince of Wales. He secured the acquittal of a number of defendants prosecuted for conspiracy or treason by the Government (1793–94), opposed the Seditious Meetings Bill (1795), in 1802 supported the Peace of Amiens, and presided at Lord Melville's trial in 1806. He was a close friend of Sheridan and Fox. (*DNB*)
7 Thomas Thomson (1768–1852) took his MA at Glasgow in 1789 and was admitted advocate in 1793. He was to contribute to the *Edinburgh Review* and occasionally acted as its editor. In 1832 he became President of the Bannatyne Club on Scott's death. He lost the Deputy Clerk Registership in 1839 because his expenditure was disapproved. This account of his career is based on Cosmo Innes, *Memoir of Thomas Thomson, Advocate*, Edinburgh, Bannatyne Club, 1854.
8 Sylvester Douglas (1743–1823), educated at Aberdeen and Leyden universities, became a barrister of Lincoln's Inn (1776), held various parliamentary seats for Ireland and England, and was a Privy Councillor of both countries; created Baron Glenbervie, an Irish peerage, in 1800. From 1797 to 1800 he was First Lord of the Treasury and subsequently held other offices.
9 Francis Horner to J.A. Murray, 13 Nov. 1804, *Memoirs of Thomson*, pp. 60–62.
10 *Ibid.*, p. 94n.
11 After one more in 1821, the reports were discontinued.
12 Frederick Sylvester, Lord Glenbervie's son (1791–1819), took an MA at Christ Church, Oxford (1813), was MP for Banbury 1812 and 1818, and became an author.
13 Lord Glenbervie to Thomas Thomson, 15 Nov. 1809, *Memoirs of Thomson*, p. 125.
14 Do. to Do., 7 Jan. 1810, *Ibid.*, p. 126.

Chapter 15: Schools, Students and Apprentices

1 The Christison family was of Scandinavian descent. Robert senior, Professor of Humanity from 1806, had formerly taught at the High School, where Henry Cockburn recalled his severity – possibly evoked by Cockburn's own indolence. Robert junior (1797–1882), one of twin sons, served as house physician to Edinburgh Infirmary from 1817–20, qualifying as MD in 1819; studied under Dr John Abernethy in London, and in 1820–21 in Paris. Appointed Professor of Medical Jurisprudence in 1822, he served for more than 50 years until 1877; in 1827 physician to the Infirmary; published a *Treatise on Poisons* (1829); medical adviser to the Crown (1829–66). In 1871 he was created a baronet. His *Life* was edited by his sons in two volumes (1886).
2 Dr Andrew Mylne later became minister of Dollar, and Principal of the Dollar Institution, which he was instrumental in founding.
3 *Life of Sir Robert Christison*, vol. I, pp. 15–16, 19.
4 *Ibid.*, vol. I, pp. 33–4.

5 Lytton Bulwer, *England and the English*, vol. I, pp. 276–7n.
6 George Combe, *The Life and Correspondence of Andrew Combe*, MD, Edinburgh, 1850, p. 12.
7 Charles Gibbon, *Life of George Combe*, vol. I, pp. 59–63.
8 *Ibid.*, pp. 64, 65–8.
9 *Life of Andrew Combe*, pp. 22–24.
10 *Ibid.*, p. 16.
11 *Ibid.*, pp. 25f.
12 *Ibid.*, pp. 24, 33f.
13 R.P. Gillies, *Memoirs of a Literary Veteran*, 3 vols, London, 1851, vol. I, pp. 195f.
14 *Ibid.*, vol. I, pp. 210f.
15 *Ibid.*, p. 212.
16 *Ibid.*, p. 216.
17 Henry Tytler (1752–1808) and his brother James (?1747–1805) were both physicians. Henry translated classics; James was a prolific writer, including much of two editions of the *Encyclopaedia Britannica*, but was often in debt and eventually had to flee to America.
18 Gillies, *Literary Veteran*, vol. I, pp. 232–3.
19 Gillies, vol. I, pp. 235f. Black later entered the church and became minister of Coylton in Ayrshire, when his writing turned to theology, though his *Life of Tasso* had brought him some fame, at least in England.
20 Gillies, vol. I, p. 255.
21 Gillies, vol. I, p. 290.
22 Gillies, vol. I, pp. 286–87.
23 [Sir] Henry Holland (1788–1873), a distinguished physician, born in Cheshire and educated at Newcastle upon Tyne and Bristol, first opted for a mercantile career and was articled in Liverpool, with two terms at Glasgow University. Finding it a wrong choice he was released to study medicine, at Edinburgh (1806–11), then in London at Guy's and St Thomas's Hospitals.
24 Maria Edgeworth to Mrs Ruxton, Jan. 1810, *Life of Maria Edgeworth*, vol. I, p. 169.
25 Gillies, *Literary Veteran*, vol. I, p. 288.
26 Simond, *Journal of a Tour*, vol. I, p. 377.
27 Gillies, *Literary Veteran*, vol. I, p. 333.
28 Alexander Murray to Cadell, 10 July 1812, *Constable and his Literary Correspondents*, vol. I, p. 326.
29 Sir Archibald Alison, *Some Account*, vol. I, pp. 37–8. Borthwick later died in a shooting accident.
30 *Ibid.*, vol. I, pp. 40–41.
31 *Ibid.*, vol. I, p. 55.
32 Anne Hogg, the unmarried daughter of Thomas Hogg, was a lady of great literary learning.
33 Benjamin Rush to his son James, 19 March 1810, *Letters of Benjamin Rush*, vol. II, p. 1038.
34 Do. to Do., 1 May 1810, *Ibid.*, vol. II, p. 1043.
35 Do. to John Adams, 8 Sept. 1810, *Ibid.*, vol. II, p. 1061; to his son James, 4 Oct. 1810, vol. II, p. 1069.
36 Do. to Trustees of the University of Pennsylvania, 30 Jan. and 1 March 1813, *Ibid.*, vol. II, pp. 1180–85.

Chapter 16: The Church and Churchmen

1 Stark, *Picture of Edinburgh*, p. 417.
2 *Ibid.*, p. 416; A. Campbell, *A Journey from Edinburgh*, vol. II, pp. 205–6.

3 Lindsay, *Georgian Edinburgh*, p. 34.
4 Youngson, *Classical Edinburgh*, pp. 189–90; David Maclagan, *St George's Church Edinburgh*, London, 1876.
5 Maclagan, *loc. cit.*
6 Mrs Grant to Mrs Brown, 21 May 1810, *Memoirs*, vol. I, pp. 258–9.
7 Rev. J. Hall, *Travels in Scotland*, vol. II, pp. 595–6.
8 *DNB*. Cockburn to John Richardson, n.d. [1806], *Letters of Lord Cockburn*, p. 9. The Tabernacle, later converted to a shop, became (says Cockburn) 'a familiar eyesore'. It was finally succeeded by a cinema.
9 *Memoirs of Thomas Chalmers*, vol. I, p. 103f.
10 Gillies, *Memoirs*, vol. I, pp. 219–20.
11 *Memoirs of Chalmers*, vol. I, p. 132, pp. 140–41.
12 David Brewster (1781–1868) studied philosophy at Edinburgh and from 1802 edited the *Edinburgh Magazine*, subsequently restyled *Edinburgh Philosophical Journal* and the *Edinburgh Journal of Science*. Although licensed as a preacher he turned instead to law and other subjects at St Andrews and Cambridge. From 1807 he was editor of the *Edinburgh Encyclopaedia*, was elected FRS and awarded several medals, invented the kaleidoscope (1816), was appointed first Director of the Royal Scottish Society of Arts (1821) and was knighted in 1832. Among later distinguished appointments he was principal of the colleges of St Salvator and St Leonard at St Andrews (1838), Vice-Chancellor of Edinburgh University (1860) and President of the Royal Society of Edinburgh (1864). He was a promoter of the British Association for Advancement of Science (1831) and of the Scottish Free Church movement (1844).
13 Thomas Thomson (1773–1852) contributed to the *Encyclopaedia Britannica*, published a *System of Chemistry* (1802), visited Sweden and published his travels (1812), and became Regius Professor of Chemistry at Glasgow (1817), later publishing numerous works. His son, also Thomas (1817–78), held important offices in India and was made an FRS in 1855, when he published *Flora Indica*.
14 *Memoirs of Chalmers*, vol. I, pp. 298, 328, 448.
15 *Dictionary of American Biography*, vol. IX, New York, 1935 (renewed 1964). Silliman (1778–1864), on his return to the USA, was to initiate public lectures at New Haven (1808) and elsewhere, was instrumental in launching Yale Medical School (1813), and became a celebrated public speaker. In 1838–40 he gave the first, famous geology and chemistry lectures at the Lowell Institute, which he had opened in 1838; in 1847 with his son-in-law he set up the college's Department of Philosophy and the Arts, and in 1848 was founder, proprietor and first editor of the *American Journal of Science and the Arts*. His extensive writings included *Elements of Chemistry* (1830–31). In 1853, after nearly fifty-four years with the college, he retired as professor emeritus. He was a gifted teacher, and carried out scientific experiments and investigation.
16 Benjamin Silliman, *A Journal of Travels in England, Holland and Scotland . . . in the Years 1805 and 1806*, 3rd edn (enlarged), 3 vols, New Haven, 1820, vol. III, p. 194 (5 Dec. 1805), p. 269 (25 April 1806).
17 *Ibid.*, vol. III, pp. 226, 228 (12 Jan. 1806).
18 Simond, *Journal of a Tour*, vol. II, pp. 56–57; Silliman, *Journal of Travels*, vol. III, p. 253.

Chapter 17: The Painters

1 Robert Brydell, *Art in Scotland, its Origin and Progress*, 1889; J.C.B. Cooksey, *Alexander Nasmyth HRSA, 1758–1840*, Paul Harris, 1991, p. 10.
2 Carr, *Caledonian Sketches*, pp. 193–4.

3 Allan Cunningham, *The Life of Sir David Wilkie*, 3 vols, London, 1843, vol. I, pp. 35ff., 40, 56ff.
4 *Ibid.*, vol. I, pp. 309, 335, 373.
5 *Letters and Papers of Andrew Robertson, AM*, etc., ed. Emily Robertson, London, 1895, pp. 41ff., 121, 129.
6 *Ibid.*, p. 133.
7 *Ibid.*, pp. 178ff. The Caledonian Asylum, for the sons of impoverished London Scots, whose boys were kitted out in a form of Scottish costume, was founded in 1823 beyond the northern outskirts of London, in a new street which was named after it.
8 James Ballantyne, *The Life of David Roberts, RA, compiled from his journals and other sources*, Edinburgh, 1866, vol. I, p. 1. Most of David Roberts's childhood was spent at Duncan's Land, an ancient stone house which survives at the foot of Gloucester Street.
9 *Ibid.*, vol. I, pp. 2ff.
10 *Ibid.*, vol. I, pp. 4ff.
11 Haydon, *Autobiography & Journals*, pp. 50, 60.
12 Pauline Chapman, *Mme Tussaud in England*, London, Quiller Press, 1992, pp. 16ff.; *Edinburgh Evening Courant*, notices between 13 May and 25 July 1803. On 28 May, when Charles was advertising his last week with 'the Invisible Girl', there was a notice of the birth of a daughter (Mary) in London, in Lincoln's Inn Fields, to the wife of John Peter Grant of Rothiemurchus.
13 Exhibition of Miss Linwood's Pictures, at Laurie's (late Bernard's) Rooms, Thistle Street, Edinburgh, 1804; NLS 3/2749 (3).

Chapter 18: The Theatre

1 Mawman, *An Excursion to the Highlands*, p. 104.
2 Southey to his wife, 14 Oct. 1805, *Life and Correspondence*, vol. II, p. 348 and n.
3 Robert Chambers, *Edinburgh Theatre Royal.*
4 *Edinburgh Evening Courant*, 6 Feb. 1808.
5 William Dunlap, *The Life of George Fred. Cooke*, 2nd edn, 2 vols, London, 1815, vol. I, pp. 345–5, vol. II, pp. 39ff.
6 This is presumably an error for Bankhouse, an inn on the old Selkirk road, about a mile south of Fountainhall.
7 Dunlap, *Life of George Cooke*, vol. II, pp. 99–101. In June 1810, after rows and drunken scenes in London, Cooke left for good following a performance of Falstaff; still drunk played in Liverpool, and was offered and eventually accepted an American engagement, sailing on 4 October. There he was successful although his career still suffered from his weakness for the bottle. In 1811 he married for the third time, but sank into a decline and died on 26 September 1812, aged only 57, looked after until the end by his wife. (Dunlap, *op. cit.*, vol. II, pp. 124, 168.)
8 Julian Charles Young, *A Memoir of Charles Mayne Young, Tragedian,* 2 vols, London, 1871, vol. I, pp. 1ff.
9 Julia Grimani's Venetian father, who became an apostate priest, would have succeeded to the title of his father the Marquis of Grimani had he only recanted. Having visited England, where he was entertained at Lansdowne House, he returned to Italy and married a nun. One of their two children was abducted as an infant, apparently in retribution for the broken vows. In his fifties Grimani remarried, the beautiful daughter of the German Herr Wagner and a Spanish lady. Returning to England, he taught at Eton, where the Prince Regent pestered the young wife with unwanted attentions, so they retreated to Paris, where their daughter Julia was born, and then Bath. Julia, well educated, was befriended by

Lord and Lady Suffolk and had two 'noble' offers of marriage before she was twenty. She preferred to go on the stage, first in Bath, then at the Haymarket, where she met Charles Young.

10 *Memoir of Young*, vol. I, p. 12.
11 *Ibid.*, vol. I, p. 137.
12 Gillies, *Memoirs*, vol. I, p. 318.
13 C.K. Sharpe to his sister Isabella, April 1808, *Sharpe Letters*, vol. I, p. 336.
14 R.W. Elliston to his wife, [summer 1808], *The Elliston Papers*, ed. George Raymond, in *Ainsworth's Magazine*, vol. IV, pt XXVI, Nov. 1843; George Raymond, *Memoir of Robert William Elliston, Comedian*, 2 vols, London, 1846, vol. I, pp. 336–7.
15 Norma Armstrong, *The Edinburgh Stage, 1715–1820*, 3 vols, Edinburgh, 1968 [Fellowship thesis for the Library Association], Vols.I & III.
16 Dibdin, *Annals of the Edinburgh Stage*, p. 259.
17 Armstrong, *The Edinburgh Stage*, vol. I; Dibdin, *Annals of the Edinburgh Stage*, pp. 258, 265; Chambers, *Edinburgh Theatre Royal.*
18 Dibdin, *Annals of the Edinburgh Stage*, p. 261; Margaret Carhart, *The Life and Work of Joanna Baillie*, Yale UP, 1923, p. 142; Chambers, *Edinburgh Theatre Royal.*
19 Dibdin, *Annals of the Edinburgh Stage*, p. 262; Walter Scott to Joanna Baillie, 22 Jan. 1810 and *post*, *Letters*, vol. I, pp. 278ff.
20 Carhart, *Joanna Baillie*, p. 144; Scott, *Letters*, *loc. cit.*
21 Carhart, *Joanna Baillie*, pp. 130–2; Dibdin, *Annals of the Edinburgh Stage*, p. 263.
22 Mrs Jordan to the Duke of Clarence [1 June 1810] and post, *Mrs Jordan and her Family* . . . ed. A. Aspinall, London, 1951, pp. 136ff.
23 [James Hogg], *The Spy*, Edinburgh, 1810–11, No.XIII, 24 Nov. 1810, p. 97.
24 Lady Clementina Davies, *Recollections of Society in France and England*, 2 vols, London, 1872, vol. I, pp. 58ff.
25 *Ibid.*, p. 63.
26 Alison, *My Life and Writings*, vol. I, p. 66.
27 Simond, *Journal of a Tour*, vol. II, p. 49 (6 Feb. 1811).
28 Lord Glenbervie to Thomas Thomson, 7 March 1809, *Memoirs of Thomson*, pp. 123–4.
29 Armstrong, *Edinburgh Stage*, vol. I; Dibdin, *Annals of Edinburgh Stage*, p. 270.
30 Chambers, *Edinburgh Theatre Royal.*
31 Lindsay, *Georgian Edinburgh*, p. 49. The village was demolished in 1800 and the land feued to Robert Burn, who shortly built Picardy Place and Forth Street. Armstrong, *Edinburgh Stage*, vol. I, p. 247.
32 A. Campbell, *A Journey from Edinburgh*, vol. II, pp. 205–6; Stark, *Picture of Edinburgh*, p. 416.
33 Stark, *Picture of Edinburgh*, p. 383.
34 The Panorama's first 'ingenious contriver' appears to have started in a humble way in an apartment of the Assembly Rooms. He had better success in London, and returned with an Edinburgh panorama shown at the foot of the Mound.
35 J.&R. Burford, *Description of a View of the City of Edinburgh and Surrounding Country, now exhibiting in the Panorama, Leicester Square.* Painted by the Proprietors . . ., London, 1826.
36 Hare, *Maria Edgeworth*, vol. I, p. 184, Maria Edgeworth to Mrs Edgeworth, Oct. 1812.
37 *Edinburgh Evening Courant*, 25 Feb. 1811; March 1808.
38 *Ibid.*, pp. 2, 4, 11 Feb. 1811. Philosophical fireworks were a method of exploding gases. An instrument made in London in 1830 is displayed at the Royal Museum of Scotland.
39 Simond, 1 Feb. 1811, *Journal of a Tour*, vol. II, p. 47.
40 Youngson, *Classical Edinburgh*, p. 249.

41 Campbell, *A Journey from Edinburgh*, vol. II, pp. 184–5; Stark, p. 372.
42 Campbell, *A Journey from Edinburgh*, vol. II,, pp. 187–9.
43 Matthew Lewis to his mother, *c.* Sept. 1804, *Life and Correspondence of M.G. Lewis*, 2 vols, London, 1839, vol. I, pp. 304–5.
44 John Braham (?1774–1856), from 1787 sang at Covent Garden, Bath and Drury Lane, toured the Continent and formed a partnership at Drury Lane with Anna (Nancy) Storace, and after her retirement in 1808 appeared at various theatres and festivals throughout the country. In 1831 with Frederick Yates he bought the Colosseum in Regent's Park and in 1835 built the St James's Theatre, both of which, together with an American tour, unfortunately proved unsuccessful. He retired in 1852.
45 Simond, *Journal of a Tour*, vol. II, p. 41, vol. I, p. 373.
46 A. Campbell, *A Journey from Edinburgh*, vol. II, p. 288.
47 Stark, *Picture of Edinburgh*, p. 382.
48 *Ibid.*, pp. 375f.
49 Carr, *Caledonian Sketches*, pp. 176–7.
50 *Ibid.*, pp. 178–9.
51 *Ibid.*, pp. 191–2.

Chapter 19: Eccentrics and Others

1 *Constable and his Correspondents*, vol. I, p. 518.
2 *Boswell, Laird of Auchinleck 1778–1782*, ed. Joseph W. Reed and F.A. Pottle, New York, McGraw Hill, 1977, p. 271.
3 Gillies, *Literary Veteran*, vol. I, pp. 258–70.
4 Francis Watt, *Book of Edinburgh Anecdote*, pp. 282–3.
5 *Life and Letters of Thomas Campbell*, vol. I, p. 240.
6 T. Campbell to Miss Mayow, 13 Feb. 1809, *Ibid.*, vol. II, p. 170.
7 Gillies, *Literary Veteran*, vol. I, p. 339.
8 *Ibid.*, vol. I, pp. 258–63.
9 *Ibid.*, vol. I, pp. 263f.
10 *Ibid.*, vol. I, p. 267.
11 *Memoirs of Susan Sibbald*, pp. 159–61.
12 Rev. James Hall, *Travels in Scotland*, vol. II, pp. 622f.
13 Daniel Stuart (1766–1846), the journalist, made a great success of the *Morning Post*, a moderate Tory paper to which besides Mackintosh and Coleridge, contributors included Wordsworth, Southey and Charles Lamb; and of the *Courier* which he took over in 1796. Mackintosh from 1818 to 1824 acted as Professor of Law and Politics at Haileybury College, and published historical works.
14 Coleridge to Thomas Poole, 21 Oct. 1801, *Collected Letters*, vol. II, pp. 770–1.
15 *Life and Letters of Thomas Campbell*, vol. I, p. 358.
16 Coleridge, *Collected Letters*, vol. I, p. 633.
17 *Ibid.*, vol. I, p. 359n; Coleridge to Poole, 13 Feb. 1801, *Ibid.*, vol. II, pp. 675–6.
18 *Ibid.*, vol. I, pp. 633, 636, vol. II,, pp. 675, 770–1, 931.
19 In 1807 Coleridge first met Scott, in London, and with his young son Hartley the three visited the Tower of London together. (*Collected Letters*, vol. III, p. 41.)
20 Coleridge to Southey, 14 Dec. 1807; to William Sotheby, [28 April 1808], *Collected Letters*, vol. III, pp. 41, 58–9.
21 Francis Horner to William Erskine, 4 Feb. 1804; Lord Webb Seymour to Horner, 11 April 1804, Horner, *Memoirs and Correspondence*, vol. I, pp. 256, 258–9; Mackintosh, *Memoirs*, vol. I, p. 199.
22 Mackintosh, *Memoirs*, vol. II, p. 272. When Miss Edgeworth visited London in the late spring of 1813, she went to Westminster Abbey with a party including Sir

James Mackintosh. Her mother wrote later, 'Days might have been spent without exhausting the information he so easily, and with such enjoyment to himself, as well as to his hearers, poured forth with quotations, appropriate anecdotes, and allusions.' (Mrs Edgeworth to Miss Ruxton, May 1813, Hare, *Life of Maria Edgeworth*, vol. I, p. 214.)

Similarly Mme de Staël in 1816, though impressed by Mackintosh's 'wonderful fertility and felicity in conversation', agreed with others that 'his flattering success in that respect debauched him from literary exertion and his history'. In other words, more talker than doer. (*The Diaries of Sylvester Douglas (Lord Glenbervie)*, ed. Francis Bickley, 2 vols, London, 1928, vol. II, p. 163.)

23 Journal of Miss Mary Berry, 7 Sept. 1808, *Extracts from the Journals and Correspondence of the Misses Berry from the Year 1783 to 1852*, ed. Lady Theresa Lewis, 3 vols, London, 1865, vol. II, p. 370.
24 Do., 7 Oct. 1808, *Ibid.*, vol. II, p. 372.
25 Ld Webb Seymour to Miss Berry, 7 Nov. 1808, *Ibid.*, vol. II, p. 373.
26 Journal of Miss Mary Berry, 17 Sept. 1809, *Ibid.*, vol. II, p. 394.
27 Kay's *Portraits*, vol. II, p. 115; *DNB*.
28 Andrew Bigelow, *Leaves from a Journal; or Sketches of Rambles in North Britain and Ireland*, Edinburgh, 1824, p. 114 (28 April 1817).

Chapter 20: Reviewers and Rivals

1 Dorothy Wordsworth to Lady Beaumont, 6 Dec. 1807, *Memorials of Coleorton*, ed. William Knight, 2 vols, Edinburgh, 1887, vol. II, pp. 20–21.
2 Byron's *Letters and Journals*, ed. Leslie A. Marquand, 11 vols, John Murray, 1973ff, vol. I, pp. 132f.
3 Byron to the Rev. John Becher, 26 Feb. 1808, *Journal*, 22 Nov. 1813, *Ibid.*, vol. I, p. 157, vol. II, p. 213.
4 Byron to Cam Hobhouse, 27 Feb. 1808, *Ibid.*, vol. I, p. 159.
5 *Ibid.*, vol. I, pp. 132, 157, 159, 177, 191, 193.
6 Coleridge to Southey, [9] Feb. 1808, *Collected Letters*, vol. IV, pp. 58–59.
7 Southey to his brother Harry, 1804, *Selections from the Letters*, vol. I, p. 297. Southey's shocked reference to 'extra-uterine gestation' concerns a discussion in the *Edinburgh Review* (vol. II, p. 408) of a paper in *Transactions of Edinburgh Royal Society* by Thomas Blizzard, FRS, Lecturer in Anatomy at the London Hospital, on an extra-uterine (fallopian or ectopic) foetus. The reader evidently considered the subject too indelicate to be aired in a public periodical.
8 Coleridge to Southey, 14 Dec. 1807, to Jeffrey, 23 May and c.16 July 1808, 14 Dec. 1808, *Collected Letters*, vol. III, pp. 41, 116, 118, 148.
9 Do. to Daniel Stuart, 14 Dec. and similarly to Humphrey Davy, 7 Dec. 1808, *Ibid.*, vol. III, pp. 141–2, 135.
10 Do. to Thomas Poole, 12 Jan. 1810, *Ibid.*, vol. III, p. 272.
11 Southey to Daniel Stuart, 27 Nov. 1807, *Letters from the Lake Poets . . . to Daniel Stuart*, p. p. , London, 1889, p. 395.
12 Gillies, *Literary Veteran*, vol. I, pp. 224ff.
13 *Ibid.*, vol. I, pp. 229–30.
14 Southey to Charles Danvers, July 1808, *Selections from the Letters*, vol. II, p. 82.
15 Sir Gilbert Elliot to James Loch, 15 May 1808, *Brougham and his Early Friends*, vol. II, p. 305.
16 Alexander Murray to Archibald Constable, 27 June 1808, *Constable and his Correspondents*, vol. I, p. 266. Mary Berry often commented on *Review* articles, for example in 1808, the one exploding William Cobbett's apparent inconsistencies in his *Weekly Journal*. (William Windham was similarly appreciative, being 'out of all

patience' with Cobbett.) In October 1809 Playfair, sharing her praise, enlightened Miss Berry about the author of the article on 'Reform', namely Jeffrey. (*Journals of the Misses Berry*, vol. II, p. 386.)

17 Murray to Constable, 3 Aug. 1808, *Constable and his Correspondents*, vol. I, p. 277. *Brougham and his Early Friends*, vol. II, p. 305. A few years later, in 1812, Murray's own politics were in question when he was narrowly elected to the chair of Oriental Languages on the death of Mr Moodie, in the teeth of strong local support for Dr Brunton. Although Murray had never taken part in politics (as he assured Dr Baird), 'I have been *accused* of being a writer (would you think of it) in the *Edinburgh Review*'. (Do. to Do. June 1812, *Constable and his Correspondents*, vol. II, pp. 320, 323–5.)

18 Redding, *Fifty Years' Recollections*, vol. I, pp. 65–7.

19 Brougham to Loch, 19 Aug. 1808, *Brougham and his Early Friends*, vol. II, p. 319.

20 Gillies, *Literary Veteran*, vol. I, pp. 322–3.

21 Lord Gower to C.K. Sharpe, 28 Jan. 1809, *Sharpe Letters*, vol. I, p. 359.

22 William Gifford (1756–1826) edited the *Quarterly Review* from 1809 to 1824.

23 Scott to Sharpe, 30 Dec. 1808, *Sharpe Letters*, vol. I, p. 350.

24 Do. to Do., 3 March 1809, *Ibid.*, vol. I, pp. 370f.

25 Redding, *Fifty Years' Recollections*, vol. I, pp. 68–9, 71–72.

26 Simond, *Journal of a Tour*, vol. II, pp. 27f.

27 George Combe, in his process of self-education, was early influenced by the *Review*, attracted by its liberal, unorthodox views and 'daring spirit' and the 'literary and political impulse' it gave to young Edinburgh. It helped stir his own ambition to write, and in 1811 he started to keep a diary, at first full of self-examination and then beginning to see a prospect for his abilities. For example, watching the passing of President Blair's funeral, and distressed at the crowds' contempt for the procession of lawyers as 'vermin', he went home to write a defence which he offered to the *Edinburgh Magazine*. (Diary of George Combe, 3 Dec. 1811, NLS MS 7402.)

28 Southey to C. Williams Wynn, 6 July 1809, *Selections from Letters*, vol. II, p. 151.

29 David Hunter to Archibald Constable, 18 March 1807, *Constable and his Correspondents*, vol. I, p. 111.

30 Scott to Sharpe, 13 Jan. 1809, *Sharpe Letters*, vol. I, p. 353.

31 Southey to Daniel Stuart, 10 Sept. 1809, *Letters from the Lake Poets*, p. 404.

32 Southey to Sir George Beaumont, 28 Sept. 1811, *Memorials of Coleorton*, vol. II, p. 143.

33 Southey to Scott, 24 Dec. 1810, *New Southey Letters*, vol. I, p. 551.

34 Coleridge to Wordsworth, Oct. 1810, *Collected Letters*, vol. IV, pp. 294–5.

35 *Ibid.*, vol. IV, p. 296.

36 Mrs Grant of Laggan, *Memoir and Correspondence*, vol. I, pp. 248, 253.

37 Journal of Mary Berry, 15 May 1808, *Journals of the Misses Berry*, vol. II, p. 349.

38 Mrs Grant to John Hatsell, 17 March 1810, *Memoir and Correspondence*, vol. I, pp. 247, 249.

39 Mrs Grant to Miss Catherine Fanshawe, 6 Oct. 1810, *Ibid.*, vol. II, p. 270.

40 Mrs Grant to Mrs Hook, 5 June 1810, *Ibid.*, vol. I, p. 263

41 Do. to Do., 10 Sept. 1811, *Ibid.*, vol. I, pp. 290–1.

42 Do. to Miss Fanshawe, 15 April 1810, *Ibid.*, vol. I, pp. 253–4.

43 Do. to Do., 13 Feb. 1809, *Ibid.*, vol. I, pp. 198–9.

44 Lord Calthorpe to William Wilberforce, 2 Sept. 1801, *Private Papers of William Wilberforce*, ed. A.M. Wilberforce, 1897, p. 103.

45 Mrs Grant to Miss Fanshawe, 13 Feb. 1809, *Memoir and Correspondence*, vol. I, p. 199.

46 Simond, *Journal of a Tour*, vol. I, pp. 371–2.

47 Mrs Grant to Mrs Brown, 21 May 1810, to Mrs Hook, 5 June 1810, *Memoir and Correspondence*, vol. I, pp. 260, 261.

48 *The Letters of Sir Walter Scott*, vol. III, 1811–1814, 1812 *passim*.

Chapter 21: The Social Surface

1 Charles Sharpe to his mother, 14 June 1808, *Sharpe Letters*, vol. I, p. 339.
2 Do, to his sister Grace, n.d. [1809], *Ibid.*, vol. I, p. 360.
3 Gillies, *Literary Veteran* vol. I, p. 306.
4 Redding, *Fifty Years' Recollections*, vol. III, pp. 111, 333.
5 Mrs Grant to Miss Fanshawe, 15 April 1810, *Memoirs*, vol. I, pp. 252–3.
6 Mrs Fletcher *Autobiography*, p. 82.
7 *Ibid.*, pp. 103f.' see also Mrs Grant to John Hatsell, 17 March 1810, *Memoir*, vol. I, p. 247. When in due course the Williamson family left Edinburgh, the Fletchers were given a warm invitation to visit Whitburn Hall whenever their travels took them through the county. The youngest Williamson daughter in 1823 married the Hon. Thomas Dundas, who became Earl of Zetland.
8 Gillies, *Literary Veteran*, vol. I, pp. 299f.
9 Simond, *Journal of a Tour*, vol. I, pp. 274, 360.
10 Mrs Grant to Mrs Hook, 14 Aug. 1811, *Memoirs*, vol. I, p. 288.
11 Mrs Fletcher *Autobiography*, pp. 102–3. Mrs Waddington, born Georgina Port (1771), was granddaughter to Mrs Delany's sister Anne, Mrs Dewes. Georgina was Mrs Delany's beloved protégée and adopted child, but after her death, from the age of seventeen had to live rather unhappily with her uncle and aunt, the Court D'Ewes, and more happily with her other uncle and aunt, Granville. Her marriage in 1789 to Benjamin Waddington, son of a Nottinghamshire clergyman, was one of convenience. Frances, b.1791, was her second daughter.

The family spent a winter in Edinburgh in 1809, partly to finish the girls' education, and Mrs Waddington was happy to renew friendship with Mrs Delany's favourite godson Dr Daniel Sandiford, then Bishop of Edinburgh. During this agreeable visit they met Scott, Mr Alison, Jeffrey, and Mrs Waddington's 'lifelong friend', 'the charming Lady Louisa Stuart', and were also able to enjoy the acting of Mrs Siddons. (Augustus J.C. Hare, *The Life and Letters of Frances Baroness Bunsen*, 2 vols, London, 1879, vol. I, pp. 78ff.)
12 Hare, *Maria Edgeworth*, vol. I, p. 157. Maria Edgeworth to Mrs Ruxton, Jan. 1810, *Ibid.*, vol. I, p. 169.
13 Mrs Fletcher *Autobiography*, p. 100.
14 Playfair to Mary Berry, 22 Sept. 1810, *Journals of the Misses Berry*, vol. II, p. 427.
15 The Argyll/Paget marriage was much written about by shocked contemporaries. See *Glenbervie Diaries*, pp. 73–4, 104; Simond, *Journal of a Tour*, vol. II, pp. 44–6, *Memoirs of the Comtesse de Boigne*, p. 150 etc.; and Ian G. Lindsay and Mary Cosh, *Inveraray and the Dukes of Argyll*, Edinburgh, 1973, pp. 310 and n.14, 398.
16 Simond, *Journal of a Tour*, vol. II, pp. 60–61.
17 *Ibid.*, vol. I, pp. 368–9.
18 *The Spy*, no. XV, 8 Dec. 1810, No.32, 6 April 1811. Both these items were said to be written by Mrs Gray.
19 Simond, *Journal of a Tour*, vol. II, p. 368.
20 *Ibid.*, vol. II, pp. 41ff.

Chapter 22: Four Marriages

1 *The Letters of Percy Bysshe Shelley*, ed. Frederick L. Jones, 3 vols, Oxford, 1964, vol. I, pp. 137n, 110; Shelley to his father, 30 Aug., 27 Sept. 1811, vol. I, pp. 139, 141.
2 Thomas Jefferson Hogg, *The Life of Percy Bysshe Shelley*, London, 1906, pp. 249f.
3 *Ibid.*, pp. 250f.
4 *Ibid.*, pp. 253f.; Thomas Peacock, 'Memoirs of Percy Bysshe Shelley', in Hogg's *The Life of Percy Bysshe Shelley*, 2 vols, London, 1933, vol. II, pp. 320–1; Walter

Edwin Peck, 'Shelley in Edinburgh', in *OEC* XI, Edinburgh, 1922, pp. 75–85; Roger Ingpen, *Shelley in England*, pp. 308ff.

5 Jefferson Hogg, *Life of Shelley*, vol. II, pp. 256ff.

6 *Ibid.*, vol. II, pp. 260ff.

7 *Ibid.*, pp. 270f.; Harriet Shelley to Mrs Nugent, 20 Oct. 1813, *Shelley Letters*, vol. I, pp. 378–9n.

8 Sharpe to Mrs Balfour, n.d. [1811], *Sharpe Letters*, vol. I, p. 379.

9 Shelley to Hogg, 26 Nov. 1813, *Shelley Letters*, vol. I, p. 379.

10 *Ibid.*, vol. I, p. 381n. To avoid any suggestion of illegality in their Scottish marriage they remarried in London on 24 March 1814, but the first rift soon appeared. When Harriet was pregnant Shelley met and fell madly in love with the sixteen-year-old Mary Wolstonecraft, just back from Scotland; while Harriet and the baby born in December were in Bath, the newly matched pair eloped to Switzerland with Mary's half-sister, Claire Clairmont, while Shelley, explaining to Harriet that his feeling for her was friendship rather than passion, kindly but unsuccessfully proposed that they all live together. (*Shelley Letters*, vol. I, pp. 381f.)

11 Alfred T. Story, *The Life of John Linnell*, 2 vols, London, 1892, vol. I, pp. 108f.

12 Mrs Edgeworth to Mrs Ruxton, Nov. 1810; Miss Edgeworth to Mrs Ruxton, Oct. 1811, *Life of Maria Edgeworth*, vol. I, pp. 176, 179.

13 Sydney Smith to Lady Holland, 3 Nov. 1810, to Jeffrey, Nov. 1810; to Do., 22 June 1811, *Letters*, vol. I, pp. 191, 194, 209.

14 Sydney Smith to Mrs Apreece, 29 Dec. 1811, *Letters*, vol. I, p. 217.

15 Humphrey Davy to his brother John, March 1812, *Fragmentary Remains, Literary and Scientific, of Sir Humphrey Davy, Bart . . .*, ed. by his brother, John Davy, London, 1858, p. 141; to Mrs Apreece, 1 March 1812, pp. 155–6.

16 Mrs Grant to Mrs L——, 16 Aug. 1812, *Memoir*, vol. II, p. 20.

17 Sharpe to Margravine of Anspach, 17 Aug. 1812, *Sharpe Letters*, vol. II, p. 8. Dr Thomas Beddoes, who married Maria Edgeworth's sister Anna, was father to the poet Thomas Lovell Beddoes. Having studied at Oxford, London and Edinburgh, he was reader in Chemistry at Oxford 1788–92, and in 1798 established the 'Pneumatic Institute' at Clifton for medical treatment by inhalation.

18 Miss Edgeworth to Margaret Ruxton, 20 July 1812, *Life of Maria Edgeworth*, vol. I, p. 182. When the Edgeworths reached London in 1813, Maria's fame with the *Edinburgh Review's* praise having preceded her, it was the Davys who were first to call, 'inviting them to dinners and parties, with dozens of people'. (Miss Edgeworth to Margaret Ruxton, May 1813, *Ibid.*, vol. I, pp. 206f.)

19 Davy to his brother John, March 1812, *Fragmentary Remains*, p. 141.

20 *Ibid.*, pp. 155–6, 171. At the time of their marriage John Davy was about to visit Edinburgh, and his brother informed him that Mrs Apreece had written to Henry Mackenzie's family, 'which she thinks the one in Edinburgh that will be most agreeable to you', while Playfair and Hall were other suggested contacts. Humphrey added that if John were interested in reviewing the French chemists Gay-Lussac and Thenard, he ought to meet Jeffrey, for 'the chemical part of the *Edinburgh Review* is vilely conducted'. (Davy to John, Dec. 1811, *Ibid.*, pp. 137, 138.)

21 *Ibid.*, pp. 222ff.

22 Sydney Smith to Lady Holland, 16 Nov. 1816, *Letters*, vol. I, p. 268 & n.

23 Do. to Lady Davy, 8 April 1818; to Lady Mary Bennet, Aug. 1822, *Ibid.*, vol. I, pp. 288, 391.

24 *Fragmentary Remains*, pp. 228ff. Davy's health deteriorated for several years, and in January 1827, not long after he was last elected FRS, he suffered a stroke. Wordsworth, whom he had met during his Institute lectures, noted his debilitated appearance on their last meeting in 1816, and for some years he had suffered autumnal 'bilious rheumatic' attacks. In 1827 for health reasons Davy went to Italy

with his brother, and having remained there until October also travelled abroad next year, still writing. In February he suffered a second stroke, was joined first by John, then by his wife, and on 29 May died in Geneva on his way back from Rome, aged only 50.

25 Sydney Smith to Lady Holland, 10 Jan. 1809, *Letters*, vol. I, p. 152.

26 Simond, *Journal of a Tour*, vol. I, p. 265.

27 Jeffrey to Horner, 20 July 1810, Cockburn, *Life of Jeffrey*, vol. II, p. 129.

28 Rev. Robert Morehead, Journal, 17 Jan. 1811, *Life and Writings*, p. 152. 'Mrs Erskine' was presumably Harry Erskine's wife. 'Mr Holland' was the 22–year-old Henry Holland (1788–1873), related to the Wedgwoods and Charles Darwin, and who in his teems had met Mrs Barbauld in Stoke Newington. He had abandoned training for a mercantile career to study medicine and joined Edinburgh's medical school in 1808, met all the most eminent inhabitants, accompanied Sir George Mackenzie's Iceland expedition in 1810, with Dr Richard Bright, with whom he had been at school, and later studied at Guy's and St Thomas's Hospitals. In 1814 he became Princess Caroline of Wales's medical attendant, and gave evidence in her support at her trial (1820). He was appointed physician in ordinary to both Prince Albert and Queen Victoria, who made him a baronet, travelled widely and published several books. (Sir Henry Holland, *Recollections of Past Life*, London, 1872; *DNB* (See ch.15 n.23.))

29 Mrs Grant to Catherine Fanshawe, 24 March 1814, *Memoir*, vol. II, pp. 40–41.

30 Sydney Smith to Jeffrey, Jan. 1812, 6 April 1813, *Letters*, vol. I, pp. 220, 236.

31 Jeffrey to J.A. Murray, 20 Aug. 1813, Cockburn, *Life of Jeffrey*, vol. II, p. 140. Visitors to Liverpool, notably from America, took care to be put in touch with William Roscoe (1753–1831). Starting his career as assistant to his market-gardener father, he qualified as an attorney in Liverpool and in 1774 was admitted to the court of King's Bench, but retired from the profession to study literature, though in 1791 he became a banker in Liverpool. He was Whig MP for the town in 1806–7. He later lost money through bank difficulties and in 1820 became bankrupt; in his ruin friends provided for him. A man of great culture, he studied botany, prompted the Liverpool Royal Institution and was its first President, collected books and prints, and published a number of works including on Pope Leo X (1805), edited Alexander Pope's works, and himself composed poetry.

32 Morehead, Journal, 16 June 1813, *Life and Writings*, p. 158.

33 Jeffrey to Thomas Thomson, 10 Aug., 29 Aug. 1813, *Memoirs of Thomas Thomson*, pp. 138, 140.

34 Jeffrey to Morehead, 28 Aug. 1813, Cockburn, *Life of Jeffrey*, vol. II, pp. 142–3, vol. I, p. 216.

35 *Ibid.*, Jeffrey's journal on voyage, vol. I, pp. 218, 225–6.

36 George Ticknor to Charles Davies, 8 Feb. 1814, Life, *Letters and Journals of George Ticknor*, ed. G.S. Hillard, 2 vols, Boston, 1909, vol. I, p. 45. In the following year Ticknor sailed for Europe with a group of other Americans, including two sons of John Quincy Adams about to join their father in St Petersburg. Delighted with England, and becoming friendly with Lord Byron, Ticknor set off for Germany with the same friends, studied at Göttingen and in 1819 returned via Paris, in London meeting Sir James Mackintosh, the Hollands and John Allen, and Lord Brougham, before travelling to Edinburgh for an extended stay in February 1815. He was by then twenty-eight.

37 Cockburn, *Life of Jeffrey*, vol. I, pp. 227–8.

38 Washington Irving, Journal, 27 Aug. 1817, *Journals and Notebooks*, vol. II, *1807–1822*, Boston, Twayne Publisher, 1981, p. 99.

39 Jeffrey to Charles Wilkes, 25 Feb. 1815, Cockburn, *Life of Jeffrey*, vol. II, p. 147.

40 *Ibid.*, vol. I, pp. 229–30.

41 *Ibid.*, vol. I, pp. 234–5.

Chapter 23: Edinburgh Shops

1 See, e.g., Robert Heron, *Observations made in a Journey*, vol. II, p. 488; John Stoddart, *Remarks on Local Scenery*, vol. I, p. 213; Charles Dibdin, *Observations on a Tour*, vol. I, p. 332.
2 Thomas Carlyle, *Reminiscences*, ed. J.A. Froude, 2 vols, London, 1881, vol. II, p. 223.
3 Carr, *Caledonian Sketches*, p. 199.
4 James Grant, Cassell's *Old and New Edinburgh*, 3 vols, London, 1883, vol. II, p. 118.
5 W.H. Marwick, 'Shops in 18th and 19th Century Edinburgh', *OEC*, XXX, 1959, pp. 119f.
6 Most of what follows is based on Josiah Livingston, *Some Edinburgh Shops*.
7 *Edinburgh Evening Courant*, 24 Sept. 1818. Melrose's shop was at South Bridge until moving to 93 George Street in the early 1840s.
8 The East India Company had gradually lost control of trade since Pitt's India Act of 1784, which established government control of policy; it lost its commercial monopoly in 1813, and from 1834 it became a managing agency for the British Government, losing even this after the Indian Mutiny of 1857.
9 *Edinburgh Evening Courant*, 24 Oct. 1818.
10 William and Robert Chambers, born 1800 and 1802, were the sons of an accomplished but unworldly man who, having set up as a draper in Peebles, was fairly ruined by allowing extended credit to the many French prisoners quartered there, who were then ordered away without ever settling their debts.
11 William Chambers, *Memoir of Robert Chambers with Autobiographic Reminiscences of William Chambers*, Edinburgh, 1872, pp. 77ff.
12 Carr, *Caledonian Sketches*, p. 124.
13 Rev. James Hall, *Travels in Scotland*, vol. I, p. 599.
14 *Edinburgh Evening Courant*, 4 Nov. 1815.
15 *Ibid.*, 29 Oct. 1818.
16 L.A. Necker de Saussure, *Travels in Scotland; descriptive of Manners, Literature, and Science*, London, 1821, p. 3.

Chapter 24: Among the Poor

1 Simond, *Journal of a Tour*, vol. I, pp. 275–6.
2 Carr, *Caledonian Sketches*, pp. 214–7.
3 *Dying Speeches, Executions etc., Scotish* [sic] *1807–35*, NLS Rosebery Collection, Ry III a 2.
4 Thomas Campbell, *Life and Letters*, vol. II, p. 306n.; Lockhart, *Life of Scott*, vol. III, pp. 156–60.
5 *Memoir of Robert Chambers*, pp. 73–4.
6 *Ibid.*, p. 75.
7 *Hawkie, the Autobiography of a Gangrel*, ed. John Southesk, 1888.

PART III

Chapter 25: The Expanding City

1 Alexander Campbell, *A Journey from Edinburgh*, vol. II, p. 179.
2 *Ibid.*, vol. II, p. 180. Alexander Campbell (1764–1824), besides tours of Scotland published music, verses and collections of Scottish songs. He practised as an organist in Edinburgh, and taught music, including to Walter Scott, besides studying medicine. (*DNB*)

3 Elizabeth Grant, *Memoirs of a Highland Lady*, vol. I, p. 23.
4 Gillies, *Literary Veteran*, vol. II, p. 33.
5 Youngson, *Classical Edinburgh*, pp. 133–4.
6 W. Forbes Gray, 'The Lands of Newington and their Owners', *OEC* vol. XXIV, pp. 152–97; Youngson, *Classical Edinburgh*, p. 272.
7 Lindsay, *Georgian Edinburgh*, p. 54.
8 Youngson, *Classical Edinburgh*, p. 211.
9 Edward Pinnington, *Sir Henry Raeburn, RA*, London, 1904, p. 84.
10 Thomas Carlyle to his mother (from 9 Jamaica Street), 16 Nov. 1821, to his brother Alexander, 21 Nov. 1821, *The Collected Letters of Thomas and Jane Welsh Carlyle*, ed. Charles Richard Saunders *et al.*, N. Carolina, 1970ff., vol. I, pp. 393, 397.
11 Lindsay, *Georgian Edinburgh*, p. 53.
12 *Ibid.*, pp. 55–6; Colvin, *Dictionary of British Architects*, pp. 421, 424.
13 Charles Nodier, *Promenade from Dieppe*, p. 80; Lindsay, *Georgian Edinburgh*, p. 51.
14 *Edinburgh Evening Courant*, 3 & 10 October, 7 November 1815.
15 Lindsay, *Georgian Edinburgh*, pp. 34–5.
16 *Ibid.*, p. 40.
17 Youngson, *Classical Edinburgh*, pp. 135ff; Lindsay, *Georgian Edinburgh*, p. 41.
18 Alexander Campbell, *A Journey from Edinburgh*, vol. II, pp. 200–2; *Edinburgh in the 1th Century*, p. 30.
19 Carr, *Caledonian Sketches*, pp. 105–7.
20 Stark, *Picture of Edinburgh*, p. 450.
21 *Diary of George Combe*, NLS MS 7402, 5 Oct. 1814.
22 Youngson, *Classical Edinburgh*, pp. 104, 212, 241.
23 *Ibid.*, p. 48.
24 George Combe to his brother Andrew, 25 March 1818, March 1819, Gibbon, *Life of George Combe*, vol. I, pp. 111, 118.
25 Sydney Smith to Lady Mary Bennet, 20 Dec. 1820, *Letters*, vol. I, p. 370.
26 Thomas Moore, Journal, 6 May 1822, *Memoirs, Journals and Correspondence of Thomas Moore*, ed. Lord John Russell, 8 vols, London, 1853, vol. III, p. 351. Moore was then in the middle of his creditor-exile, and had to return to Paris next day.
27 *Edinburgh Evening Courant*, March and April 1815; *Edinburgh Advertiser*, 21 April 1815; *Edinburgh in the 19th Century*, 1818, 1822.
28 Carlyle to his brother Alexander, 23 Dec. 1820, *Collected Letters*, vol. I, p. 298.
29 Alison, *My Life and Writings*, vol. I, p. 174.
30 *Edinburgh Annual Register*, 1819, pp. 259–60.
31 *Edinburgh Evening Courant*, 2 November 1818. Cakes and other refreshments were sold on the ground floor of the Nelson Monument, run by the widow of a naval petty officer.
32 *Edinburgh in the 1th Century*, 1821.
33 Lindsay, *Georgian Edinburgh*, pp. 41–2.

Chapter 26: A New Kind of Novel

1 Lockhart, *Life of Scott*, vol. III, p. 261, vol. IV, pp. 145–6.
2 Gillies, *Literary Veteran*, vol. II, p. 183.
3 Cockburn, *Memoirs*, p. 241.
4 Lockhart, *Life of Scott*, vol. V, pp. 95, 54ff, 117–8.
5 *Ibid.*, vol. V, pp. 122, 129ff.
6 Mrs Grant to Miss Fanshawe, 13 Dec. 1814, *Memoirs*, vol. II, p. 61; Jeffrey to Charles Wilkes, 25 Feb. 1815, Cockburn *Life of Jeffrey*, vol. II, p. 147.
7 Lord Glenbervie, Journal, 17 June 1816, *The Diaries of Sylvester Douglas (Lord Glenbervie)*, 2 vols, London, 1928, vol. II, pp. 152–3.

8 Do., Journal, 5 Jan. 1817, *Ibid.*, vol. II, p. 212.
9 Mrs Grant to Miss Fanshawe, *loc. cit.*; Washington Irving, Journal, 18 March 1824, *Journals and Notebooks*, vol. III, p. 305.
10 Mrs Grant, *loc. cit.*
11 Frances Waddington to Prof. Monk, 1815, Hare, *Life of Baroness Bunsen*, vol. I, pp. 86–8.
12 *The Life of George Crabbe*, by his Son [the Rev. George Crabbe], London, OUP (World's Classics), 1932, [first published in 1834], p. 165n.
13 Maria Edgeworth 'To the author of "Waverley" ', 23 Oct. 1814, *Life and Letters*, vol. I, pp. 226, 221; to Mrs Ruxton, Oct. 1814.
14 Elizabeth Grant, *Memoirs of a Highland Lady*, vol. II, p. 72.
15 Anne Romilly to Maria Edgeworth, 7 Nov. 1814, 15 Feb. 1815, Jan. 1815, *Romilly–Edgeworth Letters, 1813–1818*, Introd. By Samuel Henry Romilly, London, 1936, pp. 92, 101–2, 106.
16 Do. to Do., 17 Dec 1816, *Ibid.*, p. 161.
17 Mrs Hamilton to Miss J.B., 9 July 1814, 7 March 1815, *Memoirs*, pp. 181, 186–7.
18 Lord Byron to John Murray, 24 July 1814, Byron, *Letters and Journals*, vol. IV, p. 146.
19 Do. to Do., 9 April 1815, *Ibid.*, vol. IV, p. 287.
20 Sydney Smith to Jeffrey, [30] Dec. 1814, *Letters*, vol. I, p. 251 and n.
21 Mrs Brunton to Mrs Izett, 15 Aug. 1814, in Dr Alexander Brunton, 'Memoir of [Mrs] Mary Brunton', prefaced in her novel *Discipline* (1814), Edinburgh, 1849, p. 37.
22 John Quincy Adams, Diary, 2 June, 30 Aug. 1816, *Memoirs of John Quincy Adams*, comprising portions of his diary from 1785 to 1848, ed. Charles Francis Adams, Philadelphia, 1874, vol. III, pp. 372–3, 439–40. Quincy Adams tells this as of *Lord* Erskine.
23 Dorothy Wordsworth to Sara Hutchinson, 18 Feb. 1815, *Wordsworth Letters*, vol. III, p. 203.
24 Wordsworth to Southey, Jan. 1815, to Gillies, 25 April 1815, *Ibid.*, vol. III, pp. 187, 232.
25 Moore, Journal, 27 Oct. 1820, *Memoirs, Journals and Correspondence*, vol. III, p. 161.
26 Mrs Grant to Mrs Rucker, 1 May 1815, *Memoir*, vol. II, pp. 85–6. The vexed matter of 'the atrocious Queen' was at the time much under discussion, this party being strongly convinced (being Tory) of her guilt. Scott wrote off the whole affair as merely the 'most extravagant' among numerous 'fits of national excitement', remarking that such crises always ended in 'a great revulsion of opinion, attended by shame and remorse'. This tallied exactly with Mrs Grant's opinion, which noted that those who supported the Queen merely on political grounds had been put to shame. 'Indeed the party [Whig] begin to look very foolish and crestfallen.'
27 John Whishaw to Thomas Smith, 18 Feb. 1816, Lady Seymour, *The Pope of Holland House*, London, 1906, p. 143.
28 Gordon, *'Christopher North'*, vol. I, pp. 197f.
29 Lockhart, *Life of Scott*, vol. V, pp. 95–6.
30 Moore to Lady Donegal, n.d. [1816], *Memoirs, Journal and Correspondence*, vol. II, p. 97.
31 Do. to Miss Godfrey, 6 Dec. 1815, *Ibid.*, vol. II, p. 85.
32 Scott to C.K. Sharpe, 17 Feb. 1809, *Letters*, vol. II, p. 166; *Sharpe Letters*, vol. I, p. 366.
33 Lockhart, *Life of Scott*, vol. V, pp. 140ff.
34 Mrs Brunton to her brother, Dec. 1816, *loc. cit.*, p. 43.
35 Robert Mitchell to Thomas Carlyle, 12 April 1815, Carlyle to Mitchell, 12 Feb. 1817, *Collected Letters*, vol. I, pp. 46, 91.

36 Byron to Murray, 9 May 1817, *Letters and Journals*, vol. IV, p. 220.
37 Whishaw to Thomas Smith, 16 Feb, 1 March 1817, *Pope of Holland House*, pp. 166, 172–3.
38 Francis Horner to his sister , 20 May 1816, *Memoirs and Correspondence*, vol. II, p. 356.
39 Whishaw to Smith, 24 Dec. 1816, *op. cit.*, p. 162.
40 David Wilkie to his sister Helen, 30 Oct. 1817, Allan Cunningham, *The Life of Wilkie*, vol. I, pp. 482–3.
41 Henry Hallam to Lord Webb Seymour, 5 March 1818, *Correspondence of Two Brothers*, p. 224.
42 Whishaw to Thomas Smith, 6 and 16 Feb. 1817, *Pope of Holland House*, p. 166.
43 Lockhart to Jonathan Christie, 22 Dec. 1816, Andrew Lang, *Life and Letters of John Gibson Lockhart*, 2 vols, London, 1897, vol. I, p. 114.
44 *Ibid.*, vol. I, p. 191.
45 Duke of Somerset to Lord Webb Seymour, 4 Feb. 1815, *Correspondence of Two Brothers*, p. 161.
46 Lord Webb Seymour to Duke of Somerset, 17 Jan, 23 Feb. 1815, *Ibid.*, pp. 160, 163.
47 Duke of Somerset to Lord Webb Seymour, 7 March 1815, *Ibid.*, p. 164.
48 Sydney Smith to Lady Mary Bennet, [July or Aug. 1818], to Lord Grey, 28 Aug., to Lady Holland, 11 Oct. 1818, *Letters*, vol. I, pp. 296, 297, 302, 297–8.
49 Richard Rush, Journal, 29 March 1818, Richard Rush, *Residence at the Court of London*, 3rd edn, ed. By his son Benjamin Rush, London, 1872, p. 142.
50 Moore, 4 Jan. 1819, *Memoirs, Journal and Correspondence*, vol. II, p. 249; Baroness Bunsen did not read *The Heart of Midlothian* until 1836 (when she was living in Italy with her husband the Chevalier) – partly from curiosity about Scott's later novels. For her it proved how 'idle' was the 'multitude' in admitting it as his best. 'To my feelings it is the very worst I have ever read', with the single merit of being based on a historical event. 'It is *remplissage* from first to last, mostly or entirely unreadable.' The public only wanted sensation, and in this novel Scott took advantage of it, lacing the good taste displayed in *Waverley*! To each his taste. (Hare, *Life of Baroness Bunsen*, vol. II, p. 428.)
51 Norma Armstrong, *The Edinburgh Stage*, 1715–820, vol. I; Dibdin, *Annals of the Edinburgh Stage*, p. 286; see also Cooksey, *Alexander Nasmyth.*
52 Sydney Smith to Archibald Constable, 28 June 1819, to Lord Lansdowne, 24 July 1819, *Letters*, vol. I, pp. 328, 330.
53 Gillies, *Recollections of Scott*, pp. 235ff.
54 Joseph Cogswell spent every evening at Mrs Fletcher's or Mrs Grant's, who did her best to comfort his gloom, but daily reminder of his anxiety made the mercurial young man feel worse. At last, on the point of leaving Edinburgh, he saw Constable, back from Abbotsford two days earlier, who was able to reassure him that Scott was now 'quite well', a welcome reassurance on the eve of his setting off for the Continent, where he was to spend the next 15 months. (Cogswell to Ticknor, 23 March, 9 April 1819, *Life of Joseph Green Cogswell* as sketched in his letters, ed. Anna Elliot Ticknor, p.p., Cambridge, Mass., 1874, pp. 95–6. See also *Life, Letters, and Journals of George Ticknor*, vol. I, p. 282.)
55 Gillies, *loc. cit.*

Chapter 27: Scott Lionised

1 Amédée Pichot, *Voyage Historique*, vol. III, pp. 182–3.
2 Moore, Journal, 12 Nov. 1825, *Memoirs, Journal* etc., vol. V, p. 14. See also pt IV, ch.17, pp. 336–7 and n.3.
3 Lockhart, *Life of Scott*, vol. II, pp. 36–8, 104; *Constable and his Correspondents*, vol. III, pp. 47f.

4 Scott to Constable, 22 Sept. 1817; *Constable and his Correspondents*, vol. III, p. 99.
5 *Ibid.*, vol. III, p. 106; Scott to Lady Louisa Stuart, 16 Jan. 1818, Scott, *Letters*, vol. V, pp. 55–6. See also *Edinburgh Evening Courant*, 5 Feb. 1818.
6 *Constable and his Correspondence*, vol. III, pp. 106–8, 110, 121.
7 Scott to Constable, 23 March 1819, *Ibid.*, vol. III, pp. 123–4.
8 Southey to Rev. Herbert Hill, 22 March 1819, *Selections from Letters*, vol. III, pp. 126–7.
9 Lockhart, *Life of Scott*, vol. VI, pp. 172, 181, 243.
10 Byron to Coleridge, 18 Oct. 1815, *Letters and Journals*, vol. IV, p. 318.
11 Byron to John Murray, 25 March, 2 April 1817, *Letters and Journals*, vol. VI, pp. 192, 204.
12 Byron to Moore, 24 Dec. 1816, 28 Feb. 1817, to Murray, 15 Feb. 1817, *Letters and Journals*, vol. VI, pp. 160, 170, 177.
13 Byron to Cam Hobhouse, 7 March 1817, *Letters and Journals*, vol. VI, p. 182.
14 Byron to Moore, 28 Oct. 1815, *Letters and Journals*, vol. IV, pp. 323–4; to Coleridge, 18 Oct. 1815, *Ibid.*, vol. IV, p. 318. See Peter Quennell, *Byron, a Self-Portrait,* 2 vols, London, 1950, vol. II, p. 137.
15 Coleridge to an Unknown Correspondent, 20 Oct. 1824, *Collected Letters*, vol. V, pp. 379–81 & n.
16 Byron to William Bankes, 26 Feb. 1820, to John Murray, 1 March 1820, *Letters and Journals*, vol. VII, pp. 45, 48.
17 Byron to Murray, 23 April, 16 Oct. 1820, to Richard Belgrave Hoppner, 28 Oct. 1820, *Letters and Journals*, vol. VII, pp. 83, 204.
18 Byron to Murray, 12 Aug. 1820, 12 Sept. 1821, *Ibid.*, vol. VII, p. 158, vol. VIII, p. 207. Journal, 5 & 12 Jan. 1821; to Scott, 12 Jan. 1822, *Ibid.*, vol. VIII, pp. 13, 23, vol. IX, pp. 85–7.
19 Byron to Stendhal ('Henri Beyle'), 29 May 823, *Ibid.*, vol. X, pp. 189–90.
20 Mrs (Anne) Mathews, *Memoirs of Charles Mathews, Comedian*, 2 vols, London, 1838, vol. I, pp. 376–81.
21 Washington Irving, Journal, 27 Aug. 1817, *Journals and Notebooks*, vol. II, p. 98. Irving records that, calling on Scott in late August with an introductory letter from Thomas Campbell, he was received with delight by Scott, who gave him another introductory letter, to his friend the Laird of Ross Priory, for Irving's Highland tour. On his return he had hoped to visit him at Abbotsford, bur Scott was away.
22 Joseph Cogswell to C.S. Davies, 19 Feb. 1819, *Life of Cogswell*, p. 95.
23 Mrs Grant to Mrs Hook, 26 Feb. 1817, *Memoir*, vol. II, pp. 168–9.
24 Do. to Mrs Gorman, 27 July 1818, *Memoir*, vol. II, pp. 109–10.
25 Do. to Mrs Brown, 7 May 1819; *Memoir*, vol. II, p. 232; to Joseph Cogswell, 24 May 1819, *Memoirs of an American Lady*, ed. Ian Grant Wilson, 2 vols, New York, 1901, vol. II, p. 245.
26 Do. to Joseph Cogswell, 14 April 1821, *Memoirs of an American Lady*, vol. II, pp. 250–51.
27 Cecilia Lucy Brightwell, *Memorials of the Life of Amelia Opie*, 2nd edn, Norwich, 1854, pp. 174–5. The date in Miss Opie's biography is wrongly given as November 1816.
28 *The Diary of Frances Lady Shelley 1787–1817* (vol. I), ed. Richard Edgcumbe, London, 1912, p. 139.
29 *Memoirs of a Highland Lady*, vol. II, pp. 72–4. Mrs Jobson was born an Athol Stewart and claimed descent from Robert II.
30 *The Diary of Frances Lady Shelley 1818–1873* (vol. II), London, 1913, pp. 42–45.
31 *Ibid.*, pp. 46–49.
32 *Ibid.*, pp. 54–55, 59–62.
33 *Ibid.*, vol. II, pp. 72, 73.

34 *Ibid.*, vol. II, p. 73.
35 Sydney Smith to J.A. Murray, ?3 Sept. 1820, *Letters*, vol. I, p. 364.
36 *Ibid.*
37 Smith to Archibald Constable, 21 Dec. 1821, to Jeffrey, 30 Dec. 1821, *Letters*, vol. I, pp. 384, 385.
38 Whishaw to Thomas Smith, 28 Dec. 1821, Seymour, *The Pope of Holland House*, p. 240.
39 Do. to Do., 25 March 1820, *Ibid.*, p. 217.
40 John Cam Hobhouse (Lord Broughton), *Recollections of a Long Life*, ed. by his daughter, Lady Dorchester, 6 vols, London, 1909, vol. III, p. 165.
41 Whishaw to Thomas Smith, 8 April 1820; *Ibid.*, p. 218.
42 Lockhart to Jonathan Christie, 5 Dec. 1819, Lockhart, *Life and Letters*, vol. I, p. 93.
43 Do. to Do., 29 Nov. 1815; *Ibid.*, vol. I, p. 97.
44 Do. to Do., 6 Jan. 1816, *Ibid.*, vol. I, p. 104
45 Henry Edward Fox, Journal, 20 Jan. & 5 Feb. 1819, *The Journal of Henry Edward Fox 1818–30*, ed. Lord Ilchester, London, 1923, pp. 30, 33.
46 *Ibid.*, 28 Jan. 1819, 8 Oct., 12 Dec. 1820, pp. 32, 45, 48.
47 *Ibid.*, 20 Dec. 1820, 3 Jan. 1821, pp. 54, 91.
48 *Ibid.*, 23 May 1822, pp. 119–20.
49 *Ibid.*, 7 June 1822, pp. 121–2. Scott acquired his memorabilia from many sources. Humphrey Davy, when in the Tyrol, was presented by the old patriot Speckbacker, in gratitude for Davy's help in an illness, with a gun which he had 'shot 30 Bavarians in one day'. 'I have a friend that would be delighted to have any such article,' said Davy as he received the gift, 'and you may depend on its being hung up in his hall, and the story of it told for many a year to come.' The gun accordingly ended up at Abbotsford. (*Memoir of the Life of Sir Humphrey Davy, Bart*, by his brother, John Davy, 2 vols, London, 1836, vol. I, pp. 506–7.)
50 Henry Fox, Journal, 7 June 1822, *Journal of Fox*, p. 122.
51 Do., 19 June, 3, 6, 10 Aug. 1822, *Ibid.*, pp. 125, 135ff.
52 Henry did not marry Harriet Canning, his parents vigorously opposing any proposal to her. He was a susceptible young man, but only after several flights of fancy did he marry, in 1833 at the age of thirty-one, during his diplomatic career in Italy. His wife was Mary Augusta, daughter of the 8th Earl of Coventry. Unfortunately they left no children, as she habitually miscarried. Henry succeeded his father as 4th Baron Holland in 1840, and died at Naples in 1859. His life is covered in part by Sonia Keppel in *The Sovereign Lady*, Hamish Hamilton, 1974.
53 In London 'The Entry' was exhibited at the Egyptian Hall in Piccadilly, with great success, but through the hostility of Richard Payne Knight the Royal Academy refused to buy it. At the end of the season Haydon had it packed up and sent to Edinburgh by sea.
54 Benjamin Robert Haydon, *Autobiography & Journals*, p. 336.
55 *Ibid.*, pp. 340–1.
56 *Ibid.*, pp. 341–2.
57 Haydon to Wordsworth, 28 April 1820, *Benjamin Robert Haydon: Correspondence and Table-Talk with a Memoir by his Son*, Frederic Wordsworth Haydon, 2 vols, London, 1876, vol. II, p. 36.
58 Haydon, Journal, 30 March 1820, *The Diary of Benjamin Robert Haydon*, ed. Willard Bissell Pope, Harvard UP, Cambridge, Mass., 5 vols, 1960–63, vol. II, p. 268.
59 Haydon *Autobiography*, p. 340; *Diary*, 26 Nov. 1820, vol. II, p. 294.
60 Haydon *Correspondence and Table-Talk*, vol. I, p. 113ff. Southey, who could sometimes make charitable judgments, chided his friend Grosvenor Bedford in 1819

for criticising Haydon who (he said) was admitted even by those who did not like him to be 'of first-rate power in his art'. Although he acted sometimes indiscreetly, even foolishly, 'to speak of him with contempt, and call him a coward, is out of all reason'. He had broken off with Leigh Hunt for the latter's 'mischievous opinions', and in Southey's view, given the opportunity would advance Britain as far in art as it was now ahead in poetry. (Southey, *Selections from the Letters*, vol. III, p. 107.

61 Haydon, *Autobiography*, p. 344.)

62 *Ibid.*, p. 343; also in *Correspondence and Table-Talk*, vol. II, p. 117. There are variations in detail and in inclusions in the different editions.

63 *Autobiography*, p. 343. Andrew Geddes (1783–1844) had exhibited at the Royal Academy since 1806, and was especially successful at etching portraits and copying Old Masters. From 1828–31 he was in Italy, and in 1832 was made an ARA. (*DNB*)

64 *Autobiography*, p. 343.

65 Haydon to Miss Mitford, 5 Dec. 1820, *Correspondence and Table-Talk*, vol. II, p. 67 (also quoted in *Life of Mary Russell Mitford*, vol. II, p. 120).

66 *Autobiography*, p. 342.

67 *Ibid.*, pp. 342ff.

68 Diary, 7 March 1821, Diary, vol. II, p. 311.

69 *Diary*, vol. II, pp. 415ff. Haydon's autobiography and letters differ in detail, and he made corrections before publication of the former. The question is, which description was the more accurate?

70 William Chambers, *Memoir of Robert Chambers*, pp. 169ff.

Chapter 28: Periodical Warfare

1 John Murray (1778–1843), son of the publisher who founded the firm of that name; see *Oxford Companion of English Literature* and *DNB*.

2 Brougham claimed authorship of this article, though it seems to have been written at least in part by Jeffrey. This was the occasion when Lord Buchan kicked the journal into the street.

3 Scott to George Ellis, [15 Dec. 1808], *Letters*, vol. II, p. 138; Lockhart, *Life of Scott*, vol. III, pp. 109, 132.

4 The *Edinburgh Review* continued for exactly 100 years after Jeffrey's resignation in 1829. The *Quarterly* ceased in 1967.

5 William Gifford (1756–1826) was generally considered unfit for the *Quarterly* editorship, notably by Hazlitt in *The Spirit of the Age* (1825), and was revealingly bitter against younger writers. He himself translated Latin satires and edited the works of Jacobean playwrights. (*Oxford Companion to English Literature.*)

6 Southey to James Grahame, 4 Jan. 1808; to H.C. Standert, 14 Dec. 1809, *New Letters*, vol. I, pp. 469, 522.

7 Thomas De Quincey to Dorothy Wordsworth, 5 March 1809, John E. Jordan, *De Quincey to Wordsworth. A Biography of a Relationship*, Univ. of California Press, 1962, pp. 99–100.

8 Thomas Carlyle, 'Christopher North', *19th Century and After*, LXXXVII, Jan. 1920, pp. 103–17. The description, written in 1868, had been intended for Carlyle's *Reminiscences*, but was in the event omitted. The account is also quoted in his *Collected Letters*, vol. IV, pp. 234f.

9 Dorothy Wordsworth to Catherine Clarkson, 28 March 1808, *Wordsworth Letters*, vol. II, p. 260

10 Do. to De Quincey, 1 May 1809, *Wordsworth Letters*, vol. II, p. 326.

11 Wordsworth to Southey, Jan. 1815, *Wordsworth Letters*, vol. III, p. 167.

12 Jeffrey to Horner, 20 July 1810, Cockburn, *Life of Jeffrey*, vol. II, pp. 129–31.

13 Jeffrey to Charles Wilkes, Sept. 1816, 17 Feb. 1817, *Ibid.*, vol. II, pp. 161–2, 167.

14 *Ibid.*, vol. I, pp188–9.
15 Mrs Wilson to her sister, n.d., *'Christopher North,'* vol. I, p. 162.
16 Jeffrey to Horner, 21 Dec. 1809, *Horner Memoirs and Correspondence*, pp. 511–3.
17 Horner to J.A. Murray, 23 Dec. 1809, *Ibid.*, vol. I, p. 514.
18 Horner to Murray, 28 Nov. 1815, *Ibid.*, vol. I, p. 294.
19 George Ticknor to Charles Davies, 8 Feb. 1814, *Life and Letters*, vol. I, pp. 43ff.
20 Jeffrey to Samuel Rogers, 30 March 1814, *Memoirs, Journals etc., of Thomas Moore*, vol. II, p. 13.
21 Simond, *Journal of a Tour*, 1 Jan. 1811, vol. II, pp. 27f.
22 Mrs Grant to Miss Fanshawe, 22 Sept. 1809, *Memoir*, vol. I, pp. 41–2.
23 Gillies, *Memoirs*, vol. II, pp. 117ff. James Hogg, *Memoir of the Author's Life*, ed. Douglas S. Mack, Edinburgh, 1872, pp. 26ff.
24 Gillies, *Literary Veteran*, vol. II, p. 243.
25 Hogg, *Memoir*, vol. II, p. 29.
26 Mary Gordon, *'Christopher North,'* pp. 161f, 171. Scott to Joanna Baillie, 17 Jan. 1812, *Letters*, vol. III, p. 61.
27 Mrs Grant to Mrs Brown, 15 July 1815, *Memoir*, vol. II, p. 92.
28 Mrs Grant to Mrs Gorman, 12 Sept. 1816, *Ibid.*, vol. II, p. 148.
29 Sir George Douglas, *The Blackwood Group*, Edinburgh, 1897, 19–20; Hogg, *Memoir*, p. 42.
30 *Thomas Pringle His Life, Times and Poems*, ed. William Hay, Cape Town, 1912, pp. 16ff.
31 Gillies, *Literary Veteran*, vol. II, pp. 230ff.; Pringle, *loc. cit.*
32 Some chequered years followed for Pringle, shortage of friends, an unhappy marriage, and an attempt to settle in South Africa, where he lost money (but successfully published poetry). Back in London and seeking compensation, he supported Wilberforce's anti-slave trade campaign, but before that succeeded (1834), Pringle was dying of TB. He was buried in Bunhill Fields. Literary friends included Coleridge, and his death was noticed in the *Athenaeum*.

Pringle also edited the *Edinburgh Star*, Scotland's almost sole Liberal paper. His struggling, not very happy career seems hardly to justify the derision he incurred in the 'Chaldee Manuscript'. (*Pringle, ad loc.*)
33 *Blackwood's Magazine*, Nos 1–2.
34 Wilson's daughter Mary Gordon in her biography of her father describes how on evenings at Sym's house Hogg would look wistful until their host took a gold key from round his neck and unlocked 'two splendid fiddle-cases', taking the better instrument himself and offering Hogg the other. Then with a 'sublime' look he would rosin the bow and, seating himself beside Hogg, strike up with him tune after tune, each punctuated with a jovial glass, in a state of ecstasy while the rest of the party continued their conversation and laughter. (*'Christopher North'*, vol. II, p. 267.)
35 Coleridge, *Letters*, vol. IV, pp. 966ff.
36 James Hamilton, *Memoirs of the Life of James Wilson, Esq., FRSE, MWS, of Woodville*, London, 1859, pp. 19–21, 25ff, 81.
37 Gordon, *'Christopher North,'* vol. II, pp. 277–8.
38 *Ibid.*, vol. II, p. 97 & n.
39 *Blackwood's Magazine*, from October 1817; Redding, *Fifty Years' Recollections*, vol. II, p. 176.
40 Coleridge, *Biographia Literaria*, Everyman edn, 1956, pp. 282–3 & n,; *Letters*, vol. IV, p. 785 & n.
41 Coleridge to William Mudford, 19 March 1819, *Letters*, vol. IV, p. 928.
42 Wordsworth to Rev. Francis Wrangham, 19 Feb. 1819, *Letters*, vol. III, pp. 522–4 and n.
43 Wordsworth to Lord Lonsdale, 24 May 1819, *Letters*, vol. III, p. 544.

44 Scott to Jeffrey, 5 Aug., to Sharpe, 7 Aug. 1817, *Letters*, vol. III, pp. 485, 487, and in Sharpe, *Letters of Scott and Sharpe*, vol. II, p. 153; Sharpe to Scott, [Aug. 1817], [Oct. 1817], *Ibid.*, vol. II, pp. 150, 163.

45 Carlyle to Robert Mitchell, 31 March 1817, *Collected Letters*, vol. I, p. 100. The reference is to the *Quarterly Review*, XVI, October 1816, pp. 89–116. Carlyle to James Johnston, 25 Sept, 1817, *Ibid.*, vol. I, p. 109, on the *Quarterly*, XXXIII, April 1817.

46 Do. to Do., 25 Sept.1817, *Collected Letters*, vol. I, p. 109.

47 Redding, *Fifty Years' Recollections*, vol. III, p. 1.

48 *Some Letters of Lord Cockburn*, pp. 91–2; Stanley Jones, 'Hazlitt in Edinburgh: An Evening with Mr Ritchie of the *Scotsman*', *Etudes Angliaises*, Grand-Bretagne-Etats-Unis, Paris, Jan.–March (pp. 109–20) and April–June 1964 (pp. 113–27).

In 1825 McCulloch published *Principles of Political Economy*, and from 1828–37 was Professor of Political Economy at the new London University, and from 1838–64 Comptroller of the Stationery Office. Among his works on statistics and economics in the 1840s and 1850s were *A Dictionary . . . of Commerce and Commercial Navigation* (1832), and an explanation of the wages fund theory. He died in 1864.

John Ritchie (d.1870) became proprietor of the *Scotsman* after the death of his brother William in 1831, until when William and Charles Maclaren had continued joint editors. Maclaren, editor until 1845, also edited the 6th edition of *Encyclopaedia Britannica*, worked on its later editions, and published works on geology. He died in 1866. (*DNB*)

49 *Constable and his Correspondents*, vol. II, pp. 36, 311f.; *Oxford Companion to English Literature*.

50 Macvey Napier (1776–1847) had changed his name from Napier Macvey at his grandfather's request. In 1824 he became Edinburgh's first Professor of Conveyancing, and after Jeffrey's retirement in 1829 he edited the *Edinburgh Review*. In 1837 he became Clerk of Session in Edinburgh.

His own publications met with some misfortune, when he projected an edition of Raleigh's works as early as 1809, but its printing was delayed by Constable, to his annoyance, even after it was advertised in 1814, and it appeared only in 1820, incomplete, and a memoir of Raleigh only in 1840. (*DNB*)

51 *'Christopher North,'* vol. I, p. 260.; Gillies, *Literary Veteran*, vol. II, p. 236.

52 Hogg, *Memoir*, pp. 75–6; also quoted in *'Christopher North,'* vol. I, pp. 269–70; Thompson, *A Scottish Man of Feeling*, p. 357.

53 'Christopher in the Tent', in *Blackwood's*, August & September 1819.

54 After Blackwood died in 1834, Wilson carried on for about ten years, finally handing over editorship to his son-in-law William Aytoun.

55 *Noctes Ambrosianae*, No.2, April 1822.

56 Mrs Grant to Mrs Gorman, 12 June 1818, *Memoir*, vol. II, p. 203.

57 Mrs Grant to Mrs Hook, 23 Jan. 1819, *Ibid.*, vol. II, pp. 223–4.

58 Mrs Grant to Mrs Gorman, 24 May 1819, *Ibid.*, vol. II, p. 236.

59 Mrs Josiah (Bessy) Wedgwood to her sister Jessie (Mme Sismondi), 8 April 1822, Emma Darwin, *A Century of Family Letters, 1792–1866*, ed. Henrietta Litchfield, 2 vols, London, 1915, vol. I, p. 143.

60 Redding, *Fifty Years' Recollections*, vol. III, p. 16.

61 *Ibid.*, vol. III, p. 18; Wilson, in Preface to *Noctes*; *Memorials of James Hogg*, ed. by his daughter Mrs Garden, 2nd edn, 1887, pp. 132f.

62 Hogg, *Memoir*, p. 53; *Memorials of James Hogg*, pp. 135–8; Redding, *Fifty Years' Recollections*, vol. I, pp. 220–1.

63 Journal of Julian Young, in *Memoir of Charles Mayne Young*, vol. I, pp. 149–50. This was related to Julian Young at Lord Lansdowne's house, Bowood, where Moore was a frequent guest.

64 Haydon to Miss Mitford, *Correspondence and Table-Talk*, vol. II, p. 67; *Diary*, pp. 295, 297 (8 Dec. 1820 and Notes after Journey).
65 Lang, *Life of Lockhart*, pp. 124–5; Lockhart to Haydon, 11 July 1838, *Ibid.*, pp. 126ff.
66 *Ibid.*, pp. 124–5; Lockhart to Haydon, 11 July 1838, pp. 131–2.
67 *Ibid.*, p. 191.
68 Scott to Lockhart, July 1820, in Lang, *Life of Lockhart*, pp. 239f, 238.
69 Mrs Grant to Joseph Cogswell, 24 May 1819, *Memoirs of an American Lady*, p. 245.
70 Julian Young, Journal, *Memoir of Charles Mayne Young*, vol. I, pp. 139, 146.
71 Maria Edgeworth to Mrs Ruxton, 8 June 1823, *Life and Letters*, vol. II, p. 100.
72 Lang, *Life of Lockhart*, pp. 283f.

Chapter 29: The Literati in the Field

1 Statement by the Committee of the Inhabitants of the City of Edinburgh, held on 2nd December 1817, upon . . . the North Bridge Buildings, Edinburgh, 1818. Cockburn, *Memorials of his Time*, p. 298; Youngson, *Classical Edinburgh*, pp. 142–3. Attention was called, nearly for the first time, to the duty of maintaining the beauty of Edinburgh (Cockburn, p. 299). The public stand was only partially successful, as the buildings remained, though reduced in height.
2 Mrs Grant to Joseph Cogswell, 24 June 1821, *Memoirs of an American Lady*, Appendix, p. 255.
3 Cockburn, *Memorials*, p. 329.
4 Whishaw to Tom Smith, 30 March 1821, *Pope of Holland House*, p. 245.
5 *Ibid.* As Mrs Grant told Cogswell, 'Professor Seresby is prosecuting Blackwood for accusing him of ignorance in the Hebrew tongue, and Lord Archibald Hamilton, the Coryphaeus of the Scotch Whigs, prosecutes the Beacon for saying that he and his brother, the duke, deserted their part at Hamilton last year for fear of the very Radicals whom their croaking encouraged. As they actually did run away the trial is likely to be a merry one, at least his Lordship, like Falstaff, will be the cause of wit in others.' (24 June 1821, *loc. cit.)*
6 Southey to Rev. Herbert Hill, 20 April 1822, *Selected Letters*, vol. III, p. 303. James Boswell younger (1778–1822), educated at Westminster and Oxford, entered the Middle Temple but remained poor until he eventually became Commissioner of Bankrupts. Besides his work on Malone's papers he edited the third Variorum Shakespeare. He had been at school with Southey, where he was known as 'Dr Johnson' from his frequent Johnsonian quotations.

Sir Alexander Boswell (b.1775) set up a private press at the family seat at Auchinleck where he edited and republished antique poems and other works he had collected, entitled *Frondes Caducae* (1816–18). Like his younger brother he was a member of the Roxburghe Club, and published many verses, including songs in the Scottish dialect. It was he who initiated the proposal for a monument to Burns on the banks of the Doon. In 1818 he became MP for Plympton, Devon, but in 1821 accepted the Chiltern Hundreds. In July 1821 he was made a baronet in recognition of his services in keeping the peace in 1819–21 as a colonel in the Ayrshire Yeomanry.
7 Cockburn, *Memorials*, pp. 329–30 and n.
8 *The Trial of James Stuart, Esq., of Dunearn . . . on Monday, June 10, 1822*; Edinburgh, 1822.
9 *Ibid.*, pp. 27–34.
10 Cockburn, *Memorials*, pp. 338–40.
11 Lang, *Life of Lockhart*, vol. I, pp. 283ff.
12 According to Dr Robert Christison, writing years later, his uncle from Kirkcaldy, Dr Johnson, was in attendance. Lord Rosslyn got him to hide in the corner of

a nearby wood, so that he would see noting and thus avoid being involved as a witness. Christison also says that Stuart was said never to have fired a pistol before. Christison, Journal, *Life*, Oct. 1867, vol. II, pp. 344–5.

13 *Journal of Henry Edward Fox*, 10 June 1821, p. 123.

14 Sydney Smith to Jeffrey, 22 June 1822, *Letters*, vol. I, p. 390.

15 James Stuart (1775–1849) was a graduate of Edinburgh University. After the Boswell affair he visited America (1828) and his subsequent book, *Three Years in North America* (1833), was more strongly disposed towards the Americans than was usual at the time – *vide* Fanny Trollope and others. In 1836 he became inspector of factories. (*DNB*)

There are numerous sources of information on the duel and trial, including: Broadsheet, NLS RY.IIIa.2 (25), A True Account of that Fatal Duel . . . Glasgow Broadsides, L.C. folio 73 (35), Unfortunate Duel . . . Dying Speeches etc. Ry.III.a.2 (27), 'The Whole Particulars of the Trial of Mrs James Stuart . . .' The Trial of James Stuart, Esq., younger, of Dunearn before the High Court of Justiciary, at Edinburgh, on Monday, June 10, 1822, taken in short hand. Broadsides, 1819–31 (BM 1825 b.10 (19)), A True Account of the Fatal Duel . . . Sir Alexander Boswell, *Collected Poems*.

16 Southey to Rev. Herbert Hill, 20 April 1822, *Selected Letters*, p. 304.

17 *Journal of Henry Edward Fox*, *loc. cit.*

18 Mrs Wilson to her sister, 20 May 1818, *'Christopher North,'* vol. I, pp. 277–8. George Combe gives a version which differs in detail but is more colourful. 'A vile attack' on both Jeffrey and John Douglas in the April issue left Jeffrey silently ignoring it, whereas Douglas, when in Edinburgh, bought a large horse-whip, entered Blackwood's shop and there thrashed him soundly (yet another version says he did him little harm), whereupon Wilson, to whom Blackwood hastened, insisted on revenge, went along to catch Douglas at the 4 o'clock coach with his brother James and James Hogg, when Blackwood, armed with a big stick, laid into the assailant. Douglas still had his whip and the two lambasted each other until he entered the coach. (George to Andrew Combe, 15 May 1818, Gibbon, *Life of George Combe*, p. 112). Others say he was almost floored by Blackwood.

George Combe had been legal agent for Cleghorn and Pringle in their dispute with Blackwood when they left his *Edinburgh Monthly Magazine*. Combe contrived to settle the dispute out of court, and Blackwood paid £125 compensation to Cleghorn and Pringle. – *Ibid.*, p. 110.

19 Lang, *Life of Lockhart*, p. 182; *'Christopher North,'* vol. I, pp. 280–4; Jeffrey to Wilson, 13 Oct. 1818, *Ibid.*, vol. I, pp. 293–4.

20 Rev. Robert Morehead to Wilson, Oct. 1818, *'Christopher North,'* vol. I, pp. 285–91.

21 Jeffrey to Morehead, [?October] 1818, *Ibid.*, vol. I, p. 292.

22 Carlyle to his brother Alexander, 2 Jan. 1821, *Collected Letters*, vol. I, p. 302 and n.

23 The dispute and duel are described in Lang, *Life of Lockhart*, pp. 250–80; also Redding, *Fifty Years' Recollections*, vol. II, p. 217.

24 Basil Champneys, *Memoirs and Correspondence of Coventry Patmore*, 2 vols, London, 1900, vol. II, Appendices vols. II–IV. Peter Patmore (1786–1856), father of Coventry Patmore, was Hazlitt's confidant in many of the personal letters published in *Liber Amoris*. In 1841–53 he edited the *New Monthly Magazine*. See Lang and Redding, *loc. cit.*

25 Lockhart's later career was of sorrow, ill-health and some disappointment. After they settled in London, Sophia and their two sons all died untimely, and his job with the *Quarterly* was one of pressure. Mrs Somerville considered that after his bereavement he 'lost much of his asperity' and, as Dr Henry Holland recorded, he became prematurely aged by 'a disappointed and often harassed life'. Like many with an arrogant carapace he was sensitive, too much so for the tough life of an

editor. 'He felt the slavery more than the power.' (*Mary Somerville Recollections*, pp. 99ff; Sir Henry Holland, *Recollections*, p. 87.)

26 Mrs Grant to Joseph Cogswell, 14 April 1821, *Memoirs of an American Lady*, Appendix 251–2.

Chapter 30: Lifestyles

1 Susan Ferrier to Charlotte Clavering, [?autumn] 1809, *Memoir and Correspondence*, p. 68.
2 Elizabeth Hamilton to Mrs [?Churchill], 26 Nov. 1809, NLS MS 3813, 54.
3 Susan Ferrier to Charlotte Clavering, 12 Oct. 1815, *op. cit.*, p. 126.
4 Elizabeth Grant, *Highland Lady*, vol. II, p. 31.
5 Gillies, *Literary Veteran*, vol. I, p. 299.
6 Elizabeth Grant, *op. cit.*, vol. II, p. 41.
7 Mrs Grant to Mrs Hook, 1 July 1815, *Memoir*, vol. II, pp. 89–90. This was 'the fashionable – and, what is much better, the quiet – end of Princes Street . . . more properly a row.' Mrs Grant was lyrical about the view of the Old Town and castle (opposite her windows): 'a verdant little valley, once a small lake, separates it from the majestic pile of towers . . . that form the old town', besides Sir Harry Moncreiff's church, St Cuthbert's, in front of which were two tree-shaded 'quiet humble manses (for it is collegiate)'. There was even a back garden of sorts, which obviously got no sun, 'a fruitless cherry-tree . . . a hopeless stunted plum-tree . . . tolerably decent jasmine' and some non-flowering rosebushes, with a patch of grass in the middle. (Mrs Grant to Mrs Gorman, 16 July 1815, *Memoir*, vol. II, p. 93.)
8 Elizabeth Grant, *op. cit.*, vol. II, pp. 5–6, 7.
9 Betsey Fremantle, Diary, 1 June 1811, *The Wynne Diaries*, pp. 496–7.
10 *'Christopher North'*, vol. I, pp. 298–9.
11 George Combe, *Life of Andrew Combe*, pp. 90, 96.
12 *Memorials of James Hogg*, p. 66.
13 Charlotte Clavering to Susan Ferrier, n.d. [?1817], *Memoir and Correspondence of Susan Ferrier*, p. 131.
14 James Hamilton, *Memoirs of the Life of James Wilson, Esq., FRS, MWS, of Woodville*, p. 132. In 1838, with Wilson's caged birds, the family moved to the more spacious setting of George Square, where they became neighbours of James Hamilton, who was to write Wilson's biography.
15 *Diary of George Combe*, NLS MS 7402, 20 Sept. 1812, 20 Dec. 1812.
16 *Ibid.*, 5 Oct. 1814.
17 Charles Darwin to his father, [Oct. 1825], *More Letters of Charles Darwin*, ed. Francis Darwin, 2 vols, London, 1903, vol. I, p. 6.

Nn.18–32 are from Carlyle's *Collected Letters*, vol. I.

18 Thomas Carlyle to his mother, 17 Dec. 1818, *Collected Letters*, vol. I, pp. 152ff.
19 Do. to his brother Alexander, 23 Feb. 1819, to Thomas Murray, 14 April 1819, *Ibid.*, vol. I, pp. 166–7, 175.
20 Do. to his brother John, 11 Nov. 1819, *Ibid.*, vol. I, p. 205.
21 Do. to mother, 26 Jan. 1820, to Alexander, 19 April, to James Johnston, 6 May 1820, *Ibid.*, vol. I, pp. 226, 240, 245.
22 Do. to Alexander, 23 Nov. 1820, *Ibid.*, vol. I, pp. 287–8.
23 Do. to mother, 6 Dec., to Alexander, 23 Dec. 1820, *Ibid.*, vol. I, pp. 293, 297.
24 Do. to Alexander, 10 Jan. 1821, to John, 25 Jan., to Alexander, 30 Jan. 1821, *Ibid.*, vol. I, pp. 306, 312, 318.
25 Do. to John, 10 Feb. 1821, to Alexander, 19 Feb., 6 March 1821, *Ibid.*, vol. I, pp. 325, 327.

26 Do. to John, 9 March 1821, to Alexander, [24 March] 1821, *Ibid.*, vol. I, pp. 339,349.
27 Do. to mother, 21 July 1821, *Ibid.*, vol. I, p. 371.
28 Do. to Do., 16 Nov. 1821, *Ibid.*, vol. I, p. 393.
29 Do. to Alexander, 21 Nov., 4 Dec., to John, 11 Dec., to Alexander, 25 Dec. 1821, *Ibid.*, vol. I, pp. 397, 402–3, 409, 416. Moray Street is now Spey Street.
30 Do. to Alexander, 19 Dec. 1821, *Ibid.*, vol. I, p. 415.
31 Do.. to Do. 25 Dec. 1821, to his mother, 25 Dec. 1821, *Ibid.*, vol. I, pp. 416–8.
32 Jane Welsh to Carlyle, 29 Dec. 1821, *Ibid.*, vol. I, p. 420.
33 Benson Earle Hill, *Playing About, or Theatrical 'Notes and Adventures*, 2 vols, London, 1840, vol. II, pp. 57ff., 78–9.
34 *Edinburgh Evening Courant*, 25 Feb. 1826.

Chapter 31: Literary Figures (1)

1 De Quincey's affair with Peggy Simpson earned Wordsworth's disapproval, especially when he fathered an illegitimate son on her, and then to the dismay of more than Wordsworth, married her in February 1817.
2 Gillies, *Literary Veteran*, vol. II, p. 219.
3 Lang, *Life of Lockhart*, vol. I, p. 97.
4 *Ibid.*, vol. I, p. 104.
5 John Ritchie Findlay, *Personal Recollections of Thomas De Quincey*, Edinburgh, 1886, pp. 2–6.
6 Alexander H. Japp, *De Quincey Memorials* Being his and other Records here first published, 2 vols, London, 1891, vol. II, pp. 34–36. Wilson to De Quincey, 17 Dec. [1813].
7 Do. to Do., [22 March 1820], *Ibid.*, vol. II, p. 38.
8 James Hogg, *De Quincey and his Friends*, London, 1895, pp. 75–6. The quotation is from Richard Woodhouse, Barrister at Temple, who though not himself a writer met many literary celebrities from about 1820, and was especially fond of Keats. All his notebooks of personalities, full of perceptive recording, were burnt in a fire at the publishers in 1883, except the above, Sept.–Dec 1821.
9 Alexander H. Japp, *Thomas De Quincey, His Life and Writings*, London, 1890, pp. 137–9.
10 John Mitchell (1785–1859), served in the Peninsula and Holland, promoted major 1821, major-general 1855. He also wrote *The Fall of Napoleon* (1845). (*DNB*)
11 Japp, *Thomas De Quincey*, p. 139.
12 *Ibid.*, p. 143.
13 Wilson to De Quincey, [7 Feb. 1821], Japp, *De Quincey Memorials*, p. 46.
14 Lord Webb Seymour to Duke of Somerset, 28 April 1814, *Correspondence of Two Brothers*, p. 135.
15 Duke of Somerset to Lord Webb Seymour, 4 May 1814, *Ibid.*, p. 146.
16 Frederick A. Wendeborn, *A View of England*, vol. II, p. 175.
17 Mrs Wilson to her sister, 29 April 1820, *'Christopher North*,' vol. I, p. 305.
18 Wilson to John Fleming, 2 July 1820, to Mrs Grant of Laggan, [July 1820], *'Christopher North*,' vol. I, pp. 308–12.
19 Wordsworth to Wilson, 5 May 1820, *Wordsworth Letters*, vol. III, p. 594.
20 *'Christopher North*,' vol. I, pp. 313–4.
21 *Ibid.*, vol. I, pp. 316–7.
22 Mrs Grant to Cogswell, 24 June 1821 [sic], *American Lady*, Appendix, p. 254.
23 *'Christopher North*,' vol. I, p. 321.
24 Wilson to De Quincey, 5 Aug. [1820], Japp, *De Quincey Memorials*, vol. II, pp. 43–4.

25 *'Christopher North,'* vol. I, pp. 321ff.
26 *Ibid.*, vol. I, pp. 331–2.
27 David Masson, *Memories of Two Cities, Edinburgh and Aberdeen*, Edinburgh and London, 1911, pp. 111f.; Sir George Douglas, *The Blackwood Group*, pp. 27–8.
28 Wilson to John Smith, Glasgow publisher, 25 Dec. 1820, *'Christopher North,'* vol. I, p. 335.
29 Sir George Douglas, *The Blackwood Group*, p. 34. (But see ch. [9], p. [222]).
30 Wilson to De Quincey, Feb. 1821, Greville Lindop, *The Opium Eater: A Life of Thomas De Quincey*, London, 1981, p. 241.

Except where otherwise shown, nn.31–67 are from Carlyle's *Collected Letters*.

31 Carlyle to Thomas Murray, 24 Aug. 1814, vol. I, pp. 23–4.
32 Do. to Robert Mitchell, 18 Oct. 1814, vol. I, p. 29.
33 Do. to Do., 24 May 1815, vol. I, pp. 46–7.
34 Do. to James Johnston, 10 Dec. 1816, *Ibid.*, vol. I, p. 66. The eclipse was visible in Edinburgh from 7.51 p.m. to 10.07 a.m. on 19 November. (*Ibid.*)
35 *Loc. cit.*
36 This Dissertation, entitled 'Exhibiting a General view of the progress of Mathematical and Physical Science', appeared in the 5th–6th edition's supplement.
37 Carlyle to Mitchell, 12 Feb. 1817, vol. I, pp. 90. 92.
38 Do. to his mother, 17 March 1817, *Ibid.*, vol. I, p. 94.
39 Do. to Johnston,26 June 1818, *Ibid.*, vol. I, pp. 131f.
40 Do. to Mitchell, 31 March 1817, *Ibid.*, pp. 97–9.
41 Do. to Johnston, 25 Sept. 1818, *Ibid.*, vol. I, p. 109.
42 Do. to Mitchell, 6 Nov., 27 Nov. 1818, *Ibid.*, vol. I, pp. 141, 147.
43 Do. to his mother, 17 Dec. 1818, *Ibid.*, vol. I, pp. 151ff.
44 Do. to Johnston, 8 Jan. 1819, *Ibid.*, vol. I, p. 157.
45 Do. to Thomas Murray, 19 Feb., *Ibid.*, vol. I, p. 164. Professor Jameson, the first exponent in Britain of Abraham Werner's theories, later converted to the Huttonian theory.
46 To Alexander, 23 Feb. 1819, *Ibid.*, vol. I, pp. 167–8. The Swedish Dr John Jacob Berzelius (1779–1848) was a founder of modern chemistry, discovering and developing various elements, symbols and techniques; a member and then Permanent Secretary of the Stockholm Royal Academy of Science, and from 1815–32 Professor of chemistry at the Caroline Medical-Surgical Institute there. King Charles XIV created him a baron in 1835. (*Ency.Britannica*) This particular paper was published in the *Edinburgh Philosophical Journal* vol. I, June and October 1819.
47 Carlyle to Alexander, 23 Feb., 29 March 1819, *Ibid.*, vol. I, pp. 168, 171.
48 Do. to Do., 15 Dec. 1819, *Ibid.*, vol. I, p. 212.
49 Do. to Mitchell, 30 Dec. 1819, *Ibid.*, vol. I, p. 218.
50 *Ibid.*, vol. I, p. 216n.; *Reminiscences*, vol. II, pp. 23–25.
51 Do. to Mitchell, 30 Dec. 1819, *Ibid.*, vol. I, p. 218.
52 To Alexander and John, both 26 Jan. 1820, *Ibid.*, vol. I, pp. 221, 224–5.
53 Do. to Alexander, 1 March, 29 March, 19 April 1820, *Ibid.*, vol. I, pp. 229, 235, 240.
54 Do. to Johnston, 6 May 1820, *Ibid.*, vol. I, pp. 245–6, 248.
55 Do. to John Fergusson, 5 Aug. 1820, *Ibid.*, vol. I, p. 271.
56 Do. to Alexander, 23 Nov. 1820, *Ibid.*, vol. I, p. 288.
57 Do. to his mother, 6 Dec., to his father, 18 Dec., to Alexander, 23 Dec. 1820, *Ibid.*, vol. I, pp. 293, 296–7, 298.
58 Do. to Alexander, 2 Jan. 1821, *Ibid.*, vol. I, p. 301.
59 Do. to mother, 10 Jan. 1821, *Ibid.*, vol. I, p. 208.
60 Do. to John, 10 Feb. 1821, *Ibid.*, vol. I, p. 325.
61 Do. to father, 25 Feb. 1821, to his mother, [?March], *Ibid.*, vol. I, pp. 331–2, 334–5.

62 Do. to John, 9 March 1821, *Ibid.*, vol. I, p. 325.
63 Do. to Robert Mitchell, 16 March 1821, *Ibid.*, vol. I, pp. 344–5.
64 Do. to Edward Irving, 14 Aug. 1821, *Ibid.*, vol. I, p. 379. Carlyle's first letter from Jane Welsh was written on 4 June, and received four days after his return from the Haddington visit.
65 Carlyle to father, 12 Jan. 1822, to John, 30 Jan. 1822. *Collected Letters*, vol. II, pp. 4, 24.
66 Various letters to his family and to Jane Welsh, *Collected Letters*, vol. II, Feb., March 1823. The burglary is described to his mother, [16 April 1823], vol. II, p. 335.
67 *Ibid.* Carlyle writes of his attempts to write his Life of Schiller (1823) in *Two Notebooks of Thomas Carlyle*, ed. Charles Eliot Norton, New York, Crolier Club, 1898. Jane Welsh's first repudiation of his marriage proposal was on 16 September 1823 (*Collected Letters*, vol. II, pp. 426–8).
68 Coleridge, *Collected Letters*, vol. IV, pp. 668ff.; Coleridge to Francis Wrangham, 2 June 1817, *Ibid.*, vol. IV, pp. 735–6.
69 Haydon, *Autobiography*, pp. 187, 200.
70 Haydon to Miss Mitford, 1821, *Correspondence*, vol. II, pp. 75–6; *Journal of Washington Irving*, ed. Stanley T. Williams, Harvard UP, 1931, p. 81 (4 Dec. 1823).
71 Jeffrey to William Hazlitt, P.P. Howe, *The Life of Hazlitt*, London, 1922, pp. 254–5. Gregor von Feinagle (?1765–1819), born in Baden, had from 1805 been lecturing on mnemonics. In 1811 he lectured in England and Scotland, and in 1812 published *The New Art of Memory.*
72 Howe, *Life of Hazlitt*, p. 261.
73 Sarah Stoddart was the daughter of a 'disappointed' naval lieutenant; her brother John, a barrister, became Chief Justice in Malta and was knighted in 1826. He had earlier edited an unsuccessful paper, *The New Times*, and among minor works published *Remarks on the Local Scenery and Manners of Scotland* (1801).
74 William Hazlitt, *Liber Amoris*, London, 1834 (Hogarth Press, 1985).
75 Howe, *Life of Hazlitt*, pp. 340ff.; Hazlitt to P. G. Patmore, 21 April 1822, in Appendix III of Hogarth Press edition of *Liber Amoris.*
76 Most of what follows is based on Sarah Hazlitt's Journal, *The Journals of Sarah and William Hazlitt*, 1822–1831, ed. William Hallam Bonner, *University of Buffalo Studies*, vol.24 No.3, Feb. 1989, to p. 21.
77 George Cranstoun (d.1850), a friend of Scott, became Dean of the Faculty of Advocates in 1823 and a judge, as Lord Corehouse, in 1826. His sister Helen was the wife of Professor Dugald Stewart.
78 Hazlitt to Patmore, 30 March 1822, Howe, *Life of Hazlitt*, p. 341.
79 George Combe to Rev. David Welsh, 10 May 1822, Stanley Jones, 'Hazlitt in Edinburgh: An Evening with Mr Ritchie of the *Scotsman*', in *Etudes Anglaises*, Grand-Bretagne-Etats-Unis, Paris, Jan.–March and April–June 1964.
80 In May 1825 Ritchie was to publish a critical review of Hazlitt's *Spirit of the Age* in the *Scotsman*, following Hazlitt's own virulent criticism of the *Scotsman* in the *Liberal* in the year after his divorce. In 1828 Hazlitt published a thinly veiled reference to Ritchie in 'the main Chance', on self-interest in Edinburgh, quoting a 'hard-headed Scotsman' in Nicolson Street, and 'in the next street to it, and in the next street to that, and in the whole of Edinburgh'.
81 Wilson in the first *Noctes Ambrosianae*, and August 1823, quoted in Howe, *Life of Hazlitt*, p. 357; Hazlitt in 'On the Scotch Character', *Ibid.*
82 Hazlitt's later publications included *The Spirit of the Age* (1825), *Boswell Redivivus* (1827) and a four-volume *Life of Napoleon* in 1828 and 1830, the year of his death. He was a wide reader and a successful critic-cum-historian of literature, then a new field, and was the first to make a career mostly from literary criticism. His complete works, edited in the 1930s, ran to 21 volumes.

Chapter 32: Literary Figures (2)

1 Gillies, *Literary Veteran*, pp. 180–84.
2 *Ibid.*, p. 180.
3 *Constable and his Correspondents*, vol. II, p. 335.
4 Ticknor, Journal, March 1819, *Life, Letters, and Journals*, vol. I, p. 279.
5 *Life of Campbell*, vol. II, pp. 208, 212, 282ff.
6 Ticknor, *Life*, vol. I, p. 279.
7 *Life of Campbell*, vol. II, pp. 284–5.
8 Mrs Grant to Mrs Gorman, 24 April 1815, *Memoir*, vol. II, p. 78.
9 *Life of Campbell*, vol. II, p. 285.
10 *Ibid.*, vol. II, p. 286–97.
11 Scott to Campbell, 12 April 1816, *Letters*, vol. III, p. 200; *Life of Campbell*, vol. II, pp. 315–6.
12 *Life of Campbell*, vol. II, pp. 316, 395.
13 *Ibid.*, vol. II, p. 348.
14 Jeffrey to Samuel Rogers, 30 July 1819, Cockburn, *Life of Jeffrey*, vol. I, p. 258.
15 Mary Berry Journal, 7 June 1809 *et al.*, 18 May 1811, *Journals of the Misses Berry*, vol. II, pp. 381, 476f.
16 Mrs Grant to Miss Fanshawe, 30 August 1815, *Memoir*, vol. II, p. 105. *Tancred and Sigismunda* (1745) was a tragedy by the poet and playwright James Thomson (1700–48) based on a tale in *Gil Blas*. It was one of two plays produced only after his death, in 1752 with David Garrick as Tancred.
17 Cockburn, *Life of Jeffrey*, vol. I, p. 260.
18 Quoted in *Berry Journals*, vol. II, p. 470.
19 Mrs Grant to Mrs Hook, 1 Oct. [1816], *Memoir*, vol. II, p. 151.
20 Elizabeth Spence, *Sketches of the Present Manners, Customs, and Scenery of Scotland, with incidental remarks on the Scottish character*, 2 vols, London, 1811, vol. I, p. 222 (Letter XLV).
21 *Loc. cit.*
22 *Ibid.*, vol. I, p. 221.
23 Mrs Grant to Mrs Hook, 1 Oct. [1816], *Memoir*, vol. II, p. 151.
24 Mrs Brunton to Mrs Balfour, 17 Jan. 1818, from Brunton's *Memoir*, p. 47.
25 *Personal Recollections of Mary Somerville*, p. 156.
26 Mary Berry Journal, 12 May 1813, *Journals of the Misses Berry*, vol. II, p. 534.
27 *Romilly–Edgeworth Letters*, p. 41.
28 Susan Ferrier to Mrs Cornell, n.d. [c.1819], *Memoirs and Correspondence*, p. 155.
29 Susan Ferrier to her brother Walter, 10 Dec. 1810, *Ibid.*, p. 106.
30 *Ibid.*, pp. 144, 147.
31 Charles Kirkpatrick Sharpe to the Margravine of Anspach, 17 Aug. 1812, *Sharpe Letters*, vol. II, p. 8.
32 *Life and Songs of Baroness Nairne*, ed. Rev. Charles Rogers, London, 1869, pp. xxiii–iv.
33 *Ibid.*, pp. xxxvi–viii, xxxix.
34 *Ibid.*, p. 181. Colquhoun died in 1820, and his widow survived until 1833, a year longer than Scott.
35 *Ibid.*, pp. xliiff. Lord Nairne fell ill in 1829 with a severe attack of jaundice from which he never really recovered, and died in 1830. His widow and son removed first to Clifton, then to his birthplace in Ireland, and finally to Europe, but the ailing son, now Lord Nairne, died in Brussels in 1837. In 1843, at the invitation of her nephew James Oliphant, his mother returned to Gask, home of her forebears, where she lived retired, undertaking good works for the Kirk. She died after a stroke, in October 1845.
36 Gillies, *Literary Veteran*, vol. II, p. 136.

37 *Ibid.*, vol. II, p. 137–43.
38 Mrs Grant to Mrs Rucker, 3 Nov. 1814, *Memoir*, vol. II, p. 59.
39 Do. to Mrs Smith, 10 Dec. 1816, *Ibid.*, vol. II, pp. 162–3.
40 Elizabeth Grant, *Highland Lady*, vol. II, p. 55. Elizabeth Grant's memory may be at fault here. None of the various Lord Abercrombys was both 'a grave elderly friend' *and* 'unmarried'. She is possibly referring to a Baron of the Exchequer, an office not a title. She could hardly mean Scott's friend George Abercromby (1770–1843), elder son of Sir Ralph Abercromby (1738–1801), victor of Aboukir, but inheriting the title from his mother, created Baroness Abercromby of Aboukir in honour of her late husband. George Abercromby had, however, married Lord Melville's sister in 1800.
41 Elizabeth Grant, *op. cit.*, vol. II, pp. 49–51.
42 Sir Archibald Alison, *Some Account of my Life and Writings*, pp. 171–2.
43 *Ibid.*, p. 141.
44 Burgon, *Memoirs of Patrick Fraser Tytler*, pp. 20, 24; Alison, *Memoir of Patrick Fraser* Tytler, in Patrick Fraser Tytler's *History of Scotland* (vol. III), 1873.
45 Burgon, *Memoir of Tytler*, pp. 60ff.; Alison, *Memoir.*
46 Mrs Grant to Mrs Gorman, 28 May 1816, *Memoir*, vol. II, p. 135.
47 Do. to Do., 16 July 1815, *Ibid.*, vol. II, pp. 94–5.
48 Do. to Mrs Smith, 20 Nov. 1815, *Ibid.*, vol. II, p. 113.
49 Sydney Smith to Lady Holland, [May or June] 1819, *Letters*, vol. I, p. 327.
50 Do. to Jeffrey, 7 August 1819, *Ibid.*, vol. I, pp. 331–2.
51 Jefferson Hogg, *Life of Shelley*, pp. 210–11.
52 Ticknor, *Life, Letters, and Journals*, vol. I, pp. 66–7.
53 *Ibid.*, vol. I, p. 68. Ticknor (1791–1871) raised the stakes of the literary profession in America, and published a standard history of Spanish literature.
54 *Ibid.*, Journal, 10 Feb. 1819, vol. I, p. 273.
55 *Ibid.*, Journal, March 1819, vol. I, pp. 277, 275.
56 *Ibid.*, vol. I, p. 278.
57 Mrs Grant to an American friend, 24 June 1819, *Memoir*, vol. II, pp. 288–9.
58 Cogswell to Ticknor, 23 March 1819, *Life of Joseph Green Cogswell*, pp. 95–6; Ticknor, *Life, Letters, and Journals*, vol. I, pp. 281ff.
59 Ticknor, Journal, March 1819, 23 March ff., *Life, Letters, and Journals*, vol. I, pp. 282ff.
60 Southey to Rev. Herbert Hill, 22 March 1819, *Selected Letters*, vol. III, pp. 124–6, 134.

Chapter 33: The Social Background

1 Cockburn, *Memorials*, p. 92.
2 Helen Graham, Diary, 4 Jan. 1825, *Parties and Pleasures*, pp. 117–8; Scott to Joanna Baillie, 4 April 1812, *Letters*, vol. III, p. 97.
3 Elizabeth Grant, *Highland Lady*, vol. II, pp. 8–9.
4 *Ibid.*, vol. II, pp. 9ff.
5 *Ibid.*, vol. I, p. 111, vol. II, pp. 13–20.
6 *Ibid.*, vol. II, pp. 91–2.
7 Her grandfather, the Earl of Melfort, had been Secretary of State to King James VII and II and accompanied him in exile.
8 Lady Clementina Davies, *Recollections of Society*, pp. 65, 67.
9 Charles Sharpe to Scott, 10 June 1812, Scott to Sharpe, 18 June 1812, *Letters*, vol. I, pp. 547, 548.
10 Davies, *Recollections*, vol. I, p. 68.
11 *Ibid.*, vol. I, pp. 68ff.

12 *Ibid.*, vol. I, pp. 82–5.
13 Cogswell to Ticknor, 6 April 1819, *Life of Joseph Green Cogswell*, p. 106.
14 This is related by Elizabeth Grant (*Highland Lady*, vol. II, pp. 98–9), in about 1818, of Miss Maclean, prettiest daughter of the Barrack Master at Berwick. The wager was so successful that for a time 'she lived in a mob, was deluged with invitations and was temporarily taken up by the Count and Countess de Flahault. The young lady's reign was short, but 'Oh! it was glorious!' In the end she made a not particularly glamorous marriage to a Lt. Clarke, and accompanied him to Bombay.
15 Cogswell to Ticknor, 23 March and 9 April 1819, *Life*, pp. 95–6.
16 Davies, *Recollections*, pp. 88–91. Some allowance may be made for exaggeration in Clementina's details as, like so many ladies, she wrote her memoirs many years later.
17 Elizabeth Grant, *Highland Lady*, vol. II, pp. 60–61.
18 Sharpe to Scott, 7 April 1819, *Letters*, vol. II, p. 199.
19 Elizabeth Grant, *Highland Lady*, vol. II, p. 91.
20 *Ibid.*, vol. II, p. 67.
21 *Ibid.*
22 Cockburn, *Memorials*, pp. 31–2.
23 Redding, *Fifty Years' Recollections*, vol. III, pp. 37f.
24 H. Graham, Journal, 4 Feb. 1824, *Parties and Pleasures*, p. 40.
25 *Loc. cit.*
26 E. Grant, *Highland Lady*, vol. II, p. 90.
27 Christison, *Life*, vol. II, pp. 349–50.
28 *Ibid.*, vol. II, pp. 346–7.
29 *Ibid.*, vol. II, pp. 347–8.
30 *Edinburgh Advertiser*, 22 Dec. 1815.
31 Davies, *Recollections*, vol. I, pp. 75–7.
32 Rev. Daniel Sandford to his daughter Fanny, 2 Nov. 1814, *Remains*, vol. I, p. 336.
33 Davies, *Recollections*, vol. I, pp. 78–81.
34 E. Grant, *Highland Lady*, vol. II, pp. 47–8.
35 *Ibid.*, vol. II, p. 41. For Lady Molesworth see p.
36 *Ibid.*, vol. II, p. 42ff.
37 *Ibid.*, vol. II, pp. 44–5.
38 *Ibid.*, vol. II, p. 88.
39 *Ibid.*, vol. II, pp. 87–8.
40 Mrs Grant to Miss Fanshawe, 20 Nov. 1811, *Memoir*, vol. I, pp. 299–300.
41 Do. to Mrs Gorman, 25 Jan. 1819, *Ibid.*, vol. II, p. 227.
42 *Ibid.*, vol. II, p. 226.
43 Do. to Mrs Smith, 2 March 1819. *Ibid.*, vol. II, pp. 228–9. William Campbell Preston (b.1794), son of a Member of Congress for Virginia, had travelled to Europe to complete his education after travels in America. On arrival in Liverpool he had been taken seriously ill and was rescued by Washington Irving, with whom he became friendly and visited Wales and Scotland with him, afterwards travelling to the Continent. Most of his European visit, including London and Edinburgh, was never written up. He did, however, leave a blistering criticism of 'English reticence . . . a surly and ill mannered and unsympathetic manner. It is a national character resulting from the false and foolish notion that true dignity is to be always on the watch for aggression and that *nihil admirati* is elegant and aristocratic. All emotion is vulgar and ardor horrible.' That was the English. Preston's comments on the Scots would have been worth hearing. Even Washington Irving was criticised to the extent of his 'propriety, fitness, retention' and for trying to restrain Preston's own American over-exuberance. Few Americans apart from Fenimore Cooper were so dismissive. Preston fulfilled Mrs Grant's expectations

by becoming Senator for South Carolina and, in the 1840s, a distinguished speaker in Congress. (*Reminiscences of William Campbell Preston*, ed. Minnie Clare Yarborough, University of N. Carolina Press, 1933, p. 34.)

44 Mrs Grant to Mrs Smith, 2 March 1819, *Memoir*, vol. II, pp. 228–9.

45 Mrs Grant to Mrs Hook (in another hand), 15 Nov. 1820, *Ibid.*, vol. II, p. 275.

46 Mrs Grant to Mrs Brown, 30 Dec. 1820, to Mrs Hook, 17 Jan. 1821, *Ibid.*, vol. II, pp. 277, 279.

47 Mrs Grant to Mrs Hook, Mrs Brown, Miss Catherine Gorman, Mrs Smith, Mrs Izett, 19 Feb.–21 August 1821, *Ibid.*, vol. II, pp. 284–300.

48 Mrs Grant to Mrs Hook, Mrs Gorman, Mrs Brown, 28 Sept. 1821–13 Jan. 1822, *Ibid.*, vol. II, pp. 301–317.

49 *The Reminiscences of Charlotte, Lady Wake*, ed. Lucy Wake, London, 1908, pp. 68f. Charlotte Tait (b.1800), in 1822 married Charles Wake, of Courteenhall, a young army officer she had met in Edinburgh among the troops come to guard French prisoners. Her brother Archibald became Archbishop of Canterbury.

50 Jan Willison, born in 1785, was only ten years older than Constable's eldest son David. She had been educated in France, and was interned there during the war, escaping on a ship with a false passport (1807). She never married, having turned down a young French suitor in order to look after her widowed father, and from then on she lived alternately with him and with her sister at Craigcrook. She was permanently lamed by a fall in one of Edinburgh's steep streets, and walked a mile after the accident before Professor Syme diagnosed a broken leg. She was a 'never failing delight' with her liveliness and tales of her foreign adventures, though perhaps unconsciously funny rather than actually witty. Jan lived until 1870, though in later life severely deaf and senile. (*Constable and his Literary Correspondents*, vol. II, p. 99.)

51 Cockburn, *Life of Jeffrey*, vol. I, pp. 213–4.

52 Horner to his sister Fanny, 5 Sept. 1812, *Memoirs and Correspondence*, Vol II, 111.

53 Cockburn, *Life of Jeffrey*, vol. I, p. 234.

54 James Taylor, *Lord Jeffrey and Craigcrook. A History of the Castle*, Edinburgh, 1892, pp. 1–4; Jeffrey to Charles Wilkes, 7 May 1815, *Ibid.*, pp. 5–6; Cockburn, *Life of Jeffrey*, vol. II, pp. 155–6.

55 Horner to Jeffrey, 19 April 1815, *Memoirs and Correspondence*, vol. I, p. 253.

56 E. Grant, *Highland Lady*, vol. II, pp. 89–90.

57 Jeffrey to John Richardson, 24 July 1817, Cockburn's *Life of Jeffrey*, vol. II, pp. 172–3.

58 Washington Irving, Journal, 27 Aug. 1817, *Journals and Notebooks*, vol. I, p. 99.

59 Cockburn, *Life of Jeffrey*, vol. I, pp. 236–7.

60 'Peter Morris' [John Gibson Lockhart], *Peter's Letters to his Kinsfolk*, 3 vols, 3rd [i.e. 2nd] edn, Edinburgh 1819, vol. I, pp. 64ff.

61 Jeffrey to Charles Wilkes, 9 May 1818, Cockburn, *Life of Jeffrey*, vol. II, pp. 175ff., Taylor, *Jeffrey and Craigcrook*, p. 8.

62 *Ibid.* Although apparently part of the same letter, the latter gives a less idyllic impression, chiefly of the weather.

63 Henry Fox, Journal, 19 May 1822, *Fox Journal*, p. 118.

64 *Ibid.*, 8 June 1822, p. 122. Mackintosh's 'success' possibly refers to his recent election to the Rectorship of Glasgow University (Mackintosh, *Memoirs*, vol. II, p. 410).

65 *Ibid.*, 10 June 1822, pp. 123–4.

Chapter 34: The Church

1 *Fasti Ecclesiasticae Scoticanae*, vol. I, p. 42. Inglis's son John was to become Lord Justice General and Lord President, as Lord Glencorse, in the 1850s and 1860s.

2 *Peter's Letters*, vol. III, pp. 74–8.

3 *Ibid.*, vol. III, pp. 79–85; Rev. Donald Sage, *Memorabilia Domestica; or, Parish Life in the North of Scotland*, 2nd edn, Wick, 1899, p. 241.
4 Mrs Grant to Mrs Izett, 13 Jan. 1822, *Memoir*, vol. II, pp. 318–9.
5 Do. to Mrs Brown, 10 March 1822, *Ibid.*, vol. II, p. 322, to Mrs Izett, *loc. cit.*
6 *Peter's Letters*, vol. III, p. 87.
7 Christison, *Life*, vol. I, pp. 410–11.
8 Sage, *Memorabilia*, p. 175.
9 *Ibid.*, pp. 171–2.
10 Carlyle to mother, [?March] 1821, *Collected Letters*, vol. I, p. 335.
11 Hugh Miller, *My Schools and Schoolmasters*, ed. W.M. Mackenzie, Edinburgh, 1907, pp. 350–51.
12 Dr McCrie's son, another Thomas (1797–1875), also attended Edinburgh University, was ordained in 1820, became a DD of Aberdeen and LLD of Glasgow, and was later Professor of Church History and Theology at the London College of the English Presbyterian Church. (*DNB*)
13 Crabb Robinson, Diary, 9 Sept. 1821, *Diary, Reminiscences and Correspondence of Henry Crabb Robinson, Barrister-at-Law, FRS*, ed. Thomas Sadler, 3 vols, London, 1869, vol. II, p. 211.
14 Later a Baptist chapel.
15 *Remains of Sandford*, vol. I, pp. 46–8; Morehead, *Life and Writings*, pp. 162–3.
16 *Peter's Letters*, vol. III, p. 91.
17 Lindsay, *Georgian Edinburgh*, pp. 33–4.
18 Carlyle to Mitchell, 19 November 1817, *Collected Letters*, vol. I, p. 113. Dowie's, a dark, stuffy tavern in Liberton Wynd, was where Burns, Thomas Campbell, John Wilson and others met for convivial evenings. It was demolished for the building of the North Bridge approach.
19 *Peter's Letters*, vol. III, pp. 93–5.
20 Morehead, *Life and Writings*, pp. 164ff.
21 Susan Ferrier to Charlotte Clavering, n.d. [1816], *Memoirs and Correspondence*, p. 129.
22 Sage, *Memorabilia*, pp. 277–8.
23 Mrs Grant to Mrs Gorman, 28 May 1816, *Memoir*, vol. II, pp. 135–6.
24 Do, to Mrs Rucker, 29 May 1814, *Ibid.*, vol. II, pp. 46–7, to Mrs Gorman, *loc. cit.*
25 Do. to John Richardson, *Ibid.*, vol. II, p. 137.
26 James Dodds, *Thomas Chalmers. A Biographical Study*, Edinburgh, 1870, p. 123.
27 *Memoirs of Chalmers*, vol. II, p. 69; Dodds, *Thomas Chalmers*, pp. 126f.
28 Dodds, *Thomas Chalmers*, p. 133.
29 Sage, *Memorabilia*, p. 242.
30 *Ibid.*, pp. 242, 244.
31 *Ibid.*, pp. 244–50. David Boyle (1772–1853) was called to the Bar in 1793, was MP for Ayrshire from 1807–11, and became successively Solicitor-General (1807), Lord Justice Clerk (1811), Privy Councillor (1820), Lord Justice General and President of the Court of Session (1840–52). His title as judge was Lord Boyle.
32 Carlyle, *Collected Letters*, vol. I, p. 99n.; Mitchison, *History of Scotland*, pp. 320, 330–1, 355.
33 *Peter's Letters*, vol. III, pp. 98ff.
34 Carlyle to mother, 4 May 1821, *Collected Letters*, vol. I, pp. 356–7.
35 Sage, *Memorabilia*, p. 263.
36 Henry Fox, Journal, 22 May 1822, *Fox Journal*, p. 119.
37 Chalmers, *Memoirs*, vol. I, pp. 291–2.
38 *Ibid.*, vol. I, pp. 367ff.
39 Mrs Grant to Mrs Rucker, 8 Nov. 1815, *Memoir*, vol. II, pp. 108–9.
40 Dodds, *Thomas Chalmers*, pp. 116–7.
41 Mrs Grant to Mrs Hook, 26 Feb. 1817, *Memoir*, vol. II, p. 168.

42 Andrew Bigelow [of Medford, Mass.], *Leaves from a Journal*, 12 April 1817, p. 25. Bigelow, of a distinguished Massachusetts family, was asked to write up his travel diaries in 1819 for 'a southern journal'. The pieces appeared in *Analectic Magazine* and its successor, the *Philadelphia Literary Gazette*, etc.
43 *Life of George Combe*, p. 140 (1821).
44 David Walsh (1793–1845) became minister of Crossmichael in 1821, and in Glasgow 1827; an honorary DD of Glasgow 1831, Professor of Church History at Edinburgh 1831–43, and at the Free College, Edinburgh 1844–5. He published his sermons, and edited Thomas Brown's *Lectures on the Philosophy of the Human Mind* (1834). (*Life of Combe*, p. 145)
45 Bigelow, 12 & 13 April 1817, *Leaves from a Journal*, pp. 21–3.
46 Whishaw to Tom Smith, 21 Oct. 1820, *Pope of Holland House*, pp. 223–4.
47 Mrs Grant to John Richardson, 3 June, to Mrs Rucker, 4 June 1816, *Memoir*, vol. II, pp. 137–41.
48 *Peter's Letters*, vol. III, pp. 268–72.
49 William Wilberforce, Diary, quoted in Chalmers *Memoirs*, vol. II, pp. 102–3. Maria Stanley to Mrs Edward Stanley, June 1817, *Early Married Life*, p. 402. In 1818 Chalmers, corresponding with Wilberforce, commented on the Prince Regent's speech on the serious shortage of Anglican churches to serve England's increasing population. 'The habit of church-going has got most wofully into desuetude, and nothing should be overlooked which can help to restore it.' (Chalmers to Wilberforce, 9 Feb. 1818, *A Selection from the Correspondence of the late Thomas Chalmers, DD, LLD*, ed. Rev. William Hanna, Edinburgh, 1853, p. 93.)
50 Wordsworth to Crabb Robinson, 24 June 1817, *Letters*, vol. III, p. 391.
51 Cockburn, *Life of Jeffrey*, vol. I, pp. 253–4.
52 Chalmers to Rev. John Foster, 8 Nov. 1821, *Correspondence*, pp. 118–9.
53 Carlyle to Mitchell, 5 July 1817, *Collected Letters*, vol. I, p. 104, to Do., 25 May 1818, vol. I, p. 130.
54 Carlyle's system was continued long after he left Glasgow, until the unfortunate 1845 Act introduced the English poor law to Scotland. See, e.g., Rosalind Mitchison, *A History of Scotland*, pp. 387–8.
55 Chalmers *Memoirs*, vol. I, pp. 217ff.; Chalmers to Wilberforce, 9 Feb. 1818, *Selections from Correspondence*, p. 96.
56 Henry Fox, Journal, 18 May, 26 May 1822, *Fox Journal*, pp. 117–8, 120.
57 Crabb Robinson, Diary, 9 Sept. 1821, *Diary, Reminiscences*, vol. II, p. 211.
58 [Charles Shore], Lord Teignmouth, *Reminiscences of Many Years*, 2 vols, Edinburgh, 1878, vol. I, pp. 304, 313, 318–9, 323–4. Charles Shore (b. India 1796), was the eldest son of John Shore, Governor General of India in 1796 and given an Irish peerage in 1798. When at school under the Rev. Charles Jerram at Chobham, among Charles's fellow-pupils were Patrick Fraser Tytler and two successive Earls of Moray, while at Cambridge he was contemporary with Spencer Percival. After foreign travel and two visits to Dublin, where in 1821 he witnessed the King's visit (therefore did not stay to see it all again in Edinburgh), the brothers toured the Highlands. Henry Shore unfortunately died in France shortly after a rendezvous visit with their family. Charles, who succeeded to the peerage in 1834, made further visits to Scotland. He became MP for Marylebone in 1837.
59 Young, *Charles Mayne Young*, vol. I, pp. 158–61.
60 Chalmers *Memoirs*, vol. II, pp. 347ff.; Wilkie to his sister, 1 Oct. 1822, *Life*, vol. II, pp. 93–4.
61 Chalmers *Memoirs*, vol. II, pp. 356f.
62 *Ibid.*, vol. II, pp. 277, 368, 373, 401.
63 Carlyle, *Reminiscences*, ed. Charles Eliot Norton, vol. II, pp. 17–18.
64 *Ibid.*, vol. II, pp. 21–4.
65 Carlyle, *Reminiscences*, ed. J.A. Froude, 2 vols, London, 1881, vol. I, p. 115.

66 *Ibid.*, ed. Norton, pp. 61–2.
67 *Ibid.*, pp. 61–2.
68 Andrew Landale Drummond, *Edward Irving and his Circle*, 1792–1834, London, 1937, p. 30.
69 Carlyle, *Reminiscences*, ed. Froude, p. 151.
70 *Ibid.*, p. 153; Chalmers, *Memoirs*, vol. II, pp. 249, 282f.
71 Carlyle, ed. Froude, p. 160.
72 *Ibid.*, p. 215.
73 Drummond, Edward Irving, pp. 49–50; Frances Williams Wynn, *Diaries of a Lady of Quality, from 1797–1844*, ed. A. Hayward, London, 1864, pp. 110–11.
74 Mrs Oliphant, *The Life of Edward Irving, Minister of the National Scotch* Church, 2 vols, London, 1862, vol. II.
75 Drummond, *Edward Irving*, pp. 53, 90, 103f.
76 Julian Young, *Charles Mayne Young*, vol. II, pp. 113ff. This description is, in fact, borrowed almost word for word from *A Portion of the Journal kept by Thomas Raikes, Esq., from 1831 to 1847*, 4 vols, London, 1856–7, vol. II, p. 61.
77 Frances Williams Wynn, *Lady of Quality*, pp. 110–16.
78 Diary of John H. Merivale, 2 July 1823 *et al.*, 19 Jan. 1824, *Family Memorials*, compiled by Anna Merivale, p. p. , Exeter, 1884, pp. 244ff.; Edward H.A. Koch, *Leaves from the Diary of a Literary Amateur. John Herman Merivale, 1819–1844*, p.p., Hampstead, 1911.
79 Redding, *Fifty Years' Recollections*, vol. III, p. 20.
80 Mary Berry, Journal, 21 Sept. 1823, 5 Nov. 1823, *Journals and Correspondence*, vol. III, pp. 346, 348.

Chapter 35: Colleges and Schools

1 James Nasmyth, Engineer, *An Autobiography*, London, 1883, pp. 79–80, 82.
2 *Ibid.*, p. 98.
3 Nodier, *Promenade from Dieppe*, pp. 89, 96.
4 Josiah Livingston, *Our Street. Memories of Buccleuch Place*, Edinburgh, 1893, pp. 55ff.
5 James Nasmyth, *Autobiography*, pp. 89–90.
6 *Ibid.*, pp. 80–81.
7 Livingston, *Our Street*, pp. 3, 7, 29, 30, 40–41, 66, 48–9, 9, 39.
8 *Life of Christison*, vol. II, p. 413.
9 Holland, *Recollections*, p. 80.
10 *Ibid.*, pp. 29–30, 82–3.
11 *Autobiographical Recollections of George Pryme, Esq., MA*, ed. by his daughter, Alice Byre, 2 vols, Cambridge, 1870, vol. I, p. 120.
12 Miss Edgeworth to Mrs Ruxton, Jan. 1810, *Life and Letters* vol. I, p. 160; George Combe, *Life of Andrew Combe*, pp. 41f.
13 Carlyle to Mitchell, 24 May 1815, *Collected Letters*, vol. 1, pp. 46–7.
14 Wilkie to Haydon, 7 August 1817, Haydon, *Correspondence and Table-Talk*, vol. I, p. 320.
15 *Constable and his Literary Correspondents*, vol. II, pp. 31–2.
16 Edward Lytton Bulwer, *England and the English*, 2 vols, London, 1833, vol. II, p. 161.
17 Rev. William Field, *Memoirs of the Reverend Samuel Parr*, 2 vols, London, 1828, vol. II, pp. 234, 236.
18 Spencer Walpole, *The Life of Lord John Russell*, 2 vols, London, 1889, vol. II, pp. 44, 45.
19 Ticknor, Journal, March 1819, *Life, Letters, and Journals*, p. 279.
20 Carlyle to Mitchell, 12 Feb. 1817, *Collected Letters*, vol. I, p. 90.
21 *Constable and his Literary Correspondents*, vol. II, pp. 381–2.

22 John Leslie to Constable, 14 Dec. 1818, *Ibid.*, vol. II, p. 386.
23 *Ibid.*, vol. II, p. 389.
24 Carlyle to Mitchell, 31 March 1817, *Collected Letters*, vol. I, p. 97.
25 Do. to father, 2 Sept. 1818, to Mitchell, 30 August, *Ibid.*, vol. I, pp. 138, 140; to his mother, 17 Dec. 1818, p. 138; *Ibid.*, vol. I, p. 153.
26 Do. to Mitchell, 18 Nov. 1819, *Ibid.*, vol. I, p. 147.
27 Cogswell to Mrs Prescott, 18 Dec. 1818, *Life*, p. 91.
28 Carlyle to Mitchell, 17 Nov. 1818, *op. cit.*, vol. I, p. 147.
29 Do. to James Johnstone, 6 May 1820, *Ibid.*, vol. I, p. 246.
30 Elizabeth Grant, *Highland Lady*, vol. II, p. 51.
31 *Loc. cit.*
32 In 1838 Brewster became principal of the Colleges of St Salvator and St Leonard, Aberdeen, in 1860 Principal and Vice-Chancellor of Edinburgh University and in 1864 President of the Royal Society. In 1834 he joined the Scottish Free Church movement. (*DNB*)
33 Ticknor, Journal, March 1819, *Life, Letters, and Journals*, p. 280.
34 Mrs Grant to Mrs Smith, 1 Jan. 1816, *Memoir*, vol. II, p. 118.
35 Cecilia Lucy Brightwell, *Memorials of the Life of Amelia Opie*, 2nd edn, Norwich, 1854, pp. 150–1.
36 Drummond, *Edward Irving and his Circle*, p. 19.
37 Archibald Murray to Constable, 4 July, to Robert Cadell, 10 July 1812, *Constable and his Literary Correspondents*, vol. I, pp. 323–5.
38 Carlyle to Mitchell, 31 March 1817, *Collected Letters*, vol. I, p. 98.
39 *Samuel Parr Memoirs*, pp. 230, 232.
40 *Life of Christison*, vol. I, p. 10.
41 *Ibid.*, vol. I, p. 41.
42 *Ibid.*, vol. I, p. 42.
43 *Ibid.*, pp. 43–4.
44 *Ibid.*, vol. I, p. 46.
45 *OEC* XX, Appendix 30, XVI, Appendix 8. Louisfield, the house of Louis Cauvin (*c.*1754–1825), described in 1935 as 'a plain, villa-like building', was near Jock's Lodge, Duddingston. The school continued until after the Second World War, and is still referred to as Cauvin's Hospital.

Cauvin was a Freemason and a friend of Robert Burns. His son became a WS.
46 Vol. I, pp. 48–9
47 *Ibid.*, vol. I, p. 555.
48 *Ibid.*, vol. I, pp. 58–9
49 *Ibid.*, vol. 1, pp. 61–2

Chapter 36: Medicine and Surgery

1 This chapter is largely based on Douglas Guthrie, *A History of Medicine*, London and Edinburgh, 1945; Alexander Miles, *The Edinburgh School of Surgery before Lister*, London, 1918; John Struthers, *Historical Sketch of the Edinburgh Anatomical School*, Edinburgh 1867.
2 Benjamin Rush to the Trustees of the University of Pennsylvania, 20 Jan. 1813, *Letters*, p. 1180.
3 *Edinburgh University, A Sketch*, 1884; Wright St Clair, *Doctors Monro*, p. 115.
4 John Bell's works included *Elements of the Anatomy of the Human Body*, 2 vols, 1825. The number of Bells in Edinburgh's surgical world is confusing, more confounded by there being a second, unrelated family.
5 Struthers, *Edinburgh Anatomical School*, pp. 44f.

6 In 1836 Charles Bell, who had been knighted in 1831, rather misguidedly interrupted his successful London career and returned to Edinburgh to take over the chair of surgery. Hailed as 'the Magna Carta of Neurology', he was awarded the first medal of the Royal Society (1829). He died in 1842.
7 *Medical Times and Gazette*, January 1980.
8 *Edinburgh Medical & Surgical Journal*, 1805.
9 Sir Walter Scott, Journal, 5 Dec. 1825, 3 Dec. 1827, *Journal of Sir Walter Scott, 1825–1832*.
10 Miles, *Edinburgh School of Surgery*, p. 81.
11 G. Combe, *Life of Andrew Combe*, pp. 38–40.
12 *Scots Magazine*.
13 *Life of Christison*, vol. I, pp. 6–7.
14 Struthers, *Edinburgh Anatomical School*, pp. 63–5; Cresswell, *Royal College of Surgeons of Edinburgh*, pp. 203–4.
15 *Life of Christison*, vol. I, pp. 176–7.
16 Kay, *Portraits*, vol. II,, CLII, The Craft in Danger.
17 *Life of Christison*, vol. I, p. 79.
18 *Ibid.*, vol. I, p. 80.
19 Mrs Grant to Cogswell, 14 April 1821, *Memoirs of an American Lady*, vol. II, p. 252.
20 Mrs Grant to Mrs Catherine Gorman, 29 April 1821, *Memoir*, vol. II, p. 288.
21 Elizabeth Grant, *Highland Lady*, vol. II, pp. 63–4.
22 Miles, *Edinburgh School of Surgery*, pp. 148ff.
23 *Ibid.*, pp. 174ff.
24 *Life of Christison*, vol. I, pp. 75f; DNB for John Abercrombie.
25 *Life of Christison*, vol. I, pp. 84–7.
26 *Ibid.*, vol. I, pp. 113–25, 137, 141.
27 *Ibid.*, vol. I, pp. 141–7.
28 *Ibid.*, vol. I, pp. 152–6.
29 *Ibid.*, vol. I, pp. 158–60.
20 *Ibid.*, vol. I, pp. 170ff., 181ff., 275–9.

Chapter 37: Two Sides of the Law

1 Dairy of George Combe, 31 Jan. 1812, NLS MS 7402.
2 Alison, *My Life and Writings*, pp. 107f.
3 Mrs Grant to Miss Fanshawe, 20 March 1818, *Memoir*, vol. II, p. 197. One of Crawfurd's cousins was married to Dr Gregory, another to Sir George Mackenzie. 'You Anglo-Saxons', Mrs Grant told Miss Fanshawe, 'have no conception how long and fine the threads of consanguinity are drawn out in this externally cold country.' (*Ibid.*)
4 Cockburn, *Life of Jeffrey*, vol. I, pp. 200–203.
5 Gillies, *Literary Veteran*, pp. 207–8, Cockburn, *Life of Jeffrey*, vol. I, p. 200.
6 E. Grant, *Highland Lady*, vol. II, pp. 67–9.
7 Cockburn, *Memorials*, pp. 133–4; see also Brougham, *Life and Times*, p. 229.
8 Gillies, *Literary Veteran*, vol. II, p. 40.
9 Cockburn, *Memorials*, pp. 139–42.
10 *Some Letters of Lord Cockburn, with pages omitted from the Memorials of his Time*, ed. Harry A. Cockburn, Edinburgh, 1932, p. 105.
11 Cockburn, *Life of Jeffrey*, vol. I, pp. 209–12. In June 1799 Jane Cranstoun married the much older Count Purgstall. After it had been 'much rumoured in Edinburgh last winter', he suddenly returned to the city and carried her off as a bride to his estate on the borders of Styria and Hungary, 'a splendid match'. She was a sad loss

to Thomas Thomson and his circle. (Thomson to his father, 26 June 1795, Cosmo Innes, *Memorials of Thomas Thomson, Advocate*, Edinburgh, Bannatyne Club, 1854, p. 33.)

12 *Letters of Lord Cockburn*, p. 88; Cockburn, *Memorials*, vol. I, pp. 124–5.

13 Mrs Grant to John Richardson of Pitfour, 21 May 1816, *Memoir*, vol. II, p. 129.

14 E. Grant, *Highland Lady*, vol. II, p. 59.

15 *Letters of Lord Cockburn*, p. 105.

16 *DNB*.

17 *Proceedings at the Dinner given to Lord Erskine . . . the 21st February, 1820, by Francis Jeffrey, Esq.*, Edinburgh, 1820; Cockburn, *Memorials*, pp. 316–7.

18 Lady Morgan (Sydney Owenson), *The Book of the Boudoir*, 2 vols, London, 1829, vol. I, pp. 117–9.

19 Later Miss Opie went with Lord Erskine to Lady Cork's, where as so many celebrities had gone to the opera to view the Royals, it was a 'small' party of about sixteen: but then it included Dr Spurzheim, Monk Lewis, Horace Twiss, Lady Caroline Lamb . . . (Amelia Opie to her father, 16 June 1814, Brightwell, *Amelia Opie*, p. 159. Richard Rush, *Residence at the Court of London*, journal, 4 March, pp. 117–9.)

20 *Letters of Lord Cockburn*, p. 82; Richard Rush, *The Court of London from 1819 to 1825*, ed. Benjamin Rush, 3rd edn, London, 1873, pp. 28f.

21 Elliot was architect of the Regent Bridge, St Paul's Episcopal Church and the County Hall. This was demolished in 1900, and the prison, all but the Governor's house, in 1938. (Howard Colvin, *A Biographical Dictionary of British Architects, 1600–1840*, John Murray, 1995, pp. 339, 56. The Bridewell was demolished about 1884.)

22 Nodier, *Promenade from Dieppe*, p. 78.

23 [Elizabeth Fry &] Joseph John Gurney, *Notes on a visit made to some of the Prisons of Scotland and the North of England, in company with Elizabeth Fry . . .*, London, 1819, pp. 41–49.

24 Sharpe to Scott, [October] 1818, *Letters*, vol. II, p. 164.

25 *Ibid.*

26 W. Chambers, *Memoir of Robert Chambers*, pp. 92–98.

27 James Nasmyth, *Autobiography*, pp. 84–86. John Linnell (1792–1882), a man of strong libertarian principles, had come to Scotland to marry because his scruples prevented his marrying under the strict English law. A portrait and landscape painter, he had exhibited at the Royal Academy and Society of Painters in Oil and Water Colours, and became a close friend of William Blake. He entered his name for ARA in 1821 but withdrew in disgust in 1842 and later declined membership when offered.

Fifty-seven years after his appearance at the destruction of the Tolbooth, James Nasmyth met him at an Academy private view, 'a remarkable and venerable-looking old gentleman', who when James introduced himself recalled the rat incident, and confessed that he still possessed the skeleton in a 'cabinet of curiosities'. (Nasmyth, *loc. cit.*)

28 *Last Leaves from the Journal of Julian Charles Young*, AM, Rector of Ilmington, Warks, Edinburgh, 1875 (visit of 1872), p. 142.

29 Clementina Davies, *Recollections of Society*, pp. 57–8.

30 Elizabeth Spence, *Letters from the North Highlands*, pp. 19–21.

31 Nodier, *Promenade from Dieppe*, p. 85.

32 W. Chambers, *op. cit.*, p. 91.

33 *Reminiscences and Table-Talk of Samuel Rogers*, ed. G.H. Powell, London, 1903, p. 223.

34 *Memoirs of Patrick Fraser Tytler*, p. 129.

35 Mrs Christian I. Johnstone, *The Saxon and the Gael*, 4 vols, London, 1814; *Edinburgh: A Satirical Novel*, by the author of *London; or, A Month at Stevens's*, 3 vols, London, 1820, vol. III, pp. 153–4. The grandfather of these sisters, Lt.

Alexander Home, RN, had claimed the title as nearest heir-male descended from George Hume of Wedderburn, younger brother of Patrick 1st Earl of Polwarth, who had been further created Earl of Marchmont in 1697. On his death the ladies' father, Captain Francis, took up the claim. The case dragged on until 1842, when a rival case was made by Sir Hugh Hume Campbell, of Marchmont. However, as too many claimants appeared to exist, the claim was eventually dropped. (Balfour Paul, *Scots Peerage*, vol. VI, who does not, however, mention the sisters and their straitened circumstances.)

36 Mrs Grant to Mrs Gorman, 27 July 1818, *Memoirs*, vol. II, p. 208.

37 James Nasmyth, *Autobiography*, pp. 67–8.

38 Charles Dibdin, elder, *Observations on a Tour, through almost the whole of England, and a considerable part of Scotland, in a series of letters*, 2 vols, London, 1802. vol. II, p. 208.

39 Charlotte, Lady Wake, *Reminiscences*, pp. 41–2.

40 James Nasmyth, *Autobiography*, pp. 67,69.

41 *Ibid.*, pp. 70–71.

Chapter 38: Artists and Musicians

1 *Life of David Roberts*, pp. 9ff.

2 *Ibid.*, p. 10; see also Armstrong, *The Edinburgh Stage.*

3 *Life of Roberts*, pp. 11ff.

4 Clarkson Stanfield (1793–1867) had entered the merchant service in 1808 and in 1812 was pressed into the Royal Navy. In 1818 he left the sea and became a scene painter at Drury Lane. He later specialised in marine and landscape painting and was known as 'the English Vandevelde'. In 1836 he painted 'The Battle of Trafalgar', and from 1847 lived at Hampstead. (*DNB*)

5 *Life of Roberts*, pp. 18ff.

6 Cooksey, *Alexander Nasmyth*, pp. 91–2.

7 *Ibid.*, p. 92. There is no official record of such a gift, which James Nasmyth may have confused with the Calton Hill scheme award. James Nasmyth, *Autobiography*, pp. 42–3.

8 *Ibid.*, p. 94.

9 *Ibid.*, pp. 92–3.

10 Cockburn to Thomas Dick Lauder, 15 Feb. 1822, *Some Letters of Lord Cockburn*, p. 20. George Joseph Bell was brother to the surgeon Charles Bell, who had moved to London in 1805.

11 Mrs Grant to Mrs Gorman, 11 Nov. 1818, *Memoir*, vol. II, p. 215.

12 Cockburn, *Memorials*, p. 400. Williams died in 1829, 'the severest loss' to the arts in Scotland, according to Cockburn. (*Ibid.*)

13 Gillies, *Literary Veteran*, vol. II, p. 211.

14 William Allan (1782–1850), who helped to set the fashion for historical painting in Scotland, later became President of the Royal Scottish Academy, was elected RA in 1835 and knighted in 1842. Walter Scott was a great admirer.

15 Adela Geddes, *Memoir of the late Andrew Geddes, Esq., ARA*, London, 1844, *passim.*

16 *Peter's Letters*, vol. II, pp. 234f.

17 C.R. Leslie to his sister Betsey, 20 April 1821, to Washington Irving, 2 April 1820, *Autobiographical Recollections of the late Charles Robert Leslie, RA*, ed. Tom Taylor, 2 vols, London, 1860, vol. I, p. 111. Charles Robert Leslie (1794–1859) became an acknowledged expert of literary and narrative painting. In 1843 he published the classic *Life* of his friend John Constable, and his own autobiography was published in 1860. (*OCA*)

18 Scott, *Letters*, vol. VII, p. 381, October 1818.
19 Jane Schetky to her brother, 22 No.1818, *Ninety Years of Work and Play*, pp. 138–9.
20 Alexander Schetky sailed in 1823 for Sierra Leone to become Deputy Inspector of Hospitals, but sadly died of fever in 1824. When the news reached home in November, John Schetky was devastated. He was seen one morning 'pacing up and down in the studio, valise in hand', in despair how to tell his old father. But on arrival at their St Vincent Street house he found the old man ill and failing fast, and as he was on the brink of death Schetky never revealed to him Alick's death. (*Ninety Years of Work and Play*, p. 139.)
21 J.M.W. Turner to Robert Stevenson, 8 July 1819, *Collected Correspondence of J.M.W. Turner*, ed. John Gage, Oxford, 1980, pp. 79–80.
22 Gerald Finley, *Turner and George the Fourth in Edinburgh 1822*, Tate Gallery and Edinburgh UP, 1981, p. 16.
23 George Jones, RA, *Sir Francis Chantrey, RA, Recollections of his Life, Practice, and Opinions*, London, 1849, p. 80.
24 Lindsay, *Georgian Edinburgh*, pp. 41–2.
25 Moore, Journal, 23 October 1821, *Memoirs, Journals etc. of Thomas Moore*, ed. Russell, vol. III, p. 292.
26 Haydon, *Autobiography*, p. 65; David Hunter to Constable, 15 March 1807, *Constable and his Literary Correspondents*, vol. I, pp. 105–6.
27 Redding, *Recollections*, pp. 120f.; Haydon, *Autobiography*, p. 65.
28 Wilkie was rather scathing about Inveraray and its 'illusory grandeur', which 'on acquaintance dwindled into a little new-fashioned modern upstart of a Scottish town', while the castle was just 'Bond Street or Brighton'. He also saw Loch Lomond and at Blair Atholl stayed with the Duke, and at Leslie with Lord Leven. (Wilkie to his brother Thomas, 21 August 1817, Allan Cunningham, *The Life of Sir David Wilkie*, 3 vols, London, 1843, vol. I, pp. 472f.)
29 *Ibid.*, vol. I, pp. 482f.
30 *Ibid.*, vol. II, pp. 58f.; W. Wilkie Collins, *Memoirs of the Life of William Collins, Esq., RA*, with selections from his Journals and Correspondence, London, 2 vols, 1848, vol. I, pp. 128–30, 191–4, 208ff., 197.
31 Mrs Grant to Sir Walter Farquhar, 9 Oct. 1811; to John Henning, 20 Jan. 1812, *Memoir*, vol. I, pp. 292–4, 310–11; to Henning, 25 April, 20 June, 24 July 1812, to Mrs ——, New England, 23 May 1813, to Henning, 24 April, 20 Dec. 1814, vol. II, pp. 6–8, 14, 32, 42, 63.
32 Mrs S. Uwins, *A Memoir of Thomas Uwins, RA, late Keeper of the Royal Galleries and the National Gallery (etc.)*, 2 vols, London, 1858, vol. I, pp. 5ff.
33 Thomas Uwins to his brother Zechariah, 7 October 1821, *Ibid.*, vol. I, p. 90.
34 Do. to his mother, 12 Nov. 1822, *Ibid.*, vol. I, pp. 93–5.
35 Do. to Zechariah, 28 April 1823, *Ibid.*, vol. I, pp. 96–8.
36 *Ibid.*, vol. I, pp. 98ff. The visit to Italy proved a turning-point in Uwins's life. On return to England he lived in Paddington Green and other West London addresses, was elected ARA in 1833, RA in 1838, and in 1847 became Keeper of the National Gallery. In 1855, in bad health, he retired to Staines, where he died two years later.
37 E. Grant, *Highland Lady*, vol. II, pp. 94–5.
38 *Ibid.*, vol. II, pp. 67–8.
39 *Memoir and Correspondence of Susan Ferrier*, pp. 155n.
40 Cockburn, *Life of Jeffrey*, vol. I, p. 204.
41 Gillies, *Memoirs*, vol. II, p. 209.
42 Ferrier, *loc. cit.*
43 Graham, *Parties and Pleasures*, February 1824, p. 43; 19 March 1825, p. 127.
44 Cockburn, *loc. cit.*
45 E. Grant, *Highland Lady*, vol. II, p. 70.

46 Susan Ferrier to Mrs Connell, [?1821]. *Memoir*, p. 161.
47 Cockburn to Thomas Dick-Lauder, 16 Oct. 1815, *Some Letters*, p. 14.
48 Susan Ferrier to Charlotte Clavering, 12 Oct. 1815, *Memoir*, p. 126.
49 Cockburn, *Memorials*, pp. 253–4.
50 Domenico Dragonetti (1763–1846), born in Venice and largely self-taught, at eighteen was performing in the orchestra at St Mark's. In 1794 he went to London to play in opera orchestras and give recitals with Lindley. He visited Vienna, knew Beethoven and Haydn, and composed solos for his own instrument, the double bass. Robert Lindley (1777–1855), born in Rotherham, a pupil of Cervetto, was principal cellist of the opera orchestra in London (1794–1851), and was a recital partner of Dragonetti. Charles Ashley (1773–1843), a cellist, had been secretary of the Royal Society of Music since 1811. (Michael Kennedy, *Concise Oxford Dictionary of Music* (updated).)
51 *Edinburgh Advertiser*, 13 October–15 November.
52 E. Grant, *Highland Lady*, vol. II, pp. 86–7.
53 Jane Schetky to her brother, 22 November 1818, Schetky, *Ninety Years of Work and Play*, p. 109.
54 *Edinburgh, A Satirical Novel*, vol. II, p. 260.
55 George Combe, MS Diary, 28 February 1814.
56 E. Grant, *Highland Lady*, vol. II, pp. 83–5.

Chapter 39: A New Start in the Theatre

1 J. Dibdin, *The Edinburgh Stage*, p. 270.
2 Robert Chambers, *The Edinburgh Theatre Royal*,.
3 Mrs Grant to Mrs Fletcher, 4 August 1815, *Memoir*, vol. II, p. 98.
4 *Edinburgh Evening Courant*, 26 September–12 October 1815. Dates of closing and reopening the theatre during this summer and autumn are confusing.
5 *Ibid.*, 15 October 1815.
6 Mrs Grant to Mrs Gorman, 19 December 1815, *Memoir*, vol. II, p. 116.
7 Amelia Opie to her father, 1 July 1814, Brightwell, *Amelia Opie*, p. 165.
8 Chambers, *The Edinburgh Theatre Royal*; Armstrong, *Edinburgh Stage*, vol. I; Dibdin, *The Edinburgh Stage*, p. 272.
9 Charles Mathews to his wife, 13 April 1812, 13 April 1816, *Memoirs*, vol. II, p. 211.
10 Do. to Do., 13 April 1816, *Ibid.*, vol. II, pp. 388–90; 19 April 1816, pp. 391ff.
11 J. Dibdin, *The Edinburgh Stage*, pp. 273, 274.
12 *Ibid.*, pp. 274–5.
13 John W. Francis, MD, *Old New York; or, Reminiscences of the Past 60 Years* (based on a talk given to the New York Historical Society, 17 November 1857), enlarged edition, New York, 1858, pp. 221–3.
14 Elizabeth Spence, *Letters from the North Highlands*, pp. 318–9.
15 Dibdin, *The Edinburgh Stage*, p. 275.
16 The *Scotsman*, January 1817.
17 Scott to Mrs Clephane, [23 March 1817], *Letters*, vol. IV, pp. 420–21 and n.
18 Dibdin, *The Edinburgh Stage*, p. 279.
19 Gillies, *Literary Veteran*, vol. I, pp. 255, 260.
20 Dibdin, *The Edinburgh Stage*, pp. 279–81.
21 Charles Mathews to his wife, January 1818, 19 Jan. 1818, *Memoirs*, vol. II, pp. 429, 431.
22 William Blackwood to Peter Patmore, 29 January 1818, Champneys, *Memoirs of Coventry Patmore*, vol. II, app. V.

23 Dibdin, *The Edinburgh Stage*, pp. 282ff.; the *Scotsman*, 7 March and 5 Dec. 1818, quoted *loc. cit.*

24 George Combe to Andrew Combe, March 1819, Gibbon, *Life*, p. 118.

25 E. Grant, *Highland Lady*, vol. II, pp. 101–2.

26 *Ibid.*, p. 102. Elizabeth Grant, writing many years later, quite possibly confused the dates.

27 Mrs Grant to Mrs Gorman, 27 July 1818, *Memoirs*, vol. II, p. 229.

28 Sydney Smith wrote to Lord Grey that he thought often of Miss O'Neill, 'that fool Lord Normanby has not married her' (24 August 1818, *Letters*, vol. I, p. 298). In fact Lord Normanby, heir to Lord Mulgrave, a great theatre fan and author early in life of novels and romances, had just (12 August) married Lord Ravensworth's daughter.

29 Dibdin, *The Edinburgh Stage*, pp. 285–8, quoting the *Courant* and the *Scotsman*.

30 *Ibid.*, pp. 289–91.

31 *Ibid.*, p. 291; *Macready's Reminiscences, and Selections from his Diaries and Letters*, ed. Sir Frederick Pollock, 2 vols, London, 1875, vol. I, p. 181.

32 Southey, Journal, 18 August 1819, Robert Southey, *Journal of a Tour in Scotland in 1819*, London, 1929, p. 9.

33 *Diary of Frances Lady Shelley*, pp. 58–9. Catherine Stephens (1794–1882), singer and actress, made £30,000 from her voice, with which she was able to maintain her large family of relatives. From 1807–12 she appeared at Covent Garden, played Sheakespearean parts, and created Susanna in *The Marriage of Figaro* (1819), and several parts in adaptations of Scott's novels, 1816–20. Before her retirement in 1835 she played at Drury Lane and Covent Garden, highly praised by Hazlitt and Leigh Hunt. In 1838 she married the 5th Earl of Essex. (*DNB*)

34 Mathews to his wife, 20 October 1819, *Memoirs*, vol. III, p. 95.

35 Dibdin, *The Edinburgh Theatre*, pp. 294–5.

36 *Ibid.*, pp. 295–6.

37 Chambers, *Edinburgh Theatre Royal.*

38 Dibdin, *The Edinburgh Theatre*, p. 296.

39 *Ibid.*, p. 297. John William Calcraft, *An Address to the Public containing Observations on some late Criticisms connected with the Edinburgh Theatre*, Edinburgh, John Anderson, 1832.

40 Dibdin, *The Edinburgh Theatre*, p. 297.

41 Armstrong, *Edinburgh Stage*, vol. III. There seems no documentary evidence for work by Burn.

42 Dibdin, *ibid.*, pp. 336f. This version of Corri is presented in a bill of suspension and interdict which Mrs Siddons later brought against Corbet Ryder, which may not be quite true, and Corri may or may not have become bankrupt.

43 Dibdin, *The Edinburgh Theatre*, *ibid.*, pp. 338ff.; Armstrong, *Edinburgh Stage*, vol. III.

44 Mathews to his wife, 5, 9 & 12 February 1822, *Memoirs*, vol. III, pp. 258ff.

45 *Ibid.*, vol. III, p. 315; Francis, *Old New York*, p. 242. Incidentally John Francis first heard from Mathews, when he was appearing in New York in 1822, 'a pretty decisive opinion' that Sir Walter Scott was the author of 'the Novels'. This was before Scott disclosed the truth at the Ballantyne dinner, and while Coleman in the *Evening Post* in New York was still assuring everyone that the author was 'a Major, or Colonel Scott, of Canada'. (*loc. cit.*)

Chapter 40: Adventures and Curiosities

1 Robert Chambers, *Traditions of Edinburgh*, 1868, p. 303. The whole story is related on pp. 301ff.

2 —— Denovan, *The Life and Trial of James Mackoull*, 1822.

3 *A Memoir of Zerah Colburn, written by himself*, Springfield [Vermont], Mass., 1833, *Life of William Allen*, 3 vols, London, 1846, vol. II, p. 107. The account of Zerah's career is to be found in his autobiography.
4 Lady Harriet Elliot to her brother Viscount Melgund, 19 January 1814, NLS, Minto MSS 11756.
5 Rev. Daniel Sandford to his son Daniel, 28 December 1813, *Remains*, vol. I, p. 277.
6 Lord Webb Seymour to his brother the Duke of Somerset, 17 January 1814, *Correspondence of Two Brothers*, p. 127.
7 Calling on Basil Montagu with the news, Zerah met the Rev. Edward Irving, and noticed his 'cranium and countenance indicative of a strong mind'. A fairly obvious observation, perhaps.
8 A brief summary of Zerah's life is also to be found in the *Dictionary of American Biography*, ed. Allen Johnson and Dumas Malone, London, 1930, vol. IV, pp. 283–4. Two small books on gasworks and waterworks published in 1865 and 1867 under the name Zerah Colburn are not surprisingly not recorded in this *Dictionary* or in the autobiography, but the duplication of so unusual a name is curious.
9 *Edinburgh Annual Register*, 1819, p. 391; *DNB*.
10 Illustrated poster in Miscellaneous Broadsides 1819–31, British Library 1875.b.30 (43); *Edinburgh Evening Courant*, 3 Jan. 1822.
11 *Ibid.*, (4).
12 A Complete List of all the Bonny Ladies, who are assembled in Edinburgh during the Race Week, with their Names and Characters . . . together with an account of their different Prices. [n.d.] Printed for the Flying Stationers. *Ibid.* (33).
13 The account of Sadler's ascent is covered in the *Edinburgh Evening Courant*, 21, 28, and 31 October and 4 and 7 November 1815. For the summary of his career, *DNB*.
14 *Some Letters of Lord Cockburn*, pp. 14ff.
15 Miscellaneous Broadsides, *loc. cit.* (37).
16 John Howell (1788–1863), first apprentice to a bookbinder, became assistant to the bookseller Kinnear, spent 15 years in the pressroom of Stevenson, printer to the University, and thenceforward was independent, publishing and editing, bookbinding (in Thistle Street), improving the stereotyping process, and inventing the 'plough' or page-trimmer. He later moved to Rose Street, with the street sign 'Polyartist'. His obituary published in the *Scotsman* (6 April) and the *Staffs Advertiser* (18 April 1863), gives no date for his inventions, which included failed attempts to fly and to launch a submarine. Alexander Laing, in Foreword to the *Life and Adventures of John Nicol, Mariner*, London, 1937, pp. 18f., 26–29.
17 Gordon, *'Christopher North,'* vol. II, pp. 26–7.
18 *Edinburgh Evening Courant*, 30 March 1815.
19 Journal of Richard Bush, 21 June 1819, R. Bush, *The Court of London*, pp. 87ff.
20 James Nasmyth, *Autobiography*, p. 88.
21 E. Grant, *Highland Lady*, vol. II pp. 51–2.
22 Haydon, *Autobiography*, p. 340.
23 Clementina Davies, *Recollections*, vol. I, p. 65.
24 Mrs Grant to Mrs Gorman, 24 May 1819, *Memoir*, vol. II, p. 237.
25 Mrs Fletcher, *Autobiography*, p. 138.
26 *Edinburgh*, 1820, vol. I, pp. 29–31, 46, 215ff.
27 Al Alison, *My Life and Writings*, p. 60.
28 Helen Graham, Diary, 14 February 1824, *Parties and Pleasures*, p. 45.
29 *Narrative of the Life and Travels of Serjeant [Robert] Butler*, written by himself, 3rd edition, Edinburgh, 1854, p. 42. The work was written in the 1820s.
30 Carlyle to Mitchell, 11 January and 15 February 1815, *Early Letters of Thomas Carlyle*, ed. Charles Eliot Norton, 2 vols, London, 1886, vol. I, pp. 19, 58.
31 Do. to Do., 18 November 1819; to his brother Alexander, 23 November 1820, *Collected Letters*, vol. I, pp. 207, 287.

32 Do. to his brother John, 26 September 1822, *Ibid.*, vol. II, p. 169.
33 Serjeant Butler, *Narrative*, pp. 298ff.
34 Daniel Carless Webb, *Observations and Remarks during Four Excursions made to various parts of Great Britain, in the Years 1810 and 1811* . . ., London, 1812, pp. 226ff, 250.
35 Simond, *Journal of a Tour*, vol. II, pp. 52–55.
36 A version in the *Caledonian Mercury* somewhat vindicates the magistrates, who had actually had the 'apparatus' checked, claimed that the rope was indeed too long – the hangman was later dismissed – and that Johnson could have been hanging for only seconds before the carpenters axed the woodwork, had not the mob showered them with stones (including Johnson himself) that they were forced indoors. Nearly 200 panes of the church windows were smashed before the body was carried off.
37 *Letter to the Magistrates of Edinburgh, on the Execution of Robert Johnson*, by an Eye Witness, Edinburgh, 1819 (with undated press cutting), NLS 3/2737(4a); *Letter to the Rt Hon. The Lord Advocate, on the Execution of Robert Johnson, Dec. 30, 1818*, by 'Vindex', Edinburgh [1819], NLS 3/2737(5); MS note by Henry Cockburn in his own copy of the four pamphlets on Robert Johnson's execution, B.Lib. 1131 c.8–1–4; *Address to the Inhabitants of Edinburgh*, on the Outrages committed on the 30th December. Amicus Ventatis, Edinburgh, 1819, *Ib.*(4); *Letter to the Citizens of Edinburgh in which the cruel and malicious aspersions of an 'Eye-Witness' are answered, and the conduct of the magistrates is placed in its true light*, by 'Civis', Edinburgh, 1819, NLS 3/2737(4) (also in 3/2749(11)).

Chapter 41: Phrenology

1 *Encyclopaedia Britannica*, *loc. cit.*
2 George to Andrew Combe, 29 April 1818, *Life*, pp. 111–2.
3 *Ibid.*, pp. 116f. Much of what follows is recorded by Charles Gibbon in his *Life of George Combe*, pp. 120–48.
4 Advert, Luke O'Neill & Son, Canongate, 1823.
5 George Combe, *Andrew Combe*, pp. 123ff.
6 Hamilton, a metaphysician, had studied at Glasgow and Balliol College, Oxford, where he was a friend of Lockhart's. In 1816 he established his claim to a baronetcy, and through Wilson met De Quincey in Edinburgh. He too had travelled in Germany, and in 1821 was appointed Professor of Civil History at Edinburgh. He joined in the controversy against Phrenology.

Colquhoun, a son of the second baronet of Luss, had been educated at Göttingen, became an advocate in Edinburgh, and from 1815–54 was Sheriff of Dunbartonshire. He studied psychical research, produced several psychological theories, such as on the association of ideas, wrote on animal magnetism, was interested in mesmerism, and partly translated Kant. In 1836 he became Professor of Logic and Metaphysics at Edinburgh, when his lectures made a great impression. From 1829 he had been celebrated for articles on philosophy in the *Review*. In 1844 he became partly paralysed. (*DNB*)
7 Gillies, *Literary Veteran*, vol. III, pp. 93–4.

Chapter 42: The Scottish Regalia

1 Hugo Arnot, *History of Edinburgh*, 1788, p. 291.
2 Lockhart, *Life of Scott*, vol. V, pp. 249ff.; Scott to Duke of Buccleuch, 17 January 1818, *Letters*, vol. V, pp. 57, 59, 60.

3 The others were William Adam, Lord Chief Commissioner of the Jury Court, Major-General John Hope, C-in-C Scotland, James Wedderburn, Solicitor-General, William Clerk, Principal Clerk of the Jury court, Henry Jardine, Deputy Remembrancer to the Exchequer, Thomas Thomson, Deputy Clerk Register, and Walter Scott, a Principal Clerk of Session.

4 Scott to J.W. Croker, 7 February 1818, *Letters*, vol. V, pp. 74–7.

5 Alexander Maconochie to Viscount Sidmouth, 7 February 1818, *The Letters of King George IV, 1812–1830*, ed. A. Aspinall, 3 vols, Cambridge, 1938, vol. II, p. 246; John Wilson Croker to Sir Benjamin Bloomfield, 7 February 1818, *Ibid.*, vol. II, p. 245. Maconochie (1777–1861) had been Solicitor-General in 1813 and Lord Advocate from 1816. He became MP for Yarmouth in 1817 and for Kilrenny district of burghs in 1818–19. In 1819 he was raised to the Bench with the title Lord Meadowbank which had been borne by his father, who died in 1816.

6 *Description of the Regalia of Scotland*, Edinburgh, 1841; *Edinburgh Evening Courant*, 5 February 1818; *The Scottish Regalia, Anciently styled The Honours of Scotland*, compiled by W.D. Collier, Edinburgh, HMSO, 1841.

7 Scott to William Dundas, 14 February 1818, *Letters*, vol. V, p. 81; *Edinburgh Evening Courant*, 12 February 1818.

8 *Description of the Regalia*; *The Scottish Regalia.*

9 M. Audubon, *Audubon and his Journals*, 2 vols, London, 1898 (March 1827).

10 Frances Ann Kemble, *Record of a Girlhood,* 3 vols, London, 1878, vol. I, p. 255.

Chapter 43: Accolade

1 Lockhart to Hogg, 13 July 1821, *Memorials of James Hogg*, pp. 143–5; *Ibid.*, p. 148.

2 C.K. Sharpe to Lady Charlotte Campbell, [late] 1817, *Letters*, vol. II, p. 174.

3 Mrs Grant to Mrs Col. White, [summer 1822], *Memoir,* vol. III, p. 4.

4 Davy to his brother, August [printed here 1821, evidently for 1822], *Fragmentary Remains of Sir Humphrey Davy*, p. 238.

5 Jane Grant (of Rothiemurchus) to her mother, 8 August 1822; [*Letters from Jane and Mary Grant on Edinburgh visit,* August 1822], p.p. , Dublin (bound with no title, no title page or imprint), p. 4.

6 *Life of George Crabbe*, pp. 259, 262.

7 Nodier, *Promenade from Dieppe*, p. 81.

8 Gillies, *Literary Veteran*, vol. III, pp. 70, 71.

9 Robert Gilfillan, *Songs*, 2nd edn, enlarged, Edinburgh, 1836. Gilfillan (1798–1850) was Collector of Poor Rates in Leith.

10 Henry Fox, Journal, 19 July, 3 August, 10–14 August 1822, *Journal*, pp. 135ff. The 8th Earl of Lauderdale had been a close friend of Henry's father, Lord Holland, but had drifted into Toryism. In 1821 he had accepted a 'Green ribbon' (Order of the Thistle) to Lord Holland's sorrow, but Henry commented that 'he is baby enough to be captivated with any of these silly distractions' (Journal, 17 July).

11 Fox, *loc. cit.*

12 *Voyage Historique*, vol. III, p. 439.

13 *Ibid.*, vol. III, pp. 413–5.

14 *Ibid.*, vol. III, p. 266.

15 Cunningham, *Life of Wilkie*, vol. II, pp. 82–3; Wilkie Collins, *Memoirs of the Life of William Collins, Esq., RA*, with selections from his Journals and Correspondence, 2 vols, London, 1848, vol. I, pp. 197ff.

16 Norman Gash, *Mr Secretary Peel*, revised edn, Longman, 1985, pp. 301ff.

17 J. Dibdin, *Edinburgh Stage*, p. 300.

18 Jane to Elizabeth Grant, 9 August 1822, Jane and Mary Grant, *Letters on Edinburgh Visit*, pp. 10f.

19 Sir William Knighton to [a member of his family], 16 August 1822, Lady [Dorothy] Knighton, *Memoirs of Sir William Knighton, Bart, GCE, Keeper of the Privy Purse*, 2 vols, Paris, 1838, vol. I, p. 118.
20 Pichot, *Voyage Historique*, vol. III, p. 424.
21 Lockhart, *Life of Scott*, vol. III, p. 48; C. Young, *Memoir of Charles Mayne Young*, p. 154.
22 Knighton, *Memoirs*, vol. I, p. 119.
23 Lockhart, *loc. cit.* (who calls it 'Highland whisky'); Knighton, *loc. cit.* (who calls it cherry brandy). According to Pichot (vol. II, pp. 424–5) the 'cup of welcome' was presented by Scott to the King – rather unlikely in the King's own yacht? – and not vice versa.
24 Pichot, *Voyage Historique*, vol. III, p. 423.
25 Young, *Charles Mayne Young*, vol. I, p. 153.
26 Pichot, *Voyage Historique*, vol. III, p. 435.
27 Jane and Mary Grant, *Letters on Edinburgh Visit*, pp. 15ff. The exhaustively detailed *Historical Account of His Majesty's Visit to Scotland*, published by Robert Mudie immediately afterwards, provides much of the material on the occasion. Useful and based on Mudie in the Scottish National Portrait Gallery's handbook to an exhibition in 1961, *Visit of George IV to Edinburgh 1822*, compiled by the late Basil Skinner. Gerald Finley, *Turner and George the Fourth in Edinburgh 1822*.
28 Except for the High Constable of Leith, detachments of the various troops escorted all the processions during the visit.

The artist painting the Squadron was Schetky. Others busily recording the scene were the engraver W.H. Lizars, James Skene, Scott's topographical artist friend, and the young marine painter George Philip Reinagle. (*An Historical Account of His Majesty's visit to Scotland*, Edinburgh, 1822, ch. III.)
29 An iron plaque marked the spot, inscribed 'Geo.IV – O Felicem Diem'.
30 The costume worn by Baillie McFie, a well-to-do sugar refiner, is preserved at the Huntly House Museum in Edinburgh.
31 William Collins to his mother, 17 & 28 August 1822, *Memoirs of the Life*, vol. I, pp. 203ff.
32 Dr Thomas Chalmers to ——, 18 August 1822, *Memoirs*, vol. II, p. 326.
33 Pichot, *Voyage Historique*, vol. III, pp. 428–30.
34 Julian Young, *Charles Mayne Young*, vol. I, pp. 155–6.
35 Mudie, *Account of the Visit*, p. 104.
36 Alexander Macdonell of Glengarry, chieftain and brother of Sir James, and once major in the Fencibles, maintained a 'feudal' style. He was the original of Fergus MacIvor in *Waverley*. He died in a shipwreck in 1818.
37 *Some Letters of Lord Cockburn*, p. 101.
38 Pichot, *Voyage Historique*, vol. III, pp. 437–8.
39 It was on this occasion that the Company was established as the King's Bodyguard in Scotland.
40 Mary to Elizabeth Grant, 14 & 15 August 1822, Jane & Mary Grant, *Letters on Edinburgh Visit*, pp. 33–5. At the Gibsons' in Picardy Place, a window had been taken out to allow for erecting a scaffold and stage which covered the lower half of the house down to the doorstep and railings. When it rained this proved inaccessible. Mr Gibson sent for sailcloth for shelter but none could be got, and the stage proved too drenched for use. With the fine day, families and friends scattered to take places at different houses, and each provided a 'collation', much appreciated, for parties had sat for at least a couple of hours until the procession passed.
41 Mrs Fletcher, *Autobiography*, p. 151.
42 Archibald Geikie, *Life of Sir Roderick I. Murchison, Bart, KCB, FRS*, 2 vols, London, 1875, vol. I, p. 91.

43 J. Nasmyth, *Autobiography*, p. 102; Pichot, *Voyage Historique*, vol. III, pp. 430, 432–3.
44 *Ibid.*, vol. III, p. 442.
45 Mudie, *Account of the Visit*, p. 109.
46 Others present included the Duke of Dorset, the Marquess of Winchester, the Earl of Lauderdale, Lord Francis Conyngham and Sir William Knighton. (Mudie, *Account of the Visit*, p. 115.)
47 Wilkie to his sister, 23 August 1822, *Life*, vol. II, pp. 65–6.
48 Henry Fox, Journal 15 August 1822, *Journal*, p. 141.
49 Uwins to his brother David, 20 August 1822, *Memoir*, vol. I, pp. 91–3.
50 *Ibid.*, vol. I, p. 92.
51 Gash, *Mr Secretary Peel*, *loc. cit.* More usually known as Lord Castlereagh, he had succeeded his father, the first Marquess of Londonderry only the previous year.
52 Sir William Knighton, *loc. cit.* (Sunday [18 August 1822]), p. 120. The story of the Restoration treaty must have been a favourite family myth, as General Monck held the lease of Dalkeith only from 1654 to 1659.
53 Jane to Elizabeth Grant, 16 August 1822, *Letters on Edinburgh Visit*, pp. 45, 46.
54 Miss Stewart, London dressmaker, to the Grant sisters, 9 August 1822, *Ibid.*, pp. 29, 30; Mary and Jane to Elizabeth, *passim*.
55 E. Grant, *Highland Lady*, vol. II, p. 166.
56 Henry Fox, Journal, 16 August 1833, *Journal*, p. 141.
57 Lockhart, *Life of Scott*, vol. II. pp. 350; Life of Crabbe, pp. 259ff.; Lockhart to the Rev. George Crabbe (younger), 26 December 1822, quoted *ibid.*, p. 263.
58 Mrs Fletcher, *Autobiography*, p. 153.
59 *Ibid.*, p. 155. William Wolfe Tone (1791–1828) was the soldier son of the famous Irish patriot Theobald Wolfe Tone, who during his eventful career had lived in America, fought in several expeditions during the French Revolution, and had eventually been court-martialled and condemned to death, but committed suicide (1798). His son William was educated in France, joined the French army, and fought in Germany in 1813. He was also an author, and published his father's writings.
60 Lockhart, *Life of Scott*, vol. VII, p. 50; *Life of Crabbe*, p. 264.
61 *Memoirs* of William Collins, pp. 197f.; *Life of Crabbe*, p. 260.
62 *Life of Crabbe*, p. 262.
63 Henry Fox, Journal, 17 August 1822, *Journal*, p. 141. Sir George Warrender (1782–1849), 4th baronet, succeeded in 1799 and married in 1819 Anna, daughter of Viscount Falmouth. Mme de Noailles was Charlotte, daughter of the Prince de Poix, and had been married to her cousin Alfred who was killed in Russia in 1812. Sir George's house near the castle, supposedly the original of Bradwardine in *Waverley*, had been made 'comfortable and pretty'. Lord Ancram, who was there, had had a fall from his horse and had to be bled; more sadly, being Lady Londonderry's nephew, the news of her husband's suicide just arrived was a great blow to him. He now felt obliged to return to London in order to be with her.
64 Jane and Mary Grant, *Letters on Edinburgh Visit*, pp. 15ff., 31–2.
65 Jane to Elizabeth Grant, 17 August, *Ibid.*, p. 51.
66 Henry Fox, Journal, 17 August, *loc. cit.* The full account of the Levée is in Mudie, *Account of the Visit*, pp. 128ff. The King reckoned that he must have received about 2,000 persons.
67 Peel to Lord Liverpool, 17 August, Gash, Mr Secretary Peel, *ad loc.*
68 *Some Cockburn Letters*, p. 101; E. Grant, *Highland Lady*, vol. II, pp. 165–6.
69 E. Grant, *loc. cit.*
70 *Life of Crabbe*, p. 266.
71 Wilkie to his sister, 23 August, *Life*, vol. I, p. 86.
72 Julian Young, *op. cit.*, vol. I, p. 158. In 1831 Young, then Sub-Chaplain to Hampton Court Palace, recorded a dinner party with Admiral George Scott, when Theodore

Hook related at his own expense how, when presented to the King, after kissing hands he inadvertently turned his back. When everyone had stopped laughing Young capped this with the story of the laird at Holyrood. One of the party said superciliously, '*Si non e vero e ben trovato*' – at which the admiral unexpectedly back Young by saying he could vouch for it: the gentleman concerned was his own uncle. (*Ibid.*, vol. I, pp. 207–8.)

73 Mudie, *Account of the Visit*, p. 149.
74 Mrs Fletcher, *Autobiography*, p. 153.
75 Uwins to his brother David, 20 August 1822, *Memoir*, vol. I, p. 91.
76 Jane to Elizabeth Grant, 18 August, *Letters on Edinburgh visit*, p. 53.
77 *Ibid.*, p. 54; Mudie, *Account of the Visit*, pp. 151ff.; Knighton, *loc. cit.*, vol. I, p. 120.
78 Memoir of Robert Chambers, p. 176; *Letters of Scott and Sharpe to Chambers.*
79 Henry Fox, Journal, 19 August 1822, *Journal*, p. 142.
80 Uwins, *loc. cit.*
81 Henry Fox, Journal, 20 & 21 August 1822, *Journal*, p. 142.
82 Life of Wilkie, vol. II, p. 86; Mudie, *Account of the Visit*, pp. 165ff.
83 Susan Ferrier to Mrs Connell, [August 1822], *Memoir and Correspondence*, p. 162.
84 Jane, Sally Siddons and Mrs Siddons to Elizabeth Grant, 20 August, *Letters on Edinburgh Visit*, vol. I, pp. 56–7 and 'vol. II', pp. 58–9.
85 '*Christopher North*,' vol. I, p. 213 (Wilson to his wife, 29 April 1816).
86 The *Scotsman*, 17 August 1822.
87 *Ibid.*, 24 August 1822.
88 Gillies, *Literary Veteran*, vol. III, p. 71.
89 *Ibid.*, vol. III, p. 70.
90 *Visit of George IV to Edinburgh 1822*, Exhibition Catalogue, Scottish National Portrait Gallery, Edinburgh 1961; Mudie, *Account of Visit.*
91 *Some Letters of Lord Cockburn*, p. 101.
92 Susan Ferrier to Mrs Connell, [August 1822], *loc. cit.*
93 Julian Young, vol. I, p. 157; Henry Fox, Journal, 22 August, p. 143; Collins to his mother, 28 August, *Memoirs of William Collins*, vol. I, p. 207.; Mary to Elizabeth Grant, 22 August, *Letters on Edinburgh Visit*, pp. 68–70.
94 Chalmers, *Memoirs*, vol. II, pp. 326–7.
95 Gash, *Mr Secretary Peel*, *loc. cit.*
96 The full account of the procession is in Mudie, *Account of the Visit*, ch.IX.
97 Mary Grant, *loc. cit.*
98 Mary & Jane Grant, J.P. Grant to his wife, 23 August, *Letters on Edinburgh Visit*, pp. 71ff.
99 Henry Fox, Journal, 23 August, *Journal*, p. 143.
100 Mary Grant, 23 August, *Letters on Edinburgh Visit*, pp. 77–8.
101 Mudie, *Account of the Visit*, pp. 209ff. The regiments were: 3rd Dragoon Guards, Glasgow Troop of Yeomanry, Peeblesshire Yeomanry, Fifeshire Troop of Lancers, Fifeshire Yeomanry, Berwickshire Yeomanry, East, West and Midlothian Yeomanry, and Scots Greys.
102 Mary Grant, 23 August, *Letters on Edinburgh Visit*, pp. 79ff.
103 Henry Fox, *loc. cit.* William George, 18th Earl of Erroll, had in 1820 married Eliza Fitz-Clarence, a daughter of the Duke of Clarence and Mrs Jordan.
104 Mudie, *Account of the Visit*, p. 223.
105 Mary Grant, *Letters on Edinburgh Visit*, p. 86.
106 Mary Grant, *Letters on Edinburgh Visit*, pp. 86–7.
107 The *Scotsman*, 20 August 1822; Mudie, *Account of the Visit*, pp. 226ff.
108 *The Times*, 12 September 1822.
109 *Life of Crabbe*, p. 261; Mudie, *Account of the Visit*, pp. 245–6.
110 *Life of Wilkie*, vol. I, p. 87; *Life of Collins*, vol. I, p. 208; *Turner . . . in Edinburgh*, p. 24.

111 *Some Letters of Lord Cockburn*, p. 107.
112 Jane Grant, 25 & 26 August, pp. 89–92.
113 Jane Grant, 26 August, *Letters on Edinburgh Visit*, pp. 94–7; Mudie, *Account of the Visit*, pp. 253–5.
114 Susan Ferrier, *loc. cit.*
115 Henry Fox, Journal, 26 August, *Journal*, pp. 143–4.
116 *The Scotsman*, 31 August 1822; *Some Letters of Lord Cockburn*, pp. 105–6; Mudie, *Account of the Visit*, pp. 256ff.
117 Dibdin, *Edinburgh Stage*, p. 300.
118 *Ibid.*, pp. 300–02; the *Scotsman*, 31 August 1822. A detailed description is in Mudie, *Account of the Visit*, pp. 170ff.
119 Collins to his mother, 28 August, *Life*, pp. 206–7; Wilkie to his brother Thomas, 31 August, *Life*, vol. I, pp. 89–92; Mudie, *Account of the Visit*, pp. 291ff.
120 Wilkie to his sister, 15 September 1822, *Life*, vol. II, p. 92.
121 Do. to Do., 26 September 1824, *Life*, vol. I, p. 122.
122 Do. to his brother Thomas, 31 August 1822, *Life*, vol. I, pp. 89–90.
123 Collins to his mother, 28 August 1822, *Life*, vol. I, p. 208.
124 Scott to Sir William Knighton, 29 August 1822, *Memoirs of Knighton*, vol. I, p. 121; 12 September 1822, *Letters of King George IV*, vol. II, pp. 539ff.
125 Gash, *Mr Secretary Peel*, *loc. cit.*
126 Viscount Melville to King George IV, 29 August 1822, *Letters of King George IV*, vol. II, pp. 584–5.
127 *Some Letters of Lord Cockburn*, pp. 103–5.
128 *The Times*, 2 September 1822.

PART IV

Chapter 44: A Rash of New Building

1 *Improvements in Edinburgh during the year 1823*, Edinburgh, February 1824 (24 pp.) 'Extracts from an Edinburgh Journal 1823–1833', ed. D.J. Moir, *OEC*, vol. XXIX, pp. 143–84, vol. XXX, pp. 142–59, 1956, 1858. Much of what follows is based on these publications.
2 Lindsay, *Georgian Edinburgh*, p. 43; Youngson, *Classical Edinburgh*, pp. 162ff.
3 'Edinburgh Journal', 10 October 1823.
4 Lindsay, *Georgian Edinburgh*, pp. 32, 50, 61–2.
5 *Improvements in Edinburgh.*
6 *Ibid.*
7 Lindsay, *Georgian Edinburgh*, pp. 52–4, 49–50.
8 *Ibid.*, pp. 60–1.
9 *Ibid.*, pp. 56–8.
10 Burgon, *Memoirs of Patrick Fraser Tytler*, pp. 190–1.
11 John James Audubon, 26 October 1826, *The 1826 Journal of John James Audubon*, ed. Alice Ford, University of Oklahoma Press, 1967, p. 234.
12 *Remains of the Rev. Edmund Griffin, compiled by Francis Griffin, with a biographical memoir of the Deceased, by the Rev. John McVicar*, 2 vols, New York, 1831, pp. 250–1. Griffin, showing signs of tuberculosis, had been advised to travel. After visiting Europe he came to England in August 1829, was miserably lonely in London, made some tours and arrived in Edinburgh in November, where he was delighted to meet Mrs Grant of Laggan and had a memorable visit with Henry Mackenzie. He heard Dr Chalmers preach, and visited and described the courts, and the school for poor children.

13 *Edinburgh Advertiser*, 18 April 1815; *Edinburgh Evening Courant*, 29 October, 3 & 4 November 1818.
14 Benson Earle Hill, *Playing About*, p. 84.
15 Pichot, *Voyage Historique*, vol. III, p. 193, 192.
16 Karl Friedrich Schinkel, 'The English Journey', *Journal of a visit to France and Britain in 1826*, ed. David Bindman & Gottfried Riemann, Yale UP, 1993, pp. 148ff. (3–5 July 1826).
17 Colvin, *Dictionary of British Architects*, 3rd edn, p. 455.
18 Schinkel, *loc. cit.*; *Peter's Letters*, vol. III, p. 80; Southey, *Journal of a Tour*, 17 October 1819, pp. 8–9.
19 Lindsay, *Georgian Edinburgh*, p. 43; *Edinburgh in the 19th Century, ad loc.*
20 Audubon, 27 October 1826, *1826 Journal*, p. 235.
21 Youngson, *Classical Edinburgh*, p. 158.
22 *Edinburgh in the 19th Century, ad loc.* (quoting from the newspapers).
23 *Edinburgh Evening Courant*, 27 April 1815; *Edinburgh Annual Register*, 1819, p. 261.
24 Alexander Trotter, *A Plan of Communication between the New and the Old Town of Edinburgh, in the Line of the earthen Mound, and of Building upon that site, with Observations and Ground-Plans*, 2nd edn, enlarged, Edinburgh, 1829; Youngson, *Classical Edinburgh*, pp. 168ff.
25 *The West Approach Investigated; or, The History of Two Purchases on that Line*, Edinburgh, printed for W. Hunter, Hanover Street, 1830; Youngson, *Classical Edinburgh*, pp. 174ff; *Edinburgh Evening Courant*, 9 Nov. 1826.
26 Sharpe to Scott, [Aug.] 1823, *Sharpe Letters*, vol. II, pp. 269–70.
27 Do. to Do., [?Aug. 1823], *Ibid.*, vol. II, pp. 288–9.
28 Sharpe to Lord Gower, 14 June 1824, *Ibid.*, vol. II, p. 301.
29 *Life of Sir Robert Christison*, vol. II, p. 264; Sharpe to Sir Patrick Walker of Dalry, Jan. 1826, to Lady Gwydyr, 5 March 1826, *Sharpe Letters*, vol. II, pp. 355, 360.
30 Marchioness of Stafford to Sharpe, 11 Feb. 1824, *Sharpe Letters*, vol. II, p. 284; Lady Gwydyr to Sharpe, 31 Jan. [?1826], *Ibid.*, vol. II, p. 359.
31 Sharpe to editor of *Edinburgh Observer*, [1826], *Ibid.*, vol. II, pp. 371–4.
32 *Ibid.*, vol. II, pp. 374ff.
33 Lord Strathaven to Sharpe, 29 Dec. 1826; Sharpe to Scott, n.d. [1827], Scott to Sharpe, 29 Aug. 1826, *Ibid.*, vol. II, pp. 377, 392, 369–71.
34 Youngson, *Classical Edinburgh*, pp. 159–60.
35 Archibald Alison in *Edinburgh Review*, Feb. 1823.

Chapter 45: Scott in the Heights

1 *Constable and his Literary Correspondents*, vol. III, pp. 151–3, and n. on Julian Young's *Recollections* [sic].
2 *Ibid.*, vol. III, p. 162.
3 *Ibid.*, vol. III, pp. 167–8.
4 Smith to Constable, 26 January 1821, to Lady Grey, 9 February 1821, *Letters*, vol. I, pp. 373, 374.
5 Smith to Constable, 21 December 1821, to Jeffrey, 30 December 1821, *Ibid.*, vol. I, pp. 384, 385.
6 Smith to Constable, 21 June 1822, *Ibid.*, vol. I, p. 389.
7 Do. to Do., 21 January 1823, to Lady Grey, 31 January, *Ibid.*, vol. I, pp. 393, 394.
8 Scott to Constable, 23 March 1822, *Constable and his Literary Correspondents*, vol. III, pp. 206–8.
9 *Ibid.*, vol. III, pp. 216, 231–2.
10 Morehead, *Life and Writings*, 4 February 1823, pp. 174–5.
11 Smith to Lady Grey, 31 January 1823, *Letters*, p. 394.

12 Scott to Knighton, [?February] 1823, *Memoirs of Sir Wiliam Knighton*, vol. I, p. 130.
13 Morehead, *Life and Writings*, 4, 8, 11 February 1823, *loc. cit.*
14 Carlyle to Jane Welsh, 4 February 1823, Jane Welsh to Carlyle, 10 February 1823, *Collected Letters*, vol. II, pp. 283, 284–5.
15 Carlyle to his brother Alexander, 8 March 1823, to Jane Welsh, [26 March], *Ibid.*, vol. II, pp. 301, 315; Mrs Grant to Mrs Hook, April 1823, *Memoir*, vol. II, p. 17.
16 Lady Gwydyr to Sharpe, 9 April 1823, *Sharpe Letters*, vol. II, p. 251. The Caledonian Asylum was built in what was to become the Caledonian Road. It was demolished in 1903.
17 Scott to Sharpe, 27 July 1823, *Ibid.*, vol. II, p. 264.
18 Miss Edgeworth to Mrs Ruxton, 8 June 1823, *Life and Letters*, vol. II, pp. 95ff.
19 Mrs Fletcher, *Autobiography*, p. 156.
20 Lockhart to Wilson, [?August] 1823, *'Christopher North,'* vol. II, p. 58. Some years later Thomas Moore met Miss Edgeworth in London at a Rogers breakfast, where in due course one would meet everyone, and found her 'anything but agreeable' from her habit of interrupting the moment anyone started to speak, 'seldom more than a sentence behind them', and usually managing to outrun all rivals. 'With all her cleverness', this did not make up for 'this over-activity of tongue'. (Moore, 19 April 1831, *Journals and Correspondence*, vol. I, p. 187.)
21 Moore, Journal, *Ibid.*, vol. III, p. 328; Mrs Grant to Mrs Col. White [?February] 1823, *Memoir*, vol. III, pp. 9–10. John Leycester Adolphus (1795–1862), educated at Merchant Taylors' School and St John's College, Oxford, was called to the bar in 1822. (*DNB*)
22 James Skene, *Memories of Sir Walter Scott*, London, 1909, pp. 112–4.
23 Haydon to Miss Mitford, [November 1821], *Correspondence and Table-Talk*, vol. II, p. 74.
24 Do. to Do., 31 May 1824, *Correspondence and Table-Talk*, vol. II, p. 86. Miss Mitford to Miss Sephson, 22 October 1824, *Letters of Mary Russell Mitford*, 2nd ser., ed. Henry Chorley, 2 vols, London, 1872, vol. II, p. 191.
25 Mrs Somerville, *Personal Recollections*, p. 189.
26 Nathaniel Willis, *Pencillings by the Way*, London, 1835, vol. III, p. 100.
27 Mrs Grant to Mrs Smith, 6 February 1824, *Memoir*, vol. III, p. 41; Smith to Constable, 28 December 1823, *Letters*, vol. I, pp. 404–5.
28 Moore, Journal, 23 February 1822, *Journals and Correspondence*, vol. III, pp. 328–9.
29 Do., 1 and 3 April 1823, *Ibid.*, vol. IV, pp. 47–9.
30 Mrs Grant to Mrs Hook, 23 June 1824, *Memoir*, vol. III, p. 57.
31 *Constable and his Literary Correspondents*, vol. III, pp. 305–6, 329ff.
32 *Ibid.*, vol. III, pp. 274f., 301–2.
33 *Memoir of Robert Chambers*, pp. 169ff.; *Letters of Scott and Sharpe to Chambers*, pp. 9ff.
34 Scott to Sharpe, [July] 1823 & 15 July 1823, *Sharpe Letters*, vol. II, pp. 258, 259.
35 Helen Graham, Diary, Jan. 1824, *Parties and Pleasures*, pp. 36ff.
36 *Ibid.* Susan Ferrier tells this as of the castle of Threave. And when Scott called on the Grahams in George Street, as the manservant was slow in answering the door, Mrs Graham called on Helen to go down and let him in. Sir Walter patted her approvingly on the shoulder and repeated the anecdote – about Threave. No matter where it happened, it was evidently a favourite.
37 Do., diary, 3 Feb. and [Jan.] 1824, *Ibid.*, pp. 39, 37–8; 23 Feb., p. 52.
38 Do., diary, 21 Feb. 1825, *Ibid.*, pp. 119–20.
39 Sharpe to Chambers, April and June 1824, *Sharpe Letters*, vol. II, pp. 294, 302f.
40 Chambers to Sharpe, 26 Aug., 23 Oct. 1824, *Ibid.*, vol. II, pp. 310,316.
41 Sharpe to Scott, 1 [Oct.], to 'A Lady', Oct. 1825, *Ibid.*, vol. II, pp. 345, 347.
42 Chambers to Sharpe, 12 Feb. 1825, *Ibid.*, vol. II, p. 330.

Chapter 46: Carlyle Rises

Except for nn.1 and 29 (part) the references in this chapter are from Carlyle's *Collected Letters*, Vols.II, III and IV.

1 *Two Notebooks of Thomas Carlyle*, from 23 March 1822 to 18 May 1832, ed. Charles Eliot Norton; New York, Grolier Club, 1898, pp. 57–9.
2 Carlyle to his father, 4 December 1822, to Robert Mitchell, 23 December, vol. II, pp. 217–8, 243.
3 Do. to David Hope, 23 December 1822, vol. II, pp. 245–6.
4 Do. to Jane Welsh, [26 March 1823], to his father, 2 April, vol. II, pp. 315, 323.
5 Do. to his mother, [16 April 1823], vol. II, pp. 335–7.
6 Do. to William Graham, 24 April 1823, to his brother John, 10 May, to Jane Welsh, [11 May], vol. II, pp. 341, 351, 355.
7 Jane Welsh to Carlyle, 16 September 1823, vol. II, pp. 426–8; Carlyle to his brother Alexander, 21 February 1824, vol. III, pp. 34–5.
8 Do. to Jane Welsh, 7 March 1824, to Alexander, 2 March, vol. III, pp. 40–44, 40.
9 Do. to Jane Welsh, 19 May, to George Boyd, 31 May, to Jane Welsh, [5 June] 1824, vol. III, pp. 66, 74, 75–6.
10 Do. to his mother, 10 June 1824, to Jane Welsh, 23 June, vol. III, pp. 80, 83–4, 87–8, 90.
11 Do. to Jane, *loc. cit.*, vol. III, pp. 85, 91.
12 Do. to his mother, 2 July 1824, vol. III, p. 100.
13 Do. to Thomas Murray, 24 August 1824, vol. III, p. 139.
14 Jane Welsh to Carlyle, 11 August 1824, vol. III, pp. 129, 132.
15 Carlyle letters August–October 1824, *passim*; to his mother, 12 November 1824, vol. III, p. 194.
16 Do. to his brother John, 21 & 30 November, 20 December 1824, vol. III, pp. 207, 209–11, 233.
17 Do. to his brother Alexander, 14 December 1824, vol. III, pp. 220–1.
18 Do. to Jane Welsh and v.v., January 1825, vol. III, pp. 244–66.
19 Do. to John, 10 February 1825, to Jane, 28 February 1825, vol. III, pp. 277, 289.
20 Do. to Jane, 12 April, 22 May 1825, vol. III, pp. 315, 331.
21 C. to Jane, 22 May 1825, vol. III, p. 331. Nicholas Heinrich Julius (1783–1862) had been sent to Scotland officially to study the quarantine laws. In 1834–5 he visited America to report on their prison system. He published a German translation of Ticknor's *History of Spanish Literature.*
22 Jane Welsh to Carlyle, 30 July 1825 *et seq*; Carlyle to James Johnston, 26 October 1825, vol. III, p. 400.
23 John to Thomas Carlyle, 21 November 1825, vol. III, p. 421, n.
24 Carlyle to his mother, 8 January 1826, to Jane Welsh, [14 January], [23 January], Jane to Carlyle, 21 February 1826, vol. IV, pp. 3–4, 12–13, 38.
25 Letters, February–May 1826; Jane to Carlyle, [23 May 1826], vol. IV, pp. 97–8.
26 Mrs Montagu to Carlyle, 13 May 1826, vol. IV, p. 105n.
27 Jane to Carlyle, 28 June 1826, vol. IV, pp. 111–2.
28 Carlyle to William Tait, 31 July 1826, vol. IV, p. 120.
29 Carlyle to his mother, 19 October 1826, vol. IV, pp. 152–3; *Two Notebooks of Thomas Carlyle*, 3 December 1826, p. 67.

Chapter 47: Jeffrey's Progress

1 *Some Letters of Lord Cockburn*, p. 20; Cockburn's *Life of Jeffrey*, vol. I, pp. 272–3.
2 Cockburn to Charles Wilkes, 13 April 1822, *Ibid.*, vol. II, pp. 198–9; vol. I, pp. 246–7.
3 *Ibid.*, vol. I, pp. 261–2.
4 *Ibid.*, vol. I, p. 267.

5 *Ibid.*, vol. I, pp269, 273–5.
6 *Ibid.*, vol. I, pp. 247–8, vol. II, pp. 196–7.
7 Wordsworth to Lord Lonsdale, 24 January 1823; *Edinburgh Review*, XXXVII, November 1822, quoted in Wordsworth *Letters*, vol. III, p. 183 and n.
8 Cockburn, *Life of Jeffrey*, vol. I, pp. 267–9.
9 *Ibid.*, vol. I, p. 270.
10 Ticknor, Journal, March 1819, *Life etc. of Ticknor*, vol. I, pp. 277, 280.
11 Moore, Journal, 12 June 1823, *Memoirs, Journals* etc., vol. III, p. 81.
12 Carlyle, *Reminiscences*, ed. Froude, vol. II, p. 230.
13 John Cam Hobhouse (Lord Broughton), *Recollections of a Long Life*, vol. II, p. 143 (2 April 1821).
14 Helen Graham, Diary, 4 January, 18 March 1825, *Parties and Pleasures*, pp. 118, 127.
15 John Whishaw to Mrs Smith, 6 May 1826, Lady Seymour, *The Pope of Holland House*, p. 252.
16 Moore, Journal, 3 & 21 June 1823, *Memoirs, Journals* etc., vol. III, pp. 71, 88–9.
17 Smith to Jeffrey, February and 10 November 1826; *Edinburgh Review*, LXXXVIII and LXXXIX, September and December 1826; Smith *Letters*, vol. I, p. 454.
18 Smith to Lady Holland, 6 November 1827, *Letters*, vol. I, p. 472.
19 Carlyle, *Reminiscences*, vol. II, pp. 232ff.; also to his brother Alexander, 3 February 1827, Carlyle to his mother in a letter of Jane's, 17 February, *Collected Letters*, vol. IV, pp. 185, 190.
20 Carlyle, *Reminiscences*, vol. II, pp. 241, 247–8.

Chapter 48: A Calamity

1 Robert Chambers, *Remarkable Fires in Edinburgh*, pp. 52ff.
2 *Ibid.*, pp. 52–5; Alison, *Fraser Tytler*, pp. xiv–xv.
3 Burgon, *Fraser Tytler* (Miss Tytler's Narrative), p. 168.
4 Chambers, *loc. cit.*
5 James Nasmyth, *Autobiography*, p. 104.
6 Alison, *My Life and Writings*, p. 230.
7 Mrs Grant to Mrs Hook, 22 November 1824, *Memoir*, vol. III, p. 70,
8 Chambers, *loc. cit.*
9 Burgon, *Fraser Tytler*, p. 269.
10 Lang, *Life of Lockhart*, vol. I, p. 348.
11 Burgon, *loc. cit.*
12 Alison, *op. cit.*, pp. 230–31.
13 Burgon, p. 170.
14 Hugh Miller, *My Schools and Schoolmasters*, ed. W.M. Mackenzie, Edinburgh, 1907, pp. 345–7.
15 Jane Welsh to Thomas Carlyle, 18 Nov, 1824, *Collected Letters*, vol. III, p. 203.
16 Josiah Livingston, *Our Street*, pp. 26–7.
17 Helen Graham, 19 November 1824, *Parties and Pleasures*, pp. 115–6.
18 Chambers, *Remarkable Fires*, pp. 66–8.
19 Mrs Grant, *loc. cit.*
20 Chambers, *Remarkable Fires*, p. 69.
21 Mrs Grant, *loc. cit.*, vol. III, p. 71; to Mrs Smith, 26 December, vol. III, p. 78.

Chapter 49: A Crisis

1 *Constable and his Literary Correspondents*, vol. III, pp. 210ff., 267ff.
2 *Ibid.*, vol. III, pp. 306–7, 309, quoted from Lockhart, *Life of Scott*, vol. VII, pp. 351–2, vol. VI, pp. 28–32.

3 Scott to Lockhart, 17 Nov., to Robert Cadell, [22 Nov.] 1825, *Letters*, vol. IX, pp. 291–5, 301 & n.
4 Moore to Scott, 24 July 1825, to Do., [11 Nov. 1825], *Letters* (Dowden edn), pp. 537f., 541.
5 Moore, Journal, 29 October 1825, *Memoirs and Journals*, vol. IV, pp. 332–4; to Owen Rees, 18 November 1825, *Letters* (Dowden), vol. II, pp. 541–2.
6 Moore to Scott, [Feb. 1826], *Letters*, vol. II, pp. 551–2.
7 Do. to Jeffrey, 29 April 1826, *Ibid.*, vol. II, p. 558.
8 Charles Mathews to his wife, 23 Dec. 1825, *Continuation of Memoirs*, pp. 314–5.
9 Scott, *Journal*, 25 Nov. 1825, p. 14, *The Journal of Sir Walter Scott 1825–1832*, ed. W.E.K. Anderson, Oxford, Clarendon Press, 1972, p. 14.
10 *Ibid.*, 18 Dec. 1825, p. 38.
11 *Ibid.*, 16, 17, 18 Jan. 1826, pp. 61, 65–6, 60.
12 *Ibid.*, e.g. 22/29 Jan. 1826, pp. 65–6, 71; 22, 23 July 1827, pp. 331–2.
13 *Ibid.*, 11–18 May 1826, pp. 142–7; Lockhart, *Life of Scott*, vol. VIII, pp. 308ff.; Gillies, *Recollections of Scott*, p. 266; *Literary Veteran*, vol. III, pp. 109f., 123f. Gillies returned briefly to Edinburgh in 1829 to settle his affairs and pack up his Great King Street possessions, and in London launched the intended journal with George Moir and with contributions from Scott and others, with some success. He again revisited Edinburgh in 1847, and in 1851 published his three-volume *Memoirs of a Literary Veteran*. He died in 1858.
14 Miss Mitford to Haydon, 4 May, 11 July 1826, *Letters*, vol. II, p. 225.
15 Coleridge to his nephew Edward, 8 February 1826, to Daniel Stuart, 28 July, *Collected Letters*, vol. VI, pp. 562, 602.
16 Coleridge to Blackwood, 20 October 1829, *Ibid.*, vol. VI, p. 821.
17 Mrs Grant to Mrs Grant of Duthil, 2 February 1826, to Mrs Willis, 23 February, *Memoir*, vol. III, pp. 95–6, 101–2.
18 Do. to a friend in America, 16 January 1827, to Mrs Hook, 12 September 1827, *Ibid.*, vol. III, p. 111, 116.
19 Hobhouse, *Recollections*, 15 January 1827, vol. III, p. 165.
20 *Ibid.*, 17 April 1828, vol. III, p. 256.
21 *The Journal of Mrs Arbuthnot 1820–1832*, ed. Francis Bamford and the Duke of Wellington, 2 vols, London, 1950, vol. II, 56–7 (17 November 1826).
22 *Diary of Frances Lady Shelley*, vol. II, pp. 314–5.
23 Gillies, *Recollections of Scott*, p. 267; Haydon, *Diary*, 31 October 1826, vol. III, p. 164.
24 Lockhart, *Life of Scott*, p. 267, vol. IX, pp. 8ff.; Scott, *Journal*, 24 February 1827, p. 282; *Journal of Mrs Arbuthnot*, *loc. cit.*
25 Haydon, Journal, 2 March 1827, *Correspondence and Table-Talk*, vol. II, p. 337.
26 *Ibid.*, vol. II, p. 362.
27 Dorothy Wordsworth to Mary Laing, [c.10 March 1827], *Wordsworth Letters*, vol. III, p. 522.
28 John Merivale (elder), diary, [25] October 1824, *Family Memorials*, p. 254.
29 Haydon, *loc. cit.*
30 *Diary*, vol. III, pp. 85–6, 164 (27 February 1826 & 11 October 1826).
31 Do., 5 & 8 May 1828, *Ibid.*, vol. III, pp. 273–5.
32 Mrs Arbuthnot, *Journal*, 6 May 1828, pp. 186–7.
33 Dorothy Wordsworth to Mary Laing, 3 June 1828, *Wordsworth Letters*, vol. III, p. 612.
34 Gillies, *Recollections of Scott*, pp. 277, 288.
35 *Ibid.*, p. 289; Lockhart, *Life of Scott*, vol. IX, pp. 219, 312; Scott, *Journal*, 27 May 1820, pp. 591–2.
36 Scott to Lockhart, 22 Feb. 1830, *Letters*, vol. XI, p. 298 n.; Lockhart, *Life of Scott*, vol. IX, pp. 297–8; Johnson, *Scott, The Great Unknown*, vol. II, p. 1274.

Chapter 51: Stages of Friendship: Wilson, Jeffrey, Carlyle

Except where otherwise noted, references in this chapter are to the fourth volume of the Carlyles' *Collected Letters.*

1 Carlyle, *Reminiscences*, vol. I, p. 79.
2 Carlyle to Dr Julius, 4 December 1826, p. 161.
3 *'Christopher North,'* vol. II, pp. 88f.
4 Carlyle to his brother John, [7 July 1827], p. 236. John Gordon, born in Kirkcudbright, studied at Edinburgh University, took his degree in 1825 and was appointed Secretary to the Church of Scotland Education Scheme; in 1833 became the first General Secretary of the University, and was Inspector 1843–74. In 1845 he collaborated in the second *Statistical Account.* He died in 1882.
Carlyle records this evening in greater detail, with further impressions of Wilson, in his essay on 'Christopher North' intended for his *Reminiscences.*
5 Carlyle, 'Christopher North', in *19th Century and After*, LXXXVII, January 1920, pp. 103–17, written in 1868 (quoted in his *Collected Letters*, vol. IV, pp. 234–8).
6 M. Gordon, *'Christopher North.'* vol. II, pp. 303–4.
7 Carlyle, 'Christopher North', quoted *loc. cit.*, p. 242.
8 Carlyle to John, 25 October 1827, p. 271.
9 Carlyle to Mrs Montagu, 20 November 1827, p. 283.
10 M. Gordon, *'Christopher North,'* vol. II, pp. 305–6.
11 *Ibid.*, vol. II, pp. 252–3 (and see *Noctes Ambrosianae,* March 1829, vol. III).
12 *Ibid.*, vol. II, pp. 82, 267, 325 & n.
13 *Ibid.*, vol. II, pp. 159–60.
14 Carlyle, 'Christopher North', quoted *loc. cit.*, pp. 238–9.
15 M. Gordon, *op. cit.*, vol. II, pp. 175–6.
16 W.A. McVickar, *Life of the Rev. John McVickar*, pp. 152, 156 (Journal, 19 & 21 July 1830).
17 Sir Henry Taylor to Miss Fenwick, November 1835; to Southey, 5 November 1835, *Correspondence of [Sir] Henry Taylor*, ed. Edward Dowden, London, 1888, pp. 66, 67 & n.; to Do., 28 December 1835; to Lady Hislop, 16 February 1836, pp. 70–1.
18 *Edinburgh Advertiser*, quoted in *'Christopher North.'* 29 November 1831, vol. II, pp. 173–4; Mrs Wilson to her sister, n.d., *Ibid.*, vol. II, p. 175.
19 E.L. Woodward, *The Age of Reform 1815–70*, Oxford, 1938, pp. 78ff.; Gordon, *'Christopher North,'* vol. II, pp. 28–9.
20 In spite of his numerous children and grandchildren, Wilson's late years tended to be solitary, Blackwood, Hogg, and finally his wife all dying in the 1830s. In 1840 his right hand was paralysed by a stroke, but he was able to continue lecturing until another stroke in 1850 obliged him to retire. From 1840 he wrote only two *Blackwood's* papers, after for years being its most prolific contributor. In a decline, feeling depressed and useless, he died at Gloucester Place from a final stroke in 1854. (Sir George Douglas, *The Blackwood Group*, pp. 37–8.)
21 Carlyle to his mother, 11 August 1827, p. 244; Jeffrey to Carlyle, n.d., NLS MS 787.1.
22 Carlyle to John, 27 August 1827, Jane Carlyle to Mrs Montagu, 2 September 1827, pp. 249, 250.
23 Jane Carlyle to John, 13 September 1827, p. 259.
24 Carlyle to his mother, 20 October 1827, p. 262.
25 Carlyle to Alexander, 25 October 1827, p. 266, to his sister Jean, 13 November, p. 276.
26 Carlyle to James Johnston, [19 November 1827], to Mrs Montagu, 20 November 1827, pp. 278, 279–80.
27 Carlyle to Mrs Montagu, *loc. cit.*
28 To his father, 22 December 1827, to Brian Proctor, 17 January 1828, pp. 298, 303.

29 To Alexander, 26 November 1827, p. 285, to John, 29 November, p. 290.
30 To John Taylor, bookseller, 30 December 1827; to William Tait, [18 January 1828], pp. 300, 307.
31 To Proctor, 17 January 1828, p. 305.
32 To John, 1 February 1828; to Alexander, [3 February 1828] pp. 317, 321; Jane to Mrs Carlyle, 19 Feb., p. 328.
33 To John, 7 March 1828, pp. 335, 337.
34 To John, 1 February & 12 March 1828, pp. 317–8, 340.
35 To Do., 12 March 1828, p. 341. It was Maginn who wrote of 'O'Doherty' in *Noctes*, but the character was based on Captain Hamilton.
36 To John 12 March 1828, pp. 341–2.
37 To Johann Wolfgang von Goethe, 18 April, to Sir Walter Scott, 13 April 1828, pp. 344, 363–5.
38 Thomas Babington Macaulay to his mother, 15 April 1828, G.O. Trevelyan, *Life of Macaulay*, 2 vols, London, 1932 [1st edn 1876], vol. I, pp. 136ff. Macaulay was educated at Trinity College, Cambridge, had qualified as a barrister in 1824 and was to sit in Parliament from 1830. His *History* was published in 1848.
39 Jeffrey to Mrs James Craig, 21 October 1828, 8 April 1829, Cockburn, *Life of Jeffrey*, vol. II, pp. 277–8, 228–9.
40 Sydney Smith, asking John Murray in November 1828 about the state of Jeffrey's throat, continued in verse,
That throat, so vex'd by cackle and by cup,
Where wine descends, and endless words come up,
Much injured organ! Constant is thy toil;
Spits turn to do thee harm, and coppers boil.
(Smith *Letters*, vol. I, pp. 485–6.)
41 Jeffrey to John Allen, 3 January 1825, Cockburn, *Life of Jeffrey*, vol. I, p. 279.
42 Carlyle to his mother, 20 April 1828, to John, 10 June 1828, pp. 371, 382.
43 To John, October 1828, Jane to Eliza Stoddart, 21 November 1828, pp. 414, 416–7.
44 Carlyle, *Reminiscences*, vol. I, p. 85.
45 Carlyle to John, 11 August 129, *Collected Letters*, vol. V, pp. 20–21.
46 Jane to Eliza Stoddart, 11 November 1829, *Ibid.*, p. 30; Carlyle to Wilson, 19 December 1829, *Ibid.*, p. 42.
47 Jeffrey to Cockburn, 1 November 1827, Cockburn, *Life of Jeffrey*, vol. I, pp. 279–280.
48 Cockburn, *op. cit.*, vol. I, pp. 282–4.
49 *Ibid.*, vol. I, pp. 296–8.
50 *Ibid.*, vol. I, p. 285. Napier (1776–1847) had been born Napier Macvey, but changed his name at his grandfather's request. He became an FRS and, in 1837, Clerk of Session in Edinburgh. (*DNB*)

Chapter 51: Stages of Friendship: Jeffrey, Carlyle

Where not otherwise noted, letters from Carlyle are from the *Collected Letters*, Vols. V and VI.

1 Carlyle to Macvey Napier, 27 January 1830, vol. V, p. 64.
2 Carlyle, *Reminiscences*, vol. II, p. 254; *Collected Letters*, vol. V, p. 80n.; *Two Notebooks*, p. 155. Carlyle's letters to Jeffrey have unfortunately not survived.
3 Carlyle to John, 1 May 1830, p. 96; John to Carlyle, p. 101n.
4 Carlyle to William Tait, 24 July 1830, p. 125; to John, 18 September 1830, p. 163.
5 To his mother, 28 September 1828, pp. 167–8.
6 Carlyle, *Reminiscences*, vol. I, p. 86, vol. II, pp. 252–3.
7 *Reminiscences*, vol. II, pp. 254, 255.

8 Carlyle to Mrs Montagu, 27 October 1830, p. 186.
9 Carlyle to Napier, 20 January 1831, to John, 31 January, pp. 210, 213–5. William Taylor, an Oxford MA and a priest, was burned as a heretic at Smithfield in 1423.
10 Francis Horner to J.A. Murray, 3 November 1804, *Memoirs*, vol. I, pp. 286, 289.
11 Cockburn, *Life of Jeffrey*, vol. I, p. 310.
12 Cockburn, *Life of Jeffrey*, *loc. cit.*
13 Jeffrey to his niece Mary Brown, 3 December 1830, *Ibid.*, vol. I, pp. 306–7.
14 Cockburn to Sir Thomas Dick Lauder, 30 December 1830, *Some Letters*, p. 28.
15 Carlyle to John, 21 January 1831, p. 217.
16 Sydney Smith to Mrs Meynell, 3 January 1831, to J.A. Murray, [24 January 1831], *Letters*, vol. II, p. 527.
17 Cockburn, *op. cit.*, vol. I, p. 318.
18 *Life of Christison*, vol. II, p. 376.
19 Mrs Montagu to Jane Carlyle, 21 February 1831, p. 245.
20 Carlyle, *Two Notebooks*, 15 August 1831, vol. II, p. 198.
21 'Fifteen English Friends' to Goethe, ?17 July 1831, vol. V, pp. 305f.
22 Cam Hobhouse, *Recollections*, vol. IV, p. 90; John Allen to Macvey Napier, 10 March 1831, *Selections from the Correspondence of the late Macvey Napier, Esq.*, edited by his son, Macvey Napier, London, 1879, p. 111.
23 Alexander Somerville, *The Autobiography of a Working Man, 1848*, republished ed. Brian Behan, Macgibbon & Kee, 1967, pp. 99ff.
24 Cockburn, *Life of Jeffrey*, vol. I, pp. 324f., vol. II, pp. 239f.; Carlyle to Jane, 4 September 1831, p. 402.
25 Sydney Smith to Lady Grey, 6 September, 1829, 27 February 1831, *Letters*, vol. II, pp. 500, 530.
26 Carlyle to Jane, 24 August 1831, pp. 363–4.
27 Do., *loc. cit.*; to mother, 26 August 1831, p. 367.
28 To Jane, 29 August, 4 September 1831, pp. 376, 396.
29 Do., 11 & 14 September 1831, pp. 417–8, 421.
30 Do., 30 September 1831, p. 444; Cockburn, *Life of Jeffrey*, vol. I, pp. 321–3.
31 Sharpe to Scott, 9 April 1831, *Sharpe Letters*, vol. II, pp. 451ff.
32 *Edinburgh Evening Courant*, 16 April 1832.
33 *Ibid.*, 26 April 1832.
34 Sharpe to A Lady, [?4 May 1832], *Sharpe Letters*, vol. II, pp. 458–9.
35 Carlyle to John, 22 May 1832, vol. VI, p. 163.
36 Sydney Smith to J.A. Murray, 21 November 1832, *Letters*, vol. II, p. 568.
37 Cockburn, *Life of Jeffrey*, vol. I, pp. 325, 337–9; Carlyle to John, 31 July 1832, vol. VI, p. 197.
38 Carlyle to John, 31 August 1832, vol. VI, p. 223.
39 Jeffrey to Cockburn, 3 February 1833, Cockburn, *Life of Jeffrey*, vol. I, p. 341.
40 Carlyle, *Two Notebooks*, vol. II, pp. 256–7.
41 Carlyle, *Letters*, vol. VI, pp. 139–40, 143.
42 Carlyle to Napier, 28 April 1832, vol. VI, p. 148.
43 Carlyle to John, 17 October 1832, vol. VI, pp. 246, 247.

Chapter 52: De Quincey and Lesser Luminaries

1 Wilson to De Quincey, n.s. [?December] [1825], Japp, *De Quincey Memorials*, vol. II, pp. 48–9.
2 *'Christopher North,'* vol. II, pp. 157–8.
3 *Ibid.*, vol. II, p. 158.
4 Thomas Tod Stoddart, Autobiographical Sketch of the Author's Life, in his *Songs of the Seasons, and other Poems*, Kelso, 1881, pp. xxxi–ii.

5 Carlyle to Dr Julius, 4 December 1826, *Collected Letters*, vol. IV, p. 161.
6 Carlyle to John, 29 November 1827, *Ibid.*, vol. V, p. 291.
7 Japp, *Thomas De Quincey, His Life and Writings*, London, 1890, pp. 195–6, 211–2. 195–6.
8 Grevil Lindop, *The Opium Eater: A Life of Thomas De Quincey*, London, 1981, pp. 284, 288f., 299ff.
9 *Ibid.*, pp. 303ff.; Japp, *Thomas De Quincey*, pp. 212, 215–7, 223–4.
10 Charles MacFarlane, *Reminiscence of a Literary Life*, London, 1917, pp. 78–81.
11 Sir Henry Taylor to Southey, 28 December 1835, *Correspondence*, p. 67n.
12 Hogg to his wife, 1 January 1832, *Memorials*, p. 242.
13 Do. to Do., 17 February 1832, *Ibid.*, p. 258.
14 *Ibid.*, p. 242.
15 *Ibid., loc. cit.*
16 Carlyle to John, 10 January 1832, to his mother, 22 January, to John, 10 January, 16 February 1832, *Collected Letters*, vol. VI, pp. 87, 97, 126; *Two Notebooks* (21 January 1832), p. 250.
17 Carlyle, *Two Notebooks*, *loc. cit.*, pp. 250–1.
18 Hobhouse, *Recollections*, 17 March 1832, vol. IV, pp. 203, 204. Hogg was given another public reception in Peebles in 1833. In June 1831 Pringle had written inviting him to contribute to his periodical *Friendship's Offering*, then going to press – the last he was to edit – with the caution that it should be a few short pieces and not, like the last year's, 'too broad', which he could not use as unsuitable for ladies. (*Memorials of James Hogg, the Ettrick Shepherd*, ed. by his daughter Mrs Garden, 1887.) Hogg's next major work, *The Domestic Manners and Private Life of Sir Walter Scott*, completed after Scott's death, was published in 1834. In 1835 his last *Montrose Tales* were well received, but that publisher too shortly failed. Meanwhile Hogg's own health was giving way. He made a final visit to Edinburgh in April 1835, when on one occasion he was escorted from Wilson's house by Wilson and his two daughters, his son and another friend walking in front; they parted at the University. (*Memoirs*, p. 320. He died at home in November 1835.)
19 Susan Ferrier to her sister Mrs [Helen] Kinloch, [?September] 1823, *Memoir*, p. 177.
20 The Douglas Cause was the lawsuit brought by George, 7th Duke of Hamilton (son of the famous Elizabeth Gunning by her first husband the 6th Duke), to claim the estates of Archibald, Duke of Douglas, who had died in 1761 with no direct male heir. The Duke's sister, Lady Jane Douglas, had maintained that at the age of 50 she had given birth to twin sons. The lawsuit was on the grounds that the infants were not hers at all. The protracted case was at first given in favour of the Duke of Hamilton in 1767, but was reversed by the House of Lords in 1769. The case is described in *Boswell in Search of a Wife*, ed. Frank Brady & Frederick A. Pottle, Heinemann, 1957.
21 Lord (John A.) Murray (the judge) to Susan Ferrier, n.d. [1824], *Memoir of Susan Ferrier*, p. 182; Douglas, *The 'Blackwood' Group*, pp. 112f.
22 Mrs Graham to Susan Ferrier, 19 June 1824, *Memoir*, p. 182.
23 Helen Graham, Diary, 27 March 1825, *Parties and Pleasures*, pp. 129–30.
24 *Memoir of Susan Ferrier*, pp. 258ff.
25 *Constable and his Literary Correspondents*, vol. II, pp. 473ff.
26 Mrs Grant to Mrs Hook, 23 June 1824, *Memoir*, vol. III, p. 57.
27 *Constable and his Literary Correspondents*, vol. II, p. 472.
28 *Ibid., loc. cit.*; Mrs Grant to Mrs Smith, 14 July 1829, *op. cit.*, vol. III, pp. 151–2; to a friend in America, 16 July 1829, vol. III, pp. 153–4.
29 Eliza [Mrs John] Farrar, *Recollections of 70 Years*, Boston, 1866, p. 238.
30 Whishaw to Mrs Smith, 6 May 1826, Seymour, *Pope of Holland House*, p. 252.
31 *Noctes Ambrosianae*, quoted in Trevelyan, *Life of Macaulay*, vol. I, p. 129.

32 *Ibid.*, vol. I, pp. 173f.
33 Carlyle to John, 16 April 1828, *Collected Letters*, vol. IV, p. 362; *Two Notebooks*, p. 376.
34 Carlyle, *Two Notebooks, loc. cit.*
35 Crabb Robinson, *Diary Reminiscences and Correspondence*, vol. II, pp. 244–5, 246–7, 259; Trevelyan, *Life of Macaulay*, vol. I, pp. 114, 110–12. Macaulay's main achievements came later. In 1834, as member of the Supreme Council of India, his Minutes on Law and Education were influential on Indian development. On return in 1838 he embarked on his famous *History of England from 1688*, combined with a political career, sitting for Edinburgh in 1839 and 1852. His famous *Lays of Ancient Rome* (1842) had an instant and enduring popularity. His *History*, published in 1849 and 1855, was also a bestseller, so that he became rich, and was ennobled in 1857. He was unmarried, and lived quietly, and Carlyle probably had a point in implying limitations of character and in his treatment of history. He died in 1859. (*DNB*)
36 Cam Hobhouse, *Recollections* (26 May 1830), vol. IV, p. 23.
37 *Life of Rev. John McVickar*, pp. 226–7.
38 Hobhouse, *op. cit.* (3 July 1842), vol. VI, pp. 121ff.
39 Napier to Sir George Mackintosh, 22 June 1829; Mackintosh to Napier, 20 January 1830 *et al.*, *Biographical Notice of Napier*, p. 55.
40 Moore, 11 November 1829, 6 June 1829, *Memoirs, Journals*, vol. VI, pp. 90, 146.
41 *Ibid.*, 28 May 1829, vol. VI, p. 39; *Memoirs of Mackintosh*, vol. II, pp. 256ff.
42 Moore, 20 February 1830, *Memoirs, Journals*, vol. VI, p. 108.
43 *Ibid.*, 7 June 1829, vol. VI, pp. 47–8.
44 McVickar, Journal, 10 June, 21 July 1830, *Life*, pp. 134, 156.
45 Carlyle, *Two Notebooks*, 10 October 1831, vol. II, pp. 202–3.
46 Moore, 9 October 1832, *Memoirs, Journals*, vol. VI, p. 292.
47 *Ibid.*, 29 April 1831, 13 March 1833, vol. VI, pp. 202, 315.
48 Trevelyan, *Life of Macaulay*, vol. I, p. 132–3, 203.
49 *The Diaries of William Charles Macready, 1833–1851*, ed. William Toynbee, 2 vols, London, 1912 (10 July 1834), vol. I, p. 162 and n.

Chapter 53: Old Periodicals and New Ventures

1 Carlyle to James Johnston, 20 December 1823, *Collected Letters*, vol. II, p. 490.
2 Lang, *Life of Lockhart*, vol. I, pp. 356ff.
3 *Ibid.*, vol. I, p. 374; Scott to his son Walter, 5 December 1825, *Letters*, vol. IX, p. 321.
4 *Life of Lockhart*, vol. I, pp. 385–7.
5 *Constable and his Literary Correspondents*, vol. II, pp. 448ff.
6 *Biographical Notice of Napier*, pp. 61–2.
7 Jeffrey to Napier, 17 October, 5 November 1829, *Ibid.*, pp. 64–5; George Ticknor, Journal, 2 April 1838, *Life, Letters* etc., vol. II, p. 150.
8 Jeffrey to Napier, 7 February 1832, *Correspondence of Macvey Napier*, p. 126.
9 *Memoir of Robert Chambers*, pp. 138ff.
10 *Ibid.*, pp. 147–9.
11 *Ibid.*, pp. 149–58.
12 *Ibid.*, pp. 158–67.
13 *Ibid.*, pp. 167–8; *Constable* etc., vol. II, pp. 458ff. *Traditions of Edinburgh* is still in print today.
14 *Memoir of Robert Chambers*, pp. 184ff.
15 *Ibid.*, pp. 189, 202ff.
16 *Constable*, vol. II, p. 469; *Chambers, Memoir*, pp. 223f.

17 *Chambers*, pp. 225ff.
18 *Ibid.*, pp. 232ff. *Chambers's Edinburgh Journal* ran until 1938, having changed its name in 1854 to *Chambers's Journal*. The brothers produced numerous other works, notably *Chambers's Encyclopaedia* in 1859. Robert, made an honorary LLD of St Andrews in 1861, compiled an antiquarian miscellany called *The Book of Days* in 1862–4, and died in 1871. William was Lord Provost of Edinburgh in 1865–9, an honorary LLD of Edinburgh in 1872, restored St Giles', and presented Peebles with a public library. He died in 1883. (*DNB*)
19 *Ibid.*, pp. 235–6.

Chapter 54: The Social Scene: Feasts

1 Helen Graham, Diary, 24 February 1824, *Parties and Pleasures*, pp. 54–5.
2 *Ibid.*, 13 January, 24 February 1825, pp. 118, 120.
3 Charles P. Ainslie, *Life as I have found it*, Edinburgh & London, 1883, pp. 34–5.
4 Graham, Diary, 17 March 1825, *op. cit.*, p. 125.
5 Ticknor, Journal, March 1819, *Life, Letters*, vol. I, pp. 277–8.
6 Charlotte, Lady Wake, *Reminiscences* (1817), p. 68.
7 Mrs Grant to Mrs Col. White, [early February] 1823, to Mrs Smith, 10 February 1823, *Memoir*, vol. III, pp. 9, 12. James Smith (1782–1867), geologist, man of letters, merchant, specialised in glacial studies, and later, as an authority on ancient shipbuilding, wrote on St Paul's voyage and shipwreck (1848). (*DNB*)
8 Do. to Mrs Smith, 16 March 1823, *Ibid.*, vol. III, p. 16.
9 Do. to Do., 6 February 1824, to Mrs Hook, 20 February 1824, *Ibid.*, vol. III, pp. 40, 43.
10 Helen Graham, Diary, 4 February 1824, *op. cit.*, p. 40.
11 *Ibid.*, February 1824, p. 43.
12 J.J. Audubon, Journal, 14 December 1826, *1826 Journal*, p. 289.
13 Janet L. Story, *Early Reminiscences*, Glasgow, 1911, pp. 21–8.
14 Nathaniel Carter, *Letters from Europe*, 2 vols, 1827, vol. I, pp. 253–4.
15 *Ibid.*, vol. I, p. 264.
16 *Noctes Ambrosianae*, July 1829, vol. III, pp. 328–31.
17 *Ibid.*, April 1830, vol. III, pp. 433f., 443, 456; 239.
18 *Ibid.*, vol. II, p. 29.
19 Gillies, *Memoirs*, vol. II, p. 130.
20 Burgon, *Memoirs of Patrick Fraser Tytler*, p. 256.
21 Ticknor, *Journal*, March, 1819, *op. cit.*, vol. I, p. 277.
22 Adam Sedgwick to William Ainger, 19 February 1825, John Willis Clark & Thomas McKenny Hughes, *The Life and Letters of the Reverend Adam Sedgwick*, 2 vols, Cambridge, 1890, vol. I, p. 264.
23 Moore, *Memoirs, Journals* etc., October–November 1825, vol. IV, pp. 331ff., vol. V, pp. 3ff.
24 Lord Frederick Lennox, *Drafts on my Memory*, 2 vols, London, 1866, vol. I, pp. 377ff. Patrick Robertson (1794–1855), son of James Robertson, WS, was elected Dean of Faculty in 1842, became a Lord of Session on Lord Meadowbank's retirement, and was Rector of Marischal College, 1848. He died of a stroke at his Drummond Street home.
25 Carlyle to Alexander, 3 February 1827; Jane Carlyle to Mrs Carlyle, [17 February] 1827, *Collected Letters*, vol. IV, pp. 184, 188.
26 Audubon, *Journal*, 26 November 1826, p. 261.
27 *Ibid.*, 30 November 1826, pp. 267–8.
28 *Ibid.*, 27 November, 17 December, 22 December, 27 December 1826, pp. 262, 295, 308, 303.

29 Cam Hobhouse, 28 June 1832, 22 June 1843, *Recollections*, vol. IV, p. 245, vol. VI, p. 119.
30 Sedgwick to Ainger, 19 February 1825, *loc. cit.*
31 Disraeli to John Murray, 18 September 1825, *Benjamin Disraeli Letters: 1825–1834*, ed. J.A.W. Gunn etc., University of Toronto Press, 1982, p. 36.
32 Audubon, *Journal*, 20 December 1826, p. 299.
33 *Peter's Letters to his Kinsfolk*, Letter LII, vol. II, p. 316.
34 Willis, *Pencillings by the Way*, vol. III, p. 135.
35 Catherine Sinclair, *Holiday House*, Philadelphia, 1849.
36 *Remains of the Rev. Edmund Griffin*, vol. I, pp. 251–2.
37 Audubon, *Journal*, 2 November 1826, p. 249. Early in 1826 the *Edinburgh Evening Courant* reported how a dexterous thief had for some time been stealing brass handles and plates undetected, until on 2 March 'a fellow of the name of Syme' was 'catched' in the very act by police vigilance (*EEC*, 6 March 1826).
38 Griffin, *op. cit.*, vol. I, p. 251.
39 [Thomas Sibbald], *Reminiscences of a British Naval Officer*, by an Old Salt, Toronto, 1885, p. 15.
40 Frederick von Raumer, *England in 1835*, 3 vols, London, 1836, vol. II, p. 25.
41 Catherine Sinclair, *Holiday House*.

Chapter 55: The Social Scene: Personalities

1 Angus Davidson, *Miss Douglas of New York*, London, 1952, pp. 69ff., 76; *Memoirs of an American lady*, pp. xxi–ii.
2 *Ibid.*, p. 70; Scott *Letters*, to Maria Edgeworth, *c.* 14–15 Nov. 1827, vol. X, p. 312.
3 Davidson, *Miss Douglas of New York*, pp. 71–3.
4 *Ibid.*, pp. 74–5.
5 *Loc. cit.* The Basil Halls' visit covered Niagara, New Orleans, Boston, St Louis, and Hall wrote it up in *Travels in North America* in 1827–8, a three-volume work, 'pompous, painstaking and slightly supercilious' and not always accurate. (*Ibid.*)
6 *Ibid.*, p. 119; Scott, *Journal*, 1 & 2 July 1828.
7 Davidson, *Miss Douglas of New York*, p. 120. On her way south Miss Douglas met the Wordsworths, went on to visit the Continent, and when back in London in 1829 became friendly with the poetess L.E. Landon and with the Wilkies, brother and sister, who entertained her hospitably. She last met Scott in Italy, and on return to America finally married her faithful suitor Henry Cruger, in 1833. (*Ibid.*)
8 Mrs Grant to Mrs Smith, 18 July 1828, *Memoir*, vol. III, p. 137.
9 *Ibid.*, vol. III, p. 138.
10 Mrs Grant to a friend in USA, 26 April 1832, *Memoir*, vol. III, pp. 222–3. See also *DNB*.
11 McVickar, Journal, 17 July 1830, *Life*, pp. 149ff.
12 Mrs Grant to Mrs Smith, 16 May 1832, *Memoir*, vol. III, p. 24.
13 Carlyle, *Reminiscences*, vol. I, p. 269.
14 Lady Salisbury, Diary, 8 December 1836, Carola Oman, *The Gascoyne Heiress, The Life and Diaries of Frances Mary Gascoyne-Cecil, 1800–39*, Hodder & Stoughton, 1968, pp. 222–3.
15 Sydney Smith to his wife, 4 May 1826, *Letters*, vol. I, pp. 444–5.
16 [Frances Williams Wynn], *Diaries of a Lady of Quality*, p. 96.
17 Mrs Grant to Mrs Smith, 13 November 1830, *Memoir*, vol. III, pp. 182–3.
18 Morehead, Journal, 24 November 1830, *Life and Writings*, p. 218.
19 Josiah Livingston, *Our Street*, p. 32.
20 Scott and Sharpe to Robert Chambers, p. 47; Sharpe to A Lady, August 1832, *Sharpe Letters*, p. 463.

21 Do., February 1831, *Ibid.*, p. 449.
22 Moore, Journal, 29 April 1832, *Memoirs, Journals* etc., vol. VI, pp. 270–1.
23 Sharpe, *loc. cit.*, p. 448.
24 Mrs Grant to Mrs Hook, 27 November 1830, *Memoir*, vol. III, pp. 189–91.
25 Do. to Mrs Smith, 13 November 1830, *Ibid.*, vol. III, pp. 182–3. 'Poor Robert Miller' died not long afterwards, leaving (said Mrs Grant) a blank by 'his cordial good will, his harmless though ludicrous old stories, his most graphic descriptions, and his honest countenance beaming with benevolence, which has shone unclouded on me for 20 years' (to Mrs Izett, 4 March 1831, vol. III, p. 201).
26 Do. to Mrs Hook, *loc. cit.*; to Do., 23 May 1832, *Ibid.*, vol. III, p. 226.
27 McVickar, Journal, July 1830, *Life*, pp. 149ff., 155.
28 Mrs Grant to Mrs Smith, 16 March 1823, to Mrs Brown, 13 February 1823, *Memoir*, vol. III, pp. 15–16, 14.
29 [John Peter] Grant to Sir Robert Liston, 10 March 1825, Liston MSS, NLS, 161.

Except where otherwise shown, nn. 30–39 and 47–55 are from Mrs Grant's *Memoir*, vol. III.

30 Mrs Grant to Mrs Hook, 13 February 1826, vol. III, p. 97.
31 Do. to Mrs Smith, 16 December 1825, vol. III, p. 92.
32 Mrs Grant to Miss Mercer, 23 June 1826, vol. III, pp. 104–5. The site of Brae House was later to be covered by the Caledonian Railway Station.
33 Do. to Mrs Smith, 1 January & 22 April 1828, vol. III, pp. 120–1, 133.
34 Do. to Mrs Hook, 14 June 1830, vol. III, pp. 173–5.
35 Do. to Miss Mercer, 24 September 1828, vol. III, pp144–6.
36 Do. to Mrs Hook, 2 February 1829, vol. III, p. 148.
37 Do. to Do., 5 November 1829, vol. III, p. 161.
38 Do. to Mrs Smith, 19 August 1830, vol. III, pp. 176–8.
39 Do. to Do., 13 November 1830; to Mrs Hook, 27 November 1830, vol. III, pp. 182, 184, 189.
40 Ticknor, *Journal*, 27 April 1838, Life, Letters etc., vol. II, p. 163.
41 Helen Graham, Diary, 2 March 1825, *Parties and Pleasures*, p. 122.
42 Audubon, *Journal*, 19, 25, 29 November 1826, pp. 255, 259, 265–6.
43 Alison, *Memoir of Patrick Fraser Tytler*, pp. xvff.; Burgon, *Memoirs of Do.*, pp. 173ff.
44 Burgon, *op. cit.*, pp. 166–7.
45 Alison, *op. cit.*, p. xvii.
46 Burgon, *op. cit.*, pp. 167, 198, 208,212 ff.; Alison, *Patrick Fraser Tytler*. After his wife's death Tytler with his family moved to Hampstead, and continued writing, in spite of a slight stroke in 1841. Peel obtained a £200 pension for him in 1844. After his sister-housekeeper died, he married Anastasia Bonar, but his own health was now declining, and despite two winters in Dresden he died in London in 1849 and was buried in Edinburgh at Greyfriars.
47 Mrs Grant to Mrs Smith, 26 January 1831, vol. III, p. 196.
48 Do. to Dr Francis Boott, 21 February 1831, vol. III, p. 197.
49 Do. to Mrs Hook, 5 May 1831, to Mrs Izett, 4 March 1831, vol. III, pp. 203, 204, 200.
50 Do. to Mrs Brown, 3 December 1831, vol. III, p. 210 ff
51 Do to Mrs Hook, 26 January 1832, vol. III, pp. 213–4.
52 To Mrs Smith, 23 February 1832, vol. III, pp. 215–6.
53 Do. to Mrs Hook, 26 January, 16 April 1832, vol. III, pp. 214, 219.
54 Do. to Mrs Francis Boott, 25 April 1832, to Mrs Hook, 23 May 1832, vol. III, pp. 221, 226.
55 Do. to Mrs Smith, 18 & 24 September 1832, to Mrs Hook, 28 November 1832, vol. III, pp. 233, 236. Innerleithen is the locus for Scott's novel, *St Ronan's Well.*

Chapter 56: The Church: Great Preachers and Divided Issues

1 Chalmers, *Life and Writing*, vol. III, p. 15.
2 Sage, *Memorabilia Domestica*, pp. 278–9.
3 Chalmers, Journal, May 1824, *Life and Writing*, vol. III, pp. 17–18, 24.
4 *Ibid.*, vol. III, pp. 22–24.
5 *Ibid.*, vol. III, pp. 71–2, 74.
6 *Ibid.*, vol. III, pp. 76–8.
7 *Ibid.*, vol. III, pp. 75–6.
8 Sage, *op. cit.*, pp. 290–1n. Sinclair succeeded his brother in the baronetcy in 1835.
9 Chalmers, *op. cit.*, vol. III, pp. 118–9. In 1831 the Commission resolved that certain professorships, Languages, Philosophy, Mathematics, Medicine, Law or Oriental Languages, or the Principalship of the University, should not be combined with holding a living.
10 Chalmers, *op. cit.*, vol. III, pp. 100–3.
11 Mrs Grant to Mrs Hook, 12 September 1827, *Memoir*, vol. III, p. 117.
12 Chalmers, *op. cit.*, vol. III, pp. 164–5, 166–7.
13 *Ibid.*, vol. III, p. 165.
14 *Ibid.*, vol. III, pp.155, 159.
15 Charlotte Wedgwood to her sister Emma, 6 May 1827, Emma Darwin, *A Century of Family Letters, 1792–1866*, ed. Henrietta Litchfield, 2 vols, London, 1915, vol. I, p. 196.
16 Cockburn to Jeffrey, 15 August 1827, *Some Letters*, p. 22. Sir Harry's son, who inherited as Sir James, became Lord Moncrieff in 1828.
17 Dr Chalmers to Mrs Parker, 17 November 1828; to his sister Jane, 29 November 1828, *Correspondence of Thomas Chalmers*, pp. 142, 212–3.
18 James Dodds, *Thomas Chalmers*, p. 179.
19 Ticknor, *Life, Letters* etc. (March 1819), vol. I, p. 280.
20 Mrs Grant to Mrs Hook, 26 May 1827, *Memoir*, vol. III, p. 114.
21 Helen Graham, Diary, 16 November 1823, *Parties and Pleasures*, p. 31; Carlyle to his father, 22 December 1827, *Collected Letters*, vol. IV, p. 297.
22 von Raumer, *England in 1835*, vol. III, pp. 172–3.
23 Carlyle, *Collected Letters*, vol. IV, pp. 342–3; to his mother, 20 April 1828, *Ibid.*, p. 371.
24 *The Autobiography or History of the Life of John Bowes*, Glasgow, 1872, pp. 54ff.
25 von Raumer, *op. cit.*, vol. III, pp. 172–3.
26 Chalmers, Journal, 24 May 1828, *Life and Writing*, vol. III, p. 220.
27 Drummond, *Edward Irving and his Circle*, p. 115.
28 Chalmers, *Life and Writing, loc. cit.*
29 *Ibid.*, vol. III, pp. 231ff.
30 Dodds, *Thomas Chalmers*, pp. 199–210.
31 Chalmers, *Life and Writing*, vol. III, p. 245.
32 *Ibid.*, vol. III, p. 261.
33 Mrs Grant to Mrs Smith, 22 May 1830, to Miss Mercer, 31 October 1831, to a friend in the USA, 26 April 1832, *Memoir*, vol. III, pp. 171–2, 207, 224.
34 Chalmers, *Life and Writing*, vol. III, pp. 259–60, 275, 279f.
35 Dodds, *Thomas Chalmers*, pp. 211ff.
36 Mrs Grant to Mrs Hook, 17 December 1830, *Memoir*, vol. III, p. 194.
37 Chalmers, *Life and Writing*, vol. III, pp. 291ff.
38 *Ibid.*, vol. III, p. 306. Carlyle suspected that 'the old Dundas system' of influence was now so unpopular that such preferments would now go 'on public views only'. Aitken later married Jane Carlyle's friend Eliza Stoddart. Carlyle to Samuel Aitken, 28 June 1831, *Collected Letters*, vol. V, p. 293.
39 McVickar, *Life*, pp. 127–8, 149–50, 151.

40 Chalmers, *Life and Writing*, vol. III, pp. 310, 313–5.
41 *Ibid.*, vol. III, p. 290.
42 Carlyle, *Reminiscences*, vol. II, pp. 201ff.
43 Chalmers, *Life and Writing*, vol. III, pp. 290–1.
44 *Ibid.*, vol. III, pp. 349–50.
45 *Ibid.*, vol. III, pp. 340–1.
46 *Ibid.*, vol. III, pp. 298–9; Dodds, *Thomas Chalmers*, pp. 144–6.

Chapter 57: The Educational Scene Schools

1 Cockburn, *Memorials of his Time*, pp. 358–9; 'Edinburgh Journal 1823–1833', *OEC*, vol. XXIX, pp. 143–4.
2 Youngson, *Classical Edinburgh*, pp. 156–8; *Edinburgh in the 19th Century*, 1823; Lindsay, *Georgian Edinburgh*, p. 40.
3 Youngson, *loc. cit. Address from the Town Council of Edinburgh on the subject of the New Buildings for the High School* (1825–1829), NLS Ry.IV.e.4 (18).
4 *Georgian Edinburgh*, p. 41.
5 See Carlyle to Charles Tait, 13 May 1825, *Collected Letters*, vol. III, p. 324 and n. The Rev. John Williams (1792–1858) in 1827 was appointed Professor of Latin at London University, in 1833 became Archdeacon of Cardigan and in 1847 Warden of Llandovery New School. He published numerous works on the Welsh language. [*DNB*] Thomas Carlyle's friend Robert Mitchell, who also became a personal friend of Williams, became a master there.
6 Cockburn, *Life of Jeffrey*, vol. I, pp. 304–5.
7 *Reminiscences of Charlotte, Lady Wake*, p. 68.
8 *Ibid.*, p. 115; see also *Edinburgh Evening Courant*, 2 August 1827.
9 Rev. John McVickar, Journal, 19 July 1830, *Life*, p. 153.
10 Catherine Sinclair, *Holiday House*.
11 *EEC*, 24 October 1818.
12 Lindsay, *Georgian Edinburgh*, p. 4. It is now the Scottish National Gallery of Modern Art.
13 *EEC*, 20 April 1815, 31 October 1818.
14 Chalmers, *Life and Writing*, vol. III, p. 25.
15 Smiles, James Nasmyth, *Autobiography*, pp. 112–5.
16 *Constable and his Literary Correspondents*, vol. II, pp. 390ff.
17 *DNB, ad loc.*
18 Gibbon, *Life of George Combe*, pp. 163, 205–6; Frank Podmore, *Robert Owen*, 2 vols, London, 1923, vol. I, pp. 356–71.

Chapter 58: The Educational Scene: University and Medical College

1 Cockburn, *Life of Jeffrey*, vol. I, pp. 277–8.
2 J.R. McCulloch to Macvey Napier, 25 May 1825, *Correspondence of Macvey Napier*, pp. 41–2.
3 Chalmers, *Life and Writings*, vol. III, pp. 224–6; David Masson, *Memories of Two Cities, Edinburgh and Aberdeen*, Edinburgh & London, 1911, pp. 77f.
4 *Life of Christison*, vol. I, pp. 423ff.
5 Carlyle, *Collected Letters*, vol. VI, p. 168n.
6 *Life of Christison*, vol. I, pp. 406–7.
7 Andrew G. Fraser, *The Building of Old College: Adam, Playfair and the University of Edinburgh*, Edinburgh, 1989, p. 178.
8 *The Life and Letters of Charles Darwin*, ed. by his son Francis Darwin, 3 vols, London,

1887, vol. I, p. 87; Darwin to his sister Caroline, 6 January 1826, *More Letters of Charles Darwin*, vol. I, p. 8.

9 Audubon, Journal, 4 & 9 December 1826, *1826 Journal*, pp. 273–4, 281.

10 Darwin, *Life and Letters*, vol. I, pp38–40. Robert Grant became an FRS in 1826, Fullerton Professor of Physiology 1837–40, and Swiney lecturer on geology at the British Museum. He died in 1874, and bequeathed his collections to University College. (*DNB*)

11 Darwin, *Life and Letters*, vol. I, pp. 40–42.

12 Christison, *Life*, vol. I, pp. 90–91.

13 Darwin to his sister Caroline, *loc. cit.*; *More Letters*, vol. I, pp. 5–8.

14 Struthers, *Edinburgh Anatomical School*, p. 91.

15 McVickar, Journal, 19 July 1830, *Life*, p. 152.

16 Struthers, *op. cit.*, pp. 80–82.

17 *Life of Christison*, vol. I, pp279ff., 286–7.

18 *Ibid.*, vol. I, pp. 288–96.

19 *Ibid.*, vol. I, p. 304.

20 *Edinburgh Evening Courant*, 23 January 1826.

21 Dr Robert Knox to Robert Peel, draft, 3 November 1828, quoted in Cresswell, *Royal College of Surgeons of Edinburgh*, pp. 205–6.

22 *Life of Christison*, vol. I, p. 306 ff.

23 Sydney Smith to Richard Sharp, 5 January 1829, *Letters*, p. 432.

24 Robert Seton to Charles K. Sharpe, 14 January 1829, *Sharpe Letters*, p. 432.

25 Cresswell, *Royal College of Surgeons of Edinburgh*, pp. 204–5.

26 Miles, *Edinburgh School of Surgery before Lister*, pp. 161–2, 185 ff.

27 Syme's hospital was opposite the National Museum. It had been the town house of the Elliots of Minto, and between it and Horse Wynd were the former houses of Lady Galloway, Lord Kennet, Baron Stuart and Lord Covington, then tenanted by the poor. All were destroyed in the mid-19th century, Minto House in 1874 during demolition for city 'improvements'.

28 Miles, *School of Surgery*, p. 186 ff.; Wilmot Harrison, *Memorable Edinburgh Houses*, Edinburgh, 1893, p. 62.

29 Miles, *School of Surgery*, p. 132; Guthrie, *A History of Medicine*, pp. 307f.

30 pp. 191–2; Guthrie, *A History of Medicine*, p. 309.

31 Guthrie, *A History of Medicine*, p. 231.

32 *Life of Christison*, vol. I, pp. 339–40.

33 Cresswell, pp. 269ff.; *Life of Christison*, vol. I, pp. 317ff.

34 Frederick von Raumer, *England in 1835*, vol. III, pp. 106–7.

35 *Life of Christison*, vol. I, pp. 328–33.

36 *Ibid.*, vol. I, pp. 361, 370–2.

37 Carlyle to Alexander, 3 February 1827, *Collected Letters*, vol. IV, pp. 182–4.

38 *Life of Christison*, vol. I, pp. 372–8.

39 Livingston, *Our Street*, pp. 11–12, 10.

40 C.K. Sharpe to A Lady, December [1831], *Letters*, pp. 456–7.

41 Mrs Grant to Mrs Hook, 26 January 1832, to Mrs Smith, 23 February 1832, *Memoir*, vol. III, pp. 214, 216.

42 Carlyle to his mother, 10 November 1831, to John, 21 October 1831; to John, 10 January 1832, *Collected Letters*, vol. VI, pp. 42, 29, 84.

43 Jeffrey to Miss Cockburn, 21 March 1832, Cockburn, *Life of Jeffrey*, vol. II, pp. 247–8.

44 Chambers's *Edinburgh Journal*, No.1, 4 February 1832, pp. 7–8.

45 *Ibid.*, No.4, 25 February 1832, p. 29.

46 J.M.W. Turner to Robert Cadell, 22 December 1831, *Collected Correspondence of J.M.W. Turner*, ed. John Gage, Oxford, 1980, p. 145.

47 Fanny Kemble to Harriet in USA, 31 January 1832, Frances Ann Kemble, *Record of a Girlhood*, vol. II, pp. 178–9.

48 Countess Gower to Lady Caroline Lascelles, 26 July 1832, *Three Howard Sisters*, ed. Maud, Lady Leconfield, London, 1955, p. 236.
49 Susan Ferrier, *Memoir and Correspondence*, p. 261.
50 Gibbon, *Life of George Combe*, pp. 168, 176–7.
51 Combe to Rev. David Welsh, 6 April 1825, *Ibid.*, p. 178.
52 *Ibid.*, pp. 179–80.
53 *Letter from George Combe to Frederick Jeffrey, Esq.*, Edinburgh, 1826.
54 *Life of George Combe*, pp. 181–5.
55 *Ibid.*, pp. 191–8. Carlyle, irritated by the 'science', commenting on Hamilton's attacks, merely remarked that 'Combe and Hamilton are still jawing on phrenology, and this in print'. (Carlyle to John, 16 April 1828, *Collected Letters*, vol. IV, pp. 362–3.)
56 *Memoir of Thomas Uwins*, vol. I, p. 98.
57 Carlyle to James Johnston, 20 December 1823, *Collected Letters*, vol. II, p. 490. The *Journal* continued under that name until 1837, and for another ten years under a different name.
58 Mrs Stair Douglas [Janet M. Douglas], *The Life and Selections of the Correspondence of William Whewell, DD, late Master of Trinity College*, Cambridge, London, 1881, p. 107.
59 Adam Sedgwick to William Ainger, 19 February 1825, Clark & Hughes, *Reverend Adam Sedgwick*, vol. I, pp. 264, 265.
60 Moore, Journal, 20 May 1826, *Memoirs, Journal*, etc., vol. V, p. 70.
61 Audubon, Journal, 19 November 1826, *1826 Journal*, p. 256.
62 *Ibid.*, 27 November 1826, p. 263.
63 *Ibid.*, 18, 20, 21 December 1826, pp. 296, 299–300, 302.
64 *Ibid.*, 20 December 1826, pp. 299–300; to Mrs William Rathbone III, 29 November [sic] 1826, *Ibid.*, *Letters*, p. 374.
65 Gibbon, *Life of George Combe*, pp. 205–6.
66 *Ibid.*, pp. 209–10.
67 *Ibid.*, p. 213. Samuel Wilderspin (?1792–1866), who worked as a clerk in a mercantile office, had in 1820 opened an infant school at Spitalfields in London, then developed them throughout Britain, backed by publications on the education of the young. (*DNB*)
68 Combe to Dr Spurzheim, 20 January 1829, *Life of Combe*, *loc. cit.*
69 Do. to Rev. David Welsh, 12 November 1829, *op. cit.*, pp. 213f., 228–9. A pamphlet consisting of newspaper offprints was published at Combe's request, as 'Quarrel between the *Scotsman* and *Mercury*' (1829), with an explanation of his view and reproduction of the numerous letters between the parties.
70 *Life of Combe*, p. 229. In 1830 a lengthy explanatory pamphlet was published by the Commissioners for Improvements, on the knotty and protracted negotiations for the purchase of this and adjoining property for the purposes of making a new road into this side of the city. The avowed object was to demonstrate the correctness of the transactions and the 'faithfulness, economy, and prudence, combined with enlightened judgment and good taste' with which the Commissioners managed their affairs. (*The Western Approach Investigated; or, The History of Two Purchases in that Line*; NLS 6.1504(10).)
71 *Life of Combe*, pp. 231f., 236.
72 *Ibid.*, pp. 253–5.
73 *Ibid.*, pp. 256ff.
74 *Ibid.*, pp. 264, 275–6.
75 Frances Ann Kemble, *Record of a Girlhood*, vol. I, pp. 245–7, 251. Fanny met Macdonald again in 1846 in Rome, where he died in 1858. (*Loc. cit.*)
76 *Ibid.*, vol. II, p. 222.
77 *Life of Combe*, pp. 283ff.

78 *DNB*, George and Andrew Combe, *ad loc.*
79 Kemble, *op. cit.*, vol. I, p. 246.

Chapter 59: Artists and Musicians

1 Ballantyne, *Life of Roberts*, pp. 24ff.
2 *Ibid.*, p. 32.
3 *Edinburgh Evening Courant*, 11, 18, 25 February 1826.
4 Charles Kirkpatrick Sharpe to Lady Gwydyr, 5 March 1826, *Letters*, p. 362.
5 Sydney Smith to Lady Grey, February 1827, *Letters*, vol. I, p. 460.
6 William Nicholson to David Roberts, 1 May 1829, Ballantyne, *Life of Roberts*, p. 32.
7 Wilkie to Andrew Wilson, 27 September 1829, Cunningham, *Life of Wilkie*, vol. III, p. 24.
8 *Ibid.*, vol. II, p. 113, 116–7, 118ff. Wilkie to his sister, 26 September 1824, *Ibid.*, vol. II, p. 123.
9 *Ibid.*, vol. II, pp. 138ff.
10 *Ibid.*, vol. III, pp. 9, 16, 22; Susan Ferrier to Mrs Kinloch, 5 November 1829, *Memoir and Correspondence*, p. 242.
11 Cam Hobhouse, 27 March 1830, *Recollections*, vol. IV, p. 13.
12 Lady Salisbury, Diary, 19 October 1833, Carola Oman, *The Gascoyne Heiress*, p. 88.
13 Cunningham, *Life of Wilkie*, vol. III, pp41ff. Benjamin Haydon, who called on Wilkie in 1829 while he was finishing the painting, remarked how 'very curious' he found it, Wilkie having been to Italy since he began the picture and having much changed his style. Argyll, the King's head, the man on horseback with the crowd, were all in his first style 'when detail and finish were all in all to him', while the trumpeters, the costume of the Duke of Hamilton, the woman and other features were in his later style, forming a mixture 'like oil and water'. (Haydon, Diary, 30 July 1829, *Diary*, vol. III, p. 383.)
14 *Correspondence of J.M.W. Turner*, p. 116.
15 Turner to Sir Walter Scott, 20 April 1831, *Ibid.*, p. 143; to Robert Cadell, 22 December 1831, 25 February 1832, *Ibid.*, pp. 145f.
16 *Ibid.*, p. 148; *Life of Wilkie*, vol. III, p. 54.
17 Henry Cockburn to Sir Thomas Dick Lauder, 26 April 1829, *Some Letters of Lord Cockburn*, p. 25; see also Cockburn's *Memorials*, p. 400.
18 Burgon, *Memoirs of Patrick Fraser Tytler*, p. 171; *DNB*.
19 Mrs Grant to Mrs Gorman, 23 March 1825, *Memoir*, vol. III, p. 83.
20 Sharpe to Scott, [1825], *Letters*, p. 325; *DNB*.
21 Rev. D.T.K. Drummond, *Memoir of Montague Stanley, ARSA*, Edinburgh, 1848, pp. 1–55.
22 *DNB*.
23 *Journal and Correspondence of Lady Eastlake*, ed. Charles Eastlake Smith, 2 vols, London, 1895, vol. I, p. 48.
24 *Encyclopaedia Britannica, loc. cit.*
25 The information and quotations in this section for 1826 are from the University of Oklahoma Press edition (1967) of *The 1826 Journal of John James Audubon*, ed. Alice Ford. (See n.29)
26 Prideaux Selby (1788–1867), naturalist, of a prominent Northumberland family, studied at Oxford but took no degree, was active in local politics but was chiefly devoted to natural history, especially ornithology. He was a member of the Wernerian Society of Edinburgh, to which he dedicated his *Illustrations of British Ornithology*, in 19 parts from 1821 to 1834. An FRS of Edinburgh and Honorary MA of Durham University, he was a remarkable combination of sportsman, naturalist and scientist. (*DNB*)

27 In 1832 Mrs Dickie, apparently given either to drink or to extravagance, had her furniture sold by auction, when Audubon's 'spirited picture of the cats' went for £4. (J.B. Kidd to Audubon, 22 November 1832, Audubon, *1826 Journal*, p. 295n.)

28 This was 'Sauve qui Peut', now in New York.

29 *Journal of Sir Walter Scott*, 24 January 1827, pp. 268–9, and his *Letters*, vol. XII, pp. 476–7, 8 March 1827, in reply to Audubon's asking him for a letter of introduction. He expresses his ignorance of natural history, but is pleased to send good wishes, accommodation of his 'talents and manners', and belief in his 'scientific attainments'. Information on Audubon for 1827 is based on Maria Audubon's inaccurate rendering of her father's diaries, *Audubon and his Journals* (2 vols, London, 1898), and partly on *The Life and Times of J.J. Audubon, the Naturalist*, ed. Robert Buchanan, 2nd edn, London, 1869, which is more true to the original but omits more. For example, Buchanan's version of the snowy weather is altered by Maria to comparison with 'countries of northern climes'.

Audubon left Edinburgh on 5 April 1827 for Newcastle and then Paris, staying briefly with Prideaux Selby and his family at Twizel House, Belford. In October 1830 he returned to Edinburgh with his wife, Lucy, and lodged comfortably with his former landlady Mrs Dickie until 15 April 1831, when they set off again for London and Paris.

30 There were four volumes of the engravings, with an index, under the title *A Synopsis of the Birds of North America* (1839). Audubon's 1828 journal has been destroyed.

31 *A Concise and Accurate Account of the Accident that occurred at the Sale of the late Lord Eldin's Pictures, Saturday the 16th March, at 16 Picardy Place, by a Sufferer* [= John Howell, Polyartist], Edinburgh, published by John Howell, 67 Thistle Street, 1833. (NLS, Tracts relating to Edinburgh, LC 137/(12); Edinburgh Broadside, LC Fol.74.)

Chapter 60: Craftsmen and Labourers

1 A tablet reset in the pavement of Niddrie Mains Drive, on the site of the demolished Niddrie House, records 'This pavilion is Found[ed] by Andrew Waucho[pe] of Niddrie, Esq., the 8th day of October 1735 years'. (John Gifford, Colin McWilliam, David Walker, *Buildings of Scotland, Edinburgh*, Penguin Books, Harmondsworth, 1984, p. 544. And see Colvin, *Dictionary of British Architects*, 3rd edn, pp. 64, 186.)

2 This section, except where otherwise specified, is based on Hugh Miller's *My Schools and Schoolmasters*, ed. W.M. Mackenzie, Edinburgh, 1907, pp. 307–9, 319–40, 353–7.

3 This man was possibly the son of Alexander Lindsay, 23rd Earl Crawford, 1752–1825, a representative peer, who had served in the army in N. America, became Governor of Jamaica, returned to Britain 1801 and was crated full general in 1803. He settled in Lancashire where he mined coalfields inherited by his wife, whom he had married in 1780. She was Elizabeth Dalrymple, of Castleton, Derbyshire, and they had several children, of whom the eldest, James (1783–1869) succeeded to the earldom in 1825. (*The Scots Peerage*, ed. Sir James Balfour Paul, 9 vols, Edinburgh, 1903–1911, vol. III.) The 23rd Earl's death in 1825 would presumably explain the supposed claim of 'John Yearl Crawford', whose birth might well have preceded the former's marriage; though Peerages did not record illegitimate births.

However, Crawford might more likely have been the son of George, 22nd Earl, who died unmarried in 1808 when the direct line became extinct, and the title reverted to heirs-male of the 2nd Earl. This would account for Miller's belief that but for his illegitimacy John the mason could or should have succeeded to the title.

4 Hawkie, *Autobiography of a Gangrel*, p. 36.

5 Miller met and married Lydia Mackenzie Fraser, who had been living in Edinburgh as a 'young lady' lodger at the house of Burns's one-time correspondent George Thomson. At his music parties she met such interesting guests as the Ballantyne brothers James and Alexander, the Rev. Mr Thomson of Duddingston, and Mrs Grant of Laggan. Miller returned to Edinburgh in 1834, where unlike Carlyle he found 'something inspiriting in the air . . . I feel myself an inch taller'. He met and was befriended by the Dick Lauder family, and secured a job in Linlithgow.

Having married in 1837, from 1840 he edited a radical paper, *The Witness*, and wrote profusely on geology and pre-Darwinian evolutionary theories. Sadly, illness and a brain disease led him to shoot himself in 1856.

6 Alexander Somerville, *Autobiography of a Working Man*, pp. 97–8, 99ff., 117. Alexander Somerville (1811–85) was the son of a Lothian carpenter. Following army service he wrote on Corn Law reform and other economic subjects and worked with Richard Cobden. Besides his autobiography and other works he contributed to newspapers such as the *Manchester Examiner.* (*DNB*)

7 Miller, *op. cit.*, pp. 314–8. In the enquiries for the Mines Act of 1842, when a Commission on female labour was investigating Scottish pits, a collier was recorded in Inveresk parish who worked in a Musselburgh pit, son and grandson of slave workers and himself born a slave, who had never in his life been more than 20 miles from Edinburgh. See also Cockburn, *Memorials*, p. 67.

8 Smiles, *James Nasmyth, Autobiography*, pp. 91–5.

9 *Ibid.*, pp. 112ff.

10 Dodds, *Thomas Chalmers*, pp. 226–7.

11 Rev. Henry Colman, *European Life and Manners; in Familiar Letters to his Friends*, 2 vols, Boston & London, vol. I, p. 59.

12 *Ibid.*, vol. I, p. 60.

13 Audubon, Journal, 31 December 1926, *1826 Journal*, pp. 316–7.

14 *Ibid.*, 27 October 1826, pp. 235–6.

15 *Diary of Frances Lady Shelley* (July 1819), pp. 57–8.

16 Grant Thorburn, *Men and Manners in Britain; or A bone to gnaw for the Trollopes: Fidlers &c.*, New York, 1834, pp. 141f.

17 Audubon, 20 November 1826, 27 October 1826, pp. 259, 238.

18 *Ibid.*, 19 December 1826, p. 298.

19 *Death of Rose Street Miser*, Edinburgh Broadsides, NLS, LC FOL.74

20 Note by Carlyle, 17 February 1827, in *New Letters and Memorials of Jane Welsh Carlyle*; annotated by Thomas Carlyle, ed. Alexander Carlyle, 2 vols, London, 1904, pp. 18–19.

21 Gillies, *Literary Veteran*, vol. III, pp. 172–3.

22 Catherine Sinclair, *Holiday House*, p. 116.

23 *Ibid.*

24 Susanna Corder, *Life of Elizabeth Fry, compiled from her journal*, London, 1853, p. 439.

25 Dodds, *Thomas Chalmers*, pp. 228–31.

26 Morehead, *Life and Writings*, p. 201.

27 Mrs Fletcher, *Autobiography*, pp. 136–156.

28 *Edinburgh Evening Courant*, February 1826.

29 Smiles, James Nasmyth, *Autobiography*, p. 103.

30 Scott to Jane Scott, 26 March 1825, *Letters*, vol. IX, p. 49.

31 Do. to Henry Mackenzie, 2 April 1825, *Ibid.*, vol. IX, p. 60.

32 *Prospectus of the Edinburgh Oil Gas Company* (1823), NLS 6.1245 (23); *Edinburgh Oil Gas Light Company* (incorporated by Act of Parliament), 1824, NLS APS 3.83.12.

33 *Illuminating Powers of Gas from Coal and Oil* (1824), NLS 6.1245 (21).
34 *Proposals for Establishing in Edinburgh and Glasgow a Company to be entitled The Edinburgh Portable Gas Company* . . . (1825), NLS 6.081 (21).
35 Scott to Jane Scott, and to Miss Edgeworth, 23 March 1825, *Letters*, vol. IX, pp. 40–42, 44.

Chapter 61: Thieves, Confidence Tricksters and Beggars

1 Dying Speeches, Executions etc., Scottish 1807–35, NLS, Rosebery Collection, Ry.III.a.3A.
2 NLS Ry.a.2 (3) & (31).
3 *Ibid.*, (85).
3 *Ibid.*, 86 & 112v., including newspaper cuttings (June 1836) and ?*Caledonian Mercury* (?June 1836). William Broughton (1788–1853), after working at East India House, studied at Pembroke Hall, Cambridge, became chaplain to the Tower of London, DD 1836 and in the same year was appointed Archdeacon of New South Wales. In 1847 he became Bishop of Sydney. (*DNB*)
5 Chambers's *Edinburgh Journal*, 24 March 1832, vol. I, p. 59.
6 *Ibid.*, 12 May 1832, p. 115.
7 *Ibid.*, *loc. cit.*
8 *Ibid.*

Chapter 62: The Theatre

1 Jane Welsh to Thomas Carlyle, [1 July 1824], Carlyle, *Collected Letters*, vol. IV, p. 97.
2 Darwin to his father, [October 1825], *More Letters*, vol. I, pp. 6–7.
3 Moore, Journal, 12 November 1825, *Memoirs, Journals,* etc., vol. V, pp. 13–15; 9 November 1825, vol. V, pp. 12–13.
4 Audubon, Journal, 27 October & 3 November 1826, *1826 Journal*, pp. 239, 252.
5 Mathews, to his wife, 10 & 14 January 1826, 21 February 1828, 1 February 1830; *Continuation of Memoirs*, vol. I, pp. 335–6, 369, vol. II, p. 33.
6 From 1834 Mathews suffered seriously in health, managed to carry on to a last tour in the United States with his wife, but fell ill in Liverpool on his return, and died in 1835 in Plymouth.
7 *Ibid.*, vol. II, p. 37; to his wife, 1 February 1830, vol. II, p. 33.
8 *Macready's Reminiscences*, vol. I, p. 368.
9 Kemble, *Record of a Girlhood*, vol. I, pp. 229–32, 258–60, 251.
10 James Robinson Planché, *Recollections and Reflections*, London, 1901, p. 102.
11 Kemble, *Record of a Girlhood*, vol. I, pp. 125–8.
12 *Noctes Ambrosianae*, August 1830, vol. IV, pp. 110f.
13 Kemble, *Record of a Girlhood*, vol. I, pp. 125–9, 176, vol. II, pp. 162, 212ff.
14 Bayne, *Life and Letters of Hugh Miller*, vol. I, pp. 138–40.
15 *Macready's Reminiscences*, 2 March 1846 *et seq.*, vol. II, pp. 271–9.
16 *Journal and Correspondence of Lady Eastlake*, vol. I, p. 179.
17 Macready, *loc. cit.*

Chapter 63: Lawyers and Law-Breakers

1 *Remains of the Rev. Edmund Griffin*, vol. I, pp. 239–42, 244.
2 Schinkel, *The English Journey*, 4 July 1826, p. 150.
3 Alison, *My Life and Writings*, pp. 213–7.
4 *Ibid.*, pp. 220–3.

5 *Ibid.*, p. 250.
6 *Ibid.*, pp. 250, 257, 272.
7 *Ibid.*, pp. 276–7, 279–80.
8 Moore, *Memoirs, Journals*, etc., 3 & 7 November 1825, vol. V, pp. 7, 10.
9 Cockburn to Sir Thomas Dick Lauder, 1833 or 4, *Some Letters*, p. 31.
10 Alison, *My Life and Writings*, p. 281.
11 *Ibid.*, pp. 278–9.
12 Graham, *Parties and Pleasures*, February 1824, p. 43.
13 Cockburn to Jeffrey, 21 July 1830, *Some Letters*, p. 27.
14 Alison, *My Life and Writings*, pp. 289–90, 291, 294–5.
15 *Ibid.*, pp. 302ff. In 1845 Alison was elected Lord Rector of Marischal College, Aberdeen, defeating Macaulay, and in 1851 of Glasgow, defeating Palmerston. In 1852–9 he published a continuation of his *History of Europe*, and in 1852 was created a baronet.
16 Execution: NLS Edinburgh Broadsides LC FOL.74, 285.
17 Dying Speeches, Executions, etc., NLS, Rosebery Collection, Ry.III.a.2 (91).
18 *Ibid.*, (105).

Chapter 64: The Last Years of Scott

1 Janet Schetky to Charlotte Trevenen, 19 January 1827, Schetky, *90 Years of Work and Play*, p. 140. Charlotte Trevenen, the recipient of this letter, became engaged to Schetky, twenty years her senior, in 1827, but Jane died at the end of the year and the wedding was deferred until April next. In 1830 Schetky was appointed Marine Painter Extraordinary to William IV.
2 Gillies, *Recollections of Scott*, p. 266.
3 Scott to Sharpe, 17 August 1830, *Sharpe Letters*, pp. 442–4.
4 Felix Mendelssohn to his family, 30 July 1829, Sebastian Hensel, *The Mendelssohn Family (1729–1847) from Letters and Journals*, 2 vols, 1881, vol. I, pp. 196–8, 31 July, vol. I, pp. 199–200.
5 *Remains of the Rev. Edmund Griffin*, vol. I, pp. 242–3. Griffin would undoubtedly have gone on to a distinguished career, but sadly, having sailed from Liverpool on 1 April 1830 and returned to New York apparently restored to health to resume his academic career, he shortly broke down, and died on 31 August, leaving two volumes of works including poems, literary essays, and a lengthy travel journal.
6 McVickar, Journal, July 1830, *Life*, pp. 157, 182. The minister of Melrose, Rev. George Thomson, had a son, also Rev. George (?1782–1838), who between about 1811 and 1820 was librarian and tutor in Scott's household. He was a skilled fencer and vigorous horseman, despite having lost a leg in a boyhood accident. With the passing years he became increasingly eccentric. (*Fasti Eccles. Scot.*, vol. I, p. 561) Not to be confused with his namesake (1757–1851), a Fife schoolmaster's son, apprenticed to the law and from 1780 Clerk to the Trustees. This other Thomson, a keen musician, was a director of Edinburgh's first music festival in 1815, and published and collected Scottish airs. Burns had written for him from 1792. (*DNB*)
7 Coleridge to Alaric Watts, [August 1827], to William Blackwood, 20 October 1829, *Letters*, vol. VI, pp. 299, 821.
8 Mrs Grant to Mrs Smith, 17 November 1830, *Memoir*, vol. III, pp. 186–7.
9 Cam Hobhouse, 30 December 1831, *Recollections*, vol. IV, p. 160.
10 Moore, 30 October 1833, *Memoirs, Journals* etc., vol. VI, p. 349. This is presumably Dionysius Lardner (1793–1859), the Irish scientific writer, who compiled the *Cabinet Cyclopaedia* in 133 volumes (1849), and edited *The Edinburgh Cabinet Library* in 1830–44.

11 *Journal of Lady Eastlake*, 25 August, 24 February 1843, vol. I, pp. 96–7, 55.
12 Wordsworth to Scott, 7 June & 20 July 1830, Rogers to Wordsworth, n.d., Wordsworth to Rogers, 30 July 1830, *Letters*, vol. V, pp. 276, 305, 310.
13 Skene, *Memories of Sir Walter Scott*, p. 181.
14 Gillies, *Recollections of Sir Walter Scott*, pp. 266, 289–90.
15 D. Wordsworth to William Pearson, 11 August 1831; Wordsworth to Edward Quillinan, 23 August, to Scott, 29 August; Scott to Wordsworth, 2 September, D. Wordsworth to Catherine Clarkson, 9 September, to Francis Mereweather, 13 September, *Letters*, vol. V, pp. 419–30.
16 Wordsworth to Scott, 16 Sept. 1831, to Rev. Robert Jones, 26 Sept., to William Rowan Hamilton, 27 Oct., to Samuel Rogers, 7 Nov., *Letters*, vol. V, pp. 434, 435, 447f.
17 Wordsworth to Mrs Hemans, 20 Aug. 1813, *Letters*, vol. V, p. 637.
18 Southey to Mrs Bray, 13 August 1831, *Selections from the Letters*, vol. IV, p. 234.
19 Charles MacFarlane, *Reminiscences of a Literary Life*, London, 1917, pp. 26–7. MacFarlane (1799–1858) travelled in Italy from 1816–27, in Turkey from 1827–9, then settled in London as a writer and travelled again in 1847. Among his works were the eight-volume *Civil and Military History of England* (1838–44) and *The Book of Table Talk* (1838). In 1857 he entered the Charterhouse as a Poor Brother. (*DNB*)
20 *Memoirs of Sir William Knighton*, 3 October 1831, vol. II, p. 113.
21 Haydon, *Diary*, 16 October 1831, *Diary*, vol. III, p. 563.
22 Scott to Sharpe, 5 April & September 1831, Sharpe to Scott, 9 April 1831, *Sharpe Letters*, pp. 450, 455, 451.
23 Moore, Journal, 14–16 October 1831, *Memoirs, Journals* etc., vol. VI, pp. 226ff.
24 Skene, *Memories of Sir Walter Scott*, pp. 181–2.
25 Hon. Frances Mackenzie to Crabb Robinson, 24 April 1832, The *Correspondence of Henry Crabb Robinson with the Wordsworth Circle* (1808–1866), ed. Edith J. Morley, 2 vols, Oxford, 1927, vol. II, p. 228.
26 Hare, *Frances Baroness Bunsen*, vol. I, p. 373.
27 Southey to Walter Savage Landor, 26 June 1832, *Selections from Letters*, vol. IV, p. 284.
28 Do. to Mrs Hughes, 16 August, 16 September 1832, *Ibid.*, vol. IV, pp. 296, 298.
29 Haydon, *Diary*, 22 & 24 September 1832, *Diary*, vol. III, pp. 636, 637.
30 Redding, *Recollections*, vol. III, p. 26.
31 Julian Young, *Charles Mayne Young*, vol. I, p. 235.
32 Moore to Lockhart, 27 September 1832, *Letters*, vol. II, p. 755.
33 *Edinburgh Evening Courant*, 24 September 1832.
34 Mrs Grant to Mrs Hook, 28 November 1832, *Memoir*, vol. III, p. 238.
35 *Edinburgh Evening Courant*, 6 October 1832.
36 Moore, Journal, 12 October 1832, *Memoirs, Journals* etc., vol. VI, p. 294.

Epilogue: Afterwards

1 Moore, Journal, 11 Jan. 1825, *Journals and Correspondence*, vol. IV, p. 268.
2 *Ibid.*, 28 Oct. 1825, vol. IV, p. 330.
3 Carlyle to his mother, and to J.S. Mill, 12 Jan. 1833; to Alexander, 27 Jan. 1833, *Collected Letters*, vol. VI, pp. 292, 298, 308.
4 Skene, *Memories of Sir Walter Scott*, p. 224.
5 [Sir] Henry Taylor to Miss Fenwick, May 1831; Southey to Taylor, 2 March 1833, *Correspondence of [Sir] Henry Taylor*, pp. 38, 43–4.
6 Taylor to Miss Fenwick, November 1835, to Southey, 5 November, to Lady Hislop, 16 February 1836, *Correspondence*, pp. 66–7, 68, 70–1. Sir Henry Taylor (1800–86),

who briefly held a minor official post in his late teens, worked at the Colonial Office, wrote poetry and articles for the *Quarterly* and the *London Magazine*, wrote two failed tragedies, though *Philip van Arnevelde* (1834) was successful in print, and the ironical *The Statesman* on 'the art of succeeding' (1836). Not surprisingly, perhaps, rather than abolition of slavery he advocated improving the lot of slaves, and advised suppression of the West Indian republics. (*DNB*)

7 Carlyle, *Reminiscences* (Jeffrey), vol. II, p. 269.
8 Jeffrey to Mr Empson, 26 August 1832, Cockburn, *Life of Jeffrey*, vol. II, p. 255.
9 Haydon, *Diary*, 12 & 21 February, 9 & 12 March 1833, *Diary*, vol. IV, pp. 46, 49, 55, 59.
10 Haydon to his wife, 13 March 1846, *Correspondence and Table Talk*, vol. II, pp. 464, 376.
11 Ticknor, Journal, 29 Mach & 2 April 1838, *Life, Letters and Journals*, vol. II, pp. 148,150.
12 *The Letters of Charles Dickens*, ed. Madeline House and Graham Storey, Oxford, 1965, vol. II, pp. 307ff.
13 Elizabeth Rigby to Miss Browne, 14 January 1843, *Journal of Lady Eastlake*, vol. I, pp. 44, 48, 52.
14 Do., 18 February 1845, *Ibid.*, vol. I, pp. 158–9.
15 Cockburn, *Life of Jeffrey*, vol. I, pp. 357, 412, 364. *Memoirs of Mackintosh*, vol. II, p. 256.
16 Christison to Dr Bright, 31 January 1850, *Life*, vol. II, pp. 294–5.
17 Carlyle, *Table Talk*, ed. Walter Irwin (Cope's Smoke Room Booklets, No.5 (1)), Liverpool, 1890; *Reminiscences*, vol. II, pp. 272, 273.
18 Ticknor, Journal, 26 April 1838, *Life, Letters*, vol. II, p. 163.
19 Carlyle to his mother, 27 January 1833, to John, 10 February 1833, *Collected Letters*, vol. VI, pp. 311, 319.
20 Young, *Charles Mayne Young*, vol. II, p. 231.
21 Dickens to John Forster, 23 June 1841, *Letters*, vol. II, p. 308.
22 Elizabeth Rigby to Miss Browne, 14 January 1843; Journal, 22 February, 6 April, 23 May 1846, *Journal and Correspondence*, vol. I, pp. 45, 54, 64, 70–72, 107.
23 *Ibid.*, 20 March 1846, vol. I, p. 181.
24 David Masson, *Memories of London in the Forties*, Edinburgh and London, 1908, pp. 10, 42–4.
25 Elizabeth Rigby, Journal, 27 February & 3 March 1844, *Journal and Correspondence*, vol. I, pp. 116, 118.
26 *Macready's Reminiscences*, 19 June 1850, vol. II, p. 353.
27 Lady Salisbury, Diary, 19 & 21 October 1833, Oman, *The Gascoyne Heiress*, pp. 88, 89.
28 Crabb Robinson, Diary, 14 & 15 August 1837, 2 March 1838, *Diary, Reminiscences and Correspondence*, vol. III, pp. 142, 188.
29 Macvey Napier, *Selections from Correspondence*, pp. 257–8.
30 Elizabeth Rigby, Journal, 31 January 1844, *Journal and Correspondence*, vol. I, pp. 113–4.
31 *Ibid.*, vol. I, p. 275.
32 Young, *Charles Mayne Young*, vol. II, p. 234.
33 Cam Hobhouse, *Recollections*, 18 September 1834, vol. V, p. 13.
34 Hare, *Baroness Bunsen*, vol. I, p. 426.
35 Ticknor, 23 April 1838, *Life, Letters*, vol. II, p. 161.
36 Elizabeth Rigby, Journal, 5 February 1845 (in this case a view of Watson Gordon's portrait of De Quincey), 30 June 1845, *Journal and Correspondence*, vol. I, pp. 157, 163.
37 Nathaniel P. Willis, *Pencillings by the Way*, London, 1835, vol. III, p. 106.
38 Elizabeth Rigby to Miss Laura Browne, 5 November 1842, *Journal and Correspondence*, vol. I, p. 34.

39 Fanny Kemble, to Harriet St Leger, 10 August 1842, Kemble, *Records of Later Life*, 3 vols, London, 1882, vol. II, p. 260.
40 Carlyle to Jane Welsh, 20 December 1824, *Collected Letters*, vol. III, p. 233 – one of many disparaging, or rather disillusioned, comments on Campbell from June 1824.
41 *Macready's Reminiscences*, 6 July 1844, vol. II, p. 249; Mrs Fletcher to Henry Crabb Robinson, 4 July 1844, Diary, *Reminiscences & Correspondence of Crabb Robinson*, vol. II, p. 561.
42 Carlyle, *Table Talk*.
43 Macready, 10 July 1834, *Diaries*, vol. I, p. 163 and n.
44 Lady Salisbury, Diary, 24 Feb. 1838, Carola Oman, *The Gascoyne Heiress*, p. 274.
45 Henry Crabb Robinson, 21 & 22 Oct. 1838, *Diary, Reminiscences & Correspondence*, vol. II, p. 222.
46 Kemble, *Records of Later Life*, vol. II, pp. 153–5.
47 [Thomas Campbell], *Mrs Dugald Stewart*, Edinburgh, 1838.
48 Ticknor, 23 April 1838, *Life, Letters*, vol. II, p. 162.
49 Grant Thorburn, *Men and Manners in Britain*, pp. 89–90.
50 Mrs Stair Douglas, *Life and Correspondence of William Whewell*, p. 142. William Whewell to Mrs Slatter, n.d. [?1832],
51 Mrs Somerville, *Personal Recollections*, p. 273. The book was her translation of *Mécanique Céleste* (1827–30).
52 Kemble, *Records of Later Life*, vol. I, pp. 144–5.
53 Crabb Robinson, *Diary, Reminiscences* etc., vol. II, p. 254.
54 Cockburn to his daughter Elizabeth, 9 July 1848, *Some Letters of Lord Cockburn*, p. 63.
55 Hare, *Baroness Bunsen*, vol. II, p. 129.
56 [Rev.] Henry Colman, *European Life and Manners*, vol. I, pp. 217, 66.
57 *Ibid.*, vol. I, p. 74.
58 *Ibid.*, vol. I, pp. 59–60.
59 *Ibid.*, vol. I, pp. 62, 259.
60 Frederick von Raumer, *England in 1835*, vol. II, p. 28.
61 Willis, *Pencillings by the Way*, vol. III, p. 141.
62 *Chambers's Edinburgh Journal*, 5 October & 15 December 1832, vol. I, pp. 284, 364. Malcolm Cant, *Villages of Edinburgh*, vol. I, Edinburgh, John Donald Publishers Ltd, 1985, pp. 103–5. The line was in use until 1968, and in 1981 the track was converted to a bicycle path, opened in 1982.
63 Fanny Kemble to Hal, 12 Oct. 1847, *Records of Later Life*, vol. III, p. 225.
64 Macvey Napier, 12 June 1840, *Selections from Correspondence*, p. 329.
65 Colman, *European Life and Manners*, vol. I, p. 83 (25 Sept. 1843).
66 Kemble, *loc. cit.*
67 Colman, *loc. cit.*
68 Elizabeth Rigby, 30 December 1842; *Journal and Correspondence*, vol. I, p. 41.
69 Gillies, *Literary Veteran*, vol. III, p. 306.
70 Mrs Somerville, *Personal Recollections*, p. 274.
71 Colman, 1 August 1843, *European Life and Manners*, vol. I, pp. 215–6.
72 Colman, *loc. cit.*, and 15 August 1843, vol. I, p. 58.
73 Elizabeth Rigby, 2 September 1843, *Journal and Correspondence*, vol. I, p. 105.
74 Livingston, *Our Street*, pp. 2–3.
75 *Last Leaves from the Journal of Julian Charles Young*, pp. 139–40, 142.
76 *Edinburgh Evening Courant*, 5 January 1826. The Rooms were unfortunately demolished in 1967.
77 Dickens to John Forster, 23 June 1841, *Letters*, vol. II, p. 307.
78 Colman, 15 August 1843, *European Life and Manners*, vol. I, p. 56.
79 *Macready's Reminiscences*, vol. II, pp. 275–6.

SELECT BIBLIOGRAPHY

Abbreviations

DNB	*Dictionary of National Biography*
EEC	*Edinburgh Evening Courant*
NLS	National Library of Scotland
OCA	*Oxford Companion to Art*
OEC	*Book of the Old Edinburgh Club*
RCAHMS	Royal Commission on the Ancient and Historical Monuments of Scotland

Works of Reference and Background History

Book of the Old Edinburgh Club

The Buildings of Scotland: Edinburgh, Penguin Books, 1984 (John Gerrard, Colin McWilliam, David Walker)

Cassell's Old and New Edinburgh, 3 Vols, London 1883

H.M. Colvin, *A Biographical Dictionary of British Architects, 1600–1840*, 3rd edn, Yale UP, 1995

Dictionary of American Biography

Dictionary of National Biography

Encyclopaedia Britannica

Fasti Ecclesiasticae Scoticaniae

Ian G. Lindsay, *Georgian Edinburgh*, revised by David Walker, Edinburgh, Scottish Academic Press, 1973

The London Stage, 1600–1800, ed. William Van Lennep, 11 vols, S. Illinois UP, 1965–8; Index, B.R. Schneider, 1979

Rosalind Mitchison, *A History of Scotland*, Methuen, 1970

Oxford Companion to Art

Oxford Companion to English Literature

Oxford Dictionary of Music

T.C. Smout, *A History of the Scottish People 1560–1830*, Collins, 1969

The Statistical Account of Scotland, Vol. II, *The Lothians*, ed. Sir John Sinclair, Edinburgh, 1794

University of Buffalo Studies, Vol. 24

University of Edinburgh Journal, Vols. IV, VIII

The Scots Peerage, ed. Sir James Balfour Paul, 9 vols, Edinburgh 1904

E.L. Woodward, *The Age of Reform, 1815–1870*, Oxford, Clarendon Press, 2nd edn, 1962

A. J. Youngson, *The Making of Classical Edinburgh 1750–1840*, Edinburgh University Press, 1966

The Complete Peerage of England, Scotland and Ireland, ed. The Hon. Vicary Gibbs & H.A. Doubleday, 13 vols, London, 1910–59

Manuscripts

Norma Armstrong, 'The Edinburgh Stage, 1715–1820', 3 vols, Edinburgh, 1968 (Fellowship Thesis for the Library Association)

Diary of George Combe, NLS MS 7402

Edinburgh Town Council Minutes

Erskine Murray MSS, NLS 5084

Joseph Farington, Tour in England, 1792, Edinburgh Public Library, Transcript, qYDA 1861

Liston MSS 161

Innes of Stow MSS, SRO MS GD113/5

Minto MSS NLS MS 11046, 11756 [III.16.4]

Thrale MSS 1789, Rylands Library, Ryl.Eng.MS 623

NLS 3813

NLS 3/2749 (3) (Miss Linwood's Pictures)

Tracts and Pamphlets

Dying Speeches and Executions, etc., Scotish [sic], 1804–1835, Ry.III a.2; Ry.III.a.3A Edinburgh Broadsides, NLS 787.1

[Oil and gas] NLS 6.1205 (23)
APS 3.83.12
6.1245 (21)
6.081 (21)

Tracts relating to Edinburgh NLS LC 137

Western Approach Investigated . . . NLS 7.1504 (10)

NLS 3/2737 (4), (4a), (5) (execution of Robert Johnson, 1818); NLS 3/2749 (11)

NLS LC.Fol.74

NLS Ry.IV.e.4

Newspapers and periodicals

Dublin University Magazine

Edinburgh Advertiser

Edinburgh Annual Register 1819

Edinburgh Evening Courant

Edinburgh Review

Edinburgh Magazine

Etudes Anglaises, Gt Britain, Etats Unis, Paris, 1964

Scots Magazine

Scottish Historical Review

The Spy

ADAMS, JOHN QUINCY, *Memoirs of John Quincy Adams*, ed. Charles Francis Adams, Philadelphia, 1874

ALISON, SIR ARCHIBALD, *Some Account of my Life and Writings*, ed. by his daughter-in-law, Lady [Jane] Alison, 2 vols, London, 1883

ALLEN, WILLIAM, *Life of William Allen*, 3 vols, London, 1846

ARBUTHNOT, MRS, *The Journal of Mrs Arbuthnot, 1820–1832*, ed. Francis Bamford and the Duke of Wellington, 2 vols, London, 1950

ARMSTRONG, NORMA, 'The Edinburgh Stage, 1715–1820' 3 vols, Edinburgh, 1968 (Fellowship Thesis for the Library Association)

ARNOT, HUGO, *The History of Edinburgh from the Earliest Accounts to the Present Time*, Edinburgh, 1788 [1st edn, 1779]

D'ARTOIS, COMTE CHARLES [King Charles X], J. Lucas Dubreton, *Le Comte d'Artois, Charles X*, Paris, 1927

AUDUBON, JOHN JAMES,

M. Audubon, *Audubon and his Journals*, 2 vols, London, 1898

The 1826 Journal of John James Audubon, ed. Alice Ford, Univ. of Oklahoma Press, 1967

The Life and Adventures of J. J. Audubon, the Naturalist, ed. Robert Buchanan, 2nd edn, London, 1869

BAILLIE, JOANNA, Margaret Carhart, *The Life and Works of Joanna Baillie*, Yale Univ. Press, 1923

BEATTIE, JAMES, Margaret Forbes, *Beattie and his Friends*, Westminster, 1904

BERRY, ELIZABETH, *The Writing on the Walls*, Edinburgh, Cockburn Association, 1990

BERRY, THE MISSES AGNES & MARY, *Extracts from the Journals and Correspondence of the Misses Berry from the Year 1783 to 1852*, ed. Lady Theresa Lewis, 3 vols, London, 1865

BIGELOW, ANDREW, *Leaves from a Journal; or Sketches of Rambles in North Britain and Ireland*, Edinburgh, 1824

BOIGNE, COMTESSE DE, *Memoirs of the Comtesse de Boigne*, ed. Charles Nicallaud, 3 vols, London, 1907–8

BOSWELL, JAMES,

Boswell in Search of a Wife, 1766–1769, ed. Frank Brady & Frederick A. Pottle, Heinemann, 1957

Boswell for the Defence, 1769–1774, ed. William K. Wimsatt & Frederick A. Pottle, Heinemann, 1960

Boswell, The Ominous Years, 1774–1776, ed. Charles Ryskamp, Heinemann, 1963

Boswell in Extremis, 1776–1778, ed. Charles McC. Webb, Yale edn, Heinemann, 1971

Boswell, Laird of Auchinleck, 1778–1782, ed. Joseph W. Read & Frederick A. Pottle, Heinemann, 1982

Boswell, The Applause of the Jury, 1782–1785, ed. Irma S. Lustig & Frederick A. Pottle, Heinemann, 1982

Boswell, The English Experiment, 1785–1789, ed. Irma S. Lustig & Frederick A. Pottle, Heinemann, 1986

Boswell, The Great Biographer, 1789–1795, ed. Marlies K. Danziger & Frank Brady, Heinemann, 1989

The Correspondence of James Boswell with David Garrick, Edmund Burke and Edmund Malone, Private Papers of James Boswell, Vol. 4, Heinemann, 1986

The Correspondence of James Boswell and James Johnstone of Grange, ed. Ralph S. Walker, London, 1966

BOWES, JOHN, *The Autobiography or History of the Life of John Bowes*, Glasgow, 1872

BROUGHAM, HENRY LORD,

Brougham and his Early Friends, Letters to James Loch, 1798–1809, ed. R.H.M. Buddle Atkinson & G.A. Jackson, 3 vols, London, 1908

The Life and Times of Henry Lord Brougham, written by himself, 3 vols, Edinburgh, 1871

BRYDALL, ROBERT, *Art in Scotland, its Origin and Progress*, 1889

BULWER LYTTON, EDWARD, *England and the English*, 2 vols, London, 1833

BUNSEN, FRANCES, BARONESS, Augustus J.C. Hare, *The Life and Letters of Frances Bunsen*, 2 vols, London, 1879

BURKE, EDMUND, *The Correspondence of Edmund Burke*, Vol. IV, ed. John A. Woods, 1963; Vol. V, ed. Holden Furber, 1965, Cambridge Univ. Press

BURNS, ROBERT, *The Letters of Robert Burns*, 2nd edn, ed. G. Ross Roy, Vol. 1 1780–1789, Oxford, 1985

BUTLER, SERGEANT ROBERT, *Narrative of the Life of Serjeant Butler, written by himself*, 3rd edn., Edinburgh, 1854

BYRON, GEORGE GORDON, LORD,

Peter Quennell, Byron, *A Self-Portrait*, 2 vols, London, 1950

Byron's Letters and Journals, ed. Leslie A. Marquand, 11 vols, John Murray, 1973 ff.

English Bards and Scotch Reviewers, London, [1809]

CALLCOTT, MARIA, LADY, Rosamund Brunel Gotch, *Maria, Lady Callcott, The Creator of Little Arthur*, London, 1937

CAMPBELL, ALEXANDER, *A Journey from Edinburgh through Parts of North Britain*, 2 vols, London, 1802

CAMPBELL, THOMAS, *Life and Letters of Thomas Campbell*, ed. William Beattie, 3 vols, London, 1850

CARLYLE, THOMAS & JANE

The Collected Letters of Thomas and Jane Welsh Carlyle, ed. Charles Richard Saunders *et al.*, 9 vols, North Carlolina, 1970 ff.

Early Letters of Thomas Carlyle, ed. Charles Eliot Norton, 2 vols, London, 1886

New Letters and Memorials of Jane Welsh Carlyle, annotated by Thomas Carlyle, ed. Alexander Carlyle, 2 vols, London, 1903

Reminiscences, ed. J.A. Froude, 2 vols, London, 1881

Reminiscences, ed. Charles Eliot Norton

Two Notebooks of Thomas Carlyle, ed. Charles Eliot Norton, New York, Grolier Club, 1898

CARR, SIR JOHN, *Caledonian Sketches, or a Tour through Scotland in 1807*, London, 1809

CAVENDISH, HARRIET, *Hary-O, The Letters of Harriet Cavendish, 1796–1809*, ed. Ld Granville Leveson-Gower, London, 1940

CHALMERS, REV. DR THOMAS,

Memoirs of the Life and Writings of Thomas Chalmers, DD, LLD, by his son-in-law, the Rev. Thomas Hanna, LLD, 5 vols, Edinburgh, 1849

A Selection from the Correspondence of the late Thomas Chalmers, DD, LLD, ed. The Rev. William Hanna, Edinburgh, 1853

James Dodds, *Thomas Chalmers, A Biographical Study*, Edinburgh, 1870

CHAMBERS, ROBERT,

Notices of the most Remarkable Fires in Edinburgh, from 1785 to 1824 . . .

Sketch of the History of the Edinburgh Theatre Royal . . ., Edinburgh, 1859

Traditions of Edinburgh, new edn, London and Edinburgh, 1868

Chambers' Edinburgh Journal, Vol. 1, Edinburgh, 1832

CHAMBERS, WILLIAM, *Memoir of Robert Chambers with Autobiographic Remains of William Chambers*, Edinburgh, 1872

CHANTREY, SIR FRANCIS, George Jones RA, *Sir Francis Chantrey, RA, Recollections of his Life, Practice and Opinions*, London, 1849

CHRISTISON, SIR ROBERT, *The Life of Sir Robert Christison, Bart,* by his son, 2 vols, Edinburgh, 1886

COCKBURN, HENRY, LORD,

Memorials of his Time, Edinburgh, 1874

Some Letters of Lord Cockburn, with pages omitted from the Memorials of his Time, ed. Henry Cockburn, Edinburgh, 1932

COGSWELL, JOSEPH GREEN, *Life of Joseph Green Cogswell as sketched in his letters*, ed. Anne Elliot Ticknor, p.p. Cambridge, Mass., 1874

COLBURN, ZERAH, *A Life of Zerah Colburn, written by himself*, Springfield, Vermont, 1833

COLERIDGE, SAMUEL TAYLOR, *Collected Letters of Samuel Taylor Coleridge*, ed. Earl Leslie Griggs, 6 vols, Oxford, 1956–71

COLLINS, WILLIAM, Wilkie Collins, *Memoirs of the Life of William Collins, Esq., RA, with Selections from his Journals and Correspondence*, 2 vols, London, 1848

COLMAN, REV. HENRY, *European Life and Manners; in Familiar Letters to his Friends*, 2 vols, Boston and London, 1849

COMBE, ANDREW, George Combe, *The Life and Correspondence of Andrew Combe, MD*, Edinburgh, 1850

COMBE, GEORGE, Charles Gibbon, *The Life of George Combe*, 2 vols, London, 1878

COMRIE, JOHN D., *History of Scottish Medicine*, 2nd edn, 2 vols, London 1937

CONNELL, BRIAN, *Portrait of a Whig Peer*, [Lord Palmerston], London, 1957

CONSTABLE, ARCHIBALD, *Archibald Constable and his Literary Correspondents*, 3 vols, Edinburgh, 1873

COOKE, GEORGE, William Dunlap, *The Life of George Fred. Cooke*, 2nd edn, 2 vols, London, 1815

CRABBE, REV. GEORGE, *The Life of George Crabbe,* by his son, London, Oxford Univ. Press (World's Classics), 1932

CRESSWELL, CLARENDON HYDE, *The Royal College of Surgeons of Edinburgh 1505–1905*, Edinburgh, 1926

DALZELL, ANDREW, *History of the University of Edinburgh*, Edinburgh, 1862

DARWIN, CHARLES,

Emma Darwin, *A Century of Family Letters, 1792–1866*, ed. Henrietta Litchfield, 2 vols, London, 1915

The Life and Letters of Charles Darwin, ed. by his son, Francis Darwin, 3 vols, London, 1887

More Letters of Charles Darwin, ed. Francis Darwin, 2 vols, London, 1903

DAVIES, LADY CLEMENTINA, *Recollections of Society in France and England*, 2 vols, London, 1872

DAVY, SIR HUMPHREY, *Fragmentary Remains, Literary and Scientific, of Sir Humphrey Davy, Bart* . . . ed. by his brother, John Davy, London, 1858

DE QUINCEY, THOMAS,

John Ritchie Findlay, *Personal Recollections of Thomas De Quincey,* Edinburgh, 1886

James Hogg, *De Quincey and his Friends*, London, 1895

Alexander H. Japp, *De Quincey Memorials . . .* 2 vols, London, 1891

Alexander H. Japp, *Thomas De Quincey, His Life and Writings*, London, 1890

John E. Jordan, *De Quincey to Wordsworth, A Biography of a Relationship*, Univ. of California Press, 1962

Greville Lindop, *The Opium Eater: A Life of Thomas De Quincey*, London, 1981

The Collected Writings of Thomas De Quincey, new and enlarged edn, ed. David Mason, 14 vols, Edinburgh, 1890

DENOVAN, ——[Bow Street Runner], *The Life and Trial of James Mackoull*, 1822

DIBDIN, CHARLES, elder, *Observations on a Tour through almost the whole of England, and a considerable part of Scotland*, 2 vols, London, [1802]

DIBDIN, JAMES C., *Annals of the Edinburgh Stage*, Edinburgh, 1888

DICKENS, CHARLES, *The Letters of Charles Dickens*, ed. Madeline House & Graham Storey, Oxford, 1965 ff.

DISRAELI, BENJAMIN, *Benjamin Disraeli Letters: 1825–1834*, ed. J.A.W. Gunn etc., Univ. of Toronto Press, 1982

DOUGLAS, SIR GEORGE, *The Blackwood Group*, Edinburgh, 1897

DOUGLAS, HARRIET, Angus Davidson, *Miss Douglas of New York*, London, 1952

DUNDAS, HENRY, VISCOUNT MELVILLE, Cyril Matheson, *The Life of Henry Dundas, 1st Viscount Melville 1742–1811*, London, 1933

DUNLOP FAMILY, *The Dunlop Papers*, vol. III, *Letters and Journals*, ed. J.G. Dunlop, p.p., Frome/London, 1953

EASTLAKE, LADY (Elizabeth Rigby), *Journal and Correspondence of Lady Eastlake*, ed. Charles Eastlake Smith, 2 vols, London, 1895

EDGEWORTH, MARIA,

Augustus J.C. Hare, *The Life and Letters of Maria Edgeworth*, 2 vols, 1894

Romilly-Edgeworth Letters, 1813–1818, introd. by Samuel Henry Romilly, London, 1936

EDINBURGH

John Gerrard, Colin McWilliam, David Walker, *The Buildings of Scotland: Edinburgh*, Penguin Books, 1984

Edinburgh, or, The Ancient Royalty; A Sketch of Former Manners, Edinburgh, 1810

Edinburgh, A Satirical Novel, by the Author of *London; or, A Month at St Steven's*, 3 vols, London, 1820

A New History of the City of Edinburgh, 1800

Improvements in Edinburgh during the year 1823, Edinburgh, Feb. 1824

The City of Edinburgh, RCAHMS, 1911

The West Approach Investigated; or, The History of the Purchases on that Line, Edinburgh, printed for W. Hunter, 1830

ELLIOT, SIR GILBERT, EARL OF MINTO, *Life and Letters of Sir Gilbert Elliot, 1st Earl of Minto, from 1751 to 1806*, ed. by his great-niece the Countess of Minto, 3 vols, London, 1874

ELLISTON, ROBERT,

The Elliston Papers, ed. George Raymond, in *Ainsworth's Magazine*, Vol. IV, Part xxvi, Nov. 1843

George Raymond, *Memoir of Robert William Elliston, Comedian*, 2 vols, London, 1846

FARRAR, ELIZA (Mrs John Farrar), *Recollections of 70 Years*, Boston, 1866

FAUJAS DE ST FOND, BARTHOLOMEW, *Travels in England, Scotland, and the Hebrides*, 2 vols, Edinburgh, 1799

FERGUSSON, ALEXANDER, *The Hon. Henry Erskine, Lord Advocate for Scotland*, Edinburgh, 1882

FERRIER, SUSAN, *Memoirs and Correspondence of Susan Ferrier, 1752–1854*, ed. John A. Doyle, London, 1929

FLETCHER, ELIZABETH, *Autobiography of Mrs Fletcher*, ed. Mary Richardson, 3rd edn, Edinburgh, 1876

FLETCHER, HAROLD R. & WILLIAM H. BROWN, *The Royal Botanic Garden, Edinburgh, 1670–1970*, Edinburgh, 1970

FORBES, THE HON. MRS ATHOLL (Mrs Margaret Forbes), *Curiosities of a Scots Charta Chest*, Edinburgh, 1897

FOX, HENRY EDWARD (4th Baron Holland), *The Journal of Henry Edward Fox, 1818–1830*, ed. Lord Ilchester, London, 1923

FRANCIS, JOHN W., MD, *Old New York; or, Reminiscences of the Past 60 Years . . .*, New York, 1858

FRANKLIN, BENJAMIN,

The Papers of Benjamin Franklin, ed. William B. Willcox, Vols 18, 19, Yale Univ. Press 1974, 1975

J. Bennett Nolan, *Benjamin Franklin in Scotland and ireland, 1759 and 1771*, Philadelphia, 1938

FRASER, ANDREW, *The Building of Old College: Adam, Playfair and the University of Edinburgh*, Edinburgh, 1989

FRAZER, MRS, *The Practice of Cookery, Pastry, Pickling, Preserving &c.*, Edinburgh, 1791

FRY, ELIZABETH,

[Elizabeth Fry &] Joseph John Gurney, *Notes on a Visit Made to some of the Prisons of Scotland and the North of England, in company with Elizabeth Fry . . .*, London, 1819

Susanna Corder, *Life of Elizabeth Fry*, compiled from her journal, London, 1853

FYFE, W.T. *Edinburgh under Sir Walter Scott*, London, 1906

GASCOYNE-CECIL, FRANCES MARY, Carola Oman, *The Gascoyne Heiress: The Life and Diaries of Frances Mary Gascoyne-Cecil, 1800–1839*, Hodder & Stoughton, 1968

GASH, NORMAN, *Mr Secretary Peel*, revised edn, Longman, 1988

GEDDES, ANDREW, Adela Geddes, *Memoir of the late Andrew Geddes, Esq., ARA*, London, 1844

GEORGE, PRINCE OF WALES/ GEORGE IV, KING,

The Correspondence of George Prince of Wales, ed. A. Aspinall, 8 vols, Cassell, 1963–71

The Letters of King George IV, 1812–1830, ed. A. Aspinall, 3 vols, Cambridge, 1938

GILBERT, WILLIAM, *Edinburgh in the 19th Century*, Edinburgh, 1901

GILFILLAN, ROBERT, *Songs*, 2nd edn, enlarged, Edinburgh 1836

GILLIES, ROBERT P., *Memoirs of a Literary Veteran*, 3 vols, London, 1851

GLENBERVIE, LORD (Sylvester Douglas), *The Diaries of Sylvester Douglas (Lord Glenbervie)*, ed. Francis Bickley, 2 vols, London, 1928

GONTAUT, DUCHESSE DE, *Memoirs of the Duchess de Gontaut*, trans. Mrs J.W. Davis, 2 vols, London, 1894

GRAHAM, HELEN, *Parties and Pleasures, the diaries of Helen Graham 1823–1826*, ed. James Irvine, [Edinburgh], 1957

GRANT, SIR ALEXANDER, *History of the University of Edinburgh*, 2 vols, Edinburgh, 1884

GRANT, MRS (ANNE) OF LAGGAN,

Memoir and Correspondence of Mrs Grant of Laggan, ed. by her son, John Peter Grant, 3 vols, London, 1844

Memoirs of an American Lady, ed. Ian Grant Wilson, 2 vols, New York, 1901

GRANT OF ROTHIEMURCHUS, ELIZABETH, *Memoirs of a Highland Lady*, 2 vols, Edinburgh, Canongate, 1988

GRANT OF ROTHIEMURCHUS, JANE & MARY, [*Letters on Edinburgh Visit, August, 1822*], p.p., Dublin

GRIFFIN, REV. EDMUND, *Remains of the Rev. Edmund Griffin, compiled by Francis Griffin*, by the Rev. John McVicar, 2 vols, New York, 1831

GUTHRIE, DOUGLAS, *A History of Medicine*, London and Edinburgh, 1945

HALKERTON, PETER, LLD, *A Digest of the Law of Scotland relating to Marriage*, Edinburgh, 1827

HALL, REV. JAMES, *Travels in Scotland by an Unusual Route . . .*, 2 vols, London, 1807

HAMILTON, ELIZABETH, Miss Benger, *Memoirs of the late Mrs Elizabeth Hamilton*, 2 vols, London, 1818

HANWAY, MRS MARY ANNE, *A Journey to the Highlands of Scotland with occasional remarks on Dr Johnson's Tour, By a Lady*, p.p., London, [?1775]

HARRISON, WILMOT, *Memorable Edinburgh Houses*, Edinburgh, 1893

HAYDON, BENJAMIN ROBERT,

The Autobiography & Journals of Benjamin Robert Haydon, ed. Malcolm Elwin, London, 1950

Benjamin Robert Haydon, Correspondence and Table-Talk, with a Memoir by his Son, Frederic Wordsworth Haydon, 2 vols, London, 1876

The Diary of Benjamin Robert Haydon, ed. William Bissell Pope, Harvard Univ. Press, Cambridge, Mass., 5 vols, 1960–63

HAZLITT, WILLIAM & SARAH,

The Journals of Sarah and William Hazlitt, 1822–1831, ed. William Hallam Bonner, *Univ. of Buffalo Studies*, vol. 24, no. 3, Feb. 1989

P.P. Howe, *The Life of Hazlitt*, London, 1922

HAWKIE, *The Autobiography of a Gangrel*, ed. John Southesk, 1888

HERON, ROBERT, *Observations made on a Journey through the Western Counties of Scotland in the Autumn of MDCCXCII*, 2 vols, Edinburgh, 1793

HILL, BENSON EARLE, *Playing About, or Theatrical Notes and Adventures*, 2 vols, London, 1840

HOBHOUSE, JOHN CAM (Lord Broughton), *Recollections of a Long Life*, ed. by his daughter, Lady Dorchester, 6 vols, London, 1909

HOGG, JAMES,

Memoirs of the Author's Life, ed. Douglas S. Mack, Edinburgh, 1872

Memorials of James Hogg, the Ettrick Shepherd, ed. by his daughter Mrs Garden, 2nd edn, 1887

HOLLAND, SIR HENRY, *Recollections of Past Life*, London, 1872

HORNER, FRANCIS,

M. Lyell, *Francis Horner and Leonard Horner*, Edinburgh, p.p. [1890s]

Memorials and Correspondence of Francis Horner, MP, ed. Leonard Horner, 2 vols, with additions, Boston & London, 1853

HOWARD SISTERS, *Three Howard Sisters*, ed. Maud, Lady Leconfield, London, 1955

HUME, DAVID, *Letters of David Hume*, ed. J.Y.T. Grieg, 2 vols, Oxford, 1932

HUTTON, JAMES, *Theory of the Earth*, 2 vols, 1795

IRVING, EDWARD,

Andrew Lonsdale Drummond, *Edward Irving and his Circle, 1792–1837*, London, 1937

Mrs Oliphant, *The Life of Edward Irving, Minister of the National Scotch Church*, 2 vols, London, 1862

IRVING, WASHINGTON, *Journals and Notebooks*, Vol. II, *1807–1822*, Boston, Twayne Publisher, 1981

JAY, JOHN, *The Correspondence and Public Papers of John Jay*, ed. Henry P. Johnston, 4 vols, New York and London, 1890–93

JEFFREY, FRANCIS,

Henry Cockburn, *Life of Lord Jeffrey*, 2 vols, Edinburgh, 1852

James Taylor, *Lord Jeffrey and Craigcrook, A History of the Castle*, Edinburgh, 1892

JOHNSON, ROBERT, *Letter to the Magistrates of Edinburgh, on the Execution of Robert Johnson, by an Eyewitness*, Edinburgh, 1819

JOHNSTONE, MRS CHRISTIAN I., *The Saxon and the Gael*, 4 vols, Edinburgh, 1814

KAY, JOHN, *A Series of Original Portraits and Caricature Etchings*, new edn, ed. H. Paton, 2 vols, Edinburgh, 1877

KEMBLE, FRANCES ANN,

Record of a Girlhood, 3 vols, London, 1878

Records of Later Life, 3 vols, London, 1882

KNIGHTON, SIR WILLIAM, *Memoirs of Sir William Knighton, Bart, GCE, Keeper of the Privy Purse*, 2 vols, Paris, 1838

LAKE POETS, *Letters from the Lake Poets to Daniel Stuart*, p.p., London, 1889

LENNOX, FREDERICK, LORD, *Drafts on my Memory*, 2 vols, London, 1866

LESLIE, CHARLES ROBERT, *Autobiographical Recollections of the Late Charles Robert Leslie, RA*, ed. Tom Taylor, 2 vols, London, 1860

LETTERS WRITTEN FOR THE POST, AND NOT FOR THE PRESS, London, 1820

LEVESON-GOWER, G., *Private Correspondence of G. Leveson-Gower, 1781–1821*, 2 vols, London, 1916

LEWIS, MATTHEW, *Life and Correspondence of M.G. Lewis*, 2 vols, London, 1839

LINDSAY, IAN G., *Georgian Edinburgh*, revised by David Walker, Edinburgh, Scottish Academic Press, 1973

LINNELL, JOHN, Alfred T. Story, *The Life of John Linnell*, 2 vols, London, 1892

LIVINGSTON, JOSIAH,

Our Street, Memories of Buccleuch Place, Edinburgh, 1893

Some Edinburgh Shops, Edinburgh, 1894

LOCKHART, JOHN GIBSON, Andrew Lang, *Life and Letters of John Gibson Lockhart*, 2 vols, London, 1897

LUNARDI, VINCENT, *An Account of 5 Aerial Voyages in Scotland*, London, 1786

MACAULAY, THOMAS BABINGTON, G.O. Trevelyan, *Life of Macaulay*, 2 vols, London, 1932

MACDONALD, JOHN, *Memoirs of an 18th Century Footman*, introd. John Beresford, London, 1927

MACFARLANE, CHARLES, *Recollections of a Literary Life*, London, 1917

MACKENZIE, HENRY,

Anecdotes and Egotisms, 1745–1831, ed. Harold William Thompson, Oxford, 1927

Letters to Elizabeth Rose of Kilravock, ed. Horst W. Brescher, Edinburgh, 1967

Harold William Thompson, *A Scottish Man of Feeling*, Oxford, 1931

MACKINTOSH, SIR JAMES, *Memoirs of the Life of the Rt Hon. Sir James Mackintosh*, by Robert J. Mackintosh, 2 vols, London, [1835 &] 1836

MACIVER, MRS, *Cookery and Pastry, As taught and practised by Mrs MacIver, Teacher of those Arts in Edinburgh*, 2nd edn, Edinburgh, 1787

MACREADY, WILLIAM CHARLES,

The Diaries of William Charles Macready, 1833–1851, ed. William Toynbee, 2 vols, London, 1912

Macready's Reminiscences, and Selections from his Diaries and Letters, ed. Sir Frederick Pollard, 2 vols, London, 1875

MCVICKAR, REV. JOHN, W. A. McVickar, *Life of the Rev. John McVickar, STD*, New York, 1872

MASSON, DAVID,

Edinburgh Sketches and Memories, London, 1892

Memories of London in the Forties, Edinburgh and London, 1908

Memories of Two Cities, Edinburgh and Aberdeen, Edinburgh and London, 1908

MATHEWS, CHARLES,

Mrs Anne Mathews, *Memoirs of Charles Mathews, Comedian*, 2 vols, London, 1838

A Continuation of the Memoirs of Charles Mathews, Comedian . . ., 2 vols, Philadelphia, 1837

MAWMAN, JOSEPH, *An Excursion to the Highlands of Scotland and the English Lakes*, London, 1805

MEMORIALS OF COLEORTON, ed. William Knight, 2 vols, Edinburgh 1887

MENDELSSOHN, FELIX, Sebastian Hensel, *The Mendelssohn Family (1729–1847), from Letters and Journals*, 2 vols, 1881

MERIVALE, JOHN HERMAN,

Edwin H.A. Koch, *Leaves from the Diary of a Literary Amateur, John Herman Merivale, 1819–1844*, p.p. Hampstead, 1911

Family Memorials, compiled by Anna Merivale, p.p., Exeter, 1884

MILES, ALEXANDER, *The Edinburgh School of Surgery before Lister*, London, 1918

MILLER, HUGH,

Peter Bayne, *The Life and Letters of Hugh Miller*, 2 vols, London, 1871

My Schools and Schoolmasters, ed. W.M. Mackenzie, Edinburgh, 1907

MITFORD, MARY RUSSELL, *Letters of Mary Russell Mitford*, 2nd ser., ed. Henry Chorley, 2 vols, London, 1872

MOREHEAD, ROBERT, *Life and Writings of the Rev. Robert Morehead*, ed. by his son, Charles Morehead, Edinburgh, 1875

MOORE , THOMAS,

The Letters of Thomas Moore, ed. Wilfred S. Dowden, 2 vols, Oxford, 1964

Memoirs, Journal and Correspondence of Thomas Moore, ed. Lord John Russell, 8 vols, London, 1851

MORGAN, LADY (Sydney Owensen), *The Book of the Boudoir*, 2 vols, London 1829

MUDIE, ROBERT, *A Historical Account of His Majesty's Visit to Scotland*, Edinburgh 1822

MURCHISON, SIR RODERICK, Archibald Geikie, *Life of Sir Roderick T. Murchison, Bart, KCB, FRS*, 2 vols, London, 1875

MURRAY, THE HON. MRS SARAH, *A Companion and Useful Guide to the Beauties of Scotland and the Lakes*, 2 vols, p.p., 1799

NAIRNE, CAROLINE, LADY, *Life and Songs of the Baroness Nairne*, ed. Rev. Charles Rogers, London, 1869

NAPIER, MACVEY, *Selections from the Correspondence of the late Macvey Napier, Esq.*, by his son, Macvey Napier, London, 1879

NASMYTH, ALEXANDER, J.C.B. Cooksey, *Alexander Nasmyth, HRSA, 1758–1840*, Paul Harris, 1991

NASMYTH, JAMES, *James Nasmyth, Engineer, An Autobiography*, ed. Samuel Smiles, London, 1883

NEWTE, THOMAS, *Prospects and Observations; on a Tour of England and Scotland; Natural, Oeconomical, and Literary*, London, 1791

NECKER DE SAUSSURE, L.A., *Travels in Scotland descriptive of Manners, Literature, and Science*, London, 1821

NOCTES AMBROSIANAE, by John Wilson etc., with memorials and notes by R. Stretton Mackenzie, 5 vols, New York, 1875

NODIER, CHARLES, *Promenade from Dieppe to the Mountains of Scotland*, trans. from the French, Edinburgh & London, 1822

OPIE, AMELIA , Cecilia Lucy Brightwell, *Memorials of the Life of Amelia Opie*, 2nd edn, Norwich, 1854

PALMERSTON, HENRY TEMPLE, VISCOUNT,

The Hon. Evelyn Ashley, *The Life and Correspondence of Henry Temple, Viscount Palmerston*, 4 vols, London, 1879

Brian Connell, *Portrait of a Whig Peer*, London, 1957

The Letters of the 3rd Viscount Palmerston to Laurence and Elizabeth Sulivan, 1804–1863, ed. Kenneth E. Bourne, Camden 4th ser., Vol. 23, London Royal Hist. Society, 1979

PARR, REV. SAMUEL, Rev. Samuel Field, M*emoirs of the Rev. Samuel Parr*, 2 vols, London, 1828

PASTON, GEORGE [Emily Morse Symonds], *Little Memoirs of the 18th Century*, 1906

PATMORE, COVENTRY, Basil Champneys, *Memoirs and Correspondence of Coventry Patmore*, 2 vols, London, 1900

PEEL, LADY GEORGIANA, *Recollections*, London, 1920

PENNANT, THOMAS, *A Tour of Scotland, MDCCLXIX*, Warrington, 1774

PETER'S LETTERS TO HIS KINSFOLK [J.G. Lockhart], by 'Peter Morris', 3 vols, 3rd edn [2nd edn], Edinburgh, 1819

PHILO-SCOTUS [Philip Barrington Ainslie], *Reminiscences of a Scottish Gentleman*, London, 1861

PICHOT, AMEDEE, *Voyage Historique et Litteraire de Angleterre en Ecosse*, 3 vols, Paris, 1825

PIOZZI, MRS HESTER, *The Intimate Letters of Hestor Piozzi and Penelope Pennington, 1788–1821*, ed. Oswald G. Knapp, London, 1914

PLANCHE, JAMES ROBINSON, *Recollections and Reflections*, London, 1901

PLUMPTRE, JAMES, *James Plumptre's Britain, The Journal of a Tourist in the 1780s*, ed. Ian Ousby, Hutchinson, 1992

POCOCKE, THOMAS, *Tours in Scotland, 1747, 1750, 1760*, ed. Daniel William Kemp, Edinburgh, 1887

PRINGLE, THOMAS, *Thomas Pringle, His Life, Times and Poems*, ed. William Hay, Cape Town, 1912

PRYME, GEORGE, *Autobiographical Recollections of George Pryme Esq., MA*, 2 vols, Cambridge, 1870

RAEBURN, SIR HENRY, Edward Pinnington, *Sir Henry Raeburn, RA*, London, 1904

RAMSDEN, LADY GUENDOLEN, *Correspondence of Two Brothers, Edward Adolphus, 11th Duke of Somerset, and his brother, Lord Webb Seymour . . .*, London, 1906

RAIKES, THOMAS, Edward H. Koch, *A Portion of the Journal kept by Thomas Raikes, Esq., from 1831 to 1847*, 4 vols, London, 1856–7

REDDING, CYRUS, *50 Years' Recollections, Literary and Personal, with Observations on Men and Things*, 3 vols, London, 1838

REGALIA, SCOTTISH, *The Scottish Regalia, Anciently styled The Honours of Scotland*, compiled by W.D. Collier, Edinburgh, 1851

ROBERTS, DAVID, James Ballantyne, *The Life of David Roberts, RA, compiled from his journals and other sources*, Edinburgh, 1866

ROBERTSON, ANDREW, *Letters and Papers of Andrew Robertson, AM*, ed. Emily Robertson, London, 1895

ROBINSON, HENRY CRABB,
The Correspondence of Henry Crabb Robinson with the Wordsworth Circle (1808–1866), ed. Edith J. Morley, 2 vols, Oxford, 1927
Reminiscences and Correspondence of Henry Crabb Robinson, Barrister-at-Law, FRS, ed. Thomas Sadler, 3 vols, Oxford, 1869
ROGERS, REV. CHARLES, *Scotland Social and Domestic*, Grampian Club, London, 1869
ROGERS, SAMUEL,
P.A. Clayden, *Early Life of Samuel Rogers*, London, 1887
Reminiscences and Table Talk of Samuel Rogers, ed. G.H. Powell, 1903
RUSH, BENJAMIN,
The Autobiography of Benjamin Rush, ed. George W. Corner, Princeton Univ. Press, for American Philosophical Society, Vol. 25, 1948
Letters of Benjamin Rush, ed. L.H. Butterfield, 2 vols, Princeton Univ. Press, as above, Vol. V, 1951
RUSH, RICHARD,
The Court of London from 1819 to 1825, ed. Benjamin Rush, 3rd edn, London, 1873
Residence at the Court of London, 3rd edn, ed. by his son Benjamin Rush, London, 1872
RUSKIN FAMILY LETTERS, ed. Van Akin Burd, Vol. 1, *1801–1837*, Cornell UP, 1973
RUSSELL, LORD JOHN, Spencer Walpole, *The Life of Lord John Russell*, 2 vols, London, 1889
RUTLAND, DUKE OF (John Henry Manners, 5th Duke), *Journal of a Tour to the Northern Parts of Great Britain*, 3 vols, London, 1813
SAGE, REV. DONALD, M*emorabilia Domestica, or, Parish Life in the North of Scotland*, 2nd edn, Wick, 1899
ST CLAIR, R.E. WRIGHT, *Doctors Monro: A Medical Saga*, London, 1964
SANDFORD, DANIEL, *Remains of the late Rt Reverend Daniel Sandford, DD, Oxon, Bishop of Edinburgh in the Scottish Episcopal Church* . . . by the Rev. John Sandford, 2 vols, Edinburgh, 1830
SCHETKY, S.F.L., *90 Years of Work and Play: Sketches from the Public and Private Career of John Christian Schekty*, by his daughter, Edinburgh and London, 1877
SCHINKEL, KARL FRIEDRICH, *'The English Journey'. Journal of a Journey to France and England in 1826*, ed. David Bindman & Gottfried Riemann, Yale Univ. Press, 1993
SCOTT, SIR WALTER,
R.P. Gillies, *Recollections of Sir Walter Scott*, London, 1837
James Hogg, *Familiar Anecdotes of Sir Walter Scott*, ed. Douglas S. Mack, Edinburgh
Edgar Johnson, *Sir Walter Scott. The Great Unknown*, 2 vols, Hamish Hamilton, 1970
John Gibson Lockhart, *The Life of Sir Walter Scott, Bart*, 10 vols, Edinburgh, 1902
The Journal of Sir Walter Scott 1825–1832, ed. W.E.K. Anderson, Oxford, Clarendon Press, 1972
The Letters of Sir Walter Scott, ed. H.J.C. Grierson, London, 1932
SEDGEWICK, REV. ADAM, John Willis Clark & Thomas McKenny Hughes, *The Life and Letters of the Revd Adam Sedgewick*, 2 vols, Cambridge, 1890
SEGUR, COMTE DE, *Memoirs of Louis Philippe, Comte de Ségur*, ed. Eveline Cruikshanks, London, Folio Society, 1960
SEYMOUR, LADY, *The Pope of Holland House*, London, 1906

SHARPE, CHARLES KIRKPATRICK,
Letters of Sir Walter Scott and Charles Kirkpatrick Sharpe to Robert Chambers 1821–1845, Edinburgh, 1904
Letters to and from Charles Kirkpatrick Sharpe Esq., ed. Alexander Allardyce, 2 vols, Edinburgh and London, 1888
SHAW, STEBBING, *A Tour, in 1787, from London, to the Western Highlands of Scotland*, London, [1788]
SHELLEY, FRANCES, LADY, *The Diary of Frances Lady Shelley 1787–1817*, ed. Rice Edgcumbe, 2 vols, London, 1912, 1913
SHELLEY, PERCY BYSSHE,
Thomas Jefferson Hogg, *The Life of Percy Bysshe Shelley*, London, 1906
Roger Inkpen, *Shelley in England*, Appendix III
The Letters of Percy Bysshe Shelley, ed. Frederick L. Jones, 3 vols, Oxford, 1964
SHORE, CHARLES, LORD TEIGNMOUTH, *Reminiscences of Many Years*, 2 vols, Edinburgh, 1878
SIBBALD, SUSAN, *The Memoirs of Susan Sibbald (1783–1812)*, ed. by her great-grandson Francis Paget Hett, London, 1926
[SIBBALD, THOMAS], *Reminiscences of a British Naval Officer, by an Old Salt*, Toronto, 1885
SILLIMAN, BENJAMIN, *A Journal of Travels in England, Holland and Scotland . . . in the Years 1805 and 1806*, 3rd edn, (enlarged), New Haven, 1820
SIMEON, REV. CHARLES, *Memoirs of the Rev. Charles Simeon, MA, with a selection from his writings and correspondence*, ed. Rev. William Carus, 3rd edn, 1848
SIMOND, LOUIS, *Journal of a Tour and Residence in Great Britain during the years 1810 and 1811*, 2 vols, Edinburgh, 1815
SINCLAIR, CATHERINE, *Holiday House*, Philadelphia, 1849
SINCLAIR, SIR JOHN, *Memorials of the Life and Letters of the Rt Hon. Sir John Sinclair, Bart*, 2 vols, Edinburgh, 1837
SKRINE, HENRY, *Travels in the Eastern Counties, and Northern Highlands of Scotland*, London, 1813
SMITH, REV. SYDNEY,
The Letters of Sydney Smith, ed. Nowell C. Smith, 2 vols, Oxford, Clarendon Press, 1953
The Wit and Wisdom of the Rev. Sydney Smith, London, 1860
SOMERVILLE, ALEXANDER, *The Autobiography of a Working Man*, ed. Brian Behan, Macgibbon and Kee, 1967
SOMERVILLE, MARY, *Personal Recollections, from early life to old age, of Mary Somerville*, by her daughter, Martha Somerville, London, 1873
SOMERVILLE, DR THOMAS, *My Own Life and Times 1741–1814*, Edinburgh, 1961
SOUTHEY, ROBERT,
The Life and Correspondence of the late Robert Southey, ed. by his son the Rev. Charles Cuthbert Southey, 6 vols, London, 1849–50
New Letters of Robert Southey, ed. Kenneth Curry, 2 vols, Columbia UP, 1965
Selections from the Letters of Robert Southey, ed. by his son-in-law John Wood Warter, 4 vols, London, 1896
SPENCE, ELIZABETH,
Sketches of the Present Manners, Customs, and Scenery of Scotland . . ., 2 vols, London, 1811
Letters from the North Highlands, during the Summer 1816, London, 1817
SPENCER, SARAH, *Correspondence of Sarah Spencer, Lady Lyttelton, 1787–1879*, by her great-granddaughter Mrs Hugh Wyndham, London, 1912

STARK, J., *Picture of Edinburgh; containing a History and Description of the City*, Edinburgh, 1806

STANLEY, MARIA, LADY, *The Early Married Life of Maria Josepha Lady Stanley, with extracts from Sir John Stanley's 'Praeterita',* ed. Jane H. Adeane, London, 1849

STEWART, A. FRANCIS, *The Exiled Bourbons in Scotland*, Edinburgh, 1898

STEWART, DUGALD, Col. M.D. Stewart, *Memoirs of the late Dugald Stewart, Author of the Philosophy of the Human Mind*, p.p., Edinburgh, 1838

STODDART, JOHN, *Remarks on Local Scenery and Manners in Scotland during the Years 1799 and 1800*, 2 vols, London, 1801

STORY, JANET L., *Early Reminiscences*, Glasgow, 1911

STRUTHERS, JOHN, *Historical Sketch of the Edinburgh Anatomical School*, Edinburgh, 1867

STUART, JAMES, OF DUNEARN, *The Trial of James Stuart, Esq. of Dunearn . . .*, Edinburgh, 1822

STUART, LADY LOUISA, *Gleanings from an Old Portfolio*, ed. Mrs Godfrey Clark, 3 vols, p.p., Edinburgh, 1895

SVENDENSTIERNA'S TOUR, *Great Britain, 1802–30, The Travel Diary of an Industrial Spy*, trans. E.L. Dellow, David & Charles, 1973

TAYLOR, SIR HENRY, *Correspondence of [Sir] Henry Taylor*, ed. Edward Dowden, London, 1888

THOMSON, COSMO INNES, *Memoir of Thomas Thomson, Esq.*, Bannatyne Club, 1854

THORBURN, GRANT, *Men and Manners in Britain, or A bone to gnaw for the Trollopes, Fidlers &c.*, New York, 1834

THORNTON, COL. THOMAS, *A Sporting Tour through the Northern Parts of England and Great Parts of the Highlands of Scotland*, (first published 1804), London, 1896

TICKNOR, GEORGE, *Life, Letters and Journals of George Ticknor*, ed. G.S. Hillard, 2 vols, Boston, 1909

TOPHAM, EDWARD, *Letters from Edinburgh, Written in the Years 1774 and 1775 . . .*, London, 1776

TOWN COUNCIL, *Address from the Town Council on the subject of the New Buildings for the High School* (1825–29)

THE TRAVELLER'S COMPANION through the City of Edinburgh and Suburbs . . ., Edinburgh, 1794

TROTTER, ALEXANDER, *A Plan of Communication between the Old and New Town of Edinburgh, in the Line of the earthen Mound . . .*, 2nd edn enlarged, Edinburgh, 1829

TURNER, A. LOGAN, *Story of a Great Hospital: The Royal Infirmary of Edinburgh, 1729–1929*, Edinburgh, 1937

TURNER, J.M.W.,

Collected Correspondence of J.M.W. Turner, ed. John Gage, Oxford, 1980

Gerard Finlay, *Turner and George the Fourth in Edinburgh*,1872, Tate Gallery and Edinburgh Univ. Press, 1981

TUSSAUD, MADAME, Pauline Chapman, *Mme Tussaud in England*, London, Quiller Press, 1992

TYERMAN, REV. L., *The Life of the Rev. George Whitfield, BA, of Pembroke College, Oxford*, 2 vols, 2nd edn, London, 1890

TYTLER, PATRICK FRASER, Rev. John W. Burgon, *Memoirs of Patrick Fraser Tytler*, London, 1859

UWINS, THOMAS, Mrs. S, Uwins, *A Memoir of Thomas Uwins, RA, late Keeper of the Royal Galleries and the National Gallery . . .*, 2 vols, London, 1858

VON RAUMER, FREDERICK, *England in 1835*, 3 vols, London, 1836

WAKE, CHARLOTTE, LADY, *Reminiscences of Charlotte, Lady Wake*, ed. Lucy Wake, London, 1908

WATT, FRANCIS, *The Book of Edinburgh Anecdote*, Edinburgh, 1913

WEBB, DANIEL CARLESS, *Observations and Remarks during four Excursions . . . in the Years 1810 and 1811 . . .*, London, 1812

WENDEBORN, FREDERICK AUGUSTUS, *A View of England towards the Close of the 18th Century*, trans. from the German, 2 vols, London, 1791

WHARAM, ALAN, *The Treason Trials 1794*, Leicester Univ. Press, 1992

WHEWELL, WILLIAM, Mrs Stair Douglas [Janet M. Douglas], *The Life and Selections of the Correspondence of William Whewell, DD . . .*, London, 1881

WILBERFORCE, WILLIAM,

The Correspondence of William Wilberforce, ed. R.I. Wilberforce and Samuel Wilberforce, 2 vols, London, 1840

Private Papers of William Wilberforce, ed. A.M. Wilberforce, 1897

WILKIE, DAVID, Allan Cunningham, *The Life of Sir David Wilkie*, 3 vols, London, 1843

WILLIS, NATHANIEL, *Pencillings by the Way*, London, 1835

WILLIS, R.L., *Journal of a Tour from London to Elgin made about 1799, in company with Mr Brodie, younger . . .*, Edinburgh, 1897

WILSON, SIR DANIEL, *Memorials of Edinburgh in the Olden Time*, 2nd edn, 2 vols, Edinburgh, 1891

WILSON, JAMES, James Hamilton, *Memoirs of the Life of James Wilson, Esq., FRSE, MWS, of Woodville*, London, 1859

WILSON, JOHN, Mary Gordon, *'Christopher North', A Memoir of John Wilson*, 2 vols, Edinburgh, 1862

WINDHAM, WILLIAM, *The Diary of the Rt Hon. William Windham, 1784 to 1810*, ed. Mrs Henry Baring, London, 1866

WORDSWORTH, WILLIAM & DOROTHY,

The Letters of William and Dorothy Wordsworth, ed. Ernest de Selincourt, 2nd edn, revised by Charles L. Shaver, Oxford, 1967

Dorothy Wordsworth, *Recollections of a Tour made in Scotland in 1803*, Edinburgh, 1894

WYNN, FRANCES WILLIAMS, *Diary of a Lady of Quality, from 1797–1844*, ed. A. Hayward, London, 1864

WYNNE DIARIES, THE, ed. Anne Fremantle, Oxford, 1952

YOUNG, JULIAN CHARLES,

A Memoir of Charles Mayne Young, Tragedian, 2 vols, London, 1871

Last Leaves from the Journal of Julian Charles Young, Rector of Ilmington, Warks, Edinburgh, 187

INDEX

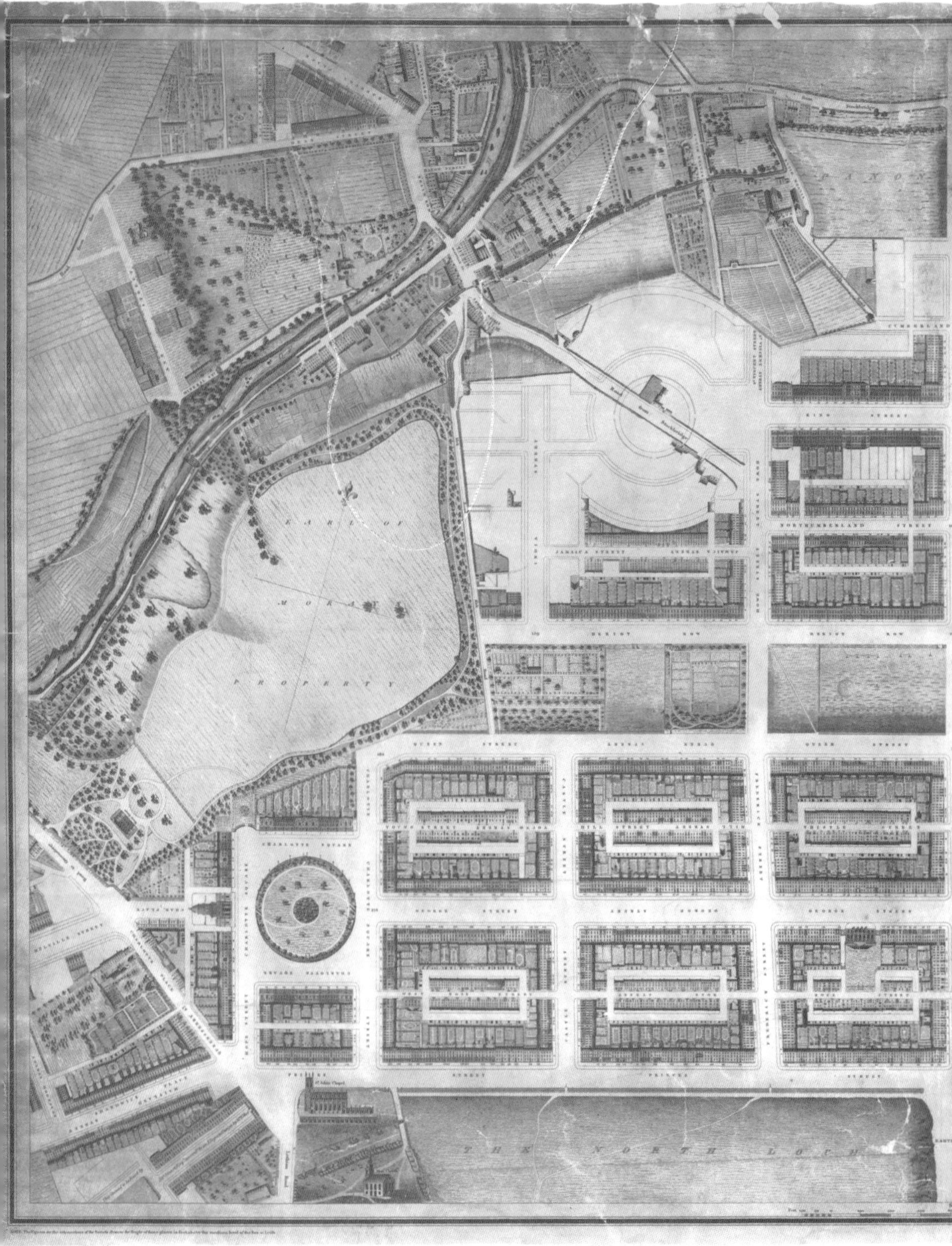

CUMBERLAND
KING STREET
NORTHUMBERLAND STREET
HOWE STREET
JAMAICA STREET
INDIA STREET
HERIOT ROW
EARL OF MORAY PROPERTY
QUEEN STREET
YOUNG STREET
CASTLE STREET
HILL STREET
FREDERICK STREET
THISTLE STREET
CHARLOTTE SQUARE
GEORGE STREET
PRINCES STREET
St. John's Chapel
Lothian Road
THE NORTH LOCH